Empire of Democracy

The Remaking of the West Since the Cold War, 1971–2017

SIMON REID-HENRY

Simon & Schuster

NEW YORK   LONDON   TORONTO   SYDNEY   NEW DELHI

Simon & Schuster
1230 Avenue of the Americas
New York, NY 10020

First Simon & Schuster hardcover edition June 2019

SIMON & SCHUSTER and colophon are registered trademarks of Simon & Schuster, Inc.

For information about special discounts for bulk purchases, please contact Simon & Schuster
Special Sales at 1-866-506-1949 or business@simonandschuster.com

The Simon & Schuster Speakers Bureau can bring authors to your live event. For more
information or to book an event contact the Simon & Schuster Speakers Bureau at
1-866-248-3049 or visit our website at www.simonspeakers.com

Interior design by Paul Dippolito

Manufactured in the United States of America

1 3 5 7 9 10 8 6 4 2

Library of Congress Cataloging-in-Publication Data

Names: Reid-Henry, Simon, author.
Title: Empire of democracy : the remaking of the West since the Cold War, 1971–2017 /
Simon Reid-Henry.
Description: First Simon & Schuster hardcover edition. | New York : Simon & Schuster, 2019.
| Includes bibliographical references and index.
Identifiers: LCCN 2019013544 (print) | LCCN 2019016633 (ebook) | ISBN 9781451684988
(E-book) | ISBN 9781451684964 (hardcover) | ISBN 9781451684971 (trade pbk.) |
ISBN 9781451684988 (ebook)
Subjects: LCSH: Democracy—Western countries—History—20th century. | Democracy—
Western countries—History—21st century. | Liberalism—Western countries—History—20th
century. | Liberalism—Western countries—History—21st century. | Cold War—Political
aspects—Western countries—History. | Western countries—Politics and government—20th
century. | Western countries—Politics and government—21st century.
Classification: LCC JC421 (ebook) | LCC JC421 .R4183 2019 (print) | DDC
320.9182/109045—dc23
LC record available at https://lccn.loc.gov/2019013544

ISBN 978-1-4516-8496-4
ISBN 978-1-4516-8498-8 (ebook)

For Katerini,
and Oscar and Elias

Contents

At the International Café,
two fools are laughing
telling jokes.
They say if you want to lie,
you want to make someone laugh
just try the word "democracy."

At the International Café,
after they've finished drinking
the fools chatted some more.
They said the moment will arrive,
when the whole earth
will be embraced by a white dove.

And a young man
sat alone on the side,
listening to the two fools talking,
saying that, if everyone on earth
was as crazy as these two,
we'd really have a day of peace sometime.

Kostas Hatzis, 'Sto Diethnes To Magazi'
(At the International Café), 1974

Introduction

> But the scene is now changed, and gradually the two ranks mingle; the divisions which once severed mankind are lowered, property is divided, power is held in common, the light of intelligence spreads, and the capacities of all classes are equally cultivated; the State becomes democratic, and the empire of democracy is slowly and peaceably introduced into the institutions and the manners of the nation.
>
> Alexis de Tocqueville, *Democracy in America*, 1831

WHAT IS THE story of democracy in our time? Not long ago the Western formula of democracy and free markets seemed unassailable. When the Cold War ended in 1989, the new "great game" played by diplomats, politicians and intellectuals alike became to promote and report on the further spread of democracy about the globe.[1] The tendency was to assume that democracy was working well still at home. The war on terror and the financial crisis have more recently framed those assumptions in a less comfortable light. By the time of the uprisings that swept across the Arab world in 2011, the dimming status of the liberal democratic formula was clear. Whatever was being demanded on the streets of Cairo it was not Western-style liberal democracy. Nor was a liberal democratic form of government any longer something that could be "built" on behalf of these nations, as the United States had attempted during the previous decade in Iraq. In the aftermath of 2011, as Syria imploded and Islamic State dug in its bloodied claws, the former call to democratic arms of the pundits in Washington was replaced by a faint piccolo whistling about "democracy in retreat." From the point of view of the West it was not long before the high drama of the Arab Spring was drowned out by a pervasive and growing cacophony of discontent at home.

The former narrative of democracy's historical spread has now been firmly replaced by one of its crisis and decline. "Never has there been such a thin line between a positive outlook for democracy and the chance that it might go off the rails," wrote the French historian Pierre Rosanvallon in 2008. "What's gone wrong with democracy?" asked London's *The Economist* a few years later in 2014.[2] Neither were looking across the Mediterranean to Tunisia or Algeria, but home to the disaffected *banlieues* of Paris, to the US Congress and the European Union. The concerns of over 4 million British voters, who in 2016 signed a petition demanding repeal of the country's recent referendum on "Brexit," or of those dumbfounded by the election of Donald J. Trump to the White House later that same year, revealed that sense of anxiety to be spreading. "Democracy has survived the twentieth century by the skin of its teeth," observed Arthur Schlesinger Jr. presciently at the end of the millennium. "It will not enjoy a free ride through the century to come."[3]

In recent years Western democracy has indeed come under threat; the basic right of citizens to habeas corpus has been pared back after centuries of struggle to flesh it out. Distrust in politics has grown. Foreign governments have been shown to have interfered in national elections. Civil liberties, including the right to privacy in the home, have been openly infringed. The growing power of political lobbies has given moneyed interests undue influence over policymaking, and has endowed a new class of politician with the ability not only to fundamentally misunderstand their constituents but to be rewarded for this. Socioeconomic inequality, which for much of the postwar era had been warded off by the welfare state, has returned.

In response to such developments, the streets of Western capitals have been marched upon by people in larger numbers than at any time since the high point of the civil rights movement half a century ago. Whether it is Occupy protesters or the *gilets jaunes*, white supremacists or national populists, a more assertive popular voice is emerging beneath the battered wing of liberal democracy and its representative institutions. Some of these movements are utopian; others demand greater rights, if only for themselves. But everywhere the clamor of popular disapproval is growing and is making its presence felt in the cordoned halls of liberal democratic debate. Democracy itself is changing before our eyes. But what is it that has changed exactly? That is the question I set out to answer in this book.

Stripped of its national particulars, modern democracy, as the influential Austrian jurist Hans Kelsen once argued, is "the restriction of freedom by a law under which all subjects are equal."[4] That is, on the face of it, a wonderfully simple formula. And yet the way different societies have over time sought to reconcile these two values—of freedom and equality—has fallen short more often than it has succeeded. Franchises were neither full nor fair for most of the nineteenth century. And many of the parliaments and constitutions thrown up in the wake of imperialism's retreat did not survive long before they too needed rebuilding in the aftermath of two catastrophic world wars.

To recognize that democracy may be different things at different times is to recognize that it is both more recent and more fragile than we tend to imagine. Our own liberal democracy has almost nothing in common with the classical democracy of Athens. Scratch beneath the surface, and it soon reveals itself to have little in common either with that form of democracy inaugurated by the French and American revolutions, which placed "representative" institutions at the heart of the nation state and its newly constituted "peoples." But if democracy changes over time it also changes from place to place. Writing in the middle of the nineteenth century, Alexis de Tocqueville famously compared democracy in France with what he had recently seen of it in America. He believed that America had come some considerable way further than France in achieving the right balance between governments that ruled from above and people as they voiced their demands from below. What was distinct about democracy in America, Tocqueville suggested, was the achievement of "the general equality of conditions." Looking to America as the crucible of democracy's future, Tocqueville saw that the "empire of democracy" was irresistible—even in aristocratic societies such as his own.

And yet republican America was no more the end of history in the mid nineteenth century than Western democracy was after the Cold War. Liberal democracy as we understand it today in fact only properly took root across the Western world in the early years of the new century. It grew from the same bloodied soil of war, revolution, and economic crisis as its principal competitor ideologies of fascism on the right and communism on the left. The term itself had relatively little traction in America until President Woodrow Wilson roused the nation to war in its name: to "make the world safe for democracy" (he meant safe for America) in 1917. And it took the experience of yet more illiberal regimes and failed democracies—by 1941, there were just eleven democracies left amidst the carnage of the Second World War—before the commitment to combining liberal values and the institutions of democratic equality was reaffirmed amid the "general political fatigue" of the postwar moment.[5]

A more consistent set of liberal democratic political institutions locked into place across the Western countries after 1945, binding them more

3

closely together as it did so. These same countries exceeded even their prewar trajectory of industrialization and they now bureaucratized as well. The resulting era of prosperity—"the Golden Age," *les trente glorieuses,* the *wirtschaftswunder,* the *miracolo economico*: most countries had a term for it—was always more golden for some than it was for others. It also unfolded in the shadow of the struggle between capitalism and the communist world: indeed, it was significantly shaped by that struggle. But it nonetheless provided an unprecedented degree of political stability and economic progress that left its mark in "the institutions and the manners," as Tocqueville put it, of the Western nations. The gap between rich and poor narrowed and for many there was a sense that the Western world's political compass was pointing in the right direction. People felt they knew where they stood and that they had a good chance of getting to where they wanted to be.

This is not at all what many now think of when they think about democracy today. For all its achievements, the modern democratic state has been hollowed out. The markets upon which the delivery of political outcomes has come to rely are volatile and encourage short-term thinking. Today's citizens are garlanded with an expanded panoply of political rights, yet they routinely lack the social protections once taken for granted by their elders. The people grow resentful of the political elite's detachment, while the public domain through which democratic voice is exercised has been parceled out to the highest bidder. A thinly scraped notion of liberty has gained the upper hand over equality. Something has changed, in short, and in the turmoil of the present it may well be changing again.

It is imperative we now try to understand the full chain of events by which our modern democracy has changed. It is of course a difficult thing to capture something like democracy in the process of transforming itself, and that much harder when we cannot meter history by the rhythm of the drums of war alone. The changes I seek to address in this book are not best measured by the number of bodies on the ground. They provide us, rather, with a different kind of drama: one forged through institutional reconfigurations, political epiphanies, and societal changes of heart. One is dealing primarily with the cold, deep seepage of ideas as they form about, and take a hold of, the present. Such changes, too, have the potential to split history apart: and, as it happens, they do leave their share of victims on the ground.

The earlier part of the twentieth century was defined by liberal democracy's struggle against its rival ideologies of fascism on the right and communism on the left: to the point of hot and cold wars alike. Tocqueville's "empire" of democracy, by which he meant its indisputable influence as an ideal, largely won those battles in the way that Western society was reassembled after the Second World War.[6] The defining issue of our own era has therefore been something else entirely: more a full-throated struggle *over* democracy itself, a struggle to reconcile democratic equality with liberal freedom in an age of capitalist globalization. To tell this story properly we must discard the conventional narrative frame of the twentieth century: for its threads weave most meaningfully together not in 1945, nor even in 1989, but in the early 1970s, the very point at which fascism and communism, as state forms, also finally began to yield their grip.[7] It is there that the changes giving shape to the political order we have all been living through first set in.

In the half-decade between 1968 and 1974 an entire era—the postwar era—came to an end and something else began: our present age. There was no single year of upheaval, though 1971, for reasons that will become clear, cusps this change. There was no singular break, either, between some uniformly experienced before and after. But amid a perfect storm of crises that befell both East and West alike, the very structure of democracy that had sustained the Western nations through the first half of the twentieth century appeared suddenly to have run its course. That wider constellation of crises included the most dramatic transformation of the world economy since the Great Depression, and a fracturing of territorial sovereignty which, for the best part of two centuries, had underpinned national and international politics alike. It included the upheaval of rapidly modernizing societies at home, whose citizens suddenly demanded of their governments what their governments could not provide. The response to these crises in the East, we know well, was more repression at home and more credit from abroad to shore up their failing regimes: a path that ultimately led to the collapse of the entire communist system. But what of the response in the West? As historians are beginning to document, something more radical happened: the West underwent "regime change."[8]

From around 1971, on the back of the social upheavals of the late 1960s, with the Nixon administration in America at its most reckless and radical groups rising across Europe; with people marching on the streets and a crisis in the international economy, the postwar consensus unraveled and the institutional arrangements of the liberal democratic order began to be reconfigured. As Part I of this book seeks to show, this played out in various ways. New class arrangements took shape as national elites transnationalized and the working class disaggregated. The international politics of the Cold War changed too, in the aftermath of Vietnam and détente, as the transatlantic alliance was rebuilt around the forces of globalization. States sought new structures of legitimacy, executive authority was augmented and individualism was encouraged as a counterweight to the decline in more social forms of citizenship. Democracy began to pivot on its axis. Freedom came to be prioritized over equality and politicians felt their way toward a system of market-oriented governance that was ever-more removed from the whims of the electorate—an undoubted advantage to governments struggling to hold on to power, but one which came at the later price of denying those same states the benefits of more active public support.

This new era of liberal governance saw a fourth pillar of political authority join the old tripartite structure of democratic rule as the institutions of the market took up their place alongside parliaments, the executive branch, and the judiciary. As the postwar institutions of democracy were challenged, new ones were found to replace them, and new—often more conservative—norms came to transform the way that they worked. Actually existing democracy was overhauled; and long before the decade was out the reinvention of the West was underway. Critically, the fall of communism between 1989 and 1991 represented a denouement to this process, rather than the beginning it is usually taken for; the now liberated countries of the East being swept up into the ongoing history of liberal reinvention in the West. Fatefully, it also provided Western political liberalism with an opportunity not only to overlook the difficulties already apparent in the new liberal democratic consensus, but in many ways to intensify their effect.

Part II of the book traces these developments until the end of the millennium, as the Western democracies sought to reboot something of the economic prosperity they had become accustomed to in the earlier postwar era. These were the years of the Clinton boom and the gradual recovery of economic dynamism in Europe. They were the heyday of economic globalization and the weightless consumerism it afforded the Western middle classes in particular. The implications of this proved significant in the forging of at least three basic elements of the post–Cold War order: first, regarding the manner in which the world economy was "constructed" (primarily around international finance), the variant of financialized globalization it led to, and the leverage that this afforded markets over states; secondly, regarding the timing and significance of the Cold War's end, the lessons of which pushed the decade's critical actors, social democrats, into a generational turn toward these newly liberalized markets as a less costly tool of distributional fairness; and thirdly, in terms of the very real social tensions that reappeared across the Western democracies during the immediate post–Cold War years.

With the world seeming to pick up speed all around, much of this went unnoticed—or at least it was not acted upon—at the time. For this was when the two Germanies were learning how to live as one nation again, and when the European Union was born at Maastricht. It was when the twentieth century seemed to deliver on so many of its technological promises—home computing and the Internet, GM food and cable television—and when it was possible to look to the world at large and, for the first time in many people's memory, not need to interpret events in terms of the struggle between communism and capitalism. It was the self-proclaimed era of being "post-" everything. And yet there was much that persisted too. Yugoslavia broke apart amid the violence in Bosnia; Eastern Europe struggled under the burden of its rapid conversion to a capitalist economy. International law took great strides forward but was written mostly by—and for—the powerful. Meanwhile, an oversized and underregulated financial market thrived beyond the oversight of national states, as did the black market and the oligarchs who profited from this.

In Part III, the book follows the story of the twin shocks that did more than anything else to define the political tenor of the new millennium. In the process they began to undermine the post-70s model of political order in the West, along with the democratic peace its citizens had come to believe was now their rightful inheritance. Both appeared in the form of a deus ex machina at first; but each was in truth exacerbated by the developments of previous decades. The first blow was struck by the events of 9/11 and, more significantly still, by the way that the United States in particular responded to this. Long-cherished civil liberties were struck down and multiculturalism began to fray. Public spaces were boarded up. The backlash of the "war on terror" profoundly shaped political developments in Europe too, though some countries held out better than others. Above all, these years began to pose the question of a failing international order, as it was conceived at the end of the Cold War. Accustomed to projecting itself outward, the West was now subject to forces determined to break back in.

The massive costs of running the war on terror, in conjunction with the seemingly inexorable turn to a non-state-based credit rather than a savings-based economy, were among the factors that led to the second major challenge of the new millennium: the financial crisis, and its long corrosive aftermath of the Great Recession. Society was now riven by a biting austerity on the one hand and an anti-immigrant backlash on the other. Governments used up what remaining reserves of popular trust they had in fighting the fires of a seemingly unquenchable crisis. Fatefully, this was also the moment when Europe was confronted by the largest refugee influx since the Second World War (many of them fleeing the havoc unleashed by the global war on terror). The social tensions sparked by some of these developments began to raise the specter of more desperate solutions drawn from the past.

Alarmed by such developments, one ninety-year-old survivor of the Warsaw ghetto took a plea of remembrance to the international press. Fear and lies are terrible things, he warned: "do not ever imagine that your world cannot collapse, as ours did."[9] Was anyone listening? In Europe, the solidarity that had underpinned the European Union's expansion for half a century entered its gravest crisis yet. In the US, the political atmosphere grew more, not less, tense under the nation's first black president. With public trust in the workings of Congress at its lowest ebb, and popular discontents soaring amid an antiliberal surge, the conditions favored an outsider in the presidential elections of 2016. What that outsider might then do only time, and power, would tell.

When a great many changes are upon us it is easy to lose one's bearings. Dramatic events prove hard to grasp during the onslaught and unthinkingly we may accede to things for which the history books will later rightly ask of us: why? My aim in treating the history of democracy in this book as something that is constantly made and remade, is in part to provide clarity over how our values and our institutions interact. It is not to deny the considerable divergence that exists between national histories—readers should in fact come away with a far better sense of how different societies have variously responded to the overarching challenges of the time. Nor is it to reify the notion of "the West," which like other catchall geographical descriptors ("Europe" or "the American century," say) is a partial and a vested claim before it is a settled fact. That the West is the relevant locus for this particular history of democracy is less because of its presumed certainties than it is for the manner of its constant reinvention.[10]

But by suggesting that a discrete era in the history of democracy opens in the economic and political upheavals of the 1970s, and that it ends in the current succession of crises across the West, I do want to suggest that there are common threads binding the Western experience together during these years, and that the relationship between liberalism, capitalism, and democracy stands at the forefront of how we are to understand this historically. These are the pillars that sustain our modern age. They were each differently aligned around the beginning of the last third of the twentieth century, and they are each shifting in relation to one another again today. Of course, all periodizations are historical constructions: wittingly or not they reproduce the politics and the perspective of those who define them.

My aim in opening this history in the early 1970s, therefore, is twofold. Most simply I seek to write against the grain of an historiography of democratic progressivism: above all the idea that democracy is an accumulation of improvements locked in after the war, that it is always heading forward in just the right way. But I also seek to open up space: for this is not a story we can tell from within the confines of any one nation alone, nor, in modern times, can we limit our narrative to just the *scale* of the nation state itself. What emerges is thus a resolutely transnational history as well. And what it attempts to capture, by breaking out of the national frame, is both the wider structure of the forces pressing in upon democracy today, and the uneven and combined effects of the various efforts to address this. The real significance of the early 1970s as a turning point emerges against this fuller backdrop.

In what follows I have not set out to offer a comprehensive history of the past few decades in the West, if such a thing is even possible. My account here necessarily focuses on some countries and certain developments more than others, and some of the elements may strike the reader as surprising (although anything else would be to assume we know this past simply because we lived through it). But to offer no explanatory "vision" at all is to consign the recent past to a succession of "isms" with little sense of intellectual priority, and that is perhaps as much a part of our present dilemma as anything else. I began writing this book in 2011, when it became clear to me that there was a real need for, and the time also seemed right to attempt, a narrative overview of the past few decades. For all that I am wary of the pitfalls, nothing that has happened since then has led me to change my mind. I am if anything more strongly of the belief that until we undertake this task we will not properly be able to address the welter of challenges that confront us once again today.

Those challenges ought not to be taken lightly. Fewer Western citizens

vote now than they did in the past, yet more believe the present generation of politicians is failing miserably at their task. We bemoan a lack
of public trust and declining sense of community, and we demand our
rights be respected. Yet few of us have the time to fulfill our obligations
to others. The fault line between left and right has for some time been
breaking up in favor of new divides: between the old (with their expensive pension plans) and the young (who are paying disproportionately
more for them); between populists and the "elite"; migrants and their
host countries, rich and poor. Class remains, but its geography, as with
that of so much else, is changing. For most of us, it is no longer seen as
a contradiction in terms to talk of public services being privately provided.
Europeans take it for granted that their courts of law and national banks
are not their nations' respective institutions of last resort. For Americans
it has become normal to pay both less in taxes and substantially more
on insurance premiums. And yet so ceaselessly do we experience these
changes that it proves hard to mark off quite when "then" was different
to "now."

My hope is that the narrative that follows will go some way to explaining what is new and what is old in the challenges before us. The last
time Western society was as unequal as now was during the interwar years,
when the idea of parliamentarianism was jettisoned in Europe in favor of
governments prepared to "do" something about the seemingly endless
succession of crises that erupted during that period. Today, as they look
to Greece, commentators are inclined to speak not of the "birthplace of
democracy" but of the "crisis of democracy." What is more they fear, and
not without reason, that the Greek crisis is in some sense also their own.

When nationalists marched in Hungary in 2015, and Viktor Orbán,
the Hungarian prime minister, spoke that summer of the threat posed
by illegal immigrants, his speech itself goose-stepped along, in the words
of one social media wag, to the theme of "fear, hate, fear, hate, fear, fear,
fear." Orbán's speech was an authoritarian populist's to make: the government was "to adopt stricter regulations . . . allowing us to detain
people who have illegally crossed Hungarian borders, and to deport them
within the shortest possible time," he said, as he pointed to a sham con-
sultation that confirmed this as the "people's will." But it was democratic
Europe's own handling of an unfolding refugee crisis, which had in those
weeks packed full the grand train station in Budapest with a mass of
bodies and their carted possessions: and *this* provided him with the tools.[11]
These are lessons that America under Donald Trump is now learning the
hard way as well.

Yet there are also signs of democratic renewal. Political parties are having more earnest discussions about their structure and purpose than in a generation. MeToo and BlackLivesMatter are just two of many movements putting injustice back at the heart of public debate. Citizens are stirring. Quite what form of democracy will emerge through the upheavals of our own time, what new answers will be found to the old and inescapable question—"how are we best to govern ourselves?"— remains to be seen. What is certain is that we are much more likely to be satisfied rather than terrified by the answers we give to that question when we properly understand the nature of the era we have been living through. If we are willing to revisit the recent past in this more critical light, then Tocqueville's penetrating description of the progress of democracy remains as pertinent today as ever before. It explains why the "empire of democracy" is still being built and why it can still go very different ways, some of which may be more appealing to us than others.

This book—a history of the political life of the Western democracies— is the first full account of the way it has been going for most of the past half-century. It places the actions of politicians squarely alongside the background thrum of ideas and the struggle over values and institutions their actions gave rise to. But equally it foregrounds the international character of the forces they were responding to. Perhaps we will one day come to think of this era—our own—as one in which the wisdom of Prometheus was traded for the rewards of a Leviathan unbound. We must in any case come to some sort of reckoning with just how it was that the basic virtues we impute to democracy could change so dramatically, and could do so in the absence of war or revolution. The struggle between equality and liberty, and the form of democracy that struggle has bequeathed us, defines the latter part of the past century and the millennium as we have experienced it to date. This book is the story of how the last great struggle of the twentieth century and the first great struggle of the twenty-first unfolded. It is a struggle that gives shape to the entire era we have just been living through.

Prologue:
Two Helicopters

"I THINK OF what happened to Greece and Rome," said President Richard Nixon in the summer of 1971. "What is left," he mused: "—only the pillars."[1] Three years later, in 1974, West Germany's Willy Brandt was every bit as despondent: "Western Europe has only twenty or thirty more years of democracy left in it," he declared, shortly before his own departure from power. "[A]fter that it will slide, engineless and rudderless, under the surrounding sea of dictatorship, and whether the dictator comes from a politburo or a junta will not make that much difference."[2] In Britain, that same summer, the former colonel and minister of disarmament Lord Chalfont took his concerns about a society in free-fall to the opinion pages of *The Times*. "Could Britain be heading for a military takeover?" he speculated, as he contemplated "the massive power and often ruthless action of the great industrial trades unions."[3]

Such fears proved, of course, to be unfounded: in Europe, it was the authoritarian regimes of Portugal, Spain, and Greece that were soon brought under democracy's wing and the Soviet bloc that began its terminal decline. But we should not underestimate the extent to which, from the late 1960s and into the early 1970s, a genuine and deeply felt concern for the future of society pervaded the Western democracies. For the first time since the height of the Second World War, the fate of the West appeared in doubt. America was mired in Vietnam, the USSR had overtaken it in the missile race, and the NATO alliance was strained. New anxieties about the planet's finite resources were gnawing away at the postwar model of economic growth and the nonaligned countries were snapping at Western heels.[4]

The greater problems, however, came from within.

★

At around midday on May 29, 1968, the streets of Paris packed with students waving banners and millions of workers out on strike in support, the towering figure of postwar French politics President Charles de Gaulle boarded a helicopter at Issy in the western suburbs of Paris and vanished into the fog. When de Gaulle did not arrive at his family home of La Boisserie later that day, as the prime minister had been informed, rumors began circulating within the government that perhaps the aging general was abdicating: "*De Gaulle, au musée!*" some of the banners on the streets had been demanding (De Gaulle to the Museum!). "*Adieu de Gaulle.*" But de Gaulle was not abdicating. Much more dramatically, he had flown by helicopter to the French garrison at Baden-Baden to consult with the commander of French forces in Germany, General Jacques Massu, a loyal member of the French old guard. Quite why remains shrouded in mystery: was it, as de Gaulle himself later declared, a tactical ploy intended to "plunge the French people, including the government, into doubt and anxiety . . . in order to regain control of the situation" in Paris?[5]

Or was it that he planned to abandon the country and to stay in Germany, or even, as some have suggested, that he was secretly reaching out to the Soviets, the better to restrain the Confédération générale du travail (CGT) and the French Communist Party he believed to be or-chestrating the protests at home? Certainly de Gaulle was worried that the fate of the Fifth Republic—*his* Republic—was at stake in the up-heavals that were rocking the country. But de Gaulle's actual Soviet policy sought openly to reconstruct the Cold War balance of power over Germany between his own nuclear France and the USSR, not to do deals in the dark between them. De Gaulle was as vocal as any foreign leader later that summer when, on Moscow's orders, the tanks rolled into Czechoslovakia and the Prague Spring was brutally crushed.[6]

Most likely, de Gaulle was simply maneuvering to buy himself a little time. Prior to his departure the government had failed to contain the greatest popular upheavals the country had seen since the war, and it was deeply split over how to respond. Prime Minister Georges Pompidou's strategy had been to offer the workers real concessions, in the hope of prising their support away from the students. But this looked to have failed when the workers themselves rejected the terms that the govern-ment had agreed with the CGT, despite the offer of a 10 percent rise in the basic wage. De Gaulle's own preferred strategy of offering the people a referendum—while it spoke the right language of "participation"—was largely ignored.

Meanwhile a battle for the streets of Paris raged on outside. With students building barricades and police smashing them down, de Gaulle spent several tense days prior to his dramatic flight holed up in the Élysée, where his closest adviser, Jacques Foccart, feared for the general's security (at one point he heard rumors that explosives were being stockpiled in the Sorbonne). Sensing things moving their way, the CGT called for a major protest on May 29. With even an establishment politician like François Mitterrand now going on record to say he was ready to form a provisional government, de Gaulle had decided enough was enough. "There is no point attacking an empty palace," he declared that morning as he made his plans to depart.[7]

Whatever the truth of those few hours, de Gaulle's secret flight from France was in many ways illustrative of what was, by now, the nub of a new and troubling problem that confronted the Western democracies: the yawning gap that had opened up between states, as they had been institutionalized after the war, and the people as they had become beneath its protective yet stifling wing. The staunchly paternalistic de Gaulle and the Paris of the sixties cultural explosion were, if anything, the very exemplification of this. Yet on his return to Paris from Baden-Baden the following day, on May 30, it looked at first as though de Gaulle had circumvented the problem, if only through the sheer calculated drama of his actions. After first meeting with a colossally aggravated Pompidou, de Gaulle acceded to his Prime Minister's insistence that he now dissolve parliament and call a snap election. Then, in the afternoon, he took to the radio to announce that he was postponing his own unpopular proposal of a referendum.

"In the last twenty-four hours I considered all eventualities without exception," de Gaulle told the French people. Against the protesters who had brought Paris to a standstill that May, he appealed to his own supporters to take to the streets, in a march that had been planned to show support for the old regime. De Gaulle used his airtime to blame the entire affair on the CGT, who had in truth struggled to control events on the streets as much as he. The Gaullist march that afternoon was larger than any of the protests to date: perhaps as many as half a million strong. And in the elections which followed, the Gaullist party was returned to power with a resounding majority, now as the Union pour la défense de la République (UDR)—the central plank of the modern French mainstream right—with a new prime minister, Couve de Murville, to lead it.

Yet if de Gaulle won the battle of 1968, his forced resignation the following year confirmed that he had just as surely lost the wider war over the future of modern France. With de Gaulle having elected to see through his earlier proposal of a referendum on constitutional reform, the campaign quickly became, after the events of the previous year, a vote of confidence in the general himself. It left de Gaulle, who championed the losing side, with no choice but to resign once the results were in. The reforms, de Gaulle had claimed before the vote, would have completed his vision of creating a modern France—and perhaps in his own mind they would have done. But the people disagreed. They had other ideas as to what their country needed. And so, shortly after midnight on April 28, 1969—in stark contrast to the high drama of the year before—it was announced that de Gaulle would be resigning the presidency of the republic, effective at midday. The general had in fact already packed his bags some days before.[8]

"General de Gaulle? He no longer exists," Georges Pompidou had commented at the height of the crisis of '68.[9] He was right in more ways than one. When de Gaulle died, in November 1970, it was not just his vision for a modern France, or indeed for Europe, that was buried with him near the family home in Colombey; something of the tenor of the postwar era, its certainties as well as its constraints, was interred with him. The juddering reality of that was also something that Pompidou, who now replaced de Gaulle as president, was himself soon to experience at first hand. Under his leadership, France recovered from the standstill of the May events, only to succumb to the more deeply seated economic malaise that was by then afflicting the democracies at large. *Le général de Gaulle est mort; la France est veuve*, declared Pompidou when he heard of the old man's death (General de Gaulle is dead; France is a widow). Again, Pompidou was right: but France was also now a widow looking forward to a whole new era in life.

★

Across the Atlantic, and under very different circumstances, the political career of a dashing young forty-something, Pierre Trudeau, was at this moment just getting going. Where the previous spring had seen the aging de Gaulle temporarily abandon the country, it had also seen 48-year-old Pierre Trudeau become the first Canadian prime minister actually to have been born in the twentieth century. The old were exiting the stage and the young pushing forward to take their place; or so it seemed. As befits the different generations they represented, not to mention their contrasting political styles, the two leaders could not have been more different. Where de Gaulle, the former soldier, was aloof and awkward even, Trudeau was the embodiment of style; a man who knew, as one biographer put it, that what the modern crowd wanted was "the expert jackknife into a pool, beautiful and brilliant young people, and stunning women in miniskirts surrounding him."[10]

As even the British *Spectator* remarked of Trudeau's arrival in 1968, it looked as if he would "catapult the country into the brilliant sunshine of the late twentieth century from the stagnant swamp of traditionalism and mediocrity in which Canadian politics had been bogged down for years." If that was stirring praise from the British establishment, it was a reminder too that Trudeau's politics were both pragmatic and staunchly postideological. He was elected because of a certain aura and a definite style; neither the first nor the last politician to win power on the basis of promises of "change," but one who perfectly embodied the character of the moment for it. Snappily dressed in sandals and open shirts, a straight-talker with a sparkling turn of phrase, Trudeau had made his name as a reformer when he rewrote Canada's criminal code as justice minister (on the matter of sexual politics, "the state has no business in the bedrooms of the nation," as he famously put it). Even more so than Kennedy, the media adored him.[11] Like moths to a flame, he attracted intellectuals and celebrities throughout his time in office.

But in Canada too, it did not take long for the euphoria of 1968 to blow itself out. Within just a few months of taking office, Trudeau found that his ambitions for a modern, open style of politics, ideas forged as a freewheeling young intellectual, did not sit easily amid the sheer grasping unavoidability of the upheavals of the time.[12] As the sixties turned into the seventies, his more pragmatic instincts took over and it was a hardened Trudeau that turned out to meet Canada's first major crisis of the era, in October 1970, when members of the separatist group the Front de libération du Québec kidnapped the British trade commissioner, Richard Cross. In doing so they inaugurated what would come to be known as the October Crisis. "We have had enough of promises of work and prosperity," their manifesto declared, when it was read out on national radio, "when in fact we will always be the diligent servants and boot-lickers of the big shots . . . we will be slaves until Quebecers, all of us, have used every means, including dynamite and guns, to drive out these big bosses of the economy and of politics . . ."[13]

Five days later and angered by the lack of official response thus far, FLQ members went further and took another hostage: this time a sitting cabinet minister named Pierre Laporte. Trudeau now had no choice but to intervene. But how far was he prepared to go, an interviewer for CBC asked him? "Just watch me!" Trudeau famously shot back from the top of Parliament Hill. First, he invoked the War Measures Act for the first time in a generation. Then he rounded up several hundred individuals with the remotest of links to the revolutionary group. Lester Pearson, the former prime minister, had been right: Trudeau had "ice water" in his veins after all.[14] But so too did the FLQ, and the strangled body of Pierre Laporte was the price paid for the two sides' intransigence. In Canada as much as in France, the vivid lights of the late 1960s were receding as a more somber political mood settled across the West.

South of the border, in the United States, the optimism of the earlier age had ended, if anything, a year or two earlier. Trudeau's election had been front-page news, when it was reported alongside coverage of the riots that erupted after Martin Luther King's assassination. While Canadians were basking in "Trudeaumania," in the afterglow of the late-sixties' euphoria, the election of Richard Nixon at the end of 1968 marked the ascendancy, by contrast, of "Nixonland": a relief to the establishment, which was roundly shaken by the events of that year, but an awakening, as if to a desperate and ringing hangover, for those who had spent much of it parading on the streets.[15] Over the next few years the teach-ins and occupations of '68 gave way to edgier protests against the Vietnam War, civil rights gave way to black power, and the hopes that a nation might be healed by the reform program of the Great Society turned to a racially tinged despair that American society would always be greater for some of its citizens than for others.

Over the next few years the national distemper descended only further. By the time Nixon's first term in office was drawing to a close, the public mood was fast approaching a point of crisis. In the spring of 1971, the streets of Washington were engulfed by more than half a million people, marching in protest at the Vietnam War. The event was the culmination of two weeks of rolling protests: an ironically named "May Day" action that antiwar activists hoped might temporarily "shut down" the government. Things had gone smoothly until, as the marchers dispersed, dissident groups made to assault government buildings where they confronted National Guard units called in to defend them. Amid the pandemonium that ensued, anyone seen to be loitering was liable to be arrested, leading many to keep wildly "running through the streets," as one participant recalled. Upward of ten thousand were taken into custody: so many that they needed to be interned at the nearby Redskins practice field.[16]

It was no small reminder of the extent to which the people and the people's authorities were at odds with one another at this, the very height of the Cold War, that the director of the CIA, Richard Helms (a man later immortalized as "the gentlemanly planner of assassinations"), observed all this and fumed.[17] Helms had headed up the nation's intelligence agency since 1962 but his office had become inundated with casework concerning not foreign military plots but a growing *civil* dissent at home (although the "European youth movement" was also adding to his workload). Just days before the Washington protests the US Supreme Court had voted to continue the controversial program of busing black students to mixed race public schools in order to overcome segregation in schools.

As was almost inevitable in these years, it sparked its own counter-reaction—in this case of white, middle-class resentment at the intrusion of the state into what many considered a matter of personal choice—and precipitated in turn yet another round of protests. Just two months before that, the Weather Underground, a radical offshoot of the Students for a Democratic Society (SDS) whose antiwar platform was the most public strand of a wider underground revolutionism, had exploded a bomb in the Capitol building causing substantial physical damage. No fatalities were recorded, except perhaps—as the *Washington Post* speculated—the cherished sixties ideal of nonviolent protest itself.[18] But then there were new ways of protesting as well.

One week later—at the precise moment Joe Frazier squared up to Muhammad Ali in the "Fight of the Century" at Madison Square Garden—a group of eight civilians, the self-appointed Citizens' Commission to Investigate the FBI, broke into the Bureau's Pennsylvania headquarters and made off with more than a thousand documents: the security guards' attention remained glued to their radio sets throughout. The activists, in a reminder that the politics of WikiLeaks has deeper roots than we tend to recall, immediately mailed their trove to various newspapers for publication. With its revelations of FBI Director J. Edgar Hoover's long-running COINTELPRO program, which aimed to spy on and disrupt domestic political organizations, it was a shocking exposé of the extent to which the American state had for some time now distrusted some of its own citizens.

The more novel and the more explosive problem, however, was the extent to which citizens any longer trusted the state. This was brought home in September, when prisoners at the Attica Correctional Facility in upstate New York took over the entire prison. The uprising had begun almost by chance, when a panicked scuffle in a corridor led a few prisoners, without having planned what they were doing, to seize a section of the prison. After years of routinely inhumane treatment—prisoners were granted only one sheet of toilet paper and were served just 63 cents worth of food each per day—they took some of their former captors hostage in the process.[19] Security breached, the revolt soon spread, as dozens and then hundreds of prisoners, some grabbing baseball bats and others donning makeshift *kaffiyehs*, took over the central hub of the prison complex and one of the exercise yards.

Given the scale of the uprising and the shockwaves it sent through the establishment, given perhaps above all the TV crews who pitched their cameras at the prison gates to broadcast the drama to households across America, the odds of the standoff being peacefully resolved, "of either side listening," were indeed "slim," as Lewis Smith, a civil rights lawyer sent in as a neutral observer, remarked upon his arrival. When a prison guard who had been beaten to a bloody pulp in the initial outbreak subsequently died of his injuries the odds lengthened further still. On September 13, Governor Nelson Rockefeller, whom the prisoners had hoped to negotiate with, turned the riot into a massacre when he sent in heavily armed state troopers with orders to "retake" the prison.[20]

In the hours that followed, and with cameras cordoned off at a safe distance outside, state troopers and reservists surged into the yard, some carrying their own personal sidearm with bullets designed to inflict maximum injury upon impact. Once inside they went on a killing spree. Prisoners were made to strip naked and crawl across the wet yard now strewn with bodies and glass. Thirty-nine people, including ten hostages, were killed as a result of state trooper gunfire (the killing of the hostages was initially and cynically blamed on the hostages themselves). The prison was soon retaken but the violence and recriminations continued behind the carefully resealed prison walls for weeks. It was "the bloodiest one-day encounter between Americans since the civil war," reported the McKay Commission, charged with looking into the events the following year.

But the prisoners' complaints, as with their earlier demands for fairer living standards, were buried out of sight. The official story—the one that Governor Nelson Rockefeller, his eye on a presidential run, was at pains to ensure the media reported—was that justice had been done and law and order restored. Attica was duly reported as a case closed: a violent bookend to the era of civil rights before it. But despite the media blackout of the riot's bloody denouement, the sense of anger and frustration that sparked it off had long since seeped outside the prison walls and into the rest of society.[21] As it did so, it shone a glancing light not just onto American society but onto the simmering discontent afflicting Western liberal democracy at large.

★

Not only in America but in Europe too the mass protests and marches that had begun in the civil rights activism of the previous decade continued in the early 1970s, but they were joined now, if their voices were not at times drowned out, by a growing cacophony of working- and middle-class protest focused on the rising cost of living. In Australia, the US embassy reported "a pervasive sense of gloom," as the country headed toward recession; in Denmark in 1973, concerns over rising prices saw more than a third of the national vote go to parties outside the political mainstream.[22] The Danes were concerned about rising inflation in neighboring Germany; the Germans for their part were worried about a possible communist takeover in Italy. That same year, in Britain, 1.6 million people took to the streets to protest at an escalating inflationary crisis that was dragging the country to its knees. As the country turned the corner of that year and came out haltingly into the half-light (it shone no brighter) of 1974 the British government was still sufficiently panicked to introduce a three-day working week to placate the trade unions. When that failed to calm things, the Heath government was forced to call an election.

Writing from London in March of that year, the *New York Times*' star political reporter James "Scotty" Reston—who had, by virtue of his profession, been witness to much of this change—sat down at his desk to write about what he now believed was a "crisis of democracy" gripping the Western world. Reston didn't buy the idea that the lackluster turnout at the first of two national elections in Britain that year was simply a consequence of the "cost of living" crisis.[23] For Reston it was the product of a wider social and political distemper. Governments were elected on boldly worded platforms. But their policies invariably collapsed within a few months, leaving them for the remainder of their time in office scrambling to find workable solutions to increasingly intractable problems. The Tories decried Europe, only then to lead Britain into it; Labour sought to restore full employment, only to embrace the market.

As Reston saw it, the British public was heaping its opprobrium not on one or other of the major political parties but on Britain's system of government itself.

Prior to the election, the Conservative leader Edward (Ted) Heath had famously asked the voters "Who governs Britain?" It was a "silly question," Reston mused, and in awarding none of the parties a workable majority the public had responded with a silly answer: "nobody." By the time the election was rerun, later in the year, neither voters nor politicians seemed to have the stamina for it any more (the Liberals went to the polls with the distinctly uninspiring slogan: "One more heave!").[24] So far as Scotty Reston was concerned, however, this quintessentially British saga painted not merely a dismal picture of democracy in Britain, it was a picture common to other countries too: Canada, West Germany, Israel, and Italy all sprang to his mind as suffering from a similar democratic malaise. "The world is now being run by Communist governments that rule by fear and force and by non-Communist governments that do not have the confidence of the majority of their people," Reston concluded.[25]

This was a criticism he directed most strongly at the leader of the free world itself. Writing the year before, with the war in Vietnam at the forefront of his mind, Reston had bemoaned what he called "a sharp decline in respect for authority in the United States . . . a decline in respect not only for the civil authority of government but also for the moral authority of the schools, the universities, the press, the church and even the family." Reston was writing these words the day after Lyndon Johnson's funeral, and he took the opportunity to vent at the state of American government, then nearing the end of the most controversial presidency in half a century. It may have been a political miracle that "Richard Nixon, with all his troubles and a Democratic party in control of Congress, somehow keeps going without any visible means of political support," he said. But that didn't change the underlying problem: "The political 'decline of the West' is no longer a subject for theoretical debate, but an ominous reality," he concluded.[26]

Reston was half-right about this: for it was a transformation not a decline of the West that was underway, and Nixon's exit was a telling case in point. In his efforts to secure reelection in 1972 Nixon had first ordered and then orchestrated a cover-up of a break-in at the Democratic National Committee headquarters in the Watergate complex of Washington, DC. While the public were more concerned about inflation and the hundreds of Americans dying every week in Vietnam, the president had managed to keep a lid on the scandal that was slowly developing.

But the Senate committee established to investigate the attempted cover-up of the burglary was closing in on the president. In October 1973, in a last-ditch effort to avoid special prosecutor Archibald Cox coming into possession of a set of White House tapes (which would surely reveal his guilt) Nixon fired Cox, sparking off a meltdown within his administration.

"You will be returning to an environment of major national crisis," Nixon's chief of staff, Alexander Haig, warned Nixon's Secretary of State Henry Kissinger who was overseas.[27] That was somewhat underestimating the extent to which the public had by now turned against the president. Nixon's documentable crime was to have hindered the judicial investigation into links between his reelection committee and the documents stolen from Watergate. His greater crime was to have broken the bonds of political integrity. As state representative and civil rights activist Julian Bond lamented in public: "The prisons of Georgia are full of people who stole $5 or $10, and [yet] this man tried to steal the Constitution of the United States."[28] With the net drawing in, and amid a near unprecedented wave of public disillusionment and anger at the state of the political class, Nixon was forced to resign.

On the day of his resignation, the formalities over and his last address given to the staff inside, the president ambled across the South Lawn of the White House, past the magnolia tree planted by Andrew Jackson, and toward the waiting presidential helicopter, *Marine One*. Nixon looked strangely relieved, if worn out: like the battery in his watch, which he later recalled had run out just that morning.[29] As he climbed up into the helicopter after Mrs. Nixon, he turned suddenly and, unsure of what to do, for one last time raised his hands in a rendition of his now infamous "V for victory" sign. Then the helicopter took off into skies that brightened just briefly. Rome had not fallen, but it had been forced to rethink its ways; the rethinking in fact had just begun. For while Watergate was over, and the president was gone, the wider political crisis was still in full flow.

★

By 1974 America was facing problems ranging from public concerns over its (actually modest) energy dependency on external producers, to international currency instability and ever-more vocal transnational protest movements. These were not all Nixon's doing, far from it. But the manner of Nixon's departure had somehow tied them all together. Where was the nation to go from here? Most immediately, Nixon was replaced by his vice president, Gerald Ford: a man who for being twice unelected, first after acceding to the vice-presidency when Spiro Agnew resigned and now to the presidency itself, hardly inspired a great deal of confidence. And as with Pompidou in France, Ford would confront such a deluge of changes during his five years in office that his entire presidency ended up submerged beneath the transformations. The Western democracies had converged around a similar set of achievements since the Second World War; now it was becoming apparent that they also shared a similar set of vulnerabilities. James Reston was not alone in noticing these.[30]

In the half decade from Charles de Gaulle's temporary departure by helicopter in 1968 to Richard Nixon's rather more permanent adieu aboard *Marine One* in 1974, a change in direction was imparted to the Western democracies: not overtly, but fundamentally. Simply stated it was the felt drama of these years that provided the necessary momentum for one model of political order in the West to be rejected in the course of the 1970s and a new one called up to replace it. We cannot, however, make sense of how—and with what consequences for our own times— governments at the time responded to this cascade of crises until we first grasp the extent to which the upheavals of the early 1970s so dramatically ruptured the postwar political framework.

PART I
Democracy Unbound (1971–)

I

The Unraveling

T HE HISTORY OF the postwar era is usually narrated as a story of economic growth; but equally it is a story of the struggle to build a more robust democratic order on the ashes of the furnace of war. In fact it is the story of a number of quite different ways of doing this. For Alva and Gunnar Myrdal, as they began to think about this task in Sweden, in 1941, surrounded by the occupied countries, there was hope to be found in looking across the Atlantic to America. Their bestselling book, *Kontakt med Amerika* (*Contact with America*) struck a chord with their fellow Swedes and soon became a hit among the resistance in neighboring Norway; it would go on to influence reformers elsewhere across the continent as well. The Myrdals then moved to America, taking with them the lessons of Scandinavia in turn.[1] Democracy did not simply return to the Western nations in 1945, in other words, along with the homeward bound troops. As these two influential Swedes had already recognized, it needed in many respects to be imagined anew.

In Europe, the task of rebuilding democracy was undertaken predominantly by the Christian and social democrats. In Italy, West Germany, Austria and the Benelux countries it was the "popular" and "people's" Christian democratic parties that led the way. Leaders like Italy's Alcide de Gasperi, a former resistance fighter and Vatican librarian, and West Germany's first chancellor, Konrad Adenauer, were distinctly ambivalent about the power of the national state and were staunch anticommunists to boot.[2] Social democrats by contrast, like the Myrdals or indeed Einar Gerhardsen, who towered (quite literally) over Norway for seventeen years, were much more comfortable integrating strands of socialist thinking into their welfarist policies: and they dominated Scandinavian politics for half a century by doing so.[3] They also spoke proudly of the nation as the *folkehemmet* (People's Home) in a way that placed the common man at the center of politics. Along with French gaullists and British liberals, though not always comfortably so, Christian and social democrats were the trailblazers in building a continental-scaled political architecture after the war.

Across the Atlantic democracy was likewise reimagined to meet the challenges of the postwar era and to ensure that something as crippling as the Great Depression never returned. American liberalism was not the same as European liberalism. Above all, it placed the demands of freedom before the claims of equality: a point reinforced in 1947–9 when Truman's "Freedom Train" toured all forty-eight states displaying the cherished documents of American liberty.[4] No less than in Europe, however, Republicans and Democrats converged after the war around one of the era's defining political ideas: "Not left, not right, but a vital center," as Arthur Schlesinger Jr. put it in 1948. This was a vision for democracy born of a new global outlook amidst the onrush of the Cold War: liberalism's defense of "the ultimate integrity of the individual," it now being argued, was the glue that could best hold capitalism and democracy together going forward.[5]

Yet if this was the basis of a new moderate center ground in America, it was moderate primarily so far as concerned the white majority population. For the main difference between Europe and America was to be found in terms of the latter's racial inheritance. Social mobility, at least for whites, was often greater in the United States even than it was in Europe.[6] But blacks experienced nothing of the sort, even after the civil rights movement. For all that Americans were more reluctant than Europeans to assign to national government the social obligations that national welfare demanded, the one place where the federal state was *not* to be prevented from performing a social function, it seemed, was in policing the bounds of the racial political order. As Cold War internationalism took shape, the social aspects of New Deal liberalism were likewise retrenched: worker democracy in particular making way for a more vociferous anticommunism.

Elsewhere the former settler colonies of Australia, New Zealand, and Canada blended basic elements of the European (or rather British) and American models. Australia inherited many of its legal principles from Great Britain, but its sheer size demanded a more federal model of government of the sort found in the United States. Welfare was more generous than in America, but labor relations were more constrained than in the United Kingdom. New Zealand too brought into its Westminster-derived parliamentary system something of the constitutionally enshrined value system of the American model, in its case setting fairness as the nation's guiding leitmotif in place of the American feeling for liberty. These societies too confronted the task of demobilizing after the war.[7] Canada meanwhile was defined by its two primary political cleavages, in the form of First Nation and linguistic minority counter-claims on the majoritarian political state.

Despite all their apparent differences, therefore, there were certain similarities common to each of the postwar democracies that with hindsight seem compelling. The reformism of the interwar period was frequently picked up again, carrying political rights and the promise of participation with it, particularly for women. Popular sovereignty was acknowledged too, although in light of the demagoguery and the total politics that derailed liberal parliaments during the interwar years, it was also now constrained.[8] Economic rights were formalized in the name of political stability. A new international architecture was created to further lock in these arrangements. Above all the postwar democracies made "democracy" itself a public concern in a way it never had been before: and defining what that meant (and who really was permitted to take part in it) largely set the parameters for how Western politics now developed.

Meanwhile material prosperity was prioritized through a renewed attention to managed economies and New Deal reformism. As economic growth returned to Europe it was spectacular but uneven. Given the extent of postwar destruction the bounce back was most dramatic at first in West Germany. But for Western Europe as a whole the growth rate was soon 4 percent a year for the period 1950 to 1970, compared to just 1.0 percent a year for the period 1913 to 1950. Even in the relatively sluggish Netherlands, the 3.5 percent average annual growth recorded between 1950 and 1975 was several times greater than it had been in the period 1910 to 1950.[9] The US too, which entered the post-45 era with an economy three times larger than any other also performed strongly to start with, for all that Western Europe's spectacular growth steadily drew them level. GIs returned home from the war and via the "GI Bill" received generous loans to rebuild both their own lives and national society alike, fueling a suburban housing boom and an expansion in the job market. American GDP grew steadily after 1947, culminating in an average of 5.3 percent growth per year during Johnson's term in office (1964–8). As in Europe, this was growth enjoyed by the middle and lower classes above all.[10]

As the immediate challenge of postwar reconstruction gave way to more ambitious plans for national development, a renewed faith in the values of democracy in the West, and a set of procedural imperatives that would characterize the functioning of that democracy, steadily began to take shape around a common set of ideas and institutions. This was the backdrop against which the transformations of the 1970s were to play out.

What Went Before

The first and most basic pillar upon which Western democracy was rebuilt after the war was the nation state, which was locked in place through a concerted focus on national economic growth. Economic development took the place of interstate rivalry as the era's principal political obsession. The new concept of "national income," or GDP, as it recorded that growth for public consumption, took on something of the importance once accorded the expanses of empire that could be shown in pink on some map. The task of securing what, in Europe especially, were often recently reinstalled national governments was also undertaken through the exercise of political constraint, as this was levied upon the institutions of democracy itself.

A not dissimilar picture emerged in the United States. As the influential US diplomat George Kennan put it, democracy itself could be dangerous when it gave rise to populist mischief: it was like "one of those prehistoric monsters with a body as long as this room and a brain the size of a pin." Hence where constitutional courts were established in countries like Italy, West Germany, and France for the purpose of ensuring that formal democracy was actively kept in line with the values and principles of society, the US relied on a more politically engaged judiciary.[11] Those safeguards being established, citizens were encouraged to play their role at election time, but to refrain from too much political engagement in the months or years in between. Not unlike prevailing attitudes to sex, when it came to democracy it was argued that you could have too much of a good thing.

Instead political differences were to be mediated through the major workers' and employers' confederations such as France's Confédération générale du travail (CGT), or Norway's Landsorganisation (LO) or the American Federation of Labor and Congress of Industrial Organizations (AFL–CIO). The result was a fragile yet stable "consensus" model of democracy, in which individual freedoms were protected from the tyranny of the majority and political passions were toned down in the name of a wider vision of social harmony. It was, as the philosopher Isaiah Berlin formulated it in 1958, a politics based on a balance of both positive and negative freedoms. It was inconceivable without the experience of the previous years of upheaval. And for all that it provided a sense of normal politics when measured against the turbulence of recent times, it was never destined to last.

Such widespread commitment to political moderation and constraint was hardly born of altruism alone, however. As postwar governments sought to manage the new social relations of production, while simultaneously reasserting their own authority in the aftermath of the war, the nation states that left 1945 behind became, almost inevitably, more centralized ones. We remember this era today, not inaccurately, as one of board meetings and briefcases, of secretariats and ministries and the milk quotas and postal routes they oversaw. Above all we remember it for the constant presence of an active, administrative state. The federal state was the primary investor in the mass suburban housing schemes, like Levittown, that cropped up in America. In Europe, state planning boards and industry agencies proliferated (something the Japanese also cottoned on to and mastered). This enabled what was perhaps the most visible manifestation of postwar reconstruction: the discipline, and indeed achievements, of national planning.

Planning was the second central pillar supporting the revival of postwar democracy at large, and it too was about securing growth first and foremost. Roosevelt's (ultimately failed) attempt to introduce a Second Bill of Rights in America—"true individual freedom cannot exist without economic security and independence," as he suggested in launching the idea in 1944—was an early recognition that the national state had to plan to provide for people's needs. But the roots of state planning ultimately lay outside existing democratic experience: the IRI, Istituto per la Ricostruzione Industriale in Italy, was founded under Mussolini to rescue failed banks in 1933. Its virtues only really took hold in the minds of Western policymakers during the war: Jean Monnet first floating the idea of what became the French Commisariat général du Plan with de Gaulle in Washington in 1945.[12] Planning came to be seen as a way to ensure that the sorts of crises that had brought democracy to its knees were henceforth avoided. Equally it was encouraged by the counterexample of the socialist countries, who for much of the era seemed to be developing as fast, if not faster, than their Western counterparts.

Unlike in the socialist countries, however, Western planning was put to the twin ends of industrial investment (which included laying the conditions for private investment as well) and the establishment of a third pillar of postwar democracy: the national welfare state (partly as a way to nullify worker discontent). Even in Italy and West Germany, two countries which had so recently experienced the reality of a totalitarian political order, but where economic policy was notably more liberal than in Britain or Sweden, the necessity for a strong state was never really in doubt when it came to social security. In a country like Britain, achievements such as the National Health Service soon became an integral part of the national identity itself: untouchable even by later arch critics of the state.

By the mid 1960s, therefore, the big-government, Western welfare state seemed unassailably popular. There was just one hitch. For all that the economies of the Western democracies had been growing fast, national spending had been growing even faster. Between 1950 and 1973 government spending as a percentage of GDP grew from 30.4 to 42 percent in Germany, from 27.6 to 38.8 percent in France, and from 34.2 to 41.5 percent in Britain.[13] In the United States the expansion of government spending, on welfare in particular, was if anything even more dramatic, its cash outlays amplified by its underinvestment in a European-style welfare infrastructure. In 1950 the federal government put 26 percent of its total budget toward welfare (admittedly in a context in which local and state authorities contributed more). By 1975 the ratio had increased to 55 percent.[14]

No less substantial increases were to be seen in Scandinavia, where Danish spending on social security doubled between 1950 and 1973 and Norwegian spending more than tripled.[15] In the good times, this forged a virtuous circle between capitalism and democracy, commitments to securing basic rights for the people being also a major source of economic growth in their own right. Hence, by the end of the 1970s in Belgium 60 percent of all university graduates took up jobs either within or directly connected to the public sector. In France, a period of service in public administration became the traditional route to more lucrative private sector jobs for graduates of elite public management schools like the École Nationale d'Administration.

In place of the national-scale Beveridge plan (1944) in Britain, American welfarism developed sectorally, through pacts like that signed between autoworkers and General Motors in the Treaty of Detroit (1950), providing those workers with a set of guaranteed health, pension, and insurance benefits in exchange for relinquishing the right to strike over certain workplace issues. The US commitment to welfare was more grudging than it was in Europe, but again the powerful presence of communism as an ideological foe helped lock it into place. In this regard welfare played a central *political* role on both sides of the Atlantic, not least as formal testimony to the fact that liberal societies too could provide sufficient measure of social solidarity. Indeed, in America no less than in Europe, the rich accepted far higher rates of taxation during this period to meet the growing social security bill than would ever be the case again: in the 1960s the top rate of income tax in the United States was a hefty 91 percent.

The extent to which such public commitments to collective prosperity were accepted by the majority of people points toward a fourth characteristic of postwar democracy: the way that social progress relied upon the paradoxical encouragement of a consumerist culture and the satisfaction (if not creation) of individual needs. This was especially apparent in America, where the logic of consumer society and the demands of the Cold War went hand in hand. If political freedoms needed sometimes to be curtailed in the name of the wider superpower struggle, went the logic, then an expanding sphere of personal consumption could at least provide some measure of relief against this. Lying behind this was the recognition that unless one could cultivate mass consumption there would be no mass production either; and no mass production meant no meaningful stand against communism. But the upside was greater freedom of choice. In Europe, as rationing became a thing of the past, and people no longer had to queue for the basics, the market now reached out to people in their homes, whether it was the Avon lady who came knocking on people's doors, or a *Reader's Digest* or *Which?* magazine that flopped through the letterbox.

What most middle-class households wanted was washing machines and white goods for the women and automobiles for the men. This reinforced some gendered expectations but it also undermined others. "You can't do any longer without electricity, espresso and Cola," one German advertisement proclaimed in the 1960s: "But you can do without cooking!"[16] Most European households did not even have a fridge to store basic cooking ingredients in the early 1950s; twenty years later and the vast majority did. A similar story was apparent with cars: America produced around 4 million vehicles per year at the start of the 1950s; it had doubled that to 8 million by the mid 1960s. Italy, Germany, France and the UK were by then producing about the same (if not a little more) between them. Cars in turn required more petrol stations and a rapidly expanding network of highways on which to drive them. National motorway networks—the A Roads, the Interstate Highway System, the Routes Nationales and the Autobahns—everywhere began to displace the railways. The countryside having just been emptied of people, who were moving to the cities, it was now being paved over in their wake.

Literally and imaginatively, horizons expanded ever further afield. Leisure travel gradually became a possibility for more than just the affluent upper classes: family holidays could begin to be planned and enjoyed. And in the months in between there was an increasing array of radio and television programs to tune in to: admittedly dominated by the major broadcasters such as RAI and the BBC, but opening onto a world of private entertainment, not just of public information broadcasting. In the US there were fewer than 17,000 television sets in 1946; by 1953 two thirds of American households owned one. Politicians saw that the freedom to choose what to buy and political freedom could be merged, to wit Nixon's famous kitchen debate with Khrushchev in 1959, where he gloated over a new range of dishwasher ("We have such things," Khrushchev snapped back).[17] As the range of basic shopping items expanded, supermarkets sprang up to display them (the Netherlands had just seven in 1961, but 520 a decade later). The rise of a more consumerist individual was soon driving the national economy forward, awakening material rather than political passions, and endowing a considerable degree of legitimacy—and stability—upon governments only too happy to take credit for the economic achievements of the age.

By the late 1960s it was hard to remember the years of rationing and reconstruction, for all that they were only two decades in the past, along with the lessons that such hardships had bestowed. It was "detergent wars" that raged now over the heads of Western consumers; and cultural wars too. De Gaulle made André Malraux minister for cultural affairs in France in 1959 specifically to defend the French cultural patrimony he feared was being lost.[18] Political transformations followed on in the wake of social change. Britain and France joined Germany in abolishing the death penalty and could look askance at the United States, which had not. Yet even in America, basic civil rights legislation had been laid down, beginning with the Voting Rights Act (1965) but later covering freedom of expression, and a measure of legal protection to homosexuals or to those who wished to divorce. In such ways, then, did the "Golden Age"—as for many it would soon, somewhat wistfully, be referred to—leap forward. Economic growth and new technological developments enabled rapid social change and vice versa. The pace of change grew faster.

For all their prior differences, therefore, at the nexus of these developments there was considerably greater convergence of political culture among and between the Western democracies than had existed even half a century before; enough at least to lend credence to the claim that together these countries rightfully made up the "free world."[19] Beneath that ideological canopy, states, markets, and society all seemed to be moving forward in step together. But the skein of consensus was being stretched all the while. As one of those who lived through this, the British liberal Edmund Fawcett, wrote: "The changes of the 1950s to 1970s were for many a welcome upheaval. Still, they were an upheaval. They raised expectations. They disturbed familiar patterns. They stored up a powerful counterreaction mixing wrathful opposition and disappointed hopes."[20] By the late 1960s, this was a counterreaction fast approaching the point of release.

"An Unheavenly Chorus"

Adrift in a new global era—"the epoch of space," as the French philosopher Michel Foucault put it in 1967—more and more people began to wonder from the mid sixties onward just where exactly they stood amid the changes underway around them.[21] Ironically, it was the very political stability of the previous decades, combined with its unprecedented socioeconomic mobility, that contributed to this sense of unease. For three decades people's lives had assumed a certain benign predictability: one's career, life plans, social environment and even cultural appetites all played out within relatively contained parameters. Now they began to experience what Swedish Prime Minister Tage Erlander mordantly dubbed "the discontent of rising expectations" (de stigande förväntningarnas missnöje).

Not infrequently this manifested in psychological terms: the fear of becoming just a faceless cog in the machine of postindustrial prosperity: the burden that growing prosperity (enabling the time) and consumerist choice (presenting the dilemma) together combined to create. And as social mobility began to desert them, people's acceptance of the social and political constraints that came with the postwar consensus began to fray.[22] More and more overt expressions of disquiet became apparent as transnational labor movements and civil rights, the unwinding of colonialism and Third World social movements, all broke in upon the West at the same time, confronting a younger generation in particular with the arbitrary nature of the choices they were offered in their lives. This realization increasingly registered as a desire to rebel against "the system" itself.

In America in 1962 the Students for a Democratic Society (SDS) put forward an early expression of this with their influential manifesto, the

Port Huron Statement. The statement took aim at the materialist values of the incumbent generation and the "racial bigotry" and Cold War technocracy this relied upon. Against this it called for the defusing of international tensions (this was the year of the Cuban Missile Crisis, after all) and a more "participatory" democracy at home. For the students, the closely informed decision-making this entailed had many attractions over "mere" representative democracy and the more passive political voice of the vote. It also had its problems, the members of one SDS group in Cleveland famously holding a twenty-four-hour meeting to decide whether they should take a day off at the beach.[23] But the desire to participate, and not simply to submit, was a powerful idea: and it was one that, in France, de Gaulle himself had recognized as an issue of relevance for workers as well.

Moreover, come the late 1960s society at large shared something of the same concerns. "The patience, the mildness, the taste for conformity that seemed prerequisites for a tolerable life were behind me," recalled the author Bruce McCall of his life growing up on the outskirts of Toronto, before emigrating to find work in New York. McCall's memoir *Thin Ice* is a laconic sketch of growing up on the margins of a golden age that had been oversold to many.[24] And it was echoed across the racial and class divide. Before the decade was over the sense that postwar democracy had not overcome all of the problems confronting the capitalist West was increasingly common: perceptions were changing for people of all ages.

The most dramatic and important reason for this was the profound impact of the civil rights movement in America and this, of course, was the contribution of America's blacks. Civil rights brought home to American liberals what had long been right before their eyes: the fact that the promises of postwar democracy had no more overcome racial segregation than had earlier efforts at enfranchising black citizens during the Reconstruction. Civil rights thus broke upon the scene as a reminder that Cold War liberalism was always racial liberalism: that the privileges enjoyed by the "silent majority" whom Nixon mobilized on his way to winning the White House in 1968, relied as well upon a quite remarkable degree of social tolerance toward domestic racial inequality.[25]

Ironically, such tensions had been intensified by the extent to which citizens were encouraged to buy into the idea that their societies were somehow now more consensus-based. Johnson's War on Poverty, which included the creation of Medicare and Medicaid, belatedly helped bring greater socioeconomic equality to America after its launch in 1964, but it did so primarily for whites. In such ways, postwar liberal democracy, inflationary in its rhetoric of freedom and opportunity, served to intensify some of the century's greatest social contradictions, as divisive struggles over what should have been mundane issues such as schools and housing soon made clear. By bringing this out into the open, civil rights presented such a powerful criticism of the New Deal era that the very notion of a collective "we" upon which it was based was tainted. The American left in particular would be hit by this, since it henceforth steered away from any attempt at building a true civic universalism, ultimately to its own disadvantage.

In Europe it was the gradual unwinding of colonialism, and the consequent challenge to European nations posed by the fallout from the era of the *Empire Windrush* that first brought the tensions in postwar liberal democracy to the fore (Europeans having previously lived out their race issues across the vast distances of empire). After that the pace of change merely picked up, with demands for gay rights and women's rights, for animal and environmental rights all following suit. All of a sudden the political establishment seemed stuck in the past. In France, workers bridled at the way they were treated like children within an industrial hierarchy that, like their political leadership, seemed to have changed little since the late 1940s and that showed no interest whatsoever in their views. In Italy and West Germany the problem was the postwar grand coalitions, which dominated the political landscape, largely skeptical of the free market in Italy, largely skeptical of the state in West Germany, but in neither case allowing any real room for new or alternative voices. In Scandinavia, Axel Sandemose's *Jantelov* still frowned upon the pursuit of individual success before that of the national community as if it were the 1930s.

By the end of the decade, the political sensibilities of the postwar years were showing their age in other ways too. The transition from a mass industrial economy to one requiring a more mobile and well-educated workforce led to more women taking up part-time work, which immediately began challenging prevailing assumptions about their domestic duties. Rising real wages and dual incomes also meant that people could now afford to buy what the Avon lady was selling; and the fact that women had their own income afforded them a growing independence. The trend would be continued in the decade to come, this time as a result of inflation eating away at the wages of their husbands. This, in turn, would play its part in shaping a critical new demographic, the disgruntled white working-class male.

The young meanwhile distinguished themselves from their parents by purchasing mass-produced fashion items—denim jeans most eagerly. They listened to popular music and bought records in increasing numbers: the Beatles and Bob Dylan, Elvis Presley and Cliff Richard. Music often had a distinctive national, even local flavor, but Dolby noise reduction became a standard technology after 1966. In 1967 the Beatles performed "All You Need Is Love" to a live global audience via satellite, the first such musical communion of its kind. Then came Jimi Hendrix with his "Axis: Bold As Love" to raise the bar once again. Meanwhile, the Carnaby Street "style" was imitated across Western Europe and embraced in the East: in both places as a gesture of rebellion, whether that was directed at middle-class parents or the bureaucracy of totalitarianism, or both.[26] Music was similarly adopted. Record sales in 1960 in America stood at $600 million but a decade later topped $1.6 billion. In West Germany, Japan and Sweden sales doubled during the course of the decade and in Australia they tripled: all to the benefit of Decca, Philips-Polygram, and EMI.[27]

The outlets for cultural expression were widening as well, often in what would once have been unimaginable ways. The radicalism of Third World revolutionaries broke in upon the suburban lifestyles of many Western students, where it mingled awkwardly with the homegrown variant of peace and love. Sex was deemed the very antithesis of politics and, practiced as such, it could only of course become intensely politicized itself. But that was the least of the era's unresolved paradoxes. A decade that began with sex, or at least the overt celebration of it, ended with the more private pleasures of drugs, which scarcely overcame the continual, nagging sense of discontent. Grace Slick of Jefferson Airplane, who had studied alongside one of Richard Nixon's daughters, later recalled how at a White House party she planned to spike the president's drink with a hallucinogen.[28]

The growing emphasis on how people spent their leisure time was changing cultural mores in other ways. Sport became professionalized, notably tennis and football; and in that way too it became commercialized. If this changed the tenor of the athletic ideal (the money put up by the new Grand Slams or pouring into US college football being a case in point) it also meant that sports now rendered visible some of the hitherto hidden fractures of society. In 1973 Billie Jean King beat Bobby Riggs in the so-called Battle of the Sexes (it was really a battle over sexism) and Frank Robinson became the first black manager of a Major League Baseball Team. Muhammad Ali (born Cassius Clay) had already raised hackles nearly a decade before by rejecting his "slave name" and joining the Nation of Islam: "I am America. I am the part you won't recognize. But get used to me," Ali famously declared. No less famously he later rejected the draft (costing him his heavyweight belt) and became an impassioned and outspoken speaker on race.

Yet religious convictions were in some ways fracturing too. As the Golden Age ran deeper into the sand, it transpired that a corresponding turn to secularization had set in as well. Religious hypocrisy may have been nothing new: Ali's own wife challenged him to explain his multiple affairs in light of his religious convictions.[29] But Christianity now fragmented and went into decline—the final "crisis of Christendom"— as a more secular age confronted the Church, and a more sectarian future, in turn, awaited the earthly world of politics. "The mainline churches in America," wrote one religious scholar, "have been in a state of depression for more than a decade."[30] In Canada and Britain, the largest Protestant churches saw a sharp decline in their membership while the loosening of Roman Catholicism in Quebec presaged the beginning of the end of French-Canadian separatism (thereby removing a very large problem for Trudeau). In the early 1960s 80 percent of Dutch citizens claimed to belong to a church; by the mid 1970s half of them claimed they did not.

Catholicism held out for longer but there too a decline in organized religious observance set in. In Belgium, attendees at Catholic Mass declined from 43 percent in 1967 to 33 percent in 1976; Church of Scotland communicants saw a drop of 11 percent between 1966 and 1972. The number of confirmations performed likewise dropped off precipitously. In Spain more than 3,000 priests, 6,000 monks, and 10,000 nuns would opt to leave Holy Orders between 1960 and 1990. If skepticism among the clergy and religious leaders as to the new social discourse around marriage and divorce, gay rights, and abortion was one aspect of this decline, it was equally—because of their great certainty on those same issues—the reason why a more conservative strand of Christian evangelism was also on the rise, above all in America.[31] Interestingly this did not help Europe's Christian democratic parties since religiosity in politics henceforth coalesced primarily around social movements, including Martin Luther King's civil rights, rather than the Church per se. Thus the moment of a transnational loosening of religious conviction was equally the moment of a distinctively remoralized form of national politics.

If religion as one source of order and stability now began breaking up amid the wider cultural floes, the bonds of community were loosening for more prosaic reasons too. For one, citizens in the postwar democracies were moving out of the country and into the city in search of work. There they were more likely to meet recently arrived immigrant workers, especially in Europe as the colonies closed shop during the 1950s and 1960s and their peoples moved to the former colonial metropole in search of work. Among those for whom this impacted most strongly was a generation of students who had been brought up in the *ennui* of the suburbs and who now found on their arrival in the city the face of difference that postcolonial revolutionists like Frantz Fanon warned them they would find when Europe's stolen "tower of opulence" came crashing down. The student-led uprisings of 1968 were the most obvious consequence of this. But the world impacted on the West no less directly as a result of the other major political "event" of the late 1960s and early 1970s: the Vietnam War. These two developments entwined not so much to overturn the old political consensus as to change the nature of political struggle itself.

"Coming Apart"

It was "1968" that first brought this out into the open. The events of that year began and in some senses ended in Paris when a series of clashes between students and police led to the University of Nanterre in western Paris being shut down. A newly formed students' movement then took their protest to the Sorbonne in the heart of the city itself. Students barricaded the streets in symbolic protest at the conformity of the modern "authoritarian welfare state" and the "repressive tolerance" of their parents' generation (a view that Eastern European radicals of the same generation would later all too happily disabuse them of).[32] It was not until French workers also went on strike in sympathy, the largest strike in French history, that the government really began to worry: by the end of May—the point at which de Gaulle felt obliged to abscond—they had effectively brought the country to a standstill. At the Berliet car factory in Lyons, workers rearranged the letters on the gate to read "Liberté." But events were not confined to France alone.[33]

Protests flared up in each of the major Western democracies. In Germany, events centered on the US-funded Free University of Berlin. German workers became even more involved than in France and the sense of rebellion was, if anything, much more intense, particularly given how fundamental to West German society the "restart" of 1945—and so the thing being rebelled against—had been.[34] In America, student rebellion on campuses like Berkeley was more directly about the question of race, and the uprisings of the year—if anything even more tumultuous than in Europe—converged in the public's mind with the clashes between radicals and the police during the Democratic National Convention in Chicago in the summer. In Britain things were calmer, the visitations of European student dignitaries and American Black Power activists aside, while in Italy it was workers, not students, who led from the front, as they took the frustrations of the era in a more militant direction altogether.

The year 1968 was thus on one level a demographic event: a glorified coming of age party for the first generation of a mass higher-education society. And the where of 1968 is in this sense as important as the what. In France there were six times more university students in 1968 than there had been in 1945; in Italy, after a law liberalizing access in 1961, enrollment had grown from 280,000 in 1960 to 700,000 in 1970.[35] Throughout the 1960s the number of students in higher education grew at around 8 percent per year in Europe. In America it doubled (to 8 million by 1970) as the "massification" of higher education caught on (more importantly it was also opened, for the first time, to African American students).

More and more of these students were studying the new "social sciences" too. By 1968 in Britain more students were reading sociology than law or economics. More still were using the insights of these disciplines to resist the idea that social knowledge should be "useful" to industrial society (one British student, Phil Cohen, contemplated breaking into the LSE library so that he could glue together pages of works by the esteemed sociologist Talcott Parsons, the better to reveal the "congealment of praxis").[36] A large number of American students enrolled simply to avoid the draft for Vietnam. Students in the late 1960s were well educated enough, in short, and in the right disciplines, to recognize the depth of the challenges of the age but not yet of a class that could expect to avoid them.

But if the uprisings of 1968 were generational in this way, they were equally a transnational phenomenon. "In our eyes," recalled Heidelberg activist Joscha Schmierer, of the late 1960s, "the shrinking world . . . coalesced into a unified world in 1968."[37] No two individuals—unlike one another as they might have been—better encapsulated this than Daniel Cohn-Bendit, the impish young student who had been central in the drama from its opening act in Nanterre, and the strikingly tall black activist Angela Davis. During the course of the year Cohn-Bendit was expelled from France, only to resurface at talks in Brussels, Berlin, Amsterdam, and even London. From Saarbrücken he then publicly vowed to return to France, marching to the German–French border along with a thousand students from Saarbrücken University to present the guard there with a bouquet of flowers. Expelled again, he next reappeared in Paris, at an event at the Sorbonne, where he mounted the dais unobserved in dark sunglasses, before removing them, to a gathering wave of recognition and standing applause and shouts of "*Les frontières on s'en fout!*" ("We don't give a shit about borders").[38]

For her part, Angela Davis, the black power activist from Birmingham, Alabama, who had studied under Adorno in West Germany, was fired from her teaching position at UCLA on account of being a member of the US Communist Party, and ultimately forced to become a fugitive after the FBI placed her on its list of most wanted persons. By then she had long been a figure of significance for West German leftists (and not only because she had attended a youth congress in Helsinki, or because, as her mentor Herbert Marcuse put it when asked to define her appeal: "She's black, she's militant, she's communist, and she's pretty"). Thanks to her political biography, her ideas—a hard, anticolonial form of communism—also circulated alongside the much-copied image of her halo-style Afro. Such transnationalism crossed the East–West divide as well. In 1968 a young Václav Havel was in New York to oversee production of one of his plays. While there he not only attended demonstrations at Columbia University but went and listened to Frank Zappa (who would later repay the compliment in Prague, in 1989).[39]

The true unity of 1968, however, was in the outward articulation of the postwar era's discontents. In this sense, 1968 *was* an avowedly political event and in ways more nuanced than we tend to recall: not least because the causes of the mobilization were frequently quite specific local injustices relating to such mundane matters as the quality of housing. The greatest political significance of the protests, however, was the demand for autonomy that most closely linked the student uprisings of that year with the parallel, and for much of the time distinct, protests waged by workers who took their own battles into the space opened up by the students. This was the moment's great political potential. And yet, as has sometimes been remarked, one of the things that ultimately distinguished the two primary strands of protest that year was that students were largely protesting against the alienating effects of an increasingly consumerist society, while workers were protesting against the exploitative conditions required to sustain those consumerist advances.

★

What then was the legacy of these months and years? Elsewhere in the world, 1968 was the point of dramatic and often violent upheavals: whether worker protests against entrenched regimes in Portugal and Spain, or the externally orchestrated civil war in Vietnam; or indeed of real revolutionary movements in Latin America and the widespread civic dissent witnessed in Havel's Prague (where Soviet tanks rolled in to crush the temerity of those seeking "socialism with a human face") and in Poland (where the uprisings of March that year genuinely challenged the regime and were accordingly met with repression and an anti-Semitic backlash in response).[40] There were important connections between these different spheres (Greek 68ers supported their compatriots against the British in Cyprus on specifically anti-imperialist grounds, for example). In Western Europe and America, by contrast, the political threat of 1968 was in some ways overplayed, both then and in the popular memory today. The reason why was best expressed by the American activist and radical Paul Potter when, three years earlier, as leader of the Students for a Democratic Society, he had challenged the crowd standing in front of him at the Washington Monument to first "name the system" if they planned on marching against it.[41]

The truth was, of course, that most of those who took to the streets later simply couldn't. This was partly because, as students, they had experienced only a very particular (and privileged) part of that system. The real struggles of the working class, of minorities and excluded citizens were some distance from the students' own more privileged world. But it was also because the system itself was undergoing a transformation: its institutional bases were reforming and the fluid "personal is political" critique of the 68ers was unable to address this. This is not to undermine the significance of the year itself as a first real caesura with the past. "Whatever else may be said of [those times], it must be conceded that they were animated by an intensely democratic vision," wrote one of them looking back years later.[42] But for all that its protagonists may have believed otherwise, 1968 was not the harbinger of the new so much as the beginning of the end of the old. It was "[t]he 'twilight of the Gods,'" as the Italian socialist Gianni De Michelis put it: "the last great collective moment . . . the end of all dreams of a new era."[43]

The gaping absence at the heart of 1968—which hoovered up like a black hole every theory of change to emerge from the year—was the very idea of *popular* sovereignty itself. This was why it was "the state" in general (and above all in "theory"), not parliaments in particular, that were seen as the source of the problem. Yet as the emergence of antiparliamentarism in West Germany implied, there *were* grounds for criticism of the postwar democratic state as a parliamentary form, had the students wished to take this debate further. In Germany the CDU-CSU coalition was so large as to swamp all but a minuscule parliamentary opposition; in France the stability that Gaullism had brought to the country now looked to some like a "presidential dictatorship"; in Scandinavia it was impossible to imagine any party that wasn't run by social democrats being returned at the polls, and the same could be said of the Christian Democrats in Italy.[44]

The events of 1968 ultimately did not challenge parliaments, or much alter their makeup in the years afterward. Its leaders cared less for collective action than they did for the individual realization of autonomy. The verdict of William O'Neill's contemporary account, *Coming Apart* (1971), captured it well. They ripped up existing notions of what the political was, or could be, but did not have much to say about what it might be replaced by. The institutions of postwar capitalist democracy, to put it in Tocqueville's terms, had survived the intellectual and cultural onslaught of 1968 largely unscathed; the "manners" of the nations, however, would never be the same again. This was its paradoxical legacy. As the workers returned to work disgruntled, and the students left university to get rather better paid jobs, it was clear the social relations of production had been left largely intact. The cultural relations of society, by contrast, were in a state of Brownian motion. And into this setting was thrust the most divisive hot war of the entire twentieth century.

Vietnam

Installed at the Hotel Pierre off New York's Central Park during the presidential transition in the winter of 1969, Richard Nixon and Henry Kissinger made an unlikely pairing at first glance. The Republican president-elect was known for his stance on domestic "law and order"; his newly appointed national security adviser, by contrast, had spent his political career to date working for Nixon's Republican opponent, then governor of New York, Nelson Rockefeller. Yet Nixon and Kissinger in fact had rather a lot in common, including a solidly antiestablishment chip on the shoulder. Nixon the bureaucracy-bashing populist and Kissinger, the "lone ranger" statesman, as the latter characterized himself in an interview with Italian journalist Oriana Fallaci, were partners in outlook if not in party political attachment.[45] Henceforth, if there were a committee, Kissinger would likely be chairing it; if there was an exchange of views, it was likely to be between the two men themselves. By October 1972, Arthur Schlesinger Jr. had dubbed them "Nixonger" in his private journals.[46] *The Times* was more acerbic, likening the result of their partnership as akin to a political coup, executed from the top.

On entering the White House, these two men, who most defiantly embodied the transition from one era to the next during these years, knew only too well that the United States was in a bind over Vietnam. At the moment the two began seriously plotting together in late 1968 it was far from clear just what exactly was to be salvaged from the wreckage of the country's involvement in South East Asia, however. The US Army had been on the back foot in Vietnam since the Tet Offensive in January 1968. Meanwhile the Soviets were confident and aggressive, as they had demonstrated by sending tanks into Prague the previous summer.[47] Nixon and Kissinger felt that the only solution was to try deescalating the situation first, and to do so by picking up the threads of Soviet–American dialogue that had been initiated under the outgoing Johnson administration. Their plan was to convert this into a more fully fledged form of détente. If relations with the Soviets could be put on a more manageable footing, Nixon reasoned, then other problems— including Vietnam—would accordingly be reduced in size. As Kissinger theorized, the key word here was "linkage." In reality the key word was "if": for the world in which the new Nixon strategy was to be applied was rapidly changing.

The stationing of American troops in South East Asia had begun gradually at first. John F. Kennedy had inherited from Eisenhower the problem of what to do with the Cold War partitioning of North and South Vietnam, but in the face of a growing guerrilla insurgency in the country, and not wanting to look "soft" on communism after his failure to oust Castro at the Bay of Pigs, he began to increase US military assistance in the region. That later trapped Johnson into following suit, beginning with military reprisals launched after US destroyers were attacked in the Bay of Tonkin in 1964, and continuing after Johnson's election to a full term at the end of that year.[48] Thereafter the "floodgates" opened, as Secretary of Defense Robert McNamara later put it.[49] The aim of all this, in the statutory Cold War gloss of the time, had initially been to support an "ally" (the corrupt administration of Ngo Dinh Diem in Saigon) in a key Cold War hotspot.[50] After Diem was removed in a US-supported coup in 1963 the US only found itself more entrenched. Yet war was to prove a costly way of maintaining the "credibility" of

America's superpower status. There were 536,100 US troops on the ground by 1968, which was more than sufficient to ensure the Soviets and Chinese set about evening up the numbers on the other side. At its peak, the war cost the US $2 billion a month, the cost in American lives itself peaking in 1968 when more than 16,500 service personnel were killed.[51]

One understands why, on taking office, Nixon wanted nothing more than to avoid getting sucked any further into the whole sorry cycle. "I'm going to stop that war. Fast," as he put it.[52] But characteristically, what Nixon actually did do, under the new doctrine of linkage, was to double down first in order to extricate himself later on better terms. While staying true to the letter of his word, therefore, and pulling out American troops in exchange for building up South Vietnamese forces ("changing the color of the corpses," as one administration official put it) he also greatly intensified the ferocity of the war and expanded it into two neighboring countries, Cambodia and Laos.[53] "We live in an age of anarchy, both abroad and at home," Nixon urged in 1970, in explaining to the nation why he was escalating the war in South East Asia. "We see mindless attacks on all the great institutions which have been created by free civilizations in the last 500 years. Even here in the United States, great universities are being systematically destroyed. Small nations all over the world find themselves under attack from within and from without."[54] This was nothing if not a thinly veiled attempt to tar civil rights and student demonstrations at home with the brush of communist subversion from abroad. It was equally a recognition of the fact that Vietnam was as much a problem for Nixon at home as it was on the actual front lines.

In the United States the draft was perhaps the single most unpopular thing about the war, especially among middle-class households for whom such forced abdication of one's freedom to choose was unusual. Nixon was nonplussed and considered the protesters to be irrational: "They hate us, the country, themselves, their wives, everything they do," he insisted, revealing he perhaps had not noticed that a great many of those same protesters wore hitched skirts and knee-high boots. What Nixon more profoundly failed to grasp was that Vietnam had by now become a major point of contention between the United States and its *Western* allies. This was the substance of the protesters' more systemic critique, and it largely passed him by.

In capitals right across the West, protests against the war thus became one of the abiding images of the era. There were peace marches in Britain and France, and most worryingly for the US State Department, they marched loudest of all in West Germany, that other Cold War front line. In Sweden, America's favorite Scandinavian, Gunnar Myrdal, who thought of America as his "spiritual fatherland," led not one but two antiwar coalitions.[55] Many of these antiwar demonstrations were not just a reaction to Vietnam, however. For West Germans, protesting about Vietnam was also a way to articulate (in terms it still was not possible to do in Germany) the legacy of their own Nazi past. The protests were a rebellion against the Cold War political order more generally, therefore, and for this reason Vietnam—for all its destructiveness—was also a moment of coming together. It was constitutive of a new politics of social movement, best exemplified by the peace movements that would soon play such a critical role in the latter stages of the Cold War.[56]

Yet Vietnam rumbled on until the last military advisers were evacuated from the rooftops of Saigon in 1975, along with a few desperate South Vietnamese collaborators. Surveying the destruction levied upon Cambodia (which descended, due to the American invasion, into a bloody civil war that would be won by Pol Pot and the Khmer Rouge) and neighboring Laos (which became the most heavily bombed country in history: a ton of ordnance was dropped there for every minute of Nixon's presidency), Vietnam was thus indeed much more than just a war.[57] It marked the point when the phrase "collateral damage" was first introduced, and when trust in Western governments reached its lowest ebb since the Second World War. It was the flexion point of seemingly "9,000 other cataclysmic events," as one '68er put it. It split the American left and divided the postwar Atlantic alliance. It sharpened the countercultural divide between "the elders" and a more critical youth.[58] And where flickers of this new and somewhat differently political era were beginning to be seen they tended to be interpreted not as opportunities but glimpsed rather as the backs of pike among the weed.

The Turning

When Martin Luther King Jr. was assassinated in April 1968, he had been attending a rally in support of striking sanitation workers in Memphis. That effort to reach out to blue-collar workers of all color, and to engage with America's powerful unions, was a critical objective of the civil rights movement, precisely because America's white working class was too little interested in the plight of colored laborers, and this was a major hurdle—as King rightly saw it—in the furtherance of greater rights for all.[59] On the back of King's assassination, the Attica riot was just one of a series of events marking a change from the civil rights strategy of openly *confronting* mainstream white society with its iniquities, to the black power strategy of seeking more actively to *resist* those iniquities. It was a transformation that conveyed, as well, a loss of faith not just in the willingness but in the capacity of the democratic state in America to address what W. E. B. Dubois had long before termed "the color line."

Angela Davis was one of those for whom these events represented a turning point. As the aims of Black Power moved center stage in the public debate over equality during Richard Nixon's first term in office, she now became more active in the clandestine activities of groups like the Black Panthers. Black Power was a more radical response to the perceived deficiencies of the alliance between black and white, rich and poor, religious and secular, that King had assembled in the name of civic rights. It was equally a response to the bursting in upon the Western cultural scene at this moment of Third World revolutionism. For activists like Stokely Carmichael, learning that anticolonialism was a struggle to be fought at home as well as abroad negated the sort of cross-class alliances that King had sought to build. It was to be replaced by violence and the gun. The civil rights slogan of "Freedom Now," which Carmichael had first declared on his release from prison in 1966 (he had been detained during a march), now made way for "Black Power."

The Black Panthers would be reduced to just a small rump in Oakland, California, by 1972: gone but not forgotten. A more enduring contribution of the Black Power movement was the way it articulated a coming challenge for America's younger generation of blacks: the fact that hardwon affirmative action policies were doomed to fail not in the imagination (King had surely won that battle) but in their application.[60] The story of the Fair Housing Act, implemented in 1968 in the immediate wake of Martin Luther King's death, is testament to their point. Stripped of its ability to pursue affirmative action and address racial segregation in housing provision it ended up a force for resegregation as much as anything else.[61] This became just one reason why, contrary to civil rights, the Black Panthers sought racial "autonomy" (though not segregation) rather than civic universalism. It was why their politics, focused on urban areas in the north, explicitly recognized the fact that what might be granted in theory (equal rights to education and transport, say) was dependent upon being meaningfully delivered in practice.

Few were the politicians of status willing to grasp, at this point, that the legal achievements recently won through civil rights were nothing but a starting point to real equality—let alone the radical "participatory" equality demanded by the student radicals. Even those politicians who grasped the point gave mixed signals, at best, as to whether this was a threat or an opportunity. "No country can lead the fight for social justice unless its commitment to its own people is credible and determined," declared then presidential hopeful Robert Kennedy in 1968, "unless it seeks jobs and not the dole for man, unless it feels anguish as long as any of its children are hungry, unless it believes in opportunity for all of its citizens, all across the land. Our future may lie beyond our vision, but it is not beyond our control."[62]

Kennedy too was assassinated that year in a hotel kitchen in California, just a few months after uttering these words: another martyr to the cause of youth; another condemnation of the politics of the past. But his instinctive (and arguably more characteristic) linking of opportunity and personal responsibility as the best way to manage the challenges of the era outlived him. It did so first of all in Chicago that same summer when riots blighted the year's Democratic National Convention. The Black Panthers were among those who traveled to Chicago in force, alongside several thousand other student protesters, including the SDS and the Youth International Party (the "Yippies"), who descended on the city to confront the politicians, not only of the Democratic Party but of the political elite in general. The clashes had an air of inevitability about them, framed in advance as a pitched battle between the generations, spiced by the anger of the recent assassinations of each side's icon: Martin Luther King and Robert Kennedy. Over 12,000 police, supported by the National Guard and units drafted in from the army, were given a clear mandate to teach the protesters a lesson. It would have taken a miracle to avoid a bloody confrontation—and this was not a year for miracles after all.

Nor was the year to follow. In 1969 in Minneapolis, in the US state of Minnesota, a former police officer, Charles Stenvig, was elected mayor, replacing Democratic incumbent and university professor Arthur Naftalin, a living embodiment of liberal-era "consensus" politics, with a more aggressive political program. Since he ran as an independent, Stenvig's success was due primarily to his political base, the "T-party." No relation to the modern Tea Party—though given its populist platform it was in many ways a precursor—the T-party used racial scaremongering to explain to whites in particular the virtues of small (but strong) government. Stenvig thus traded in outright color prejudice— he promised to "take the handcuffs off the police"—by means of proxy arguments about the virtues of "popular morality" against the empty technocratic "expertise of academic professors, business leaders and community activists."[63]

Stenvig may have been an independent, and a local politician at that, but he well embodied both the beginnings of an elite backlash and the preferred Nixon style of "law and order" policing. The longer-term effect of this new approach was to place a greater burden of incarceration upon the shoulders of black and Hispanic citizens in particular. Henceforth the benefits of corruption for the well-to-do were improved, while the prospects for escaping jail by virtue of being born into poverty worsened; this meant even more blacks behind bars.[64] Of course, whether this was by now unpopular is somewhat harder to tell: the efforts of groups like "Restore Our Alienated Rights" (ROAR) to organize boycotts of schools employing equal rights quotas in 1974 were but part of an antiwhite backlash that would in due course make itself felt at the level of the Supreme Court.[65] What is readily discernible is the extent to which American society was more divided than it had been just half a decade before. So too was Europe.

In Italy, in the early 1970s, the extraparliamentary movement Lotta Continua led, under its banner of *Vogliamo Tutto!* (We want Everything!), a wave of revolutionary strikes, street brawls, and factory takeovers in response to the Italian Communist Party's move toward the political center. As parties went one way, it seemed, the people went another. In Italy and West Germany in particular, the "extra-parliamentarism" gestured at in 1968 became, for some, the new political style. In Frankfurt, members of the radical fringe group Revolutionary Struggle (including later Foreign Minister Joschka Fischer) modeled themselves on the Italians (many of whose stories were relayed by the growing Italian exile community in Frankfurt). They made plans to infiltrate the Opel factory on the outskirts of town, some of them even finding that they quite liked constructing axles and exhaust pipes. Those German radicals who did not find satisfaction, however, began spiraling off into ever-more radical and violent groups: among them Ulrike Meinhof, Andreas Baader, and their Red Army Faction.

In 1970 Baader was in jail for an earlier offense, but a well-planned prison-break from a press interview arranged for him by Meinhof in a Berlin library (the two smoked incessantly until a guard finally opened a window allowing them to shoot their way out) marked the beginning of the years of red terror in Germany.[66] In France, counterculturals resisted the more violent urges of Italian and West German political radicalism. But Maoist revolutionary groups in Paris took inspiration from their German, Italian, and American counterparts nonetheless, and went underground as a radical insurrectionary group. After a young worker, Pierre Overney, was killed at Renault's Billancourt factory in Paris during a protest in 1972, a Maoist group kidnapped one of the factory bosses and held him in an apartment for several weeks (meanwhile the left staged a 200,000-strong march involving everyone from Jean-Paul Sartre to Jane Fonda). To the dynamic of class were soon added tensions over immigration, when anti-immigrant groups in southern France planted a bomb that killed four in the waiting room of the Algerian consulate in Marseille, sparking off in response the largest antiracist mobilization in years.[67]

The ostensibly divergent political dynamics of the time thus ultimately fed into one another, since the more that society bifurcated, the more it fed not only hardliners on the streets but hardliners within the state—as with Stenvig in the United States, or Jean-Marie Le Pen and the Front National in France. Of course, these were often local developments to begin with. But they were also a means for governments to restore the powers they were ceding elsewhere—over their failure to sustain their international standing, or to control matters of the economy—through more visible shows of policing that low-scale criminalization made possible. Only in a few places, as in Canada, was this problem avoided by virtue of there being no constitutionally enshrined "we the people" in the first place (Canadians opted instead for a linguistically pluralist model of federation).

But as even Pierre Trudeau was finding, this model too came under pressure when people suddenly started demanding other things as well. Until now politics in the Western democracies had revolved around the idea that the state could be encouraged to respond to social demands by changing the mix of its distribution of social resources. But with more and more citizens demanding not just redistribution but *recognition*—of their social, cultural and indeed sexual preferences, of their rights as communities of color or as ethnic minorities, of their social status, their sexual orientation and their elective affinities—it was not just national governments that struggled to respond but the postwar politics of "consensus" as a whole.[68] By the start of the 1970s the challenge of incorporating a more varied and demanding citizenry into an outdated institutional structure was upending the system everywhere.

Equally distinctive was the way that political upheavals in one country seemed increasingly to bleed into another. The overthrow of dictatorships along the southern European rim, for example, was sparked in part by the passage of young radical exiles from the streets of Paris heading back to their home countries in the south. Developments in those nations now became a part of the same political and cultural upwelling then enveloping the wider democratic West (though two of them, Portugal and Greece, were also already members of NATO, the Western security alliance). This was one reason why Henry Kissinger, for one, paid special attention to what was happening in southern Europe from his vantage point of the US State Department. As he recognized, what was distinct about the storm of protest gathering there was not just the dictatorial nature of the regimes it was pitted against, but the social makeup of that unrest. In contrast to the more middle-class orientation of the student uprisings, the antiwar marches and the burgeoning radicalisms of northern Europe and the United States, the protests that flared up in an arc of anger from Asturias in Spain through the factories of Genoa to the stifling heat of Athens were avowedly of the *working* class.

In that sense, at least, Kissinger's concerns were not misplaced: and the upsurge of workerist movements in southern Europe was in its way a more accurate harbinger of the struggles that would preoccupy the West in the decade to come than were the student uprisings of 1968.[69] This "southern '68" began late, and first of all in Spain. In October 1971, just days after the Attica prison riot in America, 28,000 workers occupied the vast SEAT factory in Barcelona. They were met by armed police firing tear gas and gunshots before a cavalry charge was unleashed, but it was the beginning of an agitation that would result in Franco's successor, King Juan Carlos, returning the country to a constitutional monarchy on Franco's death in 1975.[70] In Portugal, events began with a military coup that soon turned into a popular mobilization in 1974. After a further series of coups and countercoups, it was eventually Mário Soares's socialist party that emerged victorious from the elections that were held in April 1976. More remarkably they did so according to the terms of a newly codified *socialist* constitution.[71]

In Greece, again, it was the wider conjunction of political and economic upheaval, combined with the intersection of student and worker interests, that upended the military junta that had been in place since 1967. In 1973, inspired by the student protests of 1968, Greek law students barricaded themselves into the faculty building in protest at the way that the military draft was used to remove "undesirables." After a similar standoff at the Polytechnic in Athens, students constructed a flimsy radio and began to broadcast their actions to the nation. "This is the Polytechneion! People of Greece, the Polytechneion is the flag bearer of our struggle and your struggle, our common struggle against the dictatorship and for democracy!"[72] It was a dramatic snub to the regime. But no sooner had the Generals sent in the tanks to quieten things down than civilians, too, rose up in sympathy with the students. Just over a week later the president, Georgios Papadopolous, was out. By the end of the following year, in November 1974, the country went back to the polls for the first time in a decade.

Kiss, Kiss, Bang, Bang

By the middle of the decade the old order was everywhere being turned on its head: for better and for worse. Not surprisingly, it was also an age whose cultural and intellectual shibboleths were rapidly being pulled down, and the director Luis Buñuel captured better than most the nature of the crisis in cultural and intellectual affairs in his surrealist magnum opus, *The Phantom of Liberty* (1974). Buñuel's film opens with a parodic reenactment of the firing squads of Francisco Goya's iconic painting *El Tres de Mayo de 1808* (1814). Like that painting it perfectly captured the cusping of a new era in the West. In Buñuel's rendering, as the order to fire is given, defiant shouts ring out: yet these are howls not of protest or of anguish, but the ironic judgments of hindsight itself. "Down with Liberty" and "Long live chains!" cry the condemned before the crack of the fusillade. The execution party then leave to get drunk on communion wine in a nearby church, where the viewer takes leave of them, poised on the brink of necrophilia.

Needless to say, this was not Buñuel's most commercially successful film. But artistically it was the one he valued most. Events in the film take place mostly in Buñuel's own time, pivoting from one satirical takedown of mid–late-twentieth-century culture to another. And little escapes Buñuel's critical eye: Western bourgeois morality and the destructive, wasteful urges it rests upon; an already vacuous cult of celebrity; the ease with which majoritarian morality had come to pass itself off as political virtue. In Germany Rainer Fassbinder was experimenting with a less forcefully modernist form of social commentary cinema, with works such as his 1974 *Fear Eats the Soul*: the story of a middle-aged cleaner in Munich who falls in love with a Moroccan immigrant twenty years her junior, to the opprobrium of Munich's stubbornly racist post-war middle classes.

Equally trenchant critiques were directed not just at the specters of race and class but at the domestic and generational conflict of the times as well. Bertrand Blier's *Les Valseuses* (Going Places) was released the same year as *The Phantom of Liberty*, and saw a young Gérard Depardieu and Patrick Dewaere throw stones and metaphors alike, for the benefit of 5 million cinemagoers, at the stifling postindustrial landscapes of a golden age that had now ground to a halt.[73] Similar critiques of "the roiling desperation beneath the façade of contemporary life," as the *New York Times* put it, were being written and performed to critical acclaim in the United States by the likes of Edward Albee. His *A Delicate Balance* (1966) laid bare the Cold War family's domestic tensions that could erupt when modern pressures, if not close friends, move in to take over the home. It was followed, appropriately enough, by 1971's *All Over*, starring a young John Gielgud.[74] Albee was right in his portrayal of a delicate balance being fractured. Back in France, Marcel Ophüls's *The Sorrow and the Pity* (1971) exploded the myth of Resistance heroics that had long underpinned the postwar political landscape for left and right alike.[75]

The sense of disorientation this created was heightened by a growing awareness of the reality of state communism in China and the Soviet Union brought about by dissidents bearing testimony and shattering the fake-news of a more ideological age. The traffic was not all one way. In the 1970s during a visit to Warsaw West German Chancellor Willy Brandt fell to his knees in front of the memorial to those killed in the Warsaw Ghetto during the war. It demonstrated not just penance but a deliberate turn away from the past and was something no other chancellor had dared to do before. Intellectually such moments marked the point when the ideological battle of the Cold War was won. Henceforth the debate was no longer between the champions of representative democracy and their communist others, each neatly assigned to world geographical regions. The dividing line now lay within the two regimes, and for the West that meant between competing visions of democracy. This was *not* what Marx had predicted.

But it wasn't just Marxism that intellectuals were breaking with. Structuralism was out of the window too. Here too France proved a key bellwether state and Foucault, the embodiment of the modern globetrotting intellectual, its most revealing exemplar. Foucault was talking about more than just uprisings on the streets when he observed in conversation in 1971, "We must free ourselves from this cultural conservatism, as well as political conservatism."[76] And he was true to his word in the years to come: he was there at the march after Pierre Overney's funeral the following year, active in prisoner rights and refugee organizations, and a voice on almost any public issue of the moment. From his study he would also help bring about, alongside the likes of the Algerian-born Jacques Derrida, the late twentieth-century post-structuralist moment: which, in a reversal of two decades of "Americanization" of Europe, would become one of the most influential currents of intellectual thought across the other side of the Atlantic too.

This felt need to break with the past was reflected in politics too. In 1973 the newly crowned leader of the French left, and future president, François Mitterrand, published a deliberately symbolic essay, *La Rose au Poing* (The Rose in the Fist), arguing why socialism was better off without communism. The French Communist Party (PCF), "one of the most Stalinist of communist parties," might normally have been expected to say something about this. But it too was now forced to abandon the doctrine of the dictatorship of the proletariat at its 22nd Party Congress in February 1976.[77] By then Mitterrand had assembled together the pro-market leftists in the socialist party to take its place.[78] A perceptible shuffling to the right was underway across the political spectrum: "the great moving right show," as the British Marxist Stuart Hall dubbed it later in the decade.[79] The old utopias, and the political theories they rested upon, were being erased from the sand, as another of Foucault's influential images had it.

If there was a crisis of ideals underway by the early–mid 1970s, there was equally a crisis of the postwar era's assumptions and political commitments. An intellectual and imaginative space was opening up in which new questions could begin to be posed. In 1974 the American sociologist Richard Sennett bemoaned *The Fall of Public Man*. But at the same time the private spaces of the house, the family and the body now became subject to intensely political struggles. The boundaries of what could be considered political, and what not, were beginning perceptibly to change. Even time itself—whether one was fated to spend it shackled to the assembly line or contemplating one's future life more narrowly as a "career"—was now considered a political matter.[80]

One of the movements to capitalize fully on the tensions that some of these modern dilemmas sparked was the avant-garde group the Situationists. For them it wasn't just the concept of work that needed retheorizing. As Guy Debord wrote in *The Society of the Spectacle*, life needed reimagining outside of work too. Drunken and depressed, Debord would end up imagining his own life away. But he and the Situationists had marked out something important: the closing of the relatively brief era—just a couple of decades really—in which the forward march of capitalism had come to be taken for a fact, rather than a warning. Ever since 1945 the Western democracies had been resolutely progress-oriented and utilitarian in their aspirations. Learning how to think differently about a future that could no longer be predicted with confidence, how to manage society when economic growth was neither a given, nor ultimately perhaps even desirable, would be one of the defining challenges of the years to come.

And yet the quite dramatic technological progress of the era—from supersonic passenger planes to Telstar and, of course, the supercomputer—merely served to reinforce the habit of constantly pointing one's nose forward. Governments asserted their fitness to rule on the basis of being able to meet the challenges of modernity *going forward*. It was as if, by doing so, the "troublesome history" of the past—and not just the war years or the fascisms that had gripped France, Italy, and Germany but the less than salutary record of the parliamentary regimes that preceded them—could safely be forgotten.[81] This is not to say that people were free of the past. But they had come at least to *believe* that they were. Western citizens had learned to look toward the future as American settlers had once looked to the West: with every expectation that they would win it.

It was this confident worldview that was shattered in the late 1960s and early 1970s, and the great debate that now came bursting out of the cracks in between was whether there might not be, in fact, a fundamental tension between the technocracy of modern political life and the autonomous self it was based upon. Whether it was radicals reading Marcuse, mainstream intellectuals reading Daniel Bell, or a wider and more popular middle-class readership working their way through the pages of *The Technological Society* by Jacques Ellul (a book available in English from 1964 and widely read thanks to being championed by Aldous Huxley) all converged on a basic point: the overburdening bureaucracy of managed society.[82] Vietnam was the most obvious example of the problems to which such a society was prone. But the Cold War, and its imperatives of "containment, consensus and conformity," now came under greater scrutiny too.[83] In the process it became apparent upon just what fragile bases postwar democracy itself had been built.[84]

★

The general tenor of the new mood was reflected in the success of popular books like Alvin Toffler's *Future Shock* (1970). Despite, or rather because of, its warnings about the "physical and psychological" stresses that were overloading society, Toffler's book would eventually sell over 6 million copies worldwide. A cigar-chewing Orson Welles drove the point home in a 1972 documentary of the same name: "Our modern technologies have changed the degree of sophistication beyond our wildest dreams," Welles intoned as he strolled down an airport travelator. "But this technology has exacted a pretty heavy price. We live in an age of anxiety and time of stress. And with all our sophistication, we are in fact the victims of our own technological strengths—we are the victims of shock . . . a future shock . . ."

Like Orson Welles's private life, this meant many things. But above all it brought home to middle-class viewers, who could now be addressed as "the audience at home," the paradoxical fact which students and workers, in their protests, had been trying to point out all along: that the achievements and luxuries of the postwar age were based upon a degree of alienation and exploitation that had become simply unmanageable for many and intolerable for some. As the 1970s progressed, and the hopes of 1968 slid first into *New York Times* reporter James Reston's despair of 1974 and ultimately into Jimmy Carter's "malaise" of 1979, the specter of discontent returned to stalk the Western mind.[85] And if on one level this was nothing more than a logical reaction, across a broad swathe of society, to the apparent limitations of the political structures of the postwar era, it was a turning point nonetheless.

Yet for all that it was the radicals, the activists, the intellectuals, and the students who were the first to raise the questions, and in so doing to bring the underlying tensions of the postwar Golden Age out into the open, it was the way the Western elite now responded that proved crucial to the making of our own time. Those responses ultimately came to center upon the ways and means of managing modern democracy, and were accompanied by an intensity of debate normally reserved for when wars end or regimes collapse.[86] But they would first be formulated in relation to the sudden ending of the postwar boom. For into what was already a rather volatile admixture of social upheaval was now added the glycerine of a fully fledged crisis of capitalism.

2

The Crisis of Capitalism

URING THE LONG weeks of July 1971, the telex machine in Paul
Volcker's office at the US Treasury building in Washington rarely fell
silent. Endless streams of paper spewed across the desk of the young
undersecretary of the Treasury for Monetary Affairs, bringing in reports
on a wave of currency crises around the world. The threat of a trade war
between the Western democracies loomed. Some feared it might even
split the Atlantic alliance.[1] Concerns were already running high about the
standing of the capitalist world "bloc" as against the "rising" political forces
of communist-inspired Third World revolution. On the floor of the UN
General Assembly and in the corridors around, even the more moderately
opposed nonaligned nations were demanding a "new international economic order" to replace the Western-centric arrangements written into
the international economy at the end of the Second World War. Such
fears only increased as between 1971 and 1973 the international monetary
system was effectively abandoned in midflight.

Quite where this left the United States was unclear. Ever since the
time of Roosevelt the basic unit of the global economy had been the
US dollar, which was backed by—or "pegged" to—a fixed amount of
gold. This hegemony of the dollar had underpinned US military and
political authority for nearly half a century. It was in turn backed up by
the postwar Bretton Woods system, so named after the New Hampshire
retreat where the original framework for the postwar economy was
hammered out in the summer of 1944. Bretton Woods had many flaws,
but it worked to hold countries' exchange rates more or less stable against
the dollar. The system worked so long as everyone played by the
dollar-bound rules, and so long as the United States remained able to
exchange dollars for gold at a fixed price (the "gold window"). The US
gold guarantee was the anchor of the world's monetary system.

But the global economy had undergone enormous transformations during
the boom of the Golden Age. As recently as 1966 the total value of US
manufacturing production had been more than that of Europe and Japan

combined. With other countries running trade surpluses, they put more and more pressure on the dollar. In the 1970s the United States finally lost its position of global primacy and the whole system began to crumble. The inflationary financing of the Vietnam War and the Great Society programs at home, combined with the general growth in financial liquidity, forced the British, first of all, to devalue in 1967, with the Germans revaluing in 1969.[2] Dollars had begun accumulating in other countries, and it was no longer clear that, if push came to shove, the United States would be able to buy them back with a sufficient amount of gold. The Kennedy and Johnson administrations tried every possible means to mitigate this problem. But by 1971, US dollar liabilities, which had risen to $70 billion, were now backed by just $13 billion of gold. Hence at the very moment when national economies were struggling with a series of seemingly intractable economic downturns, the entire global economy was in the unfortunate position of being already dramatically overleveraged.[3]

Something had to give. And in May 1971 it did, in the form of an escalating wave of currency speculation that soon affected the whole international economy. Before long, European central banks feared the situation was getting out of control, and unilaterally decided to stop buying dollars. Instead they began buying German marks, forcing the Bundesbank to buy dollars in their place, just to keep the system afloat. But fearful of being drawn into a spiral of inflation of the sort that had precipitated the decline of the Weimar Republic half a century before, the Bundesbank shut down its currency operations: the Deutschmark now floating freely. It was followed in quick succession by the rest of Europe's central banks. Over the course of a few weeks, the world economy had gone into gridlock and the greatest currency crisis since the Great Depression was underway. For three months the markets remained in a state of limbo, not knowing how the world's treasuries and central banks—and the US Federal Reserve in particular—would respond. News outlets, meanwhile, were busily speculating about a return to the economic-cum-political madness of the 1930s.

"They Will Electrify the World"

This was the turmoil that was registering on Paul Volcker's telex machine in that July of 1971. Volcker could perhaps best be described as a conservative with radical instincts. When it came to economic policy he was also well aware of "the enormous gap between beautiful concept and practical application." Yet the revolution soon underway was his idea as much as anyone else's, blueprinted by a commission run in his name and presented to the incoming Secretary of the Treasury, John Connally, in March 1971. Connally was a voluble Texan, whose economic knowledge was often derided within the administration. He was also a consummate politician— a "couth LBJ"—and he had demanded to be brought up to speed.

The report Volcker delivered, "Contingency Planning: Options for the International Monetary Problem," imagined a preemptive response to the rapidly escalating currency instability, and included a massive devaluation of the dollar that would make American manufactures competitive again. Since the shock this was likely to transmit around the world risked a stock market collapse, Volcker also proposed a wage-price freeze at home: it would demonstrate that the United States was willing to take its share of the heat as well. After listening to the plan, Connally's "eyes widened," presumably at the implied refusal of US commitment to gold above all. He then "carefully placed [the memo] in his briefcase, as though he were a college freshman securing the answers to a big exam."[4]

The plan was unambiguously bold. But as Volcker saw it, as he pulled his ideas together in the early summer of 1971 from his office on the second-floor of the elegant, marble-clad Treasury building, the higher the stakes were felt to be the better: it would mean other countries would be more inclined to accept what he knew would be an unpalatable, if necessary, solution—a devaluation of the dollar and a move to partially floating currencies. To many in the Treasury this was far too radical an approach. But it was also just the sort of aggressive response that Nixon naturally gravitated toward at times of danger. It was perhaps no wonder, then, that within two years the New York Times would have Volcker down as "the Henry Kissinger of monetary diplomacy."[5]

Like Kissinger, Volcker had a way of seeing things through in the heat of the moment. Arthur Burns, Nixon's chairman of the Federal Reserve, was one of those against the idea from the start: "they will electrify the world," he said of Volcker's intended policies. But by the time Volcker's proposal was made public in August, the president had kicked such concerns into touch, for he had by now repackaged the whole thing as nothing less than a "New Economic Policy" for the times. Delivered to the world as a fait accompli—Nixon neglected even to warn the IMF in advance—the United States now suspended its commitment to purchasing dollars with gold forthwith. For good measure it also imposed a surcharge on imports into the United States. Just as Burns had predicted, the announcement sparked consternation everywhere, even among the

Americans who stood to do best from the deal. Such a wholesale up-ending of the system was further evidence, Burns sniped, that the Nixon administration knew practically nothing about economics. It would be a propaganda coup for the Soviets; *Pravda*, he warned, would "headline this as a sign of the collapse of capitalism."[6]

Reluctant though they may have been, the other G10 ministers saw it for what it was: the only available solution to the fact that the international economy had outgrown the frameworks laid down to govern it. Increasingly it became clear that the gold window would remain permanently closed. The era of Bretton Woods was over. During a final summit meeting at Washington's Smithsonian Institute in December, the world's financial leaders duly gave the new, semifloating exchange rate system their approval (in exchange for Connally agreeing to drop the further demand by the United States for greater burden-sharing over the costs of NATO). It was a grudging consensus that was forged, however. Europeans blamed the Americans for whipping up an international monetary storm. The Americans blamed the build-up of dollar surpluses, in export-oriented economies like Germany, for putting pressure on the system in the first place. For his part, Nixon was upbeat and referred to his plan as "the most significant monetary agreement in the history of the world." Volcker, who was a realist if nothing else, was rather less optimistic. "I hope it lasts three months," he muttered.[7]

It did, but not much more. As the election loomed, Nixon wanted more people in work, and for this he was prepared to accept a little more inflation. Arthur Burns at the Federal Reserve duly lowered US interest rates and the US economy heated up again. Other countries, who already had more than enough domestic inflation for their tastes, were not inclined to follow and pressure in the international system built up once again. Britain was the first to break ranks, in 1972, and to float unilaterally outside the recently established "bands." But Nixon professed not to care about the problems the Smithsonian Agreement was leading to: "I don't give a shit about the Lira," he declared, when informed of the currency crisis this had precipitated in Italy, as the Italian government tried desperately to hold the new line.

With Italy's woes in the back of their mind, other countries soon decided that they *did* care, however, and that, like the British, they too were better out of the new system than in it. By early 1973, therefore, it was becoming palpably clear that a move to a completely free exchange system was inevitable. A combination of the Nixon administration's electoral ambitions had provided the nudge, the emergence of new short-term financial markets had provided the means (by enabling markets to process round the clock currency trades) and new economic thinking, such as Volcker's, provided the ideas.[8] The value of national currencies would now be determined not by government intervention and management but by, and through, the financial markets.

From the point of view of US businesses, all this presaged a short-term sense of relief: a known risk is better than an unknown risk after all. "It's very rare that you can be as unqualifiedly bullish as you can now," an ambitious young economic consultant, Alan Greenspan, advised both his private clients and the newly reelected president.[9] Some of the United States' competitiveness was restored, improving the look of the economy (on paper at least) and Nixon easily won reelection in November. But the calm at the eye of the storm soon passed and currencies began wildly fluctuating once more. Thus did the economic freedom some countries believed they would find outside the Bretton Woods straitjacket turn out to be severely constrained by the defensive corrals they were now forced into by ever-more volatile international capital flows, and the speculators behind them.

For their part, ordinary citizens may not have noticed all this buffeting in the money markets and may not have minded if they had—since the consequences were hardly obvious in the short term. But as the value of the dollar in particular now began to decline, one influential group of actors *did* notice. And they minded rather a lot, because the value of every barrel of oil they sold was denominated in US dollars: the currency in which they were required to pay for their imported trucks, their electronic components, and the building materials needed to sustain their breakneck industrial development. That group of actors was the oil exporters' cartel: OPEC.[10] And it did not take long for them to voice their protest rather more strongly.

The OPEC Crisis

On the afternoon of October 6, 1973, Egyptian forces launched the first prong of a surprise attack against Israel, traversing the Suez Canal in the south, while Syrian tanks stormed through the Golan Heights to the north. The war began on the Jewish Day of Atonement, Yom Kippur, and raised tensions between the two superpowers to a level not seen since the Missile Crisis of 1962. In Washington, Kissinger saw a "three out of four chance" of Soviet troop intervention and placed US forces on high alert. The Soviets, who had 20,000 military personnel on the ground in Egypt, embarked on days of "wild, frantic work" as the US Sixth Fleet and the Soviet Mediterranean Squadron circled one another at full alert out to sea.[11] Meanwhile the Soviets were desperately prevailing upon their Egyptian and Syrian allies *not* to undertake the war, partly to sustain the wider climate of Cold War détente that suited them rather well. Egypt's Anwar Sadat would have done better to listen at this point. For though initially caught by surprise, Israel quickly regrouped to drive the Syrians out of the Golan Heights and the Egyptian army all the way back across the Suez Canal, where Ariel Sharon, an army major with a prime ministerial future, soon had a large portion of it cut off and surrounded. By October 25, the fighting itself was over. A ceasefire was agreed. Israel had stood its ground.

The true impact of the invasion for the Western powers was to come later, however. For the OPEC nations now grasped their opportunity to fight back against what they saw as the United States' politically motivated reduction in the value of the dollar. Just hours after Nixon had requested $2.2 billion from Congress for emergency aid to Israel, the Arabs embargoed all oil shipments to the United States. But more significantly, *all* of OPEC, including Iran and Venezuela, announced on October 16, a new benchmark price for oil: $5.16 per barrel—more than twice what it had been at the start of the year.[12] They then began deliberately cutting back on the supply of oil in general. "Let 'em, what can they do?" was how the ever-bullish John Connally had responded, in early 1971, to the suggestion that other countries might retaliate if the United States unilaterally closed the Gold Window and allowed the value of the dollar to fall. Now it was discovering what some of them *could* in fact do. "The industrial world will have to realize that the era of their terrific progress and even more terrific income based on cheap oil is finished," crowed the Shah of Iran.[13]

To make matters worse, the industrialized West was forced to discover this at a moment when the world was already beset by crop failures and food shortages, and commodity prices were skyrocketing. It was the dramatic changes in the price of oil, the one commodity that Western political life had come to rely on, that truly upset the cart. As with much else during the Golden Age, the price of oil had for long risen lower than the rate of inflation: an unacknowledged boon to the West, explicable because oil supply, in the immediate postwar era, was managed predominantly by Western companies. This was why OPEC had been founded in the first place: to redress this colonial inheritance by coordinating the nationalizing ambitions of those countries in which the oil was found. Already in the early 1970s it had been steadily looking for ways to increase the price of oil as more and more production was taken back into national hands. The geopolitical crisis sparked by the Yom Kippur War merely radicalized OPEC's ambitions, providing the justification for a much more assertive approach.

The postwar years of plenty were over, then. What is more, they had ended at a moment of heightened existential fears in the West. For coming as it did in the aftermath of the Club of Rome's 1972 *Limits to Growth* report, with its widely spread message about the extent of industrial society's reliance upon unsustainable resources, OPEC's dramatically revealed chokehold on the global oil supply was endowed with an almost apocalyptic air from the moment the pipelines began to run dry. Already by the 1970s Europe depended upon oil for around 60 percent of its energy production: substantially more in fact than the United States. But without wishing to threaten either the rate of profit on the one hand, or people's livelihoods on the other, governments found that their hands were now resolutely tied.

In America Nixon sought to parry the rising cost of oil by slashing environmental regulations, opening up the long-blocked Trans-Alaska pipeline and inaugurating a future social conflict over fracking without much addressing the underlying problem of the moment.[14] The tide would not in any case be stopped. In the summer of 1973 the global economy looked to have survived the worst of the breakup of Bretton Woods. By the time winter set in, growth forecasts were being slashed everywhere from Denmark to Japan. The US Federal Reserve was hardly alone in its leap from bullish optimism to downright despair. "Income will be destroyed and consumer psychology dampened, and the upward momentum the economy still has at this point in the cycle may well be lost," one of its economists noted in December.[15] Nearly every Western country saw a desperate effort to prune consumption and expenditure: be it petrol quotas and speed limits, or even, as in Britain, the working week itself (which was cut to just three days).

So far as OPEC saw things, however, it was not a lack of economic theory that was causing Western governments problems, but the fact that they were unwilling to conform to the very rules they had long dictated to others. As the promising young Arab economist, then head of OPEC's Economic and Finance Department, Adnan Al-Janabi, pointed out, the rise in the price of oil was actually *within* the historical trajectory of the gold price of oil, which had fallen prior to 1973 as the value of the dollar fell, and there were ways to adapt to this. Framed thus, OPEC's move to raise prices was as much a self-protecting correction as an act of economic aggression—the commodity equivalent, in fact, of what the United States had just done with the dollar standard.

There was an element of truth in this—not that it was likely to win Al-Janabi many converts in the West, as people queued outside bakeries for bread or worked at their desks under duvets to keep warm. But unless Western governments and corporations were willing to countenance a reduction in their own sources of profit and taxable income, the oil price rises were always going to be passed on to consumers in the end. Thus did the rising price of oil initiated by OPEC soon feed into the already rising cost of living. This was the longer-term and by far the more damaging consequence of the OPEC price rise, both because inflation ultimately comes to affect everybody in society, and because—in the early 1970s—there suddenly seemed to be no effective means for reducing inflation. So it was that an additional specter arose: this time, that of a persistent and deepening inflationary crisis, one more serious than any other inflationary episode outside of war for well over a century, and more widespread, too, by virtue of the sheer number of countries affected.[16]

The Great Inflation

"It would be necessary to go back to the 1930s and the Great Depression," wrote the American pollster Daniel Yankelovich in 1979, "to find a peacetime issue that had the country so concerned and so distraught."[17] It is not hard to see why. After decades of gently increasing inflation, wages and prices were already rising sharply at the start of the 1970s even before the decline of Bretton Woods and the OPEC oil shock arrived to magnify all this into a much larger cost of living problem. All of a sudden inflation was, in the words of the US Council of Economic Advisers, "a Hydra-headed monster, growing two new heads each time one was cut off."[18] And since unstable economies are rarely happy or healthy economies, it merely compounded the problem that inflation continued to rise even after unemployment also set in.

In West Germany inflation was running higher by 1973 than it had done since 1952, prompting the government secretly to start planning for the fact that as many as 2 million jobs might be lost in the year to come.[19] In the UK, it had reached as high as 19 percent by 1975, while economic growth remained parked at zero and the country's balance of payments deficit steadily worsened.[20] The UK was one of the countries most acutely affected, given both the labor unrest it was suffering at home and the international exposures of its economy. But average inflation for the whole of OECD Europe ran at well over 10 percent for much of the decade. And the situation was no better in America. Inflation there peaked at around 12 percent in 1974 (up from an average of around just 1 percent for the period 1958–64) with unemployment reaching around 8 percent in 1975.[21] As Pan American airlines put it simply in a 1974 advertising campaign: "Live today. Tomorrow will cost more."

By the end of the decade inflation had joined death and taxes, the *New Internationalist* quipped, as one of the few undeniable certainties of life.[22] What was especially worrying was the way that inflation now seemed to coincide with low growth and unemployment, which was the very opposite of what mainstream postwar economic theory held. It was the British Chancellor of the Exchequer Iain Macleod who coined the apposite term for this back in 1965: the problem, he said, was one of "stagflation"—an ugly word that captured an ugly situation of inflation *and* economic stagnation.[23] It had long been assumed, for the purposes of national planning, that policies to increase the one would invariably dissipate the other and that, in this way, a degree of equilibrium could be maintained. The usual trick, in fact, as Nixon had recently demonstrated, was to lower interest rates in the months leading up to elections—boosting employment, at the anticipated cost of a little more inflation—and then to right the ship during the years to follow. But with inflation and unemployment both now pushing into double digits, that trade-off no longer held, much less the political luxury of being able to *choose* between them.

Inflation was, if anything, even worse in Italy, where political instability and industrial unrest intensified the wider economic pressures. By the middle of the decade the Western democracies had plunged, to a man, into their deepest recession since the 1930s. As the recession bit harder, and still nobody could agree on the necessary course of action, desperation was beginning to set in. Even as anti-inflation coalitions were set up, confidence drained from the economy. By the start of 1975 the US stock market stood at half what it had been in 1972.[24] Unemployment soared and industrial production across the industrialized world had dropped by 10 percent.

Before the year was out, more bank failures had taken place than at any time in a generation.[25] Eleven banks failed in America, and more across Europe. The Bank of England alone was forced to bail out twenty-six British banking outfits. The British government was not, however, able to contain rising prices on the one hand *and* worker unrest on the other. With its balance of payments in disarray, Britain was soon well on its way to requesting an IMF bailout in March of the following year. New York City too found itself teetering on the brink of bankruptcy when, on the morning of October 17, 1975, police cars were mobilized to serve papers on New York City's banks. City lawyers were rushed to the Supreme Court to file a bankruptcy petition, and disaster was only staved off when Jack Bigel, an influential labor adviser, managed to persuade union leaders to post their collective retirement funds as collateral to support the city's loans.[26]

Thus did the workers save New York's financial elite (not for the first or last time). But in due course it was their own steadily rising unemployment that took over the headline news. This was especially concerning given both the extent to which Europe and America alike had enjoyed "full-employment" economies for the past two decades and the fact that this was very much what the postwar social peace had been built upon. By the 1970s there simply wasn't any collective experience of mass unemployment to look back to. There was accordingly considerably less tolerance for it. Unemployment had reached a low of just 1 percent in Germany and the Netherlands at the start of decade. By the middle of the decade it rose higher than 5 percent on average in *all* of the major north European economies, Belgium and Ireland being particularly badly affected.[27] For the workers themselves, things hadn't been this bad since the Great Depression—but back then the problem was insufficient demand causing a *deflation* in prices and bankruptcies as firms failed to make ends meet. The problem this time was that unemployment now coincided with *rising* prices. This presented a double squeeze on the value of people's incomes.

Countries were soon caught in a vicious wage-price spiral. Wage restraint had been another foundation stone of the postwar economic miracle, forged in the reconstructive ethic that emerged from the desolate landscape of 1945. Workers had come to expect gradually rising wages after two decades of economic growth. It was hard to understand that, for reasons that were at best highly abstract, this was no longer sustainable, especially in countries such as the Netherlands where workers had gone along with lower wages than they were entitled to so as to enable nationwide industrial development and modernization. As they saw it, having kept to their side of the bargain they were now being told the whole deal was off.[28] In the early 1970s they thus inclined toward following their Italian counterparts and demanding more. How else were they to purchase the items that advertisements were telling them now ranked among the necessities of life?

As fears grew that inflation might be more persistent than in the past, unions too began to push for their members to demand compensatory increases.[29] Governments on the whole—except in those countries where earlier indexing agreements made this impossible—acquiesced in these demands, at least to begin with. Yet the more that wages increased, the more the share of profit declined, and the less money there was available for investment—all of which further contributed to the economic slow-down. Higher wages thus ultimately fed through to higher costs, and the whole cycle began again.

This was the rather awkward scenario the Western democracies found themselves confronting in earnest by 1973. And if it came later to some countries, such as Australia, and earlier to others, such as the heavily hit Netherlands, it nonetheless affected all alike. Those countries with well-entrenched structures for wage bargaining—the social and Christian democratic countries for the most part—generally fared better in the years to come. In Sweden and Austria, where wage negotiations between unions and employers' federations were centrally organized, or directly overseen by the state, it was easier to limit the unhealthy spiral of wage hikes and price rises. In Germany too, where labor representatives sat on the boards of joint stock companies, there was a sufficient degree of transparency and trust in the systems of national bargaining to preserve a degree of mutual restraint in face of the mounting pressures each side confronted (unemployment also remained lower in Germany, it is true, since immigrant Turkish [and other] *gastarbeiter* laborers were the first to bear the brunt of the layoffs).

Great Britain, which lacked the means of institutionalized wage bargaining and where unions were accountable largely to themselves, fared less well, Prime Minister Edward Heath's failure to legislate his way out of the problem—combined with the particular intransigence of the miners' union—ultimately serving to bring down the Tory government of 1974.[30] What Heath and the Conservatives could not achieve through institutionalized negotiation the Labour Party that succeeded them sought to achieve through incentivization instead, this time using welfare benefits as the carrot to encourage wage restraint. However, the problem with that strategy was that it ate further into the government's finances.

Public spending had previously remained relatively constant across

Europe (if only because, for the first decade and a half after the Second World War, declining military budgets had offset rising social expenditures). Now governments everywhere turned to expansion of the welfare state as a last-ditch way of filling the void opened up by the economic downturn. Even in America, where outgoings on defense remained higher than in Europe, the share of government spending going to welfare rose steadily in the 1960s and dramatically so by the 1970s after Medicaid was established (in 1965). In Europe, social programs were likewise expanded in countries like Germany, Sweden, the Netherlands, and Denmark. Across the OECD government spending on welfare was rising dramatically, from 31 percent to 40 percent during the course of the 1970s. In Sweden it climbed as high as 59.8 percent.[31] Elsewhere labor replacement rates shot up as governments sought to soften the blow of unemployment and to maintain a basic level of confidence (most spectacularly in Denmark which saw rates rise from 25 percent for the years between 1965 and 1972 to 42 percent for the years between 1973 and 1979, and in Finland, which saw them jump from 5 to 27 percent across the same period).[32]

The result of all this, inevitably, was more public debt, especially in the United States with its massive military outlays on Vietnam. It became one more reason for governments to stay away from the once-favored expansionary fiscal policies of their predecessors: the sort of economic policy that encourages investment and consumption alike. The post–Bretton Woods move to floating currencies further internationalized the problem by making it more likely that expansionary policies at home would export inflation elsewhere.[33] What was more, this was all shaping up into the biggest fiscal squeeze of a generation at just the moment when the industrial basis of postwar economic growth—the underlying motor of the whole economy—was *itself* undergoing a profound, and unsettling, transformation.

The Crisis of the Industrial Society

What were the forces driving these economic upheavals? For all that OPEC may have plunged the Western democracies into a short-term recession, the impact was magnified considerably by a more profound transformation underway in the nature of capitalism, in the production and circulation of goods, and in the way that society itself was organized around this. Two developments in particular were critical. First, as 1968 had made clear, the age of the Fordist-style factory was coming to an end, for Westerners at least. The mass industrialism that had powered the advanced industrial economies through the first half of the century was being replaced by new and increasingly distanced models of production, sending parts of the manufacturing process to Asia—and jobs with them. This placed Western manufacturers on the receiving end of a competitive system that had thus far worked largely in their favor.

The changes hit industries and manufacturing regions that relied on older technologies, and materials like coal and steel, hardest of all. Japan sold just 403 vehicles to the United States in 1957; by 1975 it was selling around 800,000 (around 10 percent of the entire market).[34] The oil shock was part of the reason for this: the OPEC oil crisis was as much a boon to Japanese car manufacturers as it was a plague for American and European producers. But the underlying issue wasn't just about volumes: it was about *what* Japan was producing. As Ford executive Hal Sperlich later put it: "suddenly what they [Japan] had was hot and what Detroit had was not."[35] Driven forward by the relentless press of technological innovation unleashed during the Golden Age itself, the Western world's economies were tied in physically to their older manufacturing systems, through decades of accumulated factory plant and employment pools. All of this would have to be uprooted if they wished to compete in the coming era of more specialized activity: an era in which services ranked higher and patterns of work would ideally be more "flexible."

The transition to innovation-based growth was hardly made easier—indeed it was seriously complicated—by a second underlying economic fracture, and what was in fact the single most critical development of the moment: the sudden decline in productivity growth that set in during the autumn of 1973, never fully to return. Unlike the oil crisis, in whose wake it arrived, this was an actual *reversal* from the benign economic conditions of the past two decades. And since it could not be seen at the petrol pump or on the evening news its arrival, like some debilitating disease, passed more or less unremarked to begin with. But more than any other single factor it was this that would force a change in the nature of industrial output, and that would reshape the tenor of relations between workers, employers, and the state.

For market-based economies, productivity growth is the elixir that gives the whole capitalist system its cherished effect. Economists often measure it as the amount of output produced by one hour of labor: a measure that can be increased by adding technological, managerial, or knowledge-based improvements into the mix, thereby making production more efficient. For most of the postwar era, the value of what one average worker could produce in an hour had grown steadily. That meant firms' profits grew, wages could be improved, consumption expanded, and governments could rake in more by way of tax receipts. It was, as one commentator put it, the "virtuous circle that put the glow on the Golden Age."[36]

When productivity growth fell off in the autumn of 1973, that virtuous circle turned vicious: firms cut wages to maintain their falling profits; workers found they had less money to spend on nonessential items; and governments struggled on both counts to maintain their tax receipts, forcing them to tax more or spend less. The pivot downward after 1973 was dramatic. In the United States, economic growth ran 25 percent lower for the period 1973 to 1998 compared with the previous twenty-five years. In France and Germany, it ran at less than half. Meanwhile those two countries saw their annual rate of growth drop from around 5 percent to 2 percent.[37]

Such figures may not seem very dramatic, but small differences in the *rate* of change—which is what compound growth concerns—quickly translate into large differences over time. And these losses of several percentage points in just a few years were more than enough to open up a worrying disparity between government spending, which was growing rapidly, and GDP growth, which was falling in the wake of declining productivity.[38] This made politicians even more anxious. They worried, and not without reason, that if such a state of affairs continued, people would lose confidence in the ability of governments not only to balance the books but also to maintain economic order.

The fact that not one but several factors were at play here exacerbated the scale of the problem. The one-off gains of rural to urban migration, the sheer scale of the bounce back from wartime economies that needed repairing and infrastructures that needed rebuilding, the backlog of the wartime innovations that steadily came on tap to underpin peacetime production processes, the boost to productivity that came from mixing all this with steadily improving education to create a wealthy and willing labor force, all had been largely used up. In truth, the only really durable solution to the sudden loss of productivity growth in those years would not come until the arrival of mass computerization. But computers would not exist as a universally available platform technology until the 1990s.

In the meantime, the Americans and Europeans responded in different ways to the challenge of trying to nurture their economies back to life. The European approach was to target key sectors of their (somewhat smaller) economies: the French invested in aerospace, the Norwegians in oil, the Italians in textiles, and the Germans in heavy industry. Almost all of them competed with each other in the area of automobiles, where the Germans cultivated niches at the quality end of the spectrum, while the British and Italians went for scale. Industries clustered together: most famously in northern Italy, where the idea of the "industrial district" soon took off, as smaller firms realized it was in their interest to stop competing with one another and to begin to find more collaborative ways to cooperate across the product cycle.

At this point the United States had an advantage in two things, technical know-how and economies of scale, and US businesses therefore sought to harness the one to the other, via knowledge-intensive industries, so as to maximize the returns of high technology. The United States had a natural advantage here: it had long invested a great deal more in research and development in an effort to sustain its parity with the Soviet Union, and to run its space program and wider Cold War military industrial complex. It invested 8 percent of its national income in research, for example, something no European country even came close to achieving. In computing, it spent more than five times what the *whole* of Western Europe spent on research and development. The result was a more competitive industrial regime than that being developed in Europe. It also proved more willing to tolerate higher unemployment than the Europeans.

However, it was the European economies that initially seemed to have fared better in the transition to "post-Fordism." Sustained by a rich ecosystem of regional banks and regional policy directives, wedded into the steadily expanding architecture of the EEC, and channeling their products for the most part to markets not very far distant, the production base of European capitalism soon regained its balance after the shocks of the early 1970s. In America the pay-off would come later—perhaps inevitably given the extent and nature of the investments—and would be that much greater for it: Silicon Valley's own golden age lay some years ahead. But in both cases the changes were felt most of all in the short term: on the shop floor and in the domestic lives of workers.

In Europe, where firms were still more closely embedded in local communities—one thinks of Rover in Oxford, or of heavy machine industry in Alsace—employers might worry about the consequences of industrial change for "their" workers. But as industry disaggregated, it was on the whole a colder, more "businesslike" face that now confronted the modern worker. David Roderick, chairman of US Steel, summed up the new ethos in 1971: "The duty of management is to make money not steel," he declared.[39] There was a "new spirit of capitalism," as management theorists were soon insisting, and it was reimagining how workers and consumers were to be treated. A new breed of "managers"—men like Roderick, who knew models of accounting and finance better than the industries of the companies they ran—soon also emerged to take these new ideas forward.

Crucially, this new style of capitalism no longer feared uncertainty but embraced it as a logic of accumulation: the more unsure consumers were the more they could be encouraged that this or that product was for them. The arts of advertising had already shown this for the mass-consumer; but henceforth consumption would become increasingly individualized. The constant change in people's daily lives that this encouraged fed into the wider trend toward social fragmentation: "private opulence amid public squalor," as John Kenneth Galbraith famously put it in 1958. For workers themselves, be they agricultural or industrial, such changes could mean either greater opportunities to change one's career, or the loss of jobs that only recently seemed assured for life: and, inevitably, there were social as much as economic implications to all of this.

The new citizen-consumers were far from being passive subjects for one. Consumer groups and industry advocates had all helped to politicize consumption and to place it at the heart of postwar democratic politics: for some, African American women in particular, consumer politics were often the only way of acting politically (though it was also one of the primary vectors of their exclusion from society).[40] Searching for "the best buy" was also about searching for the right policy-mix, or else voting it in. Material goods came to embody broader ideas of social mobility and even, increasingly, political identity: "men were affiliated less by what they believed," observed the American Daniel Boorstin in the language of 1973, "than by what they consumed"—though it was equally true, as Betty Friedan pointed out, that a great many women were equally affiliated by their enclosure within the "comfortable concentration camps" of suburban domestic living.[41] Capitalism was thus regulated on behalf of consumers before it was regulated on behalf of abstract values such as the environment. Nonetheless, the distributional politics of access to consumer goods changed from the 1970s onward, in part highlighted by the reappearance of scarcity in such basic materials as oil, and in part by citizens' unwillingness to pay more for what many of them experienced as less.

By the end of the 1970s there was very little in the world of employment, welfare, and work that had not been transformed by the reorganization of capitalism that was underway. Added to these changes were a number of significant demographic shifts: women and immigrants alike entered the workforce, the structure of which changed to keep up, and the role of individuals in family units changed. These shifts fed into the problem of stagnating productivity growth. For all that the unemployment rate was creeping upward, it ought not to be forgotten that the United States, for example, had created 11 million new jobs—mainly taken up by women and the young—during the decade. But these being primarily service sector jobs of the coming tertiary age, they added little to the amount of output per worker.[42]

Fewer people now worked on or were meaningfully connected to the land. Food produce had to come from abroad, with the number of those employed on domestic farms falling from 33 percent in 1960 to 13 percent in 1981 in West Germany, from 8 percent to 3 percent in the United States, and from 22 percent to 9 percent in France. Mining collapsed, and industrial employment also fell in most countries. The service sector, by contrast—telecoms, real estate, professional services, and so on—grew everywhere: from 26 to 47 percent of the workforce in Spain, from 47 to 61 percent in the UK and from 50 to 62 percent in Australia. It would only keep on growing throughout the decades to come. The era of unprecedented growth had transitioned to one of "diminishing returns."[43]

As people left the country and moved to the city, urban planners struggled to keep up. Unable to meet the inflow of new workers effectively enough, cheap accommodation was thrown up on the outskirts of cities. In 1968, Ronan Point, one particularly ugly high-rise in the London borough of Newham, partially collapsed after a domestic gas explosion, yet the building remained inhabited until the 1980s. In some cases it was simply rampant corruption that lay behind the widespread failure to accommodate the new realities of demography and late capitalist work: as with Le Piagge, a project outside Florence, built to house up to 14,000 residents but which provided the 8,000 who actually moved there with relatively few services;[44] or as with the hasty construction of the University of Nanterre on the outskirts of Paris, the source of all the troubles in 1968.

In other cases it was simply social prejudice, which sharpened as the economic climate of the Golden Age began to dim. In the *banlieues* of Paris, populated by Algerians, West Africans and, critically, the poorer strata of the white working class, a form of implicit geographic segregation was established: on the one side, the new business district of La Défense, where Paris's old rule preventing no building from being higher than 100 meters was waived to allow a new generation of financial sky-scrapers to announce the city's entrance into the new global economy; on the other, the Le Corbusien horrors of the poorly serviced *projets*. America needed no lessons in urban segregation at this point. Its urban crisis was already underway, as the former northeastern and Midwestern industrial cities transformed themselves into a "rust belt" of "shattered storefronts and fire-scarred apartments." The causes of this urban hollow-ing were multiple, fusing the transformation of work with ingrained injustices of housing and race. But "[t]he faces that appear in the rundown houses, the homeless shelters, and social agencies in these urban wastelands are predictably familiar. Almost all are people of color."[45]

More surprising was the extent to which German and even Scandi-navian cities like Malmö in Sweden, where recession broke the back of its proud shipbuilding industry, also divided along ethnic lines. In Germany, the failure to incorporate the growing number of foreign workers and their families led to historically freighted fears of school ghettos (*schul-ghetto*) that would "raise the Negros of our society."[46] In Göteborg, im-migrants began arriving in growing numbers, drawn not to the Nordic economy as they had been for decades, but to its freedoms, and in flight from persecution in Eastern Europe and then gradually further afield. Increasingly they too clustered together, all of which undercut—ironically—the prevailing social democratic culture of integration into society and the labor market that had drawn them in the first place.[47]

By the early 1970s, these urbanizing populations had brought to pub-lic consciousness the twin problems of crime and alienation. The two problems conjoined and were lodged in the popular imagination through a resurgence of concerns about the social "underclass"—a new sociolog-ical category that would haunt elites as the background of every uprising and riot. Just as with its precursor of a century before—the "molten mass" of the Victorian city—the modern underclass was two things at the same time. It was a demographic reality—a persistent body of indi-viduals prevented from participating fully in work and society (though efforts to give immigrants full voting rights, as in Sweden in 1975, ame-liorated this)—and it was an imaginary construct: the product of wealth-ier citizens' fears and anxieties.

Fears of an underclass, of their resentments, and of their obvious lack of employment opportunities were frequently sufficient to associate them with another problem: crime. Germans, for example, feared what the "radical social decline" of an immigrant "subculture" implied for German society at large. On one level there is some evidence to suggest that such fears were well founded: violent crime was increasing during these years (it would begin to tail off in the early 1990s) in Europe, and much more strongly in the United States (and to a degree in Canada).[48] The more relevant statistics reveal that the effects of this violent crime were highly concentrated both locally and ethnically. What mattered was how the crime came to be perceived. And in this respect it was the social fears— and in some cases sheer paranoia—associating crime with the white working class and ethnic minorities that came to direct policy: nor were those same fears of social mixing in Germany allayed by such headlines as *Der Spiegel*'s "The Turks Are Coming: Run For Your Lives!" (1973).[49] It was nothing if not fitting that the very concept of "moral panic" was coined now, in 1972, with sociologist Stanley Cohen's study of "mod culture" (and other "folk devils").

Mods were one thing: a "cultural" intrusion only for those with sensitive eardrums. But those who were different by virtue of language, dialect, or above all the color of their skin, were something else entirely. And it was growing concerns about the rise of *this* particular underclass that led many governments in the 1970s to try to tackle the issue of social integration as if it were a problem of the members of those groups themselves. In Europe and the Antipodes, governments primarily addressed it through efforts to manage immigration, or more particularly to manage immigrants, which was certainly ironic. It was immigration, along with international trade, that made postwar Europe's economic miracle possible in the first place. Northern European economies benefited from the inflow of migrants from the southern European nations: Italians first, to Belgium to work in the mines in the late 1940s, and then to Germany in the 1950s. After them came Greeks and Spaniards in the 1960s.[50] These workers often squeezed the last drops of value out of the old heavy industries of the north, their precarious residency papers ensuring they were also the first—as in Germany—to be laid off when the new post-industrial economy arrived to beat out the old.

The economic slowdown of the early 1970s did more than simply stop up this cross-border flow of people that had characterized the previous decades. It also changed the character of the immigrants (increasingly they would come only from the Balkans and war-torn countries further afield and they would not be seasonal workers but permanent aspirants). And it gave increasing prominence to ethnic and cultural integration as a problem of government. So it was that in 1968—the year of Enoch Powell's culture-splitting "Rivers of Blood" speech—the civic requirements for obtaining

British citizenship were upended in the direction of ethnic qualification thanks to a new rule on the need to have a British parent. By 1971, the UK's Immigration Act had little-mentioned (but barbed) clauses on "repatriation." Germany already had such a definition, but its 1965 Foreigners Act was "an even more stringent measure than the National Socialist legislation it replaced: expulsion no longer depended on the behavior of the individual worker but simply on the needs of the state."[51]

France, Denmark, and Switzerland all imposed limits on foreign workers in the early 1970s, as did New Zealand in 1974. Such moves were not simply knee-jerk xenophobia (though that was certainly true in Switzerland). They were in part a recognition that governments had lost control (immigrants were no longer invited; they just came); though so too had the unions and social groups who once tried to accommodate immigrant members. They were also the first indication of the inevitable: the fact that the Western welfare state as it existed could not forever survive their incorporation (especially in a country like France which, fearful of demographic decline, had long promised "to make Frenchmen out of foreigners"). In Germany, economic contraction after the oil crisis of 1973 convinced a government already toying with closing the gates to stop recruiting foreign workers altogether (tripling the fees charged to firms for employing them, for example). Sweden began setting limits in 1972.[52]

The situation was different in America where the level of immigration was just, at this moment, beginning to increase—in part because it was a much larger country and there was still scope for a reserve supply of cheap foreign labor. But like the Europeans, American policymakers also fretted about their ability to maintain control over national economic policy in the face of immigration's increasingly international scope. The young Italian economist Ricardo Parboni summed it up best: ". . . all [Western] nations have to live through the same impossible situation: They have to carry through a basic mutation in their model of government and their mode of social control while facing at the same time a crisis from within and a crisis from without."[53]

It was precisely the dual nature of the problem that made the economic situation in the 1970s so turbulent. In 1977 steel plants in Ohio and western Pennsylvania had largely followed David Roderick's reasoning, and announced massive closures just years after extracting costly tax incentives and infrastructure improvements from local governments. Labor organizers were so outraged as to suggest—at the height of the Cold War—that they be seized and converted into community-owned outfits.[54] This was hardly realistic, even had there been a consensus for doing so, since far from being seized, companies and firms were more likely to be relocating elsewhere. This rendered seizure as a tactic rather ineffective, while creating its own problem of a growing mismatch between national workers and their increasingly international employers. In fact, firms had often grown to such a vast size that they now entered directly into strategic alliances with states, or else they formed new alliances among themselves so as to manage that growing discrepancy. From such vantage points they could prevail upon governments to assist them with their more demanding, specialized labor requirements, or simply threaten to leave if they did not.

This turned out to be a raw bargain for states to enter into (though most entered into it anyway): for with technological improvements, the largest corporations were employing fewer workers anyway. Fortune 500 companies employed no more people in total after 1970. Meanwhile the number of new (and smaller) businesses doubled, many of them providing subcontracting and consultancy services to the older, more established firms. In response to the falling rate of profit, then, the basic ecosystem of the economy was becoming more complex as firms, governments, and individuals all embarked upon a search for the benign conditions they had been enjoying until just a few years previously. The rate of product innovation grew, which was to be celebrated, offering people an ever-expanding range of items to desire. At the same time the longevity of these new products, if not their quality, declined by an almost equal measure. The political economy necessary to sustain the age of plastics had arrived. But firms and businesses were running faster to cover the same basic ground, and workers were inevitably bearing the brunt. The stage was accordingly set for a major standoff between the two.

The Crisis Bites (Capital vs. Labor)

"It is clear to me that the entire structure of our society is being challenged," observed David Rockefeller, the youngest member of the most powerful capitalist family in America, from the boardroom at Chase Manhattan Bank in 1971.[55] Students had inaugurated the upheavals of the early seventies in 1968, but it was workers who protested for longer, who remained on the streets throughout the decade. As classes and communities became polarized, governments found themselves unable to prevail upon the different factions of society in pursuit of political and economic harmony. America was rocked by racial strife and protests over Vietnam. But problems were just as apparent in Europe, and everywhere, including in Australia and New Zealand, the Keynesian consensus was in upheaval. Industrial unrest grew. As economic conditions worsened, workers and their unions and employers became steadily less willing to compromise their own interests in the name of the greater good of industrial harmony.

The first serious sign of dissent came when a wave of major strikes swept through the Netherlands and West Germany in 1966.[56] The Netherlands saw the gradual tearing up of wage agreements under pressure of disagreement on both sides. The German experience was more dramatic and, given the historical echoes, concerning. Confronted by just a mild recessionary episode in 1966–7, Ludwig Erhard's CDU-CSU coalition foundered in the face of regional elections in Bavaria: elections that saw the extreme right NDP win nearly 8 percent of the vote, replacing one of Erhard's minor coalition partners, the FDP. The establishment duly declared itself vulnerable to economic discontent (this was what was presumed to be fueling the return of a muscular nationalism) and it began publishing concerned, if not outright alarmist, reports such as "Inflation und Rezession zerstören die Demokratie" (Inflation and Recession Destroy Democracy).[57]

In Britain, such words earned the disdain of the ever-sanguine British liberal Ralf Dahrendorf, who dubbed the German government a "cartel of anxiety" (and who probably recognized that establishment commitments to democracy, per se, were not rock solid in Germany either). But worker discontent scarcely died away in the years to come.[58] Dahrendorf's own government had effectively abandoned any effort to maintain a traditional postwar era income policy under pressure from the trade unions. Wages accordingly exploded in Great Britain by 14 percent in 1970 alone. The Conservative government that succeeded Wilson's Labour government that year responded with a statutory wage policy and sought drastically to constrain the unions via the Industrial Relations Act of 1971 and the courts. That was not to the unions' liking at all, least of all, the miners.

With the oil crisis as their alibi, the unions went out on strike and ultimately threw the Conservatives from power early in 1974.[59] Miners were not the only ones unhappy at work. In 1976 six Asian women walked out of the Grunwick photo-processing plant in Willesden in London in protest at conditions (women were required to ask their male supervisors to use the toilet). The act not only added to the general sea of discontent, it brought home to predominantly white male union chiefs that the Western workforce had become much browner and more female in its makeup. They stayed on strike for two years and, when the Trades Union Congress (TUC) withdrew its support, they stopped eating to demonstrate their continued commitment.

Unrest became the norm elsewhere too. In Australia, 1974 saw a record number of industrial disputes in an economy already buckling at the knees. Two million workers went on strike, taking 6.3 million workdays with them: twice what it had been in 1971, which itself was hardly a year of industrial quiet.[60] The most visible victim of the Australian workers' discontent, improbably enough, was Frank Sinatra. During a performance in Melbourne Sinatra had fulminated, in his inimitable way, about the male "parasites" and the female "broads and hookers" of the Australian press pack following him around. In so doing he incurred the wrath of unions whose blood was already up (Melbourne, it should be recalled, was the city that had given international feminism its own anthem in Helen Reddy's "I Am Woman"). Hotel workers refused to bring room service to old "crankie Frankie," as they dubbed him; airport refuelers "black-banned" his plane, and Sinatra was put under effective siege in his room for three days. Bob Hawke, another future prime minister but at this time a national union boss, warned Sinatra that unless he publicly apologized, his stay in the country might be "indefinite."[61]

The country that truly led this wave of labor militancy was Canada, however. More even than in Italy—which had inaugurated the seventies as a decade of labor struggle with the "hot autumn" (*autunno caldo*) of 1969 coming out of Turin—more days were lost due to strikes in Canada than anywhere else: nearly 11 million working days in 1975 (ten times the figure for 1963 and enough to ensure that Trudeau lost the confidence of the people in his ability to manage the economy).[62] Canadian leaders emerged from this standoff concerned that the country was backsliding relative to other Western democracies and, as in Britain, this encouraged them to engage in a series of more radical policy solutions—wage controls, foreign investment reviews, and monetary growth targets among them.

Each of these struggles grew out of its own national context. In Italy industrial decline unleashed an outpouring of radical labor movements, from *operaismo* to the *Fazzoletti Rossi* (Red Bandanas), conducted largely outside the traditional labor movement. What in Italy was about workplace democracy and worker autonomy had in Germany a more militant bent. But what ultimately united them was an awareness that society was changing and a concern as to which parts of society were going to bear the costs of that transition. What workers were defending was not just their own incomes against inflation (for all that this was how the work-erist movements of the era were often portrayed). They were defending more generally the primary benefits, as they saw them, of a now rapidly fracturing political consensus: above all their right to autonomy. The sheer range and extent of some of the proposals put forward underscores this: Rudolf Meidner's plans for union ownership of corporate profits in Sweden, the German unions' turn to *Strukturpolitik* and codetermination, the French turn to *autogestion*, the British Labour Party's elaboration of its vermilion-hued Alternative Economic Strategy.[63] Even as faith in communism was being eroded, then, there was a distinct upsurge in democratic socialism during these years as workers and unions sought to gain control of capitalist economies.

Fatefully, this was not to last. If it was labor that initially appeared to have the upper hand in the early 1970s, it was the interests of capital that ended the decade very much on top, and the reasons ought to detain us a moment. Part of the problem, as the Grunwick women had found, was the weakness (not the historically overhyped excess) of national trade union representatives. The unions' growing concern with the bottom line of income levels was understandable. From 1951 to 1973 wages in the UK, for example, had risen by 72 percent. Then from 1975 to 1977 the average worker saw their real wage decline more sharply than at any time since the Industrial Revolution.[64] This was frighteningly dramatic, but ultimately it took their eye away from securing for their constituents an increased voice in economic decision-making: the British miners the quintessential example of the ultimately hollow victory these years represented for the Western working class at large.

Part of the problem, too, was the extent to which these struggles now played out not on the national scale but between firms and different employment sectors. National union networks and class-based solidarities gave way to competition between unions themselves and more locally driven struggles over work. Even in Italy, which was perhaps the most intense scene of radical workerism throughout the decade, increasingly acrimonious splits occurred between competing factions: between those like Antonio Negri who looked outside the factory to the home, and those like Sergio Bologna who looked still to the streets. In a positive sense, this made those struggles much broader, more "social," than before. It wasn't any longer just about class, but about communities and values. When a major strike was voted on at Ford's Dagenham plant in September 1978, it was "a forest of arms, white brown and ebony" that went up as the motion was called.[65]

But this same diversity also made it much harder to institutionalize the demands of the moment, which turned out to be crucial to determining the political form that the new democratic order adopted, and which ensured that a revolutionary moment, while it certainly hovered in the background for much of the 1970s, informing the anxieties for which the era is still remembered today, never actually arrived. Europeans thus in practice began to ape Americans in the way that job security now became the gift of the individual firm, not the state, to provide; yet hopefully they looked to Japan and its myth of lifelong, loyal employment to explain this to themselves.[66]

France was a revealing case in point. The Grenelle accords (secured at the height of the disruptions of May 1968) set the tone for the decade to come. The workers' more "utopian" demands for autonomy and better working conditions ultimately became the very thing (combined with a little heavy leaning by de Gaulle) that was used to defeat them: the workers were simply offered more "flexibility" instead, and the wage increases they won were eaten away by inflation. Thereafter French workers found they had much more control over their individual working conditions, but less recourse to the sort of collective pressure that might actually limit their further exploitation. Class struggle had not gone away or been resolved in the 1970s, it had been rearticulated and demassified. The very thing that made the uprisings of 1968 so radical—the *combination* of demands against both exploitation and alienation (the drudgery of work on "the line")—was severed. Calls for egalitarianism and emancipation, for equality and personal freedom, were henceforth kept carefully apart by the interests of capital.[67]

The ultimate reason for the workers' defeat during these years, moreover, was not just that labor was fragmenting, but that business and capital—hitherto two separate sets of interests—were themselves beginning to align against them, in defense of what *they* saw as the crucial achievements of postwar democracy, above all its political stability (which made capital growth easier). As investors and businesses alike became more and more convinced of the need to rein in the wage demands that led either to inflation (which damaged returns to capital) or higher prices (which damaged profits to industry) they looked to one another to fight back.

By the end of the decade this was apparent even in America. In 1976 a month-long strike by 165,000 Ford workers secured wage increases for the big three car manufacturers and an agreement to cut hours rather than jobs. But it also invited the wrath and a later backlash from industry and capital alike. Already by 1978 the door to Reaganism was cracked open, therefore, with the landmark Airline Deregulation Act and the slashing, by 40 percent, of the top rate of capital gains tax. The beginning of the fight back against labor in the United States was thus already well in hand under Carter; as it was in much of Europe too, somewhat before the era of neoliberalism, properly speaking, got off the ground. Capital's victory over labor was scored here in terms of a gradual restoration of the rate of profit, itself largely obtained on the back of a gradual decline in the proportion of national income being paid out in the form of wages: which for all of the strikes of the first half of the decade subsequently fell after 1974.[68] The workers had saved Manhattan; now they would be saving Berlin and a great many other national economies to boot.

West German workers were perhaps the first to feel the full effects of this, followed by the Dutch and Italians in 1975. Australian workers began to feel the pinch in 1976, followed by Canadians in 1978.[69] These workers' lost share went primarily to the owners of capital, of the technology platforms we have already noted being adopted in an effort to restore productivity growth, and to those who could charge rents on their property—be that property physical or intellectual—and who could speculate rather than toil for a living. A longer-term consequence of this would be the affordability crisis in Western cities. A more immediate consequence was the undermining of organized labor. In the United States, the AFL-CIO opted not to fight back in the face of these developments. In Britain, unions grew more radical, but they did so in decreasing proportion to the concessions they were able to exact from their capital-owning counterparts.

At the same time the governments who had for much of the postwar era sought to manage the competing demands of capital and labor now increasingly became active participants in the struggle themselves. In Australia the Gough Whitlam Labour government of 1972–5 found itself having to placate business at the expense of unions, and soon openly declared "the acquiescence of the unions" as imminent, inaugurating a more or less permanent rift in the Labour–union alliance in that country.[70] Governments like Whitlam's unintentionally presented a further problem for the postwar working class, however, since having bet the farm with welfare payments (and especially retirement promises) over previous decades, they now had no choice but to find some way to recoup their outlay—and that meant raising taxes. This began to exert its own income squeeze on workers (the average Canadian, for example, seeing their income tax go up by 20 percent between 1958 and 1985).[71] But with worker unrest preventing the restoration of profits and rendering government finances unsustainable, governments came to the conclusion that if they could not appease all of their constituents all of the time, ultimately they had no choice but to side with the interests of capital.

Amid the return of a worker militancy that initially set out to defend it, the postwar political consensus thus ultimately lost the confidence of the owners of capital who retained, still, the deciding vote over its future terms. As they saw it, democracy's promise to make the world "safe for capitalism" had been reneged upon. Since governments had failed to do this, a response was required.[72] A more active business community began to coalesce. For their part, governments sensed there was more to be gained and less to be lost by cooperating more closely with big business, and as this realization dawned they progressively loosened up the regulations on nonmanufacturing sectors such as finance. This was an historic development. But it could not have come about without a concurrent, and no less dramatic, transformation in economic thought. For a new set of ideas were needed to bind this new alliance into place.

A New Consensus Emerges

By the mid 1970s the capitalist system on which Western democracy rested was experiencing its worst crisis since the Great Depression. On the one hand were the underlying problems of inflation, currency volatility, and lost productivity growth; on the other was the related issue of worker militancy, which by the middle of the decade was preventing the restoration of profits for firms. Ultimately a solution to both sets of problems would be found not in the reregulation of capitalism, as had eventually stanched the crisis of the interwar period, but through the reimagination of the place of the market in the liberal democratic state. The management of the economy had swung one way in the 1930s; now it began swinging back the other. Under pressure from the inflationary crises of the 1970s, the great strength of Keynesianism—popular consent to economic outcomes—was revealed to have also been its Achilles heel. Governments were suddenly only too happy for others to take over the dubious privilege of responsibility for economic affairs.[73] The scene was set for alternative voices to have their say.

The sources of this transformation were multiple. In some cases, as with the failure of the commission cobbled together by the IMF—the so-called C20—which sought to draw up blueprints for a new international monetary system after the failure of Bretton Woods, they were unintended. The overwhelming pressures of the time, not least the impact of the oil crisis, doomed the efforts of the commission to failure. In light of such failures, and there now being no possibility of a return to managed international political economy, the only way forward—it seemed— was to embrace the forces of change by further deregulating the movement of capital.[74] The power of money was likewise multiplying by the day as banks and corporations became increasingly international in their operation and as they responded to the loosening up (and expansion) of global finance, in part by adopting financial innovation strategies designed to recoup their falling rate of profit. At the same time, new fora of international economic governance like the G5 were being established, and existing fora, like the OECD and the IMF, were given new roles to play: not as independent agents of stabilization but as advisory bodies and playmakers in the increasingly financialized global economy.

National governments too found themselves forced to adapt to rapidly integrating capitalist markets. And since one of the earliest, and in many ways most illuminating, settings for the emergence of new economic ideas turned out to be Germany it is worth focusing on the German experience as a way of illuminating the whole. Postwar German economics was the product both of its own experience of runaway inflation during the Weimar Republic and the United States' efforts to rebuild the German economy after the war, which prioritized the desire to avoid excessive centralization of power. On the one hand this had created the necessary intellectual and institutional space for the Christian Democrats' core concept of the "social market economy"—in which market actors were given ample freedoms within a relatively tight thicket of laws and institutions, including a strong central bank and judiciary.[75] On the other hand it was also the genesis of the quintessentially German aspiration to "stability and growth," a more disciplined approach to managing the economy that shaped German politics in the 1960s long before it became the EU's dogmatic mantra half a century later.

What set this monetarist ball rolling was the manner in which, in the early 1970s, the relationship between the Bundesbank, the German parliament, and the wider policy environment in which both were set, changed dramatically. It was then that a more pragmatic "monetarist" solution to the inflationary curse of the 1970s was adopted at the heights of German finance. The trigger was the same generalized meltdown of the Bretton Woods arrangements as other countries were experiencing during the first years of the decade, and in particular the very speculation on the lira that Nixon famously declared not to have given "a shit" about. For when the Swiss, in fear of contagion, then blocked all further speculation on the Swiss franc, the Deutschmark became the next nondollar currency on which traders sought to speculate. The stakes for Germany were now dramatic enough for Otmar Emminger, the new vice president of Germany's Bundesbank, to try to convince Germany's chancellor, Willy Brandt, to float the Deutschmark.

At this point, in early 1973, Brandt's finance minister, Helmut Schmidt, was reluctant to try such a radical, monetarist solution and effectively vetoed it on his superior's behalf. Undeterred, Emminger traveled to Bonn to speak directly with Brandt. On the day he did so, not only was Schmidt ill in bed, but Schmidt's Secretary of State Karl-Otto Pöhl could not be reached either (he was on holiday skiing). The one senior cabinet member present that day who actually *could* represent the Ministry of Finance, turned out to be personally sympathetic to Emminger's cause. This was enough for the instinctive Brandt. "If the economics ministry and the Bundesbank are in agreement then it is probably all right," he declared. Emminger's newly approved monetarist approach proved effective in restoring control over the economy, and on his return to health Schmidt was so relieved that the "greatest test of democracy since 1930," as he put it, was now over, that for the most part he simply waved through the changes that had been approved.[76]

The Bundesbank did not stop at simply adjusting to the new post-Bretton Woods exchange rate regime. Henceforth the German economy would be steered not by efforts at managing the value of the Deutschmark but by the publicly less "visible" process of monetary targeting: banks, labor and regional authorities would all now be pushed and pulled in order for the Bundesbank to first regain, and then retain, control over the money supply. Monetarism had just won an important battle against the social market "planning" model that preceded it. But it was not to everyone's liking. Germany's unions were aghast at what they saw would remove their ability to negotiate directly with the state. They accused the Bundesbank of "having no social responsibility" at all. But as the German economy began to strengthen relative to other countries—as the Deutschmark, which had not even existed as a currency until the occupation, now took on the status of nothing less than an international reserve currency—few were inclined to listen. Against perhaps his earlier instincts, Schmidt now came to the view that this brave new world in fact needed grabbing by the horns, not leaving to the "nerds [*fachidioten*] of economic policy." As he rightly observed: "Monetary policy is foreign policy and world politics."[77]

And where Schmidt's economics ministry was soon leading, more and more finance ministries, and the governments they served, were prepared to follow, beginning with Schmidt's "good friend" Giscard d'Estaing, the French finance minister. Thus did Germany's turn to monetarism quickly seep into the Franco-German heart of Europe. A former financier, Giscard d'Estaing was naturally more inclined to market-based solutions to economic problems than many of his European counterparts (who still preferred to use the levers of the state). But the French move would have to wait until 1976 before it could be properly instigated, by which time Giscard d'Estaing had ousted de Gaulle's successor, Georges Pompidou, as president and had installed as his new prime minister the former vice president of the EC Commission and "economics professor to the nation," Raymond Barre. Giscard had even authored a book that same year full of ideas for reinvigorating French democracy (most of which turned upon greater self-discipline and less state nannying). "If each breath we draw," he wrote, "each step we take, had to be the result of conscious decision, illness would soon follow."[78] Democracy, one was to infer, needed putting on a higher scientific plane. Unlike Schmidt, Giscard was all too happy to leave it to the nerds.

It thus fell to the affable yet determined Raymond Barre—"a square man in a round body," it was once said—to oversee the changes. Barre had already played an active role in promoting European monetary co-operation in the earliest days of the late Bretton Woods currency crises, at the end of the 1960s.[79] Hence while other European ministers of the economy came only slowly to believe that inflation needed tackling in a radically new way, Barre started out in office with the "laser beam" focus on economic transformation that a young Democratic president would later make famous for himself. Barre's particular contribution, no doubt facilitated by retaining the post of finance minister when he moved into the prime ministerial residence, was to hitch his own nation's domestic economy to the greater heft of the Deutschmark in an effort to shake out some of France's underperforming industries and to force more wage restraint onto French workers (who had arguably been overpaid since the massive wage hikes agreed upon in exchange for industrial peace at Grenelle at the height of May 1968). He then offered tax incentives to the stock market so as to inject a greater dynamism into the French economy. It would take until 1984 for this monetary revolution to play itself out. But already the storming of the "Bastille of French financial policy," as one historian put it, had begun.[80]

In economic terms, then, the state *dirigiste* years of the postwar era—

of nuclear power and the TGV in France—seemed a long way off by the middle of the 1970s. The monetary approach now reigned not just in Germany and France but in the Netherlands too (where the Partij van de Arbeid, PvdA, turned to it as a means to reduce the costly public sector). It was at this moment that the British, too, undertook their own change of direction. Conservative and Labour governments alike were, in some respects, the most Keynesian they had ever been in the early 1970s: first with US-style emergency wage and price freezes under Ted Heath, then with Harold Wilson's bargaining with striking workers, the consequence of which had been an expansion of the national debt. But after a run developed on the pound in 1976 the bottom finally fell out of the British economy and the incumbent Labour Party was forced to respond.

Then Prime Minister James Callaghan, who had taken over when Wilson resigned, famously declared to the party conference in Blackpool that year: "We used to think you could spend your way out of a recession . . . now we must go back to fundamentals." With that utterance, Keynesianism was effectively dead as a guiding philosophy of how to run a capitalist democracy, and that in the very country that had first given it to the world. No sooner had parliament reassembled after Blackpool that autumn than the British Treasury began following a path of public monetary targeting focused on inflation reduction first and foremost. The monetary pill had been swallowed, and Keynesianism began to heave its last.[81]

The quickening did not take long. In the short term, inflation began to come down, bringing relief and realism alike to industrial bargaining, and a more stable social contract between government, employers, and workers. Fatefully, it also caused the more radical fringes within the unions to split away, so that the stage was set for a more dramatic showdown yet to take place under the incoming Conservative government. The transition toward that showdown was hastened by the arrival of the "Winter of Discontent," when in January 1979 tens of thousands of public sector workers—famously gravediggers and rubbish collectors—went on strike in the largest mass stoppage in Britain since 1926.

For the Labour Party, it was the beginning of the end. Whatever was salvaged from the affair in terms of its promises for a renewed social contract came too late: the party had lost nearly all public support. On March 28, with the forces of Conservative, Unionist, nationalist, and Liberal opposition all leathering their knives in the dark, Callaghan's government lost a desperate late-night vote of confidence (311 to 310) in parliament, triggering a national election. And by the summer of 1979, after votes had been cast, it was the determined daughter of a greengrocer from Grantham who found herself in office, the first female prime minister in her country's history, and by a landslide. The Labor Party, by contrast, would not see power again for eighteen years, and in its postwar incarnation, was arguably never to return at all.[82]

By now the more general consequence of the turn to anti-inflationism—namely rising unemployment—was beginning to become apparent, and the arrival of the second oil shock in 1979, when oil production dropped and prices were raised in the aftermath of the Iranian revolution, prompted a more dramatic increase. However bad unemployment had seemed earlier in the decade it was nothing compared to the levels that were witnessed across the West in the later years of the decade. In Britain and the Netherlands it topped 10 million. In Germany, where unemployment had been held to just over 3 million prior to the end of the decade, twice as many people suddenly found themselves out of work within two years. What was perhaps most telling about all this, however, was the extent to which the need for unemployment "adjustments" like this was now *accepted* by all sides to the political debate, be it the Whip Inflation Now (WIN) coalition in the United States or the left's eventual rejection of the Alternative Economic Strategy in Great Britain.

Or perhaps not quite everywhere. For while monetarism was gradually adopted in exchange for higher unemployment in France, Germany, and Britain, many of those countries with more corporatist social democratic systems did try to hold the line at this point. Norway and Sweden had some success in restraining inflation without creating further unemployment. Throughout the 1970s both had been reluctant to give up on wage bargaining as the way to steer the economy; but they couldn't keep propping up failing industries or expanding the size of the public sector (which carried them into the 1980s) indefinitely. The Swedes then sought a third way: Kjell-Olof Feldt, Sweden's Social Democratic finance minister, engineered a massive currency devaluation to boost Swedish exports. Feldt hoped to provide cover for the government withdrawing itself from the ultimately unsustainable path of industry support on the one hand and wage increases on the other. For their part, the Norwegians struck lucky not only with oil but with the rising prices introduced by the second oil price rise after 1979: a gift from the Iranian revolutionists to the Nordic bourgeoisie.

For reasons of both luck and good planning, the arc of disengaging the government from its economic commitments was thus less painful in Scandinavia, and perhaps did less—for now—to undermine the underlying corporatist mindset. But it was a change of direction all the same, as both countries turned to inflation targeting as the norm: the Norwegians flexing their anti-inflationary muscles first via an austerity program in 1986; the Swedish following via the rejection of the principle of full employment amid a currency crisis at the start of the 1990s. There too it was apparent by then that Keynesianism really was no longer fit for purpose.[83] As to what was replacing it, the primary rationale for political interference in the economy had now switched (it did not go away, as some of the more avid advocates of the new consensus insisted). Rather than aiming to maximize economic growth so as to fund a more equal distribution of national profits, the aim now was to ensure that society and economy alike conformed with the new monetarist principles of tight money and disinflation. Expansionary policies, in other words, had been replaced by the more restrictive principles of discipline and austerity.

Neoliberalism Resurgent

The new consensus may have revealed its earliest shoots in Europe, but it would develop in its purest form at the other end of the decade and across the Atlantic from where it was first tentatively explored in Europe. In 1926 John Maynard Keynes had lectured in Berlin, prior to the Great Depression, on "The End of Laissez-Faire" and the necessary role of government in managing an economy. For much of the intervening years the ideas of those professional economists who argued for market-driven forms of political order were greeted as the utterings of a small cult of introverts. But Keynes's valedictory contained a warning that would in many ways foresee the end of the subsequent "Keynesian" regime that followed. For "above all," he noted, it was "the ineptitude of public administrators [that] strongly prejudiced the practical man in favor of Laissez-faire."[84] By laying bare the limits to state capacity on nearly all fronts, the 1970s were thus tailor-made for the resurgence of free-market ideas, above all in America, and above all for the man who was by then their leading proselytizer, Milton Friedman: a Brooklyn-born "radical [economic] liberal" with a product to sell.

By the middle of the decade there was a growing sense among economists that postwar US policy had not only been in the grip of an inflationary "bias" but that there had been all too much "discretion" in economic policymaking, and that this needed correcting by a far more radical liberation of the markets. Compared to the German Bundesbank, America's Federal Reserve was more hierarchical, however, and largely did as its chairman instructed: something only recently confirmed under Arthur Burns, when he had set the printing presses spinning at Nixon's behest prior to his reelection campaign in 1972 (an act that was accountable in no small part for the inflationary spiral that followed).[85] For this reason, those US-based economists, like Milton Friedman, who had been among the most vocal in their demands that politicians take up the new monetarist cause, were for much of the decade those with perhaps the least sway over actual government policy.[86]

Friedman and his fellow monetarists in the United States were deeply frustrated by this lack of influence. After all, the tectonic shift from a state interventionist regime to a monetarist one had in some ways been foreshadowed by the United States' abandonment of its international commitments under the gold standard. Moreover, the Federal Reserve had been collecting monetarist data for decades, while the Bundesbank didn't even bother until 1971.[87] But for much of the decade, America's conservative economic radicals could only point out these promising facts in vain, as they waged a proxy intellectual war on the Federal Reserve from the think tanks that were then just beginning to proliferate. Friedman himself collaborated closely with the Shadow Open Market Committee (SOMC), a parallel to the Federal Reserve's Open Market Committee set up in 1973 by the monetarist economist Allan Meltzer. The SOMC had the explicit purpose of critiquing the Keynesianism at the Federal Reserve, and from his own bully pulpit in the media, Friedman too rarely let up in criticizing the government and driving home the case for monetarism.[88]

Friedman's radical credentials were burnished by the fact that he was a long-standing member of the Mont Pèlerin Society: one of various neoliberal groupings that had sought to keep the flame of laissez-faire economics alive during the years of the Keynesian ascendancy. In the early 1960s Friedman had taken over as the society's chairman and leading public face, especially after publication of his first popular work, *Capitalism and Freedom*, in which he pointed out, among other things, that the only problem with the term conservatism was its implied rejection of radicalism.[89] Any number of Friedman's positions warranted the label radical by contrast: be it his calls for abolishing the Food and Drug Administration (FDA), or his proposals for a negative income tax (a guaranteed income to everyone below a certain level of income). And a decade of inflationary anxieties had made US policymakers and the public at large more open to the ideas of a self-confessed "kook": they were open to anything that looked as though it might rid the country of its economic malaise. Monetarism, and what the likes of Friedman proposed for it, thus provided a key opening for neoliberalism to take center stage in Western policy debate.

Neoliberalism was two things: as a set of economic ideas it was a reaction to the Keynesian consensus that dominated mid-twentieth-century politics and an effort to secure the conditions for a return to laissez-faire capitalism in the modern world; as a political movement, it was focused on bringing about a reinvention of the state—a new "constitution of liberty," as Hayek had put it in 1960—which would oversee the free operation of the market without the interference of such special interests as democracy enabled. It was, put bluntly, a solution to the challenge posed by democracy to the market; and for this reason it reappeared—at *this* point—as a potentially useful road map for transformation in challenging times, if not quite the theory of change that the right had, for the better part of a century, been looking for relative to the left.[90]

This, at any rate, is what neoliberal theory claimed. To explain its support, however, requires pointing to a number of more contingent factors. Perhaps most crucially of all, neoliberalism's central policy proposal of a smaller public sector was one that helped it win converts at a time when the public sector was bloated and financial burdens upon the state were high. Moreover, its promise of government-at-a-distance proved tempting to leaders who, alarmed by the fate of some of their colleagues, hoped to remain in power by deflecting responsibility for things, like the economy, which governments seemed no longer able to control. Rather than fighting back by promising to do more, governments could regain the upper hand precisely by promising to do less. Perhaps most simply it made it possible to believe—at a time of lost utopias—that there was at least something one could place one's faith in still: the market.

It was after Jimmy Carter's arrival in the White House in 1977 that momentum began to shift in favor of neoliberals such as Friedman. At first glance, the fact that it was under a Democratic administration that a profoundly conservative school of economic thought took hold in American political and central banking circles requires a little explaining. Carter, a deeply religious Democrat from the South, was anything but an economic radical, conservative or otherwise. But his tenure in office was an unhappy one, and as he struggled with a public growing frustrated at his lack of ability to govern effectively, he too realized that a more dramatic response needed orchestrating. Fatefully he turned to the resurgent popularity of neoliberal ideas about the economy to provide it. As he announced in 1978, in a live address to the nation, on the new "anti-inflation" program:

> Nearly 40 years ago, when the world watched to see whether his nation would survive, Winston Churchill defied those who thought Britain would fall to the Nazi threat. Churchill replied by asking his countrymen, "What kind of people do they think we are?" There are those today who say that a free economy cannot cope with inflation and that we've lost our ability to act as a nation rather than as a collection of special interests. And I reply, "What kind of people do they think we are?" I believe that our people, our economic system, and our government are equal to this task. I hope that you will prove me right.[91]

★

Carter backed up his words the following year, by which time he was confronting even more problems abroad with the Iranian Revolution and the onset of a second oil price spike (so-called OPEC II), when he appointed Paul Volcker to sit as the new chairman of the Federal Reserve in July 1979. This was to be Volcker's second influential act (Volcker II, one might say). At the start of the decade, during his stint at the Treasury, Volcker had, like many economists of his generation, been most concerned with economic stability in the round, rather than with pursuing any one particular form of stability. In the years since overseeing the breakup of Bretton Woods he had worked at the New York Federal Reserve and become increasingly swayed by the need to pursue anti-inflationism as a means to monetary stability—in the belief that the general economic climate would also benefit. By the time of his appointment as head of the United States' entire monetary system, he had overcome any of his remaining quibbles about the need to launch an all-out attack on inflation. After Carter's recall, he soon had the monetary guns loaded with powder.

It wasn't just domestic considerations he had in mind. As a part of the United States' new commitment to "setting the tone" in the new, free-floating international economy, it needed to show that the Federal Reserve could operate with iron discipline if need be: otherwise why trust in the United States to steer things along? In a fateful meeting of the Federal Open Market Committee on February 6, 1979, Volcker thus secured agreement on ramping up the federal funds rate dramatically. They would rise from 10 percent in 1979 to 19 percent in 1981, squeezing the money supply and forcing a major, system-wide correctional adjustment. German monetarism in the early 1970s had been moderate and had explicitly recognized a role for fiscal policy in sustaining social welfare goals alongside its correctional interventions. There was no such concession in the United States. By raising interest rates, Volcker was deliberately discouraging domestic investment and capital formation to such a degree as would purge the system of underperforming manufacturing plant.

The effect of this purging was to trigger a massive deflation sufficient to precipitate not one but *two* recessions in the early 1980s (and to plunge much of the Third World into a debt crisis). Unemployment in America surged to 10 million; 25,000 businesses failed in 1982 (a new postwar record), only to be superseded by the 52,000 failures recorded two years later. Savings banks and other thrift institutions also saw much of their capital wiped out by the 1980s. This affected those who remained in work as well as the unemployed, and it took with it something of the popular drive to save in the first place. Where savings and loan associations had been a critical means of funding property ownership for the poor, that meant, in turn, that other sources of housing finance now needed to be found, upsetting the temporary solutions that had been engineered to the (racially tinged) social and urban unrest of the 1960s.[92]

Inevitably this had social and political consequences: the theory, after all, had been that if African American communities had a fiscal stake in society they would be less likely to riot. It was Fannie Mae's semi-privatization in 1968, and the creation of the first secondary mortgage securities shortly after that, which had been intended to underpin a new and expanding mortgage market. That market, and those individuals tied into it via long-term financing, were now required to take on more and more risk to sustain the same level of financial assistance.[93] Farmers too were affected. Many of them had borrowed heavily at the start of the 1970s during the commodity and land price boom. They now found themselves unable to repay their loans at new and higher interest rates. Combined with a strong dollar that cut into their exports, they soon went bankrupt.[94]

In staying the course Volcker was not only kicking out inflation, then, he was also ushering in a more intensively financialized economic landscape that accorded to a critical tenet of Friedman's ideas: that central banks should target the money supply rather than interest rates. Milton Friedman observed all this with satisfaction, since it made so much of what he had been saying for over a decade seem prescient. Thereafter not only did Friedman himself become "an omnipresent generator of ideas in the American public sphere," one constantly calling for a more "radical emphasis on economic freedoms," so too did the particular brand of neoliberalism that he represented at the University of Chicago become the new normal. As none other than Irving Kristol observed: "To think economically has come to mean thinking along lines established by the so-called 'Chicago School.'"[95] For conservatives, here was a critique of consensus-era progressive liberalism with bite: the neoliberals' arguments instinctively appealed.

Neoliberalism, and its signature approach to monetarism, had thus—by the early 1980s—resoundingly won the intellectual battle of ideas over the question of how to manage the modern economy that had raged throughout the 1970s. Monetarism had emerged as a purely practical proposition at first: a solution to the entrenched problem of inflation, which central bankers in Germany in particular felt obliged to respond to. But it was the uses this powerful new tool was then put to that really mattered. What counted was not so much what "monetarism" *was* so much as *how* it was implemented: in that difference lay the reasons why Germany's Helmut Kohl, following on from Helmut Schmidt, would oversee a moderately conservative decade in Germany, while Margaret Thatcher in Britain and Ronald Reagan in America would be given scope to pursue their most radical instincts. In the process of implementing this new consensus, democracy had not become less political, however, as the monetarists claimed. It had simply become political in very different ways.

The Fall and Rise Again of US Economic Hegemony

The Cold War, for all that the likes of Friedman had little to say about it, was ever-present in the background of all this change. As an oil exporter, the Soviet Union benefited from the twin oil price hikes of the 1970s, and in 1979 became the world's largest exporter for a while. This provided the Soviet leadership with much needed hard cash that enabled them to mount their own response to the economic crises of the 1970s: importing both consumer goods to mollify the masses and technology to paper over the fact that the USSR was struggling to innovate in the new, post-Fordist age. While these were both ultimately to render state socialism even less tenable in the longer term, in the short term it served to intensify the pressures on a United States that had been all too aware for much of the decade—ever since it brought the Bretton Woods system crashing down around it—that it was not fully in control of global economic processes.

The particular problem confronting the White House by the mid–late 1970s was how to manage a *global* monetary system in which not only were national exchange rates floating against one another, they were floating in much deeper water too—since the volume of financial transactions and money flows had increased inordinately. This mattered to the United States in particular because, as Paul Volcker himself had pointed out to the president, the country's international standing rested not on whether it could put a man on the moon, but on its far more prosaic ability to sustain its own oversized spending plans (which included putting a man on the moon) by enabling and encouraging other nations to keep sending sufficient funds its way. As Volcker put it: "The available funding for our deficits has permitted the United States to carry out heavy overseas military expenditures and to undertake other foreign commitments, and to retain substantial flexibility for domestic economic policy."[96] In other words, for some time America had been able to have its own cake, economically speaking, and to eat a little cake belonging to others too: which country wouldn't want to restore *that* particular status quo?

Yet by the mid 1970s the United States' global hegemony was waning. The country had been tripped up by Vietnam, had demonstrably lost control over the Western world's oil supplies, and its promises of a military umbrella over Europe had been spurned by the likes of Charles de Gaulle. Meanwhile détente was looking to many to be a sign of weakness rather than strength. Economically too, the US was dealing not only with a decline in its share of global production, as manufacturing moved to Asia, it was no longer the world's de facto "lender of last resort" either. Here the twin developments of US geopolitical strategy and the new transnational monetarist consensus being forged by the central bankers of leading Western nations began fatefully to merge.[97] To the extent that US capitalism needed refounding on a new international basis—something the British had tried, and failed after all to achieve when they were still the world's major financial power—a thoroughgoing rethink of domestic and international policy was required. This was precisely what the US now got.

Domestically, the US banking system needed to be shown to be both stable and competitive. Where the Bundesbank would allow German banks to fail—notably Herstatt in 1974, which while it was a small bank did a lot of foreign exchange trades—the US Federal Reserve now deemed struggling US outfits like Franklin National Bank "too big to fail."[98] Appearance was all in the brave new world of international finance. And with appearances thereby spruced up, a measure of competitiveness could be more confidently restored to the US economy: hence the Securities Acts Amendments of 1975, which required the Securities and Exchange Commission, one of the flagship Depression-era legislative achievements, to now consider the impact upon competitiveness of any of the regulations it might think of imposing. This was followed, in turn, by a "big bang" of financial liberalization (traditional bank assets like mortgages could now be more easily turned into tradeable commodities that could be repackaged and sold on) and the establishment of new "futures" markets in everything ranging from cattle to corn and the roll-out of new speculative derivative products.[99]

The refounding of US monetary policy internationally, however, was a river that needed crossing, as Mao once said, in several steps. And Nixon's visit to China to meet with Mao in 1972 turned out, appropriately enough, to be the first of these. By relaxing tensions between the world's most powerful and its most populous countries, a form of rapprochement was established that enabled greater economic integration long before formal diplomatic ties were reestablished in 1979. Already in 1973 Beijing had approved $4.3 billion worth of Western technology imports. The true nature of the US–China rapprochement—namely the Bretton Woods II system and its balance of force between Chinese surpluses and US debt—would take another couple of decades, and the work of Deng's "reform and opening" policies, to materialize.[100] Before then a number of other steps on the path to reestablishing its economic hegemony had already been taken by the United States.

Arguably one of the most critical of these steps was overseen by William Simon, who as secretary of the Treasury between 1974 and 1977, most decisively put into action the Nixon–Ford objective of reestablishing the United States' economic standing, thereby consolidating the restructuring of Western capitalism around the new, post-Keynesian monetarist consensus. Indeed, where Paul Volcker had stepped forward as the chief architect of the domestic side of this strategy, it was arguably William Simon who most decisively put into action the *international* policies upon which that domestic policy would need to be based.

Simon was a chain-smoking former Wall Street trader who, were it not for his ferocious temper and "outsize ego," would have looked every bit a real-life Clark Kent. He had just served as Nixon's energy czar, but he was a bond trader by training and, like Nixon, a self-made man in his way. He was therefore in no doubt, by the time of his appointment in 1974, that the United States now needed to play the role of thief to catch a thief if the transition to a new global monetary system was to be successful. In supporting free trade among the Western democracies, in other words, the country would need to undertake no small amount of direct government intervention.

From the Smithsonian Agreement onward, the US government did just that. A steady succession of international meetings were convened in its wake, beginning with a series of closed door sessions between finance ministers of the leading economies in the library of the White House, to the C20 and G5 meetings and summits as they now convened everywhere from Kingston to Nairobi to Paris. With Nixon gone, the Treasury also saw fit to bring the IMF back into the picture and to grant it greater capacities of surveillance, the better to enforce the new consensus abroad. Disturbed by the saber-rattling of the nonaligned countries in the early 1970s, America also took the opportunity to overhaul its economic relations with the Third World, cutting back on public "development" aid and channeling such work to its private banks instead, while putting the larger emerging markets on the leash of IMF or private financing, rather than offering them bilateral loans.

As Simon announced on his return from a critical IMF meeting in Jamaica in 1976, where the IMF's new articles of agreement had just been concluded: "We have succeeded in persuading the world to agree on what is essentially a US view of the operation of the exchange system."[101] But the capstone at the center of this work was the repatriation of the Eurodollar markets that Simon secured during a secret visit to Saudi Arabia in 1974. Arriving to meet with King Faisal in the still tempestuous aftermath of the Yom Kippur War and the oil crisis, Simon offered to keep buying Saudi oil on the condition that the Saudis put their swollen financial war chests *not* into the Eurodollar markets that had billowed up in London in the sixties, as British banks built a whole new market of dollar foreign currency trades outside of the US (this is what the Saudis had been doing, and it was part of what had been putting pressure on Bretton Woods in the first place), but into US government treasuries instead.

Given the status of official relations between the two countries, Simon was to all intents and purposes trading with the enemy, in order to gain a lead over the United States' allies (though it was King Faisal who insisted on the secrecy, fearful of what his Arab partners in particular would make of this strong commitment to the United States). On returning home, Simon's Treasury thus created largely "invisible" ways to sell US bonds to the Saudis so as to keep them off the officially published auction totals.[102] It was a high-risk gamble but, successfully concealed, it provided a way to finance the US national debt well into the 1980s, a template for the future US–China monetary relationship, and an ingenious means to secure America's position as a stable market for others to invest in. It also brought the US and the House of Saud into what would prove to be a fateful embrace.

Before the 1970s were out the United States had effectively now completed, through a combination of serendipity and volition, a transformation of the former global system of fixed exchange rates to an alternative system of capitalist global integration. Already by 1975, 125 US banks, like sprawling Citibank, had branches in fifty-nine countries; more importantly still the basic structure of international finance was in place by the end of the decade.[103] And while it had been necessary to ditch gold as part of this transition, the new system was still backed by the US dollar, this time in the form of paper-based Treasury bills. The United States, or at least a critical class segment within it, was put back on the throne as master of the new estate—a remarkable achievement, for a nation that appeared to be hamstrung by the Watergate scandal and otherwise mired in a growing crisis of confidence in its leadership.[104]

The sheer heft of the new approach forced other nations to go along. Any collective capital controls that the Europeans, for example, might enter into as a counter to the US position, would have to be sufficient to defend domestic social and economic policies, and they would have to be agreed upon by so many countries that they were practically doomed from the start. The same was true of the tentative steps taken to address the apparent problem of underregulation of the banks in the new era of international finance: a problem that the various Basel Committee meetings (convened in the wake of the Herstatt Bank collapse) would continually struggle to address. The only realistic option, it came to be seen, was to work from the lowest common denominator up: setting *minimal* controls for balance of payments purposes alone, and otherwise throwing in one's lot with the direction America was now taking.

If this all sounded of a piece with the new neoliberal policy regime being put in place, it is important to remember that the roots were nonetheless separate, for all that the conjunction would prove to be a durable one. The need for all the advanced industrial economies to ensure they now adapted to international finance thus coincided with the desire of the United States to recoup its position as the central plank of some sort of global economic system, and it so happened that this was most easily undertaken *within* the emerging terrain of neoliberal policymaking.

It was in part the dawning realization of this that helped push the European nations, fatefully, toward a more formal monetary-based form of integration themselves. The European Community was the greatest single achievement to come out of Europe after the Second World War: providing, as it had done since the signing of the Treaty of Rome in 1957, both for the restoration of economic growth and for the guarantee of social peace. As a result of the pressure of inflation in the early part of the 1970s, and the differing ability of states to contain it, the European economies had split into two distinct groups: one centered around the (relatively) low-inflation Germany, the Benelux countries, and Denmark; and a more volatile group consisting of France, Italy, the UK, and Ireland. At what was a critical moment, both in the Cold War more broadly, and within the political economy of the West more specifically, the capacity of European nations to remain part of the same economic "community" was coming under pressure. The European "rescue" of the nation state was under threat. This could hardly be ignored, and a report on the status of the union, delivered by former Belgian Prime Minister Leo Tindemans to the European Council in Luxembourg in 1976, set out a number of possible responses, including—controversially—recommending that Europe now acknowledge its "two-tier" status.

The recently elected French president, Giscard d'Estaing, could hardly accept this splicing apart of Europe's Franco-German DNA, let alone his own country's relegation to second-tier status. In addition to their efforts to hitch the franc to the greater heft of the Deutschmark, he and Raymond Barre thus now conceived a plan to "relaunch" the entire European project. To pull this off would require pushing for much closer economic *convergence* among the European nations, not just more of the same old international *cooperation*. Thus did the image of a new and more ambitiously integrated Europe first begin to take shape. Critically, it was one to which Helmut Schmidt, now the new German chancellor, was also sympathetic.

Schmidt had his own reasons for seeking greater European monetary convergence: he wanted to wrest international leadership away from the dollar, and to finally quell the ongoing labor unrest in Germany. More positively, the two leaders were ardent Europeanists who saw in this relaunching of the European Community an alternative political utopia to the dictates of East versus West. Part of that vision was a distinctly social one: Giscard actively proposed not just the linking of European currencies but the pooling of foreign exchange reserves so as to build up a fiscal cushion, for use in emergencies. For the plan to work, however, required not only fellow European leaders but the independent German Bundesbank to be convinced—and this was Schmidt's challenge in particular. The Bundesbank saw Germany's preeminent economic position as a function of the Bundesbank's own careful guardianship of its fiscal discipline and economic stability. Never again could there be any democratic backsliding of the sort that occurred during the crises of the interwar era.

The first problem was overcome when Schmidt and Giscard—who enjoyed a strong personal relationship—sprang the idea on an unsuspecting audience at a European Council meeting in Copenhagen in 1978. But that left the Bundesbank still to be won over, with a skeptical and by now influential Otmar Emminger at its helm. Schmidt again opted for theatrics. On November 30, he flew to the Bundesbank headquarters in Frankfurt by military helicopter to deliver an impassioned speech outlining his plan to the German central banking elite. At the end of four heated hours, Schmidt had discoursed on everything from the Soviet threat to Germany's Nazi past. Critically, he also provided the Bundesbank with a get-out clause—the "Emminger Letter" as it would become known on its declassification some thirty years later—by which the government assured the Bundesbank that if the bank's commitment to price stability should ever be threatened by the ill-discipline of other nations, the Bundesbank was permitted *not* to intervene in order to save them.[105]

Ironically, it was the British who then made the final push required to get a European monetary system off the ground, and it was the British president of the European Commission, Roy Jenkins, who delivered it. Britain had entered the EEC after de Gaulle, who had long sought to keep it out, resigned in 1969. By then the British economy was wobbling sufficiently for Europe to seem like a place of greater refuge, even to the Conservatives. Jenkins had taken the post of EC president in 1977, after failing to succeed Harold Wilson as leader of the Labour Party. In lending his support to Giscard and Schmidt's proposed new monetary system, Jenkins saw a basis for making his own mark on what for him was the more promising European political stage. But Jenkins's activism was not to everyone's taste: as the Bank of England gleefully reported, he was becoming known in Brussels as *Roi Jean-Quinze*.[106] But his intercessions ensured that it was this most radical, monetary variant put forward by Schmidt and Giscard that prevailed, much to the consternation of his own government who saw in it the specter of a two-tier Europe now excluding *them*: a prospect the new British prime minister, James Callaghan, duly groused about to the American president as he filled him in on the bombshell dropped by the French and German leaders at Copenhagen.

The victory that Schmidt, Giscard, and Jenkins enjoyed over the likes of Callaghan, for all that it was initiated in response to the United States' increasingly bullish moves toward embracing international finance and the monetarist ethos, was ultimately a victory in part handed back to the United States. For the European Monetary System would end up locking European countries into the low-inflationary path of the monetary order that the new US strategy sought to oversee.[107] Yet again, the advance of a more laissez-faire form of economic liberalism was being driven forward by the defensive strategies of state dirigisme, as these interacted with one another on either side of the Atlantic. Roy Jenkins put it best during a speech in Florence in 1977 in which he hit back at his critics over the value—and, more importantly, the purpose—of monetary union. "Do we intend to create a European union or do we not?" he said. He went on:

> There would be little point in asking the peoples and governments of Europe to contemplate union, were it not for the fact that real and efficient sovereignty over monetary issues already eludes them to a high and increasing degree. The prospect of monetary union should be seen as part of the process of recovering the substance of sovereign power. At present we tend to cling to its shadow.[108]

★

It wasn't just states that found themselves having to adapt to increasingly fluid international financial flows. Private banks too were now standing over streams that were fast turning into great rivers, and they were also forced to respond. First, they were compelled to internationalize their operations. There had been only a hundred overseas branches of US regional banks in the 1950s; by the early 1980s there would be over eight hundred. Meanwhile the offshore Eurocurrency market—thanks in part to Arab money—expanded from $57 billion in 1970 to $575 billion in

1980. Banks had already begun to innovate with new practices and financial instruments like securities and derivatives. Now they extended these speculative operations internationally, fueled by the rewards of increasingly volatile currency markets. International bank lending therefore grew dramatically from $40 billion in 1975 to over $300 billion by 1990, while bond lending rose tenfold over the same period.[109]

Encouraged by the prospects of taking on new types of trading, banks then also began to demand deregulation of their activities. That way, they argued, more capital would be available to be reinvested (rather than tied up in liquidity requirements) and it would enable them to create new (so-called fictitious) markets. What national leader, mired in recession and public discontent at home, was likely to resist such a prospect? If national banks started doing well, the whole economy would benefit. To be sure, this raised new challenges of how to regulate the capital movements from country to country. The solution proposed at Basel in 1975 had been, in effect, a form of diplomatic triage: home states would be responsible for the solvency of their domestic banks' operations abroad, while host states were responsible for actual supervision of all banking activity on their territory.[110]

But that was only a partial answer to the problem. And as with the crisis of sterling in Great Britain, which required the world's former monetary hegemon to undergo the ignominy of calling in the IMF for assistance in 1976, it gave more of the responsibility for regulating markets to the banks themselves, rather than national governments (something that only further contributed to what one economic historian has called "the erosion of consent to economic outcomes").[111] This was precisely what neoliberals had been calling for. But it also had the effect of reinforcing the extent to which nations were now in competition not only for trade but for standing—for market "confidence"—as well. A new world was taking shape, then, as a focus on "competitiveness" began to replace the old metric of "productivity" as the measure by which national economic performance was judged.

What was more, this post-1970s realignment of US geostrategy and international finance fed directly back into the retooling of capitalist democracy at large: it was the promise of renewed international expansion that gave Volcker the confidence to later "hold the line" of his disinflationary, unemployment-raising purge at home at the start of the 1980s. Moreover, it laid the groundwork for a new distributional politics: one no longer focused on how to share among the public the fruits of economic growth, but on nurturing the returns to private capital. It was a deal that, to simplify only slightly, put industry, finance, and government together on one side, and workers on the other.

The consequences of these economic realignments would finally reveal themselves half a century later. The more immediate consequence for the United States, as it reestablished itself atop this system, was to provide it with the means to leverage its position as the safest port in any given storm. The US was no longer the world's "lender of last resort"—that was a responsibility it had relinquished—but it *was* the single most important economy. And henceforth it would use this latent strength, for all it was worth, in the coming final standoff of the Cold War.

To the Global Age

What are we to make of all these changes? It is usually overlooked in the nationally dominant histories of the era, but the transformation of Western political economy in the 1970s was avowedly more international than the usual narrative of stagflation, unemployment, and declining productivity growth tends to imply. The economic upheavals of the decade made it imperative that countries act radically to stave off domestic political crisis; and yet those responses now also impacted substantially on their trading and investment partners as well. Ironically, while it was protectionism that caught nations in the trap of the Great Depression it was now the very inverse of protectionism—the way governments and those advising them reached out to the world in the search to devise new structures for the management of democratic politics at home—that provided them with a certain escape velocity from the problems of postwar political economy. Australia's chief treasurer Frank Crean could have been speaking for most other ministers of the economy when he observed, "The world is beset by severe economic problems [and] Australia cannot insulate itself from them." The felt need underlying the policies of treasury chiefs like Crean was now precisely how to insulate their economies from the upheavals of political life.[112]

The term that became a standard fixture at the seemingly interminable international gatherings during these years was "interdependence." It would soon be replaced by "globalization" of course, which was first coined in 1974 but would not really enter the popular lexicon until the decade to follow. For now the world was, in more ways than one, stuck with interdependence. It sounds somewhat archaic today, and even then it had been around since at least Paul Valéry's interwar *Reflections on the World Today* (*Regards sur le monde actuel*) in 1931.[113] Valéry himself was no fan of the "excessive and instant interdependence" of the modern world and the term rang a yet more disturbing note in the context of the 1970s: above all for the way it conjured up the image of some powerful, almost magnetic status, which appeared to be neither controllable nor avoidable. This made it available as an imperative to national policymaking of course, and that made all the difference to the turn to monetarism and the isolation of economic policymaking from the unruly demos.

It is hard to overstate how significant this was. International developments now made themselves felt more directly in national policy contexts. The upshot was that nations would need to be more disciplined; ideally, in fact, they would begin to use similar sets of policies, the better to facilitate a smooth integration of their approaches. A race to the bottom was thus inaugurated at home and a race to the top (to universalization) was established internationally. And while the terms of that universalization remained to be settled at this point, it was clear, given that the disruptions of social variance would be frowned upon, that neo-liberalism would for the self-same reasons fare well. The political legacy of the crisis of capitalism in the 1970s, therefore, was not just that Keynesianism was dead but that the social harmony which Keynesianism sought (consensually) to protect was no longer the beneficiary of economic policymaking, but rather its resource.[114]

Perhaps for this very reason the term "interdependence" was there too, almost as a plea for help, in the citation for the 1974 Nobel Prize in economic science. The prize was split that year between two highly contrasting figures: the most influential advocate of laissez-faire capitalism, Friedrich von Hayek, and that primary architect of the Scandinavian welfare state, Gunnar Myrdal. The two men had publicly advocated radically different positions since the interwar era, when economics was becoming the profession of rank that it is today (the Nobel Prize in economics was only established in 1969; the Peace Prize by contrast had been around since 1901). Myrdal's founding role in the Scandinavian variant of Keynesianism and his centrality to the building of the welfare state in Sweden was guilty of precisely those things that Hayek was convinced would undermine freedom itself: it would lead liberal democracies down their own road to serfdom, he claimed.

Myrdal's and von Hayek's respective Nobel lectures were equally revealing of where that debate now stood by the mid–late twentieth century. Myrdal chose "the equality issue"; Hayek spoke of the moral hazard of imperfect knowledge and the dangers of trying to "control society."[115] One was a paean to what seemed already now to have been the greater social harmony of the past; the other a clarion call to clearing out the remaining obstacles, above all of the social state, to the future. Any lingering doubt there may have been after that as to what serious chalk and blackboard economists made of the present world situation, and what to do about it, was erased when, just two years later, the same prize went rather less ambivalently to the second most important free-market economist, Milton Friedman.

By then it was already clear in the airtime being afforded Friedman, in the takeover of formerly left ideas (like housing assistance) by neoliberal economists who sought to tackle the problem as one of efficiency rather than provision, and by the turn to deregulation under even social democratic and left governments, which of the two positions was making headway.[116] After years of gridlock it was the radicals who were in demand. The shutters had been flung open and the gust of new ideas— particularly from the monetarist stable—was welcomed into the dusty corridors of central banks and government finance ministries alike. By the end of the decade, the Western democratic state had largely acknowledged that its interests lay in defending the power of capital. As the socialist Kari Levitt lamented in Canada: the "silent surrender" of the state before the power of global capital was proceeding apace.

West Germany had, if unintentionally, led the way here, but one by one the other capitalist democracies became convinced of the benefits of following suit, until at the end of the decade the Americans and the British took the monetarist solution in a far more radical direction altogether. By that point the Western democracies were lumped together in a "chain gang" of economic policymaking, as they woke up to the fact that it was both difficult and costly to defend domestic economic policies—howsoever democratically agreed—from ever-greater volumes of international financial transactions and the market pressures they created.

After several decades in which it was understood that the task of managing the economy in a democracy was to secure an effective distribution of the fruits of economic growth, the underlying rationale now was the maintenance of the domestic rate of profit, vis-à-vis other nations, not the distribution of growth per se. Given that economic growth did not return to the levels it had reached during the thirty years after the war, this was sensible from a policy point of view—not least because it helped politicians to stay in power. It would prove to be substantially more controversial from the point of view of social justice, however, and for the way that it drove peacetime nations into ever-more open competition with one another. Above all it was to prove consequential in light of a third fundamental transformation of Western society during these years: the fracturing of the postwar *political* landscape.

3

The Reckoning

O N MARCH 16, 1978, the former Italian prime minister and president of the Christian Democratic Party, Aldo Moro, was kidnapped while on his way to vote on a newly assembled national cabinet. The kidnapping brought to a head several years of growing tensions over the so-called "historic compromise" between Italy's two most powerful political parties: the Christian Democrats and the Communist Party. Even had it ever been fully realized, the *compromesso storico* probably would not have been any solution to the corruption that bedeviled Italian politics. But it was significant given the extent to which it flew in the face of prevailing Cold War expectations. Moscow and Washington were united in their disapproval, and as the weeks passed and the nation held its breath, rumors began circulating as to whether one or other of the superpowers might have been involved in the kidnapping.

The idea for the compromise had first taken root with the president of the Italian Communist Party (PCI), Enrico Berlinguer, at the beginning of the decade. Berlinguer's belief that it might be possible to seek a parliamentary path to socialism was driven in part by his hopes that the current political climate made real change possible. It was also driven by fear of what failing to tack to a more moderate line within that context might mean for a modern-day communist party. Given both the prominence of radical left movements in Italy and the relaxation of Cold War tensions under détente, and the recent ousting of Chilean socialist Salvador Allende in 1973 in a US-engineered coup, both views were eminently reasonable. From early in the decade Berlinguer had therefore turned to Aldo Moro, on the moderate to progressive wing of the Christian Democrats (DC), to begin considering how a possible coalition between their two parties might work.[1]

From an international standpoint, the mere suggestion that the Christian Democrats and the Communist Party might govern alongside one another was sufficient to spark a high stakes political drama. In Rome the Holy See condemned the idea outright, while the American ambassador,

Graham Martin, a close friend of Nixon's, wrote home in deep concern at what he called Moro's "strategy of attention" toward the communists. Like West Germany Italy was right on the front lines of the Cold War in the 1970s. The United States had military bases there and the country was a key member of the Atlantic alliance. It was also, of course, the only southern European country to be a democracy at the start of the decade. America thus began cajoling and leaning on the Italians to keep the communists quiet. In 1975 two high-ranking communists were barred entry visas to the United States; the same year, the other Western powers were encouraged to make further financial aid to Italy conditional on the communists remaining out of power. For their part, the Soviets were even more aghast—especially when Berlinguer breezily suggested that Italy's membership in NATO was an advantage (the better to secure "socialism in liberty"). This was heresy, and they sent "scathing" private letters warning Berlinguer to desist. The Americans might have been worried about the growing influence of the communists; the politburo was just as concerned about Berlinguer's growing independence. The KGB soon began plotting smear campaigns to dethrone him.[2]

The Italians, however, confounded the efforts of both superpowers to influence their domestic affairs. In 1976 the PCI came second in the national elections, at 33 percent, just a few seats behind the DC on 36 percent. For the DC, which had been in power since 1945, such a narrow victory was nothing but a failure. For the communists it was an historic breakthrough of international significance. The PCI was already the largest, most effective, and popular communist party in the western hemisphere—a party of teachers and professionals as much as a party of workers.[3] Now it was also a hair's breadth away from actually running the country as part of a ruling coalition; all it lacked was nominated cabinet ministers of its own. And two years later, it was precisely while on his way to vote on the matter of who *should* make up that new cabinet that Moro was kidnapped.

But Moro had not fallen victim to some Cold War conspiracy. He had been taken by members of the Italian Red Brigades (*Brigate Rosse*): a loose grouping of red terror outfits opposed to any compromise between Italy's left and right. Moro was first taken to a secret apartment by the Brigades, where they held a "people's trial" and sentenced him to death. This was publicly announced, but still the government refused to negotiate. The Brigades were an offshoot of a somewhat wider militant movement; they took their historical inspiration—and their call to violence—from the partisan struggles of the fascist years. But they massively misjudged the public's enthusiasm for violent acts, and far from leading it to revolutionary utopia they would end up doing nothing more than undermining the wider Italian left.[4]

What they did succeed in doing was to usher in a wave of political violence, the so-called Years of Lead (*Anni di Piombo*) that blighted Italy for what remained of the 1970s and into the 1980s. As Aldo Ravelli, an aging grande borghese who had survived the concentration camps at Mauthausen to become a leading stockbroker in Milan, later observed: "Those were the years in which . . . I tested out how long it would take me to escape to Switzerland. I set out from my house in Varese, and got to the frontier on foot."[5] Moro was not so lucky. His body was eventually found, fifty-five days later, in the trunk of a Renault 4.

The Divided Society

Italy was not alone in experiencing an outbreak of political violence in the 1970s. Politicians were shot and strangled, bombs were detonated; a quite astounding number of hijackings, riots, and assassinations took place. The sources of this violence were diffuse, but the ambition was often consistent: and that was the primarily conservative desire to forge some path or other back to a presumed less complicated past. Ultimately none of this violence succeeded in bringing about lasting political change. But it did denote one of the principal features of the transition: the declining authority of national governments at a time of social and political upheaval.

In West Germany, the Baader-Meinhof group had grown in notoriety since Baader sprang from captivity in 1970. The Red Amy Faction (RAF), as they were now officially known, cloaked themselves in the veneer of anticapitalist dissent. Declaring themselves the "anti-fascist revolution" that never happened in 1945, they rather unconvincingly conflated "capitalism" and "the profit system" with National Socialism, as if they were moral equivalents. Nonetheless their self-styled "urban guerrilla" campaign of bombings, assaults, and bank robberies reached an all too convincing peak in the "German Autumn" of 1977, with a series of actions inaugurated by the kidnapping and murder of the powerful president of the German Employers' Association, Hanns Martin Schleyer. Like Moro, Schleyer too was dumped dead in a trunk, this time with a note attached: "After 43 days we have terminated Hanns-Martin Schleyer's wretched and corrupt existence . . . His death is meaningless to our pain and our rage . . . The struggle has only begun. Freedom through armed, anti-imperialist struggle."[6]

Violent radicalism had also largely fizzled out in the United States by the end of the decade, but it too left its permanent marker traces daubed across the official political portrait of the age. The Weather Underground Organization (which took its name from a Bob Dylan lyric) perhaps most closely approximated the RAF in its bombings, of the Pentagon and Capitol Hill. In contrast to the RAF, however, the Weathermen took that other great "anti" cause of the era, anti-imperialism, as their justification for political violence. They presented themselves, unsuccessfully, as a white ally of the Black Panthers. In Canada too, which by one estimate saw 500 acts of political violence before the Cold War was out (a looser definition, but a telling one all the same), the rise of indigenous activists in provinces like Ontario and British Columbia raised fears of genuine infiltration by anticolonialists from abroad.[7]

When over one hundred armed activists seized control of a small park in Kenora, Ontario, politicians feared Cuban meddling behind it: something that steeled the government and led to a forty-day siege by police. Transnationalism of this sort was threatening to rich, powerful states seeking to assert their own forms of international dialogue. But it was seen as potentially liberating to those for whom the Golden Age's benefits were yet to be realized and which, thanks to the crisis of capitalism, it now seemed they never would. It was hardly insignificant, then, that this wave of First Nations protests in Canada was initially prompted by the Trudeau government's plan to abolish all indigenous citizenship rights in favor of a new universal model of citizenship: something they feared would leave them even more marginalized than before.[8]

Many of these far left, protorevolutionary movements reached out to the violence of the wider international order in search of a political language with which to understand and to respond to the problems and the crises they confronted. Right-wing terrorism of the era, by contrast, was usually less concerned that other people get their history right than it was to keep writing them out of its own. Neo-Nazis in Germany killed 13 and wounded 220 people in a white power bomb attack on Munich's Oktoberfest in 1980. White nationalist revolutionaries, The Order, bombed a theater and a synagogue in America and killed the radio host Alan Berg in 1983. Italy's anti-Republican right bombed Bologna's railway station in August 1980, killing eighty-five. And the Mafia, never ones for being sat in the shadows for long, intensified the pitch of their own violence across the entire *mezzogiorno*.

Governments too were more willing than in the recent past to turn to force as they sought to crack down on the growing dissent. In West Germany, the "anti-radical decree" imposed by Chancellor Willy Brandt in 1972 (a poorly conceived effort to look strong on fringe elements, it required public sector employees to "show active loyalty to the Constitution") was quite possibly his most unpopular policy: and Brandt was not lacking for those.[9] When anti-Apartheid protesters assembled to denounce South Africa's Springbok rugby team in Queensland in 1971, they were unceremoniously charged by police. In Canada, indigenous and Red Power protesters marched on Parliament Hill in support of the Kenora cause, only to be violently beaten back by riot police.

At certain moments it almost seemed as if the "age of extremes" of the earlier part of the century was making its return. But in some cases, and usually for reasons of ingrained racism, governments were unwilling to crack down where perhaps they should. In 1978, in London's Bethnal Green, a young clothing worker from Wapping, Altab Ali, was brutally stabbed. The previous year the National Front had gained 19 percent of the vote in Bethnal Green and Bow in elections to the Greater London Council (GLC) and white racism was rife. Yet the government and the GLC had done little to prevent this. Ali's murder led to thousands of Bengalis, those who manned East London's sweatshops, marching in protest against the government's blind eye. Before long younger "cockney" Bengalis began to fight back.[10] So much for the spread of US-style "law and order." But for all the local drama of some of these individual actions, not to mention the frequent overreaction of the authorities, the disputes usually ended up falling back on the need of the fringe groups, the primary instigators, for money.

A quite different form of political struggle was emerging elsewhere in the form of a militant radicalism that was neither leftist nor internationalist, nor ideologically saturated to the point of irrationality. Rather it was national in origin, separatist in aim and highly pragmatic in its ambitions. The actions of the Front de Libération du Québec, not just the October Crisis that they sparked in 1971 but the wider questions of language and identity that they brought to the fore in Canadians' minds, was an early warning sign in this respect. The effort to model their name, the FLQ, on the Algerian FLN may have been a little too contrived, but they succeeded in stirring up the most profound challenge to the integrity of the Canadian nation since the Second World War.

In Ireland a clamor for independence of another sort was growing. To speak of secessionism does not capture what was properly speaking a postcolonial struggle over the sectarian nature of Northern Irish politics, which flared during the 1970s; to speak of "the Troubles" however does. The Provisional IRA's campaign of murder and bombings that kicked off at the start of the decade need not be excused to be understood in light of the prioritization of the Protestant majority over the Catholic minority from the time that Northern Ireland was established in 1920. The result, in any case, was that in the early 1970s the political structures, partially democratic as they were (indeed this was a part of the problem), broke down in Northern Ireland: and they would remain broken for several decades.[11]

The Troubles were most immediately sparked following the degeneration of a traditional Apprentice Boys' march through the streets of Derry in 1969. The British then stepped up their harassment and the IRA responded by demanding the British leave. Instead London clamped down only that much harder, precipitating a new round of tit-for-tat provocations and violent reprisals. So far as London was concerned, it was "upholding democracy and the law." Meanwhile, for Gerry Adams, writing from Long Kesh prison in 1976, the British were merely protecting their own "imperial" interests: "Violence in Ireland is the result of British Imperialism, of the British connection and the British presence," he declared.[12] Three hundred and twenty-one civilians who lost their lives in Northern Ireland in 1972, including the thirteen killed by British paratroopers on "Bloody Sunday," were among the first victims of that gap in understanding. Thereafter the IRA intensified its operations and extended them to mainland Britain, where it unleashed a wave of bombings and assassinations, including an attempt on the life of Margaret Thatcher, the prime minister, during the Conservative Party Conference in October 1984.

A rather different set of territorial-cum-political questions lay at the heart of the separatist violence that also flared up at this moment in the Basque Country of northwestern Spain. Unlike the IRA, the Basque separatist movement waged by ETA was ethnic-nationalist in provenance. However, to the extent that the IRA's conservatism stemmed from its Catholicism, it did share something with the Basque Nationalists. ETA was aggrieved by Franco's efforts to deny the cultural and linguistic independence of the region, just as the Irish Republicans were with the British. Here language and religion were the key axes of grievance and legitimation alike. So when the democratic Spanish Republic that emerged after Franco's fall refused (in a post-transition referendum of 1979) to grant the region more than just a Statute of Autonomy, ETA, which had lain dormant for many years, immediately returned to violence once more, murdering 181 people in 1979–80 alone.

Ultimately none of these groups succeeded in bringing down a government. They may have assassinated heads of state and key figures of the political establishment; they certainly tempted democratic governments into unleashing their own waves of counterterror in response, laying the basis, both juridical and ethical, for the counterterror industry that would emerge after 2001 (the Hilton Hotel bombing in Australia led directly to the foundation of the Australian Federal Police in 1979). They may even, in the case of Spain, have prompted a crisis of government and an attempted political coup. But in no single case did any such group achieve its stated objectives, much less incite the public at large to share their more radical disposition. For the most part they simply reinforced people's underlying sense that not only governments but the postwar political state itself was rotting away.

But of that there was already plenty of evidence. "Virtually everywhere among the industrialized democracies, the old order is crumbling," observed a respected inquiry into the upheavals of the previous decade, launched at the start of the 1980s.[13] In hindsight, the wave of terror that marked the 1970s was certainly more than just a blip. But it wasn't where the real revolution was to be found. That transformation took neither proclamations nor special police forces but a new breed of social survey and long-term polling data to detect. And as such surveys revealed, the underlying problem was that society *itself* was increasingly divided; long-standing coalitions were breaking up, mass parties were in decline, and voter loyalties "seemed to have been ripped from their moorings."[14] The resurfacing of violence at both ends of the political spectrum was merely one expression, then, of a more deeply epicentered political upheaval now underway. And the most consequential aspects of that transformation were playing out *within* the political mainstream.

Crises of Legitimation: The Fractured Middle

For much of the 1970s the political center ground did not feel very "mainstream" at all. De Gaulle was perhaps the first major postwar politician to find that, as society moved out from underneath its political leaders, suddenly there was little left to support them. But he was far from the last. As international and domestic politics blended with an intensity they had rarely achieved outside of wartime, politicians who sought the glory of national office in the good times now found they were held personally responsible for its failings during the bad times—even when this was for reasons quite beyond their control.

In 1974 the popular, if at times controversial, West German Chancellor Willy Brandt was forced to resign when it was revealed that one of his personal assistants, Günter Guillaume, was spying for the East Germans. Brandt was a German icon whose own life embodied the inexorable rise of the German state from devastation to Cold War powerhouse. A former radical, exiled in Norway during the war, whence he returned leaving behind the young family he had started, he finally attained the chancellorship in West Germany in 1969 after taking over at the helm of the SPD Party in 1964. And he did so in style, reaching out to the discontented youth and the radicals with his slogan: "Let's dare more democracy!" (*Wir wollen mehr Demokratie wagen*).[15] It says much about the speed of the changes underway that already, by the time of his exit in 1974, the reformist spirit of Brandt's years as chancellor, not to mention his trademark policy of *Ostpolitik*, or opening toward the East (for which he would later be awarded the Nobel Peace prize) was already wearing thin among the German electorate. For all that they had officially maintained good relations, his passing was not much lamented by the Americans either (two years after leaving office Brandt took up a new role as head of the Socialist International).

Brandt was soon joined by others in being removed from government office. In 1975 came what Australians refer to as "the dismissal." In fact a full-on constitutional crisis (a "constitutional coup" in the minds of some), it brought home the extent of the political upheavals Australia was going through. In this case, events turned on the dismissal of Prime Minister Gough Whitlam, and his Labour government with him, by the representative of the Queen of England in Australia. Whitlam's government had, since sweeping to victory in 1972, rammed through a wide range of reforms that upset both organized labor and the opposition alike. Disputes over the budget associated with this—including a loans scandal in which the government had essentially agreed to lend money to itself—had resulted in a standoff between the Labour government and the Liberal-dominated Senate. The government was in gridlock, and the specter loomed of an approaching government funding shortfall.[16]

It remains an unrepeated act, however, that the Queen's representative in Australia, a practically unknown and rather hapless officiary, Sir John Kerr, should then step in to settle the matter, dissolving both houses of parliament and triggering a new election. Officially this was a decision taken with deep concern at the state of the economy. But the result was to reset Australia to just the sort of political ground zero being established in more and more of the Western democracies, and to pave the way for an era of more radical policymaking on the right. In so doing another fundamental pillar of the postwar political system was pulled down. An opposition "must oppose, but not obstruct," as the Italian Giovanni Sartori observed in 1966. France's Raymond Aron agreed: there was nothing to be gained from turning politics into a struggle of good vs. evil other than an escalation into extremism, he observed.[17] But as the Australian political establishment panicked in the early 1970s in the face of a Labour government willing to spend the people's money, even as other nations were beginning to cut back, it was the opposition who moved in to capitalize by dramatically firing up their rhetoric. The antipodes had just been forced to confront the new Western realities.

In 1976, after just two years in office, it was the turn of British Prime Minister Harold Wilson to follow Whitlam, Brandt, and de Gaulle into earlier than planned retirement, once again amid a tightening fog of doubt. In fact, no English-speaking government in power in 1974/5 survived the displeasure of their electorate at the way their nations were sliding into chaos and political despair.[18] But Wilson's resignation was easily the most surprising. He was popular, undeniably in touch with the younger generation (as was later observed, he awarded MBEs to the Beatles in the same manner that Blair had tea with Noel Gallagher), and he was progressive: ensuring British troops stayed out of Vietnam and establishing the Open University—a "university of the air"—in Milton Keynes. He was also suffering from early stage Alzheimer's and, officially, this was why he resigned. Recent investigations have suggested that Wilson may also have been pushed: once again by a British establishment that took offense at the raising of the top rate of tax to 98 percent, and the soft stance on communism that they believed Wilson to be taking.[19]

Wilson's resignation also revealed something of the state of British society in the mid–late 1970s. Wilson was replaced by Callaghan, whose famous tin ear merely confirmed the public in their view that the government was losing control: of the unions, the Irish situation, and now its own public sector. "Crisis, what crisis?" as the *Sun* newspaper headlined his comments on his return from a summit in sunny Gaudeloupe, amid the crises and strikes, and the bitterly cold winter of 1979. The year before, a poster by advertising agency Saatchi & Saatchi had announced to the country, over a long queue of people at the dole office, that "Labour isn't working." That same year, the *Sun* newspaper switched allegiance to the Conservatives. Over boozy lunches the influential editor of the *Sun*, Larry Lamb, would now get a healthy dose of inside gossip in exchange for his paper's loyalty. Lamb's first return payment on that was the very phrase "The Winter of Discontent," which appeared as the headline the day before the 1979 election. That was in May. In December, The Clash released their hit album *London Calling*: a scathing critique of dystopian currents of the day.[20] The Ice Age really did seem to be coming, as they put it.

Of course, it was Richard Nixon's fall at the hands of the Watergate investigation that constituted perhaps *the* major political crisis of these years. In the long run, however, the greatest damage in America was more likely caused by Gerald Ford's nigh-on immediate pardon of Nixon, just a month after he himself had assumed office. It sent a clear signal that the political elite were not to be held accountable for their crimes. It planted a "seed" that would sprout more branches later on—during Iran-Contra, the Clinton affair, the Iraq dossier—and in the shadow of which a culture of "elite malfeasance" was exploited by those at the top and resented by those at the bottom: those who were much more likely to be held accountable for their actions, while their more well-to-do countrymen (and it was men, mainly) continued to "fail upward."[21]

Constitutionally speaking, by contrast, the United States had survived the worst of the upheavals: Nixon was never made to stand trial but he was successfully removed from office. Under extreme stress-testing the institutions of government had held firm. Amid the tumult of the Watergate years, important new freedoms had also been enshrined, which included the ending of the draft for men, the decision in *Roe v. Wade* to decriminalize abortion for women, the awarding of considerably greater powers of self-government for Native Americans in the Self-Determination Act, and via the 26th Amendment, the lowering of the voting age to eighteen for the young. It was certainly not *all* bad.

Nonetheless Ford had inherited a nation riven by growing racial, gender, and class strife: one that, even as it struggled to come to terms with the aftermath of the war in Vietnam, was descending into a new round of struggle at home as a series of vicious "culture wars" began. Unemployment was gathering pace and rising inflation was making the cost of living even less manageable for ordinary people; the Dow Jones industrial average meanwhile was falling. George Shultz, the former secretary of labor, spoke for many when he blurted out at a meeting of the new administration at the White House that summer: "The country

is in terrible shape, and I wish you guys in government would do something about it."[22]

The trouble was the US government had been busy doing other things.
And the Watergate cover-up was only one part of that. There was a
crisis of leadership in a much broader sense. Vice President Spiro Agnew
had resigned the year before Nixon, ostensibly in response to charges of
tax evasion though in reality he jumped before the tightening net around
the entire administration ensnared him on a host of other misdemeanors;
John Connally was put on trial for bribery; and Republican Senator
Wayne Hays was found to have employed his mistress as a $14,000-a-year
clerk ("I can't type, I can't file, I can't even answer the phone," she later
said at his trial. "Supposedly I'm on the oversight committee, I'd call it
the Out-of-Sight committee").[23]

By 1975, Americans had not only lost confidence in the presidency;
only 13 percent of them had what could be considered a "great deal" of
confidence in Congress either (a decade before, it had been 40 percent).
The same year, a Harris poll reported that just 15 percent of Americans,
which is to say very few indeed, had "a great deal of confidence" in corporate leaders either.[24] "The state of our union is not strong," Gerald Ford
declared in his first State of the Union address in January 1975, just a few
months after his turbulent summer inauguration. As presidential mandates
go this was, like Ford himself, derided at the time as distinctly underwhelming. Certainly, it was a long way from John F. Kennedy's famous
"Let us begin" address, and indeed Johnson's deliberately bookended "Let
us continue." But as with the best State of the Union addresses, it was in
fact closely in tune with popular sentiment of the time.

Merely recognizing the extent of the challenges now confronting the
country may well have been Ford's greatest achievement. For they included
much more than Watergate and Vietnam. Government really didn't seem
to be working any more. It was costing more (as welfare expanded) and
yet its foreign policy, its economy, even the public life of its cities seemed
to be failing like never before. Perhaps the problem was the failure of
American government, as some were already claiming; perhaps the Golden
Age had simply burned too brightly before it. Either way, what Ford was
able to give voice to, was something that all Americans (and not just
Americans either) had for some time been feeling: that the system itself
was not working. Writing from the Max Planck Institute in Starnberg,
West Germany, but looking to the squall of crises setting in across the
Atlantic, the German sociologist Jürgen Habermas coined the appropri-
ate term for this. The West, Habermas averred, was undergoing a "legit-

imation crisis": a crisis of its institutions, of faith in its procedures and its leaders. The performance of nations and their legitimacy were no longer two separate things. If a nation wasn't "doing" well, it was not likely to remain politically stable for long.

Habermas was a European and a progressive; more conservative-minded observers, especially in America, were even more concerned at what was afoot in Western politics. For them, the crisis of capitalist democracy, such as emerged in the 1970s, was understood as a crisis not of too little democracy but of too much. Congress, Dean Acheson famously remarked in 1971, was "not worth a damn." In fact, it was "too damn representative. It's just as stupid as the people are; just as uneducated, just as dumb, just as selfish." If this caught Acheson in one of his "low, geriatric, and waspish moods," his sentiments were nonetheless echoed in the more considered prose of what was the single most influential report on the upheavals of the decade, the Trilateral Commission's 1974 Task Force on the "Governability of Democracy." The West was suffering, the report argued, from an "excess of democracy."[25] And the central question that the political right now asked of this problem was an old one it had recently borrowed from the left: what was to be done?

The Trilateral Commission was one of several attempts by Western elites to provide a workable answer to this. Instinctively, perhaps, many of these efforts were international in character: be it the World Economic Forum (founded by the dynamic young German economist and engineer Klaus Schwab in 1971) or the G5 meetings that would soon become the gold standard of international summitry. The WEF would later become better known for its annual Davos gathering, but it was the Trilateral Commission that was originally the most influential gathering of wise men in the upheaval of the seventies. And its work warrants reviewing— for outside the more technocratic institutions of the emergent terrain of global governance, at the OECD, the GATT, and the like, this was the forum where some of the answers that would define the decades to come were being found.

Formed in 1973 by "private citizens" (actually Chase Manhattan Bank chairman David Rockefeller and Zbigniew Brzezinski, soon to be Carter's national security adviser), the Trilateral Commission was an intellectual grouping of elite US, European, and Japanese interests, whose express aim was to focus a spotlight on the "common problems" confronting Western society. Its less express, but more important, aim was to extend the process of Atlantic cooperation—read crisis response—to include the most important non-Western democracy: Japan. And, as the political scientist Stephen Gill puts it, the effect was to give the European and American "transatlantic ruling class" a firmer institutional footing going forward.[26]

The man chosen to lead the commission, Samuel Huntington, was very much among that class. Professor of government at Harvard, where he had been teaching since the age of twenty-three, and the founder of *Foreign Policy*—still one of the most influential Washington magazines today—Huntington was a heavyweight conservative. He was a controversialist by instinct: adviser to governments, liberal and authoritarian alike, and not shy to paint the world in broad thematic strokes. "In the modernizing world," Huntington had recently written in his magnum opus *Political Order in Changing Societies* (1968), "he controls the future who organizes its politics."[27] The phrasing deliberately echoed Halford Mackinder, the Victorian imperialist. And it accurately underscored his belief that political freedoms without control were tantamount to disaster: just the sort of disaster, as he saw it, that had been spreading across too much of the world of late.

This was not entirely in keeping with the sunnier, market-based Wilsonianism of the other trilateralists, who were willing to welcome almost anybody to the global club so long as they could pay the entrance fee and put another hand to the boardroom deck. In this sense trilateralism itself was indicative of the coming "big tent" conservatism of the decades ahead (a conservatism that would happily incorporate elements of the newly disgruntled left). But Huntington's pessimism was in keeping with the increasingly popular critique of the Keynesian socioeconomic model: a model that had already been softened up by the hugely influential *The Limits to Growth* report: the problem of an excess of population now being augmented by the idea of an excess of democracy.[28]

The "crisis of democracy" that Huntington and his colleagues ultimately diagnosed in 1975 did not stem just from the fear that Western politics was vulnerable to contagion from radical movements abroad. Rather, democracy had overreached itself in the West. Governments thus had only themselves to blame for the "adversary culture" and "civic irresponsibility" that was clogging up the system, adding more and more people to the welfare rolls while undermining the authority of governments in the process.[29] In short, as Huntington himself put it, it was far from clear that "the dramatic renewal of democratic spirit" that had taken place in America over the previous decade—be it civil rights or 1968—was such a good thing after all.[30]

Had Huntington been less concerned about democracy's looming size he might here have noticed its changing shape. But the real significance of the Trilateral Commission was not so much what it said as who was saying it and how. Trilateralism represented a new type of political forum in which powerful interests set about redefining the very terms of the debate. In the death knell announced by the crisis of democracy which its authors saw all around them was thus to be found, as well, the birthing water of a new era of "good governance," which in practice boiled down to the management of those factors impinging on individual liberal (read market) freedoms. At the same time, blinkered by its own analytical tropes, the Crisis of Democracy report arguably missed much of what was most significant about the changes afoot within democracy.

The real catch-22 of those years was thus precisely the fact that citizens and their leaders could each see half of the problem, and yet both tended to sharpen the problem in the way they set about responding. In 1977, the American Jewish intellectual Joseph Rothschild duly warned Europeans to take note of where this was likely to lead: "Where[ever] legitimacy has been gravely eroded, regimes and governments are obliged to devote so much energy to defending their authority, that they cannot use it productively—to their own detriment and the community's loss."[31] That was a lesson that left and right alike failed to heed. The left, concerned with defending its democratic legacy, failed to remain in power; the right, concerned with retaking control, failed to secure a democratic future. The political landscape of the West was left floundering in between.

The Decline of the Left

Initially it looked as if the social democrats might have emerged strongest of all from the upheavals of the 1970s. Trudeau, whose huge personality and towering intellect dominated Canadian politics from the start of the decade, remained in office (bar just nine months in opposition) until 1984, while Gough Whitlam's policies, if not the man himself, dominated much of the decade for Labour in Australia. Whitlam's liberal successor, Malcolm Fraser, was anyway a committed Keynesian—which was precisely what Nixon himself had declared himself to be, albeit with a rueful irony, at the start of the decade in America. In Europe, the transitions from decades of autocratic rule in Spain, Portugal, and Greece all saw the crowning not of conservative, but of left social democratic parties and coalitions before the decade was out. Italy of course, was flirting with heading even further to the left.

Back in 1951 the Socialist International had sanctioned democratic pluralism as the official stance of social democratic parties the world over, and pragmatic communists, like Palmiro Togliatti—in contrast to the dogmatism of the French communist party (PCF) under Georges Marchais—had come to accept the need for a period of social democratic "cultural hegemony" as the necessary stepping-stone to a democratic socialism.[32] By the early 1970s they were being rewarded for this at the polls. The start of that decade had likewise seen labor unions ascend to the pinnacle of their power: controlling the agenda, as in France and Great Britain, or else receiving ever-greater concessions, via codetermination laws, in exchange for not doing so in West Germany. In Sweden plans were afoot that, had they come to fruition, would eventually have seen major corporations entirely owned by the unions themselves.

For a while it did indeed seem as if Willy Brandt's declaration that "everyone wanted to be a social democrat during the Golden Age" still held true. Anthony Crosland, one of the most influential reformists within the Labour Party in the fifties and sixties, was still championing *The Future of Socialism* to the Home Counties into the seventies. Crosland was later ridiculed by revelations he had received a silver teapot (the graft!). But what he more enduringly represented was the fact that the radical, top-down left had largely ceded to the social democratic middle: the ends of socialism (public services) in Britain in particular being seen to be more important than the means (ownership of the means of production). Meanwhile, in their stronghold of Scandinavia, social democratic parties routinely monopolized elections year after year. In Denmark the social democratic share of the vote grew steadily to peak at 42 percent in 1964; in Norway it peaked at 48 percent in 1964; in Sweden it never once fell below 45 percent.[33]

This social democratic heyday came to a distinct end from the mid–late 1970s onward. First in France and in West Germany the age of Giscard d'Estaing and Helmut Schmidt brought a more liberal, conservative flavor to the heart of European politics. Then, most dramatically of all, in Sweden in 1976 the Social Democrats were thrown out of power for the first time in almost four decades. The British Labour Party was not only defeated in 1979, it received its lowest share of the national vote since 1931.[34] It soon became apparent, in fact, that social democrats everywhere were confronting a common set of problems. Most basically, they depended on the achievement of economic growth to come good on their largely redistributive ideological offering: and yet productivity growth was now at an end. They were reliant as well upon the welfare state and economic planning as the mechanisms for achieving that. The benign paternalism this implied chimed poorly in the new anti-authoritarian ethos of the time. And for all that the *folkhemmet* (people's home) may have helped ward off the threat of fascism in the 1930s, it did little to inspire confidence that social democrats had the answer to the more pressing contemporary problem of international economic volatility. Forced now to rethink the nature of the social contract when economic prosperity was no longer in their gift, most failed to do so.

Little by little the social democratic edifice cracked, as criticism of national insurance plans grew, as new poverty was revealed, and as widely touted social democratic "achievements" in everything from schools to urban planning came under critical scrutiny. In 1971 the head of Sweden's Employers' Confederation, Sture Eskilsson, wrote an influential (and leaked) memo, entitled "SAF's hemliga PM," which recommended the cultivation of right-wing alternatives to attract Sweden's youth away from the radicalism of the post-68 era. In 1976 Astrid Lindgren, the popular children's author, published *Pomperipossa i Monismanien*, a satirical (and soon popular) book as riposte to being asked to pay a 102 percent marginal tax rate. When Gunnar Sträng, the finance minister, accused her of incompetent calculation and suggested that she leave the economics to him, she shot back that they might all do best if they swapped places: she could do the financial calculations and he could write fanciful sagas, since he clearly had the knack for it. Little wonder that commentators were soon in fact lamenting "the end of the social democratic century."[35]

The less palatable truth, for many leftists at least, was that it wasn't just the social democracy of the past that was being put out to pasture; it was the political left more generally that was being left behind. The 1970s witnessed nothing less than the decline of the old left as a force in national politics. If this strikes us as obvious today, few were much inclined to see it at the time. Some simply claimed that the left–right divide had stopped mattering altogether. Others pointed to the fact that there were more social democrats in power in the 1980s than in the 1950s.[36] Both diagnoses had some basis in truth. But they each failed to grasp what was really afoot.

The change rather was taking place *within* the parties and in their policy formulas and above all in their reception among the people. The handing of the baton from Brandt to the economically more liberal Schmidt in West Germany was but one example of this. The Social

Democrats (SPD) under Brandt had been drifting steadily toward the center ever since they rejected Marxism in the 1959 Bad Godesberg program (and especially after the grand coalition with the CDU-CSU of 1966, which itself opened up space for the radical left of the Ausserparlamentarische Opposition, the extraparliamentary opposition, APO). Brandt skillfully rode out these changes on his route into power; but he was ultimately unable to stop them.

In Italy, a succession of elections in the 1980s, following on from the Moro debacle, also saw Italian parties of the left move to the right. While some historians point to the loosely aligned coalition (some even say conspiracy) that took shape in the immediate wake of Moro's death— between the socialist Bettino Craxi and the Christian Democrats Giulio Andreotti and Arnaldo Forlani, all of whom served in one another's governments—the reality may just as likely be the fading star of the old political blocs themselves: as marked by the declining influence of the Italian CD's single greatest postwar figure Amintore Fanfani, a man who had once held the sort of status in Italy that de Gaulle had commanded in France. In France, the electoral victory of François Mitterrand, far from promising a swing to the left, soon consolidated the opposite after his infamous policy U-turn of 1983. It helped to open up more political space for Le Pen on the right.[37] In Austria the same opening was afforded Jörg Haider. Progressively minded individuals, meanwhile, looked to other, more promising outlets instead: including the one social movement, environmentalism, that would assert itself as an electoral presence in the years to come.

There were exceptions of course: most notably in Spain, where the failed coup in 1978 shut out the political right for a generation and laid a basis for two decades of center-left hegemony under the Spanish Socialist Workers' Party (PSOE). But this could in part also be explained by the generational handover that Spain was undergoing. As a Spanish journalist observed on the night of the socialists' landslide in the first national elections of 1979, "This isn't [just] a victory by the left over the right. It's a victory by the young over the old."[38] Such nuances aside, the situation in most countries conformed to a similar general pattern: regardless of which way voters now headed, they *came* primarily from the left. As Willy Brandt would ruefully observe in Germany, for example, the Greens were the "SPD's lost children"—and they would end up costing them votes. The end result, politically speaking, might best be described as a swing to the right and a dip on the left. Not earth shattering, but substantive and—what is more important—long-term. By the

1980s, the only countries to buck the rising trend of right, or right-oriented, parties in Europe were the smallest ones—Belgium, Greece, Sweden and Norway—while to run the same numbers with leftist or workers' parties, rather than center-left parties, the picture was one of near total collapse.

So what exactly had gone wrong? The new political environment certainly accounted for part of the problem. But that same environment also confronted the right. In reflecting on the fortunes of the left in the 1970s, therefore, it is hard to avoid the conclusion that the left itself got certain things wrong, and this at the most critical juncture since the war. To some extent this was a case of misreading the signs. As the political turmoil of the 1970s escalated and economies teetered on the brink, some parts of the left were uninhibitedly jubilant, content in the knowledge that with capitalism seemingly in crisis they had been proven right all along. The dollar was stumbling; imperial America had been pushed out of Vietnam. What wasn't there to celebrate? It was a question they would soon be afforded the time to reflect on in peace.

But the problems were more fundamental than can be explained by tactical or strategic errors alone. The problem was ultimately not the left's wrongheaded analysis of the situation but its changing constituency and purpose. From the moment the Russian exile Aleksandr Solzhenitsyn's work on the Soviet gulags found its way into Western hands in 1974 the left had begun to suffer from a degree of existential doubt that the right was entirely unencumbered by. *Le choc Solzhenitsyn* broke especially hard across the backs of left-bank intellectuals, who could no longer plausibly deny that Soviet communism was anything but the hollow shell it had long looked like being. Just the year before, a French citizen, Jean Pasqualini, had published a dramatic memoir, *Prisoner of Mao*, about the state of affairs in communist China, where he too had been held in a Chinese labor camp for seven years. The combined effect of these testimonies was a key factor in the breakup of the European left, and the emergence, in France especially, of the new, more moderate left of *les nouvelles philosophes*.[39] It also provided the opening for what, in France, would be the more significant "antitotalitarian" movement on the left, spearheaded by the likes of François Furet and Claude Lefort, who sought to wrest the last of the "revolutionary" blinkers from French intellectuals' eyes (and to drive out Marxism with it), largely opening up the path to the more centrist left of today.[40]

This quite subtle reimagination of the purpose and historic meaning of "revolution" was not lacking in political intent: Furet's barbs were aimed squarely at the still dominant, and reactionary, PCF and helped, intellectually, to finish off what had been the second most dominant Western European communist party after the Italian PCI.[41] British socialists too embarked on a "new left" project of self-reinvention during these years, with the likes of Stuart Hall among its leading figures. But in contrast to the French, the British—outside a few intellectually articulate, but marginal redoubts—had never really held to the idea that the Soviet Union was any kind of acceptable alternative to capitalist democracies. The transformation of the left in Britain was thus less fratricidal than it was in France, where those who had once signed up to the PCF were now busy deserting it. In contrast to this, the southern European left, and the Italian and Spanish in particular, still considered themselves communists before they were socialists.

This may in itself explain why the changes confronted by the left from the mid–late 1970s ultimately played out most dramatically in Italy. In the aftermath of the Moro affair, which had seen the party retreat into minority opposition, and on the back of the crushing of Solidarity in Poland in December 1981, the still popular Enrico Berlinguer finally gave up the last of his hopes in existing communism and refused to continue making any more excuses for it. In a dramatic gesture he took to the airwaves and tentatively (yet no less heretically) declared that the "capacity of the eastern European societies, or at least some of them, to act as a driving force for renewal, has now exhausted itself." After a decade of provocation, and in a world where every nuance was watched and scrutinized by party hacks in Moscow, this was unheard of, even by Berlinguer's loose-lipped standards. *Lo strappo* (the break), as the Italian media soon dubbed it, had finally arrived; by January, *Pravda* had excommunicated Berlinguer from the moral community of socialists. And so it was telling, when Berlinguer died just a few years later in 1984, that not only did more than a million people attend his funeral, but that a certain Mikhail Gorbachev was among them.[42]

Once again the need to come to terms with international realities was pressing in upon the national scene. The extent to which one was likely to be supportive of communism, and more specifically of the Soviet Union, for example, was one issue in particular that separated the American and European left. Unlike Europe, and certainly unlike Italy, most socialists in the United States were not communists (the communist party had only around 25,000 members by the 1970s and had long since disgorged itself of any Stalinist line). But this made those who were committed members more, not less, subservient, and the Communist Party

USA continued to follow Moscow's signaling well into the 1980s. In Europe, by contrast, communist leaders like Spain's Santiago Carrillo were only too happy to break out on their own. But it was all just a little too late. European communist parties slid into electoral marginality throughout the 1980s for the simple reason that communism no longer responded to the challenges of the day, with or without the taint of the Soviet Union.

The moral bankruptcy of the USSR is one popular explanation for the decline of the Western left but far from a complete one, and conflation with the now discredited creed of Soviet communism was in fact among the least of the wider left's worries by the early 1980s. The much more significant problem it confronted—one which no amount of doctrinal tinkering could fix—was the bare and uncompromising fact that "the people"—its electoral but equally its moral constituency—were no longer anywhere to be found. The problem, simply put, was that the subject of politics itself was shifting: from "the people" to individuals, if not some more abstract notion of their "identities." The economic upheavals of the 1970s were a part of the reason behind this: as inflation had settled across the West, it had "made people vote as consumers" rather than as members of a class.[43]

But the demography of electorates had changed too, redrawing the old battle lines in the process. This became steadily more apparent over time. Thatcher's second election victory, for example, was often put down to the patriotic fervor she had conjured up over the Falkland Islands. That may be, but it was no less a product of the fact that the working class were no longer the majority bloc they once were in the cities and in the north and west, and they were certainly no longer unflinchingly Labour supporters. Many now defined themselves as middle class. They had new positions and new aspirations, and political parties would have to come and find them anew.

Where this problem was at least recognized as such, far more so than in Europe, was in the United States. There, in a comment that would prove unpopular for its bluntness, but insightful over time, the liberal economist J. K. Galbraith declared in the late 1960s that the working class was now little more than a statistical anomaly. He was not the first to have pointed this out. A decade before, C. Wright Mills, intellectual *padrino* of American leftists, had written his disciples a "Letter to the New Left," urging them to drop the "labor metaphysic" and to wake up to the fact that the desire for revolutionary change did not burn in the working-class breast any longer.[44] In 1978 a group of leading British leftists likewise wondered aloud (this was what the left primarily now did) if the forward march of labor had indeed finally been halted.[45] At this point the progressive end of Arthur Schlesinger's "Vital Center"—a center that had taken shape with Roosevelt and reigned dominant until Kennedy—buckled at the knees.

That old center ground of big-government, America-first liberalism had been a product of and a response to the Depression, to the war, and in due course to communism itself. But by the 1970s the new focus on détente was just one of a host of factors pushing Democrats in particular away from it. The loss of liberal–labor cohesion was another. As one historian put it: "Mindful of Vietnam, rather than Stalinism, and drawing on a Progressive middle-class reformist tradition, activists created a new liberal style and Democratic Party."[46] Of course, the vital center was never as coherent as might have been claimed. But the new trend toward a much greater fragmentation of the left was clear enough, and its coming was measured in everything from the fiasco of George McGovern's 1972 presidential campaign to the failure to continue institutionalizing the moral achievements of civil rights in the 1970s. The Democrats, in short, no longer knew quite what it was they really stood for. The result? They now "hemorrhaged votes for a generation."[47]

What was not recognized in America, any more than it was realized in Europe, however, was that the evacuation of the working class as the primary subject of left politics raised an additional problem that would have a bearing on any future left's strategy at least as much as its goals, and which would arguably do more to sideline political progressivism in the decades to come. This too was a problem first aired in the abortive revolution of 1968 and yet never subsequently addressed. It concerned the loss of complementarity between the ideals of freedom and those of social justice. In 1971 the political philosopher John Rawls published his *Theory of Justice*, one of the definitive works of political philosophy of the century. Here was *the* classic statement of the centrality of distributive politics to the success of "modern" society. But it was written in a language that was rapidly falling out of fashion; it was an epitaph more than the encomium it was intended to be, and thereafter the two objectives—individual freedom and social justice—would move only further apart, not least within Rawls's own highly influential intellectual output.

Unmoored from its own historical subject, buffeted by the trends of the time, and unsettled by the onrush of violence that its radical fringes had shown themselves still capable of wreaking, one can see just in what ways and to what extent the left as a force in politics found itself being pulled apart from the 1970s onward—and it is little wonder its subsequent history has been one mostly of uphill struggles. In response, that part which seriously wished to remain in power joined the center-right (a trend which would in due course lead to Bill Clinton, to Helen Clark in New Zealand, and to Tony Blair). The other part became increasingly critical and introspective in proportion to its declining influence. And the more that this left lost its voice the more it too came to bemoan the failure, not of its own politics within democracy, but the failure of democracy itself.[48]

The New Politics of Movement

That the left now found itself both divided and losing its voice was nothing if not ironic, since progressive movements were more active than they had been in a generation. But what neither the left nor the right could deny, any more than they could avoid trying to address, was the fact that the nature and form of political agency itself was changing. For well over a century the only way to do politics was to join a party at the top or to overthrow the system from below. But from out of the turbulence of the times a raft of new social movements now emerged to provide influential vehicles for pursuing political objectives alongside (if not outside of) the political system. Here there were all sorts of promising opportunities.

For a new wave of feminists, for example, the impetus to what was a major remobilization during these years was the simple fact that the Golden Age had always been decidedly more golden for their male counterparts. Swiss women were still being denied the vote until 1971, Portuguese women until 1975. It was little wonder, then, that "as French feminists eventually concluded, frying the steak of a revolutionary took as much time as frying the steak of a reactionary."[49] If not longer. In Italy women were confined by the powerful PCI to running the family as "a cell of resistance" in the wider Cold War confrontation: it was hardly the front lines.[50] In British universities women were often only employed so far as they were willing to put on "extra-mural" classes (literally, outside the walls), which was in part why women's liberation (WLM), as it developed in the UK, did so in such spaces as adult education to which women's intellectual endeavors were confined. As the British Labour feminist Anna Coote said of her party's otherwise radical economic platform, and its principal intellectual contribution to the decade, the Alternative Economic Strategy: "in spite of its radical pretensions, it is embedded in the same old-fashioned patriarchal values that inform and distort mainstream political thinking today." Child benefits, parental leave, and extending the social wage would all be more useful than economic reform alone. She was absolutely right.[51]

Only really in West Germany and the Nordic countries was feminism given the space to develop an original socialist voice, and both countries used it to call for state nurseries and equal pay.[52] In most countries, pursuing their own agenda within a wider demand for change meant that women, who were still not considered "proper material" for political office in most countries, would have to think around class as much as through it if they wished to change the world: and like many of their new social movement brothers and sisters, they frequently drew on the vernacular of postcolonial "liberation" to do so. As Angela Davis had already showed, they would have to do the same with race as well. "Young and old, rich and poor, white and black are meeting in towns and cities," reported the *Hayward*, California's daily review on the 1970 Strike for Equality, which saw half a million women mobilize in America.[53]

Post-68 more and more spaces opened up for women's organizing: indeed, a quite staggering transformation of the patriarchally defined public sphere now took place that would not be matched until the MeToo movement nearly half a century later. The White House was picketed and the Night was Reclaimed; even some of Cambridge's all-male colleges finally began admitting women from 1972. Refuge centers for victims of domestic abuse, the disrupting of Miss World competitions, clinics providing free pregnancy testing and child-care support all emerged as well.[54] Often, as with the continuing struggle of American blacks for racial equality and justice, Western women's growing political engagement involved forms of legal activism too—something the years of protest in the 1960s had laid the foundation for.[55] In America groups like the National Organization for Women (NOW), founded and led initially by Betty Friedan, pushed for equal rights amendments on the basis of collective forms of private disenfranchisement. "Each suburban wife," Friedan famously wrote in *The Feminine Mystique*, "struggled alone. As she made the beds, shopped for groceries, matched slipcover material, ate peanut butter sandwiches with her children, chauffeured Cub Scouts and Brownies, lay beside her husband at night—she was afraid to ask even of herself the silent question—'Is this all?'"[56]

As white middle-class women began to pose that question more vocally on the streets, they were often joined by black feminists, who were more seasoned community activists, and who imparted another distinctive element to the emerging feminist movement. From 1970 on, the year that French feminists, in their own legal struggles, declared *"l'année zéro,"* patriarchy also began to be written out of the laws of the land. The landmark US Supreme Court ruling in *Roe v. Wade* (1973) gave American women greater control over the right to have an abortion while marital rape laws tightened. The Equal Pay Act was extended. In Europe divorce laws, such as Britain's Divorce Reform Act (1969), were introduced, giving greater opportunity for women to initiate proceedings, and divorce was legalized for the first time in Italy in 1974 (Spanish women would have to wait until 1981). Even in Italy, by the end of the decade the Senate approved, after half a decade of concerted agitation, a "Law on the social protection of motherhood and the voluntary termination of pregnancy."[57]

Change was not always forthcoming, however. Politically, women were being taken more seriously. Legally, they were gaining control over their bodies. But patriarchy persisted, as in one mildly infamous yet revealing interview by the British chat-show host Michael Parkinson with the actress Helen Mirren: "You are, in quotes, a 'serious actor,'" he said. "But do you find that what could best be described as your equipment hinders you in that pursuit?" Women's bodies were also being reconstituted around market values. It came to matter not just whether the law said you could get an abortion, but whether you could afford a safe one. More pervasively, the changing cultural conventions around getting a job opened up new challenges in combining that with the home-keeping and child-rearing that women were still routinely expected by men to undertake well into the new millennium. As the disjunction between public and private advances grew, the movement faltered a little.

A separate strand of the new wave of feminism gave less priority to collective political concerns in favor of focusing on the cultural recuperation of sex itself. Anne Koedt's "The Myth of the Vaginal Orgasm" radically unveiled the complicity of medical knowledge with patriarchal domination. Germaine Greer's *The Female Eunuch* (1972), with its assault on such shibboleths as "the middle-class myth of love and marriage," was without doubt a singularly political book, but as one reviewer rather snootily noted, there was a good deal "more emphasis on orgasms than on increasing the number of women MPs." Broadening the battle was nonetheless an important task in confronting the often blind privilege of Western patriarchy. Some Italian feminists, like Carla Lonzi, sought outright separatism from their male counterparts (as in her influential tract "We Spit on Hegel"), but others in Turin engaged vigorously alongside their male counterparts in the city's great union battles of the decade.[58] Even in southern, conservative, and Catholic Naples, the new "civic" language coming out of the American feminist scene encouraged novel forms of social engagement.

By the end of the decade, feminists had transformed the terms of the debate: a tripling of the number of women in US state legislatures and the establishment of a first National Advisory Committee for Women under Jimmy Carter would not have come about without their concerted efforts. In 1975 the UN announced the decade for women. But too often this was just window dressing rather than real reform, and there were also some notable setbacks. In 1982 the French Constitutional Council overruled a proposed bill by the socialists insisting that no more than 75 percent of a party's candidates should be of one sex on the grounds that it infringed the Declaration of the Rights of Man.[59] In Britain, the MP Elizabeth Peacock found, on her arrival in the Houses of Parliament in 1983, that some legacies of the past even Thatcher had not yet overturned: there was only one women's loo, and nobody seemed to know where it was. The popular feminist magazine *Ms.* (1971), with its features on the Swedish welfare state, was a revelation. But it was soon swamped by *FHM* (1985), with its features on Swedish models.

The feminist movement was not the only social movement bursting onto the scene in these years. A host of other new movements were clamoring for political recognition as well. And different though these may all have been—they encompassed causes ranging from Britain's Campaign for Real Ale (CAMRA) to Franco Rocchetta's *Liga Veneta*, which sought Venetian autonomy and opposed the relocation of Mafia inmates to Venetian jails— one thing they had in common was that they each found a niche amid the fracturing of the wider political landscape.[60] Another thing they shared was a sense that transforming local problems involved reimagining the political. As one shrewd observer has put it, politics no longer mattered all of a sudden so much as *policies*. The vertical was being replaced by the horizontal; positions by positioning. And that in itself allowed a whole new range of issues to enter the mainstream political debate.

While many of these policy-based movements were local, one of the most significant to emerge was profoundly transnational in its makeup and global in its ambitions: the environmental movement. The first UN conference on environmental issues was held in Stockholm in 1972 but the movement had by then been gathering momentum for some time already. In 1968 the Italian industrialist and humanist Aurelio Peccei convened in Rome (with the help of Scottish scientist Alexander King) a group of experts, politicians, and businessmen to discuss the seemingly intractable crises of the day. The first event was a flop: we were "too foolish, too naïve," one invitee later recalled. But in 1972, with the publication of *The Limits to Growth* report on overpopulation and environmental crises, the club caught the Western world's attention. Given its somewhat improbable (and later much critiqued) extrapolations, *The Limits to Growth* was itself a little foolish and naive, perhaps. But its significance lay not in its veracity, but in the fact that it struck a chord: it would go on to sell nearly 1 million copies in the Netherlands, for example: a country with a population of just 14 million.

Britain already had a minister for the environment (established in 1970) by the time *The Limits to Growth* was published, but as environmentalism caught hold other countries followed suit: Norway in 1973, France in 1978. In Germany, Herbert Gruhl, a Bundestag deputy for the CDU (in some ways a forerunner of America's Al Gore, in many ways not), wrote a surprise bestseller, *A Planet Is Plundered* (1975). Where the Club of Rome had helped to inaugurate a global consciousness among the elite, Gruhl's book now helped to inaugurate a new political movement, initially within the umbrella of the CDU, but soon as a stand-alone party, Green Action Future (GAZ), later the German Greens. Sustainability was to be given its own political party.

It wasn't just the change in societal values that opened up space for the Greens. Like the communists, they benefited from the difficulties that the social democratic parties were encountering, opening up a space for them on the left. They also benefited from environmentalism's appeal across the political spectrum. Gruhl himself soon left the Greens to promote a more conservative and nationalist environmental politics later in the decade, while in Britain, environmentalism merged seamlessly with little Englander ruralism and concerns for landscape and heritage. Greenpeace, founded at the start of the 1970s, could cater to the radicals; Middle England was mostly content with *Mr. and Mrs. Andrews*.

At the same time, the environmentalists still had a lot to learn. Contesting their first election in 1979, the German Greens were so concerned to break with the politics of the old that they refused even to label themselves a "party" (they duly filed under the heading "Other Political Organization—the Greens"). Nonetheless, by the end of the decade they had become a serious force in German politics, more or less in proportion to the degree they now tolerated the rules of the game. That was one reason the former East German dissident Rudolf Bahro (who had resettled in the West in 1980, to become one of the Green's leading figures) quit in disgust.[61] "The Greens are almost worse than useless," he declared. "They have become so much a part of the system that capitalism would have had to invent them if they weren't here already."[62] But by then the Italian Greens had obtained going on for a million votes; in Belgium they secured 4.8 percent of the national vote at their first appearance in 1981, with their position improving thereafter; and by 1988 environmental parties had made it into ruling coalitions in both Finland and Sweden.

Environmentalism, then, was a movement just getting going. Its appeal combined the moral and goal-oriented clarity that the left had once made its own, reinvigorated by the new capacities of technology and science-based politics. It was a platform that could and would be developed on both sides of the political spectrum in the decades to come. "[W]hile everyone disagreed about politics," noted one commentator in looking back at environmentalism's emergence, "nobody was prepared to deny anything like a basic imperative to save the planet." And yet future years would prove just how easy it was to acknowledge a problem without really doing much about it: a fact that the new environmental parties' consistently low ceiling in national elections would demonstrate over the decades to come. They would also prove just how divisive a political platform environmentalism could be, as the environment became steadily more politicized—and not just in those countries, like Norway, that still wanted to hunt whales, or in Canada, which was taking full advantage of the energy crisis to ramp up oil production in Alberta.

The success of the peace movement, by contrast, was based initially on its ability to overcome political divides. There was nothing new about pacifism, of course. But peace activism, like much else in the 1970s, was influenced by the strategy of social movements and became more active as a result. Early efforts to use social values for the purpose of "rebranding" national identity were pioneered at this point by Norway and Sweden, who each expanded on their existing peace research institutes to make a name for themselves as merchants of tolerance, and to inject into a movement traditionally based on morality and conscience a measure of social scientific rationality. This was revealing of a much broader development since facts, it was now understood, could not be separated from values. But more usually, the peace movement was a grassroots affair.

It took its most recognizable form in the pan-European alliance of antinuclear groups that had been established in the 1950s but which was formalized as European Nuclear Disarmament (END)—an anti–Cold War European movement "from below"—in 1980. There were often strong national differences here: Brits, on the whole, were more critical of antiwar activists than the Dutch or the Italians (more than half of whom actively supported them, though they were also the most critical of NATO). Later protests over euro-missiles and groups hoping to ban the bomb also had their own national variants.[63] But all of them shared then CDU Chairman Helmut Kohl's later maxim that whatever missile technology held to be a safer "short range" missile, "the shorter the missile, the deader the Germans." And this younger, more active movement would crescendo, on both sides of the Atlantic, into the early 1980s, when 1 million people assembled in New York's Central Park to call for an end to the arms race.[64]

Cold War hawks interpreted the peace movement as a point of weakness in the Western alliance: a sort of Popular Front of the 1970s. Symbols like the White Dove, derived from the Soviet-funded World Peace Council, were said to be revealing of conflicted loyalties.[65] In fact, what peace protesters represented was the emergence of a transnational political consciousness in parallel with the more often discussed breakthrough of a global social consciousness during these years: a point at which concerns over security, ecology, and ethics converged across national lines. In 1971 a whole host of the era's political movements—from post-'68 *gauchistes* in West Germany and France, to local Catholic farmers—joined forces to protest against the French government's plans to expand a military base on the Larzac Plateau in southern France. Their commitment would last the entire decade until, in 1981, the new government of François Mitterrand finally agreed to abandon the project.[66] The call of peace was not everywhere unifying, however. The always-sensitive matter of the euro-missiles at times came close to splitting the North Atlantic Alliance. And disagreement over whether or not to support the renewal of Britain's nuclear defense capability really did split the Labour Party for years.

What many of these new social movements coalesced around was a new politics of identity. They were in that sense more than just a "protest cycle" for they transformed the political system itself. In America, the civil rights revolution touched off a host of "follower" minority rights movements seeking justice through active protest, be it Latinos, disabled persons, homosexuals, or others. The very terms "minorities" and "minority group" emerged at this time, as the establishment looked to find ways to address some of their arguments. Should there be a constitutional right to extra language education in US schools for second-generation Hispanics, for example? The Supreme Court was briefed on the matter in 1974.[67]

In France a similar minorities rights surge in these years had to do with the fact that earlier waves of immigrants, the Pieds-Noirs who had settled in cities like Montpellier, now had the confidence to assert more than just their basic material interests (such as housing and citizenship). They now began to demand political recognition for their rights as a specific minority group as well: as with the Cercle algérianiste (1973) or with Jacques Roseau's Rassemblement et coordination unitaire des rapatriés et spoliés (RECOURS, 1977), which set out to identify and punish electorally those Members of Parliament who had blocked compensation for Algerian immigrants.[68] Italians confronted similar issues within the nation-state: southern migrant workers who operated the lathes in northern cities like Turin were often as excluded by language (dialect), education, and racialism as to be practically from a different country altogether.[69]

Migrant struggles in other urban settings, such as Frankfurt, just before the immigration stop in 1973, were a reminder that migrant groups might win local victories, but that their voice was still excluded at the national political level. Instead, they turned their attention to local civic affairs. Guest workers in Germany often lived in housing built by the larger firms such as the United German Metal Works (Vereinigte Deutsche Metallwerke) or building contractor Holzman AG, right next to the factories themselves. Such immigrants' entire existence was thus laborized and campaigns drew attention to just how squalid conditions really were. Other workers became increasingly politically active via sit-ins, rent strikes, and transnational cooperations, as they fought against unscrupulous landlords and a one-way welfare system into which they paid, but from which they received precious little back.

As migrants' transnationalism deepened—rather more than did that of the unions who purported to represent them (preferring themselves to seek the preferential treatment of German workers, or *Inländerprimat*)—their demands became about much more than just "integration." They developed a political edge that worried the establishment and helped to turn official discourse against them. Italian workers protested at BMW in Munich in 1972, in a wildcat strike that almost turned militant, and at Ford in Cologne in 1973, in an action that was stormed by police on the grounds that it was allegedly infiltrated by radical leftists.[70] The trend was not just toward a transnationalization of national politics, however.

It corresponded as well to the increasingly global language of "human rights" and the politics of movement promoting this domestically. Minority social groups did not emerge at this point; they simply became visible by virtue of publicly demanding the rights they had been granted in postwar documents like the Universal Declaration of Human Rights. For which purpose the pioneering examples of civil rights and second wave feminism supplied examples of how the law courts, in particular, could be mobilized in their cause.

If there was one group that did this in the face of the most intensely ingrained opposition it was the gay movement, which moved beyond demands for equal treatment under the law to embrace a much wider politics of social change. After the brutal beatings at Stonewall in New York in 1969 it developed a militant wing, gay liberation, centered around groups such as the Gay Activist Alliance (also a highly democratic organization: it even used the parliamentarians' handbook *Robert's Rules of Order*), and pushed for institutional reforms, including the removal, in 1973, of homosexuality as one of the officially designated mental "disorders" in America.[71] Gradually the movement gained traction. In California, Harvey Milk became, in 1977, the first openly gay elected official in America; he championed equality and gay rights until his assassination the following year. In cities like Seattle, it was the pink pound that predominated and saw gay political activism merge with community politics, pressing for antidiscrimination at the state and municipal level.

The gay movement made important strides in other countries too. In France, gay liberation was just as vocal in groups such as the Homosexual Front for Revolutionary Action. Other strands of French gay activism were more concerned with securing "dignity."[72] Like most of the identity movements of the time, the gay and lesbian movements proved fluid across national borders, and in many ways this represented the primary force of its challenge: thus could a young Italian homosexual such as Mario Mieli learn the ropes of gay liberation in London at the start of the decade before returning to found Italy's first major gay movement in Turin a few years later. It took Australia's gay movement until the end of the decade to really get going, which it did when police violently broke up a parade in Sydney (commemorating Stonewall in America) in 1978. Sydney also proved to be a pioneering instance of intersectionality, since it was there that working-class groups (including the Builders Labourers Federation) showed solidarity in striking in support of gay activists.

To what extent was this politics of "identity" new? People had always had identities of course, and some of those—one's social class—had been the basis of political struggle for well over a century. What marked out the new politics of identity was that it sought to politicize what had previously been treated as aspects of one's personal life—one's gender, sexuality, color, ethnicity, physical or mental status—and to make that the basis of an explicitly political community.

Emerging as a legitimate critique of the failure of postwar democracy to recognize (let alone tolerate) social difference, this new politics of identity was politically charged in two ways: first it represented a desire for "authenticity"; second it carried demand for "equal recognition" beyond the economic sphere. That implied both dissent (to avoid becoming a cog in the machine) and empathy (to cultivate a political agency, beginning with others with whom one shared some element in common). Such a politics didn't cover everything, but a great many of the social movements to emerge from this new politics of identity could certainly be found somewhere on a line between the two: be it the radical feminist Combahee River Collective or the German Greens.

Ultimately it was the collective import of this transformation of the political that proved harder to fend off than each group's individual demands. A distributional politics based on some competing level of tax and spend, even a greater measure of political equality, was no longer going to cut it. President Lyndon Johnson's frustrated outburst after the riots that followed the passage of the Voting Rights Act in 1965 was an early but indicative sign of this: "I've given these people more than they could have hoped for; what do they want now?" he had thundered to an adviser. A decade later and the answer to that question was somewhat clearer. What the people wanted, and what they would only demand more strongly in the decades to come, was not just the basic goods that their parents had settled for, or even their civil rights, but a wider sense of recognition, of their rightful place in the demos *as* members of particular groups—all of which was a challenge, of course, to the white middle-class norms upon which Western democratic politics was based: a whittling away that would provide one of the leitmotifs of the new era to come. The consternation this caused the establishment merely added to their growing list of woes.

But just as the establishment had mobilized "law and order" in its response to the social disruption it perceived these groups to represent, many of them likewise followed the lessons of the feminists, and turned to law to achieve their demands. Indeed, using the law often became a way of achieving "justice" preferred to politics itself (which didn't always feel very "just" any more—and certainly wasn't always effective). Thus did these years see not only a flowering of judicial politics, as it might properly be called, as an alternative to popular mobilizations—be it Ralph Nader and Alan Morrison's Public Citizen Litigation Group (1972) or feminists' use of the courts or environmental lawyer groups—they also saw a judicialization of politics: with political outcomes now beginning to be determined in ways that did not need to involve the public's voice per se. The public would henceforth be invoked rather more than it would be consulted. And while the impetus behind this is understandable at a time when modern society was becoming technologically and institutionally more complex, there were benefits and dangers here alike.[73]

As the decade drew to a close it became increasingly clear that oil and inflation had been little more than a clearing of the way for the real changes taking place in the West. But since the general thrust of the major political movements that emerged was both antiestablishment and overwhelmingly progressive, perhaps the greatest surprise is that the political left failed successfully to incorporate them. With hindsight this appears as an historic missed opportunity. Instead, the initial achievements of the politics of movement now helped elicit a counterresponse incorporated most effectively on the right. After all, politically speaking it was not the Pieds-Noirs who made the greatest electoral gains in France, but their antithesis, the far right. In America, not only was a white backlash underway against civil rights (and black power especially) on the streets of cities like Boston, but a broader phenomenon was shaping up too: for just as blacks, and women and others for that matter, now secured a greater stake in the modern *state*, wealthy white Americans began abandoning it in droves.[74] In *this* politics, collective obligations and political compromise were out; self-reliance and political minimalism were in. Lobbies and special interest groups meanwhile were set up and welcomed into the halls of power to advocate on behalf of communities of privilege (now newly insecure amid all the mobilization) and the institutions and mechanisms of law and parliament were imagined anew in their cause. This, not Baader-Meinhof, was the real revolution coming out of the 1970s. But it required the rediscovery of political activism on the right to really set it rolling.

Governing Democracy: The Rise of the Right

By the mid 1970s, and in stark contrast to the left, the right was at the start of an historic, decades-long resurgence. Before Nixon came to power in 1968 "conservative activism seemed unthinkable." By the time of

Ronald Reagan, the most conservative president since Calvin Coolidge, it was the dominant force in Western politics. Awkward memories of the British Conservative Party's rhetorical question, "Who governs Britain?" in 1974, were now banished. By the late 1970s, it was British Conservatives, along with their European counterparts, who were well on their "long march" through the institutions of power, not the post-68 leftist radicals like Rudi Dutschke, who had first coined the phrase.[75]

In America, after half a century in which Congress had been a redoubt of the Democrats (the Republicans controlled it for just four years between 1932 and 1980), the balance of political power now began to swing the other way (the final push coming during the anti-Clinton hysteria of 1994).[76] This had significant implications: not least it locked US politics into a progressively more Republican mold at a time when it would become dramatically more expensive each year to run a congressional election campaign, and when Congress had taken on greater powers (including over matters of foreign policy). But in many ways the shift was best captured by the Australian Liberal (conservative) Party's 1975 election advertisement which, after running through the calamities and crises of the previous "three dark years" under Labour, ended simply with the—election winning—slogan: "Let's turn on the lights."[77]

It was the manner in which the lights were turned on that really did it. Conservative politicians, like Robert Muldoon in New Zealand, grasped more quickly than their opponents the implications of the new political economic situation. Muldoon threw "dancing Cossack" adverts at the public to imply that the left's generous pension promises were both farcically antiquated, and a step toward communism, and won election for it in 1975. What he and the more "pragmatic" social democrats like Germany's Helmut Schmidt (who managed to cling to power) now promoted was the idea that strong leadership would be required to force through the social discipline demanded by the new politics of deflation, while at the same time maintaining political support by deferring more and more responsibilities (and when necessary, of course, the blame) for this new politics to the market. This was a time for "young Turks" and *Macher* (people who got things done); for people who were "not for turning." In Britain, Margaret Thatcher positioned herself one move from power as she took the helm of the Tory Party in the UK in 1975.

As with the decline of the left, it was the changes *within* conservatism during these years that were to prove the crucial development. In France, one measure of that change was to be seen with the founding in 1972 of the Front National (FN). The rising star of the FN was Jean-Marie

Le Pen, a blustering provocateur who once went around with an eye patch (he claimed to have lost his eye after being beaten during a 1958 election campaign). From the mid 1970s onward the Front National rapidly gained a sizeable share of the popular vote and helped reshape the French political landscape into a tripartite and right-leaning structure of center left, center right and far right: no mean feat for a minority party, and a sign of the times to come. At the same time, as we have seen, the old Gaullist right gave way after Pompidou, to a more market-friendly right of that "Gallic Kennedy," Giscard d'Estaing.[78]

The most revealing, yet in some ways subtle, indication of the changes afoot, was again to be seen not at the edges but at the center: in the relative success of Christian democracy compared with its historic counterpart of social democracy. This was most noticeable in West Germany, where Helmut Kohl's CDU grew in influence in the 1970s even as Schmidt's social democrats clung to power (the CDU's membership more than doubled from 286,541 in 1968 to 590,482 in 1975). On many levels this was surprising. Christian democracy was, if anything, even more closely associated with the postwar political order than social democracy. Christian democrats were the architect of the basic idea of what was called "consociational" democracy—elite-driven pluralism—that guided early efforts at European integration; and it was Christian democrats who authored many of their nations' postwar constitutions and inserted distinctly Christian democratic principles into them. One might well have expected the CD parties to be among the first to fall into the cracks that had recently opened up in the Western political landscape. Yet in stark contrast to social democracy, Christian democracy would remain an influential force until much later in the century.[79]

To be sure, as with everything in the 1970s, there were wobbles for the Christian democrats. Le Pen's breakthrough on the far right was one, as it saw the Christian democratic Mouvement Républicain Populaire, MRP (Popular Republican Movement), in France finally throw in the towel in 1974, its long-time figurehead Jean Lecanuet opting to support Giscard d'Estaing instead. Within a few years that coalition too would be merged into the broader-based UDF confederation of parties of the right. The same fate confronted the Österreichische Volkspartei, ÖVP (Austrian People's Party), which after successfully presenting itself for two decades after the war as the nonsocialist catchall party, found its popularity declining in an era when social demands were changing and one could only improve the offer to some by lessening that given to others. The ÖVP would initially cede ground to the Social Democrats, the SPÖ, but only to the extent that they also drew on the support of, and so let into the game, the small but growing, right-wing Freiheitliche Partei Österreiches, FPÖ (Freedom Party of Austria). In Belgium and the Netherlands respectively, linguistic politics and denominational pillarization (*verzuiling*) put pressure on Christian democracy's former dominance, just as it had unsettled the Liberal Party in Canada. Even in Italy, the DC's stranglehold on politics was undone by the start of the 1980s as the electoral base moved away from it, first into the hands of Giovanni Spadolini's Republicans in 1981, then into those of the (at best) nominally socialist Bettino Craxi.[80]

But despite these setbacks, Christian democracy still had at least three advantages over social democracy and the left in late twentieth-century Europe that stood it—and so conservatism in general—in much better stead. First it coded, politically, for two things that were both in high demand in the 1970s: namely a liberal market and social order. Second, it was centered upon an ethics of the individual. As democratic politics swung from conformism to individualism, Christian democracy's roots in the personalism of Jacques Maritain (not that he was a fan of the tactical compromises that party-politics involved) represented its own useful third way between capitalism and communism. Even in America, although there was no Christian democratic party as such, the legacy of the Christian theologian Borden Parker Bowne was a major influence on Martin Luther King—and it was King, after all, who credited personalism with being what he called his "basic philosophical position."[81] In regarding "the person" as "a fundamentally social being" who realized him or herself "not in competition . . . but more through insertion" into social institutions, Christian democracy thus offered a politics that embraced liberal individualism.[82] This raised the potential for institution-building, including the welfare state, but it remained resolutely traditionalist in outlook, especially when it came to matters of morality. It was a middle ground that could be turned either to the left or, as was now the case, to the right, if need be.

The third advantage that Christian democracy enjoyed over social democracy was its internationalism. Christian democratic parties were invariably Atlanticist in outlook: the most committed stalwarts of NATO, they did not blink when it came to sensitive issues such as the installation of Cruise and Pershing missiles on European soil. Pro-Americanism even reigned in the French Center des Démocrates Sociaux (CDS), much to de Gaulle's dislike. This gave them an international cachet, which certainly did them no harm in the wider context of the Cold War. The fact that many Christian democratic leaders had more in common with their counterparts in other nations than with members of their own governments made it a natural organizing environment for trans-European political coordination as well: another useful string to one's bow in the political landscape of postwar Europe. Instinctively more conservative, Christian democracy survived the more radical times by going into hibernation, entering into governing coalitions in Italy and the Benelux countries as it sought to keep its own politics alive.

If survival was a victory of sorts for the moderate form of conservatism that postwar Christian democracy embodied better than any other movement, it was equally a failure, in that it ceded ground further across on the right to more vocal forms of opposition. In fact, a radical form of Christian democracy was briefly experimented with in post-Salazar Portugal in 1974 by former members of the Salazar regime. The demise of the military dictatorship in Greece in 1974 saw a more successful transition to a post-junta conservative-dominated party under New Democracy. Thereafter the far right in Greece would move out to more extreme positions or back into the New Democracy fold whenever the socialists threatened to take power (the far-right National Alignment [EP] party won 5 seats in the 1977 election, for example). But this was mostly a movement that impacted on the northern and eastern countries of the continent.[83] The BNP and the Front National, we have seen, were making powerful strides in Britain and France. The transformation and in due course resurgence of the Freedom Party of Austria (FPÖ) is perhaps the most indicative example of the changes. By incorporating new elements in the party's core beliefs, gesturing more openly in favor of libertarian free markets and offering a nod to the emergent ecological movement of the time, the party attracted new and younger cohorts. The benefits of its neopopulist makeover soon began to be reaped, culminating with Jörg Haider's "Le Pen" breakthrough moment in 1990.[84]

At its furthest reaches this new and more deeply conservative wave stretched up even into the Nordic countries (where Christian democratic parties were weak). A little like the famous Nordic lights, the turn to conservatism here was most fleeting but in its own way also most illuminating. In Sweden, after decades of social democratic ascendancy it was the conservatives who took power from 1976 and they would remain there for another six years. In Denmark the Progress Party (Fremskridtspartiet) had been established in 1972 and what would become the Norwegian Progress Party (Fremskrittspartiet) was established the year after, initially with the more illustrative name: Anders Langnes parti til sterk nedsettelse av skatter, avgifter og offentlige inngrep (the Anders Langes Party for Major Reductions in Taxes, Tariffs and Public Interventions). The Finnish Rural Party, forerunner of the present-day Finns Party, was also enjoying a heyday. The right made few moves to roll back the welfare state here, but it was a reminder that even Scandinavia was not immune to developments elsewhere. In many ways the opposite was true in Australia and New Zealand, in that there was little tradition of leftist governments introducing welfare reforms in the first place, and so no great transformation to witness. These conservative-minded, wage-earner welfare states were, in a sense, ahead of the European curve.

So too was America, where the new right was resurgent now after several decades in the shadows. Its rise was in part facilitated by the decline of confidence in liberal government that reached its nadir with Carter's ill-fated problems of American "malaise" brought on by the rising cost of oil.[85] But with the steady gathering of Ronald Reagan's New America movement—to whom middle-class suburbanites, with their "freedom forum" bookstores and their midmorning coffee meetings in Orange County tract homes, contributed substantially—perhaps it just seemed like a case of all good things come to those who wait.[86] That view certainly played well with the newly religious strand of the American right: a fact that leading progressive liberals almost entirely overlooked in their (wrong-footed) belief that the new conservatism was a passing fad. Some even wrote it off as the product of disgruntled and unenlightened groups acting in the "paranoid style."[87] In fact this new generation of conservatives were a force to be reckoned with. Not only were they less moderate than their forebears, they were also more interested in wielding social and economic power than they were in capturing the state per se.[88] For some, in fact, taking power and giving up on the state were no longer seen as contradictory objectives.

The new conservative "awakening" in America took its clearest shape in the form of the Moral Majority: a movement of conservative Christians founded in 1979, at the behest of Republican operatives, by fundamentalist preacher and host of *The Old-Time Gospel Hour* Jerry Falwell. Ostensibly "pro family and pro-American," the soon-to-be influential organization was most consistently at one with anti-"social" policies. It thus fused a hodgepodge of cultural issues—anti-homosexuality, anti–Equal Rights Amendment and anti-abortion—into a singular moral outlook, as it promoted itself through the new "electronic church" of radio and televangelism, becoming one of the first political movements to make such technologically novel "media" a central part of the way it operated. Above all, however, it proved remarkably popular: *Time* magazine even named 1976 the "Year of the Evangelical."[89] By 1980 there were 1,300 radio stations nationally with a religious format spending around $500 million a year on airtime; the same year the Christian Broadcasting Network splashed out $20 million on new "ultramodern" premises.[90]

Falwell was the heart and soul of this movement. Personally "about as menacing as the corner grocer," as the *National Review* put it in 1980, in the public domain he was nonetheless "outspoken and flamboyant" and fierce when he needed to be.[91] Within three years the Moral Majority boasted "a $10 million budget, 100,000 trained clergymen and several million volunteers."[92] And by the time of its disbanding, at the end of the 1980s, Falwell—for all that his rantings had by then left him a figure of ridicule—would not only have helped carry Reagan into power, he would have established the religious lobby as a force to be reckoned with in national politics.

By the end of the 1980s, a Religious Roundtable had been set up, mirroring the Business Roundtable. The two lobby groups were in some ways the twin flanks, the black knight and the bishop, of the new conservative renaissance. And their principal aim was to try to influence politicians.[93] Less transparent movements were by then in place too. The Family, an influential private organization devoted to "a leadership led by God," enjoyed far greater influence from the 1970s (it was founded in 1948) after "submerging" away from the public eye, in accordance with its founders' wishes, in 1966.[94] A dozen or so other evangelical lobby groups, such as Christian Voice, also established themselves in the last two years of the decade, most of them borrowing heavily from the civil rights playbook of mass mobilization. "It's like the blacks said in the 1960s," Falwell once boasted: "And this time, we're going to win."[95]

What each of these strands of conservatism characteristically offered was a "New Democracy" (as the name of the Greek political party founded after the junta itself had it) to replace what they saw as the now defunct progressive center of New Deal liberalism. The new conservative wave was both an elite and a popular phenomenon: public frustrations at the overburdened (and overbearing) liberal social-democratic state finding their prayers, often literally, answered by more radical-sounding right-wing politicians willing to call out these problems by their name— whether it was popular frustrations with mandatory school busing in America, taxes in Sweden, or immigrants in West Germany: frustrations that the left preferred to sweep under the carpet. When it wasn't being deserted (France providing the textbook case of political fission here) the left was still coming to terms with "structures"; the right, meanwhile, was knocking on doors and asking what all the trouble outside had been about.[96] For the new brand of politicians at the head of this conservative wave, the focus now shifted from thinking to doing; for the left by contrast, the direction of travel would be resolutely the other way.

Instituting the New Order

The rule of law is one of democracy's principal attributes. The nature of legal institutions fundamentally shapes the sort of democracy a society has. This was brought home in the early 1970s by the dramatic U-turn executed within the United States Supreme Court. During the late 1950s and 1960s, the Supreme Court, under Chief Justice Earl Warren, had overseen nothing short of a "progressive constitutional revolution." This was the court that threw out McCarthyism, upheld civil rights, and protected freedom of speech.[97] "For the first time," writes the legal historian Morton Horwitz, "democracy became the foundational value in American constitutional discourse." The Supreme Court ensured this by forging a balance between judicial review and democratic process, between liberty and equality.[98] The result was a true golden age of constitutional law: of *Brown v. Board of Education* on the equality side, and its creation of a new constitutional right to privacy on behalf of personal freedoms.

The need to protect, not to govern, democracy thus became a central principle of the Warren court's rulings, as it took on majority racism and challenged the court's own tradition of defending the rights of the propertied classes. This was critical for an overly powerful institution that was not, ironically, itself very democratically accountable. This was why earlier versions of the court had so readily sided with the interests of the elite. The Warren court sought to enshrine a more substantive vision of democracy: one which insisted that there could be "no effective political equality" if there was not also some measure of social and economic equality. Beyond fair elections, in which all citizens could vote, there needed to be "uninhibited, robust, and wide open" debate, and "unfettered interchange of ideas for the bringing about of political and social changes desired by the people."[99] For the Warren court, in short, it was the value of democracy itself that gave the constitution meaning.

The way it interpreted this mandate, however, increasingly ruffled feathers on the political right. Nixon himself actively campaigned against the court and some of its rulings in the 1968 election.[100] Then, once in power, he installed Warren E. Burger—a "law and order" conservative for a "law and order" president—in place of Earl Warren. Unlike the Warren court, the new Burger court, which would retain its basic complexion until 1986, was "properly conservative" as one constitutional expert put it, and it used its own power to rein in that of government. As a rather sulky dissenting judgment by Justice Black to a late Warren-era ruling on free speech put it: "if the time has come when pupils . . . can defy and flout orders of school officials to keep their minds on their own schoolwork, it is the beginning of a new revolutionary era of permissiveness in this country fostered by the judiciary."[101] The Burger-era court made sure that no such revolution would be forthcoming in the future. When the Supreme Court returned its verdict in the case of *Bakke v. Regents of the University of California*, in which a white American claimed racial discrimination on account of the university's quota system for peoples of color, it sparked a visceral debate on the relationship between race and democracy that divided the court as much as the country. Amid all the constitutional hand-wringing, the pollster Mervyn Field came up with perhaps the single most telling interjection: "It has become much more acceptable," he said of the country at large, "to be less generous."[102]

And yet the end of the constitutional progressivism displayed by the Warren court was marked by more than just the passing from an era of progressivism to an era of conservative pragmatism, "original intent," and judicial restraint (to do more, as the Warren court put it, was "to usurp a power which our democracy has lodged in its elected legislature").[103] There was a mobilization of conservative public interest law firms, initially in California, to counter the change to public law that had taken place amid the rise of the politics of movement (particularly in light of the environment).[104] Also there was a decline in the number of professional lawyers who occupied elected positions in the political system itself. In the early 1970s 51 percent of all senators were also lawyers; today only 37 percent are. Lawyers once made up 43 percent of the House; today that figure is 25 percent. The impress of law upon the executive is a particularly American phenomenon (in Britain just 14 percent of the members of the House of Commons are lawyers). But if the predominance of lawyers in politics is a problem, it is not obviously one resolved by those same lawyers instead taking up the offer to work in well-remunerated private practices, as a great many now did.

Quite aside from whatever "tone" the Supreme Court might like to set, the rapidly expanding offices of corporate law, where lawyers served the highest paying clients, slowly began to undermine the legal defense of social equality. In fact, those who now sat on the higher courts were themselves more likely to have taken one of the newly proliferating courses on "law and economics" made available by conservatives like Richard Posner at Chicago University and Henry Manne at the University of Miami—the latter a man whose personal mission was to "demolish" what he called "the myth of corporate responsibility," and whose courses for judges eventually grew into the influential Law and Economics Center (LEC). By the end of 1989, 137 federal and circuit court judges had finished the LEC's basic program. And from it these judges took with them into the world the idea that legal principles of due process and fairness were not themselves unanswerable to the logic of efficiency.[105] As some of them later ascended into the Supreme Court itself they would even take with them the idea that constitutional checks and balances—the avoidance of structural unfairness—was not itself something that should be legislated for.

In Europe a different story belied the same underlying logic. There it was more a case of a growing take-up of US judicial norms, and in particular the adoption of the American culture of constitutional review. The idea of using constitutional courts to provide a check on the power of parliament was intended—in the European context—to ensure that elected representatives would not make the sort of catastrophic mistakes they had made in the 1930s. But prior to the 1970s, constitutional review was only a part of the day-to-day procedure of democracy in Germany, Switzerland, and Austria. Not until the transitions from authoritarian rule in southern Europe (all of which also immediately adopted some form of constitutional court) did the work of constitutional courts begin to develop more bite in Europe.[106]

An important element structuring postwar democracy in Europe after 1945, for example, was the idea that rights were too important to be safeguarded by parliaments alone. Rather, "they were to be enshrined in constitutions and to be protected by courts."[107] The European Court of Human Rights was set up in 1959 to this end. But for all the novelty of its treatment of rights as prior to state law, the constitutional courts enforcing the new law were, to begin with, always *national* edifices and for some time they too lay rather dormant. In France, the French constitutional court, the *Conseil Constitutionnel*, that had been established in 1958 only really began to assert its independence after 1971 under the leadership of Louis Favoreu. Previously the *Conseil Constitutionnel* had worked to shore up the power of the executive vis-à-vis parliament.[108] Henceforth things began to run in the other direction, as it vetoed, for example, the new government's plans to nationalize industry and financial institutions in 1981. So successful did the newly revitalized constitutional court become in France that, as one expert noted, insulated as it was from political controls, it "has engendered the gradual but inevitable collapse of separation of powers doctrines."[109]

The sifting out of the state's role as protector of citizens and their rights was challenged in Germany too: first by the GDR's attempts to use a new citizenship law as a lever to gain international recognition for its sovereignty (the GDR was not recognized by the UN until 1973). As a result of this unusual piece of legal realpolitik, the West German government found it was unable to offer the protections of West German citizenship to those who had previously lived in the East. Domestically, too, the German Federal Constitutional Court found itself locking horns with the European Court of Justice over matters of jurisdiction throughout the decade. The German court insisted that it held ultimate powers of review so long as the community lacked a genuinely democratic parliament. Increasingly it came round to the position that it *could* cede matters over human rights to the European-level.[110]

This did not nullify, or always seek to oppose the process of European integration, but it did underscore the centrality of individual rights within it. The rights of the individual thus became the key unit of aggregation and contestation in the developing juridical landscape of the West and this combined, consequentially, with the proliferation of a European-level judiciary (initially set up under the Court of Justice of the European Union in 1951). By the early 1970s, a second trend had developed, in line with the revival of the wider European project, overlaying the earlier move toward national checks and balances with a distinct move toward universal, European-wide declarations and rights. At the heart of this was the growing primacy of the European Court of Justice (ECJ) itself. As the ECJ's caseload took off in the early 1970s it began to put together a supranational legal structure, a product of judicial and not parliamentary imagination. If this corresponded to, indeed even represented, the particular attraction that lawyering held for Europeans in the aftermath of the destruction of the first half of the century, it is interesting to note that it was now, at this midway point of the second half of the century, that those same "solutions" became the basis of some of the very tensions that would animate national democratic politics once more in the decades to come.[111]

On one level, this was welcome. As defenders of the move insisted at the time, and Europhiles have continued to insist since, another layer of oversight and review could hardly damage the quality of the rights now being to some extent "overprotected" as part of a wider suspicion of popular sovereignty. But it had nationalists everywhere up in arms. And not just nationalists: by locking these arrangements in beyond the reach of the nation state, Europe's new wave of legal constitutionalism not only hoisted into place the so-called "democratic deficit" between national and European-wide policymaking. It also opened the continent up to American-style liberalization since that was, in effect, what the progressively empowered European bureaucrats believed in.[112]

Britain, always the outlier, retained a greater measure of primacy for its own parliament (as did Scandinavia, to a lesser degree, when seeking national "design laws" to protect their iconic cultural pieces). But even in Britain a new culture of "checks and balances" and "separation of powers" doctrines belatedly took hold. British judges attended conferences abroad where, as one long-time observer of the British political scene put it, "they encountered the idea that a proper liberal democracy should have a constitution, whether written or not, and that that constitution, embodying the basic principles of the rule of law, should take precedence over ordinary law."[113]

British judges—drawn almost exclusively from the establishment class—may not have approved of everything that other national judiciaries, such as the post–Warren Supreme Court, were doing. But they could hardly have failed to notice the growing influence the Supreme Court in particular had upon the American domestic scene. And before long, on their side of the Atlantic too, law lords increasingly refused to be bound entirely by precedent; their powers of judicial review were resurrected, and their probing moved beyond focusing on matters of due diligence to questioning the rationale of political judgment itself. Not for nothing did *The Judge Over Your Shoulder* become a much-thumbed reference book for British political officials.[114]

It was not merely the law lords and corporate lawyers who began to change their approach to questions of justice and political order. Largely under the impress of the emergent social movements and rights activists, international lawyers also began to put aside their earlier reluctance to embrace human rights in their jurisprudence.[115] The true era of reluctance law, properly speaking a post–Cold War phenomenon, was still some years off. But already international courts and human rights instruments were beginning to gain a degree of influence and cachet they had not had before. In the process, domestic considerations became that much harder, once again, to separate off from the realm of international politics.

If law was one area of institutional change within democracy in the 1970s, the field of economics, and above all its growing significance for policymakers devoid of their own answers to the challenges of the moment, was another. Perhaps inevitably given the ongoing rumblings of the crisis of capitalism, some of the most forceful architects of the new political order to emerge at this time were not the lawyers, and not yet the politicians either, but the economists. All of a sudden it was economists who were writing the major works of political theory; it was economists who were "in demand" for their professional insights on matters large and small. And, no less significant, it was democracy that the more partisan among their number had in their sights.

In *The Limits of Liberty* (1974) Nobel Prize winner James Buchanan, for example, painted democracy as "precariously poised" between "anarchy and the Leviathan." The inflationary travails of the decade underscored what was obvious when you had politicians in search of electoral victory and people demanding ever-greater living standards, he claimed.[116] Milton Friedman, we have already seen, was enjoying greater influence since the award of his Nobel Prize, culminating in 1980 in the influential television series of his book *Capitalism and Freedom*. European economists were no less active. In France, the Association pour la liberté économique et le progrès social (ALEPS), a grouping of senior civil servants, academics and business leaders founded in 1966, was soon busily injecting a robustly positive view of liberal economic policies, and by extension a thoroughgoing critique of the nation's *étatisme* into political debate.[117]

ALEPS was itself a member of the European Hague Club, a grouping of the major private foundations on the continent that sponsored and helped to shape the research agendas befitting their worldview, just as private philanthropists had long done in America. It helped that the new economists shared an intellectual affinity, and not infrequently close personal ties, to the moneyed interests now on the march. As Roger Fauroux said of the Saint-Simon Foundation, a social liberal platform for political and economic thinking he cofounded in France in 1981, in the context of Mitterrand's move to the left: "if we wanted to take concrete actions we needed a legal framework and money."[118]

This flurry of political activity by economists was varied but not ad hoc; it was a meeting of economists increasingly in tune with the micro-economic principles (of consumer choice, preferences, and utility maxi-mization) that had taken over the macroeconomic, Keynesian landscape. Above all, what they achieved was the widespread adoption by governments of the institution of deregulation. "Deregulation," which later became a term of political art, and indeed one of the basic pillars of the new po-litical order being put in place, began partly as a functional response to the new freedom of movement that national currencies enjoyed after 1973: that and the fact that, since nobody could say with any great confidence any more quite what the market was going to do, it was as well to start enabling people to move about more freely in relation to it.

But deregulation was also a response to the growing anxiety of the corporate world that its profit lines were being squeezed in the hardened economic times. This was certainly true: but for corporations, unlike states—who were as often as not held responsible for this, their inter-vention in economic affairs now deemed a "moral hazard"—it would prove an avoidable fate. Thus, where there were just eighty-nine corpo-ration-funded political action committees (PACs) in America in 1974, by 1982 there were 1,467—most of them Republican and most of them calling for deregulation.[119] To further cut costs, these same corporations also now started moving their tax liabilities offshore into what would come to be called "tax havens." As jobs followed the same sliding scale out of the national economy, to new and cheaper manufacturing centers outside the West, it became easier to loosen one's obligations to employ-ees as well.

These were profound changes in how states would juggle their com-mitments to society and markets. If few really noticed at the time, this perhaps had something to do with the expanding scope and scale of the advertising industry, which doubled during this period, much of it focused on selling the glamour of corporate life; or with the not unrelated fact that, by the end of decade, more university students studied business than anything else.[120] Above all, however, it had to do with a steadily growing "common-sense" view that market mechanisms offered the best means of determining aggregate social choices. Private wealth trumped public finance in matters of innovation, allocation, distribution, and now too even "fairness."

Part of what drove these changes was simply the speed and efficiency with which corporations responded to the straitened economic circum-stances of the era: first by getting bigger through mergers, and then by creating political lobbies to influence government policy. In August 1971

Lewis Powell, a corporate lawyer before he too was nominated to the Supreme Court that year by Nixon, wrote a memo to the US Chamber of Commerce. Powell's intention was to "sound the alarm" about what he perceived as an "attack" by liberal regulationists on the American Free Enterprise System. "If our system is to survive," Powell wrote, "top management must be equally concerned with protecting and preserving the system itself."[121] Little wonder that the voices of more moderate economists, like Amartya Sen, whose *Collective Choice and Social Welfare* (1970) sought to show that "maximization" of anything was not the way forward, were lost to policymaking at the time.

Powell's clarion call fired the starting gun for a new era of political mobilization by businesses, one that claimed the interests of "the public" but angled over their heads to engage primarily in bartering with political elites over public resources and private freedoms. As one observer put it, American "business [now] learned how to act as a class." In 1971, the Chamber of Commerce comprised around 60,000 members. By 1982 it had 250,000 companies. In 1972, the year after Powell's memo, the Business Roundtable, an organization of CEOs "committed to the aggressive pursuit of political power for the corporation," was founded, and the same year the National Association of Manufacturers moved to Washington to tighten its own lobbying drive. In 1973, the World Trade Center opened in New York.[122] By 1978 the American Enterprise Institute, under the influence of neoconservative Irving Kristol, had increased its budget sevenfold on the start of the decade and was engaging in everything from legislative proposals, to the media, to the content of college libraries. It wasn't just market share that was driving this new activism. As a prominent corporate lawyer later appointed to the Supreme Court observed, it was more generally seen to be "time for American business to apply their great talents vigorously to the preservation of the system itself."[123]

And not just in America. The active incorporation of some of these ideas by Australian economists and the politicians they advised shows their global resonance. In 1973 the Australian Chamber of Commerce aped its American cousin and launched a nationwide "economic education campaign." In 1976 Enterprise Australia (a self-styled corporate "propaganda" body) was established. "We cannot relax," said Sir Robert Crichton-Brown, president of the Australian Institute of Directors, "until . . . we have convinced society at large that our influence is indeed for its good." The British were by then already well on the same path, with bodies like the Institute of Economic Affairs leading the way.[124] Like their counterparts manning the barricades of grassroots social movements on the left, these national outfits compared notes across their respective borders: visiting each other, copying policies and procedures, offering their advice to governments.

What these bodies almost always focused on was the need, as they saw it, for more deregulation. They had good reason to do so. Corporations benefited not only from the cutting back of rules on investment, taxation, and corporate structure. At a time of declining rate of profit, they were now also empowered to squeeze costs, or pass them on to consumers, and so to recoup in shareholder profits the value that their employees and the economy lost in production and output. "During the 1970s," wrote an American columnist at the time, "the political wing of the nation's corporate sector staged one of the most remarkable campaigns in the pursuit of power in recent history."[125] This was right, and most remarkably of all it had happened without so much as a whisper of footfall on the street. But it wasn't just the institutional procedures of law and economics that were changing. The nature of political agency itself was being transformed in the process.

Reconstituting Democracy: Freedom vs. Equality

"Every now and then the tree of liberty has to be fed with the blood of patriots," Thomas Jefferson once famously asserted. In 1982, the economist Mancur Olson—one of those thrust into the limelight during the 1970s—was busy expanding his ideas on the power of minorities to explain the economic and social stagnation of the time. It was the fault, he suggested, of "distributional coalitions," and he even went so far as to reference Jefferson's famously sanguinary comment to underscore his point. Only a revolution could shake a long-settled nation out of its torpor, he claimed. Yet what neither Olson nor many others appreciated at the time was quite the extent to which a revolution was by then already underway around them. For while Olson correctly foresaw the huge growth in free-riding and rent-seeking by minority groups that was to become a feature of liberal democratic politics, he quite failed to see that the most powerful distributional coalition to emerge out of the 1970s—the most important minority of all—was the business class itself, and they were already busy kicking the ladders away behind them.[126]

The heart of that revolution was the primacy now being accorded the value of freedom, which was variously interpreted but consistently set against its counterpart of equality. This had several consequences. First, it contributed to a waving through of the quite radical changes being put in place as if these were things that everybody should automatically agree on. Inequality was now beginning to rise in the Western nations after several decades of being brought down: but the most vocal progressives were at this point more concerned with identity and recognition than income shares. Even the Marxists, who might have been counted upon to respond, were for the most part too busy incorporating culture into their framework of economic analysis to notice. Brilliant scholar though he was, the status accorded a figure like Stuart Hall in Great Britain was not unrelated to this fact.

Second, it confronted the mass movements of inter- and postwar vintage with their new limitations. Where the old parties weren't punished simply for having been in power when the good times shuttered up, they faced new and "painful choice[s] between two identities." Did they carry on as parties of government, or give vent to the new clamor for parties of movement? Again it turned out that this was to cause far greater problems for the left than for the right. The German SPD was in some sense the one that got away here: they chose the former, and in so doing they lived to fight another day. In Britain, the so-called "gang of four" politicians (Roy Jenkins, David Owen, Shirley Williams, and Bill Rodgers) chose the latter route, splitting off from Labour to form a fringe Social Democratic Party, condemning the mother party to a decade of electoral setbacks in the process. American Democrats who had denied African Americans a voice at the national convention in Chicago in 1968 had largely incorporated these new "minority interests" by the time of the next convention in Miami in 1972: and with every four years that passed more would be added, much to the later Democratic Leadership Council's (DLC) consternation.[127] But in an economic downturn one simply could not split the difference with everyone.

The ultimate drivers of this change therefore were the people themselves. Frustrated with governments, either because of their faltering economic performance, their failed promises, their overreaching tax burdens, or simply their weakness in face of the popular dissent waged by "others," the people demanded change. They did so not "as one" but as a collective cacophony of many voices and movements. Be it for women and Greens, minority activists or disabled rights, they marched on the streets, setting up magazines, creating legal challenges in the courts or fostering grassroots activism in the local community. Whether they all got the change they desired is a moot point, but in the long run it may not matter. For what they brought about was such a reckoning with the postwar state, and with the liberal democratic principles it was based on, that there could be no going back to the political structures of before.

Crucially, what the right then did—instinctively perhaps, but fatefully also—was to hitch this new politics of the movement to their own newfound interest in the market. The blood of patriots need not be tapped if they could be assembled under a new tree altogether: as now they were, not as citizens of a state, but as individuals beneath the expanded canopy of the market. In Britain Thatcher thus redefined conservatism as an economically entrepreneurial doctrine; in America the neoconservative movement, which was soon to give birth to Reagan, placed the market at the center of an increasingly libertarian creed (it being market rules and market discipline that would distinguish libertarianism from anarchism). At the same time, the new politics of movement proved to be sometimes too easily outflanked, with many being co-opted by money themselves. "I saw the beginning of the end of a democratic LGBT movement in 1982 at the Waldorf Astoria," wrote the gay activist Andy Humm, "where the Human Rights Campaign Fund had its first big gala with tickets for $150 . . . [Former Vice President Walter] Mondale was the keynote speaker and he did not utter the word 'gay' once."[128] In Australia, the annual celebrations of its own Stonewall, of '78, soon morphed into today's multimillion-dollar Mardi Gras.

What both examples underscored was the extent to which it was the new right that had emerged not only as the party of the free market but also as a *radical* and not as a traditional force: traditionalism was now a characteristic of the left. Some of this was the result of hard graft: the business round tables and the conservative lobby groups that worked to defuse and channel popular discontent into new electoral constituencies. Some of this was serendipitous: Thatcher's rise was aided by the failure of her counterparts in Labour; Reagan was aided by the regional pivoting of American politics away from the patrimonial democrats of the East Coast to the sunbelt of West Coast technological entrepreneurialism.[129] But both these coming gales of transformation turned deliberately, and from their point of view wisely, to reforming the economy (frustrating many of those who had helped them get into power in the first place) as their political lever of choice. "The object is to change the soul," as Thatcher once put it. "But economics is the method."[130]

Thus finally did the image of the new conservatism come into view. And in contrast to the left, it carried with it the institutional means to do away with the less productive "social" functions of the state, while turning the laws and the market decidedly to its own ends. The postwar system had been assembled with a great many checks and balances against the political abuse of power; it had very few checks on the abuse of economic power. This disjuncture was to prove the underlying Achilles heel that helped undermine the old political order and consolidate the 1970s transformations.

Meanwhile, under cover of the flak screen of an emergent series of "culture wars" the real work of ring-fencing economic privilege could get underway. The little man, especially the blue-collar little man now exiting his Keynesian bubble, might have thought he was standing in the midst of a great change in his life; but for his group, the white working class, the problems were just beginning. In America especially, it was this very group, comprising men who were fearful of the downturn in their status and power as breadwinning (white) males, who would most significantly embrace the new Republican cause. After half a century of roughly equal political affiliation between women and men, blue-collar men swung heavily to vote for Reagan in 1980, while a greater proportion of women stuck with Carter.[131]

This was nothing if not ironic. Western nations were in crisis because they were capitalist nations confronting a deficit of control over the growing gap between national policies (which they were unwilling to act on alone) and novel international developments (which they were unable to act on together). But the left was riven in two and unable to explain this to anyone who mattered, and the new social movements, in their own search for greater status and recognition, proved too quick to call on the language of freedom as against the oppressions of a stultifying equality. It was the right's argument therefore—that the problems of society had been caused by too much government—which won the day. "For the first time in modern history," observed Ralf Dahrendorf with acuity and foreboding alike, "innovative thought about politics and society came from the right and not the left."[132]

"The twentieth century is witnessing the triumph of equality," declared the American foreign policy expert and later National Security adviser, Zbigniew Brzezinski in 1970.[133] With hindsight we now know that he was speaking at the very cusp of maximum equality in America. By 1973, the statistical curve of the long twentieth-century trend toward more equal national societies bottomed out, changed direction, and began heading back upward: toward greater inequality. Equality was not the future, freedom was: and in grasping this, conservatives won for themselves a far greater voice in determining how the balance between the two was to be rethought.

Even Scandinavian advocates of state welfare began shifting their attention "from a principle of the greatest possible equality to a principle of the greatest possible freedom—*freedom of choice*."[134] Here, as elsewhere, the social democratic rhetoric of equality was maintained. But it was meant now in terms of equality of opportunity, not outcome. It was valuable, in short, as a means to maximizing personal liberty. The welfare state dimmed in such a light: it became easier to bemoan its constraints and its costs; it became a collusion, if not a conspiracy, from which people needed to be "freed." By the 1980s Swedish Prime Minister Olof Palme was talking of the "authoritarian society" that lurked behind the doors of the *folkhemmet*.

Liberty and the state were thus now declared to be natural opposites, even in a democratic setting. "Out of liberty . . . stem the glories of civilized life," wrote the libertarian philosopher Murray Rothbard in 1975. "But liberty has always been threatened by the encroachments of power, power which seeks to suppress, control, cripple, tax, and exploit the fruits of liberty and production . . . And power is almost always focused upon that central repository of power and violence: the state."[135] As the man who would soon be president of the most powerful modern republic, Ronald Reagan, put it: "the very heart and soul of conservatism is libertarianism": the desire for "less government interference," "less centralized authority," "more individual freedom."[136]

Rothbard and Reagan, along with the likes of Milton Friedman, were among the more outspoken advocates of a "free" society. But their views of the dangers that a do-gooding yet unwieldy leviathan could pose to democracy were distinctly of their time. Forces on the right, be it the Austrian FPÖ, or antitax movements like those of Mogens Glistrup in Denmark and in the United States, likewise embraced the new creed. And with one or two caveats, but on the whole a dominant and major accord, popular understanding followed suit. In 1965 the *New York Times* printed sixty-six articles containing the words "free market" and 1,131 with the word "citizen." In 2008 by contrast "free market" appeared in 300 printed articles, but "citizen" appeared in only 964 articles.[137] This was probably underestimating the shift, however, since by the turn of the century to preface "market" with the adverb "free" was largely redundant. The battle by then had been won.

The left was culpable in that victory too by virtue of its own newfound interest in the sanctity of the individual. "In this grave hour in human history," declared George Meany, AFL-CIO president, to a gathering in a sweltering New York in July 1975, "when the forces arrayed against the free spirit of man are more powerful, more brutal and more lethal than ever before, the single figure who has raised highest the flame of liberty heads no state, commands no army, and leads no movement that our eyes can see."[138] When he went on immediately to talk of "a hidden movement of human beings who have no offices and have no headquarters [and] who are not represented in the great halls where nations meet," it was the shadow of Rothbard's politics, not that of the freedom-fighters, that was lingering in the wings.[139]

But in truth the libertarians were merely sharpening up a point of view that was shared by everyone on the right for whom liberty needed rescuing from the clutches of equality.[140] The temptation, and problem, for the left was that this new cult of the individual promised to replace the need to cultivate a working-class identity and its associated institutional mechanisms of mass struggle. To snipe about the individualism of the era is thus wrongly to overlook a significant and subtle reworking of the very subject of liberal democratic politics at work here. The real struggle in the years from the mid 1970s to the end of the Cold War was thus not one between states, nor even for one vision of the state over any other; it was a struggle waged, rather, *within* nations and between competing ways of creating a society of individuals.

The private individual now became *the* primary political unit: individualism had previously always been an antipolitical stance: a place of refuge from the political domain. Now the individual and his/her freedoms was politics itself, and the task of democracy was to safeguard those freedoms from the encroachments of others. The question then arises, however, as to why freedom should catch on so spectacularly as a political idea in the mid–late 1970s? The answer turns on corresponding developments in the international sphere, as the relationship between liberal ideology, the democratic nation state, and global capitalism was transformed on the international plane as well. It is to those events that we must now turn our attention.

4

A Split in the World

IN 1978 ALEKSANDR Solzhenitsyn, author of *The Gulag Archipelago*, was invited to give the year's commencement address at Harvard University. "Harvard's motto is 'VERITAS' [truth]," Solzhenitsyn began in his native Russian, his metallic voice echoed awkwardly by that of a live translator. "[But] truth seldom is pleasant . . . it is almost invariably bitter," and there would be a measure of "friendly" bitterness in his speech that day, he warned as the rain came down. But the students stayed seated. "The split in the world," he said, was not just that between East and West as rival political systems, but one "more profound and more alienating" that was to be found across them and within the human condition itself. Human rights were all well and good, but it was "human obligations" that needed defending most of all.[1]

That "goddamned horse's arse," as President Ford had taken to calling him, was at it again. Since leaving the USSR Solzhenitsyn had for several years been expected to speak out on the iniquities of life under communism. Very often he had. "[W]hat was mainly expected of me . . . was the gratitude of the exile to the great Atlantic fortress of Liberty, singing praises to its might and its virtues, which were lacking in the USSR." But Solzhenitsyn was tired of beating the same old drum. "I had kept slashing and hacking away at Communism," he later recalled, "but in these last years I had also seen in the West much that was alarmingly dangerous." When he showed his Harvard speech in advance to his translator, Irina Ilovaiskaya, she was aghast. "He will not be forgiven for this!" she said to Solzhenitsyn's wife tearfully, begging him to retract his views.[2]

He did not. Solzhenitsyn's warnings of the pitfalls of Western individualism that day were delivered, undiluted, over the heads of the students and visiting dignitaries assembled neatly in rows before him: and they were directed at the American policy and intellectual elite sitting metaphorically, if not literally, just behind. This was an elite, he said, in which mediocrity was the key to success. Solzhenitsyn's comments would later be broadcast in Russian across the Soviet Union and in full, via translation, on *Voice of America*. Criticisms of this sort were about the last thing that Americans wanted to hear from a man they had adopted as their moral rejoinder to the Soviet Union.[3] But in the way that only outsiders can be, Solzhenitsyn was on to something. For contrary to the debate that was to preoccupy the United States during the decades to come, the issue was not whether government was the solution or the problem, but the fact that a more positive vision not just of what government was for, but of what liberal society more broadly should be about, had already been separated from it.

And yet, close though he may have come to capturing what was really afflicting the Western democracies in the 1970s, Solzhenitsyn's own moralism ultimately prevented him from making the proper diagnosis. The real problem was not the dearth of all sense of human obligation, as he believed. The problem, as we have seen, was the sheer impossibility— in light of the economic and political crises of the era—of finding the right way to *institutionalize* such a vision. Modern democracy was woven into a variety of institutional forms, from the oversight exercised by the law to the advisory powers of professional economics. And the change that really mattered, in light of this, was the way that this institutional bedrock was being made to serve a more individualized model of human agency, to which the right had proved itself far better adapted.

A swerve had been imparted to democracy that involved more than just institutional change, however. It also saw a reconstituting of the very *spaces* of political activity, be it through the emergence of a new international order, the upheaval of national sovereignty, or through new sites of political agency opening up at the regional and transnational level. Under the twin pressures of Cold War geopolitics and an increasingly global international economy, a second fracturing of the Western political order took place during these years, adding to the domestic upheavals coming out of the crisis of capitalism and the breakdown of postwar democratic institutions. This twin fracturing—of the domestic political order (via the crisis of capitalism) and the international political order (via détente)—brought about in turn a further upheaval in the basic conditions of existence for modern liberal democracy: a switch from a territory-based global order to a property-based one. Here was the single most important transformation of all.

These were the real roots of the "split" that Solzhenitsyn was grasping at. National governments had been confronted by the limits of domestic policymaking and by its growing costs. In response they had found their way toward a new form of global *governance*: of ad-hoc policymaking bodies (such as the G5 and the Library Group before it) that corresponded to the post-national plane of a globalizing economy. From there they believed they could better respond to the challenges of "interdependence" by means of new forms of intergovernmentalism. This they did not do alone. Nongovernmental organizations (NGOs) soon joined them in pursuit of the same aim, while existing frameworks of transnational co-operation (most prominently, the EC) adapted their policymaking accordingly.[4]

The New International Order (Sovereignty Transformed)

If the radical movements of the era had failed, individually, to dislodge "the system," collectively they had begun to question something else: the degree to which elected governments could assume still to be the principal authority within the boundaries of their own nation states. The challenge they posed here was not, in the end, so very different from the economic unbundling of national capacity at the hands of a deregulated international economy. Each contributed, in different ways, to upending the post-Westphalian assumption that sovereignty ultimately resided with states, and that where one state's borders ended another's began. And both changes took place at a moment when a shift in Cold War geopolitical relations, which had long locked the Western democratic order into place, instead contributed for a few brief years to its loosening.

For Western states, whose very model of democracy was based upon a certain domestic consensus as to the national provision of welfare, the supremacy of national parliaments, and the anticipation of a year-on-year growth in Gross *National* Product to pay for this, the unbundling of national sovereignty, which by the end of the decade was well underway, was more than just a simple problem for the older model: it was interpreted as a fullscale rending of it. Books published with titles like *Sovereignty at Bay* (1971) and *The New Sovereigns* (1975)—the latter a book not about states but about so-called "limited" corporations—gave an indication of the anxieties that were raised by this "crisis of territoriality," as one historian has put it.[5] And yet, properly speaking, powers were not being lost so much as being transformed. And what would come to matter most was how politicians now went about trying to hang on to their sovereign privileges.

For a man like Henry Kissinger, the answer to this problem was a form of hardened pragmatism: to bend rather than to break and, if possible, to pass the costs of that bending on to others. Kissinger's solution to his country's diminishing global power was to reach for a multipolar world the United States could shape without paying for. America would become stronger, Kissinger believed, if it could position itself, with Europe at its haunches, at the center of a more *multipolar* world: with multiple sources of decision-making authority bound together, by US hands, and with a liberal capitalist thread. In return for its "offer" of managing this rapidly expanding terrain of international capital, the United States could demand not just Cold War allegiance but active support in the construction of a new empire of capital. That was not a vision that the dramatic events of the late 1970s allowed much scope for pursuing, however, as Kissinger's successor as foreign policy mandarin-in-chief, Zbigniew Brezinzski, was to find. For half a decade, from the mid 1970s onward, America was largely in response mode, with the rest of the Western democracies forced to replot their own paths accordingly.

It was as likely, during these years, to hear roundly contrasting views as to which way the geopolitical winds might be blowing. The French Marxist Henri Lefebvre, for example, also looked to the expanding international domain, the "space of the world" as he put it, for some means of resolving the national dilemmas of the moment. In Lefebvre's case, this was a way to circumvent what he saw as the irredeemable conservatism of the nation state itself: a conservatism for which the postwar consensus in Europe, and especially its ideological bulwarks of Christian and social democracy, were to blame, wedded as they both were to the expansion of the capitalist system. For Lefebvre and other Marxist writers—like the Greek Nicos Poulantzas—global capitalism was not steamrolling over states, it was being built *through* them.

What was ultimately at stake, then, in these debates was not territoriality in the abstract but the power of national government in the particular. In the 1970s this was a question raised perhaps most directly by the breaking up, and then the re-forming, of the pack ice of Cold War international relations during the era of détente. The Cold War was in many respects postwar democracy's unavoidable raison d'être, if not its shadow: be it the constant preparedness for a sudden, fatal nuclear escalation or the need to show vigilance against any and all forms of communist "subversion" (as those individuals whose names landed on one of Senator Joe McCarthy's lists in America in the 1950s could testify); or be it even the British appetite for John le Carré's watchful novels about George Smiley and the Circus. In a less well noted, yet critical, sense the Cold War was absolutely fundamental to the success of western democracy post-1945: it provided the imperative of a forced international stability from which a relatively harmonious domestic political consensus could take its cue.

That stability in turn was framed beneath the dual threat of a potential hot war on the one hand (the rejection of which was encapsulated in the founding of the United Nations and its diplomatic institutions such as the Security Council) and the specter of the Holocaust on the other (which, as the Nuremberg trials got underway, had provided the other pole). Détente is best understood in this context as a conservative effort of the superpowers and especially the United States, after several decades of expansion, to preserve the gains they had each carved out within this international arrangement. This was the other form of bipolarity that defined the mid twentieth century's world order. It was one in which both superpowers were complicit. And it revolved around a carefully balanced notion of "territorial integrity" at its heart—for if the lesson of Nuremberg was that strong states could abuse their powers, the lesson of the long slide into war in the 1930s was that economically hobbled states could equally lead to disaster.[6]

Ironically this sheer grasping unavoidability of superpower tensions did its part to sustain other national governments in their sense of territorial integrity. It was the threat of the East, after all, that created "the walled garden of western Europe," as one writer aptly put it, relieving the continent of the burden of its own security, but likewise locking individual nations into a wider political map that was less and less of their own making.[7] It was the threat of the West that justified the Warsaw Pact and the Brezhnev Doctrine that defended it. And while Europeans had often felt themselves to have been pinned down by this, other countries, especially Australia, had used the "clear choices" of the Cold War to pick their way carefully out of an equally limited past: successive Australian governments, for example, working to replace the nation's special relationship with the British to a potentially more promising one with the Americans.

All these actions worked to reinforce the primacy of state sovereignty. By the 1970s the underlying balance was beginning to be abandoned. Shocked by Vietnam into devising a morally more robust architecture governing international conflict, intellectuals like the American philosopher Michael Walzer began looking back to ancient ideas of "just war" as they sought to provide decision-makers with scenarios in which it might be ethically defensible to ignore the sovereign integrity of another nation's borders. Pioneering new human rights movements were often no longer prepared to wait for elaborate answers such as these and began providing assistance across national borders to those in need. In this they operated outside the umbrella of the United Nations system. The founding of Médicins Sans Frontières (Doctors Without Borders) in Paris in 1971 was one example; Human Rights Watch in New York in 1978 another. By the end of the decade even the Carter administration, whose first foreign policy pillar was the trilateralist one of international governance, had taken up their cause as central to its second pillar of promoting a more grassroots democratic opening around the world.

Many of these moral interventionists, like some of their new social movement forerunners, were both encouraged and provoked by radical postcolonial movements across the Third World (who as ever in this period were practicing what Western intellectuals were learning how to preach) as well as by the rise of the so-called "nonaligned nations": not a new, but an increasingly influential political bloc (today's G77) outside the bipolar Cold War framework. When the nonaligned movement's demands for a New International Economic Order were formally put before the United Nations in 1974, the rich countries countered with the need for yet more wisely stewarded international regulations. "Multipolarity" was thus in this sense also a pre-prepared defense of what looked, through the other end of the telescope, to be the perpetuation of great power privilege. And upon these countries' realization that political independence did not necessarily mean control over one's own economy, the post-1945 consecration of territorial sovereignty was thereby impaired that much more.[8]

The most transformative effects of this reworking of sovereignty for the West, however, were to be seen in the felt need to reinvent the procedures of international cooperation in light of the challenges of interdependence. And it was less the failure of détente per se than the new thinking détente made possible that mattered here. First it brought about a change in the Cold War geopolitical thinking of old. This made way for a more complex international political order that, contrary to Reagan's cold warrior grandstanding, was what accompanied and in some ways precipitated the decline of the Soviet Union. Second it helped enable the refashioning of Europe from a political to an economic project. Two very different developments, they each took root in the common desire of Western political elites to escape the troubles of the domestic arena and seek refuge in an as yet unscripted international domain. Along the way the counterpoint that the Western democracies had raised to Soviet globalism—namely enlightened technocratic nationalism (for creating wealth) combined with international cooperation (for managing the risks)—would have to be imagined anew: to wit the value of that more laissez-faire notion of individual freedom secured by the power of legal rights not democratically enabled capabilities.

After Détente (the Cold War at Home and Abroad)

As the 1972 election approached, Nixon's hopes of regaining the White House lay in tatters. A year out from the election his foreign policy relaunch, which centered upon peace in Vietnam, looked nothing so much as a butcher's closing down sale. Between 1969 and 1972 Nixon's so-called "peace plan" had seen an additional 20,000 American troops and 300,000 Asians die in Vietnam.[9] As the revelations of the My Lai Massacre hit the global headlines, and as, still, the Soviets refused to bargain, the law-and-order White House appeared to be losing control. In June 1971 Daniel Ellsberg, an employee at the RAND Corporation, leaked the Pentagon Papers to the *New York Times*. The material detailed the way the United States had defrauded the public over both its policy and purpose in Vietnam. This was followed by further revelations of the administration's secret dealings with Pakistan (in contravention of that country's publicly stated neutrality).[10]

In light of this, Nixon's trip to China and his meeting with Mao in 1972 was a stroke of political genius. It not only restored his then tattered-looking reelection hopes (though to be sure, the disastrous campaign of Democratic challenger George McGovern helped too). It also allowed him to further split the Soviet Union and China and to bring about the first Strategic Arms Limitation Talks Agreement (SALT I): two massive foreign policy achievements for which Nixon has probably not been given due credit. True, the meeting lasted less than an hour. But the point was that it happened. And if the French and the Australians, both of whom had been in Beijing shortly before Kissinger's secret preparatory meeting with Zhou Enlai, were outraged at having the thunder stolen from their own China initiatives, the Western world was arguably a safer place for it.[11]

Nonetheless, the Nixon Doctrine turned out to be a disaster for most of the countries it purported to help. Johnson had created a warfare state abroad but balanced this by means of the welfare state at home; Nixon by contrast took US-style "law and order" and applied it to the world at large. His policy of "Vietnamization" (drawing down US troops and forcing local regimes to man the battlefields) was the model for a much broader, outward-looking strategy by which the United States would encourage other proxy states to shoulder the burden of its projection of military power around the globe. This was a brilliant, if cynical, way of turning military liabilities into economic assets, since America then supplied those same nations with the weapons they would need to fight its battles. Arms sales in the 1970s were soon around tenfold what they had been during the 1960s.[12]

This then was the "peace" that détente conferred. But détente was a game-changer all the same: for it enabled the United States to recover its room for maneuver as the hegemonic power of the capitalist world. At the same time the politics of the Nixon–Kissinger understanding of détente (that military retrenchment, secured under the terms of the Paris Agreement of January 1973, should be the prelude to diplomatic advance) had also—for some of these very reasons—seen the United States relinquish its authority, in the eyes of many, as the moral standard-bearer of that democratic world. Thus would the values of Cold War political liberalism now especially need defending at home to compensate for this—hence, in part, the heightened tenor of domestic political debate.

For all that it rent and fractured the Cold War international order just as surely as the economic crisis had overturned the domestic political order, détente was destined to be a relatively short-lived phenomenon. Already by 1974, it was "discredited" as a foreign policy doctrine, as then member of the National Security Council (and future CIA Director) Robert Gates put it. Its principal architects did not themselves long outlast détente either.[13] Felled by Watergate, Nixon was out by that summer. For his part, Kissinger—whom Nixon had been planning to axe—held on under Gerald Ford, who had not the wit to install someone else. But if Kissinger remained alive, politically, this was only to afford him a front row seat in watching his earlier creations fail one by one.

The true legacy of détente, however, was to be found not in what it achieved itself but in the forces it unleashed. Kissinger probably never really imagined that the Paris Peace Agreement would hold, for all that pretending that it would had earned him the Nobel Prize.[14] But by the end of the decade, even the Nixon Doctrine he had worked so hard to "link" to détente, had blown up in his face with the flare-up of fighting in Africa. In Angola, in particular, the United States suffered the ignominy of seeing its heavily backed South African forces defeated by a better-trained Cuban army intent on keeping the flame of Guevarism alive a little longer. Finally, Kissinger had the disappointment of seeing the

Congress he had derided and run roughshod over, now expanding its sway over the executive on foreign as well as domestic policy.

At home too, the spirit of détente led to congressional limits being placed on the president's war powers over Vietnam (ultimately hastening the end of the conflict via the War Powers Act of 1973). Congress then further rapped the executive's knuckles by preventing it supplying arms to Turkey in the aftermath of the Cypriot crisis in the summer of 1974. That same year, the Senate imposed the Jackson–Vanik amendment to the Soviet trade agreement, which incensed the Soviets, and Kissinger, by insisting that Jewish dissidents be allowed to leave irrespective of the consequences to trade. By the end of the decade, the US Congress was unique among the democracies for the extent to which it controlled the nation's foreign policy. The imperial presidency had given way to Congress as a "world power" itself.[15]

Détente also highlighted some of the Cold War's underlying contradictions. One of the most basic of these was the fact that the economic and political alliances of the Western democracies no longer lined up. Trade with the Soviet bloc was growing all the time, and the front lines of the Cold War, as the Historic Compromise in Italy, or the Guillaume Affair in West Germany had shown, were as often drawn *within* the Western nations as between them. But the international tug-of-war over Italy's Historic Compromise was about more than the felt need to tamp down domestic dissent in a game of global Whac-A-Mole. It was also about reordering political sovereignty in accordance with the thinking of Cold War political realism. And in the context of détente, this became much harder to do, as the brief appearance of what came to be known as "Eurocommunism" exemplified.

The Eurocommunist movement, in which once again the Italian communist Enrico Berlinguer played a prominent role, was an effort by the communist parties of Western Europe to find that parliamentary route to socialism toward which the Socialist International had pointed them back in 1951 and which Berlinguer thought he had grasped a way to plotting. The movement rapidly gained a position of some strength in the mid–late 1970s in the aftermath of the socialist 1968. For the Prague Spring and its brutal repression had encouraged a number of Western European communist parties to become much more critical of Moscow. The Italians led the way here and the French and the Spanish communist parties in different ways joined on (the more orthodox French somewhat reluctantly and the Spanish rather more eagerly, for all that their domestic fortunes fluctuated amid the post-Franco turmoil in their country). Moscow was equally displeased with them all, of course, worried as it was that the Eurocommunists would destroy the advantage the Soviets now enjoyed over the Americans in the years after the Yom Kippur War (and which détente, they felt, had made possible for *them*). Above all Moscow was deeply irritated by the Eurocommunists' increasingly vocal criticism of the Brezhnev Doctrine, which in 1968 had affirmed that Moscow had the right to intervene in its satellite states if need be. Berlinguer himself not only approved openly of that doctrine's sworn enemy, NATO, as we have seen, he went so far as to use the 25th Congress of the Communist Party of the Soviet Union (CPSU) in Moscow to argue for "pluralism and political democracy."

Initially Moscow sought to contain these youthful enthusiasms of the Spanish and the Italians. But the Eurocommunists found that they rather enjoyed speaking their own mind after all this time.[16] In 1977, Spain's Santiago Carrillo outlined the notion of a possible "third way" between communism and capitalist democracy for his country, in what was to prove an influential tract for disoriented Western leftists at the time: *Eurocommunism and the State* (1977). As with Berlinguer's openly democratic sentiments, Carrillo's practical policy of political moderation in Spain was deliberately calculated to help secure the transition to democracy after Franco—even if this was contrary to what orthodox doctrine demanded.[17] But the Italian and Spanish communists had gone further by holding a landmark meeting in Madrid in March 1977 at which they sought to define their own *distinctive* socialist doctrine. At this the politburo's aging grandees turned purple with rage and thereafter set themselves to sabotaging the whole affair.

What these events made clear was that Moscow no longer had a "positive" strategy to take to the world struggle, for all that the years after 1975 ought to have been good ones for them, with Mao gone in 1976 and America passive after Vietnam. Instead these were the years of *zastoi*, or drift in Soviet foreign policy, when it seemed as if the USSR had lost all sense of direction amid a growing public apathy at home. The dynamism of the young Eurocommunists contrasted with this all too obviously for Eastern Europeans not to see: and that was what worried the Soviet leadership most of all. At the same time, and just as with the "historic compromise" in Italy, the Eurocommunists' embrace of democracy as an "historically universal value upon which to base an original socialist society," as Berlinguer put it, likewise disturbed the

United States.[18] And so the West too proved no more hospitable to the whole idea than did the USSR.

If détente had provided the necessary international context for the emergence of Eurocommunism, the passing of détente also signaled the end of what had been one of the most promising experiments in democratic socialism all century. It was the first, but not the last, confirmation during the late Cold War that no middle way, no compromise between communism and capitalism would be permitted, and that some other resolution to the struggle was required. A genuine movement in search of a form of parliamentary socialism had been snubbed by the two superpowers at the very moment it looked like becoming a reality. Its legacy was not quite yet settled, for its ideas would make an unexpected return in the coming drama of the Gorbachev years.[19] Before then, however, the Cold War would intensify once again, as the diplomatic initiatives of the Carter years gave way to the saber-rattling of Reagan, the Euromissiles, and the last gasp of belligerence of the Soviets in Afghanistan, and as conflicts flaring up in Southern Africa and Central America helped to lock the Cold War back into place.

For Americans what most brought home this return to a harsher international climate was not the lost opportunities of doctrinal realignment in Europe but a rather more tangible saga that began with the storming of the American embassy in Tehran on November 4, 1979. A drawn-out hostage crisis began that winter and it would last for 444 days: one day longer than the remainder of Carter's full term in office (and, as it played out in the full glare of the world's media, a large part of the reason he failed to retain it). The Americans taken hostage were for months routinely paraded before the Iranian (and watching Western) public, and subject to humiliating treatment: all of which served to make Carter look by turns both feckless and incompetent, not least when a mere sandstorm derailed an ill-advised special forces operation, codenamed Eagle's Claw, sent in to rescue them.

The underlying cause of the crisis was the rise of the radical cleric Ayatollah Ruhollah Khomeini, who had deposed the unpopular, but pro-Western Shah of Iran in July 1979. When Carter—ever the humanitarian—then offered the exiled former leader medical care in America, it proved to be the final straw for the increasingly radicalized Iranian regime and its rapidly deteriorating relationship with America. When it came to negotiating the release of the hostages, however, Carter's hands were tied. Iran was simply too important now as an oil supplier to be ignored, as the queues soon snaking their way out of American gasoline stations served to remind people. For the Soviets this was a gleeful prospect: the American empire was being made to look weak, its governing administration craven and vacillating. Moscow moved quickly to capitalize by supporting some of the latest wave of uprisings across the Third World: notably in Ethiopia, Angola and Mozambique. Most dramatically of all, in December 1979 they sent their tanks rolling across the Amu Darya into Afghanistan.

Carter was incensed when he was told of the invasion. His opinion of the Russians had changed, he said, "more drastically in the last week than even the previous two-and-a-half years." But Americans' opinion of Carter was also at an all-time low (he had just 28 percent approval in June 1979).[20] For that reason the invasion would have profound repercussions, forcing the Americans back into a hardened Cold War stance and marking the final failure of Carter's efforts to engage the world in the guise of a benign multilateralist. Here was another of the moment's lost opportunities. For in contrast to his predecessors, Carter genuinely *had* seen détente as being less about leverage and more a means to reduce global superpower tensions. The first practical outcome of this was a pronounced shift in geographical focus as to where the US sought to project its military authority: away from the global south and toward the Middle East. The consequences of this would take several decades to play out. But already, under pressure from the oil prices and the Soviet presence in the Persian Gulf, US officials were imagining a "new security relationship with Riyadh," a closer relationship with Pakistan, and a constant press on the oil-rich lands in between. Arms poured in to support the Mujahideen and the twenty-first-century geopolitical landscape began to take shape on the map.[21]

Some in America—not least the Committee on the Present Danger—no doubt saw themselves as vindicated by all this. Founded in 1976 around a lunch table in the Metropolitan Club in Washington, DC, and by such foreign-policy luminaries as Paul Nitze, George Marshall, Jeane Kirkpatrick, and Richard Perle, this high-octane group of intellectuals (not to mention volatile egos) were adamant that "our country is in a period of danger, and the danger is increasing."[22] Unconvinced the government was doing enough about it, these influential individuals now set out to reignite the Cold War by operating as an elite pressure group. Thanks in part to their needling, and his own frustrations at the behavior of the Soviets, Carter steadily increased the US strategic commitment (bringing defense spending up to at least 3 percent more than inflation per year, and persuading his NATO allies to do the same); he also invested heavily in conventional arms and moved forward with the more aggressive NATO "dual track" approach: to deploy nuclear missiles first and to negotiate after.[23] Come the early 1980s and the case of foreign policy hawks like those in the Committee on the Present Danger was largely made. Indeed, more than 30 of its 140 odd members were by then on leave of absence, serving in the new Reagan administration.[24]

Reimagining Europe

Europeans were also forced to adapt politically to the changing international order of the 1970s. The first way they did this, and it too was an offshoot of "détente," was the policy of opening to the East, or Ostpolitik, inaugurated by West Germany's Willy Brandt upon his election as chancellor in October 1969. Brandt had sighed when, immediately on sitting down in the office vacated by his predecessor Kurt Kiesinger, three letters were thrust into his hands, one for each of the three supervisory powers to whom the West German chancellor was, in those days, still required to confirm his obeisance in writing. Worse still for Brandt, the two Germanies had grown apart in all the years since the war, such that it seemed possible they might never again be one nation. Brandt resolved to do more than simply dare more democracy during his time in power: he set out to change this. As he stated in his inaugural address: "Even if two states exist in Germany, they are not foreign countries." It was the clearest gesture by a postwar German chancellor yet that something needed to be done about this.[25] No less than the Eurocommunists, Brandt was daring to challenge the lockdown of the Cold War as it impinged upon the prospects for democratic life at home.

Brandt faced considerable obstacles, however. Moscow would need convincing, as would the GDR, the Western powers, *and* those neighboring countries, Poland in particular, whose own borders were bound up in the complex postwar settlement that had been reached over the former Reich and set in stone since. To overcome these, Brandt put his faith in a trusted colleague, Egon Bahr, now secretary of the chancellor's office and an even stauncher proponent of German reunification than he was, and one whose diplomatic skill (and mordant wit) could only be an asset in the task ahead. For weeks Bahr met secretly with the Russian foreign minister, Andrei Gromyko, to flesh out the bottom line of a new basic agreement between the two German states, one which would address two fundamental and long-standing problems: the GDR's desire to be recognized as a legitimate sovereign state, and the as yet unresolved status of West Berlin.

Such were the tensions raised by even broaching this that Brandt himself was nearly unseated from power, and by his own party colleagues, several years before he was finally felled by the Guillaume Affair. On both sides of the Iron Curtain, his overtures had incensed as many as they had impressed, and in 1972 the CDU–CSU opposition thought they had successfully maneuvered to have Brandt removed in a carefully engineered vote of no-confidence. At the very last, however, they fell two votes short to pass the motion in the Bundestag (two of the opposition bloc's own deputies voting in *support* of Brandt). It was inexplicable, and would remain so for decades, until it emerged that those two deputies had been paid off by the East Germans themselves. Thus could it later be said that this was "the time the Stasi saved Brandt's government to save Ostpolitik."[26]

But save it they did. The Basic Treaty was finally approved by the Federal Constitutional Court in July 1973. By September the GDR had been welcomed as a recognized state entity into the United Nations in New York, and Brandt had his opening to the East. Was it any good? Bahr had perhaps the best answer here. "Before we had no relationship with the GDR," he quipped, "now, at least, we have a bad one."[27] Ostensibly both East and West German sensitivities over the need to retain their own vision of state sovereignty had been overcome. In reality, what had happened was that German sovereignty had just been legally tweaked; a reminder that economics was not the only force capable of prompting a reimagining of political structures.

Brandt's Ostpolitik was one way Europe was adapting itself to the domestic and international challenges of the day. Developments at the pan-European level were another. The mythology of European integration usually presents the achievement of today's EU as the belated product of postwar reconciliation: of the visions of Paul-Henri Spaak and Robert Schuman in the postwar era, and of the spirit of Altiero Spinelli's Ventotene manifesto "For a Free and United Europe" written during the war. The modern EU, however, is also a product of the way this somewhat *stalled* process of Europeanization was picked up and restarted during the 1970s, amid both economic upheaval and the changing international politics of the Cold War. In light of this, modern Europe emerges less as an endless series of cattle trades and more as a dramatic commitment to transnationalizing responsibility for domestic peace and stability at a moment of heightened international insecurity.

The upheavals of the 1970s had certainly split the European nations. New members—Denmark, Ireland, and the UK—had been admitted, ultimately, in the case of the UK, over de Gaulle's dead body. But they were not especially drawn by its vision of political integration; what they were interested in was access to the Common Market. The volatility occasioned by the breakup of Bretton Woods had come close to derailing that market, however, and it had consigned to the dustbin more ambitious plans, such as those laid out in the Werner Report (1969) formulated before the breakup of the Bretton Woods arrangements, for a more formal monetary union. An era of pragmatic triage had ensued: France's Georges Pompidou and West Germany's Willy Brandt responding to the economic upheavals of the first part of the decade by decanting European monetary relations into a series of more fluid, semifixed exchange rates: "the snake," as it had been dubbed. But the snake's failure, by the middle of the decade—as countries failed to keep their exchange rates in touch with one another—was a reminder that continued (let alone further) integration could not be an economic concern alone: the *political* institutions of European integration also needed developing.

Some leaders, notably Brandt, wanted to reboot the process of European integration therefore (and Brandt employed the aging founding father Jean Monnet to lobby for him in the background to just this end). Brandt had his reasons for this: not least, he needed a deepening of the European project to support him in his opening to the East.[28] But while some, like the Dutch, were sympathetic, the French in particular were skeptical. What ultimately induced them all to consider a reboot of European political integration was their common desire for a greater freedom of movement from America. Perturbed by Nixon's closer dealings with the Soviets over détente in the summer of 1973, European leaders had rejected Nixon's bid to launch a "new Atlantic charter" and even produced a counter statement declaring Europe a "distinct entity" in world affairs. This put European and American relations at something of a new postwar low. But equally it intensified the need for European leaders to produce an alternative vision in its place.[29]

It was the Davignon Report of 1970 that was the starting point here. Like de Gaulle's proposal of the Fouchet Plan (1961) before it, the Davignon Report, made concrete gestures in the direction of closer political union, as had the Werner Plan in the realm of monetary union, focusing in particular on foreign policy cooperation. But aside from its establishment of the forum for European Political Cooperation, inaugurated in November 1970 in Munich, a city known for its compromises, it had largely been rendered mute by the sheer extent of the upheavals of the time. It was this that prompted Giscard d'Estaing (who adored the conspiracy of behind-the-scenes diplomacy) to lobby for the establishment of a more streamlined Council for Heads of State, a body in which the leaders of the then nine core countries would meet three times a year to develop areas of common diplomatic and foreign strategy.

Now, for the first time, the Europeans had a mechanism for responding to events in real time and for setting a common political agenda. Old habits die hard, however, and the first thing the new Council for Heads of State did, inevitably, was to commission a report. Meanwhile, the European project, as it now incorporated the British, the Danes, and the Irish, set to finding some greater common ground over the issue of a "European identity," as had been called for at the Copenhagen summit of 1973.[30] This was no run-of-the-mill undertaking: the report was to consider the prospects for nothing less than the transformation of Europe's existing economic community into a formal political union. And when the new Belgian prime minister, Leo Tindemans, submitted the report that bore his name, in 1975, he lobbied strongly not only for a more unified European approach to foreign relations, but for the legal and parliamentary institutions that would allow it to do this. After all, the Americans were doing deals with everyone from the Soviets to the Chinese, and in the fallout from the Yom Kippur War they were supportive of Israel when most of Europe's interests, not to mention its oil supply, came from the Arab nations.

Tindemans himself was an ardent Christian democrat and a federalist. But the Tindemans Report's plans for an elected European parliament received a mixed response on the whole. The social democratic left played it down to avoid giving the supranational initiative to the conservatives (there was little danger of that, however, since national leaders felt they had already given up quite enough sovereignty over the economy of late). Meanwhile Tindemans's fellow federalists, who had been hoping for a full-blown constitution, felt it was far too tepid. Even so, as the economic crisis persisted, the pressure to develop a more formal European political structure continued to mount. Yet more ideas were solicited. The MacDougall Report (1977) suggested a return to the past via continental-level Keynesian demand management and tripartite bargaining. This was scuppered by employers who refused to get on board. The same year, the OECD published its McCracken Report, offering market- and price-based solutions instead. In terms of its ideas, at least, it was this version that won the day.[31]

By the time the first European elections were held in June 1979, the political structures into which a brand new set of MEPs were to be elected, and what they were representing, had been profoundly transformed. Yes, Europe now had a transnational-level electoral system. Whether that parliament of nations would have any meaningful say over matters of fiscal policy and welfare was another thing altogether. As it turned out, what the new MEPs would spend most of their time debating in the years to come was that more fluid, nonbinding notion of identity, rather than actual social and political outcomes. The shape of the proposed European Parliament had been substantially altered as well. Under pressure from France it still no legislative powers, first of all, in deference to French concerns at the prospect of a supranational parliament being seen to supersede the prerogatives of the French Assemblé Nationale (Gaullists and communists alike digging in to defend the sovereign franchise). The British House of Commons too had had its first say in the European project, vetoing its own government's suggestion that British MEPs in the new European Assembly be elected by proportional representation (always a sin in the UK).

Ultimately more questions were raised by the final shape of the parliament that Europe's governments could agree upon than answers were actually given, with each country adopting its own procedures (whether first past the post or proportional representation) and some, such as Luxembourg, even allowing voting for multiple parties. There was considerable misalignment in constituency size as well, with Luxembourgers overrepresented (they had one MEP per 60,000 citizens) and Germans comparatively underrepresented (with just one MEP per 760,000 citizens). And for all that it was an historic achievement, it was also one watered down by low voter turnouts (just 32 percent in Great Britain) and by the fact that the new assembly had no legislative powers of its own: they resided still with Giscard's Council of Ministers. A future tendency of the European Union was thus inaugurated at its 1970s rebirth, as the new parliament immediately went looking—via commissions and revisitations of existing treaties—for ways to acquire powers for itself. Nothing perhaps so well defines modern Europe as the image of a democratically elected body deploying the mechanisms of elite proceduralism in search of an expanded mandate.

Yet the real issue here was, ironically, that the failure to achieve full monetary and foreign policy union at this juncture—the lost voice, as it were, of the Werner Plan and Davignon Report—was what dampened the felt need for a genuine and democratically representative legislature, with real powers of decision-making. As the British political adviser David Marquand put it at the time, "Although large numbers of critically important decisions are now taken by the Community authorities, integration has not yet gone far enough to make the undemocratic nature of the system either obvious or intolerable."[32] This would turn out to have been doubly significant, given the domestic political drift of the moment toward the right, since the collective "voice" in which Europe's peoples wished to speak as the elections revealed, was one heavily accented with socialist and Christian democratic tones.[33] On leaving office as prime minister in 1978, Tindemans went on to form the European People's Party: the primary Christian democratic movement at the European level. The Christian democrats scored the second highest number of votes to the new assembly (26.1 percent) and took 107 in the new European parliament. It was the socialists who came first, however, with 27.6 percent of the votes cast and 113 seats (of 410 available).

Meanwhile, Giscard was busy seeking to expand the effective power of the Council of Ministers, creating that very gathering of glad-handers that a Greek economics minister would later disparage as the "adults in the room," oozing authority but lacking popular support. But Giscard knew which way the wind was blowing, and in 1978 he sought to provide a holding legitimacy by calling for a report by "three wise men" from Europe—Robert Marjolin, the former vice president of the European Commission, Edmund Dell, a former British minister for trade and perhaps the original British europhile, and former Dutch Prime Minister Barend Biesheuvel—to make recommendations on a more effective structure of governance now that the European Community was both enlarging and (democratically) expanding. The thrust of their advice was to streamline the whole operation, which was doubtless music to Giscard's ears, but it was also advice the European machine was inherently predisposed to ignore. Not that it mattered by then. As de Gaulle had long ago foreseen, and Yanis Varoufakis would later confirm, it was the meeting of heads of state at the European Council that would now become the agenda setter in the new Europe.[34]

In the midst of the upheavals of the 1970s, then, the underlying principles that would gird the relaunch of the European Project in the 1980s, and specifically in the lead-up to the Single European Act of 1986, had been laid down: political clubbishness accompanied by a liberalizing economic federalism. The ground on which Delors would later erect the single market and the euro as the primary pillar around which all other decisions would take second place had been prepared. And that ground was, in the background of events, quietly being reinforced by the procedural mechanisms of the European Community. The European Court of Justice, for example, had consolidated both its own position and the legal principle that the Treaty of Rome and EC law flowing from it took precedence over national laws and treaties: "a permanent limitation of their [member states'] sovereign rights."[35] The Treaty of Rome became steadily more like a European constitution in practice, for all that this was carefully avoided in name. And as individual plaintiffs, from Belgian air hostesses to Italian solvents manufacturers, now found, there could be considerable advantages to following European rather than domestic legal requirements: higher wages in the case of the former, better product standards in the latter.[36]

Ever the outliers, the British, under pro-European Prime Minister Ted Heath, had chosen at the start of the 1970s to make themselves a part of this "new Europe." In truth they had little choice: as a Foreign Office official engaged in the access negotiations put it, mindful of his own country's dire economic circumstances at the time, "No sensible traveler on the sinking *Titanic* would have said, 'I will only enter a lifeboat if it is well scrubbed, well painted and equipped with suitable supplies of food and drink.'"[37] It was with hindsight the equivalent of sailing willfully into iceberg-riddled waters, however, that Brussels (or at least Georges Pompidou) insisted that Britain adopt the EEC model *as it existed*, with no chance to shape the priorities or procedures upon entry. It opened a genuine cause of complaint that gave legitimacy to Britain's otherwise overplayed hand of Euroskepticism—well captured by a conservative British newspaper's claim that "Heath has done what Napoleon and Hitler tried but failed to do"—and created a sore that would never really heal.[38]

Integration was its own kind of disintegration in other ways too. "Colonialism has rarely been seen as part of the European memory landscape about post-1945 integration," remarks the historian Bo Stråth, but it should be. As he and other historians have shown, European integration and decolonization were not simply coincident.[39] In some ways they fed into one another: not least since part of the foreign policy work undertaken by "Europe" during this period focused precisely on relations with the African, Caribbean, and Pacific (ACP) states, who between them sold more than two thirds of their exports to the EEC. Out of the crises of the 1970s came, for Europeans perhaps most acutely of all, the overriding urge to flee the national domain. But at the same time the world was coming to Europe.

Thus at the very moment that the United States was reaching the limits of its much vaunted "exceptionalism" in Asia, Europe found itself coming to terms with the fallout from its own particular hubris of co-lonialism, as that now impacted back upon the metropolitan center. This was a generational challenge, thirty years after the war, and it took the form of in-migration, expectations of trade largesse, and—in the Com-monwealth—unhelpfully binding political commitments. This was most directly experienced in Portugal, where the failure of the Portuguese military to stave off independence struggles prompted the officers' revolt that brought down the old regime in 1974 (and created, in just a few years, a new headache for the United States in Southern Africa). But it was equally felt in Britain, which found that the Commonwealth nations were inching steadily away from it in their loyalties: one of the factors pushing it into its reluctant embrace with Europe.

The breakup of the old imperial bloc cut both ways, as New Zea-landers found when Britain finally acceded to the EEC in 1973. Reeling still from the oil crisis, New Zealand was immediately hit by the loss of special trading relations with the country that had taken 65 percent of all its exports as recently as 1952. The cost of oil went up and the price of lamb fell. The government stepped in with price controls and over-generous pension promises, all of which so wrecked the economy that, along with France in the years to come, New Zealand became the other early site of a radical left liberalism that had long since lost its faith in the power of government intervention.[40] Meanwhile, Australia too found itself importing more from Japan and the United States than from the UK.

North Atlantic ties were being reforged as well. Canada in particular, despite being a part of the Atlantic world Nixon wished to bring together, used these years to make a dramatic show of its independence. While British fishermen flew Canadian flags to show their support for Canada in its "turbot wars" with Spain over territorial fishing rights, Trudeau's Canada chose Europe over the Commonwealth for its export markets: establishing a bilateral Framework Agreement with Europe in 1976. This was no small snub to the UK: the Marshall Plan may be better remem-bered on the continent, but Canada had loaned one tenth of its GDP in 1946 to Great Britain, the impact being just as important for the British Isles.[41] Needless to say, Canada's shifting allegiances to the conti-nent did not go unnoticed. Nor were they unintentional: under Trudeau (reelected in 1974 and once again, after just over a year in opposition, in

1980) a new course was being charted through to the "patriation" of the Canadian constitution in 1982.

This widespread unbundling of these political structures inherited from the age of empire appeared, at first glance, to be staved off by one of the rare instances of political convergence in an era better remembered for its divergences: the signing of the Helsinki Final Act (1975), the "Helsinki Accords." In fact, the latter was nothing if not a confirmation of the growing trend. The signing was the concluding act in the inaugural meeting of the Conference for Security and Cooperation in Europe: an intergovernmental dialogue established in 1973 to improve East–West relations during the era of détente (a continental offshoot, in its way, of Brandt's hard-won victories for a future German reunification via Ostpolitik). Today (renamed as the Organization for Security and Co-operation in Europe), it is the largest stand-alone intergovernmental security agency. The CSCE's birth in the early–mid 1970s was an unlikely case of diplomatic miscegenation in which everyone pretended to go along with it for the sake of appearances, only to find that in the end they really had gone along with it after all.

On one level the Helsinki Final Act, the diplomatic pinnacle of this process, was the product of Finnish President Urho Kekkonen's desire to promote Finland's own brand of neutrality by offering to host, in the latter stages of détente, a grand summit between Eastern and Western powers. On another level, the Final Act—overseen by Pope Paul VI's diplomatic emissary, Cardinal Agostino Casaroli, a man who had been actively signing agreements between the Vatican and the communist regimes behind the Iron Curtain—is impossible to imagine at any other moment than in the still-warm afterglow of détente. Either way the result was significant: Helsinki included as signatories both the Soviet Union, which saw in it the opportunity to finalize its territorial gains in central Europe, and the United States, which wanted to secure the political gains of détente and the right to trade more.

Against these developments, Europeanization was thus but one expression of the "changing boundaries of the political" that marked these years more generally.[42] It also made clear that the executive authority that formerly resided within the postwar "national" democratic state was not withering away, it was relocating: and in at least three senses. First, national governments themselves now became more internationally oriented. Second, local and regional bodies increasingly asserted their autonomy from national political decision-making. And third, as the gap between these first two developments grew, a space for what would go by the name of *non*governmentalism opened up in between. A whole new political eco-system of NGOs, INGOs, QUANGOs, and NONGOs thus now exploded onto the scene, largely on the basis of their promise to do what states might once have been expected to do, only better, and with many of them taking their cue from another international development of the moment: the coming of age of international law and human rights.

Recalibrating the Nation

It was states that moved first and they did so not just through the restart given to Europeanization. With national governments having tried, and failed, to address their economic crises alone, they now changed tack and sought to do so collectively instead. If the way they did this appeared to bear out the worst fears of a Marxist-like Lefebvre, it also marked the dawning of a new era of global governance that sought not so much to reestablish a rules-based international system as to create a series of international talking shops in which short-term solutions could perpetually be hashed out.

This "bold" new era was inaugurated, fittingly enough, under a wintry drizzle in northern France from November 15–17, 1975. It was there, in the luxurious but cramped surroundings of the Château de Rambouillet, 30 miles from Paris (the British delegation worked out of Napoleon's bathroom), that Pompidou's successor as French prime minister Giscard d'Estaing hosted delegations from Britain, America, West Germany, Italy, and Japan, now as the "G6" (later G7 and G8) meeting of nations. What would become these meetings' characteristic combination of domestic political agendas confronting international anxieties was fully in evidence from the start. The newly installed West German leader, Helmut Schmidt, who had lent his support to the initiative, was most concerned that the British and Americans attend. This was because he saw them, alongside West Germany, as the governing triumvirate of monetary power. The Japanese prime minister, Takei Miko, was there by virtue of his country's growing industrial strength. And the Italians were invited in a superpower-supported effort to remind Moro of his international responsibilities vis-à-vis the communists at home.

On the surface, this was Giscard's show. The French president was at the peak of his powers in 1975. Riding the wave of optimism he had carried with him into the Élysée, after beating Pompidou, Giscard wanted France to play a central role in leading the Western economies back to happier times. Yet it was arguably Germany's Helmut Schmidt who had the greatest influence upon the final outcome. Schmidt was the first leader of his era really to "get" globalization. And not only had the new chancellor's efforts to expand the remit from narrowly defined monetary issues to economic problems more broadly helped persuade President Ford to attend, his ambition was infectious with the likes of Kissinger.

What also drove the West German chancellor was his concern that his democratic counterparts were underestimating the scale of the problems before them. They "lack an understanding of the complexity of problems of this, the worst crisis since the Thirties," he was heard to complain. And he was right. "There is no unity regarding the assessment of the present world economic crisis, much less the therapy."[43] But if it was Schmidt's determination to address this that enabled Rambouillet to forge a measure of Atlantic cooperation, it also helped ensure that same spirit of international economic cooperation was formulated around a German-inspired discipline. "The most urgent task is to assure the recovery of our economies," the final declaration announced in tones that made clear what the focus was to be, and which were influenced perhaps by the damp country air. "[W]e recognize the need for vigilance and adaptability in our policies. We will not allow the recovery to falter. We will not accept another outburst of inflation."[44]

For his part, Giscard ultimately failed to achieve his larger ambition of a French-authored new international monetary system: restoring the best of the stability that Bretton Woods offered, but with less of the American hegemony (an idea that would be picked up three decades later by Nicolas Sarkozy). That grand idea faltered this time round under the pressure of diplomatic differences as much as working conditions: "the Mandarins have been compressed rather than suppressed," as one wag present put it.[45] But the French president was not wrong to claim the meeting as a success, since it both reset Atlantic relations and took a positive step in the direction of big power economic diplomacy. For his part, by the time he flew home on the *Spirit of '76*, Nixon's re-liveried *Air Force One*, Ford had shown himself to be his own man, and to be reaching beyond his predecessor's foreign policy shadow. While he had made some public concessions toward the Europeans' softer position on the oil cartels, he was doubtless comforted, in private, by the fact that William Simon was already pursuing the United States' own more conciliatory back-door policy in secret.

If there was a loser from the table it was arguably Britain's Harold Wilson, who had arrived in a precarious position at home (of the original attendees to this first G6 meeting, only Miko in Japan was under more domestic pressure) and who had also gone home empty-handed. The problem for Wilson was that he needed both to demonstrate common cause with his fellow leaders (specifically regarding Rambouillet's pledges not to raise protective tariff barriers, or otherwise do anything that might undermine the fragile global trading system) and his equally pressing need to satisfy the demands of a trade union movement at home that was pushing him to do just this. Wilson thought he had overcome the dilemma by securing agreement at Rambouillet on the permissiveness of protectionist measures "in particularly acute and unusual circumstances." But as the British ambassador to Washington was told in no uncertain terms a few days later, this was not a button it was ever intended should be pressed: the concession was purely cosmetic.[46] The national political realm, in other words, was no longer isolated from the international.

As states reached out to the transnational domain, a concomitant expansion in the powers and legitimacy of *local and regional* government began to make itself felt within the confines of the domestic nation state. If this was a more peaceful expression, toward the end of the decade, of the demand for self-governance that was elsewhere being expressed through the rebirth of secessionism, it was no less of a challenge to the primacy of national democratic decision-making than were the elite tête-a-têtes now routinely underway between the members of the leading industrial democracies. As one historian rightly puts it: the hollowing out of the political center, and the preoccupation of governments themselves with macro-level challenges, "[left] ordinary citizens to sort out the world [themselves] at the local level."[47]

Nowhere did this play out with greater clarity than in California. In the sixties, California was to America as Europe was to the world: a walled garden of social democracy, "widely regarded as both model and magnet for the nation," as a resident and well-respected journalist put it, as well as for "its economic opportunities, its social outlook, and its high-quality public services and institutions."[48] The "political earthquake" that took place in 1978 over an ostensibly uncontroversial amendment to the Californian state constitution soon dramatically changed that picture, however.[49]

The amendment in question was the brainchild of a sharp-minded, hangdog-looking taxpayer advocate, Howard Jarvis, who had spent the decade gathering about him a powerful movement of people disgruntled at the way their property taxes were going up even as the nation's and the state's economic prospects seemed to be coming down. The underlying reason for the increase was the ever-ubiquitous inflation; but at a time when the state was enjoying a budget surplus, many people came to believe that it was the product of a constitutional unfairness in favor of big government spending. And since Californians, like the citizens of numerous other US states, had a legal means of raising petitions to amend the state's constitution, Jarvis and his associates had decided to take action.

The petition they tabled, Proposition 13, aimed to slash the prevailing rate of tax by 30 percent and to place a legal cap on any further increases after that. The proposition ran to just 389 words, but it attracted substantial popular support and was soon passed into law. It was widely regarded as a victory of common sense over inflexible bureaucracy. But a fundamental principle underpinning postwar democracy had been overturned in the process. And with Proposition 13 passed in California, first Michigan and then Florida and then numerous other states followed suit, intent on setting legal limits on the fiscal spending of their own local governments. Within three years twenty-two states had placed over fifty fiscal controls on their counties and schools and public-sector administrations. A passionate anti-spending fervor broke loose, with sixteen states even imposing limits on themselves.[50] In due course, the mood spread to the national level as well, as tax legislation was gradually turned into a political weapon, isolating state level governance from the federal government in the process.

What did this mean in practice? Some of the effects were soon to be seen in California. Proposition 13 turned out to be a boon to the state's wealthiest, who paid disproportionately less under the new system than the poor. That helped the state in turn to become the seedbed of a radical conservative resurgence, as it rapidly lost its primary source of funding and turned desperately to privatization and outsourcing to cope. Before long Californians were subject to cuts in education, health, mental health services, food stamps, prisons, and disabled assistance.[51] Over the next two decades, the state would build twenty new prisons but not one new university campus. At the same time, while homeowners remained subject to annual rate increases, businesses—who on the whole had access to far more capital—were not.[52] It was all enough to prompt one local journalist, a former editor of a local newspaper, the *Sacramento Bee*, to rename the state of California "Paradise Lost."[53] Wealthier Californians, of course, would probably have disputed that view.

With the scope of political agency hollowing out both below and above the level of the state, a space had therefore opened up for what would come to be known as "nongovernmental" organizations to fill the gap.

Many such groups, whether humanitarian, like the Red Cross, or inter-governmental like the International Labour Office, had existed for years. But the 1970s saw an explosion of single-issue organizations: from Amnesty (founded in 1961, but expanding) to Greenpeace (1971), BRAC (1972), the International Feminist Network (1976), and Human Rights Watch (1978). Many of these were avowedly transnational in character and did not only direct their energies at states but at corporations (Nestlé came in for particular ire) and larger political-economic structures such as "world trade." Many of them developed in parallel with the new politics of movement, providing a vehicle for citizens to express feelings and to act on a range of issues in more direct ways than they were able to do via the representative institutions of national government.

The decade also saw new institutions set up within the umbrella of the United Nations, like UN-Habitat, established in 1978 with a mandate to create a global network of mayoral politicians—doing away with the need for government-to-government conversations altogether and pro-moting more local-to-local conversations at the mayoral and technocratic level. These were not always about providing citizens with a greater say, though: on the contrary they were an expression of political elites' desire to establish new fora of governance away from the messy realities of democratic politics. And from 1970 to 1984 the number of NGOs as a whole grew at a dramatic pace, from 2,795 to 12,688—demonstrating that the real driving force was the felt need to act on a whole new political *scale*.[54] Indeed, the number of international treaties, binding governments into the international accords such groups helped to agitate for, more than tripled between 1970 and 1997.

This elaboration (and at times ceding) of the traditional responsibilities of states themselves was pressed upon governments for reasons of com-passion as much as political expediency. A politician like Kissinger may have been deaf to the demands of social and economic justice now emanating from the West's former colonial outposts, or its current sites of proxy war in Africa, but Western citizens, as we have seen, demonstrated a newfound empathy for "humanitarian" crises abroad: like Pol Pot's victims in Cambodia, following on from the US-orchestrated collapse of that country, or the Vietnamese boatpeople in the aftermath of America's failure to orchestrate a settlement there, or, somewhat closer to home, the plight of the displaced victims of the Nigerian Civil War. Spurred to act in the face of what seemed to be a proliferation of international crises, but which was probably simply a greater awareness of them than ever before, a new wave of humanitarian organizations now came into being: Africare (1971), Islamic Relief Worldwide (1972), and Pesticide Action Network (1982) among them.[55]

Science was another domain where new ways of understanding and relating to the world were creating novel forms of political consciousness. Just a decade earlier the American physicist and thinker Thomas Kuhn had first identified the power of social and intellectual communities to shape whole scientific paradigms. Now in small but animated professional fora the idea that science was in any way separate to the political was increasingly challenged. The second-ever meeting of the British Society for Social Responsibility in Science (BSSRS) in 1969 saw hundreds of scientists crammed into Friends House on London's Euston Road, to address "the abuse and moral compromise of science" in the age of Cold War technological rivalry. For some of those present, like the Nobel Prize–winning French biochemist Jacques Monod (he had observed the events of May 1968 up close from the windows of the Institut Pasteur and been ruminating ever since) science itself was to blame for "the utter destruction" of belief systems which had, "for thousands of years, served the essential function of justifying the moral code and the social structure." Many concurred that the problem, at root, was not politics but the current "fragmentation" of knowledge and society alike.[56] In truth, it may just have been the increasing emergence of the former into the latter: expert deliberation was no longer something confined within the walls of academies and learned institutes.

Such debates also help to explain, finally, the impact of the Club of Rome's widely read *The Limits to Growth* report (1972). The nuclear age had already alerted Western populations to the international nature of environmental hazards; but with a greater understanding of how problems such as river-based pollution crossed national frontiers it became more apparent just how arbitrary (and defenseless) territorial boundaries were in the face of transnational environmental challenges.[57] The ground for this changing perception had been prepared by the arrival of the age of the satellite, of course, as moon shots and images of "spaceship earth" became a part of the popular imagination. At the start of the decade, Nixon had used the spaceship earth idea repeatedly in his first inaugural, even citing the poet Archibald MacLeish: "To see the earth as it truly is, small and blue and beautiful in that eternal silence where it floats, is to see ourselves as riders on the earth together, brothers on that bright loveliness in the eternal cold—brothers who know now they are truly brothers."[58]

But imagining a transnational world was one thing; learning to live in it as brothers, or indeed sisters, was quite another. And it was precisely in an effort to resolve that question that many of these same NGOs sought to look beyond the boundaries (and the limitations) of the state for better answers than the ones national governments could provide. The fact that many were animated by an emerging concern with social and economic justice—whether news of famines or civil wars, or the plight of refugees—led them to frame this turn of political thought in terms of the pressing question of just who it was that constituted the human community, and how were they to be counted? Thus it was across the realms of ecology and public morality, and not just the economy, that the idea took hold that states alone were not able to deal with the key issues of the day. But if not the democratic nation state, then what? For some the answer was not to look to different ways and means of conducting national politics, but to refocus the very substance of politics around that sanctified political unit, the individual.

The Individual vs. the State

If the 1970s, and the global age it gave birth to, was inaugurated with the words of a modernist writer like Archibald MacLeish, they were just as famously bookended at their close by Tom Wolfe's postmodern characterization of those same years as the "me" decade: an age of self-discovery (if not selfishness) amid a rapidly changing world. In fact, the individual was crowned not only domestically during these years, but internationally too: and this was something that Jimmy Carter in particular now made central to his vision of America's role in the world. For if Carter's first foreign policy track of disarmament and détente ultimately failed in the disappointments over Afghanistan and Iran, the single-mindedness with which he pursued his second foreign policy track of human rights would ultimately do more than either of his predecessors to shake up the international political landscape of the era, by crowning as it did the individual at the center of world affairs.

In some ways the one gave on to the other. In the aftermath of Vietnam, Watergate, and détente alike, Carter was searching for a new moral and intellectual basis on which to refound US foreign policy. The Democratic Party too was desperate for a foreign policy relaunch, which is partly why Carter had emerged in the first place—from out of nowhere—as a potentially more malleable Democratic presidential candidate. It was only once he was preparing for office, in late 1976, that he picked up the language, and crusading style, of human rights advocacy as a way to reframe his administration's foreign policy. But if Carter came late to the game he did so with a singular and trademark passion of which he gave notice in his inaugural address in January 1977, declaring that: "Our commitment to human rights must be absolute."[59] Before long the United States, with the likes of Britain tagging along, was declaring its support for those who invoked the new international human rights creed left, right, and center, whether that led to the financing of dissident newspapers in Eastern Europe or counterrevolutionary paramilitaries in Central America.

For Carter, human rights—the sanctity of the individual and the primacy of freedoms from intervention and abuse—were the perfect vehicle for managing the competing political challenges of the moment. Not only did they provide legitimate grounds for continued US intervention abroad (not in the name of protecting American freedoms but, better yet, in the name of protecting *universal* human freedoms) they also provided a liberal Democratic president with a foreign policy tool that conservatives could buy into, since protecting human rights could readily be interpreted as the protection of individuals from the state. But the real reason human rights appealed—and this too was a product of the moment—was because they were taken to be largely *non*political. They required neither political institutions nor painstakingly elaborate forms of interest-group bargaining to take effect: for the most part, they simply needed to be "claimed" or "supported."

Human rights were thus the perfect cipher, *internationally*, for an era of political minimalism *nationally*. And it was one of the principal beneficiaries of this who captured the implications earlier than most. In stark contrast to Solzhenitsyn, that "other" Soviet dissident, Andrei Sakharov, quickly became a favorite both at the State Department and on the US political stage. He might have been both a secularist and a socialist, but Sakharov— for all that he never left the Soviet Union—had at least "mastered the language—'democracy' and 'human rights'—of Western liberalism."[60] He thus became for many the true "face" of human rights activism. And as he stated in the Nobel Peace Prize address his wife Elena Bonner read out for him in Stockholm in 1975 (he was banned from accepting it):

> What we need is the systematic defense of human rights and ideals, not a political struggle, which would inevitably incite people to violence, sectarianism, and frenzy . . . This constitutes a partial answer to the question of why I have (naturally) turned from world-wide problems to the defense of individual people.[61]

Sakharov's personal politics were beyond reproach. But that this nonpolitical agenda might find it hard to effect any meaningful institutional change in the world was largely irrelevant, as Sakharov plainly accepted. For him it was, as the American historian Samuel Moyn puts it, the purity of the struggle that counted. For this reason, it did not matter in the least when Carter seemed to drop the term later in his presidency. By then human rights language had taken on a life of its own among the NGO activists and, increasingly, the self-styled international "human rights lawyers" of the age.[62]

But if the popular embrace of human rights was self-consciously framed as a sort of "moral" breakthrough, located at the end of the long history of struggle for political equality, the reality was more mundane. For the sudden ascendancy of human rights in these few years—after all, "rights" had existed for centuries and were legally enshrined in many constitutions post-1945, and of course the UN Declaration of Human Rights itself— was more a product of the disruptive transnationalism of the moment than of any particular *moral* breakthrough. It had less to do with what human rights "were," in that sense, and more with what they enabled people to "do." Carter's initial foreign policy was one example of that. The continued rise of an organization like Amnesty International, which made human rights central to its agenda and was itself awarded the Nobel Prize in 1977, two years after Sakharov, was another.[63] Both hailed democracy as a normative aspiration but neither ultimately concerned itself with democratic process, much less with the collective values democracy itself presupposed.

By the second half of the decade this desire to safeguard the rights of the citizen against the state was steadily being taken up by more and more states and NGOs alike. Even in Europe's diplomatic capital of Brussels the primacy of human rights was emerging more prosaically in the various reforms—within the scope and mandate of the European Court of Justice— that the European project was undergoing: a fact that would soon lubricate the slide to a more laissez-faire vision of European union. Most significantly of all at this point, however, was the aforementioned conference at Helsinki in 1975, which sealed—unintentionally almost—a near irrevocable commitment to human rights as the institutional grail of democratic governance. The "third basket" of accords, which were added toward the end of the conference, primarily to assist the process of family reunification, could have been "written in Swahili for all I care," as Kissinger put it.[64] Yet history was to prove otherwise.

For what Helsinki most enduringly achieved, was to give a formal diplomatic stamp of approval to the new human rights discourse. The very first point of the meeting's Final Act affirmed "the right of every State to juridical equality [and] to territorial integrity."[65] The Soviets had insisted on this language in order to protect their territorial gains in Eastern Europe. Yet the consequences of their also accepting the validity of human rights claims within the boundaries of those states would in just a few years come back to strike them at their core. Not unlike a Trojan Horse, the agreements signed at Helsinki inserted a fundamental challenge into the very heart of domestic Eastern European politics: a fissile political material that could be exploited and used for cover by dissident activists from within. Helsinki was thus its own major step on the road to the fall of communism.

And yet the new rights discourse also posed a challenge for the West. Human rights imposed with increasing power a universal minimal standard of political duty upon states and a clear roster of what, at the very least, citizens of all nations should expect. There was much to be applauded here. Yet, at the same time, this was also nothing if not an open invitation to the *democratic* nations—those states especially obliged to pay attention—to ensure that what they met was the minimum, on paper, and nothing more. The ascendancy of human rights ultimately did nothing so much as to help ensure the return of a particular form of laissez-faire state power at home: for what human rights also helped facilitate was that popular consensus on the sanctity of the unobliged individual, and the value of a socially minimal state as the appropriate means of defending this, which had been developing throughout the decade.

Here too were the makings of a new democratic order: one that transcended the old left–right divide, even as it would serve the political right more effectively because of the way that it realigned the basic elements of the modern social contract as that had been experienced for the best part of two centuries. And with this structural transformation complete, the revolution could now be fully unleashed.

5

"Let Fury Have the Hour"

A s she took the campaign trail to Cardiff in 1979, Margaret Thatcher
laid out more clearly than she had done before exactly what the
British election that year was all about. "The Old Testament prophets did
not say 'Brothers, I want a consensus,'" her dropped voice intoned before
her audience; "they said 'This is my faith. This is what I passionately
believe. If you believe it too, then come with me.'"[1] And come they did.
In Italy, Guido Carli, then head of the country's National Bank, predicted
a future in which privatization would be "the funnel into which fifty, or
perhaps sixty years of Italian history are going to flow."[2] In Australia, Paul
Keating, the treasurer and later prime minister, observed, "we have to get
the private sector in with the government." Back in Britain, the birthplace
of Keynesianism, the economist John Vaizey declared the ideas of Keynes
"intellectually dead" and promptly left the Labour Party for the Conservatives.[3]

The extent of the political transformation underway was everywhere
apparent. In the United States, Herbert Stein, former chairman of the
Council of Economic Advisers under Nixon and Gerald Ford, later observed, "Nothing was more natural than the conclusion that [our] problems were caused by all these government increases and would be cured
by reversing, or at least stopping them."[4] In the Netherlands, more than
twenty years after the initial paperwork had been drawn up, a financial
liberalization bill was finally adopted by a new center-right parliament
in May 1980 intended to address just that problem. It was followed two
years later by the Wassenaar Agreement moderating wage demands of the
unions: a model soon copied elsewhere. Denmark (1979), France (1986),
Italy (1987), and Ireland (1988) would in due course remove capital restrictions as well.[5]

No two leaders took more fatefully to the task of overseeing this
political transformation than Margaret Thatcher, elected in 1979 in Britain, and Ronald Reagan, elected in 1980 in America.[6] Their two names
have become a sort of statutory shorthand for the era's turn to the mar-

ket and the transformation of citizens into private consumers. But they were much more than this. Thatcher's interjection in Cardiff—a dyed-in-the wool Labour stronghold—was not just so that she could announce where the battle lines lay; it was also so that she could redefine what the battle itself was about. For replacing the "consensus" of old what Thatcher now offered was a new "common ground": one distinctly to the right of the postwar-era "middle ground" and yet, framed thus, one that sounded inclusive all the same.[7]

As Thatcher's invocation of the Old Testament likewise suggested, what she and Reagan represented was a new type of "conviction" politician. Each had attached their convictions, fatefully, to the new pro-market politics, making economics the main aim of government and acknowledging the libertarian creed of laissez-faire as the primary mode of economics. But neither acted alone; and neither was the instigator of the revolution usually accredited them. Their particular genius was to recognize that the time was ripe for a change and to shape their countries accordingly. Both were fortunate here, for while the new economics they proposed would prove divisive in the long run, at the moment they were proposing it people were tired of the bungling of the past; they were tired, above all, of the malaise in which the western democracies seemed to be mired. They wanted results. Prosperity having been threatened by the ogre of inflation, the time was ripe for those who promised to slay the beast.

Thatcher and Reagan set out to do more than this, however. Ultimately, they each took advantage of their uniquely broad mandates for economic change to transform also the political scene in their countries. "It [became] clear," observed Jean-Claude Trichet, the French politician and a front-line player in the transformations about to be unleashed far beyond the Anglo-American sphere, "that the market economy, and its codes of conduct, constitute the basic and absolutely insurmountable rules of the game."[8] Before the decade was out, even a social democrat like Germany's Peter Glotz (a man who had thundered in Berlin at the start of the decade, amidst the fervor of antinuclear demonstrations, that "This city cannot simply stand by and watch as the right to demonstrate is smashed to bits") would feel it appropriate to declare, in 1988, that "[t]he left must stand up for consumer rights, free investment decisions, the free disposal of assets and a decentralized decision-making process."[9] These are sentiments that echo down to the present. But it was during the 1980s that they were hoisted into place as the new central pillar buttressing democratic politics in the West. Just as soon as the rubble of the old was cleared away, that is.

The Suspect State

As the new decade began, it was clear that the high-water mark of the postwar democratic state had been and gone. Yet the costs of running that state showed no signs of abating. By the early 1980s nearly a quarter of the population of all OECD countries were employed in the public sector, and almost everybody relied on the state in one way or another. This was especially true in Britain and America. During the first years of Thatcher's time in office, the state owned 40 percent of the nation's output and controlled a good deal more: everything from railways and coal mining to airports and shipbuilding.[10] There was a widespread sense, as the technological society took off, that states simply could not know enough to be rational decision-makers across so many areas of modern life. Moreover, it was felt that the state's own misguided efforts at responding to the challenges of the time had become too expensive by half. In 1981 a CBS/*NYT* poll began asking Americans whether they agreed with the claim that "when something is run by the government it is usually wasteful and inefficient." It turned out that two thirds of them did.[11]

For these Americans Ronald Reagan was the great hope that came riding in at the end of the 1970s, to the upbeat theme music from *Dallas* (1978) and *Dynasty* (1981). In the years after the Second World War, the American government had levied higher taxes on individuals, firms, and capital investment than most other Western countries. By the 1970s, its machinery of public regulation was deemed "aggressive" if not "punitive" by some.[12] Reagan promised to change all this. Whether or not he actually did ride into power on the back of "the spirit of 13" (a reference to Proposition 13), as he liked to claim, it was clear that a "seismic shift in the political balance of power" took place with his arrival.[13] "It has been said that our best years are behind us," Reagan perorated charismatically after taking office. "But I say again that America's best is still ahead."[14] As it happened, this particular line was pinched from Jimmy Carter, but nobody seemed to notice. Hope was restored; rhetoric unchained. Perhaps more prosperous times were not so far away after all?

To come good on his promise to roll back the oppressive state, the core of the Reagan administration's strategy took shape around a radical program of tax cuts and deregulation. Had Reagan been undertaking such a program in the other direction, he would probably have been painted as a revolutionary. That he was not, despite the deep swerve he now sought to impart to American history, was a sign that the political center of gravity had already shifted to the right. And sensing this, Reagan moved fast. One of his first acts, as president, for example, was to sign Executive Order 12291 by which means all existing regulations on the books would be subject to a cost-benefit review—a criterion that has little to do with whether that regulation is effective or not.

According to Murray Weidenbaum, Reagan's first chairman of the White House Council of Economic Advisers, government profligacy was wasting $100 billion a year. The Republicans' first two years in power thus saw a barrage of speeches and proposals to reduce such "wastage" (which was, seen in another light, simply dutiful government oversight). Not all of this was to be sneered at. Deregulating government services to some degree was arguably desirable at this point. But the widespread devaluing of regulation, *tout court*, since it was a basic (arguably essential) component of the postwar democratic order, was both dramatic and highly disruptive. Regulation went from being a policy tool in support of fairer social outcomes to a prime scapegoat for society's seemingly unshakeable malaise. It was a clear sign that the deregulationists, having won their spurs in the international economic arena, were now beginning to win battles on the domestic political front too.

The same broad trend was apparent with taxes. Antitax sentiment was nothing new.[15] In the 1950s, French populists had played this same fiddle both louder and more blasphemously under Pierre Poujade (who likened the French National Assembly to the "biggest brothel in Paris").[16] But it was Republican America in the 1980s, on the back of Proposition 13, that saw by far the most effective campaign to smear the very idea of "tax" at the national level, turning it into a widely accepted shorthand for state irresponsibility. At the same time, tax cuts came to be seen by conservative strategists as a policy tool in their own right. If one wanted to reduce government spending on regulation, on the environment, and on social security, and especially if one wanted to do all these things at the same time, then what better way of doing this than by "starving the beast," as Republican strategists—and above all Reagan's new head of the Office of Management and Budget, David Stockman—now liked to say. As Reagan put it in a national television address in 1981: "Well, you know, we can lecture our children about extravagance until we run out of voice and breath. Or we can cure their extravagance by simply reducing their allowance."[17]

This was precisely the rationale behind the most important piece of legislation of the first Reagan administration: the 1981 Economic Recovery Tax Act (ERTA). In announcing it Reagan was saying how ready he was to stamp his new administration's supply-side thinking upon the nation. The tax cut was sold, in accordance with the new economic thinking, by the argument that taking less of people's money in taxes meant that those tax dollars were *inevitably* freed up for investment. But this scarcely captures how radical it was. In addition to bringing down the rate of tax on the highest income earners from 70 to 50 percent, estate and corporation taxes were reduced, as were rates on capital investment and on unearned income (such as shares). Meanwhile the parallel Omnibus Budget Reconciliation Act (OBRA), presented to Congress in a hashed draft of overnight papers, went to town on entitlements and the poor.[18]

All in all, OBRA and ERTA between them oversaw the redistribution of three quarters of a trillion dollars, primarily from the poor to the rich. Already by 1984 the income of the top 0.2 percent of American taxpayers had increased by over 20 percent. For average income earners the gain was a rather more modest 3.5 percent. The poorest families (those earning less than $10,000), by contrast, saw their disposable income drop by more than 15 percent. For American citizens, it was enough to speed up the already growing income gaps between wealthier and poorer citizens. But crucially the federal state *also* saw its income drop, allowing the administration, and David Stockman in particular, to wield a merciless pen from the center of government. This was deliberate. Before long state governments were landed with funding cuts from the center and a seemingly cast-iron rationale had been forged for the next item on the administration's agenda: reducing the cost of government.

This too was addressed with vigor, and yet in spite of all the cutbacks state spending actually ballooned under Reagan, having largely been redirected from domestic programs to defense. The justification for this was, of course, the recently intensified Cold War. With Carter and his human rights nostrums gone, Pentagon strategists now looked to reheat the arms race under Reagan in an effort to burn off the Soviet economy once and for all. The Star Wars missile defense shield that resulted involved massive investment at home: so much so that it began to look every bit like a form of "military Keynesianism." This was an obvious sell to Reagan's southern and western constituency, where the next generation of military industrial corporations, and in turn the next technological wave that would drive forward the US economy, were already headquartering. But it was a contradictory one nonetheless. In fact, this late–Cold War boost in military spending was very carefully of a piece with Reagan's antistate strategy, since by creating a new and sizeable drain on ever-dwindling resources, it would only further squeeze out those areas of government spending they didn't like. Contrary to the rhetoric of the campaign trail, the whole point of Reagan's tax cuts, once in office, was not to make good his campaign trail promise that the government could afford to give people a bit of a break: the whole point was that such breaks *were not* affordable. The beast, it turned out, could be hobbled as well as squeezed.

Across the Atlantic, Margaret Thatcher was well into her own long march against the statist past by the time Reagan came into office, though domestic political considerations meant she was biding her time in a way Reagan never had to. The obstacles confronting Thatcher were greater, after all, and her electoral victory less secure. Her own rise to power within the party had also been far more fraught than Reagan's, not least as a woman in an era when almost no other female politicians made it to the front benches (Labour's Shirley Williams was the only other contemporary example, and she was hardly a natural ally). The British political system was also a more complex affair than America's: a troubled amalgam of past and present in which the state loomed substantially larger than in the United States, and was, on the whole, rather better received. There would be no starving of this particular beast.

The British public sector could, however, be sold off, piece by piece. And to achieve this, the Thatcherite strategy was to build a more popular mandate for the disassembly of the state than Reagan sought to do: not so much by reaching out to people's hearts as to their natural class-instincts. Hers was thus a very British strategy at heart. At the start of the 1980s, Britain was still an industrial state with an industrial-sized state apparatus to match. By the end of the decade over a million employees would have been transferred from the public to the private sector. State-run industries in coal, steel, railways, electricity, ports—all would be privatized as the public sector was reduced from producing around 9 percent of GDP to just 3 percent. Crucially, it wasn't only industries that were sold off. Council houses, a third of all British housing stock in 1979, were given over to their tenants (a stroke of political genius that delivered a blow to the very heart of the British Labour Party's core working-class, inner-city vote) and formerly cooperative banks were de-mutualized.[19]

None of this resulted in the great upsurge in national productivity that was promised. That could always be explained away by other reasons.

Crucially, where it *was* successful, just as in America, was in bringing about a transformation in the economic outlook of British citizens. The great British privatization drive was ultimately a function of British Conservatives' belief, in the early 1980s, that the "good person" was being crowded out by the overbearing stateliness of the "good society." And what it achieved, more than anything else, was the creation of a society of individuals who felt themselves to be stakeholders in some new national company before they were citizens. For many, the reality of going it alone proved far harsher than rhetoric supposed: by 1993 14 percent of British men would be unemployed and the number of children living in poverty would have doubled (from one in eight in 1979 to a quarter of all children). By 1997, the wages of the poor had fallen even further behind, and by the mid 1990s more than a fifth of all pensioners would find themselves living in poverty.[20]

There can be no doubt that Thatcherism transformed British society by means of economic policy. Yet here too there was precious little reduction in the size of the state, much less of state power. With every industry privatized new regulatory bodies and forms of parliamentary oversight were established; meanwhile those that were left were hardly left alone—they were hooked up instead to more direct control by the Treasury, which promptly coined new euphemisms, like "negative external borrowing requirement," to legitimize its interfering in their operations. What the newly privatized "service providers" were not subject to was democratic accountability.[21] This was, of course, precisely the point. The core ambition of Thatcherite conservatism was to isolate core branches of national policy—public services and the utilities above all—and to place them in private and "dependable" hands. The rule of government bureaucrats that had characterized the postwar democratic state, and that had been so roundly criticized, was to be replaced by the rule of economic bureaucrats. The *class* structure of British governance, by contrast, and especially the close ties between the managers of top firms, the financial institutions, and the government, was not itself to be touched. This was surely ironic, for if anything was out-of-date in the UK by the 1980s it was the persistence of the straitjacket of social class.

The state was thus not so much freed up by "the market" under Thatcher as it was made to reform itself in light of certain market principles. The bureaucratization of the National Health Service—through total commitment to plan, to "performance indicators," to ticking boxes, and to "bonuses"—was the epitome of this: market logics rammed home with a Stalinist verve. Reforms of the education sector followed suit. All of this had been alluded to in the 1979 Conservative Party manifesto. But it was present, and much more radically so (which is to say, honestly), in the "Ridley Report," leaked to *The Economist* the year before. That report had proposed "preparing the industries for partial return to the private sector more or less by stealth."[22] And in the years after Thatcher's reelection it was the original program that was pursued with determined vigor. Thatcher, in short, was bent on creating a society of investors from the beginning; and she was to prove durably tone deaf about the (predictable) social costs, over the years to come, of doing so.

At the time the British privatization program was sold as a great boon to the economy: the point at which the nation escaped from both the Scylla of imperial retreat and the Charybdis of postindustrial decline. In truth, many of the privatized industries were underpriced and sold at a loss to the taxpayer, their new (often foreign) corporate owners tempted into rent-seeking on their new assets rather than renewing them. The net profit-loss of the whole program was, according to the most thorough study to date, a transfer of "14 billion [GBP] from the taxpayer to shareholders in the privatized firms" with a further 3 billion of accountancy costs (to oversee the whole process) in additional transfers to the City of London.[23]

In exchange for this dramatic reallocation of national wealth, the British consumer was presented with a mixed bag of results. There were reductions in prices in some cases (e.g. electricity) and rises in other cases (e.g. water). Pursuant to the Transport Act (1985), which launched the privatization of the bus lines, costs became marginally better for those living in metropolitan areas, substantially higher for those in rural areas, but with the net savings due largely to the reduction in wages of bus employees. The social costs, however, came in the constant changing of timetables and redirecting of routes, which ultimately led many to give up on the buses altogether. It was a windfall for the government either way. After 1983 the Treasury's receipts from privatization were never less than a billion pounds. With the sale of British Telecom in 1988-9 they soon exceeded 7 billion.[24]

What is one to make of this British experience? In one sense, there was always something distinctively British about the Thatcherite project of renewal. As a later observer put it, the "paradoxes" of Thatcher—her liberalism and her authoritarianism, her wish to do away with the state alongside her desire to use it—"mirror those in the British constitution, where a tradition of strong Crown prerogative contends with a supposed respect for pluralist democratic institutions."[25] In Britain, far more than anywhere else, the belief was established that one could have the benefits of state dirigisme (the idea would soon be central to the Euroskepticism that united the wider Tory right) without any of its downsides.

In such an environment, the tax cuts that played such a central role in reshaping American public debate were far less important, strategically speaking, but only because Thatcher was able to take her reform program much further than Reagan without them. In this regard, the constitutional structure of American democracy, not to mention its vertical division into Federal and State government, acted as an in-built break on Reagan's wilder ambitions (though as a reminder that the United States was not as "exceptional" as might always be claimed, the same was also true in Switzerland, where the social democratic opposition and the unions were able "to block attempts at retrenchment that commanded parliamentary majorities").[26] Thatcher's deployment of the tax cut as an instrument of policy, by contrast, was more about winning elections than it was about the substance of the program itself (she brought down the top rate of tax from 83 percent to 60 percent in 1979 and then to 40 percent in 1988, while increasing VAT and National Insurance contributions). Her policies may well have contributed to hollowing out the state over time, but if they did then this was not as obviously intentional as it was in America.

Yet the end result was strikingly similar in both countries (and elsewhere). After a decade of fervent activity both states had been transformed. But they were not in any way more "efficient." Domestic discretionary spending under Reagan certainly fell during the 1980s but not overall spending.[27] By the time Reagan left office in 1989 the ratio of spending to GDP was about the same as it had been at the end of Carter's presidency: at around 21 percent.[28] In Britain, the ratio of spending to GDP under Thatcher *did* see a slight fall, but from a much higher base, down to around 39 percent.[29] In real terms, however, government spending actually *rose* for nearly every year that Thatcher was in power.[30] The achievement then was most certainly not to reduce the size of the state.

On the contrary, the Thatcher–Reagan brand of neoliberalism actively *required* the state and its levers of control. Its task was not to reduce state power but to transform it. And what it achieved, in Britain and America first of all, was to move those levers out of reach of public scrutiny and control. It was here that both Reagan and Thatcher succeeded immeasurably: above all by converting the popular mandate they had both received to get their countries working again (which meant in practice

reducing inflation) into a sufficient degree of acceptance by their electorates of a much wider program. After all, the Conservative Party in
Britain was voted into power on four consecutive occasions between
1979 and 1995 while, by 1998, as many as 56 percent of Americans agreed
with the proposition that "the best government is the one that governs
the least"; in 1973 it had only occurred to 31 percent of Americans to
think this.[31]

Neither Reagan's nor Thatcher's plans to transform the state could have
been as successful as they were without the creation of a conducive
intellectual environment, mediating the whims of the political class with
the beliefs of the electorate. Thatcher and Reagan alike were tacticians
before they were strategists, and they needed others around them to
create the ideas they would fight for. This left the door open to the likes
of Milton Friedman, who proved all too happy, of course, to fill the gap.
As he spoke one evening to a Conservative Philosophy Group event in
the 1970s, a younger Margaret Thatcher was apparently seen sitting quite
literally at Friedman's feet, "gazing at him in rapt adoration."[32] For his
part, Reagan kept Friedman on the end of a phone line (the two men,
who had first met in 1967, fascinated one another: Reagan's eyes apparently "sparkled with delight" whenever he heard Friedman talk).[33] But
both leaders listened to Friedman's core message that free enterprise was
the only antidote to communism, and that communism was still the clear
and present danger of the time. As Thatcher herself later put it, her
proudest achievement was to make Britain, in her eyes, "the first country
to attempt and to succeed in rolling back the frontiers of socialism—which
is the first cousin to communism." And her rule of thumb for doing so
was "the same rule as applies in the economic [domain]: responsibility—
personal responsibility."[34]

More significantly, a plethora of think tanks—today a standard feature
of the political landscape—began sprouting up around the New Conservatives in Britain and the New Right in America, offering nourishment
and a veneer of intellectual justification to their policies. In just the way
that Lewis Powell had envisaged for America in the early 1970s, new
foundations like the Olin Institute emerged, with the support of big
business. The American Enterprise Institute, though it had been around
for some time, also sharpened its politics considerably in the early 1980s,
turning itself into a home for a new grouping of influential neoconservatives like Irving Kristol and Jeane Kirkpatrick. Why the interest in
education? Because Reaganites were shut out of the liberal universities

and needed an alternative base from which to wage the revolution. In 1981, the Heritage Foundation, established in 1973 with money from the brewer Joseph Coors, authored what the *New York Times* described as the unofficial "manifesto" of the Reagan administration. *Mandate for Leadership* was a surprisingly popular read (it made it onto the *New York Times* bestseller list) and Reagan handed out copies of the fuller twenty-volume work with its call for cutting income tax and increasing defense spending, for mothballing affirmative action policies and spending more money on B1 bombers, at his first cabinet meeting. Of its more than 2,000 suggestions for reforming the federal government, most resolved to ways of cutting it back.

In Britain, too, the battle for ideas now spread: via informal outfits like the Bow Group (under the leadership of Geoffrey Howe), the Adam Smith Institute (founded in 1976), or the more formal and longer-lasting Institute for Economic Affairs (which had its roots in the economic program of the Mont Pèlerin Society). Leading the charge, though, was the Center for Policy Studies set up by Keith Joseph in 1974, almost from within the heart of government itself. The CPS was especially close to Thatcher, and she to it. In the early days, writes her biographer Charles Moore, she could be found sitting on the floor, wiring up the plugs: "which, in those days, due to some trade union rule," he quickly added, "were never attached to electrical goods when you bought them in a shop."[35]

Taken together, this institutional panoply worked to consolidate the new brand of economic thinking in British conservatism of the late 1970s and early 1980s and to fashion a political project capable of enacting it. But contrary to popular memory today it had been a long time in the making. From as far back as the Sundridge Park conference of 1969, organized by Conservative backbenchers under the umbrella of the Public Sector Research Unit (PSRU)—the conference where plans for a "new style of government" were first formally blueprinted within the Conservative Party—to its realization and defense in the public pronouncements of the Institute of Economic Affairs throughout the 1980s, behind the jutting shoulder pads of Margaret Thatcher's policy prescriptions was an entire intellectual industry dedicated to reimagining politics, and remaking the state.[36]

One of the ideas most strongly promoted by think tanks on both sides of the Atlantic was the importance of following private sector principles in the administration of government. Dubbed the New Public Management, though much of it was culled from earlier ideas on management and it was anything but public-spirited, the new discourse first took root at around the same time in the state of California, in Australia, and in New Zealand, as those territories' administrations sought (usually) to make tax cuts. It was then further promoted in new "management centers," such as Virginia's Center for Studies in Political Economy, founded by the libertarian Thomas Buchanan. The aim of the new public management was to place the individual at the center of government decision-making. On one level this seemed perfectly sensible, since public policy, if it was to be democratic, was supposed to form itself around aggregated individual interests. But since this meant rejecting the class and interest bargaining that had defined industrial relations for the entire postwar era, the New Public Management was not intended as an improvement to public policymaking but as a reinvention of its purpose.

On another level, the results were frequently anything but the more efficient satisfaction of individual needs since the median individual in question was a fiction. Confronted by a plethora of real world "wants," the only "rational" solution that policymakers following this approach could adopt, in practice, was to try to incentivize people to act in accordance with an ideal type. This was just a different way of telling them what to do, such that individuals became, once again, a coherent, malleable mass. What was promised as a greater freedom for all boiled down to rejigging the system in favor of those who most resembled the individuals that New Public Management sought to create. Advocates of this approach promised constitutional safeguards against "exploitation" by the government (forgetting that some people are capable of paying more taxes than others); they promised "polycentrism" of policymaking (which meant disaggregation of responsibility when things did not work out), and they promised economies of scale (which usually meant outsourcing state activity rather than trying to improve it).

But still, what they promised *sounded* good off the back of the dreary 1970s. And as these ideas caught on, but the result was not so much to push back at the conformism of the postwar democratic state as to undermine its conditions of existence: severing its tax base by undermining its publicly funded mandate, isolating the provision of public goods from regulation and oversight, and opening public entities such as schools and prisons to management by profit-seeking enterprises. Nobody could any longer deny that the winds of change had blown in. But the revolution, as Thatcher herself said, was still to be made.[37]

A New Social Contract

The great achievement of Reagan and Thatcher was to place the individual at the center of a new vision for democracy. The harshest critics, usually on the left, saw the state being stripped away by this. More acute observers saw that it was actually being remade. It wasn't that governments had unilaterally decided to stop intervening in social affairs. Social Security (pensions) and Medicaid both remained popular in America throughout the 1980s. And Thatcher did not even try to privatize the British NHS. It was more that the changing nature of employment, and the growing gaps in skills and wages this implied, made collective bargaining between unions, employers and the state—the mainstay of the post-45 welfare state—increasingly hard to achieve.

This affected some countries more than others. But almost all were faced with aging populations and rising health care costs, and one way of meeting both problems was to adopt the new trend of treating people, when they came to the state demanding their rights, not as citizens but as consumers. It was a trend made easier by the concomitant improvements in computing and data management, which now began their inexorable tug toward systematization and standardization. The computing revolution was still at a basic stage, but the fundamental step from digital to analog had been taken. And as punch-cards gave way to "systems" based on the newly invented microprocessor, data storage and manipulation afforded administrators unheard-of capacities to streamline operations. Retailers like Walmart adopted the "big box" approach to out-of-town retail centers. Governments found they could obtain more information about their citizens: policies could be targeted, individualized. They also tended to be rolled out, rather than requested.

All in all, then, it was a more distant state that looked down upon its most vulnerable citizens. And soon people began to notice the results. "I live in a market street in north London," said the expatriate writer, television presenter, and later leader of the Canadian Liberal Party, Michael Ignatieff, in 1984:

> Every Tuesday morning there is a barrow outside my door and a cluster of old age pensioners rummage through the torn curtains, buttonless shirts, stained vests, torn jackets, frayed trousers and faded dresses that the barrow man has to offer. They make a cheerful chatter outside my door, beating down the barrow man's prices, scrabbling for bargains like crows pecking

among the stubble . . . The political arguments between right and left over the future of the welfare state which rage over these old people's heads almost always take their needs entirely for granted. . . . What almost never gets asked is whether they might need something more than the means of mere survival.[38]

As Ignatieff saw, in modern liberal societies human needs extended beyond what a welfare state could provide; at the same time, "[a] theory of the human good cannot," he thought, "be premised on the absolute priority of liberty. Nor can it be based on the priority of happiness as the ultimate human virtue."[39] These were, however, precisely the "needs" that would now be created, expanded upon, and ultimately used as the popular basis on which to dismantle the welfare state of old.

Crucial to the spreading of the new liberal politics was the fact that each country had its own public sector inefficiencies that could be rectified in this way. In Greece and Italy, and to a lesser extent France, it was the pension system (and public sector workers retiring too early) that was especially problematic by the 1980s. In Italy it was the new (post-1978) National Health Service, which was bedeviled by entrenched corruption and inefficiency in the Unità Sanitarie Locali (local health units).[40] In the US and Australia it was excessive public sector wage demands. In 1983, the Australian metalworkers' union leadership, the sector which had seen the largest pay claims, was told by the treasurer that they were carrying the guilt of "100,000 dead members" around their necks. What really delivered the change, however, was the underlying fact of still rising unemployment. With fewer workers paying taxes there was less money to intervene in the market with redistributive policies, regulatory initiatives, and health and safety demands levied on behalf of the social protection of society. The appropriate role of the state now came to be seen as that of intervening in society on behalf of the market to ensure the good health of the economy. If that meant further cutting back on things like welfare, then so be it. For the British conservative writer Simon Jenkins, the British welfare state was a "domestic empire" that paralleled the overseas one and was "run in the same paternalist spirit."[41] It was time to shut up shop.

In the 1980s, in short, the aims and ideals of social welfare underwent a profound transformation. Driving these changes was a steadily gathering force of neoliberal ideas—the belief that the tottering social state of the mid twentieth century should be replaced by a narrower, more authoritative executive capable of liberating society from the shackles of its collective obligations, the better to enable people to fulfill their private desires. This required removing the state from its role in establishing the conditions of the good life. And that, in turn, called for more than just tax cuts. As one of Thatcher's closest advisers, Geoffrey Howe, reasoned in a British shadow cabinet meeting of 1975, if the British economy was to be put back on its feet, then the effects of unemployment would have to be made "harsher . . . for those elements of the labor force that were insufficiently mobile."[42] The reinvention of a new social contract called, in short, for sticks as well as carrots.

Here it was Reagan who led the way with a second but rather less advertised prong of the Reaganomics strategy: the overhaul of the Office of Management and Budget (OMB). Rather than being merely an advisory body, as it had been for decades, Reagan used it to help roll out his policies.[43] Hence why he installed the knuckle-dusting David Stockman as its head. Stockman had grown up on a small working farm in the American south but he had himself never had any employer other than the federal government. He was the inverate insider Reagan trusted to act as his modern-day Samson. And with Stockman at the helm, the Office immediately set to work pulling down as many pillars of the Johnson-era Great Society programs as possible. Initially, state funding for anyone below the poverty line was left untouched, while Food Stamps and Aid to Families with Dependent Children (AFDC) payments were cut back for anyone above the poverty line. But those whose income rose toward the poverty line—working mothers on AFDC checks, for example—soon saw their taxes raised to a marginal top rate of 60 percent (higher than that paid by most millionaires).[44]

The genius of Stockman's assault on welfare (as embodied in such legislation as the 1981 Omnibus Budget Reconciliation Act) was that it fundamentally undermined the very concept of welfare, not by abolishing it per se—Reagan would always be able to say that the basic institutions of Medicaid and Social Security remained in place—but by turning it into such a pathetic imitation of itself that it became easy to show that it was failing. Fragmented and underfunded, the American welfare state, which at best had always been "stingily funded" in comparison with Europe, had itself become just the sort of "basket case" that many of its dependants were stigmatized as being.[45] Reagan would soon have done more than simply abolish welfare, therefore. He would have left it to stand as a living ruin. And he was not done yet.

The truly "transformative" moment of Reagan's presidency came in the summer of 1981 when he stood down a wildcat strike by 13,000 members of PATCO, the air traffic controllers' union, unilaterally dismissing 11,345 employees (by recourse to the Taft–Hartley Act). Flights in the country ground to a halt and billions of dollars were lost. But Reagan had seen off the challenge from the workers. More importantly he had broken their union. The previous two decades had seen thirty-nine illegal federal work stoppages; after 1981 there would be none of any significance.[46] Seeing the opportunity, private employers quickly followed their president's lead and the ability of American labor to organize itself was drastically undermined. Wages fell further, as wage bargaining was avoided, and strikes dropped to a level not seen since the Second World War. Like the OMB, the National Labor Relations Board was now given a new mandate—to *manage* labor, not to represent it—effectively removing the last protective ditches that the preceding century had contrived to dig around working people's lives. On March 22, 1983, the Board found in a dismissal case that "a worker who left the place of employment to fetch medical assistance for another worker was voluntarily terminating employment." On June 7, 1984, it found that "an employer, or the employer's agent, taking pictures of workers involved in union activities so that the employer could have a picture 'to remember them by,' was not in any way guilty of harassing those workers."[47]

It wasn't just old myths about the welfare state that were shattered in the course of all this. New ones were erected in their place. Historically, welfare spending tended disproportionately to benefit the middle class. It was no small achievement of the conservative movement of these years, then, to foster among that middle class the view that welfare spending was *actually* primarily for the benefit of others: immigrants, blacks, and the working class in particular—and, of course, single mothers: Reagan's infamous "welfare queens." By and large, however, polls still suggested that American citizens wanted more welfare not less at this time. And yet time and again state and federal election results confirmed that they were now convinced that this was not affordable.

The wholesale redistribution of wealth and income was, for different reasons, also the primary outcome of the reform program rolled out by Thatcher in Britain. The privatizations that reached fever pitch during her second government (from 1983 to 1988) had some direct impact here. But more explicit policies, such as changes to the tax bands and the 1980 and 1982 Employment Acts, which removed certain legal immunities from unions and made striking families more vulnerable, did more to hollow out the welfare state from within. Not all employers wanted weaker unions of course. Many wanted fewer, stronger, and more reliable unions that it would be easier to negotiate with. But the general sense that unions represented an unaccountable form of power was apparent in Britain before Thatcher. And when push came to shove most people were happy to sit back and watch her finish them off.[48]

Nothing elucidated this as clearly as the miners' strike standoff in 1984–5: the bloody return match (and denouement) to the 1972 strike that had cost Thatcher's predecessor, Ted Heath, the government. "The last Conservative government was destroyed by the miners' strike," she said to her first Home Secretary, Willie Whitelaw, immediately on taking office. "We'll have another and we'll win."[49] Her response was to plan for, and then unleash, a final assault in the class struggle that had simmered in Britain for more than a decade. When miners struck in anger in 1984 at the year-on-year cuts in the workforce, the trap was effectively sprung and Thatcher went on the offensive. She spared no weapon in her cause: at Orgreave 10,000 miners were charged by 5,000 police and then put on trial for provoking a "riot"; MI5 was set to spying on the NUM; scandals were fabricated, slush funds opened up. Thatcher smeared the unions who, to be sure, at times had their own reputations more than the interests of the workers at heart. But they at least were operating largely within the law. It was little wonder Leon Brittan, the Home Secretary, wanted to avoid a public inquiry into events the following year.

The strike soon descended into a "battle of attrition" (one waged by miners' families as much as the men on the picket lines themselves). As Arthur Scargill, the NUM leader, continued driving his forces onward, miners who refused to strike in the absence of a national ballot were branded traitors. The possibility that both sides might have had a point (that the mines were indeed becoming uneconomic but so too were the regions in which they were located) was discounted at every turn. Thatcher kept up the pressure on her side, only refraining from branding the Labour Party an "enemy of democracy" after the IRA's attempt on her life in Brighton (the national feeling was becoming too divided, she was told).[50] After a year on the line, the miners finally capitulated in March 1985. Pits went on being closed; South Wales and the North East embarked on their own postindustrial malaise; and the Conservatives' legal assault on the trade unions continued—unions were sued, their funding was cut back, and in 1988 it was declared an "essential freedom" to be able to work in spite of industrial action being called.[51]

As with the PATCO standoff, the miners' strike ultimately merely added to the rising numbers of the unemployed. In January 1982, British unemployment topped 3 million for the first time since the Depression. The number of people taking early retirement, or who felt obliged (or were forced) to classify themselves as disabled, also increased dramatically. Workforce exclusion became more apparent, even if the secular (socially driven) trend to increasing female participation in the labor force helped even out the aggregate numbers of unemployed.[52]

While unemployment rose, public investment declined (by around 0.8 percent of GDP per year) and, contrary to the government's claims, the difference was not made up by private investment.[53] The share of public spending relative to GDP also rose, slightly, but it was realigned in ways that were regressive: more of it now went on social security, owing primarily to the "explosion of family disintegration and poverty" that accompanied the closure of the pits and the shedding of public sector jobs, while less went on education and housing.[54] As a result of these employment changes, by 1997–8 a full third of British households had no savings at all and just over half had less than £1,500 tucked away for a rainy day: so much for Thatcher's nation of petty shareholders. In fact, the number of individual shareholders in British corporations did rise as the privatization program picked up speed: from 3 million to over 11 million between 1979 and 1993. And as with Reagan winning over the middle class to his tax cuts, this was successfully sold at elections as a case of sharing out the national wealth. But the fuller picture revealed that those buying shares were mostly from the top 20 percent of income earners, not the middle classes, and they merely transferred their existing habits of saving (in government bonds) to the new privatized industries (something the one-off windfall from North Sea oil receipts, which might have been used to fund a twenty-first-century welfare state, was instead used to disguise).[55]

In the US and UK alike, then, the welfare state had not been thrown out by the end of the decade so much as it had been retrenched. It had been variously defunded, outsourced, means-tested, and at times even turned against itself. All of which raises the question of just what served to justify these changes? Individuals and their freedoms, yes; but also families and the normative moral template they provided. It was here that the fullness of the conservative revolution undertaken over the previous decade became most apparent. "The family is the fundamental building block and the basic unit of our society," declared Jerry Falwell in 1981, "and its continued health is a prerequisite for a healthy and prosperous nation. No nation has ever been stronger than the families within her."[56] In America, the family was made the central unit of American society, the Christian right was presented as its defender, and everything it disagreed with, from equal rights to the Cold War, was made the source of an attack upon it. Thatcher, of course, instinctively agreed. "There is no such thing as society," she famously declared. "There are individual men and women, and there are families."[57]

This mobilization of the family helped to channel the resurrection of the individual. Individuals needed to shape up, get a hold of themselves: stop "casting their problem on society," as Thatcher put it.[58] It was a political-economic as much as a moral argument. The "knowledge society" was presented as the new intellectual ecology within which people might "realize" themselves, and this in turn soon became one of the fastest-growing parts of the new services economy: everything from yoga retreats for yuppies to health foods and self-help, Jonathan Livingston Seagull–style. The private life was entered into and would become inseparable from the commercial ventures whose task it now was to enhance it. Yet another characteristic paradox of the era was thereby created: the increased political premium being placed upon the family coming just at the very moment the nuclear family was breaking up.

The ongoing transformation in home life was mirrored by the changing culture of work too: again, in a manner that centered upon the individual. The new emphasis on flexibility blurred the divide between what was career maximization, and what was simply avoiding the sack. In Britain, "Gizza job" became a much-parodied one-liner, and revealed the slide between rump employment and stigmatization at the "working poor" end of the scale. In the United States the huddles of homeless men gathered around street burners in places like Baltimore was indication that there were fates worse than that too. But even for those who had a job, the 1980s marked the end of a whole era of *industrial* democracy. Flexibilization was in, and the ability to adapt began to be prized in the way formerly reserved for productivity. The difference, however, was that now people were on their own: in the increasingly neoliberal world of Anglo-America, the economic reach of democracy had been cut back.[59]

The Revolution Spreads

What, then, were the alternatives: what other directions were open to the Western democracies at this point in the mid 1980s? Resistance to the new laissez-faire orthodoxy initially proved stronger in Europe. For continentals, American-style liberalism was always too hitched to the spirit of free enterprise, especially in France, which had no solid liberal tradition of its own (for the French, it was always "as if they were *in* liberalism but not yet *of* it," as one observer put it).[60] At the beginning of the 1980s, France, in fact, had appeared to be heading in the very opposite direction. In 1981, the charismatic French socialist François Mitterrand had successfully assembled the splinters of the post-68 left into a force sufficient to win the presidential election of that year. France was electrified, as for some time after Mitterrand's victory it looked as if this newly reunited French left might offer a viable alternative to the Anglo-American route. With the rest of the Western world seemingly turning to the right, Mitterrand turned resolutely to the left: bringing into his presidential advisory team, with a Gallic shrug at the new times, a number of sixties-era radicals—including Régis Debray, Che Guevara's comrade and author of *Revolution in the Revolution*.

Mitterrand's choices were less deliberately provocative than they were a product of the decade-long struggle to reunite communist and non-communist factions on the left. This had not been achieved without the spilling of some political blood. On his path to power, Mitterrand had first ousted his great rival, the more intellectual, less lupine, Michel Rocard, at a dramatic party showdown in Nantes in the early 1970s, before proceeding to oust the union-bashing Giscard d'Estaing at the polling booth a decade later, in a national context grown tense by rising unemployment. By then Mitterrand was desperately struggling to keep his patchwork force together. One consequence of this was that Mitterrand's platform upon taking office was essentially the same as that drawn up in 1971. More than that, his first policies—which ramped up the national deficit by more than 25 percent—struck some as little more than a throwback to the interwar period. But believing his mandate to be substantial (which a second landslide for the socialists in the legislative elections of June 1981 had seemed to suggest) Mitterrand immediately set about renationalizing industries and pulling industrial relations out of the hands of the corporations (including the promotion of new "worker councils").

Not content to stop there, Mitterrand then embarked upon a radical decentralization program, what he himself termed "the most important institutional reform since the beginning of the Third Republic": and this at the very moment Thatcher and Reagan were bleeding local authorities dry.[61] Like the man himself it was nothing if not a full-blooded alternative. But Mitterrand had gone too far. In what was later to become a familiar pattern, the markets first took a dislike to his policies, the country's credit rating began to plummet, and finally a full-blown economic crisis ensued. In the words of one valedictory, Mitterrand's high-stakes gamble had "foundered on the too-clever-by-half strategy of trying to use an international capitalist upswing to float the French Socialists' experiment."[62] In a short space of time, his entire platform became financially untenable, and Mitterrand was forced to spin the wheel about face, replacing his original economic program with a new politics of "austerity."[63]

Mitterrand's dramatic U-turn was political common sense and he was of more than sufficiently pragmatic mind to pull it off. But it was an electoral disaster for his party. Mitterrand offered his own left-wing prime minister, Pierre Mauroy, to the lions, in favor of the more reliably centrist Laurent Fabius, condemning the socialists to heavy losses in the 1986 legislative elections. Mitterrand himself survived as president (a political bruiser, he would remain in office until 1995) but he did so as a man standing alone at the top, in "cohabitation" with a conservative platform positioned securely now beneath both feet.

Once more the political landscape shuffled rightward. French support for the PCF (French Communist Party) and, perhaps more tellingly, for the trade union confederations—the CGT (General Confederation of Labor) and CFDT (French Democratic Confederation of Labor)—fell away. "In a short space of time," recalled the president of France's National Foundation of Political Sciences, René Rémond, "nearly all of the issues over which elections were fought, majorities in parliament rose and fell, which nourished debates and gave meaning and color to our political life, have ceased to evoke any passion, have lost their luster and have in some cases disappeared altogether." François Furet's declaration in 1978 that "The Revolution is Over"—a declaration which had scandalized the left bank on its publication—was now looking like timely commentary indeed. Modern France's own age of exceptionalism was over. As Furet and his fellow former radical Pierre Rosanvallon put it at the end of the decade: "We are falling into line."[64]

At the same time, there was a considerable degree of continuity in respect of the statist nature of the French turn to liberalization. "Modernization" in France was a top-down process, and politics remained for most people a bizarre form of theater played out in an altogether different world. The French governing elite had lost none of their power; like Mitterrand's cabinet, they had merely nailed their colors to another mast. The *grand corps*, France's imperial-era management bureaucracy, might now be busy squabbling among themselves for influence within the new liberal political staging ground—the *corps des mines*, for example, were fighting an intensive rearguard action against the new empowered *corps des financières*—but it was still an intracorps struggle.[65]

France had tried and failed to construct an alternative left-wing politics in an increasingly neoliberal era. But "actually existing" alternatives remained entrenched elsewhere in Europe: above all in countries governed by social and Christian democratic coalitions, where welfare meant more than just a costly conjunction of incapacity and state largesse. Christian Democrats in West Germany still spoke of "social capitalism," for example. But there, as in Italy, it was not ideology that held the welfare state afloat in the 1980s: it had as much to do with the fact that the Christian Democrats' own political base was woven into the benefits (and at times kickbacks) provided by it. There was never much temptation to try rolling it back in the way that Thatcher was doing.

That still left plenty of scope for rolling out various other neoliberal realignments of the welfare state.[66] Employer–employee cooperation in the workplace had reached a peak in Germany in the 1970s, for example, with the passing of a general codetermination law in 1976, mandating worker representation on boards of companies with more than five hundred employees. But the response that the new law met with—the banks and employers' unions said it was stealing the wealth of shareholders by passing on potential profit to the workers in the form of job security—was proof of the prevailing political climate.[67] The country's largest banks and corporations claimed it was an "unconstitutional violation of the right to property" and by the mid 1980s the governing SPD, in search of new votes, was inclined to agree.[68]

Just a few years after that and the unions were forced to relent altogether. With IG Metall, the metalworkers' union, taking the lead, they now offered to drop their demand for increased wages in exchange for guaranteed jobs. Below-minimum-wage work for the unemployed was better than nothing at all, they concluded. Little could have better captured the shifting balance of power than the response to such moves by Hans-Olaf Henkel, a successor to the ill-fated Hanns Martin Schleyer, as the new head of the German employers' association. Countries like Britain had obtained "social peace and political stability" without any bargaining at all, Henkel reasoned. So why even bother with class compromise anymore?[69]

The countries that proved most reluctant to embrace the neoliberal dogma were the Scandinavian ones, naturally enough. Industrial democracy was most deeply embedded there, and the workers were able to defend their well-entrenched positions in national policymaking. Inspired by Thatcher's experience in Britain, the Norwegian Employers Association (NAF) tried to provoke a lockout of workers in 1986. They soon found they had misjudged the strength of the Norwegian labor movement.[70] In neighboring Sweden unions reacted more positively, putting forward the idea of a standardized system of wage-earner funds which, in its original form, would have required larger firms to release 20 percent of each year's profits as stock to be owned by wage-earners collectively.

Such proposals were rejected—they were hopeful even by Scandinavian standards. Perhaps the more relevant point was that they could even have been taken seriously. Yet the winds of neoliberalism continued to blow in across the social democratic redoubts of the north. In 1991, just five years after the assassination of Olof Palme, the Swedish Social Democrats, under Ingvar Carlsson, would experience their worst defeat since the 1920s. Their valiant efforts to reduce unemployment, at the same time as cutting the top rate of income tax to 50 percent, had not been enough to please an electorate that was increasingly bourgeois in its tastes and they were unceremoniously booted from power. The Danish social democrats faced a similar problem at the start of the decade. From 1973 to 1982 foreign debt in Denmark had gone from 10.8 to 33.0 percent of GDP. In the early 1980s the government gave in trying to ring-fence its welfare programs and turned to more hard-edged methods of managing the public accounts.

Australia and New Zealand at this time were no less worried about declining international competitiveness and rising public sector borrowing. From 1973 to 1982 foreign debt as a percentage of GDP increased from 7.3 to a massive 57 percent in New Zealand. Having thus far tried to ride out the economic crises of the 1970s, they now gave in, with new governments brought to power in 1983 and 1984 respectively, determined to overhaul the public provision of welfare (if not to cut it back, as Britain and America were doing). As with the Danes, they turned to private sector management models to overhaul how the state did its business of looking after the people. Thus did the New Public Management, eventually codified in the Financial Management Improvement Program in Australia (1984) and the Public Finance Act in New Zealand (1990), make its entry in the Antipodes. And what was most notable about it (and indicative of a trend that would later appear in Europe as well) was that both countries at this time were governed by *Labour* administrations.

In Australia, Bob Hawke (with Paul Keating as his finance minister)—a friendly, feuding Brown–Blair facsimile *avant la lettre*—came to power first, in 1983, and immediately made economic stability and discipline the core of their political program. What Thatcher did with the miners over a coaling cart they did with the Australian unions consensually, via the Prices and Incomes Accord. It was a less gory but ultimately more effective approach. Of the two countries it was New Zealand, however, where the Labour government had an overwhelming majority during the years 1984 to 1990, which had the most radical economic program of any Western country during these years. The reason? Its majority meant simply that it could damn the consequences of going against its traditional pro-labor policies. The imperative to restore economic growth was now the overriding objective.[71]

Southern Europe too was undergoing profound political changes, albeit of a rather different sort. It was, after all, a *left* democratic wave that swept across southern Europe in the late 1970s and into the 1980s. In Spain and Portugal, where the new governments replaced the decades-old dictatorships of Franco and Salazar, hopes were raised (primarily, it should be said, in countries further north) of a social democratic renaissance that might counter the Anglo-American neoliberalism that now seemed a more or less inevitable fate. There were several reasons that these parties did not redeem those promises.

The first was simply the nature of the transition itself. The death of Franco in Spain in 1975 and the three-year transition to democracy overseen by his designated successor King Juan Carlos was a triumph of diplomacy and a true victory for economic liberals. But it fell short of what many radicals had been hoping for. The Spanish constitution of 1978, formed on the back of the Moncloa Pacts between the major political groupings in 1977, was a "correlation of weaknesses" in the words of the Catalan communist Vázquez Montalbán. True, as the failed coup attempt of 1981 made clear, the Francoist oligarchy may have been too debilitated to carry on. But the democratic opposition lacked sufficient vitality to make a truly revolutionary break.[72] But the transition to democracy also marked, as it did in Portugal too, a more general failure to shed the cultural constraints of a male breadwinning household that underpinned the economy under Franco and Salazar and which would structurally impinge upon modernization efforts thereafter.

If this was the left's argument to make, however, it did not care to do so. Indeed, disappointing results of the PSOE (Spanish Socialist Workers' Party) in the first fully democratic elections of 1979 prompted Felipe González, the dominant Spanish politician of his era, to make as abrupt an about-turn as Mitterrand. González interpreted the disappointing result of PSOE in the 1979 elections in Spain as a rejection of the country's, and of his party's, more radical past, rather than of him, and he threatened to resign unless the party changed course. PSOE then adopted a very different set of policies, exorcising what González now referred to as "minority currents" and thereafter embracing NATO and neoliberalism alike.[73] For its part, Portugal oscillated between socialist and social democratic government, but revised its constitution in 1989 (and again in 1992) red-penning the more leftist references, such as to "agrarian reform," of its 1976 restoration and allowing for greater privatization of state assets.[74]

In Italy, Ciriaco de Mita, the new Christian Democrat secretary from 1982, sought to do the same: though he had less success in reforming his party than Thatcher or Reagan and took the Christian Democrats to a dismal showing at the polls in 1983.[75] That finally provided the opening that Bettino Craxi had been angling for over the previous decade. Craxi's socialist affiliations ought not to confuse: he was a man very much in the Thatcher–Reagan mold. A libertarian at heart, and a staunchly self-serving one at that, in 1984 he replaced the Italian socialist party's Central Committee with a national assembly to which preselected candidates would henceforth simply be "clapped in." Then he pushed through reform of the *scala mobile*, the threshold payments system, to the cost of the workers and the delight of the business community.[76] The communists, still battered and bruised from the PCI's experimental moment in power, finally keeled over at this latest hurdle to be set in their way. Between them, Craxi and his good friend Berlusconi (the two Milanese businessmen took holidays together at Portofino) would effect a lasting shift in Italy toward a neoliberal form of politics. Christian democracy still served as the national political livery, for now, but in truth the nation had undergone a distinct change of heart and social welfare was no longer such a central concern.

By the end of the 1980s, the nature and purpose of the "social contract" had been quite dramatically transformed across the liberal democratic West. In contrast to the 1960s there was still plenty of welfare on the books. But there was a lot less state with which to deliver it. Only in

Sweden would average tax levels thereafter remain at anything over 50 percent, with Denmark, Finland, Belgium, and France just behind. Italy and Norway both had average rates of around 40 percent; Britain, Australia, and New Zealand, and the southern European states, all had rates now in the mid 30s. Switzerland, Japan, and the United States filled out the bottom of the scale with rates in the mid 20s.[77] By the late 1980s the Western welfare state, in short, looked to be going the way of the one-party state in the East. As the German sociologist, Wolfgang Streeck, summed up what for him were the good old days: "[P]olitically guaranteed full employment, collective society-wide wage formation . . . universal social rights protected from competition, tax and income policies that kept inequality within tight limits"[78]—all that was now gone.

In its place was a much tougher approach to social policy, advanced undercover of a new rhetoric of the minimal state. And yet such a picture needs nuancing as well. The transformation in the overall political direction of the Western democracies is perhaps too easily told as a story of willing sabotage by the right. The truth of the matter was that left and right alike were in a bind about how to move forward after the upheavals of the 1970s. The right was "constrained" in moving any further because the welfare state was popular; the left was unable to explain itself to the electorate because what it wanted to offer (social security above all) was no longer affordable now that unemployment, combined with lower productivity, had pushed most states into the red.[79] Ironically, then, the very partisan political landscape that had provided the backcloth to the transformation of the postwar political economy in the first place had, by the mid to late 1980s, brought both sides of the political spectrum *together* in the search for a new one.

The New Political Economy

Sometime around the early 1980s it became apparent that the economic base of democratic life in the West had changed. A new type of economy was taking shape within the Western nations. Less national in orientation, less subject to restrictive rules and regulations, it was posing new questions of politicians and captains of industry alike. Supply-side strategies and "tight money," cutting back on the social state and deregulating the economy were all part of a broad, transnational effort to overcome the legacy of "the great inflation" of the 1970s. But still governments worried whether what they were doing was enough. The specter of the "legitimation crisis" that Habermas had some time ago observed was still stalking the Western democratic state, and ensuring the return of profitability to economic activity remained the number one priority.

Central to this task, it was argued, was the need to loosen the constraints on market activity. In so doing, the shackles of the years of stagflation were finally thrown off and a new era of "casino capitalism" was inaugurated.[80] The new pecuniary ethic informed everything from government policies to the major technological breakthroughs of the time. Communications and biotechnology replaced manufacturing and chemicals, which in turn increasingly moved offshore. Technology start-ups, like Microsoft and Apple, began to make their presence felt on the national stage. The earliest affordable personal computers, using new microprocessor technology, were switched on at the start of the decade; by its end they were close to a standard item in middle-class households.

Such achievements were historic in their own right; but no less importantly they seemed to confirm the idea that competition itself was a guarantor of quality and innovation. The long years of state-subsidised research that had enabled the communications and computing revolution to take place proved easily forgotten. It was competitive rationalization and profit-incentivized entrepreneurialism that were now considered the driving force behind technological innovation. And yet, for all the obvious benefits, the GDP and labor productivity impact of computing, for example, was still low compared with other historic technological innovations. The growth rate of labor productivity in the United States for 1965 to 1990 never got to much over 1 percent.[81]

The new political economy had other downsides too: not least a degree of volatility not seen since the interwar period. Speculative bubbles formed more easily in property and stock than new productivity could be squeezed out of computing, and this took shape most damagingly in Japan, where they frequently ended in stock market crashes. Europeans were afforded a telling glimpse of a similar future in July 1982 when news bulletins showed officials moving in to seize Italy's largest private bank, Banco Ambrosiano, which at that point had over a billion dollars in overdue international loans on its books.[82] Americans were given another glimpse on Black Monday in October 1987, when stock markets reeled around the world and huge values were wiped off national stock indexes. Australia, Spain, the United States, and Canada were all hit; the UK too, as it recovered from a hurricane that had wreaked physical damage across the land. But it was New Zealand's stock market that fell the most, by a colossal 60 percent, throwing the country right back into the economic troubles it had just begun to emerge from.

What ultimately lay behind much of this economic turmoil was the precipitous, post-Volcker rise in the value of the US dollar during the first half of the decade. America's European partners groaned at the additional burden the "unprecedented" value of the dollar now added to their already moribund economies (Jacques Delors complained that it was like "a third oil shock").[83] But Reagan had even less reason to care about this than Nixon had. He took it, rather, as a sign of the strength of the nation and "a vote of confidence by the markets" in the national economy, even as businesses insisted that the influx of comparatively cheap imports was sending them into receivership.[84]

Behind the rise of the dollar lay a much more serious problem with the new political economy. This was the glaring lack of control over what were now often wildly fluctuating exchange rates. The Reagan administration tried, belatedly, to ward off trouble in 1985 by tabling the Plaza Accords, by which means the finance ministers of the G5—West Germany, Japan, Britain, France, and America—agreed to place funds to collectively devalue the dollar. But just a year later the British government heaped fuel back onto the fire with its Financial Services Act, deregulating the City of London more or less overnight.

The Big Bang as it became known injected back into the international economy most of the volatility that had just been taken out of it, as did the pursuant wave of financial speculation that began to drive the dollar downward this time, even after the managed controls agreed on in 1985 had been lifted. In 1988, at a hastily convened meeting at the Louvre in Paris, finance ministers of the now G7 met once again. This time they were forced to take the opposite tack to that taken at the Plaza Hotel, as they sought to restore the value of the dollar. A constant push to nudge prices this way or that, narrowly averted crises, and anxious, laboriously negotiated quid pro quos to stitch back together some minimal level of control over the system: this was the pattern of the international economy in the 1980s. And it was becoming apparent all the while that it mattered less how workers and businesses reacted to what governments now did than what markets had to say.

For those able to master its arcane depths, a career in finance promised alluring salaries. The problem was that finance itself did little to contribute to wider economic growth: this was in part because relatively little of the wealth it produced was taxed and in part because, for all that it encouraged the siting of Ferrari dealerships and Balenciaga outlets in and around the offices of Mayfair and La Défense, it did not actually "produce" anything itself. The growth in cross-border capital flows also limited the ability of governments to control their own macroeconomic policy (they were unable to control both interest rates and exchange rates at the same time). This was not an incidental problem. To be successful, finance relied upon exploiting a basic paradox: growing deregulation and relaxation of rules for itself along with monetary stability and fiscal discipline for national governments. And to ensure that it could rely on the right policies being put into place to provide this financial security, central banks were now, one after the other, made independent from the state: an achievement that placed financial policy one step further from the voters' control.[85]

The brave new world of international finance proclaimed its global status loudly, but it was in fact intensely local in its geography of financial centers and corporate summits populated with brash new traders excitedly discussing new and complex financial instruments. "Les City Boys," the French called their London counterparts, derisively at first but with steadily growing envy as they saw what profits their instruments, such as derivatives, could reap. And the more the financial sector was deregulated the more these instruments took on a bewildering array of forms: be it swaps, options, swaptions, or futures.

All this was risky business (the number of bank failures shot up from less than 10 to nearly 200 between 1970 and the mid 1980s) but profitable for those who succeeded.[86] At the same time the range of "assets" that could be traded expanded to include almost anything (it need not be something as tangible as a commodity any more, it could be as abstract as an idea or the probability itself of some future event happening or not). By 1991 the value of all these derivatives was estimated to be worth around $7.1 trillion. Cross-border transactions in bonds and equities expanded rapidly as well. In the United States they were worth around 9 percent of GDP in the 1980s but 89 percent just a decade later.[87]

Compared to the rise of finance the dominant trend in the material world of productive enterprises told a very different story. Between 1973 and 2000, profits in the private sector ran at 15 percent below the postwar-era average prior to 1973. They would have been even lower had wages been paid at a proportional rate to the earlier period as well.[88] Instead it was workers who were forced to subsidize the falling rate of profit earned by their companies, effectively turning the rules of the postwar political economy on its head. US firms led the way in cutting wages here, desperate as they were to compete with the newer, more efficient firms coming out of Germany and Japan.

When that failed they turned to buying up their competitors or cutting back on the quality of their product (a task which ever-more stringent guidelines paradoxically made easier). The last throw of the dice was usually to increase the scale of operations, the better to squeeze at least a little profit out of ever-narrowing margins. The ongoing expansion of Walmart—domestically at first, then overseas—was a classic example of this. Its arrival in France was taken as a sign of the inevitable victory of capitalism American-style. In fact it was the opposite: a defensive grasp for market share by an industrial giant on the ropes.

The paradox of late twentieth-century economic globalization was thus revealed in its very inception: dynamism was not restored; the reckoning was merely delayed—or more precisely it was displaced. Those firms and industries that could, found ways of protecting their market share and their profit lines (which usually meant cutting back on labor costs). Those who could not would struggle to be competitive. For all the optimism of the newsstand, of *The Economist* and the *Financial Times* in particular, it is perhaps no wonder that most of the informed chatter at conferences, round tables, and in learned economic journals was still, underneath it all, about "the deteriorating performance" of the global economy, and "these trying times."[89]

If the outcomes of the new political economy were so mixed then we are prompted to ask why it was that the 1980s heralded the crowning of laissez-faire market economics and such large-scale claims for the virtues of a market-driven social order? On one level the answer was perfectly simple, for what the model offered, through its emphasis on deregulation, on fiscal discipline as the central motif of "sound government," and on the expansion of consumer desires, was the seemingly limitless expansion of economic freedoms. Yet what this promise in turn rested on was not any desire to safeguard democracy but—which was more pressing—to save capitalism. The parallels with the way that Gorbachev in the USSR was just now seeking to respond to the global crisis of the 1970s (his predecessors having ignored the problem) are suggestive here. In the Soviet Union, however, the system would ultimately be sacrificed in order to free the worker; in the West it was the workers (or at least their wages in the first instance) that were sacrificed in order to save the system.[90] On this basis, the capitalist world economy could proceed anew.

And proceed it did. Governments stopped fretting about how to build a new distributional consensus to win votes and began focusing instead on how to win over the support of the powerful business lobbies, corporate managers, and international finance. This was, in effect, its own distributional settlement away from those whose voice no longer mattered as much; it just wasn't a very democratic one. In America, the interest rate spike had got the US economy going and the inflationary spillover had made things harder for Europe. Reaganites clapped each other on the back about "eurosclerosis." And the now nine EEC countries, suffering both from integration of the three new Mediterranean countries in the first part of the decade, and from the last of the main oil shocks in 1979–81, saw little option but to begin to emulate what America was doing. Reconciled to Volcker's turn to disinflation, governments stopped fretting about whether and how to secure credit and focused instead primarily on its price.

For their part, corporations too turned to finance to grease the wheels, inaugurating a new era of corporate takeovers by private equity firms and management consultancy advisers (the latter often called in to ward off the former). It began to matter less what the real world outcomes of any new product development was, and more its "results" for the company: and executives were handsomely remunerated with the proceeds of these (in stock and stock options) the better to ensure "they don't hesitate to make difficult decisions such as shedding divisions, closing plants or outsourcing work overseas," as one report put it.[91] States did what they could to support them. In 1985 the Bundesbank loudly trumpeted what was taken, off the back of the previous decade's upheavals, to be the achievement of the ages: inflation in Germany had reached 0 percent. The specter of the 1970s had finally been vanquished, and the wisdom of allowing finance to steer the economy was thereafter enthroned.[92] Of course, much of the trust upon which the postwar social contract relied was also lost in the process.

Who was to stop this? With the left experiencing a generational break in service, progressive counterargument to this new political economy came most strongly from the Church. In 1986 the Catholic Church published a pastoral letter on Catholic social teaching. Entitled "Economic Justice for All," it was to become a mainstay of Catholic social advocacy in the years to come. Above all it presented a biting critique not only of Reagan's domestic policies but of the international economic order in which they were set. "[P]rivate charity and voluntary action are not sufficient," it said, and it called for radical "structural" changes to government and financial institutions that they might "more equitably distribute the profits resulting from labor."[93]

The Church called people to religion to ward off what it saw as a steadily bifurcating society: the society of Gordon Gekko, as immortalized in the film *Wall Street* (1987). Most people did not turn to religion, however. Evangelical Christian conservatism as a political movement may have helped cement a new and more contrarian political style, as a part of the new democratic consensus in the first place, but the number of actually *practicing* Christians continued its decline across the West, especially in Europe. For those who could afford it, the more appropriate secular response to the precarities of laissez-faire society was to take out life insurance. For those who could not, there was little else to fall back on than some inner faith in society itself.

Civil Societies?

"I believe that it is justified to talk of a genuine turning-point in the evolution of democratic institutions which can be summed up in a simple formula," wrote the influential Italian philosopher Norberto Bobbio in 1987: "from the democratization of the state to the democratization of society." The noncommunist Italian left, a little like its counterpart in France, had, by the dying years of the Cold War, come to believe very strongly in the power of "the social." Certain influential French intellectuals had even come to see in the lessons of the nineteenth-century liberal François Guizot a precursor of the present search for a way to reconcile modern society's growing emphasis on liberty with democratic principle. But while history would prove Bobbio right about the turning point (and eventually those who looked to the nineteenth century about its precursors) the Italian was quite wrong about its "evolutionary" effects. Civil society was to be the handmaiden to something far more radical than that.

By the mid 1980s the left's efforts to re-democratize the economy had largely been given up, or else—as with Mitterrand—tried and failed. Efforts by the right to do away with the state in the name of the market, by contrast, had made substantial strides forward. But they had also revealed the present limits of the neoliberal project within democratic societies. In some ways, it was inevitable, therefore, that the champions of markets and states would each alike seek to turn to the one remaining area of contestation where there was territory to be won: the domain of civil society that lay between them. Civil society was an age-old nostrum. What was unusual about its late twentieth-century reappearance, and indeed reimagination, was that it was now considered to be a political platform of its own. "Civil society" thus emerged in the 1980s as something quite new, something that could be struggled over and won—a means to other ends.

For progressives, civil society offered a way to "house" the variously disjointed political projects for participation that had emerged in the 1960s and 1970s: a space, or more accurately, a series of "networks" and "associations," through which to forge a new wave of oppositional politics outside the traditional boundaries (and limitations) of class organizations.[94] This was like the hopefulness of a halftime pep talk to the losing side. For conservatives it offered something even more valuable than this: the promise of a return to "civility" in public affairs. As the British conservative Ferdinand Mount wrote in a 1973 essay, "The Recovery of Civility," civil society was both about "courtesy and consideration . . . modesty, restraint and moderation." This was, he thought, "an important and useful quality in politics," especially in light of the upheavals of the sixties.[95]

Much of Mount's essay was a response to Irving Kristol's book *On the Democratic Idea in America* (1972), a work that marked the beginnings of the transition from traditional conservatism to the more radical variant of *neo*conservatism in America. Kristol's argument there, and in a series of works to follow over the coming decade and a half, was that American liberalism had stretched itself too far in the 1960s. Specifically, the state had overreached itself in its Good Society programs by trying to correct for inequalities it had no real business trying to correct for in the first place. Such inequalities as existed in a market society must be natural, Kristol insisted, or else they would not have appeared in the first place.

For neoconservatives, then, civil society provided a means of disguising the underlying moralism that lay behind their own purportedly secular crusade. The state's proper functions, they claimed, had been disrupted by "interest group politics," "affirmative actions," and what the neoconservative sociologist Nathan Glazer called the "imperial judiciary" and "permanent officials" of the federal and state bureaucracy.[96] Moral decay was inevitable as a result (though it was never specified clearly why) and the thrust of the neoconservative project was accordingly not to preserve existing traditions, but to strip away the present layer of politics and uncover the more "authentic" traditions of the deeper past. Kristol accordingly spoke of the need for a "Long Trek Back" to a more self-governing and "civil" society in which morality had room to breathe. Mount's essay was dutifully subtitled "notes for the long trek back."

But did the Western rediscovery of "civil society" provide the means for embarking on such a journey? Certainly its new language of "associations," "networks," and "affiliations" soon fluttered about the warm glow that "civil society" seemed to give off, along with the voluntarist organizations and registered charities that crept in as their prime beneficiaries. Influential advocates like Peter Berger and Richard Neuhaus, in enticingly named works such as *To Empower People* (1977), called for neighborhoods, churches, and voluntary organizations to take on "wherever possible" the tasks of social provision.[97] For Benjamin Barber, in *Strong Democracy* (1984), it was not so much voluntary organizations but the new capabilities of technology and communications that could replace the old town hall meeting. Civil society in the West then, at least in the 1980s, was a somewhat elitist concept.[98]

Elsewhere in the world, by contrast, and specifically in Latin America and Eastern Europe, civil society emerged at this time in a far more popular register. In Latin America the umbrella of civil society offered a way to resist oppressive right-wing regimes without playing the radical left card, and thereby risking being tarred with the brush of the unions and communist movements in those countries. In Eastern Europe it was a way of resisting the communist regimes after the Prague Spring. It needs to be asked, then, why the sort of civil society organizations to emerge in liberal democracies were so lacking in actual transformative effect? The answer is that, whereas in the East civil society was defined by a logic of opposition, in the West it was defined by a logic of voluntarism. Civil society in Eastern Europe and Latin America arose as a critique of a particular sort of (oppressive) state; in the West, it sought to substitute *for* the institution of the state.

That the idea of liberty was essential to both variants of the new civil society discourse was testament to just how far notions of "liberty" had moved over the preceding years. The Western version of civil society remained a society of individuals. It is what allowed Thatcher to square the circle of being for "people" but also against society, allowing her to separate out the one from the other. In Britain, at least, the implications of this for democracy passed by largely unnoticed. Opening the tricentenary celebration of England's Glorious Revolution in parliament in 1988, Thatcher held that event up as having "established the enduring qualities of democracy—tolerance, respect for the law, for the impartial administration of justice."[99] This was a distinctly Tory version of democracy, and a narrow one at that: there was no "we the people" within sight of it, for one. And by digging deeply back into a presumed unchanging past, it was a means of glossing over the uses to which civil society was being put in the present.

The primary function of civil society in the 1980s was in fact the very opposite of that which Bobbio had detected. For it was used, most consistently, as an instrument in the ongoing struggle against the state, regardless of which side was brandishing it. Thus in France it offered a way of being antitotalitarian and progressive at the same time. The seed having been planted by the new left, the *deuxième gauche*, as it looked abroad in the late 1970s, it was now taken up in wordy condemnations of the domestic state at home. In Italy, by contrast, it emerged through the more quotidian means of family and business: a galvanizing presence more than a political movement, it was as much the credo of moderates in the northern movements as it was the basis of the teleocracy already being promoted by Berlusconi out of Milan and then Rome. In Britain it was a way of resisting Thatcherism in light of the ineffective opposition she encountered from the Labour Party (indeed, from any professional politicians outside her own cabinet, it sometimes seemed).

In America it was given shape through prominent accounts by liberal intellectuals of the graffiti they encountered on trains and the broken windows they were forced to observe on their way to restaurants in formerly down-and-out neighborhoods: as if the windows themselves were responsible for the exclusion of the people living there. Ironically just about the only place it did not take off was in Scandinavia: a reminder that necessity is the mother of political invention after all. In almost every other case, civil society presented itself as the promised solution to the failures of social and economic policy. Above all it purported to offer more power to choose at a time when people were losing that power to the abstract and proliferating processes of market exchange.

Against the dramatic changes of the time, and contrary to its own stated objectives, civil society thus offered an especially alluring balm: a politics based on what people were—"men and women who are citizens, producers, consumers, members of the nation and much else besides," as Michael Walzer put it—not what they ought to be. "Society" in short now became a sort of elective concept. Which was fine, of course, so long as you were in a position to choose. And yet as the French writer Georges Perec had put it in his then still widely read 1965 novel *Things*— a story that follows the travails of a young Parisian couple bent on achieving the better standard of living constantly dangled before them—

a consumer society often made it seem that these "choices" were so many, and so freighted socially and culturally, that they left even middle-class people feeling exhausted, if not "consumed" themselves.[100]

The Death of the Working Class

For those who did not carry the burden of so much choice, the new society became only a harsher, less compromising place. For the working class in particular, it had begun to seem, in the early 1980s, that there was no longer much place for them in society at all. In his 1982 book, *Farewell to the Working Class*, the French Marxist André Gorz offered a summary of the problems confronting the working class in a postindustrial society: segmented workforces and a de facto de-skilling of people who worked in trades—at the lathe or on the factory floor—that were no longer valued. The British novelist David Lodge offered a more literary take on the same theme in a series of novels, including the Booker-shortlisted *Nice Work*, lampooning modern working life through the lens of the university. What had begun in 1848, in other words, was now drawing to an end. Society was being riven in two and only one part of the new arrangement, it seemed, had come to matter—except, that was, in Scandinavia, where from the 1970s, class consciousness had "almost vanish[ed]" to the extent that there, for now, the grievances of class had largely disappeared.[101] For now.

This sense of impending decline may well explain why the 1970s had seen a great workerist moment take hold where the working class looked still to have something approaching strength in numbers. What turned Gorz himself into a household name, for example, was his 1968 text, *Strategy for Labor*, which outlined ways in which people could take control of their workplaces. This was at the time when Spanish and Portuguese workers were doing just that, of course: when, in Italy, heavily exploited southern *Meridionale* workers began to assert their own agenda at the vast factories of Fiat in the north, and when factory councils—16,000 in all across the country—were set up in cities like Turin, *la città dell'auto*, representing the pinnacle of the working class '68. At the same time, in that other great Fordist city of Detroit, workers pulled together to resist not just an industry but a whole city in decline.[102] In France, under the aegis of the CFDT (Conféderation française démocratique du travail), *autoges-tion* (worker self-management, loosely translated) was finding its way into workplaces across the country.

With hindsight all this was little more than a swansong for a working class whose best days were behind them. In Turin, Fiat won a crucial victory over the CGIL union (the communist Confederazione Generale Italiana del Lavoro) in 1980, after which it was able to push through a major restructuring program. Front of house, the new Fiat Uno was the key to getting the company back in shape. From its appearance in 1983 it would become one of the most successful automobile platforms in history: rolling off the new and more efficient factory lines in vast numbers through until 1995. The real secret of its success, however, was that it was based upon automation, and a halving of the workforce between 1981 and 1986. Despite the layoffs, which proceeded apace throughout the decade, union rates fell off almost everywhere. Those unions that remained became more and more fragmented: competing with each other for a diminishing market share, as much as against the employers. Between 1980 and 1995 the rate of unionization in France and Britain halved; in Australia it fell from 49 percent to 35 percent, in Japan from 31 to 24, and in America from 23 to 15 percent.[103]

At the root of the problem was the fact that few workers thought of themselves as part of a solidarity group in the first place: they were too preoccupied just trying to get by. It wasn't just a case of farewell to the working class, but farewell to the hopes and ideals that had made it worth thinking of oneself as politically working class in the first place. For France's Marcel Gauchet, the working class had largely done its historical job of creating a mass political society; it could now go home—the world had moved on. This would later prove precipitate. But it was true that citizens were less exclusively defined by their class than in the past. And that being so, it became harder to think about politics as an active, physical event: the taking of the street or the shouting of "Stop thief!" from the soap box—as the socialists used to do to grab the attention of passersby. Moreover, the idea that "civil society" could replace class with a more universal appeal to everyone's human rights was, ironically enough, itself something of an instance of false consciousness.

For all the rhetorical appeal and excitement aroused by the explosion of new social movements and human rights organizations in particular, much of this left the working class, in particular, cold. Tax reform and better regulation did not make enticing platforms for rights activists to pull people away from their free time. The idealism of civil society thus became a sort of auxiliary to the new social contract: individualist, technocratic, and resolutely antipathetic to the universalism of the earlier age. Its greatest achievement in the 1980s was to intensify the value placed upon law and individual freedom. But civil society movements failed to do the same for the equality that democracy also required. They may never have been intended to become handmaidens to the laissez-faire reforms the likes of Thatcher and Reagan were implementing (much less to a minimalist, yet assertive state). But that is what the rise of civil society discourse in effect brought about. It provided a cushion for the new political economy rather than a critique.

Perhaps with hindsight what matters most is not what the idea of civil society *did* do so much as what it ensured people did *not* do.[104] Placated by what the great British journalist and correspondent Alistair Cooke called "the inquisitive magic of television" people did not riot. Increasingly, after PATCO and the miners, they did not strike. Mostly they got mad and listened to music. In America this led to hip hop and rap. In Britain there was punk: and punk was a way of talking about class. But it was an effort at social rebellion that in some ways peaked too early (the late 1970s) and which ultimately failed because the artists themselves became commercially successful—as New Wave music took off—and as professionalized as the establishment they railed against.[105] Dissent was replaced by the radical (yet at times rather *haute*) disdain of satire: programs like *Monty Python, Yes, Minister*, and *Spitting Image* were perhaps especially popular in Britain. But many of these were also syndicated around the world. There were, it is true, more political forms of rejecting mainstream society elsewhere: Germany's countercultural "taz" (*die tageszeitung*) network of writers in the early 1980s, or the BZ "squatters" movement in Denmark (and the riot police they struggled with).[106] But their self-conscious embrace of a whole set of new ideas about "society" during these years did not so much address the social and cultural tensions of the time as much as it helped people grow accustomed to them. Meanwhile the pace of social change accelerated.

Dancers in the Dark

Society and not just the economy had been undergoing a major transformation in the aftermath of the upheavals of the 1970s, and by the mid to late 1980s the shape this was taking began to become clear. Class politics was on the way out now that the state, to save itself, had sided with the power of capital. Labor was abandoned on the steppes amid the retreat. And yet, for all this, the problem of social division had scarcely been resolved, much less consigned to the past: it had simply taken on a new form, and a new associated geography.

A part of this geography, in the United States no less than in Europe, was urban, where the glaring results of a decades-long crisis could be seen in the ruins of the once great American city. Whites had fled to the suburbs and left behind a desolate landscape of poisoned brownfield land and potholed roads for their black compatriots to live among. Their exit also further "busted" the value of the properties left behind, which stunted tax revenue and left the inner city a desolately underfunded place populated by blacks and the down-and-out protagonists of Bruce Springsteen's 1984 hit single "Dancing in the Dark." In Detroit this process that began in the 1950s would be almost complete by the 2000s, with only 7.8 percent of downtown Detroiters white in the 2010 US Census.[107] The result, already by the time the 1980s rolled around, was an increase in drugs and crime and social problems, not the least of which was a new and troubling epidemic of HIV/AIDS.

The response was to tackle just one part of the much larger problem. The War on Drugs, officially launched in 1971, had now become, with Nancy Reagan's privately funded "Just Say No" campaign, a white-middle-class defensive operation. White citizens were, however, the least likely to be vulnerable to the explosion of cheap crack, which hit the New York streets in 1985. The same was true of the housing crisis and the explosion in incarceration rates of nonwhite citizens: a problem compounded by the steadily more punitive approach taken in the war on drugs. "Casual drug users should be taken out and shot," declared the Los Angeles police chief, Daryl Gates, publicly. But the real causes of the problem were longer term: they were more structural than cultural, as Gates believed. Reinvestment in public services was what was needed—this much was evident even to an old Cold Warrior like Walt Rostow. Better known for advocating development policies for the Third World, Rostow was given space in the *Wall Street Journal* to outline what, if anything, might save the US economy (he suggested a massive program of public infrastructure development).[108]

The "urban crisis" in America was a long-term, secular problem, then. But accompanying it now was the more recent return to inequality and the demise of urban civic life in Europe too. For this was also the moment of the emergence of the global city, as major urban centers like Manhattan and London sought to leverage their nodal status to attract capital and highly skilled, highly mobile workers. Nations may not any longer be able to "fix" global capital but financial centers and their municipal sponsors certainly could. The effect was not to reduce inequalities but to intensify them, dusting off the streets and pushing the unwanted further out of sight. But whereas in America the geographic separation of rich and poor, black and white, was understood as a problem *in* America, not a problem *of* America, in France, to take an obviously contrasting example, the separation of Algerians and white working classes into the *banlieues* was such an obvious indictment of the claim to *solidarité, fraternité, égalité* that it repeatedly came up in national political debate.

For those who now voted for the Front National, it was just these edge-city residents of the *banlieues* who were to blame for most of the nation's ills. And the Front National increased its share of the national vote the more it pointed this out, primarily at the expense of the once powerful PCF. The still charismatically gruff Jean-Marie Le Pen was polling better than ever, and received 14.5 percent of the national vote in the 1988 presidential elections.[109] Le Pen, having earned his political stripes under Pierre Poujade in the 1950s, knew how to turn the growing insecurity to his advantage: his stock-in-trade message of *Tous pareils, tous pourris* ("They're all the same, all rotten") carried more than an echo of his own political mentor.

In response immigrant groups became ever-more active. In late 1983 many hundreds took part in a rolling protest march from Marseille to Paris, the *Marche pour l'égalité et contre le racisme*, which brought the plight of first and second generation migrants on the receiving end of these policies to national attention.[110] It was indicative of the times, however, that immigrants, and especially young immigrants, now waged their struggle not through the organizations of the old left but increasingly on their own terms, as a battle for cultural identity and legal representation, finding their voice in new cultural media and community organizations.

The same withdrawal of interest in the politics of the old left was apparent in Britain, among those who lived on the real sink estates, the ones that the Thatcher government did not even try to sell off, and which became more and more like their own downtown *banlieues*: no-go areas and repositories, as a result, of every middle-class fear imaginable. Central Manchester was almost deserted by the mid 1980s: "a largely derelict and uninhabited space" populated only by "rundown warehouses."[111] For the white working class in these estates the nearest thing to a community focal point was the local boozer.

Urban divides were one thing, and certainly hard to overlook. But a significant division of society was also taking place at the regional level: and this was harder to see at first, for all that its effects were palpable. Forty-five million people were living in poverty in Europe by the late 1980s (14 percent of the population): the figure was rising and it was concentrated in some areas more than others. The old industrial heart-lands—the Ruhr, the Clyde—declined and the metropolitan regions (London's south east, the French and Italian north) prospered. The same was apparent in Australia with the decline of the coal burners in the once bustling Latrobe Valley.

The growing numbers of people out of work did what they always do and followed the money to the cities: the *Nord-Süd-Gefälle* in Germany, the ongoing influx of *Meridionale* workers, now boosted by North African immigrants, in Italy. Working-class "Mancs" may well have considered themselves a different being altogether from Liverpool's "Scousers," for all that they lived just thirty miles away across the peatlands at the other end of the M62, but both were equally set apart by the growth and prosperity of the South East ring, centered on London. Residents in the South East enjoyed higher incomes, better housing, and greater access to services than those in the north. They may have shared a passport, but increasingly they lived in different worlds of opportunity and experience.

The popular memory of the era is one of yuppies and city residents enjoying an unprecedented financial boom. The Italian wealthy did not all live together, as the British did, in upmarket boroughs like London's Chelsea; they holidayed together in St. Moritz, while the French split their time between Paris and Juan-les-Pins on the south coast, studiously avoiding Marseille on the TGV route down. But it was true as well that in Italy they stopped building *case del popolo* altogether, and the country's division into red (northwestern, communist) and white (northeastern, Catholic) fell away. While some reveled in the antipolitics of this, and others abhorred it, most simply missed—on account of their own pre-occupations, or prejudices, or perhaps both—some of the most positive new developments to stem from it.

Chief among these was the achievement, against all the odds, of the gay community in countries from the United States to Sweden, in the face of the "new plague" of AIDS and the indifference of the governments of almost every country to their plight. *And the Band Played On* was the title of American journalist Randy Shilts's epic, if troubled, history of the epidemic that unfolded in America from California to New York and beyond. But the same story played out in Sweden too, and in Britain for that matter, where the Ministry of Health refused to sanction explicit safe sex advertising for fear of offending public decency, and where so-ciety at large was encouraged to think of it as a problem of deviant sexual identities, as opposed to risky sexual practices. The denial upon which the latter was based was the prime reason that AIDS soon became far more than just the "gay disease" it was stigmatized as being at the beginning: increasingly it became a heterosexual problem too.

And yet, for all that they were never accorded the privilege of inclusion as a "new social movement," gay groups like Gay Men's Health Crisis and ACT UP proved to be more than just identity-based social movements: they actually did more to provide Western heterosexual society with the social tools required to combat the spread of HIV, and to manage the task of living with a disease for which no cure could be found, than did most of the health systems and the institutes and ministries of public health in those countries put together. In a mass demonstration in October 1988 ACT UP organized one of its most successful mobilizations to date when it managed to barricade and shut down the American Food and Drug Administration for a day in protest at the lack of research into possible drugs. The individual was not everywhere crowned in these years therefore. Community and even some thicker notion of society lived on.

If the idea of "community" lived on, it now did so against the backdrop of a dramatically changed political landscape. In the neoliberal thinking that increasingly dominated political thought, it was democracy that had been threatening to destroy capitalism, and so it was democracy, therefore, that now needed bringing into line. Everything that happened in the 1980s needs framing in light of this: above all, the constant demands for change and to relinquish the old democratic safeguards that the "new rules of the game" put to peoples and their governments alike.[112] Under the promise of freeing up individuals to get on with their lives, society had been radically altered and the nature and purpose of government was being rethought. Yet by setting the popular terms by which they were to be judged as being the success or otherwise of their economic performance, this originally Anglo-American politics succeeded well enough—on its own terms—to convince governments across the West that this was the way forward.

Historical chance played a minor role here. When it came to the economy, the late 1980s was arguably the one moment, in the history of the postwar West, in which it appeared conceivable that the return to a laissez-faire political economy really *was* the way back to a more prosperous future. The more radical economic recipe of cutting wages and seeking competitive mergers and acquisitions had restored a degree of profitability and economic stability to the Western democracies. Set against the dismal record of the seventies, this was enough to convince many people that a corner had been turned. By the end of the decade trade volumes had increased, national level GDP growth was restored to countries like Britain and America, and the aggregate GDP of the rich Western countries grew—and would continue to grow—up until the 1990s. In Europe the last five years of the decade saw output increase by 3 percent a year and unemployment decrease by 2.5 percent.

All this was taken as welcome proof of the earlier wisdom in reining in the welfare state, of beating back the unions and introducing tax cuts, and of deregulating the economy. But such policies could only provide a short-term boost to economic activity. And in truth, the small growth—while it lasted—could just as easily be explained in terms of the sharp drop in oil prices from their late 1970s high and, in Europe at least, of rising hopes attached to the renewed momentum of European integration.[113] It could even be argued that what had really saved Western capitalism, as the British historian Donald Sassoon suggested not long afterward, was the bruised and bloodied body of the welfare state itself, which despite the best efforts of Thatcher and Reagan had largely enabled the costs of the transformation to be physically shouldered. But there were precious few politicians around prepared to make this argument by the end of the 1980s. And in the final analysis the return of economic growth was enough to bring even many of the staunchest social democrats around to the new way of thinking.

Cold War Redux

Remarkably this dramatic transformation in social and political thought would have to share top billing as the moment's primary historic act with a very different set of developments. For after a decade of steadily heightened international tensions, Cold War geopolitics was about to come crashing back in upon the domestic scene of the West. The souring of relations between Washington and Moscow had, of course, begun on the back of détente under Carter. But it was Reagan who would do most to restore a confrontational tone to Cold War international affairs. First Reagan relegitimized patriotism and gave it a Cold War outlet the better to reinforce his domestic policy platform (the army's slogan in 1980 became "Be all you can be!").[114] Then he turned to the Marines and the Mujahideen alike to foment troubles for Soviet-backed regimes.

In each case Reagan made it clear that, so far as he saw it, the Cold War was a conflict that needed winning like any other, not simply accepting—as in containment—and learning to live with it.

Yet Reagan's reheating of the conflict was largely one-way traffic. The Soviets were mired in a war of attrition in Afghanistan and experiencing a revolving door of new leaders at the top: they had neither the capacity nor the strategic clarity to really respond. That did not make things any less dangerous. In September 1983, the Soviets shot down a Korean Air Lines Boeing 747 over the Sea of Japan and a US congressman was one of the victims on board. Just a few days earlier, the Soviets' new (technologically inferior) early warning satellite system falsely detected five incoming American Minutemen missiles. The duty officer overrode the signals, but it was a frighteningly close call given the Soviets' official "launch on warning" approach. With the Soviet regime still tetchy after the uprising of the Solidarity movement in Poland in 1981, Reagan's blustering and the planned deployment of Pershing II missiles in Europe further ratcheted up the tension. Asked about the prospects for war or peace in 1983, 47 percent of Americans thought Reagan had taken them closer to war; only 26 percent thought he was leading them to peace.[115]

When the Euromissiles were finally installed at the end of 1983, Europeans resigned themselves to a retreat back into the past. The Brits drew a sigh of relief that the Americans had their back again, the Germans mostly acknowledged it was necessary (and that Günter Grass's comparison of the moment to the Wannsee Conference was overdrawn), while the French cocked a sardonic eyebrow: *Mieux un Pershing dans votre jardin qu'un soldat Russe sur votre femme*, as Parisian graffiti had it ("Better a Pershing in your garden than a Russian soldier on your wife"). An older generation of American diplomats, who had seen this play before, were intensely concerned, however. It was thus a despondent George Kennan who wrote to an old friend: "While I could, perhaps, talk usefully with the Party leadership in the Soviet Union (if not with the military one), I cannot talk that way, and I know of no one who could, with my own government."

Kennan may not have known quite how right he was: for the US Cold War machinery was divided at this point: the State Department seeking to defuse tensions; the Pentagon quietly stoking them behind the scenes.[116] This was hardly a promising context for world peace. Nor was the fact that the Soviet Union had gone through three leaders in as many years. The incoming Konstantin Chernenko was so decrepit that he could barely get out the words at Andropov's funeral in 1984 (Andropov himself having replaced Brezhnev in 1982). Chernenko lasted just a few months himself before wheezing to a halt in early 1985. Little wonder that by the mid–late 1980s the economy was no longer Western leaders' primary concern. The sense of fragility, of things teetering on the edge of a great abyss had returned.

On the death of Chernenko, however, the baton of power in the USSR was handed on to a much younger, and it would turn out dramatically more open-minded leader, Mikhail Gorbachev. Gorbachev himself was not entirely unknown to a Western audience. It was he, after all, who had attended Enrico Berlinguer's funeral in 1984: a public statement of no small significance, given Berlinguer's outcast status, by the then youngest member of the politburo. More controversially, during that same trip Gorbachev had also met privately with other Eurocommunist leaders. In fact, as it later transpired, he had over 150 books on Eurocommunism. "Afterward," he said, "this thinking, adapted to our reality, took its place in our ideology of *perestroika*."[117] But perhaps most poignantly of all, as he said to his wife at the time in light of the state of affairs back home, "We can't go on living like this."[118]

To be sure, what would soon become Gorbachev's world-changing turn away from the past took in other developments too: the nuclear meltdown at Chernobyl, still far and away the worst nuclear disaster to date. Chernobyl helped Gorbachev to grasp clearly that the world—with its new global challenges, its new fora for meeting these, and the new aspirations of its citizens—had changed, while the Soviet Union had changed all too little for nearly seventy years. It was his encounter with the Eurocommunists, however, that proved critical. Whether what he learned from the Eurocommunists was a different theory of communism or simply a study in the practice of communist heresy remains to be seen. The consequences, either way, were profound. For it was now that Gorbachev's thinking on the role of the Communist Party in world politics began to change.[119] The route from the Soviet Union thus did not pass through the Star Wars program, as Reagan liked to claim, but through Eurocommunism first, and even in due course, as we shall see, through social democracy.

But that was for the years to come. Most immediately, and within months of securing control of the politburo, Gorbachev began talking openly of the need for reform. By 1988, however, and sensing that the Western audience to whom he frequently addressed his overtures was unaware just how serious he was, he chose to cap an historic visit to the United Nations in New York, also in December 1988, with his clearest statement yet. As he stood at the podium, Gorbachev delivered a jaw-dropping speech to the floor of the General Assembly, effectively bringing to an end the Brezhnev Doctrine, the "legal" basis by which the USSR committed itself to intervening in the satellite states.

In a certain sense, then, the first proper glimpse of the fall of communism and the upheavals of 1989 was seen not at the Brandenburg Gate in 1989, but toward the end of 1988 and against the backdrop of a wintry New York skyline. The Brezhnev Doctrine was the central pillar upholding the Soviet Union's entire socialist empire. It was also a throwback to the age of the unquestioned prerogative of sovereignty—a prerogative that in the new era of human rights, of transnational social movements and expanding international trade, including between East and West, no longer really held. That age, we have seen, had already ended in the 1970s. It was Gorbachev's genius perhaps to have recognized this. And the manner in which he acted on this recognition would have far-reaching implications not just for the Soviet Union but for the empire of democracy as well.

"A new vision of the world is being established," Gorbachev declared just a few days later in his annual New Year's Eve speech to the nation at the end of 1988.[120] Speaking at the start of the year in which the Berlin Wall would come down, Gorbachev may well have been signaling his own intentions to speed up the process of reform at home. Knowingly or not, he was also giving his final blessing to forces that would transform the future of the West as well as the East.[121] And for all that the Western media again studiously overlooked his comments, Eastern European citizens most certainly did not, as first the Hungarians, and then the Poles, and in due course also the East Germans were about to reveal.

6

The Victory: Remaking Europe

"I've just arrived from Berlin," declared a jubilant Helmut Kohl on the afternoon of November 10, as he relayed the gist of events in the city, the day after the Wall fell, over a telephone line to the American president. "It is like witnessing an enormous fair. It has the atmosphere of a festival."[1] But if the atmosphere on the streets was exuberant the atmosphere behind the scenes was tense. In November and December of that year Western leaders streamed through Berlin, Strasbourg, and Brussels to hold anxious tête-a-têtes as they grappled with the situation unfolding all around them.[2]

In Poland events were the culmination of a decade-long reform process. In Hungary, memories of the 1956 uprising (and the tanks sent in to crush it) had fostered a real distance from Moscow, and it was reformers *within* the Communist Party who led the changes. By contrast, Czechoslovakians had resented their own government since the crushing of the Prague Spring in 1968, while in Yugoslavia it was nationalist resistance to the communist federation that drove the desire for self-determination. East Germany was really the only case where the sheer volume of people on the streets was enough to topple the party leadership, and even there popular protest came about at the end of a long chain of events unfolding across at least two other countries.

There was not one 1989 but several, therefore, and none of them were revolutions in the traditional sense of the term. The intellectual dissident groups Charter 77 and its spin-off VONS (Committee for the Defense of the Unjustly Prosecuted) in Czechoslovakia, the shipyard workers behind *Solidarność* in Poland, the Hungarian reformers, and the crowds that eventually gathered along the Bornholmer Strasse on the East–West German border were not, as the historian Jan-Werner Müller points out, "the people" of 1789 or even 1917: "The revolutions of 1989 were self-consciously self-limiting and pluralist." And for good reason: their protagonists knew better than most the dangers as well as the prospects of revolution.[3] They were ad hoc constellations that represented no single

social group, nor did they have a clear political platform beyond the desire just to live more normal, unencumbered lives. The dissident movements
were democratic by instinct rather than by design, and the West's ultimate
failure to recognize this was to be one of the most important factors in
determining what "lessons" were learned from the fall of communism. It
was a misreading that would shape how the most important political
development of the second half of the twentieth century was to play out.

What *tended* to be assumed in the West was that the revolutions of
1989 were straightforwardly a demand for liberal democracy and free
markets. It was further assumed that, because Eastern and central Europeans wanted both these things, they wanted, as well, the contemporary
Western balance of force between them. What was not generally recognized at the time was the extent to which the fall of communism in the
East was born of the same moment of crisis as the West had been living
through since the 1970s. Instead, Cold War liberals crowed, while social
democrats looked to the unified territory of Europe with hopes of restoring and reentrenching what they had just lost at the national level.
Neoliberal conservatives, by contrast, saw in the new Europe the chance
to expand the realm of laissez-faire and to finish off what they had begun.
Only one of these ideological groupings would successfully win the
failure of communism to its cause. To understand why, we need to set
the history of the struggles for democracy in the East alongside the
parallel history of its reinvention in the West.

Reconstituting Democracy

After seven decades of extortion and abuse, communism, it should be
remembered, fell predominantly of its own accord. By highlighting the
gap that existed between communist rhetoric and everyday reality, Eastern
and central European dissidents and reformers bravely underscored what
hollow and rotten edifices the parties of power had become. In the end,
given the decrepit and unloved status of the entire communist regime,
that was all they needed to do. In Poland *Solidarność* fatally undermined
the Communist Party as early as 1981 simply by demonstrating that it
cared more about socialist principles (and workers' interests) than the Party
itself.[4] In Hungary Miklós Németh's reformist government decided for
itself that enough was enough: but Hungary was an exception in that its
leadership was both younger and more reform-minded.

It wasn't just bureaucratic sclerosis that did for the outgoing regimes.

Already by the 1980s, as a consequence of the global economic upheavals of the 1970s, the satellite states of Eastern and central Europe were up to their eyeballs in debt. Poland's stood at $20 billion by the turn of the decade, East Germany's at $12 billion, Hungary's at $9 billion. "Cheap bread, a dry flat and a job," was what the East German leader Erich Honecker reckoned was the bare minimum needed to keep state socialism ticking over. By the early 1980s most communist regimes could no longer provide even that. Unwilling, as the West had been, to undergo regime change, they had no option but to borrow drastically. Across the Soviet bloc hard currency debt soared from $6 billion in 1970 to $90 billion in 1989. By the late 1980s merely servicing that debt used up the lion's share of each country's export earnings: 79 percent of GDP in Poland, 47 percent in Hungary. In the words of one historian: "The [entire] bloc had become a ponzi scheme."[5]

Paradoxically perhaps, for the Soviet authorities, the idea of "people's democracy" now became more important than ever. It had always meant something quite different to "liberal democracy" of course. When the Soviet leadership spoke of people's democracy they were not celebrating the value of personal and political rights; they were describing a collective identity and emphasizing personal responsibilities to that end. It was intended, if it rarely functioned, as a standing rebuke to Western individualism. More specifically it framed the ends that were said to demand the "optimal" management of society as the means, thereby providing a way for state fiat to be dressed up with the embellishments of democratic performance.

The limits of treating democracy as a rhetorical whipping rod in this way had, however, already been revealed in Berlin in 1953 (where an East German rebellion was bloodily put down in Potsdamer Platz prior to the Wall going up), in Budapest in 1956 (where Imre Nagy's appeal to the West for assistance in the Hungarian uprising was met by a deafening silence soon drowned out by the sound of Soviet tanks), and in Prague in 1968 (where the tanks once again rolled in to crush the Prague Spring). By the late 1980s those limits had been reached in another way too. For in the aftermath of the economic crisis of the 1970s the people were quite evidently not receiving the people's promised due. This was where the almost serendipitous signing of the Helsinki Accords in 1975 became so important. For it bound the Soviet states legally to respecting the "civil, economic, social, cultural and other rights and freedoms" associated with "the inherent dignity of the human person."[6] In other words, it bound them to making good on some of their promises.

239

Helsinki was a crucial opening for dissidents like Adam Michnik in Poland, Miklós Haraszti in Hungary, or Václav Havel and the members of Charter 77 in Czechoslovakia. It gave them something other than moral critique to work with. Above all they no longer needed to challenge their governments for what they refused to give the people—and thereby stand accused of waging politics outside the sanctioned domain of the Party. Instead they could hold them to account for providing those things in practice that they had formally committed to on paper.[7] The aim, in short, was to push them harder, but to push them on the basic rights their citizens were technically already endowed with and not on political procedure. "[D]aily life," wrote the American author and peace activist Jonathan Schell, could now become "a vast terrain on which totalitarianism can be opposed."[8]

It was on this terrain that political life under communism began to be reconstituted as an autonomous space—be this Václav Benda's "parallel polis" or Jacek Kuroń's realms of "social self-organization"—where civil society could realize itself beyond the reach of prying eyes and the heavy hand that accompanied them.[9] It was not, therefore, some transplanted urge to emulate the Western institutional model of strong markets and weak states that turned dissenters into dissidents, or that unified the shipyard workers at Gdańsk, or the signatories of Charter 77. It was the desire for a general state of political freedom allied to more specific *local* frustrations at the systematized corruption, cronyism, and police and security service violence of the communist regimes.

For what had been the ideological conflict par excellence, it is striking to note that the way the Cold War ended, and Eastern European communism finally fell, was one lacking in overt ideology. Yet that still leaves the question of how the fall of communism in the East came to be interpreted as such a "glorious victory" for liberalism and Western democracy. The answer to that turns upon the way the transitions themselves played out once the old regimes were gone. Ideology may be a fine thing to discard in the name of political purity, but political purity itself is hard to maintain in the face of wholesale social change. And as the dissidents soon realized, in the process of being tossed from one system to another people need something to hang on to.

The dissidents were soon joined in this realization by a host of alternative voices, "populist fundamentalists, religious zealots, and nostalgics of the pre-communist non-democratic regimes" among them.[10] Howsoever they may have begun, as the "wind of change" blew in, the realities of political pluralism turned out to be a colder front than Klaus Meine and the Scorpions imagined in their bestselling hit of 1991: the song that became, for many, the unofficial anthem of the era. As one commentator put it, "[a]pathetic, cynical, demagogic, money-riddled politics are not departures from the democratic norm: they *are* the norm."[11]

For the Hungarian intellectual Ágnes Heller—and this was after all a revolution of the intellectuals first and foremost—it was soon as if the democratic spirit seemed to be having some difficulty filling the formal institutions of democracy. This was hardly surprising: as former colonial nations could have told their Eastern and central European counterparts, rebuilding the institutional architecture of democratic society after many years of foreign rule is a mammoth task. And the Soviet Union was more than just "foreign," of course. "The problem of erecting a liberal, stable and prosperous society on the ruins of a totalitarian industrial ideocracy," said the British-Czech philosopher Ernest Gellner, "is historically absolutely new, no one knows what the answer or answers may be, or indeed whether there is one."[12]

In Poland, there were fifty separate acts reforming everything from the police to the powers of local government under Tadeusz Mazowiecki's government in 1990 after it was voted in by the country's first post-communist elections.[13] In some instances, as with East Germany, Poland and, to a certain extent, the Baltic Republics, the new governments had parliamentary or liberal democratic traditions to look back to. These were at times so old as to provide little practical help, but they did at least offer a legitimating tradition of constitutional rule. Elsewhere, as disputes in the lead-up to the framing of Russia's new 1993 constitution amply revealed, it was not always obvious which of various competing traditions (liberal universalism or national patriotism in Russia's case) the new constitutions should be based upon. But everywhere, legal traditions underpinning individual freedoms and private property had to be either rediscovered or invented anew; the social habits of a lifetime needed to be unlearned. Put another way it was not just sovereignty but subjectivity that had to be remade; not just political rights but social mores and meaning that needed to be recast.

But even before this the rule of law had to be established from out of the ruins of totalitarianism. Democratic procedures had not just to be found but defended against the alternatives, including those imposed from outside. As one constitutional authority put it: "Elections though very important cannot come before elections."[14] *Someone* had to decide where to start. The so-called Round Tables, in which dissidents and governing officials alike took part, were one such effort to respond to the challenge of doing so in a manner that was representative of society at large but fair and sufficiently decisive. But even they could not solve the most basic problem of all, which was having to make a vast number of decisions practically overnight. The key elements of a functioning political system needed putting into place and at lightning speed: banking infrastructure, political chambers, courts and constitutions.

If all this makes it only the more remarkable that, for the most part, the transition from communism was remarkably peaceful, it also explains why a specifically liberal model of democracy was imported into the postcommunist states *after* their revolutions. Transitioning out of communism required not only choosing what sort of new system to adopt, it required each country to rebuild (in some cases to build from scratch) its government infrastructure, to replace the conventions of authoritarianism with those of democracy, and to switch from communist to capitalist economic systems.[15] In light of this it was perhaps inevitable that the easiest (and probably most effective) way for Eastern Europe's new leaders to do both of these things was by borrowing Western institutions which it seemed they might need.

Only at this point did the East begin to look to the West for guidance. And the result was as great a boon to the new neoliberal consensus in the West as it was to democracy in the East. One of the clearest examples of this was the newly enshrined principle of central bank independence, for example, which had only quite recently become a part of liberal democratic "good practice" in the West, as we have seen, but which was now consolidated as a political norm by the sheer scale on which it was rolled out across the newly independent states: in Croatia in 1990, then Slovenia, Russia, Poland, and Hungary in 1991, and Slovakia and the Czech Republic when the two nations split in 1993.[16] In all of this, it was *liberal* values that were routinely established as the truly fundamental element needing to be "transferred" to the East, while their associated democratic forms and procedures were reduced to a more "instrumental significance."[17] "Democracy has captured the spirit of our times," said the newly elected President George H. W. Bush, as he spoke before the Polish National Assembly in July 1989: "[It is] the destiny of man."[18] But it was a very particular form of democracy that was now to be the fate of Eastern and central Europe, and in a different way too, of the West itself.

To understand the full implications of this, however, we need to look to what was happening in Germany. The German question was absolutely central to the wider post–Cold War settlement that was gradually being staked out. It was Germany, after all, that brought the four occupying powers—the Americans, the Soviets, the British, and the French, who since 1947 had each provided the forces on the ground to lock in the Cold War settlement—immediately back to the table to decide on the post–Cold War future. At the start of the Cold War, the division of Germany had been the foundation stone of the entire wider European settlement: a Cold Peace of entrenched lines and zones of influence, the points of all this force sharpened at the one place they all touched, in Berlin. Now, at the end of the century, democracy would have to make its way within this still bristling array of military materiel and vested interests.

Remaking the West

As 1989 turned into 1990 events began to take on a momentum of their own across Eastern Europe, and indeed into Russia and the central Asian states too. But the question that was soon at the forefront of everyone's mind was what to do about Germany. The German chancellor himself had raised the stakes here, to some extent unwittingly, when making his first public pronouncement after hearing that the East Germans were beginning to cross over the Berlin Wall. Rushing back from an official visit he was making to Poland, and speaking before an understandably restless West Berlin crowd, he had declared: "We are and will remain one nation, and we belong together!" It was a noble and for Kohl a heartfelt sentiment. But no Western leader had spoken like this for decades: even Willy Brandt had been more circumspect. The implications of what he was saying were staggering.

The idea that communism might be on the way out in East Germany, and that the GDR might be able to transition toward a more democratic society, was one thing. But the mere mention of the idea of a *unified* Germany sparked off growing unease in the capitals of the West. The French president, François Mitterrand, with whom Kohl had developed a close relationship over previous years, could be heard carping in private about Kohl's insistent references to "the unity of the German people" rather than "reunification." "What does that mean, 'unity of the German people'?" he asked Jacques Attali, his long-suffering adviser. "Does Kohl include in that the Germans in Polish Silesia or in the Czech Sudetenland?" Britain's Margaret Thatcher, her decade-long reign beginning to slip away, could be heard letting off steam rather more publicly. When the two had a moment's private conversation at the edges of a summit in Strasbourg in December, Thatcher pulled out of her handbag a map of Germany's pre-war borders, saying to Mitterrand: "They'll take all that and Czechoslovakia." She and Mitterrand alike were terrified that they might be caught in the role of passive bystanders to yet another German renaissance.[19] But both were as much in the dark as to what was actually happening as anyone else.

What *was* clear, come the end of the year, as the two superpowers belatedly entered the fray, was that the former communist states were undergoing a transition and that a new European order was in the making; that powers were being redistributed and spheres of influence rearranged, all things that had been held in place at terrible cost during the decades before. By the time the still freshly elected President Bush and Mikhail Gorbachev had their first meeting to discuss the situation in Europe from their ships moored off stormy seas in Malta, events in Europe were already shaping into the greatest transformation in international affairs for half a century. To the Americans and the Soviets alike this was a matter for concern, as much as it was an opportunity. For at this point (and by the time 1989 was out only Hungary, Poland, Romania, and East Germany had overthrown their former leaders) nobody really new what the newly independent states were moving toward.

This was one reason why the United States wanted to slow down the pace of events. After taking office in January 1989, Bush had famously opted for a "pause" in what was easily the biggest story of international affairs: the American–Soviet negotiations over missile reductions. He had met Gorbachev for the first time the previous December during Gorbachev's trip to the UN, when Reagan took them both out with him to see Governors Island in New York. But Bush did not yet have the rapport that Reagan had eventually built up with the Soviet leader (culminating when the two sat down to sign the 1987 treaty on Intermediate-Range Nuclear Forces: the first ever actual *reduction* in their nuclear armories). Bush was certainly far more circumspect than Reagan had been as to what Gorbachev actually meant by all his talk of a new world order, and the escalation of events in Eastern Europe only made him more cautious.

As many saw it, this was madness. Momentum on the ground was everything to somebody like Adam Michnik, who saw how far the dissenters in his own country of Poland had come, but who saw too that it might yet all be taken away from them. Michnik told the Americans that they were "sleepwalking through history." But Bush was cautious by nature, and following some urgent, steeple-fingered advice from Richard Nixon, loitering in the shadows as ever, Bush was even more cautious than usual in Malta: "I do not propose that we negotiate here," he said in his opening statement from the USS *Belknap*.[20] Perhaps too he was mindful that the fates of the United States and the USSR, locked as they had been into a clasp of mutual containment for four decades, were hardly separable from one another.

The Americans and the Soviets were not, however, the only players at the table seeking to influence what would have to be an entirely new political settlement for Europe, the first in more than four decades. In that sense, some of the comparisons between Malta and the Yalta conference of 1945 were warranted. In fact, very little of substance actually came out of the meeting, which went down in history rather more prosaically dubbed as the "seasick summit." But in some ways that was precisely its achievement. For what the British writer Timothy Garton Ash once observed for Britain—"[t]ake away the Berlin Wall and you are left with the English Channel"—was a problem that now held true for all of Europe's major powers.[21] The fall of the communist regime in East Germany brought red lines back into play everywhere, and not acting on those was as much of a breakthrough as any plan of action.

At the close of the Malta conference Bush flew immediately on to Brussels, to speak personally with Kohl, and to gain a better sense of how the political landscape in Germany looked. He was also buying himself a little time while he tried desperately to think what the American response should be. For now that would continue to be simply to trust in Kohl: the two politicians shared a similar instinctive approach to policymaking. But in the weeks immediately after the fall of the Berlin Wall the other members of the "four powers," each of whom still held considerable numbers of troops on the ground, sought to lay out a plan for what to do about the German question, as it was—once again—now being called.

The most critical question, of course, was exactly *how* were Eastern and Western Europe to be integrated and, more importantly, on whose terms? As the man most responsible for the whole situation, if somewhat unintentionally, Gorbachev was the first to put forward a concrete plan. After briefly floating the idea of resurrecting the old quadripartite powers agreement, under which Germany had been governed prior to the establishment of the FRG and GDR in 1949 (this was rejected out of hand by the other powers) Gorbachev turned to making the case for a more wholesale rebuilding, not just of the two Germanies but of East–West relations in general.

It was clear that he had done more than just take with good humor the proddings of some of his own politburo when they referred jokingly to his "Sinatra" doctrine on Eastern Europe: a reference to the fact that whatever Moscow said, they were now going their own way. As early as summer 1989, long before the Wall fell, Gorbachev had been ruminating about what he called a "Common European Home." By this he meant "a commonwealth of sovereign and economically interdependent nations" that would span East and West alike. If it was, on one level, merely "an attempt to preserve a semblance of Moscow's influence" it was actually not all that far from what most Europeans were hoping for: save for one thing.[22] There was not now, nor would there ever be, a place for Russia within the European home. Did Gorbachev seriously think that the likes of Hungary and Poland, having finally escaped the clutches of the Soviet empire, would bind themselves back to Moscow's designs? At times he seemed to.

The former satellite states begged to differ. And so for all that Gorbachev could count on a sympathetic ear from the likes of Felipe González and even François Mitterrand, his vision for Europe never made it further west than Berlin. A loosely federated commonwealth of the sort he was envisaging did eventually come into force, in the shape of the Commonwealth of Independent States (CIS). But it did so at the behest of Gorbachev's arch-rival Boris Yeltsin, and it would be the stick by means of which power was finally wrested from him.

It was not until the very end of the year that the Americans began to stake out their position. In some ways, the American strategy consisted in *not* setting out any grand vision. By standing back they thought they could force Gorbachev to stand down, "making it clear to people on the ground in Eastern Europe that change must come at their initiative."[23] The Americans did not want to hold up change but they did not want to provoke a counterreaction either. The lessons of that other 1989, in Tiananmen Square, where the tanks had rolled and protesters had been viciously struck down by the Chinese authorities, hung over events in Eastern Europe like a pall. In fact the regime in China was at least as concerned by events in Eastern Europe as it was by the protesters in Beijing. It had been perturbed by the enthusiasm with which Gorbachev had been greeted on a recent visit. But as the months wore on and—thanks to Gorbachev's staying hand—the likelihood of a blood-bath in Europe receded, it became increasingly clear in Washington that the uprisings should be welcomed with a rather more positive response after all.

The central issue for the Americans, however, was the substantial nuclear arsenal they had to take care of in West Germany (now the country with the highest concentration of missiles per square meter anywhere in the world). So whatever solution the Americans came up with, it had to be built around this first and foremost. As James Baker wrote in his preparatory notes for a meeting with Hans-Dietrich Genscher, the German foreign minister, and Gerhard Stoltenberg, the defense minister: "We need those wpn's [weapons] to defend our own troops."[24] With hindsight this was a remarkably narrow construal of the problem. Having spent the past four decades strategizing over Europe as a potential theater for conflict, the Americans now revealed themselves to have almost no means to deal with a European peace. The matter of nuclear and conventional force parity aside, they spoke no more than tentatively of a "Euro-Atlantic architecture" and a "new Atlanticism."[25]

The prime concern of the Americans, in short, was risk-management. And at times of risk one turns to security institutions. So it was that both NATO and the CSCE featured prominently in the American proposal that emerged: not a Common European home but a "new European architecture" (the references to Atlanticism having been dropped). If the phrase lacked something of the "heroic modernism" of Gorbachev's vision, it was also nothing if not misleading. The United States was a key part of both organizations and wished very much to keep the *old* European architecture intact.[26] What it wanted, more specifically, was Germany in NATO and a revived NATO in Europe. But that was something, as Bush knew only too well, that needed to be pursued through Kohl himself. In the meantime, by keeping Soviet troops *in* Europe, the Americans hoped to prevent the Soviets from withdrawing them to use elsewhere or simply to pocket the resource windfall.[27] They were not aware perhaps of quite how tied Gorbachev's hands already were, caught as he was between a relentless reform process abroad and a reluctant politburo at home.

Kohl, for his part, was grateful for American support. But not all of Europe's leaders felt the same. Mitterrand held out the hope that the fall of communism would allow Europeans to be rid of the superpower meddling in their affairs. At a tense meeting of the G7 in Bonn in May 1985, the French president had previously launched into a rare public tirade against the costly American Star Wars program, and the reluctant but for now loyal support of the other nations that had been garnered for it. *Pas moi* ("Not me"), he said to each point as he read it out to his astonished peers. *Pas moi.* It was followed, reports Mitterrand's biographer, by a "shocked silence."[28] In the matter of Cold War realpolitik, however, France was even more vital to America in 1989 than it was four years earlier. It was to Paris, after all, that Gorbachev made his first visit to the West in October 1985 and it was to Mitterrand that Gorbachev had said, privately, that what the USSR needed was, "in a word . . . democracy."[29]

The Bush administration was careful to show greater respect toward French sensitivities than Reagan ever did, despite Mitterrand's occasional diplomatic heavy-handedness. When, on New Year's Eve 1989, Mitterrand declared: "Europe will no longer be what we have known for half a century. . . . [After having been] dependent on the two superpowers, she will return to her own history and geography, as one returns to one's own home," the Americans were roundly displeased.[30] But Bush largely ignored the implied insult in public and moved quickly, four months later, to let a little warmth back into the Franco-American alliance—this time during a one-on-one meeting with the French president on Key Largo. Bush certainly played up the theme of "tropical hospitality" afterward. In the press conference, while confirming his desire for a "unified" Germany, he downplayed the challenge of the "external aspects" of unification and pointed to the potential for resolving those issues via the new 4+2 talks: the four powers plus the two Germanies. Mitterrand highlighted the need for a "common reflection on how to adapt the alliance to meet the requirements of the new times ahead."[31] It was not exactly the same thing but it kept open the idea that the German question might yet be solved once again.

It was Thatcher who was the most forthright in her opposition to a unified Germany. "The fact is," she had said in a widely reported speech in Bruges the previous September, 1988, "that things are going our way . . . freedom is on the offensive for the first time in my lifetime." At this point she had in her sights the integrationist moves coming from the European Community (her speech was full of barbs aimed at Jacques Delors and the rising power of the European Council in particular). "We have not successfully rolled back the frontiers of the state in Britain, only to see them reimposed at a European level," she said. In Thatcher's view what Europe needed was not more integration but stronger, firmer nation states in dialogue with one another. That did not in any way include a *unified* Germany, however: that was the European prospect she feared most of all. And the dawning realization that the one might well imply the other simply terrified her. When Helmut Kohl observed, "It is better to have a European Germany otherwise you will have a German Europe," her quick-fire response was: "It comes to the same thing."[32]

So it was that Margaret Thatcher found herself in an unlikely alliance with Mikhail Gorbachev as the two leaders most concerned to avoid a reunited Germany. The Soviets of course saw East Germany as more than just their primary satellite, and Gorbachev was not himself personally committed to their remaining separate. But East Germany was still the Soviets' primary point of leverage over an entire continent. And so with or without the Warsaw Pact—whose future now looked distinctly unpromising—Gorbachev hoped to keep the East German connection intact. Thatcher agreed. "Britain and Western Europe are not interested in the unification of Germany," she told him in a private meeting in September 1989. "The words written in the NATO communiqué may sound different, but disregard them. We do not want the unification of Germany. . . . It would . . . undermine the stability of the entire international system." She then added, by way of elaboration, "I can tell you this is also the position of the US President."[33]

Unfortunately for her, not only were events on the ground running in the direction of full reunification, but the US president's position was not what she believed it to be. And yet Thatcher also saw something that many of her contemporaries did not: the unavoidable conflation of the reunification of Germany with the economic and monetary unification of the entire continent. "Mrs. Thatcher was absolutely clear," recounts her biographer Charles Moore, "that if you have a single currency, Germany will become the great power in Europe because it will be built on their model and with their success and they will therefore dictate the terms . . ."[34]

History would prove her diagnosis to be right. But as it was, in the months after the Berlin Wall was first breached, her position at home was steadily weakening: and as Dean Acheson liked to say, 80 percent of foreign policy was "management of your domestic ability to have a policy."[35] In Thatcher's case, the economic boom her chancellor, Nigel Lawson, had orchestrated and which had carried Britain, and her government, out of the 1980s, was rapidly turning to dust. Inflation was back up to 10 percent and interest rates were nearly at 15 percent.[36] Her onetime bastion of support, British business, now saw Europe—especially an enlarged Europe—as a bright spot on the horizon. She was fast becoming stranded. And from this fact issued two fateful consequences. First, recognizing she was stranded, her own party decided the time was right to sail on without her. True, it may have been the Poll Tax that finally did for her popularity, but it was Europe that provided the knife her colleagues now drove in to the hilt. Second, and most important outside of Britain, Thatcher's demise, in conjunction with Gorbachev's isolation, cleared the way for the vision of Europe that did finally win out: that being put together by Helmut Kohl.

Initially, and despite his loose-lipped comment on the night the Wall fell, Kohl had not dared to dream of a reunified Germany. His immediate preference was for a more modest form of confederation—"two states in one nation," as he put it—and he duly set out a ten-point plan for achieving this over a number of years. Even this was felt to be such a potentially explosive idea that Kohl insisted only his closest advisers— excluding even his own foreign minister—draw it up in secret at his private residence. At the end of November, once it was ready, he sprang it as a surprise on a distinctly flabbergasted Bundestag, just as Schmidt had done before him with the EMS. But come the new year, as Kohl began to spend a little more time in Germany (the first few weeks after the autumn were a blur of international summits) he came to what would be an historic realization: that not only was full reunification what was needed, but it needed to be enacted quickly as well.

By the end of January 1990 it was also clear that Gorbachev was now the only remaining hurdle to such a plan. Bush was at least personally convinced of the idea in theory, Thatcher was isolated, and Mitterrand had come round to the notion that it might pay to get on board with Kohl's plans (primarily because of the opportunity it presented to drag out of Kohl as many concessions on other fronts as possible). Gorbachev's concerns focused on NATO more than Germany per se, but of course the two were inextricably linked, as Kohl understood. "The future ar-chitecture of Germany must fit into the future architecture of Europe as a whole," the ten-point plan had put it.[37] So it was that first the Amer-icans flew in: James Baker visiting Moscow in February to affirm, or so Gorbachev believed, that NATO would "not shift one inch eastward." Then Kohl dropped quietly into town, just as Baker left, to obtain Gor-bachev's accession to the idea of German reunification. Thus was the first stage in the cutting out of East Germany from the Soviet sphere of influence completed.

The next stage in Kohl's plan was to secure popular backing for reunification. The easiest way to do this was to make it an explicit part of the upcoming elections—the first in six decades—being held in East Germany. Kohl was not himself on the ballot of course, but his CDU Party along with its policies were. And so the East Germans were treated to a spectacle of a West German chancellor holding stump speeches on their side of the border. Kohl knew that a win for his party in the East would provide him with the level of domestic support he needed to convince his international partners of the correctness of his plans. To keep those international partners happy in the interim, Bush and Kohl agreed to push forward with the new forum—the Two Plus Four group of the USSR, France, Britain, and America (plus the two Germanies)—to discuss the various "external" aspects of reunification. At a meeting of the joint NATO and Warsaw Pact heads in Ottawa on February 10–11, a series of Two Plus Four talks were agreed to. It was largely just for show, though. Throughout it was the one plus one of Kohl and Bush who unilaterally decided what was happening, and who then worked hard to gain acceptance for their decision after the event.

Such was the manner in which the two men decided, at Camp David in late February, that a reunified Germany would, as a single entity, become a part of NATO, the GDR simply being subsumed within the existing agreements that the FRG had taken on in the previous decades. Institutionally speaking, East Germany was simply to be erased. Gorbachev was aghast when he heard, but with events spiraling out of control at home and his own position now weakened, he was amenable to being brought around. To make sure of this the Americans and Kohl promised to reform NATO (it would declare itself henceforth to be a defensive alliance that would "never be the first to use force"), and to provide the USSR with a lot of money (Kohl eventually parted with 12 billion Deutschmarks plus a further 3 billion in interest-free credit).[38]

Such guarantees helped Gorbachev sell to the Kremlin what was clearly a terrible deal for the Soviets. Meanwhile Kohl got on with the practicalities of reunification. The new country would need a single accepted legal system to begin with. In fact, the West German constitution, the Basic Law of 1949, contained a self-determination clause for use in just such a situation of merger between the two nations. It provided for a sovereign and reunited German peoples to decide a new constitution for and among themselves. In the event, the use of that clause was deemed far too risky: events were moving fast and it would take a long time to have it approved and constitutionally reviewed.[39] Fortunately there was another option, Article 23, that provided for a quicker and easier route:

the peoples of the East could also *choose* to put themselves under the jurisdiction of the Basic Law itself.

This was the other reason the East German election was so important to Kohl. But of course it was not the only option being tabled for Germany. Hans Modrow, the new transitional leader of the East German Communist Party (after Honecker and then Krenz had both resigned, unrepentant, in 1989), had assembled his own round table partners, who wanted to find a "third way" constitutional solution for a reunited Germany: one that would avoid the tendency for the constitutional arrangements of the West to lock in the interests of the bourgeoisie and that might promote a form of what New Forum member Klaus Wolfram described as "property pluralism" in Germany: a society where private and public ownership were mutually respected.[40] These were noble ambitions perhaps. But in the rush of the times, they were quite simply surpassed by popular impatience and the embodiment, in Kohl, of a clear and more tested alternative.

To ensure that East Germans availed themselves of this opportunity, Kohl once again reached into his pockets during the election, this time directing the state's largesse toward his own fellow citizens in the East with a one-off offer of monetary union as a stepping-stone—the adoption of the West German mark at an extremely generous 1:1 rate. And to make sure that *this* message was effectively conveyed, he arranged for West Germans to staff the campaign teams of the East German CDU, who he feared were not entirely to be trusted as competent in the arts of competitive elections. The results came in on 18 March. The CDU and Kohl's Alliance for Germany party won 48 percent of the vote: a massive total in multiparty elections. Within two days it was announced that economic and monetary union would take place in the summer. All this being done, in Moscow on September 12, the Two Plus Four agreement was officially signed. NATO's guarantees over Germany came into effect immediately. The following year, after the other administrative aspects of preunification had been carried out on both sides of the old borderline, the two Germanies merged: on October 3, 1991.

In a little less than two years from the fall of the Berlin Wall, the two Germanies had thus been reunited, the whole international security architecture that for four decades had been premised on their separation had been reconceived, and the end result—a single Germany united under NATO, within Europe, and organized according to West Germany's "temporary" Basic Law constitution of 1949—had come into being. None of this had even been imaginable just a few years before. But it wasn't just international security that was at stake here. The reunification of Germany also now provided the final spur to the economic reconstitution of the continent as a whole.

The New Europe

In a speech to the British Royal Institute of Strategic Affairs in July 1989, Giscard d'Estaing, the irrepressible former French president, tried, largely in vain, to draw the attention of a skeptical British audience to what was really afoot within the continent at this moment, with a speech entitled: "The Two Europes: East and West." "[T]he political, economic and strategic facts of Europe are in the throes of change," he declared, but the continent still suffers "from a peculiarity inherited from the Second World War," namely that the two superpowers believed it was *their* business— their "natural right"—to decide them.[41] This was quite wrong. "The Yalta Agreement," he suggested, "must be allowed to dissolve gradually, like aspirin in water." In its place Europe needed to build further on its ongoing integrationist project. "The future of Europe," he said, "is, first and foremost, the business of the Europeans themselves."[42]

Giscard for one recognized that the history of Western Europe's integrationist project would be central to the way Western capitalism would respond to the fall of communism. But even he could not have foreseen quite how, and to what extent, Western Europe's decade-old plans for monetary union would now converge with the plans for political reunification launched by Kohl. The outline of that convergence was already coming into view, however. Just a few months before Giscard spoke, France had become the first country to overcome all barriers to meeting the terms of the EC's new capital liberalization directive. Others soon joined it: Denmark, Belgium, even Italy. Leading out the charge for the Nordics, Sweden too declared that it was now falling into line with the "global trend."[43] Even the newly acceded countries of southern Europe joined in, though in their cases primarily because they were still new to the game and wished to show willing. Only Greece remained behind: a little-noticed sign of a future dispute.

In the tumult of events that year none of this made front-page news: what could the significance of France's dismantling its remaining capital controls possibly be compared to the political drama taking place elsewhere? But as a small step in a larger and silent revolution in European economic policy, the French government's move *was* of historic importance. It was a palpable reminder that the trend toward economic liberalization underway across the Western half of the continent was now picking up speed. More than that, it was about to take over the Eastern nations as well. The "two Europes" were thus no longer those of East and West, but those of free nations versus free markets: of north and south, of cooperation and competition. And what divided this new Europe were the very different political commitments required to build either a union that gave voice to Europe's peoples or one that spoke primarily to their desire for prosperity.

Perhaps Giscard of all people ought to have seen this, since the struggle to resolve this new dualism would place his two favored topics, finance and *La France*, back at the very center of events. But to see quite how, we need to uncover the direct line connecting the failure of Mitterrand's socialist experiment during the first two years of his presidency (1981–3) with the subsequent emergence of a unique partnership between Kohl and Mitterrand and the way in which their transnational cooperation pulled the upheavals in the East and the longer-running turn to liberalization in the West into a singular vision of the future.

Back at the beginning of the 1980s Mitterrand, we have seen, bet large on his Gallic alternative to Thatcherism: his belief that a strongly interventionist state offered a more viable route out of the troubles of the 1970s. The markets had punished him heavily for this. A run on the Banque de France began almost the instant he won the presidency in 1981 and the cost of state borrowing only escalated thereafter. With or without the additional cost of his nationalization and labor reform programs, the economy, much less the value of the franc, simply couldn't sustain the pressure: a situation best captured in the image of the French prime minister, Mauroy, chasing him down the corridors of Versailles crying of the franc's value, "I can't hold it, I can't hold it!"[44]

Almost overnight, French citizens began to feel the effects of austerity, job cuts, and reduced state spending. Amid falling wages and a government-imposed prices freeze (which even the right had never dared impose) Mitterrand was forced to reshuffle his government, largely turning his attention thereafter to international affairs: "no doubt finding it a relief," as one observer put it, "from the gloom at home."[45] But the U-turn was not complete yet. That task fell to an eager generation of influential young socialists: the likes of Jacques Delors (former banker and social minister), Laurent Fabius (the son of a rich Parisian family and a future prime minister), Pascal Lamy and Michel Camdessus (both later heads of the IMF).[46] All were convinced that the future of the French left lay in reinventing itself outside the terms of the alliance that Mitterrand and Rocard had contrived to stitch together in the still communist-influenced 1970s. More specifically, it was to be found by embracing the market.[47] In the hands of this influential grouping, the guiding principle of the French economy now became economic liberalization and the *Franc Fort*: a new and at times quixotic monetary policy that would bring the markets back on board by aiming to track and hold to the value of the seemingly impregnable Deutschmark. Thus Mitterrand's true achievement over the coming decade, if that is what it was, was to combine the rhetorical tropes of Gaullism with the more practical language *du jour* of tight money, liberal markets, and international integration.

But how to implement this vision? It was here that the recent dramatic turn in French domestic political developments began to intersect with the resurgence of interest in monetary integration at the European level (with its new market-based imagination of what European cooperation ought to consist of). The point of intersection was perhaps best expressed in the figure of Jacques Delors, particularly during his two terms as European Commission president from 1985 to 1992. Delors moved to the European Commission after having helped to oversee Mitterrand's great U-turn. In the anglophone world Delors is routinely mistaken—perhaps because of Thatcher's constant upbraiding of him—as one of the hardcore European federalists. That is false. The real Euro-federalists were those Euro MPs, led by Altiero Spinelli, who after the first European elections in 1979, grouped themselves into the so-called Crocodile Club, (named for the restaurant in Strasbourg, Au Crocodile, in which they met). While they explored a route to European federalism, Delors not only kept himself outside this majority grouping, he actually formed his own parallel group, the Amigo Club, to encourage more *intergovernmental* exchanges between his social democratic confreres.[48]

It was on the back of his prior experience in France, however, that the chief architect of *le tournant* then made two signature contributions to the post–Cold War European landscape. First, and from his position as EC president, Delors oversaw the creation of a much more proactive European Council than had hitherto existed or that Giscard had even envisaged. Delors then used the Council to drive forward the idea of monetary union as the central pillar around which the European project could be reinvigorated—the long-touted *relance*—in which the French, by playing a central role, could regain the upper hand (and be done once and for all with any accusations as to their "second tier" status). Up until the 1970s the European Council had performed a "minimum but crucial" role within the European Community, ensuring the objective of European cooperation remained on national parliaments' agendas.[49] But it never did very much more than that. Under Delors all this changed, and the Council now became a much more powerful institution within the labyrinthine European bureaucracy. For the first time in its history, Europe was being driven forward from Brussels, and not by the diplomacy of national politicians. The visions of Werner and Davignon were discarded along the way.

Long before the Cold War was over, then, the European Council was expanding its powerbase and focusing its attention on the *economic* aspects of "Europeanization." To pursue this agenda, it drew together two previously separate spheres of economic policymaking. The first encompassed the specialized committees of the European Community itself: the Monetary Committee, the Committee of Governors, the EPC, and so on, whose members—such as Karl Otto Pohl, the former Secretary of State in the German Finance Ministry (1972–7) and Jacques de Larosière, the former head of the IMF and later of the European Bank for Reconstruction and Development—were both "a network already built and a group of network builders," as one historian of European integration has put it.[50] They were also frequently current or formal central bankers, including the influential Otmar Emminger ("the Bundesbank's foreign minister," as he was known in Germany).[51] For two decades this elite group of economic policymakers made full use of the revolving doors between European institutions and national financial ministries, to dominate the very summit of European monetary politics. In so doing they would become some of the central figures in the creation of a new Europe that was itself built upon the lines of a "common monetary language."[52]

But this new monetary-oriented European consensus did not center upon a group of experts alone; it revolved secondly, and perhaps most significantly, around the authority and prestige of the principal monetary institution on the continent: the German Bundesbank. This was highly significant: the Bundesbank was an independent, nonparliamentary body with a specifically monetary mandate, a mandate made all the more relevant in the context of the ongoing inflationary crises of the 1980s, which the Bundesbank, more than any other European institution, had shown itself capable of defeating. It was not just the German government but increasingly the French and other European governments that took their economic cues from the Bundesbank. A fateful conjuncture was thus established, and not only between France and Germany, but between the new Germany and the new Europe too. Here was the true crux of the immediate post–Cold War moment.

This conjuncture was mirrored in the developing personal relationship between the two leaders, Helmut Kohl and François Mitterrand. A connection between them had first been established when Kohl, two days after his own election in 1982, had visited the French leader to stress how important the Franco-German relationship was to his administration. Mitterrand reciprocated the following year, when contrary to his own earlier position, he offered his support for Kohl on the thorny issue of the Euromissiles. Their connection soon became the other "special relationship" of the 1980s: a continental alter ego to the path being mapped out by Thatcher and Reagan.

Unlike Thatcher and Reagan, who tended to be thought of as a pair more than they actually worked as one, Mitterrand and Kohl were a genuine political double act. With Kohl at times quite consciously playing Adenauer to Mitterrand's de Gaulle, it was a partnership ultimately enshrined in the image of the two men holding hands at the memorial service for the victims of Verdun in 1984. It may well have helped, too, that both men were united in their opposition to Thatcher. Certainly there was never much love lost between Mitterrand and the British prime minister. She always spelled Mitterrand wrong (with one "r") while, as he once put it, "*Le pb* [*probléme*], *c'est le GB.*"[53] Likewise Thatcher and Kohl's relationship cooled over her demands for a rebate on Britain's payments to Europe and her instinctive tendency to hold Germany responsible for both that and the rest of the continent's ills.

It was nothing if not ironic, then, that Mitterrand and Kohl's cooperation ultimately brought them closer to one part of Thatcher's political vision (the primacy of free markets) by pursuing more vigorously than anyone else in the 1980s the part she disliked most (namely European integration). This became apparent at the critical European Council summit in Fontainebleau in the summer of 1984. Widely framed as the beginning of a "new start" for Europe, this was also the start—toward "ever closer union"—that Thatcher was adamant she did not wish to be part of. It was the start, too, of a critical tension that would remain unresolved right up to the painful Brexit negotiations thirty years later.

All too aware of what was at stake, the British arrived with an alternative document to the Spinelli Treaty on a partially federal European Union (the outcome of all those late-night dinners at Au Crocodile) that delegates were supposed to be discussing. The British version, called

Europe: The Future, pointedly claimed that the realization of the Treaty of Rome was to be found in the completion of the common market, *and nothing else*.[54] And yet the harder Britain sought to resist moves to European union, the more it also pushed Delors's own preferred option for a single market up the agenda. Bit by bit earlier ambitions for a politically federalized Europe were dropped in favor of a narrower focus on the monetary domain. In short, as the political misgivings of national leaders played out—leaders who nonetheless recognized that in times of change some greater cooperation was needed—a push toward the market set in.

With the "British problem," as Kohl had also taken to calling it, out of the way, a path was cleared for a new stage in Europe's history in the mid 1980s.[55] The destination of the European journey now a little more clearly specified, it was time for some housekeeping. Spain and Portugal were finally admitted, the budget was increased, and the road to the single market and ultimately Maastricht and the euro was embarked upon.[56] The "hour of truth" for Europe had indeed "struck," as Kohl put it a couple of years later, declaring, in a veiled insult to Thatcher, that he "could not accept that Europe should degenerate into an elevated free trade zone." It needed to be much *more* than that. The Iron Lady's reaction to that comment was positively "Krakatoan," as her press secretary Bernard Ingham described it, after experiencing the eruption first hand. Kohl's was the sort of behavior, she observed in private, "that would get you thrown out of any London club."[57]

All clubs have their rules, of course, and Thatcher was only too aware that what Mitterrand and Kohl were actually doing was increasing the demands being put upon the European Community's members. But perhaps even they did not fully grasp how far-reaching those changes would be. The Single European Act (SEA) of 1986 was the starting point, but of itself did not propose so very much more than the original Treaty of Rome: the difference was it set a timeline for removing the barriers to trade and capital movements, and, with the help of the Franco-German commitment, it was provided with sufficient political will to see it through (including beefing up the power of the European Parliament).

Most critical of all for the SEA was the support of Mitterrand and Kohl. Mitterrand, his socialist experiment now firmly behind him, wanted to tie French monetary policy to Germany's, the better to secure greater independence from the dollar. Kohl, for his part, was all too aware that the best hope for Germany to play a leading role on the international stage was in monetary policy, and by tying Germany closer to Europe he hoped to be able also to oversee a greater liberalization of the German economy (since at the first sign of grumbling from state sectors he could simply point to the EC as the culprit).[58] But the SEA would imply more than just this. It required a change in the nature and function of European states themselves. Henceforth Europe would not be comprised simply of a group of nations seeking to harmonize standards so as to enhance what markets *could* do: it would become its own form of transnationalism that took decisions on what states were *permitted* to do.[59]

This had pros as well as cons. The lifting of capital controls, for example—which the French had committed to just as Eastern Europeans began taking to the streets in 1989—certainly helped to free up the movement of capital across what were now more porous European borders. But it also meant that nations confronted a less stable tax base and so had less control over their own fiscal policy. Individuals and especially firms could move elsewhere. Increasingly, they could organize to pay their taxes elsewhere too. And the only possible counter to this was for governments to lower taxes in a bid to encourage them to stay. That, in turn, meant less money for social policy and public spending at a time when the welfare state—as we have seen—was already being squeezed dry. It became harder for national governments to support policies that were not directly conducive to enhancing profits. Redistribution and equity: these were two ends that increasingly lacked a viable means for their achievement.

Secondly, by legally binding themselves to the deregulation of the financial sector, the power of monied interests to pick and choose the national policies they supported was vastly enhanced at the expense of citizens who could not. This may well have been an "unintended" consequence of the move to monetary union, as one economic historian has put it, but it was significant nonetheless.[60] States now gave up a large measure of their control over the management of industrial and economic policy—the use of directed credit, for example—in exchange for seats at a more powerful table. In signing on to the SEA and following through with Maastricht, European governments ensured that a great many of the planner's traditional levers were "eliminated" in a single stroke.[61] Taxes and planning: these had once been two critical pillars of postwar Western democracy.

At the same time, other levers and institutions became that much more important: particularly Europe's increasingly independent central banks. It was here that the Bundesbank would play a central role. With its reputation for fiscal discipline and its constitutionally mandated commitment to keeping inflation under control, the Bundesbank proved to be a useful tool in helping to smooth the alignment between different European economies and in securing a wider market confidence in the whole project. In exchange for assuming this leading position the Bundesbank was obliged to step in when other currencies slipped. The German heart of European monetarism thus coincided with the French-led revival of the European Council under Delors. And with deflationary politics back in vogue in France after 1983, thanks to Mitterrand's survival instincts, the path toward European Monetary Union (EMU) now really opened up. "The break of 1983 was fundamental," recalled Delors sometime later.[62] It was the beginning of the long march into a European future quite different from the one first envisaged by the Treaty of Rome.

All this was hugely significant. No less than the decline of state communisms, the forging of modern, liberal market Europe was directly a part of the counterresponse to the crisis of the 1970s. Restarting the integration process was to be the European solution to recovering the elusive economic growth of the Golden Age. A radical new direction for the continent, it was wrought with the tools of a growing institutional bureaucracy and modeled upon the principles of what was believed to be the appropriate economic base for modern *stable*, as well as productive, societies. To its critics this new Europe was little more than "a neoliberal project masquerading as an attempt to build a continental democracy and construct a European identity."[63] To its supporters, it was an institutional firewall against the "European disease" of the past. Such debates were still open in the mid to late 1980s. But the fall of communism at the end of the decade helped to decide the matter in favor of market liberalization, and at that point the two histories—the liberalization of Europe in the West and the democratization of Europe in the East—would merge.

In 1988, at a meeting in Evian, where the water flows underground, Kohl and Mitterrand finalized the deal. Kohl would give his approval for the Commission to start looking into EMU, and Mitterrand, in return, would personally guarantee French acceptance of capital liberalization: hence the dismantling of French capital controls. What is perhaps most remarkable about the entire story is how Kohl managed to keep the whole deal on track during the upheavals in his own country in the year to follow. But of course, as we have seen, it was by then overwhelmingly in his interest to do so. And as Germany reunited, Mitterrand grew only more and more grateful for Kohl's efforts, since by tying Germany, and the Deutschmark in particular, into a wider European infrastructure, and ultimately by replacing the Deutschmark with a single European currency, there could be at least some measure of French control over their neighbor's economic power. As Jacques de Larosière, then governor of the Banque de France, put it in 1990: "Today I am the governor of a central bank who has decided, along with his nation, to follow fully the German monetary policy without voting on it. At least, as part of a European central bank, I'll have a vote."[64] Mitterrand the socialist had just pulled off one of the most remarkable acts of liberalization of modern times.

The Last Yards

A certain amount of geopolitical calculation was in play here. Kohl knew, like Adenauer before him, that the best way to secure Germany's future was to bind it firmly to the heart of Europe. For the powerful Bundesbank, however, the idea of European monetary integration was even less palatable than that of German monetary integration. And so it put forward a number of demands—"unconditional and nonnegotiable"—that would ensure any future European currency—if it did get off the ground—would adhere to the Bundesbank's own ground rules. These included a demand for a new European central bank that would be at least as independent as the Bundesbank itself, a monetary regime that was focused on capital liberalization as much as trade, and a gradualist, means-tested approach to membership. In short: a disciplined and a monetarist approach to European union.

And what the Bundesbank asked for, as the preliminary papers circulated in the lead-up to the Maastricht treaty reveal, the Bundesbank largely got. Monetary union (EMU) would in due course become a part of the original Treaty of Rome and the EU would take on both foreign and home affairs pillars to accompany it. The result was "a giant step toward a more united Europe," according to Max Kohnstamm, the aging Dutch diplomat and first-ever secretary of the old Coal and Steel Community.[65] In the process, part of the policy machinery binding capitalism and democracy together adjusted once more. To regain power lost at the national level, governments and central banks would cast their lot in with each other at the emergent supranational level. Even so, what they lost and gained were not quite the same thing. A greater control over monetary policy would be obtained, but the ability to pursue domestic social policies, or to make unemployment rather than inflation the focus of that policy, for example, was relinquished.

All of this was a stunning historical irony, of course. Europe's march toward supranational institutions had originally been conceived as a way of constitutionally "locking in" Western Europe's postwar democratic arrangements; it was about ensuring there would never again be any backsliding to authoritarianism. But the whole project had been re-imagined in the 1980s as central to the pursuit of national prosperity more generally. And now, at the start of the 1990s, it was monetarism—not democracy—that was locked in and presented as the "great historic opportunity of Europe," as Richard von Weizsäcker, the president of the Federal German Republic, put it when he addressed the Bundestag in May 1990.

But what was the opportunity here, exactly? As Eastern Europeans marched for political freedoms, the new European vision looked forward to an enhancement of the freedom of capital. States were repositioned as the protectors of a capitalist economy, not the other way round, and liberalization was cemented into the new institutional architecture that emerged. The old Europe's "politics of productivity" model—its commitment to popular welfare based on melding planning and consumerism together institutionally—had shown itself, in the 1970s, to have passed its sell-by date.[66] Now, a decade and a half later, it was officially consigned to the scrapheap. In the coming years government deficits would be brought down across the expanded EU-15 countries, spending would be brought into line, public sectors would be pared back and taxes, when they were raised, would be raised in the name of fiscal discipline.[67] Thus was the New Europe born, not on the ashes of communism, but upon the funeral pyre of the old social Europe in the West, and with the fuel of the postcommunist transitions lighting up its way.

The rebuilding of Europe after the fall was thus very much its own process of reconstituting society in the name of a particular brand of market-oriented liberal thinking, and one that drew upon the ongoing history of *national* political struggle in the West every bit as much as it drew on the overt politics of upheaval in the East.[68] The French left embraced this new Europe as a substitute for socialism; the Germans embraced it as a means of reunification; and the British themselves ultimately accepted it because it offered the best way to promote a market model of Europe in which its own financial services, not to mention their offshore positions, would be an asset more than a liability.

In that sense it was a case of *plus ça change*. Europe remained a bundle of compromises, in which everyone got a little of what they wanted in exchange for giving up something else they hoped they could do without. What differed was what lay beneath: the fact that the underlying norm now pointed in the direction of a market-based vision of Europe— that and the far from insignificant fact that there was no longer any communist "other" holding European nations to a redistributive social model. And yet the final stone to be laid in the construction of the New European home was, ironically, about to be provided by the final act in the fall of the house of Lenin. For it was not just the power of the politburos that was lost in the collapse of communism. On the contrary, a range of reformist ideas surfaced briefly into the light of the postcommunist moment, before they too were lost to the belief that there was no alternative to fiscal discipline, liberal markets, and minimalist social government. Nowhere was this clearer than at the very heart of the old eastern empire itself.

Eastern Exits

For his part, Mikhail Gorbachev never meant to do away with the Soviet Union. It was true that from the moment he replaced his predecessor, Konstantin Chernenko, as general secretary in 1985, he had set about making changes. But this was because he wanted it to be better than it was: to practice what it preached: "Today, we turn to the October revolution that shook the world," he told the public on December 2, 1987, "for spiritual support and instructive lessons."[69] Given the way in which state socialism worked, it was precisely this that would make him such a destructive force within it. In the words of one commentator, he was "like a modern Pandora, unleashing forces he could not control."[70] History may turn out to be kinder in judgment.

Gorbachev's commitment to the principles of Leninism was never in any doubt. In that sense he was less of a radical choice for general secretary than some at first suspected. Yet the fact that his inspirations as a politician included, as we have seen, the likes of the Italian communist Enrico Berlinguer and the Spanish socialist Felipe González, indicating that he was Europeanist by nature and intellectually attracted to their southern, reform-minded communism, was unusual. So too was the fact that, by 1987, works by "nonauthors"—be it Aleksandr Bek's *The New Appointment*, Anna Akhmatova's *Requiem*, or Anatoly Rybakov's *Children of the Arbat*—were suddenly there to be read once again. Gorbachev was a man who did what he said. Once banned films, like the anti-Stalinist allegory *Pokayanie* (Repentance), were released for mass viewing.[71] Long before it had even started, a lecture to be given on Stalinism in March 1987 had "the corridors of the Historical-Archive Institute . . . overflowing and half of Nikol'skaya street . . . blocked by students from Moscow higher education establishments."[72] Such things were unthinkable in the years before Gorbachev.

By 1990, with events having taken on a life of their own in Eastern Europe, the challenge for Gorbachev was no longer with getting his reform process up and running so much as controlling where it was going: and controlling it at home most of all. In that sense, Gorbachev, like Stalin, was more than happy to sacrifice Eastern Europe to save the sinking ship of empire at home—which in part explains his permissiveness over events in Eastern Europe between 1989 and 1991. The more sanguine among the Soviet leadership, however, already knew by now which way the wind was blowing. As Gorbachev's influential and trusted foreign policy aide Anatoly Chernyaev confided to his diary: "In a word, the total dismantling of socialism as a world phenomenon has been proceeding . . . Perhaps it is inevitable and good . . . For this is a reunification of mankind on the basis of common sense."[73]

Such reformism did not go unchallenged. Gorbachev may have cared little about aging hard-liners like East Germany's Honecker or seatwarmers like Czechoslovakia's newly installed Miloš Jakeš, as they carped and cajoled from the sidelines about his reforms.[74] But the Communist Party of the Soviet Union itself—"this colossus of conservatism . . . this dirty, mean dog," as Gorbachev himself once put it—posed a more serious problem, above all because he could never quite bring himself to abandon it.[75] This may have been why he survived in power for as long as he did: the fact that his own inconsistencies—his constant tacking between radicalism and conservatism, revolution and reform—kept his enemies perpetually wrong-footed.[76] *Perestroika* would end up producing radical reform, but did not begin intending that. *Glasnost* would end up paving the way for freedom of speech, but it did not set out to do so.[77]

Gorbachev's most persistent battle was with the state of the Soviet economy: above all, the growing debt that was undermining both communist nations and their much-hyped fraternal relations with one another. By the end of the decade these economic difficulties had reduced to a simpler choice: either the communist economies reform themselves in the way that capitalist economies had in the 1970s (this relied on rapidly cultivating belief in foreign investment *and* internal organizational capacity), or they acknowledge that the rot had set in so deeply that the only option was to start from scratch (in a sort of economic Versailles). What the communist nations got in the end was a variant on the latter with the justificatory armature of the former, as Gorbachev committed himself to an endless series of tweaks that in turn required the inflationary rhetoric of perestroika to justify them.

But what lay behind this and what ultimately drove it forward was Gorbachev's own increasing conversion to nothing other than a distinctly Western vision of social democracy. We are used to the story that social democracy withered in Western Europe once the shadow of communism had passed. This story is the invention of the left as much as the right. But on reflection the final battle for social democracy may in fact turn out to have been in Russia, during the dying days of the Soviet empire. For it was there that Gorbachev's effort to adopt Western-style social democracy as the new political system of the Soviet Union was defeated, and by Western advisers themselves as much as the politburo.

The irony of all this was unmistakable. At the very moment the West was abandoning the principles of social democracy, the leader of the Soviet Union was grasping, half in the dark as ever, for some way to embrace them. Gorbachev's constant gesturing at the "democratization of the life of the Party and society" was often written off as empty rhetoric.[78] It was not. And for all that the development of the Soviet leader's thinking, post-perestroika, tends to be overlooked in many accounts of the end of the Cold War, it is in fact both central to what happened and revealing of what did not happen. For if it is true that, as early as 1987, Gorbachev was "preparing to go far from the socialism we had and have," as the ever-perceptive Chernyaev noted in his diary, it is equally true—as one of his most informed critics notes—that "over a three-year period from 1988 to 1990 Gorbachev ceased to be a communist in any meaningful sense of that term."[79] In 1988 he had embraced the idea of competitive elections; by 1990 he was no longer convinced that a planned economy was anything other than a hoax.

The southern European transitions to democracy in the mid 1970s, and Spain's in particular, are usually cited as confirmation of a new wave of democratization in the West. In fact, their entry into the group of Western democracies was to prove a more troubled, indeed partial, affair over the longer term, as the later crisis of the euro was to reveal. Their far greater impact in the short term, however, was in the East. For they did not so much inspire the Eastern European revolutions against Moscow, as political scientists have long claimed, so much as Eurocommunism in particular, and southern European socialism in general, inspired Moscow to reform its own house: which only then provided the context in which Eastern Europe broke free. As Gorbachev himself wrote: "Cooperation with Spain is especially important for us because this is a country with positive experience of transition to a different stage of development of society. For us what matters is the Spanish experience of constructing democracy and new forms of economic life."[80]

In all of this Gorbachev, even as party head, was not merely making enormous leaps of the imagination—Spain was hardly Russia, let alone the Soviet Union. He was equally treading a perilous path. Conservatives in the politburo threw everything they had at him, and had Gorbachev backed down rather than speed up his reforms in the face of it, a very different story may have ensued. But Gorbachev did more than "pour scorn" on the arrogation of power assumed by the CPSU. He fostered contact internationally with social democrats like Willy Brandt, whom he received in Moscow in May 1985, and Hans-Jochen Vogel, leader of the German Social Democratic Party, whom he met in Germany in 1988. At home he promoted those like Aleksandr Veber, who were supporters of social democracy, within the system.

When Vogel remarked of the theses for reform that Gorbachev was taking to the 19th Party Conference that summer before his visit to the UN, that they had a distinctly "social democratic element," Gorbachev confessed that he had "no objection" to that interpretation. The seasoned US ambassador to Moscow, Jack Matlock, likewise came to the same opinion when he got around to translating those theses into English for Reagan. "Never before," Matlock wrote, "had I seen in an official Communist Party document such an extensive section on protecting the rights of citizens or such principles as the separation of powers, judicial independence, and presumption of a defendant's innocence until proven guilty." What the "theses" described, he added, was "something closer to European social democracy" than anything Soviet Russia had seen before.[81]

It was this steadily more democratic vision, then, that led Gorbachev to his optimistic idea of a "common European home" and to his no less hopeful reliance on Mitterrand to be his European interlocutor (and crutch) in that process. At first this seemed a marvelous choice. With Mitterrand's assistance, Gorbachev secured the framework for a Soviet–EEC trade agreement that came into force in 1990 (not that anyone much noticed). Far more significantly he also put in place a new Soviet Constitutional Court to provide a measure of judicial oversight and a counterweight to the once unchallenged power of the politburo. By the summer of 1991, the Union of Soviet Socialist Republics was now described in the draft party program as a looser federation of soviet states: a "voluntary . . . association." "Freedom" within those states was affirmed in every sense, and Stalin was openly condemned as a "totalitarian," the purveyor of "crimes." A variety of forms of ownership, including private, were allowed for, while "true socialists," as they were known just a few years before, were now branded "communist fundamentalists."[82]

Internationally Gorbachev dreamt even grander dreams. He began speaking of "a single international democratic space" as a prelude to a wider "global perestroika" and "the birth of a new world order"—sentiments that encouraged even a redbaiter like the American Republican Jeane Kirkpatrick to append the word "yet" to her judgment that, "[Gorbachev] has not brought democracy to the Soviet Union."[83] The Eurocommunists could scarcely believe their ears. Nor could the Soviet peoples. And yet, even as the words that some had waited whole lifetimes to hear were finally spoken, nobody much cared any more. The Soviet people were suspicious that it was all just another attempt to leverage international standing; that it had nothing really to do with them. To the extent that Gorbachev failed to convince them, the fall of communism ultimately does not register as an economic or as a military crisis, but as a simple failure of ideas: it was the legitimation crisis that the West had narrowly escaped just over a decade before. Meanwhile, Gorbachev's domestic enemies were by now paying him lip service only, biding their time while silently plotting to remove him.[84]

As 1990 came and went, rumors of a possible coup intensified, prompting Gorbachev to tack back from radicalism to conservatism, as he sought to keep his domestic opponents guessing and some measure of wind in his own political sail. But it backfired badly, losing him the trust and support of some of his closest advisers, not to mention setting the scene for his least admirable days—when he allowed a short-lived but violent crackdown on protesters in the Baltics. Gorbachev, it was clear, was desperate to retain the union. But blinded by this, by now, unrealistic desire, he failed to see that he was clinging to the flotsam of an already sunken ship.

In many ways, Gorbachev's experience here echoed that of Czechoslovakia's Václav Havel—the other political "giant" to have emerged from the rubble of communism's collapse. Havel had been lionized before the fall of the Czech regime, and his election to president in 1989 was widely celebrated around the globe, where his writing and his principled stance as a dissident had made him famous. But few were those Western politicians who had supported his initial ambition to reconstitute democracy itself. Havel wanted in fact to pass quite quickly through the "parliamentary" phase of his country's new democracy to a "post-democratic" form of politics: one based upon a more authentic realization of the human subject than parliamentary parties could provide.[85] Havel was advised to think again. And the more it became clear that the progress the Western powers wanted to see was progress in the opening up of these vast and as yet untapped markets, the more such talk crumbled into irrelevance, along with those who persisted with it. Havel's own career struggled and waned accordingly.

Lessons of the Fall

Just three years separated Gorbachev's United Nations speech in New York, where he had announced the end of the Brezhnev Doctrine, in December 1988, and his own resignation from power, affirmed with the stroke of a pen borrowed from an American journalist because his own pen no longer worked. The events of those months in Europe mattered enormously, both for Europe and for the post–Cold War "peace settlement" as it was experienced more generally around the world. But the fall of communism had also raised as many questions about liberal democracy, in Europe, America and elsewhere, as democracy was assumed to have provided answers to communism's fall. This was masked for the time being, however, by the general tone of triumphalism emanating from the West.

Such triumphalism fulfilled another purpose too. Without it one would have had to question the West's own historical record, and to have examined the structural flaws in its own ideological ramparts. The fall of communism obviated the need for all this, just as it appeared to confirm to observers, and above all the Western public, that democracy had indeed been "won" by standing firm for Western values, and that this thing called democracy was something that could now be "gifted" to others. Political liberalism, which had freed itself of any attempt to frame a positive vision for society when last challenged to do so, in the years of crisis that opened the 1970s, now appeared to have been justified in doing so. As the new liberal democratic settlement was triumphally transported east, the formerly communist countries found themselves subject not only to the reinventions of their own history, but to the recent reinventions of the West as well.

In the heady blur that was communism's demise it was taken for granted that capitalism was ticking along nicely in the West and carrying democracy with it. The tumultuous and decisive years that followed from the crises of the 1970s now slipped into a largely forgotten or at best glossed-over past. Liberal democracy had been just one rival claim among others before. Now it boldly declared itself to be everybody's future and was free to demand new ways of making the world safe for democracy once more. It was this task that brought the United States, belatedly some no doubt felt, to the front and center of the post–Cold War picture. The reunification of Europe had provided one "engine of free capital's spread on the world stage."[86] It now fell to America, and the matter of what it would do with its newfound unilateral status, to provide the other.

PART II

Novus Ordo Seclorum? (1989–)

7

America and "A World Transformed"[1]

"EASTERN EUROPE AND the Soviet Union are now experiencing one of the greatest moments in their history," wrote the economist J. K. Galbraith from his home in America in 1991. "That moment is also ours." The ending of the Cold War left the United States the sole remaining superpower. It was a privilege undreamt of by the likes of Kissinger even just a few years before. But it was also a privilege that now bestowed upon America the need to confront directly the contours of a rapidly changing world order.

For nearly half a century, American policymakers at home and abroad had been obliged to carry out their work in the shadow of a life-and-death struggle with the USSR: the heightening of Cold War tensions under Reagan had merely served to remind people of that. Now new reasons would have to be found to justify and to support the great span of security commitments the United States had entered into across the globe, and new ways of managing the Western allies—who were also now competitors—would need devising. For America, the unexpected fall of its great ideological rival precipitated a moment of national soul-searching, as the initial clarion-calls of the triumphalists died away, to be replaced by the anxieties and introspections of a burgeoning constituency of isolationists.

To begin with, as communism crumbled in the East, the general tenor of optimism in America was such that even the left refrained from spoiling the moment. "For the first time since 1945 it is possible for an American president to speak of constructing a 'new world order,'" wrote the American socialist Bruce Cumings at the start of the decade. "And for the first time since 1919, it is possible that he might succeed." In Cumings's view there were three great mistakes committed at the end of the First World War and between them they had conspired to wreck the subsequent running of the twentieth century. These were the failure of the League of Nations, the arrival of communism in Russia, and the punitive terms of peace dictated to Germany by the Allies. In the fullness of time, he was relieved now to observe, those mistakes had each resolved themselves: "Now the United Nations is reinvigorated; Germany has the 'soft' peace of reunification and the most vibrant economy in Europe; and the Bolsheviks have declared themselves to be a mistake."[2] Things were not quite this neat, of course. But if even the left could see fit to allow a little optimism back into its analysis then perhaps the political certainties of the twentieth century's age of extremes really had begun to change.

For its part, the American right was unabashedly jubilant. "[A]n exhausted Soviet Union," wrote a young and soon to be famous political aide Charles Krauthammer, was "calling off the Cold War." In a phrase that was to resonate over the years to come he declared that "Now was the unipolar moment." Of course, there were more seasoned voices who counseled their younger colleagues against such wishful thinking. George F. Kennan, the man who had, in his famous "long telegram" of 1946, introduced the very idea of "containment" and, indirectly, the phrase "the Cold War" into Western political discourse, once again warned his fellow countrymen to tread cautiously: "[This] is not a fit occasion for pretending that the end of [the Cold War] was a great triumph for anyone."[3]

The choices America now confronted were of far greater significance than the matter of whether to gloat openly or not. Not least, the solutions to the crises of the 1970s, which had carried the Western democracies forward through the 1980s, would soon be tested in an entirely new *international* context. Would they be found wanting? For America in particular, the years immediately after 1989 would bring new perils into the picture, as a unique opportunity to take stock of the state of politics at home was overlooked in favor of the opportunities—for expansion, investment, and the spreading of the virtues of the new international order—that the "unipolar moment" seemed fleetingly to provide abroad. In short, the choices that were taken as the Cold War receded into the past were to have significant repercussions for the ongoing reimagination of democracy in the West. And it fell to a man who famously disliked such choices to make them.

Testing the New Order

George Herbert Walker Bush had never been a people's politician. Unlike Reagan, under whom he had served as vice president for two consecutive terms, Bush was better described as a steady pair of hands. The first vice president to be directly elected to the presidency since Martin van Buren, he was also a politician who had lived through the twentieth century's political crises at first hand. A fighter pilot in Asia during the Second World War, a former special envoy to China, ambassador to the United Nations, and director of the CIA, he was a man of considerable world experience. Yet Bush was also a cautious individual who was, in his way, somewhat detached from the reality of modern America. During the four years he was in office, the decisions he made on behalf of his country—and indeed the globe—were to reflect this unusual mixture.

Bush took office at the start of 1989, a moment that promised no great change in world affairs, since few, at this point, had really been willing to take Gorbachev's pronouncements at face value. Bush thought it the better part of wisdom, therefore, to put in place a "pause" in the often heated Cold War realpolitik of his predecessor. As events in Europe rapidly gathered steam throughout the year, this was widely and routinely mocked. But by the end of the year, with the international order in upheaval, it was Bush who looked to have been vindicated. The US president had by then garnered, both personally and for his administration, the trust of Germany's Helmut Kohl and the respect of France's Mitterrand (something Reagan never managed), accommodating to the American position the two main players in the future rebuilding of Europe.

More importantly still, he had developed a close relationship with his Soviet counterpart, all while keeping the British "special relationship" with "that woman" on track. But Bush received a good deal less credit for all this at home than he did abroad, and his political adversaries had old "wimpy," as they referred to him, marked down for failure from the start. As 1989 drew to a close Bush was therefore looking for ways to leverage American's position—to take the dramatic yet unexpected events of the year forward on his *own* terms. And as so often in American affairs, it was events in America's self-proclaimed backyard of Central America that provided the opening, precipitating the beginnings of a more assertive post–Cold War foreign policy.

The critical moment came in December. With the streets of Berlin still jubilant in the first flush of reunification, Bush found himself flying over the Atlantic en route to his dockside summit with Gorbachev in Malta: the first face-to-face meeting between the two superpower leaders since Bush had taken office. Tensions were running high and he was receiving mixed advice from his advisers as to how to handle the new direction the Soviets seemed to be taking. As *Air Force One* tracked eastward, American intelligence now also began picking up reports that a

Nicaraguan plane carrying Soviet surface-to-air missiles had just crashed in southern El Salvador.

Under Reagan, this first test case of the new post–Cold War political order would have been grounds for a series of tit-for-tat recriminations and veiled threats between the two superpowers. But the Bush administration responded differently. "All I can gather," said James Baker after the two leaders had raised the matter aboard ship in Malta, "is that either the Nicaraguans are lying to the Soviet Union or the Soviet Union is lying to us. We would prefer to believe it is the former." Gorbachev duly backed off and Bush was free to step in. The region was still a political tinderbox, after years of CIA and Soviet meddling had left it stuffed with arms and agendas alike.[4] But Bush knew that, however pressing issues in Europe may be, the Latin American "powder keg" was a situation he could not leave to fester.

The nub of the issue was in fact Panama: a minuscule, yet strategically critical republic whose canal had for much of the previous century pumped the lifeblood of intercontinental trade back and forth between the Atlantic and Pacific oceans. Panama was a former US possession and remained, in 1989, a de facto staging post for the projection of US power across the region. Local strongman Manuel Noriega had been a useful funnel for US support to the Nicaraguan Contras, but gradually spurned his American benefactors. When members of Noriega's Panamanian Defense Forces (PDF) opened fire on a car carrying four US military officers in December, Bush seized the chance to intervene.

On December 20 the largest military action by the United States since Vietnam was green-lighted and an invasion force of 20,000 US Marines, accompanied by helicopter gunships and fighter-bombers, was mobilized for the "liberation" of Panama. The entire country was secured within just five days and Guillermo Endara, the victor in elections held earlier that year which Noriega had ignored, was duly installed (though he was given only a few hours' warning to think about it). Panama thus marked a change from passive to active in the verbalizing of Bush administration foreign policy. More than that, it gave an inkling—at the time only half-grasped by the administration itself—of a new approach to international politics writ large. As the United States then set about providing large sums of money to the opposition party that was lining up against Daniel Ortega's left-wing Sandinista party in Nicaragua, a more liberal-interventionist post–Cold War US foreign policy began to take shape: and Europe had not a thing to do with it.

What *was* central was that recently refined and enlarged notion of freedom. As Bush himself had put it in his inauguration speech at the start of the year: "We know what works: Freedom works. We know what's right: Freedom is right. We know how to secure a more just and prosperous life for man on Earth: through free markets, free speech, free elections, and the exercise of free will unhampered by the state."[5] Central America was just the beginning. For much of 1989 Bush had taken a backseat to events playing out on the world stage. With Panama and Nicaragua successfully addressed, and his relationship to Europe's leaders established, Bush was now keen to clarify the terms of the new and more active role he had glimpsed for America as post–Cold War global policeman. He would not have long to wait for the opportunity to do so.

"A World, Whole and Free"

It was, Bush would later recall, a somewhat rare moment of calm that tense summer of 1990. As the aqua-hulled *Fidelity* bobbed gently off the Maryland coast not six months after his return from Latin America, Bush and his National Security adviser Brent Scowcroft, an old and trusted friend, were enjoying a few hours' respite, happily trolling for fish in the president's beloved cigar boat. Inevitably their discussion soon turned to the matter of Iraq, their onetime ally in the cauldron of Middle Eastern politics.

Pentagon planners had long envisaged Soviet tanks rolling down through Iran. But on August 2, 1990—just half a year after the Panama affair—it was Iraqi leader Saddam Hussein who sent his tanks rolling into oil-rich Kuwait. The timing was not by chance. The invasion of a neighboring country by a Middle Eastern proxy power would have been unthinkable under the geopolitical constraints of the Cold War. Hussein was merely the first to take advantage of the new, and presently undecided, world order. As Margaret Thatcher sought particularly to impress upon her American counterpart shortly before her departure from power, he would not be the last either. Bush was also struck by the sense that the Iraqi invasion could prove to be a critical piece in the new geopolitical puzzle that was emerging, as against some of his advisers, such as Colin Powell, who were suggesting it was all just a storm in a teacup.

In truth Bush could hardly have looked at Iraq in isolation even had he wanted to, since the pace of events following those of the previous year had shown no signs of letting up. In May, as part of the ongoing negotiations over the delicate matter of settling Germany's future, Gorbachev had arrived in Washington to a "splendid" military reception (although, so far as Bush was concerned, what Gorbachev brought with him was no less splendid, since he basically now agreed that "all countries [in Europe] had the right to choose their alliances").[6] Events in Latin America, meanwhile, continued to make themselves felt in the US capital, while new and more troubling signs in some of the post-Soviet successor states arose to pepper the near-constant rounds of East–West diplomacy with problems.

The Philippines had seen an attempted coup the previous December, and when in February yet another corner of the world was thrust into the spotlight—this time Bush received a telephone call informing him that, after twenty-seven years, Nelson Mandela was to be freed in South Africa—it elicited from the president a momentary sense of relief. "Change—the amazing change," he observed in his diary that day. But he was soon back on his guard. "Who's the enemy?" he wrote again, sometime later that same month. "I keep getting asked that. It's apathy; it's the inability to predict accurately; it's dramatic change that can't be foreseen."[7]

Come the start of August, Saddam Hussein had proven Bush right about the dangers of apathy and the capacity for new threats to emerge seemingly from out of nowhere. From August 1990 on, alongside the already burning questions of Europe, the "German question," and of Latin America, was now added the Iraqi invasion of Kuwait and what was soon to become a no less entrenched Middle Eastern question as it confronted the Western powers. Indeed, the moment that Saddam's armored divisions crossed the invisible desert boundary into Kuwait it was impossible that a now singularly powerful United States, not to mention one that imported two thirds of the oil it consumed, would not respond. Bush knew it. Saddam knew it. And the rest of the world knew it as well.

It was the exact nature of that response that was the subject of Bush and Scowcroft's musing that day, as their lines tugged against the rolling swells behind them. What was permissible now that the Cold War was over? What was needed? Who should be involved? Under Reagan, America had supported Iraq, traditionally the Soviets' key ally in the region, in its long and bloody war of attrition against Iran. That war had helped keep the 1979 Iranian Revolution pinned down, much to US liberals' relief. America had also spent $3 billion arming the Mujahideen in Afghanistan, sending them out to fight the Soviets for most of the 1980s. Much of this support was channeled, as it had been in Central and South America, via the CIA. But the long decades of proxy intervention by the Cold War powers had shaped itself into an entirely unforeseen crisis in the Iraqi invasion of Kuwait. And what was needed at *this* moment—Bush and Scowcroft both knew—was a more public response than America's previous largely subversive engagements in the region. They were also acutely aware that such a response was one that the whole world, closely tuned in to international events since the fall of the Berlin Wall, would be watching.

Taken by surprise, Bush's National Security Council had been divided during their first meeting on the morning after the invasion. A frantic rewrite of a long-planned major speech on US defense policy, to be delivered in Aspen, Colorado, later that day—the knees of the president and Scowcroft jammed up against the cockpit of a plane small enough to get them into the mountain retreat—had not been very much clearer. If some detected in it a slight stiffening of the response, they were inclined to put that down to Margaret Thatcher's presence at the same event, and her meeting with Bush privately before the speech. Either way, on Bush's return to Washington the following day the White House was still playing for time. As everybody around the president realized only too well, America now desperately needed to lay out a proactive vision of global power and to start acting on it right away.

The president was the first to admit that he himself was no expert at "the vision thing." But the sniping of more hard-line officials, such as former US ambassador to the United Nations Jeane Kirkpatrick—temperamentally, at least, the Joan Collins of the American political scene—was damaging the president's popularity at home. Kirkpatrick deplored the fact that the administration, presented with the greatest shake-up of America's role in the world for fully half a century, was, as she put it, an administration with a particular aversion to "big think." Bush knew all too well, therefore, that the longer he refused to set out a new American vision for the world, the more the press pack at home would continue baying for his blood.

In fact, the president's thinking about America's role in shaping the international order had begun back in the early postwar period when he was stationed in the Pacific, putting his own life on the line in the name of then President Roosevelt's guiding vision of "Four Freedoms." It had matured, along with his political career, during the half-century of American preponderance since. His natural vision of world order was thus a distinctly paternalistic one, which was also why, for Bush, US foreign policy was always more than just the struggle *against* the communists (he was perennially frustrated that Reagan never seemed to get this): it was about threading and shaping what Churchill had referred to as the "sinews of peace" as well. Halfway through his presidential term it was this pre–Cold War dream that he now sought to conjure into existence as a post–Cold War reality. He would do so by setting out the case for what Bush's Secretary of State James Baker called "the imperative of global leadership": an idea that now morphed, after the conversation that day aboard the *Fidelity*, into the short-lived, yet instructive, idea of the project for a New World Order: an order in which "the great dream of all democracies: a true commonwealth of free nations" could be marshaled into existence.[8]

The obstacles to setting out this new American mission for the world were largely practical in the first instance. It was a vision of world order backed by American force but parlayed through the United Nations, whose status would be resurrected as its intermediary. To speak of America now leading a "partnership of nations"—as Bush would go on to do—implied states willing to follow, however. And that was a less certain proposition in 1990 than it had been for many years.[9] Just who was America to lead, and to where? Thatcher's zero-tolerance approach to minor-country upstarts as she saw them, like Saddam Hussein, was one sticking point. But the real nub of the problem was working out what Gorbachev's actual position was.

The Soviet Union after all was far from a spent force in the summer of 1990: any new vision of a US-orchestrated multilateralism would still need to be run by the Soviet premier first. And for all his positive intimations, it was not clear to the US administration whether it would be Gorbachev the reformer, or Gorbachev the man increasingly hemmed in by politburo hard-liners, who responded. Bush therefore decided he needed to speak to the Soviet leader face-to-face and talk him round before taking his plans any further forward. "The world order I see coming out of this," he said to Gorbachev, during a hastily convened meeting in Helsinki intended to secure a warrant from the Soviets, "is US and Soviet cooperation to solve not only this but other problems in the Middle East." He then handed Gorbachev a cartoon depicting the two of them as boxers, "arms raised in victory over the Cold War dragon."[10]

Gorbachev laughed when he saw it. He replied that Iraq was the real challenge, "a problem no less difficult" than that of European and German reunification. "In the Gulf, the United States is in a more difficult position," he added. That got the Americans worried that they were in for a fight over Iraq. But Gorbachev was a step ahead and already playing to his own domestic audience. The same afternoon, when handed the text of a proposal that James Baker and Eduard Shevardnadze, Baker's counterpart in Moscow, had drafted in their parallel meeting to that of the leaders, Gorbachev "read the draft carefully, asked for some minor changes, and, in a move which absolutely astounded me," Bush later recalled, "essentially said 'okay.'" The result was the US and USSR issuing a joint statement about the most dramatic and dangerous global challenge of the day, as if they were the oldest allies in the world: "We must demonstrate beyond any doubt," the statement read, "that aggression cannot and will not pay."[11]

Yet again the Soviet premier had surprised Bush by showing that not only could he keep up with the pace of events on the ground, he could step ahead of them too. But Bush was delighted regardless. No sooner had he returned home from Helsinki than he took what he had understood from Gorbachev to be a wider "great powers" mandate to the American people. Speaking of what he now more publicly referred to as a "new world order . . . struggling to be born" before a joint session of Congress on September 11, 1990, he gave some policy substance to the idea which, for all it fell well short of a "Fourteen Points" or a "Four Freedoms," his administration hoped might at least offer something of an overarching structure. The new world order that was emerging, Bush announced, was one "[f]reer from the threat of terror, stronger in the pursuit of justice, and more secure in the quest for peace. An era in which nations of the world, East and West, North and South, can prosper and live in harmony."[12]

As it happened, of course, such talk of a "new world order" of peace and security could scarcely have been a less apposite description of the decades to come. Bush's new vision of geopolitical order drew upon a curious combination of optimism about the future and nostalgia for the past: optimism in that it assumed America *would* be able to nurture into existence the rule of law and international stability that all this talk of peace and human rights must necessarily rest upon; and nostalgia in that it looked back to the institutions, not to mention the aspirations, of 1945 as the appropriate mechanisms—put on ice during the Cold War—to create it.

The president's mind made up, over the next few months the US Department of Defense worked hard to put together a major operational plan for Iraq that was in line with the new vision and that somehow kept all parties, in what was to be the most complex international coalition yet formed, not only on stage together, but working off the same script. The Israelis needed to be convinced not to take matters into their own hands (lest Saddam be granted the opportunity to split the coalition by turning it into another Arab–Israeli confrontation), the Saudis needed to be convinced to allow US forces to be based on their territory, and the Soviets' repeated efforts to broker a peace agreement with Iraq needed to be delicately rebuffed.

At home, Bush worked hard to sell the coalition build-up (and its escalating costs) to a Democrat-controlled Senate and Congress. Mid-terms were under way and budgets were a sensitive topic (Bush duly sent his highest-ranking administration officials on what they mordantly dubbed a "tin cup" tour of London, Paris, Moscow, and elsewhere). But with images beamed around the world of US hostages under Saddam's lock and key, the president was ultimately not taking no for an answer. "I've had it," he said at a party fundraiser in the final weeks of the mid-term election campaign where the matter of Iraqi hostage-taking had come up. "And what am I going to do about it? Let's just wait and see. Because I have had it with that kind of treatment of Americans."

As autumn turned to winter the normally calm Bush grew only more "angry" and "emotionally involved" in the whole affair. Lauded in the autumn for finally taking a stand, he was now being ridiculed for making it a personal battle of wills. His constant comparing of Saddam to Hitler began drawing satire as much as serious criticism. And on October 30, Congress, alarmed by his talk—and by the fact it was about to go into recess until the end of the year (and as anyone with half an inkling of military affairs knew, any attack would have to happen during the cool months of the year, which meant in effect before March)—wrote Bush a strongly worded "expression of concern." Signed by 81 Democratic members, the document reminded Bush that under the Constitution (and ever since Nixon, they might have added), only Congress has the right to declare war. They therefore asked to be kept informed of events throughout the winter months. Bush might be ready for war, but "The country and Congress," as Speaker of the House Tom Foley informed him, "are not prepared for offensive action."[13]

Bush began to fret that the new world order, upon whose successful realization he had staked his credibility as president, if not the stature of his own country as the presumptive global hegemon, was going to be lost at home, and by just the sort of politicking he had always so disliked. He had drawn a "line in the sand" over Iraq. Now he would have to draw a line before Congress to defend it. Saddam needed to be out by the end of January, he declared point blank. When he announced, just after the midterm elections, that he was giving the green light to a continuing and much larger troop increase, from a quarter to eventually half a million troops, Congress was outraged.

But Bush didn't care, and he was prepared to use up as much of his political capital as he needed to in Washington to get the job done. Everything was about this now. Instead of working to patch relations with Congress, he worked instead on getting trade and aid packages approved for loyal supporters, like Turkey's Turgut Özal, and emergency military packages of tanks and munitions to the Saudis. Meanwhile, Saddam stoked tensions as well, launching a cat-and-mouse game with Western hostages captured in Kuwait, as he shuttled them from one potential target site to another, or flirted with releasing them to buy himself more time—all to create as much of a headache for the White House as possible.

As it was, Bush's grand strategy—his effort to pick up the post–Cold War era by the scruff of the neck and set it down in a manner of America's own choosing—would fail, not because of congressional intransigence, but because of the changed realities of the international political order. For the first time in over half a century, the president was singing a new tune largely without international accompaniment. The Europeans, in particular, were far from sure that they wanted to continue living under the shadow of American power now that the Cold War was over. Thatcher was something of an exception here, and an influential one at that. She wanted direct action in the Gulf without the need to keep going back to the UN for clarification of what was, and was not, permissible. But even Thatcher no more wanted America to lead the world on its own than she wanted Germany to stand reunited and tall in Europe. Her much-cited comment to Bush, after a further UN resolution was secured at the end of August—that this was no time to go "wobbly"—has been routinely misinterpreted in this light.

This European reluctance to respond to the president's call-up had been the nub of Gorbachev's quietly delivered insight all along. Few European leaders shared Thatcher's particular brand of unilateralism, of course. But when it came to the possibility of military action against Iraq, they were even more concerned than she about how the whole thing might "look": above all, how it might play with domestic immigrant populations and in neighboring North Africa, where pro-Iraqi demonstrations were already attracting headlines. The French were particularly hesitant, leading Mitterrand to be accused of "Munich-style appeasement" by the Americans when he sent his close aide Michel Vauzelle to negotiate with Saddam. The hawks in the Bush administration became only that much more enraged when France's defense minister, Jean-Pierre Chevènement, went so far as to declare that the whole lead-up to war was simply an effort by the Americans to stave off recession at home, and to avoid confronting the economic quandary of an otherwise lame-duck trillion-dollar arsenal with no obvious purpose in life now that the Cold War was over.[14]

Needless to say, Chevènement was a socialist. But the rift between Europe and America was no less apparent elsewhere. As the Israeli-American critic Leon Hadar put it: "Washington's support for a united Europe does not seem to have taken into consideration the possibility that a united European voice will not necessarily be a sympathetic one."[15] Bush's deputy assistant secretary of defense, Alberto Coll, was soon fretting that Europe might retreat from its close reliance on America altogether. There were considerable unresolved issues needing to be settled, then, as January 1991 rolled around. But as Bush's deadline for Iraq to relinquish Kuwait approached, as Iraq continued to refuse to comply with the terms of the UN sanctions regime, and as the number of coalition troops stationed in Saudi Arabia and in warships off the Gulf rose above 500,000, it was apparent that these differences would, for now, need to be set aside.

Storm over Iraq

The deadline for Saddam passed at midnight on January 15, and Operation Desert Storm was launched in the early hours of the 17th. Bush was in scant danger of being seen to go wobbly, as Thatcher had feared. The assault was, in the language of the new age, a "mid-intensity" conflict: neither all-out war as had been strategized for against the USSR in Europe, nor the low-intensity combat pioneered in proxy conflicts across the Third World. With 500,000 combat troops in the field and 109,876 aircraft sorties flown, it might be more accurate to say it was a high-intensity conflict with low-intensity aims. The initial bombardment was massive and was, as Pentagon planners intended, immediately imprinted upon the mind of the world that watched with bated breath. Images of tracer bullets licking up into the air, and of explosions observed through the grainy-green tint of night-vision cameras, were brought to homes across the Western world via CNN news, the first and at this point the only twenty-four-hour satellite news channel. The images alone offered all the confirmation of American hegemony that Bush could have desired;

the plumes of smoke left by retreating Iraqi forces as they torched oil fields behind them merely confirmed it.

Rarely for a military operation, events on the ground went smoother than envisaged. After months of planning for a potentially hazardous ground offensive, Cheney's Defense Department was genuinely caught off guard when they realized, after just three days, that they had largely accomplished their war aims. By February 26 Arab coalition forces entered Kuwait City and a vastly overpowered Saddam could only respond by retreating to Baghdad while truculently firing off Scud missiles at Israel and Saudi Arabia. Bush himself feared it was "probably too cute by half" but ground operations ended at midnight on the 27th—exactly 100 hours after they had started.[16] The war made General Norman Schwarzkopf into the first household military name in a generation. "Talk to me, General Schwarzkopf, tell me all about it," urged Madonna from the stage of the 1991 Academy Awards show.[17] Not a man to shun the limelight, Schwarzkopf duly did, granting interviews with everyone from *Time* magazine downward. Colin Powell, then still a relatively new chairman of the Joint Chiefs of Staff, also had a good war—his star rising more quietly behind the scenes.

But it was the president who reaped the greatest reward. Immediately he ordered a parade of tanks, troops, and Patriot missiles before a crowd of several hundred thousand gathered in the capital. A few days later Schwarzkopf walked at the head of an even more glamorous ticker-tape parade along Wall Street in New York, a "paper blizzard" of confetti and balloons raining down over the troops: a stark difference from the bitter and solitary return of veterans from Vietnam a generation before.[18] Bush missed the second parade, but not the significance of the yellow ribbons hung up across America in support of the missing Kuwaiti prisoners of war who had been held by Iraq, and whom Bush had vowed to get back.

At the close of the war, Bush's own popularity was higher than it had ever been: the highest ever reached by any American president, in fact. The first man to have assumed the role of a specifically "global" leader would never be as popular again. But for now at least he had managed to put together the largest military campaign since Vietnam, had "buried" that particular memory in the process, and had gotten almost every other member of the coalition but the United States—"oil rich arabs [sic] and oil dependent Europeans and Japanese"—for the most part to pay for it (in the final reckoning the United States paid merely $4 billion out of a total bill of $61 billion).[19] From the US point of view it could hardly have been more successful.

And yet not everything was as cleanly resolved as it may have looked from the Washington Mall, beneath the jets and their flyover trails. *First*, for all that the war had indeed been "trivial" in a military sense, its legacy was to prove of the utmost importance. As one of the more insightful retrospectives pointed out, for America's military elite the war represented a critical turning point after Vietnam. Military intervention was no longer seen as taboo. Given the war's seeming success it also gave vent to a new technological utopianism that would make the unleashing of the dogs of war that much more likely in the future, at the same time as its promises of minimal "collateral damage" would change military planning irrevocably (a legacy Bush's successor Bill Clinton would exploit in Bosnia and Kosovo).[20]

Second, the "victory"—falling to America as easily as it did—fatally skewed the public's understanding of American power itself. It restored militarism to the heart of American national identity. Reagan's efforts aside—the armed forces had been largely absent from the political chemistry of US politics since Vietnam—the war in the Persian Gulf now let the US military and its patriotic train back in. And while it would take a few years for the implications to become apparent, a more militarized democracy was imaginable now in a way that, ironically, it simply had not been during the last decades of the Cold War. Coming so sharply on the heels of victory over the communists in Europe, it was as if the ambitions of the American century were being realized all at once. As Andrew Bacevich wrote in the *Wilson Quarterly*:

> In the collective public consciousness, the Persian Gulf War and the favorable conclusion of the Cold War were evidence that, despite two world wars, multiple episodes of genocide, and the mind-boggling criminality of totalitarianism, the twentieth century had turned out basically all right. The war let Americans see contemporary history not as a chronicle of hubris, miscalculation, and tragedy, but as a march of progress, its arc ever upward.[21]

Bacevich was writing after the end of the twentieth century and when the consequences of that hubris had become apparent in the very same sands of Iraq now patrolled from on high by American Stealth jets.

But already, in fact, the lineages of descent were beginning to become apparent—and above all from the *third* consequence of the war: the way that America had now irrevocably hitched itself to the wider fate of the Middle East. For all its aid and interventionism of recent decades (tanks and money to Israel, support to Iran's enemies, funding for the Mujahi-deen in Afghanistan), for all their reliance on Middle Eastern oil, Amer-ican presidents before Bush had managed to avoid becoming too *publicly* involved in the region. Now there was no choice about the matter: Bush himself had seen to that. And the ties that bound America to the Middle East would merely further tighten under the administrations of Clinton and George W. Bush. In this context, it was arguably Bush's failure to dispose of Saddam (or else to undo America's growing reliance upon oil) that doomed the first confrontation to a reprise.

By not pursuing Saddam into Iraq, but instead stationing even more troops in Saudi Arabia and elsewhere, the better to stand watch over the embargo that liberal international realpolitik required, the United States irreversibly committed itself to a decade-long saga of weapons inspections and "no-fly zones," of tacit connivance in domestic Iraqi repression for the sake of maintaining an ineffective and callous sanctions regime: a regime that affected the Iraqi people more than the government and its cronies. The plight of ordinary Iraqis was not helped, either, when Bush called on them, in a misplaced gesture of solidarity, to "take matters into their own hands."[22] This was remarkably loose-lipped for a man who had so carefully avoided saying anything that might preempt local repression in Europe and who had no intention, or capacity, to do anything to help them. When Kurds in the north and especially Shiites in the south did indeed rise up they did so alone, and they were met, predictably enough, by brutal repression.

In the aftermath of Desert Storm, the best that the Western powers could do, it seemed, was to set the whole sorry situation in aspic. Opera-tion Provide Comfort, launched already in April 1991, was just the largest of a series of humanitarian "missions" undertaken with the assistance of a pliant United Nations: all of them as noble as they were politically naive. As one observer remarked of Provide Comfort: "one is tempted to com-ment, unkindly, that not the least of its remarkable achievements was the degree of comfort it provided in the countries which organized it."[23] Ultimately such missions functioned as a way of avoiding the political problem presented by such groups as the Kurds, who sought independent nationhood, carved not just out of Iraq but out of Turkey too.

Meanwhile, with Iraq no longer a threat, the Emir of Kuwait was promptly reinstalled, along with the parliament he had himself abolished just prior to Iraq's invasion. Saudi Arabia acquiesced in US bases but seemed content to drag its heels over the reforms that Western powers demanded of it (primarily by making empty gestures toward a form of consultative council that was even less than the Polish government had been talked into making during the last years of communism).[24] And the Jordanian government continued to tread its fine line between British sponsorship and Iraqi aspersion. But these were the Middle East's problems to worry about, at least for now. For Western countries the predominant emotion was a widespread sense of relief that the first test of the post–Cold War era had been settled and survived. Meanwhile there was no shortage of international crises that demanded their attention as the Cold War continued its thaw.

Realignments and Rising Powers

It would ultimately take more than two years for the Soviet Union to break up, and for much of that time the scramble to respond to this in the West was strongly inflected by the parallel crisis that had unfolded in the Middle East. In Germany, where the first elections since reunification took place on December 3, 1990, the now footloose Willy Brandt's return from Iraq with 120 freed German hostages was a poke in the eye for Chancellor Kohl, who was otherwise trying to assure the eastern half of the country that he was the man of the moment. Two weeks later, as the Conference on Security and Cooperation in Europe (CSCE) met in Paris on December 19, Saddam Hussein released all the other German hostages, encouraging European leaders to make their own individual peace with him rather than stand with the Americans.

Of all the leaders gathered at the CSCE meeting that December, Margaret Thatcher was the least impressed by such behavior. But then she was also the least able to do anything about it, for it was during this meeting that she was ruthlessly deserted by her cabinet back home. Thatcher put a brave face on things. She still attended the dinner that evening. But it was clear she was deeply wounded. And her departure from power finally silenced one of the most decisive voices of the previous decade. Like de Gaulle in France, she had transformed the political landscape in her own country for a generation. Equally like de Gaulle, Thatcher had taken such command of the direction of her nation and enjoyed such credit for it, that when things went wrong, as they seemed to have been doing of late—the sinking of the *Herald of Free Enterprise* (187 dead) and the *Marchioness* (51 dead), the fires on the oil platform Piper Alpha (166 dead) and at King's Cross station (31 dead), the bodies laid out on the pitch at Hillsborough (96 dead)—disasters widely read as indicative of a public infrastructure cut to breaking point, she was in the end held responsible for them.[25]

A conservative, in every sense of the term, Thatcher had also helped ensure that, with the bipolar choices of the Cold War melting away, her European counterparts ultimately fell into line with the American-led future that was offered them, rather than striking out on their own. There was, therefore, a certain irony attached to the fact that one of the last public documents Margaret Thatcher put her name to as prime minister was a text—the Treaty of Paris—welcoming German reunification and a "Europe whole and free." It was also one of the last meaningful documents of the CSCE itself. As a bridging device out of the Cold War and into the new post–Cold War reality, the CSCE had helped link the economic and social project of the European Community to the political and strategic concerns of NATO. Henceforth it was the resurgent European Community that was to become the primary forum for Europe's leaders as they plotted a path forward out of the Cold War.

Meanwhile, the Americans had begun looking over the heads of their counterparts in Europe to Asia. What was needed now were trading partners more than the cumbersome paraphernalia of military allies and security alliances. After all, any aspirations the president might have to lead a new world order of peace and international cooperation came with not inconsiderable costs. And in the early 1990s the only other country capable of contributing financially to such an agenda was Japan. At the start of the 1990s the United States' Asia Pacific trade (at around $300 billion annually) was already a third greater than its transatlantic trade. And Japan's military, while constitutionally slated for defense purposes only, like Germany's, was the world's third largest.[26] Despite decent print runs for such alarmist titles as *The Coming War with Japan* (1991) what really defined the United States' new post–Cold War relationship with Japan was its economic value to the West. As one wit put it, Japan, like Germany, was now "expected to contribute economically to the maintenance of a military system which locked them into accepting American control over their own security."[27] Modifying, rather than suspending, the Cold War-era Mutual Security Treaty and insisting Japan raise its contribution to the cost of stationing US troops on Japanese soil to 50 percent was one way the Bush administration ensured this.

Asking Japan to contribute $13 billion to the Iraq War was another. Such was the sum that the government of Kaifu Toshiki was ultimately forced to raise taxes to cover it, prompting Japanese critics to complain, laconically, of "taxation without representation." Despite the historical rebuke, the US public remained unmoved. And when Bush visited Tokyo and the new government of Prime Minister Miyazawa Kiichi—a meeting at which Bush rather unceremoniously fainted—he made sure that there would be no drawdown of US troops stationed there. So far as the Bush administration was concerned, Japan was now due for bringing back into the international community. But America still wanted to make sure that its economic ambitions were kept in check as it did so. The other ASEAN members proved only too happy to go along. As relationships deepened, the United States was finding new friends off its Pacific rather than its Atlantic coast.

Seen in this light, the four-fold increase in Chinese purchases of military hardware at the turn of the decade understandably rattled some inside the American foreign policy establishment. Was this defensive posturing against other regional competitors, above all Japan, or was it posturing at America itself? For now, these were just increases from a previously low level. The real threat posed by China was the same as that coming out of Japan: namely the fact that China was a rising *economic* power. Mao's replacement, Deng, reinforced the message in early 1992, committing China to economic, but not political, reforms.

By then Bush had personally initiated a behind-the-scenes rehabilitation of the country's international standing after Tiananmen. The Asian Newly Industrializing Economies (the NIEs, or Asian "tigers" as they were known) had already shown the value to America of a low-cost, high-tech industrial regime. Now China–US economic cooperation was to offer a radical and dramatic twist to the recipe: one that would see China, and not Japan, keep America and its global ambitions afloat financially, in exchange for China leapfrogging to a position of economic preponderance in just a few years.[28] For a country that in 1989 was still primarily a peasant nation (peasants making up around 70 percent of the population) that was no mean feat.

All this was pressing and important as the Iraq War subsided and Bush's thoughts were returned to other arenas, not least the underlying importance of the need to finance the dollar as the most important plank of US economic and political hegemony alike. But as the American administration began to recognize with growing alarm, in the spring of 1991, the greatest immediate challenge to the emerging security order was not Germany or Japan, nor even China—for now. Instead it was Gorbachev, the man who in the space of just a few years had been taken to the heart of the Western public, and the sudden and disconcertingly open question in early 1991 of whether or not the popular Soviet leader was in control of the USSR anymore.

The new Soviet politics that began to take shape in 1990 was a world apart from the tried and tested party politics of the politburo years. But it was still fraught with tensions. In December 1990, Gorbachev's most trusted adviser, Eduard Shevardnadze, had resigned in frustration at the conservative pull being exerted on the leadership, leaving the Soviet premier to fall only further into the clutches of hard-liners like Vice President Gennady Yaneyev and soon-to-be Prime Minister Valentin Pavlov. "Dictatorship is coming," he scowled to the Soviet parliament as he announced his decision. No sooner had Shevardnadze left office than, on January 13, 1991, troops fired on protesters in Vilnius, killing fourteen, as they formed a human ring to protect a radio and television center during an attempted communist countercoup. A week later four were killed in a similar incident in Riga. It seemed as if Gorbachev was being overwhelmed by the hard-liners, something Bush had started to sense during their meeting in Helsinki the previous summer. Over vodka toasts at lunch, Brent Scowcroft had a candid discussion with Sergey Akhrome-yev, Gorbachev's top military aide. "I am loyal to him," Akhromeyev said, gesturing at Gorbachev, "and doing my best to help him. But I am confused."[29]

Akhromeyev, and there were many like him, was a man who simply couldn't come to terms with the profundity of the changes taking place. A year later, ultimately unable to accommodate himself to the world around him, he took his own life.[30] But the implication of what he was saying persisted. A lifetime of certainties was being shaken to its roots. Westerners looked east and saw countries being gently lapped by the soft winds of democracy; the truth was that those breezes—inside the USSR itself—felt more like a tornado of domestic political upheaval. And with the Americans preoccupied elsewhere, the storms of the Soviet collapse had raged on without them.

The darkest and in many respects most critical months of the Soviet breakup thus took place largely beyond the purview of a Western media whose lenses were now trained almost exclusively upon Operation Desert Storm in Iraq. But they were critical, nonetheless, for the subsequent deterioration of relations between a partially democratized Russia and the West. Gorbachev was now for the first time unsure of himself. In the lead-up to a party conference in April, he even toyed with abandoning the Communist Party altogether (only much later would he acknowledge that—for the sake of what Russia and the successor states would later become—he should indeed have done so, and set up instead a "democratic party of reform"). But he was unable to act decisively, caught as he was in a viselike grip between two contradictory movements: the communist old guard who could now see what Gorbachev's reforms entailed for them, and the liberal reformers who thought Gorbachev was moving too slowly and who wanted the market reforms that countries like Poland and Czechoslovakia were making. Gorbachev, in short, was trapped.

For those, like Boris Yeltsin, who grasped the significance of Gorbachev's predicament, the opportunities were immense. Born to a peasant family in the Urals, Yeltsin had been a relatively minor regional official until Gorbachev brought him to Moscow to help drive through his reforms. There he would take over the entire wheel of Gorbachev's reform process and turn it to his own political ends. Yeltsin's particular insight was to recognize early on how the very space that Gorbachev had opened up for public opinion to express itself in the Soviet Union could be used for *national*, which was to say specifically Russian, political gain. Yeltsin's dramatic resignation from the Communist Party in 1990 was a remarkable piece of political theater in pursuit of this end. And, for all he was temporarily banished to the margins of politics, it secured him considerable popularity in Moscow that he would leverage later on.[31]

As Gorbachev's popularity continued to decline, Yeltsin had merely to return to first-rank politics and to establish his own platform as that of representing the Russian and not the Soviet people. In so doing he wrong-footed Gorbachev at almost every turn. Gorbachev was suppressing the Baltics while Yeltsin championed their cause; Gorbachev was arguing for the Soviet Union's past while Yeltsin spoke of Russia's future; and Gorbachev believed that by establishing a national legislature he could absorb internal dissent, only for Yeltsin to use that legislature to foment yet more dissatisfaction and channel it to his own ends, which were, increasingly, to see Gorbachev removed.

At this point the Bush administration stepped into the Soviet diplomatic theater by taking a fateful decision. "The situation in the Soviet Union is so bad that it is hard to believe that [an] explosion can be avoided," observed Scowcroft in a memo to Bush on March 7. The Americans thus decided that it was time, as Bush put it, "to consolidate our gains."[32] What happened in Russia thereafter would be without a Western say. James Baker accordingly went to Moscow on the eve of the March 17 referendum on the future of the Soviet Union and Gorbachev's proposed new Union Treaty replacing it. The referendum recorded a moderate degree of support for Gorbachev, amid miners' strikes and general political turmoil, though it was to prove the final straw for the hard-liners in his government. Gorbachev regained sufficient control to enable Bush to waive the Jackson–Vanik amendment to the 1974 Trade Act and to restore the Soviet Union to a more or less normal trade partner.[33] But that was the last of American political involvement: thereafter, the Soviet Union would be left to disintegrate on its own.

When Yeltsin became, on June 12, 1991, the first-ever democratically elected leader (and an immensely popular one at that) of a Russian nation within a wider but much looser socialist union, Gorbachev's days were practically over, with or without the coup against him that followed in August. The coup was orchestrated by eight top Soviet officials who identified themselves as the State Committee on the State of Emergency. It gave the Western political elite a momentary shudder of concern: perhaps the wounded beast of the Soviet Union would not stay down for its death throes, as they had assumed. Perhaps the West's guard had been let down too soon? "I hope that the new rulers will be sensible enough to understand there can be no relapse into earlier policies," Kohl said to Bush in a gesture that indicated no small lack of personal concern for Gorbachev. "Let's avoid statements about rearming," said Mitterrand, likewise in damage limitation mode. For his part—and very much to his credit—the American president was more worried about what was happening to the Soviet premier himself. But he was no less concerned about the need to secure stability.

Bush was particularly concerned that the coup might now bring the Baltics fully into play and that he would be tasked with coming to their aid—against Moscow—on the very terms he had fashioned for himself over Kuwait.[34] What saved the day, ultimately, was Yeltsin's dramatic antics atop the tanks that had come to threaten his power base, the presidential palace. Yeltsin's "stand" for democracy brought him considerable goodwill in Washington, but in truth the generals' coup had been doomed from the start. Staged by an incompetent cabal of the politburo and military old guard, their chief strategy consisted of little more than seizing the moment once Gorbachev had chosen, unwisely, to take a vacation back in his native Ukraine, on the Black Sea, and forcing him to resign from there on grounds of ill health. They had no other serious plan for securing the support of either their own troops or the public.[35]

Gorbachev's subsequent return to Moscow, from where he had been held under house arrest at his villa, was no less of a failure, however. It ought to have been a moment of vindication for the returning premier.

But Gorbachev wrongly chose conservatism over radicalism. And once again he defended the now discredited Party against what he believed were just its few rotten apples—curiously insisting that the coup merely proved the need for its continued reform. In doing so he effectively sealed his own fate alongside the disgraced generals who were now under arrest. And not just with the Russian people at home: during his three days of detention two of the Baltic states had taken the opportunity to declare their independence. Ukraine, Belarus, Moldova, Georgia, Armenia, and most of the Central Asian republics soon followed them. No less significantly, the KGB was replaced by the forerunner of the modern Russian FSB on October 24—by which time there was almost nothing left of the Soviet Union to enforce.

Whatever did remain would be gone by the end of December. By then Gorbachev had sought, and largely failed, to garner the confidence of his fellow leaders. At a testy meeting of the G7 in London, just prior to the coup, Jacques Delors had interrogated Gorbachev on his economic reform program, "like a professor questioning a student." When the Soviet premier signaled that what he needed to make his reforms stick was not lecturing but a major injection of foreign aid, his official status as an "observer" at the event was used to politely turn down his requests. Instead of an economic aid package he hoped would be agreed in the region of $50–70 billion, Gorbachev was offered grain credits and technical assistance running into the tens of millions. Back home the situation only worsened for Gorbachev after the coup. The economy came to a stuttering halt and his last-ditch effort to engineer a new political structure for the Soviet republics soon collapsed alongside it. Gorbachev had become like the pacemaker who drops quietly away from the race as the finishing line approaches. From the summer of 1991 onward he was merely trying to stave off the inevitable, his efforts to remain in control of his country preventing him from actually reforming it any further.

It was the coup and its aftermath that finally flung the door wide open for Yeltsin to emerge as the dominant figure in charge of administering the last rites to communism. And Yeltsin wasted no time in seeing to it. By the end of the year he had gathered together the heads of the largest former Soviet states, the Slav republics of Ukraine and Belarus, along with Russia, to announce a successor arrangement to the Union of Soviet Socialist Republics: the pointedly worded Commonwealth of Independent States (CIS), which in due course would incorporate the majority of the former republics that Gorbachev had tried unsuccessfully to yoke to his own preferred rejig of the USSR: the

Union of Sovereign States. The Baltics having now broken away entirely, they took no part in either scheme. Since the international community already recognized them as fully independent states, they had no reason to do so.

The CIS was a federation not of popular need but of Yeltsin's devising and it served primarily as a cloak for further disunity and national decay as much as it offered a forum for addressing real problems. Indeed, far from seeking to stem the tide of political fission that had engulfed the East, Yeltsin and his fellow nationalist leaders were only too happy to stoke up resentments in order to achieve their own political ambitions. For all the initial euphoria as to the "reunification" of a continent, then, the final stage in the demise of communism had been accompanied by the rise of a divisive ethnic nationalism that would return to haunt the West later (presenting a host of difficult questions as to what to do about large minority populations who found themselves on the wrong side of a redrawn borderline).

The day he resigned as president of the Soviet Union, Gorbachev put a last call through to Bush, who was staying at Camp David. He underscored that he thought the "debate" in Russia had gone the wrong way, but he was stepping aside to make way for it all the same. He asked Bush to try to help make sure that there would be no more disintegration of his country. He explained the process of transition of his powers to those of the president of the Russian Federation. And he assured Bush that it would all go smoothly: Bush could enjoy "a quiet Christmas," Gorbachev said.

"I've written you a letter," Bush replied. "[I]n it I express my conviction that what you have done will live on in history."

"Thank you, George," Gorbachev responded. "I was glad to hear all of this today. I am saying goodbye and shaking your hands. You have said to me many important things and I appreciate it."

"All the best to you, Mikhail," Bush replied.

With that, Gorbachev hung up the phone.[36]

Domestic Tensions

The Soviet Union was officially no more. In February 1992, in a meeting held "under snowy skies" at Camp David, President Bush and Boris Yeltsin, the new Russian president, formally signed an end to seven decades of Cold War rivalry.[37] Historic though it was, the document was already an afterthought by the time the ink was dry. Yeltsin had an entire country waiting to be rebuilt at home. And Bush too had a country that he acknowledged he had largely neglected for most of the first three years of his presidency. If he hoped to stay in the White House for very much longer he needed to focus on domestic matters and fast: because for all the triumphalism of the Washington beltway pundits in the aftermath of the Gulf War, for all the president's own successes in the foreign policy domain, the dominant mood of Americans when they turned to look at their own country remained one of considerable unease. For the first time in almost half a century, Americans were without a major, existential enemy: yet this did little to stem a quite separate and growing anxiety over what was perceived as America's own state of "decline" at home.

There was one overriding reason for this: the country had arrived at the end of the Cold War in recession. The stock market crash of 1987 may well have been forgotten by most, with all that had been going on in world politics, but it had left its mark on the economy: and by 1990 the signs of the first major downturn since Reagan came to power were apparent. The hot topics of the day were declining competitiveness, rising foreign debt, and underinvestment in public services. In other words, for all that the United States may have won the Cold War it was feeling more than a little battle weary itself, and the bestsellers list, among other things, reflected this.[38] Benjamin M. Friedman's *Day of Reckoning* (1988) and, above all, Paul Kennedy's *The Rise and Fall of the Great Powers* (1987)—a book that could be seen "spilling out of briefcases in Washington," as a young Christopher Hitchens wrote home for Britain's *New Statesman*—associated, in the public's mind, the problem of imperial overstretch abroad with the decline of American productivity at home. And unhelpfully, while the one pointed to the need for higher taxes, the other suggested they were part of the problem.

The question of "whither America" had, by the late 1980s, become a perennial favorite of the political weeklies and the major syndicated newspaper columns. Walt Rostow, better known for advocating development policies for the Third World, was given space in the *Wall Street Journal* to outline what, in light of these challenges, might save the US economy at the Cold War's end. His suggestion, a massive program of domestic public infrastructure development, was not at all what most Republicans wanted to hear.[39] It was, however, in tune with what Republican voters themselves actually wanted. When James Baker started playing up the theme of "American jobs," as he tested the political waters before the upcoming presidential election, his comments gained more traction than did most of his frenetic foreign policy machinations on the international stage.

The nub of the problem, however, was that, from the White House down, almost all the major prescriptions on offer at the start of what was to prove a pivotal election year in 1992 seemed oblivious of a trend that the journal *Foreign Affairs* had noted over a year before: that the American people felt distinctly underwhelmed by the euphoria their leaders were expressing in regard to their former adversaries. It was noted:

> The sight of East Europeans opening new frontiers of political freedom, while Americans wring their hands, will probably accelerate this desire to join in the global celebration of political change. It was as if Americans as a nation had volunteered diligently for four decades in support of a political campaign, only to then have to watch the victory party on television at home.[40]

In short, Americans had woken up to the post–Cold War era shouldering the enormous costs of their postwar struggle against the Soviet Union and beginning to recognize, really for the first time, exactly how high these were. The US economy went into negative economic growth in 1991. The rate of failure of businesses in the first three years of the decade was the worst it had been since 1945.[41] America's largest companies began downsizing, which hit middle managers as well as factory-floor workers. And while unemployment increased only moderately, just about the only jobs going were, it became popular to lament, those "flipping burgers" in the local fast food restaurant. Kuwait City had been devastated under the Iraqi occupation, but decades of neglect had left parts of once great American cities like Philadelphia, parts of Washington even, looking like war zones themselves. Even in the American Sun Belt the bud had come off the rose: in California unemployment jumped from 6.1 to 9.3 percent in the year to September 1991, while the previous Christmas thousands of women and children stood in line in the cold for a free handout of a chicken and a toy.[42] There were, in short, precious few signs of a "new world order" at home in America in the early 1990s. On the first anniversary of Desert Storm, in January 1992, Bush went so far as to acknowledge that the US economy was in "free-fall."[43]

A struggling economy was one thing; escalating violence was another. More Americans had just been killed by street violence at home than were killed in Operation Desert Storm in Iraq, and it was hard to lay the blame for this anywhere other than at America's own door.[44] Race relations were tense and had become only more complicated over the previous decade as the number of Asian and Latino immigrants grew, adding to a combustible social mix in the underresourced downtown neighborhoods, where they invariably ended up taking residence. In Los Angeles, in 1991, a young black man, Rodney King, was violently beaten by police officers after being caught for speeding. Believing him to be resisting arrest, King was shot twice with a Taser before officers batoned him fifty-six times as he lay on the ground: with solid aluminium bars. Camera footage of all this, shot by a resident on a nearby balcony, was soon one of the first videos to "go viral" in a new age of media surveillance.

A year later, when the police officers involved were acquitted of any wrongdoing, Los Angeles erupted in riots. *Time* magazine called it "the worst single episode of urban unrest in American history."[45] In fact what had taken place was a series of "separate but simultaneous detonations."[46] Some black rioters attacked Koreans (they called them East Asians); others grabbed food. When 33-year-old white truck driver Reginald Denny drove his rig across downtown Florence Street, he ran right into one of the angry mobs. They pulled him out of his cab and beat him to a pulp, the attack ending when one of the assailants, Damian Monroe Williams, "took a cinderblock and bashed Denny's skull, fracturing it in 91 places and causing severe brain damage."[47] Publicly the footage was used to bookend the whole saga, tit for tat: a black beating and a black reprisal. But as the writer and social activist Mike Davis pointed out, much of the looting took place outside the city limits and blacks were not the only perpetrators.

Unlike in the Soviet Union, where the weight of economic problems was ultimately greater, what the Los Angeles riots revealed was that America's problem was not the overall size of its economic burden so much as its distribution. The complex racial and socioeconomic geography of the city was the truly critical event, but it was largely ignored in the coverage of the time—there was, after all, so much else going on— and it was likewise swept under the carpet in the official response. "Rebuild LA," the federally financed public clean-up program, did nothing to create jobs or invest in services. It did little to puncture the underlying injustices of daily life that had sparked the riots in the first place. A further problem was that the US economy was by now experiencing growing domestic dislocation brought about by the uneven regional development of its Cold War industries. The economy had been particularly distorted by the highly paid defense industry: something that initially had been good news for California, with its aerospace industry, and for the larger defense contractors along Route 128 on the East Coast. But it was bad news for most people in between.

Quite another problem altogether was the fact that the burden of America's debt had increasingly come to be felt, during the Reagan and Bush administrations, by the poorest in society most of all. The budgets of some individual states had been so heavily squeezed between rapidly growing welfare expenditures and declining federal income that forty of them had cut or frozen benefits to families with children. The poor held up placards with "WILL WORK FOR FOOD" written on them. And if it was true, as the old saying had it, that whatever was good for Detroit-based General Motors was good for the United States, then that company's $4.5 billion loss in 1991 (with the closure of twenty-one plants and the demise of 75,000 jobs) was a darkening portent for the country.[48] Detroit, once America's "arsenal of democracy," was fast becoming a wasteland.[49]

Confronted by such stark indicators of economic decline, many experts began looking abroad for answers. The obvious place to look was Japan: for while the US dollar share of total OECD GDP had dropped from half to just over a third in recent years, Japan's had leapt up to around a fifth. Japan's economy was growing at a rate of 4.5 percent in 1990 and 3.9 percent the year after; America by contrast managed just 0.2 percent growth in 1990 and suffered negative growth in 1991.[50] In 1989 Japan's Nikkei index hit a high of around 39,000, with Japan itself accounting for a massive 40 percent of all global stock market value.[51] Perhaps above all, with its orderly way of business and hierarchical society, Japan appealed to social conservatives on both sides of the American political spectrum.

Others looked to the now reunified Germany, another nation suddenly enjoying respectable economic growth, albeit for very different reasons. "Every country is unique, but some, Germany among them, are more unique than others," wrote Walter Russell Mead in an essay on the rising power of the now reunified European superstate. He was damning with faint praise. "We do not need to speculate on the shortcomings, real or alleged, in the German 'national character' to understand the nation's distinctive attributes."[52] But in fact he was also painting in reverse the American situation at home: militarily unassailable but creaking at the joints economically.

When the cultural and intellectual elite *did* look home to America, which was rare in the immediate post–Cold War euphoria, they seemed at times more concerned to channel the puritanical spirit of a John Milton rather than the liberal passion of an Alexis de Tocqueville. This included the author of perhaps the most influential work of all the political catechisms published in the late 1980s, the philosopher and classicist Allan Bloom: and his target was the upbringing of America's youth. The American education system, Bloom declared in *The Closing of the American Mind*, had "failed democracy and impoverished the souls of today's students." By students, however, he really meant *all* young Americans. In fact, it was more the case that an undemocratic education system was failing America's poor (Bloom preferred to lay the blame at Mick Jagger's door). As one recent commentator aptly suggests: "Read now, the book seems slightly unhinged. Read then, it captured a hankering for philosophical certainty in an uncertain world, as well as pandering to the perennial democratic appetite to hear the worst of itself."[53]

Such an appetite was apparent right across the country. "It seems to me that triumphalism is misplaced because at the very moment when democracy is blossoming in places like Eastern Europe, it is decaying in the United States," noted an alumnus of Stanford, speaking to a reunion of her class of 1970. "Over the past 25 years, the faith of the American people in their democratic institutions has declined by virtually any measure," she went on.[54] A first national literacy survey in 1988 revealed that Bloom was right about the parlous state of American education. In Kentucky over a third of those over twenty-five did not have a high school diploma and 40 percent of the state's adult population had at best a minimal or partial level of literacy. But even before the results were in, Bush was pressured into adopting a more proactive federal stance on literacy that resulted, in 1991, in the National Literacy Act.[55] The problem was not that Bloom was askew with his prognostications but that he chose to understand the matter of American decline in overtly moral terms. Bloom was the inheritor of the conservative belief that had emerged in the 1970s, which held that the people themselves were not to be trusted with too much democracy. Much less leftist relativism. And this ultimately did nothing less than to support US assertiveness abroad that others, if not Bloom himself, saw as the appropriate corrective.

And yet, if concerns about American domestic decline fastened initially on its educational system (a problem not only of concern with regard to citizens' participation in national economic and political life, but to their understanding and say in America's oversized role in world affairs as well) they were scarcely limited to it. Criminal prosecutions were another area of domestic policy in a state of near crisis. The rate of imprisonment of blacks and Hispanics not only greatly outstripped that of whites, for example, it resulted in knock-on social dislocation within their communities and made no small contribution to soaring levels of violence and violent crime. Since felons in America are denied the vote it was also building up a form of racial disenfranchisement by proxy. What these differences revealed was that it wasn't so much America *as a nation* that was in decline, so much as the fortunes of some of its citizens.

The politics of race pervaded much else too. In Europe, racial politics were primarily a function of the fact that non-Western migration had largely served its purpose as a source of cheap labor (it having been replaced, for the time being, by more white labor reserves from the newly liberated East: the age of the Polish plumber had arrived). But in America it had to do with the failure of even the Democratic Party to sustain its "big tent" version of liberalism in the new demographic climate: or, more precisely, the failure of US liberals either to address the problems confronting racial minorities or to reinvent their offering *away* from special interests and toward democratic citizenship writ large.[56]

Lacking any effective vehicle for social inclusion, the result could only be more policing of the problems. Thus, the more that international borders were seen to be opening up, the more dirt and trouble, it was assumed, would need weeding out at home. FBI agents "freed from anti-communist duties" abroad were put to work on the streets of US cities against violent street gangs,[57] while inner-city families were encouraged to turn in their husbands' or their sons' semi-automatics for gift certificates at Toys "R" Us.[58] Special interests now became special problems, and while this might have been taken as a case for greater universalism, at the time it was taken to imply the need for a more selective, more targeted approach to law and order than before.

To be sure, this latent willingness to police the borders of liberal society was far from an American peculiarity. The Swedish center-right fought the 1991 election on the slogan "Keep them locked in, so we can go out!"[59] But one element *was* specific to the United States. And that was the emergence of a deep-seated fracture in American political life, the reanimation of an assertively *isolationist* strand in public opinion, which would go unnoticed for a good many years, but whose impact would—eventually—be all the more devastating for it. At various points during the American Century, the United States had been something of a reluctant hegemon: content with the spoils of its power but reluctant to shoulder the costs and the commitment required to sustain it. Such sentiment was a powerful driving force, not least in mainstream liberal economic thought, which had for decades sought ways to govern less "actively" (and thereby become, in its way, a central plank of contemporary liberal democracy since the 1970s). Outside the realm of economics, it had previously been shown most explicitly in the aftermath of America's wars: in the rejection of the League of Nations, the (failed) rejection of the Marshall Plan, and in McGovern's 1972 "Come home, America" campaign, during Vietnam.

That same isolationist streak appeared now too. But what was different this time was the near-complete lack of institutional platforms, political faces, or popular vehicles through which it might let off a little steam. In what was perhaps the first indication of a growing gap between politicians of *all* political stripes, and the publics they were mandated to represent, the isolationism of the early 1990s was isolated from front-line political debate. "Washington has fallen out of touch with the voters," warned pollster Daniel Yankelovich and former Under Secretary of Commerce Sidney Harman in 1988. "To meet the challenges ahead America needs a new consensus," they insisted.[60] The trouble was, there were precious few politicians interested in constructing such a consensus at the start of the 1990s.

By contrast, a few Republican radicals gave an indication of the direction that all this *could* and would be taken in: the early successes of Pat Buchanan in the primaries, and the "primal scream" of populist anger that Newt Gingrich for one believed he detected in it, being perhaps the most notable example. But Buchanan's initially powerful challenge for the Republican nomination to the presidential election of 1992 ultimately came to nought, and the uncomfortable truth that many Americans did not feel themselves well represented by the political "status quo" was soon washed away along with his short-lived political hopes. Indeed, the increasingly partisan atmosphere that Gingrich more than anyone else was soon to bring about, in which political sides—Democrat vs. Republican—would need to be chosen regardless of the concerns raised by each, would further hide it from view. But it would remain in place. And, many years later, people would recall that they had not been given a chance to voice their desire for a smaller role for America when the opportunity had presented itself.

What *was* recognized by the political elite to be a serious problem, what ultimately knitted each of America's immediate post–Cold War challenges more tightly together than anything else, was the size of the economic hole—above all the growing budget deficit—that the country was now mired in. Such was the size of this deficit that it cast its shadow over practically every other matter and threatened at times to disqualify the victory over communism before it had been properly savored. This was a new and therefore troubling phenomenon. The US budget deficit had first widened in the 1980s, as military spending continued to leap forward in spite of the tax cuts under Reagan. Throughout the 1980s, thanks also to Reagan, it was considered unpatriotic to question the need to increase it and so the deficit grew. But with the Cold War gone the deficit now entered public debate as a "fact" of political life and it would not leave it for a good many years to come.

In fact, it was the financing of the budget deficit that was making things worse, by drawing foreign money in to fill the gap. Thus, America had also to run a current account deficit. The resulting "twin deficit" (the budget deficit and this current account deficit) was undermining America's competitiveness abroad, even as it gave it just enough room to engineer continued growth—on paper at least—of its economy at home. By early 1992, even conservatives in Bush's own party were worried about the extent of the problem. As the election year got properly under way the tone of debate became steadily more acrimonious. "The whole world seems to be entering its Hollywood period," wrote one commentator at the time, "while back where those dreams are manufactured the natives squabble fantastically and arcanely among themselves."[61] The deficit thus became the entry point for a new era of left–right acrimony, and the election of that year was to be its first staging post. Nowhere was this more apparent than with the rise to prominence of that more vocal strand of neoconservatism that had flourished during the previous decade under the canopy of the Reaganite ascendancy. And no one better characterized that particular brand of neoconservatism than the "godfather" of the movement, the former book editor and journalist Irving Kristol.

For Kristol a neoconservative was famously a liberal who had been "mugged by reality" and his trademark response to such muggings was a no less aggressive form of self-defense. As Kristol saw it, the present moment was not one for sitting idly by. "Now that the 'other' Cold War is over, the real cold war has begun," he declared, surveying what he saw as the "perversions" of "sector after sector of American life [that] has been ruthlessly corrupted by the [progressive] liberal ethos." For those such as Kristol the new domain of struggle was to be a *Kulturkampf* against the left.[62] And to fight this battle Kristol teamed up with the likes of David Horowitz (or at least Horowitz, the ex-radical, joined Kristol) to man the intellectual barricades, and the recording studios, of what soon became a more assertive, more aggressive form of politics. There they would meet, before too long, a disgruntled wing of the Republican Party with intellectual aspirations and political ambitions to match.

At this critical moment the American left was still in the doldrums, especially on its more radical "old left" fringe. Come the 1990s and American leftists either acknowledged that the game was up, as Bruce Cumings had, or else they indulged in melancholic introspection. Looking first to Europe from the editorial office of *Dissent* magazine, Irving Howe diagnosed a kind of post-communist "sobriety" across the European continent: an "indigo" mood, which "sometimes looks like a cover for depression," he said. But then he looked home to America and concluded that things were, if anything, a little worse:

> You can see the signs of this exhaustion if you pick up any of the leading intellectual journals. Some are sour (usually edited by ex-radicals) and others are timid (usually edited by quasi-liberals). Some subsist by mocking the hopes of their youth. Others avoid any long range expectations or desires. Still others narrow their focus of concern to the daily routines of politics, sometimes saying useful things, though not much more.[63]

In part this was about the now certified failure of the New Deal political legacy and the lack of any guiding, positive vision to replace it: a problem that would continue to bedevil the left for a generation. But more broadly it was about the failure of American idealism. Undermined by culture wars and widening value positions, stretched wider still by the new medium of talk show radio, and deflated from without by the apparent collapse of the modern world's great ideological categories, the nation was culturally adrift. It was this that was truly novel.

For the better part of a century, America had sought to weave morality and power together, its moral mission assuming its greatest clarity in the context of the ideological certainties of the Cold War. Yet at the very point of its victory over communism, it found that its guiding moral project had never been as confused as it was now. Here was the central irony that would suffuse some of the key political decisions of the coming decade. That "history-less, willed quality" of American popular culture captured by the essayist David Rieff seemed suddenly very much mired

in history and lacking, most critically of all, the will to drag itself forward.[64]

The New Political Realism

Ironically the first victim of this new mood was the incumbent Republican president. The first beneficiary, by contrast, was to be a more dynamic
and centrist younger left that would now begin to ape its adversaries on
the new right in ways that promised to sharpen the political debate in
the decade to come. There were numerous reasons for Bush's failure to
win reelection. He was no great campaigner for one. For much of the
election year the president jolted back and forth between his competitive
instincts and a reluctance derived, so his biographer Jon Meacham later
speculated, from the fact that "victory in a real war had sapped his energies for the often manufactured skirmishes of politics."[65] Speaking to
a town hall meeting in New Hampshire early in the year, a distracted
Bush read out from a note-card intended to summarize the day's key
message: "Message: I care," Bush announced to a somewhat bemused
audience.[66] Few believed that he really did.

With hindsight there were other reasons he lost. Across America there
was a widely felt desire to "shake things up." And when measured against
those aspirations Bush's domestic program had been distinctly underwhelming: comprising little more, in effect, than a piece of anti-discrimination
legislation, protecting the rights of the disabled in the workplace, and a
new Clean Air Act (itself a chastened piece of policy occasioned by the
spillage of the *Exxon Valdez* during his first year in office). "You don't
expect me to read this shit, do you," snapped the president to the White
House communications staff when he looked over the first speech he
was to give on domestic policy after the close of operations in Iraq.[67]
But they did expect him to read it, because it was a speech all about his
own policies to date. Had the 1992 election been about foreign policy,
this might not have mattered. But it wasn't. And this left him vulnerable
as a candidate.

Bush also confronted a host of other problems that were not of his
making. The first was that he faced not one but two challengers in the
1992 presidential election. In addition to the Democratic ticket led by
the Southern Democrats Bill Clinton and Al Gore, he confronted Ross
Perot, a short but perky Texan businessman flush from the $2.5 billion
sale of his data systems company and, when it came to campaigning, a

good deal quicker on the uptake than the president. Perot's presence made absolutely certain that it was the economy—and therefore the deficit—which was to be the central battleground in the election: a battleground thereby pitched in the one place the incumbent president had no hope of winning.

The problem posed by the Democrats, and above all a powerful new political movement within the Democratic Party itself, the New Democrats, was even greater, however. The original impetus behind the New Democrat movement was the drubbing that Reagan had given Democratic candidate Walter Mondale back in 1984. The sheer scale of Mondale's defeat (he lost in 49 of 50 states) had prompted a group of center-right Democrats to set up a new Democratic Leadership Council (DLC) in 1985 as an institutional base from which to rethink the future of the Democratic Party. Although framed as a response to Reagan it was equally a response to the rising popularity of Jesse Jackson and his minority-oriented National Rainbow Coalition (he lost the two primaries he stood for in 1984 and 1988, but secured 3 million and then 7 million votes respectively in each). The Democrats having previously embraced the new politics of movement, they were now desperately seeking a way out.

Driven forward by party strategist Al From and Senator Sam Nunn, the DLC agenda was privately funded and run without official party sanction. The reason for this soon became clear as the DLC put forward a new political platform that was all about fiscal discipline, small government, and ending welfare "indulgence." In short, the DLC was pro-business and even more pro-finance—almost more so than the Republicans. And in the years to come, to make sure that it put a new generation of politicians in power, it put together both a fighting fund (the New Democrat Network) and go-to think tanks (the PPI) for hammering out electorally appropriate policies. As Jesse Jackson himself once quipped, the DLC should properly have stood for "Democrats for the Leisure Class."[68]

The DLC's most important move was to convince the young Arkansas-born governor Bill Clinton to be its chairman. Its second most important decision was to put Al Gore alongside him as his running mate. Clinton was an energetic young senator, the same age as Bush's eldest son, and a former Rhodes scholar at Oxford. He was therefore free of the old taint of East Coast privilege that had hampered many Democratic campaigns, and he was accompanied by a no less brilliant wife, Hillary, who was every bit his equal, if not more so. Together the Clintons brought into the DLC not only a new pragmatism in Democratic politics, but a new spirit of "can-do," baby-boomer confidence. The Gores, too, were a young and energetic pairing, in which Al played Lancelot to the Clintons' Arthur and Guinevere. Together these were the most talented, and certainly the most ambitious, Democratic politicians of their generation. The press adopted a more filmic metaphor when it duly labeled them "the Young Guns."

That new spirit of confidence was apparent at Madison Square Garden in New York in the summer of 1992, as the Democrats held their nominating convention. The whole event struck a marked contrast to the wider political malaise in which the country seemed to be mired, especially with trouble once again boiling over in America's cities. Los Angeles was reeling still from the Rodney King riots of early spring, and in June Chicago's South Side erupted in violence as well. The spark was post-NBA season celebrations gone awry. But the fuel was the same as that in LA, supplied this time by the passage just two months before of the largest welfare cut in Illinois history.[69] In July, rioters cut out across a forty-block area around New York's Washington Heights after police officers killed a local youth from the Dominican Republic.

The Democrats' slickly staged convention, with its white, blue, and red balloon drops to Fleetwood Mac and its invocations that "we can do it," sought to lift America's brow up and away from all of this. The now famous rhetorical question with which Rodney King had prevailed upon the rioters back in April—"Can we all get along?"—made an appearance at the convention, in the text of civil rights leader Barbara Jordan's keynote address. But this open-armed embrace of the national underclass ultimately served just to disguise the New Democrats' *real* political agenda. The dominant tone, the electorally important one, was of white middle-class resurgence. "I am a product of that middle class," said Clinton in his acceptance speech, "and when I am president you will be forgotten no more." Somewhere on an arc linking the looted stores of South Central Los Angeles and the ticker tape and the balloons of Madison Square Garden, a new political landscape was emerging in America: and yet it left the truly marginal members of society behind once again.

Indeed, by the time the balloons in Madison Square Garden had been punctured and swept away, many of the "old" Democratic Party "interest group" nostrums had been rejected. The convention had also made clear that the "politics of old" more generally was out (a few obligatory references to Camelot and Martin Luther King notwithstanding). "The choice we offer is not Conservative or Liberal," declared Clinton to the press during the convention; "in many ways it is not even Republican or Democratic. It is different. It is new . . . I call it a New Covenant."[70]

Clinton's New Covenant promised nothing less than a "new social contract" for America. But the truth, as all this talk of the "new" suggested, was that the Democrats were actually in the process of writing down existing commitments to their usual constituencies because they didn't think there were enough votes there anymore. Supporting "minorities" with their constant litany of special causes was deemed simply to have cost the party votes. The party needed to reconnect with the rest of America: to "shoot where the ducks were," as one electoral hack put it—which meant, of course, reaching out to the white middle class.

The path to achieving this was well captured in the Democrats' election manifesto for that year: *Putting People First*. By putting people first as individuals, by "empowering" them, the claims of communities and of American "society"—of America's peoples, that is—could be allowed to fall naturally into the background. Rights implied responsibilities, of course, and a Democratic government, it was promised, would get tough with welfare cheats and "deadbeat parents." Empowerment turned out to mean in practice the redistribution of power, away from the vulnerable toward the can-do. It was the perfect political complement to the economic redistribution already under way, away from the poor and into the pockets of the rich. Clinton's constant homilies to the "forgotten middle class" were projected out as "nearly every American" but counted back in as a narrow band of swing voters the Democrats were really concerned about.[71] And they had a crystal-clear focus: to win the election above all else. Clinton was certainly keeping his eyes resolutely "on the prize," as his strategists constantly advised.[72]

The New Democrats did not merely preach the values of the economy as part of their electoral platform either. They made sure to practice their new liturgy as well, reaching out not only to the voting middle class but to what one democratic fundraiser called "the hundred-thousand people": the big donors—setting up in the process a new and significant political conjuncture between private capital and party politics on the left.[73] In so doing they narrowed their party base but drastically expanded their electoral reach. And they dressed it all up with a new, Republican-type small-town moralism. They praised new business but solicited the support of old corporate chiefs; they saluted Main Street but flirted with Wall Street. If this seemed contradictory it could also be explained away in the new political climate as pragmatism in the face of the era's "historic" challenges.

Much of this new approach to politics Clinton could take credit for engineering. But as the presumptive Democratic Party leader in 1992, he was also the fortunate beneficiary of a further piece of good luck. This was the much overlooked, but hardly insignificant, fact that the Democrats were now liberated from the internal divisions that had riven the party during the Cold War. Unlike the Republicans, who offered a clear and forthright foreign policy of anticommunism, and irrespective of the fact that some Democrats, like Henry "Scoop" Jackson, were stauncher anti-communists than any sitting Republican, the party had been routinely hamstrung in national elections by their divisions over what America should be doing abroad.

Ever since Vietnam this problem had sharpened, leaving Democrats not only split between the hawks and the doves, but further divided by the constant plethora of political innovations they devised to overcome this rift: human rights, Third Worldism, and economic aid ranking among them. There were always too many messages to get behind, too many versions of the party, too many policies purporting to be hard and soft at the same time. Republicans, by contrast, only ever had just the one message to get across and, even when the controversy of the day—as most famously with the funding scandal of Iran-Contra—was of their own making, they frequently found ways to pin at least some of the blame on Democrats precisely *because* of that singularity of vision (in the case of Iran-Contra by portraying the Democrats as having been too soft on communist agitators in the first place: "what else could we do?").

Much of this helps explain why in 1989, as the Wall began to be pulled down, 51 percent of voters trusted the Republicans best to handle national defense, while only 15 percent were prepared to put their faith in the Democrats.[74] The crucial difference, come 1992, was that public concern for strong national defense was a desire now largely *sated*—and by the Gulf War in particular. Thus, ironically, it was Bush's greatest success that allowed the Democrats to close ranks: such that even a Democratic hawk like Richard Perle (who actually served in a Republican administration) could now speak of "a real chance for significant healing within the party."[75]

More importantly, by 1992 the arc of public concern that Republicans had so successfully cultivated for the past three elections had come full circle. The American public was now primarily concerned with the *bill* they were having to foot for the anticommunist build-up the Republicans had encouraged them to support. This was why 59 percent of voters now saw "economic competitors like Japan" as a greater threat to America than "military adversaries like the Soviet Union."[76] It was why the economic experts began looking to those countries for answers. It was why the end of communism was to prove a far greater political boon to the Democrats than to the Republicans.

Bush had not been unaware of all this, of course—and he had certainly not been idle in response. The White House nearly ran out of eggs Benedict in May 1992, or so the joke went, as Bush sought to lobby one senatorial lawmaker after another to get behind the new free trade agreement (NAFTA) that he had been working on with Canada and Mexico, the better to have *some* major domestic policy achievement to his name. But that agreement would not be officially signed until after the election, and the public does not judge a leader on the future consequences of their policies. They tend to judge a leader on what happens to matter to them most at election time. And going to the polls in 1992 what mattered was the state of the economy, which was precisely where Bush was seen to be weak. His much-criticized reversal on his earlier "read my lips" pledge not to increase taxes seemed to confirm it. This had in many ways been a necessary act of statesmanship in the face of a threatened government shutdown. But the public interpreted it as a further sign of his mishandling of the economy. When the president vomited because of flu during a state banquet in Tokyo in early 1992, and then bravely continued with the occasion until eventually he collapsed on the floor, the *New York Times* observed that "Mr. Bush's bout with the flu recalled his handling of the recession. He got it after everyone else did and he kept trying to pretend it wasn't bad."[77]

The Clinton campaign by contrast *did* get it. And they played on that fact as hard and as often as they could. Of course, Clinton was not the only politician at the start of the 1990s to make economics the focal point of his approach to governing: the political ashes of the Cold War having been cleared away, a whole new generation of leaders was heading toward the front of the national stage reciting lines from the new playbook of "business leadership" rather than "international statesmanship." But Clinton's embrace of the language and the ideas of the market led the way for this approach on the left. And it gave the governor from Little Rock the entrée that he needed to turn an otherwise scandal-ridden campaign into White House–winning material.

The moment at which the election finally tilted Clinton's way was indicative of this. During a second televised debate—a new addition to the electoral process, and another step in the direction of a more media-saturated politics—held in a town hall in Richmond, Virginia, on October 15, the obvious question was put. "How has the national debt personally affected each of your lives?" a young African American woman in the audience asked the candidates. "And if it hasn't, how can you honestly find a cure for the economic problems of the common people if you have no experience in what's ailing them?"

Ross Perot—the independent candidate, whose eventual 19 percent of the vote would help put Clinton into the presidency—answered first. Bush went next and had a visibly torrid time admitting that, ensconced as he often was in the White House, he had seen very little of people's real problems. He bumbled on about the teenage pregnancies mentioned in a bulletin at a black church he had visited. But his answer didn't seem to make much sense, even to him. Seizing his opportunity, Clinton then slid off his stool and prowled to the front of the stage. He'd been governor of a small state for twelve years, he said, and he knew people who had lost their jobs: he knew them by name.

Clinton could no more name these people than could Bush, one suspects. But the difference was, he sounded as if he meant it. And he ended, with a perfect pivot that gave notice of the depth of his political talent, by adding that the debt problem was really just the beginning. "We're in the grip of a failed economic theory," he told the young woman in the audience, bringing the evening, and the election itself, squarely onto his campaign's primary talking point.[78] Thereafter Ross Perot merely played into Clinton's hands by continually insisting that America could not be a political superpower abroad if it wasn't an economic superpower at home (all the while undermining his own claim to be able to address this by virtue of a fastidious bookkeeper's insistence that it was government "red ink" that was the problem now, not the "Red Army"). Clinton, by contrast, had the wind in his sails. Along with the country's first baby-boomer president-elect, the post-70s era had now come of age in America.

8

The Great Convergence

"To discuss democracy without considering the economy . . . is an operation worthy of an ostrich." So wrote the Polish-American political scientist Adam Przeworski in 1990, as the Cold War faded into the past about him.[1] Przeworski, like many others of his generation, assumed that the role of the state in directing the economy was *the* central issue in modern politics. But as the dust settled on the upheavals brought about by the fall of communism a new watchword— "globalization"—was upending that assumption before his eyes.[2] During the last great wave of global economic expansion, a century before, the world had been pitched into turmoil. "People who were not born then will find it difficult to believe," wrote the Austrian novelist Robert Musil in his 1940 novel documenting the social and economic changes of fin-de-siècle Europe: "but the fact is that even then time was moving faster than a cavalry camel."[3]

The new wave of globalization had its roots in the economic transformations of the 1970s and seemed even more a breath of fresh air. As consumer choice for the masses expanded, the popular media reported glowingly on the sense of a shrinking globe brought about by a post–Cold War expansion in freedom of movement and capital alike. Bestsellers like *New York Times* columnist Thomas Friedman's *The World Is Flat* were soon all the rage. But in respect of open borders, Western society was not obviously more globalized at the end of that century than it had been at the start: if anything the ability of people to cross borders in search of work had been severely retrenched since the years of economic crisis and the abandonment of open-door migrant labor policies at the start of the 1970s. As late even as 2004, only 0.1 percent of Europeans lived and worked in a country other than the one they grew up in; and only 2.4 percent of Americans worked in a state other than the one where they were born.[4] The significance of borders was changing, to be sure, but they were hardly disappearing.

On the other hand, if globalization is taken as a measure of the *inte-*

gration of economic activity, rather than as a metaphor simply for its spread about the globe, then there *was* something distinct and original about the immediate post–Cold War moment. International bank lending had risen from $265 billion in the 1970s to $4.2 trillion by 1994 and trade in goods and services among the OECD nations was up from 45 to 65 percent over the same twenty-year period. Foreign exchange transactions had grown to the point where they were now sixty times larger than actual physical trade, leaving national markets not only more open but more intensely *connected* with one another than before. Corporations, we have already seen, took advantage of the new international division of labor to refashion their production lines on a global scale, such that the manufacture of everything from aircraft to sports shoes was no longer the preserve of any one country to regulate. Labels such as "Made in Italy" began to fall into disuse, while those declaring "Made in China" by contrast proliferated, indicating low-cost, high-volume turnover. This was good for Western consumers, but another nail in the coffin for Western workers.

The changes were in both cases hard to deny. Pasta, to take an Italian product that actually *was* faring rather well, had been a rarity in much of northern Europe in the 1960s, but thirty years later was so ubiquitous as to be an inflation-indexed good. Fresh fruit was by turns as cheap as it had ever been, despite the fact that strawberries now came from Kenya, not Portugal, and bananas were flown in from Costa Rica and Ecuador. But expanded consumer choice not only made Western labor markets more volatile, it also drove a pervasive privatization of the productive economy. Growth in *intra*-firm trade now outpaced that of trade between national states, and increasingly it was up to firms, not the states that "hosted" them, to decide how to move money and investment around—or whom they were going to employ and at what price.[5]

Ultimately, then, it proves most useful to think of the great surge in globalization, as the Western world experienced this in the 1990s, as the moment when many of the structural transformations set in train during the upheavals of the 1970s began to take on a compelling new shape. Cables straddled the oceans (the Iraq War, after all, was the first war to be covered live on television) and satellites breached the horizon in a thickening web of communications networks. In the 1980s, the image of bank traders taking "portable" phones to lunch with them, their curly cables patched into transmitters, conveyed the prospect of a universally interconnected future; by the 1990s that future had arrived:

genuinely mobile telephony was now already a reality for many middle-class households.

Yet for all that such developments tend to be understood as the beginnings of a process of cultural universalization, of "westernization" even, in the eyes of many critics, this new phase in the globalization of trade and capital flows proceeded more unevenly than is usually recalled: for there were losers as well as winners. Paradoxically, globalization also tended to reinforce people's identification with *local* causes and values and it thereby often entrenched local social and economic relations. The reality of major fashion retailer Benetton, which ran one of the most successful marketing campaigns of the decade, for example, was a global cost-cutting empire headquartered in the Ponzano neighborhood of Treviso. It took the Dutch much longer to adopt the Internet than the Belgians, even though their two countries border one another and share similar values. And for all the efforts of the global branding industry to universalize musical taste, by the end of the decade 93 percent of music in America, 74 percent in Japan, and 50 percent of the total volume of music sales in Europe were sales of *local* artists.[6]

Globalization in the 1990s was not therefore some great convergence of trade and economic development, as it has often been portrayed. It was a process in which rules needed to be drawn up and ideas found to justify them. In 1990 the British economist John Williamson coined one such idea, embodied in the term the "Washington Consensus," to capture the style of economic policy advice then being promoted around the world by the IMF and the World Bank. This Western liberal recipe comprised a now common listing of fiscal discipline, tax reform, trade and interest-rate liberalization, privatization, and deregulation. These were the lessons the Western democracies believed they had themselves learned when lifting their own economies out of the doldrums of the 1970s: lessons that were now taken to pass for basic economic common sense—"motherhood and apple pie," in Williamson's words.[7] They were lessons that were now put to work in the wider world, under close supervision by the United States in particular.

The imperatives of "globalization" that were discovered in these years were created, not found, in other words, and the emerging institutional pillars of a new global economic order reflected this. These were the great liberalizing projects of NAFTA, the EU, and the institutions of Williamson's Washington Consensus: the IMF, the World Bank, and the WTO. And no less significant than the market-friendly liberal regimes they were pushing for abroad was the fact that the Western states, which already considered themselves unimpeachably democratic, now came to believe that they had little to lose and everything to gain by supporting this US-based liberal international agenda. Thus, for all the *political* differences that had flared up since the 1970s, and which the tumult of the years after 1989 seemed only to confirm, in matters of the economy Western liberal democracy now began to speak with an increasingly singular voice. What Nixon had seen falling down about him back in 1971 was, by the early 1990s, rapidly being rebuilt amid an historic resurgence of laissez-faire international capitalism.

Age of Accession

As is often the case, the nature of this emergent economic order could most clearly be appreciated from the margins. In the early 1990s that meant the countries of Eastern and central Europe. And it was with Eastern Europe's incorporation into the Western market economy foremost in mind that, in 1990, the world's economic elite gathered in the relatively unknown alpine town of Davos—for what had become the traditional annual meeting of the recently established World Economic Forum. Away from the sun-decked terraces, where Europe's well-to-do sipped coffee in neon-colored overalls, Eastern Europe's economic leaders gathered in a darkened room to hammer out a vision for what the businessmen who joined them were now grandly calling the "New Europe" (but which they themselves were less sure what to think of, let alone to call). The question on the table was how the Eastern nations were to be incorporated into the West. And the near unanimous view was that the answer was contingent on their first showing progress in moving to a free-market economy.

Huddled into the same room that February were Hans Modrow of the GDR, the Czechoslovak prime minister, Marián Čalfa, President Wojciech Jaruzelski of Poland, and Prime Minister Andrei Lukanov of Bulgaria (such was the speed of the changes across the continent that the latter had been in office just twenty-four hours).[8] The first step, they agreed, was to do away with the Soviet Union's economic trading bloc, COMECON. It would be opened up to capitalist investment to begin with, and then formally disbanded the following June. The Bulgarians, as inheritors of perhaps the weakest economy around the table, were the least enamored of this idea. As Lukanov of Bulgaria recognized, abandoning COMECON, without forging a new alternative, would leave the newly postcommunist nations with no institutional fallback plan as they grappled with the challenge of incorporation into the capitalist world.

Other disagreements broke out at the meeting too. Czechoslovakia's Marián Čalfa took the opportunity to air his country's demand that the 75,000 soldiers of the USSR still stationed in Czechoslovakia now leave forthwith, a call which Moscow had to date been studiously ignoring. "They say that this is too brief a time. We say that it took one night for the [Soviet] troops to come and that one year should be enough for them to leave," said Čalfa to raucous applause.[9] Next it was the Warsaw Pact's turn to be decommissioned (though this was not formalized until a follow-up meeting in Budapest later in the month). NATO's longtime greatest foe was officially disbanded on July 1, 1991, after a final meeting overseen by Václav Havel in Prague, the very city which in 1968 had been the victim of that Pact's then considerable force. By that time the military alliance had been reduced to a mere "political consultative committee": its "funeral," in the words of Lech Wałęsa, a happy occasion—if remarkably muted, given its past importance.[10]

The Eastern and central European leaders present at Davos welcomed most of these changes, even if, like the Bulgarians, they sometimes balked at the speed at which they were occurring. It is not hard to understand why: the fact that many of the newly independent nations were also heavily indebted and in desperate need of Western assistance and expertise drastically curtailed their options. Poland's Jan Krzysztof Bielecki, for example, asked for Western forgiveness for 80 percent of the country's debt, which, within limits, the Western nations were willing to grant. Hungary, however, took a different approach altogether and studiously avoided asking for *any* debt relief (it was forced instead to raise cash by selling off state assets). In so doing its intention was to elicit not the sympathy but the confidence of Western investors—suggesting there was little about the rules of capitalism that the Eastern Europeans needed teaching.

Ostensibly what emerged from the meeting was a sense, as the French magazine *L'Expansion* put it, that, as capitalist economics came to the formerly socialist states, "Europe's Renaissance" as a unified continent was safely in hand. Denmark's prime minister, Poul Schlüter, was perhaps more prudent in observing, during a follow-up event organized in Berlin that June, that the changes set in motion may well have been "incredible," but there remained a "moral-ideological" aspect to keep in mind as well, and there were more complex lessons of history to be taken into account than he feared his colleagues had thus far stopped to consider. To attend the meeting in Berlin the Western leaders had to pass through Checkpoint Charlie, for example. And while the famous symbol of a Europe divided would be removed just the following week, the past could not—and should not—be erased quite so easily, Schlüter warned. "Socialism with a human face was the name which Alexander Dubček gave his attempt to introduce reforms in the Prague Spring of 1968," he went on. "I believe that the present situation calls for the representation of capitalism with a human face."[11] These were wise words indeed. But there were already strong indications that this might be rather too much to ask for.

Come the summer of 1990 and it was apparent that the newly post-communist nations would struggle as they sought to join the global economy. Some, like Czechoslovakia, would ultimately break apart entirely, the wealthier Czechs deciding they did not wish to be held back by the economically more backward Slovakia, resulting in the "velvet divorce" of January 1, 1993. It was a peaceful parting of the ways, but one that would be to the lasting regret of many who perhaps rightly felt it was indicative of a new impatience that had been lacking in the past. Opinion polls at the time revealed that 67 percent of Slovaks and 78 percent of Czechs were actually against the division of their country. But Václav Havel and Vladimír Mečiar, who orchestrated the separation, each preferred the look of his own political prospects in the newly seceded entities, and they chose not to listen to the people. The result was dramatic. Everything now had to be divided according to the 2:1 population ratio between the two halves of the former Czechoslovakian state: military equipment, property, even embassies.[12] Other countries, like Hungary, fared better at first in managing the new realities. But even there, difficulties were becoming apparent.

In part the problem was that no one knew quite what they were supposed to be doing anymore. As the historian Tony Judt was surely right to observe, "The much-anticipated passage from capitalism to socialism had been theorized ad nauseam in academies, universities and coffee bars from Belgrade to Berkeley; but no one had thought to offer a blueprint for the transition from socialism to capitalism."[13] The practicalities were so vast and complex as to defy any such theorizing, of course. Disposing of organizations like COMECON was the work of a minute. But the actual regional distortions of industrial plant, of labor force and of transport and communication networks that COMECON accounted for *on the ground* would take years to unpick: something the British would later learn to their cost after Brexit. It would also leave a great many people without jobs in the meantime (as engine parts made in one former bloc country, for assembly in another, no longer had a third country willing to buy the resulting car). As their protected communist-era economies deteriorated the former socialist countries often found they were without means to capitalize on the global economy either.

The formal definition of a capitalist crisis is a situation in which firms are unable to employ workers at a time of high unemployment. The irony for the East was that they were about to experience the ultimate downside of capitalism as a condition of entering into it. And their travails were to last for some time: the Baltic nations of Estonia, Lithuania, and Latvia would experience on average five years of declining GDP after 1989; Slovenia would experience three, Romania four, and Bulgaria no less than six.[14] Germany was once more the great exception here: the economic woes were largely covered by the deep pockets of the federal treasury in the West. In most cases, the postcommunist countries had to stitch their productive economies back together at a time when industry and output were collapsing.

In some instances wide-ranging, even brilliant solutions were found to almost impossible problems. Currency boards were introduced in the Baltics and eventually Bulgaria, which helped to stabilize its national monetary system by backing it with foreign exchange. Hungary meanwhile ruled that property expropriated under the former regime would not be returned (there was a strong case for restituting assets stolen under the former regime, of course, but to do so would literally bring the country to financial ruin). Instead, monetary compensation was provided, the argument being that it was better for everyone to get a little than for some to get everything they might have wanted.[15] In Germany, by contrast, the first-ever freely elected parliament of the GDR established a trusteeship, the *Treuhand*, in June 1990 that would handle the privatization of former state property and act as a curating mechanism for turning state enterprises into private companies. It was in effect a managed form of deindustrialization.

Such foresight was not everywhere forthcoming. In Ukraine, where the often-disastrous experience of other countries in the region led to a refusal to adopt any sort of economic reform at all, the problems of the past persisted and no new opportunities came knocking to suggest an escape route. In the Balkans, escalating war and ethnic violence merely added to the problems and ensured that unemployment remained high. By the mid 1990s incomes in the East were on average just 30 percent what they were in Western Europe.[16] In Bulgaria corruption was rife and the government simply slid into debt until, in 1996, hyperinflation set off a mass brain drain of the nation's most talented workers. As a group of experts later observed: "The values, principles and procedures of democracy are alive only on paper, while the political and administrative establishments persistently undermine them and create favorable conditions for state capture and corruption."[17]

Bulgaria experienced one of the least successful transitions. Events there were a reminder that the social and economic problems of transition were inseparable from the political challenges of the moment. As the novelist György Konrád put it, describing the experience of a new-found democratic malaise in Hungary:

> You can found a party, start a newspaper, establish a publishing house; you can demonstrate if you wish, and assemble in public places in great numbers; and you can talk, talk as much as you like, as long as you can get someone to listen. New faces, names and concepts emerge—and submerge. It is easy to become fashionable—and to become unfashionable. If anything deserves publicity, it will most probably get it. The press has an insatiable appetite, and viewers expect the small screen to provide them with the truth, maybe even with wisdom. Are they getting any? They are somewhat disappointed: they get as much as there is. Stocks of wisdom are low. The country presents itself. There were no masterpieces in the desk drawers. It turned out that the country was not given democracy as a gift, and moreover, it was also short of democrats.[18]

There were plenty of democrats in the western half of the continent, of course. Yet after the upheavals of the past fifteen years these were democrats of an increasingly conservative hue. This was not just about a reorientation of the political center: for much of the modern democratic era the main challenge to mainstream parties had come from the (communist) left. From now on the radical left would go into hibernation while the challenger parties would be almost entirely from the right. That challenge frequently found its footing in mainstream debate, moreover, when free-market economics (not social policy) was the chosen ground to stand upon. The effect was to intensify the pull away from managed to laissez-faire policies. And with inflation skyrocketing in the Eastern European nations it simply looked to many Western policymakers and advisers as if the East was merely lacking in this basic insight; that this was why it was now experiencing its own version of 1970s malaise. And they made sure that it was soon being fast-tracked out of it along the path the West had found for itself.

In the immediate aftermath of the anti-Gorbachev coup in 1992, for example, 150 business leaders descended upon Moscow to offer their advice on economic reforms. Understanding next to nothing of the communist past, much less the current and unstable postcommunist reality, the Western delegation did not think that a gradual transition— a finding of their feet, as the West had found its feet for more than a decade after the crises of the early 1970s—was the most appropriate way forward. Their preference rather was for a sudden and dramatic overhaul of the institutional DNA of the former Soviet countries. Only once that was in hand would Western investors be willing to jump on board with any actual investment itself. It was a forceful, and largely untested, approach to the delicate task of transition that put the size of the market long before the quality of democratic institutions in the pecking order of transition priorities. In doing so it betrayed a blind spot that would later come back to haunt the hallways of power in the West for years to come.

"'SHOCK THERAPY' FOR POLAND" announced the *New York Times* at the very end of 1989, in reference to the new set of ideas that was rolled out—just months after the fall of the Berlin Wall—in the East. One of the leading advocates of this shock therapy was an American scholar turned policy guru, Jeffrey Sachs.[19] Sachs had been influential in overseeing the economic aspects of the transition from autocracy in Bolivia: a very particular set of circumstances he fervently believed, in light of the fall of communism, now had a more universal import. Sachs's observations of what had happened in countries like Bolivia that suffered a so-called "resource curse" were replaced by the new "curse" of communist inheritance. The promise of economic growth, and the sort of liberal economic institutions that it was believed were best positioned to deliver this, would in due course also be seen as fundamental to the claims of peace-building in the Balkans: that second pillar of the Western response to postcommunism.[20]

After Poland, "front-loaded reform" programs (as the IMF's technical jargon had it) were also introduced the same year in Hungary and Yugoslavia. Bulgaria, Romania, and Czechoslovakia signed on the following year. In due course the IMF would provide 530 person-years of advice, almost exclusively in fiscal and monetary practices, and oversee the training of 12,000 officials across the region in Washington Consensus-friendly policies.[21] But if the stated purpose of these programs was to create a

Western *economic* system, it was not to say there was no political project invested in the shock therapy. Indeed, the signature feature of such reforms was the need to make uncompromisingly deep and rapid changes in the political and institutional makeup of a country, to roll back the state along the trail blazed by Thatcher and Reagan in the West the decade before, so as to afford the maximum freedom of movement to the market and to market actors.

One of the solutions proposed for Mongolia's collapsed economy, for example, was for it to specialize in making computer software: this in a country where only 4 percent of the population outside of the capital had electricity.[22] In Poland, the Balcerowicz Plan, another shock-therapy blueprint, recommended the wholesale ditching of the agricultural sector, even though agriculture still occupied a fifth of the workforce by the end of the twentieth century.[23] The plan was the brainchild of Finance Minister Leszek Balcerowicz (a homegrown advocate of rapid economic reforms) and it accompanied no less drastic upheavals in other sectors too: the removal of price controls and the cutting of all existing subsidies, while at the same time building up foreign reserves to secure the "confidence" of the markets.

It was true that confidence was needed in Eastern Europe at this point, and economic expertise to guide it. Just as in the 1920s, when an earlier generation of (mainly) British and French bankers, advisers, and "experts" had been packed off to Eastern Europe to offer advice as well as money, such reform packages were frequently welcomed by the former communist countries. But as György Konrád again observed, this time with his eyes cast firmly to the West: "It is not easy to create a firmly founded democracy in a country that is in the midst of an economic crisis: fearing the rigors of the world market, afraid that its labor and property—indeed, its whole existence—will be devalued, that the switch to a market economy will result in a new kind of insecurity and servile incertitude."[24] This proved also to be the case in those countries like Slovakia, Romania, and Ukraine, where the opposite path to the shock therapists was taken and authoritarian-inclined leaders like Slovakia's Vladimír Mečiar stubbornly refused to reform a thing. The tragic irony confronting the region in the first half of the 1990s was that so few countries were willing to adopt a more moderate middle ground.

But the heart of the problem was something else as well: the refusal of the West, and the United States above all, even to countenance a more public economic support package, without ties or conditions, of the sort that had been so successfully granted to Western Europe half a century before under the Marshall Plan. With hindsight, this was *exactly* what Eastern Europe now needed. But the US Treasury did not feel it could afford such largesse; it preferred, along with its European counterparts, to give its private bankers the responsibility; and the intellectual climate of the day was for holding a demonstratively promarket hard line. Thus *The Economist* was soon urging Gorbachev to adopt "strong man rule" at home, the better "to smash the resistance that has blocked serious economic reform."[25]

The Economist was not alone. "Whereas these countries are willing to implement reforms in order to evolve toward market-oriented economies . . ."[26] went the preamble to the new European Bank for Reconstruction and Development (EBRD), which was the institution set up largely in place of a fully fledged Marshall Plan–type offering. There was, not surprisingly, no small amount of scandal at the EBRD's inception in 1990, when it was revealed it had spent more money preparing its sumptuous new headquarters in London than it did on actual aid to Eastern and central Europe.[27]

It is hard not to detect in all this baying for economic blood a certain will to see just what sort of economic utopias might yet be pushed through in countries which were not yet fully fledged democracies. But as one prominent economic theorist put it, shock therapy—what he described as a Popperian form of "Utopian Social Engineering"[28]—not only failed to develop meaningful economic change, it also wrought enormous social havoc. *The Lancet* reported several million deaths as a direct result of the reforms, the life expectancy of Russian men actually falling from sixty-seven to sixty years between 1985 and 2007.

In light of such figures the Western response to the actual *needs* of the postcommunist countries was, in hindsight, nothing short of dismal. The former chemist and founder of the Loctite corporation, Robert H. Krieble, formed the Krieble Institute in 1989, "to promote democracy and economic freedom in the Soviet Union and Eastern Europe." Krieble himself made over eighty trips to the region, "conducting seminars, meeting with leaders and training a full-time network of over 20,000 field experts to establish political economic reform."[29] In reality most would be forced to choose between a greater degree of liberalization (open up the private sector, reduce taxes, peel back regulations) or a more comprehensive democratization of the state (requiring greater numbers of competent public-sector workers). And whether it was the advice of the EBRD, or the individual development plans worked out by Western experts for the various states themselves, the advice was always the same: choose the market, democracy will follow.

Democratization ensued in the East then only after the banner of liberalization had staked out the ground first. The countries of the East were sold the promise of functioning states and free markets as if they were one and the same thing. But if what beckoned investors to the former Soviet lands was the promise of a vast "peace dividend," what informed their investment decisions was less postcommunist reality, which was often dire, than prevailing ideas in the West about capitalist hyper-reality. As one bond trader later recalled: "The 90s was a very special period that's unlikely to be repeated for a while." All of a sudden "there were more people to sell to and there was cheaper labor."[30] For Eastern Europeans it may well have seemed as if history was "pressing a hundred years into a hundred days."[31] But Western advisers, not history, were the ones applying the torque. Nationalism was one ideology enjoying a new lease of life in the wake of communism's fall, as the Yugoslavs were soon to find to their cost. But the market was another. What it achieved was less the reconstruction of the East than the consolidation of the new liberal politics of the West.

By the mid 1990s the score sheets were in. Poland's economy was rapidly liberalized beyond even the level of the most advanced capitalist econ-omies of the time as domestic real wages fell by up to 40 percent. In Ukraine, where the nomenclature had simply changed shirts, from com-munist bureaucrats to capitalist entrepreneurs, state assets—be it drilling rights or property—continued to be kept out of the reach of ordinary citizens, as they were sold off (for a slice of the profits) to the highest bidder: usually one known to the selling party beforehand. The investment that was forthcoming thus did little to leverage, for ordinary people, the value of the often-rich resources these countries disposed of: energy, minerals, and property, not to mention a well-educated workforce.

Indeed, when measured in the aggregate, the overall effect of what Russian Premier Viktor Chernomyrdin had, by 1994, come to dub dis-paragingly as the "market economic romance," had been nothing less than to reduce the living standards of Eastern Europeans by one third (in Russia it would fall to one half and in Georgia to less than a fifth).[32] This was borne by the citizens of the former Soviet Union, for now, because they were told that a capitalist great leap forward was waiting for them just around the corner. What was more immediately waiting, for Russians in particular, was a setback in terms of democratization and the sort of devastation to economy and society that it usually takes a war to achieve. For all that the breakup of the Soviet Empire had achieved the near impossible feat of avoiding violence and bloodshed, the way that blank slate was now being built upon by the West threatened to render the achievement null and void, as countries like Poland, Slovenia, and Hungary simply took, in the words of the Hungarian historian Iván Berend, a "detour from the Periphery to the Periphery."[33]

Things were bleaker still in Russia, where Yeltsin's now increasingly heavy-handed rule at home was propped up by his seemingly indefatigable international appeal: an appeal that was itself strengthened by his commitment, as against his people's wishes, to the economic reforms the West wanted to see. Yeltsin proved himself adept at asking for money from the West, and Clinton in particular, charmed by his "charisma"—an attraction well captured in his roaring with laughter behind a no less roaringly drunk Yeltsin at a press conference in New York in 1995—was happy to oblige. But Yeltsin was less enamored of adopting the legal restraints and the institutions of economic oversight that any ethical market economy by rights requires. Instead, he gathered together his favored associates, cronies, and business partners, and proceeded to divvy up the Russian economy between them. By 2004 thirty-six Russian billionaires had siphoned off $110 billion from the national coffers: a quarter of the nation's entire GDP.[34]

Contrary to the West's stated aims of "enabling them to overcome their past," the "complete disdain for all that exists" of the Yeltsin era did not so much destroy the communist system in Russia as the reformed institutions that Gorbachev had put in place after 1989.[35] It was not the communist past that was erased but the potentially more vibrant and social democratic future that Gorbachev had envisaged. By the time the Russian parliament finally saw fit to bring Yeltsin's party to an end in 1993, the president felt strong enough to disband it. In a move that finally nailed his true colors to the mast, on October 4 Yeltsin had 5,000 loyal soldiers surround the Russian White House and set it ablaze. Long before Vladimir Putin, Russia had been returned to the good offices of autocracy in all but name, and the intensity of market reforms had helped to achieve it.

There was one further and yet more troubling outcome of the economic free-for-all promoted by the West after 1989: the ease with which free markets, former authoritarians, and criminals were able to blend seamlessly together. "The [only] private entrepreneurs being spawned in Russia today," commented Melvin Fagen, former director of the UN Economic Commission for Europe, in the *New York Times*, "are mainly black marketeers or corrupt officials who have stolen state property."[36] This was most apparent in those countries like Slovakia, Romania, Serbia, and Croatia, where totalitarianism was replaced by a form of crony capitalism.[37] Nicolae Ceauşescu had starved the people to pay off the country's debts in the 1980s; now those same people would be robbed of their inheritance by capitalist corruption instead. It was apparent too in the rise of organized crime, not—as some argued—as an unfortunate side effect of the transitions, but as integral to the political systems being put in place.[38] "A Mafia-type goods distribution system continues to exist and grow," Fagen went on. "The economic outlook is bleak for all except hustlers and fast-ruble artists."[39]

Yet few Western European leaders were prepared to see this. Had they done so they might have reassessed the slick narratives of "economic opening" and "regional integration" they had constructed for themselves out of communism's fall: the Eastern nations could only catch up, argued the experts; they could only benefit from economic liberalization. When it was clear the flight plan wasn't working, the solution was usually just to ask them to keep circling. The EC in particular refined this approach via its use of the *acquis communautaire*, the accumulated body of EU law, to arrange the different countries of the East into an elaborate series of holding patterns. "No one here is serious about enlargement [anymore]," observed a senior European Commission official in the mid 1990s.[40]

The accession of Eastern and central Europe was in the final analysis a partial achievement. Its mixed economic blessings and distinctly underwhelming democratic progress was a reality that the rhetoric of a largely boosterish Western media tended to hide. All this was dramatically different from the way that southern Europe had been integrated in the 1970s. Perhaps because the stakes were not as high—because there was not as much the West hoped to gain by their accession—the Mediterranean countries were given much greater freedom of maneuver in their transitions from authoritarian rule. Their largely agrarian economies and patronage-soaked societies were allowed to adapt and to adopt the institutions of liberal democracy and markets largely on their own terms, and to begin with they fared better for it. In the aftermath of communism, the Western democracies chose not to show their "human face," as Schlüter had urged back in the summer of 1990.

By the 1990s that face had notably hardened in some respects. Eastern

Europe was falling into a state of disarray. Meanwhile the Western half of the continent now set itself to hitching all further political integration to a parallel process of European-wide deregulation: the problems raised by geopolitics in the East would be solved by a further turn to the market in the West.[41] Eastern and central European citizens had hoped the fall of communism might introduce to their countries the consumer capitalism of the Western Golden Age; instead they found themselves a glorified experiment on behalf of the casino capitalism of the future. As the former Polish dissident Lech Wałęsa famously put it in 1989: "To our misfortune, we have won!"[42]

The European "Relaunch" (and a Crisis in the Markets)

If the transition to capitalism and democracy had turned into something of a pyrrhic victory for countries such as Poland, this still left unresolved the question of what the more fortunate nations of the continent (those whose citizens were now learning to imagine themselves as less narrowly "Western" European) thought they had won. The answer here soon took shape around the long-anticipated Treaty of European Union, to be signed at Maastricht in December 1992. Even as the institutions of the former communist world were being torn down the new European Treaty, as it was officially known, was being hashed out, the two parallel processes a specter at one another's feast. The Maastricht Treaty—the culmination of the work toward a single market that EC president Jacques Delors had set in train with the signing of the Single European Act (SEA) in 1986— provided the most dramatic example yet of just what sort of future the Western democracies were aiming for. It was far and away the most ambitious blueprint ever to be unveiled at the transnational level. And its central feature was the concrete plans that it now laid out for a full *monetary* union.

That Delors was the chief architect of Maastricht was a fact lost on few Brits at the time thanks to the unflinching clarity of the *Sun* newspaper's pithy opposition—"Up Yours, Delors!"—which it blazoned on its front page in November 1990. Delors bore the brunt of Britain's Euroskepticism, but then at the midway point of his ten years in charge of the EC (1985–1995) he not only had the wind behind him, he knew which way it was blowing. Monetary union, he argued, was just a step change in the status quo agreed with the SEA in 1986: if European nations were going to coordinate their currency movements, why not do so in a more carefully managed way with a single currency? Of course, it was precisely that sort of managerialism, over which the lines of British authority were unclear, that most irritated the *Sun* and its readers. And a great many Brits no doubt did turn to face France at the stroke of noon, as the *Sun* advised, to raise a two-fingered salute to his plans.

In fact, the plot lines of the single currency are ultimately to be traced, once again, in the interactions between the governments of Mitterrand and Kohl: this time in the context of ongoing moves toward the single market and above all its progressive removal of capital controls between nations. The French had long found the existing European Monetary System (the system of semi-fixed pegs introduced in 1979) far from optimal because the franc tended to be weaker relative to the Deutschmark, with the result that it was invariably France that appeared to bear the political costs of any adjustment required to keep the system operational. Mitterrand's decision to try more actively tracking the Deutschmark in 1983, the so-called Franc Fort policy, was a first attempt to solve this problem. Formally binding themselves to the Deutschmark, as was now proposed, would be a far more comprehensive solution. After Black Monday in 1987, which saw the largest percentage fall in US stock market history and yet another costly French revaluation, this was increasingly seen as the only option. Behind the scenes the French now finally gave up on the Franc Fort and, in January 1988, the French finance minister, Édouard Balladur, sent word to the Germans that his government was looking to obtain a more permanent fix with the Deutschmark.

This wasn't something that West Germany would necessarily be willing to agree to, however. But for different reasons the West Germans too now came to see a comprehensive monetary union as the best way forward. Critical for the Federal German Republic (FDR) was the fact that, ever since moves toward the single market had been set in motion after 1986, the challenge of managing the EMS had become all the greater (since the national policy tools enabling small adjustments within it were increasingly being removed). The German economy suffered only indirectly from this, since the Deutschmark was the strongest currency, but it was a problem all the same, precisely because the Deutschmark *was* the strongest currency: it was Germany's system, in other words, to have to watch over.

By the late 1980s the FDR's leadership was also growing tired of being blamed for Europe's currency problems. For these two reasons, and because in 1988 it was also West Germany's turn to host the rotating presidency of the Council of Ministers, German Foreign Minister Hans-Dietrich

Genscher tabled the idea for consideration: the Germans needed to show something for their period at the helm, after all. Delors was then put in charge of a commission tasked with looking into the matter and soon stamped his own liberalizing imprint upon it. The blueprint for a European Monetary Union (EMU) that emerged was in some respects influenced by the Werner Plan (1970) before it. But there would be no fiscal union here.[43] This was a plan designed largely *by* central bankers and *for* central bankers, and ensuring that it succeeded as a purely monetary proposition now trumped everything else.

What finally sealed the decision to make monetary union a central part of the forthcoming Maastricht Treaty was the fall of communism and the suddenly greatly sharpened desire—including among the British—to lock a now reunified Germany *into* Europe. If the geopolitical future had suddenly become a lot less certain after 1989, monetary union would at least remove *one* source of a future greater Germany's power: the Deutschmark. Kohl largely acquiesced in this, more preoccupied as he was with the German elections in 1990. Critically he also dropped the earlier German insistence that closer monetary union should proceed hand in hand with closer *political* union. Finally, he cajoled the Bundesbank, which was perhaps the most reluctant actor of all, into cooperating, though not without their winning some significant guarantees in the process: above all that any future European Central Bank would be modeled closely on the Bundesbank itself.[44]

Maastricht was thus the culmination of each of these multiple histories that converged through the breakup of communism. But it was also, of course, its own beginning. For once Maastricht came into force on January 1, 1993, the European Community (EC) officially ceased to exist and the modern, more closely integrated European Union (EU) was born. The treaty itself set out everything from a concrete road map toward the single currency, which would not actually be named the "euro" until 1995, to new powers for the European parliament and elements of a new common foreign and security policy among the member nations. Institutionally speaking, the step change was unprecedented. Little wonder that "the EU" now exploded onto the consciousness of European citizens in a way the European Community never had.

And yet not everyone was as enamored of the idea of Maastricht as the members of Delors's working groups. The Dutch voted against Maastricht and the French only just approved it by a wafer-thin vote, which was especially embarrassing for Mitterrand. Indeed, given that the treaty had been written for the most part not only over the heads but also often against the wishes of the citizens of those countries, it is not hard to understand why "Europeans" also began to become wary of "Europe" at this moment, with the result that a more hardened strain of Euroskepticism now developed. Ultimately, however, the hesitations of Europe's citizens did little to dent the march to a single currency after 1992. The one thing that did, temporarily, put a dent in such plans was a crisis brought on after Maastricht not in Europe's parliaments but in its financial markets.

Until the single currency came into force in 1999 European monetary policy continued to be organized within the terms of the increasingly fragile European Monetary System. Back in 1979 it had been pressure on the dollar (driving up European prices) that helped pull the major continental economies, and eventually Britain, into what was in effect a system of semifixed exchange rates. Now, at the start of the 1990s, pressure on Europe's own leading currency, the Deutschmark, threatened to bring about its demise. The huge increase in spending consequent on Germany's own recent monetary union (the convergence of the two Deutschmarks at the eye-wateringly expensive ratio of 1:1) had contributed to rising inflation. The real problem, however, was that Kohl insisted on paying for this by borrowing rather than by raising taxes: the result was a tripling of the West German deficit and an interest rate spike that cascaded across the continent via the Exchange Rate Mechanism.[45] Combined with the political uncertainty of the ongoing Maastricht approval process, the markets began to sense there might be chinks in the armor of the EMS, and speculators began testing out what looked to be the weakest links in the chain.

It was the UK economy that was hit hardest by this, on September 16, 1992, yet another "black" day, this one falling on a Wednesday: Black Wednesday. Britain had only joined the ERM in 1990, when Thatcher's ambitious Chancellor Nigel Lawson had smooth-talked her into it (after a "nasty little meeting" between himself and Geoffrey Howe, as she recalled).[46] Since then it had repeatedly fallen to the bottom level of its permissible band as Thatcher's economy came off the rails and recession in the UK gripped tighter. Interest rates were high and the pound was overvalued. To try to persuade the markets that sterling was sound, the Major government began using up some of its own foreign reserves to buy back British pounds, thereby in effect maintaining the value of sterling. This they found easy to do, since speculators like George Soros were all too happy to sell what they were still convinced was a weak currency back to them (Soros reportedly made a billion dollars out of the UK government during the crisis).[47]

On Black Wednesday itself, Britain made a last-ditch effort to ride out the crisis. The chief dealer for the Bank of England was asked to buy more sterling in four hours than he ever had before or would do after. It was, he said, a "stunningly expensive" day. But it was like buying buckets of water filled with holes, since no matter how much sterling was purchased the currency immediately began shedding its value. Meanwhile, the Bundesbank looked on, but with Helmut Schmidt's secret assurance still in its pocket (the guarantee that it need never put its domestic inflation-fighting mandate at risk in the name of supporting weaker currencies) it declared itself unwilling to apply its funds to Britain's defense. As the day wore on the whole affair was painted in the media as if some grand battle had been taking place, which, in a way, it had. The government was "firing off its biggest guns" in defense of the pound, it was reported, but before the day was over it had met with economic "slaughter." The pound had not been "saved."[48] At 7:40 the Chancellor of the Exchequer Norman Lamont—certainly no Duke of Wellington—appeared live on national television to announce what the BBC described as "[t]he most dramatic turn in government economic strategy in 25 years": Britain would be leaving the ERM forthwith.[49]

The markets were not done yet, though. Encouraged, they turned on Italy. The result there was exactly the same as it had been in Britain, and Italy too left on September 17. Then it was the turn of Spain and Portugal. And then France, where—adding to the tensions—elections were soon to take place. Unlike with the pound, this denouement to the crisis did finally bring the Bundesbank into play, the "cavalry from over the hill" that never did arrive to help Britain.[50] But it did so acrimoniously: billions upon billions were expended by France and Germany in a war of financial attrition against the markets that continued well into the following year.

By the end of July 1993, the Bank of France was spending over $32 billion a week. Edmond Alphandéry, the French finance minister, could hold out no more and he called for a crisis meeting of the ERM countries. With some politicians declaring "Maastricht is dead," the situation clearly could not be allowed to continue. An emergency nighttime meeting was called between German and French bankers in Munich on July 22. But still the Germans refused to adjust interest rates and the crisis rumbled on. All that could then be done was to move the outer bounds of permissible currency variation from 2.25 percent to 15 percent.[51]

Maastricht had not yet entered into force (it would do so on November 1, 1993). But already the new order was established. Caught between the rock of currency market speculation and the hard place of Bundesbank fiscal discipline, things would simply keep being changed until the right outcome was obtained. "The result," as the economic historian Harold James has written, was nothing if not "paradoxical": "a severe crisis that shook nerves, destroyed confidence, and was generally supposed to have made the realization of the Maastricht Treaty impossible, produced the *real* foundation for monetary Union."[52]

In many ways the death of the ERM and the crisis of the European Monetary System more generally can be seen as the opening salvo, a first skirmish within the terms of the new neoliberal consensus, between markets and democratic states. It certainly replicated many of the features of the later, far more serious crisis of the euro. And during this first round, at least, the markets won hands down. The primary response of governments was simply to accommodate to the new reality. In 1993 a new capital liberalization demand was incorporated into the very definition of "European-ness" at the Copenhagen meeting on European integration. The "Copenhagen criteria" thus became a way of ensuring that all countries who were or wished to be European had therefore, in addition to conforming to the constitutive norms of democracy, rule of law, human rights protections, and a market economy, also to enact strong capital liberalization legislation and to renounce capital controls. This being European law, they no longer had any choice in the matter.

However, the parallel financial crisis playing itself out simultaneously in Sweden between 1991 and 1993 suggested there were other ways that European nations could have handled the ERM crisis without resorting to a formula of more of the same. Sweden was one of the European Free Trade Area (EFTA) countries, along with Finland, Austria, Switzerland, and Norway. These were all relatively small, well-to-do countries who had long wanted access to the European single market, but who were also either skeptical of greater political and economic integration (as with Norway and Switzerland) or unable to align themselves more closely during the Cold War given their officially more "neutral" stances (as in the case of Finland, Sweden, and Austria). Regardless, their currencies were pegged to Europe and Sweden's krona came under intense pressure in 1992 as the economy reeled from a burst property market bubble.

What followed was Sweden's worst economic crisis since the 1930s.

The newly elected government was forced to take radical action (in this respect it was fortunate that the government was newly elected: a more ingrained one might well have been reliant on so many vested interests that it would have been reluctant to try). Its response was two-fold. First, in a move that would become familiar some years later, the government intervened to secure the banking system. But it did so by bailing out the banks with clear strings attached. Then, thanks to a demonstration of cross-party cooperation, the center-right government headed by Carl Bildt was able to offer a clear deposit guarantee for citizens and businesses alike, getting out ahead of the crisis and restoring confidence in the economy. The government later unpegged the krona and allowed the exchange rate to float naturally. Sweden turned the corner and within a year or two had already embarked upon a decade of export-led economic prosperity.[53]

In that regard it fared better than much of the rest of Europe, which struggled during the first half of the decade. In France, Renault closed its flagship factory at Boulogne-Billancourt, the island in the Seine at Sèvres that had for decades been known as the "workers' fortress"—most recently during the upheavals of 1968. It was a telling sign of the times (and was followed by the closure of Bugatti's plant in Emilia-Romagna in 1995). Since the shocks of the 1970s, unemployment had continued to creep up throughout most of Europe during the 1980s, to reach 17 percent in Finland by 1993, and 20 percent in Spain by 1994. The average rate for the EU15 was over 10 percent by 1994, a thirty-year high.[54]

Such aggregate figures disguised sharp regional variations, of course, especially in countries like Italy, with its strong division between North and South. But they could not disguise the overall trend. For in Italy too, in the aftermath of its forced exit from the ERM, alongside a wave of political scandals that greeted the 1990s as they brought the old republic down, the Italian economy began what was to be a twenty-year slide, in which consumption and labor productivity both tailed off. The picture was no better in Portugal, where nearly a third of the active labor force was already working outside the country. Britain meanwhile was officially in recession. And Denmark, like most of the other Nordic countries, was experiencing its slowest period of growth in over a decade, even as it grappled with high rates of inflation.

If Europe was intent on looking forward and on radically speeding up its project of economic integration, then it is important to recall that it was doing so at a moment, once more, of heightened economic unease. But in contrast with what it was permitting the Eastern Europeans to do, Western Europe *did* intend to fashion for itself a place of greater safety amid the turmoil of the post–Cold War years. Only once that was in place would the formerly communist nations, or some of them at least, be invited into the club. In such ways the political upheavals of the immediate post–Cold War moment in the East and the economic transformation of the West thus went hand in hand. Europe as a whole would now spend the next few years tidying up its house and preparing for the future along the lines mapped out by the single currency due to come into force in 1999. Meanwhile, the pendulum of change swung toward the United States.

The Politics of Laissez-Faire

In what seemed a world away from Europe's economic woes, the much-trumpeted arrival of Bill Clinton at the White House in January 1993 represented more than just the usual transition from one presidential administration to another. It marked the return of the Democratic Party to the White House: a place where, Jimmy Carter's four awkward years aside, they had spent precious little time since Lyndon Johnson last closed the door of the Oval Office behind him. It also marked the arrival on the US political scene of a *new* Democratic Party and a *new* brand of politics that was to reshape the entire Western political landscape during the decade to come.

The New Democrats were ecstatic about their recent electoral achievement, and they were anxious to get on with an ambitious program of domestic reform. But first, as always when the dust on the inauguration has settled, there was the education of a president to attend to. And Bill Clinton's was to be delivered at the hands of the very market actors now wreaking havoc across Europe. During the campaign Clinton had promised major investments in jobs, education, and public infrastructure. By the time he took office, the president had undertaken a Mitterrand-style U-turn, and his prior commitments to public spending had been replaced by something altogether different. The reason for the change was a crisis in the bond markets, which, Clinton now learned, a president upsets at his peril.

Specifically Clinton learned that the bond markets did not like his spending plans. And encouraged by his new economic advisers (the imposing Texas senator, businessman, and former vice-presidential candidate Lloyd Bentsen, Roger Altman from the Blackstone Group, and Robert

Rubin from Goldman Sachs) he had dropped the middle-class tax cut he had promised during the election and moved to embrace a new form of fiscal conservatism. "We're Eisenhower Republicans here [now]," Clinton was heard muttering during the transition. "We stand for lower deficits, free trade, and the bond market. Isn't that great?"[55] He was being ironic, but he was also being a realist.

Clinton had in fact never been a traditional big-spending liberal. Even during the campaign he had made clear that "[t]he most important global challenge we face, is the emergence of an increasingly interdependent and competitive global economy."[56] But at the start of the 1990s politicians in all the Western democracies were waking up to two new and uncomfortable facts and Clinton was no exception. First, it had become apparent that globalization was restricting their ability to raise money by increasing taxes, since it was less easy to work out who to tax and more tempting to tax the wealthiest of all less (to avoid them moving elsewhere). Second, that element of globalization that was most dynamic of all, the money markets, as they moved operations to the transnational sphere, increasingly lay beyond *national* governments' regulatory sphere of influence.[57]

The new economic policy that Clinton now put forward, which would underpin the next eight years of American politics, needs to be understood in light of this dawning recognition. It was a policy that, for the first time ever, deliberately took its signals from the markets rather than from the voters themselves. As Bentsen outlined to the president-elect, Clinton would have to rein in his ambitions for office in light of this fact if he wanted to avoid the fate that had befallen his predecessor. He would also have to go out of his way to actively "please" the markets, and the bond traders in particular, who did not like tax increases or large-scale government spending. "You mean to tell me that the success of my program and my reelection hinges on the Federal Reserve and a bunch of fucking bond traders?" Clinton shot back under his breath.[58] Bentsen absolutely did.

The thinking that therefore came to dominate Clinton's economic platform in office was simple. Cut the deficit; reduce government borrowing, and so free up capital for investment elsewhere in the economy. "The less money we tie up in publicly held debt, the more money we free up for private sector investment," as Clinton himself put it. "In an age of worldwide capital markets, this is the way a nation prospers."[59] Whether or not that would hold true for everyone time would tell. The reality was that Clinton's promise to focus on the economy became, in office, a somewhat narrower commitment to focusing on the financial markets. And the immediate priority, if he was to do this, was to show such discipline in fiscal matters that the Federal Reserve could confidently keep short-term interest rates low. The result was a tacit and yet highly significant agreement between the president and his chairman of the Federal Reserve, Alan Greenspan, that the first fully post–Cold War US administration would keep the world's largest economy on a fiscally conservative leash. But first, as both recognized, the US economy had to be got going again.

Clinton's first and defining budget in 1993 was thus focused on economic *growth*. And for good reason. Clinton needed *something* to show for a torrid first year of nomination knockdowns and congressional disappointments resulting from the fact that the Republicans, undergoing their own metamorphosis toward a party of partisan opposition, had decided to meet his every move with a stony wall of noncooperation. The economy was in no better shape. When Clinton took office the US recovery was still uncertain (unemployment remained high at 7.5 percent and inflation at 3.3 percent). The budget deficit had reached $290 billion and the national debt more than $3 trillion. Real wages were falling, as they had been since 1986, as competition from low-wage countries began to be felt by US firms.[60]

By January 1994, however, the economy was beginning to pick up. By then more than 1.6 million jobs had been created. Home and auto sales were up. People were beginning to refinance their homes and to spend a little of the extra money available to them. Banks were beginning to lend once again: something they hadn't done since the Savings and Loans (S&L) debacle and the tighter regulations on bank capital requirements (how much money they needed to keep in reserve in case their investments turned sour) subsequently introduced by Bush in 1989. Perhaps most importantly the bond markets Clinton had been told he needed to keep on his side seemed satisfied. In that year's State of the Union an exuberant Clinton lauded the new spirit of optimism in the country. The only thing that might spoil the party was if the Federal Reserve raised interest rates to cool off the recovery. But the Federal Reserve hadn't done that for six years.

Perhaps Clinton ought to have become suspicious when Alan Greenspan met with him in January 1994 to tell him that the Federal Reserve was worried about rising inflation, and a growing equity bubble in particular. Both concerns pointed to the specter of a possible interest rate rise. But Clinton believed the Fed was still with him on the need to get the economy going again. After all, he had kept his side of the bargain. Clinton was furious therefore when Greenspan did raise short-term interest rates on February 4. The bond markets had already been given their "pound of flesh" in the ditching of Clinton's investment strategy during the transition. Now Greenspan was demanding another pound of flesh from him because things were going *too* well. There was nothing, however, that Clinton could do about it—except to throw "purple fits" each time Greenspan raised interest rates again—something he did seven times that year.[61]

Clinton was about to become more incensed still when the unanticipated effect of Greenspan's interest rate rises hit the very bond markets he had been so careful to keep happy. In the early 1990s, bond trading was carried out on small green terminals: there was no Bloomberg, no wider net of information feeding in to help traders make reasoned decisions. All they could do was react to the basic indicators before them. And for bond traders the world over, the shock of Greenspan's interest rate rise was responded to with devastating effect. What *Fortune* described as "the great bond massacre"—the worst bond market loss in history, in fact—saw more than a trillion dollars lost by bondholders. And chaos on such a scale inevitably spread to other parts of the financial market as well. Hedge funds went bust. Banks plunged into the red. Portfolio investors lost nearly everything. "It was Armageddon," recalled one trader. "Everyone got crushed heading for the exits at the same time."[62] By the end of the year, even Orange County in California, whose borrowing had become highly leveraged as the county put off paying off its debts, was forced to declare bankruptcy.

If Clinton had been in any doubt before about the power of the markets over government, the chaos in Orange County and, hot on its heels, the even more drastic travails of the Mexican peso just over the border served as timely reminders of the fate that awaited those who did not tread with utmost care. The US economy would bounce back from this initial crisis in the markets. But the fallout from the bond market crash was every bit as definitive for the Clinton administration's thinking as the EMS crisis had been for Europe's leaders. The only real question for Clinton now, as for the Europeans before him, was not whether but *how* to accommodate his political program to the new economic realities. In other words, what Clinton had been told in theory by Bentsen had now been brought home as incontrovertible fact. Clinton's combative adviser James Carville, one of the fiscal progressives who had argued for more spending stimulus and less deficit cutting, had it about right when he quipped that he would now like to be reincarnated as the bond market in order that he could come back and intimidate everyone.[63]

Clinton's tack to a more conservative fiscal line was not simply a function of the intimidation of the markets, nor even a function of his political flip-flopping, as many—especially his critics on the left—believed. Clinton was negotiating an economic reality that was bigger than him, bigger than the new Democratic Party, and bigger even than the White House. Ultimately, it wouldn't have mattered if Clinton had been a dyed-in-the-wool Keynesian, since not only was there never much incentive for politicians only fleetingly in office to prime the pump for their successors, but now, after the massive Reagan-era tax cuts and late Cold War military build-up of the 1980s, the US government had little pump left to be primed.

The New Democrats claimed that it was the better part of wisdom to rely instead on their admittedly somewhat fickle new comrades in arms: the private investors (and bond markets in particular) and the Federal Reserve, whose hands were clasped firmly on the levers of interest rates. By leaving the markets and the Federal Reserve to fulfill the role of stimulating the economy, the administration could busy itself with weaning the federal government off the hard stuff of serious debt. The proper task for a *progressive* administration in this context, it was claimed, was to ensure that the short-term costs of such a hands-off approach to the economy fell mainly on those who could shoulder them.

Some were skeptical of this. As Herbert Stein, a long-toothed economist and former member of the president's Council of Economic Advisers under Nixon, put it, Clinton's was now the third (at least) "New Economics" in his lifetime, the first being Kennedy-era Keynesianism and the second the supply-side counterrevolution under Reagan. But if there was one thing that linked them all, Stein believed, it was an overriding confidence that the answers they had in theory would work out in practice.[64] Stein was doubtless right about this, though he was not perhaps in a position to recognize that this latest approach to the economy, being the belated fruition of the changing consensus first set in train in the 1970s, would prove to be the most dramatic of them all. He was, however, correct that newly elected governments are rarely places of modesty and caution. "Sometimes I think that we would be better off being governed by the party that just lost the election," he mused in 1994, since "they might be more humble." Humility was not something the Clinton administration could by then be realistically accused of. The tone of one of Clinton's own economic advisers confirmed both of Stein's concerns: "For decades, conservatives had tried to slay Keynes and his call for government intervention in times of economic downturn. Here in a short span, we band of Clinton economists, the so-called New Democrats, accomplished what the conservatives had for so long failed to do. . . ."[65]

It is in light of this emerging consensus on the need for fiscal austerity on both sides of the political aisle in America, and of the severe reinforcement of that message in the chaos unleashed by the bond markets, that the wider economic program guiding Clinton's first term begins to make sense. Clinton's first priority upon taking office may have been to bring the deficit under control, but he also needed to coax the economy out of recession, and that could not be done simply by battening down the hatches on government spending. He needed to show the markets he was a safe pair of hands as he steered the national debt out of choppy waters. He also needed to create new business. There were bitter disputes (between Hillary Clinton and Al Gore not least) over how to do this. Clinton resolved these dilemmas the way he resolved most problems in his life, which is to say, instinctively.

What Clinton's instincts eventually told him was not all that different to what the central bankers under Jacques Delors had told him: that the US economy needed to be opened up yet more to global economic processes: to the goods, services, and labor markets of other countries, and that the major thrust of any growth agenda needed to center upon the promotion of liberalization and free trade. Here was another dramatic change of heart in the government, as the new Clinton-era "strategic traders," as Nobel Prize–winning economist Paul Krugman later dubbed them, took over from the "supply siders" of the Republican era. It was a policy shift overseen by the president himself. But to come good on its two key aspects—the signing into law of NAFTA and later the WTO-GATT agreement—the president would first be required to go against his own party. In the process he would put the country at large firmly on a new laissez-faire path toward the future.

NAFTA came first. When it came into force in January 1994, the regional free trade agreement that President Bush had negotiated with Mexico and Canada, but especially with Mexican President Carlos Salinas de Gortari, immediately created the largest free trade area in the world, encompassing 420 million people with a combined GDP of almost $12 trillion.[66] NAFTA was a dramatic step forward toward a future of open global markets and Clinton was instinctively in favor of it. American labor unions, still the Democratic Party's primary constituency, abhorred what this implied for American jobs and were resolutely against it. But Clinton would not be budged. First the administration negotiated a couple of additional side agreements to ease tensions. Then Clinton pushed hard on the promise of jobs to be created in other areas.

In the face of Ross Perot's more resonant claim of a "giant sucking sound" of American jobs going to low-wage Mexico, getting NAFTA passed was an uphill struggle all the same. As ever with Clinton's policies, victory for the White House did not seem likely until perilously late in the day. This time it was Al Gore who led the charge, challenging Perot (whose presidential challenge had positioned him as the voice of NAFTA opposition) to a live televised debate. Gore spent days prepping for the showdown on *Larry King Live* and ended up winning the debate with ease. He got personal to do so, but he also had possession of the facts, calling Perot out on his politics of fear and pessimism. Perot had been wrong over Iraq, Gore said, when Perot had predicted 40,000 American deaths; he had been wrong over the banks that would fail if Clinton were elected, and he was wrong again on NAFTA. In "ninety dramatic minutes," as one write-up had it, Gore transformed the entire debate. Thereafter it fell to Clinton merely to promise special provisions to everyone "from broom makers to citrus growers" for the bill to eventually pass, albeit with 158 of the House's 258 Democrats voting against him.[67]

Focused on the reduction of tariff barriers, NAFTA was nothing like the wholesale institutional redevelopment under way in Europe after Maastricht. What it did do in due course was to create (some) jobs, to increase regional trade (from just short of $300 billion to just over $1 trillion), and to modestly increase American GDP. But it would also lead to wage stagnation in the United States, to the offshoring of American companies, and to changing the US–Mexican trade balance, which moved the needle in favor of Mexico. Leftists also made much of the fact that NAFTA's democratic credentials (which included a democracy clause, primarily as a ruse to keep the Cubans out) were announced at a meeting where protesters were driven off with batons. It was a reminder of the fine line that Clinton was having to tread. On the one hand he was strategically committed to promoting global free trade; on the other he was constitutionally bound to promoting a policy of economic nationalism: American jobs and American growth.

Here the administration's answer was again to double down rather than to retreat. Without engaging in more overt forms of protectionism, Clinton and the Democratic Party more generally were of the view that policies addressing the trade deficit and that promoted (a more palatable way of saying "protected") strategic industries by focusing industrial policy on educational reform and innovation were the best way to go. In other words, they opted for disruptive transformation, or what Schumpeter once called "creative destruction." Here it was the Japanese that provided both the model and the target. For decades Americans had watched their former adversary pull itself up by the bootstraps through corporatist policies and state-sponsored trade. But Japan had also done well by exploiting flexibilities in the international rules on free trade. The United States could fight back by seeking to firm up those rules. The effect of this was to close the circle, as it were: to go all in. The full weight of the United States would now be brought to bear not only upon the direction taken by its own domestic economy, but upon the global economy too.

This raised in its wake questions as to the trade-off between national democracy and a now greatly empowered free trade agenda. When a coalition of NGOs (led by Public Citizen, the Sierra Club, and Friends of the Earth) insisted that, in accordance with federal law, any federal policy likely to have implications for the environment (which a free trade area encompassing half a billion people surely was) properly required an Environmental Impact Statement to be legal, the government responded by having their case thrown out by the federal appeals court.[68] NAFTA was about infrastructure, law, and the environment too, in other words. Neoliberal economic policymaking had a very wide net to throw.

Reining in the deficit and opening up the US economy to free trade from the outside were two of the signature achievements of the first Clinton administration, and the president expended a great deal of political capital winching these new pillars of the economy into place. The third, and the most important pillar of his first term's agenda, however, was a more serious commitment to economic deregulation than even Reagan had overseen. Telecommunications came first—the building of Gore's much touted "information superhighway"—providing a springboard for more lightly regulated emergent electronics and telecoms industries (and the bubble economy in which they would eventually become ensnared). Then came deregulation of the electricity sector itself, upon which telecoms was dependent, and on through finance to biotech and beyond (the first GM food, the Flavr Savr Tomato, was approved by the FDA in 1994).

Deregulation soon became something of a one-size-fits-all policy plaster for industries that were deemed to be underperforming. When the US Congress turned strongly Republican after the midterm elections of 1994, deregulation further became one of the few policy areas Democrats and Republicans agreed on: which meant of course that this was one area that moved forward when others got entrenched in political infighting. So much of the potential good that Bush had done after the late 1980s S&L crisis (namely to put regulation back on the agenda, after Reagan, and to force banks to toe a more responsible line) was wound back once again. If Clinton was consciously addressing the unforeseen consequences of that Bush-era policy (namely the fact that banks as a result stopped lending so much, hence the recession) he also confirmed that modern government was about setting the terms for the economy first and worrying about the social consequences later. In a sense, the economy was now firmly positioned above the people in the pecking order of national government.

What all this deregulation ultimately achieved was not so much a reignition of the economy or new business but an intensified fight for *existing* market share. No sooner were new genetic crop technologies commercialized, for example, than the major industrial farms began rolling them out—3.6 million planted acres by the year 2000—in an effort to gain a competitive advantage: but Americans weren't *eating* more. In such an environment, anyone who feared the growing specter of monopolies was shot down by an increasingly active lobby sector. The Telecommunications Act of 1996, for example, handed a major victory to the larger telecoms corporations: the very ones financing the lobbyists, of course. In finance, there not being much left of pre-1970s-era legislation to roll back anymore, attention now focused on pre-war-era legislation such as that erected in the wake of the Great Depression.[69] The pinnacle would be reached at the end of the decade with the repeal of the 1933 Glass-Steagall regulations separating commercial and main street banking.

None of this looked much like traditional Democratic policy fare: not least since it tended to benefit the very rich (the top 1 percent for the most part) and because it threatened to defund the government's own tax base further down the line. Above all it concentrated big businesses and investors on short-term bottom lines rather than long-term sustainability. But since they were also now freed up to cash out their holdings if they wished, they no longer needed to worry about how their investments performed over a longer term. All this was fuel heaped onto the fire of what was soon a "roaring" but also a somewhat unhinged economy: an economy in which profits were growing, but where workers were not sharing in the benefits, the profits being quickly reinvested in other ventures across an increasingly speculative economy rather than going to higher wages.[70]

As the decade wore on it became clear that the Clinton White House was not at all what the left had imagined it would be amid the ticker-tape euphoria of Madison Square Garden back in 1992. So substantial was the change that it forced Republicans to shift their strategy too. Between 1993 and 1996 Republican and Democratic economic policy in certain respects changed places: Democrats were now the fiscal conservatives in favor of trade and trickle-down economics (in place of investment and protection of special interests like labor). Meanwhile, Republicans who had long argued, in utilitarian terms, that tax cuts should go mainly to the rich (whence everyone would ultimately benefit thanks to the economic growth the rich would then unleash) now found themselves arguing for their ever-cherished tax cuts in the name of distributive justice and just deserts. After Clinton's economic policy had finally succeeded in erasing the public deficit, in 1999, the chairman of the House Committee on Ways and Means, Bill Archer, could only see fit to observe that "The only reason for this surplus is because taxpayers are paying too much."[71]

Clinton's embrace of fiscal conservatism upended not only the economics but the politics of the decade as well. On the one hand he was applying a tight fiscal discipline to the state, yet on the other he never failed to hype the economic free-for-all of a deregulated open market.[72] The techniques of political spin thus now truly came of age in America, as political branding moved in to fill the gap between hype and reality. Some tried to justify the new approach as one of "progressive fiscal conservatism," which was just the sort of oxymoronic neologism that Clinton liked creating. But a sizeable number of more progressive Democrats would never forgive the extent to which Clinton turned the Democratic Party into a vehicle for unleashing private wealth and intensifying the already alarming gap between rich and poor.

What was not up for debate, come the middle of the decade, was the fact that Clinton had hitched the American economy more strongly to the forces of a globalizing economy than it had been before. For some, the president included, this was a victory to be celebrated and a new basis for American hegemony in the world. As Clinton's chairman of the Council of Economic Advisers Joseph Stiglitz put it, "[w]ith globalization came the spread of American-style capitalism to all reaches of the world."[73] But for others, workers in particular, the New Democrats' promarket policies equally brought globalization, and its demands, to America. And globalization, of this sort, was a fundamental challenge not just to the working class, but to the institutional basis of national democracy itself.

Converging Paths

Responding to that paradox was, of course, precisely what the European project was now all about. To read party manifestos and planning documents from practically any of the European democracies from this era is to read a constant series of references to the "challenge" of internationalization upon the rights of domestic citizens. For small states in particular—the sort of state that Europe had in abundance—the challenges were especially acute. "By the turn of the century . . ." wrote the Austrian socialists in a series of "Proposals for Discussion on the Future of Austria" in 1989, "the scope of action for a small state like Austria will be influenced by external factors." Swedes and Finns thought likewise, and none of them had the political upheavals of the moment especially in mind. Their concerns, rather, as the Swedish SAP put it, were that "the internationalization of capital is . . . limiting the ability of the Government, the Bank of Sweden and the Swedish Riksdag [the national legislature] to accomplish the national objectives defined by the democratic process."[74]

If the Swedes were worried in this way, then perhaps national democracy really wasn't any longer capable of holding the forces of globalization at bay. And in that scenario the only real solution was to speed up the retreat to regional safety. This was indeed why the Swedish government wanted to maintain some kind of formal link to Europe as the new EU embarked on its flagship program of monetary integration: in the result, the Swedes voted in favor of EU membership in November 1994. By then so too had most of the other European Free Trade Association (EFTA) countries: Austria voting in favor in June, and Finland in October. The Norwegians and the Swiss by contrast opted to go it alone (along with Iceland and Liechtenstein).

But it was not just smaller states who wished to tighten the knot among themselves. In France, even a Gaullist like Jacques Chirac, the former prime minister and now mayor of Paris, felt obliged to declare in 1992, "I accept the Maastricht Treaty without enthusiasm, but without soul-searching."[75] Formerly a staunch opponent of EMU, as he circled in on the presidential elections of 1995, Chirac would gradually resign himself and his party to the paradox that to survive in the modern, globalizing era, a state that wished to remain independent needed to give up some of its sovereignty to do so. The ERM crisis had done nothing to dampen Western Europeans' growing recognition of this fact, or, in truth, to undermine its wisdom.

Accordingly, the overwhelming focus of those Western European nations committed to the euro in the early to mid 1990s was on tightening belts and finding the means to meet the strict convergence criteria laid out in Maastricht for membership in the eurozone. But it was accompanied by a simultaneous concern, shared by all the newly constituted EU nations, to slow down the process of integration with the East— offering membership of NATO as a temporary tidbit, if that was possible, and loans where it was not. Holding off these other nations was, for the time being, deemed essential, because for all that it was clear that the EU would eventually *have* to let its former communist neighbors into the European club, the prevailing view was that first there needed to be much closer cooperation within the core itself.

The burning question was how. In America the earlier demise of the Keynesian consensus had been confirmed by the rise of the New Democrats. In Europe that same gaping hole had come to be filled by the new project of monetary union, which would proceed with or without those member states, like the British, who could not countenance giving up their national coin. But even after Maastricht the question of what *sort* of monetary union was still a radically open one. Would the new European economic policy regime prioritize low interest rates or high employment? Would it be about public spending or fighting inflation? What sort of economic base, in practice, would the new Europe be erected upon? The foundations had been sketched out by other countries acknowledging the primary influence of Germany, and the Bundesbank in particular, on the basic structure of monetary union. But each country had its own reasons for buying into EMU. And the different parties within them frequently envisaged different futures being built upon that same base.

In Germany itself, the Social Democratic Party (SPD) duly supported Kohl's CDU during the process of ratifying Maastricht in December 1993, but its members were not all of like mind as to how the single currency, in particular, should be run. Some feared that interest rates would be used to support the interests of capital and (international) business, rather than the (usually more local) issue of employment. But the bigger issue was that Germany's Social Democrats were torn.[76] They supported European integration in general, and many looked to the EU as the relevant arena for the rebuilding of the social democratic project. But they were wary of the extent to which this would actually be feasible (rightly, it would turn out) and concerned (also rightly) that what they might be left with would be neither national nor transnational tools for delivering on their promises of redistribution and social protection.

As Germany came to different views about how best to resolve this tension, the seeds of a bitter personal struggle between the SPD's more pragmatic Gerhard Schröder and its more radically minded Oskar Lafontaine were sown. The two were the most important German politicians on the left at the time. For Schröder, a rather dismal performance of the SPD in the national elections of 1994 and the Berlin elections of 1995 meant it was now time for the SPD to bring itself up to date. For Lafontaine there were older promises that needed keeping first. But both were caught in the same basic bind: more welfare meant higher government spending, and that in turn meant less international competitiveness and a greater likelihood of laying off workers. The New Europe precipitated a transformation of the left elsewhere in the continent as well.

In southern Europe, the desire to move rapidly out of the still-recent autocratic past ensured that there was a broad-based support for "Europe," whatever policies it happened to be offering. Parties in Italy and Spain had only to demonstrate that Europeanization (even when that meant monetary integration) equalled economic modernization to convince even the most ardent supporters of state largesse and economic patronage that there was something in it for them. Thus the Spanish left—which under Felipe González had been far and away the dominant political force in the country since the fall of Franco—had already broken with Keynesianism in the 1980s when it was confronted by high inflation and a growing public deficit. The Spanish had also been looking across the border to France, and to what seemed to be the more successful counterexample of Great Britain: and they had by now concluded that there was little future left in national Keynesian approaches to the economy anyway.

Thus did each of the major European social democratic parties begin to make their peace with the more market-friendly platform represented by European monetary convergence. With the Spanish government unable to come to an agreement with the unions over an appropriate social pact for

the country (in which workers might continue to receive some social protections while the government went after the primary aim of reducing
inflation), joining the ERM was increasingly seen as the only remaining
alternative. After Spain's currency crisis in the early 1990s, and the associated
loss of a parliamentary majority for the Spanish Socialist Workers' Party
(PSOE), there were other voices in government—many of them the voices
of small business—in favor of closely controlled exchange rates. The offer
of Delors's generous structural funds was the final element required to buy
the PSOE out of its earlier commitments to national employment over
international monetary convergence. As was also the case in Austria, in
Finland, in Spain, and in the Netherlands, yet another U-turn in social
democratic policy had been more or less seamlessly executed.[77]

In the Netherlands, the Dutch social democratic Partij van de Arbeid
(PvdA) came to the conclusion, a little like the French, of better the devil
you know: that a new European Central Bank organized along German
lines was preferable to a new Europe dominated by the Bundesbank and
the Deutschmark.[78] As ever, then, it was domestic politics that determined
the reasons why different countries joined the European bandwagon and
acquiesced in monetary union. This included, for example, the decision
by social democratic Finland to participate in the then relatively advanced
stage of EMU in 1998, in contrast with the rest of their Nordic counterparts. For the Finns, who had only joined the EU in 1995, there were
two immediate reasons for this. First, a major economic recession had left
the old welfarist economic policies discredited. Second, Russia was by
then looking to be heading in a less liberal direction and there was a
desire to stand a little less alone. What was at stake in each of these decisions was nothing less than the future of social democracy as a once
broad-based commitment to government spending and discretionary national policies. And the fact that social democrats and economic liberals
were meeting in open combat over the question of what *sort* of monetary
integration was best for the continent was an indication of how far social
democratic parties in Europe had already begun to reinvent themselves.

But it was not just social democrats who were having to reinvent
themselves in relation to monetary integration. The continent's Christian
democratic parties too became staunch supporters of EMU. It was less of
an ideological stretch for them to become so, of course. But the implication was significant nonetheless, for it meant that the mainstreaming of a
more liberal Europe was more or less guaranteed. As Kohl himself once
said: "we didn't create Europe to leave it to the socialists." The corollary
of that was that it had now been handed over to the monetarists and the

fiscal disciplinarians—those who promised steady-state growth without the turmoil of union barricades and voting blocs and who vowed to be rid of the curse of inflation no matter what the cost.

From January 1994 the process of economic convergence began to tighten. To ensure price stability across the European area, countries were expected to bring their economic policies more closely into line with the European norm agreed upon by the finance ministers of each country. This included increased convergence of monetary policies. It also included plans for a new Growth and Stability Pact, which came into force in 1997. The Bundesbank was particularly concerned about the need to fight inflation in each of the national territories that were now linked to each other via the European System of Central Banks (ESCB). It was particularly worried that Greece and Italy might cut taxes and embark on national spending sprees as a way of getting around the convergence criteria. The Growth and Stability Pact thus had some states more closely in mind than others, and it was a first step toward enforcing budgetary discipline within the euro area, establishing a new rule by which governments were to keep their budget deficits to within 3 percent of the overall size of the economy.

The post-Maastricht move toward greater integration was not just about European monetary union. European nations were also turning more and more to the EU's judicial institutions to cope. European national law now converged at a single point in Strasbourg: the European Court of Justice (ECJ). It was in Strasbourg that the large-scale judicial work to implement the SEA after 1986 had steadily introduced a form of de facto transnationalism with which national governments were expected to comply. Since the 1970s the ECJ had by now largely come to be seen as a de facto European constitutional court—one whose growth at times seemed self-generating as it conferred upon itself additional competencies.[79] It was the 1990s that saw a real surge in ECJ rulings, however: more than all preceding decades put together. And it was revealing of the European Union's current preferences that these focused on matters of competition law in particular.[80] Once again, this was a relatively silent revolution within the European polity, but a crucial development nonetheless. For it meant that at the very point when Europe's economies were converging around the liberal economic principles hashed out by some countries the decade before, with their focus on monetary rather than fiscal policy, it was these principles that the ECJ served to lock in constitutionally.[81]

347

A further significant milestone was passed in 1995 when the Schengen area came into force, bringing about the abolition, in effect, of the internal borders between participating national states (initially five, but soon nearly all EU member states). It was now possible to travel without a passport from Gozo in Malta to the town of Schengen in Luxembourg, where the agreement had first been signed ten years before: appropriately enough not on land, but on the pleasure boat the *Princesse Marie-Astrid*, on the waters of the Moselle. Along with the radical proposition to proceed to a single currency coming out of Maastricht, the Schengen Agreement was the second most profound European decision of the decade. Border posts were carted away, pillar boxes were taken down, and blue European Union plaques were put up in their place. It was hardly the radical makeover of the continent's landscape of the sort that had seen tanks roll in during the bad years, or statues of dictators toppled during the good ones. But the reality it conveyed was no less historic, since these changes ultimately afforded free movement and the right to work where they wished to more than 400 million people across the continent.

Though it would become one of the most cherished aspects of EU citizenship for Europeans, Schengen also had at its heart a more stony-faced approach to the outside world. If borders within Europe were to come down, those around its outer edges would need to become that much harder in turn. As ever the UK opted to sit on the sidelines in this matter by retaining its own border controls. This was the Conservative Party's sop, at a moment it was running out of juicier bones to throw to the electorate, to domestic fears about the loss of British sovereignty (though the agreement in fact always allowed for temporary reimposition of border controls if deemed necessary—ultimately for a period of up to two years). The concern in Britain was loss of national control over asylum policy, which now inevitably required relocating to the European level. Other outliers, such as Norway which was a member of the EFTA, were more concerned about what their own citizens had access to, and would eventually opt to join the Schengen area, when the agreement—initially conceived as something quite separate from the European Union—was incorporated into the wider EU architecture by the Treaty of Amsterdam in 1999.

There were more prosaic changes affecting everyday aspects of work and life too. The signing of Maastricht was accompanied by the enclosure of European airspace as a singular entity, for example, such that national firms, like Air France, found themselves unable to operate across European "space" in quite the same way anymore. Air France practically went bust overnight as a result. But right across the continent, independent regulators in a large number of spheres (from food standards agencies to telecoms) all took oversight responsibilities out of the hands of elected governments and placed them in those of autonomous agencies (in the case of Air France, the EC did the opposite, allowing the government to bail the company out, until the ECJ later overruled this).[82]

Investors swore by this and helped to champion the process, not surprisingly, since it meant their investments were no longer so directly vulnerable to popular whims and demands. The number of independent regulators thus grew dramatically during the decade, as capital-starved governments desperate to bring their national economies into line with the new international convergence criteria sought to do whatever they could to entice the market to look kindly upon the display cases of their domestic economies. The new mantra for European governments was that doing less and offering the appearance of "impartiality" was the key to obtaining "creditworthiness."[83] That in turn was the secret to securing the investment and economic growth that all other government policy relied upon. It sounded a lot like the sort of argument that had been heard of late coming out of America.

There was good reason for this. Europeans were taking a different route, but ultimately they were heading toward a similar destination and these were the European Community's great contributions toward that end: conditions and conditionalities, rules and regulations, procedures and protocols, courts and covenants. These were among the key elements of the new liberal Western order that both sides of the Atlantic were now pushing forward together as a *collective* project: be this driven by businesses, as with the Transatlantic Business Dialogue (TABD, 1995) or by governments, as with the OECD and the Transatlantic Economic Partnership (TEP, 1998), or indeed by the EU itself.

Each new element had its part to play in managing the challenges now confronting national democratic societies in a globalizing world. Individually, each made sense in light of sector-specific challenges. But all were equally, if not always intentionally, part of a new doctrine that promoted market freedoms first and foremost: a doctrine first directly applied to the work of reconstructing the ruins of the Soviet Empire but which, by the middle of the decade, was being most enthusiastically put into place in the heart of the West itself.

Other Vistas

In Canada too a slide toward the same neoliberal economic policy regime had by now set in, albeit for different reasons, under its new prime minister, Brian Mulroney. It too was leaving its social democratic past behind. The 1988 election, which had first brought Mulroney to power, was essentially a referendum on free trade, as encapsulated in the then NAFTA proposal, and on whether Canada wished to look a little more like America after all. Once in office, the new prime minister set limits to welfare expenditure via means-testing, he reduced personal, corporate, and estate taxes, and he looked to liberalize Canadian trade with other countries. On top of this he remained committed to high interest rates in accordance with the Western liberal anti-inflationary creed. And yet despite or possibly because of this, unemployment remained high in Canada, just as it had everywhere else that such policies had been implemented. Mulroney was a harbinger of the new in another sense too, since he not only transformed the political economic landscape, but he also transformed the party-political landscape, breaking progressive conservatism apart and making partisanship more apparent. In these senses at least, though not in all others, Canada really was becoming a little bit more like America.

A similar story could be seen playing itself out in New Zealand. In 1984, the country had been on the brink of bankruptcy while unemployment exceeded 12 percent—as bad as during the Depression years. With the economy in meltdown, Prime Minister Robert Muldoon of the conservative New Zealand National Party called a snap election, which he lost to the New Zealand Labour Party. At this moment, the NZLP was—somewhat ahead of its European counterparts—busy getting rid of its prior policy commitments and reinventing itself as a fiscally conservative, promarket party. It was New Zealand's incoming Finance Minister Roger Douglas who played the critical role here. In the space of just a few years Douglas drove through a "revolutionary restructuring"[84] of the economy which amounted, in the words of one historian, to an economic "Blitzkrieg." In 1985 the NZLP floated the dollar. In 1987 it began large-scale privatizations after the State-Owned Enterprises Act. Financial markets were deregulated and price controls were abolished. Trade barriers were reduced and state-owned steel, telecoms, and rail services were privatized. The same year the top rate of income tax was reduced from 66 percent to 32 percent.

At the same time Rogernomics, as this latest variant of the laissez-faire approach came to be called, was distinct from its Atlantic counterparts: not least it initially had a greater concern with equity—or in New Zealand parlance, with "fairness"—than did most policies introduced under Thatcher or Reagan. With the turn of the decade, however, and the coming to power of the National Party in 1990, the basic policy thrust of Rogernomics continued but it now did so with less effort being made to limit its distributional impacts. Welfare was thus substantially retrenched and, under the Employment Contracts Act of 1991, the ability of unions to negotiate as collective entities was undermined. In many ways, New Zealand was granted the worst of both worlds.

Australia took a softer route to, again, a broadly similar destination. After 1983, Labour Prime Minister Bob Hawke and his Finance Minister Michael Keating oversaw a raft of dramatic turnarounds in economic policy: exchange rates were allowed to float, the National Bank of Australia was given independence, and tariffs were steadily reduced—all with a view to creating a more liberal market economy. Hawke was eventually shunted out of power by Paul Keating as frustration gripped the younger man and their long-simmering personal rivalry finally bubbled over. But not before businesses had been awarded a bigger slice of national profits than labor, thanks to deregulation in numerous sectors and the opening up of the economy to international capital and trade. What followed was a competitive grab for market share in the newly deregulated economy, and a fit of overexuberant lending, corruption, and abuse of office—followed, of course, by a crash.

To put the crash in perspective, between March 1990 and May 1991 American employers, in the midst of that country's post–Cold War recession, had laid off 1.5 percent of their workforce; Australian employers laid off 3.9 percent in the same period. Two state banks went out of business while the four largest banks in Australia wrote off A$17 billion between them from 1989 to 1993. If it was the recession that Keating was candid enough to admit Australians "had to have," it was nonetheless a reminder that the new normal was a volatile one and that not everybody's interests were equally well protected.[85]

By the time the middle of the decade was approaching, however, it was South Africa that provided the clearest example of the extent to which the market was now prioritized over democratic institutions and their constitutional safeguards: and this at the very moment of democracy's supposedly global triumph. Upon his release from twenty-seven years of prison, much of it spent on Robben Island, on February 11, 1990, Nelson Mandela had been adamant that political freedom would not be a reality in his country until there was also economic redistribution—of land in particular—from minority whites to the majority black population. But redistribution was not the direction other Western leaders thought Mandela should be traveling in. And by the time the ANC swept to its historic election victory in 1994 it was clear that it was a radically probusiness and not Mandela's original redistributive agenda that had won out.

How could this have been? Political negotiations between the old regime under South African President F. W. de Klerk and Mandela had gone smoothly enough, and the world's media had naturally focused on the restoration of civil liberties. But Mandela's warning on the need for economic as well as political freedom had been resolutely undermined at every step of the way in the more meaningful, behind the scenes, economic negotiations. In 1992, for example, two years after the World Economic Forum had announced the birth of a New Europe at Davos, WEF director Klaus Schwab invited de Klerk, Nelson Mandela, and Zulu Chief Mangosuthu Buthelezi to meet for the first time at the forum's private offices in Geneva, and to do so with representatives of the business community in South Africa. Mandela spoke of what he called "the truly phenomenal process of renewal which our planet is experiencing [. . .] a future in which the peoples in all countries will govern themselves under open and plural democratic systems."[86]

Yet what was more seriously discussed at the meeting was whether the economic policies of the transition should focus upon wealth redistribution or wealth creation. Caught by the glare of publicity directed toward the front-of-stage encounter between the leaders of the different sides, the ANC activists with their Make Democracy Work! manifesto were blindsided by their economically more literate opposition, who now locked in such standard liberalizing reforms as central bank independence in a way that made the promises of the manifesto moot. By 1996, under the growing influence of Thabo Mbeki, the ANC announced a shock therapy program of the sort that had been devised for Eastern Europe, signaling to international investors that the new government was prepared to maintain macroeconomic stability over and above the demands of its own citizens for employment, infrastructure, and social services. A new round of state privatization followed.

The Economy, Stupid

The convergence, by the mid 1990s, of so many different countries upon a similar set of responses to the economic challenges of the 1970s was in part just a case of similarly motivated governments feeding from the same trough of ideas. Convergence in this sense had an element of contingency about it. Yet this was also a development whose overall shape and timing were given a definite push to embed the rules of a more laissez-faire economy into the institutional architecture of the West.

Again, there was no single author of the convergence. Such rules might come from the Château de la Muette, the Paris-based headquarters of the OECD in the 16th arrondissement, where, beginning in the early 1990s, the Western states agreed between themselves not only to continue removing such barriers to the movement of capital as still existed between them (as France and in a different way Denmark had led the way in doing in the 1980s) but to reduce their "formal legal rights" to control the movement of capital altogether in the future.[87] Or they might be found in the long-awaited conclusion of the GATT negotiating rounds, which had begun life focused on addressing the problem of barriers to market entry (as the basis for a future World Trade Organization, which came into effect in 1995, to be headquartered in Geneva) but which now wished to concern itself with the management and regulation of trade in almost every respect. Pharmaceutical companies likewise grew rich helping to shape the international standards that governed their ability to make money on lifesaving medicines, in this instance via lobbying over the treatment of intellectual property rights in the GATT-TRIPS agreement.

As these developments showed, the one consistently prioritized element, as agreements were drawn up, negotiations concluded, and policy regimes locked in for a generation, were the codified, seemingly universal norms of private property. The owners of wealth needed not just free markets to move their capital around—to make it productive—they needed enhanced rights of ownership and access if profits were to be maximized and the gains protected. The public realm was opened up; private capital was locked down. Everything else, from social protections to environmental regulations, and the obligations of international development and social justice, took an avowedly second place. Less advanced, less liberal countries were now "partners in transition"; poor countries were "emerging markets." They mattered to the extent that they provided opportunities for others: something that three of the new countries to join the OECD in the 1990s (Mexico, the Czech Republic, and Hungary) immediately found to their cost upon accession. Struck by the stringency of the organization's capital liberalization demands, their economies plunged into recession.[88] Is it any wonder that democracy did not take root in Eastern and central Europe with quite the ease that was expected back in 1989?

But for the OECD these countries' "commitment to a democratic political system" was now officially taken as secondary to their commitment to "economic growth and liberty." It was hardly alone. In 1991 the Asia-Pacific Economic Cooperation zone (APEC) had declared the Pacific Rim a "liberalized free trade area"; the EU declared itself a "single market" in 1992; and in 1994 NAFTA declared the Americas a hemispheric "zone of free trade." It was not so much the individual agreements as their collective force which mattered. For what was collectively put in place by such processes were economic spaces that were less regulated and whose rules were largely written in the shadows of public debate. At a moment of global opening, then, the Western democracies had, ironically it must be said, overseen an historic reenclosure of the commons; the safeguards that had been so hard won in the three decades or so following the Second World War were prized away. As one of this era's most widely read chroniclers observed, globalization was indeed not just a "trend" or a "fad": it was "the international system [itself] that has replaced the cold-war system."[89] Liberal democracy and American hegemony had each in their way done well out of the fall of communism. But as the decade wore on, it was becoming clear that capitalism was faring best of all.

9

A Democratic Peace?

A S THE FIRST half of the decade drew to a close, the United States had found its footing and its young president, whose position had seemed so precarious during his first twelve months in office, was warming to the glow of a greater popularity at home. Clinton's approval ratings were tracking steeply and steadily up, from just 37 percent during his first and difficult year in office to a peak of 73 percent at the end of 1998. By 1995 he had not only survived an entrenched Republican revolt against him but had successfully stared down their policy of non-cooperation in Congress, during a budget-deal stand-off in which, for neither the first nor the last time, the government officially shut down. He had overseen his nation's commitment to a series of historic trade deals and won sufficient minor victories against the Republicans to earn himself the moniker, once again, of "the comeback kid." But despite all these successes at home, Clinton was finding it much harder than Bush before him to promote America's interests abroad.

Outside the economic domain, talk was less of a new world order than it was of a new world disorder. Ethnic nationalism was tearing apart the Balkans, while elsewhere the problem was not so much an aggressive irredentism as it was of failed states collapsing and taking with them anyone in the way, US marines included. "Get ready for fifty new countries in the world in the next fifty years," Daniel Patrick Moynihan warned his compatriots in 1993. "Most of them will be born in bloodshed."[1] As the world was indeed forced to confront first a genocide in Rwanda, in 1994, and then ethnic cleansing in the former Yugoslavia later that same year, Moynihan was not the only Washington insider articulating such concerns. "To the surprise and dismay of our fellow citizens," said the Hon. Tom Lantos before the US House of Representatives in June 1994, "we have found that the post-cold war world is neither tranquil nor peaceful nor secure."[2]

Indeed, for all the hopes in Washington or at the United Nations building on East 42nd Street in New York, that the ending of the Cold

War might usher in the balm of a widespread "democratic peace," the post–Cold War era was for many people nothing of the sort. Globally, interstate conflict dropped to an historic and persistent low. And yet, as if in some cruel post–Cold War riposte, *intra*state conflict, civil war, was just now reaching its murderous peak.[3] Civilians accounted for over 80 percent of all deaths in wars in the 1990s. At the height of the First World War they had made up less than 10 percent.[4] Little wonder that by the mid 1990s the international news seemed filled with endless reports of local strongmen seizing power in the vacuum left behind by the retreating Cold War superpowers; of warlords in sub-Saharan Africa turning circles in armored pickups while running their countries into the ground; and of Latin American caudillos and strongmen cutting deals with drug barons while stuffing the proceeds into ballot boxes. Meanwhile, a new strand of anti-Americanism could be heard being chanted angrily, everywhere from the dockyards of Port-au-Prince to the streets of Tehran and Tikrit.

Inevitably, these post–Cold War discontents precipitated, for the victorious Western nations, a debate over their international obligations. The idea of a liberal world order could only have been imagined in the post–Cold War moment. Yet for all the United States' attempts to give shape to it, that world order had thus far resisted categorization, much less control. The growing sense of international unease that resulted further raised the question of whether or not the Western democracies had a right, perhaps even a duty, to intervene in events elsewhere in the name of their own national security interests. The world's wealthiest countries had never existed in a vacuum, of course. But one of the primary conceits of the Golden Age had been the assumption that democratic societies enjoyed, by virtue of their privileged position, a monopoly on the right to determine their own future. The more that countries now opened up to one another through globalization and trade, and the more that politics in the West was shaped by events elsewhere, the less that conceit held. After the Iraq War, in particular, a new age of global news reporting had been ushered in, bringing home pictures of far-off crises more frequently than ever before.

Alongside the boosterism of a globalizing economic age, foreign policy experts and journalists were soon peddling a parallel, and unsettling, trope of international anarchy. According to the influential American journalist and political scientist Robert Kaplan, whose bestselling book *The New World Disorder* had the ear of the US president, anarchy and its principal geographical referent, the "failed state," represented the new clear and present danger to the national security and democratic integrity of the West, and to the United States in particular. After several years of hearing that they should sit back and enjoy the new era of peace and tranquility, Western citizens were now being told that the barbarians were still at the gates. France's inveterate public mouthpiece Bernard Henri-Lévy warned, in the pages of *La pureté dangereuse*, of the ills that lay in wait for the Western democracies if they did not take the proliferation of "new" domestic civil wars elsewhere in the world seriously. *Mourir pour Sarajevo?* he asked his readers in 1994. It was not a choice that French or even American citizens had much desire to make.

The New Internationalism

For Britain's then representative to the UN, Sir David Hannay, there was no choice, once the rubble from the fall of communism had been cleared away, but to engage more actively in the wider world. "It's the UN or it's the jungle," Hannay declared in 1994, pointing to what was to be one of the two primary means of engaging that wider world going forward: a reinvigorated, or so he hoped, United Nations system.[5] The principal alternative to the UN, the other way of engaging, was a new form of transnational governance just then emerging in face of the growing range of issues that fell beyond the scope of national governments. The fact that both the UN and the transnationalists ultimately failed was little lamented at the time. But it would have a dramatic impact on the Western democracies: for their failure was a victory for the anxious and the fearful who would influence foreign policy in the 2000s.

As the Cold War receded into the past, it was to the UN that most Western citizens instinctively looked. The UN was the most widely recognized world organization and far and away the most legitimate in the eyes of most of the world's people. It was also, however, a system in need of substantial rebuilding. Ever since the 1970s, when détente had upended the Cold War, pushing East and West into more bi-, tri-, and multilateral forms of diplomacy beyond its reach, and the failure of the New International Economic Order program saw many of the G77 nations lose heart in it, the UN had found itself in a position of declining influence. Bringing the UN back into the center of events in the post–Cold War era would require a clear sense of mission and someone to lead it. From 1992, in the figure of the Egyptian politician and diplomat Boutros Boutros-Ghali, it looked initially to have both.

"This organization must never again be crippled as it was in the era that has now passed," the newly crowned Boutros-Ghali said in 1992, demonstrating the independent streak that the US had disliked and for which it had sought to prevent his election to the top post.[6] Boutros-Ghali had taken the UN helm after a succession of ineffective secretaries general, and in his landmark document for reform of the post–Cold War international landscape, "Agenda for Peace," he laid out a new vision for the UN. The whole purpose of the organization, he believed, should no longer be confined to just "keeping the peace": it should be concerned with helping to make a better peace in the world, above all by promoting "human rights." Thus did the UN hierarchy greet the new world order at the end of the Cold War with a new and more activist mission. It set out, as Boutros-Ghali put it, to foster "social progress and better standards of life in larger freedom."[7]

But it was not in fact obvious whether the UN had *more* of a future now that the superpower rivalry had subsided or *less*. For all that the superpowers' dreaded weapon of the veto had hobbled UN decision-making throughout the entire Cold War, the organization also owed its very purpose to that rivalry. "[T]he entrance of the United States and the USSR into a permanent organization is more important than the organization itself," the British civil servant Charles Webster had observed from his seat at the drafters' table of the UN Charter in 1944.[8] Also Boutros-Ghali's confidence had to a large extent been engendered by the success of the coalition forces in Iraq: a mission that only involved the UN on a superficial level. Desert Storm was a victory presaged upon a unique (and, it would prove, unrepeatable) degree of international cooperation, not UN sponsorship. Moreover, Iraq's annexation of Kuwait represented a relatively straightforward case of interstate aggression, while the vast majority of the cases the UN would be forced to address in the years to come would be intranational civil wars—a type of conflict of which it had little experience (and where Boutros-Ghali himself had an unfortunate record).

The UN, though not Boutros-Ghali, found an unlikely rescuer at this point. For as it had served the United States to keep the UN out of the management of serious international crises for the past twenty years, so it now served it to bring the UN back in. Conservatives in America did not like the idea of their country being beholden to any other authority, but they didn't think it was America's task to clear up the seeming proliferation of international crises either. The UN was duly called up to duty once more. But it was the UN of the Security Council, not the

General Assembly or the Office of the Secretary General, that was the focus of its post–Cold War rebirth. The UN thus now took on a more direct role in postconflict activities, but not at all in the way that Boutros-Ghali had imagined.

In two years, from 1991 to 1993, the UN launched fifteen new peace-keeping operations (almost as many as the seventeen it had launched in the *entire* preceding forty-six years of its history).[9] The deliberations of the Security Council now also leapt into life. By 1994 the UN had more than 70,000 military personnel deployed at any one moment, as compared to just under 10,000 in 1988. Its peacekeeping budget increased from $230 million to $3.6 billion. Yet as the UN secretariat would admit, by the mid 1990s "peacekeeping" was anything but a straightforward objective. The questions it posed were legion: where did peacekeeping end and nation-building begin, for example? And who got to decide? Meanwhile, the UN was further involved in "preventive diplomacy" regarding twenty-eight separate disputes in 1994 compared with just eleven in 1988.[10] It was possible to see why many countries, including powerful ones like China, saw it as little more than a rubber stamp outfit for a Western liberal vision of the world.

At the same time as it engaged in an ever-more expansively defined notion of "peace-making," the UN also remained firmly with one hand tied behind its back: reliant upon the agreement of the permanent members of the Security Council before it could act. And that meant of course that America needed to be on board with whatever the UN did. Institutionally, the Security Council was still "fifteen men on a powder keg," as *The Economist*'s man at the UN, Andrew Boyd, had described it. But for the moment the United States alone held the fuses. And nowhere was this clearer than with Resolution 687, imposed on Iraq after the Persian Gulf War: the resolution which marked the beginning of the long geopolitical tail leading up to the second invasion of Iraq in 2003.

With the passing of Resolution 687 the Security Council had effectively drawn a line in the sand by "criminalizing" the Iraqi regime—"no less than the war guilt clause did Germany in the Treaty of Versailles," as one international lawyer, José E. Álvarez, warned.[11] The resolution further imposed, Álvarez continued, "without benefit of due process or opportunity for rebuttal by Iraq, extensive financial liability for any and all consequences of the Persian Gulf War, reaching far beyond that permitted under then existing international law."[12] There may well have been good reasons for all this from America's point of view. But it is not hard to understand why Iraq would choose, in light of this treatment, to continue to provoke its perceived tormentor—especially given that, for better or worse, Iraq was, like every other sovereign state, itself a member of the body formally overseeing its punishment. It was an international version of the "law and orderism" developed in the Western democracies to contain the internal dissent of the 1970s. And it was to meet with similarly unconstructive results.

The UN did not emerge out of its post–Cold War reconstruction in quite the progressive shape that Boutros-Ghali had imagined for it, then. The power of the Security Council had been reinvigorated, in general, but this was used largely as a foil for American power in particular (for all that China and Russia now began to exercise the veto with more deliberate intent than before). Meanwhile, the more democratic chamber of the UN, the General Assembly, had continued to show that when it came to matters of real significance it was little better than a talking shop. But if the UN was, for now at least, not the solution required to address the problems of a world order in a state of dramatic flux—and perhaps it was simply too static and too tied to its great power roots to ever be the answer required—an alternative approach was in the process of being formed.

Despite what the merchants of anarchy implied in their accounts of a world falling into disorder, other, more positive transformations of the state were at work in the early 1990s. Driven by the communications revolution that economic globalization was spearheading, the Western state was disaggregating into "functionally distinct" parts not only within national borders, as we have seen, but *across* them too. For a young Harvard lawyer and later director of Policy Planning at the US State Department, Anne-Marie Slaughter, this presaged nothing less than a new era of "transgovernmentalism." Lawyers like Slaughter were indeed sharing notes with their counterparts in other nations; government regulators, judges, regional legislatures, and even national executives were doing likewise. And it was in the "dense web of relations" that came out of all this that a new transgovernmental order was being built.

Slaughter, it turned out, was onto something important here. But this "real" new world order of her more positive imagining did not conform to the liberal internationalism of President Bush's New World Order (which required a clear rule-making authority, such as the United States, not to mention the willingness of other nations to go along—neither of which conditions existed). Nor did it conform to the "new medievalism" of states undergoing variously terminal forms of political fission and each heading their own way (as hard-nosed realists would have it). What was happening was something in between: neither global government, nor global anarchy, but a new world of "global governance networks link[ing] Microsoft, the Roman Catholic Church, and Amnesty International to the European Union, the United Nations, and Catalonia," as Slaughter put it in the journal *Foreign Affairs*.[13]

In short, the same sort of transnational relationships that had become important in the economic realm were now beginning to reshape the international political realm too. And if a great many leaders and certainly national citizens were overlooking this, then this was only because the work of securities regulators, antitrust environmental officials, and the like was, as Slaughter put it, so "mundane": not unimportant but invisible. Regardless, what these new institutional internationalists were creating would prove to be stupendous. For as a collective they were doing nothing less than reshaping politics at home *and* abroad. Civilizations were not "clashing" as foreign policy experts like Samuel Huntington, Robert Kagan, and others were pointing out, they were much busier just "communicating." The watchword here was not anarchy but comity, since they were also doing so on the basis of Western democratic values, not to mention Western technology and institutions. National and international judges were in the midst of a dramatic new wave of constitutionalism, of the sort not seen since lawyers like Hugo Preuss and Hans Kelsen last helped rebuild the liberal order in the aftermath of the First World War. Across Eastern Europe fledgling constitutional courts were being set to work. National supreme and high courts everywhere were accessing and learning from one another's jurisprudence.

As ever on transnational matters it was the Europeans who led the way. Before they had taken any steps to establish the appropriate legal footing for a *European* central bank, the European Court of Justice (ECJ) had been in (not always amicable) dialogue with national courts over their respective jurisdiction. Since 1978 European Supreme Court judges had been meeting with one another to harmonize practices every three years. And the Americas were not that far behind. In October 1995 the supreme courts of twenty-five American nations met in Washington to draft a charter for their new Organization of the Supreme Courts of the Americas (OCSA).[14] There would and could be no world court; but there could be a well-managed transnational system of integrated courts at a range of different levels, from the local to the national to the regional.

Similar developments were at work in the realm of international regulation. Whether it was the European Union's efforts, post-Maastricht, to harmonize their police and security forces and the criminal law enforcement procedures that went with this, or environmental activists seeking to harmonize national environment agencies, the modern regulatory state was being forced to go global, as the phrase soon had it. The material consequence of all this work could be seen in the growing volume of bilateral and multilateral treaties and memoranda of understanding piling up in offices around the world. The EU and America were already cooperating closely on antitrust laws, for example. In light of the financial crisis of 1987, central bankers of the leading financial powers had convened in 1988 to create the Basel Committee on Banking Supervision. Securities commissioners and insurance regulators had been meeting under the auspices of the International Organization of Securities Commissions since 1983, and in 1998 went further to adopt a set of principles that became the accepted international standards. For proponents like Slaughter, all this heralded not only a more cooperative spirit, but the possibility of doing away altogether with the old domestic political divisions of right versus left.

There was just one catch. While all of this activity certainly had the potential to be accountable, reasoned, and perhaps even wise in the face of the intense international challenges of the moment, was it actually *democratic*? There was indeed a groundswell of cooperative activity between experts and legislators the world over, and most intensely within and between the nations of the West. But the success of these endeavors would ultimately hinge not just upon what they managed to agree between themselves but on whether or not, in the fullness of time, people came to believe it had all been carried out in their name. And that, in turn, would depend upon whether Western citizens were interested enough to hold not just their governments, but these individual agencies and commissions, accountable for what they were doing; whether, in fact, they were even aware of what they were doing. Mostly, it turned out, they were not.

Transgovernmentalism then, for all that it seemed to make so much sense to an elite, East Coast American lawyer like Slaughter, never really surfaced as the new political paradigm that, with a bit more thought and public engagement, perhaps it could have been. In 1995 a New Transatlantic Agenda (NTA) was signed by Clinton and Spanish Prime Minister Felipe González at an EU–US summit in Madrid. The NTA was intended to foster closer cooperation on a range of critical issues, from terrorism to drug trafficking to disease, and was a pet project of the US president himself. Ten years later, however, the number of transatlantic disputes had grown, not lessened—exacerbated by spats relating to the Clinton administration's decision to impose third-party sanctions on anybody trading with Cuban businesses (a sop to an influential domestic electorate, the Cuban-Americans, but a slap in the face to its allies across the ocean and businesses like Sol Meliá hotels and Pernod Ricard).

Perhaps sensing which way the wind was blowing, neither conservatives nor progressives on either side of the Atlantic continued to invest their energies much in trying to make this transgovernmental domain a sufficiently "political" one, such that citizens themselves might actually care what became of it. So far as most politicians on the new right and the new left were concerned, the preferred alternative was in expanding the institutions of the market and handing over the determination of international problems to the enlightened voluntarism of individuals: the 1990s were good years for the international humanitarian system and the NGOs founded back in the 1970s. Those who retained a faith in planning would soon find their own preferred alternative in a more assertive brand of moralized foreign policy: one whose inauguration, primed by the shocking images of genocide in Rwanda, awaited merely another spectacle sufficiently dire and dramatic to rouse it.

Specters of the Past

Dear Mimmy,

Yesterday the people in front of parliament tried peacefully to cross the Vrbanka bridge. But they were shot at. Who? How? Why? A girl, a medical student from Dubrovnik, was KILLED. Her blood spilled onto the bridge.

In her final moments all she said was: "Is this Sarajevo?" HORRIBLE, HORRIBLE!

NO ONE AND NOTHING HERE IS NORMAL![15]

So read the diary of eleven-year-old Zlata Filipović, a resident of Sarajevo, as she marked yet another gruesome milestone in the siege of her city. In the early 1990s, while America was preoccupied with the Middle East, Europeans were increasingly concerned about a civil war—or rather a series of interwoven civil wars—in the Balkans. The fall of the Iron Curtain had been cause for so much jubilation. Not so for the breakaway nations of the former Yugoslavia. For them it was as if "the Berlin wall crumbled down upon their heads," as the Croatian writer Igor Štiks put it.[16]

Over the course of the 1990s an entire region from Zagreb to Skopje was reduced to rubble and smoke plumes as Serbs, Croats, and Muslims, who had contrived to live peaceably with one another for generations, harangued, victimized, and ultimately turned to killing one another. They did so from village to village, and from door to door, as much as along any clearly defined battle lines. As the European Union would soon recognize, in many ways there simply were no clearly defined front lines. For Western observers, Yugoslavia became a source of lurid fascination precisely because it seemed to be going in the opposite direction of liberal democracy's apparent victory elsewhere: not so much the end of history as a turning of the clock back into the past.

The violence first broke out in Slovenia and Croatia, which were the first two republics to declare independence from the federal Yugoslavia: a structure that had stubbornly stumbled on into the post–Cold War light of day under President Ante Marković. Rather like Gorbachev, however, Marković was a man with greater support outside his country than within: not least because Western leaders saw him as a reliable pair of hands to manage the substantial foreign debts Yugoslavia still owed them. But Marković, also like Gorbachev, found himself the head of a country fast being erased from beneath him, as fighting spread to Bosnia, where inflammatory Serbian broadcasts on Radio Knin and politicians like Lazar Macura stoked a new and yet more lethal round of infighting. Once started, the tit-for-tat of grievance and reprisal proved a hard and vicious circle to close. Organized-crime syndicates brought in a steady supply of weapons for protonationalist movements to carry out their violence. And the international community proved itself incapable of stepping in to intervene, despite mounting evidence of what was going on.

By the summer of 1992 the scale of ethnic cleansing was brought home to the West by gaunt faces over their watery soup in the Omarska concentration camp: a place officially termed an "investigation" center for Muslim captives at Prijedor in northern Bosnia.[17] The British *Guardian* newspaper supplied the first eyewitness account of the camp's real purpose on August 7, 1992. "The internees are horribly thin, raw-boned; some are almost cadaverous, with skin like parchment folded around their arms; their faces are lantern-jawed, and their eyes are haunted by the empty stare of the prisoner who does not know what will happen to him next."[18] The *Guardian's* testimony would not be the last. The bloodshed reached its peak three years later at Srebrenica, where an undermanned Dutch peacekeeping force stationed in the small salt-mining town in Eastern Srpksa was forced to acquiesce in the handing over of the Bosniak civilians who had sheltered there. The men were separated from the women and children, who were driven away in buses. The men, who remained, around 7,000 of them in all, were shot and then tipped into freshly dug pits.

Confronted by the resurgence of ethnic cleansing on their own doorstep, the temptation to write off the Balkans' complex struggles as so much deep-rooted savagery proved too great for most Western commentators to resist. Like many others, Britain's new prime minister, John Major, saw the problems as rooted in ethnic animosities from the past. "The conflict in Bosnia [is] a product of impersonal and inevitable forces beyond anyone's control," he said as he sought to wash Britain's hands of it. It was a case of ethnic nationalism gone mad. Those who didn't seek to locate the problems in the past opted to bury them in the naturalizing metaphors of geography: Madeleine Albright pointed to the old communist "ground thawing" as the reason why "all the worms were crawling out."[19] Such accounts were a convenient way of implying that the resurgence of ethnic cleansing was a problem that had been found rather than created. In fact, neither religion nor ethnicity had given the peoples of the Balkans reason to live in anything other than a relatively peaceful coexistence until the politicians first in Belgrade and then in the capitals of the republics sought to gain territory.

The stoking of ethnic rivalries proved an easy way to popularity for politicians on the make (albeit dipping into the coffers of the former Bank of Yugoslavia helped too). The tensions had begun during the years after Tito's death in 1981. But it really took off after the collapse of communism, and the chief ringleader at this circus was Serbia's Slobodan Milošević. Milošević wanted something more than just greater influence in the old corridors of federal power in Belgrade. And a part of the tragedy of the Yugoslav Wars was that it took the Western powers such a long time to recognize that his true ambition was that of securing a "greater Serbia," if need be by murdering his way through the ethnic tapestry of the republics adjoining Serbia. From Milošević's point of view, ethnic cleansing was simply the rational application of force required to achieve these nationalist aims. The old habit of moving people to fit the lines on some map had returned.

So too had European leaders' tendency to prevaricate. For all that it insisted that the violence in the former Yugoslavia was a problem it was more than capable of sorting out, the European response was shambolic. The European Community initially saw the breakup of Yugoslavia as an opportunity to demonstrate its own, independent regional security credentials. And with the brokering of the Brioni Agreement, bringing to an end the first round of postindependence fighting in Slovenia, it seemed to have succeeded. But Brioni proved a weak dam against the pressure-cooker of what was already a much wider regional conflict. Indeed, no sooner was the ink dry on a settlement for Slovenia (the fortunate in-heritor of a relatively ethnically homogeneous population) than more fighting erupted in Croatia. But the Europeans refused to ramp up their response to the escalation of events on the ground: the EC's Lord Car-rington and the UN's American diplomat Cyrus Vance were thus destined to be overwhelmed by the scale of the problem.

The heart of the matter, however, was that Europeans—and European leaders such as Major, Chirac, Kohl, and the European Commission above all—could not see what exactly they had to gain by doing very much more: not until several years later at least. The brute fact was that, for all the talk of a "spillover" of violence into neighboring regions, especially perhaps Turkey, the Balkans were not a political or strategic concern to the West (in the way that the heavily armed successor states of the for-mer USSR were). As was noted by one of the more insightful outside observers, the journalist Misha Glenny, Western policymakers had already singled out Hungary, Poland, and Czechoslovakia specifically for rapid integration into the market structures of the West: as a region, the Balkans was of little economic interest.[20]

But Western diplomats, it is easy to forget, were also stretched to the limit during the early years of the Balkan crisis, with developments in the Gulf and across the Soviet Union, not to mention over Maastricht at home. This goes some way to explaining the disjointed solutions put forward for the Balkan crisis: the inviolability of borders being insisted upon in the case of Serbia and its minorities even as the right to seces-sion from Serbia and independence for the Albanian nationalities was also acknowledged. As the conflict escalated, such questions began to divide Western policymakers as much as regional actors, including a somewhat implacable Greece, which had its own eyes on the Republic of Macedonia, which it considered a threat to its territorial integrity (northern Greece is also called Macedonia).

For their part, the French and British never really wanted to recognize Slovenia and Croatia as independent states; newly reunified Germany, by contrast, did. When the Germans finally got their way, it changed the nature of events on the ground dramatically, as a formerly domestic conflict was immediately redefined, overnight, as an *international* war. This was the cue for the United Nations under Boutros-Ghali to send in one of its new peacekeeping forces in the form of UNPROFOR. Peacekeeping was perhaps putting it strongly. For the next three years, UNPROFOR did little to stop the killing, which went on at a carefully monitored and internationally condemned—but never actually prevented—pace. It may even have prolonged it. Sarajevo fell under siege to Radovan Karadžić, and the Vance–Owen plan, which sought to redivide the old Federal Yugoslavia along more ethnically dominant lines, seemed only to reward the Serbs for their aggression. The NATO-sponsored no-fly zone, hampered by a "dual key" system that required approval from both NATO *and* the UN before air strikes could be launched, did little to prevent the worst of the village-to-village fighting.

It is hard to avoid the conclusion today, therefore, that the Yugoslav Wars held up a distinctly unflattering mirror to the West at a moment when it had more freedom of movement internationally than at any time before or since. Greece and Turkey took the wars as an excuse to re-animate their longstanding rivalry. Northern European nations proved distinctly unwelcoming to southern refugees (over half of Bosnia-Herzegovina's 4.4 million inhabitants would be displaced during the wars). America, however, for all that Secretary of State James Baker declared the US "had no dog in this fight," was more active—behind the scenes at least. As early as 1992 Clinton proposed putting time-limited military options such as "lift and strike" on the table (the French and the British refused to allow this) and in an era when Muslim did not mean suspect to US foreign policymakers there is some evidence to suggest it was clandestinely re-arming the Bosniaks under siege.[21] But NATO confined itself exclusively to air operations and the UN forces on the ground were, while often warmly received, so lightly armed as to be little more than camouflaged comforters.

The ethnic struggles in Yugoslavia did, however, contribute to a substantial rethink in the aftermath of the Cold War that would prove of significance. For Western policymakers national security was now less a function of the ability to deter invasion or military strike from abroad, and more about remaking former adversaries in one's own image. "Borders matter less," as NATO Secretary General Javier Solana would later put it, "and the main challenge for the coming twenty years will be how best to spread prosperity, democracy and stability beyond our borders."[22] In practice, in the 1990s, this was a new policy projected onto Eastern Europe, the former Soviet Union, and the Balkans. These were the testing grounds of Western Europe's new understanding of the security of its own position in the world. "Security" now became a discursive construct in its own right; something that at times might need to be wrested from others.

Peacekeeping aside, the major strategic idea driving the actions of the Europeans was the so-called politics of "enlargement," as the reunification of Europe had now come to be called. Enlargement to the East continued to be the primary vehicle for elaborating a European-wide defense and security policy. And NATO and the EU remained the primary engines. The assumption was still that other countries *did* of course want to join the West but that they should be required to adopt liberal democratic norms and market structures to do so. The mid 1990s saw not only the drawing up of elaborate accession criteria for membership in NATO and the EU but the projection of the same criteria onto those who had no hope of joining: those, such as the Balkans, who simply wanted, or needed, Western support.

Thus was the geopolitical reckoning of the post–Cold War moment finally set in motion, as European and American leaders became involved once again in the domestic affairs of others without seriously imagining that this relationship might ultimately become a two-way affair. Ever since the 1970s the West had been more forcefully challenged from outside its own borders than ever before. Yet its collective response to this amounted to nothing more than the belief that the poverty and suffering of other nations could be adequately confronted with the faintest flicker of self-interest to light the way.

The once loudly trumpeted post–Cold War "peace dividend" proving elusive, it was substituted for with moral triage, in other words. And that triage was itself girded by a powerful—yet poorly defined—conflation of the norms of democracy and the claims of human rights. On the surface there was little not to like here, since to speak of democracy and human rights offered grounds for a scaling back on the high levels of military spending that had come to be taken as the norm. In 1995 Belgium and the Netherlands thus phased out military conscription; France undertook a large-scale downsizing of its military in 1996. Few countries anyway made their 2 percent of GDP military spending commitments advised under NATO, and those that did now reduced them. Meanwhile NATO was busily reinventing itself as a political as much as a military organization.

Driving this change was a growing sense, in part coming out of places like the Balkans, that it was the nature of domestic institutions, not military apparel, which determined the level of international threat. Accordingly, the solution required was a vast new program of promoting these

Western "norms" whether or not they were actually desired, or even appropriate in some cases. Had this move to demilitarization been undertaken without a corresponding evangelism on behalf of a particular set of norms it would probably have been a welcome and valuable contribution to longer-term peace. As it was, it was the right idea, wrongly executed, at a highly unpropitious time.

Problems from Hell

All this soon became a particular problem for Clinton, who was finding that the spirit of cooperation and multilateralism which had enabled his predecessor to launch operations Desert Shield and Desert Storm was disintegrating. No sooner was Gorbachev gone than Russia, under Yeltsin, rediscovered its power of veto in the Security Council, followed swiftly by China. As a result America found its post–Cold War freedom of movement becoming steadily more constrained. Elsewhere, fewer and fewer nations were willing to bear the costs of multilateral interventions on behalf of "peace and democracy."

Like the Europeans the Clinton administration initially made much of the fact that it was moving on from the old Cold War strategy of "containment" of the Soviet Union to one of "enlargement" of its own democratic creed.[23] In practice this boiled down to promoting a range of activities from electoral observation to business round tables: for which purpose US financial aid had already escalated rapidly after 1989. By the mid 1990s it was spending around $600 million annually on democracy promotion work abroad.[24] But it was discovering at the same time that there were very real *limits* to its international authority. Nothing brought this home more clearly than the first in a series of "problems from hell," as UN envoy Samantha Power later put it, which broke out in the autumn of 1993. Just weeks before leaving office President Bush had been so moved by pictures of starving children in war-torn Somalia that he sent American troops to assist a UN-sponsored humanitarian mission. He may also have felt moved to act as a way of avoiding getting embroiled elsewhere: in the more complicated waters of Bosnia, for example. Countries like Somalia were deemed not to have complicated histories.

Little could have been further from the truth. The civil war—which UN Operation Restore Hope was there to "peacekeep"—was the inevitable result of the implosion of the various ethnic groups that had, via their respective guerrilla militias, been snapping at the heels of the unpopular Siad Barre regime throughout the 1980s. American citizens might have been innocent in their ignorance of this, but their government was hardly free of complicity: since 1979 the United States had provided military aid to the Siad regime in response to the perceived threat of Soviet engagements in Afghanistan. When a helicopter sent in to rescue the US embassy staff made a neighborly detour to pick up the Soviets too, the fate of so many parts of the world left by the two superpowers was captured in the act.[25]

There was unfinished business then, when the US marines landed at night on the beaches of Mogadishu on December 10, 1992, to be greeted not by an enemy but—in a sign of the new global era—by television lights.[26] The situation deteriorated rapidly soon after, however, during Clinton's first year in office. In October a US Black Hawk helicopter was shot down in a firefight with rebels. Within hours, television pictures beamed back images of the captured helicopter pilot being paraded through the streets of the city; the naked body of his dead comrade was dragged about, kicked and spat upon by Somali fighters. American news audiences were horrified. "How did an operation that began with American soldiers feeding starving Somalis end with an American soldier's corpse being dragged through the streets of Mogadishu by Somalis starving only for revenge?" asked one journalist. Or as an emergency worker put it when interviewed on national television: "If I have to choose between pictures of starving Somali babies or dead American soldiers . . . well, I don't want to see any more dead Americans. Sorry. It's time to bring the boys home."[27]

To its critics the debacle in Somalia revealed the Clinton administration to be floundering on foreign policy: an impression not helped by a "briefing" session held before Congress two days later, in the stuffy basement of the Capitol Rotunda, by his national security team. Instead of laying out a response, Warren Christopher and Les Aspin let it be known they were interested in hearing "suggestions." It was, said Newt Gingrich, "the most dismal performance by a national security official in modern times."[28]

Somalia was soon eclipsed by another problem, this time in Haiti. Again the source of the crisis was a long-running issue inherited from the Bush era. Following a military coup that overthrew Jean-Bertrand Aristide in 1991, Haitians had been fleeing the island nation on rickety rafts trying to get to Cuba. In response to the humanitarian crisis a UN-brokered accord had set October 31, 1993, as the deadline for Aristide to be returned to power. When US engineers and technicians arrived on the USS *Harlan County* in advance of the approaching deadline they were jeered at and threatened by junta mobs until Clinton ordered the ship, unable to dock, to be turned around.

The moment the *Harlan County* turned about, Clinton appeared to have lost control of his foreign policy agenda, and the media and his Republican opponents wasted no time in pointing this out. Clinton's role as commander-in-chief had already got off to a rocky start when he took on the issue of gays in the military at the start of his term: his first visit aboard the USS *Theodore Roosevelt* resulted in mutterings about his having dodged the draft. By the following year, 1994, Clinton felt he simply had no choice but to revisit the Haitian situation—and more successfully this time—if he wanted to restore his standing as commander-in-chief.

And he did just that. This time the Pentagon drew up plans for an actual US invasion, although, ever one to keep his options open, Clinton simultaneously sent former president Jimmy Carter on a mission to secure the peaceful removal of the junta. It resulted in something of a near-miss disaster, with Carter still leading negotiations in Haiti while US forces were on their way. But in a last-minute turnaround, this time by the junta, the 20,000 US troops approaching Haiti narrowly avoided going to war.[29]

Two things of significance emerged from out of the storm clouds that October in American foreign policy terms. The first was a new willingness, of the president, to use force to back up his nation's ambitions. Clinton had turned the cheek twice. He would not be doing so again. The second thing that came out of it was the fact that, henceforth, what was now called the "Mogadishu line"—the point at which the West would or would not get involved in conflicts—would be drawn according to *domestic* US political opinion and not local need on the ground. The desire never again to be complicit with the forces of evil, as Western powers had found themselves in the 1930s, was thus affirmed in the same moment the ability to take such decisions was removed.

The first and in many ways definitive exemplification of that came just a few months after the Somalia and Haiti episodes, when Hutu extremists in Rwanda shot down their president's plane as it flew back into the capital of Kigali from peace negotiations seeking an end to the ongoing civil war. Within hours a killing spree was unleashed against the Hutus' primary ethnic rivals, the Tutsis. For the next hundred days Rwanda descended into a blood-soaked hell on earth as more than 800,000 Tutsis and others were slaughtered wherever they were found.

Rwanda made a mockery of Clinton's campaign stump speech calling for a UN rapid deployment force that would be "standing at the borders of countries threatened by aggression, preventing mass violence against civilian populations, providing humanitarian relief and combatting terrorism."[30] It made a mockery of Boutros-Ghali's promise for a more active and engaged UN. Above all it revealed the limits of the Western will to care in the new post–Cold War international era, making it quite clear what forces it was—in this case a racialized disdain for African lives—that shaped those limits. It also tipped the scales of America's willingness to take more concerted military action in the Balkans, where Clinton would find not only the means to silence his foreign policy critics at home, but the basis too for a new liberal internationalism.

The Bosnia Solution

Meanwhile the fighting had hardly let up in the former Yugoslavia, particularly in Bosnia, the most ethnically mixed of the former republics. But in light of the genocide in Rwanda, and the unsettling guilt over the failure to intervene that it provoked, the second shelling of a civilian marketplace in Sarajevo in August 1995—coming so soon after the Srebrenica massacre of July—prodded the United States to call for a more resolute NATO intervention. Four years earlier Desert Storm had demonstrated the unprecedented power of democracies acting in unilateral mode. But in the years between, an average of 330 shells a day had landed on the city of Sarajevo during its forty-six-month siege, and snipers, like the one who took "potshots" at Zlata Filipović's family home—they nicknamed him "Jovo"—had terrorized the city with impunity. That was now set to end.

Clinton was all too aware he had been vacillating on Bosnia, much to the consternation of his European allies. Whatever "wisps of resolve" the president might one day possess, sniped *The Times* of London, would invariably disappear "halfway down Pennsylvania Avenue, blown away by Congressional muttering." Clinton found it harder to push the issue away after the election of Jacques Chirac in May 1995. In his blunderbuss manner, Chirac immediately began goading the president to act. After the Srebrenica massacre in July, Chirac jumped on the telephone to Clinton to propose that a rapid reaction force go in to retake the town: the United States could limit itself to just flying them in if Clinton preferred. "Then what do we do?" Clinton replied. Chirac did not have a good answer. But Sarajevo had in truth convinced Clinton that the

French president, "le bulldozer" as the French called him, was right. America could not stay out of the Bosnia imbroglio any longer.[31]

Clinton had other concerns too. Bosnia was making a mockery not only of European foreign policy but of NATO—which America had made considerable efforts to keep going since the end of the Cold War. Relations with Russia were no warmer over NATO than they had been two years earlier. And so Clinton was keen to find a way to give NATO a role in the conflict in the former Yugoslavia that Yeltsin could get involved in as well. Since the Russians were strongly against the use of NATO as an instrument of war in a region that was, after all, previously well within the Soviet orbit, the logical alternative was to get them involved in a NATO-led peacekeeping operation instead.

With Clinton's mind made up, National Security Advisor Anthony Lake and Richard Holbrooke, then Assistant Secretary of State for European affairs, and a respected if brusque man, set about crafting a policy that would use force, or the threat of it, to drag the various warring parties to the peace table. First they ditched the "dual key" system limiting missile strikes that had made it so hard for NATO to act decisively. Then, in a manner that suggested the United States was finding its authoritative voice again, they told the Europeans to get on board with the new plan or to step out of the way. Finally they set about the harder work of trying to get the warring parties to come together. The shelling of the marketplace in Sarajevo was the moment that the new plan came together. Two days later NATO responded with a massive bombardment of Serbian positions in and around Sarajevo. When they had run out of second order targets, they expanded the bombing further afield. It was the largest operation in the organization's history, and it left nobody in any doubt that the US president now meant business. But where would this newfound resolve take the Bosnian imbroglio?

The answer to that became clear at the start of November, when three unlikely figures disembarked at a US airfield in the heart of Montgomery County, Ohio. For the next few days Bosnian President Alija Izetbegović, Croatia's Franjo Tudjman, and Serbian President Slobodan Milošević hunkered down in the heart of Dayton, where the NASCAR racers meet, to hammer out a peace settlement. Overseen by Holbrooke and Secretary of State Warren Christopher, the talks went on for three weeks. Clinton kept his distance. The agreement that was reached was ultimately extracted, like so many teeth, from leaders who could barely conceal their disdain for each other, let alone their US hosts. But reached it was, not least because Milošević, perhaps the critical figure, was suffering desperately from the UN sanctions regime and was prepared to give things up to have those sanctions lifted. Either way it would prove to be one of the major foreign policy victories of the Clinton presidency.

A peace plan requires troops on the ground to enforce it, and America was now required to commit to the 60,000-strong force—just for a year, Clinton insisted, somewhat disingenuously, on announcing the deal. Such had been the upheaval and the intimate nature of the violence that there could be no happy or simple ending. With partition now a fact on the ground, the image of many thousands of Serbs from Sarajevo, "literally digging up the relics and bones of their fathers and mothers to drag them into Serb-held territory," was a reminder of the human cost. There were endless problems as the new NATO Implementation Force (IFOR) sought to bring about the book-length terms of the peace agreement. Was the ancient town of Mostar, whose famous bridge had been destroyed during the war, to be a carefully divided city or should it be rejoined at its hip across the River Neretva? What was the international community to do with the leaders who had brought so much ruin down upon the heads of their peoples and yet who now would enjoy a new status as heads of recognized, democratic states?

The consequences for the West of the Bosnian saga would not end there. Two of the 9/11 hijackers fought in the Yugoslav Wars: two among the many who had traveled to the republic from across the Middle East to defend their Muslim counterparts. Clinton was happy to claim credit for finally bringing the conflict to a halt but in the same stroke he also affixed America to the longer history of suffering in the region and made it in some ways responsible for its outcome. US troops would not be coming home within a year, as Clinton first promised, and the NATO bombardments of 1995 would not be the last US-sponsored interventions in that part of the world.

There was a catch here, then, that the Clinton administration in particular was slow to realize. But American foreign policy writers like Walter Russell Mead, Samuel Huntington, Michael Mandelbaum, and Charles Kupchan were all offering a variant of it: namely that America and the world were already linked far more closely than Americans tended to realize. The evidence had been coming in for years. But to the Cold War creep of the United States' security commitments was now added its newfound post–Cold War promotion of democracy, often to the seemingly most marginal groups and places: the PUK, the SDPI, the

HVO, the 55th Arab Brigade. Who had heard of most of these? And yet they had all heard of America.

These were longer-term problems, however. In the short term, the Dayton Agreement represented the final chapter in the post–Cold War story of international realignment. It helped set the United States and its European allies on a new footing, and reestablished American authority over the wider international system. It gave a new sense of mission and purpose to NATO and so, in another sense, ensured that the institutions of Cold War internationalism persisted into the foreseeable future. And, of course, it got the Russians involved in working alongside US forces stationed in the region to uphold the settlement. Dayton also had some considerable significance on the domestic political front. Not only did it present a clear foreign policy "achievement" for a president who had been accused for much of his tenure in office of letting American power slip embarrassingly away; the inclusion of the neoconservative Richard Perle at the peace talks was also a way of securing greater bipartisan agreement over what America was doing internationally.

One not insignificant result of this was that, despite the ongoing partisanship in domestic politics, Republicans and Democrats were closer in their views that America needed to play a more robust role internationally than they had been for a generation. The domestic pegs of the post-9/11 expansion of American militarism were thus in some senses now knocked into their holes by the Bosnian solution. "In substance and style," as two US foreign policy experts would later put it, "the leader of the free world was back."[32] This brought the Democrats closer to the usually more hawkish Republicans on the matter of when liberal democratic societies were permitted to use force elsewhere.

That, in turn, created problems for the Republicans. The more serious among their potential presidential contenders for the 1996 race—Colin Powell, Dick Cheney, James Baker—were all foreign policy big-hitters and largely onside with the newly proactive president. This left a door open for self-styled radicals like Pat Buchanan (again), Newt Gingrich, and other UN-detesting isolationists to make headway on the right, cementing its move to a more radical stance. Since most people actually supported what the president had achieved in countries like Bosnia, the political sweet spot to be found here was by turning to domestic scapegoats—"foreigners" living at "home" in America—instead. If this revealed the existence of a latent, America-first sentiment lurking within the less well-remunerated reaches of the working population, it equally garnered sufficient votes for Buchanan to beat the Republican front-runner, and eventual candidate Bob Dole, in the early 1996 New Hampshire primary. The consequences would begin to become apparent some two decades later.

Also of longer-term significance, these foreign-policy realignments triggered an internal rupture within the Republican Party. A breakaway grouping now formed, as tends to happen at moments of policy impasse. This time a group of foreign-policy focused Republicans (including William Kristol, former chief of staff to Vice President Dan Quayle, and Robert Kagan, an influential political analyst and writer) began calling for what they called a neo-Reaganite foreign policy. They demanded a larger role for America in the world, believing that America was safest when it dictated terms to others, not when it just sat back and hoped things would work out in its favor (as mainstream Republicans seemed to now think) or flitted here and there in damage-limitation mode (as they sought to characterize the new Clintonite approach). It was either too little too late to influence the 1996 election, or perhaps the time for their ideas had not yet come. But they would not have so very long to wait. One election cycle down the road and the neoconservative moment would have fully arrived.[33] Clinton was not done yet though.

The Utopian Moment

From a position of authority often comes the desire to administer a greater justice in the world. Hegemony must be sold as much as it sometimes needs defending. And from the Middle East, to Bosnia and Kosovo, the 1990s represented a high point in the Western way of bringing peace to a troubled world. Clinton for one was personally invested in some of the causes; a great many others—such as Norway's Thorvald Stoltenberg or Britain's Paddy Ashdown—were no less invested and more directly involved in bringing it about. But the nature of what they were doing served a double purpose, even if that purpose was often hidden from themselves at the time: as surely it was when it came to peace in the Middle East.

As ever when America wishes to let fly the doves of peace, as it did after the war in Iraq, it was the Israel–Palestine conflict that would become the focus of its attentions. Before the dust had even settled on Operation Desert Storm, Bush had set his old friend James Baker to shuttling about the globe in rapid, Kissingerian strokes, as he sought to bring about the Madrid discussions (October 1991)—the first-ever talks between Israel and all of its Arab neighbors. The event was not a resounding success—though it did at least repay some debts the United States had accrued with the Arab states in the region during the Gulf War. Rather it was the parallel, back-channel discussions that led to the Oslo Accords (September 1993) that broke more promising ground (though they too would hit a roadblock in the failure of the Camp David summit and the return to violence that accompanied the Second Intifada). Meanwhile, the United States and Israel continued to lock arms around the shared assumption that "Arabs only understand force," as one foreign policy guru put it.[34] America thus continued to supply the region with substantially more military hardware than economic aid in the years to come. The prospects for a longer-term peace waxed and waned accordingly.

Nonetheless Clinton had been genuinely inspired by the famous handshake between Yitzhak Rabin and Yasser Arafat on the White House lawn in 1993, and he believed he had made a real difference to its having taken place. It was a belief that fed into his more active approach to Bosnia the following year. States were henceforth put on notice that sovereignty was no longer a right but a privilege. Confirmation of the new approach came toward the end of the decade in neighboring Kosovo. By 1999 Milošević, who like Saddam had been forced back into his box after the NATO-led intervention, had nonetheless remained in power and was soon back to his unpleasant ways. In March 1999 news began circulating that several dozen Albanians had been killed by his forces in the village of Račak in Kosovo, some of them clearly executed. As reports filtered through of similar bouts of targeted killings elsewhere, and the specter of inaction in the face of mass killings once again raised its head, Western leaders were minded to act more decisively. This time it took just weeks, rather than years, before NATO unleashed massive airpower on the Serbian forces. The unconditional flexing of muscle left Milošević in no doubt this time just exactly where he stood. On June 9 Belgrade capitulated and agreed to withdraw its forces from Kosovo.

What was equally beyond doubt was that there had been "a changing of the guard" in the Clinton administration.[35] That was a signal that the president had undergone a change of heart as well. In both cases the new mood was a preference to deploy American soldiery and matériel in order to stamp out bad behavior before local problems started making bigger problems for anyone else. Tentative at the beginning of the decade, Clinton was resolute toward its end as intervening in other countries for "humanitarian" reasons became an increasingly appealing (and remarkably uncontroversial) casus belli for the Western powers. And why not: coupled to human rights on the one hand and a sort of liberal developmentalism on the other, waging peace via humanitarian intervention would prove to be a sweet spot of international diplomacy that few Western leaders could resist. For the United States in particular it provided the means to reassert its claims of hegemonic protection for other nations without the long shadow of communism.

Perhaps the first indication of the extent to which these aims had merged with the underlying desire to keep America in a position of unassailable international authority was Operation Desert Fox, launched in Iraq in 1998. Three days of cruise missile strikes by the United States (now acting "on behalf" of the UN) rained down on Iraq as if America were "world policeman," as Russian Ambassador Sergei Lavrov snapped.[36] Gone was any rhetoric of "democracy promotion." There was no emancipatory vision of "enlarging" the community of democratic nations here. Domestic political considerations and even Iraqi civil society were scarcely considered: instead it was about the power that could be unleashed by one state in the name of the rights of individual people, of global citizens, wherever in the world they might be.

What Desert Fox was once again about, in other words, was promoting particular sorts of societies in the name of a particular vision of societal order. In that sense at least, Clinton had solved the problem of America's international mission—"the theory of the case," it had been dubbed within his administration—which had so vexed his first years in power. In the end, no grand doctrine had been found to replace the old Cold War umbrella of "containment," as first articulated by George Kennan. In that sense, the Kennan Sweepstakes, as Clinton's inner circle jokingly referred to the constant effort to find a new phrase, never found a clear winner. But something more valuable for the United States *had* been found: not a doctrine, but a rationale, a generally accepted means of making itself of interest to the internal affairs of other countries when it wanted to.[37]

Two other things emerged out of the Yugoslav Wars that would bear upon the nature of Western democratic politics. The first was the way the meaning of democracy was once again narrowed as it was projected abroad in the new "interventionist" liberal politics. In 1997 Madeleine Albright, who had provoked Colin Powell in the lead-up to Desert Storm by saying, "What's the point of having this superb military you're always talking about if we can't use it?" (as Powell famously said afterward, "I thought I would have an aneurysm"), replaced Warren Christopher as Secretary of State.[38] Under her guidance the norms of liberal democracy would now be spread more forthrightly as a package of rules and procedures, and NATO was to be a key tool in that process. Albright had long been one of the more hawkish over Bosnia, and one of the least warmly disposed to the UN Secretary General. She would soon also be making the case for intervention in Iraq.

The second thing to emerge from this period concerned the related matter of US hegemony within the new liberal order. What the Clinton administration had discovered for itself over the skies of Bosnia, and later Kosovo, was an answer to the claim that its interventions abroad were little more than "foreign policy as social work," as a former Democrat, Michael Mandelbaum, a foreign policy expert who had famously belittled the Clinton camp, said.[39] Now the projection of a more muscular form of humanitarianism abroad could be sold as a way of keeping America safe at home: it merely had to be resolute enough, to be approved but not run by the UN, and to involve aerial power and not troops on the ground (here was where NATO now found itself with a renewed role and mandate). The implications were substantial. For the first time since the end of the Cold War, America had a means for intervening when, and only when—but also almost *always* when—it wished.

Come Kosovo, when that policy was put into action on the ground, it was clear that a certain confidence had returned to the Western democracies. At some point during the previous few years a new liberal internationalism had been born. That new internationalism was not the governmental transnationalism that had briefly surfaced as a possibility earlier in the decade. It was not an internationalism centered on the UN, either, for all that the US—for now—elected to at least work *through* the UN. It had taken shape, rather, as a classically Clintonite neologism—military humanitarianism—an approach not just to the world's problems but to the political challenges of dealing with that world as they were raised within the political sphere at home. It was a policy approach that had emerged out of Iraq and stretched its wings over Bosnia, but which really took flight during the Kosovo crisis in 1999. By then it was almost as if the anxieties and uncertainties of the immediate post–Cold War years having proven formative, the existing democracies were at last turning a harder face to the outside world.

One of the first victims of the new American clarity in international affairs was Boutros Boutros-Ghali, the UN secretary general. The United States had decided it could not tolerate a man who was seen to have dithered while Rome burned. They wanted a more interventionist-minded figure, and they found him in Kofi Annan, the man who did finally push the button to intervene with force upon the siege of Sarajevo. Via its power of the veto in the Security Council the United States ensured that it was Annan who was installed in Boutros-Ghali's place: the first and only time a standing UN Secretary General has been ousted by use of the veto. It was yet another reminder that, if the United States' short-lived interest in UN diplomacy was now over, there was still a role for the Security Council, so long as it did "the right thing." The Security Council now consolidated its preeminence within the UN system, and as David M. Malone, the Canadian diplomat and former representative to the UN, observed, it completed in the process its transformation from "a politico-military mode in which it mediated between warring states, to a mode in which it sits at the apex of a global legal-regulatory architecture."[40] Here was the real transnationalism of the age.[41]

As the Cold War faded from memory, democracy was on the rise as a global norm, as any number of indicators, including the rise in the number of requests to the UN for electoral assistance, suggests: from seven in 1989 to eighty-nine in 1995.[42] By the turn of the millennium, "governance," "public sector reform," and "leadership development" would together consume around half the UN's budget.[43] But while the money kept being thrown at it, for America at least the idea of "democratic enlargement" as a foreign policy ambition soon fell into quiet disuse: as marked in the rhetorical slippage from the Bush–Clinton notion of "democratic enlargement" to Albright's "assertive multilateralism" to the "indispensable nation" of Clinton's second term, to what would in due course reemerge as the notion of "forward engagement" during Al Gore's ill-fated 2000 campaign.

But it was not international developments that lay behind this. Rather, it was what had by now come to pass closer to home. Prosperity had returned to the West. And it brought with it a new sense of optimism missing during the last few years of upheaval. If that left certain international problems, such as those in the former Yugoslavia, ultimately unresolved, then perhaps that was just the way things were now. Western citizens, in any case, seemed tired of other people's problems: the internationalism of the 1970s and 1980s, of Live Aid and Médicins sans Frontières, and the immediate post–Cold War enthusiasm for bringing democracy to the furthest corners of the world had died away. Deep down, many wanted nothing more than to enjoy the economic prosperity that seemed, all of a sudden, to have returned.

10

The New Prosperity

"FOR THE FIRST time in all history, more people on this planet live under democracy than dictatorship," Bill Clinton announced in his second inaugural address in 1997. It was a bold claim of the sort that the American president, flush from success at Dayton and in the Middle East, and now the first full, two-term Democrat since FDR, felt within rights to be using at the start of his "legacy" term. Like much that sounds too good to be true, it immediately got the fact-checkers at the *New York Times* to work. He was right, they soon confirmed, flapping the official final score: 3.1 billion who did to 2.66 billion who did not.[1] But what really mattered for most Western citizens, and Americans above all, was that their own economic fortunes also seemed to be expanding. Clinton himself was in no doubt that this was the actual reason he had been reinstalled as president.

By making the right choices about government, the president argued, further into his address, "the forces of the Information Age and the global society" can "unleash the limitless potential of all our people." After decades of moderate to low economic growth, of wage restraint and diminished expectations, *this* was what people had been waiting to hear. Right across America there were signs that people were catching on to the thermals of a remarkable uplift. Certainly, few felt obliged to call in the fact-checkers when Clinton went on to insist that "Once again, our economy is the strongest on Earth." Government was not the problem, Clinton intoned, in a pointed effort to echo Reagan's famous line. But nor was government the solution. "We—the American people—we are the solution." Clinton's tone was celebratory, and insistent: a lot like the times themselves. Finally, the boom-time feeling was back—and there could not have been a more fitting president to lead it.

The Boom

The nineties boom would ultimately shape the tenor of politics within all the Western economies. But it was experienced first, and most dramatically, in America. Ever since the United States had stumbled into the post–Cold War era in a recessionary funk in 1991, the speed and extent of the recovery, recalled Nobel Prize–winning economist Joseph Stiglitz, recently drafted in to head up Clinton's Council of Economic Advisers, "seemed to defy what was universally taught in economics courses around the world."[2]

The economy had actually turned the corner in 1992: too late for Bush to cash in on the upswing and too early for Clinton yet to appreciate his historic good fortune. It began expanding in 1993. But it was not until the second half of the decade that the extent of the upswing became apparent (productivity growth for the second half of the decade dramatically outperformed that of the first half). By 1996 it wasn't only Murdoch-owned presses spinning out headline after hyperventilating headline. "Is this a great time or what?" asked a set of commercials for telecoms giant MCI in 1996. In 1998 America's *Wired* magazine declared the past half-decade to have been the "five greatest years for humanity ever."[3]

When the G7 (with Russia included, for now, as a full member of the liberal international order) met in Denver in 1997, the transformation in America's fortunes could not have been more apparent. Memories of recession seemed distant. The United States was easily the leading Western economy: it had created 12 million new jobs while the Europeans and Japanese were still shedding them; and the year-on-year increase in GDP was now the highest it had been since the Kennedy–Johnson era. Remarkably, inflation had also come down to levels near that of the postwar Golden Age. To top it all off, the long-running, secular decline in the value of real wages that had eroded most people's purchasing power since the 1970s was held at bay for a few years; some groups even saw a small increase in the value of their take-home pay.

What was more, the US economy seemed to be doing better not only in quantitative, aggregate terms, but in qualitative terms as well. Compared to the gloom of the 1970s, there was a remarkable sense of optimism, of adventure in the air. Talk was rife of a "new economy," technology driven, dynamic, and daring. Investment in IT was growing fast, and manufacturing had been replaced by services; the assembly line by creative content management. As Treasury Secretary Larry Summers observed: "It's unbelievable what has happened since 1990. It's almost a new world in economic terms since then." And what accounted for that new world, Summers concluded, was the return of the entrepreneurial spirit: "[U]nlike in most other countries," as he put it, "bankers in America will give money to guys without ties."[4]

It wasn't quite that simple, of course. But it was true that with productivity growth returning at last—as Americans gained more output per hours worked—US citizens found a little more money in their back pockets when they went to the shops, a little more confidence among the financial institutions who had once been reluctant to lend them money, and a lot more reason to go out and spend on more than just the necessities.

Much of what they invested in was stocks and shares. Between 1994 and 1999 the value of stock market assets held by households in America increased by around $9 trillion. Americans also began spending a lot more on consumer goods and on eating out. They invested in bricks and mortar. And the growth in incomes and spending meant a growth in the government's own tax revenue, which kept confidence in the economy high. It was as if, or so the real estate and media tycoon Mortimer Zuckerman put it, "Everything that should be up is up—GDP, capital spending, incomes, the stock market, employment, exports, consumer and business confidence. Everything that should be down is down—unemployment, inflation, and interest rates." Zuckerman duly predicted a "Second American Century."[5]

The boom also brought about a transformation in the relationship between society and the economy at large. By the end of the decade, with 60 million Americans owning stocks and shares privately, and 125 million as shareholders in investment funds moving pension plans out of safer treasuries and into riskier but more lucrative assets, people began thinking of themselves as asset-holders, as investors.[6] This drove an unprecedented growth in the American stock market. People proved willing to pay more for less in the expectation that less was going through the roof anyway. They were also encouraged by the hype around the Internet and new technology. The economy seemed glamorous and glitzy again, as CEOs of dynamic new media and technology conglomerates, often from Silicon Valley, attended gala events and fundraisers in Manhattan and downtown Los Angeles.

The scale of the new prosperity was such that it reached even many of those groups who had benefited least from economic growth over the previous few decades. Unemployment among African American groups, for example, fell from 14.1 percent to 7.8 percent between 1993 and 1999; that among Latinos fell from 11.3 percent to 6.5 percent.[7] Both were still well above the national average, to be sure, but these groups were seeing a larger slice of the income pie at least (housing remained a structural barrier). The latter half of the 1990s, in short, was the moment when mass democracy was replaced by mass participation in the market: and as far as most people were concerned, things either felt the same or they felt quite a bit better.

There were naysayers, of course. Some grouched about a new form of "market populism": of collective hysteria by a society that had let the trappings of wealth go to its head. It was true. Part of what was inflating the stock market was a widespread growth in fraud and corporate malpractice. "The rules had become so ambiguous and the lack of enforcement of rules of fiduciary duty and integrity had become so pervasive," observed then–Attorney General Eliot Spitzer of New York, "that everybody was playing improperly."[8] Spitzer was perhaps not the best spokesperson on the matter of integrity of accounts, but his point was basically sound. Markets were no longer just mediums of economic exchange, as another critic put it, but mediums of political consent. Why criticize the market when "markets were a friend of the little guy."[9]

In 1998 Pulitzer Prize–winning Daniel Yergin and Joseph Stanislaw published the era's new testament: a bestselling and glowing history of the rise and rise again of global capitalism, *The Commanding Heights*. America was shown as embarking on a long-nurtured historic payoff: the lessons of the past finally bringing in the trophies now that US capitalism, leaner of musculature than before, was running its competitors into the dust. Yergin and Stanislaw's historic playbook was characteristic of the confidence of the time. People borrowed heavily against the rising value of their homes, for which they were assisted by the introduction of high-loan-to-value (HLTV) mortgages in 1995. Others tried their hand at day-trading in a stock market that seemed on aggregate, or so the Dow Jones strongly suggested, to be heading constantly upward.[10]

Of course, such a pervasive turn to the market required changes in habits and lifestyle. Society and business alike incorporated the logic of flexibility, opportunity, technology, and credit in their affairs. CNBC aired its "CEO wealthometer" for digestion in hotel lobbies and on running machines around the nation. *Newsweek* insisted in its headlines that "Markets R Us." There was an unmistakable sense that people had grasped what "market freedom" meant, and that they were enjoying it to the full.[11] The "financialization of everyday life" proceeded apace and the "new economy" was seen to be somehow immune to the problems of the past. "In a knowledge-based economy there are no constraints to growth," declared the Princeton economist Paul Krugman in 2001.[12] And that, or so it seemed, was that.

The New Economy

One is immediately prompted to ask just what *was* the real cause of the boom in America? It certainly was not the investments in jobs, education, and public infrastructure that Clinton had promised in the lead-up to the election.[13] Two things in fact proved critical. First was that Clinton focused, as we have seen, on getting the deficit under control, beginning with the Deficit Reduction Act of 1993. When Clinton first took office, the deficit had stood at $290 billion and rising fast. By the time he left in 2001 it had been converted into a $237 billion surplus. To achieve this, he brought money into government by reversing the worst of the Reagan-era tax cuts, raising taxes elsewhere, and paring back the welfare rolls (passing on the costs of food stamps to privately run soup kitchens, among others). His government also no longer had to spend quite so much on the military now that the Cold War was over.[14]

The second critical factor was US manufacturing, for all that this was never as closely prioritized as it might have been: a missed opportunity, perhaps, in light of the coming of the twenty-first-century economy driven by AI and the Internet. It was the strength of US manufacturing that had first enabled the American economy to turn a corner at the start of the decade. And it was manufacturing (even of advanced products such as computer terminals) within the new technology industries, rather than the share options and stock market floats of technology service companies like AOL, which was driving the growth in productivity by the end of the decade. The heart of the boom was American workers, for all that they were largely overlooked still as an electoral demographic.

Perhaps the most remarkable characteristic of the new economy was something that had not been seen since the 1960s. As the decade progressed the value of real wages for some American workers began to go up. For most of the previous forty years they had been declining (and the push to recover them had been, as we have seen, one of the structural drivers of the political changes afoot). When Clinton took office, wages had never lagged so far behind productivity. But with the boom driving business on, firms needed to hire more employees. And with unemployment levels generally declining during these years, workers were able to exert a little traction over how much they were paid.[15] For economists what was all the more remarkable was the fact that this decline in unemployment (from 7.5 percent to 4.0 percent between 1993 and 2000) was *not* accompanied by a resurgence of inflation (which orthodox economic theory would expect, given that businesses tend to pass on the costs of their rising wages bill to consumers).

It would later become apparent that globalization was part of the reason here: for in the now more integrated US economy, American firms were simply less able to pass on costs as they became uncompetitive relative to foreign firms. American workers faced similar constraints because of increasing influxes of immigrant workers willing to work for less, which was perhaps why they did not demand more than they were already demanding.[16] More Americans were in work, therefore, but they were perhaps more fearful than ever of being out of it. Alan Greenspan liked to speak of the "irrational exuberance" of employers and stock market investors. Workers, by contrast, were acting both more cautiously and a good deal more rationally: 50 percent of all firms surveyed in 1993–5, and 65 percent of manufacturing firms, threatened to move abroad when confronted by worker proposals to unionize.[17]

So the new economy did not do so very much to improve the position of labor *relative* to capital, for all the short-term gains in workers' take-home pay. Structurally speaking, workers remained largely unprotected against the vicissitudes of market volatility, and many of them, single mothers in particular, faced a difficult juggling act matching moderately improving wages with declining welfare and child support benefits. Corporations by contrast *did* fare well. They now had access to a better-educated workforce that was still pliant, they were paying less in taxes, and—as their profit margins increased as a result—they were encouraged to cash out value through share issues. That in turn freed up yet more capital for them to invest further and expand.

The new economy was a boom, above all else, for the top 10 percent of the income scale: the owners of capital (be it in stocks, shares, real estate, or inheritance) whose rapidly expanding wealth did not so much trickle down to the rest of society as hold everyone else aloft on puppet strings. The top 1 percent now took home 45 percent of all national income (it had been just 7.7 percent in 1973).[18] The lower middle classes and the workers continued, for the most part, to hold about the same position they had at the start of the decade, with one primary difference: they were now both able, and encouraged, to borrow money at an unprecedented rate. The Joneses were still in sight; you just had to take out another credit card to keep up with them.

To make sure that corporations kept investing and workers kept borrowing, Clinton knew that he needed to keep the supply of credit in the US economy flowing. In policy terms this required a capital-friendly (i.e., loosely regulated) macroeconomic environment. The puppet strings were not made of gossamer, then, but of those ever-expanding, self-indulgent credit lines. Above all they were tied to the central plank of finance that bound this whole system together. The financial sector had been growing dramatically since the late 1970s. But the nineties was the decade in which it truly "reigned supreme."[19] To increase the ability of finance to animate and to coordinate the movement of the wider economy the US government had freed up the ability of capital to invest and to maximize its chances of gaining a profit. That was achieved in a number of ways, including via large reductions in capital gains taxes (taxes on the value of shares and real estate), which encouraged yet more stock inflation and property speculation.

Above all, it was achieved by peeling back the regulatory architecture that limited what financial markets could do. Clinton's commitment to this new agenda was well encapsulated by the introduction of the Reverse Plaza Accords of 1995, which by amending the late 1980s Plaza Accords currency regime, ostensibly bailed out a stagnating Japanese economy. It did so, however, in such a way as to fuel both a massive influx of liquidity into the US economy and into US technology shares in particular, as well as—via Asian markets—into US government securities. By the time it came to repealing, via the Financial Services Modernization Act of 1999, the Depression-era Glass-Steagall regulations on banking practices, the administration was "one hundred percent behind the project of financial deregulation." As the official view of the administration declared of the former financial safeguards, which had been put in place specifically to avoid the sort of financial turmoil that had devastated the country in the 1930s: "those rules are not needed today."[20]

Thanks to the bulked-up role of finance in the US economy, the self-generating aspect of the boom was already in hand. But the Federal Reserve too played a crucial supporting role. Alan Greenspan remained its chairman throughout the 1990s. He had once been famously ticked off by President Bush with the mordant line, "I reappointed him and he disappointed me."[21] By contrast, and despite the rather rocky start to their relationship, Greenspan was to be Clinton's savior. It was Greenspan's Federal Reserve in the 1990s that ensured that the gap between short-term borrowing costs and long-term lending income would now be "unusually wide" and that in many ways *allowed* finance to come to dominate the entire economy.[22] Greenspan abetted the boom in other ways too. During his time in office, he increasingly came to think he could control the excesses of the market by the enunciation of a few carefully chosen words alone.[23] He did not therefore ask the Fed to raise interest rates as the boom turned into a bubble. He anticipated that markets would correct themselves.

This deliberate government-sponsored rise of finance had a transformative effect upon the wider workings of Western capitalist democracy. Seen over a longer time frame, the pendulum in national economic policymaking had now swung almost to the opposite end of where it had been in the 1970s, with its prudent citizens and governments happy to take on high levels of public debt. The mantra now was to keep public debt low—hence Clinton's willing embrace of the deficit hawk badge—but to substitute for it with private (i.e., personal) debt. In conjunction with the freeze on wages that corporations had undergone in order to secure profitability over previous decades, levels of personal debt had rocketed dramatically. The easiest way to cash in on a house, for example, was to remortgage it; and banks were now actively pushing other consumer credit lines as well, posting out credit cards to land on doormats throughout the land. The result was dramatic. On the one hand, the government was further liberated from the burden of stimulating the economy and maintaining a desirable level of economic growth; instead, citizens themselves now took on this role through their private spending and investment. On the other hand, there was less pressure to negotiate for higher wages—less pressure to change the system from below—so long as the credit kept coming.

If this was the heart of the new economy in America it was not limited to the United States alone. Similar processes of financial deregulation were at play across the Anglophone liberal market economies. They were transforming in the process the extent to which the market was able to leave its mark on the relationship between governments and citizens. Scholars dubbed this "privatized Keynesianism": a willing but unevenly balanced compact between active citizens and an increasingly passive state. Before, it was governments who would borrow money to calibrate the economy; now private citizens were encouraged to do so instead.[24]

This was the real political importance of credit in the context of the late twentieth century's deregulated markets. Credit was, or at least it appeared to be, the collective means to fulfill, literally, everyone's ends. In an increasingly "flexible" and volatile job market citizens could remain optimistic—could keep up the all-important "consumer confidence"—because they were given every opportunity to believe they could afford to spend beyond their means. There was a strong but pervasive pressure, therefore, though it never took the form of overt policy, for firms and even individuals to switch their sources of incomes from goods and services to assets, further fueling the financialization that was driving the boom forward. There was a strong incentive for everybody to wade into the waters of a more marketized society.

So it was, then, that at the very moment the Western democracies were celebrating the post-Fordist "service economy" as the late-century embodiment, par excellence, of the liberal democratic good life, that economy was itself being underwritten by a financial bazaar, in which assets were prioritized and high levels of personal debt were permissible. Mortgage-to-income ratios went down; the proportion of salaries paid not in cash but in share options went up.[25] Oil prices were held low, but house prices were allowed to inflate. All this was arcane and ephemeral to most people's lives. And yet the undoubted greater market "freedoms" it enabled were embraced as a powerful means of self-realization by almost everyone, irrespective of which social class or ethnic and racial group they belonged to.

And why not? For the first time in a generation, Western citizens could contemplate social mobility again. They could make plans and think a little more creatively about what to do with their lives and their careers. That made them, in turn, less willing than before to identify with a predetermined set of characteristics (much less the homilies) of the fixed political identities of old. Why remain what you were born? The right to choose who you were had begun to supersede the desire to secure the more tangible rights that belonged to you as the member of a particular group. Whether or not people were progovernment or not, most by now agreed—left and right, Democrat and Republican alike—that one thing government could do a bit less of was to tell people what a good society was supposed to look like. "[W]ho is to judge what is virtue and what is vice?" as the moral philosopher Michael Sandel, a popular guest at the White House and at one point a long-listed candidate for the Supreme Court, once put it. The president himself was more specific: "The era of big government is over," he declared.[26]

The Information Revolution

Luckily a new era appeared to be dawning just in time to replace it. This had less to do with Clinton's, or anyone else's, policies, than it did with the growing evidence that Western society was in the middle of a second great industrial revolution. Knowledge and technology—the basic elements of the first industrial revolution—had long gone hand in hand. Now, with the power of computing that had come on stream in the 1990s, they merged. This was most obvious in daily life in terms of the unprecedented availability of consumer technology—everything from the routine appearance of personal computers in people's homes, and Microsoft's ubiquitous Windows platform with it, to the rise of gadgets and gaming.

The rise in demand for such products added a further cascade into the seemingly unstoppable current of the boom. Microsoft reportedly paid over $8 million for the opening bars of the Rolling Stones song "Start Me Up" to launch their industry-standard, Windows 95 package (complete with CD-ROMs still) in the summer of 1995. "After years of development and months of the most intense hype ever to attend a product launch," wrote the British *Guardian* in attendance, Microsoft's Bill Gates ("complete with pudding basin haircut") was confident that the new Windows was going to "unlock the potential of personal computing."[27] Such boosterism was not confined to Microsoft alone. Standard & Poor's stock price index rose to unheard-of levels in the middle to late years of the decade, well above the level of growth in the real economy and of actual earnings within firms, as corporations themselves began to borrow at unprecedented rates.[28]

Silicon Valley, which had long been a center of technological innovation, now itself became a household name. Companies like Cisco, Hewlett-Packard, and Sun Microsystems turned telephone lines into mass data networks. Usually, before doing so, they received large injections of venture capital funding. The quality and processing speed of microchips, as manufactured by companies such as Intel and Pentium, were going up, and their cost was coming down. New platforms that would enable further developments, and that assembled their own new technological ecosystems, with more potential innovation down the line, began to emerge too. At Stanford, two graduate students, Larry Page and Sergey Brin, began developing a page rank algorithm that would in due course morph into Google, the most famous of all Silicon Valley's offspring. The one place computers could not really be seen, ironically, was in statistics relating to productivity growth. New consumer-based technologies were revolutionizing the American economy; they were not making it that much more productive.

But consumer technology was just one part of a wider information revolution that—hype or no hype—really *was* reshaping the way Western society lived, worked, and communicated. Perhaps most basically, by the 1990s the question of technology and of a technologized economy and society had come to have a profound influence on the very nature of politics itself. Under the banner of the "information society," with its accompanying rubric of "networks" and "speed," liberal society moved forward toward the new millennium with confidence. The technology revolution in communications, biology, and synthetics created a profoundly important domain in which to think about society more generally. In doing so, however, technology also projected onto *political* thought the notion that competition was a political virtue and that innovation was inherently liberating. Here were the first signs of a new techno-utopianism in the making.

"Innovation" was one of the most cherished values of the decade. As the economy turned the corner of the century, information technology suddenly started making a real impact on people's lives; the long gestation was over, warp speed had been attained. A Democratic Leadership Council report on the benefits of the new economy spoke of "voice recognition, expert systems, smart cards, e-books, cheap storage devices, new display devices and video software, intelligent transportation systems, 'third generation' wireless communication devices, and robots."[29] In contrast to the techno-utopianism of the 1950s, with its images of flying cars and Jetson-style abodes, there was little on the DLC's list that would not soon be a reality. At the same time, existing realities were altered. Dolly the Sheep (named after Dolly Parton) became the first transgenic mammal in 1997. By then an ambitious project to map the entire human genome was under way. Having begun in 1990 it would declare completion in 2003: next barrier, please.

All this was remarkable. The Internet had still been a military research program at the start of the decade; before the century was out it had become a standard feature in classrooms across the West as well as in wealthier and middle-class homes, the familiar *boing-whir-pling* of modems "going online" as ubiquitous a part of the era's soundscape as was the clacking of the secretarial typewriter in an earlier time (within less than a decade, of course, it would be increasingly rare ever to be *off*line in the West). To this emergent techno-soundscape had been added the ringtones of the better-known mobile phone providers: Orange, Nokia, and AT&T. Their handheld devices were yet another standard addition to life's new "essentials" as the century came to a close. Social media was not far behind.

As with computers, this new generation of communications technology demanded renewal and repurchase (or upgrading as it was now called) every few years at the latest. On one level there was nothing especially new about the centrality of technology to people's lives: the home telephone was once as revolutionary as the Internet (and hushed conversations by the phone in the hall arguably more relevant than blurted ones "on the train"). But as the Spanish sociologist Manuel Castells argued in his *The Information Age* trilogy—one of the decade's intellectual talking points on both sides of the Atlantic—it was not "knowledge" that mattered anymore, but information coupled to technology, and above all the harnessing of information technology with the age-old structure of the network. The era of the network had arrived, though it had not quite left good old "gossip" behind, as such portraits tended to imply.

Castells was far from the only thinker at this time to try to make sense of contemporary society in terms of a network. Like painters in a previous era, the more that late twentieth-century thinkers found new ways of conceiving society, the more that any one intellectual canvas made most sense when hung alongside another: be it those of the Frenchman Bruno Latour, one of the postmodern academy's new darlings, or of the more prosaic American Hudson Institute. In its Workforce 2000 project, the Hudson Institute sought to relocate the basic unit of production from "the worker" to the "network structure": a network "made up of other organizations that are its suppliers, customers, regulators, and financial backers." Then there were influential economists, like Robert Reich, who rightly observed that firms were now but one part of wider "global webs" while products were "international composites"—imparting a somewhat ephemeral feel to a noun once routinely prefaced with the word "end." As Reich himself put it: "what is traded between nations is less often finished products than specialized problem-solving . . . and brokerage . . . all of which combine to create value."[30] He might have added "exchange value" here, rather than "use value"—to put it in Marxian terms. For there was something potentially dehumanizing in much of this. But it was efficiency that counted most of all, not social purpose.

Of all the era's technological sages, it was Castells who painted on the grandest scale. What had been happening these past two decades, he averred, was more profound even than the printing revolution that inaugurated the Reformation. Everything from the black market to the Sydney Mardi Gras was brought together in an analysis that framed the modern-day social network as the central actor in a political struggle. In place of classes or even states, society was now organized through information technology across space. Looking to the future, Castells offered a vision that focused less on the dehumanizing effects of robotics and labor de-skilling than on the redemptive possibilities of all this. Vertical organizational hierarchies (whether employers' relationship to their employees, or of governments to citizens) would not immediately disappear, but they would gradually become redundant in light of the new social forces of a networked society—for whom identity rather than social status was the key axis of political power.[31]

In reality the "new economy" that Castells proffered as one part of his analysis turned out to be nothing less than a primary source of that political power itself. Global financial markets were networks, after all, as were the fiber-optic cables linking terminals and traders via webs of digital money. Technology platforms were no longer parallel and perhaps mutually generative of economies of scale; they were increasingly merging into a seamless whole. Yet this was to overlook the continued relevance of the old divide between state and market, as it played out even within the realm of high technology. In due course the idea of networked relations would be associated as much with the US military's embrace of "network-centric warfare" or corporations' soon rather more self-conscious embrace of the "networked firm" and its associated practice of "transfer-price fixing" (or tax avoidance, in plain English) with emancipatory political possibilities.

The basic research that lay behind the arrival of the Internet at the start of the decade was a good example of the reason why. Publicly funded in the first instance, it soon became the milch cow of the private sector. As the race heated up to map the human genome, the American firm Celera Genomics took the publicly funded data provided by the Human Genome Project and fast-tracked the analysis by processing the data with a new "shotgun sequencing" technique. This was textbook capitalist innovation at work, as was Celera's desire to immediately copyright the results—effectively privatizing key biological structures within the human genome. Clinton and Blair, as the leaders of the two nations most heavily involved, begged to differ: "raw fundamental data on the human genome, including the human DNA sequence and its variations, should be made freely available to scientists everywhere," they said in a March 2000 statement.[32]

It was a "finger wagged" at the efforts of the private sector to reap the rewards of public research. But it was a reminder too of just how political technology had become. And mostly the prodding came from the private sector. For example, health ministries would come to be shaped by the nature and cost of health-care innovations more than anything else in the years to come, aging populations included. But where to draw the line between public need and private reward? This was to be one of the most important debates of the decade and would reveal a great deal about the assumptions of the era. Above all it revealed that governments and the private sector often actually agreed on the fundamental importance of market-based measures of value. Clinton and Blair's careful use of the term "raw data" was revealing here. For it suggested that they saw the hard work of producing it as akin merely to stumbling upon a naturally occurring resource. The public sector was increasingly taken for granted; the private sector had never been taken more seriously.

The most significant aspect of the arrival of the information age in the 1990s thus turned out not to be its technological "novelty" (the intelligent homes and the microsensors in cars) but the social and political systems for *managing* that technology. As the information age began to take hold, as the vast expansion in knowledge it enabled became data that required processing and sorting, one of the few really effective means of separating what mattered from what was just "noise" was the market and its underlying ethic of competition. Increasingly, social and political needs were prioritized according to the metric of market value as well. What the rise of the information society did for the market, then, was to give it, belatedly, something approximating a soul (a soul that would later turn out to be the mirror image of the observer).

The information revolution, and the market-based techniques that developed for managing it, soon extended to all aspects of life (like congestion charges on cars entering cities or the emergence of security rings of steel, such as the City of London rolled out during the IRA's early–mid decade wave of terror, and whose elaboration was in fact based upon the technology of the earlier scheme).[33] The social life of cities was not dead, as old-style liberals feared, but it was increasingly being remade in accordance with the logic of maximizing the free flow of capital and wealth. The intellectual space of the market had encroached upon the material spaces of an urbanizing Western society, and social space—the space of community attachment and impromptu solidarities—was forced to vacate the premises to make room. It thus became a subversive act to be "socially minded," as in the emergence of previously unfathomable acts of protest, such as "guerrilla gardening" in parts of larger cities.

But if one aspect of the new economy was the belief that competition was a better arbiter of social need than political solidarity, a second aspect concerned a more deeply seated transition at the heart of democracy itself. As capitalism had increasingly come to influence the nature of the democratic political vision, and with distribution no longer the primary focus of political struggle, politics became less about struggling over outcomes and more about optimization of the means. This meant seeking solutions that were deemed "doable," rather than unrealistically "desirable." Perhaps above all it meant the emergence of a more professionalized, seemingly rationalized account of the purpose and meaning of life. And nowhere was this more clearly captured than in the rise to prominence of management studies, and the ideal of "management" itself, in corporate and political life alike.

For those on the left, like French critics Luc Boltanski and Eve Chiapello, the rise of "management discourse" was nothing less than a "new ideological configuration"—a transformation in the "spirit of capitalism" itself. It was a way to refit global capitalism after the end of the Cold War, now that strong ideological justifications, one way or the other, had lost their bite. What was needed instead was a wide-ranging justification that good capitalism made good sense. Formalizing the various innovations that had been adopted over the previous decades in response to the crisis of the 1970s was one way of doing this. And management discourse was at the heart of that process of formalization.[34]

Like works of "moral instruction" in an age gone by, the new management literature set about establishing what was good practice and what was not. There was very little consideration of what made capitalism a force for "good" or otherwise. The question rather was about what *sort* of good could best be leveraged via capitalism. The cart was swinging about to take its place before the horse. This was not just about maximizing profits: indeed, it was recognized that in the modern age, profit itself "is not a very inspiring goal."[35] Instead, and it was this that was both more radical and ultimately more convincing, the capitalist process had *itself* to become a desirable way of life; it had to provide meaning. But that meaning was increasingly provided through the promotion of the values of an ever-more entrepreneurial capitalism: flexibility, adjustment, investment, and competition.

In the new network society the struggle was no less constant than it had been before, for all that the signature claim of the times was that the Western world was now somehow postideological. On the contrary, echoes of a neo-Darwinian order fluttered in through the shutters of the new capitalist ideal home, and the continued rise of the "career" as the central object for individuals to "manage" in the course of their lives embodied both the promissory notes of this new age and its attendant anxieties. But something important *had* changed. The old model of economic growth, in which workers provided the value for capitalist growth and were compensated by the state, which met their basic needs, was now replaced by a laissez-faire model of growth based on finance, technology, and efficiency savings. A new era of neoliberal hegemony was replacing the more socially invested "dispensations" of the moderately progressive "vital center" in America, and of the age of social democratic and Christian democratic hegemony in Europe.[36] After the 1980s perhaps this was inevitable. What was truly surprising, however, was that it was social democrats who were the ones in power and overseeing the change.

American Anglo

To outside observers, particularly on the European left, the US Democrats looked like a political project in close step with the country around them. "This party's trains are running on time," as a delegate to the 1992 convention had put it.[37] Various upheavals along the way—not infrequently caused by the president's own lapses of sexual and financial good sense— had at times threatened to upset that promissory note: by early 1998 news that Clinton had been having an affair with a White House intern, Monica Lewinsky, was about to break. But on matters of the economy the Clinton administration's record looked to be unimpeachable—in contrast, it would soon turn out, to the president. The country was now well into the longest economic expansion (a record 115 months) in its history, unemployment was falling to what would, by 1999, be its lowest level in thirty years, and America's welfare rolls had been halved.

In Britain, where the trains are famous for never running on time, such smooth running of the Democratic Party's rolling stock was bound to pique a certain interest. The British left had been watching events in

America for a while. In the late 1980s and into the 1990s the Labour Party was desperately concerned about its seeming unelectability and increasingly it looked to events in the United States for guidance. This was in many ways ironic, since it was Neil Kinnock—whose political horizons rarely extended beyond the British Isles—who first set the ball rolling. The turning point was a broadside unleashed by Kinnock to his own party faithful in the seaside town of Bournemouth in 1985. "Thank you, comrades," it began, harmlessly enough, in his lilting Welsh tones. But Kinnock was soon into the meat of an historic takedown of the old party ways:

> 463 resolutions have been submitted to this Conference on policy issues, committed honestly, earnestly, and a lot of thought has gone into them. Of those 463, 300 refer to something called the next Labour Government and they refer to what they want that next Labour Government to do . . . But there is of course a pre-condition to honoring those or any other undertaking that we give. That pre-condition is unavoidable, total and insurmountable, and it is a pre-condition that in this movement we do not want to surmount. It is the pre-condition that we win a general election.

Kinnock ultimately failed to drag his party to electoral success. But under his successor John Smith, and then—following Smith's sudden death in 1994, even more resolutely under Tony Blair—Labour not only threw any remaining talk of building a socialist society out of the nearest window, it gave up on the more social democratic claim that workers' rights needed special protection relative to other sectors of society. For a labor party, especially one in the throes of a new industrial revolution—"a time of shifts in the whole structure of the world economy . . . of new needs among the peoples of the world and new aspirations," as Kinnock had quite presciently put it—this was not a small change of direction. And it demanded acts of considerable bureaucratic butchery to pull it off.

The bloodletting really began after Labour's fourth electoral failure in a row in 1992, and it went on until the junking of the party's hallowed Clause 4, in 1995, which permanently removed any aspiration it had to the common ownership of the means of production. But from this act also emerged a newly minted party machine: New Labour.[38] Ditching Clause 4 was important as a symbol of the new times, as much as it was a practical gesture. Labour delegates greeted its excision at the Party

Conference that year with foot-thumping; but perhaps there was a flush of renewed hope at the polls. Certainly, the sorts of ideas that now took its place—roomy words like "social justice" and the "commitment" to reduce "unjust" inequalities "where possible"—were revealing of what the Brits had learned from the Americans about political doublespeak.[39]

As with the New Democrats so then with New Labour, which now looked to embrace rather than retreat from globalization, and so abandoned its opposition to Britain being a part of Europe and the proposed single currency. The party had so thoroughly reinvented itself that it no longer seemed to matter to it that the EC had declared inflation to be the number one economic enemy, not unemployment.[40] In truth all of Europe's socialist parties were on the cusp of reinventing themselves for the times. But the British Labour Party prided itself on being the boldest and the best of these as it looked to break with every left-wing policy shibboleth from the past. It was arguably within its rights to do so. In 1997 the party swept to power in a landslide election, winning 418 seats to the Conservatives' 165—with 78 of Labour's new seats coming in the traditional Tory heartlands of suburban England.

It was not just a new Labour Party, but a new Britain that was emerging in fact. Electorally speaking Blair's campaign, no less than Clinton's, perfectly split the difference between the most important swing voters: the optimistic middle classes hoping for a greater share in the coming post–Cold War prosperity, and those who were more anxious about a global future and wanted some sort of state buffer put in place. In one sense, then, Blair had done exactly what Kinnock had called for. In another sense, he hadn't had to. "The left may lament the fact that Labour's core support is not turning out to vote," observed one commentator at the time; "—the truth is Labour's core support, in that traditional sense, barely exists at all."[41] Blair to his credit recognized this, and he made "education, education, education" the mantra of the campaign to show that he did. A great many traditional voters may not like the present, the party had argued in the run-up to the election, but if they didn't want to go back to the past, then who else did they plan on putting into office? The key point, as New Labour's saccharine election anthem reminded the British public, was that from here on in, things could only get better.

Pitched at the beginning of a slight uplift in the economy, that was a message that would prove to have been fortunately timed: again, just like Clinton's. But "better for whom?" was the real question. People in search of an answer to that were usually directed toward the phrase "the

Third Way," coined by the sociologist Anthony Giddens. Social responsibility, community values, equality of opportunity, and accountability in government and society alike: these were the core values of the Third Way philosophy that New Labour's governing triumvirate of Blair, Brown, and Peter Mandelson subscribed to. While some wits likened the Third Way to the Loch Ness Monster (much talked about, but rarely seen) the reality of Third Way politics was soon clear enough to see in the policies put forward by New Labour. Economic growth and wealth were to be maximized, just as the market liberals insisted, but these were also—in theory at least—to be a means to more socially just, egalitarian ends.

The paradoxes of this were unveiled early on when Mandelson, then head of the Department for Trade and Investment, sparked a near scandal during a trip to California in 1998. Confronted by the boss of Hewlett-Packard, who felt sufficiently informed to demand of him, "Why on earth should we come and invest in Britain when you have a New Labour government introducing socialism . . . ?" Mandelson replied by calmly assuring him that New Labour was "intensely relaxed about people getting filthy rich."[42] Mandelson famously later stylized himself as the Third Man: a characteristic pun on both the Third Way political project and his own place within it. But the influence of the "second man" of the New Labour project, Blair's Chancellor Gordon Brown, was of much greater significance in terms of shaping New Labour's new economics of fiscal conservatism and financial liberalization.

Brown cut a scholarly jib for a politician (though he had lost an eye playing rugby when at school) and he was certainly a serious student of Alan Greenspan's free-market economics.[43] He had also accompanied Blair to Washington back in January 1993 specifically to learn from the Clinton transition team how they had gone about transforming their politics.[44] Blair liked to play showman up front, as befitted the private agreement over who should be prime minister first that the two men, Blair and Brown, had come to in the Granita restaurant in fashionable and gentrifying Islington, near where the Blairs lived. But the real heart of the New Labour project once in power beat within Number 11 Downing Street. It was from here that the economic base of the entire program was constructed (and just as jealously guarded). Mandelson's comments too mattered, because they were about more than what New Labour thought about money. They were about the vision of society that the Third Way was hoping to bring about.

Who would have imagined, even just a few years before, that it would be a Labour government, that from the late 1990s onward would oversee the longest period of low inflation since the war, earning the confidence of the City and the financial markets in the process? New Labour gave vent to its more progressive side as well, introducing a national minimum wage that saw the income of the poorest tenth of the population grow by 15 percent between 1997 and 2003. They put more youngsters through school and lifted 600,000 children and a million pensioners out of poverty. They made entry to museums and cultural exhibits free. They upgraded social housing and cut waiting lists in hospitals. "London at the end of the twentieth century," wrote one observer, "appeared to have recovered its Swinging Sixties sheen."[45]

The extent and originality of the political and intellectual ambition behind all this ought not to be underestimated. Here was a genuine attempt to address problems like social exclusion without the paternalism of state interference and without leaving things to the vagaries of the market alone. This was why community building and its institutional attachments of mayors, devolved assemblies, and even public–private partnerships were so important to the Blair–Brown approach to government. But when the scores were later in, New Labour's real achievement would ultimately be shown to have been the electoral one of splitting the difference, not the political one of forging common ground: dishing out "Asbos" (Anti-Social Behavior Orders), after all, was hardly the best way of building bridges between classes and communities. Instead of addressing the underlying social divides and resentments, New Labour simply promised everyone a greater share in the nation's growing prosperity. Instead of fretting over issues of access and distribution they embraced innovation and change. They kept hold of the old vernacular of emancipation but reworked it now to mean the challenge and opportunity of "change" itself.

New Labour thus made the old liberal cry of "enrich yourself!" very much their own. And with progressive politics accordingly reframed, it was not long before they began to sway other social democratic parties (helped by their seemingly unstoppable popular appeal). Among those paying attention were Germany's social democrats, who, like New Labour, had been out of power and licking their wounds since the early 1980s. Unlike New Labour, however, Germany's social democrats had to confront the legacy of a man who had successfully overseen the reunification of Europe's once most-powerful nation.

The Third Way Rises

It should be a "farewell without tears," said East Germany's last prime minister, Lothar de Maizière, to Helmut Kohl as the two men stood in the Reichstag building at the final hour of the GDR's existence. For that reason an emotional de Maizière declined Kohl's invitation to stand with him at the window before the crowds below on October 2, 1990.[46] By the time Kohl himself finally stepped down in 1997, after sixteen years at the helm, the question was more whether things had turned out as citizens of the two Germanies might have imagined? There had inevitably been bumps along the way. In 1990 Kohl's right-hand man, Wolfgang Schäuble, who had represented West Germany during the reunification negotiations, and who would be one of the most influential voices in the decision to move the capital from Bonn to Berlin, was shot during a political rally, leaving him confined to a wheelchair.

Kohl successfully won reelection in 1994, however, and by the time he was finally voted out, he had overseen an historic transformation: the peaceful reunification of his country. With Maastricht, he had further realized Adenauer's ambition of placing that reunified Germany back at the heart of a reinvigorated Europe, and set course for the realization of the single currency (managing also to place the Bundesbank at the very heart of that model). He had also done what he could to address the awkward negotiations of reconciliation and the opening up of Stasi files to those against whom the files had been kept: problems that were handled more smoothly in East Germany than in some of the other former satellite states.

But Kohl's promises of a greater German future had proved burdensome for wealthier West German citizens in particular: the figure of the *jammerossi*, the needy and whining East German, became a metaphorical cliché as West Germans grew tired of being constantly enjoined to build the *Aufschwung Ost* (Eastern Boom): that term becoming as well the name of a techno disco, whose incessant beat no doubt made it a meaningful choice for many Germans. It came at a cost as well: some economists at the time likened reunification to the case of "mass migration of low-skilled agents holding no capital into a foreign country."[47] The promises of a better future also proved fraught for the East. For East Germans there was suddenly competition within the new state from the West for jobs, and the old welfare of the GDR was gone. Above all there was reconstruction exhaustion everywhere. Kohl, one might say, had reunified Germany so fully, and with such enthusiasm, that it was inevitable he would one day be held accountable for its failure to be everything he had promised. His very achievement in a way, then, was also his eventual downfall.

As a result it was Gerhard Schröder and his Social Democratic Party who swept into power to replace Kohl in 1997. His promises of a modern and pragmatic center ground (he was dubbed "ClintonBlair" during the campaign)—die Neue Mitte, the New Middle—seemed as if it was the right next step for Germany to be taking. And Schröder ran a good campaign hammering this message home. Kohl had been a good chancellor, he repeated over and again. Had been. If this scripted his own election from the start as a turning point for Germany—the end of the Kohl era, and the final end of the Bonn republic—this was perhaps warranted. Though Germany's history since the early 1970s can be neatly divided in two, there is a case that it ought in some ways to be divided in three: the final division falling here, in 1997, and not just in 1989. Yet while the new SPD would do much to overhaul Germany's economy and welfare—for better and for worse—it would never fully address the issues of national identity or civil society which would remain, into the millennium, the unaddressed legacy of 1989.

Clearly, Britain was not a straightforward "model" for how to reimagine social democracy for a country like Germany on the cusp of the twenty-first century. But the rise to near dominance of New Labour in Britain was a model of how to turn the necessity of accommodation to global financial capital into the virtue of political pragmatism: and it was recognized as such by Schröder. Accordingly, Schröder began speaking, after the election, not only of the promises of a globalizing age, but to proffer—and here London truly was the leading light—the balm of financialization as a fix for the crushing welfare commitments he believed were weighing Germany down. A year after he was elected Chancellor of Germany in 1998 Schröder became better positioned to do something about this, when he was made head of the German Social Democratic Party too. The place had become available when Oskar Lafontaine finally resigned at the end of his long-simmering bust-up with Schröder (officially citing "bad team play," though it was clear it was the probusiness direction Schröder was insisting on that Lafontaine could no longer stomach).[48]

Observing this, Blair—whose press had long painted Lafontaine as Europe's remaining "red" bogeyman (he wasn't)—wasted little time trying to link up with Schröder, and to lock in British–German relations going into the new century. He immediately sent Mandelson to hold a series of bilateral ministerials with Schröder's most trusted aide, Bodo Hombach. The result was the Blair–Schröder manifesto, "Europe: The Third Way/Die Neue Mitte," of 1998, which in many ways captured the essence of the new social democratic wave suddenly spreading back across the continent. "Social democrats are in government in almost all the countries of the Union," it began. "[B]ut only because, while retaining its traditional values, [social democracy] has begun in a credible way to renew its ideas and modernize its programs."[49] This was true. Social democratic parties now ruled the four largest states in Europe and, in coalition, they were in power in most of the rest of Europe. If there was a moment that third-way social democracy had arrived, it was now.[50]

But what sort of social democracy was this? The ideological kernel of the third way, we have already seen, was to be pro-equality of opportunity, not equality of outcome as social democratic parties traditionally were by virtue of their redistributive politics. It sought to encourage everyone to achieve more, rather than to set limits on the privileges of some in order to remove the burdens that fell disproportionately on others. The third way's fundamentally correct insight was that one needed to embrace globalization rather than try to ring-fence national society off from it. And "modernizing" European social democrats in the north and south of the continent sought to outdo themselves in declaring that there was no choice but to face up to this "reality."[51] In 1999 the Greek Social Democrat George Papandreou put it as well as any other: "Today, we take market relationships for granted."[52]

The roots of this new left realism in Europe ultimately lay in the convergence of two things. First was the onslaught of globalization and the perceived success of accommodating to this being enjoyed by the New Democrats in America and New Labour in Great Britain. What those two parties seemed to have found was an electorally credible recipe for removing the burden under which parties of the left had labored since the 1970s: namely how to convince workers that the modern, global, and financialized market could in any way still be controlled. The answer was simply to stop trying and instead to focus on preparing citizens to participate more fully in it: to which end the flurry of new terms focused on reconstructing how people now thought of themselves: "flexible," "adaptable," "self-reliant." Firms, as well as employees, needed more "freedom," it was said.

The second reason for this new way of thinking, and this was in stark contrast to the success of New Labour and the New Democrats, was the seemingly inexorable slide in the electoral position of the continent's social democratic left in the immediate post–Cold War years. With communism gone, social democracy seemed initially to have slunk off into the gaping hole the USSR left behind. In France, for example, Mitterrand had continued to hold sway until 1995 but only by leaning ever more strongly to the right. In West Germany the inevitable economic downturn presaged by reunification, as we have seen, sparked a similar slide to the right. In Italy, the Communist Party—which for much of the 1980s had been losing out to the Christian Democrats—finally imploded in the corruption scandals revealed by *Mani Pulite* (clean hands), changing its name in the end to the Democratic Party of the Left: a name under which it then steadily lost yet more ground to Silvio Berlusconi's Forza Italia.

There was thus some truth in the claim that the first few years after the fall of communism were marked by a "rush for the exits" on the political left, as the literary critic Terry Eagleton—one of those happy to sit it out on deck—put it: "[r]adical ideas withered as radical change seemed increasingly implausible."[53] But that was only half right: because of radical change there was plenty and the seeds of a remarkable comeback were already being sown. Moreover, among the leading figures of the new European center-left there was now an effort to progress their ideas *internationally*, just as the Christian Democrats had done through the European People's Party in the decades before. This cooperation had its roots in the earliest exchanges of ideas between the New Democrats in America and New Labour in Britain at the start of the decade. But it deepened in 1997, in a meeting at the British prime minister's country retreat of Chequers. There a more specifically transcontinental version of the Third Way philosophy of government was officially outlined.

At Chequers, with an air of satisfaction, Tony Blair pulled a scrap of paper from his pocket, as he said to the Democratic Party's key strategist, Al From: "Opportunity, responsibility, community. These are the notes from our first meeting during the Clinton transition."[54] Subsequent meetings on both sides of the Atlantic between US Democrats and other prominent leaders of the new European left—Italy's Romano Prodi, Germany's Gerhard Schröder, Sweden's Göran Persson, and the long-standing Dutch prime minister Wim Kok—confirmed that the continent too was beginning to embrace the same distinctly Anglophone political recipe. But not before the right had cleared the way by itself failing to capitalize on that immediate post–Cold War moment.

Continental Drift

The tide began to turn on the continent from around 1995. In that year, Jacques Chirac had taken the French presidency from François Mitterrand in a flurry: "policy on the run, arms in the air, rictus smile freezing his face," as a British observer recorded it.[55] Chirac had promised pretty much anything to anyone in a closely fought battle with Édouard Balladur at the Matignon. But the promises required to get him there, in the face of a resurgent far right, which had just propelled Jean-Marie Le Pen to 15 percent of the vote in the first round of the election, meant that he arrived without any real strategy or plan. "Now our [real] problems start," Chirac's new prime minister, Alain Juppé, quipped to his staff after his appointment as they surveyed a country of high unemployment, low self-esteem, and an economy 50 billion francs deeper into the red than was feared.[56]

The problems in fact had begun sometime before. And they were not limited to France alone. In Germany, the new economy and its associated boom had restored profitability but, as in France, while there were new jobs there were not any *more* jobs. Even in Sweden, which had undergone large-scale deregulation in the late 1980s, the bursting of the housing bubble had plunged the country into its deepest recession since 1945 (the value of tangible assets fell by 30 percent).[57] Italy, by contrast, was among the most celebrated examples of the new economy in Europe—if only because it seemed to represent such a break with its recent, dysfunctional past. As the *Observer*'s correspondent William Scobie captured it, "Suddenly this is a land of upward mobility, of vital computerized industry, bustling young business managers and slick middle-aged tycoons who have abjured their sixties' ideals in the sacred cause of profit." But dig beneath the clichés; dig for example into lists of directors, and it was still very much— as one of the more informed observers pointed out—an economy dominated by a few elite families: the Agnelli, the Pirelli, the Borletti, Zanussi, and Cuccia. It was they who still ran the major corporations and manufactures, covering everything from finance to cement.[58]

In Eastern Europe, the former communist elite (the nearest equivalent to a conservative old guard) were even quicker to dig their fingernails into the state in place of providing it with answers. The newly democratic half of the continent was in fact, by the middle of the decade, in a considerably worse state economically than it had been before the fall of communism, as it grappled with the twin challenges of leaving behind the communist past and catching up with the new liberalization agenda of the West. Across the region economic growth and wages had declined, inflation had spiraled, and unemployment ranged from 10 percent in the Czech Republic to as high as 20 percent in Hungary.[59] The euphoria of the fall of communism having subsided, the scale of the economic challenge confronting both of the former halves of Europe was beginning to surface.

But just as in America and in Britain, it was this that now created the opportunity for the continent's social democrats to stage their unexpected return to power—so long as they were prepared to ditch the cumbersome idea of equality and sign up to the promise of individual freedom endowed by a neoliberal political economy. Throughout the 1980s and into the 1990s, before Schröder's meetings with Blair, the German SPD had been feeling its way toward this: testing its redistributive politics at the polls, where it found them increasingly wanting. In response it gradually lowered its demands for taxes. This turn to fiscal conservatism was perhaps most pronounced in Germany, but a similar trend could be seen across Europe.

In 1987 the former Dutch labor prime minister, Jan Pronk, once an old-style internationalist, authored a report, "Schuivende Panelen," suggesting the PvdA drop its long-standing demand for a shorter working week and instead embrace the European monetary agenda. This was exactly what the PvdA then did in the subsequent 1989 election.[60] Meanwhile, the leader of the Finnish social democrats, Paavo Lipponen, made the same point, only clearer still, in publicly announcing via the *Financial Times*: "We need a real paradigm change. . . . We have to get more flexibility and reduce labor costs and social security costs." The problem, he said, was a "lack of competition." Whether or not that was true it was certainly what Finns wanted to hear. Lipponen was voted into power in 1995.[61] The same applied in Italy, where Romano Prodi was elected in 1996 at the head of a reconstructed (which was to say liberalized) Italian left: the Olive Tree coalition.

This embrace of the new politics occurred at a fateful time. As the European economy began to pick up, those social democrats who had learned to sing its praises were rewarded with the keys to national office. Blair's election victory in 1997 was the most dramatic incarnation of this, given the years of conservative hegemony under Margaret Thatcher. But even in France the socialist candidate Lionel Jospin won in a landslide in that year's legislative elections called by Chirac—who after two years as president had still found no answer to the country's problems. Jospin was in truth more of an old-school social democrat. But he brought with him into the prime minister's office a new generation of younger, less haughty socialists: the likes of Martine Aubry (the daughter of Jacques Delors) and Dominique Strauss-Kahn. A new period of cohabitation began, but this time with the left snapping at the heels of the right.[62] If Chirac managed to put a surprisingly bright face on what had actually been the first loss by a president in snap legislative elections in over a century, it was perhaps because he sensed the true mettle of most of those he was now cohabiting with. Even Jospin was forced to toe the line. "I forbid you to speak ill of our benefactor," he quipped to colleagues at one of their first cabinet meetings.[63]

By now European social democrats had resolutely ditched the working class in favor of the consumerist middle classes. And with the economy picking up—not as quickly as in America, but noticeably all the same (even France, which had lagged, saw a return of economic growth, rising exports, and a million new jobs toward the end of the decade)—their promise of a brighter future began to ring true.[64] Just as in Britain and America, continental social democrats now reinvented themselves on the back of the new prosperity as election-winning machines and not as cross-class coalitions. That reinvention was to be both their star to ascend, for a while, and the black hole into which they would ultimately disappear.

The high point of this European Third Way—as a political project at least—was reached in 1999, at an international conference held in Florence under the banner of "Progressive Governance for the 21st Century." Such a self-consciously ostentatious meeting of social democratic grandees took place, fittingly, in the "Room of Five Hundred"—seat of the short-lived Florentine Republic—in the Palazzo Vecchio.[65] Lionel Jospin appeared at the event as the lone, old-style leftist among his fellow "modernized" social democrats. In France simply being against liberalism still counted, for better or worse, as a form of progressivism. And it was on precisely this basis that he sounded the sole note of disagreement. "If . . . the Third Way involves finding a middle way between social democracy and neoliberalism," he said, "then this approach is not mine."[66] Clinton, who was also in attendance, deftly swatted him away in his closing comments: I agree with Jospin, he effectively said, but I am more in agreement with Tony Blair.[67] By Clinton's standards, that was a ringing dismissal.

Jospin plotted his response for the next year's meeting in Germany. By then, however, as Germany's *Die Zeit* quipped, interest in the whole idea of the Third Way was waning, and to such a degree that "there probably would not be enough 'progressive governments' in the future to hold another [meeting]."[68] But perhaps the absence, for really the first time in a century, of a serious leftist vision of internationalism did not matter at this moment: at least not to the extent that the post–Cold War years were a boon for the idea of "Europe" instead. For many this now served quite happily as a less politicized version of the same thing. The politics of identity was duly crowned at the transnational level as well. In the new European political landscape, politics of the old "distributive" sort seemed only to muddy the waters: to taint the return of prosperity with the leaden tincture of the past. The absence of an alternative trans-national vision would cost the left, not to mention European citizens, dearly in the years to come. For now, though, the European left was too happy celebrating its national electoral victories to notice: the disagree-ments in Florence were forgotten; and more pressing developments would soon lead Europeans at large to forget what all the fuss over the politics of the new left was about. Its legacy, however, would not be so easily erased.

The New Europe: "Freedom, Security, and Justice"

Come the end of the 1990s the European economy, at least, was in bet-ter shape than it had been for many years. The continent was enjoying the benefits of having cut back on trade barriers and regulations. It now boasted everything from the largest and most profitable pharmaceutical giants (Glaxo and Novartis) to major players in the ongoing telecoms boom (Siemens, Ericsson, Nokia, and Alcatel Alsthom). GDP growth reached 3 percent across the continent in 1994, and it would remain at around 2.5 percent for the rest of the decade: this was getting toward levels last seen during the 1950s and 1960s.[69] From 1998 the European Central Bank (ECB), the institution that the Germans had insisted a European single currency required, was in position and soon to be fos-tering its own brand of European "community" by ensuring errant Gaullists and Romans alike kept within the bounds of the European Monetary System. That system itself locked "irrevocably" into place the following year.[70] Henceforth you wanted your economy to look like Germany's or else you were likely to be penalized for it. Membership of the euro now came to define "Western" Europe in the post–Cold War age, even as the EU itself expanded east.

This was revealing in two senses. First, it gestured toward a two-track

Europe (with a core of eurozone countries and a wider zone of EU aspirants). When this became the EU's reality in the decade to come, it made the politics of transnationalism that much easier to implement from Brussels, but it also created a more complicated picture on the ground. The constant insistence that Eastern Europe change this or that, without any fiscal transfer or serious effort to assist those countries from the West, fostered confusion and resentment alike. But these were concerns for later. Second, and more immediately, it marked a turn toward a "larger and more liquid market" within the European core.[71]

Corporations found it easier to get credit. Firms were more likely to engage in mergers and acquisitions. The European Commission, from when it started to hear cases on mergers between firms in 1990, leaned decidedly in favor of big business, approving more than 94 percent of these mergers—including that of Swedish Electrolux's takeover of Italian Zanussi to become the world leader in white goods manufacture.[72] Investors were given larger corporate palaces in which to put their money. The European political economy began to approximate that of America's, in which finance ruled. Banks underwent a period of growth on the back of this: and in all the EC's hearings during this period not a single bank merger (out of a total of 187) was questioned.[73]

The idea that competition was a better arbiter of social need than collectively determined preferences, and the closely related shift from government to governance, had taken shape as the new double helix at the heart of European democracy. After the wobbles of the early ratification process, and the EMS crisis that followed, the years following Maastricht were to be the single market's heyday: the long march toward the single currency kept the agenda focused; the forces of nationalism were dented as New Left social democrats came to power singing the promises of globalization; and new countries joined up. By then national economies right across the continent were looking substantially healthier. These were the years that the "internal market" enjoyed its widest political support and took its greatest strides forward. With the profederalist, promarket (Christian democratic) European People's Party in power, even in countries like the UK, Europe could not integrate fast enough.

The pace of development was certainly remarkable. Possibly too much so: because it was on the basis of this prosperity that the EU felt secure enough now to expand its membership from nine to twenty-seven countries. Successful expansion required a further narrowing of institutional focus. More than two hundred pieces of European legislation had been created since the SEA in 1986 on areas ranging from tax policy to business regulations. But with the "Four Freedoms" of 1993 the single market (enabling free movement of goods, workers, services, and capital) had just one central focus: the expansion of European capitalism. And it would be simplifying only slightly to say that, wherever states had legislation on the books that hindered any of these goals, it would need to be removed: variations in national legislation were to be flattened out to make way for a uniform "European legal order." The European Court of Justice, of course, was on hand to provide guidance and instruction.

The effects of this were not as uniform as detractors sometimes liked to claim. In 1999, when the European Council took over the running of the Schengen system, it also approved the UK having access to the Schengen Information System (SIS) and to police and judicial cooperation with Schengen members, without it being part of the Schengen Agreement. Ireland followed suit the following year. Britain was perhaps a singular case here, but it was revealing nonetheless of the multiple layers through which "Europe" now existed: a part of the EU, but not of the euro, within EFTA but outside the Schengen Agreement. Somewhat differently, for the Czech Republic, "Europe" increasingly became a way of leveraging political and economic benefits, but also an external force structuring its own domestic political reforms. While foreign investment "surged" into the Czech Republic along with €9 billion of structural funds that Prague would receive from Brussels between 2004 and 2009, Czech membership of the European Union had a centralizing effect on the Czech government (since somebody needed to oversee the EU directive mandating dispersal of political powers to the euro-compatible "regions").[74]

The real transformation was not that of a "European" elite imposing itself upon the national "communities" of the continent—two problematic ascriptions which would henceforth join together in mortal and misleading combat. More significant by far were the ideological and political transformations of the nation-states themselves, as *national* elites prepared finally to move from a customs union to a proper economic community. All the tools they needed to do this had in fact been there since the Treaty of Rome. What had changed was the calculus of risk versus reward: or, as one of the principal intellectual minds behind thinking about customs unions, Jacob Viner, had put it, the opportunity cost of *not* moving forward with an internal market. There was no great ideological imperative, then, for all the rhetoric and the incessant talk about an area of "freedom, security and justice," but rather a simple cost-benefit calculation that the representatives of European capital now took.

Thus it was not the bureaucrats but economists like Jacob Viner, James Meade, and others who were the fathers of the final push to integration.[75] And *their* stall had first been set out in the Cecchini Report of 1988, "The Cost of Non-Europe"—the first of many elaborate technical arguments for integration—which confirmed "what those engaged in building Europe have always known: that the failure to achieve a single market has been costing European industry dearly."[76]* That subsequent reports were frequently written by free-market private advisers was neither surprising nor insignificant. Indeed, as the 1990s progressed, the project of European integration was one driven by financial interests in place of the heavy industry, and its lobby groups, that drove forward the project's earlier years. By the end of the decade this new "Europe" seemed to have an unstoppable air about it. It was little short of a modern-day *Rechtsgemeinschaft* (or "juridical state").[77] But a juridical state of what sort?

In fact, there were two separate European visions abutting one another here: a *market* model and a *social* model, and each pointed to very different futures. The first was focused upon the centerpiece of the new European project: the euro. The ECB, with its mandate to manage the euro, was a supremely important institution here—one in which every citizen of Europe had an interest and a stake, whether they realized it or not (for the most part they did *not* realize this). "If the ECB fails to restrain inflation, millions of Europeans who have made long-term investments in euro-denominated assets will suffer a substantial loss," said one observer of the basic conundrum. "But if the ECB is too zealous in restraining inflation, European business will retrench and workers will lose their jobs."[78] Tellingly, the bank charged with managing this dilemma was to be headquartered not in Brussels but in Frankfurt—in close proximity to Germany's own Bundesbank. There were similarities in institutional design too. Not least the ECB was to be free of the ultimate responsibility for maintaining the stability it was empowered to keep.

Above all, and despite the extent to which its decisions could shape the lives of ordinary citizens across participating nations in the eurozone,

---

* The most recent report, *The Cost of Non-Europe in the Single Market* [Cecchini Revisited], put the benefits of further integration at "potential gains between 651 billion and 1.1 trillion per year."

the ECB was to be shielded as far as possible from any actual democratic oversight by those same people: they could not name independents to sit on its board, nor have access to the "confidential" nature of its deliberations, nor make their views known via their representatives at the European Council. The ECB, and the wider European Central Bank System of which it formed part, was shielded from outside thinking too. Where once university departments provided a large measure of the intellectual guidance deployed within institutions like central banks, the latter now beefed up their *own* research departments—staffed by employees already inducted into the bank's particular culture. The number of internal PhDs in central banks grew from around 300 to 700 between 1990 and 2003.[79]

There was good reason for this: high finance was now high politics too, and national democratic structures were having to adapt. For the northern, advanced economies of Europe the whole point of the euro was the wider architectural edifice of fiscal governance that it brought with it. This was why Germany in particular had pushed so hard for the Stability and Growth Pact, which finally came into force in 1997 as that "set of rules designed to ensure that countries in the European Union pursue sound public finances and coordinate their fiscal policies." Germany was fearful that outer countries (it had Greece and Italy in particular in mind) would not live up to their anti-inflationary commitments, and so it wanted some kind of institutional lock on the ability of these countries to spend beyond their means. On one level this was sensible enough. But it had the potential to wreak havoc if mishandled in a crisis. Nobody thought such a crisis was very likely, however.

Yet those weaker economies were intent on joining for a reason, of course: above all they wanted to hitch their weaker economies to the backs of the strong. For these predominantly southern nations—to whom was extended the Stabilization and Accession program, as a carrot to go along with the stick of Stability and Growth—what really mattered was the symbolism of being "in" rather than "out." Thus the eleven nations (plus Greece one year later) who eventually formed the euro area all deemed it worthwhile to make the necessary adjustments for joining the euro: trimming sails in the case of France and Germany, sucking in guts and braving the storm in the case of Italy, Spain, and Greece—which would need until 2001 before it was quite ready. Purists from the northern European left might sneer at how socialists engaged in this effort now flouted their fiscal discipline as a mark of electoral pragmatism, but for Greeks, and perhaps especially Italians, membership of the euro "was a badge of pride and a source of strength."[80]

It wasn't just north–south relations that figured here. Expansion eastward remained a paramount issue, and by the end of the decade it too had become increasingly subject to the logic of the new European fiscal model as well. The promise of possible entry into the eurozone offered a primary means of extending the culture of fiscal discipline into Eastern and central Europe—all of whom opted for independent central banks on the Western model. Investment in central Europe thus became a key element in the wider European economy as a whole.[81] Before the decade was out, and often in stark contrast to where some countries had begun the decade, the entire continent had oriented itself around the centrality of the euro and the wider project of monetary union. And to meet this need, a functioning central executive had, somewhat against the odds, been put together, centered on the ECB and its directives.

One wonders what the nations from the communist bloc made of all this. After all, it was they who experienced this first model most directly. It was in fact in these countries that the extent to which this vision was a vision of national elites became most clear. Between 1992 and June 1994 Russia privatized 14,000 medium-sized enterprises, pushing the private sector from 13 to more than 60 percent of total employment. If this puts Thatcher's work in perspective, it also helps explain how Russia's GDP fell around 40 percent between 1990 and 1998, since there was little by way of organization or productive endeavor in the way this was done.[82] The effect of "reforms" in many cases was simply to generate rents for elites able to capture the system. At least as important as the much-discussed imposition of an aggressive Western culture of the market was the fact that there was no real culture of the market in Russia (or at least of its rule-bound behaviors), which opened the door to the oligarchs.[83] The civil society movements that had done so much to bring about the fall of communism and to ensure the peaceful transition of power also now fragmented into a thousand different splinters.

It is hard to overestimate the scale of the transformation, especially at the individual level. The case of one Pole, Bogdan Lapinski, is revealing here. Lapinski was a trained psychologist in Poland when he applied in 1989 for a job at IKEA—looking for a little extra cash in difficult times. On being called to interview he found that the position in question was on the company's board of directors. This was "quite common," he later recalled. Markets arrived, and liberal institutions were developed;

but it was a "DIY kind of liberalism," and not always conducive to nation-building either.[84] But that is not necessarily a problem for national elites. A similar story played out in Romania. Initially, the emergence of newly established social democratic parties (of Ion Iliescu) and Christian Democrat parties (led by Emil Constantinescu) in the early 1990s managed to override sharp ethnic-regional divisions. But Romania was also snubbed by the West more often than were the Baltics or the Eastern European nations, and so it tended to lurch more from one crisis to another on its own. Quite what liberalism was worth in this context soon began to be questioned, stoking the return of xenophobic and antiliberal sentiment.[85]

Rapid dissolution was not the signature experience everywhere. Hungary endured a decade of "social patience" in the years after 1989, Attila Ágh observed from Budapest a decade later. It was a telling phrase and one that fitted many of the post-communist nations' actual experience once the euphoria of transition had subsided. Where Hungary did lead was in terms of its expansion of the private sector and capital liberalization. Hungary had long since signed an Association Agreement with the EU (in 1971); and with a nod to the Nordic economies, it now created CEFTA, with the other Visegrád nations (in 1993); joined the OECD in 1995 and also signed up to the Washington Consensus with a hard-hitting adjustment package introduced that year. In short, Hungary did all that it could to lock itself into the West. In the process, however, trade unions were rendered weak or dissolved and large sectors of society found themselves poorly represented in the new political system. Hungary found *itself* stuck, unable to go back but unable to really improve the quality of its democracy, this being the very gap into which Viktor Orbán, after an unhappy first stint in power in the 1990s, would later reappear in decidedly more pronationalist livery.[86]

Old regional and ethnic divides were reappearing elsewhere. Most Eastern and central European nations remained strongly provincial still (especially a country like Serbia, in which regions and their leaders operated on grounds of patronage). Poland, which was not as ravaged by war as Serbia, resisted the tendency to ethnic fracture, but partly at the expense of a growing economic divide between a prosperous West and a more backward East. The failure in Catholic Poland of a successful Christian democratic party to take root along Western lines is equally revealing of the difficulties of building inclusive national visions. In Poland, as much as anywhere else, a more populist, antiliberal ethos was soon emerging in between the cracks. In the East, in short, the institutions of democracy proved easier to put into place than many had at first feared; but as to whether these were sufficient to underpin a liberal politics and not just a liberal economics was another matter altogether.

Before the decade was out these political failings were soon undermining the economic reforms that had been so unevenly introduced. As one Bulgarian woman recalled of the communist past and her current capitalist present: all "those years I was forced to write about unemployment and exploitation . . . But I didn't believe a word of it." In 2014 this multilingual and highly educated woman could not get a job anywhere. "I thought it was all lies," she said. "Can you imagine that all that time I was actually writing the truth."[87] Anyone then living in Slovenia, which fared much better than most of the central and Eastern European nations, might have struggled to recognize that picture. Citizens of Prague, by contrast, now routinely visited by stag parties and sex tourists, might have thought her troubles were the least of it. It was all a reminder of just what divergent paths the countries of the East had been set along.

A second vision for Europe also emerged at this time. It grew out of the parallel debate over the social functions of the new Europe, which had begun in earnest at around the same time as the first concrete moves toward monetary union were taken after 1987. After Maastricht the EU had been organized into three "pillars": the core European Communities pillar, the Common Foreign and Security Policy (CFSP), and Justice and Home Affairs (JHA). But social policy, such as that concerning migration, often bled across the three. The thinking behind these various pillars never quite caught on in the way that the economic rationale for the EU had done. And it was partly in the effort to put that right that Europe's leaders called for a new intergovernmental conference to be held in Amsterdam in 1997. The primary outcome of that meeting—of what was rather grandly called the "Treaty" of Amsterdam (it was not nearly so set in stone as that suggested)—was an amendment to Maastricht in which certain powers of social policymaking would be transferred from the national to the European level.

Beyond that it was a free-for-all—"an awful piece of treaty drafting," as one retrospective put it—that did nothing so much as reveal the ongoing tensions not only between different nations within the union, but between competing visions of how they should relate to one another.[88] The Germans wanted greater cooperation on immigration matters; the Nordics wanted pollution controls; the French wanted employment policies. An unemployment chapter was included but, typically, was granted little more than window-dressing status.[89] As an act of professional diplomacy, concluding the treaty had proven more straightforward than Maastricht before it, but primarily because very little serious policy was actually at stake. Joschka Fischer, as ever, was about the only politician proposing serious political reforms (this time a kind of federal social model that was more in tune with the vision for Europe of an Altiero Spinelli in his Ventotene days, but hopelessly out of tune with the majority of those present). But the outcome was limited, because Kohl vetoed many of the more far-reaching proposals at the last minute, fearing political repercussions at home.

In some ways the purpose, when read between the lines, of the meeting of numerous heads of state in Nice three years later, in December 2000, was about resolving the status of European social policy raised, but left hanging, in the Amsterdam Treaty: and about doing so before the new countries to the East joined in what was being billed as the "big bang" expansion of 2004 (when ten predominantly Eastern and central European countries, including Poland, would finally be let into the EU). And it was to be a rather more bruising affair: the Spanish newspaper *El País* dubbed it *"la batalla de Niza."* Two main issues confronted the gathered heads of the participating fifteen nations at Nice. The immediate question was about the forthcoming expansion east, and the addition of around 75 million new members to the community that this would involve. But the deeper question that the meeting provoked was about the lack of a constitutional framework within the EU as it *already* existed, and which had already proven hard enough to negotiate among the existing core. The lure of the greater international political clout promised by an EU of twenty-five proved too great, however, and substantive questions of democracy and constitutionalism were played down in favor of a Charter of Fundamental Rights (which the British managed to ensure was not incorporated into the treaty, thus rendering it largely of symbolic value) and an expansion in the scale of the European judiciary to support this.

For the most part, therefore, substantive social issues were ignored or glossed over. It was as if the only problems confronting Europe were technical ones relating to national implementation of the *acquis communautaire*—the body of legislation the European project had thus far accumulated in its wake—and communication of the results of this: not the high levels of unemployment that still marred some of the countries, or the problems that confronted ethnic minorities. There was certainly little by way of a modern "social question" as such being posed and not all existing EU members opened up their job markets right away to the new members (the UK being an unlikely exception). All the talk of European comity thus struck many as distinctly hollow. But most of the politicians at Nice were more worried about their respective national influence at the constitutional bargaining table. France wanted decision-making parity with Germany, for example, despite having 20 million fewer citizens. And when it came to the thorniest issue of all, introducing qualified majority voting on all council decisions, the big countries like the UK and France refused to give up their power of veto. The Irish, to many a bureaucrat's consternation, then vetoed the whole treaty in a referendum the following year. They did so in part because of the issue of abortion rights but mainly because of the way the treaty was associated with expansion east. "Enough was enough," was the recurring theme of debate—but the European project marched on regardless.

This was to prove fateful. When Europe was first imagined as a coal and steel community, and then later as a wider economic area, questions of democracy were not even part of the discussion. That did not make it "undemocratic," because it was assumed that such things were properly addressed at the national level. But likewise it was never intended that Europe should do any particular work on "behalf" of democracy either. The primary concern was to ensure the survival of the nation-state, and national democracy as part of that. Now, however, in keeping with the wider shift toward thinking about democracy as a series of transposable procedures, rather than the outcome of political contestation, European leaders were seeking to lock in a very particular model of democracy as their own universal norm. That meant that the particular model of integration that Europe was at this very point pursuing—a liberal, market-based integration—now started to matter very much *for* democracy. This too became clearer in the 1990s. For European politicians, it was easier to do business with one another if markets were now the primary subject of politics.

With the messier struggle over social policy pushed to the background, the European project now proceeded as a dual policy of single-market integration for the fifteen (soon to be twenty-five) and eurozone membership for the Western European core (minus the UK). Together, the single market and the single currency now acted as a lowest common denominator holding out the promise of more cohesive policymaking but at the cost of overlooking the less universalizable issues of class and nation. The latter two problems had not gone away: they simply did not fit very well into the new model and were therefore to a certain extent ignored. To the extent they were included it was as a function of the belief that successfully managing the markets gives one sufficient control over social policy. This was the very opposite of the way that politicians had thought just a few decades ago. The outcome of the search for a "European democracy" had thus ended up as nothing less than a means for constitutionalizing the primacy of the market by proxy. The liberal vision of democracy as a particular sort of claim on freedom had become the European norm.

Indeed, as successive treaties and referenda and constitutional court decisions steadily built "Europe" into more and more of a constitutional entity, as the different governmental branches of the European bureaucracy laid down at Maastricht developed and were complemented by yet more European Court of Justice hearings, it became clear to European citizens and not just their technocrats that something historically quite unprecedented was taking shape before their eyes. "There is no other place or time in world history where there has existed as rich and as lengthy an elite debate about constitutional reform as what we have seen in Europe over the past decade," observed the political scientist Andrew Moravcsik in 2002.[90] He was right. But to what end?

While the boom lasted, which for most of the 1990s it did, this question did not matter. The effort to turn European integration into a project for the expansion of market liberalism appeared to be the right way to go. There was support from the lower middle classes, who for now had what seemed like realistic hopes of keeping their new and, in some cases, rather better jobs, or of getting better ones later if they desired. There was also broad support among Europe's upper middle classes, to whom social democrats had committed themselves in their own pursuit of power. Most of the post–Cold War European governments to emerge out of this conjunction felt more in control of their destiny than they had in a long while. But these late-twentieth-century social democrats had shackled their electoral fortunes to the persistence of a buoyant economy. The moment that disappeared they would find they now had no other leg to stand on. Their citizens would then also discover that their countries no longer had a viable left to count upon.

I I

Farewell to All That

ON A TROUBLED and lonely late-night flight across the country on *Air Force One* in September 1995, President Clinton "ambled back to the press Cabin," reported one of the journalists present, and confided to the rest of the press pack that the country seemed to him in something of a "funk";[1] not down, by a long way, but out of kilter. In Europe as well, amidst the new prosperity, there could be no denying the almost palpable sense that public life had somehow lost its soul. Something strange had transpired amid the post–Cold War peace dividend and what seemed to many Westerners, at the height of the 1990s, as the economic boom of ages. Confidence in democracy was not growing stronger; it was ebbing slowly away.

One basic indicator of these underlying concerns was a sharpening erosion of civic trust. In 1964, 78 percent of Americans believed they could "trust" Washington to do what was right; by 1994 that number had fallen to just 19 percent.[2] In fact it wasn't just the system but its representatives that were facing an historic decline in popular faith. Faith in democratic principles remained strong but surveys repeatedly placed politicians and political parties near the bottom of the pile of trustworthiness. Even in Sweden, where 60 percent of respondents to an election study in 1968 said they thought that political parties were interested in people's opinions, not just their votes, it transpired that by 1994 only 25 percent of Swedes still thought this.[3] The decline in respect for the political class fostered a more general disengagement from politics as well, since where political trust was lower, voter turnout tended to be lower also. After 1990 voter turnout in national elections declined nearly everywhere, until it reached its lowest postwar average of 62 percent in 2001. Political polls told their own story too: beginning in the 1990s, fewer and fewer people were prepared to take part in them.[4]

Part of the reason for this was that political leaders had become less reliant on popular bases of support and more reliant on a demonstrable record of competence in the "managerial" style. In the process governments had adopted less ideological, more technocratic, approaches to policymaking. On the continent, the EU was frequently made the scapegoat for this process, its governing bodies presumed to have climbed so far away from the national electorate that they could not possibly see or hear them. But the fact that the same trend was equally visible at the national and municipal level suggests this was not the full story. Polls consistently revealed that American voters, from the mid 1990s, supported more government assistance to the needy, even as most government programs of the time were actually cutting *back* on such support.[5] Another part of the problem was that the trust that had come to count "politically" had changed as well. What mattered now was the degree of confidence that markets expressed in the willingness and ability of national governments to provide economic stability and security. Generally the more successful post–Cold War politicians to emerge were those willing to side with the interests of capital over those of their own party constituencies. The people gathering together in "mass" organizations became of steadily less importance to them, or to the media, or to the lobbyists whom politicians courted when they wished to get things done.

To make up for this loss of popular voice, politicians had—intuitively for the most part—shifted the terms of debate away from "issues." They had especially learned to avoid that most fundamental issue of the distribution of power and resource, since this involved taking from some voters in order to give to others. Politics had instead become much more about "values" and, perhaps above all, about charisma, since these could appeal in principle to a greater number of people. As one British diplomat observed at the turn of the decade: "Not so long ago, candidates were elected in much of Europe on the strength of their policies and platforms. . . . These days it's personality that counts."[6] The emphasis now, it was widely acknowledged, was on "TV blitzes, capped teeth, dyed hair and 'up-close' portraits of aspiring first couples." An older generation of politicians relied on "kitchen cabinets" of informal advisers; the new generation were more likely to be photographed in front of their kitchen cabinets than they were to actually organize one. And from this performance-obsessed environment emerged the new generation of leaders that enchanted and disappointed alike.

For some of this new crop of politicians, like Britain's Tony Blair and Germany's Gerhard Schröder, the new art of politics as theater came naturally. Others like Australia's more wooden John Howard would learn (successfully—he was elected four times) to adapt. Either way, by the final years of the millennium it had become almost imperative for any politician who seriously wanted to be given the keys to national office to stress that one was "not" really a career politician at all. As Tony Blair famously—and with that singular lack of irony that also now character- ized the political art—announced to the BBC during his first term as PM: "I never grew up as a politician. I don't feel myself a politician even now."[7] Not even Orwell could have done much with that. In such a milieu, the chances of voting into power those who would pursue a longer-term set of objectives to the ones they were being told would get them elected in the first place decreased substantially. Was it any surprise that people's interest, let alone their "belief" in politics, was beginning to wane?

The Hollow State

Both the extent and the limits of this process are neatly encapsulated in the brief, little remembered, yet illuminating political career of Steve Forbes, the American magazine magnate. Steve Forbes had what media circles liked to refer to as "name recognition" when he decided to stand for the Republican nomination to the 1996 presidential election. This was no worse a justification than the one Forbes himself supplied: "In their late forties, Forbes men's hormones seem to change," he explained. "Pop started riding motorcycles. I would say running for president quali- fies." If this was a rather folksy rationale on which to be standing for public office, it was in many ways a part of Forbes's objective and, in truth, his appeal.

The core value of Forbes's campaign was its simplicity, as embodied in the one serious policy idea he presented to the American public, the idea of a flat rate tax: a single tax band for everyone. Forbes's big idea gained no little traction. He was soon running at 15 percent in the polls (only a little lower than his proposed tax rate) and second in the race behind the big-hitting leader of the Republican Senate, Bob Dole. Like most independent candidates, Forbes invested his own wealth in his ul- timately unsuccessful campaign. Four years later he was at it again, this time having dropped the flat tax in hope of focusing more on his religious credentials.

Forbes failed to win the nomination that year as well, and thereafter withdrew from front-line politics, but not before he had successfully helped to reinvigorate both the antitax movement and the religious right in the United States. Along the way he helped accustom the electorate

to the new politics of personality: ironically without having much charisma himself. Nowhere was this more apparent than when, during his
2000 nomination campaign, he had his former pastor vouch for the depth
of his religious convictions and the authenticity of his now "politicizing"
them. "He gave really a remarkable speech on the subject of religion,
ethics and spirituality on the one hand and corporate life and free enterprise on the other," said the Reverend Al Niese of St. John on the
Mountain, Bernardsville, New Jersey, to the press. "It was wonderfully
witty initially and then marvelously deep and thoughtful. He really seemed
to be comfortable with his voice here."[8] Opportunism was nothing new,
but this was a new compaction in the politics of the surface. Forbes may
have failed, but he had quite correctly caught which way the wind was
blowing.

So too in Italy had the media impresario and former lounge singer
Silvio Berlusconi. In the early 1990s the perma-tanned Berlusconi, having consolidated his media empire, established a new type of party, Forza
Italia. Formed without a "people" in mind to represent, Forza Italia was
a "pure" political gesture: a means above all else of securing power for
its charismatic founder. Its exhibition of assorted policies was hung together around this core platform almost as an afterthought. Opportunism
incarnate, the success of Forza Italia is explicable only against the backdrop of the public cynicism unleashed amidst the historic rupture in
Italy's postwar Second Republic that was brought about by the massive
Tangentopoli scandals of the early 1990s.

Tangentopoli was the name given to the previous corrupt political
system in Italy, uncovered by a series of judicial investigations into Italian
politics, known as *Mani Pulite*. Such was the extent of the investigations
(and of the corruption) that, at one point, two thirds of all parliamentarians were under investigation. It was enough to shake the Italian
public out of its tacit acceptance of the endemic cronyism into which
the country had settled. The politics of *raccomandazione* (patronage) had
rotted the Italian government to the core: as one observer put it, in a
resource-scarce economy the dominant Christian Democratic party had
turned power itself into a growth industry.[9] At the time the *Tangentopoli*
scandal broke most Italian ministers of justice had for some time been
more concerned to rein in the power of the investigating judges than to
address the very serious misgivings people had with the conduct of local
magistrates in cases, for example, where employees sought compensation,
or where families sought fair divorce settlements.[10]

It was legitimate grievances over just such issues that afforded Berlusconi the opening he needed. The effective demise of the two major parties, the Socialists and the Christian Democrats, the sense of a new beginning provided by the ejection of many of the older generation of politicians from the former era, and the holding in April 1993 of an eight-part referenda on such constitutional matters as the abolition of former ministries and the regulation of public banks allowed him to build his new party on the ashes of the former system. In the days of "clean hands" anything that was new looked good in comparison to the old. Within a year Berlusconi had led Forza Italia to power in the elections of March 1994. But Berlusconi wasn't the only one to capitalize on the vacuum at the center of Italian politics. The Christian Democrat Mario Segni, something of a loose cannon himself, instituted a referendum to limit the system of preferences by which the old parties had ruled: it passed with 95 percent voting in favor. This move from proportional representation to first-past-the-post broke the hold of the old parties, who had dominated the prior coalition-based politics. But doing so at a time when they were themselves felled by the *Tangentopoli* scandals, it also opened the way to new, single-issue parties, like Umberto Ossi's Northern League movement, which rose on the back of promises of tax cuts and freedom from meddling Roman politicians. Contrasted with what had been happening in Eastern Europe in recent years, the likes of Ossi now promised an antipolitics of a rather different sort.

Berlusconi's first government was raucous and short-lived—and all the more so because the Christian Democrats and the Italian communists, who had long acted as the moral compass within Italian politics, were each now so resoundingly out of favor. It had been no small matter when, just days after the fall of the Berlin Wall, the then leader of the Partito Comunista Italiano (PCI), Achille Occhetto, changed the name of the communist party to the Democratic Party of the Left. For despite its original professed aim of bringing about the end of bourgeois democratic culture, the Italian PCI, as we have seen, had actually become, over the years, an effective and reliable defender of the public interest, especially during the Years of Lead. The PCI's support of a form of mass politics, education, and public activism was a vision of politics that rested firmly on the idea of social equality—and its loss was one of the unintentional consequences of the fallout from *Tangentopoli*: some of what was good from the past erased in the process of drawing a line firmly beneath it.

Henceforth in Italy it was the more negative liberties—freedom *from* the Roman elite, from corruption, from the communists themselves, and from government bureaucracy and inefficiency—that were promoted by the plethora of new and smaller parties that took over the old parties' seats. This was no flash in the pan: Italy would still be in the throes of a broad-spectrum populism more than two decades later. And it was why the central political terrain vacated by the old parties would hereafter be dominated by governments, such as that under Lamberto Dini (himself appointed by the Italian president in the wake of the collapse of Berlusconi's first government), in which senior banking and civil service officials played front-line roles.

Here was the original stand-off between the populists and the technocrats in Europe. But Berlusconi was not done yet. After all, his student wing was called Students for Freedom and its watchword was "efficiency."[11] He had done his electoral calculations and Berlusconi would return at the start of the new millennium to head up a new coalition of the improbable: anchored this time in a more populist, libertarian platform that took the name *La Casa delle Libertà* (The House of Freedoms). For all that Forza Italia was often labeled in the foreign media as a "postpolitical" party, it was in fact political in a new way. Berlusconi's secret weapon was his control of the media (as satirized by novelists such as Andrea Camilleri) and his utter lack of scruples. But he was also an effective coalition builder, and that made him less the self-serving ogre that his critics wanted others to see, and more the politician whose time had come.[12]

Berlusconi and Forbes were not the only politically ambitious mavericks to be tapping into the growing demand for single-issue politics in the 1990s. The political situation in Australia at this time offered a similar window onto the new issues-based politics helping to prize away parties from their rather taken-for-granted publics. In 1996 a young firebrand named Pauline Hanson stood on the mainstream Liberal Party's ticket in that year's elections and looked set to take a Labour stronghold for the Liberals in Ipswich. Hanson's extreme anti-immigrant views, however, led to her being deselected by the Liberal Party prior to the election. She went on to win the seat anyway, but as an independent candidate, turning the election into a referendum on state support for Aborigines, and making it just a little clearer as to what sort of issues the public, who felt their majoritarian status to be at stake, wanted to focus upon.

"I believe we are in danger of being swamped by Asians," Hanson declared in her maiden speech to parliament in September 1996. "They have their own culture and religion, form ghettos, and do not assimilate."

A year later her One Nation party was up and running and drawing older, rural voters away from the governing coalition, cracking open a cultural split that tore right through the middle of the Australian nation. In Britain too, the libertarian and equally anti-immigrant UKIP was formed in 1993; these were also the years of the Front National's great strides forward in France, and of the Norwegian Progress Party's transformation into a serious electoral presence (often gaining more than 10 percent of the national vote), closely followed by its sister Progress Party in Denmark. In Austria the formerly liberal Freedom Party (FPÖ) had since the late 1980s become, under Jörg Haider's leadership, an increasingly anti-immigrant far-right party (with one or two policy sops to female voters), and it was rewarded with a record 27 percent of the vote in 1999.[13]

What would soon be a plethora of single-issue parties, of which blood-and-soil nationalists were but a part, was not, however, the beginnings of a renewed democratic plurality, as many on the right—desperate for a way back into politics, a new "mission" of the sort the Third Way left seemed to have found—suggested at the time. Far from it, they created new social cleavages and pushed the old parties of mass movement toward more negative campaigning in response. That in turn created another divide between the old parties of mass movement and the people they sought to win to their cause. Electoral volatility was in part dependent on whether countries had proportional representation or first-past-the-post political systems (the latter tending to be more stable). But it was also a function of this upheaval in the old party-political landscape, and an indication of the extent to which many citizens felt the state no longer fully represented them. The "demos" was dividing. Aware that something was wrong, Canada's annual Royal Commission made the question of what was happening to the state, and state–citizen relations above all, a major focus of one of its inquiries back in the 1980s.[14] And yet the answers to the present dilemma were to be found not in reflection, at this moment, but in the instincts of a citizenry that no longer knew quite where it stood.

Accordingly, the issues that such parties and political campaigns promoted ranged across all aspects of the political spectrum, from animal rights campaigners to anti-globalization protesters. Parties of the left found themselves struggling in this sort of atmosphere. Where they tried to speak the words of populist protest, they came out sounding wrong. When the French actor and comedian Michel Gérard Colucci announced that he would run for president in the 1981 elections, and even gained the support of the satirical magazine *Charlie Hebdo* to do so, the mainstream media had simply refused to take him seriously: and this despite "Coluche," as he was popularly known, running at 16 percent in the polls. Coluche's campaign may have begun as a joke but it was fueled by a sincere critique of party politics as usual. It also ended when he withdrew after his manager was murdered amidst a growing political backlash: "it's starting to be a pain in the ass," he joked. But in truth he was devastated. Left-wing populism thus never really made it out of the blocks, even though workers and the lower middle classes bore a disproportionate burden of the costs of restructuring during the 1980s.

The right, however, proved more adept at managing the deepening sense of mistrust in mainstream politics. Come the 1990s and here were the makings of its own solution to the post–Cold War democratic "funk." By then, a new convergence—of right-wing parties and working-class voters—was now open to exploration by cherry-picking issues of contention and isolating them from their context. In the early 1990s, for example, the anti-immigrant Belgium MP Filip Dewinter's Vlaams Blok tightened its grip on the Flemish vote in Belgium by presenting the controversial 1992 "70 Point Plan." The full title of the plan was: *Immigration: the solutions. 70 proposals for the solution of the problem of aliens.* The document was inspired by Le Pen's *Fifty Measures to Help Manage the Problem of Immigration.* In Holland Pim Fortuyn's party Pim Fortuyn List also rose to prominence during the second half of the decade on a similarly skewed platform. These parties were proof that the Western working classes would vote for parties of the (far) right if appealed to in the right way. The left had missed a trick, it seemed, and in so doing it had also lost a little more of the confidence of some of those who ought to have been its natural constituents.

Where these new parties were also characteristic of the times was in their popular references to strong-handed governments: to saying what needed to be said and to making "tough choices"—a trait they shared with the new social democrats as much as anything else. At one end of the spectrum this leaned toward fascism—as with the welcoming hand Berlusconi extended to neofascist Gianfranco Fini as he searched in the late 1990s for that governing coalition of freedoms that would light his path back to power. At the other end it led to constant invocations of the "challenge" of globalization as justification for political platforms that differed from one another only by virtue of their alternative suggestions for reducing government spending (as if spending the public's money was all governments did). In both cases it raised a new challenge for

politics, which was how to give more of government away without losing control at the center. This was in some ways *the* central challenge of
the decade, and the various efforts to resolve it would leave their mark
upon the upheavals to follow.

One immediate consequence, and a favorite response of the new breed
of anti-political politicians, was to speak of the importance of "depoliticization." This was not a word amenable to soaring rhetoric, which in
some ways was precisely the point. Politics could not solve people's
problems, Tony Blair liked to say. Only people could. The purpose of
government therefore was to help people to help themselves: "Working
with communities engaged in making their own solutions," as he put it
in one of his earliest speeches as prime minister.[15] And yet it was not
Britain's New Labour but America's Republicans that would fully explore
the potential of that insight: above all the Georgia Republican and Speaker
of the House from 1995 to 1999, Newt Gingrich.

Gingrich was a deceptively divisive—and critical—figure: a policy
radical and Christian conservative whose humble origins as a geography
teacher belied the polarizing effect he had already had within Congress
for well over a decade before his promotion to Speaker of the House in
January 1995. That promotion came on the back of the Republican
landslide achieved in the midterm congressional elections of 1994: a
landslide in which Gingrich had played a leading role. Six weeks before
the elections were due to take place, and surrounded by "a phalanx of
Republican hopefuls" on the steps of the Capitol building in Washington,
Gingrich had pointed the United States firmly in the direction of political polarization by launching what would come to be known as the
Contract with America.

On one level the Contract's actual platform was straightforward: Gingrich merely pulled together information from Republican candidates
and focus groups (carried out by Pat Buchanan and Ross Perot's former
pollster Frank Luntz) to identify the core issues Republicans should be
standing for. The Contract duly promised to lower taxes and shrink
government, to rein in welfare, get tough on crime, and to stand up for
"family values."[16] And while it could not simply "wish" these things into
being, certain parts of the Contract *were* enacted in some form or other
(notably the Personal Responsibility Act, which made it into the 1996
Clinton Personal Responsibility and Work Opportunity Reconciliation
Act). More significantly, what the Contract succeeded in doing was to
"nationalize" the congressional midterm elections of that year, and to do

so by hitting the detonator on whatever was left of the American political middle ground and the scope for consensus politics it enabled.[17]

In reality the Contract was much more than this. It was its own political movement designed to dial into and to capitalize on voter disaffection *between* national elections.[18] As Gingrich himself put it: "A
campaign promise is one thing, a signed contract is quite another."
Gingrich's plan was to hold his own party accountable, in writing, to an
ever-more partisan political agenda. Above all, it was an effort to bring
the Republican Party to the people as a movement, now, rather than as
a party: this was its true innovation. "We have listened to what you want
and we hear you loud and clear," the Contract preamble announced to
the American people. But the "popular" nature of its proposals was a
façade, since half of its policies were not about voter issues at all but
about elite Republicans' plans for reshaping the state. The Contract thus
not only proposed cutting taxes, it also cut out certain caucuses within
Congress itself (including the Congressional Black Caucus) and abolished
standing committees on issues of Democratic interest (the Post Office
and Civil Service and District of Columbia included). More generally it
made the work of subcommittees more dependent upon the party line,
locking in a period of more ingrained partisanship.[19]

To be sure, *some* of this reform impetus (not least the insistence that
Congress be subject to the laws it imposed upon the rest of the country—
laws regarding sexual harassment, for example) was a positive development.
But the more lasting result was to further hollow out the capacity of
Congress by laying the foundations for a more partisan legislature in
the future: something Gingrich's rhetoric as speaker merely reinforced.
Thereafter Clinton's remaining domestic legislative program had little
hope of passing—unless, that was, he reformed it in the direction that
corporate consultants said was "good politics." Hence it was the Contract
that truly sounded the death knell of Clinton's planned $16 billion
assistance package to the poorest families with dependent children, and
that cut his intended boost of social security for the middle class. In
due course it would prove to be the beginning of the end of "welfare
as we know it."[20]

American progressives were more than a little irked, therefore, when
in 1995 Clinton stood alongside the newly victorious Gingrich, smiling
and shaking hands for a photo op. For liberal firebrand Thomas Frank
this was "the most important symbolic moment of the decade."[21] In
reality it wasn't so much Clinton's program as the space for democratic
debate itself that had been swept up and tidied away by Gingrich's in-

spired power-grab. And so it was, in that sense, not remarkable at all: it was just more of the new politics as usual.

Political Estrangement

As the likes of Gingrich were only too aware, one of the principal driving forces behind these changes was the trend toward the privatization of government functions: after all, it was this that provided them with the means to wage politics no longer just against but increasingly now outside the democratic institutions of the state. At the start of the century Lenin had staked the Soviet Union's future on social planning; by the century's end the liberal democracies were no less committed—as a matter of presumed philosophy—to rolling back the last vestiges of the era of the social state. Not only in Britain and America, but notably also by now in Germany, Sweden, Canada, Denmark, and New Zealand, the privatization of the public sector continued apace into the 1990s. But whereas in the 1980s there had been a distinctly antistate agenda to the process, by now privatization was carrying the newly disaggregated state with it.

In the UK, New Labour's bit-part privatizations of the remnants of the British public sector were couched in terms of the potential savings to citizens themselves. This avowed need to reduce the public sector, to make it "efficient," combined fiscal prudence with political entrepreneurialism. The national economy (one of the few "public goods" still routinely applauded) would be the first beneficiary; the "people," by association, would reap their just rewards later. If this seemed like a miraculously simple solution to the century-long struggle between the demands of capital and the needs of labor it was no less revealing that it emerged at the very moment the distinction itself had stopped mattering (it was usually *labor* parties, after all, overseeing all of this). The flies in this soup would become apparent over the years—they would be found, for one, in those same parties' dwindling electoral wins—as people realized that good service was not something easily obtainable on the cheap, regardless of whether it was the public or the private sector providing it.

Political entrepreneurialism was something that could be taken too far, however. As politics became more expensive, politicians running for office recused themselves from their traditional "bases" of economic support, be it unions or mass party organizations, in order to go looking for financial support elsewhere. By the end of the century campaign spending was more than twice what it had been in the early 1980s and rising. In America the number of major private donors (corporate CEOs primarily, donating the largest individual sums) quadrupled between 1990 and 2010 from 6,456 to 26,783. Meanwhile the total amount of money the major parties raised from them grew from around $110 million in 1990 to well over $500 million just a decade later.[22] The initiative process, allowing citizens in some states to propose laws for popular consideration, was supposed to be a way to give a voice back to citizens in those (mainly western) US states that permitted the tabling of state-wide ballots. But a proposal to reduce long-distance access charges in Nebraska in 1998 was successfully defeated in just such a referendum thanks to a $5.3 million war chest provided by AT&T and was a reminder, if any were needed, that money talks loudest of all.[23]

This was exactly the problem that Italy, somewhat further down the road perhaps, had been suffering from for years. As a British expatriate there observed:

Today the parties, much reduced in membership, are further away from society and much more the privileged distributors of the resources of the state. The slippery slope of corruption beckons to all. In the face of these developments, the ordinary citizen castigates the political class, but secretly (or openly) desires to climb on, or at least hang on, to one of the many clientelist ladders which constitute the hidden, inner mechanisms of very many "democratic" states.[24]

Of course, the idea that parties had received most of their funding from membership dues beforehand was nothing more than a convenient myth (in France there had been no rules on party financing until 1988 and in the UK parties were not even legally recognized entities until 1998). But if the demand was always there the supply of money was not. From the 1990s on, with the injection of bigger money—much bigger—into elections, corruption was soon on the rise.[25]

With corruption came a rise in political scandal in the 1990s as well: be it the veritable earthquake of *Tangentopoli* in Italy, or the Luchaire affair concerning arms-to-Iran in France; be it tabloid scandalizing of parliamentary privileges in Britain or abuse-of-office inquiries in Belgium and Spain. But reform was not always in the direction of a more "transparent" politics. In 1995, then Prime Minister Édouard Balladur "reformed" the system just prior to his presidential bid in order to create a funding loophole for his own campaign. Individual politicians were frequently strung up by such scandals, but the growing proximity of political office and corporate power survived intact.[26] When the former West German Economics Minister Martin Bangemann left the European Commission in 1999, amid a series of fraud inquiries into the Santer Commission, it proved no problem for him to then join the Spanish telecommunications giant Telefónica, despite having previously been commissioner for Industrial Affairs, Information, and Telecommunications.[27]

Bangemann was not the only minister to find remuneration in areas of his former political portfolio. On leaving office Britain's Peter Sutherland joined oil and consultancy giants BP and Goldman Sachs while France's former president of the European Commission François-Xavier Ortoli took over as head of Total Oil. The latter company, it was soon revealed, had prior to Ortoli's arrival paid millions of francs to all of the French political parties to secure their silence in its corporate misdemeanors (which included siphoning off company assets to key figures within the corporation). A 2003 public trial further revealed that the Élysée had itself long used the dominant position of Elf Aquitaine, which merged with TotalFina in 2000, in the African state of Gabon to pursue its own security and surveillance activities in the region.[28]

But corruption, for all the periodic flashes of indignation it aroused, was not the only consequence of the yawning separation between the citizens of Western democracies and their representatives in office. A bigger problem, since it indicated a decrease in support for democracy among the citizenry at large, was to be found in the declining level of participation in national elections. This had become apparent in the 1970s, but the process was gathering pace by the 1990s as the first signs of genuine voter apathy began to arise. Of fifteen European democracies only Belgium, Norway, and the Netherlands were seeing more people turn out to vote by the late 1990s. Elsewhere the trend was downward. In Austria, Finland, and Germany the decline was dramatic. It was more modest in southern Europe, where democracy had been more recently rekindled. But even there historic lows in electoral turnout were recorded in Spain and Greece by 2000.

They were followed by low electoral turnouts in the UK in 2001, and by France, Portugal, and Ireland in 2002 and then Switzerland the following year. For all that there was also a rise in political partisanship during these years, this was not in most cases managing to sustain the voter turnout either—least of all in America. When Barry Goldwater lined up against Lyndon Johnson in America in 1964, 96 percent of registered voters decided the outcome. Bush v. Gore in 2000 was similarly acrimonious. Yet this time only 47 percent voted.[29] To the extent that popular disgruntlement did not find its expression at the polls, this was a worrying sign that precious few, with hindsight, bothered much to think about.

The same trend was even more marked in those countries to have most recently regained the vote. Observing the state of democracy in central and Eastern Europe since the fall of communism, the Czech-born French historian (and former aide to Václav Havel) Jacques Rupnik saw little more than "a steady decline of voter participation, the huge gap between citizens and political elites, low trust in parliamentary and state institutions and the rise of populist and nationalist challenges to liberal democracy." Eastern Europe had indeed faithfully imitated the Western model, its "signs of fatigue, even of crisis" included. Havel summed it up best: "We fought for a different political system from the one we ended up [with]," he said.[30]

Voter turnout was declining, then; and so too was political party membership, long the bellwether of an active citizenry during the post-war era. In the mid 1960s the percentage of national electorates who were party members was around the mid teens. By the end of the 1990s it was less than 6 percent, a third as much. This didn't mean people were no longer politically active: protest actions, from signing petitions to complaining about minor political malpractice, were all on the rise. But these were largely negative traits. European democracy had for the entire twentieth century been a democracy of the party, and that invariably laid more positive demands upon citizens. It had also been forged by the instruments of mass participation, the trade unions above all. Yet membership in trade unions had hollowed out, thanks in part to the legal assault of the Thatcher–Reagan years, as well as to the disaggregation of the workplace itself.

During Clinton's years in office union rates in America declined from 16.8 to 13.5 percent. Political action committees (PACs) replaced union and party bases as the major source of campaign funds for candidates, and as a result they came to have more of a say in key issues of strategy and personnel.[31] The problem for the unions was not just politics, of course, but the fact that the industries and trades they represented were disappearing or relocating to China and other low-cost manufacturing countries (including the cheaper but still well-educated labor pool in Eastern and central Europe).

Either way the trend was clear. From 1980 to 2003 union membership as a percentage of the entire workforce fell from 34.9 to 22.6 percent in

432

Germany, helped by the disciplining effect of reunification, which forced former East German workers to make themselves more competitive with those in the West. During this same period union rates fell from 18.3 to 8.3 percent in France, where they had always been historically weak, and from 50.1 to 29.3 percent in the UK, where once they had been strong. In Australia they fell from 65 percent in the late 1970s to 15 percent in the early 2010s, largely because unions had become increasingly redundant regarding constraints on workers' incomes and welfare, ever since the days of the Hawke–Keating Prices and Incomes Accord in the 1980s.[32]

British unions adapted by focusing on their public sector "elite" workers; German unions by contrast continued to represent the more traditional manufacturing (and male) demographic but in their case at the expense of taking on the interests of the many new types of worker being created in the information age, who were excluded now as the immigrants had been before them. In Italy the unions stayed with their former workers and became pension advocates within the political system, rather than an adversarial component of that system.[33] In almost all cases, their base was fragmenting and membership numbers were declining: from 1990 to 1999 membership fell by a quarter in the UK, by nearly a third in Germany, and by around a sixth in Italy.[34]

After the rise of alternative and single-issue movements, then, this decline of public participation was a second major challenge to the traditional party system that had for years dominated in the Western democracies. Given that parliamentary and presidential systems of rule alike had been organized around the major class-interest parties throughout the postwar era; given too that the managed disagreement and productive opposition they enabled were each central to the democratic oversight of power and to the legitimacy of government mandates, this was critical. As Germany's postwar Basic Law had made explicit, at least a part of the purpose of political parties lay in their "forming of the political will" of the people (Article 21). Beginning in the 1970s that virtuous circle had become a vicious one. Now political parties were being cut adrift, both by their failing capacity to engage ordinary folk, and by the lack of interest shown in them by their own leaders: be it Blair's open-armed turn to the City of London and Australian media baron Rupert Murdoch (who owned much of the conservative half of the press in Britain) or Washington's bipartisan embrace of the lobby.[35]

The base was now less valuable than the purse, in other words. "Millionaires have not replaced members or trade unions . . ." wrote an observer in late century, "[b]ut the actions necessary to attract new, wealthy business donors may well deter these other types of supporter." But what were the causes of this? In part, it was simply that the scramble for the political center ground that the new prosperity made possible (and above all its recuperation of the "forgotten" middle classes) meant that different parties mostly now offered variations on the same laissez-faire policies (just as their predecessors had, for a while, mostly hewn to more or less the same *Keynesian* ideas). As to the consequences, the recovery of European social democratic parties at the polls (on the back of their radically more liberal economic platforms) was one. Another was the fact that there were now more coalition governments, or cohabitations of various sorts, in power across the continent. In America, Republicans and Democrats similarly disagreed vehemently over just about everything but who their core voters were—and this was ultimately why Clinton guessed, quite rightly, that he could cave in to the Contract Republicans and get away with it at the next election. In Britain there was substantially less difference between what modern Conservatives and New Labour offered the British electorate than there had been between their "Clause Four" and "One Nation" predecessors.

All this left the swing voters who occupied that contested central ground needing to be won over by mass campaigns and expensive advertisements. Political success, in an unintended confirmation of the Schumpeterian ideal, had become about maximizing marginal returns. For a while at least, "getting out the base" was no longer the priority, and "the party" plunged only further into decline. In the United States this was exacerbated by the success of "outsiders" like Carter and Clinton, who had rendered party platforms a near-irrelevance compared to what the candidate and his or her staff themselves believed.[36] In Australia it was more recent, but every bit as noticeable, that the newly elected Howard government received, in 1999, the lowest incoming vote since 1931.[37] Meanwhile the likes of Blair—with his doctrine of the international community, announced in Chicago in 1999—cavorted on the international stage in a studied approximation of the presidential style of politics. "Citizens change from participants into spectators," wrote one political observer, "while the elites win more and more space in which to pursue their own particular interests."[38]

In some ways this was nothing more than a growing professionalization of politics in an era when to be "professional" was an increasingly laudable aim. And this was part cause of, and part response to, the need to address "problems" such as declining voter turnout and waning party identities. But it wasn't just that a new breed of professional politician

had arrived. A whole new ethos had arrived with them. The most successful politicians of the age now brought a panoply of "special advisers" (the
Brits soon dubbed them "Spads") who replaced the party hacks of old (with
their yuletide promises of a bucket of coal and a Christmas turkey). Together
with the spin doctors and the in-house pollsters, and with more and more
think tanks, the modern political scene was being transformed. Elections
were becoming little more than "circuses of marketing and management,
from spectacles of fund-raising to spectacles of targeted voter 'mobilization.'"[39]
Politics, as a result, was becoming a more top-heavy, cliquey affair.[40]

Yet the changes under way were not just about what politicians were
doing. Society, as we have seen, had been radically transformed over the
previous two decades. People's political identities were changing. They
pursued different lives and more varied careers and the problems they
confronted were often more complex than before. Electorates were more
educated, independently minded, and women especially were more likely
to assert their own political preferences independently of family. People
were more likely to support "postmaterialist" parties like the German
greens, on the left, or knee-jerk antimodernization and ethno-regionalist
parties, like the Northern League in Italy, on the right; or indeed, in a
reminder that communism wasn't quite dead, the separatist grouping of
Herri Batasuna in the Basque country. In the 1990s, Western citizens held
a very different set of values from the people who had forged the political landscape into which most of them had been born, and this undercut the class-based dividing lines that had shaped their parents'
preferences and the nature of the parties they voted for.

In light of all this, it would have been a miracle for parties whose
roots often went back to the late nineteenth century to maintain their
own traditions and their current support base. Exceptions were Fine Gael
and Fianna Fáil in Ireland: two parties shaped out of the civil war at the
start of the twentieth century. Another, perhaps not unrelated exception,
was religion, which for all the secularization of society had left Catholic
and Christian democratic party loyalties largely unaffected.

For the most part, though, the era of Golden Age party loyalty was
gone for good, the social cleavages they had followed having largely
melted away. By the end of the millennium, in fact, only around 5.5
percent of the electorate was party affiliated. And this wasn't just a national
phenomenon. Turnout in European elections was down and would continue falling well into the 2000s. In 1979 over 60 percent of the electorate voted in every country (apart from the euro-grudging UK). By 2009
it was as low as 21 percent in Slovakia and 24.5 percent in Poland.[41]

Electorates were turning their back not just on parties and politicians, but on the electoral system itself. But if this said a lot about the changing bases of the postwar liberal democratic order, if it seemed to confirm that the institutions of mass democracy were disappearing, it said little about what was replacing them.

La Pensée Unique

It was, the former vice chairman of the Board of Governors of the Federal Reserve, Alan Blinder, confessed, a rather "devilish" thought. But it had occurred to him anyway, and now he was airing it in the pages of the highly influential *Foreign Affairs* magazine: "Is government too political?" Blinder asked his global audience. Of course, policymaking in a democracy "must be political—that is, legitimized by popular support rather than by technical analyses." But all the same, could it be that a line between democracy and effective government had been drawn "in the wrong place?" If so, then it was time now to move that line in the direction of the technocrats, the central bankers, the regulators, the courts. Government, Blinder suggested, might do better if it learned from well-managed institutions like the Federal Reserve, which oversaw the ever-more complex running and occasional crisis of the modern capitalist state, blissfully unencumbered by the rat race of electoral politics.[42]

By the late 1990s, even as a new brand of charismatic politician strode to the center of the stage, such promises of "good governance" and "efficiency" were everywhere beginning to replace the old problem of "representativeness" as the central dilemma of democratic life. Politicians no longer listened quite so much to the plight of the outcast or the maligned for the simple reason that the "people" were so atomized they could not articulate their demands. They could only respond as individuals, which governments took as proof of the fact that they wanted to be treated as individuals as well. In this brave new world, citizens were no longer seen as an "electorate" so much as "stakeholders" and they had lost some of their ability to demand accountability as a result.[43] Mid-twentieth-century mass democracy implied a highly visible potential power—a sword of Damocles suspended above the politician's head. The new politics involved giving up that power in the hope that one's own vested interests would be the ones that got to count.

But of course some vested interests are more influential than others, a fact not lost on Tony Blair when he confided in 1999, to the UK

Venture Capitalists Association, that he had "scars on his back" after two years of trying to push through public service reform.[44] Blair's comments provoked an outcry from doctors and teachers. But nobody paid them much attention. Since the introduction of internal party changes such as One Person One Vote earlier in the decade, neither they nor their unions had anything like the influence they once did over the party; and at the height of the Murdoch age the media was hardly pro–public service either. Hence while they may have landed a few more blows against Blair, they failed to have any significant impact on the government's turn to the City of London for support.

To the extent that the gap between politicians and the electorate was growing then it was logical that private citizens, companies, public institutions, and communities alike would all seek to influence particular actors within the system more directly.[45] After all, the ability to do this was precisely what made lobbies like the Venture Capitalists Association so valuable. But it also opened them up to an underlying problem. Since lobbies were prepared to represent people's interests as consumers, but not as citizens per se, well-motivated minorities had become increasingly capable of holding the entire political system hostage.

Lobbies could be resisted, of course, but it took concerted effort and at times even courage by politicians to do so. And that was not always in evidence. One moment when such courage *was* forthcoming was after the Port Arthur massacre in Tasmania in April 1996, when a lone gunman managed to claim fifty-three victims before he was finally apprehended.[46] Australian Prime Minister John Howard immediately announced that he would seek to ban all automatic and semiautomatic weapons. In the face of intense opposition from the gun lobby—at one point he appeared before a crowd of 3,000 pro-gun supporters to speak to them in a bulletproof vest—Howard succeeded in introducing a national gun amnesty that brought in the better part of a million firearms for destruction. Gun-related murders fell by 7.5 percent a year on average thereafter.[47] But Howard's was a rare victory against what was, for the most part, the growing power of lobby groups and special interests over a political system that had turned its back on mass politics. In the US the National Rifle Association remained as entrenched a feature of national policy-making as ever.

In the late 1990s, gun libertarians were but one part of a much larger political species seeking to influence policy outcomes: whether prohunting Tories in Britain, or French business lobbies, or Spanish *corrida* traditionalists. All hailed from a growth curve that saw private institutions increasingly replace public funded bodies in the political life of the West. Conservative lobbies were at the heart of this but the lobby system was not just the preserve of the right. The political left too was turning to the lobby to get its voice heard in government, especially now that it was desperately seeking to lock in some of the social benefits under threat. Needless to say, since the financing of lobbies was overwhelmingly provided by corporations the odds were not stacked in its favor.[48]

For their part companies had now stopped using the lobby simply to limit how much they were taxed (the original impetus behind their revival in the United States, as Lewis Powell had envisaged it in 1971) and were using it instead to go after more far-reaching legislation that supported the interests of their particular economic sector or investment plans. Despite all the rhetoric that government should keep its nose out of their business, the truth of it was that they wanted government as a "partner" more than anything else.[49] This wasn't just an American proclivity, as well-funded representatives of Airbus, Thales, BAE Systems, and others—all assembled in Brussels to lay siege to the growing European bureaucracy—were only too happy to testify, as they often did. It wasn't just the work of corporations either: the China lobby and the Israel lobby were two of the most powerful in Washington.

There were those who sought to resist this. One powerful parallel trend at the time, particularly in Europe, sought to hand more control over the political process to independent bodies like regulators, insurers, dispute settlement boards, tribunals, and expert panels, or judiciaries. This was well-meaning for the most part. But the effect of setting experts against experts was to leave the one group that was most affected, that is ordinary people, with even less control over the agreements and policies that shaped their lives. It made their vote for any one particular government or party seem less "relevant" in determining their political fate. It was not so much apathy that lay behind declining voter turnouts then but a sensible reading of the facts. The same was true in America, where pursuant to a Supreme Court ruling of 1984, the fourth branch of government, federal agencies, were given greater freedom to pass their own rules and procedures.

While Congress at this time passed new laws numbering in the dozens each year, government agencies enacted literally hundreds of binding rules a year: mostly effectively, but almost all entirely without accountability as well. The prospect thus arose of citizens being pulled into "the vortex of an administrative state that allows little challenge or appeal" and which, in almost Kafka-like terms, they struggled even to comprehend.[50] Across the liberal democracies the number of regulatory agencies grew at a dramatically faster rate from the 1990s. Neoliberalism was rolling back parts of the state, but it was hardly leading to debureaucratization of government: if anything, quite the opposite.[51] This was especially apparent in Europe. For example, European energy regulators had become so numerous by the century's end that they had established their own club, the Council of European Energy Regulators, in 2000. Telecoms regulators numbered 113 in Europe by 2001: a ratio of around four per country. Consistency was, not surprisingly, a scarce commodity to come by, but that opened up almost as many opportunities for profiteering as the regulatory agencies themselves managed to close down.

In 1999 American businessman Ronald Lauder hauled the Czech Republic before two arbitration panels over changes in the media regulatory environment that he alleged had damaged his investment in the nation's first private television channel. The two cases, one heard in America (where Lauder was resident) and the other in the Netherlands (where his investment company was based), reached conclusions that were "diametrically opposed." From one the Czech Republic was ordered to pay damages; the other absolved it of any wrongdoing.[52] What was becoming less clear all the while was where the buck of responsibility actually stopped. This was particularly so when firms and corporations were encouraged, as were the media in Australia, for example, to regulate themselves.[53]

The same applied to central banks.[54] In the late 1980s, there had been only around a dozen independent central banks. Before the century was out there would be well over a hundred.[55] As both the number and the policy scope of independent central banks grew, they came to comprise nothing less than a new and largely independent transnational elite—whose authority was reinforced by their achieving, around the mid 1990s, a remarkable degree of internal agreement over what healthy economies should look like. National politicians, rarely knowing much better, were obliged to sign up to these international experts' primary mission of price stability.[56] This was structurally exactly as Anne-Marie Slaughter had imagined it; politically, the outcome was anything but. As Federal Reserve Chairman Alan Greenspan remarked, "[a] central bank in a democratic society is a magnet for many of the tensions that such a society confronts."[57] And yet for all that they now found themselves at the heart of democratic society in this way, *independent* central banks were never intended to be loci of democratic deliberation: quite the opposite in fact.

When the European Central Bank opened its doors in 1999, the very idea of a single, continent-wide central bank was so ambitious that its inauguration even prompted Milton Friedman to write to one of the new members of the ECB's board, former Bundesbank board member Otmar Issing, congratulating him on his appointment to an "impossible job" and predicting the collapse of the whole endeavor within five years. But against the odds Issing and his colleagues succeeded spectacularly at getting both the bank and the euro in place in time for its January 1, 1999, launch. And they did so thanks in no small part to a level of institutional discipline that Friedman can only have admired.[58] What they achieved was in many ways a double first: a banking structure that was not only institutionally transnational in scale, but also almost uniquely immune to the special pleading of politicians and electorates. "I am polite," the first ECB president, Wim Duisenberg, later said, in response to calls from eurozone ministers for him to change policy in a slowdown: "You might say, I hear but I don't listen."[59] A UK Treasury official was even more blunt: "Parliament is incapable of exercising its financial responsibilities: we must do it for them."

The repetition of this new fiscal liturgy soon became a common refrain. In Canada, where the economy wobbled in the mid 1990s after the Mexican financial crisis of 1994, the Canadian government found itself articulating the need to strengthen its "credibility" before the international markets. Mulroney's government promised deep cuts in its federal spending, not to please its own electorate but to curry favor with the markets. This gave rise to further domestic retrenchment when the Finance Ministry, under Paul Martin, then moved to shore up its own influence within the government as if it took its cues from the banks, not the parliamentary benches.[60] What central bankers began, then, it often fell to the more economically literate politicians, namely finance ministers, to finish, as with Paul Martin in Canada or Gordon Brown in Britain.

To the extent that politicians too had learned to think of their public not as citizens but as consumers, then this was because doing so accorded with the general philosophy that politics should be less "political" and because consumption was the one thing that governments committed (not least by their newly independent central banks) to a low inflationary, tight-spending regime needed to promote. Of course, since the new tight-money orthodoxy meant that the national pump was rarely being primed anywhere anymore, governments needed to entice the horses to pull buckets up instead. And it was *this* that led the likes of Clinton, Blair, and Schröder to shift their gaze, in the mid–late 1990s, from the market *back* to the societies in which markets must ultimately be embedded, and to bring about a wholesale reform of the welfare system in which they believed their constituents' hooves were ensnared.

Social Responsibility

Nowhere were the consequences of the new thinking in government more dramatic than in the transformation of the Western welfare state that took place during these years. Of course, there had always been variations in the nature of welfare provision and its funding. Basic differences existed still between the liberal model of means-tested welfare in the US, UK, and Canada; the conservative corporatist approach in which social insurance schemes predominated in countries like Germany, Italy, Austria, and the Netherlands; and the social democratic model of universal coverage typified by Scandinavia. But in the 1990s welfare states were subjected to such a concerted and common assault that they would all, if at different speeds and in different ways, soon be heading in the same direction.[61]

The first country to make the move here was America. After their victory in the midterms, and with Newt Gingrich safely ensconced as the new Speaker of the House, the Republicans (or more precisely that "phalanx" of intellectuals under Gingrich who were the driving force of the Contract with America movement) had made welfare reform central to their mission to overhaul the federal government: which is to say they sought to devolve power away from the federal government in Washington toward the states (most of which were run, at this point, by Republican governors).[62] For several months Clinton had resisted this, refusing to sign a great many of the Republicans' block grant requests. Then in 1996, just as his reelection campaign was about to get started in earnest, he gave in, signing what was more or less the Republicans' standing plan for welfare reform: the Personal Responsibility and Work Opportunity Reconciliation Act (PRWORA).

Clinton's liberal advisers were aghast. Job seekers would henceforth be enrolled into mandatory programs where before they might have been entitled to benefits. This was a profound change not simply in the mechanism of welfare provision but in its entire purpose. The emphasis was no longer on giving people the means to subsist outside of the labor market for short periods, or on trying to fix the fact that some of them became trapped in the system—usually against their will. Instead it was about ensuring their maximum participation in it. The new euphemism for all this—"workforce activation"—said it all.

The reasoning here was that the generosity of benefits was to be reduced to such a point that recipients would be "willing" to take part-time, or even substandard jobs on pain of losing their benefits altogether. Aid to Families with Dependent Children (AFDC) was cut back; means testing was tightened (immigrants found it harder to access social services as a result, while poor families had to demonstrate they were even poorer so as to keep accessing food stamps). To ensure compliance, individual states were required to cut their welfare rolls by 50 percent by the year 2002 or they too would be penalized.[63] States varied in how they responded: Minnesota offered relatively generous cash incentives and retraining efforts; Texas and Wisconsin demanded more compliance by welfare recipients and gave them, on the whole, less in return.

This new and distinctly less forgiving welfare landscape was the price of Gingrich's victory over Clinton (and Clinton's victory of triangulation was, in turn, the price of his reelection). A young black mother from Little Rock, Lillie Harden, became the face of the new reform. She stood next to Clinton on the White House lawn as he signed the Welfare Reform Act as "testament" to what incentivization could do for a former self-styled welfare queen. But she died twelve years later after suffering a stroke in 2002, unable to qualify for Medicaid or to afford her monthly prescriptions.[64] Supporters of the new "workfare" politics pointed to the efficiency savings for the federal government (though its total financial outlay for benefits programs was now capped anyway). And as the welfare rolls predictably fell, these same supporters also pointed to the declining numbers of people on welfare: a peculiarly blunt, and in many ways insensitive, metric by which to measure success, but one that now became fetishized, like so many other quantitative indicators, and stripped of all the necessary context required to understand it.

The most immediate consequence of this successful overhaul of welfare was an increase in the particular forms of precarity that defined the post-1970s-era workforce: of single parenting and part-time jobs, of the difficulty of returning to work after incarceration (a particular problem for America's black men). That it did this while purporting to be a demonstration of how "competition-based" social policy could best meet modern social needs was doubly pernicious, yet explicable to the extent that the new workfare state was characteristic of the times: a transnational policy regime, not unlike central banking, tied not to any one individual state, but to the interests of the dominant classes in each of those states. Hence whether the agents of these changes were the architects of PRWORA in America (1996), or of the dismantling of the universal Canada Assistance Plan and its replacement by the Health and Social Transfer program (1996), or even Tony Abbott's more straight-talking "Work for the Dole" (1998) program in Australia didn't really matter.[65] In every case the direction was a more punitive approach to labor-market management orchestrated by the state on behalf of the interests of corporate capital (which, of course, it now took for its own).

The same year that Abbott made his move in Australia, the Blair government put forward its own "New Deal" (1998) in Britain: a program whose very name aspired to the grandiosity of American reformism in an earlier era. It was almost as if Blair consciously wished to compete with Clinton's overhaul of "welfare as we know it." And yet Blair was actually bolder in many ways, for he sought to give his workfare program a moral spin as well: specifically, the need to "balance" rights and responsibilities in the modern age. Blair wanted to make the new approach to welfare not merely a necessary adjustment to the realities of a globalizing world, but its moral center of gravity as well. So far as Blair saw it, you could still rely on the support of the state in the late twentieth century: but you had to *earn* that support first, which was fine in principle, but tended in practice to mean that you had to be the "right" sort of citizen and to act in the "right" sort of way.

What Blair had really contributed to the new welfare paradigm was not progressive-era secularism so much as a good dose of Victorian-era moralism. In France, by contrast, it was the imperatives of government spending that provided the more pressing justification for welfare reform. The "troubles" that Alain Juppé knew he faced in 1995, upon taking up his appointment as prime minister, revolved around the need to square the circle of high unemployment (and the mass protests this was occasioning on the streets), a government committed to keeping inflation low (which meant also low growth and so *continued* unemployment), and deficit reduction: and this at a moment when welfare spending was higher than ever (registering an accumulated deficit that would reach 300 billion francs by 1997).[66]

Juppé was nothing if not a superlative technocrat, however, and he attacked this nearly impossible task with relish, reforming welfare and cutting government spending drastically. The result was even more protests, the largest seen on the streets of France since May 1968, and before long a major political crisis. Not yet as firmly ensconced in the office of the

443

presidency as he might like to be, this had Chirac running scared: hence, the snap election he called to try to resolve the situation. Juppé was, as Chirac knew he would be, unceremoniously thrown out of office. But Chirac himself survived (albeit with the tightest mandate in a century). The real surprise was that it was the newly elected socialists who then decided to finish what Juppé had started.

But if incoming socialist prime minister Lionel Jospin reluctantly learned to ape the doublespeak that his counterparts in Britain and America had been perfecting—he spoke of *réalisme de gauche* (left realism) and "competitiveness within a context of social justice and equality"— French socialists nonetheless took themselves to represent a distinct alternative, within Europe, to the dominant Anglo-German axis of antilabor reforms.[67] Certainly the French set greater store by the need to regulate market functions than did the British or the Germans: Jospin's most progressive move was to increase the *contribution sociale généralisée*, a tax on an individual's global wealth, including property and assets, from 3.4 to 7.5 percent, raising the effective burden of tax for the rich most of all.[68] But the socialists still felt it necessary to point out that France was to be "a society of work, not charity." The public dividing line really had moved, if not in the way that Alan Blinder had surmised. Accordingly they cut taxes, got the unions to accept a moderate pay deal, and increased the sale of state assets.[69] France Telecom was partially sold off in 1997, to handpicked domestic investors like Bouygues, and to foreign telecoms operators like Deutsche Telekom and Sprint.

Again, there were limits to how far the French were prepared to go in the Anglo-American direction. Air France, when needed, was bailed out. Électricité de France and Gaz de France workers retained their public service employment status, with public service conditions imposed by the state on those private providers who were allowed to compete in power provision. And the reduction of the working week did seem to bring some return of productivity back to the economy, despite widely voiced howls of consternation from the right. But welfare provision would henceforth become substantially more punitive, less universal, and officially less desirable than it had been before. In France, then, a quid pro quo had taken shape: the government had given up on state ownership and control of basic services (one or two flagships aside) but it still wished to retain an influence over the operations of the market and its impact upon the lives of its citizens.[70] As any businessman could have told the French government, however, when you are selling your own stake in something, you are not retaining control, you are giving it up. The result,

in France, would be a distinctly sluggish economy and disgruntled workforce for some time to come.

Even as national circumstances differed, the challenges confronting the
Western world's welfare states had certain basic features in common in
the 1990s: aging populations, radically transformed labor markets, and the
entry of women into the workplace had all transformed the calculus that
welfare provision relied on. The Scandinavian countries, where promises
of universal coverage and social protection were backed up by acceptance
of high rates of taxation, adapted most easily.

In Sweden, in the wake of the country's financial crisis and recession
during the early part of the decade, there was a greater social constituency
for cutting back on certain of these guarantees. Moves were made to
lower salary replacement rates for the sick from 90 to 75 percent, for
example, in an effort—probably needed, since Sweden was spending
roughly twice any other European country on sick pay—to incentivize
people to go back to work. But unlike in America it made sure that
those being nudged back into the labor force were supported, rather than
simply barked at, through education and training and efforts to make
sure there were better-paying jobs than the part-time "burger flipping"
bonanza unleashed in the United States. This was not uncontroversial in
Sweden: the left in particular decried the attack on the traditional commitment to social protection. But as was the hallmark of the left at this
moment, it turned out they had nothing better to offer, not least since
the costs of Sweden's fiscal consolidation program were disproportionately
paid for by the wealthy (the top fifth of income earners meeting 43
percent of the costs, the bottom fifth just 11 percent).[71]

Norway, by contrast, largely carried on as before, at least for now—
boosted by its safety blanket of oil receipts from the North Sea and the
introduction (in 1990) of a Sovereign Wealth Fund investing a percentage
of the country's oil receipts abroad, which was by now bringing in its
own healthy return (in stark contrast to UK oil receipts during the decade). But all the Scandinavian countries also benefited, Denmark and
Finland included, by the fact that they already had service-oriented
economies with—and this was more important than oil—high levels of
female participation in the labor force. They did not need to be sold a
line about the need to be flexible since they were already juggling work
and family with the support of the state. Labor conditions were such that
people did not mind working later in life, and child support policies
meant that women did not leave the labor force earlier (the norm in

more liberal countries was that they dropped out after having children). The opposite was the case in countries like Italy and Spain, where traditional gender roles often forced women to choose between a family and a career in the first place, and where the young were routinely housed by their parents well into their forties.

Germany was caught somewhere between the continental and, increasingly, the Anglo-American neoliberal approach. Farsighted organizations like the Friedrich Ebert Stiftung proposed a "new German model" for the twenty-first century, but for most of the 1990s Germany was still dealing with the aftermath of reunification and the challenges not of democratization in the East so much as of liberalization from the West. After reunification social expenditure in Eastern Germany had rocketed, paid for mainly by West Germany in order to manage the transition (it was still paying for a third of the East's consumption and investment in 1996). If this was a considerable cost, it had to be borne in mind that in many senses the welfare state had "enabled" German reunification to proceed successfully. That did not make it any less controversial. Graffiti declaring "I want my wall back" began to spring up in Berlin.[72]

The Wall was not going back up, of course, but it was not until the two German systems had begun to merge more fully, in the mid 1990s, that the idea of reforming the welfare state was even feasible. Throughout the late Kohl years the German system had remained more universalist in approach, despite being steadily overwhelmed by the fallout from reunification, by the arrival of mass immigration and low-cost competition from Eastern Europe, and by a sharp growth in unemployment. But if Kohl had no idea which way to turn in the face of this onslaught and his government's dwindling coffers, the man who had now replaced him, Gerhard Schröder, certainly did. In 2002, after a decade of rising unemployment, and with 4.2 million unemployed, Germany finally gave in to the need for radical overhaul of its employment system with the controversial Hartz labor reforms introduced by the Schröder government in 2002.

It was a "watershed" moment for Germany, as one newspaper put it. In truth given that Germany was now finishing a process that America had begun, the implications were even broader in scope. The Hartz reforms were practically a new welfare state by committee: the most important welfare reform in Germany since the war. Chaired by the Volkswagen employment director who gave the reforms his name, Peter Hartz, the reforms laid out the, by now, classic workfare strategy: job centers and welfare offices were merged; the sick and the unemployed were rolled into databases (sixteen-page questionnaires were sent out to 3.8 million households); government departments then got to work on addressing the numbers (sometimes forgetting there were people behind them).[73]

A second battle soon erupted for Hartz, however, this time at his own company of Volkswagen. By 2004, Volkswagen was mired in a protracted dispute with IG Metall, the metalworkers' union representing the major-ity of Germany's manual workers. It was the latest in a series of confron-tations sparked by restless manufacturers (Opel, Daimler Chrysler, Siemens, and now VW) threatening either to lower wages, increase hours, or cut jobs altogether and move operations to the East. Part of the reason Ger-man cars were so expensive was precisely that their employment costs were so high: it made the companies proud and tightly welded affairs, and their cars reflected this. Hartz—like most managers—was concerned about falling profitability and adamant this could not continue, and the resolution he engineered at VW ultimately came to stand, a little like his reforms, as a watershed moment in the history of the German economy.[74]

With hindsight what Hartz achieved was a mixed victory on both fronts. VW survived, its workers' wages were not cut, and German unions (who represented the highest-earning employees anywhere) came to learn that the world had changed around them: that it had become a much more competitive place. Nationally, Hartz's reforms were also successful in freeing up the labor market, lowering unemployment, and in reducing benefit claimants. But the fact that "Hartz" became a pejorative adjective for the remaining long-term unemployed—like R'miste in France and Chav in Britain—suggested that the reforms placed the burden of ad-justment squarely on the backs of the poor. Over time the Hartz reforms would contribute to rising inequality in Germany. They even drove one activist to embark on a hunger strike.[75]

If Germany had no choice but to reform its welfare system, Peter Hartz's struggles were a reminder that there were still choices regarding how countries went about doing so. In Italy, Berlusconi aside, a long overdue tightening of the rules was carried out, cutting early pensions that were part of a bloated public sector bill and the product of patron-age as much as equity or good sense, and making it harder for self-employed workers to skirt the tax system. Similarly, in Holland, the welfare picture was "adjusted" by means of tax cuts targeted at ordinary wage earners (this had the additional virtue of making Dutch workers more willing to moderate their demands for increased wages, thereby maintaining employment in a tight labor market).[76] Despite Mulroney's efforts to tilt his country southward, Canada also managed to find room for a more progressive slant to its welfare overhaul: old age pensions for the relatively affluent were cut back in order to free up more money for the poorest pensioners.[77]

Ultimately those countries that saw the biggest changes were the southern European nations. This was because, for much of the 1990s, they were desperately rallying their economies in an effort to meet the EU's Stability and Growth Pact (SGP) criteria for membership in the eurozone. Countries like Greece, Italy, and Spain still relied heavily on the role of the family and had set huge store (and coming expense) by generous pension provisions to accommodate it. That had to change. "Baby pensions" for early public service retirees were accordingly abolished and social security and labor market rules were tightened in Italy. In Spain, where recession saw unemployment leap to a record 25 percent, governments and employees signed off on the Toledo pact, liberalizing the labor market and creating an "explosion" of temporary and revolving job contracts.[78]

As in Germany, in Spain the problem of unemployment was solved, but scarcely the problem of job insecurity. Indeed, the reforms would work to casualize the Spanish labor force over the years to come, pushing its youngest workers out into the world in search of more solid careers. By contrast the hard landing from welfare largesse to workfarist discipline was most effectively softened in Denmark. Unemployment there fell from 8.1 percent in 1994 to 5.6 percent in 2003—not dramatically, but consistently and without the need for the long arm of the state to interfere, à la Hartz. Most of this growth was in the private sector, but it was achieved, by careful managing—counseling, training, and educational initiatives were developed along with job rotation policies—and without undermining a more egalitarian wage structure in society at large.[79] For their part, Eastern and central European countries were of course transitioning from universal yet poor quality provision under communism. Accordingly they mixed and matched a little from the other European models (while generally, along with Ireland and Luxembourg, keeping their social spending quite low).

Some of these individual policy reforms were successful; many more were not. But in an environment of large-scale change to longstanding social and political assumptions, the authors of the tome *Reinventing Government: How the Entrepreneurial Spirit Is Transforming the Public Sector* had it just about right. Welfare was no longer about the collective provision of individual needs; it was about reshaping private incentives, forcibly if need be, to reduce collective costs. At the same time, employment in the West—for all that the "new economy" rhetoric framed itself as the leading edge of capitalist development—was, if anything, even more precarious than it had been just a few decades before. This was because politicians were now thinking less about how to create the conditions for mass employment, and more about how to maintain the rate of profit while managing the *un*employment that came with this. This was a particular problem for the young, as Spanish youth could attest. But older workers were also being forced out of the labor market amid all this flexibilization and found themselves struggling—since they were increasingly deemed "too old" to rejoin it—to get by within the terms of the new social contract.

Before the millennium was out and in response to the challenges of high unemployment, low growth, and economic restructuring, the Western democracies had, in their different ways, not only redesigned their economic base but adapted their institutional shape and structure—and possibly even their purpose—to match. The reigning liberal democratic order had been transposed from a system of public demand management, orchestrated through the institutions of mass democracy, to one of private consumption management, orchestrated through the market.[80] As Clinton's and Schröder's economic reforms underscored, it was business and the financial elites who exerted the greatest influence on the system now, and who best articulated the needs that politicians felt compelled to respond to. What it meant to be a citizen was changing.[81]

The New Citizens

The trend to declining popular participation in public life was observable beyond the overtly political sphere. What was more it could be seen at all ages, be it the decline of Boys' Brigade members in Scotland or of the old *Centro Primo Maggio* in Verona province—a communist party social club, which transformed itself first into a modern social center, and then into a sports club.[82] But where had people gone, if they weren't any longer members of political parties, or unions, or social clubs? Were they all now, as the American sociologist Robert Putnam famously observed in his 1995 essay (and later bestselling book), simply "bowling alone"? In fact, people had not vacated the public realm; but they were thinking and acting as public citizens differently: more individually, more voluntaristically. And the result was a notable decline in *civic* engagement.

The evidence was certainly striking: since 1973 the number of Americans who had, in the last year, "attended a public meeting on town or school affairs" had fallen by a third.[83] As Putnam concluded, "Americans' direct engagement in politics and government has fallen steadily and sharply over the last generation."[84] But people more generally were not joining sports clubs, or literary societies, or helping out at their local school as much as they used to do. Instead they were doing a shift at the local soup kitchen or Restaurants du Coeur (founded across France's major cities in the mid 1980s by none other than failed presidential candidate "Coluche"). One study estimated the total voluntary labor time devoted to these charitable works in France at 700,000 hours a year in 1990, or equivalent to 3.4 percent of all paid jobs.[85]

In a curious return of the international scene to domestic shores, these were often inspired by a distinctly humanitarian passion rather than a political ethic, and so it is little surprise they should often have been overseen by the Red Cross or Oxfam. And while these programs filled in for the civic engagement of earlier times, they did not endow a specific solidarity or sense of community that true civic engagement did. Where people *were* coming together now, it was in passive, nonideological organizations—of the sort that brings football fans into a common identity, but one that falls short of community—and in small private gatherings which, as the sociologist Robert Wuthnow demonstrated, may not be public gatherings so much as "occasions for individuals to focus on themselves in the presence of others."[86] Trust was on the decline; people had largely stopped meeting socially with their neighbors. More people asked dog walkers to take out their pets; eventually they would entrust Alexa to look after the dog at home.

Citizens were also encouraged in their retreat from civic engagement by the private sector, which sought to offer them a commercialized form of citizenship in place of the political one they were losing. Public institutions were given over to market providers who promised to offer a better variety of services for less money. Citizens were sold the pleasures of personalized entertainment and leisure time, with the underlying promise of taking control over their lives at home as well as at work. But they were also pushed into it, in a way that Putnam never really considered—he speculated that the transferral of women into the workplace might be the primary driver, which a glance at Scandinavia would have confirmed could not be the case—by the removal of welfare provision, public services, and even public spaces, and by the commercialization of all three. Whether it was the Aid to Families with Dependent

450

Children checks that the Contract with America had banished, or the more general decrease in public provision in Europe and Australia (where Howard, for all his foresight on gun control, was now leading the charge), the decline of public institutions combined with the lure of private freedoms encouraged a sense that one was better off by doing things oneself.

But one wasn't and what was more, one couldn't. Britain's (infamous) Child Support Agency, launched by the Conservative government in 1993, was intended to ensure that fathers paid the maintenance required of them by law after divorce. But given the mandate of maximizing returns to the Department for Work and Pensions it became little more than an aggressive debt-collecting agency on behalf of the state as much as their former partners.[87] The more that the life of work was subcontracted and flexibilized, the less recourse to social protections citizens now had. Their growing invocation of individual rights in response likewise combined to leave them adrift of society, and its collective obligations, at large. Was it any wonder that people felt estranged?

And yet citizens did have a special role to play in the new democratic order: because among the few tangible ways citizens still had of shaping their wider circumstances, by far the most effective was to draw upon personal credit. Resorting to the market to leverage what scant forms of political equality could be found there had long been a necessary tactic for African Americans and for minority groups more generally. Credit now made this tactic available for whites and the more recently disenfranchised lower middle classes in particular. It worked just as well for the paying of maintenance demands as it did for ensuring that one's house was equipped with the latest technology. Thus, at a time when average incomes were stagnating or falling (for all that the US economy grew by 3 percent as a whole in 1993, the income of median families fell that year by 1 percent) credit was for many becoming one of life's essentials.[88]

But the function of credit was not just to satisfy individuals' wants such as we have seen. Credit granted to the individual had two important public functions as well. First, by borrowing on credit cards, or through taking up mortgages so as to free up income for other things, individuals were—in the broadest sense—subsidizing governments as *they* sought to cut back on funding for basic public service provision. Second, the collective accumulation of private debt that this amounted to was a solution to the primary economic problem of anti-inflationary policies (the principal solution that had been manufactured by Western democracies to the crises of the 1970s)—namely the problem of low consumer demand. It was its own form of stimulus (as irreversible and as "one-off" in its way as was the rural–urban transition in the immediate postwar period).

Since rising wages were largely a thing of the past in the post–Cold War economy, the "political" task of citizens was no longer to moderate their wage demands while keeping up consumption, but to keep spending money by agreeing to hold higher levels of private debt. The government's job, meanwhile, was to assist them in this and to assist the providers of credit in supplying their citizens with this capacity. The status (and to some extent, fate) of citizenship was thus hitched to the wider state of the economy. Moreover, it positioned personal needs and desires to take over as the engine room of continued growth in the financial sector in the 1990s (large levels of unsecured debt requiring elaborate systems of risk deferral and debt management to sustain them, in turn creating new opportunities for financial innovation). At first glance, what wasn't to like?

"Finance is fun," declared an ad for a new Internet start-up in the *New York Times* in 1999. But the real point was that finance and the market were also increasingly unavoidable. There was thus a certain unintended irony in management theorist Charles Handy's 1994 declaration that "We are all in business these days." For indeed, by 1995, individuals had invested $100 billion in the US stock market. Yet at the same time, more and more people dipped into their saving and pensions income to finance their lifestyles in the present.[89] By such means citizens kept demand in the economy going and they helped pay for the public services that governments now no longer wished to. But they were also storing up problems for themselves, and others, further down the line.

In no small part because of these policies, household debt had reached just over 97 percent of disposable income by the end of the millennium. If this was almost unthinkable even just a decade before, it was indicative not only of a newly financialized basis of day-to-day life, but of a new attitude to risk that had developed in its wake. Sociologists now wrote tracts about the "Risk Society" and the mantra of cost-benefit analysis permeated society at large: hospitals, schools, and local governments alike.[90] Risk could not be avoided in a modern technologically advanced society, but it could be managed. Of course there was evidence to the contrary: crises such as foot and mouth disease in Europe and the 1995 heat wave that left 739 dead in Chicago brought that home, primarily at the expense of trust in central government. The collapse of Barings Bank in 1995 and the Shell Brent Spar disaster likewise underscored the need to manage the escalation of risk in the corporate sector as well.[91]

On a more day-to-day level, to be at one with the management of risk was a way to reestablish the appearance of control in an increasingly fast-moving and fraught society. "Risk" was not an unwanted externality to be avoided but a basic property of most things: food at the supermarket was fresher but it might sell out unless you got there early enough; electronic goods *would* break down eventually, so people stopped planning on having them for long. To approach life not as a series of barriers to be overcome (getting the right education, putting money aside for a rainy day) but as a constant dynamic of risks and contingencies to be managed, was nothing if not a profound generational change. It made it apparent that a great many Western citizens were not just prepared but eager to take chances in life: to indebt themselves down the line to take advantage of the here and now.

Others found themselves no less swamped by all the changes. This registered most strongly of all in that central social institution: the family. The family, as Margaret Thatcher knew, was a political institution as well. As historians have begun to show, the location of the family within the wider political landscape of states, civil societies, the individual, and the market—and the different sinews that one political regime may forge (or break) between them, relative to another—is central to understanding the wider fabric of political life. In the case of the Western democracies in the post–Cold War era a number of changes had taken place.

First, the family had become a mediating institution between states (and their variously generous welfare provisions) and individuals, who might sometimes seek to flee the family in the name of greater freedoms—a new career, a new life—elsewhere, but who at other times had to retreat into it to survive (especially in the southern European states during their years of high unemployment). Second, the family had become less of a "productive" unit within capitalism itself: something which freed up labor for higher-value production elsewhere, but which equally freed the family from one of its basic social functions: the reproduction of the labor force. Fertility rates duly dropped, increasing the pressure on welfare states. Third, the moral role of the family—particularly in Christian democratic societies—changed, as more secular (and it might be added less patriarchal) mores began to take over.

The transformation of family life, and gender relations, was perhaps most dramatic in Spain (and the other southern Mediterranean countries).

In 1970, 71 percent of people over sixty-five lived with a member of their family; by 1992 only 32 percent did. Domestic gender relations were changing almost as fast, and not everyone was inclined to think this a good thing. In 1997 a sixty-year-old Andalusian woman, Ana Orantes, became a cause célèbre after she described, in a widely viewed documentary interview, how despite her being regularly beaten by her husband, the Spanish courts had ruled they should remain living together. The Spanish public took pity and held Orantes up as representative of the changes society still needed to make. A few days later her husband, by contrast, took revenge: tying her to a chair and setting her alight.[92]

There were substantial variations between countries in the upheaval to which family life was subjected. For reasons both of welfare and gender norms (among other things), Ana Orantes would not have suffered the same fate in Bergen in the 1990s, had she married an abusive husband there. A slightly more common feature, however, was the shifting function and meaning attached to the physical space of the family home. The availability of credit fuels commodification and when governments come to rely upon credit to sustain their national economic growth then homes are more likely to be turned into assets, and duly traded as an element of domestic and public economics alike. Accordingly, homes stopped being the sanctuary that people strove to "keep" (this may not have unduly worried many women who were usually expected to do the keeping) and instead became collateralized assets: the savings that once provided security for a rainy day now willingly "exposed" to secure a better "return." A housing boom beckoned.

With safety nets removed and nothing but their own appetite and capacity for work to keep them in house and home, people were now required to adjust themselves to the idea that risk was a constant presence in daily life. They responded, in due course, by reinserting themselves into a different public domain. The very last years of the decade thus saw the first, tentative openings of a new social media universe, whose primary purpose was to capitalize on this: the lost friends site SixDegrees .com went online in 1997 and Craigslist was incorporated in 1999. That was soon followed by AOL's Instant Messenger. By the end of the millennium there were still only 100 million people worldwide with access to the Internet. But Friendster (2002), MySpace (2003), and Facebook (2004) all followed as the Internet both exploded and adapted itself to the age of social media. The UK-based Friends Reunited had 3,000 members in the year 2000; a year later it had 2.5 million. The Internet was no longer just for work. For a brief moment the new dot-coms seemed to be the very locus of Western modernity and its rapidly re-forming social dependencies.

Socializing the self now became a way of life for many, with people uploading personal profiles and showcasing professional networks, or writing weblogs for others to read about one's skill in juggling the new work–life balance. "We are witnessing an erosion not only of privacy but of the sense that privacy of the individual is important," as one technology writer rather more durably observed.[93] But so too, for many more, did somewhat older concerns return as well: not least the threat of losing one's job amid all this remaking of the self and society. Of course, such anxieties could also be managed, and ideally by individuals as well: sales of antidepressant drugs began to rise rapidly at the end of the decade. Had people realized how much firms were also taking out of their pension funds to reinvest in the stock market (one study of S&P 500 companies identified a funding shortfall in their employees' pension entitlements of as much as $323 billion); had they seen, more broadly, that the money saved from the welfare they were losing was fueling a new economy bubble whose "shortfalls" would soon become further individualized losses, they might have ordered something stronger.[94] As it was, the 1990s were not on the whole a time for slowing down, or for holding back.

The Transformation of the Public Sphere

The great convergence of markets and societies that the liberal democracies had so roundly celebrated at the start of the decade was on its way to becoming a great divergence of peoples by the end. Inequality within nations was rising as the prosperity gains of the decade went primarily toward the rich, especially those who owned the largest companies or held shares in them, or those who owned the land whose value was rising as others sought to invest in bricks and mortar. This end of society was catered to by celebrity architects like Richard Rogers and I. M. Pei, who built towering, curvaceous temples to wealth, redefining the urban landscape and reinforcing the trend to rising property prices in the process. Meanwhile welfare retrenchment and the ongoing reskilling of the economy made it hard for working-class citizens, usually in rural or second-tier cities (in the French littoral, the British North, the German South, or the American Midwest) to adapt to the pace of change. It also made it harder for them to afford its consequences, let alone the luxuries of life.

In one small, but revealing, indication of this emergent twin-track economy the late 1990s saw both the most *expensive* film (the $200 million *Titanic*) and one of the most successful *low-budget* films (the $60,000 *The Blair Witch Project*) ever produced. Both became box office hits. But it was *The Blair Witch Project* that spoke most directly to the era's concerns. When the film's producers manufactured evidence of its central premise online to create a fuller sense of "realism," the matter of what was, and was not, trustworthy information in a networked world was broken wide open. The "raw, unpolished menace" of *Blair Witch* was a small, but early crack in the façade of public knowledge.[95] But it wasn't just what was happening to information. The basic fabric of society was changing as well.

The fact that inequality was rising was one thing; but the way that this transformation was increasingly embedded in the landscape of modern (especially urban) life was another thing altogether. Public spheres are not inherently democratic, nor are the public spaces upon which they may be built (as any glance at the vast pomposity of fascist architecture of the 1930s will attest). But good public spheres and functioning public spaces are critical to democracy and they require constant nurture and renewal. However, the nature and purpose of public space was up for grabs in the post–Cold War years.

Already by the middle of the decade the signs did not look good. In 1995 the French film *La Haine* grittily chronicled a day in the lives of three French teenagers from the *banlieues* of Paris in the aftermath of a riot. The film was released after a real wave of violence that afflicted the French capital in one of its darkest years: a gas bomb went off on the RER line at the Saint-Michel Métro station, killing eight people and injuring over sixty; it was followed, three weeks later, by another bomb planted at the Arc de Triomphe and a wave of further bomb threats followed. The atmosphere was clouded too by the austerity measures Alain Juppé had introduced that year. "I can remember flying to Manchester from Paris on Christmas Eve that year," recalled a British correspondent, "leaving behind an almost empty airport, and a morose country. It was one of the few times that I have left Paris feeling glad to be out of it."[96]

But above all the atmosphere in France was suffused with the sense of a barely contained anger and alienation that was captured in pitch-perfect monotone by *La Haine*'s improbably young director, Mathieu Kassovitz. The film brought home to an older, less cognizant generation the reality of France's own urban crisis: the housing projects and estates pushed—like their occupants—to the edge of the city.[97] Just two years before a black youth, Makomé M'Bowolé, really had been shot in the head under police custody (an act referenced in the film's dramatic finale). The police even had a euphemism for such "slip-ups": they called them *bavures* (blunders). Juppé, a little humbled, screened a private viewing for his cabinet. Predictably, Jean-Marie Le Pen called for "yobs" like those in the film to be "sent to jail."[98]

That did little to quell the unrest—but then this was not just a French problem alone. The following year, the British film *Trainspotting*, based on an Irvine Welsh novel, was released, portraying the travails of a Scottish underclass excluded from everywhere they went, be it parks or public urinals, spaces they instead put to inventive uses. The film's eponymous (and deeply ironic) tagline "choose life" soon became a favorite put-down for Generation X-ers everywhere. In America, the indie film renaissance that was partly inspired by the same post–Cold War climate of *ennui* proved less edgy than its European counterpart, and was more likely to offer commentary on middle-class suburban futility, as in films like *American Beauty* (1999) or the prescient reality-TV satire *The Truman Show* (1998). But the pulse it touched was the same: amidst a constant barrage of change the future seemed increasingly out of focus.

A common thrust to most of these films was that people were merely *adapting* to the great social changes of the time, rather than seeking to challenge them. That was echoed in the dominant artistic trends of the time as well: as Seattle grunge rockers Nirvana had it, the point was just to "come as you are." This was "kind of confusing I guess," Kurt Cobain proffered as an explanation for the lyrics to their breakthrough hit. But its celebration of the self made it an instinctively clear critique of the past all the same. In terms of popular culture more broadly there was a sense of being profoundly "post" something—the Cold War usually—and this dominated the aesthetic and creative imagination. This merely intensified the lack of clarity about the future.

Literary and cultural critics had long been post- many things, of course (poststructuralism, post-Marxism, postmodernism) and the litany of the prefixed suffix would continue for years to come (postsecular, posttruth and so on). But the high art that most people noticed in the post–Cold War era—the unmade beds and surgically halved bovines of Young British Artists (YBAs) like Tracey Emin, Damien Hirst, and Sarah Lucas, or Marc Quinn's sculptures made from his own frozen blood—was consistently geared toward shock, material fetishism, and money. The work of many of these artists was most radical when it focused, as did the likes of American Cindy Sherman, on social crises like the AIDS epidemic (a number of artists, including Keith Haring and Robert Mapplethorpe, themselves died of AIDS in the 1990s).

But it was also often conservative, as with its fascination for "preserving" items (sometimes literally, in formaldehyde) and for documenting change rather than challenging social structures.[99] This wasn't helped in the United States by conservative members of Congress lobbying for the National Endowment of the Arts budget to be cut for its support of sometimes challenging works, as well as for the introduction of a "decency clause." New York "shouldn't have to pay for sick stuff," as then Mayor Giuliani insisted when the YBAs, and especially Chris Ofili's elephant dung, crashed into town with their artistic shock and awe in 1999.[100]

But the curiously indefinable quality to art during the decade—what it was "about"—was again often just this sense of there being so many social and cultural changes one needed to get the measure of. It wasn't just that artistic media were changing, with the embrace of installation and video, digital technology, or the trope of viewer participation pioneered by French artist Dominique Gonzalez-Foerster. Like everything else, the art world and its referents were becoming more global too: Chinese, African, Thai, Indian artists, all were increasingly being exhibited in their own right as Western public art began to be challenged from without.[101] The art friezes and biennales were becoming more popular than ever at the very moment when they were less clear what they were about—other than "voice" and "viewpoint." That was probably precisely why art had become so popular again. Art, like the social life it sought to represent, was not sure where it was heading.

Not everyone was so disoriented, however. Public space in particular was not being abandoned, so much as reinvented in accordance with the logic of the market. After several decades of the sort of urban decline that lay behind the suffocated lives of those living in London's high-rises or Los Angeles's Skid Row, the increase in economic fortunes of the Western democracies during the 1990s was a cue not only for the rapidly rising prices fetched by artworks on the auction block, but for municipal authorities to set about rebuilding the urban landscapes in whose cracked surfaces artist's studios cropped up on a good day, alongside muggings on a bad one.

In the 1990s the redevelopment of urban space became the new municipal obsession everywhere from Sydney to Vancouver to Copenhagen.

Sometimes, as in Copenhagen, these makeovers were successful. On visiting Spain, the American urban critic Sharon Zukin was prompted to observe: "Even a brief visit to Barcelona confirms the observation that public space is still important. . . . Public space is not only a visible means of integrating social diversity. It is also what tourists and visitors see of the city; it is the living room of the young, the old, and the poor."[102] But as Zukin was all too aware, what public space was "for" depended on who controlled it. And that now increasingly being private capital, the new mantra of "culture-led redevelopment" was often little more than a euphemism for corporate reinvestment.

Western Sydney was given a much-needed overhaul in the 1990s as the authorities sought to stake a claim for "global city" status prior to the Olympics. But this also entailed its public services being privatized to the point where, as one planner put it, "public space has now largely become a managed thoroughfare to the private domain."[103] In somewhere like Vancouver's gas lamp district, this had the effect of planting fronds of luxuriant wealth deliberately where they would hang over the grit of poverty at their feet. Gentrification of this sort was the decade's counterpart to the "white flight" from inner-city areas in the 1970s and 1980s: and frequently it built on the same abandoned spaces. Younger professionals now moved back *into* the cities, resurrecting old industrial buildings and setting up coffee shops on the corner, but still usually not mixing with the locals.

The rising property prices that ultimately provided this impetus to gentrification transformed urban space in another way too, for they drove main streets and small businesses back out the other way: to airless shopping malls and "out-of-town" superstores, where, as Joan Didion memorably chronicled, the enforced air-conditioning invariably brought on in its visitors "an aqueous suspension: not only of light, but of judgment."[104] If property prices were the motor here, though, it was government policies that imparted the direction of travel. Be it Giuliani in New York or former Prime Minister Pierre Mauroy, now installed as the Mayor of Lille in France, government policy of the era was a near constant reminder of just whose interests the new urban politics was serving. "As the nation divides," remarked two concerned planners in the wake of the Rodney King riots of 1992, "it reduces its capacity to address the fundamental requirements of national aspirations for a just and economically equitable society."[105]

That was planning-speak for the racial and class-based disenfranchisement that urban raconteurs like Los Angelino Mike Davis had been painstakingly documenting since the 1980s. Talk of *The Death and Life of Great American Cities* had been a constant concern since at least 1981, when the influential writer and activist Jane Jacobs published her book of the same name. But the new urban fall, as depicted by the Marxist critic Mike Davis, was different. It was orchestrated for one: Los Angeles standing in as the paradigmatic case for any number of cities where the root causes of homelessness were overlooked in preference for the quicker installation of "bus benches" that ensured no tired tramp might disruptively curl up and sleep, and where the relocation of the wealthy to high-wildfire-risk suburbs took underfunded fire services with them (leaving the poorer areas of downtown Los Angeles devoid of adequate coverage). There was little sense of public common ground to be seen here.

The more radically minded saw in all this nothing less than "the annihilation of space by law." They decried the probusiness zoning regulations and the antihomeless ethos that city authorities took such relish in, the American architect Michael Sorkin famously condemning much of the new architecture as *Variations on a Theme Park*; others took New York mayor Rudolph Giuliani to task for using white middle-class disgruntlement as political cover for his veritable cleansing of the city's minority and countercultural currents.[106] In a turn of phrase that would soon receive a wider airing, more and more mayors called for their cities to be "secured" from crime and violence, which in practice usually meant from undesirables, as if both of these things were separate somehow to the flooding of public space with private money. Either way there was less and less genuinely public space from which to sit and view the problem, and less and less funding for those bothered to do so.

Another hard reality, especially for the left, was that the metropolis was no longer "a factory for the production of the common," as radicals like Michael Hardt and Antonio Negri proclaimed. In Eastern Europe, the public spaces whose occupation by the crowds had finally brought communism to its knees lay deserted once again, the people having retreated into the private interior of their own homes. The public squares of Gdańsk, Tallinn, and Warsaw were instead handed over to speculative corporate developments. In Bratislava and Kiev, parks, playgrounds, and even small slices of land between residential projects, the latter once the breathing space of public life under communism, were seized by private interests as well.[107] There was, of course, considerable pent-up demand for a creative infusion into the drab public spaces of the communist era. But much of what was actually built was the product of Western investment banks' own imagining, most proactively of all Dutch Bank ING, which financed large projects by big-name architects in cities like Prague, Warsaw, and Budapest.[108] It was not always aesthetically much more pleasing than the edifices thrown up under communism.

In North America, public space was being no less hastily redesigned according to a capitalist monotone and its scrupulously repetitive features left a rather anemic effect on the user. Corporate plazas sprouted up that looked the same whether they were located in downtown Atlanta or Phoenix or Toronto. They took over in "new cities" like Montpellier in southern France. In Rotterdam, the techniques that Giuliani had pioneered in New York were applied, with a twist, by populist parties seeking legislatively to remove the immigrant communities of the city.[109] Such policies often brought a curious silence to places where trams once clacked and newspaper stands pitched headlines rather than advertising taglines onto the streets (this was even true when those same redevelopments actually featured new tram systems, as in Montpellier). Occasional gems stood out, though, such as Frank Gehry's Guggenheim Museum in Bilbao—giving the formerly struggling city a classic postindustrial makeover, and a more welcome one than Madrid's "thrusting" Torre Picasso, thrown up in the late eighties money and modernization splurge.[110]

Faced with the challenge of rekindling run-down urban environments, municipal planners did all they could to aid the gentrification of formerly derelict districts as well: often plumping for public space "improvement" strategies, as in Newcastle in the UK, or throwing up "magnet" buildings to showcase who the new spaces were for. The thinking here was "build it, and they will come." And a new public architecture quickly took its cue from this, grateful at the beginning of the decade for the funds, but eager by the end to show off the scale of commission it could now command (the search for which increasingly led it to turn its attentions to the oil-rich Arab states and the Far East). Showpiece buildings, individual visions, one-off investments: daring and bold structures were a routine testament by the century's end not only to innovative new construction materials but to a new vision of the role of public architecture in the social life of the city. It was a world away from the mass planning of the postwar era, and even for that matter from the postmodern grandiloquence of public architecture in the 1980s.

As land rents steepened and prices rose it was also increasingly corporate in funding, purpose, and style. The urban redevelopment programs that characterized the decade were usually initiated by self-styled redevelopment authorities (former docklands, as in Dublin and most famously around London's Canary Wharf, were a perennial favorite) to whom were devolved fast-track powers that privileged the corporate milieu. Where major sports facilities were redeveloped they were invariably also now "branded," because that was where the money was. This made sport more expensive, as the cost of securing the quadrennial Olympic Games attests: $66 million for the Barcelona Olympics in 1992, $1.5 billion for Athens in 2004.[111] In due course universities followed suit, leveraging their central location into profitable building works at the expense of their educational mission. In the largest cities, public rights of access were curtailed in favor of statement works of "art." The city stopped being a place where people might meet and mingle and became instead a space where movement and flow to and from work were prioritized (the parlous state of twentieth-century transport systems notwithstanding). The point was not to be exposed to difference, even within the terms of the multiculturalist mantra; the point was simply to live better by consuming more seamlessly.

Of course, there are many things that can color a city and a good number of the changes in urban public life were positive. In Belfast, the cessation of violence that followed the Downing Street Declaration of 1993 *did* provide the opening for a self-consciously "multicultural" urban regeneration (partly underpinned by the British taxpayer): this in the city where police wire had once been strung out across main thoroughfares. In Berlin the substantial tracts of derelict land left behind when the Wall and its security zone were removed were still there by the middle of the decade: "an isolated, undeveloped yawning gap," in the words of one resident.[112] But from 1995 onward, spaces such as the Prachtgleis esplanade bordering the Potsdamer Platz were turned into pleasantly laid-back green escapes. People had not stopped caring for public spaces or enjoying the serendipity of public encounter. They still used public spaces politically, as shown by the Belgians who turned out in public squares across Brussels to protest at the secessionist demands of Flemish and Walloon nationalists, and the Italians who crowded into the Piazza Santa Croce in Florence to stand against terrorism after the Uffizi bombing in 1993.[113]

Partly in response to some of these developments, citizens were also learning to group themselves together to defend the shrinking public realm.[114] It was perhaps inevitable that "local communities" emerged as one of the more proactive sites of resistance to urban redevelopment: nobody else was going to do it for them, after all. But local communities, for all their richness and value—and experimentations with "communicative" forms of planning were one of the signature contributions of the moment—were not quite fully animated publics. They were not representative of society at large either. After all, most Western citizens still lived outside the large urban centers that monopolized political interest and private investment.

The country was thus in some ways "the new inner city" by now, certainly in the United States. But who was listening to its concerns? Investment went into urban areas, and into self-professed "global" cities first and foremost—which was why, of course, the new mayors and municipal leaders to whom governments were devolving authority all fell over themselves to assert their global (that is, business friendly) characteristics. These were the spaces that provided international capital with the local footholds it needed as a base. Much of everything else—including the rural hinterlands of the American Midwest or the commuter belts of most European cities—was just the view from 38,000 feet. Amid all this change there had rarely been a greater need to "coordinate" the public life of cities and the provision of private homes and spaces. And yet never had the top-down "regulatory style" been less in vogue.[115]

Where there *was* a genuine renaissance of sorts in the public sphere, though whether this was too little too late would remain to be seen, was in the domain of the environment. Environmental planning, from the mundane (such as recycling) to the grand (such as land-use repurposing), not only spruced up often derelict regions and districts, but fed into the dawning environmental consciousness that marked what has been this era's greatest, if still imperfect, legacy. There were profound difficulties to be overcome in turning national societies into ecologically sustainable ones. Most legislation on how public land was to be used, for example, focused on who had right of access *to* the land and what they could build or do *upon* it; there was little by way of guidance as to what ultimate ends such land was actually "for," particularly if those ends were as unspecific as "improving the environment."

Gradually over the decade this changed, as governments moved to put forward more specific environmental policies. This was not always under pressure from below. The UK government published its first environmental strategy, *This Common Inheritance*, as early as 1990 (thanks to the efforts of then Environment Secretary Chris Patten). In Germany environmental protection was already a high priority (the country was a leader in decoupling economic growth from emissions and pollutants) but the hardwiring of environmental protection into its amended Basic Law constitution of 1994 pushed Germany to the very front of the pack, whence it began spending up to 1.5 percent of GDP annually on environmental protection.[116] In Europe, driven often by proactive EC legislation, Scandinavian countries also led on environmental protection (Sweden pioneering the use of carbon taxes, and feeding some of the proceeds into income tax reductions), while southern European countries for the most part lagged behind.

The more significant laggard by far was the United States, where it wasn't so much that economic growth could not be decoupled from environmental damage, as that economic growth could not be decoupled from oil. Where once the United States led on environmental debates, by the 1990s the environment was reduced to yet another feeding trough for partisan disagreement. The world's most powerful nation now became the least proactive on the single most critical issue of the time. The *Exxon Valdez* disaster precipitated the Oil Pollution Act (1990) at the start of the decade, but that was in many ways the last moment of environmental foresight by the American political elite; the years after saw nothing like the welter of public-policy initiatives that characterized the late 1960s and early 1970s. Of course, Al Gore's prominent role in the vice presidency helped promote a more pro-environmental *image* in the 1990s. But while the 1992 Rio Earth Summit translated into a new sustainability agenda in America, the fact that this was ultimately devolved to the community level was indication, as in the UK, that the problem was being passed on, rather than addressed.[117]

In Canada too, the federal state was not always prepared (or even able) to act as a trustee of the environment. The legacy of the sixties and seventies there had been a host of regulations on what people could not do (as embodied in the Canadian Environmental Protection Act). Such regulations had resulted in major improvements in air and water quality. But unlike in Germany, where environmental protection was made central to all policy areas, Environment Canada found itself trumped by other government agencies whenever its portfolio overlapped (which it almost always did). In Canada, as in America, government policy lagged behind popular consensus—a policy gap that underpinned a halfhearted approach to CO_2 emission reductions, for example (and that would in due course make the infamous Cold War "missile gap" of the 1960s seem harmless by comparison).

The problem, of course, is that it takes time to turn round large ships of state, especially in democratic nations, and it ought to be acknowledged that the post–Cold War years were in many ways remarkable for the speed with which a world formerly locked into a superpower conflict turned its attention from those concerns to matters such as the quality of its air and water and what to do about plastic bottles. Across the liberal democracies, the 1990s saw a step change: environmental ISO standards were adopted, cap-and-trade systems experimented with, and efforts made to identify pollutants and to name and shame industries that contravened them. For all that countries were moving at different speeds to get there, there could be no doubting the fact that a turning point in the relationship of Western modernity to its physical environment had taken place.

And yet it was to be this second-wave environmentalism's fate that it came to public prominence when the belief that the market was the best mechanism for allocating costs and benefits was in vogue, when even the socially minded conservatism that lay behind moderately progressive policy documents like Britain's *This Common Inheritance* could be happily translated into the neoliberal idioms of the day.[118] Indeed the extent to which environmental problems required joined-up national and transnational solutions *and* engaged citizens (be it to address climate change, biodiversity reduction, or water pollution) was becoming apparent (to citizens as much as to science) at the very point when national states were approaching their own moment of crisis.

12

Blueprints for the New Millennium

I F POLITICAL LIFE in the Western democracies was rushing forward in the last years of the twentieth century, for the most part it did so peaceably. With the market the arbiter of ever-more choices, the struggles of ideological extremism seemed something from a bygone age. Across the Western world the reigning liberal blueprint was that of societies governed at a distance: a blueprint discovered amid the turmoil of the 1970s and locked into place, in the aftermath of communism's fall, by that expanding panoply of rights that was now accepted, by all parties to the debate, as the ends to which politics should most efficiently supply the means.

As people looked forward more than they had done in decades, public opinion was buoyant; the general atmosphere was upbeat. To the extent that there *were* any real anxieties about the arrival of the millennium, these related primarily to what the "Y2K" bug might hold in store for societies now wedded to a digital superstructure. But even these concerns passed quietly into history. In the event, the millennium cleaved more closely to the passing of a year-end graduation ceremony than it did to the social and political fears articulated in the novelist Upton Sinclair's fictional version of the millennium.

In Sinclair's account, written from the vantage point of 1907, the arrival of the twenty-first century was marked by the opening of "yet another" monument to capitalist luxury, the Pleasure Palace—a fantastical skyscraper serviced by flight craft and boarding decks and towering half a mile over Central Park. But no sooner did the Pleasure Palace's grand clock turn midnight than it was blown apart by a catastrophic and deliberately engineered explosion. For all that Sinclair's vision was not so very far from a reality that would soon engulf the Western world, the millennial moment itself was experienced neither as an end-of-times catastrophe, nor quite as the beginning of a brave new world, but rather with the overwhelming sense that Western societies had been liberated by virtue of their own prosperity from the iron grip of the past. Between text messages shared and images "beamed" live around the world ("streaming" was not yet a meaningful term of art) the millennium was celebrated as a great rolling Mexican wave, making its way around the earth in twenty-four segments of simultaneous euphoria.

If this sense of the millennium as a shared global moment prompted memories of 1989, there was at least one difference to which Sinclair— a staunch critic of capitalism—would probably have been attuned. For while the fall of communism was an event screened predominantly on public broadcast channels around the world, the TVs flicked on to catch the fireworks going off in Hong Kong or over Sydney Harbour Bridge were, in stark contrast, much more likely to be shown on a privately owned channel, which was probably a different channel from the one viewed next door. Television had tracked in the intervening decade from an era of mass broadcasting to one of multiple competing networks, and it had put people on different cultural diets in the process. In that sense it was not at all unlike political life itself. The Western world was now disabused of any pretensions to collective thinking, to aggregating the whole; it was free to move forward instead as a constellation of individual (or at most communitarian) interests. It was "disenchanted." The national security state seemed, for the moment, an outdated relic of the Cold War. The social security state, meanwhile, had been cut back.

This all raised the question of what was actually left of the twentieth-century state and of what citizenship affiliation to the "nation" meant: the state, that is, as something more than just a professionalized political core on the one hand, and a "large-scale provider of services" on the other. There was no doubt that the mainstream blueprint for the road ahead was now a liberal one. Western politicians took it for granted that capitalism and democracy sat happily together. But other visions were articulated during these years, some of them quite starkly opposed to the liberal utopia of integrating capitalist democracies. Abroad there were the examples of authoritarian capitalism in China, now surging ahead. Closer to home there was the ongoing and increasingly nationalist fallout from state communism in Russia.

But in truth the strains were already visible in the liberal blueprint for democracy, first in a burgeoning anticapitalist movement which, for all that it did not yet quite know what it was for, was at least capable of articulating a clarity of opposition against the promarket center that for nearly two decades had been all but lacking. A less visible but soon to be even more influential critique was also developing on the neoconservative right, particularly in America. Elsewhere, it was less a case of movements building than of pressures. In smaller European countries like Austria and the Netherlands, the return of nationalist thinking was forcing a rethink even for governing parties of the Christian democratic mainstream. In France the emphasis on officially sanctioned secularism, or *laïcité*, was alienating many of its non-Christian (more devout) minorities. These and other minority voices would now come to have their say too, gesturing toward some of the principal countercurrents that would so dramatically shape the early twenty-first-century political landscape. And if they were relatively unformed still, prior to the turn of the century, the state of play among these different groups nonetheless provides a sense of the social forces that would jostle for influence in the years to come.

Toward the Millennium (the State of the Nations)

For its part, the United States was catapulted into the twenty-first century on the horns of two historic political controversies. The first was a full-blown presidential scandal, as a majority Republican Congress had the sitting president impeached for his sexual misdemeanors. The second, a year later, was the Supreme Court's decisive intervention in the outcome of the gridlocked national election between Republican candidate George W. Bush and Democratic contender Al Gore. Between these two controversies much more than just the passing of the old century took place.

The decision to bring impeachment charges against Clinton was based on a technicality: Clinton's behavior had long veered toward the unprofessional, and Republicans had been looking to unseat him since the day he took office. But the president's failure to acknowledge, under oath, the nature of his relations with White House intern Monica Lewinsky—the matter of his famous insistence that "I did not have sexual relations with that woman"—opened him to the technical charge of impeachment. And Republicans were adamant that this time, after earlier inconclusive testimonies before a federal grand jury into the nature of his financial relationships, and probes into his various personal affairs (first Paula Jones, then Lewinsky), the president would not be able to wriggle off the hook.

As they sought to hound him out of office, however, what began as a personal scandal ended up underscoring the tensions between the public and their nominated representatives. "The people of California's 37th Congressional District elected me to fight for better education, to fight for safer streets, to fight for the protection of Social Security," intoned Juanita Millender-McDonald, the Democratic representative from California, as she took to the floor to speak on November 12, 1998. "Instead I have had to spend the crucial last weeks of this Congress wading through more than 4,000 pages of what amounts to little more than pornography."[1] But when the Senate made its decision in the hearing, it was all too aware that this was not the first presidential scandal and that the more relevant issue was public confidence in the political system, which had been growing weaker ever since Watergate. In having Clinton acquitted, it hoped to draw a line under both issues. If anything, it merely reinforced the lingering suspicion that politicians were now largely unaccountable.

As the battle-weary Clinton passed the baton to his two-time running mate Al Gore, the partisan split in American politics showed few signs of abating. The 2000 election campaign, in which Gore faced off against Republican nominee George W. Bush (son of George H. W. Bush), was equally acrimonious. It was also incredibly closely fought. On election night the networks repeatedly miscalled the winner in several different states. This happened a number of times in the decisive race in Florida. At one point during the night, Gore had privately conceded the presidency to Bush, on the basis of the Florida count. He later changed his mind when the final result was close enough for a recount. Hordes of lawyers were called up by each side and sent out to do battle. For thirty-six days, the American people waited to hear the outcome. The case batted back and forth between law offices, electoral stations, the Florida court system, and the Supreme Court. Meanwhile the wait for a result went on: "among the most confusing, exhilarating, nerve-racking, educational, divisive, uplifting, and depressing [moments] in our political history as a nation," as the lawyer Alan Dershowitz put it.[2]

It was the role of the Supreme Court in finally settling the matter (and not the much-touted fact that Bush was eventually "elected" with less of the popular vote than his rival) that ultimately proved both unusual and decisive. The judiciary is supposed to keep out of electoral politics. But the Supreme Court not only got involved, it effectively decided the outcome, in a 5–4 decision—along partisan lines—to shut down the ongoing vote recount. The decision was widely denounced as "lawless," "bad constitutional law," "partisan," and "illegitimate" by legal professionals, none of which mattered in the least to the outcome. Where it did matter was in what it revealed, alongside the impeachment process, of the shifting relationship between the American people and their public officials. As Justice Stephen Breyer observed in his dissenting opinion: "The Court was wrong to take this case," he said. "The political implications are momentous." And:

> By halting the manual recount, and thus ensuring that the uncounted legal votes will not be counted by any standard, this Court crafts a remedy out of proportion to the asserted harm. . . . [The decision] runs the risk of undermining the public's confidence in the Court itself. . . . That confidence is a public treasure. It has been built slowly over many years. . . . It is a vitally necessary ingredient of any successful effort to protect basic liberty and, indeed, the rule of law itself. . . .[3]

Such comments revealed just what an outsized place the Supreme Court had come to hold in the firmament of American democracy. In this sense, the nature of the challenges confronting US democracy at the turn of the millennium were unique. Over the course of the previous century, a court which had once defended the interests of the elite had been browbeaten into becoming a crusading progressive court, and since the 1970s had slid back once more into a tool of conservative hegemony. This mattered to the extent that the US Constitution gave the Supreme Court a powerful influence in domestic policymaking. It further mattered because both major political parties had learned to use the court to deliver "the advances [that] popular politics fail to deliver" (with Republicans in particular now routinely using the court to equate "the rights of property with the rights of dissent").[4]

Breyer's comments were also to prove a telling harbinger of the controversies soon to rock the American political landscape. Something of the moral character of government had also been lost, as he saw it, along with "the nation's confidence in the judge as the impartial guardian of the rule of law." Yet this had not been lost because of poor decision-making or legal gerrymandering, as Breyer's dissenting opinion suggested. It had been lost, once again, because of the underlying transformation of that political landscape over the preceding two decades, as a result of the way that law *could* now be turned to political ends, and as popular democracy had been peeled back in the name of securing "good" governance—all things that Breyer himself would acknowledge, some years later, in *The Court and the World*, a valedictory volume penned after his eventual retirement from the bench.

Yet one wonders too just what exactly "the nation" that Breyer wished to invoke in his dissent actually meant at the close of the century. More than three quarters of Americans still declared themselves "very proud" of their country.[5] But this was an expression of that distinctly American form of national belonging that goes by the name of patriotism. Patriotism could demand allegiance. But self-referential as it is, patriotism is not well suited to fostering collective solutions to the challenges of a multicultural society—the very thing, when voter demographics were later broken down, that had caused such a close-run vote in the first place. The underlying problem that Clinton's impeachment hearing and the Supreme Court decision in *Bush v. Gore* had underscored was precisely the fact that the demos itself was divided. And this being the case, the way was open to a much more selective interpretation of exactly who the political "we" was.

America was not the only place seeing a resurgence of the national question at the turn of the twenty-first century. The matter of what statehood demanded, of the grounds upon which it could and should be fought for, was the nub of the problem, and sharply so, in the case of Northern Ireland. But here, for the first time in a long while, the political runes were more encouraging. In contrast to the direction America appeared to be heading in, the Good Friday Agreement, which came into force in December 1999, the very last month of the century, suggested more positive ways of addressing divided political sentiments through innovative cooperative agreements.

As one of its main sponsors, the Good Friday Agreement also provided President Clinton with a rare moment of positive news coverage during his last months in office.[6] It was eventually signed after several decades of armed struggle and two years of multiparty talks made possible by the Downing Street Declaration signed by John Major and Irish Taoiseach Albert Reynolds in London in 1993. The peace process was given a final push by Blair's active championing of meaningful talks alongside the restoration of the cease-fire by the IRA in 1997. It envisaged a power-sharing arrangement whereby both communities, Catholics and Protestants, would be represented in a Northern Ireland Assembly: not a democratic settlement, as routinely portrayed at the time, but a peaceful one at least.

Back during the critical first months of 1998, when the agreement was negotiated, tensions were still rife: Unionists feared that any cease-fire was meaningless without decommissioning of IRA arms; loyalist paramilitaries suspected their views were not being taken seriously. Talks had all but broken down when the Secretary of State for Northern Ireland, Mo Mowlam, took the unprecedented step of visiting Ulster Unionists held in the Maze prison, the real center of power behind the Unionist parties at the negotiating table, to talk them into staying the course. Mowlam made this visit without informing the prime minister or his team. And for good reason, as it turned out: as Blair's then chief of staff recalled, "If she had asked us we would certainly have said no. But in the event she was right and we were wrong."[7] The turnout for the following month's referendum, to ratify the deal, was 81 percent. North and south of the border alike voted overwhelmingly to support it.

The Irish question thus, in a sense, now became just another part of the wider resolution to the national question as New Labour sought to allay growing tensions between the constituent nations of the UK by experimenting with varying degrees of regional autonomy and decentralization. In 1997, referenda had been held in Scotland and Wales, following which the Blair government put forward a proposal of "devolution" of political powers to the kingdoms of the union: Scotland got a parliament and the Welsh got an assembly (they might have got more had they insisted). Northern Ireland got less by way of real legislative independence (in contrast to Scotland, which gained some powers of taxation and local government). But then Downing Street was of the view that they should probably be happy with the Good Friday Agreement.

France too underwent a degree of decentralization, via a constitutional amendment in 2002, and for not dissimilar reasons—offering greater independence to Corsica, where a protonationalist movement had made trouble since 1975, for all that it did little to convince most Corsicans that they really were better off without the assistance of the Matignon (in a referendum the following year the island rejected the offer). Where French devolution differed was in its unwritten ambitions on the mainland. The first was Prime Minister Jean-Pierre Raffarin's belief that devolving more powers to the territorial regions might finally break the back of the large public sector unions and the Parisian capture of national politics. The second, an effort to confront declining voter turnouts, was implicitly conveyed in Jacques Chirac's characteristic contribution to the debate. France, he said, did not need "the corset of centralization to stand up straight."[8] On the French mainland, devolution went ahead the following year.

Spain and Italy also confronted well-funded and, at times, violent secessionist movements calling for regional autonomy in the mid to late 1990s. The Italians responded, courtesy of Berlusconi's need for a workable coalition, by inviting the troublemakers, in the form of the Lega Nord, into government. The Spanish—whose 1978 constitution had already accorded the autonomous regions greater independence than in almost any other modern democratic state—drew a line and did the opposite. It was revealed in the mid 1990s that the government, rather like the British in Northern Ireland, had long sanctioned the covert use of force. Secessionism had survived the arrival of democracy in Spain, it transpired, and so too had the state's recourse to violent means. Secretly funded by the interior ministry, the GAL counterterror group carried out murders and kidnappings across the border in France in the mid 1980s. And for his involvement in the dirty war against ETA that ensued, and a wider series of corruption scandals (inaugurating a period, not unlike Italy's own postcorruption reckoning, known as *la crispación*), PSOE's once favored son, Felipe González, would pay with his job.

Significantly, however, none of these pressures for political devolution, not even the more overt secessionist ones, were based upon the appeal of a rugged nationalism. Most now rested on an *economic* case of some sort or other (the territorial secession of the poor in this sense mirroring the more pervasive and ongoing economic secessionism of the rich). This was most especially the case in Catalonia, but also in Canada, where long-simmering frustration at the federal–province relationship (and the manner in which Quebec in particular seemed to be taking Ottawa for a ride on this) saw the emergence in western Canada of the right-wing Reform Party. Founded in 1987 on the back of the declining price of oil from the region, they now wanted much more by way of laissez-faire policies from the federal government and were prepared to let Quebec secede from the confederation if that was the necessary price.[9] Trudeau's earlier lockdown on Canadian federalism appeared to be in doubt.

Elsewhere, and despite the preemptive giveaway of devolution, renewed calls for Scottish independence continued to be voiced more loudly into the millennium, driven by possible North Sea revenues and the promise of EU regional development policies. The Lega Nord, meanwhile, based its arguments on the financial drain that southern layabouts in the Mezzogiorno made upon the northern taxpayer's purse. Even the Catalans, who *did* have an authentic national tradition based upon a living language, increasingly framed the advantages of secession from Spain as an economic win-win, just as the Czechs had before them. And while the Irish didn't, the economic boom that had come to the south of the island during the previous decade did much to cast the sectarian rivalries of Northern Ireland in a decidedly outdated light (and was one reason the Irish Republic now ceded its prior claims to the six Northern Irish counties as part of the Good Friday deal).

Nationalist movements during the 1990s had taken a rather unusual detour, then, across the liberal democratic world. As the success of movements like Pauline Hanson's One Nation movement in Australia, and Jean-Marie Le Pen's Front National in France revealed, nationalism was far from being the spent force of the twentieth century that many thought to have seen the last of in Bosnia. To some extent one could even say that the Europeans, with their instinctive preference for bureaucracy and institution building, had rediscovered the essence of it—the bonds of cultural ties, collective identity, and the promise of a better future—through the making of a regional polity: the EU having been the savior of the European nation-state, not its executioner. America, with its self-proclaimed "exceptionalism," had rediscovered it at the other end of the telescope: through the local patriotism of groups who did not feel themselves well represented by Washington's political circus, but who believed that thinking this made them more "authentic" Americans all the same.

Accordingly, the national question such as it had presented itself during the 1990s was defused, at the turn of the century, in the way that it always had been: which is to say, by economic adjustments of one sort or another to the states that were the ultimate object of capture by nationalist movements. As tensions increased between regions and cultures in the years to come, particularly in Europe, this would change, and nationalism would return to the front pages of the newspapers in its more potent guise once again. But for the time being the matter appeared settled. And on this basis the whole question as to the purpose and function of the modern democratic nation state was, for many, assumed to have been settled. The purpose of national governments was to oversee "economic integration" in Europe, "multiculturalism" in America, a more genuinely "one nation" in Australia (as against the claims of the party of that name). The Western democracies were becoming ever "closer neighbors." Tensions defused, the liberal blueprint was kept on track; market expansion continued apace. But where did all this leave democracy?

The Liberal Blueprint

Political liberalism in the post-1970s era rested upon two basic pillars. The first was the elective preference, adopted by the major parties of left and right, for "avoid[ing] politics by governing through the market."[10] This concerned more than just the newfound desire to put the levers of the state to work on behalf of the interests of a resurgent capitalist class (though that was how the right preferred to interpret it). Nor was it simply a means to more effective, nimble (and potentially less harmful) states working in partnership with active and aspiring citizens (though that was how the new left preferred to interpret it).

It had been shaped, rather, in response to the quite specific challenges of the post-1970s economic environment. Yet it had developed over the years into a more general model of liberal democratic governance in which governments chose steadily to devolve both power and responsibility to citizens, regions, markets, independent agencies, and more besides, in return for these agents' forbearance as much as their active support. This was, from the point of view of governments, a significant achievement. There could be no "crisis of legitimacy" anymore because the state itself no longer aspired to take the risks that would precipitate such a crisis in the first place. But this had also led to a number of very different ways of thinking about democracy in the West.

Not least under the impress of social and technological change (and "globalization" in particular) Western leaders no longer looked to the old-style, vertical organicism of patrimonial nationalism or party allegiance to mobilize their parties or their base. For the most part, politicians of the present era had instead learned to ensure the provision of the second pillar supporting modern political liberalism: the rights that their citizens-cum-stakeholders now expected as a matter of course.

The language of rights had blossomed in the 1970s, as we have seen, as part of the more general antipolitical utopianism of that moment. By the late 1990s it had, somewhat paradoxically, come to supply the basic discursive bedrock of national politics right across the liberal democratic West. Yet it warrants asking just what, exactly, these rights implied for citizens: because what they in effect coded for was a new vocabulary of individual liberty, understood not as a natural right or a claim against the state, nor even solely as the defense of the privileges of property, but as a means of securing and promoting the general good of the individual within liberal democratic societies. Human rights had taken shape over the previous decades against this background of individually orientated legal instrumentalism. And if the decades that followed were the age of human rights across the West, they were equally an age of political and "negative" rights (the right to be free from interference) before they were an age of "positive" socioeconomic rights.

Through the Additional Protocols to the Geneva Convention signed in 1977, the civilian as a somewhat apolitical category had been reified and the liberal democratic state charged with the protection of individuals at home and abroad. The "negative" human rights underpinning this bled not only into international politics (such as Reagan-era democracy promotion) but into the escalating number of human rights NGOs soon commonplace across Europe in the 1980s as well. There they intersected with the emergent Europeanist vision of supranationalism that had achieved its critical milestone at Maastricht in 1992, displacing such formerly prominent "civil society" institutions as the antinuclear movement in the public imagination of what it meant to hold states accountable to their principal duties.[11]

By the 1990s, the politics of rights provided an organizing framework for almost anything, from the environment (Ontario instituted in 1994 an Environmental Bill of Rights including rights to petition for the enforcement of environmental laws) to freedom of speech. It immediately began changing the debate. When, at the end of the decade the French writer, philosopher, and former politician Roger Garaudy was convicted by the European Court of Justice of disputing crimes against humanity in his 1995 book *The Founding Myths of Modern Israel*, the first thing he did was to appeal to the European Court of Human Rights (ECtHR), to have the judgment overturned. As it happened the ECtHR determined, in a unanimous vote, that the book was indeed "incompatible with democracy and human rights" and that the sentence, which included suspended prison terms, should stand.[12] But at issue was less the outcome than the normative status of rights against which the outcome was decided. Not to be outdone the ECJ too strode into the gap left open by often surprisingly mute nation-states, repeatedly "scolding" Luxembourg, among other countries, for its restrictive national citizenship laws.[13]

If these were welcome domestic implications to human rights, there were international implications too as rights treaties and rights "instruments" came to trump the former substrate of rules governing international relations: the primacy of state sovereignty. A tapestry of treaties now formed the binding cloth of international relations with a densely woven fabric of guidelines and norms. The output was immense; international lawyers had not been this busy for half a century. But there was no constitutional moment in any of this. Instead the law of contract simply replaced the law of duty. Relations between states were now to be performed as a constant pursuit not of interest-mediation but, as the Finnish international lawyer Martti Koskenniemi noted, of "compliance." And since "achieving compliance is all that counts," that in turn meant a logic that was "not really about cooperation but conquest."[14] But conquest in the name of what? The answer to that, of course, took lawyers straight back to the newly crowned "individual person" and the distinctively modern conception of human rights upon whose throne this figure sat.

There was a catch, however, both internationally and on the home front. The reason that human rights had emerged so rapidly to define the new international era was precisely because, in keeping with the professed anti-ideological spirit of the times, they "lacked a political blueprint." Here was the Western achievement writ large. And this was why rights ultimately also merged so functionally with the liberal *economic* imperative of governing at a distance. Yet for all the protestations that human rights offered a way out of the ideological violence of a century now receding from view, they *did* in fact contain a basic political blueprint. Human rights were a liberal invention that prized freedom over equality. And fundamentally they allowed political liberalism, for several crucial decades, to avoid confronting its own lack of a more positive vision for what society should be.[15] That had been a boon ever since the 1970s; it was now to reveal its more problematic nature.

By the end of the decade, and in part as a function of these institutional developments, an important inversion in the earlier democratic order had taken place. Postwar liberal democracy had been founded upon the negotiated compromise between workers and capitalists. As the preamble to the 1945 ordinance establishing the French social security system put it, this "compromise" was enshrined in the capacity of national welfare states to deliver security for the poor and not just the rich.[16] And as with America's social security the means of that model was economic redistribution, but the intended aim was always political security.

While there was nothing necessary about the relationship of the welfare state to democracy, the form of democracy that Western nations espoused was therefore one whose political levers were constructed around this foundational commitment to nurturing society. Removing the state's capacity to control those basic levers was in effect to excise the state from *its* end of the social contract. When Britain's Lord Falconer declared, just prior to the end of the century, that "depoliticizing of key decision-making is a vital element in bringing power closer to the people," the problem was not so much that he was wrong, as that he was being willfully ignorant of what taking power away from the state also meant *for* "the people."[17]

Falconer did, however, have a trump card to call to his defense, and it was the very human rights that underpinned his belief that "the people" were somehow separate from "society." Individual rights and the promise of governing at a distance now supplied such a closely knit pairing that the reliance of both upon wider *representative* accountability (and not least a sufficient level of equality from which base the particular rights and obligations deemed to matter might be chosen) was overlooked. The insurmountable logic of their twin appeal was thus once more confirmed. And yet even as the politial elite overlooked this, it was becoming all the more apparent to the very minorities whose exclusion from the polity such an invocation of rights seemed unable to prevent.

Minority Report

Arguably the central issue for Western democracy at the turn of the millennium, and a critical aspect of the national question, was the fact that citizens were having to learn how to share their democracy, and more immediately their prosperity, with others with whom—rightly or wrongly—they did not feel they shared a common history. This was the darker background beat to the frontline story of prosperity that rings loudest still in the popular memory of the decade. And it had been there all along. When thousands of Albanians fleeing Yugoslavia's descent into war in the early 1990s arrived at the Italian coast in the summer of 1991, authorities herded them into the city's old football stadium to await deportation. It was a harbinger of the tensions to come. "The dream of the Albanians has dissolved, but so too has that of the Italians!" wrote the *Corriere della Sera*'s Enzo Biagi on witnessing the scenes. "The fifth industrial power in the world has not been capable, in three days, of distributing ten thousand cups of coffee. . . . Those plastic sacks of water thrown from above to the dehydrated immigrants, those sandwiches scattered by the soldiers into the scrambling mob—it was like being at the zoo."[18]

If Italy thus found itself on the front lines of a new geography of identity and belonging—a dividing line that would only sharpen come the refugee crisis of the mid 2010s—the problem was not Italy's alone to confront. Immigration flows into Europe were uneven. In 1992 the UK received 32,000 asylum applications while Germany received 438,000.[19] But they were rising everywhere, and they were resented across the continent. For four days in 1992 extremists threw rocks and firebombs at a refuge for Roma asylum seekers in Rostock in Germany. An arson attack on the home of a Turkish family the same year killed three people in Mölln.[20] Britain sheltered behind the sea and its own stricter immigration policy. But in 1999 anti-immigrant sentiment fueled sporadic violence there too, including an attack on asylum seekers in Dover. "How long before we kick the whole lot out?" the *Sun* newspaper demanded to know, as it ran with an indignant story of a Roma beggar "earning" over £30,000.[21]

Things did not get any better as the decade came to a close. In 1997 nearly one third of Europeans sampled considered themselves to be "very" or "quite racist." Despite the EU promoting a "European Year Against Racism" in 1997, fewer people were convinced that fighting racism was as important as controlling immigrant arrivals.[22] In 2000 the EU Monitoring Center on Racism and Xenophobia reported evidence of 259 racist murders during the previous five years. The same year a riot in Almería in Spain saw Moroccan villagers attacked by a crowd of hundreds over four days. The police largely stood by and watched. In a poll carried out just a few years before, two thirds of French people seemed to agree that there were "too many Arabs" in their country.[23] A year later the number of racist attacks was up 33 percent in Germany and had doubled in the UK.[24]

The problem was not just cultural resentment unleashed by economic competition; and it was not just a function of the number of immigrants present, since the worst attacks often occurred where immigrant numbers were lowest. It was not just about "recent arrivals" either, since attacks on long-standing communities, not least Jews, comprised an important part of the overall numbers. It was a problem, in part, of often quite antiquated national rules and procedures for dealing with immigrant populations. Germany was a case in point. Germany had ended its *Gastarbeiter* agreements in 1973, when the boom ended. But many had stayed on and their families had since joined them. By 1996 there were over 7 million foreigners in Germany. They had limited civil rights, worked for the lowest wages, and were frequently housed in low-standard public accommodations. Legal constraints made it hard for them to become naturalized citizens.

It was a problem too of domestic economics. Many French immigrants, predominantly from North Africa, had come in the aftermath of the Algerian War. Under republican ideology they were officially tolerated, so long as they conformed to national values, but they were also socially and economically excluded. Immigrants like the Pieds-Noirs had begun contesting their political exclusion in the 1970s, but when the recession bit deeply in the early 1990s they now found they were also losing their welfare benefits and increasingly subject to police harassment. In 1996, as part of Chirac's more aggressive policy of repatriation, French police "splintered a church door" to forcibly remove 220 African asylum seekers on hunger strike inside, demanding their right to asylum. After being separated by color, blacks being presumed illegal immigrants, they were sent home. "The application of the law is nonnegotiable" was all that Michel Pricard, a member of Chirac's RPF party, had to say about it.[25] The British meanwhile held to their own tried and tested solution. Immigrants being viewed as distinctly problematic were, so far as possible, kept out. The same applied to asylum seekers, most of whom were officially classified as "economic migrants" and sent home again at the first opportunity. In 1997, only 19 percent of applicants were granted permission to stay.[26]

The need for asylum was something that was growing all the time. In Europe, prior to the Yugoslavian Wars, only relatively small numbers of foreigners had claimed asylum. By the end of the decade the number of applications ran into hundreds of thousands. Internal economic migration also grew during the decade, as a result of European integration policies and the freedom of movement permitted within the Schengen Area. This prompted xenophobic resentments as local working-class tradesmen, for example, were outpriced by predominantly Eastern European plumbers, builders and electricians, all of whom were willing to work for less. Ultimately, many of those same Eastern European workers would find themselves muttering similar curses when, as Eastern European countries joined the EU, they lost their cost advantages over the West. Their home countries, meanwhile, began to complain about the outsourcing of jobs to even lower-cost countries like India and China, just as their Western European counterparts had recently moaned about Eastern Europeans taking *their* jobs.

Not dissimilar stories could be heard in America, where asylum applications rose to 150,000 per year by the end of the decade and Congress was on its way to making it a felony to be an undocumented immigrant (this in a society where, by 2005, millions already were). In Australia, where rising Asian immigration since the ending of the White Australia Policy in the 1970s had now eclipsed that coming from Britain, similar policies were flirted with.[27] In Canada, economic migration programs were beefed up, by contrast, so as to admit greater numbers of skilled workers. But here too admissions of refugee and asylum seekers were kept down.[28] The Canadian government was in effect "privatizing" its immigration system—allowing the social makeup of the citizenry to be determined by business demand, in place of the "tap on, tap off" employment regulation that the federal government had pursued over the previous decades.[29]

With legal immigration becoming increasingly constrained—and here the United States and Germany led the way—illegal immigration also inevitably increased toward the end of the millennium. Soon much tighter physical controls were brought in to tackle this problem. Europe's southern Mediterranean border was always deemed its most vulnerable point of entry. And in the late 1990s Italy, Spain, and France each intensified their patrols and other efforts to deter migrants. In America the Mexican–American border was tightened, but not the Canadian border. Meanwhile immigration controls expanded away from the physical border itself, both inwardly, in terms of policing operations within cities like Los Angeles, and by pushing border control functions outward, down to Mexico's own southern border. The Europeans soon cottoned on to the same trick too, establishing migrant processing centers in North Africa.

All this was not just about the question of how to manage new arrivals. Part of the problem in America was that the status of minority rights domestically was not making much noticeable progress either. For all its activism over the election the US Supreme Court had been conspicuously less active over the previous decade when it came to defending the liberties of minority groups—even though the state of minority urban living and the race issue were among the most pressing social problems the country faced. The Rodney King riots had been an early expression of this. But they were also, it was often overlooked, a reminder that much of the resentment lay *between* immigrant groups in addition to the old black–white divide.

The declining status of minorities took a more procedural form in 1994. While the media focused on the high-circus police chase of O. J. Simpson in his white Ford Bronco, Californians quietly passed Prop 187, denying health and social services to illegal immigrants. On one level this was a classic majority response at a time of perceived resource scarcity, not least of declining state budgets (it was also later struck down by the federal district court). But it was equally a sign of the times to come. California, Washington, and Florida all banned affirmative action policies in the 1990s; Michigan, Nebraska, Colorado, Arizona, New Hampshire, and Oklahoma followed suit in the decade after that, most of these changes having been introduced by voter referendum.[30] None of it did very much for interethnic understanding. African Americans grumbled at the growing dominance of Latinos and both looked on with dismay as the growth in average family income of Asian groups outpaced everyone, whites included.

For all the celebration of multiculturalism then, the American nation entered the millennium distinctly fragmented along lines not only of race but also of class. Even something as seemingly "apolitical" (it was anything but, of course) as a census reclassification was enough to cause dispute. At the end of the decade the Clinton administration proposed a more multifaceted series of racial categories for people to select in the coming 2000 census. It was a tacit acknowledgment that mixed-race families were a growing presence in the nation and that their children needed recognizing as such (the degree to which one was "white" was a legal category to which many blacks turned to improve their situation).

To American conservatives like Stephan Thernstrom, however, the new census categories threatened to turn that dilemma on its head. "The fear now," Thernstrom said, "is that whites will try to pass as blacks," the better to avail themselves of affirmative action policies.[31] The category problem, that "a white woman can give birth to a black baby but a black woman cannot give birth to a white baby," was, as he saw it, a fundamental injustice perpetrated against whites. For Thernstrom all this was just a boon for the civil rights lobbies—whose membership, he observed, can but grow over time. A no less entrenched problem for blacks themselves, it might have been said, was the way that race continued to intersect ever more strongly with class. It was this that did most to turn host nations into vilifiers (almost regardless of whether they were Christian, social, or liberal democratic) and immigrants in search of a better life into supposed threats (one of the last things the Spanish did during negotiations over the Amsterdam Treaty in Europe was to have a line inserted on the need to cooperate on migration surveillance). It did so because for certain groups the presence of immigrant populations really *was* perceived as a threat.

The arrival of immigrants and asylum seekers made a mockery of the official line on "multiculturalism" in America, or on "ever closer union" in Europe, since immigrants were invariably channeled into urban areas and poorer communities where it was harder to assimilate. Greeks abused Albanians, Brits resented Poles, Italians put Ethiopians into positions of near servitude, and the French grew testy once again with Algerians. Outside of elite, cosmopolitan circles, the liberal claim that market expansion and democratic deepening went hand in hand with social peace was nothing like as obvious as it was claimed. Working-class fears that immigrants were "taking all the jobs" were nothing new. But now they were channeled, paradoxically, into resentment of the welfare system that strove to provide for them both: a system that was now seen as both unfair and complicit with the presence of foreigners, and which was therefore hated by those it sought to assist.

The consequence was that many working-class people were on the same side as governments seeking to reduce benefits. This was one reason why, in the UK, the government felt obliged to increase the rate of prosecutions for welfare fraud from around 1,500 to 6,000 cases in the new century, while prosecutions for tax fraud remained around a couple of hundred every year, an inversion of priorities seen in New Zealand and Australia as well.[32] The extent of transformation in popular understanding of what democracy was, and how it worked, was now revealed, and it hung on the greater premium accorded individual freedom. It was no longer the capitalists that were seen to exploit workers; it was nonworkers ("welfare takers" and "immigrants") who exploited the state and the state that passed the buck on to "its" workers.[33] And the more that minorities were excluded in this way, the more the lower middle class feared them, and the more they tuned in to the voices of those who would turn the clock back to a past when those others were presumed not to exist.

Forms of the (Modern) Right

The years after the fall of communism had been imagined as a time when the world would turn to the ways of the West, not one where the rest of the world's peoples would come to the West. By the end of the decade the social tensions unleashed by the refusal to address this reality had begun to give succor to populists and xenophobes; it put a little wind back in the sails of a listless far right. Indeed, it was the populists who began to reap the greatest rewards from a pervasive, but too infrequently acknowledged, anti-immigrant backlash in the post–Cold War years.

In Germany the years immediately after reunification saw a return to prominence of the *Republikaner* (Republicans) party, a far-right party founded in the 1980s by a former member of the Waffen-SS. The *Republikaner* gained a degree of popularity in Berlin, which bore the brunt of the social tensions unleashed by rising immigration. But like their most immediate rivals on the right, the German People's Union (DVU), while the *Republikaner* did well in state and metropolitan elections they never made serious inroads in the Bundestag. The question was whether they actually needed to. As the tiny British National Party also found in Britain at this time: call the tune and you can name the price. Thanks to the *Republikaner* in part, the German parliament amended its constitution in 1993 to make it harder for immigrants to obtain welfare. In Britain the government just made it harder for immigrants to get a job in the first place.

The *Republikaner* ran on a slogan that the BNP might have thought would work well for them—"the boat is full." For Jean-Marie Le Pen, who still dominated the far right in France, it was always "France for the French." The politician turned soldier turned politician once again, Le Pen was finally, in the 1990s, enjoying the popularity that he believed his policies deserved. And unlike his German counterparts he *was* able to translate this into major successes at the polls. He did so by adding a new and telling element to the anti-immigrant rhetorical stable: *Europe* as the enemy. Foreigners might be breaching the walls, Le Pen argued, but it was the Eurocrats who had ripped away the defenses from the turrets in the first place. It was all one great conspiracy for those gathered within. Here was an early airing of the struggle between the populists and the technocrats.

Laying down the new anti-European card was a trick that Austria's Jörg Haider was also learning to play at this moment, and it proved perhaps especially useful in a country that had neither the level of immigration nor the social problems of France. "We Austrians should answer not to the EU, not to Maastricht, not to some international idea or other, but to this our Homeland," Haider boomed. His FPÖ party, we have seen, had already become steadily more popular as the decade wore on precisely because it hitched its anti-immigrant arguments to a concern for "the little people" on the one side, and everything from "criminals" and "drug users" to the "foreign rabble" on the other. In 1994 Haider recorded 23 percent of the national vote and in 1999, when the party's success peaked, he achieved 27 percent—running the socialists to a close second place.[34] This same combination proved most effective of all in Switzerland, hardly a country plagued by poverty. There the far right had become, by 1999, the country's second-largest party with 23 percent of the national vote.

Outside of the BNP, as they looked to inherit the mantle of Oswald Mosley, the debate in Britain focused more on Little Englander-ism. In some ways this blunted the far right's radical appeal relative to other countries on the continent. But it also allowed it to sink roots across the *Daily Telegraph*–reading countryside, which meant that it influenced national political parties only that much more. UKIP was the most significant political child to emerge in Britain from this fusion of anti-immigrant and anti-European rhetoric. But for all it painted Britain as somehow distinct, its trumped-up islander mentality was more continentally rooted than it might like to admit.

Exactly the same mentality could be found in Denmark, where Pia Kjærsgaard was in the throes of leading the Danish People's Party into a governing coalition for the first time in 2001. In Holland too, in the wake of Pim Fortuyn's assassination, the anti-immigrant party that took his name experienced a short-lived electoral boost. In the Nordic countries, in contrast to Britain and the Low Countries, there was an authentic and still living fascist culture to draw upon. Hence in Sweden, the ironically named Swedish Democrats were carrying neofascism from the streets and into the polling booth. Famously, as they marched more openly into public debate, one of their number was bashed by a shopping bag wielded by an old lady as they strutted past. But hers was a rare act of bravery. Many were silent before the fascists' arguments until they had become too mainstream to ignore.

The story of Christian democracy in the post–Cold War years paints an important, countervailing picture to these developments on the far right— and it is where answers to the question of how social change and democratic politics were re-entwined in these years are ultimately to be found. Almost single-handedly, in fact, it was Christian democracy that provided a mainstream, centrist political response to the challenges of the new political environment after the Cold War and into the new millennium: not least since as a movement it had always been constitutionally opposed to raw nationalism. For all that it did not do much more than update its policies of the postwar era, it did at least listen to what the electorate were trying to say, and it had a moral tenor that the secularism of social and Anglo-American democratic parties (for all the professed religiosity of American presidents) simply lacked. Rather than focus on the quicksilver of a boom economy, and its trickle-down solutions to social problems, Europe's Christian democrats instead dug trenches behind which to confront the changing dynamics of a world in the throes of major transformation. And for that they were rewarded with greater staying power at the polls.

At the end of the Cold War, this did not look to have been in the script. The trend toward secularization and urbanization, the growing disaffection with "Europe" among working-class voters, all should have condemned the Christian democrats to the dustbin of history in the aftermath of 1989. It was true the 1990s were difficult years: resurgent in Germany, divided in Belgium, dominant in Luxembourg, and dead on arrival in France, Christian democracy was also now challenged from within in the East, where it became a label of convenience for more primordially conservative and nationalist forces in a country like Hungary.

But Europe's Christian democrats also found that when they adapted their messages to the concerns of the times, their social conservatism blended quite naturally with neoliberal economic policies. This was confirmed at a meeting in Toulouse in 1997, where the Christian democrats' older vision of a "social market economy" was now ditched in favor of a distinctly more laissez-faire "European social model." It also put them in the same pen, and the same quandary when later stalked by the forces of radical opposition, as the social democrats. Five years earlier, in Athens, a similar meeting had confirmed the importance of economic growth in providing for "social justice"; now it was "social responsibility" that was to serve the ends of "economic dynamism and adapting to the global market."[35] Geography aside, Blair by now could have happily picked up the CDU torch in Germany.

As European integration gathered speed in the 1990s Christian democrats found their most supportive footing at the European level. Consisting of just the Christian democratic parties of Germany, France, Italy, Belgium, Luxembourg, Holland, and Ireland at the time of the first European-wide elections in 1979, by the end of the millennium the European People's Party would comprise 74 member parties from 38 countries.[36] In other words Christian democracy learned to build coalitions, in which it foregrounded the notions of "freedom and responsibility" at a time when other parties seemed to be prioritizing *either* one or the other (Blair may in fact have been an exception to this). They were also assisted by the fact that, as Europe expanded east and north, it took in more and more countries with strong Catholic or religious conservative parties.

This was not because there were always local Christian democratic parties leaping into action on the ashes of communism. Postcommunist Poland, for all that it was 90 percent Catholic and still had a sizeable rural workforce, should have been prime Christian democrat territory, and yet no party bearing the name ever succeeded in taking off. The same, to a lesser extent, was true in Spain and Ireland.[37] What happened, rather, was that Christian democracy opened its arms to conservative all-comers, many of whom joined up, just as southern Europe had to social democracy in the 1980s, the better to have a stable of some sort to call home. What the Christian democrats thus lost in terms of their association with the European project in the core countries of Europe they regained elsewhere—for now—as Europe expanded. And what Europeans gained— also for now—was a countervailing force to that of the far right, which otherwise would likely have put down deeper roots somewhat earlier than it did. But now Christian as well as social democracy had bought itself short-term electoral gains at the cost of a longer-term cause. And this would in due course come back to haunt it.

There was no Christian democratic movement as such in America. But then again, one advantage of the American two-party system was that it retained, long into the post–Cold War era, a much greater degree of fixity than could be said about the European political landscape. And it left little room for the far right or the far left to secure a portion of the electorate. Of course, one of the major disadvantages of the two-party system was precisely the extent to which the two major parties could themselves be captured by more intemperate political voices: a problem that was to plague the Republican Party in the years to come.

For the most part right-wing populism was channeled into distinctly local cultural manifestations after the Cold War—rallies and Confederate boot sales—while the leftists focused their efforts on the national and the international stage. Far-right violence still existed, as epitomized by Timothy McVeigh in Oklahoma City in 1995. But public perception was focused overwhelmingly on a restrictive media diet of "lone wolves," which said little about the wider cultural templates, be it white supremacism or even antifederalism, which multiple cases of violence were based on. In a report carried out some years later, the Department of Homeland Security found that far-right extremists had been involved in over 560 homicides between 1990 and 2010.[38] One struggles to imagine the post-9/11-era press giving quite so little coverage to similar bouts of radical-Islam sponsored violence.

Politically speaking we must look elsewhere to find the movements on the right gaining momentum in the United States during these years. In sharp distinction to Europe, where the parties had come to prominence on the back of a deep groundswell of resentment, the resurgence of the radical (though not far) right in America was not a mass phenomenon. On the contrary it was an elite-driven process and nurtured primarily within metropolitan political institutions. This was not the West Coast conservatism of the Reagan years, with its close ties to the religious right and to new industry. This was a predominantly East Coast coalition of second-generation political grandees with the big business interests they had fostered in the years since they were out of power.

Contract with America had been an early sign of the renewed momentum of the right in the early to mid 1990s. But as the decade drew on it was a reinvented neoconservative movement that proved to be the more influential force in national politics. Neoconservatism was nothing new to America. It had been, as we have seen, a "distinct and very significant" voice on the US right since the 1970s, when it first took off under such leading lights as William Kristol and Norman Podhoretz. Initially conceived as a response to the perceived leftward turn of American liberalism, neo-conservatism had—like America itself—undergone something of a transformation in the decades since. By the end of the millennium it was a movement focused much more strongly on international affairs: above all on the specific issue of the previous Republican administration's unfinished business in Iraq. And in outpourings from institutions like the American Enterprise Institute, in publications like the *Weekly Standard*, and via organized programs like the Project for the New American Century (PNAC) neoconservatives framed an aggressive vision of America in the world, which would prove influential in the years to come.[39]

It would prove influential because it linked America's standing in the world to its success (or otherwise) at home. If Clinton had beaten Dole, went the neoconservative thinking, then perhaps that had something to do with the lack of a clear Republican vision of America's role in the world. All of a sudden the lingering views of a "coming anarchy" and a "clash of civilizations"—those bestselling portraits of a world fragmenting into dangerous pockets, or "belts" of disorder and disruption—were transformed into the intellectual matériel behind a reinvigorated foreign policy activism. Foreign policy was actually a very small part of the original ten-point program of the Contract Republicans and this was where the neocons thought they had something to say.

In most of what they did say, the matter of unfinished business in Iraq was a constant referent, present in almost every proposal or delineation of new threats. "Saddam is a convicted killer still in possession of a loaded gun," Paul Wolfowitz insisted in 1996, on the matter of Iraq holding up the work of UN weapons inspectors.[40] But so too was there a distinct sense that neoconservatives wanted more than just to set about "Rebuilding America's Defenses," as the title of the PNAC's most influential report had it. The PNAC was, officially speaking, a think tank: headed by none other than William Kristol, inevitably enough. But around it gathered a constellation of powerful (and in the current climate, disaffected) intellectuals and politicians, including former big-hitting administration officials like Paul Wolfowitz, Dick Cheney, Donald Rumsfeld, and John Bolton (all of whom would yet see a return to the front line).

The project's legacy was to set the post–Cold War world in a new and harsher light: one far removed from the optimism of the response to the fall of the Berlin Wall just a few years earlier. The basic thrust of their platform was that America would need to keep both its friends and foes firmly in their place in its overriding mission to maintain the conditions for a successful expansion of a global free market upon which American prosperity relied. To speak of "zones of peace" was, for them, thus also to declare territories—including the American "homeland" (a term which it now used with pride)—which would require defending, and, in all likelihood, policing too. It was not a banishment of the realpolitik of old, therefore, but its reconstitution around a new set of "global" values whose author, executor, and bailiff were in every case the United States. Even Clinton, in his newly interventionist guise, found himself completely outflanked by this.

In 1998 the PNAC group began to spend large sums on full-page editorials making the case for overthrowing Saddam. It was a remarkable reversal by some of the same people who had chosen not to continue the war against Saddam in 1991, but the case was made with such persistence that even Clinton, by the time he spoke with the Pentagon on contingency plans for another build-up of force in the Gulf in 1998, felt obliged to declare, "If we fail to respond today, Saddam and all those who would follow in his footsteps will be emboldened by tomorrow by the knowledge that they can act with impunity. . . ."[41]

It was something of a setback, and a surprise to the president's team, when the following day key members of his cabinet, including Madeleine Albright, spoke before a meeting of 6,000 members of the public at Ohio State University to sell the case for possible action in the Gulf. The event was broadcast live on CNN in the hopes of reaching Saddam's own ears: an intended show of public support for action it was hoped might force him into line. What the administration got instead were chants of derision from protesters: "One, two, three, four—we don't want your racist war!" Albright was aghast: the whole thing was a "fiasco," she said. But it was Republican Congressman John Boehner who delivered the more telling verdict: "This is a matter of global security and international peace and they turned it into the Oprah Winfrey show." Of course, he could hardly have imagined that within two decades there would be a chorus of supporters calling precisely for the American presidency to be turned over to Oprah Winfrey, much less that he himself would have helped to bring this about.

Back in 1998, the solution that Clinton found to this particular problem of the gap between popular interest, his own now self-professed commitment to dealing with Saddam, and the proscriptions of international law, went by the name of Operation Desert Fox. Fighting at a distance (via cruise missiles and smart bombs) had become the preferred Western way of war over previous years. But as Clinton now discovered this had the effect, in turn, of further narrowing the political and moral distance that must be traveled before military actions are approved. And Desert Fox did not, in fact, go very far in mollifying the neoconservatives, any more than did congressional passage, in the summer of 1998, of the Iraq Liberation Act, codifying the aim of regime change into US law.

The reason for this was simple. The source of the neocons' radicalism was resentment. Many of them had supported Clinton at the start of his time in office, and—to simplify only slightly—none of them had gotten any jobs out of doing so.[42] To their longstanding mistrust of American liberalism was thus added personal disaffection. But the fact that the neoconservatives were not swayed *either* by the knee-jerk anti-Clintonism of the Contract Republicans meant that they were, and would remain through the Bush years to come, a free-floating and dangerous grouping within the context of American policy discourse. The future they mapped out was one best outlined by Richard Boucher, a State Department spokesman, who declared in a Thanksgiving address in London in 2002, the year before the invasion of Iraq finally took place: "I declare myself an unabashed, simplistic American. I believe in Freedom as a right, a responsibility, a destiny, a force that cannot be vanquished. And, in my line of work, it is more than a faith: freedom is a foreign policy. The United States will defend freedom relentlessly . . . to me that is what it is all about—plain and simple."[43]

The Anticapitalist Left

But whose freedom did Boucher have in mind? This was *the* question animating the other side of the political spectrum, the radical left, in the last years of the century. Just as the neoconservative right now saw the international stage as the terrain that needed fighting over, so too did the anticapitalist left think in terms of "global" trends—both of them fatefully ceding the domestic political terrain to the nationalists and the populists in the process. No movement better embodied the anticapitalist left, of course, than the signature political movement of the late 1990s: the antiglobalization movement.

At its most visible this "movement of movements" coalesced at the turn of the millennium into a series of mass protests at major events on the liberal globalization agenda: the meetings of the G6 group of countries, the so-called Washington Consensus organizations of the WTO, the IMF, and the World Bank, and at milestones in the orchestration of regional trading blocs. But it drew sustenance from a wider global civil society movement that was beginning to think of itself as a meaningful political identity.[44] If this left was distinctly international it was also almost entirely divorced from the national left, which had either adopted the third-way conciliation with the right, or retreated into abstract hypercritique, and which in both cases had left itself short of arguments that could speak to the concerns of those who did not have the luxury of principled opposition.

As with the right, the antiglobalization movement had been gradually coalescing since the very start of the decade; its roots reached back even further than that, to the Green movement and the Third World solidarity networks that emerged out of the imbroglio of the seventies. Action groups had coalesced around specific issues, most dramatically in West Germany (including major protests against the Star Wars system in Bonn in 1985 and the IMF in West Berlin in 1988). Many of them took place outside the West as well, as with Subcomandante Marcos's Zapatista uprising in Chiapas in southern Mexico: a short-lived, media-savvy struggle timed to coincide with Mexico's entry into NAFTA, and a reminder that it was no longer Western left-bank intellectuals who got to shape the terms of oppositional discourse.

Instead radical ideas now reverberated around the echo chamber of an emergent global community based on the 1970s-era realization that it could communicate with itself outside the old national-cultural confines.

As the liberal trade agenda was pushed forward at an accelerating pace throughout the 1990s, this oppositional movement likewise shifted gears. Even so, it was not until "the battle of Seattle" in November 1999 that the movement truly came to global attention. At that year's World Trade Organization meeting, more than 40,000 people turned out to protest against further trade liberalization measures. Well-publicized clashes with riot police, using tear gas and batons, were beamed around the world. Delegates—including Kofi Annan—were trapped in hotel rooms, the streets between their hotels and the meeting itself blocked with the bodies of protesters. The whole affair soon became an indelible snapshot of a new generational stand-off: this time between corporate and cooperative visions regarding the nature of Western democracy's relationship to global capitalism.

The anticapitalist movement's great problem as a movement was that it never really achieved any greater *specificity*. This was unfortunate, but it was also self-inflicted. In many respects the movement was not against globalization per se, after all. For this reason the label was one that its corporate opponents, not to mention the mainstream proliberalization media, regularly used against them. The antiglobalization movement was in fact against corporate power most specifically. But it failed to articulate this to a wider audience because it was also, as the American lawyer Adam Warner put it, "a faction the likes of which the world has never seen." And yet that faction was richly diverse internally: young and old, blue collar and white collar, black and white.[45] Sustained by a burgeoning global conscience it was the unforeseen embodiment of Manuel Castells' "network society"—a counternetwork feeding off its own autonomous power. And for all that it was international in scope, its operations were increasingly tinged with a strategic localism. As one of the organizers of Seattle later recalled:

> I don't think the WTO realized when they planned this for Seattle that they were setting down in one of the most heavily unionized cities in the United States. There are 120,000 union members in Seattle and more than 400,000 AFL-CIO members in Washington State. Add to that members of nonaffiliated unions like the teachers, who are backing us, and close to 80,000 retirees, and you're talking about a real base to work from.[46]

However, for those tasked with policing them, and for the media who then covered their actions, the movement proved to be quite easily divided into two basic groups: peaceful protesters on the one side, and anarchists on the other. This was another misrepresentation of anti-globalizers, of course, but one aided by the many self-declared anarchists among them. As the American political commentator Barbara Epstein put it, one could be fairly sure that most of these were not anarchists in the traditional sense of the term. They were not reading Bakunin at night nor preaching Kropotkin by day. They were anti-authoritarians first and egalitarians last.[47] And while this sort of anarchism could be useful, it had its limits. "Telling the truth to power is or should be a part of radical politics but it is not a substitute for strategy and planning," as Epstein put it.[48] If the antiglobalization movement thus found its deepest roots in the nonviolent protest movements and civil disobedience movements of the post-1970s left, it also shared something of those movements' Achilles' heels as well: how many people, really, would be prepared to get arrested in any one place in support of any one partic-ular issue?

Fortunately, or unfortunately, the movement had an answer of sorts to this that Epstein did not consider. And it was there in the book that became the unofficial "manifesto" of the movement: *No Logo*, published in 1999 by the young Canadian journalist Naomi Klein. The movement's great strength, Klein explained in a different text, was its likeness to a "swarm of mosquitoes." If this captured something of the anarchist model of small self-contained groups coming together to mass forces when under threat, it also overlooked the other thing that the antiglobalization movement provided for its younger (and more dynamic) cohorts at least: a political identity outside the mainstream political left and right, which for many in the Anglo-American, and increasingly French, world was no longer a formula they identified with.

Klein herself was famously described as a "teenager fixated on brand names," until immersion in her project provided her with a more polit-ical identity.[49] But the wider fascination with "brands" was genuine and it captured something of the antiglobalization movement's central paradox: the way that antiglobalization as a "movement" could mesh, in the West, with "underground music" in Italy[50] or with skate parks in Toronto; the way activists were often seen organizing themselves on Apple-based computers. But here too was where the movement encountered its own Achilles' heel. All movements need representatives, and those who would represent the antiglobalizers were often the leaders of the civil society organizations that had been growing apace since the 1980s.

The problem was, as the writer Paul Kivel pointed out in 2004, that the higher-level civil society organizations often needed financial backing from somewhere, and that allowed the ruling classes not only to "co-opt leadership from grassroots communities" but "to make the funding, accounting, and evaluation components of the work so time-consuming and onerous that social justice work is virtually impossible under these conditions."[51] Klein's analysis was that there was "no space" that was not taken over by the corporation. The question now being asked was whether that applied to dissent itself. The French socialist of 1968 vintage, Daniel Bensaïd, certainly sounded decidedly out of ideas when he declared that slogans like "our world is not for sale," "the world is not a commodity," or indeed "no logo" marked a phase of "big refusal and stoical resistance."[52] On one level they marked nothing more than the branding of left opposition itself.

Not everyone on the left was willing to concede that the movement had to have its representatives, however, or that it was destined to be outsmarted in face of the corporate behemoth it confronted. Chief among them was Italy's still active generation of '68ers. As the American English professor and interlocutor of the Italian left Michael Hardt put it in 1996, if the revolutionary politics of an earlier age was based upon German philosophy, English economics, and French politics, "In our time . . . revolutionary thinking might be said to draw on French philosophy, U.S. economics, and Italian politics."[53] His pithy summary was not inaccurate. But what was the substance of the politics? "Postmodern political disenchantment," according to one commentator. For antiglobalization's Italian vanguard, it was also—or at least it *should* be—anticapitalist in its analysis, and techno-anarchist in its own politics.

The two strands were well represented by the Paduan-born Italian Marxist Antonio Negri, the figurehead of the Italian revolutionary left at this point. Formerly one of the leaders of the *Potere Operaio* (workers' power) movement in the late 1960s, in 1979 Negri had been arrested for his involvement in the political violence of the *Anni di Piombo* (Years of Lead). Convicted of involvement in two murders and remanded in an Italian jail, while serving time he was nonetheless elected to the Italian legislature (for the Radical Party) in 1993. Immediately claiming parliamentary immunity, he used his temporary freedom to flee to France, where he lived and taught for fourteen years until agreeing to return and serve out his sentence in 1997. Like all good Italian revolutionaries, jail did not prevent him turning out his most important work: in this case a book coauthored with Hardt and published under the title of *Empire*.

Written over the previous half-decade, *Empire* soon became a surprise bestseller when it was published in 2000. Sweeping in its diagnoses of a world transformed into a postnational capitalist dystopia, it struck a chord—either despite or because of its arcane prose—with a younger, radicalized generation of students. For these would-be revolutionists it was probably the Wachowskis' *Matrix* trilogy that offered the necessary visual synthesis of *Empire*'s basic point: that a machinelike capitalist order was its own form of power, and one in which everyone found themselves complicit. *Empire* was, in many ways, the intellectual bookend to Klein's *No Logo* of the same year—the sort of weighty philosophical tome that anchored convictions and steeled belief. So it was fitting, if tragic, that the first fatality at an antiglobalization protest, 23-year-old Carlo Giuliani, took place not at the other end of the world but in Genoa, in 2001, where the largest demonstration since Seattle was met with heavy-handed policing, and the battle lines were dug a little deeper.

Trouble Across the Water

Global capital, meanwhile, had its own problems to worry about. In the 1990s the East Asian economies—the "tigers"—were the best-performing regional economy outside the West. Most of the world's so-called "emerging markets" were to be found there and Western money had been flowing in as investors sought to take advantage. The East Asian economies had been encouraged by the major global financial institutions to liberalize their economies and to adopt the macroeconomic approach spearheaded by the West over the previous two decades. And by and large they had done so. But they had also accumulated heavy debts in the process and were reliant on continued high levels of growth to meet the escalating costs of servicing those debts.

In 1997 the wheels finally came off the wagon, as country after country fell into economic difficulty. Speculation grew rife that devaluations would soon be necessary, and investors began selling off East Asian currencies as quickly as they could: first Thailand, then the Philippines and Indonesia, then Malaysia, and Taiwan and even South Korea. Each currency soon fell off a cliff in terms of its value. Banks tottered, stock markets crashed, real estate booms went bust overnight, and shares in national companies declined. It was the biggest upset in global finance for two decades and the worst prior to the great recession of 2007–8. And it mattered to the West in two important respects.

First, and most immediately, it mattered because it demonstrated that financial markets were now truly global. Domestic and international markets had become so heavily entwined that "for all intents and purposes," as one commentator put it, "there was one global financial system, [and] that included all the developed countries and many developing and formerly communist countries."[54] The implications of this applied to Western economies no less than it applied to emerging markets. Western pensioners' income was probably invested as much in Chilean or South Korean technology companies as any other and their bank deposits could be held in a bank that was now owned abroad. Meanwhile, the spending commitments of Western governments, whether on welfare or trains, were largely enabled off the back of the willingness of emerging nations, China especially, to invest: or in the case of the United States, to keep buying their own treasury bonds.[55] A crash in Asia was therefore of immediate interest to domestic policy-making in Western states.

But secondly it mattered because of the way that the triumvirate power of business, banking, and political leaders responded to the crisis. One commentator dubbed the combined experience of financial crises "the rebirth of doubt," and, to be sure, each of the primary institutions that comprise the global liberal financial architecture did begin to think a little more seriously about the risks as well as the benefits of high capital mobility. At this point the Asian crisis could have been taken as a wake-up call to the dominant liberal vision of global free-market capitalism, particularly in Australia, which narrowly escaped being dragged in (largely on the basis that currency crises didn't happen to "Western" countries). New Zealand by contrast did slip into recession, largely on account of its central bank's fierce independence, allowing it to tighten money (for reasons of stability) during the crisis.[56]

It was taken as confirmation once more that the West, at least—in contrast to all these others—was on the right path. After all, the crisis was eventually contained and the lessons that finance ministries and central bankers learned from the crisis suggested that the fault ultimately lay in Asia itself. Asian countries had undertaken the right capital account liberalization policies but in the wrong order; their politicians had made bad calls in response. Where 1989 had left off in the making of a distinctly Western hubris, the crisis of 1998 now picked up. And as the former status quo was returned to East Asia, and fires were dampened elsewhere (first in Russia, which defaulted in 1998, and then in Brazil the following year), a collective sigh of relief was breathed.

The overriding conclusion that was arrived at and, fatefully, locked in for a generation, was that economic liberalization worked, so long as democratic leaders (or any others for that matter) responded to its swings and troughs with the appropriate measure of resilience, of fiscal discipline, and of steady-handedness at the tiller. That these same commitments of managerial virtue may have negative social and political consequences was a fact largely glossed over. The IMF, under the leadership of Michel Camdessus, only eased off the throttle on its post–Cold War capital account liberalization policies in 1998, at the point the Asian crisis spread to Russia (the point when, as Executive Director Willy Kiekens confessed sometime later, the liberalization program rather "blew up in our faces").[57]

There could be little doubting that the overwhelming political priority of the age was now rooted firmly in the defense of the post-'70s laissez-faire variant of global capitalism. To be sure, there was plenty of disagreement "inside the tent," as the influential American economist Jeffrey Frieden observed, "but few questioned the general superiority of markets as mechanisms of economic allocation."[58] Even the US army was happy to go along. The "security state" could now usefully be replaced by the "competition state," suggested James R. Golden, a US colonel and presidential economic adviser.[59] The ultimate lesson that was confirmed coming out of the Asian crisis was that it was markets that needed protecting, not people. The primary aim of governments was "protecting capital."[60] So long as politicians and other decision-makers did that, all would be well.

As the century drew to a close the principle of "democracy promotion"—once so vociferously a part of liberal foreign policy—was no longer argued for in quite the same terms. It was now frequently dropped in favor of exporting the neoliberal values of "fiscal prudence," "discipline," and "government restraint." Of course, this was precisely what the protesters at Seattle had been arguing against. And if their arguments expressed a certain naivete about the workings of liberal democracy in the modern world, they were at least more willing than many to recognize that the globalization of capital had costs as well as benefits for the state. In any case it was clear, as left and right put forward their competing visions of global order, that the struggle over democracy was no longer a struggle confined to the national level alone. Equally it now played out in terms of corporate reach, citizenship status, and national and international regulations.

For a moment in the late 1990s it was as if the Western world was a suspension of indivisible elements, all jostling for institutional and political supremacy on a conveyor belt that had them heading in largely the same direction. In the antipodes Australia had at last risen to its long-sought-after global status, the much-heralded "Australian moment" attributed to a combination of liberal economic reforms combined with a social democratic communitarianism; New Zealand was enjoying the ripening macroeconomic fruits of its own neoliberal revolution earlier in the decade, and was serenely untroubled by the financial turmoil on the other side of the Pacific.

In Canada, postwar "boomers"—"nationalist in politics, international in style"—had defined the terms of political debate since the early 1970s. But a new generation was beginning to redefine both the demographics and the values of that political inheritance.[61] In September 2000, at his father's near-regal state funeral, a young Justin Trudeau stepped forward to offer a reading. "Friends, Romans, countrymen . . ." the younger Trudeau began, his eulogy viewed by a record nationwide audience. It was, it would later become apparent, a statement of political intent as much as an expression of personal grief.

Across the Atlantic it was the European Union that perhaps most sharply embodied the dilemmas of the moment, as it reached the high point of its popularity and momentum at the end of the decade: a point at which it then commissioned a constitutional treaty that was roundly (and predictably) rejected. For its part, Washington had "every reason to be satisfied with the overall balance sheet of the nineties," as one critic put it.

> The USSR had been knocked out of the ring, Europe and Japan kept in check, China drawn into increasingly close trade relations, the UN reduced to little more than a permissions office; and all this accomplished to the tune of the most emollient of ideologies, whose every second word was international understanding and democratic goodwill. Peace, justice and freedom were spreading around the world.[62]

Seen in this light the Empire of Democracy looked strong at the turn of the millennium. And yet as the rumblings from the margins of society—on left and right alike—suggested, the old collective resentments were not quite spent either. Indeed, the years to come would see questions of nation and class come crashing back to the very center of Western politics, each brought into play by what were to be the two major shocks of the decade. The Western democracies, beginning with America, were about to be swept into a powerful vortex of events that would fundamentally challenge the post-1970s liberal democratic order.

The very first of those shocks was just a few months away.

PART III
Victory without Peace (2001–)

13

The Assault on Freedom

"THE LAST WEEK is a great blur with no divisions between night and day," observed the Australian novelist Peter Carey from his home in New York a week after the attacks of September 11, 2001. "Time is broken. The events of the first day bleed into the next and all the powerful emotions and disturbing sights are now so hard to put in proper sequence."[1] Staggered as the attacks were, many news networks already had cameras trained on the burning north building when the second plane struck the south—an audacity of intended spectacle that brought the world to a momentary standstill.[2]

Almost everybody would remember where they were when they heard or first glimpsed the news. Few would forget the details as they unfolded during the day: of calls patched out from those trapped above the flames; of firemen still inside searching as the first tower fell because their radio equipment was faulty and they had not received the order to evacuate. The ghastly, cinematic quality of events in New York—the ash that covered Fifth Avenue and fell as far away as Brooklyn, the letterheads and memos and office papers that littered the neighboring streets for days after—seared the imagination of a generation. Worst of all was the smell: the acrid smell of burnt metal, like "singed hair," and the stench of the smoldering "pile" that lingered weeks after.[3]

Many however did forget the other locations: a plane that crashed into a field after the passengers failed in their bid to retake control; the western corner of the Pentagon wrought, by the impact of American Airlines' Flight 77, into a mass of blackened rubble.

Since taking office in January, the incoming President George W. Bush had confirmed suspicions that his would be a lackluster presidency. Now his administration moved quickly to downplay early signs of unpreparedness before the attacks. Warnings, it seemed, had trickled in over the summer. Reports had been passed up the chain of command that the radicalized Saudi heir, Osama bin Laden, and his al-Qaeda network were intending to strike the United States, perhaps on American soil. The president had been alerted. These facts were kept from the public in the immediate aftermath of the attacks. There would be time for blame later. For now, there were more immediate problems to deal with. The public was jumpy. The New York stock exchange and the Federal Reserve had shut. America's borders had been closed and its airspace sealed. The first task for the new president was reassuring a nation in shock that life, American life, would go on. But what did that mean at the start of the twenty-first century? The years to come would be a profound reckoning on that score; and an awakening once more to the fact that democracy can be threatened from within at the same time as it is threatened from without.

As the shocks reverberated around the world messages of sympathy and support flowed in. "We are all traumatized by this terrible tragedy," declared the UN's Kofi Annan, whose own offices in midtown New York were evacuated when the second tower was struck. Germany's Gerhard Schröder announced that the attacks were "a declaration of war against the civilized world."[4] Australia's John Howard, who was in Washington, DC, when he heard the news, pulled open the curtain of his room at the Willard Hotel to see the Pentagon ablaze. That evening he sat in the visitors' gallery of the House to show solidarity; the next day he invoked the ANZUS alliance (requiring Australia, New Zealand, and the United States to come to each other's aid in the event of attack) and declared: "Australia will provide all support that might be requested of us by the United States in any action that might be taken."[5] NATO too placed itself at the American president's disposal (for all that the Bush administration had scarcely acknowledged it during his first nine months in office).

The British responded most effusively of all. Publicly they substituted "God Save the Queen" with "The Star Spangled Banner" during the changing of the guard at Buckingham Palace. Privately, Prime Minister Tony Blair maneuvered to play a leading role in supporting, and perhaps shaping, the US response, whatever that might now be. It was the British who, the following day, flew their top intelligence forces into Washington—with the national lockdown still in place, the only non-military patrol flight to carve its way into American airspace that day. On board were Richard Dearlove, the grandmaster of British intelligence, Eliza Manningham-Buller, then deputy chief of MI5, and David Manning, Blair's foreign policy adviser.

Officially the British delegation had come to convey their condolences.

Unofficially they were there to convey a warning, framed as a diplomatic expression of hope, that America would react to these catastrophic events with caution. It was already known that Afghanistan was where bin Laden had based himself while planning the attacks. It was also widely known that the embers of the first President Bush's unfinished business in Iraq still glowed in the hearts of those former officials who had returned to public service in the younger Bush's administration. "I hope we can all agree," said David Manning over dinner at the CIA's headquarters in Langley, Virginia, "that we should concentrate on Afghanistan, and not launch any attacks on Iraq."

In the days and weeks to come other nations too weighed in behind what they hoped would be a carefully measured response. There was little love lost for Saddam Hussein anywhere. But it was clear that radical terror networks like bin Laden's posed a more complex danger than the matter of whether or not they were sponsored by one or other "rogue" state. In keeping with the liberal internationalism the Western democracies had spent the previous decade building up, most countries wanted any perpetrators still unaccounted for brought to legal justice if possible. Most hoped to avoid a military response altogether (Israel, India, and the US public being the exceptions to this).[6] Meanwhile the rest of the world held its breath and waited to see what a twenty-first-century Gulliver would do when roused. It was obvious to everyone that whoever did find themselves on the receiving end of America's vengeance would pay a very high price. What was not yet apparent, though it soon would be, was the extent to which the response to 9/11 would also redefine the parameters of democratic life at home in the West.

It is vital to take stock of 9/11, therefore, in the context of the larger history we have been traversing. There was not, contrary to the bellicose rhetoric of the US foreign policy community, a "before 9/11 and an after 9/11." What 9/11 *did* do was to intensify some of the contradictions inherent to post-70s era liberal democracy. More immediately, it gave succor to some of the more radical conservative visions of domestic and foreign policy that had emerged in the 1990s. It was inevitable that American citizens wanted more protection all of a sudden, even if they did not want more "state" as the price of supplying it. But the way the Western nations, and the United States in particular, sought to resolve that particular tension arguably created more problems in the long run than it resolved.

For one, the question of what should be the appropriate means and limits of executive power in a democracy was blown wide open after nearly half a century of being closed down. For another, a thornier trade-off was now posed between those competing values of freedom and security. "You're either with us or you're with the terrorists," Bush proclaimed fatefully as his administration geared up to launch a "war" on terror that would know no bounds nor limits nor price. This was, of course, a game that bin Laden himself, who within days of the attacks had moved into hiding deep in the Tora Bora mountains of Afghanistan, was only too happy to play. "These events have divided the world into two camps, the camp of the faithful and the camp of infidels," he said later that year, in a televised address on Qatar's Al Jazeera television network.

And yet it was not, of course, a game in which bin Laden was in any sense an equal player. Just five weeks after four planes were brought down over America the first twelve-man American Special Forces team crossed into Afghanistan near Mazar-e-Sharif and the US war machine powered into action behind them. Ostensibly in pursuit of Osama bin Laden, in truth they were the vanguard of a much broader, more ambitious, and for liberal democracy in general, more dangerous objective: the remaking of global order in the image of might, not right. The military response to 9/11 had begun.

The Response

Long before the first bombs fell on Afghanistan a welter of political and legal work had already been undertaken. "They've roused a mighty giant," the newly incumbent President Bush declared in one of his earliest speeches to the nation.[7] But during the first crucial hours after the twin towers were struck it was Vice President Dick Cheney who proved the most prepared for the unimaginable and who steered the reeling ship of state. One wonders, with hindsight, how Clinton and Gore might have handled this situation differently. It was not long since the heated presidential campaign of 2000, when Al Gore out-hawked Bush on the need to deploy US forces abroad in defense of democratic values at home. But Gore, like Clinton, thought that there was already a rationale rooted in the "international community" for doing this. Cheney, who as a congressman in the 1980s had participated in top-secret contingency plans for maintaining the US chain of command in the event of nuclear war, believed a whole new basis for American intervention needed creating.

That basis began to be put in place on the morning of 9/11 itself, several hundred feet under the White House, where Cheney translated his experience born of an earlier era's threat into handling the administration's emergency phase of the response: the closing of airspace, orders to shoot down further planes, what to do about visiting dignitaries (including John Howard), and how to respond to the press. He also began planning a more strategic response as well. The sense within the Bush administration, but especially in the office of the vice president and the president (both of whom now demanded to review all possible intelligence reports concerning future threats), was that—as things stood—they were being asked to fight with one hand tied behind their back. There was "too much international law, too many civil liberties, too many constraints on the President's war powers, too many rights for defendants, and too many rules against lethal covert actions" to mount an effective response to a crisis of this scale, it was later said.[8]

Cheney was not acting alone, however. The vice president was part of a wider grouping of conservative foreign policy hawks, which included Donald Rumsfeld and Colin Powell, whom Bush had brought into government with him. In some cases this was simply because they had worked for his father. These were the disgruntled Republicans, like Paul Wolfowitz, who had authored the infamous Defense Planning Guidance (DPG) document of 1992, and who had since spread themselves across most of the more forthright foreign policy think tanks and "committees" operating in Washington in the years between. Now they were back in office and nothing in the present moment of danger was going to disabuse them of their view that American power needed reasserting in the world; in fact it had confirmed it. The inner core of the Bush administration now began to make plans "to work sort of on the dark side, if you will," as Cheney put it in the administration's chillingly folksy vernacular.[9]

Little more beyond that was said in public during the first days. But within the White House there was feverish activity and a closing of ranks around the president by a committed group of conservative lawyers, advisers, and senior staff under Cheney's control brought in specifically to shore up the executive. This included the vice president's combative and dogmatic legal counsel David Addington and a former Addington appointee at the Pentagon, Jim Haynes. Cheney made sure that Addington was brought with him into the Emergency Operations Center beneath the White House on September 11, and Addington was soon coordinating the first salvo in the White House's response: the legal ramparts of a twenty-first-century democracy at war.[10]

This team under Cheney worked as if they were aides-de-camp already in the midst of battle. Intellectually the transition to war—one still active at the time of writing—had been made with barely a flicker of a second thought. And just as quickly, they began rewriting some of the rules laid down by the US constitution so that the president could exercise greater war powers than it had been customary to grant the executive branch alone. A week after the attacks Robert Mueller III, the head of the FBI, came with a report outlining progress in the FBI's investigation to date. He underscored in particular the need for proper commitment to judicial procedure. This being not at all what the administration wanted to hear, Bush's attorney general, John Ashcroft, batted his concerns aside.

The CIA meanwhile came forward with memoranda demanding it be granted greater powers (or as the CIA saw it, given back the powers Frank Church had taken from them in the 1970s) to launch a "covert war." This was looked on much more favorably by the administration. "We'll all probably be prosecuted," said then CIA director Cofer Black, with a certain patriotic relish as he prepared an intelligence note for the president to sign, in which the CIA laid out its requests. Even covert actions ordinarily require congressional approval, but in the state of emergency the Bush administration had declared after 9/11, congressional approval was now "pared down" so that it consisted of four elected representatives, who furthermore would retain their anonymity. Before long the White House had put together a dual strategy to effect not only a response to the attacks but a complete transformation of the presidency into a war cabinet.

After listing aimlessly in the first months of his presidency, the Bush administration was thus, within days of 9/11, moving forward with a singular poise, as a process of institutional and legal rescripting of US citizens' basic liberties was set in train under the imperative of protecting Americans and safeguarding American values. Ironically, Bush's own approval ratings now shot up for the first time. Bush himself was no details man, of course—prior to 9/11 his staff had to schedule intelligence briefings in five-minute slots, lest the president should lose attention—but he grasped the new narrative of a war presidency with instinctive willingness and immediately embraced the role of commander-in-chief.

In public the president continued to speak of a Manichean world divided into good and evil. Having already challenged people to stand with America or stand on the side of the terrorists, he then went further, in his first-ever State of the Union in January, to introduce the notion of an "axis of evil": countries who should consider themselves on the United States' watch list. This had the advantage of being a worldview he already held. As he had said some months before 9/11, "[Before] it was us versus them. And it was clear who them was. Today, we're not so sure who they are, but we know they're there."[11] The US satirical weekly the *Onion* quickly foresaw where this sort of worldview was headed in the post-9/11 context: "US Vows To Defeat Whoever It Is We're At War With," it emblazoned on its front page late in 2001.

But who was the "we" here? As one skeptical reader in the *Washington Post* put it some years later in 2006: "If al-Qaeda had attacked Sydney in September 2001, Australia would not have invaded Afghanistan."[12] Al-Qaeda had not attacked Australia, of course, and it had not attacked Clinton's America either; it had attacked an America run by the untested mettle of a new Republican administration staffed by old Republican radicals. And so the question inevitably arises as to where the imperative driving this overhaul of foreign and domestic policy was really coming from. Cheney and the rest of "the Vulcans" as they were dubbed—Paul Wolfowitz, Richard Armitage, Donald Rumsfeld, Condoleezza Rice— whose foreign policy experience stretched back to the Nixon adminis- tration in many cases, and who were the ones who really authored the foreign policy decisions attributed to Bush, were certainly crucial.[13] But tactical moves to rewrite the rules of engagement at home are not the same as strategic visions of what to do next.

In fact, the Bush administration *did* have its own strategy, but it was an old one. It consisted of using the might of the US military to promote democracy in other parts of the world, especially in those areas, like the Middle East, deemed critical to the projection of US power more broadly, not to bring democracy to those nations, but in order to safeguard the security of American liberal democracy at home. This was presented to the world still as a part of the post–Cold War democratic or liberal peace. But it was more broadly about US hegemony in the world. And the Bush administration's signature contribution to it, now, was to flip the transmission switch from the liberal humanitarian mode in which Amer- ican power had operated over the previous decade to a liberal imperial mode in which it was much more willing to use military firepower as a lever in this process. It was a vision that came, of course, from the neo- conservative school of thought.

Though with hindsight the Bush administration would come to be remembered as the neoconservative administration par excellence—more so even than Reagan had been with his Star Wars programs abroad and his tax cuts and deregulation drives at home—there was nothing inevitable about the Bush administration's fateful turn to neonconservative thinking. Neoconservatives after all wanted an active, even aggressive role for America in the world and as a candidate Bush had looked to all intents and purposes like an isolationist. Had it not been for September 11, the era of Trumpian "America First" policies may well have come a decade earlier, and under Bush. Back in 2000, with Clinton still at the helm, neoconservative intellectuals in Washington saw sufficiently little promise in the Bush campaign that they had initially gravitated toward Trump's later nemesis John McCain in the Republican primaries. As William Kristol himself put it, "When McCain talks about remoralizing America, he talks in terms of reinvigorating patriotism."[14] Bush did nothing of the sort. McCain was a former fighter pilot and prisoner of war; Bush was a draft dodger and a former alcoholic.

But there were, in fact, always two George W. Bushes. There was the maladroit, folksy buffoon: the one who, so far as the neocons saw it, as they looked on with dismay in the first months of his administration, took too soft a line on North Korea, did little to increase defense spending, and who apologized meekly to the Chinese when a US spy plane collided with a Chinese fighter jet in April. This was the constrained George W. Bush; the one who sang to the tune of the realist politics and mainstream Republican homilies of his father's hand-me-down advisers. In the aftermath of 9/11, however, the other more idealist and single-minded Bush—the Bush who in a rare flicker of his underlying evangelical candor had spoken in 1999, in the context of US foreign policy, of freedom as "the soul's right to breathe"—was shaken back into life. It was, in the words of one observer, an "astonishing transformation."[15] And the neocons had taken note of it.

Central to the neoconservative vision was the primacy of freedom not just as a political value but as a motor of history. Freedom for the neocons was as class had been for Marx: a central organizing concept around which all else needed rearranging to fit. Unlike Marx's analysis of class, however, neoconservatives saw freedom not as a process of struggle, but as a thing, a resource. For America that meant not merely protecting it at home but actively promoting it abroad. And it was these ideas, of the "transformative power of freedom," as Natan Sharansky put it, that appealed to Bush as he looked for ways forward amid the turmoil of the first few days and weeks. In particular it underpinned his growing conviction that a hegemonic power such as America could and perhaps even should act with imperial single-mindedness: and it would still be seen as a benevolent force for good, "a veritable global public good," in doing so.[16]

If neocons themselves were coy about using the term "imperialism" to describe this, it scarcely mattered, since their convictions on most other matters were imperialist in all but name. This included their view both that the UN was not merely an obstacle to unilateral engagement but a part of the problem (because it granted legitimacy to dubious political regimes and put countries like Somalia on equal footing with others), and that international law was ultimately just a hindrance to effective international diplomacy. And the moment that the president also came to believe, after 9/11, that the United States did have a "right" to strike "preemptively" against other nations before catastrophe struck at home, was the moment that the neoconservative ascendancy touched down in the heart of the Oval Office as well.

The historical significance of this can hardly be understated. The idea of preemptive intervention had been put forward in the Defense Planning Guidance (DPG) document that Bush's father had rejected as being not merely radical but livewire and borderline dangerous. But Bush senior was acting in a moment of national euphoria and patriotic triumph and, ever the true conservative, he was trying to dampen expectations not inflame them. His son by contrast was caught in the midst of the gravest national crisis in more than half a century, was aware that confidence needed restoring, and he now made this rather radical reinvention of the age-old doctrine of American exceptionalism the linchpin of his new policy.

Bush turned to the neoconservatives largely for contingent reasons therefore: in part through his own latently suppressed instincts; in part out of the desperate need for a method to respond to the suddenly enveloping madness; and in part out of a lack of better alternatives of his own. But once he had adopted the neoconservative line, this man who had worked his way out of problems with alcohol, who understood the idea of "staying the course" as a moral imperative, not as an historical lesson, would not deviate from it for an instant for the remainder of his time in office. And prosecuting this "war on terror" would become not so much the defining feature of his presidency as the very substance of that presidency itself.

The great irony in all of this was the fact that the neocons had never seriously considered terrorism as a factor in world politics. This was significant to the extent that it also determined why the US response took the shape of a more conventional war footing. More specifically, the neocons, and those in the administration like Vice President Cheney who shared their views, wanted a rerun of the Cold War that many of them had earned their political stripes fighting. They needed an enemy they understood and knew how to fight and so they did all they could to fashion that enemy in the form of what they now called "Islamic extremism" or, in more colorful moments, "Islamo-fascism."

Thus would the coming war on terror be every bit as political, and indeed cultural, as the Cold War before it had been. And like the Cold War it would be a war fought against a clearly scripted *ideological* enemy, with religious markers made to stand in for now defunct political ones. It was to be extensive in reach and indeterminate in duration, a "long war" and a "global war" at the same time: all of which would provide the US administration with the flexibility needed to fight it. And of course it would require sacrifice at home too, if not in lives, at least in the democratic way of life, and what now came to be seen as that naive garden of innocence that the 1990s had brought about.

In another climate all this might have been more openly contested from the start. One reason it was not, and least of all within the administration, was owing to the critical roles played by Cheney and Donald Rumsfeld. Rumsfeld, secretary of defense, was not a card-carrying neoconservative. But he was a former chair of the Committee on the Present Danger, like many self-identified neoconservatives, and he was on the board of Freedom House, another of the movement's institutional strongholds in Washington. Rumsfeld did not share the neoconservatives' more utopian visions, however, such as the idea that it was incumbent upon America to promote freedom elsewhere. For him the critical thing was asserting American power to protect its *own* interests. That made him the perfect foil for their ideas (for what Rumsfeld suggested in pared down military strategic terms, Bush could usually see a larger, utopian endpoint to).

It was Dick Cheney who provided the most effective conduit for neoconservative ideas. His understanding of the Middle East as a region came in large part from neoconservative scholars writing in publications like the *Weekly Standard*. Cheney did not consider himself to be a neoconservative. But by 2003 he had ordered thirty copies of the neocon *Weekly Standard* to be delivered to the White House each week. Perhaps more significantly he made sure that the many discussions now taking place about how to respond to 9/11 remained focused on the Middle East.[17] Elsewhere within the administration other neocons began to influence the way that intelligence was interpreted and disseminated. In September 2002 Paul Wolfowitz, deputy secretary of defense and co-lead on the controversial 1992 DPG, and Douglas Feith, undersecretary of defense for policy, oversaw the creation of the Office of Special Plans, which reported to Scooter Libby in Cheney's office. The information it put together on Iraq, usually from sources such as Ahmed Chalabi's Iraqi National Congress, was not sent to the security or intelligence agencies, where it might have been vetted, but instead sent straight for discussion by the administration's inner core.[18]

But the Bush administration was aided by one other critical source, as it looked to turn a terrorist attack at home into a case for war abroad. For the underlying notion of launching preemptive wars on states that had not themselves attacked the United States—the argument upon which the entire Bush administration's response now rested—was not merely the product of hard-core neocons' imagining. The ground here had been prepared by two other "liberal hawks," namely British Prime Minister Tony Blair and UN Secretary General Kofi Annan, each of whom had put forward their own grand doctrines of sovereign "responsibility"— exposing states who failed to comply to possible military action from the international community—in 1999 and 2000 respectively.

Annan and Blair both had in mind a situation in which mass civilian atrocities were perpetrated within a rogue or failed state. They were liberal, not imperial, interventionists. But they had blurred the line none-theless. And legally the underlying argument was the same. It ensured that there was sufficient flexibility, internationally, for Bush and his team to now rewrite the rules abroad, to launch his "visionary foreign policy against international terrorism," just as they were doing at home. "Our war begins with al-Qaeda," Bush insisted, "but it does not end there." With approval for $40 billion from Congress and the requisite "cursory diplomacy" out of the way, the war on terror proper could begin.[19] The conflict would, of course, be more costly than anybody could imagine, the matter of a few billion dollars soon paling into insignificance. It would also do greater damage to the formal and informal ties that had thus far bound the post–Cold War era together than even the United States might have wished for. Above all, once started, it would prove practically im-possible to stop.

Democracy at War

Before even the heat of the pile had gone out in New York, the world's most powerful democracy was embarked on a global offensive, the likes of which had not been seen since the height of the Vietnam War. This was not Bosnia, it was a thousand Bosnias unleashed wherever the world's most powerful liberal democracy saw fit. On October 7 the first bombs fell on Kandahar and Operation Enduring Freedom was green-lighted, with al-Qaeda and the Taliban, who had made the mistake of "harboring" them, in its sights. Aware of the need to keep allies as much as Afghan civilians on his side, Bush was quick to point out the following day that "at the same time, our good Nation" also dropped 37,000 kits of food and medicine, as if that somehow answered any outstanding legal or moral question marks over the operation.[20] As if the Department of Defense had any idea who picked them up.

First, Special Operations forces went into action in the north—the signature "light footprint" approach it was hoped would be the defining feature of the conflict to come. Meanwhile the CIA focused on trying to provoke anti-Taliban splits among tribal regions in the south. Adopting this "dual strategy" had been something of a compromise position between those wishing to throw support behind the Northern Alliance forces in the north and those, better apprised of the state and reliability of those forces, who preferred to give the CIA's strategy of bribes and provocations time to work in the south. The latter included the Musharraf regime in Islamabad, Pakistan, and his influence was one reason the initial bombing—aside from there being relatively few "hard targets" in Afghanistan in the first place—was too conservative for Rumsfeld's taste.[21]

After several weeks of only modest gains Rumsfeld thus asked General Tommy Franks to step up the campaign in the north. With over a hundred sorties now being flown a day, including B-52s dropping "some of the heaviest arms in the American subnuclear arsenal," Northern Alliance fighters, spotted by American special forces, pressed into Kabul on the evening of November 13.[22] Very few Taliban fighters had stayed behind to defend it. Bin Laden himself had last been in the city on November 8, to attend a memorial service for an Uzbek militant leader killed in an airstrike the day before.

Otherwise the world's most wanted man spent the first weeks of the war constantly on the move. From Kabul bin Laden fled first to Jalalabad, leaving there by convoy before that too fell to the advancing coalition and Northern Alliance forces on November 14. From Jalalabad bin Laden headed up into the Tora Bora mountains. When fighting closed in on the caves around bin Laden's position, US Central Command made what was arguably a crucial mistake: it opted to have Pakistani forces go in (there were by now around a thousand Marines on the ground) with the Americans providing air support only. Sometime before the 17th, bin Laden saw his moment and disappeared.

If this was a major blow to the stated aims of the war (it was less a blow to their real aim of course) better news was at least coming from elsewhere. With Kandahar and Kabul now "secured," and the fighting in the Tora Bora effectively over, the Americans had Hamid Karzai—an exile in the Chalabi mold—sworn in as the "consensus" leader of a new interim government. Though careful to avoid too much triumphalism, the White House nonetheless felt some sort of progress report was required, and in late January it presented its verdict in the form of a public information document. "The Global War on Terrorism: The First 100 Days" actually said less about what sort of "military success" had been achieved than it did about *how* it had been achieved: "Supported by the collective will of the world," the military campaign had been "lightning quick"—an adaptable strategy that put "less than 3,000 troops on the ground."[23] If the effect was in part to underscore the sheer scale and cutting-edge capacity of American military power, it was also, and just as importantly, a prescription and a prologue to the next phase in the war. America wasn't done yet.

Two things in particular emerged from "The Global War on Terrorism: The First 100 Days" that would be of significance. The first was the effort to normalize if not to conceal, within narratives of "coalition" support, the intensely radical nature of Bush's neocon-inspired doctrine of military preemption. Second, the "cutting-edge military strategy," with its constant references to "twenty-first-century technology" and its invocation of the fact that there had not been a single American casualty during the campaign was celebrated as if the violence of war was now some sort of humanitarian triumph. More shrewdly it was used to create "a low-risk power vacuum around American [military] planning."[24] Rumsfeld and his war planners were all too aware that modern democracies simply do not tolerate large numbers of casualties: hence the refusal to go into the Tora Bora after bin Laden. The entire success of the war on terror, as a longer-term prospect, rested on demonstrating right from the start that the burden of its fatalities would be borne by others. Afghanistan was, in that sense, a deliberate and a well-executed testing ground.

In a crude sense, it had in fact never been safer to fight as an American soldier. Even when the war escalated to Iraq and the violent insurgency of the 2003–5 years had set in, heavily mobilized American forces at war lost 1,874 "on duty" soldiers during 2004. In 1980, at the start of the last Cold War decade, by contrast, the nation suffered 2,393 active duty military deaths—many through accident rather than hostile action.[25] But the difference was also in large part because the risks of combat, thanks to the nature of the technologies deployed, had been displaced onto others, making the "footprint" of the twenty-first-century American military at war anything but light (or likely to be well received). This did not undermine the psychological burden of fighting, but it did change the mortality effect. On the day that Hamid Karzai was to be inaugurated a convoy of tribal elders on their way to take part in the celebrations was blown apart by US navy jets and gunships. Fifty people were killed in their vehicles and more died after the few survivors sought refuge in a nearby village. It turned out that the tip-off had been manufactured by a local Pashtun warlord in the pay of the CIA who was exploiting the post-conflict anarchy in Afghanistan to build up his own power base.[26]

This was one of the first times America would find itself taking the wrong lives in the name of its gift of "freedom" after 9/11, but it wouldn't be the last. And though it wasn't keeping count, others were. Moreover, as the numerous internecine conflicts and nebulous local fronts underscored, the politics of Afghanistan were highly complex, and US military planners understood barely the half of it. Lack of knowledge on the ground was compounded by a near complete ignorance of the wider region (despite it being the primary obsession of the neocon movement). But with such a disparity of force in the field, ignorance also made simplification of the task that much easier. Within a year the ragged tribal hodgepodge of Afghanistan had been converted into a "nation" and the Bush administration was busy justifying the intervention of its troops in the style of a League of Nations mandate.

The threat of global terrorism was likewise reconstructed during these first months until it looked more like the sort of thing the US military could physically attack. In the offices of the Pentagon, new strategic maps were created in which whole swathes of the earth were flattened down, first into "zones of nonintegration"—a description that functioned both as an "analysis" of the problem and a warning—and then into "battle zones." The full political implications of this work would become clearer in February of the following year, when Colin Powell stood before the UN Security Council and rapped on his chart about the existence of weapons of mass destruction (WMD) in Iraq. But long before then, out of this concocted regional geography and the military-strategic conclusions drawn from it at the Pentagon and the Department of Defense, a whole new "landscape of terrorism" was being "constructed," as the cultural critic Michael Shapiro put it, as desertscapes interspersed with khaki and smoke became the routine backdrop to news bulletins across the West.

Already in the week after 9/11, when parallels were still being drawn with Pearl Harbor rather than Saigon, a covert legal strategy that would underpin the assault on what Rumsfeld would later call the "unknown unknowns" posing a threat to US national security had begun to be elaborated in secret. Under David Addington's direction, the president's lawyers were at work providing a justificatory architecture for the ad-ministration's war plans: and this new legal edifice was to be rolled out domestically as well as in US interventions abroad. This required no little legal rewriting of its own.

At the Justice Department, John Yoo, a legal counsel, got to work addressing and revising the president's powers in wartime. He and others conformed to the basic rationale that guided the entire inner circle around the president, and that was framed around Addington's own unorthodox reading of the constitution. As Addington saw it, in times of national emergency, the president was permitted to disregard almost all legal con-straints that might prevent him responding as he saw fit in the nation's interest. Of course, those restraints had been put there, equally in the nation's interest, to ensure that executive power operated within limits. But by turning the terrorist attacks of 9/11 into an act of war, by mak-ing the current crisis a rerun of the Cold War and a clash of state-based ideologies, the president's lawyers found a way to circumvent those constraints. That it was a strategy fundamentally mismatched to the threat it wished to respond to would only later become apparent.

The focus of all this legal work, the "New Paradigm" it was called, would in due course bring about an expansion of executive power not seen in a democratic nation since the Second World War. As early as September 14, just as Congress was about to vote to authorize Bush to go to war against the perpetrators of the attacks, White House counsel Alberto Gonzalez sought to add a last-minute demand that Congress also permit the president to wage war against terrorists at home too. Congress denied him, but the administration was not about to give up that easily. Bush's legal team—the War Council as they were now known—were already at work on a series of legal memos that would provide de facto, and in *secret*, what Congress had been asked to grant de jure.[27]

On September 21 Bush's lawyers overturned the long-standing con-straint of *Posse comitatus* (the Reconstruction-era stipulation that the federal government not be allowed to deploy soldiers domestically), asserting instead that, *at times of national emergency*, "if the President decided the threat justified deploying the military inside the country" he could do so. On September 25, the Office issued yet another secret legal memo, this time permitting the president to take whatever military action he deemed necessary abroad, including using preemptive strikes.[28] Other memos put restrictions on domestic surveillance and Fourth Amendment protections on ice, as behind the scenes a remarkable set of powers continued to be transferred to the president. When the next head of the Office of Legal Counsel, Jack Goldsmith, took over in 2003 the extent of this overhaul immediately struck him; it was, he said later, "the biggest legal mess I had ever seen in my life."[29] But that legal mess nonetheless had a crystal-clear objective, and it was one that by 2003 was largely met: to take the nation to war "in a way and at an hour of our choosing," as Bush put it.

Little by little, then, often without quite realizing it, the Western world adjusted itself to a state of constant siege. The silent markers of political tension, of a sort that had not been felt since the height of the Cold War, blanketed daily life once more. If this time the fighting was "hot," it was also mercifully far removed. "On the one side we witnessed images of [political leaders'] embodied resolve in high resolution," a critic of the war observed, "on the other, nighttime shadows with nobody in sight."[30] Only it wasn't all that far removed. Back home, as the scale of the deployment increased in preparation for the war's transition into Iraq, American soldiers trained in mock-up Arab cities in Nevada where they practiced kicking down doors and forcing families onto their knees, and where their colleagues learned to shoot from remote-controlled drones at suspicious-looking convoys.

It wasn't long before the first captives of the war on terror were being brought home too. On November 13, President Bush had signed into law Military Order Number 1 on the "Detention, Treatment, and Trial of Certain Non-Citizens in the War Against Terrorism." The immediate reference to "non-citizens" was telling, and the opening salvo in a new lexicon of subcivilian categories of personhood that the Bush administration would first introduce—frequently in contravention of existing international legal duties, including the Geneva Conventions—and then use to prosecute its underlying war aims. Such individuals would be those "with respect to whom I determine," declared Bush, in deeply Orwellian tones. The "principles of law" and "rules of evidence" as they apply in the United States would not apply to them, therefore. Such individuals were to be detained, but not necessarily to be tried, nor were they to be allowed any legal means to protest against their situation, be it in a US court or indeed "any court of any foreign nation." This was more than just breathtakingly sweeping rhetoric. It was a near unprecedented rewriting of the rulebook of international law, and it was authored by a *democratic* leader.

Individuals who found themselves falling into this category (which meant first falling into the hands of the US military, or those of the local bandits who usually handed them over) began to be transported out of Afghanistan and across the Atlantic to arrive at the newly prepared facilities for holding them at Guantánamo Bay, Cuba. They arrived, manacled to each other in orange jumpsuits and blacked-out masks; in effect they could be held indefinitely even though no evidence against them could, in point of fact, be brought to bear. What was more, they would not be able to contest their detention: eight centuries of habeas corpus now became a victim of the war on terror. Perhaps the most dramatic thing of all was that the US military was happy for all this to be noted down by the world's press.[31] *Pour encourager les autres.*

Like so much in the first months after September 11, this was the brainchild of the US Justice Department. After first considering the island enclaves of Tinian, Wake, and Midway in the Pacific, Guantánamo was ultimately chosen because it was believed that it provided close access to the detainees (as well, it should be pointed out, as a reminder to Americans of just how "real" the war on terror was). The fact that it was an American-run base stationed on *Cuban* sovereign territory meant that it also provided—or so at least it was claimed—both immunity from American domestic laws and an "anomalous" relationship to international law more broadly: an ambiguity that could and would be exploited. "Every civilian death is a tragedy," the conservative lawyer Alan Dershowitz observed, "but some are more tragic than others."[32] In short some lives counted for more than others and in the Manichean politics being espoused by the US president they were to be treated as such. A long-burning and carefully guarded light had just gone out in the heartland of liberal democracy.

The Long March to Iraq

During the course of 2002 it became increasingly clear to the world exactly why the United States had been copying across the aims of the ground offensive in Afghanistan onto a much broader canvas. It was already the closest thing to an international "open secret" that America had unfinished business in Iraq after 1991. In the intervening years it had become even more invested—to its constant frustration—in the issue of Israel–Palestine. The war on terror having brought its armed forces back to the region, America now wanted to revisit the entire Middle Eastern question and to do so by removing Iraq from the equation. And from this point on, the new logic of the war on terror merged with the neocon agenda embodied by the Project for a New American Century.

It wasn't as if the United States had left Iraq alone in the meantime. The West had been waging a "low intensity" war of sporadic missile strikes against Saddam Hussein for much of the 1990s and a higher-burning war on the Iraqi people through the UN sanctions regime.[33] Those two fronts would now merge, and powerfully so, as the war on terror swept into the country. The assault was to involve a "coalition" of forces, once again, and would be spearheaded by the US and the UK. Preparations for the war in Iraq had been under way since the very first weeks after September 11, and they in turn built on earlier contingency preparations dusted off from the US Defense Department's vaults. None of this could disguise the fact that moving into Iraq was a dramatic detour from the original mandate of the response to 9/11.

It is remarkable that neither Bush nor Blair reckoned on the level of public opposition to the war in Iraq that they encountered. For Blair, given that he was placing UK forces in danger in support of another nation's war aims, it was not obvious, least of all to the British public, quite what he sought to gain. The answer, as suggested in a 2002 note Blair penned privately to Bush and which was later made available during the Chilcot Inquiry, turns on a combination of character and political strategy. It turns on his character in that, for all he had shown himself tireless in support of peace in Northern Ireland, Blair was also endowed with a missionary streak for which he had sought international legitimacy via his doctrine of the international community: "this thing is deep," as he later testified under oath, "and we have to confront it."[34] In other words, one was justified reaching into Iraq to root out an evil that was, in many respects, entirely separate from the Baathist political regime in that country.

It also turned on political strategy in that it was clear to Blair that Bush was going ahead with the invasion regardless. As Blair put it in his letter in 2002: "I will be with you, whatever. . . . The danger is, as ever with these things, unintended consequences. . . . If we win quickly, everyone will be our friend. If we don't . . . recriminations will start fast."³⁵ For Blair, then, it was better to be able to restrain Bush by insisting, at least, that the path to war be shepherded through the United Nations. But that hardly guaranteed a watertight casus belli. No more watertight was the coalition's official legal case for the war, which ultimately rested upon what came to be called the "dodgy dossier": a speculative intelligence report provided by an unnamed Iraqi source, upon whose evidence the British and American claims of Saddam's willingness and capacity to develop "weapons of mass destruction" ultimately relied.

There being no clear link to al-Qaeda, there was no reason to be in Iraq, as even the usually compliant Security Council had pointed out, and so the dossier turned out to be absolutely crucial. Yet it was an argument, not an evidentiary case. And the British intelligence agencies having been pushed into painting a general "picture" of Iraqi malfeasance, the British Parliament and the American Congress were browbeaten into accepting it. Meanwhile, the sheer scale of popular resistance to the escalation of the Afghanistan conflict was ignored. For Bush and Blair, Iraq was akin to the crossing of the Rubicon.

Just a month before the start of the war, as many as 50 million citizens marched for peace around the world. Everywhere from Athens to Rome to Tokyo to Sydney a global public fashioned itself to declare that this was not a war in their name. Nearer to the intended conflict, a firestorm of protests was set off from Benghazi to Tehran. In the UK around 2 million people took to the streets of London, the largest peace rally in the nation's history: nuns, nurses, taxi drivers, and even the George Orwell Society were among them.³⁶ Banners mixed good humor with serious intent. "Notts County Supporters Say Make Love Not War (And a Home Win Against Bristol Would Be Nice)."³⁷ Almost as noteworthy as the numbers that turned out was the sheer range of organizations behind the protest: led by the Stop the War Coalition, it included over 450 separate civil society groups, from Greenpeace to the Muslim Association for Great Britain, to the third largest political party, the Liberal Democrats.

There were international diplomatic calls for giving more time to weapons inspections. But Bush remained silent while Blair merely shrugged off the criticism. "I ask the marchers to understand this . . ." he said (oblivious to the fact that they were asking *him* to understand). "I do not seek unpopularity as a badge of honor, but sometimes it is the price of leadership and the cost of conviction." That weekend a poll revealed only 29 percent of Britons were in favor of war. If this was, curiously, a huge victory for democracy in respect of public voice, it was also a terrible defeat in light of the ease with which a political elite, whose course was already set on war, felt free to ignore it. Indeed, while the scale of the marches prompted comparisons with the antiwar and civil rights demonstrations of the 1960s, it was the differences that were more revealing. As the British radical Hilary Wainwright, veteran of many a Vietnam march, averred: "We saw there were mechanisms for political change within the system [then]. Now there's no longer that sense that movements trigger parliamentary change."[38] Democracy was in a dangerous place.

Wainwright was far from alone, it turned out, as the clock to war ticked down and the political fallout heated up. "I have resigned from the cabinet because I believe that a fundamental principle of Labour's foreign policy has been violated," declared former Foreign Secretary and standing leader of the House of Commons Robin Cook, to a silenced Commons, who had not known of his plans. "The threshold for war should always be high. [But] what has come to trouble me most in recent weeks is the suspicion that if the hanging chads in Florida had gone the other way, and Al Gore had been elected, we would not now be about to commit British troops to the Middle East."[39]

Blair's willful refusal to listen to the voice of the people served to underscore the gap that had opened up between electorates and their executives, and the power of the "inner state" that had taken shape in the postdemocratic climate of the 1990s. What Cook observed before taking his final bow he might equally have said of the state of the British political community at large (in many ways he was): "If we believe in an international community based on binding rules and institutions, we cannot simply set them aside when they produce results that are inconvenient to us."[40] But even such a high-profile resignation as his could not stop the move to war by the British and American governments.

While the British government ignored such entreaties and focused on fine-tuning the legal case for presentation to the UN, the American military pressed on with the planning. And if it remained unclear what Blair hoped to get from Bush, it was perfectly clear by now what Bush saw in having Blair tag along: for he helped provide a useful veneer of judiciousness to the whole process, his jeans and blue-jumpered walks with Bush at Camp David adding gravity and a certain soul-searched patience to the moment (a search evidently called off the moment the cameras departed).

But both men were equally committed to making sure the war went ahead. In the United States, the Department of Homeland Security raised the domestic terror threat level to "orange" (part of a new color-coded threat system) to browbeat the public into going along. All this time, UN weapons inspectors under Hans Blix had continued their painstaking and dangerous work: Iraq was "cooperating," said Blix. But from the Pentagon's Defense Policy Board Richard Perle countered that Blix was "being seriously deceived." As Perle went on: "It reminds me of the way the Nazis hoodwinked Red Cross officials."[41] The inspectors had been set up for a fall, of course. As Perle knew only too well, they were only ever going to uncover evidence of Iraqi obstructionism. And obstruction in the Bush administration's worldview was the evidence of guilt needed to push the war machine on and into Iraq.

American Empire?

As the war got under way on March 20, 2003, Rumsfeld sought explicitly to outdo the spectacle of ten years previously. This was not to be a reprise of that war; it was to be its denouement. The focus was accordingly on what would come to be known as "shock and awe." As a presidential candidate, Bush had criticized Clinton in the 1990s for "pounding sand" with ineffective airstrikes. As president, Bush now pounded cities and critical infrastructure. It was deliberately, and quite consciously, the eye for the eye of New York. It was state terror, rained down from above—a terror that was to be as relentlessly filmed and mediatized as were the attacks of September 11 themselves. Terror and virtue were once again reconnected in their original sovereign form.[42] Political violence was back where it belonged: in the crosshairs of a Tomahawk targeting system.

As in Afghanistan the invasion turned out to be easily won. As just short of 150,000 coalition troops, consisting primarily of British and American forces, headed north from Kuwait, the British peeling off east to surround Basra and the Americans pushing on toward the north and Baghdad, the almost equal numbers of Iraqi forces, and above all Hussein's Republican Guard, largely melted away. And likewise, as with Afghanistan, the first few months saw a period of relative calm, as the occupying forces went on their patrols and Iraqis accustomed themselves to life after Saddam.

Back in Washington the Joint Chiefs congratulated themselves on a job well done. On April 16, the American country singer Darryl Worley performed his newly released, and deliberately timed, hit song "Have

You Forgotten?" to an audience at the Pentagon that included Rumsfeld, chairman of the Joint Chiefs, and Air Force General Richard Myers. Dressed in jeans and a black T-shirt, Worley brought Rumsfeld to tears and the Pentagon staffers to a standing ovation. As he said to the American Forces Press Service, "Now, it's been called a prowar song. If that means that I support my president and the conflict that we just took care of over there, then I guess that's what it is if that's what it has to be. But it's a whole lot more to me. It's a pro-America song. It's a promilitary song." On May 1 Bush landed on the deck of the USS *Abraham Lincoln* in the bucket seat of a Navy S-3B Viking to announce to the world that "the United States and our allies have prevailed." A large banner behind him declared "Mission Accomplished." And yet on the ground, and even compared to the situation in Afghanistan, which was itself sharply deteriorating, May in Iraq presaged what was to be a hollow victory for all.[43]

From almost that moment on, the vacuum that the invasion had opened up—and would soon reveal itself to have had no serious plans for addressing—gradually gave way to jockeying for power among Iraq's ethnic groups. And that in turn gave way to violence. As the news cameras panned away from the aerial assault the gist of a different narrative began to emerge. For the Americans found that they were not greeted with "flowers and sweets," as the Iraqi exile Kanan Makiya had suggested they would be. They were greeted instead by roadside bombs and the faces of a people who were "bitter, disillusioned and brutalized."[44]

The rapidly escalating violence in Iraq was aggravated by the ill-thought-out attempt by the Americans to take charge of the postconflict situation by establishing a Coalition Provisional Authority under Paul Bremer. The authority seemed to have based itself on the occupying mandate applied to Berlin after the Second World War. It had almost no understanding of local political dynamics, much less the historic grievances that the Iraqi people bore, and nearly every move it tried made a bad situation worse.

Two of Bremer's policies would prove fateful. First, the program of de-Baathification that was encouraged most strongly by the Pentagon simply removed the few remaining sources of institutional capacity and means of administering the country from before the war. Second, the decision to postpone elections indefinitely undermined Iraqi trust in the Americans' ultimate intentions. "Why if the US just want to leave have they canceled the elections? This is a kind of tyranny," one irate money changer in Najaf put it when cornered by a Western journalist.[45] It was one thing to promote Iraqi freedom as a cynical guise for more self-serving American interests. But Bush's commitments to the spread of freedom *were* genuine, and the success of Iraq as a "model democracy" in the region *was* central to America's own genuine strategic aims; which makes the lack of postconflict planning all the more bemusing.

If some of the blame for that can be laid at Rumsfeld's feet (for him the demonstration of US military superiority was the prime objective and he saw it as mission accomplished) this hardly changes the fact that the situation on the ground would now be a whole new problem for America in addition to the (ongoing) threat from al-Qaeda. And such was the lack of promising news in Iraq for the rest of that first year that the announcement of Saddam's discovery in a rat-hole in the southern village of al-Auda was widely presented as some great new hope in what was by then a darkening sea of violence.

Things were to get substantially worse, and the year to come would be only more notable for its bloodshed. In March 2004 four private security contractors were lynched and dragged through the streets. Already by then the placement of IEDs by the side of the road had become another of the conflict's characteristic yet deadly set pieces. As early as the summer of 2003 the United Nations headquarters had been hit by a suicide bomb, killing dozens, including the UN Special Envoy to Iraq Sérgio Vieira de Mello. And suicide bombings at markets, checkpoints, and outside public buildings escalated in the year to come.

Contrary to the insistence of US Central Command that this growing insurgency was an organized counterattack of sorts, it was, as war reporter Jason Burke pointed out, nothing of the sort. It was so lethal and such a barrier to political dialogue precisely because it *had* no center. As he described it from the front lines, it was "a network": not so much a structure as a "lack of structure" and one that gave the insurgents "a formidable ability to adapt and evolve." Here was the networked society revisited and reimagined in a way that the techno-utopianism of the 1990s had scarcely fathomed but which had been latent within it all along. As Burke described it in British-run Fallujah, which UK forces were finding to be one of the centers of the postconflict violence: "The city was rent by the firefights and score-settling that went with the fe-rocious and fast-moving maneuvering for power between sheikhs and a variety of tribal and political factions all looking to exploit the collapse of Saddam's regime."[46]

With the situation in Iraq deteriorating throughout the year, the Co-alition Provisional Authority (CPA) and its international community partners increasingly retreated into the Green Zone of Baghdad—the "emerald city" as the new Iraqi East Berlin was somewhat hopefully called. Recognizing that there was little more that could be done, the overriding priority now became to hand over power and responsibility to something that would at least look like a viable Iraqi government. The Bush administration's plans to make Iraq the flagstone of a model democracy in the region, upon whose back they would project influence across the entire region, had by now melted away, like one of the many tarnished and blackened wrecks now littering the Iraqi landscape.

In another sense, however, the imbroglio in Iraq had been just the success that Rumsfeld and others had hoped for. This did not mean that the United States had gone to Iraq for its oil, as London's left-wing Mayor Ken Livingstone insisted. It was not just "[t]rumpets of democracy; drums of gasoline," as one wag had it.[47] To be sure, Iraqi oil was an undoubted economic asset for the United States to be able to control: only a fool would deny this. And it was indeed a consideration for US military planners that asserting control over a critical part of the global oil supply was most easily done while the US military still had the hegemonic muscle to do so. But this captures only a part of the Bush administration's larger strategy which was, if anything, more ambitious still.

What the Bush administration really hoped to achieve in Iraq was to take advantage of a moment when public acceptance of American military action abroad was probably at its highest point for a generation. There was a born-again religious conviction lingering behind some of this (something Blair of course shared). But this was channeled in Bush's neoconservative administration to distinctly national gains (whereas Blair always remained committed to the form of liberal internationalism he had first set out in the late 1990s). Blair was not always simply following Bush's lead, therefore; and if the UK's position over Iraq was particularly fraught, this was precisely because its ambitions were less straightforward than Bush's straight-up nationalism.

Freed of any larger moral worldview, the Pentagon's plan was to use its recently discovered "window" to demonstrate to the world—and to America's democratic allies in particular—that its superpower status was still worth having. By giving full vent to the capacity of its military, the administration sought to demonstrate just how far ahead of any possible rivals it was. The technological revolution that the US military (and for now the US military alone) had undergone since the closing years of the Cold War—the Revolution in Military Affairs, as it was known within military planning circles—was a stick of such weight and precision that nobody should doubt it. And in contrast to eight years of Democratic rule, the current administration had no qualms about using it.

This was of course precisely what Rumsfeld had been at such pains to demonstrate both in Afghanistan and over Iraq. And since most liberal democracies had declared themselves desirous of being rid of a threat like al-Qaeda, while none of them—the UK aside—showed much interest in committing to this end militarily, the United States was afforded something of a hegemonic reprise. Just as during the Cold War there was a "general interest" among the liberal democracies in accommodating oneself to America and its military, so too in the post–Cold War order could they once more be assembled together, outwardly at least, beneath its protective wing.

The geopolitical implications of all this were enormous. Much was made of America's "long-term" commitment to Afghanistan. But the real long-term commitments that mattered were being made with Pakistan ("The United States should be willing to make the difficult long-term commitment to the future of Pakistan," observed the Key Recommendations report on the 9/11 Commission delivered to Congress in 2004) and with Saudi Arabia ("The problems in the U.S.–Saudi relationship must be confronted, openly"). So the United States went about locking into place a political and infrastructural base from which it would negotiate the thorny path of deepening ties with these two allies, whose governments stood for much of what the war on terror was ostensibly against, by virtue of a "flexible" multilateralism that involved a "contact group of leading coalition governments."[48]

Beyond its nearest neighbors Mexico and Canada, that special relation the UK, and yes-men states like Poland, post–Cold War multilateralism was now actively pushed by the US toward its own (overplayed) security needs. International agreements were discarded or left unfinished (including the Doha round of development financing, which had been the primary means of compensating the lost decade inflicted upon the Global South in the 1980s). Global compacts and rights instruments were airbrushed away and a new style of international diplomacy emerged: one more concerned with the details of extradition agreements and the sharing of terror-related intelligence. As America now embarked upon a unilateral rescripting of the international order in pursuit of a phantom-like enemy, the only real rationale for that conflict quickly became no more than the vested interests now profiting from it: because somebody, after all, had to build and to maintain the vast new databases envisaged by the war on terror; someone had to construct the new biometric border systems; someone had to develop new systems of critical infrastructure security; someone had to decide what was at risk and what, therefore, was "worth" protecting.

"What has made American leadership so freshly self-assured in the use of force?" asked a law professor, Jedediah Purdy, some years later. The answer ultimately lay in these considerations of grand strategy. But Purdy was surely right to ask also what this augured for democracy at home. The mass protests against the war had been a clear sign that not everybody stood behind the US commitment to war. And Purdy's fear that war was in general "bad for democracy," as he put it, did not seem to be misplaced as 2001 turned into 2002. "I fear this danger is even greater when the declared enemy is nameless, faceless and placeless. . . . In such a situation fear and belligerence feed on and intensify each other."[49] In this, regretfully, he was to be proven right. In America the political indifference of the 1990s had given way to the "intense patriotism" of the post-September 11 era. But it was soon also accompanied by something else. Fear now pervaded almost everything in America, and it did so with a cloying intensity that spread a good deal further than the ash of 9/11.

The Imperial "Homeland"

On October 17, 2001, a white powder detected in the incoming mail of Senate Majority Leader Tom Daschle was revealed to be a lethal form of anthrax. It was a sharp reminder, to a still disoriented nation, that there might be more threats out there from al-Qaeda or even other terrorist groups. The next day contamination alarms went off in the White House. Four days after that further traces of anthrax spores were believed to have been discovered on the White House letter-opening machine. "Officials . . . say it is nearly impossible to exaggerate the sense of mortal and existential anger that dominated the thinking of the upper rungs of the Bush administration during those months," wrote the reporter Jane Mayer some years later.[50] Inevitably, that sense of fear and anger was soon transmitted to the public as well.

Half a century before, Clinton Rossiter's classic work *Constitutional Dictatorship* (1948) had shown that the line dividing democracies from dictatorships was drawn in legal and institutional ink alone, not by a fixed escarpment on some map of moral imagining, and that in times of emergency the one could in fact readily approximate the other. It was an insight that had been put to the test amid the law-and-order response to the "crisis of democracy" of the 1970s, and it was to be tested again as the Bush administration set to work enhancing the powers of the presidential office on the domestic front, rolling back civil guarantees in the name of security (the prime "public good" that the administration took as its democratically sanctified mandate to ensure). As Bush himself put it: "I'm the commander see, I don't need to explain, I do not need to explain why I say things. That's the interesting thing about being the president." Or again, in 2006: "I'm the decider, and I decide what is best."[51]

The Bush administration was not acting without precedent here. America was in a state of emergency and there were constitutional procedures that allowed a president to take on greater powers at such time. But amid the general state of insecurity after the attacks, the administration went further than this. It pushed through a barrage of legal changes to enshrine norms of democracy that did not protect so much as undermine the freedoms they endowed. In October came the USA PATRIOT Act (Uniting and Strengthening America by Providing Appropriate Tools Required to Intercept and Obstruct Terrorism Act): the first and, in many ways, critical legal maneuver of a new era in which collective "security" now trumped popular freedoms.

Amidst the anxiety of the moment, the Patriot Act was drafted (all 362 pages of it) and passed through Congress with precious little debate (many congressmen had not even managed to read it). Yet its reforms were far-reaching: it permitted investigation of US citizens for criminal matters without probable cause (in the event that the investigating authority deemed terrorism/intelligence to be the reason for the investigation) and relaxed wiretapping and surveillance standards established in the aftermath of Watergate. The FBI, for example, though it had been given the right to search through financial records in the 1980s by the use of National Security Letters (NSLs), had always first to prove that its suspicions were credible. The Patriot Act relaxed this standard. In the year before 9/11 there were 8,500 NSL requests; between 2003 and 2005 there were 143,074 requests.[52]

This drew fiery counterpunches from some. Senator Patrick Leahy warned that the Patriot Act was "bending or even shredding" constitutional rights. The American Civil Liberties Union declared that it granted the federal government "extraordinary new powers unchecked by meaningful judicial review" and protested that it brought groups from WTO protesters to animal rights organization PETA into the definition of terrorist (on the basis of "minor acts of vandalism"). Hundreds of local councils passed resolutions protesting against it.[53] Librarians launched a campaign to prevent some of its provisions from allowing public library reading records to be perused and Senator Bernie Sanders of Vermont launched a "right to read without government surveillance" campaign.

But the Bush administration had its defenders as well. The conservative legal scholars Eric Posner and Adrian Vermeule thought that the uproar was all just "tyrannophobic" nonsense. "The United States has never had a true dictator, or even come close to having one. . . . By now, 233 years after independence, these risks should be close to zero."[54] Fears that the United States was heading toward dictatorship were not only "irrational," they were "interfer[ing] with needed institutional reform." But the Patriot Act was not the only legislation infringing on civil liberties passed in the aftermath of 9/11.

The following year the National Security Entry-Exit Registration System (2002) began criminalizing immigration and refugee policies, and some Pakistani refugees responded by fleeing to Canada. The Domestic Security Enhancement Act of 2003 contained new law-enforcement mechanisms beyond even those in the Patriot Act. When news of the DSEA was leaked, the legislation was called off by the Justice Department. But some of its provisions were quietly passed anyway, including as riders to the House version of the Intelligence Reform and Terrorism Prevention Act of 2004 (IRTPA), proposed in late 2004.[55]

Some of the Bush administration's more drastic proposals were thus watered down as a result of popular outcry. But they were an early reminder that invocations of freedom could also serve to justify executive limitations upon it. During the Truman administration the McCarran Internal Security Act had required communist organizations to register directly with the Attorney General and a "Security Index" had been compiled, in secret, featuring the names of citizens who were to be detained in the event of a state of national emergency.[56] Now a new era of lists and public witch-hunts was dawning, as legislation enacted in the name of security ultimately did little more than redistribute *insecurity* along lines of race and class.

The fact that much of this legislation was passed while America was under an official State of Emergency limited the extent to which democratic oversight could be applied to it. But America was not alone among the Western democracies in passing far-reaching new antiterrorism laws. All told, 140 countries passed antiterror legislation in the aftermath of

9/11.[57] Canada passed the Anti-Terrorism Act in 2001, allowing the federal government to bypass the courts and determine itself if a group was terroristic or not, along with the by now statutory right to detain people (for up to seventy-two hours). Later updates, such as the Public Safety Act, introduced other, now standard, features of the post-9/11 security landscape like the "no fly" list. The former director of the Center for Strategic and International Studies (CSIS), Reid Morgan, suggested that Canadians were simply trying to keep up with the Americans. With shared borders, to some extent no doubt they were. But they were also wary of the economic implications of not playing the new game.

This fed directly into the formation, led by then Prime Minister Paul Martin with his Mexican and American counterparts, of the NAFTA-imprinted Security and Prosperity Partnership of North America—a trilateral dialogue that harked back to the trilateralism of the 1970s as it looked forward to a more politically freighted era of international trade in the new age of terror. This was a new multilateralism of antiterrorism, and it meant that international standards agreed upon within these relatively closed fora could be quickly downloaded and hardwired into successive national legislative frameworks.

It took effort and circumstance to resist this trend. France avoided putting into place any major antiterror legislation until 2006 and would not make itself more secure until after the Charlie Hebdo attacks. Sweden likewise introduced soft versions of most of the usual legislative responses, albeit with increased safeguards, and in the context of open public debate. In Germany, where a number of the 9/11 attackers had lived prior to moving to the United States for their final training, more moderate reforms to the antiterrorist legislation took place, including the ramping up of surveillance and detention capacities. But what was interesting about the German response was the way that the German Constitutional Court pushed back when criticism was raised that the new interventions went too far (as with legislation allowing German authorities to shoot down any planes believed to have been commandeered for terrorist purposes and its plans to monitor and store personal data): the state would not be allowed to use its pursuit of security to infringe what the constitution determined were basic human liberties.[58]

Arguably it was the UK response that was the most revealing of all. The UK after all had not been attacked. And it already had extensive antiterror legislation on the books as a result of the Irish troubles (updated just the year before, in 2000). Nonetheless in 2001 the Blair government brought in a new Anti-Terrorism, Crime and Security Act (ATCSA), which introduced, in effect, an officially sanctioned notion of a "suspect community." It betrayed the characteristic worrying "thief to catch a thief" mentality on display in the United States. Said Tony Blair in defense of the Act: "Here in this country and in other nations round the world, laws will be changed, not to deny basic liberties but to prevent their abuse and protect the most basic liberty of all: freedom from terror." Home Office minister Lord Rooker was perhaps even more to the point in November 2001: "The terrorists rewrote the rule book, and we have to do the same."[59]

They did just that. In order to reserve the right to detain foreign nationals suspected of involvement in terrorism, the Act required the government to opt out of Article 5 of the European Convention on Human Rights, stating that "everybody has the right to liberty and security of the person." Suspects could now be lassoed by interminable "control orders" and even placed under "house arrest." ATCSA was as controversial among civil liberties groups in the UK as the Patriot Act had been in America. The secretary of state was being granted much greater powers to control foreigners and national citizens alike, they argued. The House of Lords even waded in to the controversy, declaring the derogation unlawful. As Lord Hoffmann put it on the upper chamber's behalf: "The real threat to the life of the nation . . . comes not from terrorism but from laws such as these."[60]

Britain's knee-jerk legislation to an attack that had not occurred on its soil contravened the European Convention on Human Rights. But Europe itself was not far behind in hoisting up the legislative drawbridge. Its own Draft Framework on Combating Terrorism (2002) was written with no less latitude than Britain's or America's. And as antiterrorism increasingly blurred with criminal law, addressing it became a standard function of policing and social policy. A gnat was about to be fired upon with a shotgun. In 2004 and then again in 2005 the EU would update its antiterror legislation again. Organizations like Europol were brought into the antiterror framework, in a mirror of the development of the octopus-like Homeland Security infrastructure in the US. And a Counter-Terrorism Action Plan (2005), full of active verbs—"prevent," "protect," "pursue," "respond"—was rolled out.

For supporters of the hardened approach to governing liberal democracies, this legislative emphasis was necessary. They cited the precautionary principle that it was better to be safe than sorry. But safe against what? Some countries (notably Canada and Australia) sought to lay down a definition of what terrorism was; most opted for the politically more flexible strategy of "we know it when we see it."[61] It is interesting, with hindsight, how many of the arguments used to support the legislative counterresponse to 9/11 were similar in tone to those used to defend the original doctrine of "militant democracy" (*streitbare demokratie*) in postwar West Germany, where executive safeguards were introduced to hedge against the possibility that a majority could once again vote in a totalitarian regime.

Now, it was argued, such safeguards (be it banning a party or preventing certain individuals from enjoying their freedom of speech) were required again if liberal democracy was to be safeguarded from *international* terror. As the Italian lawyer Giovanni Capoccia put it, "the old neutral model of liberal democracy, according to which all political views are entitled to the same rights of expression and association, has given way to a general consensus that restrictions on basic rights designed to preserve democracy are legitimate."[62]

But whose rights, really, did this refer to? The voices of liberal public opinion writing in *The Nation* or on PBS spoke in universals when they condemned the Bush administration's policies as a "war on our rights" and a "war on our freedoms." But the new legalism was not equally borne by all citizens in the polity.[63] Nor were public freedoms defended with quite the same vigor as private freedoms. As a poll taken in May 2001 had confirmed, 52 percent of Americans entered into the post-9/11 era already feeling the federal government to be "so large and powerful that it poses an immediate threat to the rights and freedoms of ordinary citizens." Now it seemed the proof was in.

This was at least partly why the Bush administration felt compelled to enhance its powers in secret, which inevitably created more of the *sort* of big state that citizens were right to be worried about. When Bush sought to push forward his legislative agenda in public, as with the Terrorist Surveillance Program, it was roundly deplored. The National Security Agency (NSA) was behaving "like big brother run amok," snorted Senator Edward Kennedy at that initiative. Far from the emergence of a big brother state, what was happening was in fact the opposite.[64] The post-9/11 legislative assault on American liberties was about a *weak* president acting within a *weakened* system, and for this reason the purpose of surveillance was not to intimidate the people but to recover some of the state capacity that had been eroded over previous decades, and which the arrival of this new threat had suddenly exposed.

In that sense what 9/11 brought about was a twin crisis within

American democracy. First, within months of 9/11 there was a crisis over the division of powers, as the executive branch began to supersede the authority of the other branches of government. But this was hitched, secondly, to the longer-running *public* crisis in the question of what government was "for." Western citizens wanted small government: they had shown this in so many ways in the course of the 1980s and 1990s and they were not inclined to depart from the view after 9/11. But after 9/11 they also wanted more by way of protection of their liberties as well, something they now realized their government was less able to provide than before. And what linked these two *real* crises was the fact that what citizens now wanted, above all else, was security.

The Administration of Fear

Within days of the attacks in New York in 2001, the site of the attacks on the Twin Towers was designated, evocatively but inaccurately, as "ground zero." It was a term, with its roots in nuclear ballistics, that deliberately scripted the attack as "unprecedented" for Americans—erasing the long histories of interconnection (not least with the Middle East) that had led to it—and that helped, furthermore, to justify the unprecedented violence of the response. At the same time it provided a basic foothold from which a new nationalist imagery could be constructed too: the American homeland. The traditional American vocabulary of "civil" and "national" institutions was replaced by a terminology drawn from British colonialism, when institutions like the "home office" needed distinguishing from their colonial counterparts.[65]

The purpose was in part to foster national belonging and togetherness at a time of crisis and mourning. But the new identification of the nation with a homeland also helped justify the new security architecture that the Bush administration had begun rolling out. Writing in 2003 the American historian Amy Kaplan warned of the possible dangers that lay ahead on this path. She wrote:

> If every facet of civilian life is subject to terrorist attack, if a commercial airliner can be turned into a deadly bomb, then every facet of domestic life—in the double sense of the word as private and national—must be both protected and mobilized against these threats. Homeland security calls for vast new intrusions of government, military, and intelligence forces,

not just to secure the homeland from external threats, but to become an integral part of the workings of home, a home in a continual state of emergency.[66]

On the international front Bush had by then, of course, made full use of the institutions of national security. Indeed, for all the uproar among his administration's critics that the "imperial presidency" had returned and a new age of "American empire" was upon the West—"there is no more dangerous thing for a democracy than a foreign policy based on a presidential preventive war," inveighed an aging Arthur Schlesinger—in fact very little had changed.[67] The *National* Security Act of 1947 was always, after all, the outward expression of the *Social* Security Act of 1935. It is this powerful sense of the interrelatedness of domestic security with foreign policy that makes the Bush administration's activism abroad after 2001 rather more of a piece with the policies of liberal interventionism that had been the order of the day since Roosevelt. It is also why Obama, who was in so many ways the antithesis of Bush, would largely continue his predecessor's foreign policy almost without blinking.

Where Bush truly innovated, however, was in the way he took the institutional materiel of the national security state, which for half a century had been directed abroad, and in exactly the manner that Kaplan diagnosed began to apply it at home. At the heart of this effort to make the American "homeland" secure was the establishment of a new department that would consolidate the new national identity: the Department for Homeland Security.

Back in the 1930s Harold Laski, a trusted ear so far as Roosevelt was concerned, had stated that "without economic security, liberty is not worth having."[68] That was in many ways one of the founding sentiments of the social security state itself. In building the new architecture of a homeland security state, the Bush administration now took the same insight, but replaced the economic security of the little man—about which they were little concerned—with a raw, physical security. As Tom Ridge announced at his swearing-in ceremony as the new Homeland Security chief, in the East Room of the White House, less than a month after 9/11:

> We will work to ensure that the essential liberty of the American people is protected, that terrorists will not take away our way of life. It's called Homeland Security. While the effort will begin here, it will require the involvement of America at every level. Everyone in the homeland must

play a part. I ask the American people for their patience, their awareness and their resolve. This job calls for a national effort. We've seen it before, whether it was building the Trans-Continental Railroad, fighting World War II, or putting a man on the moon.[69]

Officially the mandate for the new Department of Homeland Security was "to design a comprehensive, coordinated national strategy to fight terror here at home." It was to overhaul vital systems—water, electricity, transportation, critical infrastructure—and to ensure that "America is going to be prepared" for the next one.[70] While this was trumpeted as the twenty-first century's equivalent of sending men into space, the costs of rendering everyday life subject to the insistent logic of security were less prominently announced. "For security reasons" almost anything could now be asked of a nation's citizens, or canceled, or temporarily removed from public access. But this was not the Cold War redux, since the new security politics took precisely the condition of radical insecurity, of "unknown unknowns" in Rumsfeld's words, as its primary object. Security had now to become total.

The securitization of everyday life was perhaps most noticeable in the separation of people from their public spaces. Two days after 9/11 the John Hancock Tower in Boston closed its top-floor viewing gallery and turned it over to Class A office use: to protect the public. Across almost every major city in the West, a massive retrenchment of public space got under way. Open spaces were cordoned off, or rezoned for crowd management purposes. "Crowds" became a threat in themselves. In just a few years the very sense of what it felt like to walk through a city changed. Obelisk-like sculptures and art installations were set up with the dual purpose of warding people away. "One hallmark of a democratic society is the ability of citizens to gather and to move freely about the city," complained an urban design expert at MIT.[71] But open spaces outside public buildings now became subject to fine-grained surveillance and the canalization of a public conceived by city planners as a threatening mass, not a democratic throng. An already burgeoning CCTV society now gained universal coverage.

The effect was not just to be seen over dim alleyways or in crime-prone areas. A flat sign—"Police Line Do Not Cross"—soon marred, in yellow and black, the view of the White House from Pennsylvania Avenue, as security officials—in light of attacks in the mail—pushed the perimeter further outward. It was a fitting metaphor for what was happening more generally. In London, the football team Arsenal installed giant-sized letters A-R-S-E-N-A-L outside its new Emirates Stadium in Highbury, their location being not just for branding purposes but car-bomb prevention. Across the other side of town, in well-to-do Grosvenor Square, residents began to pack up their homes and move away from the US embassy neighborhood, after many people began to feel as if they were living in a terrorist target zone. In Oslo, the US embassy, with the connivance of local police security forces, set up surveillance cameras in a civilian property over the street, in order to observe, unofficially, all comings and goings. In each of these cases it was not public need that drove planning decisions anymore but "professional threat assessments."[72] In America much of the money for this came from the Department of Homeland Security (DHS). Homeland Security spent more than $635 billion in its first decade, much of it monies granted to private security firms and contractors.[73]

The consequence was as complete as it was inevitable: public space was further closed down, Jersey-barriered, or bollarded off. It was rendered more uniform—more "manageable"—and more predictable. Public architecture—which had already begun addressing itself to a highly se-lective "public," as we have seen, now began to lose its meaning entirely. In America even the Supreme Court eventually shut up shop to the people. On May 3, 2010, it would close its great six-and-a-half-ton bronze doors to the public for good. Visitors could no longer walk under the words "Equal Justice Under Law" engraved over the main porticoed entrance, but instead were guided in via what was by now the ubiquitous bag-scan entrance set somewhere off to the side (all as part of a $135 million security overhaul).[74] The collective result was what one critic described as the emergence of the "national security city"—an approach to urban design that was diverting the city "from its human tasks by the architecture of manufactured fear."[75]

But security concerns reached out into other aspects of life too, in-cluding commerce. As ever in war, the civil sector was enrolled into the war effort almost immediately. It was probably inevitable that the routine of air travel would never be the same again. But in the aftermath of September 11 a new Transport Security Administration was created and before long it had "behavior detention officers" in place at airports: em-ployees who were specially trained to read physiological evidence of fear in passengers' body language. As the TSA put it: "Behavior analysis is based on the fear of being discovered. People who are trying to get away with something display signs of stress through involuntary physical and physi-ological behaviors."[76] As indeed do those who feel they are being watched.

Other aspects of civil transport became subject to federal compliance too. Schemes already in place at the American Trucking Association (ATA), which aimed to teach truck drivers what to do if they encountered an emergency on the roads, were adapted after 9/11 to encourage surveillance not just by truckers, but maintenance crews, toll collectors, and almost any other transport personnel. That scheme was given an extra $40 million by the Department of Homeland Security to "recognize and report suspicious activity." Its line was: "All of those eyes out there on our nation's highways, they see things that don't fit into the picture somehow. We want them to watch out for unusual activity and call the Highway Watch call center."[77]

Private transport too came to be shaped by the new paradigm of domestic security. Sales of SUVs—large, increasingly military-styled vehicles—soon accounted for 25 percent of all car sales in the US. Why? "[T]he SUV is an urban assault vehicle. The driver is transformed into a trooper, combating an increasingly dangerous world," wrote one industry observer. "This sense of security felt when driving the SUV continues when it is not being driven. The SUV's symbols of strength, power, command, and security become an important part of the self-sign. . . . With the identification of enemies within our borders, this vehicle has become a way of protecting members of the middle class from any threat to their lifestyle."[78]

Before long even more mundane areas of national life such as public health became "securitized" and here too the consequences were a heightening of the sense of insecurity, and a growth in private sector industry. In response to the anthrax scare of late 2001 a new Bioterrorism Act was passed in 2002. Within four years it had funneled more than $40 billion into new biodefense research. These programs were themselves later brought back under the wing of the Department of Homeland Security, by which time the end result was simply an increase in domestic (offensive) bioweapons research.

Like so much else, public health scares were recategorized as "threats" and this in turn encouraged further tightening of the new security architecture. When swine flu broke out in Mexico in 2009, it immediately fed into narratives about the "threat" of immigration along the US–Mexico border. "Illegal aliens are the carriers of the new strain of human–swine avian flu from Mexico," declared one misinformed commentator on an American radio station. "If we lived in saner times, the borders would be closed immediately. [C]ould this be a terrorist attack through Mexico?"[79] In fact, the first cases were well away from the border. Moreover, for all that swine flu was portrayed as "Mexican swine flu" in the media, it was later traced to a US-owned pig farm (which had itself relocated there to take advantage of cheaper wages).

If this was rather extreme rhetoric, it would become only more common over the years. There was some truth, then, to the argument put forward by political commentator Corey Robin that "security is an ideal language for suppressing rights because it combines a universality and neutrality in rhetoric with a particularity and partiality in practice." Indeed, the "vigilant" surveillance mantra of the post-9/11 mania for security always had particular individuals, particular "weak points," in sight. Minority groups became an object of the war on terror. On the one hand they were the most vulnerable groups in society: they had the most to lose from the lockdown on public space and facilities, yet they were also the most plagued by the new security restrictions.

In the UK Muslim communities were enrolled into the new counter-terror "Prevent" program and tasked with reporting on suspicious activities in their own neighborhoods. In the US, military recruiters looking for soldiers for Iraq did their briskest trade in poorer and especially nonwhite neighborhoods. From 2001 to 2005 the number of Latino recruits to the army increased by 26 percent, the attraction being salaries that, while low, were above the average for their racial group.[80] The FBI was more active in immigrant communities as well. In 2004 a group of Yemeni-Americans in Lackawanna, the so-called "Buffalo six," were identified on the basis of previous visits to Afghanistan as a dangerous sleeper cell. Despite there being no evidence of any credible risk, the group were placed under intensive surveillance by the FBI. When one of the men sent an email concerning a "big meal" he would have at his wedding, all six were arrested and ultimately charged (all entered plea bargains, changing their original plea from "not guilty" to "guilty"). No concrete evidence was ever found; the hope was that something would turn up under questioning.[81]

The searching presence of the state was even felt by minority groups that were not under any suspicion at all. The territorial integrity of the nation having been violated for the first time since Pearl Harbor, the borders were always going to be a subject of intense political debate. It wasn't long before the conservative Congressional Immigration Reform Caucus, among others, had come to the opinion that "The time is right to call for troops on the border in order to protect our national security interests." Numerous federal politicians joined in the call, arguing, like Tom Tancredo (R-Colo.), that "The defense of the nation begins with the defense of its borders."[82]

Tightening up the nation's borders had been an official policy objective since the pre-9/11 Hart-Rudman Report of 2001, the largest overhaul of National Security since the National Security Act of 1947 (it lumped terrorism and border control together some months before 9/11). But in revisiting it the following year, the authors—in addition to the expected focus on terrorism—also pointed to what was now seen as the major catch-22 in closing down the nation's borders: not the human rights infringements but the potential loss of trade. "The obvious solution . . . might seem to be increased funding for border controls . . . But efforts to bolster regulatory, enforcement and security operations at busy borders may result in a cure worse than the disease. Such endeavors place governments on a collision course with easy trade, which is key to the sustained expansion and integration of the global economy."[83]

The proposed solution to this was new systems like Nexus on the northern border: an electronic border pass system that prioritized regular business travelers while other drivers waited in a queue.[84] On the southern, more racially freighted border, it saw the police brought into a closer working relationship with immigration enforcement. This was increased further with the passage of legislation such as the Clear Law Enforcement for Criminal Alien Removal Act of 2005 and the Homeland Security Enhancement Act of 2005.

This wasn't just an American proclivity. The twenty-two-point US–Mexico Border Partnership Action Plan signed by presidents Fox and Bush in Monterrey in March 2002 saw some of these border control policies devolved to Mexico, which was tasked with tightening its own southern borders.[85] More so, in Europe of the late 1990s, there had been a tightening of the border all along the southern rim in response to Schengen, and it was now followed by a tightening of rhetoric. British Conservatives went to the polls in 2005 with the rather sinister, slightly breathy nod to anti-immigrant sentiment, "Are you thinking what we're thinking?" Spain was more directly impacted by immigration and ditched sly rhetoric for pointed hardware: investing heavily in maritime border control, it developed a system—the Integrated System of External Vigilance (SIVE)—that was soon being eyed as a possible technological solution for the rest of the European Union's borders.

In the post-9/11 context even the tranquil seas of the Mediterranean were becoming a fraught high-security zone, in which European and

NATO-led international patrols were carried out with increasing frequency against migrants making ever-more desperate crossings to reach Europe. NATO's "Active Endeavour" operation in the Mediterranean was actually an extension of the Afghanistan mission Enduring Freedom, "with the aim of providing a deterrent presence against the 'threat' of terrorism in [the] strategic waters of the Mediterranean."[86] But its purpose, as NGOs routinely pointed out, was quite specifically to deter the growing numbers of illegal immigrants into Europe.

Such a deterrent effect was precisely what supporters of the policy liked about it. The European Parliament managed to wring an improbable pathos from the new doctrine of security when it used the policy to speak of the salve of "greater cooperation" and national solidarity. By 2006 the EU's own border patrol agency, Frontex, was leading operations to tighten up the continent's exposed southern flanks, but Frontex officers soon suffered from the same catch-22 as America's border patrol officials. Hence the maritime Operation Hermes, first run by Frontex in 2008, was deemed to be a failure because the European governments that participated could not get Libya to take back the refugees they had rounded up at sea. After much lobbying and a €5 billion bilateral agreement (to compensate for what Gaddafi called "colonial wrongs"), Operation Hermes was run again in 2009, and this time deemed a great success.

Many of the effects of the turn to security as an element of state policy (a policy intended to be visible and thereby to engender a public response) were more mundane than this, but all the more pervasive for it. In this sense at least the global reach of the war on terror, and perhaps above all its crossings and intersections with domestic and civilian life, was always much wider than the intense media scrutiny on the primary theater of the Middle East implied. Expatriate Tamils living in London, for example, found their immigration status jeopardized the moment that the Liberation Tigers of Tamil Eelam (LTTE) came into British antiterrorism officers' line of sight (as if its record as a violent secessionist movement in Sri Lanka were not enough).[87] One didn't need to be overtly under suspicion to be affected, either: sometimes, merely to have recently arrived would be sufficient.

In Croydon, for example, asylum applicants lined up in their hundreds at Lunar House, the twenty-story home of the Immigration and Nationality Directorate, the building where within-country asylum applicants (a much greater number than those who arrive at border controls and ports) were required to present themselves. Administrative staff working in the building were kept separate (for security reasons, of course) from their own management, who enjoyed distinctly more commodious working conditions than the cramped, cold environment where the front-line decisions on asylum were actually taken (chairs, for example, were required to be screwed to floors). Such applicants had in many cases arrived from countries that were caught up in the "war on terror," but would be made to wait all day (this time without any chairs). As one of them observed: "The whole system is wanting to send a message to the countries of origin: 'Britain doesn't want you.'" Another reported an official coming out to loudly berate a pregnant woman, who was leaning against an object for support, to stand up straight in line.[88]

What was actually being achieved by the new emphasis on security was therefore in many respects its polar opposite. Societies were becoming more, not less, fractured, and in due course they would become more, not less, vulnerable to those who would take advantage of those divides. But by the time this began to be properly debated, it was almost too late: the politics of security had been given a free hand, and the extremists now had every reason they needed to swing into action. By then, fatefully, the wars in Afghanistan and Iraq were no longer the only fronts of the war on terror to have opened up.

Blowback

On March 11, 2004, Europe experienced its deadliest terrorist attack since the Lockerbie bombing of 1988. Devices timed to detonate by mobile phone exploded within minutes of each other on four commuter trains making their way into major stations in central Madrid, killing 191 people and injuring more than 1,800. Three more devices were later found that had failed to go off. As the investigation homed in on the main suspects, seven of the group responsible blew themselves up in the Madrid suburb of Leganés. Others were later brought to trial, twenty-one convicted and seven acquitted, while some were never accounted for.

The Madrid bombings were not, in fact, the first backlash from the war on terror. Not only had some Europeans traveled to Afghanistan and Pakistan to take part in the ground fighting, but Western civilians, mostly Australians, had been caught up in a series of attacks in Indonesia. The most prominent were those carried out by locally organized groups against nightclubs in Bali in 2002, where more than 200 people were killed. Over the next two years the Marriott Hotel and the Australian embassy in Jakarta were also both attacked. In 2003 attacks took place in Casablanca, Morocco, and in Istanbul, Turkey. What was interpreted in the media at the time as a growing wave of domestic terrorism revealed the spread not of radical Islam, but of the methodology of terror and the ease with which that methodology could affix itself to any number of local grievances. Most of the attacks were directly shaped by local or at most national histories—frequently with a postcolonial undercurrent. Where international dimensions came into play, the most common factor was the outrage sparked by the invasion of Iraq.

The same was true of the 2004 attacks in Madrid. Despite intensive efforts by Spanish police and security services to prove it, no connection was ever found to al-Qaeda or even to Afghanistan (which had, in point of fact, been a training ground for a wide range of terrorist causes, and not specifically Islamic terrorism, over the previous decade and a half). If there was a precipitating factor beyond a local clustering of youths attracted, again for complex reasons, to jihad, it was once again the invasion of Iraq: an action the Spanish government had strongly supported. However disparate, and in their own lives desperate, some of the perpetrators were, the attacks nonetheless brought home a new phenomenon for early twenty-first-century liberal democracies, and a new term to describe it: radicalization.[89] It would soon be a standard feature of the Western political and media landscape.

In November 2004 the Dutch filmmaker Theo van Gogh was stopped while riding his bicycle in Amsterdam and shot. A note was pinned to his chest with a knife. His assailant, Mohammed Bouyeri, had addressed the note not to van Gogh but to the Somali-born refugee and Dutch MP Ayaan Hirsi Ali, who had been outspoken and "uncompromising" in her criticism of Islam. This was seemingly an act of civil aggression then, not so much of global jihad: a cultural disgruntlement elevated to the level of violence by the uncompromising, black-and-white rhetoric of the times.

Unlike in America, the day-to-day reality of the war on terror in Europe was experienced in these years not as a perpetual anxiety of possible attack but as a progressive loosening of old assumptions by new assailants, of counterterrorist responses, and of steadily more partisan positions. "In this new and violent phase," wrote the seasoned journalist Jason Burke, now assigned from the war in Iraq to the home front on the continent, "Europe was crucial." It was now, he observed some years later, "that the 9/11 Wars came closest to being a genuine global conflict."[90] What that meant for Europe more specifically was that the fallout of the events of September 11 had come to rest upon the shifting sands of Western multiculturalism.

Indeed, if there was one consistent victim of the terrorist attacks in Europe in the early twenty-first century, it was the multiculturalism that had been the backbone to Europe's social model, which had already come under strain in the 1990s, and which was now openly challenged in the court of public opinion. For one, the events of 2001, and above all the response to them, brought religion to the fore in a way it simply had not been before and it forced questions of belief alongside more secular debates about political citizenship, often uncomfortably so. Second, it did this within a growing cultural antagonism to be found everywhere from Sarcelles to Molenbeek. There was no single pattern to this, since different European countries had their own model of integration. Some, like the French, were more assimilationist, others like the Dutch, based their vision of multiculturalism on a model of mutual coexistence. But each was now challenged in its own particular way as governments sought to respond to the new "threat" to liberal democracy.

In France the government imposed a ban in 2004 on Muslim girls wearing a headscarf, or hijab, in school. The scarf was a powerful religious symbol, and the ban a no less potent political assertion of French civic identity. The French civic model of *laïcité*, which holds Church and State strictly apart, maps onto the distinction between public and private life. This made public expression of religious identity particularly fraught, especially when the substance of the religious practice in question was one marked by visual signs, as with the headscarf. In Denmark religious communities were kept institutionally separate: there was neither the multiculturalism of the British model nor the universalism of the French model. There was, however, a growing distrust of immigration, and the events of 2001 brought religion to the front lines of those debates. Not as much, however, as the publication by the newspaper *Jyllands-Posten* in 2005 of cartoons depicting the prophet Mohammed in various scenes of ridicule.

The editor of *Jyllands-Posten*, Fleming Rose, wrote in a text accompanying the pictures that Islam, like every religion, had to be tolerant of ridicule. Anything else was contrary to the democratic imperative of freedom of expression. There was precious little by way of immediate response to this, until a Danish cleric took the images with him to the Organization of the Islamic Conference being held in Mecca, which duly published a condemnation. But still the "cartoon crisis" refused to light. Then, in a way that indicated how immigration debates were now "European" at least as much as they were national, Vebjørn Selbekk, a 36-year-old magazine editor in Norway, reprinted all twelve of the cartoons "in the name of freedom of speech."

This time it lit. Saudi Arabia withdrew its ambassador to Denmark. Violent protests ensued for weeks, including at Norwegian and Danish embassies around the world. In a distinctly Norwegian twist to the usual tale, the Norwegian Muslim Al-Jinnah Foundation (World Peace Organization) demanded a police inquiry be opened against Selbekk not only for insulting Muslims but for "placing Norwegian lives abroad in danger." Selbekk publicly apologized, the Norwegian Islamic Advice Organization accepted, and the issue was largely closed, in Norway at least. A year later the police terminated the investigation as not constituting a criminally prosecutable offense. Elsewhere, however, the cartoon crisis had opened what would be a long-running debate with more casualties to come, including in 2015 a cold-blooded murder spree carried out by armed gunmen in the editorial room of the French magazine *Charlie Hebdo*.

In Britain multiculturalism had been challenged by a tightening of asylum laws throughout the 1990s, first with the Asylum and Immigration Appeals Act (1993) and then with the Asylum and Immigration Act (1996). But while asylum applications peaked the year after 9/11 (at around 84,000 applications) Britain already had a sizeable minority ethnic population of around 4.6 million at the 2001 census (around 8 percent of the population). This was twice what it had been in 1991: a fact especially noted in the major cities, where ethnic minorities were concentrated. More controversial than the numbers coming in, at least for now, was the debate over what was happening with those whose applications had been denied but who had not yet left the country: a number that by 2005 was around a quarter of a million. Social workers attached to their cases pointed to their lack of adequate treatment; but most simply worried that there might be some sort of link between these disgruntled and free-floating "persons" and homegrown terrorism.

The greater concern was that Britain's ethnic minority groups, and especially its Muslim minority (at 3 percent of the population), experienced lower rates of employment—despite being a young and well-educated group—and it was this that was likely to leave them feeling disgruntled. It was structural forms of exclusion not minority-driven agendas that created a more constant seedbed of alienation as a possible route into radicalization. And in truth, it was a testament to the desire of these groups to participate in national life, if not to assimilate, that this seedbed never proved a more fertile recruiting agent to radical Islam than it did.[91]

For the British public it was mostly just enough simply to see the involvement of a few young Muslim faces in violent attacks. Two British men were killed as early as October 2001 by a missile strike in Afghanistan after traveling there to take up arms with the Taliban. In December, Richard Reid, a convert to Islam, tried to detonate his shoe on a transatlantic flight to Miami. Then in 2003 two British men attacked a nightclub in Tel Aviv wearing suicide vests. By then a game of cat and mouse had begun between British intelligence services and those identified as operating within an expanding public repertoire of "sleeper cells" and "self-starters." The security services spoke of radicalization but in truth—as they admitted—they had no idea really what that implied. They also, quite rightly this time, suspected that whatever it was it was part of a much larger picture.

Again, however, a large part of that bigger picture was the social and economic position young Muslim men found themselves in as a disregarded minority. Where the security services saw radicalism as something projected in upon "susceptible" individuals by extremist clerics, the truth was more that radicalism was something reached for as a way *out* of traditionally conservative families by young adults caught squarely on the horns of their own cultural roots and the wider demands of a relentlessly modernizing society. The security services looked to imams and Islamic cultural centers to track the nodes in a presumed Islamic extremist network; meanwhile, the meetings that mattered—such as between those who in 2005 would carry out the largest attack on British soil—took place in cafes and in their own living rooms in front of the TV.[92]

In July the inevitable happened. Four men blew themselves up on the London public transport system (three underground as they fanned out on different trains from King's Cross; one on the top floor of a red London double-decker bus). Fifty-two people were killed, 770 were wounded. Two weeks later a replica attack, using timed devices, failed when the bombs did not go off as planned. The government responded, using a script drawn straight from the American response to 9/11, with the heavy hand of the Terrorism Act (2005), now the fourth terrorism bill since 2001. The government wished to see greater emergency powers granted to the executive and for the legislative branch to rein in its concerns. Blair himself routinely threatened and cajoled in public to make sure the government got its way. "If the Government undermines the judiciary," said Lord Carlile, a deputy high court judge, in response to one of Blair's missives, "then the judiciary might be tempted to undermine the Government. . . . If we get into that state of affairs we undermine democracy. That is something the judiciary won't do, and the Government would be foolish to do it."[93]

But the Blair government was at least prepared to try its luck a little. Blair himself wanted again to extend to ninety days the length of time that suspects could be held without trial. The House of Commons this time resisted. In "unprecedented times" the task, it was now said, was "reconciling liberty with security." The problem was, of course, that neither the times nor really the threat was unprecedented. And liberty would not be "reconciled" with security, much less "protected," by calling simply for more of the latter.[94] To the extent that this raised the prospect of the death of the multicultural model, then, not everyone was unduly perturbed.

Conservatives of course had always been suspicious of multiculturalism— Britain had become a "mongrel race," said Conservative MP John Townsend in 2001—and they did not necessarily share in its aims. But the left too was forced to acknowledge it had focused too little on how religious and ethnic minority identity and majoritarian ideas of Britishness might be best made to work together (rather than simply criticizing the fact that they didn't, while avoiding the thornier problem of how to reconcile certain religious practices with secular human rights standards). In the end it was the Conservatives who gained the upper hand, and from the mid 2000s onward, under both Labour and Tory governments, the official understanding of British citizenship would be hardened, while minority groups and new arrivals were graded on the extent to which they "achieved" it.[95]

Europe in general then responded to the cultural and religious challenge of the post-9/11 era by raising the flag of "civic values" and, in effect, asking minorities to do more to oversee their own harmonious integration. This move overlooked the fact that a growing number of the ethnic minorities were born in Europe, and—as in the US—interethnic strife was usually more significant than minority–majority troubles. It was neither sufficient nor, really, respectful enough to win much support among minority groups. Nor was it anything like firm enough for those who would pull up the drawbridges altogether: the propagators of new myths about "Eurabia's" decline and the loss of supposedly "European" Christian values.

A Prison Archipelago

So-called "Western values" were equally being undermined from within. Already in October 2002, the war not yet one year old, the US Joint Chiefs of Staff were presented with proposals on the interrogation process at Guantánamo. The recommendations suggested that increasingly "aggressive" techniques be used on recalcitrant subjects.[96] To provide further leverage, resisting interrogation was now defined as an act of hostility, as incredibly suicide would be later on, as the number of self-inflicted fatalities—no mean feat given the micromanagement of captives' lives— crept upward. Such was the logic of the new prison system to be adopted by the twenty-first century's liberal democracies at war. Yet for all that Guantánamo's "exceptional sovereignty" was a fiction being sold by the Bush administration for the purposes of "taking the gloves off" it was equally one bought by the vast majority of international actors, including Human Rights Watch, who protested but otherwise resigned themselves to this "accident of geography." Johan Steyn, a UK law lord, described it as a "legal black hole."[97]

But it wasn't just the ongoing human rights violations at Guantánamo that marked the antidemocratic character of the response to 9/11. As disturbing pictures of prisoner abuse began to emerge from Abu Ghraib in 2004, glimpses were afforded of a much wider and more troubling network of supposedly "off stage" detention sites—in bases in Afghanistan, on military ships moored in the Caribbean basin, and on island enclaves like British-run Diego Garcia in the Indian Ocean. A similar pattern of prisoner abuse and human rights denials was common to all, but the photographs of prisoner abuse and humiliation taken at Abu Ghraib made far and away the greatest impact.

Equally alarming was the practice that linked a large number of these sites and that was, in many ways, the most frightening aspect of the West's dalliance with the dark side: the program of "extraordinary renditions," which ferried prisoners from one site to the next and which—like the proverbial Alice in Wonderland's rabbit hole—had the power to transport certain individuals in just a few hours from normal life in the West to a dank and narrowly dug pit in Egypt. This was the experience of Canadian Maher Arar, who was living an ordinary life one minute, as he sought to transit through John F. Kennedy airport, and who then was a captive within this system, kept in a "coffin-like" cell in Syria and routinely beaten for months on end.[98]

Across the ocean, two Egyptians, Muhammad al-Zery and Ahmed Agiza, were likewise swept up by the system: not captured on any battlefield but taken from Sweden by the US back to Egypt, where they were kept for some time outside Egyptian law. "Rereading the Declaration of Independence can be an uncomfortable exercise in the early twenty-first century," wrote former Clinton speechwriter Ted Widmer in his book *Ark of the Liberties*, "for in a certain late afternoon light it can read like a declaration against ourselves."[99]

As Bush began his second term, Americans continued to debate intensely whether the civil liberties they had forgone were worth the protection their government assured them it was now providing. Five years after 9/11 it continued to be the case that the civil liberties of some—of foreigners, ethnic minorities, and migrants in particular—continued to be the ones most under threat. Five years on and it was those at the margins of democracy that had become the most vulnerable to the logic of security pursued in the name of a white majority. The official line remained, as it did for President Bush during his second inaugural speech, the primacy of freedom itself: "Some, I know, have questioned the global appeal of liberty—though this time in history, four decades defined by the swiftest advance of freedom ever seen, is an odd time for doubt," the president intoned. But no matter. "Liberty will come to those who love it."[100]

But if people worried about some of the signs of a decline in the sanctity and the unity, rather than the security, of the public realm it was precisely what was happening in the shadows, in the name of this "fire" of liberty being lit around the world, that gave particular cause for concern. For these actions, while they were taking place in a proliferating series of "dark spaces" around the globe, had been brought into being by laws passed in the United States, and by an ostensibly democratic government to boot. The real challenge that all this posed to Western citizens, and to Americans in particular, ultimately lay in the extent to which any of it was quite so abnormal or so far out of reach as the condemnation of those like Ted Widmer supposed.

It was in this respect that the scale and state of refugee detention centers everywhere from Australia to the Spanish enclaves of Ceuta and Melilla in North Africa represented a striking example of how the decline in military standards was bleeding back into civilian life. One offshore detention site for returned migrants in North Africa was named *Guantanamíto* (little Guantánamo) in reference to the US detention facility. Conditions at the Nauru island facility "regional processing center" established in 2001 by the Howard government (to enable Australia to process "boat people" before they got anywhere near Australian territory) were appalling. Overcrowding, poor health facilities, and abuse by staff in an atmosphere reminiscent, according to one former nurse, of a "detention camp," led to numerous hunger strikes and suicides.[101]

These were facilities run by public bodies established by democratic governments. They were treated with all the permissiveness of emergency social policy in wartime, and yet for the most part they were addressing mundane, bread-and-butter problems of liberal democratic governance: in this case, how to manage immigration and asylum—how to welcome people to their own shores; people who had traveled far and wide in search of a better life. It was no less remarkable that this turn to a more routinely punitive form of politics did not mark the law's absence, or its denial. The law, rather, was central to its execution. Hence, the British Home Secretary's assertion that "complicity" with torture (outsourcing the actual blows to be inflicted to the secret services of less squeamish nations) was not the same as participation in it. Then there was Bush's quip that he would have to consult his lawyer when asked if what the United States was doing was acceptable. Lawyers and the law were indeed a central pillar of the new state of war.

And yet, unlike in Weimar Germany, where the law truly did lead to the whims of the Führer, and for all that some lawyers were prepared to advise on whether waterboarding constituted a form of torture or not, there were branches of the law that stood firm. This was apparent in the case of *Rasul v. Bush*, the first of what became a series of landmark Supreme Court cases, in which two Australians and twelve Kuwaitis from among the Guantánamo Bay detainees, with assistance from the Center for Constitutional Rights (CCR), filed petition for writ of habeas corpus: suits under federal law challenging the legality of their detention. In 2004 the court ruled by a six to three majority that US courts, who had initially rejected the application, did indeed have jurisdiction to consider such challenges. The law was beginning to catch up with the Bush administration's misdemeanors.

This was not to everyone's taste of course and the battle was not yet won. Justice Antonin Scalia, who wrote the dissenting opinion, insisted that the ruling wrongly "extends the scope of the habeas statute to the four corners of the earth." Three times he made the point that the court's ruling in *Rasul* was "inconvenient" to the executive, that it "springs a trap on the executive" and that "actions and events far away" will be brought back to the courts of the land to haunt it. When informed of the Supreme Court ruling, the administration moved to set up a system of military tribunals at Guantánamo, followed by a new Detainee Treatment Act, to preemptively keep their claims from reaching US courts (despite their now possessing a confirmed legal right of petition): once again, shrouding them in yet more law, rather than taking that law away.

More remarkably still, and despite the intense public debates about infringements of civil liberties, the treatment of detainees, and the gradually emerging revelations of the rendition program, did not elicit especially strong public disapproval. Until evidence of clear prisoner mistreatment emerged out of Abu Ghraib, very few Americans disagreed with the legal mugging to which detainees at Guantánamo (and elsewhere) had been subjected. A Gallup poll in 2002 showed that only 4 percent of Americans disapproved of the detainees' treatment.[102] Those who took the issue forward were a small group of pro bono lawyers, some of them, like Britain's Clive Stafford Smith, old hands at death row cases, others based around the Center for Constitutional Rights in New York, and of course the courts themselves.

In the UK the government's initial attempt in 2001 to extend detention without trial was dismissed by the High Court on the grounds that it targeted noncitizens specifically (in a case of "can't be fairer than that," the government then tried again, having now extended the request to all citizens). In America it was the Supreme Court that struck back most effectively at the Bush administration once again in 2006, when it declared the military tribunals were themselves inadequate to serve as military trials (though it was less vocal on the extent to which they fell foul of the Geneva Conventions). The ruling removed the assumption of immunity by US military staff engaged in the detention and interrogation of the detainees. The latter, it was now confirmed by the Department of Defense, were for the most part simply unlucky to have ended up there. And yet in the Kafka-esque logic of the day, for having been there they were also now deemed too dangerous to send home.

For the most part, as the Bush administration entered the middle of its second term, the most serious instances of executive overreach had been reined in. Bush's wrists had been slapped by the Supreme Court; the public shaming of American and British and other secret services had begun to force a degree of (sometimes reluctant) oversight upon their actions. Anyone looking back over the previous six years might well have seen something resembling a legal battlefield stretching out before them: pockmarked, seamed, and cratered with old laws torn apart by the recent legislative salvos. They would also have recognized, by the sound of guns all around, that this legislative war was not yet over and the outcome of the conflict was still very much undecided. As a village elder from Kandahar, who was wrongly accused of being a senior Taliban commander, told his American captors shortly before he was, in contrast to so many, released from Guantánamo after just two years: "This is me you brought [here] but I have six sons [and] ten uncles who will be against you. . . . I don't care about myself . . . [but] if you want to build Afghanistan you can't build it this way. . . . I will tell anybody who asks me this is *zulm* [arbitrary rule or tyranny]."[103]

There was no small amount of anger in the political capitals of the West as well. Perhaps it was not too late for a more moderate turn in the age of terror and security that had so quickly, and so suddenly, defined the new century to date. But few governments seemed willing to explore it just yet. As one US State Department official put it in response to a question about the limits of power in a democracy: "that's not the way the world works anymore. We're an empire now, we create our own reality. And while you're studying that reality—judiciously as you will— we'll act again, creating other new realities which you can study, too, and that's how things will sort out. We're history's actors . . ."[104]

Western belligerence reached its peak in the years between 2001 and 2006. Already by then another reckoning, at home and abroad, had begun to set in.

14

In the Shadow of War

O<small>N THE DAY</small> of the 9/11 attacks, with shopping channels suspending sales, shareholders holding their breath and employees rushing out onto the streets, or phoning through to check on the whereabouts of friends and loved ones, the mayor of New York was fearful, among other things, of the impact on his city's economy. "Go to restaurants, go to shows, go out and spend money," Mayor Giuliani advised almost immediately afterward.[1] He was not alone in his concern to ensure that the attacks would not upset the normal functioning of the market. Traders the world over breathed a sigh of relief when they saw the Federal Reserve post a solemn but welcome sign on its Internet window later that day—"The Federal Reserve System is open and operating." Western politicians were no less reassured.

Their relief was to prove short-lived. For wars and markets do not go well together. And as with the overreaction to 9/11 in the realm of civil liberties, it was less the attacks themselves than the *response* to them that would do most to undermine the normal functioning of the Western economy, especially in the United States. The winning of the first battles in Afghanistan and Iraq had proven easy; maintaining a military presence in those nations would not be anything like as straightforward—or as cost-effective—as the Pentagon initially believed. Those two occupations were just the beginning. Very soon the sheer outlay required to keep up with the United States' expanding military commitments could only be covered "on the credit card," as a noted economist at the time put it. Once veteran support and other associated costs were taken into account (and bearing in mind, too, that spending on *Vietnam* veteran support had not yet even peaked: this was due sometime in the 2010s), an escalating, decades-long fiscal burden was in effect committed to in the years after 9/11.[2] It would soon demand its own price as well.

The timing of the war's escalation, as it moved into Iraq, was significant in another way too: because by 2003 the US was experiencing the onset of the worst recession in a decade.[3] Together these two developments—the recession and the war—would leverage the economy to such an extent that the financial crisis of 2007–8 was almost an inevitability. To fully understand the role played by the global war on terror in the longer run story of democracy, therefore, we need to reckon not only with its political and juridical radicalism, but with its profoundly important economic dimensions too. In contrast to previous conflicts, the war on terror would be funded not by taxes but out of congressional "temporary special appropriations." When Donald Rumsfeld was replaced by Robert Gates in 2006, the latter took one look at the Department of Defense's approach to funding over the previous years and balked at what he would later denounce as the military's "culture of endless money."[4]

That culture was not the military's alone, however. In what would become another characteristic feature of the post-9/11 wars, the central role played by *private* military and security operations was no less critical to the war effort. For those industries and contractors supplying the means for the Western democracies to make themselves more secure, the war on terror was to prove a veritable gold rush. This not only intensified the socioeconomic inequality that had returned amid the boom years of the 1990s, it further removed some of the last remaining means of actually addressing it. This was the true hidden cost of the war. As the Nobel economist Joseph Stiglitz would later calculate, "For roughly a sixth the cost of the Iraq war you could have put the social security system on firm financial footing for the next fifty to seventy years." The failure to reckon with this astounding observation, at the time, created divisions that eventually spiraled well beyond the capacity of the political mainstream to control.

The War Economy

On the front lines of the war on terror, the contractors responsible for some of the worst abuses at Abu Ghraib were but one small part of a much larger "coalition of the billing," which by the mid 2000s constituted, in effect, a second pillar of the US war machine. By the summer of 2003, there were already as many as 20,000 private security personnel in Iraq. In Afghanistan, there would eventually be three times *more* private contractors than there were US servicemen and women. While the rest of the US economy plummeted after 2002, the shares of private security contractors (PSCs) soared by around 50 percent. As an official from the

Defense Security Cooperation Agency put it: "the war on terror is the Full Employment Act for these guys."[5]

For the US military, there were however numerous advantages in putting the king's shilling out for tender in this way, the nonapplicability of military law to private security contractors being one of them. PSCs offered one means for democracies to fight, as Cheney had insisted, on the dark side of the law. Moreover, they provided a way to bridge the growing gap between renewed domestic pressure to downsize military forces (if not always spending) and the military imperatives stemming from the global escalation of the conflict. By the summer of 2004 there were more than 15,000 employees of the South African firm Erinys protecting pipelines in Iraq, for example, and many more queuing up to do so.[6] That same year, London-based Aegis Security was awarded a contract by the US Department of Defense to cover security for all Iraqi reconstruction projects. This was viewed as essential by the Department of Defense, as the true costs of its poorly thought out (let alone delivered) postconflict reconstruction plan for Iraq became apparent. But outsourcing the war in this way, combined with the rest of its costs, was not cheap: $3 trillion in total already by 2008, according to one of the more reliable estimates.

The war on terror was big business then. But it was business that primarily the government paid for. As *Time* magazine observed: "Washington subway billboards—especially those near the Pentagon—are crammed with huge glossy photographs of multibillion-dollar weapon systems that defense contractors want the government to buy."[7] Luckily for them the government usually did. The Revolution in Military Affairs that had defined America's new "light footprint" approach to warfare since the 1990s had been intended to save money; in reality it had created such a dependency on high-tech weapons and coordination systems that planners at both the Pentagon and Defense were now harnessed to the rapidly escalating cost of new technology platforms. The rush to war had further locked in US commitments to structuring its offensive capabilities in this way, catching Congress and auditors by surprise. "We're in the wake of this speedboat," said Rep. Marcy Kaptur (D-Ohio), a member of the House Appropriations Defense Subcommittee, after being briefed by Aegis and the Corps of Engineers on a congressional factfinder to Iraq.[8] "We can't even catch up to the contracts."

There was precious little hope of regulating them, therefore. With "cost-plus" financing models (in which the American military covered all costs plus a percentage of any additional spending) and a growing insurgency

on the ground in Iraq stretching initial estimates of duration and personnel almost before the ink on the contracts was dry, the war's price
tag kept growing. After a decade the Pentagon gingerly announced that
they were in the region of $1 trillion, though it didn't like to be too
precise. Nonsense, said the experts. Once the costs of Homeland Security,
of veterans' care, of R&D were added on, not to mention the exorbitant
costs of servicing the loans the US government had taken on to pay for
it all, the true cost was nearly five times as much. That worked out at
around $16,000 per person, or $64,000 per American family per year.
And that in turn was before the costs of tightened spending in health,
education, Medicare, and work programs to help meet the military expenditures from day one of the war were factored in.

All this was of particular concern to the president, who was determined
not to repeat the mistakes of his father (Bush Sr., we will recall, having
missed out on reelection by presiding over an economic recession). As
the younger President Bush himself said in an address to the nation at
the end of 2001: "Americans will always remember" the economy was
"one of my first priorities."[9] This was rather to overlook exactly what it
means for a nation to be running a war economy into the red in the
way his administration was. For while the economics of war can go one
of two ways, they tend, on the whole, to go one way most of the time.
They tend to indebt nations and to scythe off economic growth at the
knees.

Of course, there are always examples where the leveling effect of war
clears out a nation's redundant plant and capital, in a literal form of
creative destruction, making way for new and more productive technologies to take the place of the old. That was certainly the case for France
after the Second World War, and in a different way for the United States
as well: its war spending helping it to pull out of the Depression.[10] But
one has to be both lucky and victorious, or to be more or less prepared
to start again from scratch, as Germany was forced to do, to enjoy those
beneficial side effects. One needs both mass investment at home and
generous markets abroad.

The US could count on neither of these conditions in 2001. But it
could turn, as a source of offset income, to the sale of arms to recently
acquired allies in the war on terror: which meant, in practice, anyone
willing to use them against "terrorists." Arms sales increased substantially
after 9/11 as domestic restrictions on US weapons sales lifted, along with
long-standing arms embargoes, so that more nations might fulfill their
obligations in the war on terror. It was as if Nixon's policy of linkage

were at work once again. Pakistan, in particular, saw a return to the days of General Zia in terms of its relationship to the US (this time under Pervez Musharraf). Nuclear-test sanctions recently imposed on Pakistan and India in 1998 under Clinton (after a series of nuclear detonations) were now swiftly repealed. By 2006 Pakistan had become the United States' primary trading partner: the recipient of $3.5 billion worth of arms, including American F-16s (which, to put it in perspective, was equivalent to the total volume of sales to the country over the previous half century).[11]

Britain scarcely covered itself in glory, either. In 2006 the Blair government pushed ahead on a major arms deal with Saudi Arabia, in spite of widespread public opposition. It did not improve the public mood that this took place only after a last-minute cancellation by the UK's Serious Fraud Office of an investigation it was running into arms supplier BAE systems. The probe was stopped on grounds of "national security"—the government citing the likelihood of the Saudis refusing to share war on terror intelligence (its threat to pull out of the deal was, of course, the more credible reason). France did the same, swooping in to provide military helicopters to Libya the moment that the arms embargo there was lifted in 2004.[12] Boosting exports was one thing, however—morally dubious yet hardly without historic precedent. More significant by far was the fact that the opening salvos of the war on terror were also being fought against the backdrop of a gradually deepening recession.

It was often forgotten amid the drama that followed, but just months before 9/11 the US stock market had crashed on the bursting of the global dot-com bubble. The attacks merely worsened the economic situation. Container shipping tailed off briefly, limiting the supply of goods, and consumer confidence quickly dropped to its lowest level since 1993. Unemployment rose and mass layoffs began to be seen. Other sectors of the domestic economy were soon teetering on the edge as well and the White House, whatever the tone of its public rhetoric, was worried. Reagan had burnished his credentials by facing down the airport unions and presiding over their collapse; Bush now looked likely to preside over the collapse of the entire airline industry, which had seen a 30 percent drop-off after September 2001, and in which two major airlines were teetering on the brink of bankruptcy. These signals were enough for Congress, at the White House's prompting, to take decisive action. Within ten days of the 9/11 attacks, $40 billion had been found for "security and recovery" and an additional $15 billion to help the airline industry.[13]

This was small beer in comparison to the sums that would be found to support the war effort later, but they were significant enough as the first steps on a decade-long period of eye-wateringly large congressional "emergency" appropriations.

Remarkably, none of this led Bush to reconsider his long-proposed tax cuts: the biggest tax cuts in a generation. "The terrorists who attacked the United States on September 11 targeted our economy as well," Bush declared in a radio address to the nation on September 22. But that was only all the more reason, he argued, to keep on with the economic program he had first laid out as a candidate, featuring $40 billion in tax rebates in 2001 rising to $70 billion the year after. Meanwhile interest rates were kept low and consumer spending was kept inflated. In a video-taped message in December 2001 Osama bin Laden had said that America may not be beatable militarily, but "there is another way through hitting the economic structure."[14] He was right. Bush was playing such a dangerous game with the economy—laying a form of debt-fueled military Keynesianism on top of a modern consumer spending bubble—that he risked fulfilling bin Laden's prediction for him.

With military spending soaring and the two Bush tax cuts of 2001 and 2002 shrinking the federal budget, the US government soon had no choice but to start borrowing more from abroad. The government debt ballooned; federal debt would increase by a quarter owing to war-related expenses alone over the coming decade. The tax cuts added only that much more. This was radical—and risky—in the extreme. It was also historic. The US had never cut taxes going into a war before. And the only other time the country had financed a war by debt alone was when the colonies borrowed from France during the Revolutionary War: hardly a comparable situation.[15] Now America was putting itself in the position where it would be borrowing from its real economic rivals (China in particular) to sustain a war of its choosing against a political enemy that was, in truth, scarcely to be seen.

There were other worrying portents for the economy as well. The fallout from the ground wars in Afghanistan, Iraq, and Pakistan increased the price of oil, the very resource the US was hoping to secure. The specter of the 1970s energy crises loomed large once again, as the cost of a barrel of oil, which had been around $30 at the start of the Iraq War, surged upward to $140 a barrel by 2007–8. That pushed the Federal Reserve to lower interest rates for much of the intervening period: something that would, in due course, help to exacerbate the consumer spending spree (an important cause of the financial crisis to come). Bush himself then further amplified the problems for the economy by cutting back on regulation, ensuring the housing and asset bubble that had carried over from the Clinton era was stoked up once more. By 2003 US net saving had reached its lowest level in half a century.[16] For an economy that had grown increasingly reliant on debt to sustain itself, these were each highly provocative policy prescriptions. Taken together they were an act of economic recklessness.

These United States of Europe

The flow of political traffic for much of the 1990s, the force of political innovation and change, had been eastward across the Atlantic. By the mid 2000s, it now seemed as if the relative standing of Europe and America had been reversed. Liberal Europe stood triumphant in the early years of the century. It did so less on account of any inherent cultural superiority—as Jacques Chirac liked to suggest, not least when denying the Americans the support they craved over Iraq—than on account of the strength of its economy. Continental Europe had long looked to America for its cues; more recently it had borrowed from the UK for its tools. But with the war wreaking less havoc in Europe than it was in America, increasingly it began to strike out on its own. One of the first and most popular acts of government by the newly elected Spanish prime minister, José Luis Rodríguez Zapatero, in 2004 (in addition to his "fifty-fifty" cabinet of men and women) was to remove Spanish troops from coalition forces in Iraq.

In the early years of the decade, moreover, it seemed that the political momentum of the 1990s had been retained, if not intensified. The election of Zapatero had brought yet another promarket socialist to power. And wherever it prioritized the market, Christian democracy too appeared to be making a comeback. With the election of the Christian Democratic Party (KrF) under Kjell Magne Bondevik in 1997 the Norwegians had embarked upon what would be their longest period since 1945 (the short-lived first Jens Stoltenberg government of 2000–2001 notwithstanding) without a Labour prime minister. In 2005 Germans voted the CDU's Angela Merkel into office for the first of four consecutive governments. Elsewhere, the Dutch were beginning to look more like the British as their social market economy began prioritizing the market over the social and as this was paid for by the ratcheting up of a real-estate bubble and the outsourcing of public sector jobs to low-wage service providers. In

2007 the French elected Nicolas Sarkozy because, as the center-left Jean-Marie Colombani writing in *Le Monde* was forced to acknowledge, "the country wants to be more dynamic, more offensive, more efficient."[17]

The Dutch turn to expanding low-wage, part-time employment also bespoke a certain confidence in the underlying strength of the economy. Indeed, Europeans in general—and for really the first time since the 1970s—were beginning to feel that they might be doing better, economically speaking, than any of their Western counterparts. Traditionally, when accused of being less productive, continental Europeans could always point to their healthier relationship to work. Thus, the French worked around 1,562 hours per year, compared with Americans' 1,877, and they took more paid holiday as well. Brits meanwhile had accustomed themselves, as in most matters, to something in between. They took an average of twenty-three paid days of holiday a year compared with thirty in Sweden and less than ten in America.[18]

But now the European model of embracing the market with fewer safeguards than before, albeit with a greater desire still to manage the collective outcome, was appearing to fare better in terms of brute productivity too. European GDP per hour had nearly caught up with the American level by the new millennium: Europeans were not only working less, they were working more effectively too. They had come to own more American businesses than Americans owned European businesses. And they were, contrary to American self-perceptions, more entrepreneurial as well—with a greater number of small- and medium-sized businesses starting up. Company law changes in the Netherlands in 2004, for example, changed shareholders' voting rights in accordance with the long-term value of firms rather than their short-term profits. Germans entered into a similar debate in the lead-up to national elections in 2005.[19]

The steady expansion of the European Union and its single market had been a major driving force behind these developments: wherever liberalization of national economic policy seemed to move too quickly or go too far, national leaders were able to take cover by blaming it on the faceless bureaucrats in Brussels (conveniently overlooking the fact that it was national politicians who created those European policies in the first place, by means of their participation in the European Council). This was how parties as varied as German Greens, Italian ex-Communists, British Social Democrats, and Spanish conservatives could all get behind a longer-term project in which the overriding aim was to make national life more "profitable," through a dual process that aimed to "cut back on collective provision," as one critic put it, while "commodify[ing] social protection." All the while those same leaders could profess the value of the European social model.[20] For each of them the European project was both master and foil at one and the same time.

But what was that project, exactly, and how had it unfolded in the years since the Maastricht–Nice heyday of the 1990s? There had been some important strides forward: the Austrian government was sanctioned by the rest of the EU in 2000 when the Austrian People's Party allowed Haider's anti-immigrant Freedom Party into coalition with it. But a closer European political union had been effectively ruled out by British resistance toward any moves in the direction of a greater federalism. And with the creation of the euro and the establishment of the European Central Bank (ECB) to oversee it from 1999, the route to closer union was now mostly confined to discussion of the economic case. It was the "new clergy of technocrats, doctors of the single-market law," in the words of one French critic, who increasingly ruled the European roost, and their primary instrument was the carefully monitored "convergence criteria."[21]

If the single currency was to be a reality then harmonizing European economic indicators was essential. The downside was that it left national governments with fewer ways of adjusting their macroeconomic positions than before, other than to "wring concessions from labor," as Susan Watkins, editor of the British *New Left Review*, put it. This was seen by the left as a victory for Anglo-American laissez-faire by the back door. As Watkins saw it, even the largest eurozone economies were now "forced to adjust to the Anglo-Saxon shareholder agenda of low-wage, unprotected labor and marketized services."[22] Certainly, without any effort to harmonize tax regimes between nations the way was clear for a race to the bottom in terms of cutting back on costly social service provision. But while there was a short-lived effort to move in just this direction of greater harmonization between France and Germany led by Oskar Lafontaine, this ultimately contributed to his losing out to Schröder in his ill-fated leadership bid.

More generally, the consequence was that European capital found a little of that extra value vis-à-vis the United States, albeit at the expense once again of the workers. The result was large demonstrations by workers in France, Germany, Austria, and Italy in 2004. But the fight against wage stagnation had lost something of its political bite by now. Meanwhile, the savings that governments made on their welfare outlays were used, especially in Britain, to finance tax-breaks for the financial firms that states were now desperate to attract. Whether or not this was fully realized at the time, the struggle over the future of democracy in Europe was moving increasingly to the *European* scale. And it was this that made the proposed Constitutional Treaty put together under the leadership of Giscard d'Estaing, and then—on the basis of his team's recommendations—a Treaty Document for a United States of Europe, an important moment in the history of European politics.

The European Treaty, as it became known, was intended to be the capstone on half a century of progressively deepening economic and political cooperation. There already existed a European identity; the ambition now—ten years after Maastricht, and arguably ten years too late—was to develop a European public. The whole project soon lurched into difficulties, however, the moment it was put to the citizens of the nations it hoped to gather together. French and Dutch voters were granted referenda by nervous politicians—in what looked like being a replay of the plebiscitary game of cat and mouse over the ratification of Maastricht. This time however both France and Denmark voted "no" to the treaty.

The elites who had worked so hard to put the European Treaty together were apoplectic, but there were a number of reasons why the treaty had failed to pass muster. The text itself was wordy and woolly. Moreover, its contents had been drip-fed to the public: the first two parts grandiloquently announced at a meeting of the European Council in Thessaloniki; the third part, which turned out to be a fairly comprehensive hardwiring of liberal market policies into the constitution (and 322 of the final text's 448 articles), was more quietly announced two months later. Was it any wonder, then, that the European public was disinclined to take simply at face value what was purportedly on offer? The treaty established NATO as indissolubly part of Europe, for example, despite the fact that NATO contained two non-European nations and left a few European ones out (Austria, Cyprus, Finland, Ireland, Malta, Sweden).[23]

The failure of the constitution to obtain the active support of Europe's peoples brought with it what some European experts called "the bursting of the constitution bubble," albeit this was a bubble in which arguably the European Commission alone had been living.[24] Critics insisted that the result left the Commission standing naked at the heart of Europe, like the emperor deprived of his clothes. It had "put in question the fundamental structures of the European Union," declared the French socialist Bernard Cassen. "They will need to be razed to the ground in order to build a democratic, social Europe." Cassen might almost have got his way, in fact. For as Jean-Claude Juncker confessed to *Le Monde* just days before the French referendum (also a no vote), there was, in fact, no "plan B." What it did have, though, was a "Plan D"—*Plan D for Democracy, Dialogue and Debate*—which surfaced late in 2005, and which largely confirmed the Commission's self-sustaining belief that Europe was a democratic entity for the simple reason that it declared itself to be.

Read in the aftermath of the rejection of the Constitutional Treaty, *Plan D* reads largely as an exercise in Lear-like incomprehension. Why did Europe's citizens not appreciate all that the Commission actually did for them? This perplexity was to define, in fact, the relationship between Brussels and the regions, the Eurocrats and the people, for a good many years to come. But the truth was that the problem lay not in Europe's perennially overanalyzed democratic deficit, nor in the practical institutional problems of creating a supranational democratic polity. The problem lay in what had been happening all this time to the more basic and certainly more immediate democracy that European citizens were encountering within their *own* nation states. In this one sense, at least, the problem of Europe and the problem of the nations were identical: both now lacked the confidence and the goodwill of citizens whose support they had previously taken for granted.

The depth of the problem that was unfolding was further revealed by the extent to which Europe's leaders were losing faith in the people in return. In 2008 a watered-down version of the rejected Constitutional Treaty was served up in the form of the Lisbon Treaty, this time with the word "constitution" conspicuously dropped. Since it required an amendment to the Irish constitution to pass, it was Irish voters who were granted a referendum on it this time around. And like the French and the Dutch in 2005, they too used their referendum to reject it. Said one voter: "We Irish voters found it to be an impenetrable read and an impossible thing to get our collective heads around. The treaty was purposefully drafted to defy our understanding."[25]

Once more, Europe's leaders could barely contain their frustration. The French Foreign Minister Bernard Kouchner—the memory of the no vote in France just three years before still very much on his mind—took the trouble to observe, prior to the vote, that it would be "very, very annoying for the right-thinking people [*la pensée honnête*] if we could not count on the Irish, who themselves have counted heavily on Europe's money." Giscard himself simply waited until after the vote to declare: "The Irish must be allowed to express themselves again." The newly installed Nicolas Sarkozy in France agreed. "It is of course a great disappointment, for all those who wanted to achieve greater democracy, greater political effectiveness and greater clarity and transparency in decision-making in the

EU," said Hans-Gert Pöttering of the European Parliament, "that the majority of Irish could not be convinced of the need for these reforms of the EU." It was a telling slip: there had been no reforms on the table. This was a stop–go referendum. And the Irish had said stop.

The Irish were duly presented in Brussels as the ragbags of Europe. It was all just "populist" bigotry, the European elite complained. "We cannot allow the huge majority of Europe to be duped by a minority of a minority of a minority," concluded Axel Schäfer, deputy leader of the SPD in the German Bundestag. What the Irish had dared to do, in short, was to voice their democratic opinion. In the neoliberal mindset, which most of Europe's leaders now adhered to, that simply wasn't how things were supposed to be done. Governability required consent. And consent, or so the responses to Ireland's effrontery revealed, meant going with the flow. Citizens could vote so long as they voted in the manner expected of them. Consensual democracy there was. But deliberative? "The illusion that the EU . . . could still emerge as an independent power, offering a more humanitarian, social-democratic alternative to the US, should be laid to rest," observed a left-wing commentator. Sarkozy himself, on the right, was more sanguine: "It is the EU that has given you your mobile phones and cheap air fares," he told a group of young French voters in 2005[26]—so "get into line" being the implication. Which with cheap airfares now coming on tap they duly did.

Countries further to the east had long experienced a more burdensome version of this gap between the EU's promises and its practices. Treated like junior partners, Romania and Bulgaria were promised membership in 2008, if they kept reforming well; but they didn't get membership that year. The EU's approach to the Balkans since the wars in the 1990s was even worse. Just as the wars had been allowed to fester for so long because Europe, not the peoples of the Balkans, were convinced that it was all about territory and there had to be a "territorial" settlement, so since then the Balkans had been squeezed between a rock and a hard place by Brussels insisting that the Balkans were better off in the West (that this way it was safer for all), while avoiding the fiscal costs of allowing people from the region to enter Europe. Brussels had also helped to stir up the national antipathies it claimed to wish to smooth over, by selecting some countries out for special treatment over others: Slovenia and Croatia in particular. In 2003 the Balkans were given a new deal: they would now be considered for entry to the EU, but to earn that right they would have to keep their own citizens from too easily moving there. Macedonians and Albanians might need to produce up to thirteen different types of documentation to get to Germany, for example. Meanwhile capital flowed easily the other way, with around 90 percent of banking in south Eastern Europe eventually owned by Western banks.[27]

Democracy Lite

Who spoke for democracy in all of this? "The actual weakness of democracy is the consequence not of a frontal attack but of a judgment that democracy can be managed and, when necessary, ignored," observed the American Sheldon Wolin bitterly in 2004.[28] He was right. Liberal freedoms had been granted the upper hand over democracy for several decades, and yet now they seemed to require an ever-firmer hand to secure them, even *if* that compromised basic democratic rights. And was liberalism any longer even what it once was imagined to be?

As the war on terror dragged on, and the security and surveillance state insinuated itself into the daily workings of democratic life, the freedoms of liberal society were arguably less assured than for a generation. Some liberals expressed the view that in order now to protect these freedoms at home the United States in particular was justified in asserting a form of "empire lite" abroad: it was implied that this was acceptable and that it had its appropriately humanitarian elements as well. Others feared that security may now have replaced even human rights as "the only ideal left."[29] Yet what was emerging all the while was nothing if not a form of *democracy* lite at home, structured around the principal agent not of the citizen but of the consumer. And it too relied upon a moral economy of voluntarism, rather than of political obligation.

At stake in these struggles lay the sort of social protections that were once proclaimed on banners as meaningful political goals, protections which enabled people to enjoy their freedoms, but which, since the 1970s, were considered so expensive as to rank among the luxuries of life. Already retrenched for most of the previous two decades, they now had to be cut back further. The Bush administration oversaw a total federal budget not very different in size to Nixon's, for example, but a much larger proportion of that government spending was on "mandatory" outlays such as social security.[30] As the cost of war escalated this came to be seen less as a socioeconomic obligation and more as a liability needing to be cut. To make ends meet, the United States thus began outsourcing yet more tasks of government to the private sector.

US contracting of government services duly accelerated from around

$200 billion in 2000 to $550 billion in 2011, much of this on so-called IDIQ ("Indefinite Delivery, Indefinite Quantity") contracts.[31] "By some estimates," observed the *Washington Post* laconically some years later, "there are [now] twice as many people doing government work under contract as there are government workers."[32] Institutional overhang was a problem here too. At the high point of the post-9/11 war on terror government contracts were still bound by the terms of the 1933 Buy American Act, prohibiting them from purchasing government services abroad. That meant recouping the lack of tax dollar income by charging US citizens for basic government services. Tolls and parking services proved especially popular, in this regard; the government of Orlando in Florida even privatized its 911 emergency services.[33]

Of course, Buy American restrictions did not apply to the private sector. Between 2001, when China first entered the WTO, and 2014, millions of American jobs were outsourced to China. US multinationals shut down 2.9 million jobs during the 2000s, replacing them with 2.4 million new jobs overseas. In 2006, in a reminder that Ross Perot's point was relevant still, Electrolux shut down its historic plant in Greenville, Michigan, moving its operations to Juárez, Mexico.[34] The growing fiscal pressure exerted by the war on terror thus made itself felt within the private sector as well as the public sector, and in the increasing overlap between them.

It wasn't Perot's "giant sucking sound" that was behind this, however, so much as the swooshing sound of "revolving doors" between government and big business. The advancement of one former government employee, Darleen Druyun, well represented the basic trend. In 2003 Druyun "supervised, directed, and oversaw the management of the Air Force's weapons acquisition program before she moved through the revolving door to become Boeing's Deputy General Manager for Missile Defense Systems." Boeing was also the destination of choice for Richard Perle, who was chairman of the Defense Policy Board in 2003 when he expressed his support for the Boeing Tanker deal: a deal which "came just sixteen months after Boeing committed to invest $20 million with Perle's own venture capital firm, Trireme Partners." That same year, while 22,785 individuals were referred for prosecution for official corruption, only twelve such referrals were lodged for revolving-door offenses, and just two of those resulted in a prosecution.[35]

Europeans were less exposed to the direct costs of the war effort, it was true, but the outsourcing of government services to private contractors expanded rapidly there too, and they were no less susceptible to the lack of effective oversight.[36] Government outsourcing in Denmark was heading toward 20 percent of GDP by the end of the decade. And while there were differences of approach (the Nordic countries tended to purchase inputs from the private sector, while the British and the Germans preferred to have private entities actually run government services) the trend was with few exceptions (Australia being one) toward a fracturing of government service amid a rhetoric of purported savings. In Germany in 2002, for example, the federal government engaged a private consortium to build and run a road toll system to begin in 2003. "Overly optimistic" predictions meant it was not operational until 2005, and then only on a reduced scale. Indicative of the degree of "public–private" cooperation that such a model was capable of promoting, the German government sued for lack of results (in response to which the private consortium immediately sued back).[37]

In Britain the private sector was now comprehensively at the heart of government. "Public–private partnerships," "private finance initiatives," "reform," "choice," and "best value" were the banners beneath which much of what Margaret Thatcher had left untouched was now removed from public control by her political "sons" in New Labour, who would remain in power until 2010.[38] Before long the private sector, which just two decades before had been largely separate from government, now had a greater share of the responsibility for running prisons, health services, transport, and basic infrastructure needs than many governments themselves. In 2002, 2006, and again in 2011 a contract to run the Irish, Scottish, and Welsh censuses was awarded to CACI UK, whose parent company provided interrogators to the Abu Ghraib prison in 2003 and whose data was ostensibly subject to the Patriot Act. A public boycott campaign was enacted in Scotland and Ireland. And despite reassurances by the Central Statistics Office, the public remained worried that the personal data they submitted on their census returns might, by some legal loophole or other, find its way via a US-headquartered company into the hands of the FBI.[39]

Had British citizens known the extent to which the government lacked control over its own information gathering they may have been less (or indeed more) concerned. As it was, many understandably took the fact that their data was being handled by an arms contractor as sufficient cause for concern. The real threat was not to citizens in the first instance but to the governments that were doing the outsourcing. "As more and more state functions are subcontracted to the private sector, so the state begins to lose competence to do things which once it managed very well," observed a well-regarded British political scientist in 2004. The result, he said, was that gradually government "loses touch" with how to do things, is thereby forced to "subcontract further and buy consultancy services to tell it how to do its own job," and ends up becoming "a kind of institutional idiot, its every ill-informed move being anticipated in advance and therefore discounted by smart actors."[40]

A near breakdown of the British rail network during 2000 to 2002 was one consequence of this. With a plethora of subcontractors owning or running different parts of what could only function well when subject to some form of nationwide oversight (as any experiment with a toy railway and more than one child will confirm) the buck for responsibility could be passed ad infinitum. Meanwhile, people arrived late for work—whatsoever the nature of the leaves on the track—and when they complained at the exorbitant fares charged by then Virgin Rail, the Minister of State for Transport, Lord Macdonald, suggested they simply assert their right as consumers and drive to work instead.[41] But service provision is not the same as profit. And since the upshot of Macdonald's claim was the idea that the state should not, or simply no longer *could*, do anything about such situations, the persistent trend to government outsourcing continued: why wouldn't the private sector want to get involved in the thorny work of politics and public service provision when businesses, like Virgin in this case, had no more to fear than the fact that citizens, like customers, could apparently "vote with their feet" and choose not to go to work at all.

The aspects of the public service provision market that offered the greatest opportunities to the corporations, however, were not those associated with outright privatization and operational responsibility, but those that turned government services into a tradable commodity that could be captured and then further parceled out. The US Internal Revenue Service outsourced tax collection in 2006. In Europe it was France, Italy, and Germany—each playing "catch-up"—that led the way (though the UK kept its head above water, privatizing its environmental management wing of Atomic Energy (UKAEA), along with its share in Eurostar). All told, state assets worth half a trillion dollars were outsourced by OECD countries from 2000 to 2007, usually driven by stock market valuations, always overseen by private consultants, often involving changes in the public laws of the nation.[42]

For employees directly in the pay of governments, this meant that they were obliged to accept low wages (which frequently failed even to keep pace with inflation) while the private sector consultants brought in to shave even more costs from the process of governing could charge exorbitant fees for doing so. Disgruntlement rankled within the corridors of government. Taxpayers ended up footing the bill for the growing flock of profit-making entities that circled about governments, enjoying the elevated profits provided by the thermals. No less importantly, states now found themselves seeking just the sort of "flexibility" that global firms, back in the 1980s, had long since decided was necessary to be able to survive in a free-market world. The ecosystem of modern governance was transformed: governments either adapted, or they went the way of the dodo. Outsourced as they were, the task of governments—just as had happened to firms before them—was now to focus primarily on which "brand" of governance they went in for:[43] that and delivering value to their new "stakeholders."

Ultimately none of this was "just" about business, it was about politics. The ship of state was turning on its axis and private sector associations were on hand to shape its new direction. Their agenda was straightforward and, on its own terms, an understandable one: the state should be made to look like the firm.[44] But while this certainly did bring about some efficiencies (albeit at the expense of others) it offered absolutely no vehicle for the expression of popular sovereignty. The problem, wrote the opinion columnist, and later Labour Party communications chief, Seamus Milne, in April 2004, was that "there is no clear way for voters to make their views felt because the main opposition party either agrees with the government, as on the war, or—in the case of privatization—is even more extreme."[45]

It was also, in due course, about corruption: not as a product of personal immorality or greed, but as an unavoidable part of the system. Government regulations of business had been progressively peeled back for years. But now the private sector pushed on into government itself. And most remarkably, this all enjoyed widespread public support. People had wanted the government off their backs, and that is largely what they got. Yet they also got the unavoidable counterpart to this, which was declining levels of trust in fellow citizens and in the government, and an increasingly powerful private sector now looking over their shoulder instead. For a while—and certainly during its heyday in the 1990s—this arrangement had seemed to work very well. Then, at the start of the new millennium, came a wave of major corporate scandals that suggested the outsourcing of government to the private sector was perhaps not quite the solution it was presented as being.

The most dramatic corporate scandal at the start of the decade was the collapse of the Houston-based company Enron. Enron was the perfect symbol of the deregulated, "innovative" company "of the future": a small outfit turned mega corporation whose slew of awards for its innovative approach to business proved to be a somewhat ironic judgment on a company brought down by systematic accountancy fraud. Enron had initially been set up as an electricity company but its real profits came from financial engineering. In 2001 it was the seventh largest US corporation, in large part because of its paper wealth as a futures and derivatives broker, which benefited from a progressively deregulated environment that its advisers (who remarkably enough were also its auditors), Arthur Andersen, helped supply.[46]

Enron's fall in 2001 was the first and most obviously visible consequence of a new round of aggressive deregulation, centered this time upon the Commodity Futures Modernization Act (CFMA, cosponsored in 2000 by the Republican Phil Gramm, the man who had just the year before put his name to Clinton's Gramm–Leach–Bliley Act, repealing the Glass-Steagall protections of the Depression era). The CFMA contained within it the so-called "Enron loophole," allowing it to engage in aggressive energy derivative trading, and the seeds of the company's spiral into self-destruction.[47] Enron's contacts in government, which included the two most recent presidents, further ensured its exemption from government regulations. Just prior to its fall the company was paying out to senior members of the Bush administration, and no fewer than 212 of the 248 members of Congress who sat on relevant House or Senate commissions had been recipients of either Enron or Arthur Andersen money.

Enron was portrayed as a bad apple. But the months to come would reveal that it was not at all uncharacteristic of the state of Western market economies. World.com collapsed later in 2001, submitting the largest bankruptcy filing in US history. By then more than half of the ten biggest bankruptcies in US history had occurred over the previous eighteen months.[48] They were followed by Arthur Andersen in 2002 and then a spate of further corruption, fraud, and misinformation scandals, many of them uncovered by the New York Attorney General Eliot Spitzer. In 2004 UnitedHealth, the largest health-care corporation in America, agreed to pay out $20 million in fines for negligently and deliberately delaying its processing of claims and payouts. This did little to warm the hearts of American patients. But people were scarcely shocked anymore: and it didn't deter the British government from seeking advice from the same company on its own plans for restructuring NHS services.[49]

Europe was itself soon knee-deep in scandals: Parmalat, Shell, Vivendi,

Ahold, Rover, Gescartera. The list went on. In every case the story conformed to a common pattern. Private profits were stoked by transferring costs to the public purse, usually with the witting assistance of the state. In the case of the American bankruptcies, even the US Pension Benefit Guaranty Corporation, which existed to indemnify workers holding corporate pension schemes in such events, was by 2004 itself $21 billion in debt.[50] In Europe, workers' basic pensions were being sliced up, invested, and put at risk—while they were made to pay the costs. In 2004 the American car-parts supplier Federal-Mogul collapsed, halving the pension benefits of 20,000 British workers invested in the pension schemes of its UK subsidiaries. To pay for these losses in financialized pension funds (usually incurred by wayward management) it was workers who were then sacked. The same held across other sectors too. "Private citizens are sending less mail than they used to," wrote a British reporter from Holland, "but that's only part of the story of postal decline. The price of driving down the cost of bulk mailing for a handful of big organizations is being paid for by the replacement of decently paid postmen with casual labor and the erosion of daily deliveries."[51]

In 2009, in America, the logical consequences of all this came to a head and were, remarkably it must be said, given firm legislative backing. That year the initial lawsuit was filed that would end up before the bench of the US Supreme Court as the ruling in *Citizens United*. The suit, first brought by a political action committee (PAC), successfully challenged the existing federal ban on corporations paying for political adverts immediately prior to elections. The dissenting minority argued that the effect would be to crowd out a variety of opinions, leaving public debate around elections in the hands of monied interests. The deluge of campaign finance in the first election to follow the ruling (2012) largely bore out the minority's views.[52] By then the horse had bolted from the stable.

By the end of the decade even the US Supreme Court was struggling to defend a notion of the public realm as one truly accessible to all individuals, regardless of race or creed or economic status. To the overt civil liberties infringements was now also added a distortion of economic freedoms in favor of the rich, whose powers over the public domain were enhanced; whose security in their own private property was fortified; and to whom politicians would now be yet further inclined to turn in their journey to the center of power.

The heights of the age of neoliberalism were reached during these years, as freedom became a fetish and equality a relic of the past. It was not just the market that was being promoted over the state—as a great many critics on the left wrongly insisted—but class interests that were being entrenched in new institutional settings and in public law. In fact, as the wave of corporate scandals attested, capitalism did *not* prosper under Bush or Blair or Schröder or Berlusconi in the manner widely believed. The free market was instead being turned into a more predatory form of political economy. It was digging out the very ground beneath itself and taking sizeable chunks of what was left of democracy with it. It was beginning to seem as if the profit motive was chiming a little too closely with the war that was rumbling on all the while in the background. And it was bequeathing a society not just of exploitation and competition, but one in which some lives—for all their formal political equality—were deemed to count more than others. In 2005 the storm waters came rushing in to reveal just how threadbare this institutional fabric of society had become.

Rising Waters

"It's like luxury camping," New Orleans resident John Crouch told a reporter from the *Washington Post* two weeks after Hurricane Katrina slammed into the Gulf Coast of the United States in 2005. He and another resident from well-to-do St. Charles Avenue, Andy Guzman, had set up on watch duty, with an assortment of shotguns and three dogs for company, in their neighbor's Greek Revival mansion. For the best part of a fortnight the men had lived well off their supplies of Cornish hens and jumbo shrimp, before starting on the champagne kept cool in the ice chest. For these two wealthy New Orleans residents, the aftermath of Katrina had the unmistakable air of boyhood adventure.

The story for those who lived just a few blocks away, in the poorer and lower-lying districts of the city, could hardly have been more different. Bodies lay unrecovered in the water, while victims stranded on the roofs of blown-out clapboard houses were hounded by private security contractors brought in to ensure public order (some later billing the federal government $950 per man per day for their services). One of those stranded, 46-year-old Gussie Glapion, eventually escaped with only her dog, Osa, and a single white microwave to her name. Terrified by the stories she had heard of armed gangs roaming about the makeshift Convention Center refuge, she decided to risk camping in the open. She would survive the next few weeks to give her own account of the aftermath of Hurricane Katrina. But she would lose both the microwave and her beloved dog.[53]

There were two sets of reasons for the social disaster that took shape in the wake of Hurricane Katrina, both of them quite separate from the storm's own furies of wind and water. The first was the uneven social geography of the city. Those most vulnerable to the rising waters were the city's black residents, who had been channeled into renting homes on the cheaper land beneath the levees: those levees in turn had been built because they were the most profitable way to reclaim greater areas of land for city development—areas of land that previous generations had left to nature precisely because, as wetlands, they provided the rest of the city with storm surge protection. When the banks burst, they were the first in line.

But the city's evacuation plans—based upon models of citizen behavior focused on white families with access to a personal vehicle—did not consider that the predominantly black residents of the city's poorer neighborhoods were almost entirely reliant on *public* transport. The social problems of New Orleans were racially inscribed therefore, but they had almost nothing to do with the gaudy images of black looting beamed out by Fox News and CNN helicopters circling overhead.[54] As one resident put it, "All the police officers rode by. Nobody stopped to tell us nothing, all they did was show us their guns and stick them out the window. As much as they like to put people in the back of their car, [after the hurricane] they didn't put nobody in the back of their car."[55]

The second reason also predated Katrina by at least several years, and it concerned the manner in which FEMA, the Federal Emergency Management Agency, had been folded into the stegosauran bureaucracy of Homeland Security in the aftermath of September 11. "The topic today is an adversary that poses a threat, a serious threat, to the security of the United States of America," Donald Rumsfeld had said to his audience at the Pentagon the day before 9/11. "This adversary is one of the world's last bastions of central planning. . . . With brutal consistency, it stifles free thought and crushes new ideas. It disrupts the defense of the United States and places the lives of men and women in uniform at risk. . . . The adversary [is] Pentagon bureaucracy."[56] The arrival of the war on terror the following day had not stopped the Bush administration from pushing on with its committed war against this domestic enemy. By 2004 few areas of the American federal system had been left untouched. FEMA was no exception. And in its ham-fisted, feckless response to the disaster that unfolded in New Orleans after Katrina, it revealed that this internal war being waged in America was not ultimately against bureaucracy, but against the things that bureaucracy had been erected in the first place to promote: namely the amelioration of racial and class differences.

In 2004 FEMA outsourced its hurricane disaster planning to a private contractor, Innovative Emergency Management, and ended up overlooking the basics of disaster preparedness in its drive for value for money. In 2005 more than 75 percent of its emergency preparedness grants for 2006 were slated for terrorism preparedness, not natural disaster. Michael Chertoff, the new Homeland Security secretary, had been warned of the imbalance just days before Katrina struck. But, like Bush before 9/11, he chose not to listen. Nor did FEMA acquit itself admirably afterward: it later confessed that it had only learned of the 3,000 people trapped in the New Orleans Convention Center on September 1 after several days of media coverage. Government officials from every department involved sought to deflect responsibility for a response that would ultimately cost around $100 billion. Right-wing commentators, in their wisdom, pointed to the "wrath of God" as it had descended upon the "decadent" nightlife of the city. In truth, it was the prioritization of American infrastructure and private property over the lives of (black) citizens that was the problem.[57]

New Orleans became the weathervane, but it was typical of a great many American cities. Wealthier, and generally whiter, citizens had historically secured cleaner and safer environments, leaving the poorer, largely Hispanic and black residents to make do in dirtier, more hazardous parts of town. This was not just a case of white-flight from the "problems" of the city centers (problems created by virtue of the chronic underfunding by predominantly white local governments of those very locations). In cities like New Orleans and Los Angeles it was about who could and who could not avoid urban hazards. There had been no Katrina-scale event to reveal it, but every year in Los Angeles, the way wealthy residents who chose to build luxury villas in the fire belt around the city were plucked to safety by helicopter during annual forest fires, while downtown *Angelenos* faced substantially higher risks of burning to death in their apartment, on account of underfunded inner-city fire services, told a similar tale.[58]

The social dividing lines were not always those of race and class either. During Chicago's heat wave of 1995, the long-standing mystery of why more than 700 people died in just one short, hot week that summer (more than twice the number of those killed by Hurricane Andrew three years before) was only solved when it was recognized that a great many of the dead had simply been too afraid to leave their houses and venture out onto the streets, or they too—like the *Angelenos*—had been herded into districts lacking in sufficient emergency service coverage. Their deaths were structurally determined in other words, though they were no less individual tragedies for that.[59]

Natural disasters had the effect of throwing a sudden, sharp light upon the underlying changes in American society. The problem confronting African Americans was again the most obvious case in point. They more than any other group were subject to the harsh reality that the "land of the free" had become the country with the highest incarceration rates (one in every eleven African American men being subject to some form of penal control). More blacks were being imprisoned than whites than had been the case in the late 1970s, despite rates of arrest that were broadly comparable. Blacks were in fact eight times more likely to be incarcerated than whites. And conviction for a felony being something that also excluded a person from voting, by the end of the century more than one black man in six was unable to vote. This was not despite democracy in America; it was because of the way that American democracy worked. Above all, it was because of the historical collision of slavery with specifically *capitalist* democracy.

But this was not the legacy of the past, as was frequently assumed: it was constantly recreated in the present. And if numerous institutional means of reproducing racial divisions within the nation had been devised, this was in some sense because such divisions continued to be required by the dominant political economy of the nation. It took the insights of a French-American sociologist, Loïc Wacquant, to show it. Come the turn of the century, the "ghetto," which had replaced the plantation and Jim Crow as the dominant institutionalized form of racial inequality, was now being substituted for by a new prison regime; and it was one for which civil rights offered little defense because it was not black citizens' ability to vote that mattered in this new regime but their status as economic subjects.

Young black men who, by virtue of their continuing social and geographical exclusion, were denied access to work had long been the subject of white majority fears of "urban crime" and "social demise." Statistically speaking they were more likely to be assumed guilty of criminal activity, more likely to be jailed for it, and so more likely to find themselves enrolled into postincarceration work schemes, where they had no choice but to take the lowest-paying jobs. And here was where the new regime came into play. The US penal system no longer disciplined black prisoners, it actively disciplined black ex-prisoners as well: blacks were, in Wacquant's language, the subject of the prison system's "extrapenalogical" functions. And it was here that racial politics bled into class politics too, since by forcibly holding black wages down, white working-class wages would likewise be encouraged to stay low.[60]

Katrina also revealed the incessant ways in which the war on terror seeped into everyday life: above all the intersection between what a then junior senator from Illinois, Barack Obama, derided at the time as a white-middle-class blindness to those that fell outside the bracket. "What's happening down in New Orleans? Where's your dollar? Where's your Stafford Act money? Makes no sense. Tells me that somehow, the people down in New Orleans they don't care about as much," he said in a speech to ministers in Hampton, Virginia, resonant with a drawl he was soon to drop. Obama was later criticized for his comments.[61] But how else to explain the ease with which US National Guard forces could set about "retaking" the city as if they were living in a war zone? It took a racially motivated slur to interpret the sight of poor people of color roaming the streets because they had lost their homes as the willful rampaging of organized social terror. New Orleans, said the brigadier general of Louisiana's National Guard, was "going to look like Little Somalia. We're going to go out and take this city back. This will be a combat operation to get this city under control."[62]

A week after Katrina, Abdulrahman Zeitoun, a Syrian immigrant who worked in New Orleans, was arrested at home and taken to a temporary supermax jail in the city's former Union Terminal. Zeitoun, whose case became the basis of novelist Dave Eggers's account of the response to Katrina, was later told he had been charged with being a member of a terrorist organization, although no evidence was produced. He was not permitted to call his wife to tell her where he was; for a month she had to assume, therefore, that he had been killed. Before he was released he was stripped, anally probed, and thrown into a cage in a manner of treatment modeled explicitly on practices developed at Guantánamo. Katrina was indeed, as one historian notes, the moment the wars came home. And Zeitoun, a modern-day Dreyfus in his way, was in a certain sense among the luckier ones. Ronald Madison, unarmed but mentally disabled, was shot in the back by police; another African American, James Lisette, was shot and killed as he crossed a bridge with some companions searching for food.

For anyone surveying the broken scene of New Orleans in the aftermath of Hurricane Katrina, it might well have seemed that Iraq was being built in the image of the West after all. The devastation looked

Third World and, as one observer put it, the response looked Third World as well. To think this, however, would have been to mistake as tragedy and institutional incompetence what was in fact a more structural series of problems at the heart of America's system of democracy: the convergence of America's racial politics with its political economy. If this had been under way for several decades, the reason was only just beginning to come to light. For as historians have begun to show, it was the political desire of those years to enhance white middle-class welfare, combined with the refusal to pay for this by increasing taxes, that demanded the necessary savings be found by means of an artificially depressed wage regime. The costs associated with *this* solution to the breakdown in postwar liberal democracy were then, inevitably enough, absorbed by the one group that had the least opportunity to resist it electorally: America's blacks.[63]

Every major black riot over the previous thirty years had been in some way or other about this. But it took the cleansing vengeance of a natural disaster to bring the issue to white middle-class attention (and it would require further follow-up, some years later, of the underlying message that "Black Lives Matter" to fully push that message home). In making this connection visible at the time, Katrina ultimately represented the beginning of the end of the Bush presidency as a force in American political life. It also provided a window onto the fractured state of society in the early twenty-first century more generally. But we must delve still deeper into those fractures if we hope to make any sense of the remarkable political and economic upheavals to come, particularly as they soon began rippling out of America to elsewhere.

Social Fractures / New Alignments

"As this summer's brief charade of concern for toilers in the minimum wage basement of the economy demonstrated," the American writer JoAnn Wypijeski began her postmortem of America's 2006 midterm elections, "$13.25 (compared with the federal minimum of $5.15) would be a 'good wage' in the parlance of politicians and editorialists who will never have to live on it. Its annualized full-time value, $27,600, a squeak over poverty for a family of four, better indicates how bad 'good' has become." By the mid 2000s the American economy, as experienced by those who toiled on its factory lines, at its Walmarts, across its highways or in its retail complexes, was in bad shape. Work was precarious, people were indebted, good health was neither to be taken for granted nor lost if one wanted to avoid costly repercussions. Turnover rates were so high that in the course of a working life most American workers were likely to experience being laid off: something that three to four decades before would have been almost unheard of.[64]

As with the uneven lurch forward of the economy in the mid 1980s, this expressed itself geographically as much as socially. Layoffs had been destructive of entire communities in cities like Detroit. But not even jobs in the technology sector were immune to the cutbacks. Robotics and automation were de-skilling everyone, and the brute fact was that Western economies simply did not create enough meaningful work anymore. Members of Congress were focused more on matters of stock options and assets than addressing this problem, or meeting the monthly bills of those who were living it, and in this case big business followed their lead. Rather than negotiate better conditions with unionized mechanics at its maintenance center in Indianapolis, for example, United Airlines simply allowed the unit to falter and then shut it down. As Reagan's former assistant secretary of the Treasury put it, the scale of job losses in the US in the early years of the century had "more in common with a country undergoing saturation bombing than with a 'supereconomy.'"[65]

Well might it have been a former Reaganite to have spotted this. The genius of the Republican Party since the early 1980s had been to tap into the resentment that these conditions caused (despite the fact that Republican policies were among the things causing them), first by deploying the language of "just deserts" that had formerly been the left's vocabulary of choice and second by offering such a strong confirmation of the legitimacy of middle America's cultural grievances—fears about abortion, religion, sexuality, media falsehoods, and immigration in the main—that most problems, including the economic ones that drove many of those grievances, could be translated into it. That left the Republicans free to continue promoting more, not less, probusiness legislation.

Since 2000, and despite the distractions of fighting a multipronged war, Republicans had successfully passed some of the most probusiness legislation ever to make it onto the books, including the Class Action Fairness Act, the Bankruptcy Abuse Prevention and Consumer Protection Act, and the Estate Tax Relief Act. The cumulative effect of these policies was to reward the wealthy to a deficit equivalent of 2 percent of GDP, effectively reducing federal and social spending by the same amount.[66] None of this cost the Republicans much by way of the gains they had made in 2000 when Bush had run as a "compassionate conservative."

Precisely because the situation of American workers was so perilous, all it took was a few well-articulated promises on security, and on the "values" that mattered most to them, to bring many of them to vote Republican.

The New Democrats no longer had a viable means of countering this. For one, it had become an unshakable pledge of Democrats' own imagining to maintain the "balanced budgets" Clinton had done so well from, electorally speaking, in more lucrative times. "The president can give away the Treasury to the super-rich and run up colossal debts as he invades the world," said one commentator, "but the Democrats are now sworn to a path of anti-Keynesianism rectitude that would have made Calvin Coolidge blush."[67] For another, Democrats were so desperate to prevent the swing vote they had won over in the previous decade, the "Reagan Democrats," from flocking back to the Republicans that they made themselves more and more accommodating to the demands of big business: all in the hope that this would bring them traction on the airwaves, at work, and in the bar. It didn't. Democrats instead took hope from the recapture of Congress in the 2006 midterms. Some even compared it to the Republican midterm revolution of 1994. It wasn't. The public was tired of war by then, tired of the cost of war, and tired of the Bush administration in particular. But they would not enthusiastically embrace the Democrats until the Democrats began to offer something by way of a serious alternative.

This problem was the same one, in its essentials, as could be heard in rural valleys and depressed former industrial regions across Europe as well: in the *neue Länder* of East Germany, in cities like Nottingham in the British Midlands, or on the dusty plains of Spanish Andalusia. The working class had grown tired of being lectured to by a political elite they believed to have long since given up listening to them. The reliance of democratic governments of all political stripe upon the techniques of governing at a distance—upon independent judiciaries to legislate for social and political behaviors, upon independent central banks to set economic policy, and upon intergovernmental agreements that received intense media scrutiny but left little room for popular input—lent credence to this view.

Shortly after Bush's second election victory in 2004, his predecessor Bill Clinton offered a judgment in the *Financial Times* that was half right, half wrong, and utterly indicative of the state of self-delusion the left was in. Democrats were "crazy," he said, "not to engage the American heartland in a conversation about religion and values."[68] Clinton was suggesting in short that the Democrats should now ape the cultural half of the Republican strategy as well, showing itself to be effective at getting abortion down and speaking about moral concerns. In truth, as their own polls suggested, people were hurting most in their wallets. And they were lashing out because of the misinformation they were being fed as to why this was so.

But was the European version any longer an alternative to this? True, Europe had enjoyed a brief moment of returning prosperity in the early–mid 2000s. But that had proven to be short-lived. As the decade wore on, economic growth in the US, in Canada, in Ireland, in Australia, and even in Britain began to overtake it.[69] It did not matter to the populace of European countries that this brute growth being enjoyed in the anglophone countries was being fueled by asset prices and consumer debt; that it was, in its way, a runaway train waiting to jump from the rails. What mattered was that the statistics they were shown indicated that Americans were around 30 percent richer, that eurozone growth was declining while US growth in particular was accelerating, and that employment remained higher.[70] Europe's unemployment rate meanwhile had hovered at around 9 percent for almost the whole of the previous decade (compared with between 5 and 6 percent in the US and UK). The result was to push European leaders into a fateful redoubling of their promarket, laissez-faire prescriptions.

Germany provided perhaps the most revealing crystallization of the consequences of this thinking. Schröder had come to power in 1998 promising to reduce unemployment. By the time of the next elections in 2002, however, unemployment had risen to nearly 10 percent and Schröder's response, as we have seen, was to expand the role of incentives in the labor market. While Schröder's Agenda 2010 reforms—including the Hartz labor reforms—were successful in lowering unemployment and in reducing the overall number of benefit claimants, they also contributed to rising inequality. Facing growing social unrest Schröder jumped before he was pushed, calling elections a year early in 2005. This was unconstitutional, but the German Supreme Court waved the elections through anyway on the grounds that all the political parties were in favor (though that hardly answered the question of precedent).

In the ensuing and bitterly fought election Schröder lost, after failing to piece together a coalition, and the Christian Democrats—now led by former East German, and Wolfgang Schäuble protégé, Angela Merkel—reentered German politics. The gamble Schröder had taken to ensure his own survival had failed dramatically, and its consequences landed as heavily on his party as they did on him. Indeed, where Schröder's election in 1998 drew the final line under the old Cold War politics of left versus right in Europe's central nation, his departure in 2005 drew a line under the post–Cold War European left more broadly: for Schröder had ultimately lost by refusing to form a coalition of and *with* the left.

This put Angela Merkel, the daughter of a clergyman and a young chemist in the GDR when the Wall had fallen, not only in office, but firmly in the driving seat of German politics. Merkel was exceptionally bright, but she was the opposite of a career politician. This marked her out starkly from Margaret Thatcher, the only European female politician to have attained comparable status. Merkel was, if anything, all the more mold-breaking for it. A woman who had largely entered into politics because it seemed the right thing to do at the time, she was also now the first person from a former socialist country of the East to be leading a nation in the West. She had left her youth behind her, but not her social convictions. These she combined with a ruthlessly pragmatic streak (an almost unavoidable trait in the coalition politics that rule the German parliament). First she had used this to take command of a CDU party in full post-scandal meltdown in the years 2000 to 2002.[71] Now in power she soon proved only too willing to continue Schröder's tacit politics of wage repression.

After all it was this, not technological or productivity gains, that enabled Germany once again to become an export powerhouse. And Germany, Europe's largest economy, albeit one still struggling to get going again, now stood on the front lines of the big bang expansion of the EU to the East. Moreover, the once dominant German SPD was now the junior partner and would remain so for the foreseeable future in a new center-right coalition.[72] This was all the more remarkable, however, since as a 2007 poll revealed, 86 percent of Germans considered themselves to be on the center or the left; 82 percent wanted the retirement age to return to sixty-five; and 68 percent wanted a universal minimum wage. The strategy in Germany then, as distinct from the US, was not to leverage the cultural antipathies of the working class, but simply to deny the voters the alternatives.

The rise of Nicolas Sarkozy in France tells a similar story and one that would in due course converge with Merkel's. Sarkozy was elected in 2007 on a turnout of 84 percent: an event portrayed by his supporters as a resounding victory for democracy. "What a victory!" declared

Le Figaro. "History will record this beautiful day in April," said *Le Monde*, "with its long queue of electors, old, young, couples with their children, all patient, all mobilized."[73] But what the French working class got was not a greater say in politics. They got the "hyperpresidency" of an imperial-nostalgic Sarkozy and the hard-line figure of Rachida Dati at the newly merged Justice and Interior Ministry. Dati's ministry now introduced benchmarks for prosecutions and arrests, and dramatically loosened the definitions of various crimes, including that of providing collective assistance to undocumented foreigners which now constituted the act of an "organized gang." It further reduced the age of responsibility for criminal offenses to sixteen, and by the summer the police were busy on the streets meeting their target—25,000 removals already in 2007—and they knew where to go.[74]

The French public also got a fair few of the media personalities they recognized from chat shows and the commentary pages as members of the new government. Whereas in the US the revolving door of politics shepherded its users from government into the halls of corporate offices, in France it revolved between government and the media. Sarkozy's cabinet thus included Bernard Kouchner, Jean-Louis Borloo, François Fillon, and Laurent Solly. The big corporations were not entirely excluded from this happy ménage: between them the Rothschilds and the arms manufacturer Dassault owned major shares of the presses and the media houses (including *Le Figaro*, *Le Monde*, and even *Libération*) while the heir to Bouygues Telecom held a controlling stake in the TV channel TF1. As one of the more honorably independent journalists, Serge Halimi, put it, the rest may consider themselves "the heirs of Bob Woodward" but in truth they were little more than "the bibs protecting Martin Bouygues's shirt."[75]

This was predominantly a center right tie-in, one that helped drive home the need for continuing the policy of fiscal discipline (and its downward pressure on wages) and the need to stand strong abroad (while continuing to invest in the arms required to do so); it was also one to which, history records, the left offered little more than a passing flap of resistance. Here France did indeed line up alongside Germany, Britain, and the rest of the continent. If liberalism remained a more problematic concept, as even Sarkozy's hypertenure was demonstrating, that was in part what led to a continued sense of restlessness.[76] For all its lack of progress at the polls, the French left was now so busy gilding the lily of renovation and "change," observed the French publisher Eric Hazan, that it was trapped in a constant problem of its own invention. For the would-be radical left, and above all its intellectuals, Hazan said, "there is always the same difficulty to navigate: how to make people believe that their aim is to change everything, when what they [really] want is precisely for nothing to change."[77]

For the past decade the European social democratic left had enjoyed their strongest run at the polls. But as these developments indicated, the European right was just now beginning to rebuild itself into a force to be reckoned with: above all by reaching out to a portion of the working class. Conservative political ideas had remained dominant throughout the era of Third Way leftism. But only now could right-wing parties count on being able to tap into that larger, more vocal base that had supported parties of the left for so much of the postwar era. And the layout of political parties reflected this. In the years since the turn of the millennium, Italy's left-of-center Olive Tree coalition had capitulated to Berlusconi's Forza Italia. Social democrats were soon thrown out of power in Greece, Norway, and Denmark, with the Netherlands' Labor-led government following them in 2002 in the wake of a scandal pointing to the Dutch military's possible complicity in the Srebrenica Massacre. The same year Lionel Jospin in France had come a humiliating third to Chirac and Jean-Marie Le Pen in the presidential elections, opening the way to Sarkozy's now surging, and much more forthright, unification of the right.[78]

Ever the anomaly in Europe, Britain's New Labour remained in power for now (it would do so up until 2010). This was despite the widespread antipathy that Blair had provoked by his bullish stance over Iraq. But its continued electoral success was not so much because of its social democratic commitments, as it was testimony to a deeply fractured Conservative opposition in Britain: one still coming to terms with the way New Labour had pulled the cloak of Thatcherism from Tory shoulders and taken it for its own. The final years during which Gordon Brown clung to power as prime minister were due largely to his decade of service in the chancellorship and the general sense, after the economic upheavals of 2007–8, that a steady hand was needed at the wheel in a time of economic crisis. And that, in fairness, he certainly was.

As could occasionally be seen under Brown, the arguments of the left had not completely died away. The independently authored 1999 EU Commission report "Beyond Unemployment" sought to present a more positive vision for European employment prospects beyond the by now usual trade-off between welfare retrenchment and worker precarity (which was not of course a trade-off properly speaking, since both pointed policy in the same direction). "In the name of individual liberty," wrote its lead author Alain Supiot in the journal *Esprit*, all sorts of unloved freedoms were being foisted upon working people: "the freedom to be paid less than the standard rate, to do a 15-hour day, to work on Sundays instead of spending the day with one's children."[79] What was needed instead was a new pact based upon freedom and responsibility. To be a worker ought to carry status. It ought to be something that society valued, in every sense of the word.

These were arguments echoed by the European Trade Union conference which, frustrated with the inability of the EU to beef up its offering of social protections (in contrast to its steadily hardening commitments to border patrols), put forward its own idea of a European-wide social fund.[80] Like most such initiatives in the climate of the time, such ideas were not seriously taken up. Instead of taxing corporate wealth, the European Court of Justice ruled in 2005 that companies would be able to offset losses in one European country against profits in another: a decision the *Wall Street Journal* decreed could cost European governments "billions."[81] But other voices were beginning to bubble up to the surface as well. In the summer of Sarkozy's election, a large procession of illegal immigrants and their confreres converged at Belleville in Paris singing:

> *The sans-papiers are in the street*
> *Sarkozy's in his armchair*
> *The dossiers are in the drawers*
> *We've had enough, we've had enough.*

In Germany too, the Hartz IV reforms continued to kick up a storm of protest and to make labor the new critical site of struggle, once again, regarding the problems of race and immigration.

The United States was also experiencing a burgeoning immigrants' rights movement during these years, and again this was in part because there was no clear party to represent them. In 2006, hundreds of thousands marched down Wilshire Boulevard in Los Angeles, through downtown Chicago, and in other cities across the US in protest at the introduction of a rule that would make it illegal for people to assist undocumented migrants—precisely the dragnet that Sarkozy himself later adopted. This was eventually defeated in the Senate, but the motion to make it illegal to be undocumented passed: a firm step on a road that, already by 2013, would lead to the oppressive (and secretive) Criminal Alien Removal Initiative (CARI)—a pilot program rolled out in, of all places, New Orleans.[82] In the flush of a nationwide social justice mobilization, the likes of which the country had not seen for many years, activists proclaimed the 2006 movement in America as a "new civil rights movement." A Day Without Immigrants was called, in which the undocumented were encouraged not to perform their usual labor, to reveal collectively how much the economy relied on them.

By Labor Day, however, much of the popular enthusiasm had gone out of the movement. Congress's ears had pricked up, but its gaze remained fixed on the money supply in what was, after all, an election year, and it ultimately resolved to extend the US–Mexico border fence.[83] Suitably encouraged, vigilante "minutemen" groups took it upon themselves to offer voluntary patrols in support.[84] Calls for an immigration "amnesty" thus proved too much, even for mainstream Democratic supporters of the movement, who offered instead the rather Orwellian notion of "earned citizenship." It was as if they had not understood the problem at all. The war had engendered a decline not only in the social and civic bonds that Robert Putnam famously lamented, but in civic respect pure and simple.

It was a revealing commentary on the state of Western civic-mindedness that, when the Iraqi artist Wafaa Bilal set up an online installation in 2007, in which he slept and worked under the glare of a camera wired up to the Internet and connected to a mouse-operated paintball gun, he found that he was shot 60,000 times by the anonymous visitors observing him in the installation's chat room. Bilal had emigrated to the US via a refugee camp in 1991. His brother remained behind and had been killed by a missile at a checkpoint in their hometown of Kufa. The installation, entitled *Domestic Tension*, was Bilal's response to the dehumanization taking place in his country of birth, but it also responded to the seemingly numb mediatization of "society" at large in the country that was now his home. It won him the *Chicago Tribune*'s Artist of the Year award. And it well revealed the true depth of the social fault lines, for all that the public for now largely hid these from itself.[85]

The Obama Moment

For George W. Bush it must have seemed, in the summer of the election year of 2008, that the specter of his father's political ghost had returned after all. US spending on Iraq was just peaking, at 4.3 percent of GDP. The shrinking gap between rising military expenditures and declining federal tax receipts, both of which he had initiated, had begun to squeeze the life out of the economy.[86] Oil prices had leapt up, hurting average American citizens at the petrol pump, and muting domestic demand. Businesses were finding it harder to keep going, customers to pay the bills. And then, as the election itself approached, the country finally began to lurch into what was to become the greatest financial crisis since the Great Depression.

In normal times a president might have turned to fiscal policy to alleviate some of these pressures: and had Bush done so he might at least have given the next Republican candidate, Senator John McCain, a fighting chance in the election. But with the huge budget deficit that his administration had created, he was wary of doing this and instead chose to bank more heavily still on the international financial markets. For all the spotlight that was cast on the election to follow—the break-out of populism and the surfacing of racial politics at the heart of the presidential election, the reactivation of the culture wars—it was Bush's economic policies that lost it for the Republicans, and in many ways lost the Republican Party for a generation to come (their return to office eight years later after all was as the accompanying train of a radical, independent candidate).

The Bush administration had ultimately run the American economy so hard and fast it had ended up breaking it. Against this, the rags-to-riches story of Barack Obama's rise—the prospect of a first black president, and a relative newcomer to Washington—seemed unique in nearly every respect. Perhaps recognizing this, Obama played a good deal less on his personal biography than was assumed at the time. What he instinctively seemed to have recognized was that there was a wider desire for change: which is why he soon had the word blazoned across every podium he spoke from during the campaign trail. After eight years of war and fiscal irresponsibility, the truth was that it resonated with audiences looking in on the US debate from around the democratic world as well. And yet, for all the eloquence of his words, quite *what* Obama planned on changing was never clearly specified.

Bush, by contrast, was notable during the campaign largely for his absence. Even the most loyal of Republican strategists now feared his legacy had turned toxic and they were desperate, for the sake of the campaign, to avoid it. Unfortunately for them, the Republican ticket of John McCain, the former pilot and prisoner of war, and his eventual—for many, inexplicably chosen—running mate, Sarah Palin, made their own contributions to the party's demise with rather more lasting effect. As some saw it, putting a woman on the ticket as the vice-presidential candidate was a stroke of genius. And with respect to gender it was. But Palin, with her self-styled "hockey mom–pit bull" image and her hometown libertarian homilies, turned out to have been a disastrous choice. The McCain–Palin campaign made for good TV but it did not make for good politics.

Yet the Republican campaign *was* an intensely political affair, and one in which serious battles were being fought. Not least, it became, for a while, the front line between an increasingly populist "outsider" strand of conservatism that movements like the Tea Party for now represented, and the remnants of a conservative mainstream that had once played their role as responsible members of a governing center-ground. What amounted to a somewhat clumsy effort by the mainstream Republican Party to incorporate the younger, brasher politics of the movement backfired, however. The East Coast media elite seemed to take a cruel pleasure out of grilling Palin (who had never traveled abroad) on her foreign policy inexperience and in revealing, one by one, her almost total lack of constitutional and basic policy knowledge (they soon homed in also on her near complete absence of concern about that fact). But her absence of concern was more revealing than many of them took it to be at the time.

So too was the small-town, antiestablishment populism that was rising within the Tea Party. This was a constituency that Palin was cannily positioning herself to represent. It was also one that was moving to take over from the neocons the mantle of being the principal radical force in American politics. Unlike the neocons, however, who reoriented the Republicans around highly conservative "values" (even as they were themselves invariably establishment figures), the Tea Party—by anchoring itself, a little awkwardly it must be said, to the "no taxation without representation" line of the original Boston Tea Party—was more exclusively focused on economic issues pitched in a populist vein. Where neoconservatism had led America into the war on terror, the Tea Party had emerged from out of the war on terror. And for preaching its isolationist creed Tea Partyers were as much a liability to the modern, war-mortgaged Republican mainstream as they were to the Democrats.

Indeed, the Tea Party took Bush himself to be almost as bad as his Democratic counterparts. "What use is a Republican to us, if all they do is vote with Democrats?" one of the founders of the movement, Christina Botteri, put it.[87] The Tea Party thus sold itself on a ticket of change no less explicit than that captured in the more elite, considered prose of Obama: and for all the jokes at Palin's expense, it would arguably fare better in the longer term than Obama's own brand of revisionist liberalism—the government bailouts that soon followed the foreclosures and mortgage defaults already engulfing the nation during the election year serving as the Occam's razor between them. It would fare better too than many of its ostensible supporters, including the campaign's now obligatory "real American" reference point, Joseph Wurzelbacher, better known as Joe the Plumber.

Despite her efforts, Palin did not ultimately represent the Tea Party more than *anyone* could be said to have "represented" the Tea Party. But she did benefit, in a way the Republican Party would not, from the political momentum that the big (very big) money behind it—money from such deep wells as the Koch brothers and Steve Forbes—could muster (much of which was channeled via the movement's institutional forerunner, the rather shadowy FreedomWorks lobby). This was the beginning of a critical convergence between major conservative donors and news media (like Fox News) in the cause of radical conservatism. More immediately, it was this that ultimately explained her inclusion on the vice-presidential ticket in the first place, since she offered McCain's team a means to reach out to conservative radicals—little realizing that the "Tea Party Death Star," as *Rolling Stone* dubbed it, was likely to be as destructive to their own electoral plans as to the opposition (though the peak of its impact would come with the midterms in 2010).

For all that the Republicans ran a flawed campaign in 2008, they still had one potential ace up their sleeves as the nation went to the polls: would Middle America vote for a black president? Here was the silent, unspoken core of the entire campaign. Obama himself studiously avoided the issue; and perhaps he was right to do so. For somewhat against the odds, against the birthers impugning his origins and the vitriol of the Tea Party, against the vise-like grip held by the Clintonites on the Democrats as well, Obama swept into office on a landslide greater even than Ronald Reagan's and second only to FDR's in 1932, a crowd of 90,000 turning up to his final campaign speech at Manassas, Virginia.[88] It was the changing complexion of that crowd, as much as the eloquence of the man who stood before it, that was truly significant. Bush had walked away with the 2004 election on the back of a nation in fear: and in the language of pollsters on the back of the strength of the vote of the "hockey mom," who wanted her family protected. Obama clinched the 2008 election on the back of a nation in search of hope, and on the strength of the surging Latino vote in particular.

The election of Barack Obama was indicative of a generational change as well. Swathes of younger voters had registered for the first time, many of them captured by the Democratic Party's savvy new media and grass-roots campaign. In contrast to the Republicans, Obama's team used the then new social media highly effectively. First, they netted vast numbers of small donations ($45 million of the $55 million raised in February— all without a single fundraiser event—came from individuals, not PACs). Then they used that money to fund voter-registration efforts and to mobilize blue-collar votes through early balloting (to ensure that people who could not take time off work would not miss the polling booths on election day).[89] Perhaps above all, Americans were simply tired by now of the war and its constant incursion into their lives. Recognizing this, Obama needed to do little else than to run on a solidly anti-Bush campaign, hounding the sitting president, who rarely turned out to defend himself, on his war record and its consequences.[90]

But for all the euphoria of the election night itself, the nation's first black president would be forced to take office under not one cloud but two. The crowds that packed the Washington monument from one side to the other were deceptive in this regard, as they were also soon to be disappointed. Because for all that Obama's advisers instructed him to "maintain an emphasis on changing Washington" as his campaign's central message—a sop to Tea Partyers and disgruntled Democrats alike—the new president would soon find that he was opposed on all sides and change was a lot harder to bring about than he might have imagined. If it wasn't the fact that the logo he stood on to make his speech was paid for by the billionaire Republican-funding Koch brothers, it was the extent of the political opposition's personal antipathy toward him. The Onion's spoof "shock" headline, "Black man given world's worst job," was in that sense not at all far from the truth.

The first shadow was cast by the sheer scale of his own promises. The second shadow was one for which he bore no responsibility, for all that it would condemn his administration to the worst case of partisan congressional gridlock any postwar president had yet confronted. This was the fury of a Republican Party lashing out at the president personally as the nearest available scapegoat for its own problems. It was this that would force Obama to govern—for all his popularity—largely by executive decree and therefore without a popular mandate, making too many of his policies too vulnerable to being rolled back should the political mood change after he left office.

But more even than the dug-in stubbornness of a fired-up Republican base, the new American president found himself, before he had even properly assembled his transition team, having to respond to what was very quickly shaping up to be the greatest economic crisis since the Depression. The American economy had been undergoing a sort of seizure in the background of the electoral campaign. By the time Obama finally stepped into the Oval Office in January 2009 the crisis was being felt in layoffs and bankruptcies right around the world. Banks were collapsing all around the new president, mortgage foreclosures were ascending through the roof, and the US economy was in a tailspin that would take the better part of his two full terms in office to overcome.

The speed with which the global economy had suddenly seized up caught not only Obama but almost all the world's leaders and many of the world's greatest economists by surprise. Britain's Queen Elizabeth II was sufficiently irked by this to ask, on a visit to the London School of Economics in late 2008, "Why did nobody notice it?" She was right to have been irked, for with hindsight it should not have caught anyone by surprise. War and debt have long been two of the main reasons democracies slide into crisis. For several years now the Western nations had been living with both of them.[91] What was more, however, and this was what Obama had to get to grips with during the transition, the Western nations also had a massively top-heavy and resolutely *non*national global financial system: one whose vast flows of capital around the world, organized mostly between private nonstate actors and overseen by independent nongovernment regulators, far exceeded the problems posed by the nation's own fiscal situation. And it was at the intersection of all three of these factors that the greatest financial crisis since the Great Depression was now under way.

15

The Great Recession

THE TREMORS HAD been felt all year, but few were those who predicted the catastrophe yet to come. In March 2008, Bear Stearns, the fifth largest US investment bank, needed rescuing in a Federal Reserve–backed deal. Other savings and investment banks had already found themselves in trouble. BNP Paribas, Switzerland's UBS, IndyMac Bank, HBOS, and HSBC had all been struggling because of their exposure to the collapsing US housing market since 2007. In September of that year Britain's Northern Rock could no longer meet its debts, collapsing and sparking off scenes of a bank run. Throughout 2008, as anxiety spread throughout the global financial system, it became harder and harder to secure fresh funding. By the summer of 2008, the US Treasury was forced to extend credit lines to the federal mortgage providers Fannie Mae and Freddie Mac (which together owned or guaranteed $5 trillion worth of US homes). As the Bush administration rushed through the Housing and Economic Recovery Act in July to address the collapse of the subprime mortgage sector, it was already clear that serious trouble was brewing.

It was in September, with the US election in full swing, that the real earthquake began. On September 7, the US government was forced to take over Fannie Mae and Freddie Mac entirely (loading their $5 trillion of liabilities onto the American taxpayer). Just a week later, on Monday, September 15, Lehman Brothers collapsed, the largest bankruptcy in history. At that point Lehman held $639 billion dollars in assets and employed over 25,000 people worldwide. Its fall led to the loss of nearly $10 trillion on global capital markets and cast a cloud of uncertainty across the entire financial system. As with the collapse of Bear Stearns in March, it was as if Lehman had simply "evaporated over [the] weekend."[1] The same day that Lehman collapsed, the credit rating of insurer AIG was slashed and it found itself having to pay out not only on mortgage foreclosures but on collateral owed to its trading partners as well. Widely understood as a "pillar of American capitalism"—it was, after all, the largest insurance company in the world with branches in 130 different countries—AIG suddenly needed $85 billion in government assistance to stop it from going under.[2]

The response to this massive escalation of financial market events was at first a stunned silence. The morning he heard that AIG had been taken over, former vice chairman of the US Federal Reserve Board Alan Blinder walked into the class he was now teaching at Princeton, scratched his head, and informed his students: "Last night the Federal Reserve, which has never [even] regulated an insurance company, nationalized one!"[3] An eerie mood briefly took over the normally bullish traders and the central bankers who stood watch over their shoulder. Nationalizations were not what US capitalism did. Then the panic set in. Wachovia bank crashed, as did Washington Mutual, the largest thrift organization in America. Investment bank Merrill Lynch narrowly avoided going the same way.

What also went, along with the careers of redundant twenty-somethings carting their boxes out in the morning after the collapse of their respective banks, was the confidence that the financial markets rely upon. This might very well have been the greatest problem of all. As one British investor put it: "Banking is like religion: It's *all* about trust and confidence."[4] Yet now no financial institution knew which counterpart it could trust. With everyone holding on to their money, the entire payment system of the modern world was teetering on the edge of collapse.[5] Interbank lending, the blood supply of the financial system, dried up. The world economy went into cardiac arrest. For the next two years, as the financial crisis gave on to a long and severe recession, economic growth and employment crashed harder and deeper than they had in seventy years and confidence was nowhere to be seen. Anxiety and despair were the new cardinal emotions, and they soon bled out of the markets and lodged themselves firmly in the public mood, with dramatic consequences for democracy.

The Crisis Strikes

What had happened? In the summer of 2007 the Bank for International Settlements (BIS) had issued a warning. "Years of loose monetary policy," it said, "have fueled a giant global credit bubble, leaving us vulnerable to another 1930s slump." In itself this was hardly surprising: over the previous three decades, as we have seen, people expected access to ever more credit and for the most part governments and regulators wanting small outlays and contented electorates were only too happy to allow banks to provide this.[6] But the real issue was just how large the financial markets that provided this credit had grown. National governments operate in the hundreds of billions of dollars. By 2007 the financial system traded daily in the trillions, to a large extent as a result of the policies pursued by governments, regulators, and private banks alike since the early 1970s. This was why the financial crisis first manifested itself so dramatically wherever those vast quantities of capital touched base with the real world, where oversight was often lacking. This was why the financial crisis—for all it became a truly global event—first came to investors' and economic analysts' attention in relation to the progressively overleveraged housing market in the United States.[7]

The American housing market had first become attractive to investors seeking to improve their returns in the weak market conditions that settled in the wake of the post-2001 recession. As a result of the process of deregulation that began under Carter and Reagan, and that Clinton and Bush Jr. had completed, the US financial market was also one of the least stringently overseen, allowing risky financial practices to run amok: something in which the credit-rating agencies, who were supposed now to stand in for government regulators, were themselves complicit. Households were encouraged to play their part in the system too, primarily by taking out mortgage equity withdrawals (at a volume of $800 billion per year by 2006). Median household debt rose by more than a third between 2001 and 2004: a dramatic escalation in unpropitious economic times, and yet one that people were only too happy to go along with since it freed up a bit more cash for day-to-day spending. Since people felt relatively better off thanks to the deep reserves of credit they could draw upon, they also stopped worrying quite so much about saving. These were understandable, if shortsighted, decisions that people made to get by in the modern credit-driven economy. The real problem, however, was what was brewing in the background.

For on the back of this escalating US housing market, and the many millions of household economies reliant upon it, was built a further financial trading system: the critical element of the problem. Within this setup investors were encouraged to increase their leverage on already inflated assets, and on the back of this they began to trade a variety of mortgage-backed securities and derivative financial products ever more aggressively among themselves. There was no one actor in this system: that was the whole problem. It was a product, and perfect paradigm, of the increasingly globalized financial system itself. The rising quantity of mortgage debt in the US thus became steadily securitized: a misleading financial term of art denoting simply that this debt became "tradable." This had the effect of turning the roofs above people's heads into an asset class. And that drew a further glut of international savings into the brew.[8] American homeowners were thus not the only ones increasingly reliant on a steady flow of credit. Critical pillars of the financial system at large had also become steadily more leveraged, as with the dramatic rise of "collateralized" debt obligations (CDOs), which enabled rapid turnover of trades and the selling-on of debt-related financial products.

The housing market was one bubble in the Bush-era economy, then, but there were others too—including in the bond markets that had enjoyed relatively free rein since Clinton's time in office. And ultimately what linked all of these elements was the ability of banks and investors to access ever more dollars: in other words, the liquidity of the system itself. But when the underlying housing market inevitably dried up, banks suddenly found they needed to unwind their exposures across the board. As they did so, people—working-class Americans in the first instance— suddenly found they owed more on their homes than those homes were now worth. Looking to America, just as he had done in the early 1970s, the German public intellectual Jürgen Habermas was struck this time not by its crisis of legitimation but by a "seemingly endless loop of melancholic Hopperian images" presented by "long rows of abandoned houses in Florida and elsewhere with 'Foreclosure' signs on their front lawns." When this same striking reality of foreclosures hit the secondary investment market, and banks needed to find out how much they actually owed, they quickly realized that they had no idea. That was when the first wave of the financial crisis hit: the credit crunch.

As the steadily growing roll-call of fallen banks attested, the crunch was both sudden and severe. Almost overnight, consumers, banks, and countries alike were forced to stop spending and to set about trying to deleverage themselves. The impact of this sudden stop in the economy's basic gearing was massive. As in all recessions, once the supply of credit dries up in this way, consumption too invariably declines, and the main street economy is slowed to a halt. This was exactly what happened in late 2008. Companies responded by reducing their inventory, and when that proved insufficient, by reducing their workforce. As manufacturing too collapsed, and more people were laid off, the wider economy slowed even more, this time without the elixir of liquidity—the drug to which Western democracies had turned time and again since the 1970s—to save it. That, in turn, drove investors to seek sanctuary in sovereign states: a process that would in due course mark the beginnings of the European sovereign debt saga. What had begun as a problem of balance sheets was now a very material, and painful, problem the world over. Companies and countries alike found that the supply chains which linked them now yanked them into trouble too.

To describe all this as the beginnings of a financial "crisis" is to understate how dramatically it broke upon the West at the time: for it was a near evisceration of capitalism as known and practiced. To describe it therefore as the work of a few rogue traders or greedy banks alone is that much more misleading. The credit crisis was not the work just of reckless investors: it was the result of the very structures by which capitalist democracy had come to organize itself since the 1970s. The basic underlying cause was the budget deficits from the late 1970s, the financial deregulation that had followed in their wake, and the outsized growth of transnational finance ever since. What began as a response to the large problems in the *real* economy posed in the early 1970s, above all inflation and unemployment, led on in its turn to an almost entirely *fictitious* economy: the basis of the Clinton boom. The financial sector was allowed to grow beyond almost all limits, while the state progressively unburdened itself of the regulatory tools that would be needed if such a casino economy was ever to run into trouble. Now the return flow was about to be felt on Main Street once again.

There were more proximate reasons which account for why the crisis epicentered in the US. These included the US government's deliberate policy of low interest rates (which had made it less daunting to borrow ever-larger sums). Those low interest rates had been intended to keep the US economy afloat, despite the escalating costs of the war on terror, but they also opened the way for the inexcusably reckless lending practices (allowing mortgages, for example, to be pushed onto ever less creditworthy customers) that banks were routinely undertaking. It included the failure of the four major regulatory agencies, including the Federal Reserve, to fulfill their mandate sufficiently. Perhaps not irrelevantly, when the crisis broke these were each also headed by Bush appointees in a conservative free-market mold: "a deregulation-minded bunch," recalled Alan Blinder, "who probably also got swept up in the euphoria of the day."[9]

These were macroeconomic failings, then, but as often as not they had political causes and real consequences, for the poor and the marginal in particular. Nearly ten million US citizens faced foreclosures on their homes between 2006 and 2014. African Americans were particularly hard hit: their net household wealth relative to whites would slide back to Cold War levels.[10] Because the meltdown was so complex in its fundamentals (itself a function of the sheer scale to which the financial industry had grown) the response that governments mounted came across as so technical and arcane, so resolutely focused on obscure market indicators, that, fatefully, citizens never really felt that their losses and their suffering were seriously taken into account. For all that governments and central banks, particularly in the US, must ultimately be seen as having successfully stabilized the economy (a fact we should *not* take for granted), it was this mismatch that would ensure the financial crisis and its fallout became such a watershed event. For it was to drive a wedge between elected governments and their citizenry. It would eventually awaken the electorate from their post–Cold War slumber into an angry and demanding crowd.

One way of reading the crisis, therefore, is as a rediscovery of the limits (and salience) of national sovereignty and governmental intervention amid a wider breakdown in the dominant consensus of economic liberalism. Suddenly in 2008, after three decades of being told that markets operate most efficiently when left alone, now states were plunging their hands deeply into economic affairs in the manner of emergency surgeons. Similarly, after years of exercising their international freedom of movement, it did not take long for international banks to turn in desperation to their "home" states, where they found, to their delight, that national taxpayers would be asked to bail them out. But if that solved a part of the problem, for the banks, two much larger problems emerged from this that would shape the fallout from the crisis in the years to come.

The first was a problem found: the discovery of just how embedded within the vast quantities of capital sluicing around the world every day modern Western governments had become. Over the previous three decades the banks that governments now committed to bailing out had become far larger, more extensive operations than many national leaders seemed to have reckoned with: total bank assets in the EU in 2011, for example, were €46.8 trillion: 370 percent of the combined output of all the EU nations.[11] The second, by contrast, was a problem made. This was the grim-faced determination to defend, via the burden of bank bailouts, each national parcel of the wider global financial system as if it were somehow distinct. And yet the truth of it was that this was no longer a viable option. There could be no going back—which begs the question, at the very least, of how an underregulated global financial system had become such a central component of liberal democratic politics in the first place.

The Long Road to Crisis (the "Great Moderation")

On Labor Day weekend, 2007, the brightest minds in the US Federal Reserve system headed to Jackson, Wyoming, for their annual policy retreat. The long-planned topic of the meeting was the housing market. Ben Bernanke, who had taken over from Alan Greenspan as the chairman of the Federal Reserve the year before, observed—with a wry comment—how timely the issue had suddenly become. A student of the Great Depression, he would later win recognition when the crisis broke for his proactive instincts (at least compared to his European colleagues). But he did not at this point seem particularly inclined to take remedial action. He used the occasion to underscore the generally productive relations, as he saw it, between housing finance and the American economy: presenting the vipers' nest of mortgage products that existed in the US at that moment as evidence, not of a growing problem, but of the country's "sophisticated" housing market. The full extent of the crisis that was brewing had not yet dawned on America's central bankers.

One governor who could not make the event, owing to illness, was Edward M. Gramlich. This was doubly tragic, not only because Gramlich did not long survive the illness that had kept him at home that weekend, but because he was one of the few US central bankers prepared to acknowledge the likely scale of the problem. Gramlich had in fact warned Alan Greenspan, the former Federal Reserve chairman, since around the start of the decade, of the dangers—of boom and bust—that such a "sophisticated" housing market conferred upon the economy at large. The ideologically laissez-faire, libertarian Greenspan had dismissed his concerns. But the recent blow-up in subprime mortgages, Gramlich's precirculated speech was due to remark, now looked like being a classic bust in the making. And that was just the start of it: "when the dust clears," Gramlich had warned in a freshly published book, there would be "financial carnage" to pay for the extent to which the problem had been left to grow so large.[12]

Other lone voices had pointed out the dangers of failing to properly regulate the housing market. Sheila Bair, a Treasury official who had previously worked with Gramlich, spent much of the first few years of the century asking for a code of "best practices" to be drawn up and enforced. From the consumer side too, the directors of a housing advocacy group in California had urged Greenspan to use his "bully pulpit" to push for higher standards in mortgage financing. Likewise in 2005 the Chief Economist of the IMF, Raghuram Rajan, also at Jackson Hole, laid out a warning of just the sort of scenario that was now unfolding. But Greenspan had rebuffed them all. When the states of Georgia and North Carolina took matters into their own hands and tried to address the most abusive mortgage lending practices directly, they were rebuked by the Office of the Comptroller of the Currency, one of the four main federal regulatory boards.[13]

The Federal Reserve's reluctance to step in needs contextualizing of course. It was the mindset as much as the money that was the problem. Reporting back on a lecture he had given to a gathering of bankers in the Bahamas in 2006, the influential economic historian Niall Ferguson was reputedly thrown out on his ear for warning of the thin ice that international finance was then standing on. "One of the most experienced investors attending the conference went so far as to suggest to the organizers that they 'dispense altogether with an outside speaker next year, and instead offer a screening of *Mary Poppins*,'" Ferguson later recalled.[14] Fatefully, the regulators thought the same. And it is against this background—a "lusty chorus of 'supercalifragilistic,'" as Ferguson dubbed it—that the salience of the two principal dynamics at the heart of the credit crisis and the global recession that followed in its wake needs to be understood. The first of these was the structural centrality of debt to the entire political system. The second was the intellectual bias among policymakers in favor of a financial system that was treated as if it was entirely a technical affair, and not in the least bit political.

The first and most basic cause of the credit crisis, then, was that self-same pressing problem of the past four decades: the long-term, secular decline in the rate of profit after 1973 and the gradual, creeping turn to credit to alleviate this: a development which helped fuel in turn the expansion of global finance. The deepest taproots of the crisis were in this sense sunk in the solutions that were devised amid the last economic crisis of the 1970s. With profit margins under pressure, Western manufacturers and corporations alike had increasingly turned to finance—leveraged via a mass roll-out of consumer credit schemes—as a way to boost profits and to defend their market position from more competitive entities abroad. From the late 1960s General Motors, for example, had relied more and more heavily on its financial arm, General Motors Acceptance Corporation. Similarly, at General Electric, the financing offered to consumers to help them buy its products gave birth to GE Capital, worth 42 percent of group profits by the year 2000.[15]

Banks had done exactly the same. Between 1997 and 2009 banks' share of total financial sector assets had fallen from around 56 percent to 24 percent. As people put less of their money into banks as savings (their pension monies were increasingly now tied up in private pension funds after all) and companies looked less to banks to meet their liquidity needs (they looked instead to the markets) banks had found they needed to sip at the cup of international finance as well. The subsequent agonizing of the liberals—as to the Faustian bargain struck when Main Street banks went to Wall Street for their dinner—thus overlooks the systemic reasons why this barrier *had* to be broken down in the first place. The Clinton-era repeal of the Glass-Steagall regulations that had kept investment and savings banks separated since the Great Depression had exacerbated this problem. But Glass-Steagall alone would not have prevented the credit crisis: once the pressures of financialization had reached such a tipping point as they had by the early 2000s, the banks arguably had no option but to adapt themselves to the rules of a financialized economy. It was this that had added yet further levels to the inverted pyramid that was the modern Western economy, particularly the more financialized economies such as Britain and America.

In the context of this finance-driven credit economy two other factors played a hand as well: one was the background factor of rising inequality and the other, related problem was the growing significance of private debt to national economic growth. Growing inequality ensured that, on a day-to-day basis, there was greater pressure on individuals in a consumerist society to keep up with the Joneses, such that they began to demand more and more of the credit that companies and banks were now supplying. This too was a product of the post-1970s political economy. Not for nothing was MasterCard born in 1979 (a development of the Master Charge card first introduced in 1976).[16] And for a long while the turn to credit seemed to make sense. It had been this private sector debt (in contrast to the public sector borrowing of the pre-1970s era) that had kept Western economies ticking over ever since. The "problem" of markets in a democratic society had thus been solved first by re-inventing the state in the 1970s, and then by reinventing society in the

1980s and 1990s. Now the problem of markets, finally, would have to be addressed head on. Or would it?

It was here that the second political factor came in. For while the reasons citizens were seeking such debt might well have been an amalgam of individual choices, it not only met with government approval, it was actively encouraged. With government spending squeezed, with taxes systematically lowered, and with a still substantial welfare bill to meet (no matter how much states had tried to cut back on benefits) governments had become reliant, in effect, upon citizens taking on more of the debt themselves. In such a world, institutionally locked into place as it had been in the 1990s, individuals were thus variously prodded by their erstwhile protectors toward the credit window that marked their own entry into the financial system.[17]

It becomes perhaps a little more understandable, therefore, why the Fed could leave its meeting in Jackson Hole resolved largely just to continue, in the words of Ben Bernanke, "following these developments closely." Of course, the point that Gramlich and others had been trying to make was that this was precisely what the Fed had been doing wrong all along. Under the permissive chairmanship of Alan Greenspan in particular, it had for too long simply been following events, not setting the tone, much less the rules.[18] But in this the Fed was nothing if not indicative of the second set of factors flowing into and shaping the crisis: the intellectual consensus that saw market volatility as a problem to be managed rather than the outcome of political or regulatory oversight.

Again there were two aspects to this. The first was the post-1970s commitment to low inflation that girded the liberal democratic approach to "governing at a distance." The second was the seeming success of this approach from the 1980s onward, which had translated into its own de facto orthodoxy—in the words of Greenspan himself, the view that "markets know best." Of course, there was one primary weakness with an anti-inflationary approach to the economy, and this most pronounced in Europe: its tendency to stifle economic productivity. But with credit markets effectively driving economic growth and inflationary targeting offering the appearance of a certain directional thrust, the world's central bankers had by the early twenty-first century become increasingly confident in their own ability to manage markets with the deftest of hands. So much so that they now considered it almost inappropriate to use the somewhat heavier arsenal in their possession.

The problem, then, was not just that markets were underregulated but that this was how the financial authorities wished them to be. Here Ben

Bernanke, who took over from Greenspan as chairman of the Federal Reserve in 2006, had helped set the tone as well. In a much-remarked speech from 2004 Bernanke had saluted the strategy of disciplined public money and low inflation and lent his institutional imprimatur to the claim that the post-1970s era had seen such successes in the field of central banking that it ought to go down in history as the era of the "great moderation." The Federal Reserve, Bernanke said, had not only been successful at beating back the inflationary chaos of the 1970s, it had ushered in a new period of profound macroeconomic stability, he claimed. To this way of thinking, the vast profits generated by the nineties "new economy" boom, and the dot-com and housing bubbles that followed in its wake, were not to be taken as a sign of instability, merely as an indicator of the benefits that "inflation targeting" itself could realize for the economy.[19]

These were reformist neoliberal claims that treated monetary policy as an art, "not an ironclad policy rule in the Friedman sense," as Bernanke put it.[20] But they cleaved to the same core belief nonetheless: the mistaken idea that money is not political and that markets know best. More than just a theoretical explanation of what the economy had been doing, therefore, and (thanks to the likes of the Fed) why it had been allowed to keep doing it for several decades; more than just a retrospective celebration, Bernanke's notion of a "great moderation" was also an explanation and justificatory framework for more of the same. Just as capitalism had vanquished communism, so too had tight money and central bank discipline, or so it was claimed, now vanquished the profligacy and the waste of capitalist inflation. Moreover, given the extent to which the Federal Reserve set the tone for markets and regulators elsewhere in the world, it was also a prescription as to how economies ought to be run more generally, and a gloss over the intense political implications contained within that prescription. This had proven especially significant given how truly global the post–Cold War financial system had become, how resolutely *non*–state based it had become, and the additional challenges of regulation and response this brought with it.

In a dual process that had started at the beginning of the 1990s, under Alan Greenspan's tenure at the Federal Reserve specifically, policymakers had gradually "abdicated control over credit to the market," in the words of one expert, because this was easier than "an affluent society [having] to face the political challenges posed by the end of affluence." This drew, once again, on the wrong lessons that were learned from the monetary crises of the early 1970s, the solution to which had been more market liberalization. That solution, which was itself a part of the reason for the inflationary crises of the decade to follow, was not in turn rejected but desperately clung to instead. Only in the 1980s was it seen to require a more disciplined approach to enforcing. The neoliberal paradox of "enforced liberalization" thus took shape and served, as we have seen, to constrain national governments' decision-making from then on.

By the late 1990s and 2000s, such fine-tuning of the financial markets' activity as was routinely undertaken by central banks and market actors in pursuit of this apparent ideal had itself increasingly "synched": the whole process being put in effect on autopilot.[21] This was why some, like Clinton's Treasury Secretary Robert Rubin (1995–9), had already begun to argue by the turn of the century that the Fed itself was in many ways "redundant." Rubin certainly had a point: if policymakers were simply fine-tuning interest rates up and down in an effort to "validate" prior moves made by the market then it wasn't at all clear which was the tail and which the dog in terms of their relationship.[22] Wall Street had long thought that this was exactly how it ought to be. The point was that now politicians agreed. After all, as one former EU adviser put it, doing so offered "a means of paying for a Scandinavian-style welfare system with American levels of tax."[23]

In good times—and there had been plenty of those over the previous decade—this led some to think that a well-organized partnership, between markets and the agencies intended to be steering them, had fallen into place. It was the very opposite of the theatrics launched by Paul Volcker in his massive overnight interest rate hike of 1981. Government intervention was not even called for anymore. The logic of fin-de-siècle global finance ran the opposite way: the less the contusion, the less the disruption, the more fluid the glide between market policymaking and autonomous market activity the better: in short, the greater the degree of predictability in Federal Reserve policy, the less jumpy the markets (which is to say the major investors) were likely to be, and the less need there was in turn for anything other than gentle adjustments by the Fed. All this was presented as "transparency." It was also taken by financial regulators as a winning argument regarding the virtue of unfettered markets.[24]

In fact, the system this helped usher into existence was anything but transparent. Contrary to the Federal Reserve's effort to erase the line of agency between markets and policy actions, as if the one could almost become the other, in the market itself, and especially in the heavily bundled, high-volume securities trades that dominated international finance, quite what was being bought and sold became almost impossible to understand. Transparency was, in fact, nowhere to be seen in the thicket of packaged-up and rebundled financial "products" that were widely available come the mid 2000s. As the French finance minister Christine Lagarde reportedly quipped, you would need a PhD to even understand the trades being offered, and even then it was doubtful that those offering the trades knew the likely end result of their financial alchemy.

The difficulty of doing so was only further magnified by the reliance of the system upon another critical aspect of the modern financial economy: interbank loan rates. Interbank loan rates were a fundamental pillar of the global financial system, which worked to link different national financial systems together. But they could also fluctuate depending on what was "known" (or not known) about particular markets: with the result that fears of a possible problem could very quickly turn into a real problem if everyone reacted the same way. The digitalization of money further exacerbated this by virtue of speeding everything up and by removing a technical barrier to volume expansion. Nobody could reasonably have denied that the whole system had the potential to explode. Even so everyone believed that it had too many parts, involved too many well-informed people, for it to go wrong *as* a system. Such belief was supported by yet another wrong lesson learned: the presumed successful response to the "Asian" financial crises of the 1990s which "contained" the problem and led policymakers to believe there really was a national girding to global finance (there wasn't). The significance of all that "confidence" now became clear. In the meantime, it flattered the major financial powers' GDP and allowed them to keep their spending promises to the voters.

To these longer-term developments pushing the Western economies toward the cliff-edge of financial crisis in 2007–8 were then added the economic policies of the Bush administration. Bush had two overriding macroeconomic concerns during his first term in office: to ensure a soft landing from the previous dot-com bubble that had burst at the turn of the century, and to demonstrate that the US economy had not been negatively affected by "the terrorists." As one commentator observed: "It became a national security priority to inflate the purchasing power of US consumers." Inevitably, of course, both these priorities led to a deepening focus on cheap money at the Fed and to its further inflating the housing bubble (not to mention the more general reliance of the economy upon a constant and growing supply of cheap credit).[25]

In evaluating these policies we must not forget, either, Bush's genuine conviction of the moral unassailability of a "property owning" nation— the "ownership society," as he began to call it when running for reelection in 2004.[26] For Bush, this translated into a general desire for policies geared toward improving home ownership. In light of the response to 9/11 and the credit crisis it is easy to overlook the significance of the younger Bush's evangelical streak as it defined his administration's policy, from international funding for AIDS to "big tent Republican" social security programs at home, and everything in between. Bush was, in some ways, a Republican LBJ. It certainly seems that Bush genuinely thought the freeze in social mobility in America could be resolved by the liberal application of a good dose of home ownership. Of course, if subprime credit also had the beneficial effect, from his administration's point of view, of simulating the *effect* of actual redistribution toward the poor, while leaving *actual* profits of the capitalist class and the national budget untouched, then that was so much the better.[27]

Similarly, the mortgage practices that underpinned the post-2000s housing boom may have recently become predatory, but they rested on well-meaning legislation dating back to 1977 (the Community Reinvestment Act) and 1980 (the Depository Institutions Deregulation and Monetary Control Act). The former encouraged lenders to do more to meet the credit needs of poor communities; the latter allowed them to charge higher interest rates instead of asking for more weighty deposits up-front. And once again the hard coin that linked the well-meaning effort to extend housing credit to poorer communities in the earlier era with the predatory system in the later era was the economic policy shortcut of competitive deregulation.

Here the culprit to have started it all may well have been Thatcher's Britain, whose early moves on deregulation put pressure on the American economy to respond (not least when she deregulated the City of London in an effort to prise business away from New York). Chancellor Brown then finished what Thatcher had begun by freeing up the Bank of England in 1997—adding for good measure a new and extremely light-touch regulatory agency, the Financial Services Authority (FSA), to relieve the government not only of determining its own monetary policy but of overseeing it as well (at the same time as removing the Bank of England's own powers of regulation). American central bankers, feeling the pressure to likewise ease up on the extent to which they curtailed their own finance industry's freedom of movement, soon responded in kind—and Greenspan of course was the perfect choice for undertaking this.[28]

In many ways then, the economics of the Bush administration merely built upon the thirty-year slide to deregulation that had emerged in the wake of (and partly as a solution to the problems with) the post-1970s anti-inflationary consensus. The appetite having been stoked under Reagan, the regulatory safety catches having been removed under Clinton, the way was cleared, in the post–Cold War years, for the "electronic herd" of the shadow-banking sector to embark upon its feeding frenzy under Bush. As the Citigroup CEO Chuck Prince put it before the crash: "When the music stops . . . things will be complicated. But as long as the music is playing you've got to get up and dance. We're still dancing."[29]

The further ingredient that the Bush administration added to this already combustible mix was, as we saw in the previous chapter, its remarkable decision to run a war economy on a low tax basis. For when the tax cuts failed to get the economy going again, after the dot-com recession, the emphasis was instead put on monetary policy to do so. Here Greenspan's Federal Reserve performed its most obliging service to Bush: cutting interest rates to make it cheaper to borrow and kick-starting the housing boom once again. The final contribution of the Bush administration was somewhat more avoidable, and that was the ballooning US current account deficit. The deficit, which had begun growing during the 1990s, soared after 2001, reaching $811 billion (or 6.1 percent of GDP) by 2006. "At that point," as one economist notes, the "US was absorbing nearly 80 percent of the international savings that crossed borders."[30] Other countries were busy buying up US debt, in other words. But was this because the US was overspending or because other countries were too concerned with saving? On that critical distinction the fate of the US economy turned.

As Ben Bernanke saw things, the principal underlying cause of the US deficit was not America's fault at all but other countries' (and especially China's) propensity to save. Bernanke wasn't literally saying that America's structural imbalance was China's fault. His point was subtler: it was that the entry of China into the capitalist world economy in the 1990s brought in hundreds of millions of new workers who were earning more than their still developing economy could yet find things for them to spend it on: hence they were accumulating savings that needed to be invested somewhere. Just like the comforting myth of the "great moderation" before it, however, Bernanke's "savings glut" thesis was not just a technical account of macroeconomic developments: it was also a way to justify the lack of control that politicians now had over the debt economy. That too now proved to have been a fateful misconception.

Bailing out the Banks

For the first half of 2008, Europeans looked to America and assumed they were safe from its troubles, thanks to tighter regulation, less "savage" capitalism, and fewer of the social problems that led to such predatory mortgages in the first place. To speak of the possibility of a similar crisis in a European country, insisted José Luis Rodríguez Zapatero, the Spanish prime minister, was "inelegant and unpatriotic."[31] The French in particular felt they were immune from the troubles that had struck the United States, because their banking system was more prudent. To some extent there was truth in this: French mortgage lenders demanded far more conservative debt-to-income levels than their American counterparts. In 2005 Jacques Chirac had thus felt secure in his latest jibe that American-style "ultraliberalism" was "as disastrous as communism."[32] The collapse of Britain's Northern Rock in late 2007, setting off the first bank run in the country for 150 years and forcing the government to take the mortage house into public ownership, seemed merely further proof of the failings of Anglo-American capitalism.[33]

But the French economy at large was far less immune to the transatlantic rupturing of global finance than Chirac might have presumed, as BNP Paribas's own wobble in the summer of 2007 confirmed. The previous decade had, after all, seen France finally take up its seat at the neoliberal table. Lionel Jospin, Chirac's socialist prime minister, began the process back in the late 1990s, eagerly privatizing companies and bringing millions of French citizens into the shareholding twenty-first century. Executive pay had increased along American lines too, leaving French corporate bosses among the best remunerated on the continent. In due course a somewhat inevitable rise in financial scandals began to eclipse the hoary old state-enterprise scandals of the past.[34] Above all French banks, like so many other European banks, now made their money off very short-term dollar funding: and that made them heavily dependent on what was happening in America. France, in other words, was vulnerable enough. There was disappointment but little surprise then, when in early 2008 French bank Société Générale reported losses of $7 billion incurred in bad positions by a rogue trader, prompting panic on the markets as the bank began desperately trying to unwind them amid the wider global fallout.[35]

Soon it was not just French banks that were in trouble. By late September 2008 Belgian–Dutch banking and insurance giant Fortis required the governments of the Netherlands, Belgium, and Luxembourg to take over half of its operations. It then emerged that Germany's second largest mortgage lender, Hypo Real Estate, was also in trouble, while the British government was forced to nationalize mortgage provider Bradford & Bingley (selling off its branches to Spanish bank Santander). In October, France and Belgium moved to backstop Dexia, a municipality lender, with €6.4 billion, while the Irish government extended its deposit guarantee to all Irish banking concerns. Later that same week the Dutch government took over the rest of Fortis's operations in the Netherlands, it having taken less than a week for the earlier partial nationalization to be seen as far from sufficient.

It wasn't just the financial powerhouses of Western Europe that were hit, however. Latvia's economy shrank by 13 percent over the next three years; Iceland's by the same in just two years. Poland would be forced to turn to the IMF for support while the economies of Portugal, Hungary, and Romania all went into reverse. Inside the Western European eurozone, countries were cushioned to a degree—for now at least—by virtue of being bound to the same mast and because their financial institutions had recourse to loan facilities from the ECB (which had begun making credit available since the summer of 2007, with the first wobble at BNP Paribas). Though it would later become one of the central stages on which the politics of the financial crisis played out, the euro initially acted for the member countries as a "shock absorber" for the crisis—something its many critics would later forget.[36]

Italy and Spain began struggling too, but not because—as with the UK—they had an oversized financial sector vulnerable to American "sneezes." Italy also had less household (or individual) debt and Spain had relatively less national debt as a percentage of GDP than the UK. But what Italy *did* have was a very large public debt and Spain, like Ireland, was an economy overinflated by the by-now familiar recipe of a private credit and housing market bubble. The additional vulnerability that Spain and Italy shared was that both had distinctly fragile labor markets too, which in Spain resulted in high levels of youth unemployment and widespread overuse of part-time contracts and which, in Italy, was because women tended to be left out of the labor force, in contrast to most other modern liberal democracies.[37] These were national propensities exacerbated by the way domestic economies intersected with global financial markets, of course. Spanish economic growth, unlike the labor market, was strong because it was driven by foreign investment not domestic production. But this was also why Spain had a housing bubble.

As the first phase of the financial crisis unfolded in Europe over the year to come, it was just such points of intersection between domestic economies and global markets that quickly turned what had recently seemed like opportunities into vulnerabilities. As with the ERM crisis at the start of the 1990s, the sheer variation in the problems confronting the Continent's national economies made the prospects for a coordinated response rather dim. Even though the crisis struck Europe a little later than the United States, it was this that ensured it was in Europe that confidence evaporated most quickly and most devastatingly of all.

If confidence remained a little higher in America that was largely because it was there that the first *concerted* response to the crisis began to be pieced together in the autumn of 2008. What US policymakers achieved must go down as a far greater success than is generally allowed even today: for what turned into the great recession could very easily have been an even *more* destructive crisis than that which followed the crash of 1929. The initial challenge that US economic policymakers confronted was the fact that large-scale assistance to banks that were no longer solvent could only be provided by the Treasury, with money allocated by Congress. Since President Bush and Treasury Secretary Hank Paulson hoped to get American banks back on their feet without nationalizing them, that meant that US citizens (or at least their congressional representatives) needed to sign off on the astronomical costs of bailing out those banks. Until they came up with a plan for how to do that, the banks had been drip-fed just enough taxpayer money to keep them going.[38]

Such hesitancy was understandable. At the time, in the summer and early autumn of 2008, it was scarcely imaginable quite how unorthodox monetary policy was going to become in future years—let alone that the US would have to more or less reinvent itself as a provider of unthinkably vast quantities of global liquidity to all comers, be they American banking and financial concerns or not. And there was almost no time to think strategically. The global financial system had been profoundly transformed; the era of market fine-tuning, of the great moderation, had been upended in just a few weeks. In the US in particular, the old-style interventionary state was back, for all that this remained entirely out of keeping with the dominant rhetoric on both sides of the political spectrum. Notwithstanding this continued belief that markets know best, the US government was mobilizing the economy on such a scale as would have made a newly crowned socialist revolution look conservative by comparison. Investment houses, like Morgan Stanley and Goldman Sachs, were reanointed as "banks" so that they could receive federal support; some banks like Citigroup sold large stakes to the Treasury. Insurers, mortgage lenders, and mutual funds were taken into government "conservatorship."[39]

Increasingly it became clear that something more even than all these massive but ad hoc responses was needed. And it must have come as some relief for Ben Bernanke and the Federal Reserve, who led the first phase of the response, when, in late summer 2008, the Treasury under Hank Paulson moved to take ownership of a more full-throated approach. The Treasury had been relatively quiet thus far, in part because, compared to the Fed, it had little money of its own to spend. Its key resource was the public money it could acquire if Congress so approved. And Paulson had wisely called for working papers on just this scenario after Bear Stearns's collapse earlier in the year. He might soon have regretted it, however. For it had given him a sense of just what vast sums of money would be required to shore up the financial system: a figure in excess of half a trillion dollars, and that was before the Lehman wrecking ball had swung. It was not going to be an easy sell.

Winning Congress over to what was ultimately to become the Troubled Assets Relief Program (TARP) was made no easier by Paulson's somewhat flippant publishing of an initial plan online on Saturday, September 20, the weekend after Lehman fell. Paulson's plan was published as a mere three-page memo, in which he asked for full discretion, with no judicial oversight, in the use of an unprecedented $700 billion of public funds. This was incredible. Congress refused outright and Paulson was sent back to the drawing board. He returned by the end of the following week with a more palatable plan that would allow the government to share in any eventual profits. Congress initially rejected that plan too. Republicans thought it gave away the farm; Democrats thought it let bankers off scot-free. The stalemate looked set to continue.

But when the stock market fell a hair-raising 9 percent the following day, wiping out more than $1.25 trillion in one swoop, the House was given the opportunity to rethink how far it wished to keep grinding its usual axes while the republic of money burned all around. At this point, the billionaire Warren Buffett showed what more decisive action looked like as he invested $5 billion of his own money in troubled Goldman Sachs, telling Congress in no uncertain terms in the process that "failure to agree on the bailout could result in an 'economic Pearl Harbor.'" Suitably cowed by events, Congress readily approved Paulson's marginally reamended plan on the Friday. It was by now the biggest intervention in the financial system since the Depression—and Bush promptly signed it into law as the Emergency Economic Stabilization Act (EESA) on October 3.[40]

This was, of course, not the end of things but the beginning. As it had been presented so far, these publicly raised TARP funds were to be used to buy up all *troubled* assets, which included refinancing the mortgages of those who faced foreclosure. After giving the matter some more thought Paulson now changed strategies and aimed at injecting capital into the financial system more broadly. He shifted focus, in other words, onto restoring market confidence, rather than economic assistance directed purely at those banks that were going under, though this was not at all what Congress had just voted for. If some were troubled by this excess of government largesse toward the market, others regarded it, none too kindly, as a back-door form of nationalization.

In fact private owners were not forced to suffer losses (as in Scandinavia in the 1990s) as a condition for infusion of public funds. Neither were the remaining stock owners required to provide new capital alongside the support received from the government. Indeed, the government agreed *not* to hold any voting rights in exchange for its share options in companies, and the potential 5 percent return that Paulson's modified program offered to the taxpayer as one of its key selling points was put into perspective by the fact that George Soros had, in a similar type of deal concluded just days before, asked for 10 percent.[41] This was remarkable, and said everything about who was going to be expected to pay for the financial crisis. But it was at least decisive, in stark contrast to Europe, and for being so it was welcome enough.

Against the odds, TARP, which was soon just the headline act of an entire "alphabet soup" of creative facilities—everything from the Federal Deposit Insurance Corporation's (FDIC's) Temporary Loan Guarantee Program to the Fed's innovation of "stress testing" the banks—proved to be a success in stemming the fires of the financial crisis. Yet it is hardly surprising that it also proved highly unpopular, both with Congress and more importantly with the public. It was this that would ensure the fallout of the crisis became so intensely political. It ensured that when President Obama took office (in what must have seemed one of the longest transition periods imaginable) he had no alternative other than to pick up the pieces of a rescue plan that was not of his making and which was already fatally conceived in the public's mind as little more than a golden parachute for those bankers who had caused the problems in the first place (though there were conditions in place to prevent such parachutes and though the problem was actually wider than this).

This distinctly negative and partial view of the federal government's response to the crisis (the "bailing out" of the banks, as it had gone down in popular parlance) would remain lodged in the public's mind in the years to come. It was taken as an arch instance of modern government's technocratic disrespect for the will, much less the feelings, of the people. This was to have serious implications for American politics. A moderately progressive Democratic administration and a mainstream conservative Republican administration were both now tainted with the same brush. Both had been forced to sign off on the same U-turn in neoliberal policymaking and neither side would thereafter be able to live down a growing popular suspicion of arch hypocrisy. Obama, for all his eloquence, was not able to shift this perspective. He was however able to own the second part of the response, which centered upon the need for an economic stimulus to get the economy up and running again. It was his planning for this that defined the central narrative of the transition period from Bush to Obama.

Global Problems, National Solutions

Barack Obama was not just the first black president to have held the office. He was also the youngest and least-experienced president to have taken office in decades. And yet he had arrived in Washington to the most daunting in-tray since FDR. Whatever Obama had promised on the campaign trail was, for the time being, irrelevant to the problems he now confronted. He had been elected on a platform that committed him to an ambitious list of generational reforms, from health care to immigration reform. But it was the economy, now in free fall, that would dominate his administration's agenda. Hundreds of thousands of jobs were being lost each month, people were losing their homes, and US industry was caving in on itself. On coming into office, Obama immediately signed his first executive order, rescinding the detention of prisoners at Guantánamo Bay. It was perhaps a sign that he knew the economy would dominate his program and that he had better, therefore, make this one single gesture that *did* carry over from his election promises while he still could. (It was also indicative of the political strife to come that Guantánamo would still be open some eight years later when Obama left office.)

Obama's response to the financial crisis had two main planks: first to get the economy going again and second to address the underlying problems of insufficient regulation of the financial industry. With respect to the *first* task his approach was to continue the basic response laid out under Bush and to secure congressional support (which he would do at the end of his first month in office, albeit, in a sign of times to come, without a single Republican vote) for the next stage of that program: a $787 billion fiscal stimulus. Finding some way to kick-start the rather lifeless economy again was certainly needed. And with its tax cuts (of a more progressive variety than Bush had gone in for), new spending on welfare and infrastructure, and local government assistance, the American Recovery and Reinvestment Act (ARRA) was an impressive achievement in this regard. It was followed by a further round of eye-wateringly large monetary injections into the system that would become known as quantitative easing (QE). Delivered in a series of "rounds" between 2008 and 2012, QE involved the Federal Reserve purchasing large quantities of Treasury bills and other longer-term assets in an effort to force change in the rates at which banks lent: the ultimate goal being to try to encourage banks—short of nationalizing them and forcing them to do so—to start lending again.

QE, like TARP before it, was a complex and technical affair and for all that it was absolutely critical to the way the financial system—and thereby the entire economy—was put back on its feet, it garnered relatively little public "buy in" as a policy: there were no great dam-building projects of the kind FDR had been able to point to; no killer photo opportunities: just a silent avoidance of the sheer destruction that was very nearly unleashed. The one issue that did attract close public scrutiny, by contrast, was the *second* plank to Obama's response: the thornier matter of how to regulate the financial industry going forward. This too was something to which the Obama administration had begun turning its attention during the transition phase, and as it did so it looked to the past for inspiration. "Ah, finally an adult," clapped *Newsweek* on hearing of the announcement that Obama had called up the now white-haired Paul Volcker to head a new recovery advisory board.

At eighty-one years of age, and on this his third financial crisis, Volcker had grown more impatient than his younger self with what he called "a certain circularity in all this business." This made him, at the point of his latest resurrection, all for no-nonsense regulation of the banks.[42] But in what was to become a characteristic trait of his presidency, Obama had also appointed to his team two very differently minded individuals: the mercurial Larry Summers (as director of the National Economic Council) and the often foul-mouthed Timothy Geithner (who in his former role as governor of the New York Federal Reserve, had helped oversee much of the TARP program) as Treasury secretary. It would take Volcker a year to win his battles with them. Geithner and Summers were both reluctant to entertain the full-scale overhaul of financial regulation Volcker believed was necessary. "They considered me too old," as he recalled. The real problem was that they believed too strongly that markets ought not to be regulated and Obama was too new, and too dependent upon Wall Street politically, to do more than want to split the difference between them.[43]

The compromise that they eventually reached became the Dodd–Frank Wall Street Reform and Consumer Protection Act (2010), which amended the original bailout plan by reducing the total amount of TARP monies to $475 billion. It also incorporated the so-called "Volcker rule" on separating main street from investment functions (a partial return to the common-sense position established nearly eighty years earlier and only recently repealed under President Clinton). But the Act ran to just short of 2,300 pages. And with 225 new rules engaging eleven federal agencies, it was far from being loophole proof; in fact it was an invitation to further exploitation by the financial lobbyists. Nor was it likely to reduce the uncertainty that was a part of the underlying problem. As for Volcker, having got his rule, albeit somewhat watered down, he now lost the ear of the president on most other matters thereafter. It turned out that there simply wasn't the willingness within the administration—or more specifically, there wasn't the willingness to take such a fight to Congress—for attempting any of the more far-reaching reform proposals that were put forward. There were no Pecora-style hearings as had been held in 1933 in the aftermath of the financial crash of 1929. The political environment in America in the late 2000s was simply not up to such far-reaching self-examination.

This was an ill portent for the rest of the Obama administration's plans for governing—something the epic struggle over health care was already demonstrating. But these were problems whose shape and size had not yet become apparent. The focus for now was still on the economy. And while the public had lost almost all faith in the federal and central banking nexus—which had, truth be told, snatched the US economy from out of the jaws of a second Great Depression and limited the impact of the financial crisis to being that of a great, drawn-out recession—it was at least mollified by the fact that the US economy now gradually began to show some signs of life again.

A few green shoots did little to help those 5 million US workers who had been made unemployed since 2008, however, and who had received relatively little by way of government assistance since. In late 2007 monthly job losses were running at 46,000 per month; a year later in 2008 they had ballooned to 651,000 per month.[44] Unemployment on that scale required active government intervention. But it did at least restore a certain optimism in the major institutional drivers of economic growth. And there were some other green shoots that could be divined, for those willing to look. For the true impact of the Obama administration's continuation of the response was ultimately less that it had saved US capitalism (the Treasury and Federal Reserve had done that before Obama took office) and more that it had broken the unwritten rule that governments no longer had a meaningful role to play in economic affairs. This was, on both fronts it must be said, in rather stark contrast to Europe.

The US response to the financial crisis was riddled with inconsistencies, profinancial bias and pork-barrel politics (something the Tea Party would soon have a field day with). Yet the European response, by comparison, managed to make all this seem like the very paradigm of decisiveness and efficiency. Taken as a whole Europe had an even larger banking sector than the US: and, fatefully, banks were held in greater esteem in European governmental circles than they were across the Atlantic. But as the crisis broke, and it became apparent that this was as much a European problem as it was a problem headquartered in the US, European leaders were unconscionably slow to put together a coordinated response. It was not until the massive stock market falls of early October 2008, and after they had witnessed the better coordinated US response (in contrast to their own "squabbling"), that Nicolas Sarkozy, who then held the EC presidency, was first prompted to call an emergency meeting of EU heads of state. When they did meet, over the weekend in the Élysée Palace in Paris, Britain's prime minister, Gordon Brown, hailed the resulting commitment to a coordinated response "an important day for Europe." This was perhaps unsurprising, since the bank recapitalization program he had just implemented in the UK provided the basis for the type of response they had been discussing. But it would all come to nothing just the same.[45]

In what was to become a leitmotif of the European front of the crisis, the reason for this was because the markets turned out to be less than impressed with what Europe's leaders had come up with. After all, despite a general level of agreement on the sort of response required, there was no concrete effort to coordinate actual policies at the European level, despite it being obvious that the crisis was not nationally bound. Europe's leaders simply went home and sought to implement their "vow to respond" as best they could on their own home turf. When the markets reopened on the Monday after the weekend meeting, stock indexes from Paris to Frankfurt plunged steeply in disappointment. In Iceland, share trading had to be stopped altogether. "If the $700 billion mortgage bailout plan in the US was supposed to calm global investors," Bloomberg News observed, "someone forgot to tell Europe."[46]

Inevitably the financial crisis raised more complex problems for European politicians than their counterparts in America, Canada, or Australasia (the latter of which would escape relatively unscathed). Even as they sat around the table in Paris, individual leaders were signing off on policy responses over the phone to their respective treasury departments at home. And those responses differed substantially. Gordon Brown had already taken the UK one way, for example, but Ireland took a very different route by promising—fatefully it would turn out—a blanket guarantee to all Irish banking concerns (incurring the wrath of Downing Street in the process). Iceland went to the opposite extreme by refusing to bail out foreign bank investors and foreign depositors at all (this time incurring the wrath of a great many of the British middle class who had put their money in online banks based in Iceland). The Swiss put every chip on their own major bank: UBS.

By far the most significant national response was Germany's. Like Brown, Angela Merkel had already laid out her own package of domestic policy responses before Sarkozy's weekend meeting. Hearing that this had not seemed to calm popular fears she then went further and told German savers that their deposits were safe: "the government gives its assurance," she said—only too aware of the specter of bank runs in the 1920s.[47] Gordon Brown was furious. But there were other, more pragmatic, reasons for Germany's unwillingness to go along with a more coordinated European response at the outset. For one, Germany was to Europe a little as China was to the US. Its barrowloads of savings were invested right across the continent: in the Irish housing market, in Greek ports, in British banking conglomerates. A decade and a half after reunification and Germany was both deeply integrated with the rest of Europe's national economies and highly leveraged upon them—the ambition of Mitterrand and Kohl having prevailed in a way that neither of them ever foresaw.

Further complicating a properly European-wide response was the fact that the sort of deep searching of pockets just undertaken in the US ran up against the treasured golden rule of the eurozone: the Stability and Growth Pact (SGP). This was shortsighted for it was stimulus not fiscal discipline that was needed. Remarkably, even though the usually disciplinarian Germans were, at this point, among those insisting that the "exceptional circumstances" clause be invoked—which made provision for the SGP's iron-clad 3 percent band to be loosened in extreme situations—the European Council resolutely refused to allow member states to deviate from the commitments they had made since Maastricht. "Budget policies must continue to be in line with the revised Stability and Growth Pact," it proclaimed sternly.[48] When Christine Lagarde, the French finance minister, sought to offer preventive liquidity financing to French banks, Neelie Kroes, the EU competition minister, blocked the move. "We have to apply the same criteria to everyone . . . support should be sufficient to offset the negative impact of the current financial crisis and no more," declared one of her officials.[49] The French government, as it happened, was trying to do just that: to support all six of its main street banks at the same time (so as to ensure they were not tempted to tighten credit to individual borrowers themselves).

Of course, Kroes would say that she was only concerned with maintaining European "discipline." But the EU was deceiving itself if it thought that a crisis on this scale might autocorrect according to previously laid down "good governance" criteria and without the need for creative and responsible interventions by individual states. The crisis ought to have been the proving ground for the EC to show why it was worth having all that expensive bureaucracy sitting in Brussels and Luxembourg. And yet it would not be until late November 2008, a full month after TARP was approved in the US, that the European Commission under José Manuel Barroso put forward anything even resembling a coordinated response, announced as the European Economic Recovery Plan (EERP). The nomenclature was a hopeful nod to the European Recovery Program (ERP)—or Marshall Plan—of 1947 and it proposed a €200-billion fiscal stimulus program of tax cuts and spending increases financed by member countries.

It was insufficient. Also, Barroso avoided assuming common responsibility for recapitalizing the banks. Instead the primary message coming out of Brussels and Frankfurt in the immediate wake of the crisis was a misconceived insistence that contracts would be honored, that banks would not be allowed to fail, and that governments would now be expected to bear any cross required of them in pursuit of this end. The reality was that banks were not restored in many cases, but simply kept on very expensive long-term life support, all of which drained much needed capital away from the rest of the nation's economic life. The basic arc of the crisis in Europe unfolded in the wake of this particularly damaging instance of what the *Financial Times* journalist Martin Sandbu characterized as "magical thinking."[50]

Such magical thinking was not only politically unpalatable, it would also prove fateful. For if European leaders' first mistake was to fail to move quickly enough, as the US had done, they now compounded that with a second mistake: which was to continue trying to get banks to lend and businesses to hire when it was obvious they couldn't. The result was banks that barely functioned and Europe missed its chance to address the structural causes of the problem when it could. For as realization first fully began to dawn in 2009 of just how bad things were, and confidence evaporated even more, Europe's financial policymakers found themselves trapped. Unwilling to change tack to fit the new and even more unpromising conditions, they doubled down. The stimulus approach having been halfheartedly tried, and failed, instead the focus now became about trying to stop spending money.

Europe's leaders instead began to channel their commitment to resolving the crisis in a new and very particular direction: fiscal restraint. The narrative for this seeped initially out of Germany in 2009, which was worried about growing deficits being taken on by governments as they bailed out the financial system. Merkel had faced even greater problems than Obama in the US or Brown in the UK in getting a stimulus passed. In the end, her CDU-SPD grand coalition brokered a deal that accepted some stimulus measures in exchange for locking in a constitutional commitment to balancing regional budgets in Germany. The background to this was, of course, the unspoken tensions in the Federal Republic since reunification: above all the resentment that had built up in western Länder— all that talk of the *jammerossi*—which now came back in a destructive countermove. No more borrowing was the mantra. The specter of the Hartz reforms reappeared at the national level: the German nation and not just its low-wage workers would need to show discipline.[51] Given the Bundesbank's importance to the entire approach being adopted by the eurozone, Germany's domestic politics soon locked in at the European level too. As it did so the makings of a new narrative for addressing the financial crisis had been established: the basic problem was no longer seen to be one of failed banks but of excess public debt. The politics of the sovereign debt crisis were falling into place.

To the extent that this approach caught on at the European level it was not just because it resonated with the institutional culture at the ECB and elsewhere, but also because it seemed to offer a degree of clarity amidst the confusion as to what exactly was happening and why. When Peer Steinbrück, the German finance minister, spoke off the cuff of "liquidation" of the banks, with reference to a mooted bailout, for example, his comments provoked howls of disgust from the right.[52] Yet in Britain there was no less sniping about "socialism for bankers" (public money being expropriated to defend private property rights), this time from the left. The banking sector was hardly any more taken by the political implications of the bailouts, seeing them as "a throwback to the 1970s and 1980s." A British trader feared the industry would now become "more conservative" and "less global" as a result.[53] In the gentle words of a bewildered senior LSE professor, the world had indeed become a rather "topsy-turvy" place.[54]

And yet the underlying problem was clear enough. The response in Europe simply proved too fragmented to tackle this head on. Rather than letting the worst of the banks fail, picking up the pieces, and moving on with more sensible rules pertaining to the nexus between finance and the state, Europe's leaders instead clung foolishly to their initial and flawed approach. By passing the costs of this miscalculation on to the taxpayer they then further undermined their own democratic legitimacy in the process. In hindsight Obama's failing in the US, such as it was, lay in not being able to explain to the electorate why the US was putting so much money up to backstop not just American banks but the wider financial system itself, including foreign banks; the far less excusable failing in Europe was the refusal to make publicly clear that there *were* alternatives to the contractionary hard-edged debt-reduction approach that prioritized national banks over the international system and would end up costing the electorate only that much more.

The difference in those two approaches was ultimately why the story of the financial crisis after 2009 became a tale of two recessions: the US recovery, with the Fed now actively backstopping the international banking system via massive liquidity injections, and Europe's temporary halt in the crisis, followed by the continent's plunge beneath the cold waters of recession once again after the "double dip" recession of 2011. Compounding the irony was the moral debt that Europeans now, in fact, owed to the US. After all it was the US that was largely keeping the European economy afloat in the meantime, by virtue of the money it was pumping into the system through the so-called swap lines, by which means the

Federal Reserve loaned money to Europe's central banks so that they in turn could lend it on to their own private banks. In light of this it was not just ironic that Europe's leaders continued largely to blame the whole thing on the Americans: the US, Peer Steinbrück gleefully declared, "will lose its status as the superpower of the world financial system."[55] It was a sign of the extent to which the transatlantic alliance was fracturing anew amidst the economic upheavals. What was more, the financial crisis was not by any means the only international challenge to come out of 2008.

Hegemonic Overtures

On August 10, as Western leaders looked with growing alarm to what was happening in the markets, the president of Georgia, Mikheil Saakashvili, ordered his forces to secure the ground in the two breakaway Georgian republics of Abkhazia and South Ossetia. Ever since the Rose Revolution in 2003 Georgia had been considered "an outpost of Euro-Atlanticism" by the West and was even being considered for NATO membership. The US having initially ceded the task of containing Moscow's post–Cold War ambitions in the South Caucasus to Turkey, it had since been forced to step up the pressure after Moscow and Ankara developed rather more cooperative terms in the 2000s. Georgia was to be a testing ground for this new alignment of forces. An uneasy truce had held in the two separatist republics since the early 1990s. And it was in all likelihood Moscow itself that provoked the recent disturbances, the better to lure Saakashvili into a conflict he was unlikely to win, thereby enabling Moscow to push back at NATO's encirclement.

Moscow was indeed quick to launch a well-prepared counterattack in response. Within days Russian forces were approaching Tbilisi, the capital of Georgia. At this point, Sarkozy too entered the field. Taking advantage of the fact that France then also held the six-month EU Commission presidency (one of the peculiarities of the EU is its biannual rotating presidency), and keen to win for himself a little international glory, he offered to broker a "peace deal" between Russia and Georgia in order to stop the bloodshed (there had already been over eight hundred fatalities). The EU peace treaty would later come back to haunt the Western powers. It granted significantly greater advantage to the Russian position, for all that the brief war had been a strike against NATO as much as against Georgia. It showed Putin (then functioning as Medvedev's prime minister—if Medvedev was not actually serving as Putin's president) that he could push the Western alliance quite far if need be (Russian forces did not withdraw from the oil-exporting port town of Poti). It also afforded Moscow an early opportunity to experiment with the practice of cyberwar that Russia would later hone to perfection.[56]

"The Georgian crisis," observed *The Economist*, "has exposed a tectonic shift in the balance of power. It is not just that Russia is back. The crisis has also confirmed Europe's sense of an America in decline."[57] To the extent that this was true it was an observation that would be put on hold, somewhat fatefully, for a few more years to come. The true legacy of the Georgian affair would thus not be revealed until six years on, in 2014, across the wintry flatlands of the Crimea. For now, it provided a useful canvas against which Sarkozy could define and sharpen his international image. And emboldened by what he had achieved in Georgia, on September 23, in an address to the United Nations General Assembly, he felt confident enough to extrapolate the lessons of this newfound taste for grand diplomacy to the fast-developing situation of the financial crisis. "Let us rebuild together a regulated capitalism," he declared boldly, "in which whole swathes of financial activity are not left to the sole judgment of market operators."[58]

Sarkozy, it would appear, was relishing the prospect of the "Statesman of the Year" award he was to receive later that same evening in New York, and which would be presented by none other than Henry Kissinger. At the event Kissinger offered a glowing appraisal of Sarkozy's "courage and timing." And after leaving the award ceremony Sarkozy did not disappoint. Just two weeks later, speaking this time in the Smithsonian building in Washington, he had Christine Lagarde, his finance minister, openly challenge the Americans again. Sarkozy, like many others, blamed the emerging financial crisis on the US almost exclusively. It was sufficient reason now to reject not only the US dollar as the dominant global currency but the political hegemony that America derived from that fact. Just how big was Sarkozy thinking? A "rebalancing" from American-led capitalism was in order, Lagarde replied. "I am leaving tomorrow for Washington," Sarkozy declared before the French public just before the G20 meeting in Washington, "to explain that the dollar . . . can no longer claim to be the only currency in the world. What was true in 1945 cannot be true today."[59]

Of course, "Sarko," as he was known in France, would soon move on to other concerns, as the crisis wound its way into Europe. And while he might not go so far as to seek to actively rebuild bridges with the Americans, he did at least return France to NATO's integrated command, from which it had long been absent. For her part Lagarde would move outside of national politics by taking the top job at the IMF, about to be made available after Dominique Strauss-Kahn's fall from grace in a New York hotel room. But in that moment in the autumn of 2008, when the opportunity appeared to present itself, the French attempt to wrest global financial leadership from the hands of the US, while unrealistic, was taken seriously. "Suddenly we were like Pariahs," recalled a Washington official of the moment. "We were not in the condition to even put forward a suggestion. People were yelling at us and we ourselves knew we bore the responsibility."[60]

It was inevitable that Sarkozy would be the first to grab the opportunity. He may have lacked strategic longevity, but Sarkozy was second to none in the energy with which he pursued any one project of the moment (including the actress and singer Carla Bruni; amidst the international turmoil he became engaged to her in 2008 after a two-month courtship).[61] But his great gamble largely fizzled out, because the idea that European leaders might speak in some singular European voice at this moment was a near impossibility. Instead it would take a young and at this moment freshly departed inspector of finances, Emmanuel Macron, to bring "Greater France" narratives more successfully to international attention (and he, in characteristically willful fashion, had just left his role in government at this point to join up with investment bank Rothschild & Cie: a career move against the flow of the times if ever there was one).

Where Sarkozy failed, another group of leaders did succeed in taking a step forward in the matter of global financial leadership, and that was the members of the recently convened G20. The G20 had been born—through the initiative of, among others, Canadian Prime Minister Paul Martin—very much as one of those technocratic conventions that Anne-Marie Slaughter had envisioned in the 1990s, and from out of the same moment too. Now it was to be repurposed. Recognizing that the crisis was truly global in scope, President Bush finally acquiesced in the idea that the G20 nations might also use the G20 as a head-of-state forum, in just the manner that the G7/8 had long operated.[62] Under pressure from Gordon Brown he agreed to convene such a meeting in November, in Washington, DC, and under the auspices of the IMF (Bush was concerned that the meeting remain focused on the crisis). The invitation to grandstanding was substantial for the newly promoted nations, which included the likes of India and Brazil. Not surprisingly, that first G20 meeting in Washington, on November 15, 2008, did not achieve very much.

Yet it was revealing all the same. The fact that Bush had finally acquiesced in holding such a meeting was a tacit acknowledgment that the world was shifting—and this at such a critical time—toward a more multipolar model of international order. This was sensible: the financial crisis affected them as much as anyone else, and they had financial reserves that would be useful in putting out the fires. The G20 nations accounted for no less than 85 percent of global GDP. Orchestrating the process was also a hegemon's first line of defense. At Pittsburgh the following year, the G20 would be designated the "premier forum for our international economic cooperation," as a communiqué put it. But if this was a decision that spread the locus of global power noticeably more widely, it also—just as crucially—retained a role for America at its heart: since for all that the economic standing of the American state had fallen, the primacy of the dollar remained.[63]

Critically, for the US, the financial crisis had *not* fundamentally upset the Bretton Woods II international monetary system, as it was sometimes referred to, which had de facto replaced the earlier Bretton Woods system that Nixon brought down in 1971. This referred to the arrangement by which the US was able to run a massive current account deficit on the basis of large capital inflows from emerging markets, and China most of all. This arrangement had wobbled in 2008. Russia's response to the crisis was to pull out a lot of its money from certain US debt classes. China initially did the same but quite soon it reversed tack. China held over $922 billion in US Treasuries in 2007. Selling those would have been catastrophic. But where else was it going to put all the money? China didn't have a good enough answer: the two economic superpowers thus remained tied together at the waist for now.[64]

The US was not quite out of dangerous waters yet. Rumors surfaced again the following year that the Gulf States were conspiring with Russia, China, Japan, and America's new monetary adversary, Nicolas Sarkozy's France.[65] The head of China's central bank, Zhou Xiaochuan, proposed moving to a more "neutral" global monetary unit, perhaps using something like the IMF's Special Drawing Rights (SDRs) instead. But these moves came to nothing: partly because of the diplomatic barriers to securing sufficient agreement, but mainly due to the fact that the dollar was still the currency in which liquidity was measured in the global financial system. And liquidity was what every central banker wanted to ensure his or her national enterprises had access to.[66]

Opening up responsibility for managing the global economy to the G20 was, in that sense, a perfectly executed fallback for the US as it sought to retain its global hegemony amidst the upheaval all around. It would prove its practical value too at the next G20 meeting. The decision to convene again in London had been taken at Prime Minister Gordon Brown's insistence. Brown was desperate to channel the spirit of Keynes and to revive his own flagging political fortunes. He would ultimately succeed in neither. But thanks to his persistence and grasp of the fundamentals, the London meeting *did* deliver rather more by way of concrete results. The headline agreement centered upon a new trillion-dollar financing arrangement for the IMF. This had been negotiated at the cost of further reassignment of voting rights away from Europe and America toward the emerging market economies. And China found it had a new and convenient platform for gently asserting its considerable weight.[67] But it helped to stabilize the economy internationally.

To be sure there would be plenty of bumps in the road ahead. The Chinese soon began to worry about America's turn to quantitative easing and what that meant for their own domestic economy; the Americans would moan about China's refusal to allow the value of the yuan to rise. But the Treasury no longer feared that the Chinese might seek swiftly to turn the screw on the US by virtue of the leverage their vast dollar holdings gave them (the Chinese *were* concerned to limit their exposure to the US economy, but in a more graduated manner). And this restoration of a certain consensus around the current international monetary system proved critical for the recovery of American capitalism after the crisis. It meant that America's financial policymakers at the Fed, the Treasury, and in the White House itself could sleep just a little more easily. America had largely weathered the storm. Europe, by contrast, was about to find its political ambitions plunged into the darkness of austerity and government default, and Sarkozy's short-lived initiative uncovered for what it was: a flicker of political brilliantine surfacing unnoticed amid the flood.

The Crisis Spreads

"Like soldiers falling into step," so the *Los Angeles Times* reported in late 2008, European leaders were themselves gearing up for action.[68] And yet, as we have seen, from the perspective of the following year that would prove to have been a fleeting reality. No sooner had Sarkozy's initiative failed than the European stage was reduced to jockeying for the bragging rights as to who had done most to influence the Americans. Silvio Berlusconi boasted that he was the one who had convinced Bush of the need for a bailout in the first place, while Britain's Gordon Brown, in a Freudian slip during Prime Minister's Questions, referred to having saved the world (he meant, of course, the banks). His opposite number, David Cameron, visibly delighted in responding. "Well, it's now on the record," Cameron lashed, his finger jabbing the dispatch box. "He's so busy talking about saving the world he's forgotten about the businesses of the country he should be running!"[69]

That was one thing that Germany's Angela Merkel could not be accused of. If there was one European leader who had the means to influence developments at the European level it was her. The more her counterparts bickered, the more stable Germany appeared; the more the euro tumbled, the stronger the hand of the Bundesbank, the power of whose loans stood behind it; the more that political instability racked other nations of the eurozone, the more that credit flowed into German banks, where it could be lent out again cheaply to German businesses, cushioning the country against the chokehold on growth affecting almost everywhere else.

The euro crisis thus gifted Germany, somewhat improbably, the means to consolidate its post–Cold War position in the heart of Europe as a regional monetary, rather than a military, hegemon. This could have gone two ways: by 2010 plans were afoot in Schäuble's foreign ministry for a European monetary fund that might have helped to quench some of the fires; but Merkel was not of the same West German pro-European mold as Schäuble and rather than grant Brussels any more power she opted to bring in the IMF instead.[70] What ended up being exported, in place of a relatively constructive German model for trans-European emergency financing, was a bitter struggle over the German commitment to fiscal discipline. In the process the politics of the eurozone became, for the next few years, a game of high stakes combat, with some countries threatening to leave and Germany daring them to try. Until one country finally did.

Already by late 2009 government debt had increased dramatically in almost all countries across the wider EU. This was partly as a result of the costs of the bailouts themselves, but it was equally a function of shrinking government revenue: with economies in full-blown recession there was less money to collect in taxes and more outgoings to deal with. It was also a consequence of there being no committed European-wide stimulus of the sort the US economy was receiving. The ECB could, at this point, have avoided the gradual tightening of the sovereign-debt noose around Europe's more peripheral economies by buying up a tranche of the bonds issued by those governments. In this way it could have acted as a form of lender of last resort, just as the Federal Reserve had taken to doing in the United States. That would have changed the market "meaning" of the debt it was so concerned about. But instead it merely fixated on getting governments themselves to commit to paying it all off. Already in 2008 Romania had wobbled and Iceland and Hungary both needed emergency loans from the IMF to shore up their leaky public finances, primarily because they simply couldn't do so themselves. But the full scale of the problem only really became apparent the following year, when the newly elected socialist government, PASOK, came to power in Greece.

On first discovering the somewhat parlous state of the Greek economic position, PASOK had taken the dramatic step of publicly declaring to the world that the previous New Democracy (conservative) government had deliberately misreported its accounts. This was true: its public deficit having been reported as 2.8 percent in 2009, it was subsequently revealed to be nearer 13 percent of GDP. Misreporting was one thing, but Greece's problems were also structural to the extent that national currency devaluations were no longer possible within the eurozone, of which Greece was a member. Membership of the eurozone had been a strain on its fringe countries. With generally higher levels of inflation, Portugal, Italy, and Greece had to try to hold their heads above the water of exchange rates that were ultimately too high for them, making it harder for them to compete internationally. When rates did fall, as the euro locked in at the start of the decade, Greek policymakers in particular failed to use that chance to invest in productive parts of the economy. Instead they adopted the easier route—one European leaders acquiesced in—of allowing the low interest rates of the eurozone to fuel their own mini credit boom.

In a different time, PASOK's revelations may have been welcome, perhaps even useful as a gesture toward moving beyond this. But these were dangerous times to be making announcements on just how far into the red the Greek economy was. Along with the failure to correctly report its accounts, corruption, tax evasion, patrimonialism in government, and a lack of rules on government interventions in the economy all added to the problem in Greece. But what really kick-started the Greek crisis, and with it the second phase of the financial crisis in Europe—the European sovereign debt crisis—was the fact that the markets, the modern democratic state's fickle life-partner, now shrank away from the Greek government, increasing its borrowing costs, and this at the very moment when a large repayment on some of Greece's existing debt was due.

The critical date was May 19, 2010: the first in what would become a familiar series of looming payment deadlines and dramatic escalations of tempers and fears alike. Greece was due to pay off just over €8 billion of debt by that date, and yet it was easily €25 billion in the red. Normally this might not matter: governments routinely restructure their finances and roll over some of the various debts that they owe. But in the current context of market-wariness this was not an option for the Greek government. Panic began to set in and not just in Greece. On Friday, May 7 the ECB's Jean-Claude Trichet "thundered" to the politicians at the European Council that failure to act would bring about another Lehman collapse, and upon all of Europe's heads this time.[71] Trichet was a hardline central banker who valued the defense of the ECB's independence and its tight money "values" above all other considerations, and his leadership of the ECB through until 2011 would leave a heavy imprint on the events to follow. For if the Greeks were guilty of having brought themselves to the brink, it was the way that EU leaders, alarmed by Trichet's scaremongering, stepped in to "rescue" Greece that really tipped them over the edge.

Three mistakes in particular stood out. First, the fundamental nature of Greece's debt problem was misdiagnosed and the wrong solution to it was embarked upon (and never relinquished): namely, to make Greece repay its debts at any cost, even when it soon became clear it simply could not. Debt restructuring was not considered. Nor was a managed default, of the sort that had taken place before, most recently in Argentina—such defaults were painful but less so than what the Greek people were soon going through. Second, in their overwrought efforts to "contain" the crisis in Greece, and simultaneously to use Greece as a model for how to deal with the problem elsewhere (other peripheral economies be warned) eurozone leaders in Frankfurt, Brussels, and Berlin ended up stoking the very fears of contagion they sought to banish by their scriptural commitment to showing discipline and budgetary constraint. Third, the punitive conditions ultimately imposed in *each* of these countries (though especially in Greece) not only proved counterproductive but also brought into play a much wider crisis of trust in the collective integrity that the euro had been intended to secure. The response of the eurozone leaders was to foster the very divisions within Europe that the euro was intended to overcome. That in turn left the euro a currency increasingly without a cause.

★

The first of these errors became apparent soon after PASOK's bombshell on the state of Greek finances exploded, setting off a yet more dangerous firestorm in its wake. Immediately the cost of Greek government borrowing surged, followed by public sector strikes and what was to become a familiar spectacle in Europe of credit rating downgrades, rising interest rates on loans, and forced government cutbacks on pensions and wages. None of this was enough to restore market confidence. As Greece's condition deteriorated, with high debts and a high and rising deficit, it was clear that the country was now heading irretrievably into the red.

And yet the possibility that a eurozone country would be deemed insolvent was not something that Jean-Claude Trichet at the ECB was prepared to countenance. He was adamant that Greece would not be allowed to default.[72] Thus was the cardinal error that had first been made in the bank bailouts of 2008 repeated: the fundamental refusal to write down bad debt or to consider that private actors, such as banks, should be made to bear some of the costs (even though creditors had lent knowing full well the risks). Instead, in an act of hubristic denial, Greece was to be treated as if it was suffering just a few self-inflicted spending issues, and *those* would best be dealt with by lending the Greeks even more and teaching them how to act responsibly.

At this point the IMF's own staff warned against such an approach: they pointed out that Greece was insolvent, not illiquid, and that lending it more money was akin to throwing good money after bad. But the head of the IMF, Dominique Strauss-Kahn, was at this point harboring ambitions in the upcoming presidential elections in France, and was seemingly unwilling to risk the disfavor either of his fellow European elites or the French bankers, who along with German banks turned out to be among Greece's largest creditors. Strauss-Kahn simply overruled them.[73] Denied also the option of turning to the ECB in April, Greece therefore found itself instead having to seek a bailout, for €30 billion, from the other eurozone nations.

Yet this proved insufficient to quell the market unease that was preventing Greece from resuming normal sovereign accountancy, at which point all eyes turned to the newly formed, and soon infamous, "troika"— the European Commission, the ECB, and the IMF—and to Germany's Angela Merkel in particular. In the years to come the troika, especially in Greece, would come to epitomize the very essence of unelected rule by the technocrats. The *real* problem with the troika was the opposite: it had no clear center of authority. A stand-in for the coordinated response that Europe had not yet managed to put together, it was also a solution to Merkel's problem of how to involve the ECB without unduly exposing her own country to fiscal jeopardy by virtue of its sizeable commitments to it. It is worth remembering that domestically Merkel had limited room for maneuver here: Germany's experience of reunification left its banking and political leaders acutely wary of a continental-sized "transfer union" (of the sort that had seen West Germany end up more or less permanently transferring around 4 percent of its GDP to the East each year).

In seeking the political cover she needed to go against these instincts, and to ensure that the IMF was involved alongside the ECB in the shape of the troika—thereby putting her own preferred shape on the nature of the European response—Merkel committed the EU to the second of its errors. "This is our historic task," the chancellor declared before the Bundestag on May 19, 2010, as she sought approval for what would become a much larger bailout package of €110 billion for Greece, agreed after crunch talks in Berlin in the previous weeks. "If the euro fails, then Europe will fail."[74] The economic strategy henceforth would be to keep lending to countries in trouble but not to address the reasons why: to "extend and pretend" in the jargon of the time. The political strategy this in turn relied upon was that lines had to be drawn and defended, which was almost the opposite of what the now fast-moving situation required.

The fear oiling Merkel's argument was that of financial contagion: the specter of a sovereign Lehman was wreaking its own havoc across the continent by now. Irish and Portuguese spreads had reached as dire a state as Greece's, indicating market unease with respect to those countries and amping up the tensions still further.[75] Yet their situations were quite different (centering on a housing bubble in the case of Ireland). Moreover, Greece's financial exposures were nothing like those of an investment bank, and though it might conceivably default, such a collapse could not possibly hit the markets with the same force as the Lehman collapse had. But this scarcely mattered now that talk of such an eventuality was out. Merely raising the possibility as a political fact had created a new market risk to be factored in. And this was precisely the signal that investors, by now wary of nearly everything European states were telling them, responded to. Within days of the Greek showdown in May bond yields of other, presumed fragile governments began to spike as well.

The third mistake that Europe's leaders made was the nature of the loan conditions imposed on the "Greek bailout." They were brutal. Germany had insisted on punitively high repayment rates (again, let Greece be a lesson to others). The hypocrisy was astronomical. Not only had excessive lending to Greece been roundly applauded by Trichet and the ECB, just three years before, as a sign of the eurozone's great success (the fault in that sense lying with all parties to the arrangement and not just Greece).[76] It was also conveniently overlooked by eurozone leaders, and Germany in particular, that they *too* had concealed the fragility of their accounts at the start of the crisis.[77] The decision thus to try to punish Greece for its errors was all the more unjust considering that, in reality, the bailout funds did not end up in Greece at all, but were channeled through to Greece's creditors—including German banks—so that they might avoid any undue losses. Little of the loan money ever made it to Greece, therefore; but Greek taxpayers would be footing the bill for its repayment nonetheless.

Six months after the Greek crisis came the next staging post on the path of the sovereign debt crisis. Ireland was the opposite of Greece: a eurozone star performer, fiscally prudent and aboveboard in its financial accounting. This was the famous Irish Tiger economy. What Ireland shared with Greece going into 2008, however, was a current account deficit, which had grown over the previous decade as Irish banks borrowed heavily on surging international markets to raise the capital they were pumping into a highly profitable domestic housing boom. But what really did for Ireland was the open-ended bank bailout introduced by the Irish government after the crisis in 2008 which soon sent its deficit spiraling past that even of Greece. The Irish government was considering changing strategy, from bailing "out" banks like Anglo-Irish to bailing them "in," thereby also forcing losses on creditors and not just the public. But the ECB was having none of it. Dublin too was now required to apply for assistance from the EC's new financial stability fund (the EFSF), the sheer stigma of which ensured that Ireland's borrowing costs, like Greece's, now also went through the roof.[78]

The same then happened in Portugal, which shortly after Ireland was also bullied into taking eurozone rescue money by the ECB and adopting the same sort of package Greece and Ireland had just taken. By now Europe's peripheral nations were stigmatized by belonging to some newly imagined group: the financial crisis's axis-of-vulnerability, the PIIGS (Portugal, Ireland, Iceland, Greece, and Spain). Portugal was notable for the way that it also became a much-scrutinized test case regarding the wisdom of financial austerity, with the intention being to demonstrate the path of German-style rectitude as against the purported problems of governmental excess in vagabond countries like Greece. Portugal's willing executioner, Finance Minister Vítor Gaspar (he would become known as Portugal's "architect of austerity"), announced in October 2012 that the country faced a "critical moment" and for that reason he was proposing a cut of nearly 11 percent to government spending and huge wage cuts to meet it. As with many of the cast now assembling themselves as leading figures in this European drama, Gaspar was himself a former technocrat, a Brussels insider, but he was now promoted to be the Commission's "star pupil" in the southern rim. Portuguese unions were not so sure: they immediately called for a massive strike while the Constitutional Court sought to block some of his measures. Within six months the unemployment rate had hit 16.4 percent.[79]

Despite mounting evidence of the human cost in health, welfare, and social cohesion—and even despite the specter of an imminent double-dip recession that was looming large as 2010 came to a close—the European Commission and the ECB refused to deviate from the course they had now charted. Government borrowing was to be brought down to below the limit of 3 percent, the figure agreed upon back in the 1990s and that had proven hard for many countries to meet even during the best of times. Of course, it helped, in staying the course, that none of those pushing for it at the ECB or in the European Council were directly accountable to an electorate. But the perverse scenario then also arose that the more the eurozone austerity proved not to be working the more Brussels pushed for ever-greater means of enforcing its application. This did little to warm people to the long-nurtured institutions of the EU. It was as if a lifetime of hard-earned political capital in the European project was being used up in a few rogue lunges at windmills most Europeans could not see.

But still the machinery of response plowed on (in part because Europe's political leaders—Merkel in particular—were genuinely committed to saving the euro). It was as if the Cold War policy framework of "containment" was being applied to the European south. Indeed, for someone like Wolfgang Schäuble, Germany's hard-line finance minister, who had earned his stripes during the heightened tensions of the late Cold War years, that might have been precisely what was happening.[80] The troika's approach was in a certain sense a reprise of what West Germany did to East Germany a quarter of a century before, with the ECB and the IMF now the preferred tools of state reconstruction, in place of the Treuhand (the agency that had overseen privatization of former state assets in the

East back when Schäuble was West German interior minister, and the architect behind it). Ironically, if there are parallels here they illustrate that there were limits to how much austerity West Germany could impose on East Germany because they were part of the same country: Greece was not. This time Schäuble and the troika could play much harder ball.

And they did. In 2011, the EC awarded itself new powers to impose and "monitor" the performance of individual countries; it demanded that the terms of the old Stability and Growth Pact be incorporated into member states' national legislation so as to make them more binding, "preferably at a constitutional level," and it imposed new legislation to strengthen "enforcement" of its rules.[81] To many people it looked as if the EU had simply resolved to interpret the steadily escalating crisis all around it as an opportunity to lock down the post-Maastricht-era regime of liberal market "governance"—indeed, after meeting in Brussels on October 26, EU leaders proposed a ten-point plan to just that end.[82] What it more profoundly revealed was the extent to which eurozone leaders and their banks alike were by now themselves locked into a policy of more of the same: more "fiscal discipline" and more mutual surveillance. The EU thus began firing off a series of instructions to its member states to complete the "structural reforms" and "liberalizing of labor markets" not achieved in its earlier round of market liberalization a decade before: and to do so quickly, before the gathering storm set in.

Discipline and Punish

The storm duly announced itself in late 2010 and early 2011 in the economic growth forecasts that revealed Europe to be slipping back into the recession from which it had only just begun to emerge. This time, Europeans had only the policy errors of their own leaders to thank. The banks that had stoked up the financial crisis in the first place, by leveraging themselves to the hilt, had not been restructured or reformed. Much less had they been allowed to fail. Instead they had been pumped back to a semblance of life, with vast quantities of public money, to linger as expensive but largely nonfunctioning "zombie banks," as the phrase now had it.

On top of this, and unlike in America—where the Fed had not only engaged in a series of stimulus measures but had kept interest rates low to encourage lending and investment—the ECB had, at the very first flickers of life from the eurozone economy, eased off on its stimulus spending. It further elected to raise interest rates twice in early to mid 2011. This was a political gambit by the ECB. Trichet had resolved to try to force responsibility for getting state budgets in order more firmly back onto national states themselves. It backfired terribly. Instead, banks that were just starting to loosen up their balance sheets and to start lending again to cash-starved businesses immediately recorked the bottle. GDP growth forecasts were slashed from what had been a weak but improving 0.8 percent to just 0.3 percent for 2012.

From late 2011 onward, the eurozone was now set to endure a further two years of economic stagnation—even longer in some cases—and those worst hit by this second dip were the "beneficiaries" of the eurozone's rescue packages. Through their blinkered focus on debt consolidation the eurozone leaders had thus ultimately created a self-fulfilling prophecy since it was those countries with the biggest deficits that found it hardest, given the much tighter credit conditions brought about by the ECB, to dig themselves out of a hole. They were now not alone, however. Since their banks were among the most heavily invested in Greece, French and Austrian economies also began to show signs of faltering. Britain, under a new Conservative government from 2010, soon joined them. In fact, after adding to the ECB's myopia on fiscal contraction, with a curious fixation on austerity all of its own, Britain would have the worst performing economy of all.

By 2014 any comparisons that might have been made between the eurozone as a whole and the US did not paint a flattering picture of Europe's economy. Eurozone unemployment was by then at 12.1 percent; in the US it was 6.7 percent. The colossally uneven distribution of that unemployment was even more painful to contemplate. In Greece and Spain unemployment was 27.8 and 26.7 percent respectively; for Greek and Spanish youths, it was an unbearable (and frankly unsustainable) 59.2 percent and 57.4 percent. As the costs of the initial efforts to stanch the crisis began to mount, national economies slumped to miserable depths. In Greece health-care spending shrank by 40 percent; in Portugal, the number of unionized private sector workers reduced from 1.9 million to 300,000. As the crisis ravaged Cypriot banks, Russian backers entered onto the scene—sending fears down EU leaders' spines that their hard-won bailout money was going to the oligarchs—and causing capital controls to be introduced in Europe for the first time in the postwar era.[83]

Popular discontent over governments' apparent willingness to tolerate the unprecedented scale of public losses that the bailouts implied was apparent even before 2008 was out: not least when the individuals many held responsible for the problem turned out to be still receiving their Christmas bonus. "Finance is a war machine for privatization," declared the Italian-born writer Maurizio Lazzarato. As he and many others increasingly came to see it, the bailouts and the bonuses were mere bagatelles: governments were not so much worried about saving the banks but about saving the system itself. That was quite correct, and in the process the property rights of the owners of capital had trumped European citizens' social rights. That, of course, was nothing new: what *was* new was that the defense of those property rights had trumped even traditional sovereign prerogatives. The US had self-limited by virtue of its undue reticence when it came to the question of reform; European nations had simply self-abnegated, insisting that market stability come before social stability.[84] Perhaps it was little wonder, then, that as the crisis dragged on, it was the language of class struggle that was being discovered anew, sometimes in the most surprising of places. As the billionaire investor Warren Buffett put it: "There's class warfare, all right, but it's my class, the rich class, that's making war, and we're winning."[85]

But how were they winning? The answer was in part, of course, through the Janus-faced appeal of credit itself, which took real wealth from the poor in exchange for a short-term greater purchasing power, while giving somebody else the means to save in the long term. Credit enabled a flow of wealth upward, under the rhetoric of distributing it downward. It was cost-free class warfare, in Buffett's terms, and for many years it had received the blessing of the poor themselves. Even so, such a status of manufactured consent was shortly to change as the recession bit deeper. Rising unemployment meant governments needed to find more money to support the jobless while getting less income in the form of tax. Governments and citizens alike were being forced to deleverage.

In Spain, the year began with the sorry announcement that unemployment had hit 3 million, a twelve-year high. Meanwhile its property market was about to nosedive. Even Germany was predicting its economy would probably shrink by over 2 percent during the year to come, its worst performance since 1945. In Britain and Denmark main street companies continued to go bust while Honda, which was hardly a local business start-up, suspended production in its UK factory for four months just to try to survive. Ireland announced its economy would shrink by 6 percent, showing the Germans that there were fates worse than theirs after all. And in Europe too, just as in America, behind all the macroeconomic figures that now blazed habitually across national newspapers, were the people who were affected by these job losses: people who were now turning off lights, cutting down on the monthly food bill, and wondering whether there would soon be any jobs left to apply for at all.

These were not Western problems alone, of course. As the financial crisis dragged the world into a long, deep malaise, similar problems were apparent right around the globe. Everywhere from Peru to Japan, the Philippines to India, corporations were laying off workers, banks needed rescuing, and taxpayers were being saddled with a future of suffocating obligations. In March 2009, as Ben Bernanke acknowledged that the world had now slipped into the worst recession since the Great Depression, the economic outlook appeared grim. New Zealand's economy shrank at its fastest rate in seventeen years; Canada's quicker than at any time since 1991. In June, Switzerland announced that it was officially now in recession, while in October Germany—Europe's biggest exporter—further announced that its trade surplus had fallen by 47 percent. Alongside this litany of financial destruction ran hoary narratives of the parallel unraveling of corporate frauds. In Texas, billionaire and cricket promoter Allen Stanford was charged over an $8 billion investment fraud. In Germany, the head of Deutsche Bahn was fired upon revelations the company had been spying on its employees.

Amid this economic funk—of a sort that made Carter's troubles in the turbulent years of *his* administration seem like a cakewalk—politicians sought desperately to project a confident outlook. In America, key officials in the Obama administration took their "confidence" on the record in interviews and unspecific asides, announcing that they were sure the corner was going to be turned any time now. In France, Sarkozy was as frenetic as ever; and this time he had devised (yet another) Plan de Relance, which comprised specific bailouts for the auto industry (though these may have ultimately only further entrenched its problems by beefing up the national production of generally older cars, as opposed to the more modern vehicles French firms had made in Eastern Europe). For good measure, he also launched a Sovereign Wealth Fund to support strategic French firms.[86] The Italian and Spanish prime ministers outdid each other insisting that all was as it should be. Meanwhile, Obama made frantic back channel reassurances to the Chinese that the investments they held in the US were "safe."[87]

So had anywhere actually escaped unscathed? It is a relative question of course. But the answer is also relatively simple. Those countries that had healthy public finances, generous social safety nets, and effective (and transparent) systems of labor relations found that they had the means to cushion the blows of the recession that followed on from the initial shock of the crisis. Outside Europe this meant that Australia had a relatively "good" crisis, its banks having steered clear of the subprime mania that afflicted the Atlantic economies (it was also lucky enough to be a major resource exporter to China). But steering clear of the rocks took more than just luck. When Norwegian banks encountered problems raising liquidity after 2008, the government could offer a guarantee, buttressed by the vast sovereign wealth fund that had been built up over the previous decade, using proceeds from North Sea oil. (The Thatcher government, it should be recalled, had used *its* North Sea windfall to fund tax cuts for the wealthy.) Not surprisingly citizens in these countries were the very ones comporting themselves with the confidence that seemed to be in such short supply everywhere else.

Perhaps it was not such a surprise that by 2012 the most competitive EU nations were all Scandinavian ones, with still relatively generous welfare states: Sweden, Finland, and Denmark.[88] What this implied was that the supposedly single European market now had an increasingly national tapestry. What was more, the same pattern became discernible within the single currency, with businesses of the harder creditor nations treated preferentially (by banks among other things) to those from the debtor nations on the periphery: the very ones that needed the loans in the first place.[89] The euro had been an admirable effort to level the playing field between the big beasts and the bottom feeders; it had unintentionally now created the situation in which the unresolved tensions of the post-70s era *within* each of Europe's nations had begun to erode the original ideals of Ventotene: to cooperate as individual nations in the realization of mutual benefits. It was the basis too for a series of more politically flammable struggles to come, between the very differently positioned peoples of Europe, who were no longer so sure that the national bonds they shared with others were as binding as they were told.

A Time of Austerity

All of this captures something of the extent to which the "global" financial crisis, and the great recession that followed, was experienced quite differently from country to country, even within the West. But it says little about the intensely uneven consequences of it for ordinary people *within* those same Western countries, where they were more or less left to fend for themselves. The true impact of the crisis was thus not instantaneous at all: it was slow and arduous, and if there was one consistent element to the way it was experienced between different countries, it was the fact that it was borne by the working class above all. A basic sense of the scale of the public disaster that was unleashed emerges from putting the long-term unemployment rate in the US in the years after 2007–8 in historical perspective. For sixty years prior to the financial crisis, no more than 13 percent of the unemployed in America remained out of work for more than six months. By April 2010 that same, rolling figure had leapt to 45 percent.[90]

In Europe, unemployment was higher and more likely to be longer-term prior to the crisis; but the number of people experiencing long-term unemployment also rose here, to just under half of all unemployed and around 4–5 percent of the *entire* working population by 2010 (about the same overall volume as the United States). Those still in work found they were also given fewer hours *to* work on the whole, lending rather a different perspective to the recently crowned achievement of the reduced 35-hour working week in France.[91] Every single country in the eurozone emerged from 2007–8 with its rate of profit (for business) restored at the expense of declining wages for those lucky enough to be employed. The share of GDP going to wages declined by as much as 18 percent in Latvia between 2009 and 2015, and by more than 13 percent in each of Greece, Cyprus, and Lithuania (despite the Baltics being held up as a success of austerity-engineered exit from the recession).[92]

The consequences of this can best be summarized in three words rarely heard outside university seminar rooms prior to 2007, but which were soon to become mainstays of breakfast news bulletins and lunchtime conversations: inequality, austerity, and precarity. All functioned as descriptors of social injustice but together they gave insight into the dynamics of that injustice, since it was the application of the second, in the context of the first, that ultimately gave on to the third. Inequality having made its historic return some years before, the years 2010 onward were the moment that austerity took center stage. As a policy regime, austerity was not simply a *description* of hardships needing to be endured. It was a method of redistributing those hardships within national territories. If governments could not control the international markets, or the credit-rating agencies that determined the macroeconomic environment in which they operated, they could at least manage the fallout domestically. After a period of several decades in which European states had progressively renounced the power to distribute the gains of economic growth (in exchange for a greater freedom from the responsibility) they now discovered that one of the few prerogatives still left to them to shape outcomes was the means of redistributing the *costs* of its decline.

Austerity as a deliberate strategy of last resort was deployed widely, and variously, across Europe in the years after the financial crisis: in the Baltics, where it was combined with EU structural funds, and in the peripheral economies, especially Ireland, Portugal, Spain, and Greece, where it was imposed with ECB warnings that support would be turned off without it.[93] In Britain it was used more consciously as the means to deliver a wider strategy of class retrenchment. Under the new Tory government that came to power in May 2010, a more deliberate approach to managing the fallout from the crisis was adopted than had been pursued by New Labour under Gordon Brown. The new cabinet was overseen by David Cameron, a young Etonian and former director of corporate affairs at the Carlton media company, working in close partnership with his own Richelieu, the new Chancellor George Osborne (an alumnus of Westminster School). Both were Tories of the Thatcherite mold, but they had learned their trade in the age of Blair: they knew how to wear open-necked shirts and to deliver a soundbite for the cameras.

Under their leadership the Conservatives had finally dug themselves out from under the Blair landslide of 1997. The election was hardly an ideological turnover: it owed more to declining electoral turnout and voter malaise than any overtly pressing desire to let the Tories back in. The new government had made it into office with the support of just 24 percent of eligible voters.[94] But after three electoral losses in a row, the British Tories now returned to power with considerably more energy than the old Labour government could muster. They were also determined to reconnect with the authentic legacy of the Thatcher years and to repeal some of the progressive baggage, as they saw it, of New Labour's reformulation of that legacy as a program of "markets with social policy."

At the core of their critique of the country's postcrisis woes was a belief that the previous government's cardinal sin was to have "maxed out" the country's credit card, leaving the country to wallow in its present financial misery. This was bad economics (misunderstanding the link between public debt and money creation) and it was bad politics (New Labour had not been excessive in anything: they were resolutely middle of the road and had continued winning elections after the Iraq debacle precisely because the economy remained buoyant).[95] In any case, it is unlikely that this argument won them the election. That had more to do with the long tail of Blair's own declining status in the wake of that unpopular war and his eventual handover to a man, in Gordon Brown, who had grown so unpopular that he practically gifted the election to the Tories.

But the Tory narrative of New Labour's decade of overspending was fundamentally wrong as history. Public debt had gone up because the government's bailouts had been the bare minimum required to save the economy. The economic rationale for deficit spending of this sort, in times of economic slowdown, was anyway as worn as old oak. Meanwhile, the real causes of the crisis and the downturn—deregulation of the financial industry and the structural distortions of the mainstream economy that ensued—were all things the Tories were continuing to recommend. Fatefully, for Britain's voters, this turned out not to matter. What mattered was that the Tories were not in power when the crisis struck and that they seemed to have a clear plan.

That basic plan was outlined in an emergency budget called by the new Chancellor just six weeks after the election. At heart it argued that the financial crisis and ensuing recession were the consequence not of financial market volatility but of there *still* being too much government intrusion into economic affairs. Austerity now entered the scene as the mechanism by which they would root out the last of this, by ensuring markets were allowed to clear themselves. Since this required a level of discipline that the Labour Party was ill-equipped to oversee, the Tories' return was justified: they were the nation's only responsible political agents.

Such a proposal sounded all the right notes at a time when the media was a daily digest of financial excess. But the new budget was more of a paradigm shift than was perhaps recognized at the time, since its ramifications would affect nearly every aspect of government and every budget thereafter—it was "class war waged with a calculator," in the words of one critic.[96] Osborne promised to "pay for the past" and "plan for the future" by reining in the UK budget deficit. And in doing so, as he set this out during the new government's first emergency budget in May 2010, he was not wrong to point out—and was himself politically keenly aware—that, "fear about the sustainability of sovereign debt is the greatest risk to the recovery of European economies."[97]

Osborne's plan, more specifically, was thus to use that fear to balance the national books, and to do so within five years. That was ambitious enough. What was more remarkable was that he planned to do this almost entirely through monetary and not fiscal policy (in practice, by making budget cuts and reinflating asset bubbles, rather than by public investment). "Expansionary fiscal contraction" was the governing—and self-evidently contradictory—neologism that encapsulated the Osborne program. It was unprecedented in its ambitions, and brutal in its shock delivery. But not everything about it was new. Osborne also cashed in on the favored rhetorical tropes of a decade of Third Way social democracy to justify his program: combining Clinton's fiscal prudery with Blair's "tough but fair" mantra in such a way as to direct macroeconomic policy back toward the regressive strategies of the 1980s.

As Osborne soon found on arrival in Number 11, however, there was not in fact much left to cut from domestic government spending by 2010. A dogged man, he anyway found the means to remove a further £6 billion for the year to come. There were also not many more financial powers that the government could remove from itself to independent bodies, but the Tories again showed their creative side here, immediately establishing a new Office of Budget Responsibility after the election— a body with more than a wisp of Reaganite fancy about it—which was granted the mandate of reporting back to the cabinet, and ultimately policing the boundaries of government spending. Cameron and Osborne thereby found the means to frame their economic policies as being "in line" with independently arrived at conclusions. However painful things may be, this strategy argued, the public could rest assured that the government was merely doing what needed to be done.

Rather as the turn to independent central banking had removed government responsibility for monetary policy, so now Britain's fiscal room for maneuver was also greatly narrowed. For Cameron's cabinet, whose policies were devoted to cutting back on the size of government, that was not a constraint to be concerned about, of course. But for any subsequent government wishing to expand spending on welfare, social policy, or on prisons, it would function as a powerful straitjacket. The minimal state had just acquired a further institutional lock-in. British democracy's already conservative nature was being set fast for future generations as well.

But so too had a state increasingly subject to elite capture (as distinct from simply being run by elites) dug the trenches a little deeper around its executive core. Of Osborne's £70 billion in cuts to state spending, half would be found not by cutting back on the costs of *central* government but by retrenching cash benefits and cutting back on local government *employment*. As a result of these policies, and within just a few years, there would be five times as many working families below the poverty line in Great Britain as there had been at the start of the 1970s. After a period of reversal under New Labour, urban poverty returned with a vengeance, with one in ten households forced to live in damp homes, in no small part because 9 percent of the nation's households could not afford to pay for heating.[98]

Even those escaping life on the impervious slab of a British council estate were now hit by a 10 percent decline in real wages. This decline in real wages was ultimately more damaging than unemployment, which rose less under Osborne than many predicted owing to an expansion in part-time and "zero hours" contracts (i.e. keeping people "technically" employed). This allowed the government to claim its books were looking more balanced, but equally it meant that more people were employed at a lower rate and with less job security than before. At the same time, the national unemployment rate of some 2 million was now twice the level that had caused even the steady-handed Heath government to panic in the winter of 1972–73—and it was heavily weighted in the north.[99] If this was in part testimony to a growing public tolerance for unemployment, it was also evidence of the distributional ambitions of Osborne's program of balancing the books through austerity, inescapably weighted as it was toward the London-based "well-to-do." It was a remarkable political assault on the British working class, in other words. And Osborne was not done yet. In the lead-up to the next election, in 2015, he would emphasize austerity by promising to reduce spending further: back to levels not seen since 1958.[100]

The success of Osborne's policies, despite the pain they caused, was certainly testament to the political skills of the two former Bullingdon Club members (an Oxford drinking society) at the heart of the new Tory government. It was also testament to the British public's desire to take their chances with anything other than a New Labour government. But above all it was a function of something far simpler than this: fear. After all, as citizens were frequently reminded, national income had shrunk by a quarter in Greece by 2013, suicide had become the second leading cause of death in Spain after natural causes, while across Europe there were more than 15 million young people neither in work nor education. As an adviser to the European Commission president put it, "A lost generation is in the making."[101]

But while muffling the dissent of the losers, Osborne was also courting the winners. The Conservatives had been long out of power and they needed to secure their position. Under Cameron and Osborne income taxes were thus raised only lightly for the rich and disproportionately less than they were raised for the poor. Corporation tax was cut to 20 percent (in 1984 it had been 52 percent with few questions asked) while the top rate of income tax was cut, saving those earning over £1 million—at the stroke of a pen—a little over £100,000 a year. As a political strategy this would prove highly successful: the party would be twice reelected at the time of writing. As public economics it was a disaster.

If the rich enjoyed being courted by the likes of Britain's new Tory government this was partly because they were now doing better even than they had done before the crisis. The definitive achievement of the postwar Golden Age was its reduction in the gap that separated rich from poor: a fact which had less to do with wage increases for the poor and more to do with tax policy, which in its most progressive years had allowed the market to set pretax income levels and the state to undertake posttax redistribution according to socially determined need. Since the 1970s the top 1 percent of income earners had received a growing share of overall income. Wage repression, capital liberalization, and a race to the bottom among post-Reagan-era national governments seeking to lower the tax burden on the owners of capital in particular all contributed to an increase in the share of national income going to capital (and nonwage income, like stocks and shares) rather than labor.

This privileging of the owners of capital relative to workers had been especially marked in the Anglo-American economies (US, UK, Canada, Australia). But it could be seen wherever the Keynesian-era model of state redistribution had been rolled back (which was to say, more or less everywhere: even, to degrees, in Scandinavia). But more importantly still was the growing differential in total wealth (including assets like property and other investments). By 2010 the top 10 percent of wealth holders in the US owned three quarters of all national wealth. The years just prior to the financial crisis were thus the most unequal period in the West since the 1920s; by the time the credit crunch struck almost all the fairness gains of the Golden Age had been erased.[102] Across Europe 10 percent of the workforce was unemployed by 2011, with youth unemployment running at twice that figure. On the periphery it was even worse.[103] Both figures were rising.

What proved almost as significant, politically speaking, was that the level of wealth at the top (the other end of the problem of inequality) had *not* been leveled out by the recession. On the contrary, in the aftermath of the financial crisis the status of wealth had rarely been as high. By 2013 95 percent of the economic growth generated by the recovery in the US had been absorbed by the top 1 percent of income earners: an increasingly plutocratic age was beckoning.[104] It was as if the bold public statements and decisive action of individuals like Warren Buffett, Bill Gates, George Soros—household names all—somehow further showed up the ineptitude of states as they stepped up to the plate to address the fallout from the crisis. The media, tired of stories of financial doom and gloom, purred with delight at having their stories to report on. "US Billionaires to Give Away Fortunes to Charity," announced London's *Guardian* in August 2010, and it was soon lapping at the same trough by having the Rockefeller Foundation "sponsor" some of its own online web content. "Spanx Mogul Sara Blakely Becomes First Female Billionaire to Join Gates-Buffett Giving Pledge," declared *Forbes* magazine. There was perhaps too little questioning as to exactly how some of this money was made, where it was stored, and how much tax, among other things, was paid on it. Such questions would be asked in due course, but it would require the nudge of a new era of corporate leaks and whistleblowing scandals to bring it about and they had not, at this point, broken loose.

There are no hard-and-fast rules as to what happens when a model of political society, which for all it trumpets the values of democratic equality, acts consistently against those values in its actual policies. The crisis was far from over. The politics of austerity had reignited a language of class and injustice that had lain dormant for some time. Those who would be required to pay for the bailouts contemplated the poisoned chalice before them with a new appreciation of just what power it was that the transnational elite wielded over them. At the same time that elite too began to chafe at the discomfiting glare of popular opinion. Might not the gap between rich and poor, fretted Sir Ronald Cohen, a doyen of the British financial scene, after all "ignite a violent reaction"?[105]

It was a question he was not alone in pondering.

16

Back to the Streets

LIKE ALL REVOLUTIONS, the uprisings that swept across the Arab world in the spring of 2011 seemed "impossible beforehand and inevitable afterward."[1] When a young Tunisian, Mohamed Bouazizi, burned himself to death in public in an act of protest, decades of pent-up anger were unleashed at the region's autocrats. For young Arabs in particular, Bouazizi's death epitomized a whole generation's frustration at their trampled freedoms and dubious prospects in life; at the cost of living (sharpened by recent food price spikes); and above all at the "inveterate government corruption and repression" that tied all these grievances together.[2] It was the spark to a rapidly gathering flame.

It was to prove the beginning of a dramatic few years in the West as well. Until now, the political fallout from the financial crisis had been slight. There had been a shift to the right in Spain, Sweden, Britain; a shift to the left in France and America. The record elsewhere was more mixed. In Italy and the Nordic nations, traditional majorities declined. In the Netherlands and most consequentially of all in Germany coalitions proved harder to form. In Greece and Spain elections were won by such small margins that the winning parties failed to form coalitions at all and repeat elections were required.

In Belgium it took 541 days for the parties elected in June 2010 to finally cobble together a workable majority—a year and a half without a functioning leadership. At play was often simply the punishing of whichever party had been in power when the crisis hit. But it gradually also became clear that the much remarked upon political apathy and declining electoral turnouts of recent years were not such an accurate marker of the public mood after all. Sentiments were hardening, and opinion polls increasingly told a different story: of a public that felt itself excluded and that was rapidly growing more restless as a result.

This was why, for Europeans in particular, the spectacle of a vast democratic uprising taking place across the Mediterranean was not merely a nostalgic reprise of the prodemocracy movements that shook Eastern

Europe free from communism in 1989. For many it was a call to action. Witnessed at a time of austerity-driven discontent at home, the Arab Spring perhaps should have served, for Western elites, as a reminder that sustained gaps between expectations and reality tend to bring political unrest in their wake. Instead it was taken as a belated opportunity to crow once more about the inevitable "spread" of democracy around the globe. Ultimately it was the events of 1968 and not 1989 that echoed loudest of all, since it reminded Western citizens that a more visceral politics existed, and it was still to be found out there on the streets.

The Voice of the People (Partisans I)

Throughout the long summer of 2011, Western citizens did something they had not done in a very long time: from Syntagma Square in Athens to Zuccotti Park in New York City they began occupying public squares. Their reasons for doing so were not everywhere the same: the deliberative circles that convened in Spain's public plazas contrasted strongly with the syncopated anger of race and austerity riots in the UK. But the one thread that linked them all was a wish to send to the political leaders of each country a very clear message. The years of "*Enrichissez-vous!*" ("Get rich!") were over. A new mantra of "*Indignez-vous!*" ("Time for outrage!") was taking its place. The slogan came from a short and self-explanatory tract by the former French Resistance fighter Stéphane Hessel published in late 2010. It would go on to sell over 3 million copies, and soon set something of a trend. *L'oligarchie ça suffit, vive la démocratie* (Enough of Oligarchy, Long Live Democracy) was the title of another tract, by journalist Hervé Kempf.

It was the impact of austerity that had finally flung these movements out into the open. Spain especially had been hard hit by the crisis. The austerity measures overseen by the two postcrisis governments, first that of the socialist (PSOE) José Luis Rodríguez Zapatero, a wonkish Tony Blair with saving graces, and then, from 2011, the right-wing Partido Popular (PP) of the more headmasterly Mariano Rajoy, had seen ordinary Spaniards experience dramatic cuts in health, education, and welfare spending. Strikes had been staged, including a general strike in September 2010 as the euro crisis heated up. When these had been ignored by politicians a hint of condescension was added to the corruption with which they were already associated. Amid disgruntled calls for *¡Democracia Real YA!* ("Real Democracy NOW!") Spanish citizens took to vent-ing their frustration in more direct ways instead. The battle lines between "citizens" and "the system" that would define Europe's coming political struggle were beginning to emerge.

The movement that initially came to represent these interests called itself *los Indignados*. One poll showed that as many as 72 percent of Spaniards claimed to share the grievances of the *Indignados*, but it was predominantly Spain's youth who drove things forward. It was they who had disproportionately borne the costs of the postcrisis austerity policies. "They don't represent us," was the *Indignados* cry. They saw there to be little choice between a mainstream "neoliberal left" and a mainstream "neoliberal right," to which end the chant *Juventud sin Futuro* (Youth with No Future) became another of their slogans. In 2011, with regional elections due to take place on May 22, and yet with elected politicians seemingly unwilling to listen, activists arranged for coordinated sit-ins to take over the central plazas in nearly every major Spanish city. They were to take place exactly one week before the elections.[3]

The scale of the action caught Madrid's political establishment by surprise: thousands gathered in the city's grand central square, Puerta del Sol. The mood there was fervent and earnest; improvised general assemblies were held across the country and popular votes were taken on everything from political strategy to how to organize the impromptu camps that had emerged. The people's voice would be listened to here. Since there was no real attempt to translate their actions into an especially coherent agenda, however, the mainstream press, which thronged about the encampments during the first days, quickly lost patience. Like the government frantically trying to evict them, it too soon came to see the protesters as doing little more than just "getting in the way." Within months the movement had fizzled out. But not before a new paradigm of peaceful protest had been established (or at least rediscovered). A group of American tourists wandering through the encampment in Barcelona's Plaça de Catalunya were so taken aback that all they could think to observe was: "this would never happen in the USA."[4]

At that point it appeared unlikely to happen in Britain either. But by high summer an uglier face of protest had also emerged in cities across the UK. In response to the police killing of a black youth, Mark Duggan, on August 4 in Tottenham in London, a weeklong spate of riots spread across the country, from Coventry to Birmingham to Wolverhampton and Manchester. Some of the riots began as peaceful marches but ended with looting and violence. In all, five people were killed. By August 15 more than 3,000 arrests had been made. Coming on the back of the protests in Spain and Greece and with the uprisings still playing out across Arab North Africa, the appearance now of what the *Guardian* had renamed "the worst civil disturbance in a generation" only added to the sense that a wave of social unrest was afoot.[5]

Further memories of 1968 were brought to the fore when Prime Minister David Cameron was recalled from his summer vacation to deal with the burning cars and youths smashing windows. His return was not to be as successful as de Gaulle's dramatic reentry by helicopter during the height of the Paris uprisings in 1968. But as the unrest spread to Manchester, Birmingham, and Nottingham, Cameron nonetheless went on the offensive, promising to "fight back." He did so not just by admitting the water cannon as permissible in response, but by intensifying his rhetorical assault. There are pockets of our society, he said, that were "frankly sick," though that hardly quelled the flames of unrest. Rather than addressing the stereotyping of Britain's marginalized youth, Cameron instead fired up a nationwide moral panic out of the preexisting social panic. The Cameron government was so convinced that the riots were all just the work of "vermin" and "feral" elements of society they seemed to forget that many of those "sick pockets" were also just people fed up with empty pockets. Cameron was certainly in no danger of thinking that the consumerism the looting represented was a condition encouraged by the budgets of his own government.

As the London School of Economics concluded afterward (in the absence of a public inquiry that Cameron refused to call) the true causes of the riots were opportunism, social inequality, and the growing aggressiveness of community policing: that, and the deepening reliance of the nation on its property market, pushing gentrification, and the prices that go with it, ever further up and into the faces of those who had no means now of reaching the next rung on *their* ladder. What was the government doing? asked one professor of social work, barely containing his anger. "Are you lifting up marginal people? Or are you editing them out?"[6]

It was precisely the sense that governments were choosing the latter of those two options that brought about what globally was to prove the most popular eruption of all in 2011. On September 17, inspired by the Indignados movement in Spain, a group of protesters set up camp in Zuccotti Park, the privately owned plaza in the heart of Wall Street. Nestled beneath Mark di Suvero's towering ferric sculpture, *Joie de Vivre*, the protesters unfurled the slogan "We are the 99%": a reference to the majority of the population denied the privileges of the rich. Its confident brandishing of a by now well-known statistical fact was a revelation of how widespread the debate over inequality had become, ever since the money long said to be impossible to find (at least for social programs) had been placed, in vast quantities, on the banks' troubled balance sheets. But Occupyers, like the Indignados before them, explicitly resisted being pigeonholed as a particular "type" of movement, and so they refused to name what it was they really wanted. The host of leftist intellectuals who descended upon Zuccotti Park in their droves to speak to the gathering before them were no more forthcoming. The Slovenian philosopher and darling of the radical left, Slavoj Žižek, inevitably made an appearance, as did Californian writer Rebecca Solnit, who urged protesters to "throw out the masters' tools."

In truth, the places taken over by Occupy were more important than its political agenda or its global reach. As cameo appearances by leftist intellectuals suggested, the demonstrations were intensively "theorized"— a fact their much-hyped spontaneity should not obscure. Every social relation requires its own form of space, Henri Lefebvre had observed back in the 1970s, providing one of the many intellectual maxims guiding the organizers of the protests. The camp was "the fundamental bio-political paradigm of the West," declared another of the moment's obligatory reference points, in 1998: the voguish Italian philosopher Giorgio Agamben. He certainly did not have in mind upper-middle-class protesters in tents perched on the stoop of mammon when he wrote those words, but there were some unavoidable conceptual parallels between the death camps of his highly influential studies and the camps of an alternative politics being assembled under the rubric of Occupy. For what the latter raised was the question of what happens when liberal democracy reaches some kind of limit point: when it comes to the act of casting off those it no longer values.

When the Zuccotti Park protesters were evicted on November 15— exactly half a year after the Indignados had been cleared out in Madrid— their removal was framed in the euphemistic language of public safety. "Sanitary conditions" had become unacceptable since "cleaning personnel" were denied access to the camp, it was claimed. But by then Occupy, like the Indignados before it, had made its point. It had, moreover, crystallized the common element of popular resistance that linked many of the other social protests gathering force in cities across the West. And it had provided that with the one thing that liberal democratic society knew instinctively how to manage: a single, powerful brand. On the basis of what was—for all the high-theoretical, second-order retakes—ultimately just a simple injunction to act, a sense of injustice articulated, and a slogan, its spread was nothing short of remarkable. Occupy New York became Occupy Philadelphia and Occupy Oakland and then, almost overnight, a resolutely global phenomenon.

Soon public squares were being seized in the name of the Occupy banner, everywhere from Paris to Tokyo to Buenos Aires. But there was never any set format, and there were plenty of surprising variations. Ironically, in Italy, which had seen some of the first anti-austerity protests by students in 2008, the Occupy movement was strangely muted: testimony, as one Italian activist reflected, to Silvio Berlusconi's monopoly of discontent—"saving from the popular blame the EU and the 1%" alike.[7] In London, the Occupy movement likewise took an unexpected turn. Camps were first set up at the London Stock Exchange and, after their promptly anticipated eviction, they relocated to the steps of St. Paul's Cathedral nearby.

In the words of Canon Chancellor Giles Fraser, under whose pastoral eye they reconvened, the street protests in Britain now adopted a more peaceful guise. St. Paul's provided, after all, "a natural and compelling stage" for their arguments of social equality to be heard. But this did not stop the police submitting a further eviction order. The cathedral chapter of the church was then forced to vote on what to do, and in eventually acquiescing to the eviction, precipitated the resignation of Fraser, who chose instead to stand by his somewhat ragbag new flock. The fallout, within the church, ultimately led to the installation of a new archbishop: one more willing to speak "moral purpose to the bankers," as Fraser himself put it laconically. Archbishop Justin Welby was certainly that man. "Occupy reflects a deep-seated sense that there is something wrong, and we need to think very hard about what's wrong," he was soon heard pointing out.

In bringing such a man to the fore it was just possible, Fraser would later reflect, that Occupy in London had a greater impact on the venerable old Church of England than it ever did on the financial sector.[8] That was a reminder that the politics of protest were a response to more than just the financial crisis and its long train of austerity. Its grievances had been longer in the making. At the same time this only brought home once more the central dilemma that confronted the new protest movements: what did they really want? In the words of one of Occupy's key figures, the anarchist David Graeber, that was the wrong question and needed rejecting altogether. "In the big picture it hardly matters," he observed, "whether one seeks to reorganize the world around bureaucratic efficiency or market rationality: all the fundamental assumptions remain the same."[9]

Perhaps because of this refusal to specify an alternative, and spread by the new social media of Twitter and Facebook, Occupy quickly became a global movement. Yet even as it spread beyond the Atlantic world, Occupy at heart always sought to articulate the inadequacies of liberal democracy as it had become, and to do so by seizing upon its most visible hollows: that anemic corporate architecture of central business districts and their appended global city status which had taken shape in the decades before. The protesters had no desire to "take" these spaces, simply to demonstrate, by their actions, a more human, corporal counter-narrative. In the words of one activist, what they wanted was "to be doing what they were [already] doing." *Taking control.* Assuming, in the words of an earlier generation, their "right to the city."

But was the establishment willing to cede this to them? Judith Butler, another of the intellectuals who appeared at Zuccotti Park, was on the money here: "They say [ours] are impossible demands, and impossible demands, they say, are not possible. [But] we are not just demanding economic justice and social equality, we are assembling in public . . . making democracy, enacting the phrase 'we the people'!" As Butler had crystallized, the politics of Occupy was a politics *of* democracy, not a politics *in* democracy: it didn't matter what the establishment did. Here instead was habeas corpus in action. As the Occupy protesters saw it, the body was once again, finally, being returned to the public sphere.

The realities of this were both moving and a little awkward: gauche even. To witness the "human amplifiers" that repeated in unison Butler's every muffled line so that it fanned out to the larger gathering was certainly moving, in an age that had largely forgotten popular displays of ritual. And this was where Occupy derived its political power. But while not caring what your adversaries think may have been liberating for a left whose arguments had long fallen on deaf ears, in the hands of the mob such insouciance can quickly become exclusionary itself. This was why some established voices on the left began to worry that the horse of popular protest, having finally bolted through the barn door, had forgotten to take the carriage of the rest of society with it. The protests had "failed to coalesce around a solidaristic alternative," said the American radical Nancy Fraser in language that was a part of the reason why.[10]

The *real* problem with Occupy in short was not whether its demands were clearly articulated or not. It was simply that it failed to turn from a protest into a mass movement on behalf of something or some positively defined group in particular. This was where the difference between Occupy and Podemos in Spain was perhaps most revealing. In Spain, almost against the desires of the Indignados themselves, the momentum of the initial actions on May 15 eventually boiled down and thickened into a political program that became a party: Podemos (We Can). One of the leading figures of the soon-to-be new political movement, Íñigo Errejón, had witnessed the May 15 protests at first hand. But he and fellow intellectual Pablo Iglesias, a ponytailed lecturer in political science already making a name for himself on left-wing media channels and in public debates, recognized that something more needed to be done.

Iglesias and Errejón accordingly hatched a plan, in August 2013, to build a left-wing anticapitalist party with its sights set resolutely on winning the next election. It was hugely ambitious, and even they were not sure it might succeed. But it was also precisely what the large amorphous gatherings of 2011 had to this point studiously avoided: actually trying to win an election.[11] The new party, with its participatory democratic procedures in which policies devised by meeting group "circles" would be selected or not by voting in online forums, was unveiled in January 2014. By the end of May it had secured its first three MEPs. In the national election held in December the following year, it came third overall, with 20 percent of the vote and 69 seats in parliament, only a little behind second-placed PSOE.

In the United States, by contrast, as the living in tents pitched on bare streets grew uncomfortable and the media grew less interested, the entire platform began to collapse. It looked like the demands of Stéphane Hessel having been gratified—the people *had* been enraged—enthusiasm then waned. The reasons are worth reflecting upon. For one, their failure was not necessarily their own fault. What the wave of street protests in 2011 confronted, was the problem of how to agitate democratically against a democracy that had come over the previous forty years to abhor disorder, and in which politics had become a technocratically determined art. What made politics impossible, in Judith Butler's words, was the fact that it was no longer allowed to be in any way "messy"—which rather excluded all forms of politics that were not already well entrenched and well funded.

This had left people searching outside the narrow bounds of elite liberal democratic politics. The progressive left was still divided, despite this being in many ways *its* moment: was it best to vote, to sign a petition, to march, or to otherwise deploy the weapons of the weak? There were in fact two struggles opening up for the left here. One was over the visceral need to reclaim the public sphere from decades of private encroachment. The other was intellectual and was to be waged over what was left of representative democracy. Occupy only ever addressed the former, but the title of a best-selling 2015 election guide, *None of the Above*, by a popular young television presenter in the UK, revealed there was a need to address the latter as well.

The danger was that without the more credible program that the new movements insisted it was beneath them to provide, an angrier side to democracy was more likely to be let out of the bag. Did the Indignados hope to influence the national Spanish elections due later that year, in late 2011? "Not interested," was the reply of one activist.[12] Here was the very disavowal of the system that the less constructively minded— presented, as they were about to be, with a refugee crisis of historic proportions and a second return of Islamist terror to Western shores— would soon be in a far better position to exploit. But not before Europe's leaders in particular now plunged the continent back into even greater political turmoil.

"The Lure of Technocracy"[13]

In October 2010, the evening sun setting out to sea, Angela Merkel and Nicolas Sarkozy walked deep in conversation with one another along the promenade at the French coastal resort of Deauville in Normandy. A little like the surprise agreement setting Europe on a path to monetary convergence that Giscard d'Estaing and Helmut Schmidt had sprung on their European partners in 1978, what Merkel and Sarkozy were discussing that evening were the terms of what they hoped would be a new deal for Europe, to end the constant rounds of speculation and crisis that had engulfed the continent for two years now.

The thrust of the idea was a good one: to recognize that the sovereign debts of countries like Greece needed to be restructured, rather than continuing to pile them up, and to insist that private creditors bear some of the costs of this. In short Merkel and Sarkozy were acknowledging that the strategy needed to shift from one of "bailing out" to "bailing in." Inevitably Trichet, when he heard, was outraged: the markets wouldn't buy it for a minute, he fumed. "You're going to destroy the euro," he shouted at the French delegation when he was informed of the plan in Luxembourg. Timothy Geithner, the US Treasury secretary, was no better pleased when, while staying at a hotel in Cape Cod, he took a call telling him the news. "I was like fucking apoplectic about it," he later observed.[14]

What Merkel and Sarkozy had agreed at Deauville was all the more remarkable, given the testy relationship between its two authors. Theirs was an uneasy partnership on which to be bidding for a relaunch of the old Franco-German heart of European policymaking. For Sarkozy, Merkel was, as he once put it, "a scientist, almost like a German cliché, planning everything, going step by step, unemotional, not a show horse." So far as Merkel was concerned, Sarkozy irritated her no end: she thought of him as a curly-haired Mr. Bean and despaired of his inability to do anything other than to talk. But good sense had for once been allowed to prevail. It allowed Merkel to take a step toward the more comprehensive, constitutionally locked in solution she had always favored, and Sarkozy to show that he was giving the French a bit of a breather from German discipline.[15]

The Deauville agreement might have made life much easier in countries under the thumb of the sovereign debt crisis and it should have brought a lot more stability to the way in which Europe was responding: not least it proposed properly institutionalizing the new fire-fighting fund, the European Financial Stability Facility (EFSF). But trust was already far too low and Merkel and Sarkozy should have recognized this. Instead the whole thing backfired terribly. Not just Europe's leaders but the markets too were caught by surprise and (unlike the MEPs who in 1978 could be bullied by Giscard and Schmidt) they let their concerns be known. Soon the spreads on Greek and German government bonds, which had begun to come down after several years of austerity, leapt back up. The crisis reignited.

For all the talk that capitalism was in crisis it was abidingly clear that it was democracy that was experiencing what Merkel described as a truly "existential" moment.[16] Indeed, thanks in part to the spectacular way that Deauville blew up in the faces of Merkel and Sarkozy alike—as Trichet rightly (though for the wrong reasons) predicted—the political aspects of the euro crisis now fully came to the fore, not least since Trichet himself now went on the attack from the boardroom of the ECB and set about drastically tightening up credit conditions: as Ireland would shortly be the first country to find. And yet, as politicians convened for what was to become round two of the financial crisis in Europe, they did so in a Europe that had changed as well.

The question of what kind of polity the EU wanted to be had last been raised, and answered, in the resounding rejection of the European "constitution" in 2005. Now the question was being raised a good deal more directly. With Germany able to borrow at far more generous rates than countries like Greece and Portugal, despite their sharing a common currency, it was inevitable that old national divides would reopen. The problem wasn't so much that countries couldn't agree, it was that increasingly they had less in common to agree upon. When asked what he thought of EU funding for deprived areas, one Greek responded that it was "A mess. They'll make us give it back with interest."[17]

What was left of Europe was reverting to a battle of wills. Germany sidestepped the Commission, and certainly the parliament, with bilateral agreements to ensure that the monies it sanctioned for errant countries like Italy were used in the "right" sort of way. The ECB likewise often pursued its own bilateral agenda. For the citizens of those countries this "right" way increasingly felt wrong. "We have been crushed as a people," said Anastasia Dotsi, a retired bank clerk in October 2011, as rubbish fires smoldered in the streets around her while the Greek government passed the latest round of austerity measures. "They've pushed us to become extremists."[18] But in truth the pushing had only just begun.

In November 2011, Silvio Berlusconi's car drew up to the presidential palace where he was due to tender his resignation. Outside, police "struggled to control a large, hostile crowd which booed and jeered as his convoy swept by." Some shouted "buffoon" while others did a conga dance in celebration. But it was not, as one observer noted, "the will of the people" that had toppled him from power.[19] It was the power of the troika acting for once in unison. And their act of regime change had been set in motion some months earlier that year. In the summer of 2011, still fuming, the ECB's Jean-Claude Trichet wrote to the governments of Spain and Italy with, in effect, a demand that both governments do more to improve their "sovereign signature" (i.e. to stop "worrying" the markets by their levels of debt—as if this was in any way the ECB's prerogative to demand). They were to do so, furthermore, by introducing a wish list of the ECB's preferred conservative reforms centered upon lowering government spending and raising taxes—such things, in other words, as it should be elected governments' sole privilege to put before the people to decide.

The ECB gave both governments a clear time frame within which this political overhaul by decree was to be accomplished: one month for José Luis Rodríguez Zapatero in Spain; "as soon as possible" for Berlusconi in Italy.[20] Trichet's letters were never intended to be published. Neither Italy nor Spain was in a eurozone rescue package after all. But queries over the state of both countries' finances having been raised, their cost of borrowing was surging as market pressure built. Spain and Italy ultimately had no choice but to acquiesce and introduced many of the kind of reforms the ECB was demanding. Satisfied its will had been done, the ECB then duly began buying up their debt so as to alleviate the pressure of the bond markets. "There was a time in much of Europe when generals (or worse) took it upon themselves to protect the national interest from dithering politicians," Martin Sandbu of the *Financial Times* observed of this sorry tale. "It is less bloody when central bankers do it, but nearly as noxious to democracy."[21]

But as Sandbu was among those to document, Brussels was not done yet. Next it was Berlusconi who, like Richard III, was felled while still casting about for his horse. This time it was his fellow eurozone leaders Merkel and Sarkozy who more directly piled on the pressure, whispering in the ear of Giorgio Napolitano, the Italian president, to have Berlusconi removed. For this purpose they sought to bring the Americans on board too. As Timothy Geithner recalled of the G20 meeting in Cannes in November 2011, "[t]he Europeans basically approach[ed] us softly, indirectly, before the thing saying, 'We basically want you to join us in forcing Berlusconi out.'"[22] Then Merkel and Sarkozy had ECB teams put out the word that a replacement government led by Mario Monti would be one favorably looked upon.

The reason for this was simple: Europe itself now stood in danger of falling apart. Italy was critical to the entire eurozone—as precarious as Greece, but far larger and more important. It was the sovereign equivalent of a bank that was too large to fail. And so as Merkel and Sarkozy in particular saw things, it was imperative that the eurozone's response succeed in Italy. Monti was the perfect choice for that: skilled, a man Merkel "[could] work with"—though that would later change—and ultimately of the same view that what was needed was a little domestic discipline. By December 5 Monti had been put into office and had shepherded his first "austerity-and-growth" package through the Italian Senate. For the Italians it was nothing less than the fiscal equivalent of "shock and awe": high profile tax raids, a raising of the pensionable age, tax hikes, and caps on cash payments.[23]

Before long Greece too was to be pushed along the same basic path. Greece still was not being allowed to default (it being much easier for those northern banks who had bought up many of its bonds, not to confront the potential losses they would then face).[24] But the situation was becoming intolerable for the Greek people. In late October 2011 George Papandreou defiantly put the terms of a further loan program to the Greeks in the form of a referendum, unwilling to agree to it without the people's consent. The eurozone leaders, many of them meeting at the time for the G20 in Cannes, interpreted his act as a desperate "gamble." They resented the fact that it created further panic in global markets, and in doing so put the spotlight on Italy and Spain too. Furious, Merkel and Sarkozy summoned Papandreou to Cannes, to meet both them and the IMF's Christine Lagarde (at the film festival center overlooking the harbor). In an effort to put the pressure back on Papandreou, they demanded that at the very least he change the referendum, making it not about whether Greeks wanted to accept the new loan package or not, but on whether they wanted to stay in the eurozone or not.[25]

It would be an understatement to say that tempers were fraying. But this was an incredible overreach of two national leaders' prerogatives with respect to another elected leader. Returning from Cannes, and unwilling—as the British later would not be—to risk derailing the entire system altogether—Papandreou had no choice but to drop the referendum plan. Utterly broken as a politician he had no choice but to have a new loan package simply clapped through in parliament, offering his own job as an incentive, just to have the deed done. Having thereby fallen on *his* sword, in a way Berlusconi refused to do, he was replaced by the technocrat Lucas Papademos at the head of a new government of "national unity."[26]

Again, the new prime minister was not a coincidental choice, and cries on the left of "regime change" were not far off the mark. Papademos was a former vice president of the ECB while Monti, who also combined the roles of prime minister and minister of economy and finance upon his swearing in, was the former European Competition Commissioner. The representatives of the liberal market vision of Europe were being installed along the continent's southern rim. The consequences were profound. Greece's dominant labor party, PASOK, was destroyed in the May elections of 2012 that followed Papandreou's departure. Instead it was Syriza on the far left, led by the animated Alexis Tsipras, and neo-fascist Golden Dawn on the far right that both made gains at PASOK's expense. The Greek political landscape now became increasingly polarized: a telling harbinger of polarization elsewhere on the Continent.

What the Greeks got under Papademos, that they hadn't had under Papandreou, was a strained coalition of the two main governing parties. For all their historic antagonisms, the two main parties now had to work together, or rather to work with the EU, to ensure that the second major bailout, the one that Papandreou had refused to endorse, went through.

Having achieved this, Papademos resigned after five months to allow a "renewed popular mandate" to take over the reins of implementing the austerity measures his administration had committed to. The axe having begun to fall in 2012, the people would then eventually, three years later, be consulted as to whether or not they wished to stand beneath it.[27]

Papademos left the scene successful in Europe's eyes but unloved in Greece: he would later be severely wounded by a letter bomb, posted by the anarchist group Conspiracy of the Cells of Fire, which he opened in his car while being driven home one evening in 2017. In Italy, by contrast, the more popular Mario Monti brought with him an entire cabinet of technocrats and immediately got to work raising taxes, reforming labor regulations, and slashing spending, offering to take a cut in his own salary to show his willingness to cooperate while criticizing the northern European "creditocracy."[28] Before his own eighteen months in power were up, Monti had decided he would stand in the coming election, on a new coalition ticket, With Monti for Italy, comprising a new political party, Civic Choice, that he had taken the time to build up while in charge of the government.

Papademos in Greece and Monti in Italy were not the first technocratic governments of the postcrisis years, and as Europe's troubles rumbled on they would not be the last. Hungary already had one; subsequent caretaker governments would be found in Spain, Macedonia, Bulgaria, the Czech Republic, Croatia, Turkey, and Portugal. By 2010 an incredible nine of the eurozone's national leaders had been removed from office.[29] Desperate times had called forth desperate responses among Europe's policy elite, especially in the uneasy Franco-German axis at its heart that was now busily backtracking after the disastrous agreement at Deauville. Remarkable decisions had been taken and uneasy precedents set.

As the Czech case revealed, the installation of new governments was not always at the behest of the troika, and in 2012 the "Merkozy" relation cooled even before Sarkozy was replaced by the socialist François Hollande in elections that May. A certain perspective is warranted as well. Italy was served better under Monti's government than it ever had been under Berlusconi, and Greece's government under Papandreou helped to stave off a possible default. But these two technocratic administrations also made it possible for domestic and European authorities to take leave of the responsibility of imposing austerity. This appealed to Europe's northern leaders, Merkel especially, and the governing members of the Eurogroup. But it also left both countries prone to the rise of more antiestablishment parties, whose first order of business would be restoring the will of the people and finding someone else to blame.[30]

The problems were also not as specific to the "Club Med" countries as the eurozone leaders might have liked to believe. The sovereign debt crisis was initially contained within just a handful of countries on the European periphery but by late 2011 a much wider and more threatening *European* crisis was looming in its place. "This is not just a recession, but a real and fundamental crisis," warned the French economist Nicolas Baverez. More than half a century of moves toward greater integration were being unwound. "There is a tension in the political system and doubt about democratic institutions that we have not experienced since the fall of the Soviet Union," Baverez added.[31] All of a sudden, Europe faced three problems simultaneously.

Most immediately it faced panic once more in its financial markets as the spike in government bond yields that had forced Berlusconi out, and brought Monti in to replace him, began to be seen even on French government bonds as well. For political reasons it was unlikely that such a core European country would suffer the level of speculation that had brought Greece and then very nearly Italy to its knees. But the spectacle of Nicolas Sarkozy being harangued to do more to cut government spending by the EU's hard-line Finnish economic and monetary policy commissioner, Olli Rehn, put a new perspective on events in the Mediterranean.[32] Perhaps more worrying for Sarkozy was the growing speculation as to whether France had (once again) "fallen out" of the "first rank of euro nations." There was now, so far as the markets were concerned, an "in" group of countries (Germany, Austria, the Netherlands, and Finland) and an "out" group (Greece, Portugal, Ireland, Italy, and Spain). The rest, including France, were floating in limbo in between, much like the euro itself.[33]

Secondly, with unemployment across the EU now 6 million higher in 2011 than it had been just three years earlier, a rising antiausterity backlash was beginning to make itself felt.[34] This had begun in the spring of 2011 but was in full voice and rapidly collecting its own political scalps by the following year. In Ireland, in February, Fine Gael came to power thanks to public anger at the austerity imposed under the outgoing Fianna Fáil administration. Portugal's prime minister resigned in March when the opposition party refused to sign off on yet more budget cuts. In Spain, Zapatero called early elections in November after struggling to contain the growing popular dissent on the streets. The same occurred in Slovenia, after a failed referendum on the government's handling of the crisis, and in Slovakia, where prime minister Iveta Radičová lost her job in a 2012 coalition reshuffle required to secure emergency European Financial Stability Facility (EFSF) support. In the Netherlands Mark Rutte's government—in a trend that would become commonplace for centrist parties clinging both to power and the fiscal disciplinary line—required support from Geert Wilders's far-right party to stay in office. Flemish nationalists were flexing their muscles in Belgium, where they would prevent the formation of a national government for a year, storing up major problems for Belgium in the future.[35]

Thirdly, and indeed inevitably, the single currency began to wobble. When even France had come under market pressure in November 2011, there were renewed calls for the ECB to step in and act as a lender of last resort (France after all was supposed to be one of the creditor nations backing "weaker" ones like Italy and Spain). Yet again Trichet insisted this was not possible. The result was more confusion, failed half-solutions, and panic in the bond markets, spreading this time to Austria. Both countries were then duly downgraded by the credit ratings agencies, those other unelected bodies that had come to play such a prominent role in the unfolding of the euro crisis. At this point, the high point of the crisis, anything could have happened. The European banking system was seizing up amid intensified bond market speculation and growing political acrimony; half-grasped solutions were either poorly rolled out several months too late or, as with the "fiscal compact" (more austerity), poorly conceived to begin with.[36]

It is no surprise, then, that many at the time saw in this the specter of the single currency's demise. It was inevitable, they said, in a currency union that covered such diverse national economies. But for all that Europe's leaders were struggling to contain the crisis, there were other actors with vested interests in keeping the eurozone together: China among them. Part of Europe's ambition for the euro had always been as a way of dislodging US monetary hegemony in favor of a triumvirate of global pillar currencies (the dollar, the euro, and the renminbi). As Michel Rocard had put it at the time, the euro would lead to a Europe that "the US would listen to, and not neglect amid the cacophony of a crowd of irrelevant dwarfs." The Chinese, with their own eye on the US dollar, were only too happy for Europe to keep thinking this, and they now emerged as among the most willing purchasers of unwanted euros amid the crisis, and perhaps, in their way, as the EU's midnight savior. They had other reasons too, of course: buying euros was a way to diversify out of their exclusive (and whatever Obama said to try calming their fears they now realized excessive) reliance on the no longer quite so solid US dollar.[37] To that extent, saving the euro also meant furthering the renminbi.

But ultimately, it was not until 2012 when ECB head Mario Draghi pledged that the bank would do "whatever it takes" to keep the single currency together, and as the EU held a series of summit meetings to try to sever the Gordian knot tying banks and sovereign states together, that the worst of the crisis was over. The eurozone governments now finally saw fit to create a "banking union" that would bring national bank supervisory powers to the ECB and in due course provide a collective fund—financed by levies on the banks—for the restructuring of those that had clearly failed. That this could have been done much earlier and by ensuring a euro-wide management of the crisis in place of the ultimately shortsighted obsessions with disciplining "rogue" nations was treated as if it was now beside the point.

All told, by the early–mid 2010s the financial crisis had left Europe a far more acrimonious place than it had been for decades. Writing in the *Frankfurter Allgemeine Zeitung* in December 2011, Konstantinos Simitis, the former Greek prime minister, penned a stern warning to his German counterparts: "Solidarity is a concept that certain countries in the Union are not comfortable with. They associate it with an interpretation that concentrates exclusively on the need to support those countries that are not fulfilling their obligations."[38] But the ECB, with Germany standing behind it, was not to be budged. For Otmar Issing, Germany's most influential central banker, and the architect behind the single currency's monetary policies, "The demand that the stronger countries should, in pursuit of the common interest, support the weaker ones is a perversion of the oft-quoted notion of 'financial solidarity.' . . . A political union worthy of the name cannot be set up by stealth under the guise of fiscal transfers in the cause of common money."[39]

Issing's comments exposed the jeopardy that the move to a monetary union without a corresponding fiscal let alone banking union had bequeathed: the transnational solidarity that it was intended to lock into place had become the path to dissolution. To some extent this basic oversight in the development of the euro had been hidden for its first years in operation, both by the credit-fueled boom of the previous decade, which allowed all European countries, and not just the Greeks, to juggle accounts and pretend that their economies were more nearly harmonized than they were, and by the refusal of a growing chorus of Euroskeptics to transfer sufficient powers to Brussels to oversee this.[40] The financial crisis had brought all of this out into the open. But it had also forced Europe's leaders to ask of themselves for the first time since Maastricht, where it was—beyond simply "ever closer union," since that no longer seemed an option—they wanted to go.

There was precious little concord here. When the socialist François Hollande took over from Nicolas Sarkozy in May 2012 he immediately sided with Monti in the latter's efforts to propose euro area fiscal (and not just monetary) cooperation, in the form of the banking union that Germany had long resisted. Inevitably that put him at greater odds with Merkel than even Sarkozy had been. Obama too had seized on Monti's idea, and in a sign of his own growing frustration with European leaders' failure to address the crisis, presented it to her as a fait accompli, much to Merkel's annoyance. "If the euro area were viewed as a single country, it would appear as a sound and balanced economy," Monti suggested at the next G20 meeting in Los Cabos, delighted that Obama was supporting him on this.[41] That sounded expensive to the German ear.

Above all it was political dynamite for Merkel at home as she struggled to hold her coalition together. "More Europe" for Monti was not at all the same thing as "more Europe" for Merkel. And the German chancellor was no doubt relieved that Monti's own domestic powers were waning as his time in office drew to a close. But that scarcely removed the underlying problem, which was why many front-row participants in the eurozone's struggles, like Germany's other towering central banker, Karl Otto Pöhl, grew more and more worried about the possible consequences that disagreements like this might portend. "We are witnessing a return to the same types of conflicts as in the 1970s and 1980s, in terms of the disagreement between the stability policies followed in Germany and those pursued by other countries," he observed.[42]

Pöhl was right, in a way. The euro, as we have seen, had only been agreed to by Germany on the basis that the German preoccupation with stability might thereby become a European-wide preoccupation as well. It had, but not in the way intended. German stability did now preoccupy the other European nations, but not as their savior so much as their oppressor. It may have been true, as one wit put it, that "the member states are willing, for a price, to help one another out of a hole—but [they] desperately want to retain their sovereign power to dig themselves into the hole in the first place."[43] Yet that merely underscored the fact that it was sovereignty that was at stake: the political consequences of which, as southern European nations had discovered, were considerably

more serious. It scarcely came as a surprise that with caretaker governments in Italy and Spain, with the ECB being delegated (or rather
offloaded with) new powers to set the fiscal priorities of national governments, and with member states professing all the time that they would
love to solve their countries' problems except that their hands were tied,
populist and demagogic parties claiming "popular sovereignty" unabashedly in the name of "the people" grew stronger in their wake.

In Greece, before Papademos had even called for elections in the spring
of 2012, surveys revealed 3 percent of the population were intending to
vote for neo-Nazi, anti-Europe party Golden Dawn. In Italy, more jovi-
ally, comedian Beppe Grillo founded a protest party—the Five Star
Movement—that would soon grow to count on more than a fifth of the
electorate, and by 2016 would have captured the coveted post of Mayor
of Rome on its way to surging into power. This was doubly tragic with
hindsight. Sarkozy, Merkel, Draghi, even Barroso—all had plenty of opportunities to devise more forward-looking solutions to the Greek crisis
in particular: solutions that may have shared the risk, which is surely the
principle of a single currency, rather than impoverishing the southern
member states.[44] But it wasn't just the south that was growing tired of
the center. In 2011 the Finns Party, a ragbag populist party, gained 19
percent of the national vote in Finland. Timo Soini, the Finns' leader,
had made opposing the EU bailouts a central plank of his party's manifesto.

What was really at stake in the crisis, as these quintessentially transnational problems played out in already tense national theaters, was the
issue of interdependency, trust, and collective responsibility: in short,
the political counterpart to the already advanced economic integration
that now could not be undone for better, probably only for worse.
"Europe's politicians have almost without noticing it translated an economic conflict between classes (creditors and debtors) into a political
conflict between nations," observed the ever-shrewd Free Lunch column
in the *Financial Times*.[45] They had also merged the two. In 2012 polls
recorded that, for the first time, 60 percent of Europeans felt more
mistrust than trust in the EU.[46] They had also lost faith in the future.
Sixty-four percent of respondents to a Eurobarometer survey in 2012
thought "the life of today's children" would be harder.[47]

But the most pressing problem was that of the legitimacy of European
governments in the present. To respond to the crisis Europe's leaders had
delegated decisions to nonelected institutions like the Eurogroup, the
ECB, the managers of the EFSF, and the ECOFIN group of finance
ministers. Parliaments were barely considered let alone consulted on the

hugely consequential decisions being taken almost by the day. Indeed they stood largely mute. The euro crisis was in many ways its own referendum on the status of transnational democracy. It was certainly a verdict on how far Europe had come along this path. And while for some the answer to that question was not far enough; for others, the answer, seeing the mission creep of the technocrats all around them, was too far altogether.

The Radical Right (Partisans II)

At the height of the long, fraught summer of 2011, as the euro crisis peaked and uncertainty on the Continent reached its postwar high, a young Norwegian exploded a rental van filled with a homemade fertilizer bomb inside the executive government quarter in Oslo. He then jumped into another vehicle, and drove out of town to a nearby fjord, where, armed with numerous weapons, he set about massacring sixty-nine students at a residential summer camp. Shrouded in the international media coverage that focused on the horrific details of the crime, the political motives behind Anders Behring Breivik's actions were frequently overlooked. In the aftermath of the attack, Norway did indeed meet terror with "more democracy," as Jens Stoltenberg, the Labor prime minister, who was among its intended victims, had promised would be the country's response. But the trial held the following year, and the public response to it, showed greater interest in Breivik's mental condition than in his political views.

Breivik's murderous work was not just an act of violence against immigration and Muslims, however. It was an act intended to strike at the core of the political party that Breivik held responsible and at its alienating—for him—politics of multiculturalism and liberal bureaucratic rule. The youngsters killed were all members of the Labor Party's Workers' Youth League, and former Labor leader Gro Harlem Brundtland was expected to have been speaking on the island that day. Breivik wanted not just to cleanse Norway of immigrants, he wanted to cleanse the political system as well. It was this rejection of the political system that made Breivik's act part of a wider jigsaw of growing resentment and antipolitical acrimony. As Daniel Poohl, the Swedish director of the far-right watchdog Expo, put it: Breivik was no "lone wolf" but part of a wider political environment that assembled Islam and Marxism, or rather immigrants and states, into a composite threat that required attacking democracy itself to be rid of them both.[48]

Francesco Speroni, a member of Italy's Lega Nord (itself with 8 percent of the national vote), rather proved Poohl's point when he responded, after the attacks, that "Breivik's ideas are in defense of Western civilization."[49] In Germany, just the year before, Thilo Sarrazin published a book, *Germany Is Abolishing Itself*, that revived Darwinian fears of a German race being outbred by immigrants, and especially Turks. The book was a best-seller. Among its readers were many of those who gathered in public squares in Dresden and Leipzig under the banner of Pegida (Patriotic Europeans Against the Islamisation of the Occident [West])—a new movement that set up shop to protest at Angela Merkel's policies and to remind its wider German audience that *Wir sind das Volk!* (We are the People).[50]

This trend to blaming immigrants was nothing new. As we have seen, it had been a staple of European social discourse since the end of the postwar boom in the early 1970s. Only now it was even more misdirected. As a result of the politics of austerity and wage repression, a great many immigrants were in fact heading home. In Spain, whose massive population boom in the early 2000s (to the tune of around 7 million people) had been largely driven by immigration, the year 2008 still saw 310,000 new arrivals; by 2012 more than 140,000 were leaving. Demography was indeed political; but it was also often wrongly politic*ized*, and by the right in particular.

German workers, by contrast, had no right to blame immigrants for the stagnation in their salaries: their gripes properly lay with the Hartz labor reforms and the power of German manufacturers and corporations. The latter had done the best out of any national sector from the Single Market, in part because they could use the export markets it provided as a means to bully their own workers into submission. Moreover, it was the repressed wages of German workers that had, via the profits of German corporations, been lent out across the continent by the Bundesbank, to end up as the credit monies loaned to countries in the south. This gave them, if anything, grounds for a certain solidarity, not antagonism, with their Greek counterparts. But this was not an analysis that the left was quick enough to make and its former constituency of the workers were thereby amenable to being co-opted by the right, be it Golden Dawn in Athens or Pegida in Berlin.

In fact, as the left might also have been quicker to point out, the problem right across the EU was not the number of immigrants coming (or even going, for that matter) but the speed at which the native population was growing old. Across the EU-27 there were 6 million more over-sixty-fives (an increase of 9 percent) in 2006 than there had been in 2001. The nuclear family was also in decline, with 40 percent of marriages now ending in divorce.[51] These were the real social fault lines of the age. But they made for far less dramatic politics and so were not something that parties like Germany's Alternative für Deutschland (AfD) were much prepared to consider. This was unfortunate: sickness, ill health, and old age made up the vast majority of welfare expenditures: unemployment benefits, by contrast, were minimal (the difference being in the order of 67 percent to 5 percent). A politics based around these facts might have been more attuned to the real needs of the moment.

Breivik's cold-blooded murder was driven by a demonic misreading of the Continent's political history and its demographic present, including so-called *Eurabist* theories of the growing Muslim capacity to outbreed Caucasian first-comers. But his act took place at the juncture of a set of very real pressures and fault lines that provided the conduits and the gullies along which xenophobic and neonationalist sentiments had long gathered and down which they were now beginning to run. Immigrants and refugees were the focus for this, as they had been since the 1970s. But the driving force lay elsewhere: first, in the long disgruntlement of white-collar workers in the face of underemployment and livelihood precarity; second, in the perceived failure of mainstream parties to deal with this fact, rendering them vulnerable to a narrative of "betrayal." Fear and anger alike thus drove the far right forward. The violence itself was self-referential, providing that "macabre form of certainty," as the anthropologist Arjun Appadurai put it, that was otherwise lacking in the seeming new world disorder.[52] And, of course, it was precisely these two things that the euro crisis was now amplifying dramatically.

Scandinavia would have struck many as a rather surprising home for such a prominent right-wing extremist milieu. Surely if anywhere was free of the worker insecurity it fed off, it was the plump welfare states of Sweden, Norway, and Denmark? But precisely because these relatively small nations had such generous welfare provisions they were also regions experiencing some of the highest immigration rates. It made sense after all: if you were moving to a country where you would be likely to be among the very poorest, then a country that provided you with the best means to escape that poverty made a compelling choice. Finland, Sweden, and Norway also saw higher levels of asylum applications and accepted a greater number (Sweden most of all Europe in 2014) relative to the size of their own population. All accommodated substantially more asylum cases than the much larger countries of France and Britain *combined*.[53]

But immigration and asylum rates were up right across the Continent, something European citizens were constantly reminded of thanks to an unquenchable media fixation. A perfect storm was thus created when fighting in Syria, which turned devastatingly violent in 2011, sent people fleeing from that country en masse toward Europe (though in fewer numbers, in truth, than arrived and stayed in neighboring Arab countries). As this inflow of desperate people collided with the uncertainty, rising unemployment, and the precarity of Europe's own domestic economies, fear and misunderstanding began to feed off one another. This was especially true in Europe's fringe nations, such as Hungary, Albania, and Greece, and across Italy to Spain, where crossings by land and sea were easier and where domestic economies were already fractured by the euro crisis. Europe's leaders remained obsessed with the diplomatic circus that accompanied the troubled response to the economic aspects of the crisis. Meanwhile a social time bomb was ticking away before their eyes at home.

The first indications of this came with a rise in the popularity of far-right political parties across a swathe of European countries. In Hungary, the rise of the nationalist party Jobbik was making the mainstream but solidly conservative Fidesz party in opposition look distinctly progressive. Meanwhile in Poland, the conservative Law and Justice Party was in power and was busy imposing its moral opinions on the public: Lech Kaczyński, the president from 2005 until his death in 2010, in a crash-landing at Smolensk airport in Russia, had twice banned gay pride marches as mayor of Warsaw. The question of immigrants and minority groups in Eastern and central Europe was an especially vexed and long-running one; a regretful inheritance of the population movements and boundary redrawing of the earlier twentieth century. This had often left large minorities from other nations, with whom ties of trust and common feeling were weak, stranded alongside a different national culture. It was one reason why liberal democracy had struggled in the years since communism's fall and was struggling now most of all.

But the storm was gathering elsewhere in Europe too. In Britain, the British National Party held court in over fifty local council seats, the English Defense League began marching in 2010, and in the beery wake of both the more electorally significant UK Independence Party was surging and would do well in elections in 2013. Austria's Freedom Party, after struggling in government from 2000 and falling out of power, if not out of love with itself, after the EU imposed sanctions, now also made a successful return to front-line politics. By 2011 it was polling well with the young in particular. Part of the reason for its revived success was its adoption of a distinctly "protectionist" platform: borrowing from the Swedish *folkhemmet* concept the mantle of *heimat*, with the promise of a vigorous national identity combined with social welfare. Meanwhile, Le Pen's Front National, now under the leadership of his daughter Marine, continued the strong showing it had enjoyed in the 1990s, and secured a fifth of the national vote in the presidential elections of 2012 in France.

Eastern and central Europe saw a rise in less well-organized but more aggressive far-right political groupings, such as Attack in Bulgaria and the xenophobic and anti-Semitic Greater Romania Party, which had enjoyed considerable electoral success since the start of the century. In Scandinavia the Swedish Democrats, a party that liked to sponsor concerts by Ultima Thule (a band on the White Power circuit), entered into parliament in 2010 with twenty MPs, which doubled in the next election, to become Sweden's third largest party.[54] They rose yet further in the polls after that. Across the border in Norway, the Norwegian right-wing Progress Party (FrP) was also on its way to its best-ever showing in the polls, seemingly unaffected by the fact that Anders Behring Breivik had formerly been a member of the party, and in 2014 they would take over the Finance Department in a coalition government with the Conservatives, sending the outgoing Labour leader Jens Stoltenberg off to head up a NATO alliance that was itself about to witness more interesting times than it had seen in half a century.

Elsewhere Geert Wilders's party in Holland was struggling, but he still managed to bring down the government headed up by Mark Rutte of the economically liberal Freedom Party (VVD) when he resigned from a series of coalition negotiations in 2012 in protest at the terms of a new round of austerity measures, which he blamed on the EU. The greater drama was in fact taking place in Belgium, where the explicitly secessionist conservative New Flemish Alliance (NVA) was the reason it took that country so long to form a government: the party effectively held the country to ransom, after its surprise national victory, until it secured greater rights for Dutch speakers. It was hardly punished at the polls. Four years later it was the party of government (this time stringing out coalition negotiations for only five months to get its way).

The resurgence of the far right was a Europe-wide phenomenon, then. It was not just Podemos and its progressive, ponytailed leaders that gained a foothold in the European elections of 2014. In fact, the euphoria of 2011 having subsided, the majority of electoral gains now being made across the Continent were by parties of the far right. At the European level they experienced a 50 percent increase in votes and, across various parties, now numbered 79 MEPs. Significantly, those MEPS were being sent to Brussels by *people*: a survey in Norway in 2011 revealed that immigration was the most important issue for 50 percent of Progress Party voters.

The European Parliament, however, continued as if it was all just business as usual, though one wonders if the 60 million ethnic and religious minorities living in Europe, fully 12 percent of the population, agreed on this.[55] What they could see more clearly than their parliamentary representatives was just how interlaced was the extreme right of the neo-Nazis and anti-jihadists, with the parliamentary far right of Geert Wilders and the Sweden Democrats, and the rightward-tending mainstream of once respectable conservatism: well exemplified by David Cameron's flirtation with the populist Law and Justice Party in Poland in his European engagements, and Nicolas Sarkozy's expulsion of the Roma from France as he sought to pick up votes from the Front National.

This convergence of views was paradoxical: for while the rise of the far right was based upon a strongly local, communitarian "moral" voice (nativist would be the more precise term), it was now taking flight as a distinctly *transnational* force. This was partly a product of technology. The "environment" within which Breivik had shaped his noxious views was of course the Internet, which was a boon to extremism everywhere. Parties were one thing, but an echo chamber of the like-minded was quite another. It was over the Internet that "radicalization" of extreme right views surged forward in the 2000s, to be ignited with the twin crises of financial implosion and rising immigration. In reality it was the problem of marginalization and discrimination, and of feelings of a lack of respect amplified by prevailing social prejudice, that stood behind the rise of extreme right views. It was perhaps not surprising to learn that 31 percent of British National Party voters thought blacks were intellectually inferior (relative to 13 percent of the rest of the British population); what was *more* revealing was that 47 percent thought employers should favor whites like themselves (relative to 12 percent nationally).[56] As much of a problem as the echo chamber of the Internet, therefore, it was a problem of there being no *informed* counternarrative on offer for these people to listen to.

To the extent that this was a function of declining public debate, the problem of the rise of the far right was thus about more than immigration alone. It was also not just limited to countries with particular immigration "problems."[57] In Canada in 2015, an anti-immigrant, anti-Islamic group, *La Meute* (the wolf pack), was founded in Quebec by Canadian armed forces veterans. One of the few countries to buck the trend was New Zealand. This was not because of a lack of domestic far-right discourse: the New Zealand National Front had been founded in the early 1980s as an offshoot of the British National Front. It had to do, rather, with the cross-party defusing of the matter of immigration, and the quality of public debate surrounding this issue. As a result, the Ministry of Business, Innovation and Employment (MBIE) was able to report in 2015 that 67 percent of New Zealanders saw immigrants as *good* for the economy.[58]

The Populist Return

New Zealand, however, was the exception. As the Great Recession bit deeper, most countries were witnessing the resurgence of a more populist strand to politics. This was a new and systemic challenge to the "quiet virtues" of liberal democracy, and the lessons of Breivik need revisiting in its light.[59] Breivik was no neo-Nazi, as many claimed; his actions were neofascist if anything, offering up a purifying nationalism that fused an idealized vision of the people, the *volk*, with the heroic mission of a national community. As he himself wrote, neither the bomb nor the shootings on Utøya were Plan A: the attacks were merely "a sub-task as well as [they were] a marketing method for the distribution of [my] compendium." It was "[g]ruesome but necessary," he acknowledged. But the goal was to get his compendium—his mishmash of inflammatory misunderstandings—out there.

As the success of the Swedish Democrats in neighboring Sweden amply demonstrated, the populism that had marked its entry upon the liberal democratic scene, with the antitax parties launched by the likes of Mogens Glistrup in the 1970s, had now been squarely replaced by a more fervent, ethnic nationalism. This is why comparisons to the 1930s and to the ideology of self-ascribed "saviors" are inappropriate. What was afoot was more nuanced in its expression and responded to a different set of stressors than had inflamed European politics during the interwar years. One parallel did hold up, however, and that was the sense that liberal democratic governments had abandoned their responsibilities (indeed, every time a caretaker government was formed at the behest of the EC this was pretty much what liberal democratic governments were admitting to doing). In light of this it was little wonder that more extreme populist parties emerged that appealed to disgruntled elements of the working class, to those feeling their sovereignty had somehow been "lost," and to those cultural and "identitarian" values that many voters, of all classes, felt the recent embrace of technocracy had resolutely ignored. Little wonder, in light of this, that their impact on the Western political landscape would be out of all proportion to their size.

There were other sources of resentment to be channeled as well. At a time when liberal centrist states seemed not only to be abandoning their citizens to the market but actively binding them into vassalage via the bailouts, a new generation of right-wing populists emerged, who were prepared to ditch their earlier embrace of libertarian free-market doctrines to promote instead the values of what France's FN termed "*préférence nationale*": a protectionist stance that soon found its inevitable echo in the mainstream parties some years after (one thinks of Gordon Brown's "British jobs" line), with its crowning achievement the election of the anti–free trader Donald Trump in America.[60]

But this moment first took shape elsewhere, in Hungary, where Fidesz leader and former prime minister Viktor Orbán swept into power in April 2010 with an unprecedented "super majority" in an election which also saw the far-right Jobbik party take over 12 percent of parliamentary seats. Just two years before, the Hungarian socialists had obtained over 42 percent of the national vote. No longer. Orbán's landslide upended the right–left balance of parliament that had stood since the fall of communism. Orbán immediately used his large mandate to shore up a conservative, antipluralist culture at home and to launch an assault on Western liberal navel-gazing abroad. Yet how unusual, rhetorically speaking, was this? Orbán's overt ridiculing of "liberal blah blah" found a later echo in Blair's dismissal of what he termed "flabby liberalism."[61] That both also championed a Christian foundation to politics was a reminder of the appeal of the more morally tinged platform that each (albeit differently) represented.

The difference, of course, was that Orbán was only too happy to use those aspects of the arrangement that served his purposes, while breezily discarding the rest: as he liked to assert publicly, "the new state that we are building is an illiberal state." Orbán certainly got busy constructing:

his adoption of a formal constitution for Hungary was perhaps long overdue (all other former communist countries having already taken this step). But it was also a way of hardwiring his particular administration's values and worldview into the democratic legal structure of the nation. A subsequent amendment in 2013 pushed things further by restraining the powers of the Constitutional Court, resulting in a pan-European outcry. By then it was perhaps more accurate to say that what Orbán was doing was executing a slide from his own initial, openly promoted idea of "illiberal democracy" to a form of populist autocracy. As he put it, the race was on around the world to rediscover how best to organize the state to make nations successful.[62]

Orbán knew the game he was playing. He had influence in the coalition politics of the European Parliament, which was why relatively few backed up their criticisms with threats of any more concrete sanction (as they had against the Austrian government in 2000). The case against Orbán was only further muddied by the difficulty of drawing a clear line beneath how far was too far. This was ultimately what made Orbán significant: he was only doing what Western politicians had been doing in their droves all along, albeit with a different agenda: he was simply rolling back the state. At the same time, he was squaring off against (by moving closer to) Hungary's own far right, the Jobbik party, whose proto-fascist politics of social decline and national renewal provided the mold within which the state could later be rolled back out again.

Most basically of all, Orbán was also skillfully riding the background wave of popular discontent. He thereby positioned himself at the heart of the two most dynamic trends on the continent: populism and the resurgent far right. Distinct from right-wing extremists, and even from the anti-immigrant parties in the Nordic regions, right-wing populists in central and Eastern Europe centered their politics upon the one collective resource that it was everyone's right to feel had been in some way or other denied them: the nation. Orbán was not alone here. National grievance (and its alter ego, the promise of national greatness) was likewise skillfully being leveraged by Recep Erdoğan in Turkey. As he put it to the Turkish people in 2013: "We are the people!" (and to his critics he added the aside, "Who are you?").[63] Populists had a claimed purity of purpose and a moral agenda (Hungary's fourth constitutional amendment of 2013 added the sanctity of the family as a judicial fact, for example) but above this was a vision rooted in the traditional values of a presumed self-evident national group. In all these respects, this put them at a distinct angle of disinclination from the liberal democratic "politics as technocratic competence" line of the EU. The sphere of contestation in liberal democratic politics was thus moving from the 99 percent of the Occupy movement to the 100 percent of the populists who claimed that they—and by extension no one else—were the real citizenry that mattered.[64] The volume of protest was amped up accordingly.

At the level of states the greatest challenge posed by populism to the European embodiment of the liberal democratic order was not their "exclusionary nationalism"—Britain's peculiarly anti-European sentiments had long been catered for, after all—and variegated opt-ins and opt-outs had been devised for nations ranging from Norway to Switzerland to Iceland to Ireland. It was their antisystem politics and what that implied for a democratic culture that, in Europe, had become deeply bureaucratized as a consequence of the transnational development of the EU.[65]

Europe was now contending with political movements attractive to those frustrated with the perceived failure of existing political parties, and yet who were ultimately committed to using their newfound platforms to *further* peel back the state and its (protective) institutions. If the people who supported these movements did not care about that, then this was in part because they felt that at least their views were now being listened to. And those views always resonated locally—this too was in essence the basis of populism's wider appeal. The populist parties had learned to offer more than just one narrative so as to accommodate those desires. But they still offered always just one *type* of narrative: they dealt in singular "truths," not pluralist ones.[66] The earth was theirs, and theirs alone to inherit.

Once again, populism had its left voices too, of course, and while weaker and less effective, they were not limited to those aging leftists who gazed with misty-eyed wonder at Hugo Chávez in Venezuela. Contrary to the right, left populists were more concerned to *include* than to exclude other groups—but the effect was often to polarize politics just the same. The left too promised the restoration of a mythical "popular sovereignty" and they were no keener to retain "the system" in doing this than were their right-wing counterparts. Many eschewed the idea of holding power themselves, but their critique was sometimes turned against them. Orbán in particular was adept at adapting legitimate critiques of democracy from below, stripping them of their respect for plurality, and then using them as a means of disciplining the demos from above. Democratic arguments could thereby become a step on the way to antidemocratic governments; Austria's Jörg Haider too had long claimed that only he truly embodied the will of the Austrian people. Again, that didn't leave much room for anyone else.

The geography of populism in the postcrisis West was thus a more complex, multifaceted affair than it had been the last time, nearly a century before, it had been a mass phenomenon to be taken seriously. Not least it ranged across the political spectrum. The reincarnated left of Britain's New Labour under Jeremy Corbyn was driven by a grassroots campaign that called itself "Momentum." Others described its members as Corbyn's "shock troops." It was an unfair caricature, but it held enough grains of truth about the group's sometimes egregious overstepping of its mandate to catch on. In Italy, Beppe Grillo's Five Star Movement (*Movimiento 5 Stelle*) was not a consistently populist program, but it certainly had its moments: "Everyone counts for one," wrote Grillo in 2010, by which time it was long since established that, no sooner had the people been counted, than Grillo now embodied their will.[67] That was a sleight of hand willfully misinterpreting how "representative" democracy was intended to function. And it left populist movements surprisingly open to arguments from the far right and far left alike.

What populist discourse ultimately achieved, however, was the same that it always achieves: to encourage hamstrung leaders of the mainstream political parties to retreat to a careless and inflammatory rhetoric. This most usually expressed itself in the form of protonationalism, as politicians moved to head off the more vocal right by trimming sails toward it. In the UK this led directly, via the oversized influence of UKIP, to the calamity of Brexit. In Norway it led to a center–far right coalition that soon set to work unpicking the welfare state and the sovereign wealth fund that in difficult times needed to be relied upon. It encouraged national politicians from Spain to Greece to treat the EU as a repository of blame for any domestic policies they found hard to own themselves: a trend that would reach one conclusion with Euroskeptic parties coming to prominence in the European elections of 2014, and another with the final stand-off in the long-running Greek drama between the radical antiausterity party Syriza, led by former communist Alexis Tsipras.

"New elections change nothing," grouched Wolfgang Schäuble as Syriza surged to victory in January 2015. But this time elections did, and the next six months would see the radical young Greek party, with Tsipras aided by the motorcycle-riding Yanis Varoufakis at the finance ministry, push back at the troika's refusal to deviate from the path of austerity. Syriza had a good dose of global public opinion on their side by now and they were prepared to lock horns. In an effort to show them where the real power lay, the ECB aggressively cut off their financing; the Greeks responded by recording and then making available the negotiations they were subject to behind closed doors. Would the Greeks accept the latest, punishing offer after a new crisis meeting in June? Syriza put it to another referendum to decide. The resounding answer was *Oxi!* The Greek nation had stood firm, but it was growing ever more desperate within.[68]

The Western model of representative democracy thus now found itself under siege from above and below at the same time. From above came the moral hazard of technocratic overreach; from below came the specter of boots on the street. The battle was perhaps most formally joined when, with little fanfare but a certain historical freighting nonetheless, Mario Monti and Herman Van Rompuy proposed a high-level meeting of fellow technocrats to discuss the rise of populism in Europe.[69] Surveying the darkening political atmosphere in Europe in the aftermath of the recession and the euro crisis, the Italian writer Carlo Bastasin was likewise prompted to record his fears. "Many citizens are abandoning the European project, seduced by the sound of nationalist sirens and voicing the anger and frustration of national idols."

What all three recognized was that Europe's broken promises were allowing the voices of the partisans to sing louder. Except that it was not just the promise of Europe that was broken; and it was not just Europe's partisans chanting in its wake. A young Australian writing in *The Spectator* of his own country's technocratic overreach, observed piquantly:

> More often than not, bureaucrats wield real power. The ATO official, the Centrelink functionary, the ASIC apparatchik, even the good men and women—or should that be women and men?—of the Workplace Gender Equality Agency: all of them exert significant authority over ordinary Australians going about their lives. . . . The metastasis of federal officialdom appears unstoppable.[70]

Government "by nerds," said another, was "one step from tyranny."[71] The fightback was entering the mainstream.

The Insurgency Within

When the aging yet prodigious sixties radical, father of modern linguistics, and scourge of the American right Noam Chomsky recorded his thoughts on the gathering of this wider crisis confronting the Western democracies, and the US in particular, the result was a docu-

mentary film entitled *Requiem for the American Dream*. This seemed
unnecessarily downbeat. The situation in America looked rather more
hopeful than it did in Europe in the years after 2011. The American
economy had pulled out of the recession quicker than feared, in large
part because Obama and his team at the Treasury and Federal Reserve
had been prepared to be more pragmatic—more flexible—than the
Europeans, who remained shackled by the dictates of the Stability and
Growth Pact still (and who frustrated the foul-mouthed Geithner no
end: "I completely underweighted the idea that they would just flail
around for three years. I thought it was just inconceivable," he later
said).[72] But few thought it conceivable the US economy might turn
around so quickly either. Perhaps the age of Obama had brought a
sense of hope after all?

Anyone strolling up the steps of Congress and into the House chamber in session would quickly have been disabused of any such thoughts,
however, at least with regard to the political system. For in America, it
was the politicians who had become the partisans. Right from the very
start of Obama's first term, the ideological divisions that had marred
Congress since the early 1990s and the days of the Contract with America resurfaced dramatically after 2008. In trying to understand America
in the years after the financial crisis, the fundamental paradox that needs
to be grappled with is how a political-economic situation that might
well be imagined to have been a boon to the Democratic Party and to
the left more generally (as it had been in the aftermath of the Great
Depression) turned out in fact to be a blessing for the right. This was
not an unalloyed victory for conservatives to be sure: influence came at
the cost of real power. But the fact was that the US political landscape
had been blown apart by war and economic crisis; and the pieces were
picked up and reassembled most effectively on the right.

This was even more surprising given the state of the US Republican
Party. The forced necessity of intervening in the economy had helped to
legitimize many Democratic policies. But for Republicans, the fact that
the American government, under a Republican administration, had needed
to nationalize and restructure some of the world's largest companies and
banks; that it had been forced to oversee a takeover of American Chrysler by a foreign manufacturer, Fiat; that it had needed to break some banks
up and orchestrate mergers of others, and to then step in with the single
largest commitment of public funds in history was not merely a disaster
but an earthquake. Bush stumbled out of office disorientated and forlorn,

perhaps secretly relieved that his wars of choice would now be partially buried beneath the tsunami of the financial crisis. But for his party the troubles were just beginning. Civil war now broke out in the Republican Party.

Obama, by contrast, had entered the White House not so much on a landslide but on something more valuable still: a wave of hope and political ambition. If this was indicative of a deepening popular willingness to reset the political clock, Obama's years in office would in fact play out dramatically differently from the way that he, and perhaps above all those who voted for him, imagined. Before an unprecedented gathering of close to 2 million Americans, Obama inaugurated his presidency by recalling the words of George Washington, calling for "a new responsibility" to meet the "gathering clouds and raging storms."[73] But before the dust had even settled on his eloquent appeal to a nation in conflict, two questions in particular were being asked of Obama the president. First, how could such seeming momentum dissipate so quickly? Second, how different, first from the Clintonites, and then from Bush—against both of whom the senator from Illinois had defined himself to date— would Obama actually prove to be?

The two questions were of course related. First, the Obama presidency lost momentum for reasons beyond the new president's control. Despite Democratic control of both the Senate and the House, Obama confronted a Republican Party entrenched behind a wall of noncooperation from the start of his administration. And with the terminally ill Ted Kennedy's death and the loss of his seat in late 2009 even the nominal advantage of a Democratic congressional majority began to crumble. The last vestiges of Democratic control of the House were then ripped away by the Republican landslide in the midterms of 2010. Obama's honeymoon was soon over but his troubled first term as president owed much to his own choices as well. True to his pragmatic character, the man who came to Washington as the outsider immediately chose to build his presidency by working within the existing system. This was noble, given the spirit of the times. It was also doomed to fail.

The immediate downside of Obama's cooperative spirit was that he ended up continuing many of the unpopular policies of his predecessor. It wasn't just the failure to close Guantánamo. Obama promised to rein in the expansive use of executive power pioneered by Cheney and Bush, but this rang hollow in light of Congress's refusal to work with him and his own, soon-discovered, penchant for governing by executive order (he often had no choice) and to maintaining state secrecy (likewise, given what the Bush administration had set in train). Obama in fact proved to be an even harder securitarian than Bush when it came to punishing whistle-blowing and perceived infractions of patriotic discipline within the federal bureaucracy: not for nothing was his administration nicknamed "the Obamians." And he amplified, rather than scaling back, a program of targeted assassinations. Usually these were carried out by armed drones. But in the case of the raid, and summary execution, of Osama bin Laden in his Abbottabad compound in Pakistan on May 2, 2011, a team of Navy SEALs was sent in to pull the trigger up close.

The promise having been so great it was perhaps only inevitable that Obama would prove both a disappointment to his liberal supporters, and an apostate to the opposition. He had come promising change but encountered, as his speechwriter and White House staffer Ben Rhodes put it, "the world as it is." Within a year of his inauguration, Obama was struggling on all fronts. More surprisingly, the Republicans, who had seemed to write themselves out of national politics in the later stages of 2008, were making a comeback. Rather like a balloon with the air being let out of it, the Republicans after 2008 rode on a wave of pent-up energy.

The Republican resurgence was chaotic and divisive. But it did two things with undeniable force that would soon transform the US political landscape. First it fully broke the neoconservative hold—intellectually and in terms of leading personnel—on the Republican Party. That opened up space for new voices, those with their own support bases at the grass roots, as Sarah Palin with the Tea Party had already shown was a possible route to power. Second it tapped into popular resentments at the cost of the bailout (which while it had been created by the Republicans would be a Democrat administration's problem to deal with) and it succeeded in channeling that anger into opposition. In a close approximation of the situation in Europe, then, the centrist Obama was caught firmly in the crossfire of an assault from within and one from without the American political system. The Republicans' genius, by contrast, was to have now given themselves a voice in both.

It was not, however, a very disciplined voice. And party apparatchiks looked on for a while in disdain, before deciding they had no choice but to throw themselves into the mêlée too. For the likes of Newt Gingrich this was boilerplate wrestling. But the loudly celebrated Republican successes in the midterms of 2010 would prove the calm before the real storm. It would be years before the party finally emerged out of the torrent of forces unleashed within, and all the while its traditional demographic base would be slipping away. New voices emerged as the party settled in to something akin to a domestic equivalent of the multipolar world order. But none could garner the influence to dominate the party as a whole. Despite their success in the midterms and their iron grip on the core domestic policy debate—something that the congressional tailspin of partisan gridlock merely aided—Republicans fared poorly in the general elections to come. But perhaps that didn't matter. Their impact on domestic politics was by then inordinate for a party in opposition.

Things came to a head in 2011. Despite the setbacks imposed by the financial crisis, for more than two years Obama had driven forward an ambitious policy agenda at home and this left him exposed. On one level it was a testament to his political courage: Obama used almost all the remaining political capital he had left after the financial crisis to get the Patient Protection and Affordable Care Act passed. He had confronted a Republican Party more vicious in their resistance even than they had been under Newt Gingrich during Clinton's first presidential term, rousing popular sentiment against what they preposterously called the "death panels" Obama was lining up. They had beaten Clinton then, and in a way Obama used that experience as the template for his own approach, since he did almost the opposite of Clinton. He thus avoided coming up with a detailed plan, but he did move to try and pass something as quickly as possible.[74]

It worked. But no sooner had health care been signed into law in early 2010 than the president was pushing on with reforming the nation's energy mix and overhauling its flawed immigration policy. Both were issues almost as sensitive politically as health care. On immigration, even Obama's faithful adviser Rahm Emanuel believed it would be pushing the Republicans too far. It was "political malfeasance," he said.[75] And the result was that, at the very point when Europe's crisis was reaching its peak, a new fiscal bomb blew up in the US too, with Congress firmly in gridlock over the rapidly approaching debt ceiling: the federally mandated limit of government borrowing whose renewal required congressional approval.

The debt ceiling had been a recurring problem going back decades, and traditionally was simply increased each year as required (running a country tending to become more, not less, expensive over time). In the 1990s, however, in an effort to box Clinton's government programs into a corner, the Republicans had made this pro forma practice subject to

677

congressional oversight. That provided the trigger for a now quite powerfully positioned Republican opposition, in July 2011, to make their move on Obama. With Republicans in control of Congress and the annual borrowing limit approaching, they sprang the trap, the only two options thereafter being a default on the debt (the Treasury would have to stop paying interest on the debt of the single bedrock—US Treasury bonds—at the root of the global financial industry) or face massive defunding of existing federal programs.

Coming not three years after the financial crisis it was a remarkable act of political arson. The demand was conveyed by John Boehner, the new speaker of the House. But Obama refused to blink, so that in the end breaking through the debt ceiling was avoided only by a last-minute deal—the Budget Control Act of 2011. The Act mandated that, if agreement could not be reached over the second tranche of the cuts that had just been committed to in order to trim the budget, an automatic sequester of funds from various government programs would kick in to the tune of $65 billion. It was, in the words of one news outlet, a "fiscal doomsday device," which in January 2012 saw federal bodies like the Defense Department preparing leave notices (albeit they were never sent) for its entire 800,000 civilian workforce.[76]

It was also a perfect illustration of a basic barrier confronting the realization of progressive policies in the United States: that America's fiscal imbalances were almost entirely the fault of the Republicans, yet those imbalances created problems almost entirely for the Democrats (since it was *their* political program that was usually the one requiring money to be spent, and since they had for so long been forced to work within the envelope of the Republicans' fiscal commitments). Even just to get his second post-crisis economic stimulus package passed, Obama had been forced by the Republicans into extending the Bush tax cuts another year: a quid pro quo that sharpened the wider plunge into the red and tightened the timescale on the inevitable fiscal crunch. Furthermore, most of what stood to be jeopardized by such showdowns as the "fiscal cliff" standoff were Democratic achievements, like the emergency employment compensation program.

This was the state of American democracy in the aftermath of the great recession, then. Congress was no longer, if it ever had been, a place where visions were hammered out against the anvil of constituency demands and legislative due process; it was a place where heels were dug in and party lines held aloft like weapons. The solution developed over previous decades to address that failing congressional system, namely recourse to the fiat politics of the Supreme Court, was also a solution that had now run its course—the awkward skein of the "juristocracy," as some commentators took to calling it, unable to paper over the cracks of a failed constitutional structure: something the coming fiasco over the nomination of Brett Kavanaugh would later confirm.[77] A creeping, if for now benign, presidentialism was making headway in its wake.

It wasn't just the main branches of government but the nation itself that was more divided than at any time over the previous half century. America's political class had riven itself in two over a matter, the provision of basic health care for its own people, that was routine in other parts of the world. Income and wealth inequality alike were much greater in the US, which more than any other of the Western democracies had sought over the previous decades to find ways of living without publicly institutionalized forms of collective obligation. Punitive policing and an opioid epidemic were two monuments to that achievement. Voter suppression was another. Obama took it as his presidential mission to try to bring the country together. As he would later, poignantly, say in the wake of yet another shooting incident between blacks and the police: "We are not as divided as we seem." And yet after the constant failure to address the urban crisis in the north and race relations in the south, with every shooting and televised instance of "stop and search" abuse, the country was begging to tell a different story. Obama won reelection in 2012, partly because of the lack of charisma of his challenger, Mitt Romney. It did not mean that everything was going well for the country, or indeed Obama's own administration.

Part of the problem was the gulf that had grown between a national myth rooted in the claim of "we the people" and a political system that had never fully succeeded in accommodating its own rich tapestry of identities and opinions. The identity politics pursued by the American left since the early 1980s had arguably simply exacerbated the problem. So was it fair to expect that, under a black president, from the Democratic Party to boot, political debate might become less acrimonious? Indeed, under Obama, both parties were guilty of practicing noncooperation as a deliberate political art: the laying of deep mines beneath the enemy's stronghold, waiting to be triggered at the next election. Back in the 1980s, Democrats, stung by Reagan's landslide, mauled his nomination of Robert Bork for the Supreme Court; Newt Gingrich then repaid the compliment with interest once he became speaker of the House and the Republicans subsequently "perfected the strategy." As one observer put it aptly: "When the Republican leader of the Senate declares his number one job is to make certain the president's agenda so utterly fails as to doom his reelection chances, you're not starting from a productive place."[78]

The Bush administration had fanned the flames of this process by hitting back at congressional oversight for much of the previous decade, pushing at the legal limits on executive power in an effort to find some form of override switch. But this breakdown in political institutions wasn't just limited to struggles between Congress and the presidency. The Supreme Court too was riven politically—the number of its decisions recorded as unanimous dropping over time, as split decisions (usually with long, scathing dissents attached by the losing end of the bench) became more common. The more fundamental division, however, lay in society itself. It wasn't so much that political views within the populace had become more extreme: hard evidence on that was ambiguous at best. It was the fact that there was no longer a single identity, no "we the people," that anybody could hold up as the appropriate yardstick.

Amplified by the extended reach of new media, the culture wars, meanwhile, leapt back into life as never before, as tirades blared out across the raucous and indiscriminate airwaves of shock-jock radio and Fox television. The tenor of these debates suggested a public and a party system divided along a clear liberal–conservative split. The reality was of a widening array of political sensibilities that did not always coincide along a simple left–right axis. In fact, they did not permanently do anything. Hispanic groups might align with promarket reformists, or join hands with old-style social democrats at one of California's immigration amnesty events.[79] There was movement in American politics, and lots of it. But there was not much sense of direction. Instead there was just a falling away of the center: and this was arguably the Democrats' doing more than it was the fault of the Republicans. After all, it was the strength of a diverse Democratic Party prior to the 1970s that had held the spectrum of American viewpoints together. Its decline and turn to a more monotonic message of middle-class prosperity left America's rebels increasingly without a party to support.

Where there *was* momentum, by contrast, was in the roll-back—already—of the reforms put in place to deal with the financial crisis. Dodd–Frank had belatedly been passed in 2011, along with its famous Volcker rule. But Dodd–Frank contained within its thousands of pages the marker of the many pushbacks and regulatory loopholes the financial lobby had managed to secure. It seemed to suggest that, even after such a shock, the rule of money in politics, and of the lobby that oversaw it, was if anything stronger. By the time Dodd–Frank was signed into law more than 850 businesses, trade groups, and other corporate representatives had sought to bend it to their own interests via the paid intermediary of more than 3,000 lobbyists.[80] The same trend was apparent in the paradoxical prospect of a gun control lobby that grew more powerful even as a series of terrible shootings rocked the nation. The shooting of twenty children between the ages of six and seven, along with seven staff members, at Sandy Hook Elementary School in Connecticut was not the first, and it would not be the last such tragedy. Each one inspired outpourings of grief and renewed debate; but the power of the National Rifle Association ensured that guns were still kept in about a third of all households and the issue remained stubbornly unaddressed.

The true influence of money in politics was most apparent in the 2010 Supreme Court ruling in *Citizens United v. Federal Election Commission*. In a ruling over a take-down film, *Hillary: The Movie*, in the run-up to the 2008 Democratic primaries, the court revisited an earlier decision on financing and free speech, to declare that corporations had as much democratic right as individuals to spend as they wished on candidates' campaigns: its argument, in effect, was that such campaign donations were to be protected as a form of free speech. In a scolding fury the liberal Justice John P. Stevens read his dissent from the bench: it put American democracy "up for sale," he thundered in Brandeisian tones. The title of the ruling, derived from the conservative pressure group that brought the case, was thus nothing if not misleading. It was corporate money and the lobby system that were granted a unity of cause. Not only Justice Stevens but Obama too was incensed, so much so that he took the unusual step of lashing out at the decision personally, in his state of the union address in 2010. And he would have more to say to the court in public again during the long and tortuous decision over his health-care bill before the first term was out.[81]

Yet the president did not himself stand separate to and above the nature of the political system around him. It is an enduring feature of American democracy that its greatest asset, its system of checks and balances, is the very thing that provides the cracks and whorls into which the lobby system, which represents the interests of those with money, can affix itself. Obama's presidency in many ways provided the perfect example of this. In winning the nomination in 2008 he gave no quarter to the Clintons in their Rolodex mastery of campaign support. It meant his administration, once in power, was badly positioned to rein things in. Together lobbying and electoral politicking thus captured the modus operandi of contemporary liberal democracy. The one tapped into new fault lines; the other largely exploited them.

Lobbying and polling together constituted the core techniques of the professional, elite mode of politics that dominated the running of early twenty-first-century democratic life. Increasingly influential and well-remunerated advisers made careers out of an ever-more dynamic inter-action between politics and the people, even as they did little to address real grievances, much less society's structural problems. In his more sober, toned-down 2012 inaugural, Obama pledged to tackle inequality, for example. Yet the fact remained that in 2012, after four years already of an African American president, the unemployment rate among blacks and Latinos was 13.4 and 11 percent respectively, while the national average was substantially lower, at 7.8 percent. Those same groups also still had to wait in line longer to vote in their districts.[82]

The desire to politicize such gaping holes between political promise and social reality was what ultimately—and fatefully—tied together the demands of Occupy protesters with those of the Tea Party. For all their differences, both movements were fueled by the now widespread public distrust of the institutions of government and citizens' loss of faith in their elected leaders. A Pew poll taken in 2013 revealed that approval ratings for Congress had by then fallen to less than 10 percent. When Evan Bayh, a Democratic Senator, retired in 2010 he articulated exactly what many Americans were thinking: "There is much too much parti-sanship and not enough progress," he said. "Even at a time of enormous national challenge, the people's business is not getting done . . ."[83]

In short, what was driving the increasingly temperamental mood in American politics was not so much the failings of government as the seeming inability of government to do anything about those failings. American democracy, and not just American politics, was in gridlock because it had been hollowed out. This was both novel and dangerous. Liberal democracy had always survived its crises in the past by adapting itself to changed circumstances and shifting values. But now the "Establishment"—a term that started to be used more often in Anglo-American political circles, and invariably as a form of censure—was proving itself to be incapable of this. In such situations, the running may often be taken up by others.

★

Were these specifically American complaints, however? The political landscape in Canada was also more polarized than ever before: and in contrast to developments in the United States this *did* take the form of a liberal–conservative split. Just as the US was moving on from the Bush years with Obama, Canada, observed one disgruntled professor, was going the way of the US. "Canadians should get used to a world in which Liberal governments are a thing of the past," insisted another. That they should have to do so was not by chance. This had been the explicit ambition of the Bush-esque, former right-wing lobbyist Stephen Harper, the Conservative Party leader who dominated Canadian politics as prime minister from 2006 to 2015.[84]

During his time as Canada's leader, Harper went so far as to build up the left-wing opposition, the New Democratic Party (NDP), so as to create a more polarized climate in which—he believed—his pro-market policies would dominate. Thereby, went his reasoning, a century of Liberal Party hegemony would be written out of history. He seemed to have got his way with the collapse of the Liberal vote under another professor, Michael Ignatieff, in 2011, under whose leadership the party limped home with just thirty-four seats, forcing the former academic's immediate resignation.[85] The rise of a young Justin Trudeau, the son of former premier Pierre Trudeau, carrying the fortunes of his father's party with him, would soon correct that misunderstanding, at the same time as it brought Canada into the mainstream of "issue"-based politics that now characterized liberal democratic nations more generally. But in some ways, as with the many thousands who had been made redundant during the recession and now returned to work, but work of a lesser status and lower pay, the damage had by then already been done.

Anyone picking up a political magazine or a newspaper could now read calls for Western democracies like Australia to imitate the softly authoritarian island state of Singapore, or for Europe to imitate Switzerland as a pragmatic, managerial "info-state." It was as if the only choice was between political polarization or "enlightened" technocracy. In Australia, the steady arrival of immigrants was being used to whip up a "with us or against us" storm, as if foreigners were terrorists and Australia, as a nation, had any excuse to be making such distinctions. Conservatives saw members of Parliament leave to set up their own more "ideologically pure" parties; independents like protectionist Nick Xenophon surged in the polls. But arguably the most salient political fact (the despicable treatment of asylum seekers in its island prisons aside) was the fact that in 2014 a poll revealed 40 percent of Australians no longer felt democracy was the best form of government to have.[86]

The underlying sentiment was echoed across the democratic West. It was accompanied by a contemporary twist on Mancur Olson's late Golden Age observation that this was somehow what democracy, left to its own devices, naturally resolved to: that without the imperatives of war or revolution people would always end up disagreeing about more or less everything. This somewhat overlooked the extent to which the era's popular political views were now actively being encouraged by those with a vested interest in them: by media companies seeking market share, by politicians looking to turn shallow platforms into election-winning majorities, by political donors seeking a return on their investment.

Observing the liberal democracies back in the middle of the twentieth century the British thinker R. H. Tawney had once written: "Democracy is unstable as a political system as long as it remains a political system and nothing more . . ." For Tawney, democracy, if it was truly to be realized and defended, needed to be embraced as a set of values too. Trust ranked highly among those values, and yet trust—of others, of the political system—now seemed at an all-time low. If anything, it looked as if liberal democratic society had turned its back on the commitments that political trust requires, which is to say of personal sacrifice and political accountability, and that it was merrily heading in the other direction.

Or would means yet be found to bring a measure of accountability?

The Whistle-Blowers

"WIKILEAKS: THEY'RE PUTTING LIVES AT RISK."[87] The words themselves garnered no great smiles. But spelled out as they were, in political cartoonist Steve Bell's rendering, against an emerald-blue sky shading to a dusky yellow, and by a squadron of American B-52 bombers flying in attack formation, a certain tragicomic irony was indeed appended to them. Above all what they captured was the battle that had been joined between governments and a group of young data hackers who did not so much grab as write the headlines, in late 2010, for a consortium of major papers—the *New York Times*, the *Guardian*, *Der Spiegel*, *Le Monde*, and *El País*—who had agreed to band together, to fact-check, process, and to publish them simultaneously.

What the letters therefore also spelled out was the latest front in the war on terror, the battle for the public right to information, which was also now core to the post–financial crisis fallout, and the most recent phase of the struggle over liberal democracy itself. WikiLeaks was something of a dual-edged sword here. For while it certainly gave succor to the populists in their antisystemic tirades at the technocratic elite, it also foregrounded the fact that the politics of knowledge concerned not just its "transparency" but the extent to which it should be collectively owned and discussed. It was a reminder, too, that the politics of knowledge and truth was no longer a nationally circumscribed discussion.

In many ways, the actual story behind WikiLeaks, the group founded by the Australian digital activist Julian Assange, was even more colorful than Steve Bell's drawings. The hypersecretive group first sprang to global attention in late 2010 with the release of a series of documents and video evidence on the US conduct of its wars in Afghanistan and Iraq. The leaks sparked huge controversy (with revelations of unethical conduct and evidence of the true scale of civilian deaths). They also sparked off a global "culture war" that had been brewing ever since security had become the prime concern of Western governments in the aftermath of September 11.[88]

For the post–Cold War "Matrix" generation, WikiLeaks was a literal rage against the machine. Its actions confronted the twin powers of corporate control and government secrecy in the name of a digital commons. To its detractors, however, including the US State Department, the group were little more than destructive anarchists—a nonprofit "charity" gone mad—wreaking a willful, antisocial havoc. For Assange himself, the point was transparency, and exposure was the means to achieve it. "A worldwide movement of mass leaking is the most cost-effective political intervention," as he put it in an early email to the 1971 Pentagon Papers whistle-blower Daniel Ellsberg, for confronting a system of "governance by conspiracy and fear."[89] Assange wanted Ellsberg to become the public face of his new organization; Ellsberg didn't much like what he saw and ignored Assange's overtures.

That was in 2006. By 2010 WikiLeaks had gone its own way. It had not only released an unprecedented volume of classified material into the public domain ("so much . . . that leak hardly seems to suffice as metaphor," wrote *Time* magazine's Barton Gellman, thinking more of a word like "flood"). It had sparked a more pervasive debate about the continued legitimacy of hierarchical structures of power in a Western democracy. Should governments really be allowed their state secrets in the name of the "common good"—could they be trusted to know what that common good was or to handle secrets responsibly? Or was it time for citizens to wrest back a greater say in the running of their lives, and not just in the election of leaders to do that for them?

WikiLeaks framed its actions in terms of "the defense of freedom of speech," and thereby of democracy itself. It was, in effect, a form of left libertarianism—the current moment's answer to the right libertarianism of the 1970s. Assange saw his group's task as updating the conditions of freedom of speech for a heavily mediatized era. This was partly why, for very different reasons, its ambitions were not all that far removed from those behind the Citizens United case, granting corporations, too, the right to partake in a more modern, complex vision of freedom of political speech. But WikiLeaks, for all the controversies that surrounded it, and that would eventually chase Assange into hiding at the Ecuadorian embassy in London on indictment for rape, was challenged most of all by itself. Unable to create a radical equality of information-rich citizens merely by providing some of the materials they might need, the organization turned increasingly from a horizontal supplier of raw information to a rather more traditional-looking editorial outfit, selecting the news it saw fit to print.[90]

The response, by governments around the world, was stronger "floodgates." Ironically, therefore, a culture of state secrecy was compounded by WikiLeaks, not challenged by it, and it pushed Western democracies to pursue more of the apparatus of paranoia that they so strongly criticized in less liberal counterparts like Russia and China. The Obama administration was already committed to continuing the state-run surveillance programs set up under Bush. On being informed in 2009 of Bush's dragnet program of electronic surveillance by Mary DeRosa, the National Security Council's top lawyer, and Caroline Krass, her deputy, Obama reportedly declared himself "comfortable with what you're telling me."[91] The point was not to shut down the program that cost taxpayers billions of dollars, but to make sure it operated within the rules. The means, ends, and ultimate legitimacy of the rules themselves, however, were never brought into question.

But now Obama also introduced something new to the practice of keeping state secrets: a preemptive "crackdown" on any attempts to reveal them. By 2015 the Obama administration had brought three times as many criminal charges against government leakers as all previous presidents combined (in actual numbers, nine compared to three). Was this a sign of a more ruthless president? Not really. It was more the atmosphere of the lockdown and the message it sent. There had been, as the journalist Charlie Savage detailed in his insider account of the administration, no one event that pushed the Obama White House to adopt a more punitive line on state discipline: of equating leaking with treason (the US having no Official Secrets Act, unlike the UK for example); of labeling reporters coconspirators in the act of that treason; of pushing back at the First Amendment protection allowing reporters to protect their sources.[92] What had emerged instead was a culture of fear—mild compared with similar tactics deployed elsewhere in the world, but real nonetheless—that was driven by the administration's own concerns as to what real transparency might do to rock the boat of an already shaken government legitimacy.

That culture soon bore its own victims with it: Bradley Manning, the original source for WikiLeaks, and Shamai Leibowitz were among those whistle-blowers on whom capital sentences were slapped down. Thomas Drake was another, financially ruined securing his own defense. And then there was the most famous of them all. "Lots of Americans were disturbed to learn from Edward Snowden that the government is keeping track of their every phone call and text message," wrote the *Washington Post*'s Steven Pearlstein in January 2014 shortly after Snowden's departure for Moscow, via Latin America. "But they might have also wondered why a thirty-year-old government contractor in Honolulu, with security clearance that was approved by another private contractor, had routine access to some of the government's most sensitive secrets." The answer was because this had been deemed more efficient—though the attractions of awarding contracts to provide for the nation's security to the lowest bidder now appeared in a somewhat different light. After Snowden's revelations, the security company he worked for (Booz Allen Hamilton, one of the oldest government contractors and recently used to run top-security clearance work formerly handled by the FBI) were themselves sued by the US government for "pushing through clearances without sufficient investigation in order to qualify for performance bonuses."[93]

But the bigger casualty in all this was not state secrets, nor even the "truth," though to be sure there was less "routine" information emerging into the light of day than before (and this despite the new trend toward "bulk" dumps of leaked material). What was lost, once again, were the vestiges of trust citizens and their governments relied upon. What remained, after several years of data releases, denials, and acrimonious prosecutions—much of it concerning the as yet undigested fallout of the

9/11 wars—was that governments were seen to be less competent, less reliable, and less honest in their running of the state, while citizens were considered by their governments as incapable of reacting to such unflattering revelations maturely.[94]

This declining sense of trust within society was the background to two further and important developments. The first was that left and right now converged upon a resolutely *antistate* ethos. WikiLeaks and the Tea Party were in that sense not as distinct as they first appeared. This new antistate ethos centered as much on a politics of despair as of hope. "[L]eft-wing disgust at the monopolization of politics by big business interests joins right-wing rejection of big government to celebrate nonpolitical virtue," observed a left-leaning British political scientist.[95] The conservative Ross Douthat noted a similar trend at work in the US: there, as he saw it, leftist critique of big business had joined rightist critique of big government in a politics of us versus them. Democrats, after all, were now closer to big business than many Republicans, while the Republican candidates lining up for the 2012 elections sought to burnish their populist credentials by making a show of looking out for the little man on the street.

Meanwhile voters themselves were growing tired of both wings of the traditional electoral spectrum, both of whom, it was felt, were elites who stood apart (and clear of the consequences) from the difficulties ordinary citizens faced. Americans in particular found themselves in a confusing place. They were antigovernment, but no longer quite so antiregulation—having seen the possible consequences of a deregulated society in the financial crisis. They were concerned about growing inequity but no less inclined to vote for a Republican Party that would lower taxes on the rich further still. They were more riven by racial divides, overlaid and reinforced now by the class inequalities of the recession, than they had been in a generation. They were less swayed by policies that pointed to some notion of the "common good" than those that fitted their own particular worldview. They were more partisan (prior to Bush the partisan divide in presidential approval ratings was never more than 70 percent; under Bush and Obama it was rarely anything less). And they were more divided by age, with younger voters more left wing in their orientation than their baby-boomer parents.[96] But what they were not, in *any* way, was clearer about where to take all of this.

There was no revolutionary spirit, no vision of change, in other words. The mood instead was of a constellation of unnamed fears. This was hardly surprising, given the eagerness with which the state now prosecuted those with the courage of their convictions. Against this, it fell to nongovernmental pro-bono lawyers—the sort who had previously worked for prisoners on death row—to lead the charge for social justice. Thus, it was groups like the New York–based Center for Constitutional Rights, or "crusading" judges like Spain's Baltasar Garzón, who made a name for themselves defending the basic rights and liberties that it was once the privilege of democratic governments to take to the polls. In April 2009, Garzón, who had first come to prominence investigating crimes from the Franco era, before going on to examine his own government's secret war against ETA, filed a suit against the Bush administration for its alleged torture of detainees at Guantánamo. Several weeks before, he had tried to use the universal jurisdiction clause that had seen Chilean dictator Augusto Pinochet extradited and brought to trial to indict six former members of the Bush administration, including ex–US Attorney General Alberto Gonzales.

There was more than a faint echo here of that early 1970s breakout of legal activism of various sorts (long before "human rights lawyers" became the international face of that trend): the moment when, amid Vietnam and the upheavals of the age of Nixon, the political system seemed to fail in America and more effective, reliable alternatives were sought.[97] But then, as now, while the lawyers could secure justice and bring a measure of oversight to liberal democratic governments in the years during which they had run amok, one thing they could not do was to restore the public spirit of the democratic communities that the laws were designed to protect. While citizens may have found some measure of relief in public interest suits seeking to clarify where the line actually lay between right and wrong, between militant democracy and illiberal democracy, they remained profoundly uneasy. So perhaps it was not surprising, after all, that they found themselves listening to promises of salvation from those who would shut out the problem altogether. It was certainly understandable that growing numbers of them wished to retreat behind the ideological ramparts of "secure borders," as if in an effort to ring-fence the gains of the past: to "stop all the clocks" and "arrest that man who said he winked!"[98]

Here then were the roots of the second major trend to play out in the light of declining public trust: the return of a form of national patriotism born of insecurity. In Britain, long before the country's vote to exit from the EU, it began to find expression in the fetishization of national sovereignty and the nation's "islander" status. In France it could be seen in an amplification of a more crusading form of *laïcité* (secularism). It was embodied in the resurgence of national stereotypes pertaining to "lazy" Greeks and "imperial" Germans, as the ongoing crisis of the eurozone divided the continent into a creditor north and a debtor south. The popularity of "Europe" in Spanish opinion polls plummeted from 77 percent in 2010 to just 46 percent in 2013. In France, it fell from 63 percent to 41 percent.[99]

As people hunkered down, walls were everywhere being thrown up: intellectually, institutionally, and even physically. Fences were constructed along Europe's southeastern borderlands; satellites rerouted for surveillance over the Mediterranean. In the US, the governors of southern states talked of bricking up the border with Mexico. In due course so too would presidential candidates. All this may well have been tipped with xenophobia, but it was not driven by it. The simple fact was that people felt insecure. The protections they were calling for, while they disregarded minorities' rights, were at the same time no more than a genuine effort to replace those protections that they felt had been removed from them. It was an exclusionary form of "we" they called for; but there was no doubt that it was some form of solidarity that was hankered after.

And yet even as fences were being thrown up at the borders of nation states, the deepest divides of all were growing—for the first time in four decades—*within* nation states themselves. This was borne out statistically, as newly compiled data began to be published showing how dramatically inequality had returned to the Western democracies. In 2014 a French economic historian, Thomas Piketty, became the most unlikely publishing sensation of the century when his major tome *Capital in the Twenty-First Century* documented how the rich were now doing substantially better than the poor. But it was borne out socially and culturally as well. The former *Observer* editor Will Hutton described the British as "a lost tribe— disoriented, brooding and suspicious."[100]

The fact was that after the bank bailouts and the years of austerity ordinary people were looking for something to blame other than just the bankers. And increasingly they were settling on a whole elite: the "cosmopolitan" class and the barbarians that class had brought, in the form of immigration, to the gate. They felt this all the more intensely because, for a good decade prior to the financial crash, they had been encouraged to believe they were living in a new golden age; a new "belle époque." In fact, they had been living, it turned out, in a gilded age. But it was not just middle Englanders who were inclined to such sentiments:

they were being aired across the Western democracies at large. And the consequences were revealing themselves in a fluid yet pervasive sense of social disaggregation.

In countries like Hungary and Poland, the new dividing lines were drawn along ethnic-nationalist lines. In the UK it was geographical, as wealthy southerners grew further apart from northerners and as calls for Scottish independence resurfaced despite the concessions only recently granted via devolution. In Greece, it was between the radicals, the far-right neo-Nazis, and the anarchists, and a generation of failed mainstream politicians, whose present foibles belied the deep public support that these post-Junta parties—irredeemable symbols of modern democracy—once represented. Scandinavia, with its emphasis on *samhold*, was again doing better than most. But even here new divides were opening up as immigrants gradually set their sights north while governments failed to adjust accordingly. In America, it was between a disenfranchised minority of blacks and Latinos and a majority of whites with the air of a cussed minority: the one genuinely circumscribed, the other merely feeling threatened. That these were tensions mediated through the front lines of a police force too ill-mannered (and ill-trained) to address the problem and which frequently ended up exacerbating it, hardly helped.

It was therefore not only trust that was now lacking but also a belief, at times with good reason, in the underlying sense of justice and fairness that democracies require to nourish that trust. In light of growing social insecurity and anxiety, mixed with a widening gap between the included and the excluded, it wasn't just police forces that were reported to be acting more aggressively; governments hounded out of the country citizens they now labeled traitors; auditors became the nightwatchmen not of better public standards but of litigation by those powerful enough to bring suits. Younger, more utopian voices decried all this, writing fiery books with restorative titles like *The New Zealand Project*. Yet as one reviewer of that particular work put it: was anyone actually listening?[101] Amid the general cacophony the answer was quite possibly no.

All this was the culmination of a process that had begun back in the 1970s in the institutionalization of that era's prioritization of individual freedoms over collective equality. It had ended with freedom itself divided. Politics in this state did not so much allow differences of opinion to be worked out as it tended to reinforce them. Surveying the scene with concern, there was for some the distant echo not merely of the 1970s but of the democratic slide of the 1930s. "Not all efforts to reclaim the private from the political yield successful outcomes," wrote a US historian in 2010, with reference to the 1930s, yet with his eye fixed firmly on the world around him:

> We may want the market but end up with the Mafia . . . we get the informal economy of once public institutions: private police forces, glittering hotels in wasted cities, enclaves of gentrification in urban ghettos. Renouncing the possibility of using politics to shape civil society, we nonetheless inherit politics as force to contain the conflicts we can no longer resolve.[102]

17

Crisis upon Crisis

WHETHER OR NOT it will later be recalled as a crisis of democracy or a crisis primarily of liberal values, in the years that fell between the resurfacing of the people's voice amidst the drama of 2011, and the election of Donald J. Trump in America in 2016, the Western nations were variously reminded of what "politics as force" looked like. Mostly, it should be said, they pulled back from the edge. But exposure to height can itself be enough to induce panic and irrational thoughts. The "Voice of the People," a global opinion poll, revealed in 2006 that, while 79 percent of people still agreed that democracy was the best form of government, only one third felt the people's voice was actually being heard, much less followed, by the authorities in their countries.[1] That left a yawning challenge for politicians: a gap that if it was not bridged by public confidence and political accountability, was likely to be filled by something else.

The distinctive sense of *ennui* that had haunted the Western democracies during the 1990s began to turn, during these later years, first into anxiety and insecurity and then into something more volatile, as citizens gave up on the public ties that bind. In Canada, by 2012, less than half of young people thought democracy any better than other forms of government. As the millennial generation came of age, with no recollection of the Cold War, or of the upheavals that had marked the changes in Western democracy since the 1970s, the question was not whether institutions were being run in the right or wrong way but whether the whole circus of representative rule was worth the bother. An Australian poll in 2016 found that only 42 percent of eighteen- to twenty-nine-year-olds thought democracy was "the most preferable form of government." In America only 30 percent of millennials thought it was essential to live in a democracy. In the 1930s, by contrast, fully 75 percent of people had thought this: not that it was desirable but that it was *essential*.

Of course, it is hardly surprising that with liberal values in a state of flux, the institutions of democracy were coming in for closer scrutiny.

What turned introspection into revolt, however, was the collision of two powerful yet initially independent dynamics that had been building up for several years. On the one hand was the rapidly developing struggle between the forces of liberalism and antiliberalism *within* the Western nations. In countries like Hungary, Poland, and Slovakia self-styled "illiberal democrats"—a new and troubling regime type—were busily consolidating their power and upending liberal democracy in their countries. Indeed, much of what these regimes said—about immigrants, the need for greater social protections for the "little" people, and against the machinations of liberal, technocratic forms of rule—was not all that far from what a great many British, Americans, French, Spanish, and others also thought and were now increasingly saying.[2]

Western governments would not be allowed to wrestle with these problems in peace, however, since they were now confronted as well by a series of *international* crises. All of a sudden the liberal democracies found themselves outmaneuvered not just at home but abroad, as their once lofty ambitions for a liberal international order came crashing down. First came the resurgence of Russia as an orchestrating factor behind a gathering antiliberal surge. Then, for Europeans, came the overspill of a refugee crisis from the Middle Eastern conflict: a serendipitous event, in part, but one that intensified the crisis of liberal values at home. The wider international context for that struggle was one in which Russian and American proxies squared off against each other more directly than they had done since the height of the Cold War; in which the UN Security Council was split down the middle and paralyzed; and in which the balance of power internationally was tracking slowly, but surely, from West to East.

Yet this was no return of a Cold War–style bipolar conflict. For one, the international system, to the extent that it *was* a "system," was far more diverse than it had been during even the late twentieth century. For another, it no longer consisted of states acting alongside other states. Neologisms such as "multiplex" were coined to try to capture this. As with the economy, foreign policy was now something that needed hammering out not just between states acting within international organizations but through a host of those other international actors who had taken root in the upheavals of the 1970s and which had become vastly more influential in the post–Cold War era: NGOs, private actors, and international firms, voluntary and sector-specific organizations.[3]

To the extent that these international dimensions and the new actors defining them were critical, it was for the way that they now added further tension to the insecurity, the sense of reckoning within the Western democracies. The years after 2011, a lot like the years after 1968, had seen a whole complex of crises which needed to be reckoned with and resolved. This new moment of fracture was marked for the Western democracies, already reeling from war and crisis, not by adaptation to the forces of globalization, nor by one singular geopolitical event, but by a gathering distrust in the institutions of democracy itself. The relationship between democracy and capitalism already having come under the spotlight, the effect of this new round of crises was to set that other relationship between democracy and political liberalism in a dramatic and at times uncomfortable light. Long-held taboos were lifted and the political scene became suddenly, radically, more open: just as it last had been in the 1970s.

The antiliberal moment had arrived.

The Russian Return

It was Russia that offered the first, and in many ways the most telling, window onto democracy's travails. The slide toward autocracy in Russia, after the brief democratic opening contrived by Gorbachev, had begun long before Vladimir Putin came to power. It began with Boris Yeltsin, whose last years had seen him resort more openly to rule by presidential fiat (even as the international community seemed less alarmed by this than they were by his drinking).[4] For both reasons, when Yeltsin picked out of relative obscurity the former KGB operative Vladimir Putin to replace him, the Russia he left behind was a mess. Putin was dropped first into the post of prime minister in the summer of 1999 and then, after Yeltsin's "unexpected" retirement at the end of that year, into the role of acting president. Thereafter Putin needed no further encouragement. He made sure of winning his first election in a landslide, in March 2000, by stoking up the threat of Islamic terrorism in the months before polling day, then brutally launching an assault against Islamic "rebels" in Chechnya the better to reap the patriotic vote. It was the hardest-fought election Putin would ever have to win.

As Russia's new leader made clear in his first televised presidential address, he intended to use the authority now invested in him to bring a sense of order and international prestige back to Russian affairs. He gestured only halfheartedly at the rule of law as part of this vision; democracy itself was given even lower billing. For Putin, the law was a cold tool in the service of raw power. He was more strongly motivated by the moral values of an Orthodox Russian patriotism and the discipline of the communist years; and he would never forget how he had watched with dismay from his KGB posting in East Germany as his beloved nation fell apart. As president, two decades later, Putin was at pains to ensure he embodied that vision of a vigorous conservative patriotism— as pictures of him fly fishing and hunting stripped to the waist, or genuflecting before the Russian Patriarch, Aleksy II, were intended to convey.

The most common grievance at the disorder of the Yeltsin years was not Russia's declining prestige abroad, however: it was the oligarchs, the young billionaires who had profited most from the roulette wheel of Yeltsin's post-Soviet casino economy, and whom many held responsible for it. Putin immediately addressed the system that rewarded them for their contacts and their bribes. But he did not outlaw it so much as alter its terms, clearing out those who disagreed with him and who made the mistake of showing it: be it Boris Berezovsky (who fled like many to London) or Mikhail Khodorkovsky (who found himself serving eight years in Siberia).[5] Corruption was not diminished but turned into a tool with which Putin could manage his oligarchic barons: rewarding them when desired, unleashing fraud allegations and tax investigations to hound them out of the country when necessary. For Putin the advantage with this approach was that it played to nationalist sentiment as well, since it allowed him to force out the foreign business concerns—operations like Britain's Shell oil company—who had rushed to do business on the untapped economic frontier with Russia in the 1990s. They now found that the frontier had its own rules.

While Putin was by these means turning the Russian economy into a form of "state capitalism" he was also turning Russian democracy into his own personal puppet show. The two houses of the Russian parliament, the Duma and the Council of the Federation, were subjected to a greater measure of control, beginning in 2003, when Putin's parliamentary bloc "United Russia" gained a majority foothold in the Duma. In 2004 Putin was granted the right to select the leaders of the Federal Republics. That same year the former Soviet states of Estonia, Latvia, and Lithuania were successfully joining up to the EU. Meanwhile, in Moscow, civil organizations now had to register with a new public chamber Putin had set up to monitor and control their affairs. International charities were officially rebranded as "foreign agents." Desirous of labeling this new political program, Putin's advisers willingly came up with terms such as "managed democracy" or "sovereign democracy."[6] It was in reality more accurately described as a form of "illiberal democracy": a system constituted via superficially rigorous elections, yet where liberal freedoms and the rule of law were effectively curtailed.

Journalists who dared to report critically on any of this were given short shrift. By the start of the millennium, the last independent national television broadcaster, NTV, had been taken over by the (increasingly Putin-allied) Gazprom conglomerate. Putin then added to his media arsenal the pro-Kremlin international media house Russia Today, which would interface with Western media to project a glowing image abroad. In October 2006, the journalist Anna Politkovskaya, who had accused Putin of "state terrorism" during the campaign in Chechnya, was shot as she entered the lift in her block of flats. That made her the forty-fifth journalist documented as murdered since the fall of communism, according to the independent Committee to Protect Journalists. For the most part, however, the preferred approach was to subject journalists to constant harassment.

The independent newspaper Anna Politkovskaya worked for, *Novaya Gazeta*, was continually harassed, despite its having a circulation of just 100,000.[7] Another media house, RBC, was taken over by new editors after a string of anti-Putin reports. Counseled on how critical they were now allowed to be, RBC's journalists were told by their new bosses: "If you drive over the solid double line, they take away your license. . . . Unfortunately, nobody knows where the solid double line is."[8] The members of punk rock band Pussy Riot later famously demonstrated what happened to those who willfully veered into the middle of that road, when they were imprisoned in 2012 for gatecrashing a ceremony in Moscow's cathedral to perform a song with the words, "Mother Mary, please drive Putin away." Leaders of any meaningful political opposition danced with death constantly. In 2015, Boris Nemtsov, leader of the liberal opposition, was gunned down outside the Kremlin.

During his earliest years in power, the only thing stopping Putin, it seemed, were the constitutionally imposed term limits upon the presidency. In 2007, the year before his second term was up, he found an enterprising solution to this too. Despite toying for a while, via numerous well-orchestrated "popular" demands for him to continue in office, with amending the constitution directly, he opted instead for installing Dmitry Medvedev as his successor, on the understanding that Medvedev then nominate Putin in turn as prime minister. Here was a Granita agreement, the famous pact by which Britain's Tony Blair and Gordon Brown agreed to assist each other into power, with considerably more bite. With the government thereby under his control, and with the economy surging (thanks to a spike in global oil prices, not because it was in any sense a functioning, productive system—it was still less than a tenth the size of America's) Putin now began to turn his attentions abroad.[9] He had already been given increased leeway here in his ongoing intervention in Chechnya by the United States and the European Council who, for a time, were happy to support anyone in the name of driving out "terror."

Putin did not want Western indulgence, however. He wanted parity: especially after the humiliation, as he saw it, of his country in the 1990s. Putin had also quietly seethed at the liberal democratic cheerleading of the Rose Revolution in Georgia in 2000, and even more so at the Orange Revolution in Ukraine in 2004: a snub to Russia's reassertion of influence over the former republics. In 2007 he began to push back, suspending Russia's commitments to the Treaty on Conventional Armed Forces in Europe. Then in 2008 came the Georgia intervention: the first open use of Russian forces abroad since the Cold War. By 2012, he was back in the presidency, this time with two freshly extended six-year terms before him. Now he could set his sights higher.

In February 2014, Putin pulled off his most dramatic foreign policy gamble yet: the annexation of the Crimean peninsula. The operation was a stunning success that once more took the West almost entirely by surprise. In February, as the Winter Olympics were under way further east on the Black Sea in Sochi, Putin began stuffing troops and reservists into the military bases Russia was permitted by treaty to operate in the Crimean peninsula. With that phase of the operation complete, checkpoints were suddenly thrown up at the two road crossings from mainland Ukraine. Almost overnight the peninsula was sealed off from Ukraine and the Crimean parliament was reconvened with a member of Putin's United Russia party at the helm. Russia had just seized a large part of a neighboring country's territory by sheer threat of force, and in full view of the international community.

To be sure, a large number of Russian-speaking Ukrainians quite openly wished to be a part of Russia. There was little doubt either that the invasion was popular on the streets of Moscow. But Putin's move was unprecedented in the snub it delivered to the liberal international order. What had prompted him to do it? There were numerous factors at play. Facing a growing restlessness at home since he had returned to the presidency kept warm for him by Medvedev in 2012, and under a cloud of corruption scandals, Putin was doubtless searching for a distraction abroad.

In this respect it was an opportunity characteristically seized in a moment that seemed available: no larger strategic ambition was needed, nor was there one, than to snub the West for nationalist gain.

But what also prompted him was the threat posed by the Occupy-style Maidan revolution that had taken hold in Ukraine: a reminder of how fluid events actually were between East and West. For months the Maidan protesters had been noisily occupying central Kiev until, at the start of February, they had forced Ukraine's pro-Moscow president, Viktor Yanukovych, to flee the country when he refused to sign an EU association agreement (the by now routine standard first stage on the ladder to full EU membership). In the spring of 2014, with the memory of the color revolutions of the early–mid 2000s still in his mind (Georgia in 2003, Ukraine in 2004, Kyrgyzstan in 2005), and even more so the Russian version of the 2011 wave of social protests, which in Moscow were directed at the perceived rigging of the legislative elections that year, Putin decided that it was time to nip events in the bud.[10] To move into the Crimea was thus a geopolitical gamble framed in light of Putin's ongoing dismemberment of democracy at home.

For the West the rise of Putin's Russia posed a number of challenges. First his Crimean annexation plunged Russia and the Western powers to new lows in their post–Cold War relationship, since intervening in other nations was a right that the Western powers preferred to reserve for themselves. Second it opened up deeper splits in a transatlantic alliance already strained after the Iraq War. What was Europe doing about Ukraine (and Syria for that matter) so far as the US was concerned? "Fuck the EU!" was the answer of Victoria Nuland, the US Assistant Secretary of State.[11] Given the ongoing aftershocks of the financial crisis, the standoff could hardly have come at a worse time. This was a moment when economies needed opening up to one another, and when the imbroglio in the Middle East—the Syria War having by 2014 become a much wider geopolitical flash point—needed careful diplomacy not tit-for-tat baring of geopolitical teeth. The West needed to be working together as one, but individual countries were increasingly tempted to strike out on their own.

At the same time, Putin's actions were as displeasing to the Chinese (who preferred authoritarianism to be conducted in a more orderly manner, and who abhorred the upsets that his adventurism caused on the global markets) as they were to the West.[12] The Ukraine intervention thus ultimately served to reveal the extent to which the new world order was a multipolar one and that the West's claims to sit atop that system were but one of a series of competing claims. Above all it exposed the West's own imperial rhetoric—of bombs for peace—that had long been used to justify its international encroachments. When Putin meddled against "terrorists" in Chechnya he could point to the actions of George W. Bush in Iraq. When he invaded Georgia, he got nearly everything he wanted in the peace deal he brokered with Europe because Nicolas Sarkozy was desperate to burnish his spurs as an international statesman. When he cracked down on media reporting in Russia he could point to the treatment of whistle-blowers in the US, publicly welcoming Edward Snowden to Russian soil in a coup de théâtre he visibly enjoyed.

The only Western politician to really call Putin's bluff was Angela Merkel, who Putin wrongly calculated would fold in the face of his threat to shut off Russian gas supplies. Merkel did not fold. In fact, the sanctions regime she helped to place on Russia bit harder than any other reprimand Putin had received from the West. But in some ways the horse had already bolted because the real threat posed by Russia at this point was not the geostrategic one; nor even was it the way that Putin was arming government forces in Syria against the Western-backed rebels. The greater threat was that Putin's successful creed of antiliberal politics might just begin to catch on at home.

Turkey was another state using the struggles of the Western democracies to present a more "decisive" alternative to liberalism in the near abroad. In 2014 Recep Erdoğan, who had served as prime minister since 2003, assumed the office of president. Like Putin he had merged democratic procedures and national populist sentiment shrewdly, gradually ring-fencing his own powerbase against the media and political opposition. In the summer of 2016 there was a highly convenient coup attempt, believed by many to have been staged by Erdoğan, that provided the alibi he needed to orchestrate a crackdown on his political opponents. Several hundred would-be conspirators died in a night of tense flare-ups, and several thousand military personnel were arrested by state security, bringing the last remaining alternative seat of power in Turkey to heel. Erdoğan then pushed through with a long planned constitutional reform package, abolishing the office of prime minster and converting the country from a parliamentary into a presidential system. In the spring of 2017, under the auspices of an open referendum, Erdoğan and his ruling Justice and Development Party claimed victory. Erdoğan moved to reinstall the death penalty and looked forward to remaining in power until 2029. Even Putin could not fail but to have been impressed.

For all the hopes raised at the start of the millennium that the future heralded an era of gradually opening borders and the expansion of liberal democratic norms around the globe—that liberal blueprint that had so recently seemed so self-assured—the reality was fast turning into something else. Turkey and Russia were two nations that happened to most closely encircle—historically as much as geographically—the Atlantic core of Western liberal democracy. But by the mid 2010s it was hard to see them just as errant exceptions to some benign liberal norm. Larger authoritarian forces lingered further offstage, in China above all, whose economic influence over the US in particular meant that the Western democracies had already been forced to acknowledge the *right* of these authoritarian alternatives to exist. This was one major source of difference between the current international climate and the Cold War of old. The struggle was no longer between communism and capitalism as two universal systems that each claimed to be the only viable political order. Now the struggle was between multiple forms of capitalist regime, only some of which were democratic, and fewer still were properly liberal.

Given the prominence and the belligerence of Russia in this antiliberal wave, in Washington and the capitals of Europe the value of the NATO alliance began tentatively to be explored once again. Formed back in 1944 NATO had already reinvented itself once, in the years after the Cold War, as a force for international stabilization: the outer guard of the transatlantic liberal order and a tool for expanding that order as well. Now it turned defensive again. In 2014 the chairmanship was given over to Jens Stoltenberg, Norway's former prime minister. Stoltenberg was a safe pair of hands to back up the economic sanctions on Russia imposed by Europe and the US in particular, and the Americans were careful to install a fluent Russian speaker, Rose Gottemoeller, as his deputy. NATO would later go further and expel Russian diplomats from its own offices in response to evidence of Russian state involvement in the poisoning of former agents living in the UK.

But in truth, the risks of failing to meet such challenges were not military but political in the first instance. And those challenges themselves were as likely to be found now *within* NATO's bounds as they were beyond. The European and American far right, in particular, were emboldened by what they saw in the gathering force of illiberal if nominally democratic regimes such as Russia and Turkey. Increasingly, as with the Front National in France, Europe's right-wing movements were funded by them as well. In public they voiced their support for democratic values still, while privately they began to dream how a firmer hand might assist their long frustrated political programs.

Despite having been a member of the EU since 2004, Viktor Orbán in Hungary, as we have seen, had already quite openly rewritten the Hungarian constitution. Since then he had also reformed the civil service law, allowing him to put party hacks in ostensibly neutral bureaucratic posts. As with Putin, Orbán had further hitched this populist platform to the promise of an authentic nationalism that could meet the twin challenge to Hungarians of liberal decadence (coming from Europe) and Islamification (coming from the migrants now streaming into Europe across Hungary's borders). And as with the pretext that America's adventurism in Iraq gave to Putin in Georgia, so too were some of Orbán's less palatable suggestions—like removing refugees to "camps" offshore in North Africa—given a degree of political cover by the fact that such ideas were also being considered by more liberal European governments.[13] The truth was, the European Parliament's largest political bloc, the Christian democrats, had been excusing the antagonisms of their more outspoken member for years.

By the mid 2010s there were indications that the slide to authoritarian nationalism was picking up elsewhere as well. After Hungary, it was the turn of Romania to begin dismantling some of its democratic checks and balances. Perhaps this was predictable given its checkered postcommunist history. But Romania, like Bulgaria, where there were equally ominous signs, was (since 2007) also a member of the EU. So too, since 2004, were the Visegrád nations, where one of the refrains increasingly to be heard in public debate was that the multicultural model behind Western identity pluralism was "broken." There was a ring of truth to this: multicultural tolerance was certainly not flourishing across the West. But that was partly because it was so rarely defended.[14] Now this failure of the liberal imagination was turned back upon the West. By rejecting the inauthenticity of any sort of expert, judicial-type solution, citizens could be directed instead to more *authentic* (and more exclusive) visions of nationhood.

Next it was Miloš Zeman, President of the Czech Republic, who began probing the limits of what was possible *within* the European Union. Zeman not only sanctioned the "hate-mongering" Bloc Against Islam in his country, he attended one of its antirefugee rallies, on the twenty-sixth anniversary of the Velvet Revolution. In neighboring Slovakia, left-leaning Prime Minister Robert Fico helped to sanction such behavior with his own antiimmigrant sentiments—"there is no space for Islam in Slovakia," he said—while Marian Kotleba's Nazi-sympathizing far-right party won fourteen seats in the 2016 elections (he would later be charged with extremism).[15] Remarkably, these were countries that were once the shining examples of the postcommunist transition to democracy. Hungary and Czechoslovakia had been the liberal front-runners in that now distant moment.

So too, even more significantly, was Poland, one of the largest and most central members of the EU. In Poland, the Catholic Church had been bent to the ear of the dissidents in the 1980s; now it was deployed in support of more conservative national visions. In 2015 Poland's newly elected Law and Justice Party of Jarosław Kaczyński also took to rewriting the constitution in a less liberal direction, excising individual freedoms in the name of cultural conservativism and greater state influence over the courts and the media. Why did social progress have to be in the direction of "a new mix of cultures and races, a world of cyclists and vegetarians?" Polish foreign minister Witold Waszczykowski demanded to know. For good measure Kaczyński then whipped up a storm of recidivist fervor, excoriating independently minded Poles (journalists in particular) as "Poles of the worst sort . . . [Poles] with treason in their genes."[16]

This was a challenge not just to media freedom in Poland, but to the EU's political values of "justice, freedom, and security" more broadly. How could it possibly stand? To the extent that liberalism and democracy could now be spliced quite effectively apart the answer was perfectly well. In the modern era, it would not wash—least of all within striking distance of the "bloodlands" of Eastern Europe—to announce oneself as a fully fledged autocrat. But by ceding the distinct values of liberalism and its Western institutional architecture, its superfluity of rights instruments and its endless talking shops at Davos and TEDx-appropriated town halls, by returning what was not needed to retain power, in other words, and by holding on instead to the bare rhetoric of democracy—which for all it was practiced as a form of popular nationalism, retained the cachet of political legitimacy—would-be authoritarians had found a way to organize themselves as antiliberal parliamentarians.[17]

Neither a reprise of early twentieth-century fascism nor a "slide" back into mid-twentieth-century totalitarianism (the two discourses of critique liberals had retained from the Cold War era), the polities in which the antiliberal surge sank its deepest roots thus espoused the core values of democracy—sufficiently neutered—while doing away with liberal freedoms and political equality. The balance between freedom and democracy that Western liberal democracies had struggled for forty years to maintain was now rejected altogether. Capitalism was retained as desirable; democracy was reduced to the role of necessary institutional interface. For its part, liberalism was divided: market liberalism, and such legal artifice as was required to sustain an executive over and above it, was retained; the political liberalism of democratic institutions and civil rights and the social liberalism of diversity, tolerance, and fairness were discarded. The liberal democracies had agonized for decades over how much of the one (democratic equality) could be reduced in favor of maximizing the other (liberal freedoms)—the road along which these calculations were made carved by the imperatives of capitalist growth. Now they were being shown where the end of that road was to be found, by those polities prepared to experiment a lot more radically.

Remarkably, the actions of these antiliberal regimes received only a mild ticking off in the broadsheets of Western Europe, preoccupied as it was still by the fallout from the financial crisis. Meanwhile right-wing populists like Marine Le Pen and Norbert Hofer applauded a little more vocally than they might have dared before. By turning the liberal democracies' inflationary rhetoric of individual rights against them, by adopting their half-truths of political spin, and drawing attention to their own injustices of social exclusion and "needs must" austerity, the leaders of the antiliberal surge had made it hard for the West to criticize them. Like the prizefighter who hugs his opponent to keep inside of his most powerful hooks and uppercuts, twenty-first-century antiliberals rendered themselves immune to the criticism of the West. Their novel brand of antiliberalism was all the more potent precisely because it was located right under liberal democracy's stumbling embrace. But it was not the only antiliberal force of the moment. Similar currents were emerging elsewhere.

Democracy in Retreat

By the time Obama's second administration was drawing to a close, the war on terror was more than a decade old; Vietnam was beginning to look like a limited conflict in comparison. Had there been any progress? Obama had succeeded in shutting down the US occupation of Iraq to focus on Afghanistan. He had also begun drawing down the number of US troops on the ground, in favor of a counterinsurgency (COIN) strategy that more accurately acknowledged this was no war of state-based armies. But the conflict had also changed shape. Obama having been at pains to excise all official references to the phrase the "global war on terror," it had become instead an amorphous "everywhere war," one that permitted a silent escalation in both the scale and lethality of operations (for all that Obama, the Nobel laureate, continued to speak the language of perpetual peace). This made success and failure alike harder to judge. Above all, it made it difficult to imagine there being any end to the war in sight.

With hindsight, the turning point was the kill or capture mission that finally "got" Osama bin Laden. Thereafter public engagement in America's deployments of military force abroad waned and, the leaking of classified materials notwithstanding, the military found it easier to get on with their work under less scrutiny. Combating Islamism now became more or less synonymous with the running of a global police operation. And while there was certainly little to be admired in a radical Islamic political theology that banned all talk of human rights, that held conflict to be a sacred act and women a threat to public morality, the manner of the Western assault against it had become the beginning of a slippery slope toward illiberal positions at home. Given the antiliberal challenge brewing offstage all the while, this was to prove a fateful conjuncture.

There were different reasons for the slide. The targeted killing program that Obama escalated was a function of the new technology of military drones that began to be used in 2006. But it was equally a function of Obama's campaign commitment to reducing America's troop presence in the Middle East—which required that it was replaced by some other form of "forward" pressure, as military strategists say. Legal doctrine, as we have seen, had long adjusted itself to the lack of a clear dichotomy between war and peace, but military "pressure" that was not "war" was a further step into the dark. Obama had sought to square the circle of these commitments with his robust defense of the "just war" doctrine delivered in bold defiance at the award of his Nobel Peace Prize in 2010. In doing so he certainly showed himself a more thoughtful commander-in-chief than his predecessor, not to mention his successor. But he ultimately refined, rather than resisted, the use of lethal force. Moreover, his twentieth-century justifications were increasingly out of date.

As plenty of aides attested, Obama was "not squeamish" about the use of force in pursuit of American interests. But in this perhaps he was simply of his time. For whether or not the public any longer bought the military's claims that drone strikes were surgical, and that they allowed the precision targeting of ringleaders in the fight against terrorism, the reality was that such attacks were largely uncontroversial (for all that they fell in many instances not only outside the moral boundaries of the laws of war but outside war zones themselves). Obama had a legal code drawn up to cover the program but this scarcely addressed the issue. That there was considerable public acceptance for the government's "kills lists" was hardly a comforting fact either. Extrajudicial detention under a state of exception declared by Bush had slid, under his successor, into extrajudicial killing by what was once again an openly "exceptionalist" state.

The ongoing silent escalation of America's struggle against radical Islam thus continued apace as the nation's "lethal bureaucracy" expanded after 2008.[18] By 2010 the United States was spending over $60 billion annually on drone R&D and procurement. By 2012 there were over 354 confirmed strikes in the Pakistan border territories alone, with at least 2,500 casualties—one fifth of which were civilians. The geography of these strike zones was not surprising: the areas where international law was at its patchiest were also the areas where targets could be most easily eradicated by a Predator or Reaper drone—Federally Administered Tribal Areas (FATA) in Pakistan, Gaza, Yemen, Somalia, Afghanistan, Libya, and Iraq. But as the war on terror expanded into Africa, and other parts of the world, as the number of "foreign terrorist groups" the US claimed to be fighting grew (from twenty-eight in 2002, to forty-four in 2009, to sixty-one by 2017) the rut became that much harder to escape from. The investigative journalist Glenn Greenwald had it right when he delved into the details of all this. "At this point," he wrote in 2014 in the *Intercept*, "it is literally inconceivable to imagine the US not at war." The administration did not disagree. Its highest representatives now spoke openly, and in strategic terms, of a "generational struggle." As Leon Panetta, the former secretary of defense, observed: "I think we're looking at kind of a 30-year war."[19]

Already, however, the geography of this interminable conflict was coinciding with political developments closer to home. In 2011, much of North Africa had turned away from the optimism of the Arab Spring and was now in the midst of a "bloody and inconclusive" winter.[20] Now came yet another antidemocratic backlash: and yet another challenge, coming out of that moment, for the Western powers to try to address. Libya, where NATO forces under the command of the French had intervened on humanitarian grounds, was caught in a tense stalemate between revolutionary forces and political factions. Civil unrest was intensifying in Syria too. But unlike in Libya, there would be no intervention in Syria, "humanitarian" or otherwise (there would however be substantial humanitarian *assistance* provided). Together, the Russians and the Chinese, two of the five permanent members of the UN Security Council, had drawn a line in the sand after what they interpreted as the mission creep of a humanitarian intervention turned state-building exercise in Libya. Cruise missiles rained down on the former; a deathly silence held over the latter: and Bashar Assad, the Syrian president, was not one to let such an opportunity go to waste.

By 2012 Syria was embroiled in a bloody civil war, its death toll counted in the tens of thousands and rising fast. Egypt was again controlled by the army; Bahrain was back under the thumb of King Hamad. Libya was an unstable and divided nation of powerful militias. Impoverished and tribally racked Yemen was a new and bitter front in the war on terror and the site of intense American drone atacks. At this point even Tunisia's more irenic Jasmine Revolution hung precariously in the balance, while leaders who remained in power in countries like Saudi Arabia and Morocco were clearly hopeful that the limited reforms they had agreed to would be enough to buy off dissent. What had gone wrong? Western leaders understood it as a failure of these countries to adopt individual liberal values: it was as if they were hemmed in by a cultural flaw that no amount of bravery by the young could correct for. More likely was a failure of Western realpolitik that refused to acknowledge the long histories of sectarian politics exacerbated by decades of colonial rule.

This was one reason why the short-lived promise of a moderate Muslim leadership in the region, in the form of the Muslim Brotherhood, was snuffed out and the Egyptian army were able to regain control. Just as Iran's potentially more positive role as a regional Islamic hegemon had, since 1979, been kept dogmatically (and unconstructively) in abeyance, so too was this opportunity to allow a more balanced political patchwork to take shape in the region thrown away. "The protesters wanted a better world," observed the German journalist Michael Lüders ruefully. "They got [Egyptian military president] Sisi and Islamic State."[21] But as the conflict in Syria from 2011 would underscore, the basic misconception that had informed Western policy in the Middle East since the 1970s was in no danger of standing corrected. It was, rather, about to witness its bloody confirmation.

The popular uprisings that had begun in early 2011 in Syria, and the government crackdown that followed, quickly assumed a strongly sectarian character (a product of Bashar al-Assad, an Alawite, having continued his father's approach of bribing the Sunni middle classes with trading and business privileges). No sooner did the conflict in Syria turn sectarian than Assad cracked down brutally and the violence escalated. The Western media reported that Assad was fighting a "moderate" or "civil society" opposition. In truth what he confronted was a ragbag of self-serving local militias. Western powers insisted on arming such groups, something that Russia and China, still smarting over Libya, did not appreciate at all. Before long Syria had become the sort of proxy war more characteristic of the Cold War than of the twenty-first century, with one half of the permanent members of the UN Security Council (Russia and China) arming the government, and the other half (Britain, France, and America) arming the "rebels."

In fact, Western aims—with the support of Turkey and the Gulf Arab states—were more self-interested than the staged humanitarianism of their "assistance" was intended to show. For what they sought, despite all the denials, was regime change: to cleave Iran from its one major ally in the region, and to deprive Putin of an important entry point into the Middle East. Putin, of course, was all too aware of this (and if he wasn't he soon had Hillary Clinton, as Obama's Secretary of State, reminding him he would "pay dearly" for supporting Assad). The Iranians knew full well what was going on as well—and they rightly predicted, when their presence at the second of two UN peace conferences held in Geneva in early 2014 was denied, that the talks were doomed to fail. Amid "extraordinarily ill-tempered scenes" they duly did.[22]

Western policy in Syria was naive, then, but it was also self-defeating. On the one hand, by insisting that Assad had to go they closed the door to the sort of diplomatic solution that only a few brave voices like the British humanitarian Alex de Waal, with experience of ethnic conflict, were saying was the only possible solution. That in turn allowed Assad to outfox them, willingly giving over the arid northeastern expanses of his country to the rebels while he dug in and kept his grip firmly on the economically valuable southern and coastal areas instead. On the other hand, the Western powers were so set on getting US troops, though not military bases, out of the Middle East that they continued to let a bad situation fester. For Obama in particular, removing those troops had been his campaign promise. This was affirmed in his West Point speech in 2009, when he insisted that Afghanistan was not another Vietnam. But the matter of just where, exactly, he would finally reveal his much maligned "red lines" over Syria to stand became, for a while, a running joke.

Yet it was a tragic joke all the same, because Obama's refusal to put US troops on the ground ultimately brought about the West's next great adversary in the region, and the most drastically antiliberal force yet: Islamic State.[23]

The Islamic State in Iraq, as it initially called itself, had emerged in the late 2000s as an assortment of disgruntled and frustrated former officers, soldiers, and security personnel from Saddam's regime, combined with inmates of the American-run prison system. To begin with they confined their activity to Iraq. It was the complete collapse of the Syrian state next door that allowed the group to expand, to draw in a mass of Sunnis, angered by the fighting there, and to begin receiving financial support from wealthy Arab state backers who had funded nearly every Wahhabist-type regime over the previous two decades (and yet which the US refused openly to condemn).

The group soon felt confident enough to rename itself Islamic State in Iraq and Sham (*Sham* being the Levant). Led by Ibrahim al-Badri (better known as Abu Bakr al-Baghdadi) ISIS made spectacular territorial gains across Syria such that, by the summer of 2014, it had officially declared itself a transborder Caliphate. With its sophisticated control of media, the group now outshone al-Qaeda as the most important anti-Western radical Islamic movement. And it grew only stronger, not so much despite the aerial strikes carried out by the United States, but because of the ongoing policy of arming proxy fighters in the region—the so-called "good jihadis," who were to be sent out to battle the "bad" ones, but who just as often ended up turning either themselves or their expensive weapons systems over to the distinctly more effective fighting force that was ISIS.[24] At the same time, ISIS drew in thousands of young and angry Muslims across the Western world, from as far away as London and Sydney.

Aside from the general revulsion that the group and its carefully curated television footage evoked in liberal households across the West, the real consequence of the rise of Islamic State was threefold. First, it shone a light on the utter failure of US policy in the region, which for all the multiple conflicts and peace processes had not fundamentally changed since the 1970s. Keep the Saudis and their vast oil reserves on board (despite the fact that nearly every group the US found itself fighting in the region was inspired by the Saudi brand of Wahhabism); support Israel (no matter how much suffering it inflicted on the Palestinians and howsoever its knee-jerk militarism provoked other powers in the region); and keep Iran firmly locked out of the picture on account of its largely noncommittal nuclear ambitions (regardless of the fact that Iran was the best available regional counterweight to the disruptive forces of Saudi religious hegemony). These were the three flawed pillars upon which so much American blood and treasure had been lost over the course of three decades, and because of which flowed the growing counterforce of anti-Western sentiment. At its root was less the religious extremism of the Muslim faith than the no less politicized work of the Israel lobby in the United States and of the characteristically Christian inability to understand other world religions as equal in politics as well as faith.

The second consequence was the way the Western powers were held in abeyance over Syria. In the course of 2014 alone, Putin not only blocked the Western powers over the Middle East, he also set up his own parallel system of no-fly zones and aerial strikes, and he had moved to expand his influence in Central Asia via intervention in Ukraine. Coming as it did so close on the heels of the financial crisis (which had already expanded the international franchise from the G8 to the G20) this merely confirmed the wider shift in the international political order, away from Western supremacy. That shift had been exacerbated, rather than resisted, by the geopolitical overreach of the ongoing war on terror, and by the failure of Obama in eight years successfully to unravel it, though at times he had tried. But this was not all the West had to worry about. As the death toll in Syria leapt into the hundreds of thousands, Europeans were about to come face-to-face with an exodus of refugees from the conflict, which had overwhelmed the capacity of neighboring Lebanon and Turkey to absorb.

It was here that ISIS posed its third, and ultimately most significant, *political* challenge. ISIS was the clearest attempt by a modern political movement yet—clearer even than fascism during the interwar era, albeit less successful—to force a rigid political identity upon its subjects. But it had most in common with the antiliberal authoritarianisms growing up under the liberal democracies' own wing. It was more extreme, of course: with ISIS there was no middle ground, no diversity, no tolerance of pluralism; much less was there any sense that the Caliphate's political identity was open to change. It posed itself (falsely since it was very much a product of its time) as a timeless polity gathering in its flock, via *Hijrah*, from across the world. But in reality, there was conformity, or there was death. It was the religious countercall to the favored cry of midcentury revolutionists: *Socialismo o Muerte!*

Yet perversely, the extremes hid something that ISIS held in common with more secular antiliberals as well: for this vision was based on the political regulation and censure of identity—the primacy of a politics of identity and self-realization being a central strand to liberal politics since the break with the postwar era. ISIS claimed God and a universal righteousness the way populists claimed the nation and its bloodlines: which is to say, exclusively and for themselves only. Yet the temptation to censure was there within democracy as well. After all, as Bush had begun the war on terror by declaring, either you are with us or you are with the terrorists. Quite how the "us" was to remain an open and tolerant identity in that arrangement was never especially clear. The tensions that such a worldview gave rise to, however, were soon clear for all to see, as the next crisis to engulf the Western democracies now struck in the form of refugees spilling out of the battle zones of the Middle East.

The Limits to Europe (the Refugee Crisis)

In the summer of 2015, amid appalling images of people clambering half-drowned out of inflatable orange dinghies to be herded into makeshift camps, the image of a Syrian toddler, Aylan Kurdi, photographed lying facedown in the sand, his lifeless arms lapping uselessly at his sides, not only went "viral," as people now liked to say: it announced the pinnacle of a moral and existential crisis the Continent had not witnessed in decades. Along with endless lines of the desperate and the distressed, razor-wire fences were once again being thrown up on European soil, and once again people were dying in the effort to get across. Now military-grade "rescue" boats were being used to deter the flows of people taking their chance across the Mediterranean, forcing them to take more precarious routes instead. Some of this was brought to the attention of European citizens, including reports of the more than 800 people who died when their boat capsized off the coast of Libya—the worst ever modern disaster on that sea.[25] But much of it went unnoticed: as when a refugee encampment outside the Spanish enclave of Melilla in northern Morocco was forcibly cleared by Moroccan police, resulting in several would-be migrants dying before they had even, properly speaking, had the chance to set off.

All told, well over a million refugees crossed into Europe in 2015: a human train that arrived not just by sea but by land too (through Turkey and the Balkans mostly, until the cold shoulder they received nudged them into longer, harder routes across the mountains to the north). On their way they unwittingly provided antiliberals like Erdoğan and Orbán with succor in their hardline calls to political order. The influx of people was more than four times what it had been the year before, and 100,000 of them were unaccompanied minors. European nations had been struggling to deal with the growing number of economic migrants even before the refugee crisis (many of whom a just immigration regime would have categorized as economic *refugees* anyway). But the march of bodies in 2015 was unprecedented. The current wave came from three primary sources: Syria mainly, followed by Afghanistan and Iraq. The Western democracies were scarcely without blame for their plight; as the UNHCR's António Guterres pointed out, two-thirds of all the world's refugees were Muslims.

As the scale of the crisis hit home, calls for a "comprehensive, long-term strategy" were voiced across the liberal world. Few were surprised when the response proved as piecemeal as that wrung from leaders at the height of the euro crisis four years before. In part, this was excusable on account of the highly *uneven* flows of refugees, with the vast majority arriving in the south, whose countries were if anything much less well equipped to manage than more northerly states such as Ireland, where the deal that governed how they were to be dealt with, the Dublin II accord, was struck. Countries including Ireland and the Visegrád nations proved predictably reluctant to share the burden of asylum applications. In 2015, 476,000 asylum claims were lodged in Germany; just a few thousand in Great Britain and Portugal.

It was obvious what refugees wanted, however: they were desperate but not stupid, as the uneven geography of asylum claims suggested. Against an EU average of 260 asylum applications per 100,000 of the population, the greatest number by far, excluding Hungary, which was simply the nearest port of call, went to Sweden (1,667), Austria (1,027), Norway (602), Finland (591), and Germany (587). Poland and Spain by contrast each received just 32 asylum claims per 100,000 of their domestic population. What the refugees wanted was host countries with still-functioning and generous welfare protections, where there might be some hope of a job, and a life to replace their old one, and where the gap between the wealthiest and poorest in society was not as stark as it was in a country like the UK, which received a low volume of applications despite the political rhetoric (just 60). That way they stood a better chance of integrating and achieving a moderate standard of living, starting as they would be from the very bottom. It was the same calculation made by economic migrants during the last years of the postwar economic boom. However, circumstances could hardly have been more different.

If the British public had been fully aware just how unpopular a choice their nation was they might have been piqued into presenting a more generous face. As it was, the sheer volume of overall flow was what captured headlines and featured in the soundbites of politicians on the make. Inevitably the pressure soon began to raise tensions *between* European states as well. Plans for a formal quota system were pushed by Germany's Angela Merkel but routinely rejected by Britain's David Cameron. Given the UK's active involvement in the Syrian conflict, and the scale of displaced persons it had created, Cameron's commitment to settle 20,000 Syrian refugees over the next five years was as insulting as it was shortsighted. But he was not the only national leader reluctant to open his country's arms. François Hollande was no better: as winter arrived in 2016 he ordered the "Jungle," a camp where 10,000 refugees sheltered from the cold, to be disbanded before the end of the year.

The "Jungle," racially overlain as that description was, in many ways provided the most telling image of a Continent that seemed to have lost its way. A forty-acre encampment of tents pitched onto a former landfill site outside Calais, it had provided a home, of sorts, to displaced persons since the mid 1990s, as desperate refugees from Iraq's Kurdish minority and from Afghanistan arrived there seeking a way to Great Britain. Sangatte as it was then called was closed—at British behest—by the French in the early 2000s. But with the influx of refugees from Syria it had reopened again as an informal encampment. It was a reminder, if any were needed, that not everything was new in this crisis. It also showed that the Jungle was not just a haphazard destination: for many it was the endpoint of a carefully charted migration route, along what was known as the "invisible railroad" that bisected the Continent as it headed north from Italy and Greece.[26] Like pilgrims of an earlier age, heading north this time rather than south but still in search of inner peace.

Perhaps it was the growing presence of such round-the-clock movements, of small groups of strangers crossing roads and moving on, that was the reason opinion polls in 2015 revealed a native population growing less concerned about the economy and much more concerned about migration.[27] Pushed to at least do *something* before that year's winter set in, in September 2015 EU leaders, whose combined population was half a billion, finally signed off on an official "burden-sharing" scheme: an update of the earlier Dublin regulations (now called Dublin III). It was woefully inadequate, covering just 160,000 refugees, primarily those already stationed in Italy and Greece. This did little to defuse tensions in Turkey and Hungary on the front line of arrivals. It did little to foster Europe's much-trumpeted values of community spirit and "ever greater union" either: the Czech Republic took just twelve refugees; Poland and Hungary none. Meanwhile, more than that number were dying every day in the effort to make it onto European soil. The EU felt obliged to file charges against the three nations. But given their increasingly anti-liberal stance, it wasn't clear those nations very much cared anymore. The EU was anyway then considering what to do about Austria's recent threats to Italy that it would close the Brenner Pass if the latter did not keep migrants on *its* side of the border.

Yet again the one leader to buck the trend was Germany's Angela Merkel. Her stance (indeed that of the German Christian Democrats more generally) is perhaps best read as a decent approximation of mainstream Europe's more general stance on immigration. The official line in Germany since the early 1980s had been that Germany was *not* a country of immigration (*Deutschland ist kein Einwanderungsland*). Schmidt and Kohl had insisted on this throughout their long reigns in office (though quite what that meant for "guestworkers" who had arrived in the 1950s and 1960s one wonders). The post-98 Schröder government's Nationality Act, while it belatedly brought Germany into line with other European nations, also made compromises with the "Germany First" mantra of the past. Significantly, therefore, Germany would not have a corresponding Immigration Act until after 9/11, by which time the usual post-9/11 exemptions (language tests, security tests) were applied.

When Merkel first came to power in 2005 she brought a greater degree of compassion to this arrangement, introducing a relatively more open approach to immigration (and the assimilation of Muslims already resident). Then, in the post–financial crisis of 2010 she swung more firmly back to the right, declaring that "multiculturalism has absolutely failed." These were also the years when her Foreign Minister Wolfgang Schäuble was playing hardball with the Greeks, daring them to leave the euro if they couldn't stand the heat of the budgetary discipline he made sure the troika continued to insist on.[28] Now, and perhaps aware of what the Greek crisis had done for her own image, she opened up again. On September 4, after a dramatic series of events involving refugee marches and leaked memos from government departments implying her administration was losing control, Merkel upped the ante, overruled her own Interior Minister Thomas de Maizière, and announced a dramatic plan to accept 1 million refugees. "*Wir schaffen das*," she insisted, in a catchphrase that was equal parts lauded and lampooned. *We can do this*.

Germans were encouraged to welcome refugees into their homes, and tens of thousands of them responded enthusiastically—a stark contrast to not only fellow Europeans' inhospitality but that of Americans as well. The US had taken fewer than 2,000 Syrian refugees in the first four years of the conflict, and only escalated that, provisionally, to 70,000 a year after 2015.[29] To be sure there were more pragmatic aspects to Merkel's humanitarian calculus: it did not hurt that the German economy was doing substantially better than the rest of Europe, and its booming man-ufacturing industry could do with another influx of cheap labor. Accord-ing to one estimate there were something like 600,000 jobs needing to be filled in 2015.[30]

Since it wasn't just "German" homes Merkel was opening up but, thanks to Europe's open borders, the homes of Germany's neighboring countries as well, her fellow leaders did not thank her for her gesture, humanitarian or otherwise. Indeed, in contrast to the German economy, the rest of Europe's job market and working classes were not in need of replenishment. Offering up a very deliberate recalibration of the sort of number that was "appropriate," François Hollande offered to help Merkel with resettling around 1,000 of her target. It was a first ominous sign of the fate that awaited Merkel's grand gesture, which soon descended into horse-trading between the various European nations as they sought to strike a desperate deal with antiliberal Turkey (which, perversely, was also the one nation which had thus far "done" something by allowing Mid-dle Eastern refugees, families from Yemen, for example, to escape there).

Turkey thus again turned out to be critical to events in Europe: not least since a further 3 million refugees waited to go to Europe from within its borders. The "deal" that was eventually struck with Erdoğan in 2016 was a classic statement of the wider state of play of liberal and antiliberal forces. First, it looked to Turkey to house refugees on its soil (rather than allowing them to take to the sea and to cross over to Greece, whose islands along the Turkish coast were by now full refugee camps). But Ankara, already angered by the way that EU maritime patrols were driving the refugees along *land* routes, and therefore into Turkey first of all (a division Russia had been happily exploiting by bombing close to the Turkish border in 2015) was determined to strike a hard deal. In the end it took what was effectively a bribe to Erdoğan of €6 billion of European taxpayers' money, in the form of aid, to seal it.[31] As human rights NGOs like Amnesty International were pointing out, however, Turkey was hardly a "safe haven" for asylum seekers, given the populist nationalism of Erdoğan's rhetoric. More than this, the deal gave Erdoğan a trump card to play whenever he did not get his way with Europe over practically any other matter: including the granting of visa-free travel across Europe to Turkish nationals and Turkey's ultimate accession. He could simply threaten to open the borders to refugees once again.[32]

If the refugee deal became, perversely, a feather in the antiliberals' cap, it also caused Merkel no end of problems at home. Not all Germans, it turned out, were as open-minded as she had hoped. This was brought home to her on the weekend of September 12, 2015, when some 40,000 refugees were scheduled to arrive. Aghast at the short-term numbers, some branded Merkel "mutti Teresa"—a play on Mother Teresa that used an already common derogatory nickname for her in German: *mutti*. At some of the refugee centers she visited others called her far worse than that. Her party did badly in regional elections the following year, and would lose a quarter of its vote at the next national elections in 2017. Merkel's long era of Christian Democratic hegemony was coming to an end. But with the Social Democrats somewhat in the wilderness still, this raised the question of exactly what was likely to replace it.[33]

One answer to that was supplied by the Alternative für Deutschland, the far-right party founded just three years before, which now began to surge in the polls. It soon had a sizeable foothold in the regional Länder parliaments: 15.1 percent in Baden-Württemberg, 12.5 percent in Rhineland-Palatinate, and 24 percent in Saxony-Anhalt. In 2017 the AfD would do even better, coming third in the national elections and, with ninety-four parliamentary seats, entering the Bundestag as the largest opposition party. It was the first time a far-right party had achieved such an influential position since 1945. It was the CDU/CSU's worst showing for just as long. And it offered the wheelchair-bound Wolfgang Schäuble a last great battle to fight as president of a deeply divided Bundestag.

This was the Schäuble who, with Merkel, had been dressed up in Nazi uniform by Greek cartoonists because of the bludgeoning austerity which as finance minister he long enforced over their country. But the caricature was wrongly drawn. For Schäuble was now moved to the Bundestag precisely to "maintain order" in the face of the AfD's entry into it. Schäuble was the German politician who should have been chancellor so many times had not ill fate, and most recently his fiscal disciplinarianism (which even German bankers and corporate leaders thought was a bit much), not conspired to deflate his popularity at just the wrong moment. But hard-nosed disciplinarian that he was, his recently burnished tough stance on the Greeks would serve him well in the new job (not least since it served him well in the pages of the influential German tabloid *Bild*, read by many of the AfD's supporters). So far as Merkel was concerned what mattered just as much was the fact that he was not just a disciplinarian, he was also a staunch defender of Europe (at least in its German, ordo-liberal guise). So perhaps this last challenge, as president of the Bundestag and not chancellor, was what his years in office had been preparing him for: for it was not just Germany but Europe also that called to be defended. And that task now required policing the lines of the German parliament itself.[34]

What animated this divide between the complicated humanitarianism driving Merkel's dramatic gesture and the more straight-up xenophobia of her critics, was the very limits of a European model of liberal democracy that refused, still, to address the underlying political aspects of the problems it confronted. The refugee crisis had merely laid bare the Continent's triple crisis of institutions, political identity, and population. The failure of *institutions* was apparent in the sheer inadequacy of the Dublin III agreement, which soon collapsed under the weight of its own triviality. In Luxembourg too, the European Court of Justice had not been established with the intention of hearing complaints from member states such as Fico's Slovakia arguing for their refusal to take in any refugees at all. But that was how it was now being looked to. Europe's leaders hoped that the old institutional architecture would hold up amidst the current onslaught. Mostly, they did not seek to reform it. It was easier, in this case, just to shut the door.

But where did Europe's governments think that refugees, who had spent months in a dance with death to reach their destinations, were going to go when they were denied asylum—as most in fact were? The answer was frequently that they went underground. At this point they submerged silently and without trace into the dark pool of underworld crime that merely exacerbated other social problems and made any claims as to potential "savings" by standing firm against the flood debatable to say the least. By 2017 even Sweden estimated that 12,000 rejected asylum seekers were living in the country illegally. It was probably a lot less than in other countries, but at least the Swedes were keeping a record; certainly their citizens were keeping note.

An irony was to be found here in the second element of Europe's crisis: namely the matter of *population*. For with its declining population and its economy in dire straits, not to mention with its richest citizens squirreling their wealth away offshore, an influx of young, willing, and diverse labor was exactly what Europe needed to replenish its industrial development and its tax base. The Paris-based OECD was predicting that Europe would need at least 50 million immigrants to maintain its position by the year 2060. But there was little evidence of this in the public discourse on refugees. And this in many ways led inevitably on to the third aspect of the crisis confronting Europe: namely its crisis of *political identity*.

What was "Europe" now, after all? The euro crisis revealed Europe's leaders to have few answers to this question. Just as György Konrád had observed of the former communist nations in 1989, the drawers had been turned out for inspection and shown, on this matter, to be empty. Confronted now by a crisis of humanity on its doorstep, in addition to its economic woes, Europe was again struggling to respond because its leaders no longer had a clear vision of what it was Europeans were striving toward. This was in stark contrast to the thousands risking their lives to reach it. What dominated official discussions in Brussels and in Europe's capitals instead were zero-sum calculations of "how many" people a country could sustain—regardless of the fact that this was a relative question that hinged upon how well existing political and economic institutions, including the welfare state, functioned.

It was the very lack of constructive answers to questions such as these that accounted for why a growing number of Europeans, be it AfD voters in Germany, or unemployed Spanish construction workers, were flirting with new forms of populist nationalism. It was why, by 2016, it was not just the European coast guard that was patrolling the Mediterranean, but civilian anti-immigrant outfits like Defend Europe's C-Star patrol, funded by the rather shadowy Gefira Foundation, one of just many "identitarian" groups that wanted to close Europe's borders and which mimicked the growing number of NGO boats operating in the region, only for very different ends. It was its own form of dark humanitarianism. Where one set of dividing lines was sharpening in the German Bundestag, then, another was being drawn out at sea, as some groups worked to welcome migrants in (since their governments did not seem to be doing enough) while others, like the C-Star patrol, worked to send them back (since their governments did not seem to be doing enough).

These identitarian groups were gifted ever more reasons to garner popular support. As ISIS propaganda took hold via the Internet, the small but carefully executed terror operations of al-Qaeda began to look antiquated by comparison to those of a new wave of ISIS-orchestrated attacks on European soil. Indeed, it was remarkable how few seemed to mention the name of an organization that half a decade before had been on everyone's lips. Instead, a wave of lower-grade but ultimately more damaging attacks on civilians, using mundane civilian items such as delivery vans as their weapon, became the new domestic front of the war on terror. In Sweden, France, Spain, Britain—the death toll began increasing once again as images racked up of trucks, vans, and cars careening into shoppers and pedestrians. The death tolls were highest in France and Spain—a truck that plowed through families and couples out strolling along the Promenade des Anglais in Nice on July 14, 2016; a van driven at speed down La Rambla shopping street in Barcelona on August 17, 2017—but the tactic, of ramming and stabbing, was everywhere the same. And it ensured that ISIS and the refugee crisis likewise converged in the public's imagination, encouraged as it now was, by feckless leaders, to imagine refugees as the Trojan Horses of terror and low wage competition.

It was perhaps not surprising that Europe's unemployed and its own neglected classes, who were still feeling the pinch after five years of austerity, were only too happy to be given somebody obvious to blame at this point. And ISIS being remote, it was those fleeing its clutches who ended up bearing the brunt of their latent anger; for the cacophony of protest that had been unleashed in 2011 had still not yet assembled itself properly into a movement of political reform. It had merely grown angrier and more frustrated—both with a system that seemed to ignore it and with those who had newly arrived to compete with it. Britain's Prime Minister Tony Blair, for all his failings, knew better than most how to take the pulse of a people. It was not insignificant, then, that in his view: "The one incontrovertible characteristic of politics today is its propensity for revolt," he said. No one was interested in fixing anything. All they wanted to do was "rip it [up]."[35]

A Very Bad Year

Anyone contemplating the travails of liberal democracy in the winter of 2015—amid the excruciatingly inadequate climate agreement reached between world leaders in Paris, and the brutal terrorist attacks that killed 130 people and injured 368 more in the same city—might well have been prompted to ask of that year's unending slew of disturbance and disaster whether things could realistically get any worse. The answer was a ringing affirmative; 2016 did not have the epochal significance that a 1933 or a 1989 had but it will be remembered for two defining events on either side of the Atlantic. Both helped hammer home the fact that a new moment of upheaval, a new moment of revolt, was upon the West once again.

First was the decision of Great Britain to leave the EU, ensuring that at the very moment of the continent's greatest need Europe's leaders would be entirely distracted by a matter that was as trivial as it was un-necessary and (so it would turn out) excruciatingly complex. Second, and much more resoundingly still, was the election of Donald Trump in America. Both had their immediate causes and their longer-run stressors; but both were also something of a belated admission that Western polit-ical liberalism had proven unable to mount a sufficiently positive response to the challenges of the day. As events began to snowball, one major newspaper, the *New York Times International Edition*, saw fit to run a sub-scription offer that year with the tagline: "Whatever happens next, we'll help you make sense of it."[36]

For its part, Washington's *Foreign Affairs* journal addressed the year's events by means of a cover story on "How Democracies Fail"; the World Economic Forum asked its members "Is Democracy in Danger?"; while in Athens, of all places, a specially convened "Democracy Forum" went some way to answering that by talking down democracy's "pessimistic report card." In fact each of these headline takes missed something im-portant about that year's events, for they did not represent a spurning of democracy so much as a quite dramatic *re*-enchantment of politics—albeit this had not taken the form that the Western liberal elite wanted to see. The Brexit referendum and the election of Donald Trump did represent, however, a clear-cut *recovery* of political voice that corresponded to the loss of trust in politics, of faith in civic society, and of the gnawing anx-iety of a world in disarray that had been developing in the years before.[37] What was not yet clear was in which direction this reanimated politics was heading.

In Britain, the year 2016 began calmly, as if the troubles roiling elsewhere had temporarily blown themselves out. In February, the British Prime Minister David Cameron found himself in Brussels, negotiating that "better deal" for Britain in Europe that he had promised long before in the warm glow of a prime minister's first years in office. That promise had been made all the way back in 2013 and might have been forgotten but for the fact that, in an effort to quell the internal dissent that habitually greets a prime minister's later years, and to head off the rising threat of UKIP, he had made it central to his party's 2015 election manifesto.

Cameron was all too aware that the question of "Europe" was a red flag to hard-line Tories' ears. But he was too impetuous and too overconfident to resist trying to settle, once and for all, the issue that had split his party for a generation. Ever since its accession to the then EEC in 1972 the Tory Party had been divided over whether Britain belonged inside or outside the Union: more divided, in fact, than the British people themselves. The wounds of four decades ago were about to be reopened. But there was no turning back now. Would Cameron heal the Tory Party's divisions, or would he divide the country in the act of trying?

Returning from Brussels in February, Cameron initially seemed to think he had made a good fist from what he must have known was a bad hand. He returned with a package that implied fewer financial obligations for the UK, greater independence over the setting of immigration policy, and a resounding opt-out from the EU's official mantra of "ever closer union." This belated form of prenuptial now in place, as the terms on which Britain might remain a part of the European Union, the British people were to be given the choice: in the neologisms of the time was it to be Brexit or Bremain? On June 23 they went to the polls to decide. It was not the first time they had been given the choice; in 1975, too, there had been a national referendum on membership of the EEC. But that time, in the context of an economic crisis at home, Europe seemed a safer place to be. Was that how Europe still looked, four decades later?

At 4.00 a.m. the next morning, when it was announced that the vote was for leaving the EU, a disconcerted British woman—who had voted for just that—declared herself "shocked" at the result. Hours later she rang in to the nation's prime-time morning radio station Radio 4, perhaps seeking the solace of a public confession (few things, after all, are more British than Radio 4). She was aghast at what she had done, she said. It had all been just a "protest vote"—except that she had not been alone. And if a protest vote was what it truly was, then the number of people making it had turned that protest into a full-scale revolution. The vote stilled the nation into the kind of silence normally reserved for the Cenotaph. It sparked off volatility in global currency markets, causing banks to reassess positions, and credit agencies to rethink their valuations of the country: ironically, Fitch now downgraded it on account of the probable *lower* immigration rates to come. Banks began factoring in the likelihood that, if Scotland now reactivated its calls for secession, the UK would soon no longer exist.

This was presumably not what the people thought they would be getting when they voted for Brexit. Britain had lost its last triple AAA rating, and those who had already downgraded it now did so further. Even the normally upbeat Blair was caught in a moment of melancholy as he surveyed the wreckage of what the country had done:

> In the long run this [the EU] is essentially an alliance of values: liberty, democracy, and the rule of law. As the world changes and opens up across boundaries of nation and culture, which values will govern the twenty-first century? Today, for the first time in my adult life, it is not clear that the resolution of this question will be benign.[38]

The Chancellor, George Osborne—seemingly relieved that the people might now remember a different economic disaster than the one he had overseen—admitted there would be even more austerity, and tax increases too, this time. But he reported this with all the concern of someone who knew he would probably not be around in government long enough to have to deal with it. His instincts were correct. Cameron felt he had no choice but to resign and immediately fell on his sword; the axe swung for Osborne at a snap election called the following year. Far from taking back control for the country, what the Conservatives had achieved was to hand it over to a highly uncertain future.

As for the British population, fully 7 percent of those who voted to Leave immediately regretted it and said they had since changed their minds (while 4 percent of those who voted to Remain changed theirs). The net difference of 3 percent made for an effective margin of just 400,000 votes in the final outcome and led to calls for a second referendum. These were routinely ignored (so much for the will of the people) but they did at least raise a new debate over the matter of what Brexit had really been about. And that turned out not to have been Europe after all—not, at least, if the huge spike in people typing the question "What is the EU?" into their Internet searches the morning *after* the referendum is any guide to their motivations.

What Brexit was really about was Britain. Above all it was about the fact that large swathes of the country were effectively separate from London and the prosperous South East while there was no sufficiently positive vision of British *political* identity (contra its culturalism) to hold in check the gnawing disgruntlements that stemmed from this. Half a decade of austerity had steadily exacerbated this problem and left the population of regions like Yorkshire and the Humber and the West Midlands especially resentful. Brexit sanctioned that resentment and provided it with an outlet. As the Secretary of State for Justice, former chief whip and Brexit mastermind Michael Gove said: "the British people have had enough of experts." The Brexit referendum was not simply "one of the biggest democratic exercises in British history," as his government insisted, it was a referendum on the state of democracy in Britain.[39]

Yet it is true that it was neither racism nor poverty that drove Britons to vote themselves out of Europe. The divide split more along lines of age than of class, and what accounted for *this* was the way Britain was losing its identity as it adapted to a smaller role on the world stage. Those Britons who voted for Brexit did so out of a misplaced sense that the country was somehow special. Ironically it had been special *within* the EU—it was the invisible peg against German dominance, it had the benefits of the single market, the clout of collective trade deals, and none of the tie-ins of the euro and the Stability and Growth Pact.[40] Despite its colossal expense to the British and European taxpayer, Brexit ultimately solved none of Britain's problems: all of which preceded it, most of which were made worse by it, and plenty of which had less to do with the EU than they had to do with the state of public debate in England.

There was, however, a way in which Brexit *was* about Europe. While Brexiteers made much of the EU's so-called democratic deficit (the "gap" between EU decisions and national implementation), the core problem with the EU was the fact that it did not seem prepared to use the democracy it *did* have. Once again, this ceded the running to those who were prepared to use that democracy for all it was worth: even to the extent of turning it against itself. And for these voices, Brexit was the sort of triumph that the liberals had enjoyed when the Wall came down three decades before. "Long live free nations!" declared Marine Le Pen, in the wake of the Brexit result. "Long live the United Kingdom! Long live France!"[41] In the wake of Brexit, the crisis of the eurozone, which had become a crisis of the European Union, now threatened to become a crisis in which it was not Europe, as Angela Merkel had insisted, that was at stake, but the liberal democratic nation state itself.

Ironically, one person who recognized this and who, like Marine Le Pen, had been following Britain's European referendum very closely, was Vladimir Putin. He had been following it more closely in fact than the British government at the time realized. For several years Putin had been expanding his successful domestic program of media manipulation into an international one, including an effort the previous year to hack into French state television and broadcast pro-ISIS material in an effort to sow fear and drive voters into the hands of Le Pen's Front National.[42] On the day of the Brexit vote, and from the offices of his Internet Research Agency (IRA) in Moscow, the Russian government had again overseen a major disinformation campaign: with dormant social media accounts suddenly activated, spewing out, for the most part, pro-Leave propaganda. To vote Leave was, after all, the most disruptive of the two possible outcomes, and the one thing Putin wanted above all else was to sow disruption across the West. Against the common and comforting conceit that liberal democracies, though they may sometimes get themselves in a pickle, ultimately muddle through, came the realization that muddling through was no longer necessarily in their hands alone to achieve.

The public temper, all this while, was no more settled in America. While Brits went to the polls in June to determine their fate in Europe, Americans were embroiled in the most acrimonious round of presidential primaries in decades. On the Democratic side the front-running and the best funded candidate was Hillary Clinton, who had narrowly lost the nomination to Barack Obama eight years before. Winning the Democratic nomination had once seemed guaranteed for Clinton. But her campaign ran into a major series of hurdles from late 2015. Above all was the surprising strength of *grassroots* opposition on the left, from the candidate for "democratic socialism," Bernie Sanders. Perhaps this wasn't surprising. Sanders was a septuagenarian senator fired up by a strong and well-mobilized youth base: in other words he was a sign that the establishment cachet Clinton had spent a career building up was being rejected. He was therefore also a sign that the upheaval the Republican Party had gone through in recent years was now also about to engulf the left. The struggle between Sanders and Clinton for the nomination was frequently ill-tempered and did little to warm any undecided voters to the Democratic cause. Obama tried to steer a careful line between the two viscerally opposed incumbents, though one wonders what hope he felt either of them offered for consolidating his *own* legacy.

This was not, for once, a matter just of presidential ego. Obama had sought to address the social tensions that had grown only more fraught in America since the 1970s: between different groups in society, between the people and the elite, between the state and the federal government. As these began to rupture the political landscape during his presidency at times it seemed the most he could do was simply ride out the convulsion. It was hard to imagine Black Lives Matter under a different president, and yet as the US neared the point, demographically, when a majority of the working class would be black (the point was due in 2032) what did that say about the status of racial equality? Were there sufficient grassroots movements (of the sort that had brought him to power) capable of continuing the fight against racial injustice when he had left office? This made the matter of who Obama's successor was to be of the greatest importance for America and not just the president alone.

At the end of his two terms nobody could deny that Obama had been one of his country's "great" presidents, if only for what he represented. But he had arrived largely as an outsider, and he had not—while in office—done much to build up the prospects of his own party in power. Most of what he had achieved, thanks to ingrained Republican opposition, had been forced through by executive order (on climate change) or behind-closed-door negotiations (Obamacare) and this fact set a rather worrying precedent. At the regional level (state legislatures and the like) Democrats lost 1,000 seats during Obama's time in office. Many insiders observed that Obama was frequently "aloof" from Congress. Because he had failed to secure bipartisan agreement for many of his policies, too many of his achievements were vulnerable to subsequent repeal, should a president come along who wished to undo the United States' commitment to the Paris climate deal, for example. Of course, that was partly due to the historic dumbing-down and sheer truculence of the current party of opposition.[43]

For its part, in keeping with the trend of the previous half decade, the Republican primary in 2015 was a pageant of ill-assorted candidates, the largest number ever, whose policies demonstrated how out of touch with reality the modern Republican Party had become. More so even than the Democrats the Republican primary soon descended into a bitter two-way struggle, this time pitting everyone from Marco Rubio and Ted Cruz to Carly Fiorina and Ben Carson against the most dynamite candidate of them all: Donald J. Trump. As with Hillary Clinton the one truly establishment candidate, Jeb Bush—the governor of Florida and brother and son of the two previous Republican presidents— never got a look in. In making his stand for president the property tycoon and media celebrity Donald Trump was the outsider to beat all outsiders—a "menace to American conservatism," as the conservative *National Review* put it in January 2016—and an all the more effective candidate for it.[44] Unlike previous outsiders (one thinks of Perot, Buchanan, Forbes) Trump knew that he needed the party's endorsement to succeed. But that was about as far as his commitment to the ideals of Republicanism went. The fact that he actually secured the nomination was ultimately due less to him and more to the growing partisanship, first raised under Gingrich and since taken to new heights by a Republican Party in its post–Tea Party fury during the Obama administration. For *that* Republican Party there were some—Reince Priebus, then Republican chair, being perhaps the most significant case in point—prepared to take a gamble on Trump.

What mainstream Republicans did not get until too late were the very real politics Trump represented: the fact that he had moved to the left of them on some issues (to the left even of Democrats on things such as free trade agreements and ditching the mega donors) while veering strongly right on others. To those stuck in the old left–right mindset none of this made sense: it was mindless, which for the most part was how Trump was portrayed. But this ignored the freedom of movement that such inconsistency afforded him. For like no US politician before, Trump really wasn't constrained by the rules of the game. Much less was he constrained by the truth. It didn't matter a jot when his lies were called out. He simply reverted to a defense first deployed by a man he shared not a little in common with: Silvio Berlusconi. *Sono stato frainteso*, as the latter used to say when challenged: I've been misunderstood. Which is what the people felt too.

Trump thus secured the Republican nomination mainly because he consistently confounded his opponents. Each time they thought he could not be any wilder in his ignorant exaggerations and his lies he did just that. And in this regard there *was* one thing that Trump "got" that none of the other presidential candidates did (with perhaps the partial exception of Bernie Sanders). This was the fact that, in the insecurity of the moment, people were happy to seek refuge even in ignorance of simple truths. Allan Bloom, it turned out, had made his famous prediction a generation too soon. The "closing of the American mind" was now: twenty years after the rot that so astounded him first set in. Yet still people refused to believe that Trump might actually win. This was all going to die down, his opponents insisted after he finally clinched the Republican nomination: the bluff and the bluster would be replaced by a more "realistic" campaign aimed at securing the White House. He would become more "presidential." There was more than something in journalist Salena Zito's comment that, while Trump's supporters "take him seriously but not literally . . . the press takes him literally but not seriously."[45]

In fact, Trump had no such intention of moderating his campaign after the nomination. He refused to release his tax returns, as *all* presidential hopefuls customarily did. He was overtly racist in suggesting the "Mexican" judge investigating him for fraud was probably incompetent. His infringements were soon too many to enumerate, but this only lowered expectations, making it easier for him to get away with more. He promised to repeal NAFTA, the crowning glory of the party he now represented. He said he would build a wall—"a beautiful wall"—to keep out foreigners. He promised to fight against free trade. He smiled as his supporters chanted "Lock her up, lock her up" in reference to Hillary Clinton, who had gained the Democratic nomination, and he physically and boorishly sought to intimidate her during their televised debates. He broke the seal on any number of public taboos and showed no regret when recordings of him discussing sexual conquests and using denigrating language about women were released. He embraced white supremacist views and installed members of the racist alt-right (which rejected mainstream conservatism as insufficiently attentive to the needs of white identity) like Steve Bannon, the editor of Breitbart News, in the heart of his campaign. Bannon would later become Trump's chief strategist, and later still, as the administration melted down, his chief adversary.

Just as in the primaries, however, none of this mattered because Trump had successfully veered onto the terrain of populist nationalism, of the sort that had already gained considerable traction among European nations. The greatest challenge this posed at first was to the Republican Party, whose strategy since Reagan had consistently emphasized free markets, low government spending, and social conservatism. Trump ditched this for protectionism and for denigrating American achievement (rather than crowing about it, as Reagan did), the better to promise a national rebirth that was hitched not to greater freedoms for the individual, but to a greater *collective* security against illegitimate ("un-American") others. All that mattered, he declared in May, "is the unification of the people, because the other people don't mean anything." Here was the classic populist move. Immigrants, those of different sexual preference and race, those who disagreed: they were not to count.[46]

Contrary to bemused editorials in the coastal broadsheets, Trump very much had *not* come out of nowhere, therefore. His platform was essentially a "little man" Jacksonian one reinvented—as with his slogan "America First"—for modern times. He actively incited a majoritarian identity crisis and offered as a salve to this his own brand of populist conservative nationalism: strong defenses at home, an "unyielding" stance toward US adversaries abroad, and a general disregard for the existing "rules" of the game.[47] Above all, he promised to hold "them" accountable, thereby articulating the very desire that "ordinary" Americans had been nurturing since the time of Watergate.

So just where had Trump come from? The Trump "phenomenon" is ultimately best explained by the convergence of three separate factors. *First* was the long-run transformation of American conservatism (and the failure of the Republican Party to react to this). The postwar party had rebuilt itself from the top down: its leading lights were not its presidents but its men of ideas. This was why it had always been a party available to capture by influential groups like the neocons or the supply-siders before them. But a groundswell against this elite, metropolitan version of the party was becoming apparent already under Bush Sr., when the gay-bashing former Nixon aide Pat Buchanan ran against him in 1992 (and did much better, we may recall, than anyone was predicting: ultimately securing 3 million votes in the primaries). Trump had learned from Buchanan. Indeed, the three basic prongs of his platform were pretty much identical: anti-immigration, economic nationalism, and patriotic aggrandizement (America First).

If this was a platform thoroughly wedded to a reductive, not to mention antiquated, myth of sovereign independence it was given a more modern "redemptive" twist by the *second* development feeding into Trump's runaway campaign: the rise of a form of neolibertarianism. It was not just radicals on the left who had taken heart from the upheavals of 2011. So too had libertarians like the Tea Partiers and some of the more influential (and wealthy) billionaires, such as the Koch brothers, who backed conservatives financially. Of particular relevance for Trump was the tech entrepreneur Peter Thiel. Given Silicon Valley's generally dismissive stance on Trump, Thiel's support—announced on the night of his nomination in a speech at the Republican National Convention—was a major coup, and in due course Thiel would become one of Trump's major financial backers.

For all their perceived differences Trump and Thiel were revealing of a wider trend, for they both shared a strongly antipolitical streak. Neither was for small government: both thought the power of the state should be maximized; it was democratic debate and political pluralism they despised and wanted reduced. In his 2009 essay "Education of a Libertarian," Thiel declared that he no longer believed freedom and democracy were "compatible"—and he preached an "escape from politics in all its forms" in response.[48] In practice this meant there should be less democracy to hold back capitalist overachievers like himself: the appeal of Trump became clear. The genius of Thiel's endorsement, however, came in his understanding of Trump as a "much needed dose of humility in our politics."[49]

Here was a dual use statement that read one way for the masses, and another way for the elites: and it comprised the *third* and final enabling element behind Trump's success. Trump's signature contribution was to find a way to put the two most powerful elements of the conservative political insurgency together: plutocratic elites with populist masses. For years, the more the Republican Party had looked to the international sphere to burnish its credentials, and the more it had sought to curry favor with economic elites to pay for this, the more it had alienated a small but vocal stream within the American right. Now Trump was whistling them back in.

Trump was a singularly inexperienced political shepherd however—and no matter how well his political inexperience "played," he still had to get his campaign over the line. History may well confirm that he was aided here by a remarkable run of sheer political luck. First, Clinton ran a disastrous and ill-fated campaign that largely failed to galvanize the electorate. Clinton was of course tainted with the elite liberal brush, as Sanders had savagely revealed in the primaries. Her own conduct didn't help either: a corporate lawyer before entering politics herself, she had clocked up $22 million in paid speeches since leaving it. More damaging still was her ill-received "basket of deplorables" comment, by which she alienated the very disgruntled Americans she should have been reaching out to. Even so, Clinton was not responsible for the misogyny directed at her, nor for the last-minute cloud of suspicion cast over her campaign by the utterly inexplicable decision of the director of the FBI, James Comey, to announce he was reopening an investigation into Clinton's use of a private email server when Secretary of State (only then to retract this).

Trump also benefited from a growing backlash against the liberal internationalism of the post–Cold War decades. The Western public had grown tired of fighting what it saw as other people's wars. Americans in particular had been told, for more than a decade and a half, to be watchful, to be afraid: and so they had grown fearful just as they had been instructed. Inevitably they had become a little less civic-minded too, a little less patient in the process—particularly as the injustice of the financial crisis began turning their latent and unspecified fears into something more closely resembling popular anger. Unlike the Democratic Party there was a gathering of neo-Republicans looking to capitalize on this politics of emotion and entice it over to the right.[50]

As in Britain then it was certainly not class alone that explained Trump's election. It was as much the alignment of interests between a long-neglected white working class (who for twenty years had been losing their political voice domestically, as unions disbanded and the Democratic Party was no longer seen to represent them) with a lower middle class (who for about the same time had been also losing out, in their case to globalization). While these latter were better educated they were prepared to ditch civics for personal redress. "Every Trump voter is most certainly not a white supremacist," observed the black writer Ta-Nehisi Coates with measured regret some months later. "But every Trump voter felt it acceptable to hand the fate of the country over to one."[51] The title of his postelection book, *We Were Eight Years in Power*, exposed the final reason voters turned their anger into a vote for a white supremacist presidential candidate: for eight years they had felt overflown by the soaring cadence of a black man preaching postrace liturgies from the bully pulpit.

Even so, Trump's campaign was close to coming off the rails in the weeks before the election, until the entry of one factor that the polls could not possibly have taken into account—and that was the appearance once again, almost against belief, of Vladimir Putin. As investigations that would dog Trump throughout his time in office later began piecing together, Trump's campaign had been actively assisted from Moscow. Some of Trump's closest aides—including at least one member of his family, it turned out—had significant contact with Russian agents in the year prior to the election. And the Russian ability to wage cyber warfare was deployed on behalf of Trump in the form of media disinformation, pro-Trump propaganda, and possibly even shared intelligence.

It was astounding even to consider. But Trump's son-in-law Jared Kushner *did* hold at least two meetings, later undeclared on his White House security clearance form, with a member of the Soviet embassy,

Sergey Kislyak, with a view to setting up a backchannel between Moscow and the Trump campaign. Quite aside from the question of actual collusion was the extent to which Trump refused point-blank to criticize Putin or to make any disclosure regarding his long-standing involvement in deals with Russian businesses. Later it would be hard not to come away with the view that Trump was in Putin's debt, if not actually in his pocket. But at the time of the election, on November 8, the sheer idea of it was so preposterous that few could find it in themselves to take it seriously. As the *New York Times* later put it with regard to Trump's tech-world campaign strategy: the principle of "move fast and break things" held firm.[52] Democracy cracked, but Trump moved on.

Interregnum

The evidence that Russia was meddling in the US election was one of two longer-term legacies to outlive the US election of 2016. The other one was the deepening loss of trust not just in political leaders but in the system itself. It had now become commonplace to talk of an era of "post-truth." Truth, according to the British philosopher Bernard Williams, is a composite of two distinct "virtues": accuracy and sincerity. Read in such a light, it becomes easier to understand why the American electorate struggled to separate Trump's willful lies from Clinton's labored half-truths: the one was singularly uninterested in accuracy but came across as sincere; the other was objectively more accurate, but insincerely so. Williams's greater insight applied to the social and political landscape to which the two presidential candidates addressed themselves: the growing divide between demands for more truthfulness, on the one hand, and the creeping belief that there was no longer an objective truth about any social fact. The decline of local newspapers, the growing number of citizens who built their understanding of the world from Facebook and Twitter feeds, as opposed to public media with reputations for objectivity, merely reinforced the trend.

But this was not America's cross to bear alone. In the lead-up to the Brexit vote in Britain, a popular young Labour MP, Jo Cox, was murdered in broad daylight as she arrived to hold a constituency surgery. That same morning, the pro-Brexit UKIP had unveiled its infamous "Breaking Point" poster, ostensibly showing immigrants flooding into the country along a border point. It was the culmination of the attempt to make Brexit about immigration above all else, and precisely the sort of wild-eyed exaggeration that her murderer—who was heard shouting, "This is for Britain" and "Keep Britain Independent," as he repeatedly shot and stabbed her on the street—had been inspired by. Yet the immigrants the poster suggested were queuing up to get into Britain were in fact Syrian refugees attempting to reach Slovakia who had nothing to do with the UK. This was post-truth bloodily personified, because for all its factual inaccuracy—indeed for all that it was neither accurate *nor* sincere—it fitted perfectly into the reigning narrative of Brexit, and it was the poster's political *logic*, not the truth of it per se, that counted.

This then was the context in which Trump and the wider populist explosion in Europe could take place. It was not the populists' ideas that were new, but an enabling political environment in which trust had been eroded. After all, Putin was not the only one sowing seeds of misinformation: the Democratic National Committee, it later transpired, had done all that it could legally do to undermine one of its own candidates for nomination, Bernie Sanders. This was ultimately what linked Brexit and Trump: not the coincidence of their timing. It was what accounted for the gap in polls revealing people to still want democracy, but no longer really to believe in it. Every liberal democracy by now had its own version of this basic divide between a clamoring for the truth and the recognition that few really wished to deal with that truth once uncovered. The long-drawn-out Chilcot Inquiry into the false premises of the Iraq War in Britain, which was published finally in the months between the Brexit vote and Trump's nomination, was merely the most disappointing example.

Trump's eventual election was for many nothing less than a "national trauma" and it was followed by days of shock and disbelief. But as the black intellectual Robin D. G. Kelley observed, it was one for which all of America bore some responsibility. Antiliberals everywhere could barely contain their delight at their sudden good fortune. Europe's right-wing populists flew to New York for the obligatory photo-op too. Farage, Le Pen—all took their turns waiting in the lobby of Trump Tower, just to be welcomed for a few moments in the corporate-plated suites above. Yet something more significant was at play than just a gathering of the populist passerines into some premigratory flock. On the back of the undermining of truth in politics, the crass ethnic nationalism that Trump, Le Pen, Wilders, and others offered as the one "positive" element in their usually unremittingly negative campaigns provided them with a moral currency of its own. Nationalism, it seemed, could be both the bludgeon and the balm for a liberal democratic politics in crisis mode. And it allowed the likes of Trump to provide an outlet for the pent-up frustration and self-loathing under which a large portion of Westerners had been toiling. Now they could direct their anger elsewhere.

"History does not repeat, but it does instruct," declared the American historian and public intellectual Timothy Snyder in a widely read pamphlet published just weeks after Trump's inauguration. For all that it never once mentioned the newly elected president of the United States by name, *On Tyranny* threw barbs at him from every page. Snyder was not alone in his sense of resignation. "This is a time of growing fears in Europe and the United States," warned Roger Cohen from Berlin, in a piece entitled "Daydreaming in Germany." "Ghosts have stirred. Humanity never quite grows out of the buffoon's attractions: the scapegoats he offers; the fast money; the rush of violence; the throb of nation and flag; the adrenaline of the mob; the glorious future that will, he insists, avenge past humiliations."[53]

In office, Trump was not, in point of fact, the fascist that each of these authors portrayed him as being. But as president he did come to practice an antidemocratic style; and as president of the world's most powerful country, that was danger enough. The patchy crowd who turned out at his inauguration—compared to the million and more who had greeted Obama just eight years before—was revealing of his lack of a *truly* popular mandate. Those who turned up were treated to a rendition of the guiding philosophy beneath which Trump would henceforth assemble his frequently impetuous policies: "America First." It was not an original slogan. It had been the property of Nazi sympathizers like Charles Lindbergh before him—as if Trump were willingly taunting his detractors.

Not surprisingly, it provoked mixed reactions across the world: whether it was anger in China (it "will only further sink the hearts of leaders in Beijing," it was said), bitterness in Karachi ("America played a part in making the Third World. . . . Now Americans can stay at home and live the experience"), and cynicism in London ("this is an hour of sheer despair").[54] Above all it provoked dismay at home. Several weeks later, after Trump had delivered a particularly poorly judged memorial speech (one that he himself called a "home run"), the *New York Times* lamented: "Great. Terrific. Phenomenal. Tremendous. Fabulous. Beautiful. How Trump has hollowed out these words. How arid, even nauseating he has made them."[55]

But the Twitter Presidency surged on regardless. Before even taking office, in November 2016, Trump had awoken one day to a Fox News report that college students were burning the American flag. Within half an hour he had tweeted out, "Nobody should be allowed to burn the American flag—if they do, there must be consequences—perhaps loss of citizenship or year in jail!" In January, now in power, he clocked off one day to watch Bill O'Reilly's 8 p.m. show, also on Fox News, and saw a guest call the violent crime rate in Chicago sheer "carnage." By 9:25 p.m. Trump had tweeted: "If Chicago doesn't fix the horrible 'carnage' going on . . . I will send in the Feds!"[56] Among his first acts, enacted via executive orders, were to commence construction of the much-berated "wall" along the southern border with Mexico, to immediately "ban" immigration from seven Islamic countries, and to seek to have lifted the international sanctions regime on Russia that Merkel had brokered, for no obvious *national* political gain.

In everything Trump was impetuosity personified. The Yale professor of English David Bromwich wrote that the president had no faith in words because words, unlike deeds, were disposable. He was the antithesis of deliberation as well. John Yoo, the lawyer who had advised Bush to invade Afghanistan and Iraq and to open the interrogation center at Guantánamo, and who had encouraged Obama to draw on the same sources of constitutional authority to undertake drone strikes and foreign electronic surveillance, announced: "Even I have grave concerns about Mr. Trump's uses of presidential power."[57]

Under Trump's feckless eye the private realm felt as encroached upon as the public sphere. One reason gay and lesbian couples were suddenly getting married in the dying weeks before the inauguration (23 percent more in November than the same month the previous year) was because of their "fears" of what a Trump presidency would mean for their ability to remain living under the same roof.[58] Liberals loudly decried such a slide back into the prejudices of the past. Conservatives meanwhile tried to retain a sense of self-interested perspective. With his eyes on the meltdown in Trump's National Security Council, and unswayed by the liberals' recourse to comparisons with the 1930s, the conservative David Brooks observed: "Mussolini supposedly made the trains run on time, but this group couldn't manage fascism in a phone booth."[59]

Others were less sanguine and fearful of the chaos that Trump clearly *was* capable of creating, precisely because of the ineptitude of his administration: the twenty-four-hour policymaking by CAPITALIZED 140-character injunction; his insistence that the visa ban on Muslims was both proportionate and nondiscriminatory (it was neither); his failure to condemn a series of painful domestic shootings as anything other than the work of "deranged" individuals; his rants against "fake news," which depleted further still the public's faith in government while fostering a lack of respect for an open media, indeed for any sort of open society at all; his actively threatening to "totally destroy" North Korea with "fire and fury," which echoed the worst of Nixon's "will in spades," and then some. Congress, observed Thomas Wright, the director of the Project on International Order and Strategy at the Brookings Institution in 2017, had a real dilemma before it. "They now have to choose between safeguarding the republic and protecting the president."[60] Within Congress, as it happened, both sides of the aisle seemed for once in agreement that the best way to avoid this dilemma was if the federal bureaucracy could manage to run itself for a while without the president's assistance. American democracy, it seemed, could rediscover its agency after all.

18

Epilogue: The End of an Era?

A S THE FALLOUT from 2016 continued to make itself felt in the years to come, it was almost as if the Western democracies had been brought back full circle to the 1970s. A similar sense of urgency about the unknown pervaded society, though the "democratic surge" that some detected four and a half decades before had this time been replaced by an "antiliberal surge" that was clear for all to see. There is a "genuine crisis of legitimacy," the head of the British prime minister's policy unit declared shortly after Trump's election. And on this matter at least, the populists were in accord: "The European Union is dead, but it does not know this yet," crowed France's Marine Le Pen in early 2017. Twelve months of the Trump presidency later and the *New York Times* observed sadly in its year-end valedictory: "peace feels fragile, truth is blurred and spectacle has taken over."[1]

Of course, it was not the 1970s again, much less the 1930s. What had opened up, rather, was a broad-based questioning of the assumptions of liberal democratic life. If this encompassed elements of both those previous moments, it also contained much that was new. The similarity with the 1970s was to be found not in a return to the past but in the reappearance of a sense of transition. When Jean Fourastié published his retrospective account of the postwar Golden Age in 1979, the thirty glorious years of economic growth that began after the war had only recently ended; our own age was just beginning. The four and a half decades since then have been less glorious, but they have been every bit as coherent as an era—the formidable forties, perhaps? Whatever we decide to call them, we are taking our leave of the past once again.

Few today disagree that the liberal democratic order is in disarray and that it has lost the confidence of many. It is not hard to understand why. Economic stagnation and high unemployment, combined with what has now been several decades of rising inequality, are the normal state of affairs for Western societies. The threat of terrorism, howsoever mismanaged or overplayed, has been a constant and troubling shadow in the background of public life, reanimating racial and ethnic tensions at a time of growing disquiet. Trust is at a historic low ebb, faith in government is wavering, and yet still Western leaders declare themselves unable to think of anything better than a little more of the same. Today the institutions of democracy seem unfit for the scale of the problems at hand, while the calling of referenda by elites, and the populist simplifications thrown up in response, prove a partial and inhospitable shelter all of their own. There being, finally, no convincing alternatives on offer, the people have begun to look for one themselves.

It is at moments of moral crisis such as this that democracy may shift upon its axis. It is when people converge in public, see the political architecture that has been devised for them differently, and set about rebuilding it, one piece at a time, in another image. First the broken furniture may be exchanged, a partition wall here and there may be removed; in time extensions and structural work may be considered. Usually this happens one problem at a time, under awnings set up in the background of day-to-day events. But every so often it is undertaken openly and with clamoring intent. Seen over the longer term, this episodic loosing of social force may presage either progress or retreat. But in every case, at the moment they are most involved, people will glance up briefly, see nothing but stars above, and with the roof lifted, set to rebuilding the pillars of political life itself.

It is with such a prospect once more in the offing that the narrative of this book closes. The story does not end here, of course. Rather, this is where the history of the past four and a half decades begins: with a reckoning of how the "empire of democracy," as Tocqueville long ago put it, has developed during this time. Has it fared well? Has it spread justly? What about it do we wish to keep? What is it that needs to change? We are told that the present "moment" is a "surprising," even a "crazy" one.[2] But at times of popular intervention the rulebooks always begin to show their age—as indeed they must—as the fundamental elements of political life are struggled over anew, and untested norms welded into place. Democracy's "redemptive" and "pragmatic" sides are in the throes of one of their occasional realignments.[3] But for all that there is confusion, while the structural work is contemplated, costed, and reviewed, certain things at least have become more apparent.

One thing that has become clearer is just how difficult it was for Western citizens, in the years since the 1970s, to unhitch their support for democracy from the condition of prosperity and rising expectations that was for much of the postwar era its most gratifying and correlative feature. Democracy may well be easier to pursue in the good times, and we have seen that the two postwar democratic epochs to date were constructed as cathedrals of prosperity: the mass-prosperity of the post-war era and the wealth-prosperity of the post-70s age. But democracy would have been a short-lived phenomenon if all of its promises boiled down merely to greater material improvement. It has always promised a measure of control over one's own destiny as well. This is why the other matter to have been posed with particular clarity in the past few years is the fundamental question of popular sovereignty: what it is and what it is for. The problems of governing liberal democracies at arm's length, in the name of greater economic freedom, have begun to show themselves. There has been a corresponding upsurge in people seeking to "take back control" over the larger and at times disconcerting forces that shape their lives. It seems that where the experience of twentieth-century totalitarianism taught us unequivocally that too much equality can be a dangerous thing, the early twenty-first century is already teaching us that libertarian disregard is likewise a shortcut to serfdom.

The third postwar era we are just now embarking upon, if it is to succeed, will need to base itself on a better rationale than the value presently attributed to democracy's raison d'être: the encasement of personal freedom by wealth and property alone. But the underlying question is the same one it has always been: how best to organize the rights of the person with capitalist variety and equality of political voice. The solutions of the 1970s presented but one possible way of answering that. At that point the Western democracies embarked upon a program of political minimalism that reduced state capacity and amplified market freedoms, while reimagining society as an "opt-in" arrangement: something much better suited to the new institutional architecture. This silent revolution emerged in response to the crises that overwhelmed the Western democracies in the early 1970s, and it was afforded the presumed blessings of history, fatefully, by the events of 1989. Today, after nearly forty years of political minimalism (which, it must be stressed, is *not* the same as small or weak government), we are knee-deep in the problems those "solutions" created in their turn.

Today we are forced to address the more immediate crises that these problems present us with, at the same time as we circle back to correct some of the mistakes that we have made along the way. Yet we confront, as well, two newly intersecting issues that amplify the problem. For one, the challenge of democratic renewal is even harder today than it was in the 1970s because four and half decades of governing "at a distance" have deeply eroded our public institutional commitments to democracy. For another, new challenges (be it climate change, aging populations, super-bugs, or robotics) continue crowding in around the basic problem.[4] To solve the latter suite of issues liberal democracies will somehow have to recuperate the former capacities they have lost. The huge challenge that clearly represents goes some way to explaining why the public temper is currently as disaffected as it is.

This raises a number of pressing questions. Is Europe today irredeem-ably the "hollow shell" some believe it to have become, now that thanks to the European debt crisis the political imperatives and cross-class coa-litions that sustained its expansionary project for decades are no longer? Or will new pan-European movements emerge to pick up the baton from the Christian and social democrats whose support is in decline? Is America on the cusp of sliding into "illiberal democracy" or irrelevance (or both) as others fear, or will the constitutional safeguards that guided the nation through the Watergate crisis forty-four years earlier prove robust once again? Will popular commitments to democratic norms today prove sufficient, once roused, to address the scope of these challenges at the scale that they demand? Are Europeans ready to bear dual public commitments to one another nationally *and* transnationally, as some of their philosophers suggest?[5]

Democracy's Crises

In his *Reflections on the End of an Era* the influential American theologian and public intellectual Reinhold Niebuhr wrote concernedly, in 1934, of the turning point of his day. Niebuhr had no truck with utopianism; but modern liberalism, he said, had no answer to the challenges of the rise of fascism and communism either: it was weak-willed, socially naive, and institutionally hampered. His was intended as a sympathetic critique. Yet it was echoed across the Atlantic—as Niebuhr was all too aware—by influential figures, like Carl Schmitt, who had no desire to salvage de-mocracy, but to see it replaced by more efficacious embodiments of the popular will, as in the figure of the Führer.[6] Ultimately, the antidemocratic moment of the 1930s was weathered and liberal democracy enshrined once again in 1945. But the drastic scale of the violence and devastation wrought across so much of the globe during those years stands as a warning still today. Certainly it was to prove a formative moment for the likes of Niebuhr, who helped to provide the intellectual impetus for the reconstruction of democracy after the war.[7]

At the same time, while it is right that we acknowledge democracy's inherent fragility, we must also reckon with its strengths; and we should be wary of stretched analogies. Democratic institutions may be prone to withering on the vine, but that does not mean that they will. Ultimately what happens in democracies boils down to the question of how public preferences are given meaningful institutional expression, such that the circle between political structures and social values may be a virtuous one. If the current democratic order was once again forged anew in the crises of the 1970s this is because it was the democracies that moved first and most radically, in response to a constellation of crises that ruptured the postwar political and economic order, not their authoritarian counterparts, as it had been in the 1930s. Yet the present moment of crisis presents us with a return, if not a sharpening, of disgruntlement at the perceived inefficiencies of democratic rule. As popular faith in democracy dwindles, a series of interlinked problems are emerging: these are apparent at the national and the international level alike.

At the national level, perhaps the most important problem has been the loss of moral legitimacy that democratic institutions came to hold in the postwar era. In part, the causes of this are secular and longer term: in a globalizing world, modern democratic governance has of necessity become so complex that it can be hard to see just how any one part of the system fits in with another. Europeans are thus asked to elect local, national, *and* European MPs, all of whom might be representatives of different political parties, and whose policies take effect at a tangent to other parts of the system—rights and the law, institutional norms, civil services, and binding international agreements. They are expected to understand the implications of central bank policies. It becomes impossible to know with certainty exactly how to effect change, or that one's desire even to do so actually "matters." Uncertainty has become institutionalized. Voter apathy and popular discontent inevitably follow. Such disengagement has been exacerbated by the (often justified) sense of exclusion wrought by the rise of money in politics and the lobby system, leaving citizens feeling more like passive spectators than engaged publics.

But the roots of the moral crisis are to be found at a more existential level as well. Writing in the immediate aftermath of the Cold War, the historian Charles Maier noted at the time "a profound shift of public attitude along three dimensions: a sudden sense of historical dislocation, a disaffection with the political leadership of all parties, and a recurring skepticism about doctrines of social progress."[8] All three hung together, Maier claimed, but equally—we might say with hindsight—they hung around, for each is only all the more apparent today. Of *historical dislocation*, and above all the sense that grander times had recently passed, there is today not only the Golden Age to look back to and lament, but the failed promises of the age of convergence, as I have described it, and the promises of liberal globalization more broadly. When we inquire into what it is that we feel may have passed, the answer usually comes in the form of a reminder that any democratic order that seeks to flourish must be willing to hold the capitalist system itself to account.

Of *political disaffection* it is hard to know whether the populist revolt against Europe or the Trump ascendancy in America is the more obvious sign. Either way both were indicative of a widespread suspicion of the political elite that had been erupting in the form of Ross Perot, of the Tea Party, of the Swedish Democrats, and the rise of Jobbik in Hungary, long before these all finally coalesced into a widespread antiliberal moment during the recession. Our failure to rouse ourselves to meet the most basic needs of refugees arriving at our borders is also, in this respect, a prime indicator of just how disaffected we have become; perversely our very guilt on this last matter seems also to have contributed to the wider redirected truculence.

This leads on, in its way, to Maier's third complaint: of *skepticism in social progress*, for which one could look to anything from the failure of the progressive left to rouse itself properly for three decades, to the exhausted recourse to techno-utopianism (for the globalists) and protectionism (for the "little people"). As each of these critiques articulates all too clearly, the crisis of democratic governments today is equally a crisis of institutional capacity as it is one of moral legitimacy. The sharp political conflicts raised by the upheavals of the past few years—*who* was ultimately going to pay for the bank bailouts; *which* immigrants should be admitted and on what terms?—have overwhelmed the executive branch of governments who find that they have given away the tools they need to respond. With parliamentary politics increasingly mired in partisan deadlock it was perhaps inevitable that more and more executives would turn to extraparliamentary forms of policymaking instead: the judiciary has been one beneficiary of this process of depoliticization (with human rights to guarantee your freedoms, why put up with a messy and corrupt parliamentary democracy offering the same?); but the institutions of market governance have been another; and the populists in their echo chamber a third.

Sharpening these problems is the fact that parliaments too have been weakened during the past forty years, and often merit the disapproval directed their way. Elections may well be fundamental to democracy, but they are not its limit, and electioneering, duly fetishized, spread during the post-1970s era to become a twenty-four-hour, year-round affair. Politicians became so busy running for office they found they had less and less time to run the office itself properly. Driven by the short-term needs of modern, market societies—the call to passivity of the "great moderation," the demands for consumer credit so as to forestall more awkward distributional questions, the juggling of the many private suppliers of what were once central state functions—liberal democratic leaders have little chance to think strategically about the real challenges of the day. Nor do their citizens, as they are buffeted less by the onrush of globalization than by the way they are forced to confront this on their own. Their leaders then project the insecurity people inevitably feel into exogenous threats that demand to be addressed: short-term tactics in a game of political survival.

The result is that "real" politics has come to be conducted in an antipolitical register while "politics as usual" is reduced to mere spectacle, a fact that further enhances the turn to extrapolitical procedures in the first place. The usual solution to this problem has been to call for more transparency. But if the quality of democracy is not enhanced by procedural integrity alone (a claim often pursued by the libertarians and political minimalists) it is not enhanced when it is turned over to ill-informed masses either. Deliberative capacity and institutional capability are both required: and that gives due privilege to technocrats and citizens alike. Integrity is as important as transparency, and in fact a degree of political closure *is* required to give trust something to latch on to.

One consequence of the refusal to accept this has been an avowed turn away from the twentieth-century politics of moderated conflict toward the antipolitics of the refuseniks or the total politics of the authoritarians. The effect has been to undermine democracy's core value in the modern age: the consensual management of difference. After all, democracy is not simply, or even primarily, about political rights or even political procedures, though it may rely on these things. As a political system its success rests upon its ability to function as a form of legitimate coercion, through the collective assignment of political and material resources and of capabilities; and not by governments alone, but by markets and social institutions as well.[9] Democracy is a function, in other words, of a wider prevailing commitment to reconciling pluralism with political justice.

The current upheavals of the capitalist system, of parliamentary institutions and liberal values, constitute a crisis of this very commitment. In that sense it is distinct from the last great crisis in the West, of legitimation or governability (depending on one's point of view) in the early–mid 1970s, and different in turn to the interwar crisis before that. It does not help to overgeneralize, however. Amid the undeniably widespread sense of upheaval and the underlying commonalities of its cause, there exist a multitude of national and regional variations. As the sociologist Peter Hall put it: "If every democracy is unhappy, each is unhappy in its own way."[10] But equally it does not help to think of the challenges confronting the Western democracies as internally constituted alone. The wider power structure in which their specific problems are embedded matters as well. Indeed, it is the manner of their interleaving with that wider structure which raises the other salient element of democracy's current crisis: the international domain.

Two problems confront the Western democracies here. In the first place is the unraveling of the liberal vision of economic globalization to which the United States and its democratic allies determined, in the 1970s, to hitch their fate. Relieved of the Cold War as an imperative for collective action (admittedly of a certain militarized sort), the people were given globalization instead. This sated their drives, channeled their distemper, and relieved politicians once again—or so it seemed—of the need to address fundamental problems in the management of their societies. It also contributed to the development of forms of market governance that privilege the international economy, while confining and undermining political democracy at the level of the nation state.

As much of what I have chosen to write about here I hope makes clear, the nation state was not withering away during the 1990s, as so many claimed, and nor is it today. Rather it was being reconfigured, hollowed out, and the space opened up for more exclusionary forms of nationalism to take root within that emptied nest: and this was happening in dialogue with a global revanchism that prioritized an international order based upon the rights of property as above the rights of states (let alone societies). This has led to no small amount of misdirected anger. For globalization *itself* is not the problem: it is the removal from democratic oversight of the property-based system through which it is pursued that is the problem. The travails of the euro aside, the EU is a remarkable achievement whose demonstrated capacity to address some of the avowedly transnational challenges of the late twentieth- and early twenty-first-century era demonstrates what societies acting together can achieve. But it equally reveals the problems of failing to institutionalize the social and economic rights of populations, in addition to their freedom to move and to trade.

Is this what people really want? The failure of Europe's leaders to secure a "constitution" for Europe in the early 2000s is often taken to suggest that it is not. The response in the UK to the 2016 vote to leave the EU suggests a different story, however. After all, the European citizens of those nations who participated in the earlier referenda to approve a proposed European constitution could just as easily not have bothered: including the French and the Dutch who ultimately rejected it. The problem confronting European and American intergovernmentalism alike is not in any case best described as a "democratic deficit," as we have seen, but as a "democratic gap." It is a problem not of structurally unaccountable decision-making, but of there being too many processes that lie *beyond* the purview of democratic oversight altogether: environmental controls and finance, to pluck just two historically salient examples from this era, among them.

Ironically, while the current US president for one has been only too happy to throw his weight behind the protectionist chanting that emerged after the financial crisis, he has been positively glowing, at the same time, in his praise for the other element of the international challenge: the resurgent, and deeply transnational, antiliberal discourse we are witnessing around the globe. This is deeply ironic, since the current wave of antiliberalism emerged in the vacuum created by the decline of US hegemony, and by the retreat of the Western democracies more broadly from the geopolitical dominance they enjoyed in the postwar years.

The Iraq War and the "war on terror" must shoulder some of the blame here. But so too does that much longer-running effort of American "realists," both liberal internationalists and neoconservatives alike, to construct an international economic regime dedicated primarily to the law of private property not the law of social justice. The roots of the current disorder must therefore surely be seen to lie in these postwar political developments also. Convinced that democracy followed where capitalism led, Western leaders later focused on maximizing the returns from this capitalist franchise in the immediate post–Cold War moment, rather than embedding liberal social values in the global institutional architecture: one which, for a few years, was indeed their dominium to order. The return flow on that particular historical investment is today all too apparent.

A Silent Revolution

The past four and a half decades have been much more than just a long run-up to the present moment of crisis. On the contrary, democracy *itself* has been continuously reimagined in light of the challenges that marked the beginning of the era. This work of reinvention provided a certain intellectual and institutional cohesion to much of what followed; it gave shape, as I hope to have shown, to the entire era. Several aspects of this history stand out. Perhaps most significantly the nature of political subjectivity has changed. In the aftermath of 1968, politics moved from the domain of "ideological activism" into two parallel areas that were opened up by the political-economic developments of the time: first, the elective channels of domestic social movements and, secondly, the emergence of a new liberal internationalism (be it humanitarian organizations founded by disgruntled '68ers, or the more professionalized wing of state-based socioeconomic internationalism).

Each of these developments helped define the tenor of the new democratic order taking root already in the 1970s: of politics as choice and solidarities as identity-based, in which rights replaced duties and political commitments were subject to the means–end calculus of utilitarian philosophies largely done with the idea of political "virtue." It was as if the more that society became secularized, the more that politics became rudimentarily moralized: the rise of conservative corporate evangelism in the US in the mid–late 1970s representing, perhaps, the pervading metaphor of both. This was bound up with a related change in the nature of political agency, which previously had centered on class and now centered, from the 1970s onward, on identity.

One consequence of the turn to a politics of movement and expression was the fact that, as the American commentator Fareed Zakaria put it, democracy went from being "a form of government to a way of life."[11] At that point political institutions come to matter less than the provision of an equality of access to political resource. Along with their commitment to aping the uncritically promarket stance of their more radicalized Republican counterparts, this hobbled the left because it took away the working-class subject it had long represented (hence the US Democrats' embrace of "minorities"). The rise of a precariat, in place of a working class, largely passed this new left by, given the limited terms of their political vision.

Instead it was the ethnic nationalism of the right that ultimately caught the attention of these malcontents. By then, however, citizenship had changed too. No longer "one" thing, it was now a more fractured phenomenon. A person might claim health care as one sort of (workplace) citizen, and political rights as another sort of (birthplace) citizen; meanwhile, their welfare entitlements might be derived from a third category of (status) citizenship while their fiscal obligations to the state (via taxes) were worked out in a fourth and further register of overlapping labor regimes and reciprocity agreements.[12] Is it any wonder that more exclusionary, because willfully more rudimentary, forms of nationalism re-emerged amidst this thicket of overlapping attachments? The unintended (and unfair) outcome of the left's decades-long commitment to identity politics thus proved itself to have been of ultimate advantage to the right.

A further transformation has taken place in the relationship between the market and the state. Since the 1970s (and again in the 1990s), the chase for lost productivity growth fueled a slew of policies that allowed inequality to rise once again in an effort to restore the prior rate of profit. These decades have seen stagnant wages for the lower middle classes, the social detachment of the rich, and a fraying of the basic distributive commitment to share out a portion of the national pie. No one would describe Europe as a "walled garden" any longer. School-children aside, nobody could rightly describe America as the land of "liberty and justice for all." No one says of Australia that it is welcoming of immigrants and stragglers. Competition has been tougher; comforts for all have been replaced by luxuries for the few and their usually uncosted burdens upon the rest.

In the form this struggle ultimately took, territorial nationalism came to stand as the antithesis to economic globalism. In the process, not just political consensus but value pluralism became harder to achieve. To be sure, it was easier to be pluralist within the more limited confines of homogeneous societies, and this was one reason it began to be challenged in the early 1970s through immigration and was always a flawed conceit in the racially divided United States. But pluralism in its essence is both more, and less, than the acceptance of "others." It is the disposition to cede *voluntarily* certain of one's own privileges.

If Western democracies in the current era lack an effective defense against the decline of such solidarity as we had before, then it is partly because, having turned to a more neoliberal variant of capitalism in the 1970s, they also created the perfect conditions for a more plutocratic form of political order: one that reinforced the trend to siloization. Elites are encouraged to be "tolerant" of those who look or act differently (yet another elective attribute prioritized this time under the banner of "multiculturalism") but little more. They are rarely challenged. And so they are frequently no more than indifferent to those who are deemed simply to be less "aspirational." Social life dims a little at the top as well. It is not clear if this is a winning formula for elites any more than it is for the rest.

And yet post–financial crisis, it is not just the upward mobility to which earlier generations had become accustomed that has come to a halt (if it has not actually been stolen by the wealthiest of all). Many people are now experiencing a rapid fall backward. The costs of the financial crisis in Europe and especially in America have been disproportionately borne by the least well off. The loading up of public debt that accompanied the bailing out of the banks has reinforced existing social fault lines. In Europe this has put an unbearable strain on already struggling welfare states; in America, which never had the level of social protections that European democracies built up, it has lit a touchpaper underneath long-simmering social tensions. The atmosphere is febrile. Society is riven and torn.

The state too has worn thin all this time. It has been challenged in successive waves of retrenchment: first, in the 1970s, the basic assumption that the state should be the arbiter of social changes was challenged in the breakup of the old distributional consensus and the new market-based approach to governing at a distance put in its place. This focused primarily on the state's capacity to regulate the economy. It was followed, in the 1990s, by a second wave of retrenchment, centered upon the role of the state in defining the public character of society: whether it was the progressive state's embrace of equality of opportunity over outcome, or the conservative state's embrace of the marketplace as the arbiter of cultural worth. In both cases societies were offered less interference by the state (in exchange, usually, for being given fewer resources as well). Then, in the years after 9/11 and the financial crisis, a third wave of retrenchment amplified the powers of the executive core while further downgrading the "civil" capacities of the state, such as the duty to respect people's privacy.

The result is that the one retrenchment of the state that the twentieth-century experience of totalitarianism teaches us is desirable (reining in

747

the state's powers of executive force and its ability to disregard due process) is the one retrenchment yet to be undertaken in a twenty-first-century liberal democracy. The further problem with the current democratic state is that it is no longer just "one" thing either. As economic processes became more universal in their prescriptions states disaggregated in response: the possible utopia of transgovernmentalism briefly glimpsed in the early 1990s has become (because the public were not invited to take part in it at the right time) the technocratic monster of today. Political sovereignty was orphaned at the moment it should have been discovering extended family members elsewhere. As collective political platforms disappeared, people became not only less inclined than before to want to participate in the selection of representatives, they found the very act of politics itself an increasing distraction.

This was the premise that political minimalism thrived upon as it variously took root across the liberal democracies from the 1970s onward. What most characterized that political minimalism was its grounding in the popular rejection of political participation as a solution to the challenge of the technical and institutional complexity of modern life. As two authors rightly put it in 2015: "Asked to inform themselves about the important political issues of the day, most citizens politely decline. If forced to hold an informed opinion on every law and regulation, many would gladly mount the barricades to defend their right not to rule themselves in such a burdensome manner."[13] Ever since the crises that began colliding into one another from 2011 onward, the costs of this political disengagement have become clear.

Donald Trump was a reminder that a country like the US was, by 2016, less "democratic" than it had been before—and not because of what was happening in the White House (Trump himself was as much the expression of the problem as its cause). The US was less democratic because this is what the people themselves had unthinkingly brought about for many years. The American Cornel West was no doubt right that Trump so "shattered" the political establishment in America because each of the two main political parties had for too long remained "wedded to the rule of Big Money and to the reign of meretricious politicians."[14] But as Trump's first year in office suggested, not least the success that his tax cut had in mobilizing the Republican base, the rule of money and a meretricious politics were two things that Trump, of all people, was if anything only going to reinforce. The successful nomination of Brett Kavanaugh to the Supreme Court in Trump's second year in office merely confirmed this, tightening the conservative grip on an already wayward component of American democracy. *Therein* lay the real danger of the moment: his intensification of already existing problems.

Far from the United States' shores it was, ironically, the last remaining redoubts of social democracy—whose obituary had been written many times during the previous four decades—which fared best of all in these years. What were their secrets to share? Never a product of the good times, and only partly of oil or small homogeneous societies, social democracy was in fact a politics of hard graft and desperate times: specifically, of the interwar years in continental Europe. It was successful elsewhere on the Continent until, for the reasons explored here, its achievements were variously rolled back and repealed. In that sense it is as much what Scandinavia has avoided that matters here. What was living in social democracy today—to answer the pressing question posed by British historian Tony Judt, just months before he died in 2010—was social democracy's core ethic of political compromise in the name of collective justice.[15]

This does not make it immune to the forces of political discontent, as the rise of the xenophobic Swedish Democrats and the breakdown in the consensus notion of *samhold* in Scandinavia have reinforced. Nor is nostalgia of any help. In a globalizing age Sweden's problems may be Europe's problems as much as anything else; but social democracy has its own flaws to reckon with here as well. As to what was dead (the other part of Judt's question), the answer to that was the now outdated institutional apparatus social democracy retains still, in a world where the old class allegiances that underpinned sectoral bargaining and collective compromise no longer hold. A return to the twentieth-century past is clearly not the solution to the incredible challenges of the twenty-first-century present. But that fact alone is insufficient reason to consign the whole experience to the dustbin.

On the contrary, political compromise and collective justice, no matter what the immediate circumstances and ambitions, will always be required in any form of democracy worthy of the name. After all, something needs to stand for the pillars of a more hopeful democratic architecture; what Nixon saw falling down all around him in 1971 needs putting back up. And what the last few decades teach us more than anything else is that what really matters in democracy is the forming and the testing of ideas, including something approximating a general education in them, that takes place along the way to fairly putting some individuals in, and some out, of power. The problem thus ultimately lies not with the populists and the antiliberals, any more than it does with immigration, or globalization, or any other of the apparent plagues of the moment. It lies with the various ways that liberalism, democracy, and capitalism have been forged together in the post-70s era, in a transnationalizing moment and in light of a series of common social and political-economic challenges. But where does recognition of this leave us today and in the future?

Of Peoples and Publics: Democracy's Futures

Restoring democracy today requires that we know what tools we have at our disposal. Arguably the most important tool is the willingness and capacity to work toward different goals within the bounds of common civic norms. Democracy is no more, and no less, than a reflection of the will of a people agreeing to bind themselves to such norms. If the people are angry, resentful, and confused then so too will be the democratic system they constitute. Forgetting this is one reason why some of the most complacent, yet widespread, explanations for democracy's current travails see that the true threat to democracy lies elsewhere, in its tendency to unthinking *excess*.

Amid a wave of plebiscites and political referenda, we are today routinely told that the people are uninformed; their votes are liabilities. Brexit, said Mark Leonard, the director of the European Council on Foreign Relations, was the crowning moment of "demotic democracy."[16] This is the view of those who, not unlike Tocqueville himself, fear the herd-like behavior of the "masses" and their "demagogic" instincts as the dark side of political emancipation. Others, like political philosopher Jason Brennan, take the opposite tack and claim that people have so little say with their one single vote there is no point participating in the first place.

For still others, this is just a "hatred of democracy": the sleight of hand by which those who purport to defend "democracy" do so by gainsaying a narrow and particular form of it in the name of "repress[ing] the catastrophe of democratic civilization." Perhaps the solution here is to be found in various forms of "counterdemocracy," and some are certainly swayed by the promise of more direct participation: hence the rise in referenda. But for others still the best solutions are precisely the ones articulated by those who promise to lead the masses to ends they can only guess at (until the guessing game is outlawed).[17] The threat posed by the rise of illiberal regimes today, therefore, is not that of some "wave" spreading over the West, it is that they will continue to stoke *existing* anxieties and exacerbate *existing* flaws within the democratic countries, in just the ways that Vladimir Putin has mastered.

Perhaps we are best served by taking the opposite tack to all of these voices and reaching instead for some better institutional means of expressing the modest virtues that democracy demands. After all, if one of the current challenges confronting democracy is the fact that it has become all things to all people, then this may be the best way both to honor it and to safeguard its future; not least it would provide the means to take back from the merchants of envy and fear that constituency of citizens who rightly wish to belong and to be heard when they speak up for their own. This requires, paradoxically, acknowledging that democracy is *less* than we usually claim it to be: that it does not guarantee prosperity, that it offers no formula, in and of itself, for the good life, and that it will vary from culture to culture. This still leaves it a lot more than just the worst system apart from all the others, as Churchill famously observed. It makes it the gateway to better systems in the future (something the others avowedly are not).

At present, however, we are hampered in pursuing this because our politics has foundered between the national and international scale. We genuinely don't know which way to turn, between national institutions that have been hollowed out and international ones that have not yet been built up. Some, like Germany's Wolfgang Streeck, favor relocating all sovereign powers back to the national level. Yet repatriating political rule in this way may be hard to distinguish from the populists' own claims that the natives must always come first. Britain's desperate struggle to figure out how to "repatriate" the powers it had granted to Brussels, in the two years following on from its vote to exit the EU, suggests that such a prospect may not even be realistic.

Others, like Greece's Yanis Varoufakis who would found a trans-continental social movement, point to the international arena as the solution to national problems, perhaps correctly realizing that the only way for democracy is up. They duly set course to do battle with the transnational elite on their own privileged terrain. Still others pin their hopes on the micropolitical level of local affairs, in the belief that communitarian values might serve as a crutch for more demanding democratic ones, at least until better times return. Ernesto Cortés Jr., cochair of the Industrial Areas Foundation, an influential community-organizing network in America, thus insists it is *only* possible to work at the municipal scale: "there's just too much money at the national level," he observed in 2018, "it's hopeless."[18]

Seen thus, the Western democracies would appear to have arrived at something of a turning point. The solutions found not just to the problems of democracy in the 1970s but to those of the 1930s before that (namely judicial review, constrained popular channels, parliamentary restraint, government at a distance) have themselves become the cause of a present and debilitating impasse. Even now the people aren't really trusted, and yet more than ever popular mobilization is needed to break through the gridlock. The problem is not the scale of political action at all, then, so much as the mismatch at every level between people's individual political agency and their means for realizing this autonomously.

The fact that recent years have seen a recentralization of executive power on the one hand alongside a dismemberment of state capacity on the other is a testament to this and the starting point of any organized response. The relevant question here is how to deepen (and in some cases to restore) the institutional capacity of democracy without pandering to either demagogic or monopoly power. To do this we need to think of popular sovereignty as more than just a property of the *national* electorate: granting democratic power to transnational organizations is not necessarily "giving it away"; likewise narrowing the demos along racial or class lines is not necessarily "taking it back." We need both to restore popular consent *and* render it accountable to the interests of society at large. Figuring that out is the first challenge that awaits us.

If there is a crisis of democracy today it is as much because of what has been done (and not done) to its institutions and values over the past four decades as it is of democracy's own inherent flaws (of which there are plenty). This means that there is scope enough for the undoing of what is wrong and the redoing of what may be right. The nature of social problems and collective needs changed substantially in the course of the second half of the twentieth century, and without the right institutional innovations it is no surprise that democracies have struggled to keep up. It is also worth bearing in mind that other political regimes foundered more catastrophically, and that fascism and state communism proved not to have the answers to the challenge of political modernity at all. Their demise is worth celebrating still. Democracy remains, then, the most adaptable political system by far. But democratic society also requires of its citizens a certain level of contribution if it is successfully to manage what will always be an unevenness of social attributes and a scarcity of economic resources.

And there are certain tensions within liberal democracy today that will need to be acknowledged if they are to be addressed. In light of this we should be wary of where some promised solutions might lead. It was, after all, against the "absurd, conventional untruth of political equality dressed out in the garb of collective irresponsibility" that Mussolini argued in 1935, citing Renan, for a more "organized, centralized, and authoritative democracy," as some are doing once again today. Mussolini called upon the liberal faith to acknowledge that the game was up and to "shut the doors of its deserted temples."[19] The democracy that is rooted not just in freedom but in equality is the greatest of all those temples. It was abandoned at great cost in the interwar era and resurrected at even greater cost in the political reconstruction of total war. Tempted away once more by the siren song of political individualism, the temple is growing empty once again. This is why some detect, in the "crisis of parliamentary democracy" today, certain chilling echoes of the interwar period.

Perhaps the most concerning fact, however, is that now, as then, the most convincing strongmen do not dispute democracy but argue simply for a more "authentic" form of it. The weakened democracy we have contrived for ourselves in recent decades may prove a poorly dug-in defense against such claims. The struggle that has defined our times truly has been the struggle not *for* but *over* democracy itself. The challenge today is to understand and explain why capitalist prosperity failed to offer an antidote to the rise of illiberalism at home and abroad, and to find ways of doing democracy better so that the people themselves may separate good accounts of political order from the bad. Ironically, in contrast to some of those taking to the streets, this may require that we learn to have *more* patience rather than less, since the structural changes needed will take time if they are to be undertaken properly. In a world of click-bait and social media feeds, patience may well be the hardest virtue of all to recover. But if democracy is to be defended, the challenge begins here all the same: in the realm of the mind. This bodes both good and ill.

"Never since the end of World War II, and perhaps since the Russian Revolution," wrote the American intellectual Mark Lilla in 2014, "has political thinking in the West been so shallow and clueless."[20] That must change and in contrast to the patience of our actions it must change fast. There are signs it is beginning to do so. Ironically it may now be from its enemies that the more hopeful metaphor we need can be picked up and dusted off. Democracy is indeed a temple to be tended to and respected—a housing for power and for constant reflection upon it—as much as it is a form of popular power itself. But that temple needs reconstructing today if its potential is to be realized. Its unique role in safeguarding human freedom and equality needs reprising. Its capacity to endow the greatest number of people with the means to achieve their ambitions needs rediscovering. Its ability to put politics at the service of all people needs reinventing once again. Its future still beckons us all.

Acknowledgments

A BOOK LIKE THIS owes its existence to a great many people. First of all are the many scholars from whose work I have learned and drawn: far more than I have been able to acknowledge here. I am also extremely grateful to the various institutions who have hosted me. To understand properly what has been afoot in our democracy has required working across a range of disciplines, not to mention subdisciplines—including history, political economy, political science, international relations, sociology, and law—and navigating this is a task in which I have been assisted by others. For helping me enter their world as a fellow scholar, and not just a "visiting" one, I am grateful to Mark Mazower and the History Department at Columbia University, along with Eileen Gillooly and the Heyman Center for the Humanities, where I spent some of 2013–14. In Oslo, Kristian Berg Harpviken and his colleagues, mostly in international relations and political science, at the Peace Research Institute Oslo (PRIO) have been unstintingly helpful and generous supporters of myself and this book project in particular. For 2016–17 they gave me a desk at which to write and bookshelves to fill, at a time when I needed both. I am grateful as well to the staff at the Norwegian Institute for International Affairs, where I was able to spend some weeks sharing ideas, between those visits in 2015.

My home institution of Queen Mary, University of London, remains a place where I can count some of the very best scholars as the closest of friends. From my own School of Geography, in particular, I would like to thank Adrian Smith, Miles Ogborn, Catherine Nash, Alastair Owens, Alison Blunt, Jane Wills, Tim Brown, Sam Halvorsen, and Philippa Williams, all of whom have helped me, knowingly or not, in the course of writing this book. Across campus I have been variously assisted by Julian Jackson in the School of History, Rick Saull and Engin Isin in the School of Politics and International Relations, Valsamis Mitsilegas, Eric Heinze, Isobel Roele, Neve Gordon, and Eva Nanopoulos in the School of Law, and Maks del Mar and his Centre for Law and Society in a

Global Context. In connection with a Distinguished Visiting Fellowship at QMUL, Harvard's Charles Maier was a generous interlocutor during 2016–17. For the opportunity to arrange that visit and, more recently, to help take forward the interdisciplinary work of the new Institute for Humanities and Social Sciences, I am grateful to Matthew Hilton and the QMUL Faculty of Humanities and Social Sciences. Also (then) at Harvard I am grateful to Sam Moyn for including me in some of the work being undertaken by a new and brilliant generation of young historians and for generously supporting some of my own research at the edges of that endeavor. Within geography I must thank Derek Gregory, who, over dinner in Oslo, gave me the encouragement I needed in 2012 to get on and do this; Gerry Kearns, Danny Dorling, Stuart Elden, David Nally, and Matt Sparke have each offered specific and useful guidance in the years since.

I have been fortunate to receive funding from a variety of sources. The Leverhulme Trust has been a generous supporter of my work, and the writing of this book has spanned and benefited from a Philip Leverhulme Prize (2011) and a Philip Leverhulme Fellowship (2014–16). Both those awards were to carry out other work, but this project would never have enjoyed the continuity it required without them. The writing has also been directly supported by the Norwegian Writers Association (NFFO), who provided generous stipendiary assistance for much of 2012 (Grant: 16511). Fritt Ord (Norwegian PEN) also kindly supported me that same year when otherwise I might have had to give the whole thing up (Grant: 1110-61-40). All have been patient and generous. I am grateful to PRIO for an internal project development grant to assist me in further developing some of the ideas within this book, and to those who engaged with me in the process.

This work has, inevitably, been a huge investment of time: but not just my own. I am beholden to Kristin Sandvik and Ole Jacob Sending, two friends and brilliant scholars in their own fields of law and international relations with whom I am lucky enough to have collaborated (and who were unlucky enough to be handed large chunks of prose to read by way of thanks). For offering detailed comments on different versions of this manuscript I am also grateful to Nils Gilman, whose interventions were critical to getting me started again at a point when work and health alike were faltering. Thanks too to Martin Conway, David Ekbladh, Jason Miklian, Kristoffer Lidén, Maria Gabrielsen, Henrik Syse, Greg Reichberg, Neve Gordon, Matt Sparke, Noam Maggor, Shereen Fernandez, David Jacobsen, Kristian Hoelscher, Magnus Marsdal, Nadia Urbinati, and Colin

Holmes for insightful feedback. None of the above are responsible for the product that results. Family and friends have likewise been a source of much support. I am thankful in particular to my parents, Jan and Duncan, for their own attentive readings when in truth they had other things to occupy their attention, and to Ola Storeng and Joan Piorkowski for detailed comments and suggestions. "Sto Diethnes to Magazi" appears by permission of Kostas Hatzis; translation by Theodoros Rakopoulos.

I am once again enormously grateful for the support and encouragement of my agent, Georgina Capel, and her team in London. In the UK and for taking on this book, twice, I also once again owe a debt of gratitude to Nick Davies at Hodder, then Canongate, and now again back at Hodder (John Murray Press). If Nick could slow down the ascent of his career it would be a pleasure to see through one whole book with him. Joe Zigmond, who took over the work of editing this book in 2017, picked up a huge manuscript without flinching and asked me if there was more to come: his poker face is not to be underestimated, nor are his acuity, patience, and grasp of the material, each of which has been astonishing to observe. At John Murray, Martin Bryant was a superlative copyeditor and Caroline Westmore calmly shepherded us all over the finishing line. My thanks are also due to Howard Davies for proofreading and to Douglas Matthews for compiling the index. In the US it has been a pleasure to work with Ben Loehnen, who has been unfailingly supportive of "Moby Dick's" advance throughout.

When I started this book I was just married and did not yet have two incredible sons. I certainly had no idea that I would give the best years of my thirties to nurturing a whale as well as a family; I hope there has been enough of me left over for them all. This book is dedicated to Oscar and Elias and to my darling wife, Katerini, as ever. They have been my strength and inspiration alike. The boys are still figuring out letters, but I look forward to their comments in due course.

SRH
Cambridge, October 2018

Notes

Introduction

1. This game has been played on several fronts at the same time. Alongside a liberal triumphalism, the first two decades of the post–Cold War era saw a return of what Jan-Werner Müller characterizes as the *Feindwissenschaft* of newly mooted enemies of the West: be this Samuel Huntington's *Clash of Civilizations*, or more recent polemics of radical Islam. The effect is to *claim* a displacement of the dangerous political passions of the Western twentieth century outside of the West. Fascism may still exist, but not here, so we are told (see Jan-Werner Müller, "European Intellectual History as Contemporary History," *Journal of Contemporary History*, 46 (3), pp. 574–90, p. 585).

2. Pierre Rosanvallon, *La légitimité démocratique* (Seuil, 2008), p. 317. See also Daniel Bensaïd, "Permanent Scandal," Chapter 3 in Giorgio Agamben (et al.), *Democracy in What State?* (Columbia University Press, 2011), p. 19 for discussion; "What's Gone Wrong With Democracy?," *The Economist*, March 1, 2014.

3. Arthur Schlesinger Jr., "Has Democracy a Future?," *Foreign Affairs*, September–October 1997, p. 11.

4. Hans Kelsen, "Foundations of Democracy," *Ethics*, Vol. 66 (1), Part II (October 1955), pp. 1–101.

5. See Daniel Rodgers, *Contested Truths: Keywords in American Politics Since Independence* (Harvard, 1998), p. 182; failed experiments: see Sheri Berman, "Against the Technocrats," *Dissent* magazine, Winter 2018; eleven democracies: see John Keane, *The Life and Death of Democracy* (Simon & Schuster, 2009), p. xxiii; the postwar moment and "fatigue": see Judith Shklar, *After Utopia: The Decline of Political Faith* (Princeton, 1969), p. ix.

6. On the darker side of Tocqueville, liberalism, and empire: see especially Cheryl B. Welch, "Colonial Violence and the Rhetoric of Evasion: Tocqueville on Algeria," *Political Theory*, 3.2 (April 2003): 235–64; Demin Duan, "Reconsidering Tocqueville's Imperialism," *Ethical Perspectives*, 17.3 (2010): 415–47; and Jennifer Pitts, "Empire and Democracy: Tocqueville and the Algeria Question," *Journal of Political Philosophy*, 8.3 (September 2000): 295–318.

7. Fascism and communism were neither moral nor ideological equivalents, nor were they each preformed "rivals" to liberalism (and to liberal democracy) as is too often portrayed. They were at least in part (along with anticolonial nationalism) responses to the failings of early twentieth-century liberalism, just as later twentieth-century liberalism was in part a response to their failings. To see the struggle between them as simply a war of attrition between good and evil, and to imagine that struggle only took place at a singular, flat point in time, is to underestimate the modulations each undertook in

relation to the other. See, inter alia, Marcel Gauchet, *L'Avènement de la démocratie* (Editions Gallimard), Vols. II and III esp.; and Mark Mazower, *Dark Continent: Europe's Twentieth Century* (Vintage, 2000 [1998]), Chapter 1 esp.

8. Adam Tooze and Stefan Eich, "The Great Inflation," in Anselm Doering-Manteuffel, Lutz Raphael, and Thomas Schlemmer (eds), *Vorgeschichte der Gegenwart. Dimensionen des Strukturbruchs nach dem Boom* (Göttingen: Vandenhoeck & Ruprecht, 2015). They refer here specifically to a crisis of "capitalist governance," though this was experienced as a crisis of democracy as well.

9. Stanisław Aronson, "I Survived the Warsaw Ghetto. Here Are the Lessons I'd Like to Pass On," *Guardian*, September 5, 2018.

10. On the geography of the "West," its internal and external construction, see Hans-Jürgen Puhle, "Trajectories and Transformations of Western Democracies: 1950s–2000s," pp. 153–70 in Paul Nolte, *Transatlantic Democracy in the Twentieth Century: Transfer and Transformation* (De Gruyter Oldenbourg, 2016), p. 155.

11. Andrew Stroehlein, Human Rights Watch Media Director, Twitter account, July 28, 2015; Orbán's speech was to the 26th Bálványos Summer Open University and Student Camp, July 25, 2015: http://www.kormany.hu/en/the-prime-minister/the-prime-minister-s-speeches/prime-minister-viktor-orban-s-presentation-at-the-26th-balvanyos-summer-open-university-and-student-camp.

Prologue

1. Cited in Niall Ferguson, "Crisis, What Crisis?," Introduction to Niall Ferguson, Charles S. Maier, Erez Manela, and Daniel J. Sargent (eds), *The Shock of the Global: The 1970s in Perspective* (Harvard, 2011), p. 14. See also: Thomas Borstelmann, *The 1970s: A New Global History, from Civil Rights to Inequality* (Princeton, 2011), p. 57.

2. Cited in Michel Crozier, Samuel P. Huntington, Joji Watanuki, *The Crisis of Democracy: Report on the Governability of Democracies to the Trilateral Commission* (New York University Press, 1975), p. 2.

3. Cited in Andrew Glyn, *Capitalism Unleashed: Finance, Globalization, and Welfare* (OUP, 2007), p. 7.

4. Daniel Sargent, *A Superpower Transformed: The Remaking of American Foreign Relations in the 1970s* (OUP, 2015), pp. 60–1. The USSR boasted 1,500 ICBMs by 1970, up from just 400 in 1966. Across the same period the Western arsenal remained largely the same, at around 1,000.

5. "De Gaulle, au musée," and to "plunge the French people," cited in Robert Gildea, *France Since 1945* (OUP, 2009 [2002]), pp. 62–3.

6. On the flight from France: Robert Gildea, *France Since 1945*, p. 63; on the (frankly unrealistic) speculations of Soviet contacts: see Paul-François Paoli, "Moscou dans l'ombre du Général," *Le Figaro*, June 19, 2008, and Henri-Christian Giraud, "L'accord secret du Baden-Baden: Comment de Gaulle et les Soviétiques ont mis fin à Mai 68" (Rocher, 2008); the definitive (and more sober) account is in Julian Jackson, *A Certain Idea of France: The Life of Charles de Gaulle* (Penguin, 2018), p. 676; for his actual Soviet diplomacy, see ibid., pp. 728–34, as well as for a detailed chronicle of the events of May 29–30; response to Prague Spring: Anton W. DePorte, "De Gaulle's Europe: Playing the Russian Card," *French Politics & Society*, 8.4 (Fall 1990): 25–40, p. 38.

7. De Gaulle's real intentions, rumors and details at the Élysée palace, and "There is no

point attacking . . .": see Jackson, op. cit., pp. 725–9; on the "existential" crisis this posed: see Anne Sa'adah, *Contemporary France: A Democratic Education* (Rowman & Littlefield, 2003), p. 100.

8. Resignation: Jackson, *A Certain Idea of France*, pp. 751–2.

9. Nicholas Atkin, *The French Fifth Republic* (Palgrave, 2004), p. 108.

10. John English, *Just Watch Me: The Life of Pierre Elliott Trudeau, 1968–2000*, Vol. II (Vintage, 2009), p. 19.

11. "catapult the country": ibid., p. 5; "the state has no business": cited in Robert Bothwell, *The Penguin History of Canada* (Penguin, 2008), p. 419; Trudeau's style: Margaret Conrad, *A Concise History of Canada* (Cambridge University Press, 2012), p. 247.

12. John English, *Just Watch Me*, pp. 43–7.

13. See ibid., pp. 76–104 esp.; "The October Crisis": CBC Digital Archives, available at: https://www.cbc.ca/archives/topic/the-october-crisis-civil-liberties-suspended.

14. P. E. Trudeau, "Notes for a National Broadcast, October 16, 1970," Canadian Privy Council Office, Library and Archives Canada. See also Claude Bélanger, "Chronology of the October Crisis," Marionopolis College, available at: http://faculty.marianopolis .edu/c.belanger/quebechistory/chronos/october.htm; "ice water": in John English, *Just Watch Me*, p. 6.

15. Adlai Stevenson, speaking of Nixon's then record as vice president in 1956: see Rick Pearlstein, *Nixonland: The Rise of a President and the Fracturing of America* (Simon & Schuster, 2008), p. 46; for the contemporary resonance, see Douglas E. Schoen, *The Nixon Effect: How Richard Nixon's Presidency Fundamentally Changed American Politics* (Encounter Books, 2016).

16. See Richard Halloran, "7000 Arrested in Capital War Protest; 150 are Hurt as Clashes Disrupt Traffic," *New York Times*, May 4, 1971.

17. See Jefferson Morley, "The Gentlemanly Planner of Assassinations," *Slate* magazine, November 1, 2002. The author of the phrase was Helms's biographer Thomas Powers in *Richard Helms and the CIA: The Man Who Kept the Secrets* (Alfred A. Knopf, 1979).

18. The *Washington Post* conveyed this opinion in the form of a cartoon: http://blogs.weta .org/boundarystones/2013/03/04/bomb-rocks-us-capitol.

19. Living conditions and the start of the uprising: Heather Ann Thompson, *Blood in the Water: The Attica Prison Uprising of 1971 and Its Legacy* (Pantheon, 2016), pp. 8 and 52–4.

20. Lewis Steel, "Inside the Attica Prison Uprising," *Salon*, September 10, 2016; see also Larry Getlen, "The True Story of the Attica Prison Riot," *New York Post*, August 20, 2016.

21. McKay Commission, cited in Clyde Haberman, "The Somber Shadows of Attica," *New York Times*, September 14, 2012; for other details see Malcolm Bell, *The Attica Turkey Shoot: Carnage, Cover-Up, and the Pursuit of Justice* (Grove Press, 1985).

22. Cited in George Megalogenis, *The Australian Moment* (Hamish Hamilton, 2012), p. 57.

23. James Reston, "The Crisis of Democracy," *New York Times*, March 3, 1974; the "cost of living" had of course been making itself felt for some time. See Keith Joseph, "Cost of Living," *Hansard*, July 28, 1965.

24. Cited in Steve Richards, "What Happens if Nobody Wins the UK Election?," *Guardian*, February 6, 2015.

25. James Reston, "The Crisis of Democracy," *New York Times*, March 3, 1974.

26. Ibid.; see also Thomas Borstelmann, *The 1970s: A New Global History* (Princeton University Press, 2013), reprint edn., pp. 8–9.

27. Maurice Isserman and Michael Kazin, *America Divided: The Civil War of the 1960s* (OUP, 2008), Chapter 14 esp.; John O'Farrell, "With the Saturday Night Massacre Nixon Miscalculated. Will Trump?," *Politico*, February 3, 2018.

28. Cited in James T. Patterson, *Restless Giant: The United States from Watergate to Bush v. Gore* (OUP, 2007), p. 2.

29. Associated Press Reporters, "Nixon in His Own Words: Forgotten 1983 Watergate Interview to Be Released," *Guardian*, August 5, 2014.

30. See Paul Nolte, *Transatlantic Democracy in the Twentieth Century: Transfer and Transformation* (De Gruyter Oldenbourg, 2016).

Chapter 1: The Unraveling

1. *Kontakt med Amerika*: Wendy Wall, *Inventing the American Way: The Politics of Consensus from the New Deal to the Civil Rights Movement* (OUP, 2008), pp. 98–9.

2. Jan-Werner Müller, *Contesting Democracy: Political Ideas in Twentieth Century Europe* (Yale, 2011), pp. 132–44 esp; and Jan-Werner Müller, "Toward a New History of Christian Democracy," *Journal of Political Ideologies*, 18.2 (2013): 243–55.

3. Religion, however, remained a better predictor of electoral behavior than class until the 1980s. See Martin Conway, "The Rise and Fall of Western Europe's Democratic Age," *Contemporary European History*, 13.1 (2004): 67–88.

4. David Reynolds, *America: Empire of Liberty* (Penguin, 2009), p. 408.

5. Arthur M. Schlesinger Jr., "Not Left, Not Right, but a Vital Center," *New York Review of Books*, April 4, 1948; "ultimate integrity": Arthur M. Schlesinger Jr., *The Vital Center* (Houghton Mifflin Company, 1949), p. ix.

6. Martin Conway, "The Rise and Fall of Western Europe's Democratic Age," p. 79.

7. David Hackett Fischer, *Fairness and Freedom: A History of Two Open Societies* (OUP, 2012); James J. Sheehan, *Where Have All the Soldiers Gone? The Transformation of Modern Europe* (Mariner Books, 2009).

8. Tom Buchanan and Martin Conway, "The Politics of Democracy in Twentieth-Century Europe: Introduction," *European History Quarterly*, 32.1 (2002): 7–12.

9. Figures from Tony Judt, *Postwar* (Pimlico, 2007 [2005]), p. 325.

10. US Census Bureau, Historical Income Tables, Families, 1947–2017, Table F-2, at: https://www.census.gov/data/tables/time-series/demo/income-poverty/historical-income-families.html; Jeffrey Anderson, "Economic Growth By President," Hudson Institute, August 8, 2016.

11. On consensus: David Dutton, *British Politics Since 1945: The Rise and Fall of Consensus* (Wiley-Blackwell, 1991); Kennan, cited in Perry Anderson, "Imperium," *New Left Review* 83 (September–October 2013), p. 31; courts: Lech Garlicki, "Constitutional Courts versus Supreme Courts," *International Journal of Constitutional Law*, 5.1 (2007): 44–68.

12. Roosevelt: David Reynolds, *America: Empire of Liberty* (Penguin, 2009), p. 391, and Cass Sunstein, *The Second Bill of Rights: FDR's Unfinished Revolution and Why We Need it More Than Ever* (Basic Books, 2004); French planning: Charles P. Kindleberger, "French Planning," in Max F. Millikan (ed.), *National Economic Planning* (National Bureau of Economic Research, 1967), pp. 279–303; *The Economist*, "End of an IRI," June 22, 2000.

13. See David Miles, Gareth Myles, and Ian Preston, *The Economics of Public Spending* (OUP, 1994), p. 269.

14. Alfred Skolnik and Sophie R. Dales, "Social Welfare Expenditures: 1950–1975," *Social Security Bulletin*, January 1976, p. 4.

15. Judt, *Postwar*, p. 361.

16. Cited in Mazower, *Dark Continent: Europe's Twentieth Century* (Vintage Books, 2000 [1998]), p. 303.

17. Lizabeth Cohen, *A Consumer's Republic: The Politics of Mass Consumption in Postwar America* (Vintage, 2004), pp. 292–345.

18. Richard Pells, *Not like Us: How Europeans Have Loved, Hated, and Transformed American Culture since World War II* (Basic Books, 1997).

19. On convergence, see: Victoria de Grazia, *Irresistible Empire: America's Advance Through Twentieth-Century Europe* (Harvard Belknap Press, 2005); see also Pells, *Not Like Us*, Chapter 7 esp., p. 241; and Larry Siedentop, *Democracy in Europe* (Allen Lane, 2001), Chapter 9 esp.

20. Fawcett, *Liberalism: The Life of an Idea* (Princeton University Press, 2014), p. 368.

21. Michel Foucault, "Of Other Spaces: Utopias and Heterotopias," *Diacritics*, 16.1 (1986): 22–7, p. 22. The subtitle here is a reworking of E. E. Schattschneider. "The flaw in the pluralist heaven," wrote Schattschneider in 1960, "is that the heavenly chorus sings with a strong upper-class accent," in *The Semisovereign People: A Realist's View of Democracy in America* (Holt, Rinehart and Winston, 1960), p. 35.

22. In Britain, the Conservative Keith Joseph later came to a similar formulation to account for the end of consensus, in "Escaping the Chrysalis of Statism," *Contemporary Record*, Vol. 1 (1987): 26–31.

23. Paul Berman, *A Tale of Two Utopias: The Political Journey of the Generation of 1968* (W. W. Norton, 1996), p. 56. See also Michael Kazin, "The Port Huron Statement at Fifty," *Dissent* magazine, Spring 2012.

24. Bruce McCall, *Thin Ice: Coming of Age in Canada* (Toronto, 1997). Here he is writing in the 1990s but speaking of growing up in the fifties and sixties. Cited in Bothwell, *Penguin History of Canada*, p. 405.

25. Peniel E. Joseph, "Rethinking the Black Power Era," *Journal of Southern History*, 75.3 (August 2009): 707–16, p. 707.

26. Judt, *Postwar*, p. 396.

27. Pekka Gronow, *International History of the Recording Industry* (Continuum, 1999), p. 135.

28. Richard Vinen, *The Long '68: Radical Protest and Its Enemies* (Penguin, 2018), p. 43.

29. Sean Gregory, "The Real Reason Muhammed Ali Converted to Islam," *Time* magazine, June 2, 2017.

30. Christendom: Warren H. Carroll, *The Crisis of Christendom: 1815–2015*, Vol. 6 (Christendom Press, 2013); "mainline churches": Benton Johnson, "Taking Stock: Reflections on the End of Another Era," *Journal for the Scientific Study of Religion*, 21.3 (September 1982): 189–200, p. 190.

31. Hugh McLeod, *The Religious Crisis of the 1960s* (OUP, 2007); on Scotland, Belgium: Callum G. Brown, "What Was the Religious Crisis of the 1960s?," *Journal of Religious History*, 34.4 (December 2010): 468–79, pp. 469–71. On Spain: John Hooper, *The New Spaniards* (Penguin, 2006), 2nd edn, p. 94. See also Suzanne Berger, "Religious Transformation and the Future of Politics," Chapter 3 in Charles Maier (ed.), *Changing Boundaries of the Political: Essays on the Evolving Balance Between the State and Society, Public and Private in Europe* (CUP, 2010), p. 108.

32. The phrases are Herbert Marcuse's, in Jan-Werner Müller, *Contesting Democracy: Political Ideas in Twentieth-Century Europe* (Yale, 2013), p. 177. The classic reference on 1968 as a "moral rebellion" of the well-to-do is Paul Berman, *A Tale of Two Utopias: The Political Journey of the Generation of 1968* (W. W. Norton, 1995).

33. See Judt, *Postwar*, pp. 409–10, and Julian Jackson, "Rethinking May '68," in Julian Jackson, Anna-Louise Milne, and James S. Williams (eds), *May 1968: Rethinking France's Last Revolution* (Palgrave, 2011), pp. 6–11.

34. Vinen, *The Long '68*, p. 169.

35. Corrado de Francesco, "The Growth and Crisis of Italian Higher Education during the 1960s and 1970s," *Higher Education*, 7.2 (1978): 193–212, pp. 193–4.

36. Vinen, *The Long '68*, pp. 64–8.

37. Belinda J. Davis et al., *Changing the World, Changing Oneself: Political Protest and Collective Identities in West Germany and the US in the 1960s and 1970s* (Berghahn, 2012), Introduction, p. ix.

38. Richard Ivan Jobs, "The Grand Tour of Daniel Cohn-Bendit and the Europeanism of 1968," in Julian Jackson et al., *May 68: Rethinking France's Last Revolution*, pp. 233–5.

39. Paul Berman, *A Tale of Two Utopias*; on Davis: Detlef Siegfried, Chapter 10, "White Negroes," in Belinda J. Davis et al., *Changing the World, Changing Oneself*, p. 202.

40. Jan-Werner Müller, *Contesting Democracy*, p. 172.

41. Potter, http://www.sdsrebels.com/potter.htm; Greek activists: Robert Gildea and James Mark, "Conclusion: Europe's 1968," in Robert Gildea, James Mark, and Anette Warring, *Europe's 1968: Voices of Revolt* (OUP, 2017), p. 326.

42. Stuart Ewen, *PR!: A Social History of Spin* (Basic Books, 1998), p. 405.

43. Mark Mazower, *Dark Continent*, p. 350. It was perhaps more specifically the twilight of Cold War liberalism: Michael Kazin, "Martin Luther King, Jr. and the Meanings of the 1960s," *American Historical Review*, 114.4 (October 2009): 980–99, pp. 980–1.

44. Some of these examples, and the quote, are from Jan-Werner Müller, *Contesting Democracy*, p. 183.

45. Nixon and Kissinger, similarities and difference: Robert S. Litwak, *Détente and the Nixon Doctrine: American Foreign Policy and the Pursuit of Stability, 1969–1976* (CUP, 2009), p. 66.

46. Arthur Schlesinger, *Journals 1952–2000* (Atlantic Books, 2014), entry for October 29, 1972. He was following Isaiah Berlin on this.

47. Litwak, *Détente and the Nixon Doctrine*, p. 64.

48. Fredrik Logevall, "The Indochina Wars and the Cold War, 1945–75," Chapter 14 in Melvyn P. Leffler and Odd Arne Westad (eds), *The Cambridge History of the Cold War*, Vol. II: *Crisis and Détente* (CUP, 2016), p. 296.

49. Robert McNamara, *In Retrospect: The Tragedy and Lessons of Vietnam* (New York, 1996), p. 155.

50. Ibid., pp. 29–41.

51. Sargent, *A Superpower Transformed*, pp. 48–9.

52. Cited in Fredrik Logevall, "The Indochina Wars and the Cold War, 1945–75," p. 299.

53. Walter Lafeber, *America, Russia and the Cold War*, 8th edn. (McGraw Hill, 1997), p. 261.

54. Specifically, Nixon was explaining why he was sending ground troops into Cambodia: Richard Nixon, "Address to the Nation on the Situation in Southeast Asia," April 30, 1970. Online by Gerhard Peters and John T. Woolley, The American Presidency Project. http://www.presidency.ucsb.edu/ws/?pid=2490.

55. Örjan Appelqvist and Stellan Andersson, *The Essential Gunnar Myrdal* (New York, 2005), p. 247.

56. Jeremy Suri, "Counter-cultures: The Rebellions Against the Cold War Order, 1965–1975," in Melvyn P. Leffler and Odd Arne Westad (eds), *The Cambridge History of the Cold War*, Vol. II: *Crisis and Détente* (CUP, 2016), pp. 464–5; Vietnam as a way to address the Nazi past: see Belinda Davis et al., "Introduction," in *Changing Oneself, Changing the World*, p. xiii.

57. Lafeber, *America, Russia and the Cold War*, pp. 261–2.

58. Vinen, *The Long '68*, p. 323.

59. Ibid., p. 272.

60. See Mark Lilla, *The Once and Future Liberal: After Identity Politics* (HarperCollins, 2017), p. 10.

61. See "Scant Progress on Housing Bias," *International New York Times*, April 10, 2018.

62. Speech at the Society of Professional Journalists' dinner, Ramada Inn, Tualatin, Oregon, April 17, 1968.

63. For quotes see Iric Nathanson, "Remembering Charlie Stenvig and the Minnesota T-Party," *MinnPost*, March 16, 2010, and Jeffrey T. Manuel and Andrew Urban, "You Can't Legislate the Heart: Minneapolis Mayor Charlie Stenvig and the Politics of Law and Order," *American Studies*, 49.3/4 (Fall/Winter 2008): 195–219.

64. See Elizabeth Hinton, *From the War on Poverty to the War on Crime: The Making of Mass Incarceration in America* (Harvard University Press, 2016).

65. Sean Wilentz, *The Age of Reagan: A History 1974–2008* (HarperPerennial, 2008), p. 43.

66. Paul Hockenos, *Joschka Fischer and the Making of the Berlin Republic* (OUP, 2008), pp. 100–6.

67. Paul Berman, *A Tale of Two Utopias*, pp. 268–70; Overney details and Algerian anti-racism: Daniel A. Gordon, *Immigrants and Intellectuals: May '68 and the Rise of Anti-Racism in France* (Merlin Press, 2012), pp. 142–8.

68. See Peter Kerr, *Postwar British Politics: From Conflict to Consensus* (Routledge, 2001); David Dutton, *British Politics Since 1945: The Rise and Fall of Consensus* (Wiley Blackwell, 1991); and Denis Kavanagh and Peter Morris, *Consensus Politics: From Attlee to Major* (John Wiley, 1994), 2nd edn. For the American side of the story see: Huntington, "Paradigms of American Politics: Beyond the One, the Two and the Many," *Political Science Quarterly*, 89.1 (March 1974): 1–23; and Wendy Wall, *Inventing the "American Way": The Politics of Consensus from the New Deal to the Civil Rights Movement* (OUP, 2009).

69. Daniel A. Gordon, *Immigrants and Intellectuals*, pp. 150–8.

70. See Gerd Rainer Horn, *The Spirit of '68: Rebellion in Western Europe, 1958–1976* (OUP, 2008), p. 99 for SEAT, other details passim.

71. Ibid. See also Donald Sassoon, *One Hundred Years of Socialism* (I. B. Tauris, 2010), pp. 594–644.

72. See, "44 Years Since the Athens Polytechnic Uprising," ReInform.nl, November 17, 2017.

73. Emile Chabal, "French Political Culture in the 1970s: Liberalism, Identity Politics, and the Modest State," *Geschichte und Gesellschaft*, 42 (2016): 243–65, p. 264.

74. Bruce Weber, "Edward Albee, Trenchant Playwright Who Laid Bare Modern Life, Dies at 88," *New York Times*, September 16, 2016.

75. Ophüls: in Julian Jackson, "Rethinking May '68," in Julian Jackson et al., *May 68: Rethinking France's Last Revolution*, p. 8.

76. John K. Simon, "A Conversation with Michel Foucault," *Partisan Review*, 38.2 (1971):196–201.

77. Robert Gildea, *France Since 1945* (OUP, 2009 [2002]), p. 213.

78. M. Bracke, (2008), "French Responses to the Prague Spring: Connections, (Mis)perception and Appropriation," *Europe-Asia Studies*, 60.10 (2008): 1735–47.

79. Stuart Hall, "The Great Moving Right Show," *Marxism Today*, January 1979, pp. 14–20.

80. For a helpful reflection see Charles S. Maier, "The Politics of Time: Changing Paradigms of Collective Time in the Modern Era," Chapter 4 in Charles S. Maier (ed.), *The Changing Boundaries of the Political: Essays on the Evolving Balance Between the State and Society, Public and Private in Europe* (CUP, 1987).

81. Martin Conway, "Democracy in Postwar Europe: The Triumph of a Political Model," *European History Quarterly*, 32(1) (2002): 59–84, p. 63.

82. Jon Agar, "What happened in the 1960s," *British Journal for the History of Science*, 41(4) (December 2008): 567–600, p. 585.

83. Ibid., p. 596.

84. In a useful overview that decentralizes 1960s historiography, see J. M. Neale, "The Sixties as History: A Review of the Political Historiography," *Reviews in American History*, 33.1 (March 2005): 133–52.

85. It should be noted that Carter himself did not use the term "malaise," which soon circled around his dramatic 1979 speech on America's crisis of confidence: Jimmy Carter, "Address to the Nation on Energy and National Goals: 'The Malaise Speech,'" July 15, 1979; online by Gerhard Peters and John T. Woolley, The American Presidency Project. http://www.presidency.ucsb.edu/ws/?pid=32596.

86. See Tom Buchanan and Martin Conway, "The Politics of Democracy in Twentieth-Century Europe: Introduction," *European History Quarterly*, 32.1 (2002): 7–12.

Chapter 2: The Crisis of Capitalism

1. See William L. Silber, *Volcker: The Triumph of Persistence* (Bloomsbury, 2013), Preface for Volcker's office; on the threat of trade war: see Mark Gilbert, *European Integration: A Concise History*, p. 99.

2. Up until 1966 the total value of US manufacturing production was always more than that of Western Europe and Japan combined; after 1975 it was less. See Ricardo Parboni, *The Dollar and Its Rivals: Recession, Inflation, and International Finance* (Verso, 1981), p. 7; on revaluations see Charles S. Maier, "Inflation and Stagnation as Politics and History," in Leon N. Lindberg and Charles S. Maier (eds), *The Politics of Inflation and Economic Stagnation* (The Brookings Institute, 1985), p. 18.

3. On gold liabilities, see Beth Yarbrough and Robert Yarbrough, *The World Economy: Trade and Finance* (Thomson Learning, 1994), 3rd edn, p. 641. On the growing crisis of the dollar see Barry Eichengreen, *Globalizing Capital: A History of the International Monetary System* (Princeton, 2008), 2nd edn, pp. 126–32.

4. Cited in Silber, *Volcker*, p. 76; on Connally: Robert Solomon, *The International Monetary System, 1945–1976: An Insider's View* (Harper & Row, 1977), p. 191.

5. Silber, *Volcker*, p. 115.

6. Robert H. Ferrell (ed.), *Inside the Nixon Administration: The Secret Diary of Arthur Burns, 1969–1974* (University of Kansas Press, 2010), p. 66; *Pravda*, Arthur Burns, in Silber, *Volcker*, pp. 82–9.

7. Cited in Silber, *Volcker*, p. 103; on NATO, see Robert Solomon, *The International Monetary System, 1945–1976: An Insider's View* (Harper & Row, 1977), p. 191.

8. On the driving factors and interpretations of this: see Daniel Sargent, "The Cold War and the International Political Economy in the 1970s," *Cold War History*, 13.3 (2013): 393–425, pp. 400–2.

9. Levinson, *An Extraordinary Time: The End of the Postwar Boom and the Return of the Ordinary Economy* (Basic Books, 2016), p. 65.

10. On the reasons why OPEC cared: see Levinson, *An Extraordinary Time*, pp. 65–7.

11. Soviet Captain Yevgeni Semenov, cited in Abraham Rabinovich, "The Little-Known US-Soviet Confrontation During Yom Kippur War," *Public Radio International*, October 26, 2012.

12. Levinson, *An Extraordinary Time*, p. 73.

13. Cited in Sargent, "The Cold War and the International Political Economy in the 1970s," p. 403.

14. Meg Jacobs, *Panic at the Pump: The Energy Crisis and the Transformation of American Politics in the 1970s* (Hill and Wang, 2016), p. 66.

15. Cited in Levinson, *An Extraordinary Time*, p. 78.

16. Tooze and Eich, "The Great Inflation," prepublication offprint, op. cit., p. 2.

17. Cited in Roberto Romani, "American Consumers Facing Inflation, 1965–1979: The Economists' Accounts," *Rivista di Storia Economica*, a. XXVIII, n.2 (Agosto 2012): 319–50, p. 319.

18. Michael D. Bordo and Athanasios Orphanides (eds), *The Great Inflation: The Rebirth of Modern Central Banking* (University of Chicago Press, 2013).

19. Levinson, *An Extraordinary Time*, p. 78.

20. See Edward Nelson, "The Great Inflation of the Seventies: What Really Happened," Federal Reserve Bank of St. Louis, Working Paper 2004-001, p. 5. For a comparison of CPI figures see: http://www.global-rates.com/economic-indicators/inflation/1975.aspx.

21. Arthur Burns, "The Anguish of Central Banking," the 1979 Per Jacobsson Lecture, Belgrade, Yugoslavia, September 30, 1979, p. 8.

22. "Inflation and OPEC," *New Internationalist*, August 2, 1980.

23. See Silber, *Volcker*, p. 74.

24. These data from Jeffry A. Frieden, *Global Capitalism: Its Rise and Fall in the Twentieth Century* (W. W. Norton, 2006), p. 366. Of course, low inflation could be every bit as salient a political issue, and anxiety about high inflation specifically carried strong political implications as to what the possible means of addressing inflation "as" a problem were to be. On the politics of high vs. low inflation see Jonathan Kirshner, "The Political Economy of Low Inflation," *Journal of Economic Surveys*, 15.1 (2001): 41–70.

25. Stanley Strachan, "Bank Failures Rise to Record Levels," *New York Times*, November 16, 1975.

26. Ralph Blumenthal, "Recalling New York at the Brink of Bankruptcy," *New York Times*, December 5, 2002.

27. See Barry Eichengreen, *The European Economy Since 1945* (Princeton, 2008), p. 266.

28. See Robert J. Flanagan, David W. Soskice, and Lloyd Ulman, *Unionism, Economic Stabilization and Incomes Policy: European Experience* (Brookings Institution, 1983), esp. Chapter 3.

29. Eichengreen, *The European Economy Since 1945*, p. 222.

30. Ibid., pp. 268–70.

31. Andrew Glyn, *Capitalism Unleashed: Finance, Globalization, and Welfare* (OUP, 2007), p. 17. The data are for the years 1971–80.

32. Data from Eichengreen, *The European Economy Since 1945*, Table 9.5, p. 271.

33. Exporting inflation: Charles S. Maier, "Inflation and Stagnation as Politics and History," p. 19.

34. Mathias Holweg and Nick Oliver, *Crisis, Resilience and Survival: Lessons from the Global Auto Industry* (Cambridge, 2015), p. 15.

35. Cited ibid., p. 16.

36. Levinson, *An Extraordinary Time*, p. 79: the examples of that virtuous circle are also elaborated from here.

37. For the United States this was from 4 percent for the period 1950–73 to less than 3 percent for the latter period. Productivity growth not only declined dramatically during the 1970s, it never really returned to the levels that had been seen after the war (see table 1. Real Annual GDP growth rates, 1950–73; 1973–98 in Angus Maddison, *The World Economy: A Millennial Perspective* [OECD, 2001]); see also Diane Coyle, *GDP: A Brief but Affectionate History* (Princeton, 2015), p. 45.

38. GDP spending had been relatively constant in the 1950s, as rising social expenditures were offset by declining military budgets after the war. It began to rise in the 1960s but was positively blooming in the 1970s as the social programs like Medicaid and food stamps established in the 1960s came to fruition. Across the OECD as a whole it rose from 31 percent to 40 percent from 1971 to 1980, while in Sweden it was as high as 59.8 percent: see Glyn, *Capitalism Unleashed*, p. 17.

39. Cited in Howard M. Wachtel, *The Money Mandarins: The Making of a Supranational Economic Order* (Routledge, 1990), p. 154.

40. On this "second wave" consumer activism, see Lizabeth Cohen, *A Consumer's Republic: The Politics of Mass Consumption in Postwar America* (Vintage, 2003), Chapters 2–6 esp.

41. Daniel Boorstin, *The Americans: The Democratic Experience* (Vintage, 1974 [1973]), pp. 89–90; Betty Friedan, *The Feminine Mystique* (Penguin, 2010 [1963]), pp. 244–5.

42. Charles S. Maier, "Inflation and Stagnation as Politics and History," pp. 12–13.

43. David Harvey, *The Condition of Post-Modernity: An Enquiry into the Origins of Cultural Change* (Routledge, 1991), p. 157; "diminishing returns": Maier, "Inflation and Stagnation as Politics and History," p. 17.

44. Paul Ginsborg, *Italy and Its Discontents: 1980–2001* (Penguin, 2003), p. 61.

45. America's urban crisis and quotations: Thomas Sugrue, *The Origins of the Urban Crisis: Race and Inequality in Postwar Detroit* (Princeton, 2014), rev. edn, p. 3.

46. Raika Espahangizi, "Migration and Urban Transformations: Frankfurt in the 1960s and 1970s," *Journal of Contemporary History*, 49.1 (2014): 183–208, p. 204.

47. Daniel Rauhut, "Integration of Immigrants in Sweden 1945–1975," *Finnish Yearbook of Population Research*, XLV (2010): 103–22.

48. See Stephen Pinker, *The Better Angels of Our Nature: Why Violence Has Declined* (Penguin, 2011); see also the annual UNODC, *Global Study on Homicide* (various years).

49. Raika Espahangizi, "Migration and Urban Transformations," pp. 183 and 204.

50. Tony Judt, *Postwar*, p. 334.

51. Noël O'Sullivan, *European Political Thought Since 1945* (Palgrave, 2004), p. 10.

52. Halting immigration: Rainer Münz and Ralf E. Ulrich, "Changing Patterns of Immigration to Germany, 1945–1997," *UC Davis Working Paper* (n.d.); "Frenchmen out of foreigners": Patrick R. Ireland, "Race, Immigration, and Hate," in Anthony Daley (ed.),

The Mitterrand Era: Policy Alternatives and Political Mobilization in France (New York University Press, 1996).

53. Parboni, *The Dollar and Its Rivals*, p. 54. Parboni references "European" here; but his point speaks more broadly.

54. Joshua Zeitz, "Rejecting the Center: Radical Grassroots Politics in the 1970s—Second Wave Feminism as a Case Study," *Journal of Contemporary History*, 43.4 (October 2008): 673–88, p. 676.

55. Cited in Nancy Maclean, "The Hidden History of Affirmative Action: Working Women's Struggles in the 1970s and the Gender of Class," *Feminist Studies*, 25.1 (Spring 1999): 42–78, p. 43.

56. Maier, "'Malaise': The Crisis of Capitalism in the 1970s," in Ferguson et al. (eds), *The Shock of the Global*, p. 30. Strikes only later impacted the US, and never with quite the same intensity.

57. On Erhard's fall, see Peter A. Johnson, *The Government of Money: Monetarism in Germany and the United States* (Cornell, 1998), pp. 54–5.

58. Ibid., p. 54; on the later US sentiments, see Alfred E. Kahn, "Market Power Inflation: A Conceptual Overview," in Gardiner C. Means (et al.), *The Roots of Inflation: The International Crisis* (Burt Franklin, 1975).

59. See Ton Notermans, *Money, Markets, and the State: Social Democratic Economic Policies Since 1918* (Cambridge, 2007), p. 192.

60. Figures: George Megalogenis, *The Australian Moment* (Hamish Hamilton, 2012).

61. Sinatra's visit: "The Siege of Sinatra," *Sun Herald*, April 22, 2002.

62. Robert Bothwell, *The Penguin History of Canada* (Penguin, 2008), p. 429. On Italy's industrial unrest, especially between 1969 and 1973, see Nicola Pizzolato, "A New Revolutionary Practice: Operaisti and the 'Refusal of Work' in 1970s Italy," *Estudos Históricos*, Rio de Janeiro, 30.61 (Maio–Agosto 2017): 449–64.

63. For workerist proposals: see Leo Panitch and Sam Gindin, *The Making of Global Capitalism: The Political Economy of American Empire* (Verso, 2013), pp. 138–44; on Italy: Patrick Cuninghame, "Mapping the Terrain of Struggle: Autonomous Movements in 1970s Italy," *Viewpoint Magazine*, 5.1 (November 2015).

64. See Richard Sandbrook, *Never Had It So Good* (Abacus, 2005), p. 110, and Tara Martin López, *The Winter of Discontent: Myth, Memory and History* (Liverpool University Press, 2014), p. 205.

65. Forest of arms: ibid., p. 76; Italy: Cuninghame, "Mapping the Terrain of Struggle."

66. Bo Stråth, *Europe's Utopias of Peace: 1815, 1919, 1951* (Bloomsbury, 2016), p. 374; communities and values: Rowbotham, Foreword to Tara Martin López, *The Winter of Discontent*, p. x.

67. See Boris Gobille, "Exploitation, Alienation and the Social Division of Labour in the May–June Movement in France," Chapter 3 in Julian Jackson et al. (eds), *May 1968: Rethinking France's Last Revolution*, pp. 34–46.

68. See Panitch and Gindin, *The Making of Global Capitalism*, pp. 165–6; on the '76 strike and accords, see William K. Stevens, "Auto Workers and Ford Reach Tentative Accord in 21 Day Strike," *New York Times*, October 6, 1976.

69. Figures and labor share more generally: see Levinson, p. 141.

70. Ashley Lavalle, "The Ties that Unwind: Social Democratic Parties and Unions in Australia and Britain," *Labour History*, 98 (2010): 55–75, pp. 58–9.

71. See Levinson, *An Extraordinary Time*, p. 150.

72. On this point, and "safe for capitalism," see Panitch and Gindin, *The Making of Global Capitalism*, p. 133.

73. On the significance of political consent under Keynesianism, see John H. Goldthorpe, "Political Economy After the Postwar Era," Chapter 11 in Charles S. Maier (ed.), *The Changing Boundaries of the Political*, pp. 364–6 esp.; on the subsequent challenge to the role assigned popular consent to economic outcomes, see Gretta Krippner, *Capitalizing on Crisis* (Harvard University Press, 2011), Chapter 6 esp.

74. The failure of monetary reform at the IMF, see John Williamson, *The Failure of World Monetary Reform, 1971–74* (New York University Press, 1977). See also Robert Solomon, *The International Monetary System, 1945–1976: An Insider's Perspective* (Harper & Row, 1976), pp. 235–66.

75. See Johnson, *The Government of Money*, pp. 51–6. My account of Europe's turn to monetarism is drawn from Johnson, supplemented also by Ton Notermans, *Money, Markets, and the State*, pp. 175–95.

76. On the Lira, and the German response to the Bretton Woods crisis, along with Emminger's mission and "If the economics ministry and": see Johnson, *The Government of Money*, pp. 81–3.

77. Johnson, *The Government of Money*, pp. 84–104; "[*fachidioten*]" and "Monetary policy is foreign policy": cited in E. Benning, "The Road to Rambouillet," in Emmanuel Mourlon-Druol and Federico Rom (eds), *International Summitry and Global Governance: The Rise of the G7 and the European Council, 1974–1991* (Routledge, 2014), p. 44. On monetarism's "victory" see Otmar Issing, "Is Monetarism Dead?," *The International Economy* (Spring, 2010): 35–7, p. 36.

78. The French turn: ibid., pp. 68–9 esp.; "If each breath we draw": cited in Mark Gilbert, *European Integration: A Concise History* (Rowman & Littlefield, 2011), p. 106.

79. Ariane Bernard, "Raymond Barre, 83, Former French Premier Dies," *New York Times*, August 27, 2007; on Barre's role from late 1960s to late 1970s: see Harold James and Mario Draghi, *Making the European Monetary Union* (Harvard, 2014), pp. 64–9 and pp. 125–32.

80. Michael Loriaux, *France After Hegemony: International Change and Financial Reform* (Cornell, 1992), p. 1.

81. On Callaghan's speech, see David Dutton, *British Politics Since 1945*, p. 75; see also Jim Tomlinson, "Tale of a Death Exaggerated: How Keynesian Policies Survived the 1970s," *Contemporary British History*, 21.4 (December 2007): 429–48.

82. Notermans, *Money, Markets, and the State*, pp. 191–3 and Tara Martin López, *The Winter of Discontent*, pp. 174–6.

83. Notermans, *Money, Markets, and the State*, p. 196.

84. J. M. Keynes, *The End of Laissez-Faire* (BN Publishing, n.d.), p. 19.

85. It was not, then, the Federal Reserve's independence or otherwise that was the issue here, or that determined how monetarism was implemented in the US: it was its hierarchical nature internally. As Johnson points out, we understand very little of the politics of monetarism if we do not grasp how it was for personal political reasons that monetarists, who first came out against central bank independence, eventually became staunch advocates of independence. Johnson, *The Government of Money*, p. 28.

86. See Johnson, *The Government of Money*, Chapter 5.

87. Ibid., p. 74.

88. Robert J. Samuelson, "Economist Allan Meltzer: 1928–2017," *Washington Post*, May 16,

2017; David Fettig, "Shadowing the Shadows," Federal Reserve Bank of Minneapolis, June 1, 1993.

89. See Angus Burgin, *The Great Persuasion: Reinventing Free Markets Since the Depression* (Harvard, 2012), pp. 176–7.

90. See Jeremy Gilbert, *Common Ground: Democracy and Collectivity in an Age of Individualism* (Pluto Press, 2013), Preface; for Hayek, see his book of the same name, F. A. Hayek, *The Constitution of Liberty*, Definitive Edition, Collected Works of F. A. Hayek (University of Chicago Press, 2011 [1960]).

91. See Tooze and Eich, "The Great Inflation," prepublication offprint, op. cit., p. 17.

92. Panitch and Gindin, *The Making of Global Capitalism*, pp. 173–4.

93. Ibid., p. 140.

94. See William Poole and David C. Wheelock, "Stable Prices, Stable Economy," *The Regional Economist*, St. Louis Fed., January 2008, p. 9.

95. Burgin, *The Great Persuasion*, pp. 198–9; on conservatives and neoliberals: Daniel Steinmetz-Jenkins, "Introduction," *H-Diplo Roundtable Review*, Vol. XIX (38) (2018); and Jacob Hamburger and Daniel Steinmetz-Jenkins, "Why Did Neoconservatives Join Forces with Neoliberals?," *Global Intellectual History*, Prepubn at: DOI: 10.1080/238018 83.2018.1423740.

96. Harold James, *International Monetary Cooperation Since Bretton Woods* (IMF, 1999), p. 8.

97. Panitch and Gindin, *The Making of Global Capitalism*, pp. 144–5.

98. Emmanuel Mourlon-Druol, "Trust Is Good, Control Is Better: The 1974 Herstatt Bank Crisis and Its Implications for International Monetary Reform," *Business History*, 57.2 (2015): 311–34, p. 313; too big to fail: Panitch and Gindin, *The Making of Global Capitalism*, p. 153.

99. For these examples: ibid., pp. 149–51.

100. Chen Jian, "China and the Cold War after Mao," in Melvyn P. Leffler and Odd Arne Westad (eds), *The Cambridge History of the Cold War*, Vol. III, *Endings* (CUP, 2015 [2010]), pp. 181–6.

101. Cited in Panitch and Gindin, *The Making of Global Capitalism*, p. 155.

102. Andrea Wong, "The Untold Story Behind Saudi Arabia's 41-Year US Debt Secret," *Bloomberg News*, May 31, 2016; see also David E. Spiro, *The Hidden Hand of American Hegemony: Petrodollar Recycling and International Markets* (Cornell, 1991).

103. Howard M. Wachtel, *The Money Mandarins: The Making of a Supranational Economic Order* (Pluto Press, 1990), pp. 112–13.

104. Panitch and Gindin, *The Making of Global Capitalism*, p. 144.

105. David Marsh, *The Euro: The Politics of the New Global Currency* (Yale, 2009); see also David Marsh, "Germany's 30-Year-old EMS Secret Is Revealed," *Guardian*, November 30, 2008, and Barry Eichengreen, *The European Economy Since 1945*, pp. 286–8; see also the transcript of the meeting now published at: http://www.margaretthatcher.org /document/111554.

106. Roi Jean-Quinze, cited in James and Draghi, *Making the European Monetary Union*, p. 149.

107. Notermans, *Money, Markets and the State*, p. 169.

108. Cited in Gilbert, *European Integration*, p. 108

109. Ethan B. Kapstein, *Governing the Global Economy: International Finance and the State* (Harvard, 1996), pp. 4 (banks and bonds) and 20 (overseas branches).

110. On the issues of regulation, including German banks, see Kapstein, *Governing the Global Economy*, pp. 6–7 and 21.

111. For "Erosion of popular consent" see Greta Krippner, *Capitalizing on Crisis*, p. 147; on banks as regulators, see Kapstein, *Governing the Global Economy*, p. 23.

112. Cited in Megalogenis, *The Australian Moment*, p. 56. For a recent argument elaborating on this effort to "insulate" markets from politics, see Quinn Slobodian, *Globalists: The End of Empire and the Birth of Neoliberalism* (Harvard, 2018), p. 7.

113. Claude Lefort, *Peace as an Absolute Value*, UNESCO Courier, n.p.

114. My thinking here takes as its starting point an argument put forward by Charles S. Maier in "'Malaise': The Crisis of Capitalism in the 1970s," in Ferguson et al. (eds), *The Shock of the Global*, p. 42.

115. Nobel lectures, both can be accessed here: https://www.nobelprize.org/nobel_prizes /economic-sciences/laureates/.

116. Daniel Stedman-Jones, *Masters of the Universe: Hayek, Friedman and the Birth of Neoliberal Politics* (Princeton, 2012), pp. 247–77.

Chapter 3: The Reckoning

1. On the roots of the *compromesso storico*, see Joan Barth Urban, *Moscow and the Italian Communist Party: From Togliatti to Berlinguer* (I. B. Tauris, 1986), pp. 268–70. See also Roberto Fornasier, "The DC and the PCI in the Seventies: A Complex Relationship Supervised by the United States," *Bulletin of Italian Politics*, 4.2 (2012): 209–29.

2. On cajoling: Fornasier, "The DC and the PCI in the Seventies," p. 24; "socialism in liberty" and KGB plots: Christopher Andrew and Vasili Mitrokhin, *The Mitrokhin Archive: The KGB in Europe and the West* (Penguin, 2000), new edn, Chapter 18, "Eurocommunism."

3. Fornasier, "The DC and the PCI in the Seventies," p. 210, and Ronald Koven, "'Historic Compromise' Stronger in Italy," *Washington Post*, May 18, 1978.

4. David Broder, "Historically Compromised," *Jacobin Magazine* (Spring 2018).

5. Cited in Ginsborg, *A History of Contemporary Italy*, p. 39.

6. Paul Hockenos, *Joschka Fischer and the Making of the Berlin Republic: An Alternative History of Postwar Germany* (Oxford, 2007), p. 127.

7. Lance W. Roberts, *Recent Social Trends in Canada, 1960–2000* (McGill, 1995), p. 271. In fact, where there *was* infiltration, as in Australia, this was not by anticolonial radicals but in that case Yugoslav agents seeking to frame highly vocal immigrant Croat communities in a clear case of state-based counterterror. See Paul Daley, "Catholic Extremism Fears in 1970s Australia Made Croats 'the Muslims of Their Time,'" *Guardian*, July 29, 2016.

8. Scott Rutherford, "Canada's Other Red Scare: Rights, Decolonization, and Indigenous Political Protest in the Global Sixties," PhD thesis, Queen's University, Kingston, Ontario (February 2011).

9. Hélène Miard-Delacroix, *Willy Brandt: Life of a Statesman* (I. B. Tauris, 2016), p. 151.

10. Dan Jones, "Blood on the Streets: Commemorating Altab Ali Day," Altab Ali Foundation (n.d.).

11. Irish Troubles: Richard Bourke, *Peace in Ireland: The War of Ideas* (Pimlico, 2012), pp. 4–11.

12. Cited in ibid., pp. 23 and 183.

13. Cited in Russell Dalton, Scott Flanagan, and Paul Allen Beck (eds), *Electoral Change in Advanced Industrial Democracies: Realignment or Dealignment?* (Princeton, 1984), p. 451; see

also Sheri Berman, "The Life of the Party," *Comparative Politics*, 30.1 (October 1997): 101–22.

14. Sheri Berman, "The Life of the Party," p. 101.

15. Brandt's policy was announced in 1969 and targeted at the young. See the German Historical Institute's Documents and Images Project: http://ghdi.ghi-dc.org/sub_doc ument.cfm?document_id=901.

16. Megalogenis, *The Australian Moment*, p. 81.

17. In Giovanni Sartori, "Opposition and Control: Problems and Prospects," *Government and Opposition*, 1.2 (1966): 149–54, p. 151. On Aron and Sartori together see Michal Kubát, *Political Opposition in Theory and Central European Practice* (Peter Lang, 2019), p. 54.

18. English-speaking governments: Ian Macfarlane, *The Search for Stability*, 2006 Boyer lectures, *ABC Radio* (November/December 2006).

19. Jonathan Freedland in "Enough of This Cover-Up: The Wilson Plot Was Our Watergate," *Guardian*, March 15, 2006; for the official version see Mark Duntan, "Harold Wilson's Resignation, March 16, 1976," *National Archives Blog*, March 16, 2016.

20. López, *The Winter of Discontent*, pp. 19–22 and 26.

21. For the loss of moral accountability argument, and the quotes here, see Nils Gilman, "Wanted: a Self-Draining Swamp," *American Interest*, January 1, 2018; see also Seymour M. Hersh, "The Pardon: Nixon, Ford, Haig, and the Transfer of Power," *The Atlantic* (August 1983).

22. George Shultz, cited in James T. Patterson, *Restless Giant: The United States from Watergate to Bush v. Gore* (OUP, 2007), p. 8.

23. Marion Clark and Rudy Maxa, "Closed Session Romance on the Hill," *Washington Post*, May 23, 1976.

24. Howard Zinn, *A People's History of the United States* (Routledge, 2003), 3rd edn, pp. 557–8; see also Seymour Martin Lipset, "Interpreting the Polls," in *Advances in Consumer Research*, Vol. 3, Cincinnati, OH, Association for Consumer Research, pp. 17–23; "confidence," cited in Panitch and Gindin, *The Making of Global Capitalism*, p. 142.

25. Dean Acheson, Oral history interview with Dean Acheson, Washington, DC, June 30, 1971, by Theodore A. Wilson and Richard McKinzie (Harry S. Truman Presidential Library); on his "waspish" moods, see Robert L. Beisner, *Dean Acheson: A Life in the Cold War* (OUP, 2009), p. 313; Michael Crozier, Samuel P. Huntington, and Joji Watanuki, *The Crisis of Democracy: Report on the Governability of Democracies to the Trilateral Commission* (New York, 1975).

26. Stephen Gill in "The New Constitutionalism," *Iskra*, December 18, 2011 (ed. and trans. by Iraklis Oikonomou); on trilateralism more generally: Gene Berkman, *The Trilateral Commission and the New World Order* (Renaissance Bookservice, 1995), pp. 206–8.

27. Samuel Huntington, *Political Order in Changing Societies* (Yale University Press, 1968), p. 461.

28. As *The Limits to Growth* report suggested: "Indeed, if European enterprises look more healthy than European churches and schools, this is also because they rely more on the old model of social control" (p. 30). This point is made, along with the above citation, in Maria Markantonatou, "From *The Limits to Growth* to 'Degrowth' in the Crises of the 1970s and 2008," Working Paper 05/2013 der DFG-KollegforscherInnengruppe Postwachstumsgesellschaften, p. 19.

29. Crozier et al., *The Crisis of Democracy*, pp. 6 and 16.

30. Cited in Maier, "'Malaise': The Crisis of Capitalism in the 1970s," in Ferguson et al. (eds), *The Shock of the Global*, p. 40.

31. Joseph Rothschild, "Observations on Political Legitimacy in Contemporary Europe," *Political Science Quarterly*, 92.3 (Autumn 1977): 487–501, p. 500.

32. Stefan Berger, "Democracy and Social Democracy," *European History Quarterly*, 32.1 (2002): 13–37, pp. 28–9.

33. Figures from Judt, *Postwar*, p. 364.

34. Martin Linton, in "Labour's Next Moves Forward," Fabian Society Pamphlet No. 531, p. 2.

35. Francis Sejerstad, *The Age of Social Democracy: Norway and Sweden in the Twentieth Century* (Princeton, 2011), pp. 333 and 322.

36. Donald Sassoon, *One Hundred Years of Socialism: The West European Left in the Twentieth Century* (I. B. Tauris, 2013), p. 648. As Wolfgang Merkel has shown, the average share of the vote of social democratic and labor parties during the years 1945–73 was 31.7 percent; for the years 1974–90 it was almost exactly the same: 31.5 percent.

37. Sheri Berman, "The Life of the Party," p. 109.

38. John Hooper, *The New Spaniards* (Penguin, 2006), 2nd edn, p. 46.

39. O'Sullivan, *European Political Thought Since 1945*, p. 72.

40. Emile Chabal, *A Divided Republic: Nation, State and Citizenship in Contemporary France* (Cambridge, 2015), pp. 164–6.

41. Michael Scott Christofferson, *French Intellectuals Against the Left: The Antitotalitarian Moment of the 1970s* (Berghan, 2004).

42. Ginsborg, *A History of Contemporary Italy*, p. 157.

43. Mazower, *Dark Continent*, p. 328.

44. C. Wright Mills, "Letter to the New Left," *New Left Review*, No. 5 (September–October 1960), pp. 18–23.

45. So declared Eric Hobsbawm in 1978, beginning a subsequently collected debate in Martin Jacques and Francis Mulhern (eds), *The Forward March of Labour Halted?* (Verso, 1981).

46. Jeffrey Bloodworth, *Losing the Center: The Decline of American Liberalism, 1968–1992* (Kentucky, 2013), "Introduction: Liberalism Gone With the Wind."

47. Bloodworth, *Losing the Center*, "Introduction: Liberalism Gone With the Wind."

48. And it would only be with the very belated learning of that lesson in the aftermath of the crisis of 2007–8 that *this* left found its way back, eventually, to any meaningful understanding of transformational politics.

49. Jan-Werner Müller, *Contesting Democracy*, p. 198. These were not the only concerns they confronted. "The only position for women in SNCC [the Student Nonviolent Coordinating Committee]," said leader Stokely Carmichael to two female members, "is prone"; "Fuck her! Take her off the stage! Rape her in a back alley!" shouted male members at an antiwar demonstration in January 1969 as two female Students for a Democratic Society (SDS) veterans sought to raise gender issues on stage. See Zeitz, "Rejecting the Center: Radical Grassroots Politics in the 1970s—Second Wave Feminism as a Case Study," *Journal of Contemporary History*, 43.4 (2008): 673–88, p. 678.

50. Yasmine Ergas, "Feminism and the Italian Party System: Women's Politics in a Decade of Turmoil, 1968–79," *Comparative Politics*, 14.3 (April 1982): 153–279, p. 257.

51. Anna Coote, cited in López, *The Winter of Discontent*, pp. 42–3.

52. See Susan Bassnett, *Feminist Experiences: The Women's Movement in Four Cultures* (Routledge, 2012), Chapter 2, esp. for the German experience.

53. Cited in Zeitz, "Rejecting the Center," p. 677.

54. Elizabeth Bird, "Women's Studies and the Women's Movement in Britain: Origins and Evolution, 1970–2000," *Women's History Review*, 12.2 (2003): 263–388, pp. 263–6.

55. On the continuation and modulation of 1960s-era political protest into the 1970s, see Stephen Tuck, "'We Are Taking Up Where the Movement of the 1960s Left Off': The Proliferation and Power of African American Protest During the 1970s," *Journal of Contemporary History*, 43.4 (October 2008): 637–54, pp. 638–42 esp.

56. Betty Friedan, *The Feminine Mystique* (W. W. Norton, 2001), p. 57.

57. Italian achievements: Maud Bracke, *Women and the Reinvention of the Political: Feminism in Italy, 1968–1983* (Routledge, 2014), Chapter 1 esp.

58. Ibid.

59. Siân Reynolds, "Lateness, Amnesia and Unfinished Business: Gender and Democracy in Twentieth Century Europe," *European History Quarterly*, 32.1 (2002): 85–109, p. 100.

60. For these examples see Judt, *Postwar*, pp. 486 and 704.

61. Berman, "The Life of the Party," pp. 109–15.

62. Cited in Edmund L. Andrews, "Rudolf Bahro Is Dead at 62; Dissident in Both Germanys," *New York Times*, December 11, 1997.

63. On the national variants, see Maria Eleonora Guasconi, "Public Opinion and the Euromissile Crisis," in Leopoldo Nuti, Frédéric Bozo, Marie-Pierre Rey, and Bernd Rother (eds), *The Euromissile Crisis and the End of the Cold War* (Stanford, 2015), pp. 280–4.

64. Christopher Maynard, *The Shadow: George H. W. Bush and the End of the Cold War* (Texas A&M, 2009), p. 31; on END see Gillian Wylie, "Social Movements and International Change: the Case of 'Détente from Below,'" *International Journal of Peace Studies*, 4.2 (1999): 61–82.

65. For peace movements as popular front see the work of Jeffrey Herf, as discussed in Holger Nehring, "The Last Battle of the Cold War," in Leopoldo Nuti, Frédéric Bozo, Marie-Pierre Rey, and Bernd Rother (eds), *The Euromissile Crisis and the End of the Cold War* (Stanford, 2015), pp. 309–10; on symbols and loyalties, p. 317.

66. Robert Gildea and Andrew Tompkins, "The Transnational in the Local: The Larzac Plateau as a Site of Transnational Activism since 1970," *Journal of Contemporary History*, 50.3 (2015): 581–605.

67. John D. Skrentny, *The Minority Rights Revolution* (Harvard, 2009), pp. 3–4.

68. Emile Chabal, "French Political Culture in the 1970s: Liberalism, Identity Politics, and the Modest State," *Geschichte und Gesellschaft*, 42 (2016): 243–65, p. 262.

69. Olga Sparschuh, "Citizens and Non-Citizens: The Relevance of Citizenship in Labour Migration within Italy and to Germany from the 1950s to 1970s," *Journal of Contemporary History*, 49.1 (2014): 28–53.

70. German migrants: Raika Espahangizi, "Migration and Urban Transformations: Frankfurt in the 1960s and 1970s," *Journal of Contemporary History*, 49.1 (2014): 183–208; BMW strikes: Sparschuh, op. cit., pp. 46–7; on this, Ford, and *Inländerprimat:* see Simon Goeke, "The Multinational Working Class? Political Activism and Labour Migration in West Germany During the 1960s and 1970s," *Journal of Contemporary History*, 49.1 (2014): 160–82, pp. 161 and 178 esp.

71. Simon Hall, "Protest Movements in the 1970s: The Long 1960s," *Journal of Contemporary History*, 43.4 (2008): 655–72, p. 657.

72. Julian Jackson, *Living in Arcadia: Homosexuality, Politics, and Morality in France from the Liberation to AIDS* (Chicago, 2009).

73. See Gordon Silverstein, *Law's Allure: How Law Shapes, Constrains, Saves and Kills Politics* (Cambridge, 2009), pp. 7–10.

74. As some scholars argue, White America jumped ship on liberalism before later in the decade discovering neoliberalism as a more anodyne language for retaining white (read property-based) interests. On the 1970s response to the new movements, see N. D. B. Connolly, "A White Story," *Dissent* magazine, January 2018; on the relations between property and racial identity, see Cheryl Harris, "Whiteness as Property," *Harvard Law Review*, 106.8 (June 1994): 1707–91.

75. Earl M. Maltz, *The Chief Justiceship of Warren Burger, 1969–1988* (South Carolina, 2000), p. 7; Dutschke of course drew the phrase from his own reading.

76. Anderson, "Homeland," *New Left Review*, 81 (May–June 2013): 5–32, p. 7; for a visualization of the transformation of party control see: https://web.education.wisc.edu /nwhillman/index.php/2017/02/01/party-control-in-congress-and-state-legislatures/.

77. Cited in Megalogenis, *The Australian Moment*, p. 86.

78. Emile Chabal, *France Since the 1970s: History, Politics and Memory in an Age of Uncertainty* (Bloomsbury, 2014), p. 41; on Giscard d'Estaing: Jonathan Fenby, *The History of Modern France: From the Revolution to the War with Terror* (Simon & Schuster UK, 2016), pp. 407–9.

79. Steven van Hecke and Emmanuel Gerard (eds), *Christian Democratic Parties in Europe Since the End of the Cold War* (Leuven University Press, 2004), p. 70 for German data and the Introduction in general.

80. Hanley (ed.), *Christian Democracy in Europe: A Comparative Perspective* (Continuum, 1994), passim. One could also have included Germany here, where generational change drove the more traditionalist CDU-CSU coalition out of power in 1969. They would return but with a reformed makeup. In Belgium, the Christian Democrats split in 1968 along linguistic lines (Flemish/Walloon) over the issue of the division of the Catholic University of Louvain.

81. See: http://plato.stanford.edu/entries/personalism/.

82. David Hanley, "Introduction: Christian Democracy as a Political Phenomenon," in Hanley (ed.), *Christian Democracy in Europe*, p. 4.

83. Thomas C. Davis, "The Iberian Peninsula and Greece," Chapter 10 in Hans-Georg Betz and Stefan Immerfall (eds), *The New Politics of the Right: Neo-populist Parties and Movements in Established Democracies* (St. Martin's Press, 1998), pp. 166–7.

84. On Austria, see: Max Riedlsperger, "The Freedom Party of Austria," in Hans-Georg Betz and Stefan Immerfall (eds), *The New Politics of the Right*, passim.

85. The rise of the right was facilitated in part, too, by the much-chronicled backlash against the moral relativism and big society liberalism of the sixties. But it also had more authentic (middle-class) "grass roots" itself.

86. On the middle class, see Lisa McGirr, *Suburban Warriors: The Origins of the New American Right* (Princeton, NJ, 2001), p. 4. The impact of these grassroots mobilizations was, as McGirr puts it, profound: they "became the ground forces of a conservative revival— one that transformed conservatism from a marginal force preoccupied with communism in the early 1960s into a viable electoral contender by the decade's end."

87. Richard Hofstadter's book was just the clearest example of this. See Richard Hofstadter, *The Paranoid Style in American Politics (and other essays)* (Harvard, 1996 [1964]).

88. This was a point that Tocqueville himself once made. Christianity, he said, becomes a particularly potent force politically precisely "among those who have given up the

campaign to capture the state." See Samuel Moyn, *Christian Human Rights* (Pennsylvania, 2015), p. 157.

89. Steven Tuck, "Introduction: Reconsidering the 1970s—The 1960s to a Disco Beat?," *Journal of Contemporary History*, 43.4 (2008): 617–20, p. 619.

90. Not all agreed. Famously Billy Graham, spiritual adviser to many a US president, refused on the grounds that preachers should keep themselves above the political fray. Catholic and Jewish leaders were equally skeptical from the start. The televangelism details here are from Eileen Oginitz, "New Electronic Revival Tent," *Chicago Tribune*, January 13, 1980, Section 1, p. 5.

91. See the PBS documentary *God in America*, and associated material at: http://www.pbs .org/godinamerica/people/jerry-falwell.html.

92. Peter Applebome, "Jerry Falwell, Moral Majority Founder, Dies at 73," *New York Times*, May 16, 2007.

93. Eileen Ogintz, "New Electronic Revival Tent," p. 5.

94. Jeff Sharlett, *The Family: The Secret Fundamentalism at the Heart of American Power* (Harper-Collins, 2008).

95. Jerry Falwell: cited in Doug Banwart, "Jerry Falwell, the Rise of the Moral Majority, and the 1980 Election," *Western Illinois Historical Review*, Vol. 5 (Spring 2013), p. 148.

96. A useful account of the directions taken here can be found in Jacob Collins, "An Anthropological Turn? The Unseen Paradigm in Modern French Thought," *New Left Review*, 78 (November–December 2012): 31–60.

97. Morton J. Horwitz, *The Warren Court and the Pursuit of Justice* (Hill and Wang, 1998), p. xi.

98. Ibid., p. xii.

99. Ibid., pp. 82 and 98.

100. In fact, even before Nixon's election, the Warren court's time was up. Warren himself resigned well in advance of the election, the better to give Johnson time to appoint his successor. The plan backfired. Johnson initially chose the strongly liberal Associate Justice Abe Fortas. But Republicans dug such trenches about his nomination process that he ended up having to resign. This left liberals with two less seats in the court, not just one. See Earl M. Maltz, *The Chief Justiceship of Warren Burger, 1969–1988*, pp. 7–8.

101. Justice Black, cited in Horwitz, *The Warren Court*, p. 105; the constitutional expert in question was Henry Abraham.

102. *Bakke v. Regents of California*: Geoffrey Hodgson, *The World Turned Right Side Up* (Houghton Mifflin, 1996), pp. 154–7.

103. Justice O'Connor, dissenting in a 1982 decision: see http://supremecourtopinions.wustl .edu/files/opinion_pdfs/1981/80-1735.pdf.

104. Steven M. Teles, *The Rise of the Conservative Legal Movement: The Battle for Control of the Law* (Princeton, 2010), p. 61.

105. On legal inculcation see Yves Smith, *Econned* (Griffin, 2011), pp. 124–6.

106. Alec Sweet Stone, "Constitutional Courts and Parliamentary Democracy," *West European Politics*, 25.1 (2002): 77–100, p. 79.

107. Jan-Werner Müller, "The Triumph of What (if Anything): Rethinking Political Ideologies and Political Institutions in Twentieth-Century Europe," *Journal of Political Ideologies*, 14.2 (June 2009): 211–26, p. 219. See also his "The Forgotten Twentieth Century," *Project Syndicate*, November 29, 2011.

108. Martin Shapiro and Alec Stone, "The New Constitutional Politics of Europe," *Comparative Political Studies*, 26.4 (January 1994): 397–420; see also Cheryl Saunders, "The Interesting Times of Louis Favoreu," *International Journal of Constitutional Law*, 5.1 (January 2007): 1–16.
109. Alec Stone Sweet, "Constitutional Courts and Parliamentary Democracy," pp. 85–93.
110. Sebastian Gehrig, "Cold War Identities: Citizenship, Constitutional Reform, and International Law between East and West Germany: 1967–75," *Journal of Contemporary History*, 49.4 (2014): 794–814; the Federal Constitutional Court: Peter Lindseth, "The Critical Promise of the New European Law," *Contemporary European History*, 21.3 (2012): 457–75, pp. 470–1.
111. See, for example, R. Daniel Keleman and Alec Stone Sweet, "Assessing the Transformation of Europe: A View from Political Science," Draft Ms; see also Karen Alter, "The European Court's Political Power Across Time and Space," Northwestern University School of Law Scholarly Commons, *Faculty Working Papers* (2009), No. 175.
112. The first turning point here came in the early 1960s when it was established in the ECJ that individual citizens had recourse to EC law against their own national states: it would be another forty years before its operations were next reviewed. By then EU law would have long become accustomed to enjoying "direct effect" or "supremacy" over national law.
113. Anthony King, *Who Governs Britain?* (Pelican, 2015), p. 259.
114. Ibid., pp. 259–63. *The Judge Over Your Shoulder* was first published in 1998; on design laws: Jens Schovsbo and Stina Teilmann-Lock, "We Wanted More Arne Jacobsen Chairs But All We Got Was Boxes—Experiences from the Protection of Designs in Scandinavia from 1970 Till the Directive" (April 13, 2016), *International Review of Intellectual Property and Competition Law* (Autumn 2016).
115. Samuel Moyn, *The Last Utopia: Human Rights in History* (Harvard, 2011), pp. 179–80.
116. David Runciman, *The Confidence Trap* (Princeton, 2013), p. 208: whence "poised" is Runciman and "anarchy" is Buchanan; on inflationary travails: see James M. Buchanan and Richard E. Wagner, *Democracy in Deficit: The Political Legacy of Lord Keynes* (New York, 1977).
117. Chabal, *France Since the 1970s*, p. 14.
118. Cited in Laurent Bonelli, "Enquête sur la Fondation Saint-Simon," *Le Monde Diplomatique*, September 1998, pp. 26–7.
119. David Harvey, *A Brief History of Neoliberalism* (Oxford, 2007), p. 49.
120. Borstelmann, *The 1970s*, pp. 144 and 131.
121. Cited in Jefferson Decker, *The Other Rights Revolution: Conservative Lawyers and the Remaking of American Government* (OUP, 2016), pp. 39–41, p. 44.
122. These data, quotes: Harvey, *A Brief History*, pp. 43 and 47; and Mark Blyth, *Great Transformations: Economic Ideas and Institutional Change in the Twentieth Century* (Cambridge, 2002), p. 43.
123. Cited in Panitch and Gindin, *The Making of Global Capitalism*, p. 143.
124. Alex Carey, *Taking the Risk Out of Democracy: Corporate Propaganda versus Freedom and Liberty* (University of Illinois Press, 1994), pp. 87–8; quote p. 104.
125. Edsall, cited in Harvey, *A Brief History*, p. 54.
126. Mancur Olson, *The Rise and Decline of Nations* (Yale, 1982); Ralf Dahrendorf similarly remarks on the Jefferson point in *The Modern Social Conflict: An Essay on the Politics of Liberty* (California, 1988), pp. 126–7.

127. Painful choices and German SPD: Sheri Berman, "The Life of the Party: Review Article," *Comparative Politics*, 30.1 (October 1997): 101–22, p. 109; US Democrats: Maier, "Malaise," in Ferguson et al. (eds), *The Shock of the Global*, p. 39.

128. Cited in Ruth Spencer, "Gay Rights: Five Activists Reflect on the History of the Movement in the US," *Guardian*, May 8, 2012.

129. See for example Daniel K. Williams, "Jerry Falwell's Sunbelt Politics: The Regional Origins of the Moral Majority," *Journal of Policy History*, 22.2 (2010): 125–47.

130. Margaret Thatcher, interview with Ronald Butt, *Sunday Times*, May 3, 1981, Margaret Thatcher Foundation: https://www.margaretthatcher.org/document/104475.

131. Joshua Zeitz, "Rejecting the Center: Radical Grassroots Politics in the 1970s—Second-Wave Feminism as a Case Study," *Journal of Contemporary History*, 43.4 (2008): 673–88, p. 675.

132. Ralf Dahrendorf, *The Modern Social Conflict*, p. 140.

133. Zbigniew Brzezinski, *Between Two Ages: America's Role in the Technetronic Era* (Viking Press, 1970).

134. Cited: Sejerstad, *The Age of Social Democracy*, p. 429; see also Nathalie Blanc-Noel, "Resolving the Dilemma Between Equality and Liberty: The Swedish Political System," *Eastern Journal of European Studies*, 4.1 (June 2013): 25–40.

135. Murray Rothbard cited in Gerard Casey, *Murray Rothbard: Major Conservative and Libertarian Thinkers*, Vol. 15 (Bloomsbury Academic, 2013), pp. 103–4.

136. Reagan cited in Borstelmann, *The 1970s*, p. 131.

137. Cited in Yves Smith, *Econned*, p. 112.

138. George Meany, "The Voice of Freedom," full text available at: https://archive.org/stream/SolzhenitsynTheVoiceOfFreedom/SVF2_djvu.txt/, np.

139. Ibid.

140. A point made in Norberto Bobbio, *Liberalism and Democracy* (Verso, 2006 [1990]), p. 89.

Chapter 4: A Split in the World

1. Aleksandr Solzhenitsyn, "The Exhausted West," Transcript of Speech, *Harvard Review* (July–August 1978), pp. 20–6.

2. Aleksander Solzhenitsyn, "My Harvard Speech in Retrospect," *National Review*, June 25, 2018.

3. Lee Congdon, "Solzhenitsyn Wasn't Western," *American Conservative*, September 17, 2014.

4. Territory-based global order to a property-based global order: my thinking on the switch that takes place at this time is influenced mostly by the vast geographical literature on these topics but was sparked—in its historical specificity—by reading Charles Maier's "Consigning the Twentieth Century to History: Alternative Narratives for the Modern Era," *American Historical Review* (June 2000), pp. 807–31. See also Stuart Corbridge and John Agnew, *Mastering Space: Territory and International Political Economy* (Routledge, 1995) and John Gerard Ruggie, "Territoriality and Beyond: Problematizing Modernity in International Relations," *International Organization*, 47 (1993), pp. 139–74 (in which "unbundling" now seems too passive a metaphor). An important recent attempt to explore a similar switch in terms of Carl Schmitt's distinction between *imperium* and *dominium* can be found in Quinn Slobodian, *Globalists: The End of Empire and the Birth of Neoliberalism* (Harvard, 2018).

5. Charles Maier's "Consigning the Twentieth Century to History: Alternative Narratives for the Modern Era," *American Historical Review* (June 2000): 807–31, p. 816.

6. Stuart Elden, *Terror and Territory: The Spatial Extent of Sovereignty* (Minnesota, 2009), p. 177. Elden refers to this as the "delicate compromise . . . between the injunctions against war and the holocaust."

7. Martin Conway, "The Rise and Fall of Western Europe's Democratic Age," p. 78.

8. Stuart Elden, *Terror and Territory*, p. 177.

9. Lafeber, *America, Russia and the Cold War*, p. 265.

10. See Litwak, *Détente and the Nixon Doctrine*, p. 87.

11. John C. Cairns, "France, Europe and the 'Design of the World 1974–7,'" *International Journal*, 32.2 (1977): 253–71; Litwak, *Détente and the Nixon Doctrine*, p. 137.

12. Lafeber, *America, Russia and the Cold War*, p. 261.

13. Robert Gates, *From the Shadows: The Ultimate Insider's Story of Five Presidents and How They Won the Cold War* (Simon & Schuster, 1997), Touchstone edn, p. 49.

14. This is Larry Berman's argument, as discussed in Greg Grandin, *Kissinger's Shadow* (Metropolitan Books, 2015), pp. 90–2.

15. Thomas M. Franck and Edward Weisband, *Foreign Policy by Congress* (OUP, 1979).

16. Silvio Pons, "The Rise and Fall of Eurocommunism," Chapter 3 in Melvyn P. Leffler and Odd Arne Westad (eds), *The Cambridge History of the Cold War*, Vol. II, *Endings* (Cambridge, 2015), 4th edn, p. 53; on Eurocommunism more generally, see Silvio Pons, *The Global Revolution: A History of International Communism, 1917–1991* (OUP, 2014), pp. 284–93.

17. Howard Machin (ed.), *National Communism in Western Europe: A Third Way for Socialism?* (Methuen, 1983), see especially the chapter by Paul Preston.

18. Vladislav M. Zubok, "Soviet Foreign Policy from Détente to Gorbachev, 1975–1985," Chapter 5 in Leffler and Westad (eds), *The Cambridge History of the Cold War*, Vol. III, p. 93; Berlinguer's Moscow speech, Silvio Pons, op. cit., p. 62.

19. See William Taubman, *Gorbachev: His Life and Times* (Simon & Schuster, 2017), Chapter 4 esp.

20. Cited in Sargent, *A Superpower Transformed*, p. 261; approval ratings, ibid., p. 281.

21. Ibid., p. 287.

22. CPD Executive Committee, "Common Sense and the Common Danger: Policy Statement of the Committee on the Present Danger," cited in Nicholas Blackbourn, "The Sum of Their Fears: The Committee on the Present Danger, the Demise of Détente, and Threat of Inflation, 1976–1980," PhD Thesis, University of St. Andrews (2016).

23. Olav Njølstad, "The Collapse of Superpower Détente, 1975–1980," Chapter 7 in Leffler and Westad (eds), *The Cambridge History of the Cold War*, Vol. III, pp. 148–51 esp.

24. See https://www.nytimes.com/1981/11/23/us/group-goes-from-exile-to-influence.html. In this sense, the parallel rise of political realism in the domain of foreign policy thinking had proven just as important as the parallel neoliberal turn in domestic economic policymaking: see Nicholas Guilhot, *After the Enlightenment: Political Realism and International Relations in the Mid-Twentieth Century* (Cambridge, 2017).

25. Hélène Miard-Delacroix, *Willy Brandt: Life of a Statesman* (I. B. Tauris, 2016), p. 116.

26. For the quote, here, and this account of Ostpolitik's diplomatic maneuverings, see Hélène Miard-Delacroix, *Willy Brandt*, pp. 117–30 passim.

27. Cited in Hélène Miard-Delacroix, *Willy Brandt*, p. 134.

28. See Stråth, *Europe's Utopias of Peace*, p. 368.

29. See Special to the *New York Times*, "Text of Kissinger's Speech at AP Meeting Here on US Relations With Europe," *New York Times*, April 24, 1974; on the European response see Mark Gilbert, *European Integration: A Concise History*, p. 101; "drifted apart": F. P. Bakker, *The Liberalization of Capital Movements in Europe, 1958–1994* (Kluwer, 1996), p. 136.

30. See Stråth, *Europe's Utopias of Peace*, p. 378.

31. Ibid., pp. 378–9.

32. Cited in Gilbert, *European Integration*, p. 113.

33. The matter of European "voice" being the preamble to the optimistic Paris Summit of 1972.

34. On de Gaulle, see Gilbert, *European Integration*, p. 86.

35. Cited in Anthony King, *The British Constitution* (OUP, 2007), p. 97.

36. For both these examples see Gilbert, *European Integration*, p. 112.

37. Cited in ibid., p. 92.

38. Cited in ibid., p. 93.

39. This is the argument of historians such as Georg Kreis and Guido Thiemeyer. See Hagen Schulz-Forberg and Bo Stråth, *The Political History of European Integration: The Hypocrisy of Democracy-Through-Market* (Routledge, 2012), p. 128.

40. See David Hackett Fischer, *Fairness and Freedom: A History of Two Open Societies* (OUP, 2007).

41. Robert Bothwell, *The Penguin History of Canada* (Penguin, 2008), p. 374.

42. Charles S. Maier (ed.), *Changing Boundaries of the Political* (Cambridge, 2010).

43. Schmidt, cited in Elizabeth Benning, "The Road to Rambouillet and the Creation of the Group of Five," in Emmanuel Mourlon-Druol and Federico Romero (eds), *International Summitry and Global Governance* (Routledge, 2014), pp. 39–63.

44. Cited in *Bulletin of the European Communities*, No. 11 (1975), "The Rambouillet Declaration," p. 88.

45. See: UK Embassy Paris to FCO, "Rambouillet: the French View," November 25, 1975, PREM 16/838, Margaret Thatcher Archive, p. 2.

46. Robert D. Putnam and Nicholas Bayne, *Hanging Together: The Seven-Power Summits* (Heinemann, 1984), p. 34.

47. Joshua Zeitz, "Rejecting the Center: Radical Grassroots Politics in the 1970s—Second-Wave Feminism as a Case Study," *Journal of Contemporary History*, 43 (4), pp. 673–88, p. 675.

48. Peter Schrag, *Paradise Lost: California's Experience, America's Future* (The New Press, 1998), p. 7.

49. Stephen Moore, "Proposition 13 Then, Now and Forever," CATO Institute, July 30, 1998, n.p.

50. Thomas R. Swartz and John E. Peck (eds), *The Changing Face of Fiscal Federalism* (Routledge, 1990), pp. 8–9.

51. Detail from Douglas Amy, *Government Is Good: An Unapologetic Defense of a Vital Institution* (Dog Ear Publishing, 2011), p. 8.

52. Jason Felch and Jack Dolan, "Corporations Get Edge in Prop. 13 Quirk," *LA Times*, May 5, 2013.

53. Peter Schrag, *Paradise Lost*.

54. This figure from the Union of International Associations, cited in Akire Iriye, Jürgen Osterhammel, Wilfried Loth, Thomas W. Zeiler, and J. R. Mcneill, *Global Interdependence: The World After 1945* (Harvard, 2014), p. 751.

55. See: https://www.ngoadvisor.net/ngos-a-long-and-turbulent-history/.

56. Jon Agar, "What Happened in the 1960s," *British Journal for the History of Science*, 41.4 (2008): 567–600, pp. 570 and 572. Jacques Monod also cited here.

57. Ibid., p. 572: and as reported in a widely discussed Harris poll of 1972, where "great confidence" in those "running science" had dropped from 56 percent to 37 percent.

58. Richard Nixon: "Inaugural Address," January 20, 1969: http://www.presidency.ucsb.edu /ws/?pid=1941.

59. Cited in Samuel Moyn, *The Last Utopia: Human Rights in History* (Harvard, 2011), p. 155.

60. Lee Congdon, "Solzhenitsyn Wasn't Western," *The American Conservative*, September 17, 2014.

61. Cited in Moyn, *The Last Utopia*, p. 139.

62. Ibid., p. 158.

63. Ibid., p. 132.

64. Kissinger, cited ibid., p. 150.

65. The Helsinki Final Act: available at: https://www.osce.org/helsinki-final-act?down load=true.

Chapter 5: "Let Fury Have the Hour"

1. Cited in Dutton, *British Politics Since 1945*, p. 77; the chapter title here "Let Fury Have the Hour" is taken from the documentary of the same name, by Antonino D'Ambrosio, on artistic responses to the "insane individualism" of the era.

2. Guido Carli, cited in Paul Ginsborg, *Italy and Its Discontents: 1980–2001* (Penguin, 2003), p. 223.

3. Keating, cited in Megalogenis, *The Australian Moment*, p. 166; on Vaizey, this was in 1979: see Mark Mazower, *Dark Continent*, p. 331. Vaizey had some choice words for those who would deny this, deriding them as "bombastic polytechnic lecturers regurgitating inaccurately the half-baked ideas of sentimental Marxists that Tawney would not have let in to his lecture room": see "Letters to the Editor," *The Times*, December 3, 1980.

4. Cited in Daniel Yergin and Joseph Stanislaw, *The Commanding Heights: The Battle for the World Economy* (Simon & Schuster, 2002), p. 47.

5. In the Netherlands, this was the law on external financial relations; on this and other liberalization policies see Age F. P. Bakker, *The Liberalization of Capital Movements in Europe, 1958–1994* (Kluwer, 1996), p. 133, pp. 149–51.

6. See Norberto Bobbio, *The Future of Democracy* (Polity, 2009), pp. 115–16 and Jürgen Habermas, *The Lure of Technocracy* (Polity, 2015), pp. 85–90.

7. Richard Toye, "From 'Consensus' to 'Common Ground': The Rhetoric of the Postwar Settlement and Its Collapse," *Journal of Contemporary History*, 48.1 (2013): 3–23, p. 21.

8. Cited in Rawi Abdelal, *Capital Rules: The Construction of Global Finance* (Harvard, 2007), p. 62.

9. Cited in Sassoon, *One Hundred Years of Socialism*, p. 735; "This city cannot simply stand by": cited in Carla MacDougall, "We Too Are Berliners," Chapter 5 in Belinda Davis, Wilfried Mausbach, Martin Klimke, and Carla MacDougall, *Changing Oneself, Changing the World*.

10. Simon Jenkins, *Thatcher & Sons: A Revolution in Three Acts* (Penguin, 2007), p. 87.

11. Morgan and Campbell, *The Delegated Welfare State: Medicare, Markets, and the Governance of Social Policy* (Oxford, 2011), p. 82. The figure is around the same today.

12. Ibid., p. 83.

13. William C. Berman, *America's Right Turn*, p. 1.

14. Cited in Daniel T. Rodgers, *Age of Fracture* (Belknap, 2011), p. 23.

15. These metaphors were not casual, nor were they uncommon. The state is invariably a wanton beast or an errant child in these descriptions: "draining its lifeblood" (Grover Norquist), "the way parents control spendthrift children" (Milton Friedman).

16. Specifically in the Union de Défense des Commerçants et Artisans, which under Pierre Poujade in the 1950s, and on behalf of "the good little people of France," excoriated the "thieving" state and the "rubbishy pederast" of parliament. See Fenby, *The History of Modern France*, p. 337.

17. See Bruce Bartlett, "The New Republican Tax Policy," "Economix: Explaining the Science of Everyday Life," *New York Times*, November 20, 2012; on Stockman's role, see the (infamous) but excellent piece by William Greider, "The Education of David Stockman," *The Atlantic*, December 1981.

18. On OBRA's sketchy presentation, see Karl Gerard Brandt, *Ronald Reagan and the House Democrats: Gridlock, Partisanship, and the Fiscal Crisis* (University of Missouri Press, 2009), p. 47.

19. Over a million council houses were sold in the 1980s. This was the biggest windfall for the Conservative government financially: while attention has often focused on the privatized *industries*, council house receipts were worth more than all other privatized industries together.

20. John Hills and Kitty Stewart, *A More Equal Society? New Labour, Poverty, Inequality and Exclusion* (Policy Press, 2004), pp. 1–3.

21. Jenkins, *Thatcher & Sons*, p. 94. See also Parboni, *The Dollar and Its Rivals*, p. 12.

22. "Final Report of the Nationalized Industries Policy Group: Confidential," PG/10/77/38, July 8, 1977, p. 15. Margaret Thatcher Archive, London.

23. Massimo Florio, *The Great Divestiture: Evaluating the Welfare Impact of the British Privatizations, 1979–1997* (MIT Press, 2004), p. 163.

24. Richard Vinen, *Thatcher's Britain: The Politics and Social Upheaval of the 1980s* (Simon & Schuster UK, 2010), p. 197.

25. Jenkins, *Thatcher & Sons*, p. 5.

26. Evelyne Huber and John D. Stephens, *Development and Crisis of the Welfare State: Parties and Policies in Global Markets* (Chicago, 2001), p. 310.

27. It fell from 4.5 percent in 1981 to 3.3 percent in 1988. See Bruce Bartlett, "The New Republican Tax Policy," *New York Times*, November 20, 2012.

28. It was 21.7 percent in 1980 compared to 21.3 percent in 1988 (ibid.).

29. From 45.1 percent, when Thatcher entered government, to 39.2 percent in 1989–90, so still nearly double the US figure.

30. See Simon Rogers, "How Britain Changed under Margaret Thatcher in 15 charts," *Guardian*, April 8, 2013.

31. Godfrey Hodgson, *More Equal Than Others: America from Nixon to the New Century* (Princeton, 2009), p. 2.

32. As observed by Simon Jenkins, *Thatcher & Sons*, p. 42.

33. Reagan and Friedman, Angus Burgin, *The Great Persuasion: Reinventing Free Markets Since the Depression* (Harvard, 2012), p. 207.

34. Interview with Stine Dabrowski, *Svenska TV4*, 1995, at 9 minutes.

35. Charles Moore, "The E.U. and the Nation State: Who's Winning?," *The Margaret Thatcher Lecture*, Center for Policy Studies, October 23, 2012, p. 1.

36. "The New Style of Government" was the name of its most influential document.

37. Cited in Jenkins, *Thatcher & Sons*, p. 88.

38. Ignatieff, *The Needs of Strangers* (Picador, 2000), p. 9.

39. Ibid., p. 15.

40. Ginsborg, *A History of Contemporary Italy*, pp. 392–3.

41. Megalogenis, *The Australian Moment*, p. 132; Jenkins, *Thatcher & Sons*, p. 87.

42. Cited in Vinen, *Thatcher's Britain*, p. 124.

43. David Mathiasen, "The Evolution of the Office of Management and Budget under Reagan," *Public Budgeting and Finance*, 8.3 (1988): 3–14.

44. Berman, *America's Right Turn*, p. 95.

45. Ibid.

46. Figures from Joseph A. McMartin, "The Strike That Busted Unions," *New York Times*, August 2, 2011; see also Stedman Jones, *Masters of the Universe: Hayek, Friedman and the Birth of Neoliberalism* (Princeton, 2014), p. 267.

47. Mark Blyth, *Great Transformations: Economic Ideas and Institutional Change in the Twentieth Century* (CUP, 2002), pp. 182–3.

48. Vinen, *Thatcher's Britain*, pp. 154–78.

49. Thatcher, cited in Donald MacIntyre, "How the Miners' Strike of 1984/5 Changed Britain Forever," *New Statesman*, June 11, 2014.

50. See Seamus Milne, "During the Miners' Strike Thatcher's Secret State Was the Real Enemy Within," *Guardian*, October 3, 2014; and "A War Nobody Deserved to Win," *Guardian*, Editorial, March 7, 2009.

51. Stephen Cavalier, "The Legal Legacy of the Miners' Strike," *Capital & Class*, 29.3 (2005): 65–70, pp. 66–9.

52. Florio, *The Great Divestiture*, p. 98.

53. Ibid., pp. 93–5.

54. Ibid., p. 37.

55. Vinen, *Thatcher's Britain*, p. 164.

56. Cited in Banwart, "Jerry Falwell: The Rise of the Moral Majority," *Western Illinois Historical Review*, V (Spring 2013): 133–57, p. 142.

57. Margaret Thatcher, in *Women's Own*, October 31, 1987.

58. This is the less well recalled continuation of Thatcher's *Women's Own* speech.

59. The notion is used in a slightly different context by Charles Maier, in his "Malaise," Chapter 2 in Ferguson et al. (eds), *The Shock of the Global*.

60. Mark Lilla, cited in O'Sullivan, *European Thought Since 1945*, p. 93.

61. Cited in: Vivien A. Schmidt, *Democratizing France: The Political and Administrative History of Decentralization* (CUP, 1990), p. 105.

62. Ronald Tiersky, cited in Gilbert, *European Integration: A Concise History*, p. 119.

63. Nick Hewlett and Elaine Fantham, *Modern French Politics: Analysing Conflict and Consensus Since 1945* (Polity, 1998), p. 64. The socialists' electoral manifesto was drawn essentially from the Common Program of Government (*Program Comun*) statement of 1972, which unified the communist and noncommunist left, and soon began to look more like a millstone than a platform for sustainable change.

64. Ibid., pp. 60–1.

65. See Douglas A. Yates, "The French Oil Industry and the Corps des Mines in Africa," Chatham House meeting summary, March 2, 2012, and Vivien Schmidt, *From State to Market? The Transformation of French Business and Government* (Cambridge, 1996).

66. Jamie Peck and Adam Tickell, "Neoliberalizing Space," *Antipode*, 34.3 (July 2002): 380–404.
67. This was the Mitbestimmungsgesetz 1976 (Co-determination Act, 1976). See M. C. Jensen and W. Meckling, "Rights and Production Functions: An Application to Labor-Managed Firms and Codetermination," *Journal of Business*, 52.4 (1979): 469–506, p. 469.
68. Ewan McGaughey, "The Codetermination Bargains: The History of German Corporate and Labor Law," London School of Economics and Political Science, LSE Library (2015), p. 39.
69. In Asbjorn Wahl, *The Rise and Fall of the Welfare State* (Pluto Press, 2011), p. 71.
70. Ibid., p. 73.
71. Herman Schwartz, "Small States in Big Trouble: State Reorganization in Australia, Denmark, New Zealand, and Sweden in the 1980s," *World Politics*, 46.4 (July 1994): 527–55.
72. Cited in Jaime Palomera, "The Political Economy of Spain: A Brief History (1939–2014)," *Working Paper for the ERC Greco Project*, Universitat de Barcelona (March 2015).
73. Herbert Kitschelt, *The Transformation of European Social Democracy* (Cambridge, 1994), pp. 222–3. In Spain, as in France, intellectuals underwent a "dramatic and decisive re-alignment." See Sunil Khilnani, *Arguing Revolution: The Intellectual Left in Postwar France* (Yale University Press, 1993), p. 121.
74. Tony Judt, *Postwar*, Chapter 26 esp.; see also Kitschelt, *The Transformation of European Social Democracy*, pp. 288–9.
75. Ginsborg, *Italy and Its Discontents*, p. 149. The CDs went from 38.9 percent to 32.9 percent of the vote.
76. Ibid., p. 152.
77. These tax figures are the average for the 1990s.
78. Wolfgang Streeck, *Buying Time: The Delayed Crisis of Democratic Capitalism* (Verso, 2014), p. 28.
79. Huber and Stephens, *Development and Crisis of the Welfare State*, p. 305.
80. Susan Strange, *Casino Capitalism*, new edn (Manchester, 1997).
81. It oscillated between 0.9 and 1.3 percent. See Jochen Dehio et al., "ICT and Earlier Technological Revolutions," in Jochen Dehio, Roland Döhrn, Rainer Graskamp, Klaus Löbbe, Hans Dietrich von Loeffelholz, Waike Moos, and Michael Rothgang, *New Economy: The German Perspective* (Duncker & Humblot, 2002), p. 49. See also David Audretsch and Paul J. J. Welfens (eds), *The New Economy and Economic Growth in Europe and the US* (Springer Berlin, 2002).
82. Ethan Barnaby Kapstein, "Between Power and Purpose: Central Bankers and the Politics of Regulatory Convergence," *International Organization*, 46.1 (Winter 1992): 265–87, p. 268.
83. Cited in Robert Solomon, *Money on the Move: The Revolution in International Finance Since 1980* (Princeton, 2015), p. 11.
84. As Robert Solomon, then his chief international economist at the Federal Reserve Board, later put it. See Solomon, *Money on the Move*, p. 21.
85. See Martin Marcussen, "The Fifth Age of Central Banking," Copenhagen Business School; Paper Presented at the Conference "Frontiers of Regulation," University of Bath (August 2006).
86. Harvey, *The Condition of Postmodernity*, p. 169.

87. Solomon, *Money on the Move*, p. 111.

88. The average annual growth of real wages between 1973 and 2000 for private sector and nonsupervisory workers was zero. See Brenner, *Economics of Global Turbulence* (Verso, 2005), p. xxviii.

89. Christopher J. Niggle, "Review: Casino Capitalism by Susan Strange," *Review of Social Economy*, 45.2 (October 1987): 215–18, p. 215.

90. Brenner, *Economics of Global Turbulence*, p. xxii; see also Vinen, *A History in Fragments: Europe in the Twentieth Century* (Abacus, 2014 [2000]), p. 522.

91. See: https://www.americanprogress.org/issues/labor/news/2012/07/09/11898/5-facts -about-overseas-outsourcing/.

92. An argument made in Tooze and Eich, "The Great Inflation," op. cit.

93. See the Berkley Center, "Economic Justice for All: Pastoral Letter on Catholic Social Teaching and the U.S Economy," November 1, 1986, p. 43.

94. See Jean Cohen, "Trust, voluntary association and workable democracy: the contemporary American discourse of civil society," in Mark E. Warren, *Democracy and Trust* (Cambridge, 1999), pp. 208–48, p. 215.

95. Ferdinand Mount, "The Recovery of Civility," *Encounter* magazine, July 1973, pp. 31–3. This was in fact a response to Irving Kristol's *On the Democratic Idea in America*, in which Kristol spoke of the need for a "Long Trek Back."

96. Cited in Vincent P. Franklin, *African Americans and Jews in the Twentieth Century: Studies in Convergence and Conflict* (Missouri,1998), p. 170.

97. Cited in Virginia Hodgkinson and Michael Foley (eds), *The Civil Society Reader* (Tufts, 2003), "Introduction," p. xxi. See also for Barber, and Berger and Neuhaus.

98. See Mary Ann Glendon, *The Current State of the Civil Society Debate* (Institute for American Values, 1997).

99. Cited in Ellen Meiksins Wood, *Democracy Against Capitalism* (Cambridge, 1995), p. 231.

100. Walzer: cited in Hodgkinson and Foley, *The Civil Society Reader*, p. xxi; elective concept: Judt, *Postwar*, p. 537; Perec: Mazower, *Dark Continent*, p. 304.

101. "almost vanish[ed]": Francis Sejerstad, *The Age of Social Democracy*, p. 488.

102. Ginsborg, *A History of Contemporary Italy*, p. 88. On Turin and Detroit see Nicola Pizzolato, *Challenging Global Capitalism: Labor Migration, Radical Struggle, and Urban Change in Detroit and Turin* (AIAA, 2013).

103. See Wahl, *The Rise and Fall of the Welfare State*, p. 69.

104. See Vinen, *History in Fragments*, p. 526.

105. D. Simonelli, "Anarchy, Pop and Violence: Punk Rock Subculture and the Rhetoric of Class, 1976–78," *Contemporary British History*, 16.2 (2002): 121–41.

106. Sabine von Dirke, *"All Power to the Imagination": The West German Counterculture from the Student Movement to the Greens* (University of Nebraska Press, 1997). As a British journalist later recalled, while the first half of the decade was open war, "sometime in the mid-80s everything became becalmed. The fiercest political battles had been fought and won": Jason Cowley, "England Was Convulsed by a Social and Political Revolution," *Guardian*, April 19, 2009.

107. Thomas Sugrue, *The Origins of the Urban Crisis: Race and Inequality in Postwar Detroit* (Princeton, 2014), Preface to the 2014 edition, p. xvi.

108. Leo Panitch and Ralph Miliband, "The New World Order and the Socialist Agenda," *Socialist Register*, 28 (1992): 1–25, p. 7.

109. The actual number of votes was 4,376,742. See "The Front National Since the 1970s," in Emile Chabal (ed.), *France Since the 1970s*, p. 41.

110. Emile Chabal, Introduction in ibid., p. 9.

111. Mike Savage, *Social Class in the Twenty-First Century* (Pelican, 2015), Chapter 8 esp.

112. See Bobbio, *The Future of Democracy*, p. 114.

113. Sassoon, *One Hundred Years of Socialism*, p. 455.

114. See Mark Lilla, *The Once and Future Liberal*, p. 40.

115. Maria Eleonora Guasconi, "Public Opinion and the Euromissile Crisis," in Leopoldo Nuti, Frédéric Bozo, Marie-Pierre Rey, and Berno Rother (eds), *The Euromissile Crisis and the End of the Cold War* (Stanford University Press, 2015), p. 280. See also Vladislav Zubok, "Soviet Foreign Policy from Détente to Gorbachev," in Leffler and Westad (eds), *The Cambridge History of the Cold War*, Vol. III, pp. 108–11 esp.

116. See Nicholas Thompson, *The Hawk and the Dove: Paul Nitze, George Kennan and the History of the Cold War* (Picador, 2009), pp. 291–4; on the US at cross-purposes: see William Burr, "A Question of Confidence," in Leopoldo Nuti, Frédéric Bozo, Marie-Pierre Rey, and Berno Rother (eds), *The Euromissile Crisis and the End of the Cold War* (Stanford University Press, 2015).

117. Cited in Olav Njølstad (ed.), *The Last Decade of the Cold War: From Conflict Escalation to Conflict Transformation* (Routledge, 2004), pp. 176–7. See also Edward Cody, "Euro-communists are Gratified by Gorbachev's Changes," *Washington Post*, May 13, 1988.

118. Cited in Sargent, *A Superpower Transformed*, p. 305.

119. See Silvio Pons, "The Legacy of Eurocommunism and Gorbachev," unpublished manuscript, n.d.

120. Cited in Melvyn Leffler, *For the Soul of Mankind: The United States, the Soviet Union, and the Cold War* (Farrar, Straus & Giroux, 2008), p. 422. See also Foreign Broadcast Information Service (Daily Reports), January 3, 1989, pp. 41–5.

121. Peter Baker, "Mikhail Gorbachev Brought Democracy to Russia and Was Despised for It," *New York Times*, September 16, 2017.

Chapter 6: The Victory: Remaking Europe

1. Memorandum of Telephone Conversation, 9335, November 10, 1989. Also cited in Leffler, *For the Soul of Mankind*, p. 435.

2. George Lawson, Chris Armbruster, and Michael Cox (eds), *The Global 1989: Continuity and Change in World Politics* (Cambridge, 2010).

3. Andrew Arato, "Lefort, the Philosopher of 1989," *Constellations*, 19.1 (2012): 23–9, p. 23.

4. The Party of course then spouted those principles even more loudly in response, but it did so to a steadily declining membership: from 3.1 million in 1980 to 2.1 million in 1984. Party membership figures from Mazower, *Dark Continent*, p. 370.

5. Ferguson et al. (eds), *The Shock of the Global*, p. 89.

6. Cited in Gale Stokes, *The Walls Came Tumbling Down: The Collapse of Communism in Eastern Europe* (OUP, 1993), p. 24.

7. Cf. Judt, *Postwar*, p. 569.

8. Cited in Jan-Werner Müller, *Contesting Democracy: Political Ideas in Twentieth-Century Europe* (Yale University Press, 2011), p. 230.

9. These two examples are from Barbara Falk, "1989 and Post-Cold War Policymaking:

Were the 'Wrong' Lessons Learned from the Fall of Communism?," *International Journal of Politics, Culture and Society*, 22.3 (2009): 291–313, p. 302.

10. Vladimir Tismaneanu and Bogdan C. Iacob (eds), *The End and the Beginning: The Revolutions of 1989 and the Resurgence of History* (Central European University Press, 2012), p. 22.

11. Michael Mandelbaum in *Postcommunism: Four Perspectives* (Council on Foreign Relations, 1996), p. 9.

12. Ernest Gellner, "Return of a Native," *Political Quarterly*, 67.1 (1996): 4–13, p. 12.

13. R. J. Crampton, *Eastern Europe in the Twentieth Century—and After* (Routledge 1997), p. 447.

14. Arato, "Lefort, the Philosopher of 1989," p. 26.

15. See the Preface to Timothy J. Colton and Robert Legvold (eds), *After the Soviet Union: From Empire to Nations* (W. W. Norton, 1993), p. 11.

16. See Narodowy Bank Polski, "The History of Central Banking in Poland." At: https://www.nbp.pl/homen.aspx?f=/en/onbp/informacje/historia_bankowosci.html.

17. Andrew Arato, *Civil Society, Constitution, and Legitimacy* (Rowman & Littlefield, 2000), p. 9.

18. George H. W. Bush, "Remarks to the Polish National Assembly," Warsaw, July 10, 1989, in Jim McGrath, *Heartbeat: George Bush in His Own Words* (Simon & Schuster, 2001), p. 36.

19. Quotes and anecdote: Philip Short, *Mitterrand: A Study in Ambiguity* (Vintage, 2014), pp. 478–9.

20. Sleepwalking: Michael Meyer, *The Year That Changed the World: The Untold Story Behind the Fall of the Berlin Wall* (Scribner, 2009), p. 63; not negotiate: Mary Louise Sarotte, *1989: The Struggle to Create Post–Cold War Europe* (Princeton University Press, 2011), p. 78.

21. See Mary Kaldor, *Europe from Below: An East-West Dialogue* (Verso, 1991), p. 124.

22. Philip Short, *Mitterrand*, p. 481.

23. Mary Louise Sarotte, *1989: The Struggle to Create Post–Cold War Europe* (Princeton University Press, 2011), p. 16.

24. Baker: cited in ibid., p. 27.

25. Cited in James E. Cronin, *Global Rules: America, Britain and a Disordered World* (Yale University Press, 2014), p. 190.

26. Sarotte, *1989: The Struggle to Create Post–Cold War Europe*, p. 7.

27. New European architecture, and Baker in Berlin: Short, *Mitterrand*, p. 481.

28. Short, *Mitterrand*, p. 403.

29. Ibid., p. 400.

30. Details, quotations this paragraph: ibid., p. 482.

31. See "News Conference of President Bush and President François Mitterrand of France in Key Largo, Florida, April 19, 1990," *Public Papers of the Presidents of the United States: George Bush*, April 19, 1990, pp. 523–6.

32. The fact is: Margaret Thatcher, "Speech to the College of Europe," September 20, 1988 (Margaret Thatcher Archive); Rolled back the frontiers: cited in John Palmer, "Thatcher Sets Face Against United Europe," *Guardian*, September 21, 1988; Better to have: cited in Charles Moore, *Evening Standard*, October 6, 2015, p. 23.

33. Thatcher to Gorbachev, cited in Sarotte, *1989: The Struggle to Create Post–Cold War Europe*, p. 28.

34. Charles Moore, *Evening Standard*, October 6, 2015, p. 23.

35. Cited in Charles A. Kupchan and Peter L. Trubowitz, "Grand Strategy for a Divided America," *Foreign Affairs*, 86.4 (July/August 2007), p. 82.

36. Data from Andrew Moravcsik, *The Choice for Europe: Social Purpose and State Power from Messina to Maastricht* (Routledge, 1998), p. 420.

37. Helmut Kohl, "Ten-Point Plan for German Unity" (1989), point 6, see: http://german historydocs.ghi-dc.org/docpage.cfm?docpage_id=117/.

38. Sarotte, *1989: The Struggle to Create Post–Cold War Europe*, p. 176.

39. Ibid., p. 130.

40. Ibid., pp. 115–17. For the Wolfram quote, see p. 116.

41. Valéry Giscard d'Estaing, "The Two Europes, East and West," *International Affairs*, 65.4 (Autumn 1989): 653–8, p. 653.

42. Ibid., p. 654.

43. As reported (approvingly) by Standard & Poor's: see Rawi Abdelal, *Capital Rules* (Harvard University Press, 2009), p. 184.

44. Cited in Eich and Tooze, "The Great Inflation," p. 22. See also Harold James and Mario Draghi, *Making the European Monetary Union*.

45. Fenby, *The History of Modern France*, p. 414; cf. Hewlett and Fantham, *Modern French Politics*, p. 65.

46. See Abdelal, *Capital Rules*, Chapter 4, and pp. 59–60 esp.; see also Jonah Levy, *Tocqueville's Revenge: State, Society and Economy in Contemporary France* (Harvard, 1999), Chapter 1 and Chapter 7.

47. Cited in Abdelal, *Capital Rules*, p. 60.

48. See Kenneth F. H. Dyson, Ivo Maes, *Architects of the Euro: Intellectuals in the Making of European Monetary Union* (OUP, 2016), p. 227; see also Bo Stråth, *Europe's Utopias of Peace*, p. 379.

49. Emmanuel Mourlon-Druol, *A Europe Made of Money: The Emergence of the European Monetary System* (Cornell University Press, 2012), p. 268.

50. Emmanuel Mourlon-Druol, *A Europe Made of Money*, p. 263.

51. Ibid., pp. 262–70 passim; On Emminger, this was reported in *Der Tagesspiegell*, August 1, 1991, see: https://www.bundesbank.de/resource/blob/710142/abed889e8504ec0838fc 9dea16a7b43e/mL/quotes-about-otmar-emminger-data.pdf.

52. Mourlon-Druol, *A Europe Made of Money*, p. 264.

53. Charles Moore, *Margaret Thatcher: The Authorized Biography*, Vol. II (Penguin, 2016); for "one r," p. 379, and "Le pb," p. 399.

54. Ibid., pp. 394–5.

55. Ibid., p. 380.

56. Short, *Mitterrand*, p. 382.

57. See Moore, *Margaret Thatcher*, Vol. II, p. 401.

58. See Eichengreen, *The European Economy Since 1945*, pp. 338–9.

59. See Mark Thatcher, "Supranational Neo-liberalization," in Mark Thatcher (ed.), *Resilient Liberalism in Europe's Political Economy* (CUP, 2013).

60. Eichengreen, *The European Economy Since 1945*, p. 345.

61. Ibid.

62. Cited in Abdelal, *Capital Rules*, p. 64.

63. According to Mark Gilbert, "Constructing Europe," *European History Quarterly*, 43.1 (2013): 96–106, p. 103.

64. Cited in Abdelal, *Capital Rules*, p. 77.

65. BBC Home, "1992: Maastricht treaties make EU official," February 7.

66. Jan-Werner Müller, *Contesting Democracy*, p. 146.

67. For some of the detail on this, see Eichengreen, *The European Economy Since 1945*, pp. 368–9.

68. See Stephen Gill, "New constitutionalism, democratisation and global political economy," *Global Change, Peace & Security*, 10.1 (1998): 23–38.

69. Cited Leffler, *For the Soul of Mankind*, p. 416.

70. Jeffrey A. Engel, *The Fall of the Berlin Wall: The Revolutionary Legacy of 1989* (OUP, 2009), p. 7; see also Vladimir Kontorovich, "Economists, Soviet economic reforms, and the collapse" (Department of Economics, Haverford, Typescript, November 2001).

71. Cf. Robert William Davies, *Soviet History in the Gorbachev Revolution* (Indiana, 1989), pp. 8–9.

72. Cited ibid., p. 9.

73. National Security Archive, *The Diary of Anatoly Chernyaev*, trans. Anna Melyakova, ed. Svetlana Savranskaya (NSA, 2009): entry for October 5, 1989, p. 36.

74. Stokes, *The Walls Came Tumbling Down*, pp. 22–9 and 153.

75. Cited in Jan-Werner Müller, *Contesting Democracy*, p. 234.

76. See Chris Armbruster, "One bright moment in an age of war," Chapter 9 in George Lawson, Chris Armbruster, and Michael Cox (eds), *The Global 1989: Continuity and Change in World Politics* (Cambridge, 2010), p. 202.

77. Archie Brown, *The Rise and Fall of Communism* (Vintage, 2010), pp. 41–4.

78. Cited in: Kiron Skinner, Bruce Bueno de Mesquita, Serhiy Kudelia, and Condoleezza Rice, *The Strategy of Campaigning* (University of Michigan Press, 2007), p. 215.

79. Chernyaev, cited in Archie Brown, "Did Gorbachev as Secretary Become a Social Democrat?," *Europe-Asia Studies*, 65.2 (2013): 198–220, p. 201; the critic is also Brown, p. 202.

80. Cited ibid., p. 210; see also Silvio Pons, "The Legacy of Eurocommunism and Gorbachev," unpublished manuscript.

81. Brown, "Gorbachev as Social Democrat," p. 208. The same argument can be found in William Taubman, *Gorbachev: His Life and Times* (Simon & Schuster, 2017), Chapter 17.

82. Brown, "Did Gorbachev as Secretary Become a Social Democrat," pp. 309–10.

83. Democratic space: cited in Ian Clark, *The Post–Cold War Order: The Spoils of Peace* (OUP, 1992), p. 182; global perestroika and birth: cited in Engel, *The Fall of the Berlin Wall*, p. 24; Jeane Kirkpatrick, "Beyond the Cold War," *Foreign Affairs*, 69/1 (1989/1990): 1–16, p. 2.

84. Francesco Benvenuti and Silvio Pons, "The End of Soviet Communism," Chapter 12 in Silvio Pons and Federico Romero (eds), *Reinterpreting the End of the Cold War* (Frank Cass, 2005), pp. 212–19 esp.

85. Jan Werner Müller, *Contesting Democracy*, p. 232.

86. Rawi Abdelal, *Capital Rules*, p. 84; Gorbachev's pen: Robert V. Daniels, *The End of the Communist Revolution* (Routledge, 2002), pp. 51–5.

Chapter 7: America and "A World Transformed"

1. The phrase is George H. W. Bush's, from his coedited book, George H. W. Bush and Brent Scowcroft, *A World Transformed* (Vintage, 1999).

2. Bruce Cumings, "Trilateralism and the New World Order," *World Policy Journal*, 8.2 (1991): 195–222, p. 195.

3. Cited in Jordan Michael Smith, "Kennan's Opposite," *The American Conservative*, Janu-

ary 9, 2012. Containment became the backbone of American military strategy throughout the Cold War. But while Kennan was widely given credit for this he was actually among the strategy's staunchest critics, in part because the policy had been misunderstood, he claimed: he intended it to be understood as a political not military doctrine. It was the response to Kennan's article by Walter Lipmann that coined the phrase "the cold war." See also Fareed Zakaria, "Divining Russia," *New York Times*, April 7, 1996, and Nicholas Thompson, *The Hawk and the Dove: Paul Nitze, George Kennan, and the History of the Cold War* (Picador, 2010).

4. See Robert A. Pastor, "The Bush Administration and Latin America: The pragmatic style and the regionalist option," *Journal of Interamerican Studies and World Affairs*, 33.3 (1991): 1–34, pp. 3–5 esp. On Gorbachev's forward-looking thinking at the time of Malta, see Jon Meacham, *Destiny and Power: The American Odyssey of George Herbert Walker Bush* (Random House, 2015), p. 385.

5. George H. W. Bush, "Inaugural Address," January 20, 1989, at: http://www.presidency.ucsb.edu/ws/index.php?pid=16610.

6. Meacham, *Destiny and Power*, p. 403.

7. Cited ibid., p. 402.

8. As described in Aspen some weeks before. But the outline was already there. It just required the discussion that day in Kennebunkport to crystallize the idea around a particular phrase. See George H. W. Bush, "Remarks at the Aspen Institute Symposium in Aspen, Colorado," at: http://www.presidency.ucsb.edu/ws/?pid=18731.

9. George H. W. Bush, "Address Before a Joint Session of the Congress on the Persian Gulf Crisis and the Federal Budget Deficit," September 11, 1990, at: http://www.presidency.ucsb.edu/ws/?pid=18820.

10. George H. W. Bush and Brent Scowcroft, *A World Transformed* (Vintage, 1999), p. 364.

11. Ibid., p. 368.

12. George H. W. Bush, "Address Before a Joint Session of the Congress on the Persian Gulf Crisis and the Federal Budget Deficit," September 11, 1990, at: http://www.presidency.ucsb.edu/ws/?pid=18820.

13. Cited in: Michael F. Cairo, *The Gulf: The Bush Presidencies and the Middle East* (University of Kentucky Press, 2012), p. 63.

14. Meacham, *Destiny and Power*, p. 429.

15. Leon Hadar, *Quagmire: America in the Middle East* (Cato Institute, 1992), p. 122.

16. H. W. Brands, "George Bush and the Gulf War of 1991," *Presidential Studies Quarterly*, 34.1 (March 2004): 113–131; see also: US Office of the Historian, "The Gulf War, 1991," at: http://history.state.gov/milestones/1989-1992/gulf-war/; Jerome V. Martin, Lt. Col., USAF, *Victory from Above*, Research Report No. AU-ARI-92-8 (Maxwell Air Force Base, Ala.: Air University Press, 1994), p. 63; Too cute: cited in Bush and Scowcroft, *A World Transformed*, p. 486.

17. Scott Forsyth, "Hollywood's War on the World: The New World Order as Movie," *Socialist Register*, 28 (1992): 270–85.

18. See William J. Eaton and Beth Hawkins, "200,000 Cheer Victory Parade Through Capital," *Los Angeles Times*, June 9, 1991; Josh Getlin and Scot J. Paltrow, "Paper Blizzard Welcomes Gulf Troops in N.Y.," *Los Angeles Times*, June 11, 1991.

19. Michael H. Hunt, *The American Ascendancy: How the United States Gained and Wielded Global Dominance* (North Carolina, 2007), p. 299.

20. For these points see the brilliant essay by Andrew J. Bacevich, "A Less Than Splendid

Little War," *Wilson Quarterly* (Winter 2014); see also William Pfaff, "Power For What?," *New York Review of Books*, April 8, 1999.

21. Bacevich, ibid.

22. Cited in "The War in the Gulf: Bush Statement," *New York Times*, February 16, 1991.

23. Adam Roberts, "Humanitarian War: Military Intervention and Human Rights," *International Affairs*, 69.3 (1993): 429–49, p. 438.

24. On the postwar reshuffling, see Peter Mansfield, *A History of the Middle East* (Penguin, 2013), pp. 412–13.

25. Simon Jenkins, *Thatcher & Sons*, p. 137.

26. See Gerard Toal, "The New East-West Conflict?," *Area*, 25.2 (1993): 127–35.

27. Toal, "The New East-West Conflict?," p. 129.

28. See e.g., Qimao Chen, "New Approaches in China's Foreign Policy: the post–Cold War era," *Asian Survey*, 33.3 (1993): 237–51.

29. Bush and Scowcroft, *A World Transformed*, p. 218.

30. Ibid., p. 537.

31. See Archie Brown, *The Rise and Fall of Communism* (Vintage, 2010), p. 496: for the rest of that year Yeltsin was ill in hospital, and out of the party.

32. Bush and Scowcroft, *A World Transformed*, p. 500.

33. Ibid., p. 162.

34. Ibid., pp. 518–36.

35. Brown, *The Rise and Fall of Communism*, pp. 304–5.

36. Cited in David Reynolds, *America: Empire of Liberty* (Penguin, 2010), pp. 537–8; Gorbachev interrogated: Bush and Scowcrift, op. cit., p. 507; his fall: Louis Sell, *From Washington to Moscow: US–Soviet Relations and the Collapse of the USSR* (Duke University Press, 2016), Chapter 18.

37. Michael Wines, "Bush and Yeltsin Declare Formal End to Cold War; Agree to Exchange Visits," *New York Times*, February 2, 1992.

38. Charles William Maynes, "Coping with the '90s," in Francis Xavier Sutton, *A World to Make: Development in Perspective* (Routledge, 1990), p. 216.

39. Panitch and Miliband, "The New World Order and the Socialist Agenda," *Socialist Register*, 28 (1992): 1–25, p. 7.

40. Norman J. Ornstein and Mark Schmitt, "Dateline Campaign '92: Post–Cold War Politics," *Foreign Affairs*, 79 (Summer 1990): 169–86, p. 183.

41. See Brenner, *The Boom and the Bubble* (Verso, 2003), p. 68.

42. Mike Davis, "A Tale of Two Riots," *Daily Kos*, April 5, 2012.

43. Panitch and Miliband, "The New World Order," p. 7.

44. George F. Will, *Suddenly: The American Idea Abroad and at Home, 1986–1990* (Free Press, 1992).

45. Madison Gray, "The L.A. Riots: 15 Years After Rodney King," *Time* magazine (2007).

46. Mike Davis, "A Tale of Two Riots."

47. Madison Gray, "The L.A. Riots: 15 Years After Rodney King," *Time* magazine (2007).

48. Panitch and Miliband, "The New World Order," p. 8.

49. See Thomas J. Sugrue, *The Origins of the Urban Crisis: Race and Inequality in Postwar Detroit* (Princeton, 2014).

50. Data from B. Guy Peters, "Economic Policy," in Gillian Peele and Christopher Bailey, *Developments in American Politics*, 3 (Palgrave, 1998), p. 211.

51. David Runciman, *The Confidence Trap: A History of Democracy in Crisis from World War I to the Present* (Princeton University Press, 2012), p. 243.

52. Walter Russell Mead, "The Once and Future Reich," *World Policy Journal,* 7.4 (Fall 1990): 593–638, p. 596.

53. Runciman, *The Confidence Trap,* p. 230, wherein Mick Jagger also appears.

54. This was Terry Karl, professor of political science at Stanford, speaking at a class of '70 sponsored event in 1995.

55. This at the national education "summit" in Charlottesville that year.

56. See Mark Lilla, *The Once and Future Liberal: After Identity Politics* (HarperCollins, 2017); compare Leo Casey, "The Perils of Universalism," *Dissent* magazine, Winter 2018, and Shuja Haider, "From Identity Politics to Universalism: A response to Leo Casey," *Dissent* magazine, March 22, 2018.

57. "FBI to Fight Street Gangs," *Intelligence Newsletter,* Issue 185, January 15, 1992.

58. Geároid Ó'Tuathail and Timothy Luke, "Present at the (Dis)integration: Deterritorialization and Reterritorialization in the New Wor(l)d Order," *Annals of the Association of American Geographers,* 84.3 (1994): 381–98, p. 381.

59. Cited in Mark Mazower, *Dark Continent,* p. 344.

60. Sidney Harman and Daniel Yankelovich, *Starting With the People* (Houghton Mifflin, 1988).

61. David Rieff, "A Global Culture?," *World Policy Journal,* 10.4 (1993): 73–81, p. 81.

62. For Kristol and quotes here see Ellen Schrecker (ed.), *Cold War Triumphalism: The Misuse of History After the Fall of Communism* (New Press, 2006), p. 6.

63. Irving Howe, "Two Cheers for Utopia," "Afterword" in Nicolaus Mills (ed.), *Legacy of "Dissent": Forty Years of Writing from "Dissent" Magazine* (Simon & Schuster, 1995), p. 459.

64. David Rieff, "A Global Culture?," p. 78.

65. Meacham, *Destiny and Power,* p. 469.

66. Ibid., p. 499.

67. Cited in ibid., p. 471.

68. Robert Dreyfuss, "How the DLC Does It," *The American Prospect,* December 19, 2001.

69. Michael J. Rosenfeld, "Celebration, politics, selective looting and riots: A micro level study of the Bulls Riot of 1992 in Chicago," *Social Problems,* 44.4 (1997): 483–502. On New York: James Dao, "Angered by Police Killing, a Neighborhood Erupts," *New York Times,* July 7, 1992.

70. Cited in Joan Didion, *Political Fictions* (Vintage, 2002), p. 120.

71. Both these citations, ibid., p. 146.

72. Cited ibid., p. 124.

73. Ibid., pp. 151–2.

74. Ornstein and Schmitt, "Dateline Campaign '92: Post–Cold War Politics," pp. 169–86.

75. Cited ibid., p. 175.

76. As sampled in an "Americans Talk Security poll," ibid., p. 171.

77. Cited in Meacham, *Destiny and Power,* p. 497.

78. Bill Clinton, *My Life* (Hutchinson, 2004), pp. 435–7.

Chapter 8: The Great Convergence

1. Adam Przeworski, *The State and the Economy Under Capitalism* (Harwood Academic, 1990), p. 102. The ostrich in question, it should be noted, is Bobbio and his account of liberalism and democracy as necessary counterpoints: the first to guarantee basic liberties, the

latter to ensure their consensual distribution. Their happy coincidence does nothing to mitigate poverty, says Przeworski. It is an important point and precisely the reason why liberalism and democracy require understanding alongside capitalism too.

2. Scholte, cited in Wendy Larner and William Walters, "Globalization as Governmentality," *Alternatives: Global, Local, Political*, 29.5 (2004): 495–514, p. 502. The original use of the term is usually dated to an article by Theodore Levitt, "The globalization of markets," in the *Harvard Business Review* in 1983.

3. Robert Musil, *The Man Without Qualities* (Picador, 2017 [1940]).

4. These two examples from Marieke de Mooij, *Global Marketing and Advertising: Understanding Cultural Paradoxes* (Sage, 2013), pp. 3–4.

5. These and other data in these paragraphs are from arguably the best short single summary of globalization from the point of view of the 1990s, John Gerard Ruggie's "Globalization and the Embedded Liberalism Compromise: the end of an era?," MPIfG Working Paper 97/1, Max Planck Institute for the Study of Societies (1997). It was of course the midway point of an era.

6. These two examples from Marieke de Mooij, *Global Marketing and Advertising*, pp. 3–4.

7. See John Williamson, "Did the Washington Consensus fail?," Speech given at the Center for Strategic and International Studies, Washington, DC, *Peterson Institute for International Economics*, November 6, 2002.

8. "The World Economic Forum: A Partner in Shaping History—The First 40 Years, 1971–2010," *World Economic Forum*, Geneva, 2009, p. 94.

9. Jim Hoagland, "Jaruzelski Rules Out Rapid Withdrawal of Soviet Troops in Poland," *Washington Post*, February 5, 1990.

10. Warsaw Pact: Steven Greenhouse, "Death Knell Rings For Warsaw Pact," *New York Times*, July 2, 1991.

11. "The World Economic Forum: A Partner in Shaping History—The First 40 Years, 1971–2010," *World Economic Forum*, Geneva, 2009, p. 105.

12. Velvet divorce: Angus Roxburgh, "Slovakia: Life After the Velvet Divorce," *New Statesman*, March 6, 2014.

13. Tony Judt, *Postwar*, p. 685.

14. Werner Baer and Joseph LeRoy Love (eds), *Liberalization and Its Consequences: A Comparative Perspective on Latin America and Eastern Europe* (Edward Elgar, 2000), p. 143.

15. Nigel Swain, "Getting Land in Central Europe," in Ray Abrahams (ed.), *After Socialism: Land Reform and Social Change in Eastern Europe* (Berghahn Books, 1996), p. 214.

16. James Roaf, Ruben Atoyan, Bikas Joshi, Krzysztof Krogulski, "25 Years of Transition: Post-Communist Europe and the IMF," Regional Economic Issues Special Report, *International Monetary Fund*, Washington, DC, October 2014, p. 5.

17. Nikolay Nikolov (et al.), "Bulgaria: Lost in Translation," *OpenDemocracy.net*, December 10, 2013.

18. Kaldor, *Europe from Below*, p. 51.

19. Times Leader, " 'Shock Therapy' for Poland: Jolt Might Be Too Damaging," *New York Times*, December 26, 1989; for a retrospective evaluation, one year after the January 1 shock therapy program began: Stephen Greenhouse, "Paths to Capitalism: Remaking Eastern Europe—A Special Report; Year of Economic Tumult Looms for Eastern Europe," *New York Times*, December 31, 1990.

20. On the geo-economic rationale of this neoliberal turn see Adrian Smith, "Imagining geographies of the 'new Europe': geo-economic power and the new European archi-

tecture of integration," *Political Geography*, 21 (2002): 647–70; see also Michael W. Doyle, "A Liberal View: Preserving and Expanding the Liberal Pacific Union," in T. V. Paul (ed.), *International Order and the Future of World Politics* (Cambridge, 1999), pp. 41–66.

21. Roaf et al., "25 Years of Transition," p. 9.

22. The example is discussed at length in Erik S. Reinert, *How Rich Countries Got Rich . . . and Why Poor Countries Stay Poor* (Constable, 2007), p. 177.

23. Judt, *Postwar*, p. 687.

24. György Konrád, "From Communism to Democracy," in Kaldor (ed.), *Europe from Below*, pp. 51–2.

25. Cited in Naomi Klein, *The Shock Doctrine* (Penguin, 2008), p. 220.

26. Adrian Smith, "Imagining geographies of the 'new Europe': geo-economic power and the new European architecture of integration," *Political Geography*, 21.5 (June 2002): 647-70, p. 652.

27. Ibid., p. 653.

28. Klein, *The Shock Doctrine*, p. 115.

29. Cited from: https://prabook.com/web/robert_h.krieble/423788.

30. Mohamad El-Erain, the CEO of PIMCO, the world's largest bond fund in 2012, cited in Uri Berliner, "Back to the Economy of the 90s? Not so Fast," New Public Radio, December 25, 2012.

31. Falin, cited Sarotte, *1989: The Struggle to Create Post-Communist Europe*, p. 203.

32. Market economic romance: cited in Kristina Spohr Readman, *Germany and the Baltic Problem After the Cold War: The Development of a New Ostpolitik, 1989–2000* (Routledge, 2012), p. 116; data from http://www.europe.canterbury.ac.nz/courses/euro223/dun ford%26smith.pdf, p. 176; see also Bob Deacon et al., *Social Justice, Social Policy and Citizenship in Eastern Europe* (Aldershot, 1992).

33. Iván T. Berend, *Central and Eastern Europe 1944–1993: Detour from the Periphery to the Periphery* (Cambridge University Press, 1996).

34. Judt, *Postwar*, p. 689.

35. "complete disdain": from the SEED preamble: http://www.seedact.com/seed-act-fs-act.

36. Melvin Fagen, "Russia: Shock Therapy Isn't the Way to Promote Democracy," *New York Times*, May 12, 1992.

37. Cited in Padraic Kenney, *The Burdens of Freedom: Eastern Europe Since 1989* (Zed Books, 2006), pp. 100–20.

38. See Fred Halliday, "Third World Socialism: 1989 and After," Chapter 5 in Lawson et al. (eds), *The Global 1989*, pp. 132–4.

39. Melvin Fagen, "Russia: Shock Therapy Isn't the Way to Promote Democracy," *New York Times*, May 12, 1992.

40. Cited in Judt, *Postwar*, p. 720.

41. See Wolfgang Streeck and Philippe C. Schmitter, "From national corporatism to transnational pluralism: Organized Interests in the Single European Market," *Politics and Society*, 19.2 (1991): 133–64; and Stephan Liebfried and Paul Pierson (eds), "The Prospects for a Social Europe," Program for the Study of Germany and Europe, Working Paper Series 1.4, *Center for European Studies*, Harvard (1994); and Wolfgang Streeck, "More Uncertainties: German Unions Facing 1992," *Industrial Relations*, 30.3 (1992): 317–49.

42. Cited in Tadeusz Kowalik, "Why the Social Democratic Option Failed: Poland's Experience of Systemic Change," Chapter 9 in Andrew Glyn (ed.), *Social Democracy in Neoliberal Times: The Left and Economic Policy Since 1980* (OUP, 2001), p. 223.

43. Bo Stråth, *Europe's Utopias of Peace: 1815, 1919, 1951* (Bloomsbury, 2016), pp. 367–8; Elena Danescu, "The Werner Report of 1970: Blueprint for EMU in the EU?," Paper for Panel on "Architects of the Euro," University of Miami, May 2017; Gilles Thirion, "European Fiscal Union: Economic Rationale and Design Challenges," *CEPS Working Document* 2017/01 (January 2017), p. 1.

44. See Dorothee Heisenberg, "From the Single Market to the Single Currency," Chapter 10 in Desmond Dinan (ed.), *Origins and Evolution of the European Union*, 2nd edn (OUP, 2014), pp. 236–42 esp.; the same story is dealt with in Eichengreen, *The European Economy Since 1945*, pp. 346–55.

45. Eichengreen, *The European Economy*, p. 358.

46. Cited in Simon Jenkins, *Thatcher & Sons*, p. 138.

47. Philip Inman, "Black Wednesday 20 Years On: How the Day Unfolded," *Guardian*, September 13, 2012.

48. See the BBC news bulletin in Philip Inman, ibid.

49. On the ERM crisis in general, a number of useful papers are archived at the Peterson Institute for International Economics (piie.com); I have also drawn on Eichengreen, *The European Economy*, pp. 358–66 esp.; Philip Inman (ibid.); Willem Buiter, Giancarlo M. Corsetti, and Paolo A. Pesenti, "Interpreting the ERM Crisis: Country-Specific and Systemic Issues," *Princeton Studies in International Finance*, No. 84 (March 1998); and Shirley Law and Arnaldo Silvio Rabolini, "The European Monetary System Crisis, 1992–1993" (Graduate Institute Geneva, ppt. presentation), which is particularly useful on proximate and nonproximate causes.

50. BBC News, Inman, ibid.

51. Quotes and details from James and Draghi, *Making the European Monetary Union*, pp. 376–8.

52. Ibid., p. 380 (my emphasis).

53. Lars Jonung, "Financial Crisis and Crisis Management in Sweden: Lessons for Today," *ADBI Working Paper Series*, No. 165 (November 2009).

54. Olivier Blanchard, "European Unemployment: The Evolution of Facts and Ideas," Massachusetts Institute of Technology, *Department of Economic Working Papers Series*, 05–24 (October 2005), p. 3.

55. Cited in Bob Woodward, *The Agenda: Inside the Clinton White House* (Simon & Schuster, 2005), p. 165.

56. Cited in Derek Chollet and James Goldgeier, *America Between the Wars: From 11/9 to 9/11* (Public Affairs, 2002), p. 74.

57. See Ruggie, "Globalization and the Embedded Liberalism Compromise," np. Of course, there was the Bank for International Settlements, and other accords would be forthcoming too, but this "terrain" of global finance was never the dominion of national governments as international trade once was.

58. Cited in Woodward, *The Agenda*, p. 73.

59. Clinton, speaking in 1998, cited in Jonathan Chait, "Clinton's Bequest," *American Prospect*, December 6, 1999.

60. See Peele and Bailey, *Developments in American Politics*, Vol. 3, p. 8.

61. Gerald Epstein, *Financialization and the World Economy* (Edward Elgar, 2006), p. 140.

62. Paul Griffiths, head of fixed income at Aberdeen Asset Management, in Michael Mackenzie, Robin Wigglesworth, and Stephen Foley, "Markets: The Ghosts of '94," *Financial Times*, March 19, 2013.

63. In "Government Bonds: Who's Scary Now?," *The Economist*, October 22, 2016.

64. Herbert Stein, *Presidential Economics: The Making of Economic Policy from Roosevelt to Clinton* (AEI Press, 1994), pp. 445–8.

65. Joseph Stiglitz, *The Roaring Nineties: Why We're Paying the Price for the Greediest Decade in History* (Penguin, 2004), p. 41.

66. Ibid., p. 20.

67. John F. Harris, *The Survivor: Bill Clinton in the White House* (Random House, 2006), p. 101.

68. NAFTA and the Environment: Greg Miller, "Court Is Asked to Overturn NAFTA Ruling," *Los Angeles Times*, August 25, 1993; Christina J. Bruff, "NAFTA meets NEPA: Trade and the Environment in the 1990s," *Natural Resources Journal*, 34.1 (1994), p. 179.

69. On Deregulation, see Stiglitz, *The Roaring Nineties*, pp. 87–114; biotech figures, Congressional Research Service, "Agricultural Biotechnology: Background, Regulation, and Policy Issues," Report 7-5700, July 20, 2015.

70. Stiglitz, *The Roaring Nineties*, p. 171.

71. See Chait, "Clinton's Bequest," n.p. The original Archer quote here appears in Richard W. Stevenson, "GOP Renews Push for a Big Tax Cut, Citing the Surplus," *New York Times*, July 11, 1999.

72. Harris, *The Survivor*, p. 87.

73. Stiglitz, *The Roaring Nineties*, p. 4.

74. Examples and quotes: Sassoon, *One Hundred Years of Socialism*, p. 742.

75. Cited in Craig Parsons, *A Certain Idea of Europe* (Cornell University Press, 2006), p. 202.

76. See Notermans, "The German Social Democrats and Monetary Union," Chapter 4 in Ton Notermans (ed.), *Social Democracy and Monetary Union* (Berghahn Books, 2001), pp. 71–96.

77. Carles Boix, "European Monetary Union and the Spanish Left," Chapter 5 in Notermans (ed.), *Social Democracy and Monetary Union*, pp. 116–17.

78. Notermans, Introduction, in Notermans (ed.), *Social Democracy and Monetary Union*, pp. 7–8.

79. Chris Thornhill, *A Sociology of Transnational Constitutions: Social Foundations of the Postnational Legal Structure* (Cambridge University Press, 2016), p. 376.

80. See Chapters 2 and 10 in Barry Rodger (ed.), *Article 234 and Competition Law: An analysis* (Kluwer Law International, 2008).

81. The literature on the ECJ is vast. See inter alia, Joseph Weiler, "The Transformation of Europe," *Yale Law Journal*, 100 (8), pp. 2403–83, and Alec Stone Sweet, *The Judicial Construction of Europe* (OUP, 2004).

82. Shawn Donnelly, *Reshaping Economic and Monetary Union: Membership Rules and Budget Policies in Germany, France and Spain* (Manchester University Press, 2004), p. 86; John Dowling, "EU Court Rules 2bn Bailout to Air France Was Illegal," *Irish Independent*, June 26, 1998.

83. Independent Regulatory Agencies (IRAs) are discussed in Roberts, *Logic of Discipline*, pp. 98–101.

84. David Hackett Fischer, *Fairness and Freedom*, pp. 444–74.

85. Megalogenis, *The Australian Moment*, pp. 189–231.

86. See WEF, "The World Economic Forum: A Partner in Shaping History—The First 40 Years, 1971–2010," *World Economic Forum*, Geneva, 2009, p. 97.

87. Abdelal, *Capital Rules*, p. 106.

88. Ibid., p. 108.

89. In Thomas L. Friedman, *The Lexus and Olive Tree* (Anchor Books, 2000), p. ix (Foreword to the Anchor edition).

Chapter 9: A Democratic Peace?

1. Daniel Patrick Moynihan, cited in Shashi Tharoor, "Confronting Ancient Animosities," *Washington Post*, January 25, 1998.

2. The Hon. Tom Lantos, Testimony Before the House of Representatives Subcomittee on International Security, International Affairs, and Human Rights, Thursday, June 9, 1994, in *Challenges to US Security in the 1990s*, US Govt Printing Office, Washington, DC, 1994, p. 94.

3. See the UCDP/PRIO Armed Conflict dataset, at: https://www.prio.org/Data /Armed-Conflict/UCDP-PRIO/.

4. Michael Mann, *The Dark Side of Democracy: Explaining Ethnic Cleansing* (Cambridge, 2005), p. 4.

5. Barbara Crossette, "U.N. Falters in Post–Cold War Peacekeeping, but Sees Role as Essential," *New York Times*, December 5, 1994.

6. Boutros Boutros-Ghali, "An Agenda for Peace: Preventive Diplomacy, Peacemaking and Peace-keeping, United Nations," A/47/277—S/24111, June 17, 1992, New York, p. 1.

7. "Introduction," ibid.

8. Cited in Mark Mazower, *No Enchanted Palace: The End of Empire and the Ideological Origins of the United Nations* (Princeton University Press, 2013), p. 14.

9. David Malone, *The UN Security Council: From the Cold War to the 21st Century* (Lynne Rienner, 2004), p. 6.

10. Council on Foreign Relations, "UN Agenda for Peace Supplement," January 3, 1995.

11. Jose E. Álvarez, "Hegemonic International Law Revisited," *American Journal of International Law*, 97.4 (2003): 873–88, p. 885.

12. Ibid., p. 886.

13. Anne-Marie Slaughter, "The Real New World Order," *Foreign Affairs* (September–October 1997): 183–97, p. 184. All other quotes here from this article.

14. Ibid., p. 189.

15. Cited in Alastair Finlan, *The Collapse of Yugoslavia 1991–1999* (Osprey Publishing, 2004), p. 72. Her diary entry was for Monday April 6, 1992.

16. Igor Štiks: cited in Jacques Rupnik, "From the revolutions of 1989 to democracy fatigue in Eastern Europe," Chapter 6 in Rupnik (ed.), *1989 As a Political World Event* (Routledge, 2013).

17. Quotes and outline here from Finlan, *The Collapse of Yugoslavia*, pp. 13–24.

18. Ed Vulliamy, "Shame of Camp Omarska," *Guardian*, August 7, 1992.

19. John Major, cited in Mark Mazower, *The Balkans* (Phoenix, 2002), p. 143; Madeleine Albright, cited in Chollett and Goldgeier, *America Between the Wars*, p. 56; see also Joseph S. Nye Jr., "What New World Order?," *Foreign Affairs* (Spring 1992).

20. Misha Glenny, *The Fall of Yugoslavia* (Penguin, 1996), 3rd edn, p. 235.

21. Alastair Finlan, *The Collapse of Yugoslavia, 1991–1999*, p. 65.

22. Javier Solana (then EU High Representative for the Common Foreign and Security Policy) in "Freedom of Borders," speech delivered at the Veerstichting Symposium, Leiden, the Netherlands, October 2004 (EU SO265/04).

23. Rick Travis, "The Promotion of Democracy at the End of the Twentieth Century," Chapter 10 in James M. Scott (ed.), *After the End: Making US Foreign Policy in the Post–Cold War World* (Duke, 1999).

24. Thomas Carothers, *Aiding Democracy Abroad: The Learning Curve* (Carnegie, 1999), p. 6.

25. Ibid., p. 332.

26. Adam Roberts, "Humanitarian War: Military Intervention and Human Rights," *International Affairs*, 69.3 (1993): 429–49, p. 440.

27. Both cited in Peter J. Schraeder, "From Ally to Orphan," Chapter 13 in James M. Scott (ed.), *After the End*, p. 330.

28. Chollet and Goldgeier, *America Between the Wars*, p. 76.

29. John F. Harris, *The Survivor: Bill Clinton in the White House* (Random House, 2006), pp. 139–41.

30. Cited in Jennifer Sterling-Folker, "Between a Rock and a Hard Place," Chapter 11 in James M. Scott (ed.), *After the End*, p. 280.

31. These quotes: Harris, *The Survivor*, p. 196.

32. Chollet and Goldgeier, *America Between the Wars*, pp. 129–30.

33. See ibid., pp. 139–42.

34. William Pfaff, *The Irony of Manifest Destiny: The Tragedy of America's Foreign Policy* (Bloomsbury, 2010), p. 85.

35. Mark Mazower, *Governing the World: The History of an Idea* (Allen Lane, 2012), p. 386.

36. Lavrov, cited in David L. Bosco, *Five to Rule Them All: The UN Security Council and the Making of the Modern World* (OUP, 2009), p. 208.

37. Kennan: in Rick Travis, "The Promotion of Democracy," op. cit., p. 256.

38. Reluctant warrior, *The Observer* Special Feature, "War on Terrorism," September 30, 2001.

39. By foreign policy scholar Michael Mandelbaum.

40. David M. Malone, *The International Struggle Over Iraq* (OUP, 2007), p. 2. The Persian Gulf War was seen as an example of the success of the UNSC as a collective security mechanism; see, generally: Thomas M. Franck and Faiza Patel, "UN Police Action in Lieu of War: The Old Order Changeth," *American Journal of International Law*, 85.1 (1991): 63–74, p. 63.

41. Boutros-Boutros Ghali, "Empowering the United Nations," *Foreign Affairs* (Winter 1992/1993).

42. Laura Zanotti, "Governmentalizing the Post-Cold War International Regime: The UN Debate on Democratization and Good Governance," *Alternatives*, 30 (2005): 461–87.

43. Ibid.

Chapter 10: The New Prosperity

1. This anecdote from Arthur J. Schlesinger Jr., "Has Democracy a Future," *Foreign Affairs* (September/October 1997), p. 2.

2. Stiglitz, *The Roaring Nineties*, p. xvii.

3. MCI and *Wired* examples: from *One Market Under God* (Vintage, 2002).

4. Daniel Yergin and Joseph Stanislaw, *The Commanding Heights: The Battle for the World Economy* (Simon & Schuster, 2002), p. 352.

5. Cited in Bailey, "Economic Policy," in Gillian Peele, Christopher J. Bailey, Bruce Cain, and B. Guy Peters (eds), *Developments in American Politics* 4, p. 164; data from ibid., p. 166.

6. B. Guy Peters, "Economic Policy," in Gillian Peele, Christopher J. Bailey, Bruce Cain, and B. Guy Peters (eds), *Developments in American Politics 3*, p. 213.

7. Ibid.

8. Cited in Charles R. Geisst, *Wall Street: A History* (OUP, 2012), p. 369.

9. Thomas Frank, *One Market Under God*, p. xiv.

10. Michael A. Bernstein, "Cold War Triumphalism and the Deformation of the American Economy," in Ellen Shrecker (ed.), *Cold War Triumphalism: The Misuse of History After the Fall of Communism*, p. 139.

11. Thomas Frank, *One Market Under God*, pp. 20–31.

12. Cited in Christopher J. Bailey, "Economic Policy," in *Developments in American Politics 4*, p. 167.

13. Robert Pollin, *Contours of Descent: US Economic Fractures and the Landscape of Global Austerity* (Verso, 2005), p. 21.

14. Pollin, *Contours of Descent*, pp. 26–35.

15. Ibid., p. 44.

16. Ibid., p. 50.

17. Kate Bronfenbenner, US Dept of Labor, cited in Pollin, *Contours of Descent*, p. 55.

18. Income shares: https://data.worldbank.org/indicator/SI.DST.10TH.10?locations =US&view=chart.

19. Stiglitz, *The Roaring Nineties*, p. xxi.

20. See "Economic Report of the President," 107th Congress 1st Session (2001), United States Government Printing Office, Washington, DC, p. 47.

21. Cited in Ethan S. Harris, *Ben Bernanke's Fed: The Federal Reserve After Greenspan* (Harvard Business Review Press, 2008), p. 44.

22. "Economic Report of the President," p. 89.

23. Stiglitz, *The Roaring Nineties*, pp. 56–9.

24. Colin Crouch, *The Strange Non-Death of Neoliberalism* (Polity, 2011), p. 114.

25. See ibid., p. 115.

26. Cited in Michael H. Hunt, *The American Ascendancy*, p. 273.

27. "Windows 95: The Hype and Beyond," *Guardian*, Friday August 25, 1995.

28. Pollin, *Contours of Descent*, pp. 38–40.

29. Cited in William H. Chafe, Harvard Sitkoff, and Beth Bailey (eds), *A History of Our Time: Readings on Postwar America* (OUP, 2003), 6th edn, p. 426.

30. The Hudson Institute Workforce 2000 Project: see Brad Roberts, *Order and Disorder after the Cold War* (MIT Press, 1995), p. 299.

31. Manuel Castells, *The Rise of the Network Society: Economy, Society and Culture*, Vol. 1 (Blackwell, 1996).

32. Ricki Lewis, "Clinton, Blair Stoke Debate on Gene Data," *Scientist*, April 3, 2000.

33. Jon Coaffee, "Rings of Steel, Rings of Concrete and Rings of Confidence: Designing Out Terrorism in Central London Pre and Post 9/11," *International Journal of Urban and Regional Research*, 28.1 (2004): 201–11.

34. These quotes and the discussion of the new management discourse come from Luc Boltanski and Eve Chiapello, *The New Spirit of Capitalism* (Verso, 2005), trans. Gregory Elliott, pp. 57–102.

35. Ibid., p. 63.

36. On dispensations, see Mark Lilla, *The Once and Future Liberal: After Identity Politics* (HarperCollins, 2017), p. 8.

NOTES

37. Cited in Didion, *Political Fictions*, p. 150.

38. Significant points on this journey include *Aims and Values* (1988) and *Looking to the Future* (1990).

39. See Sassoon, *One Hundred Years of Socialism*, pp. 738–9.

40. Ibid., p. 739.

41. "UK Politics: What Is the Third Way?," BBC News, September 27, 1999.

42. Michael White, "Peter Mandelson has not lost the knack of infuriating his enemies," *Guardian*, January 26, 2012.

43. Ibid.

44. Curtis Atkins, "The Third Way International," *Jacobin* magazine, November 2016.

45. Judt, *Postwar*, p. 735.

46. Noel D. Cary, "'Farewell Without Tears': Diplomats, Dissidents, and the Demise of East Germany," *Journal of Modern History*, Vol. 73 (September 2001): 369–90, p. 369.

47. Fabio Canova, Morten O. Ravn, "The Macroeconomic Effects of German Unification: Real Adjustments and the Welfare State," *Review of Economic Dynamics*, 3.3 (2000): 423–60. *Aufschwung Ost* and the *jammerossi*: Philip Ther, *Europe Since 1989: A History* (Princeton, 2016), pp. 262–3.

48. Peter Schwarz, "The Resignation of German Finance Minister Oskar Lafontaine," World Socialist Web Site, March 17, 1999.

49. Tony Blair and Gerhard Schröder, "Europe: The Third Way/Die Neue Mitte," Friedrich Ebert Stiftung (June 1998).

50. Sassoon, *One Hundred Years of Socialism*, p. xv.

51. See Richard Gillespie and William Paterson (eds), *Rethinking Social Democracy in Western Europe* (Routledge, 1993).

52. In a lecture to the Weatherhead Center at Harvard University, cited in Moravcsik, *Europe Without Illusions: The Paul Henri Spaak Lectures, 1994–1999* (University Press of America, 2005), p. 105.

53. Terry Eagleton, "Indomitable," *London Review of Books* (March 2011), pp. 13–14.

54. Cited in Atkins, "The Third Way International."

55. Fenby, *Modern France*, p. 423.

56. Ibid., p. 424.

57. See Lars Jonung, "Financial Crisis and Crisis Management in Sweden. Lessons for Today," ADBI Working Paper Series (November 2009), No. 165.

58. Ginsborg, *Italy and Its Discontents*, pp. 31–40; William Scobie quote: ibid., p. 31.

59. Hemereijck et al., "European Welfare States," in Paul M. Heywood, Eric Jones, Martin Rhodes, and Ulrich Sedelmeier, *Developments in European Politics* (Palgrave, 2006), p. 273.

60. Sassoon, *One Hundred Years of Socialism*, p. 741; cf. Notermans, *Social Democracy and Monetary Union*, p. 234. I have tried to obtain an English version of the report but apparently none exists (personal communication with Jan Pronk, March 15, 2016).

61. Sassoon, *One Hundred Years of Socialism*, p. 742.

62. Fenby, *Modern France*, pp. 427–8.

63. Cited in ibid., p. 428.

64. See Panos Minogiannis, *European Integration and Health Policy: The Artful Dance of Economics and History* (Transaction, 2003), p. 193.

65. The room was commissioned by Fra Girolamo Savonarola, who had ousted the Medici and who, for four years, sought to make Florence a more democratic seat of power— hence the 500 deputies to be housed in the room. Savonarola would later be arrested,

NOTES

37. Cited in Didion, *Political Fictions*, p. 150.

38. Significant points on this journey include *Aims and Values* (1988) and *Looking to the Future* (1990).

39. See Sassoon, *One Hundred Years of Socialism*, pp. 738–9.

40. Ibid., p. 739.

41. "UK Politics: What Is the Third Way?," BBC News, September 27, 1999.

42. Michael White, "Peter Mandelson has not lost the knack of infuriating his enemies," *Guardian*, January 26, 2012.

43. Ibid.

44. Curtis Atkins, "The Third Way International," *Jacobin* magazine, November 2016.

45. Judt, *Postwar*, p. 735.

46. Noel D. Cary, "'Farewell Without Tears': Diplomats, Dissidents, and the Demise of East Germany," *Journal of Modern History*, Vol. 73 (September 2001): 369–90, p. 369.

47. Fabio Canova, Morten O. Ravn, "The Macroeconomic Effects of German Unification: Real Adjustments and the Welfare State," *Review of Economic Dynamics*, 3.3 (2000): 423–60. *Aufschwung Ost* and the *jammerossi*: Philip Ther, *Europe Since 1989: A History* (Princeton, 2016), pp. 262–3.

48. Peter Schwarz, "The Resignation of German Finance Minister Oskar Lafontaine," World Socialist Web Site, March 17, 1999.

49. Tony Blair and Gerhard Schröder, "Europe: The Third Way/Die Neue Mitte," Friedrich Ebert Stiftung (June 1998).

50. Sassoon, *One Hundred Years of Socialism*, p. xv.

51. See Richard Gillespie and William Paterson (eds), *Rethinking Social Democracy in Western Europe* (Routledge, 1993).

52. In a lecture to the Weatherhead Center at Harvard University, cited in Moravcsik, *Europe Without Illusions: The Paul Henri Spaak Lectures, 1994–1999* (University Press of America, 2005), p. 105.

53. Terry Eagleton, "Indomitable," *London Review of Books* (March 2011), pp. 13–14.

54. Cited in Atkins, "The Third Way International."

55. Fenby, *Modern France*, p. 423.

56. Ibid., p. 424.

57. See Lars Jonung, "Financial Crisis and Crisis Management in Sweden. Lessons for Today," ADBI Working Paper Series (November 2009), No. 165.

58. Ginsborg, *Italy and Its Discontents*, pp. 31–40; William Scobie quote: ibid., p. 31.

59. Hemereijck et al., "European Welfare States," in Paul M. Heywood, Eric Jones, Martin Rhodes, and Ulrich Sedelmeier, *Developments in European Politics* (Palgrave, 2006), p. 273.

60. Sassoon, *One Hundred Years of Socialism*, p. 741; cf. Notermans, *Social Democracy and Monetary Union*, p. 234. I have tried to obtain an English version of the report but apparently none exists (personal communication with Jan Pronk, March 15, 2016).

61. Sassoon, *One Hundred Years of Socialism*, p. 742.

62. Fenby, *Modern France*, pp. 427–8.

63. Cited in ibid., p. 428.

64. See Panos Minogiannis, *European Integration and Health Policy: The Artful Dance of Economics and History* (Transaction, 2003), p. 193.

65. The room was commissioned by Fra Girolamo Savonarola, who had ousted the Medici and who, for four years, sought to make Florence a more democratic seat of power— hence the 500 deputies to be housed in the room. Savonarola would later be arrested,

801

hanged, and burned at the stake as punishment for "preaching new things." Progressives be warned.

66. Cited in Atkins, "The Third Way International."

67. Bill Clinton, "Remarks at a Dinner for the Conference on Progressive Governance for the 21st Century in Florence, Italy" (November 20, 1999), The American Presidency Project: William J. Clinton.

68. Peter Schwarz, "The 'Third Way' Loses Its Allure: Clinton, European Leaders Head Up Progressive Governance Conference in Berlin," World Socialist Web Site, June 8, 2000.

69. William I. Hitchcock, *The Struggle for Europe: The History of the Continent Since 1945* (Profile Books, 2004), p. 446.

70. Eichengreen, *The European Economy Since 1945*, p. 370.

71. Ibid., p. 375.

72. Ginsborg, *Italy and Its Discontents*, p. 14.

73. Mark Thatcher, "Supranational Neo-liberalization," in Vivien A. Schmidt, *Resilient Liberalism in Europe's Political Economy* (Cambridge, 2006), p. 192: the period being 1990–2009.

74. See Mark Gilbert, *European Integration*, p. 101.

75. Gilles Grin, *The Battle of the Single European Market* (Routledge, 2004).

76. Commission of the European Communities, "Europe 1992 The Ultimate Challenge" (Brussels SEC 88 524 Final), Brussels, April 13, 1988, p. 1.

77. Michael Geyler, "From Pan-Europe to the Single Currency: Recent Studies in the History of European Integration," *Contemporary European History*, 15.2 (May 2006): 273–89, p. 287.

78. Roberts, *Logic of Discipline*, p. 24.

79. Ibid., p. 35.

80. Mark Gilbert, "Constructing Europe," *European History Quarterly*, 43.1 (2013): 96–106, p. 99.

81. Iván T. Berend, *Europe Since 1980* (Cambridge, 2010).

82. See David W. Lovell (ed.), *The Transition: Evaluating the Postcommunist Experience* (Ashgate, 2002), p. 9.

83. Werner Baer and Joseph L. Love (eds), "Introduction" to Werner Baer and Joseph L. Love (eds), *Liberalization and Its Consequences: A Comparative Perspective on Latin America and Eastern Europe* (Edward Elgar, 2000).

84. John Feffer, *Aftershock: A Journey into Eastern Europe's Broken Dreams* (Zed, 2017), pp. 8 and 34.

85. Daniel Chirot, "How Much Does the Past Count?," Chapter 5 in Werner Baer and Joseph L. Love (eds), *Liberalization and Its Consequences*, p. 103 esp.

86. Attila Ágh, "The Dual Challenge and the Reform of the Hungarian Socialist Party," paper presented to ECPR Joint Session, Workshop 11, Third Ways in Europe; Béla Greskovits, "Hungary's Post-Communist Development," Chapter 6 in Werner Baer and Joseph L. Love (eds), *Liberalization and Its Consequences*; see esp pp. 130–40, passim.

87. Cited in William A. Plez, *A People's History of Modern Europe* (Pluto Press, 2016), Chapter 16.

88. Jean-Claude Piris and Giorgio Magazna, "The Amsterdam Treaty: Overview and Institutional Aspects," *Fordham International Law Journal*, 22.6 (1998): 32–47, p. 39.

89. Andrew Moravcsik and Kalypso Nicolaïdis, "Explaining the Treaty of Amsterdam: Interests, Influence, Institutions," *Journal of Common Market Studies*, 31.1 (March 1999): 59–85.

90. See for example Andrew Moravcsik (ed.), *Europe without Illusions*, p. 127.

Chapter 11: Farewell to All That

1. Harris, *The Survivor*, p. 203.
2. Poll data: Hunt, *The American Ascendancy: How the United States Gained and Wielded Global Dominance* (University of North Carolina Press, 2007), p. 297.
3. Sören Holmberg, "Down and Down We Go: Political Trust in Sweden," Chapter 5 in Pippa Norris (ed.), *Critical Citizens: Global Support for Democratic Government*, p. 105.
4. Lowest postwar average: Peter Mair, *Ruling the Void: The Hollowing of Western Democracy* (Verso, 2013), p. 26; Polls: Jill Lepore, "Politics and the New Machine: What the turn from polls to data science means for democracy," *New Yorker*, November 16, 2015; see also for the 1990s: "Polling Is Ubiquitous, But Is It Bad for Democracy?," *NPR*, February 11, 2016.
5. "Trends in Political Values and Core Attitudes: 1987–2007," *Pew Research Center*, March 22, 2007.
6. Cited in Heywood et al., *Developments in European Politics*, p. 163.
7. Cited in Mair, *Ruling the Void*, p. 4.
8. John F. Dickerson, "Forbes Gets His Calling," *Time* magazine, June 24, 2011.
9. John Agnew, "Remaking Italy? Place Configurations and Italian Electoral Politics under the 'Second Republic,'" *Modern Italy*, 12.1 (March 2007): 17–38, p. 17; the wit in question is cited in Judith Chubb, *Patronage, Power and Poverty in Southern Italy: A Tale of Two Cities* (Cambridge University Press, 1983), p. 91.
10. Ginsborg, *Italy and its Discontents*, p. 231.
11. Ibid., p. 162.
12. Colin Crouch, *Post-Democracy* (Polity, 2004), p. 4; on Berlusconi's political skills: see John Agnew, "Remaking Italy?."
13. Hanson: George Megalogenis, *The Australian Moment: How We Were Made for These Times* (Viking, 2012), pp. 279–80; Haider: Jonathan Hopkin, "Elections and Elections Systems," Chapter 6 in Erik Jones et al. (eds), *Developments in European Politics 2*, pp. 81–99.
14. Philip Resnick, "State and Civil Society in Canada: The limits of a Royal Commission," *Canadian Journal of Political Science*, 20.2 (June 1987): 379–401; on the broader Canadian context, see generally the work of Alan Cairns: Gerald Kernerman, and Philip Resnick (eds), *Insiders and Outsiders: Alan Cairns and the Reshaping of Canadian Citizenship* (UBC Press, 2005).
15. Tony Blair, "Bringing Britain Together," *British Political Speech Archives*, London 1997.
16. Luntz: see Didion, *Political Fictions*, p. 181; family values: Eric Schickler, "Congress" in Peele (ed.), *Developments in American Politics 4*, pp. 97–8.
17. Jennifer Harper, "Nationalizing the Election," *Washington Times*, September 25, 2014.
18. Ibid.; and James Fallows, "Washington and the Contract With America," *The Atlantic*, October 1994.
19. James Fallows, "Washington and the Contract With America."
20. Didion, *Political Fictions*, pp. 180–1; AFDC and Social Security figures also from here, p. 183.
21. Thomas Frank, *One Market Under God*, p. 314.
22. Lee Drutman, "The Political One Percent of the One Percent," Sunlight Foundation, December 13, 2011.
23. Larry J. Sabato, Bruce A. Larson, Howard R. Ernst, *Dangerous Democracy? The Battle Over Ballot Initiatives in America* (Rowman & Littlefield, 2001), p. 78.

24. Paul Ginsborg, *Democracy: Crisis and Renewal* (Profile, 2008), p. 30.

25. Crouch, *Post-Democracy*, p. 76.

26. Ben Clift and Justin Fisher, "Comparative Party Finance Reform: The Cases of Britain and France," *Party Politics*, 10.6 (November 2004): 677–99.

27. See Heywood and Krastev, "Political Scandals and Corruption," Chapter 9 in Heywood and Jones (eds), *Developments in European Politics*, p. 168; see also David Cronin, "Anti-Fraud Office closes Bangemann probe," *Politico*, November 13, 2002.

28. Jon Henley, "Gigantic Sleaze Scandal Winds Up as Former Elf Oil Chiefs Are Jailed," *Guardian*, November 13, 2003.

29. Mair, *Ruling the Void*, pp. 24–6; Goldwater: Coggan, *The Last Vote: The Threats to Western Democracy* (Allen Lane, 2013), p. 42; Bush v. Gore, IDEA voter turnout database. Available at: http://www.idea.int/vt/countryview.cfm?id=231.

30. Jacques Rupnik, *1989 as a Political World Event*, p. 63.

31. Herrnson, in Peele and Bailey (eds), *Developments in American Politics 2*, p. 69.

32. Figures in Sassoon, *One Hundred Years of Socialism*, p. xxii; for Australia, see Simon Copland, "Redeeming Australian Labor," *Jacobin* magazine, August 2016.

33. See Crouch, *Post-Democracy*, pp. 114–15.

34. Data from Jones and Heywood (eds), *Developments in European Politics 2*, p. 207.

35. Mair, *Ruling the Void*, passim.

36. Amy Burke, "Party Decline," *American Prospect*, May–June 1998.

37. Scott Bennett, "The Decline in Support for Australian Major Parties and the Prospect of Minority Government," Parliament of Australia, Politics and Public Administration Group, February 16, 1999.

38. Mair, *Ruling the Void*, p. 98.

39. Wendy Brown, cited in Alessandro Ferrara, "Judging Democracy in the 21st Century: Crisis or Transformation?," *No Foundations: An Interdisciplinary Journal of Law and Justice*, 10: 1–22, p. 1.

40. Jonathan Hopkin and Caterina Paolucci, "The Business Firm Model of Party Organization: Cases from Spain and Italy," *European Journal of Political Research*, 35.3 (1999): 307–39.

41. Paul M. Heywood and Chris Wood, "Culture versus Institutions: social capital, trust and corruption," Chapter 9 in Jones and Heywood (eds), *Developments in European Politics 2*.

42. Alan S. Blinder, "Is Government Too Political?," *Foreign Affairs*, November/December 1997.

43. The distinction is in Mair, *Ruling the Void*, p. 8.

44. "UK Politics: Blair risks row over public sector," BBC News, July 7, 1999.

45. Data from World Survey Data, assembled in Paul Heywood and Chris Wood, "Culture Versus Institutions: social capital, trust and corruption," Chapter 9 in Jones and Heywood (eds), *Developments in European Politics 2*.

46. Megalogenis, *The Australian Moment*, p. 273.

47. Matthew Grimson, "Port Arthur Massacre: The Shooting Spree That Changed Australia's Gun Laws," NBC News, April 28, 2016.

48. By 2000s American corporations would come to provide over three quarters of all lobby financing; see "The Washington wishing-well: The unstoppable rise in lobbying by American business is bad for business itself," *The Economist*, June 13, 2015.

49. Lee Drutman, "How Corporate Lobbyists Conquered American Democracy," *The Atlantic*, April 20, 2015.

50. Jonathan Turley, "The Rise of the Fourth Branch of Government," *Washington Post*, May 24, 2013. The quote is from 2013; the sentiment is hardly so recent.

51. Jacint Jordana, David Levi-Fleur, and Xavier Fernandez i Marin, "The Global Diffusion of Regulatory Agencies: Channels of Transfer and Stages of Diffusion," *Comparative Political Studies*, 44.10 (May 2011): 1343–69.

52. Roberts, *Logic of Discipline*, pp. 101–10.

53. Ian Bartle and Peter Vass, "Self-Regulation and the Regulatory State: A Survey of Policy and Practice," *CRI Research Report*, 17, University of Bath School of Management (October 2005), p. 13.

54. Peter Mair picked up on one half of this in his exegesis of the decline of party politics. "Disengagement is mutual, and for all the rhetoric that echoes on both sides, it is general," he said (in *Ruling the Void*, p. 77). But disengagement between people and state on the one side was matched by engagement between markets and states on the other.

55. See Roberts, *Logic of Discipline*, p. 31.

56. Juliet Johnson, *Priests of Prosperity: How Central Bankers Transformed the Postcommunist World* (Cornell, 2016), Chapter 1 esp.

57. Alan Greenspan, "Remarks by Chairman Alan Greenspan at the Annual Dinner and Francis Boyer Lecture of the American Enterprise Institute for Public Policy Research, Washington, DC, December 5, 1996," Federal Reserve Board, at: https://www.federal reserve.gov/boarddocs/speeches/1996/19961205.htm.

58. Guido Montani, "Ottmar Issing: an economist and architect of supranational institutions," *Il Politico*, 2011, anno LXXVI, n1, pp. 11–24, p. 12.

59. Roberts, *Logic of Discipline*, p. 25.

60. Roberts, *Logic of Discipline*, pp. 47 and 54.

61. For one account of these changes, centered mainly on the issue of debt (though it clearly extends to more than this), see Colin Crouch, "Privatized Keynesianism: An Unacknowledged Policy Regime," *British Journal of Politics and International Relations*, 11.3 (2009): 382–99, pp. 382–4.

62. See Richard P. Nathan and Thomas L. Gais, "Is Devolution Working? Federal and State Roles in Welfare," *Brookings Report*, Friday June 1, 2001.

63. Jonah D. Levy (ed.), *The State after Statism: New State Activities in the Age of Liberalization* (Harvard, 2006), pp. 39–41.

64. Victoria Massie, "Lillie Harden Was Bill Clinton's Welfare Success Story. Welfare Reform Failed Her," *Vox* magazine, August 23, 2016.

65. Jamie Peck, *Workfare States* (Guilford Press, 2001); see also Jamie Peck, "The rise of the workfare state," *Kurswechsel. Zeitschrift des Beirat für Gesellschafts-, Wirtschafts- und Umweltpolitische Alternativen*, 18.3 (2003): 75–87.

66. Deficit figure cited in Jonah D. Levy, "Social Policy in the Age of High Unemployment," Chapter 10 in Peter Hall (ed.), *Developments in French Politics 2*, p. 199.

67. Ben Clift, "The Jospin Way," *Political Quarterly*, 72.2 (2001): 170–9, pp. 170–2.

68. See Levy, "Social Policy in the Age of High Unemployment," p. 204.

69. Fenby, *Modern France*, p. 429.

70. See Ben Clift, "The Jospin Way."

71. Jonah D. Levy, *The State after Statism*, pp. 19–21.

72. Frank Vandenbroucke, "European Social Democracy and the Third Way: Convergence, Divisions, and Shared Questions," in S. White (ed.), *New Labour* (Palgrave Macmillan, 2001), p. 161; on liberalization and democratization: Wolfgang Streeck, *Re-Forming Cap-*

italism: Institutional Change in the German Political Economy (OUP, 2010); German social expenditure: Lutz Leisering, "Germany—Reform from Within," in Pete Alcock and Gary Craig (eds), *International Social Policy: Welfare Regimes in the Developed World* (Palgrave, 2001); on the transfers from West to East: see Alfred Pfaller, *The German Welfare State after National Unification* (Bonn, 1997): http://library.fes.de/fulltext/stabsabteilung/00073 .htm; reunification and the welfare state: Richard Hauser, "Problems of the German Welfare State after Unification," *Oxford Review of Economic Policy*, 11.3 (1995): 44–58.

73. Ben Knight, "'Hartz Reforms': How a Benefits Shakeup Changed Germany," *Guardian*, January 1, 2013.

74. "Hartz's Second Front," *The Economist*, September 16, 2004.

75. Ibid.

76. Levy, *The State after Statism*, p. 28.

77. Ibid., p. 18; see also John Myles and Paul Pierson, "Friedman's Revenge: The Reform of 'Liberal' Welfare States in Canada and the United States," *Politics & Society*, 25.4 (December 1997): 443–72.

78. Details from Heywood and Jones (eds), *Developments in European Politics*, pp. 270–1.

79. Ibid., p. 268.

80. The contrast here is Crouchian, though I would foreground the role of consumption (that he replaces with debt) since it is that, and not debt itself, that provides the desired end.

81. See Colin Crouch, "Privatized Keynesianism," pp. 389–92.

82. In Ginsborg, *Italy and Its Discontents*, p. 127; in the UK, the Scouts and Guides saw a major overhaul in 2002, and resurgent numbers after that. But by then it was about parents responding to the lack of public opportunities.

83. Robert Putnam, *Bowling Alone: The Collapse and Revival of American Community* (Simon & Schuster, 2001), p. 67.

84. Ibid.

85. Boltanski and Chiapello, *The New Spirit of Capitalism*, p. 350.

86. Cited in Putnam, *Bowling Alone*, p. 71.

87. Crouch, *Post-Democracy*, p. 86.

88. Jason DeParle, "Census Sees Falling Income and More Poor," *New York Times*, October 7, 1994.

89. Cited in Thomas Frank, *One Market Under God*, p. 5; stock market figure: Bernstein, "Cold War Triumphalism and the Deformation of the American Economy," in Ellen Shrecker (ed.), *Cold War Triumphalism*, p. 139.

90. This refers to the English edition (the original German edition of *The Risk Society* was published in 1986).

91. Michael Power, "The Risk Management of Everything: Rethinking the Politics of Uncertainty," Demos Report, 2004, p. 11.

92. John Hooper, *The New Spaniards* (Penguin, 2006), 2nd rev. edn, pp. 136 and 138–9. For helpful reflections on the politics of the family, see Paul Ginsborg, "The Politics of the Family in Twentieth-Century Europe," *Contemporary European History*, 9.3 (November 2000): 411–44.

93. https://fivebooks.com/best-books/nicholas-carr-on-impact-of-the-information-age/.

94. Stiglitz, *The Roaring Nineties*, p. 187.

95. Rebecca Hawkes, "Why Did the World Think the Blair Witch Project Really Happened," *Daily Telegraph*, July 25, 2016.

96. The journalist was Andrew Hussey, "La Haine 20 Years On: What Has Changed?," *Observer*, May 3, 2015.

97. Ibid.

98. Ginette Vincendeau, "La Haine and After: Arts, Politics and the Banlieue," *Criterion Collection*, May 8, 2012.

99. "The New York Art World: the 1990s," The Artstor Blog, December 13, 2016.

100. Ralph Blumenthal and Carol Vogel, "Museum Says Giuliani Knew of Show in July and Was Silent," *New York Times*, October 5, 1999.

101. See Linda Yablonsky, "The Art of the Curious Nineties," *ArtNews*, January 29, 2015.

102. Sharon Zukin, "Politics and aesthetics of public space: The 'American' model," pp. 37–42 in *Ciutat Real, Ciutat Ideal*, Pep Subiros (ed.) (Barcelona: Center de Cultura Contemporània, 1999).

103. Cited in Brendan Gleeson, "Desocializing Space: The Decline of the Public Realm in Western Sydney," *Social and Cultural Geography*, 7.1 (2006): 19–34.

104. Joan Didion, "On the Mall," in *The White Album* (Fourth Estate, 2017).

105. Edward J. Blakely and David L. Ames, "Changing Places: American Planning Policy for the 1990s," *Journal of Urban Affairs*, 14.3/4 (October 1992): 423–46, p. 423.

106. In this case Don Mitchell in *The Right to the City: Social Justice and the Fight for Public Space* (Guilford, 2003); and Neil Smith, *The New Urban Frontier: Gentrification and the Revanchist City* (Routledge, 1996).

107. Kiril Stanilov (ed.), *The Post-Socialist City: Urban Form and Space Transformations in Central and Eastern Europe after Socialism* (Springer, 2010).

108. Kimberly E. Zarecor, "Architecture in Eastern Europe and the Former Soviet Union," in Elie G. Haddad and David Rifkind (eds), *A Critical History of Contemporary Architecture, 1960–2010* (Ashgate/Gower, 2014), pp. 255–74.

109. The work is by Uitermark and Duyvendak (2008), but the comparison is made by Tom Slater here: http://www.geos.ed.ac.uk/homes/tslater/revanchist.pdf.

110. Torre Picasso: John Hooper, *The New Spaniards*, p. 52.

111. Jon Coaffee and David Murakami Wood, "Security Is Coming Home: Rethinking Scale and Constructing Resilience in the Global Urban Response to Terrorist Risk," *International Relations*, 20.4 (2006): 503–17, p. 513.

112. See http://www.publicspace.org/en/works/c088-tilla-durieux-park.

113. Lyn Hollen Lees, "Urban Public Space and Imagined Communities in the 1980s and 1990s," *Journal of Urban History*, 20.4 (August 1994): 443–65, p. 444.

114. Michael B. Teitz, "American Planning in the 1990s: Evolution, Debate and Challenge," *Urban Studies*, 33.4/5 (1996): 649–71.

115. Ibid., p. 651.

116. The OECD Environment Program, Environmental Performance Review of Germany (2012).

117. Michael E. Kraft, "US Environmental Policy and Politics: From the 1960s to the 1990s," *Journal of Policy History*, 12.1 (2000): 17–38.

118. See Philip Allmendinger and Huw Thomas, *Urban Planning and the British New Right* (Routledge, 1998), p. 22.

Chapter 12: Blueprints for the New Millennium

1. Cited US Government Publishing Office, *Congressional Record—Extensions of Remarks* (November 12, 1998), p. E2333.
2. Cited in William H. Chaff and Harvard Sitkoff (eds), *A History of Our Time: Readings on Postwar America* (OUP, 1999), p. 413.
3. Cited in Thom Hartmann, *Unequal Protection: How Corporations Became "People" and How You Can Fight Back* (Berrett-Koehler, 2010), p. 160.
4. Roberto Unger, *What Should Legal Analysis Become* (Verso, 1996), p. 73; and Sam Moyn, "Resisting the Juristocracy," *Dissent* magazine, October 5, 2018.
5. See Judt, *Postwar*, p. 799.
6. William Hazleton, "Encouragement from the Sidelines: Clinton's Role in the Good Friday Agreement," *Irish Studies in International Affairs*, 11 (2000): 103–19.
7. "Good Friday Agreement," BBC History, April 10, 1998.
8. Cited in Paul Webster, "Two Centuries On, a French Devolution Dawns," *Guardian*, October 17, 2002.
9. Margaret Conrad, *A Concise History of Canada* (CUP, 2012), Chapter 10.
10. Greta Krippner, *Capitalizing on Crisis*, p. 61.
11. Moyn, *The Last Utopia*, pp. 217–18; see also Nicholas Guilhot, *The Democracy Makers: Human Rights and the Politics of Global Order* (Columbia University Press, 2005).
12. European Court of Human Rights, "Press Release issued by the Registrar, 'Inadmissibility decision in the case of Garaudy v. France'" (no. 65831/01) (July 2003), p. 2.
13. Marc Morjé Howard, *The Politics of Citizenship in Europe* (Cambridge, 2009), p. 82.
14. Martti Koskenniemi, "Miserable Comforters: International Relations as New Natural Law," *European Journal of International Relations*, 15.3 (2009): 395–422, p. 410.
15. Moyn, *The Last Utopia*, p. 221; I should acknowledge here too Moyn's illuminating lecture on Judith Shklar's *After Utopia*, delivered at Queen Mary in the winter of 2018, which has influenced my thinking on this point.
16. See Jonah D. Levy, "French Social Policy in the Age of High Unemployment," in Alain Guyomarch et al. (eds), *Developments in French Politics 2*, p. 191.
17. Speech to the Institute for Public Policy Research (2003), cited in Gee, "The Persistent Politics of Judicial Selection," in Anja Seibert-Fohr, *Judicial Independence in Transition* (Springer, 2012), p. 140.
18. Cited in Ginsborg, *Italy and its Discontents*, p. 63.
19. Randall Hansen and Desmond King, "Illiberalism and the New Politics of Asylum: Liberalism's Dark Side," *Political Quarterly*, 71.4 (October 2000): 396–403, p. 400.
20. Charles Hawley and Daryl Lindsey, "Twenty Years after Rostock: Racism and Xenophobia Still Prevalent in Germany," Spiegel Online International, August 24, 2012.
21. Hansen and King, "Illiberalism and the New Politics of Asylum," pp. 396 and 400.
22. European Monitoring Center on Xenophobia and Racism, "Giving Europe a Soul," Annual Report on Activities (1998).
23. Hitchcock, *The Struggle for Europe*, pp. 411–12.
24. European Monitoring Center on Xenophobia and Racism, "Giving Europe a Soul."
25. Kenneth Neil Cukier, "French Police Raid on Illegals May Ignite Political Firestorm," *Christian Science Monitor*, August 26, 1996.
26. Hitchcock, *The Struggle for Europe*, pp. 416–24.
27. Idean Salehyan and Marc R. Rosenblum, "International Relations, Domestic Politics,

and Asylum Admissions in the United States," *Political Research Quarterly*, 61.1 (March 2008): 104–21, p. 104.

28. A. E. Challinor, "Canada's Immigration Policy: A Focus on Human Capital," Migration Policy Institute, September 15, 2011.

29. Alan B. Simmons, "Canadian Immigration Policy in the Early 1990s," *Canadian Journal of Sociology*, 19.4 (Autumn 1994): 525–34.

30. Drew Desilver, "Supreme Court Says States Can Ban Affirmative Action; 8 Already Have," Pew Research Center, April 22, 2014.

31. Cited in William H. Chaff and Harvard Sitkoff (eds), *A History of Our Time: Readings on Postwar America* (OUP, 1999), p. 434.

32. Lisa Marriott, "Justice and the Justice System," *Griffith Law Review*, 22.2 (2013): 403–29. On the UK my thanks to Daniel Dorling.

33. Rosanvallon, *The Society of Equals*, p. 218.

34. For these quotes, Judt, *Postwar*, p. 743.

35. Stefan Zotti, "The European People's Party: Identity and Integration," in Werner Fasslabend and Josef Pröll (eds), *The European People's Party: Successes and Future Challenges* (Verlag Noir, 2010), p. 28.

36. Jan-Werner Müller, "The End of Christian Democracy," *Foreign Affairs*, July 15, 2014.

37. Christian Passin, "Poland: Common Roots—Separate Paths," in Werner Fasslabend and Josef Pröll (eds), *The European People's Party: Successes and Future Challenges* (Verlag Noir, 2010); see also Tim Bale and Aleks Szczerbiak, "Why is there no Christian Democracy in Poland," *Party Politics*, 14.4 (July 2008): 479–500.

38. Steven Chermak, Joshua Freilich, Michael Suttmoeller, "The Organizational Dynamics of Far-Right Hate Groups in the United States: Comparing violent to nonviolent organizations," *Studies in Conflict & Terrorism*, 36.3 (2013): 193–218.

39. Justin Vaïsse, *Why Neoconservatism Still Matters* (Lowy Institute, 2010), pp. 1–3.

40. Cited in Chollett and Goldgeier, *America Between the Wars*, p. 188.

41. Cited in ibid., p. 196.

42. See Chollett and Goldgeier, *America Between the Wars*.

43. Cited in Odd Arne Westad, *The Global Cold War*, p. 405.

44. Albeit the global citizenship that resulted was frequently but a "ghostly shadow" of real citizenship since it did not involve *political* relationships. See David Miller, "The Idea of Global Citizenship," *Nuffield's Working Papers Series in Politics*, February 16, 2011.

45. Adam Warner, "A Brief History of the Anti-Globalization Movement," *University of Miami International and Comparative Law Review*, 12.2 (2005): 237–68, p. 237.

46. Cited in John Nichols, "Raising a Ruckus," *Nation*, November 18, 1999.

47. Wikipedia seems the appropriate source in this case: https://en.wikipedia.org/wiki/Anti-globalization_movement/. It seems worth mentioning, too, that Klein's (see paragraphs below) book was also variously described as "Essential millennial reading" (*Limb by Limb*) and "The Bible for anti-corporate militancy" (*Select*)—both these verdicts regarding the ten-year anniversary edition from Picador.

48. Barbara Epstein, "Anarchism and the Anti-Globalization Movement," *Monthly Review*, September 1, 2001.

49. Katherine Viner, "Hand to Brand Combat," *Guardian*, September 23, 2000.

50. See Andrea Fumagalli, "Histoire du Mouvement Antiglobalization en Italie," *Multitudes*, Vol. 3 (2002): 163–75.

51. Paul Kivel, *You Call this Democracy? Who Benefits, Who Pays and Who Really Decides* (Apex Press, 2004), p. 122.

52. Daniel Bensaïd, "The Return of Strategy," *International Viewpoint*, February 2007; see also Daniel Finn, "The Roads to Power: Capitalist Democracy and Socialist Strategy," *Irish Left Review*, July 5, 2013.

53. Cited in Jan-Werner Müller, "The Paradoxes of Postwar Italian Thought," *History of European Ideas*, 39.1 (2013): 79–102, p. 81.

54. Jeffry A. Frieden, *Global Capitalism: Its Fall and Rise in the Twentieth Century* (W. W. Norton, 2007), p. 385.

55. Barry Eichengreen, *Globalizing Capital: A History of the International Monetary System* (Princeton University Press, 2008), Chapter 6 esp.

56. Megalogenis, *The Australian Moment*, pp. 285–6.

57. Cited in Abdelal, *Capital Rules*, p. 159.

58. Frieden, *Global Capitalism*, p. 400.

59. Roberts (ed.), *Order and Disorder after the Cold War*, p. 293.

60. Roberts, *Logic of Discipline*, p. 97.

61. Bothwell, *The Penguin History of Canada*, p. 408.

62. Perry Anderson, "Force and Consent," *New Left Review*, 17 (September–October 2005): 5–30, p. 11.

Chapter 13: The Assault on Freedom

1. Cited in David Campbell, "Time Is Broken," *Theory & Event*, 5.4 (2001), np.

2. "Perry Anderson, "Homeland," *New Left Review*, 81 (May–June 2013): 5–32, p. 5.

3. These descriptions from Neil Smith, "Ten Years After," *Geographical Journal*, 177:3 (September 2011), pp. 203–7; Bob Ó Mhurcú, "The Worst Thing Was the Smell," thejournal.ie, September 10, 2011; and David Biello, "What Was in the World Trade Center Plume?," *Scientific American*, September 7, 2011.

4. Jason Burke, *The 9/11 Wars* (Allen Lane, 2011), p. 27.

5. In so doing also affirming what was to be the closest partnership ever between Australia and America, second only to the one the US had with Britain: Anne Summers, "The Day that Shook Howard's World," *Sydney Morning Herald*, February 17, 2007.

6. In Neil Smith, "Scales of Terror," p. 633.

7. George W. Bush, "Remarks at the Swearing-In Ceremony for Tom Ridge as Director of the Office of Homeland Security," *American Presidency Project*, October 8, 2001, at: http://www.presidency.ucsb.edu/ws/index.php?pid=62592.

8. Jane Meyer, *The Dark Side: The Inside Story of How the War on Terror Turned into a War on American Ideals* (Anchor, 2009), p. 7.

9. Ibid., p. 9; see also Cheney, *In My Time: A Personal and Political Memoir* (Simon & Schuster, 2012), p. 335.

10. Meyer, *The Dark Side*, p. 53. For detail on the Bush administration's legal team, see Chapter 4 esp.

11. BBC News, "Bush: The First 100 Days," April 30, 2001.

12. Alasdair Roberts, *The Collapse of Fortress Bush: The Crisis of Authority in American Government* (NYU, 2008), p. 106.

13. "The Vulcans": James Mann, *Rise of the Vulcans: The History of Bush's War Cabinet* (Penguin, 2004).

14. Cited in Justin Vaïsse, *Neoconservatism: The Biography of a Movement* (Harvard University Press, 2011), p. 229.

15. Vaïsse, *Neoconservatism*, p. 243.

16. Ibid., p. 234.

17. Ibid., p. 227.

18. Ibid., p. 250.

19. George W. Bush, "The Global War on Terrorism: The First 100 Days," *US Department of State Archives*, January 20, 2009, p. 1; "Our war begins," "cursory diplomacy," and congressional funds: Burke, *The 9/11 Wars*, pp. 47, 52, and 48.

20. George W. Bush, "Remarks at the Swearing-In Ceremony for Tom Ridge as Director of the Office of Homeland Security," *American Presidency Project*, October 8, 2001.

21. Jason Burke, *The 9/11 Wars*, pp. 51–72.

22. Ibid., p. 57.

23. George W. Bush, "The Global War on Terrorism: The First 100 Days," *US Department of State Archives*, January 20, 2009.

24. Perry Anderson, "Force and Consent," p. 13.

25. Data from US Census Bureau, Statistical Abstract of the United States, 2012, Table 516: Active Duty Military Deaths by Manner of Death, 1980 to 2010, p. 338.

26. From Jason Burke, *The 9/11 Wars*, pp. 71–2.

27. Cheney, *In My Time*, p. 332.

28. Jane Meyer, *The Dark Side*, p. 64.

29. Jack Goldsmith, *The Terror Presidency: Law and Judgment Inside the Bush Administration* (W. W. Norton, 2009); citation from Meyer, *The Dark Side*, p. 70.

30. James Der Derian, "The War of Networks," *Theory & Event*, 5.4 (2001).

31. "Military Order of November 13, 2001," *U.S. Federal Register*, 66.222: 57831–6, November 16, 2001.

32. Alan Dershowitz, "'Civilian Casualty'? That's a Gray Area," *Los Angeles Times*, July 22, 2006. See also, in more critical vein, Derek Gregory, "The Death of the Civilian?," *Environment and Planning D: Society and Space*, 24 (October 2006): 633–8.

33. Burke, *The 9/11 Wars*, p. 98.

34. Tony Blair, "Evidence of the Rt Hon. Tony Blair," The Iraq Inquiry, National Archives, January 21, 2011, p. 6.

35. Mark Hosenball, "Blair Had Qualms on Iraq War, But Promised Bush Support 'Whatever,'" *Reuters*, July 6, 2016.

36. "Iraq War Ten Years On: Mass Protest that Defined a Generation," *Guardian*, February 15, 2013.

37. Ibid.

38. Ibid.

39. This from his speech in the House of Commons. As he added: "I have heard it said that Iraq has had not months but twelve years in which to disarm, and our patience is exhausted. Yet it is over thirty years since resolution 242 called on Israel to withdraw from the occupied territories." Touché.

40. Robin Cook, "Why I Had to Leave the Cabinet," *Guardian*, March 18, 2003.

41. Jonathan Stein, Tim Dickinson, "Lie by Lie: A Timeline of How We Got into Iraq," *Mother Jones*, September/October 2006.

42. See Stuart Elden, *Terror and Territory: The Spatial Extent of Sovereignty* (Minnesota, 2009), pp. xxii–xxiii.

43. In Gerard Toal, "'Just Out Looking for a Fight': American Affect and the Invasion of Iraq," *Antipode: A Radical Journal of Geography*, 35.5 (2003): 856–70, p. 856. Bush did not ever actually say "mission accomplished," but his speech became known as this after a banner declaring the words was sprawled across the aircraft carrier as he landed. The death toll of American servicemen and women had, of course, only just begun.

44. Burke, *The 9/11 Wars*, p. 98.

45. Ibid., p. 113.

46. Cited ibid., p. 129. On the Iraq War to 2004, see also pp. 109–29 esp.

47. Kevin Philips, *American Theocracy: The Peril and Politics of Radical Religion, Oil, and Borrowed Money in the 21st Century* (Viking, 2006), p. 68.

48. Richard F. Grimmett, CRS Report for Congress: "Terrorism: Key Recommendations of the 9/11 Commission and Recent Major Commissions and Inquiries," August 11, 2004, p. 5.

49. Jedediah Purdy, *Being America: Liberty, Commerce, and Violence in an American World* (Vintage, 2007), p. xii.

50. Jane Mayer, *The Dark Side*, p. 4.

51. Bob Woodward, *Bush at War* (Simon & Schuster, 2002), pp. 145–6; and Jack M. Balkin and Sanford Levinson, "Constitutional Dictatorship: Its Dangers and Its Design," *Yale Faculty Scholarship Series*, Paper 221 (January 2010), p. 1790.

52. *Congressional Record—Senate*, Vol. 153, Pt. 6 (March 28, 2007), 8084–6.

53. Cited in Roberts, *The Collapse of Fortress Bush*, p. 36; ACLU, cited in ACLU, "USA Patriot Act Boosts Government Powers While Cutting Back on Traditional Checks and Balances," November 1, 2001.

54. Cited in Balkin and Levinson, "Constitutional Dictatorship," p. 1793.

55. Timothy Scahill, "The Domestic Security Enhancement Act of 2003: A Glimpse into a Post-PATRIOT Act Approach to Combating Domestic Terrorism," *New Centennial Review*, 6.1 (Spring 2006): 69–94, pp. 70–1.

56. See Mark Neocleous, *Critique of Security* (Edinburgh University Press, 2008), p. 110.

57. See Human Rights Watch, "In the Name of Security: Counterterrorism Laws Worldwide Since September 11" (June 29, 2012).

58. On Sweden: Iain Cameron, "The Influence of 9/11 on Swedish Anti-terrorism Policy and Measures," Chapter 12 in David Jenkins, Amanda Jacobsen, and Anders Henriksen, *The Long Decade: How 9/11 Changed the Law* (OUP, 2014); on Germany see "Germany's Anti-Terror Law Ten Years On," *Deutsche Welle*, January 9, 2012; on Canada see "The Government of Canada's response to the terrorist attacks of 9/11," Public Safety Canada (December 2015); and Reg Whitaker, "Keeping Up With the Neighbors: Canadian Responses to 9/11 in Historical and Comparative Context," *Osgoode Hall Law Journal*, 41.2/3 (Summer/Fall 2003): 241–65; on France see "Counter-Terrorism in France," *France Diplomatie* (nd).

59. "Anti-terrorism, Crime and Security Bill," *Daily Hansard*, November 27, 2001, Column 143.

60. Lord Hoffmann, cited in Clare Dyer et al., "'Judges' Verdict on Terror Law Provokes Constitutional Crisis," *Guardian*, December 17, 2004.

61. See Ashley Carver, "Parliamentary Attempts to Define Terrorism in Canada and Australia," *Journal of Applied Security Research*, 11.2 (2016): 124–38.

62. Giovanni Capoccia, "Militant Democracy: The Institutional Bases of Democratic Self-Preservation," *Annual Review of Law and Social Science*, 9 (2013): 207–26, p. 207.

63. David Cole, "The War on Civil Liberties," *Nation,* June 29, 2011; Richard Leone and Greg Anrig, *The War on Our Freedoms: Civil Liberties in an Age of Terrorism* (Public Affairs, 2003). See also David Cole, "Their Liberties, Our Security: Democracy and Double Standards," *International Journal of Legal Information,* 21 (2003): 290–311.

64. Cited in Roberts, *The Collapse of Fortress Bush,* p. 47; "like big brother": also from here.

65. Amy Kaplan, "Homeland insecurities: some reflections on language and space," *Radical History Review,* 85.1 (2003): 82–93.

66. Ibid., p. 90.

67. Arthur Schlesinger Jr., "Bush's Thousand Days," *Washington Post,* April 24, 2006.

68. Cited in Neocleous, *Critique of Security,* p. 83.

69. Tom Ridge, Inauguration as Homeland Security Chief (October 8, 2001).

70. John Woolley, Gerhard Peters, "Remarks at the Swearing-In Ceremony for Tom Ridge as Director of the Office of Homeland Security," American Presidency Project, October 8, 2001.

71. Susan Silberberg, "Access Denied: How Security Is Transforming Public Space," *Conversation,* November 17, 2014.

72. Cited ibid.

73. "Fighting for US Federal Budget that Works for All Americans: US Security Spending Since 9/11," National Priorities Project, May 26, 2011.

74. Two of the Justices, Stephen G. Breyer and Ruth Bader Ginsburg, had vehemently dissented from the plan: see Philip Kennicott. "Closing Main Doors to the Supreme Court Sends Troubling Message," *Washington Post,* May 4, 2010.

75. Cited in Stephen Graham, *Cities, War and Terrorism: Toward an Urban Geopolitics* (John Wiley, 2004), p. 248.

76. Lauren Martin, "Bombs, Bodies, and Biopolitics: Securitizing the Subject at the Airport Security Checkpoint," *Social & Cultural Geography,* 11.1 (2010): 17–35, p. 25.

77. Louise Amoore, "Vigilant Visualities: The Watchful Politics of the War on Terror," *Security Dialogue,* 38.2 (June 2007): 215–32, p. 216.

78. Cited in Stephen Graham, "Cities as Strategic Sites," in Stephen Graham (ed.), *Cities, War and Terrorism,* p. 51.

79. Cited in Matthew Sparke and Dimitar Anguelov, "H1N1, Globalization and the Epidemiology of Inequality," *Health and Place,* 18.4 (July 2012): 726–36, p. 728.

80. Michael Shapiro, "The New Violent Cartography," *Security Dialogue,* 38 (2007): 291–313, p. 3–5. At the same time, the average household income of new recruits was above average and has gone up since 9/11. Recruits to the US Army end up on the whole better educated than the average as well. The incentives to those lacking publicly funded education or employment opportunities is clear.

81. Matthew Purdy and Lowell Bergman, "Unclear Danger: Inside the Lackawanna Terror Case," *New York Times,* October 12, 2003.

82. Quotes cited in Louise Amoore and Marieke de Goede (eds), *Risk and the War on Terror* (Routledge, 2008), p. 141.

83. Cited in Matthew Coleman, "A Geopolitics of Engagement," *Geopolitics,* 12.4 (2007): 607–34, p. 613.

84. See https://georgewbush-whitehouse.archives.gov/infocus/usmxborder/02.html.

85. Coleman, "A Geopolitics of Engagement," p. 621.

86. According to the NGO WatchtheMed: http://www.watchthemed.net/index.php/page /index/1.

87. Suthaharan Nadarajah, "Disciplining the Diaspora," Chapter 6 in Alan Ingram and Klaus Dodds (eds), *Security and Insecurity: Geographies of the War on Terror* (Routledge, 2009).

88. Nick Gill, "Asylum, Immigration and the Circulation of Unease at Lunar House," Chapter 8 in Ingram and Dodds (eds), *Security and Insecurity*, p. 159.

89. Jason Burke, *The 9/11 Wars*, p. 162.

90. Ibid., pp. 179–81.

91. Data here from Gillian Peele, "The Politics of Multicultural Britain," *Developments in British Politics 8*, pp. 195–9.

92. Burke, pp. 192–6.

93. Lord Carlile, cited in *Developments in British Politics 8*, p. 223.

94. The UK Home Office: "Countering International Terrorism: The United Kingdom's Strategy," July 10, 2006.

95. Gillian Peele, "The Politics of Multicultural Britain," p. 209.

96. See Derek Gregory, "Vanishing Points," Chapter 11 of Derek Gregory and Allan Pred (eds), *Violent Geographies: Fear, Terror and Political Violence* (Routledge, 2013), prepublication print, p. 21.

97. Cited in Simon Reid-Henry, "Exceptional Sovereignty? Guantánamo Bay and the Re-Colonial Present," *Antipode: A Journal of Radical Geography*, 39.4 (2007): 627–48, p. 631.

98. Stephen Grey, *Ghost Plane* (C. Hurst & Co, 2006), pp. 16–17; on his "coffin-like" cell: Roberts, *The Collapse of Fortress Bush*, p. 54.

99. Dwight Garner, "American Abroad, Examining What We've Done in the Name of Freedom," *New York Times*, July 9, 2008.

100. George W. Bush, "Second Inaugural Address," January 20, 2005, online by Gerhard Peters and John T. Woolley, The American Presidency Project, http://www.presidency .ucsb.edu/ws/?pid=58745.

101. Ben Doherty, "Offshore Detention Whistleblower Loses Job After Condemning 'Atrocity' of Camps," *Guardian*, June 21, 2016.

102. Cited in Roberts, *The Collapse of Fortress Bush*, p. 51.

103. Cited in Burke, *The 9/11 Wars*, p. 94.

104. Ron Suskind, "Faith, Certainty and the Presidency of George W. Bush," *New York Times* magazine, October 17, 2004.

Chapter 14: In the Shadow of War

1. "Go to restaurants" and these examples: Neil Smith, "Scales of Terror," pp. 632–3.

2. "on the credit card": Linda Bilmes, "Fighting ISIL: How Much Will It Cost?," *Boston Globe*, October 7, 2014.

3. Stiglitz, *The Roaring Nineties*, p. 7.

4. Cited in Craig Whitlock, "Pentagon to Cut Thousands of Jobs Defense Secretary Says," *Washington Post*, August 10, 2010.

5. "coalition of the billing": the phrase is moral philosopher Peter Singer's. On private security contracting see also John Buckley and George Kassimeris (eds), *The Ashgate Research Companion to Modern Warfare* (Routledge, 2016), pp. 193–4. As the director-general of the British Association of Private Security Companies (BAPSC) similarly put it, "In Iraq in 2003 and 2004 money was basically free": see Edwin Lane, "The Rise of the UK's Private Security Companies," BBC News, November 2010.

6. Pratap Chatterjee, "Controversial Commando Wins Iraq Contract," CorpWatch, June 9, 2004.

7. Mark Thompson, "The $5 Trillion War on Terror," *Time* magazine, June 29, 2011.

8. Steve Fainaru, "U.S. Pays Millions in Cost Overruns for Security in Iraq," *Washington Post*, August 12, 2007.

9. George W. Bush, "Remarks at the Swearing-In Ceremony for Tom Ridge as Director of the Office of Homeland Security," October 8, 2001, online at: http://www.presidency.ucsb.edu/ws/index.php?pid=62592.

10. See Joshua Goldstein, "War and Economic History," in Joel Mokyr (ed.), *The Oxford Encyclopedia of Economic History* (OUP, 2003).

11. Richard F. Grimmett, "US Arms Sales to Pakistan," Library of Congress, Washington, DC, Congressional Research Service, 2009, p. 1.

12. Mark Phythian, "The Politics of the Contemporary Trade in Major Conventional Weapons," in Kassimeris and Buckley (eds), *The Ashgate Research Companion to Modern Warfare*, pp. 176–9.

13. Roberts, *The Collapse of Fortress Bush*, pp. 88–92.

14. Bush's radio speech: "The President's Radio Address," September 22, 2001, online at: www.presidency.ucsb.edu/ws/?pid=25000; economic program: "Remarks at the Swearing-In Ceremony for Tom Ridge as Director of the Office of Homeland Security," October 8, 2001; Bin Laden: cited in Joshua S. Goldstein, *The Real Price of War: How You Pay for the War on Terror* (New York University Press, 2005).

15. Linda J. Bilmes and Joseph E. Stiglitz, "America's Costly War Machine," *Los Angeles Times*, September 18, 2011.

16. Oil prices: Bilmes and Stiglitz, ibid.; net saving: Roberts, *The Collapse of Fortress Bush*, p. 92.

17. Cited in Emilie Bickerton, "Sarkozy's Fifth Column," *New Left Review*, 47 (September–October 2007), pp. 143–52, p. 143.

18. Figures from Tony Judt, *Reappraisals: Reflections on the Forgotten Twentieth Century* (Random House, 2008), p. 395.

19. Alain Supiot, "Law and Labour: A World Market of Norms," *New Left Review*, 39 (May–June 2006), p. 120.

20. Robin Blackburn, "Capital and Social Europe," *New Left Review*, 34 (July–August 2005), p. 87.

21. In the words, that is, of Alain Supiot, cited in Susan Watkins, "Continental Tremors," *New Left Review*, 33 (May–June 2005), p. 8.

22. Susan Watkins, ibid., p. 13.

23. Bernard Cassen, "Attac Against the Treaty," *New Left Review*, 33 (May–June 2005), pp. 30–1.

24. Hagen Schulz-Forberg and Bo Stråth, *The Political History of European Integration: The Hypocrisy of Democracy-Through-Market* (Routledge, 2012), pp. 134–5.

25. Cited in Kristin Ross, "Democracy for Sale," Chapter 7 in Giorgio Agamben and Alain Badiou (eds), *Democracy in What State?* (Columbia University Press, 2012), p. 84. All quotes in the following passage—Kouchner, Giscard, Sarkozy, Pöttering, and Schäffer—from here: pp. 84–6.

26. Susan Watkins, "Continental Tremors," p. 21.

27. For some of these insights: Dusan Reljic, comments on "Managing Borders" as part of the event "Border Politics in the Western Balkans and Turkey," attended by the author at the EUISS in Paris, March 2018.

28. Sheldon Wolin, *Politics and Vision*, p. 601.
29. Michael Ignatieff, *Empire Lite: Nation-Building in Bosnia, Kosovo, Afghanistan* (Vintage, 2004 [2003]); the only ideal: Nicholas Guilhot, *After the Enlightenment: Political Realism and International Relations in the Mid-Twentieth Century* (Cambridge, 2017), p. 2.
30. Roberts, *The Collapse of Fortress Bush*, p. 166.
31. The figure is probably larger, since this excludes classified contracting. Booz Allen Hamilton, for example, reported $5.8 billion in contracts from the US government, while the US government reported only $4 billion going to Booz Allen Hamilton: Chris Isidore, "Uncle Sam's Outsourcing Tab: $517 billion," CNN Money, June 10, 2013.
32. Steven Pearlstein, "The Federal Outsourcing Boom and Why It's Failing Americans," *Washington Post*, January 31, 2014.
33. School of Public and Environmental Affairs, "Government Outsourcing: A Practical Guide for State and Local Governments," Report of an Expert Panel, January 2014.
34. Alex Lach, "5 Facts About Overseas Outsourcing: Trends Continue to Grow as American Workers Suffer," Center for American Progress, July 9, 2012.
35. Scott H. Amey, "The Politics of Contracting," Project on Government Oversight, June 29, 2004.
36. Across the OECD, outsourcing rose by on average 1.5 percent during the decade: see OECD iLibrary, "Government at a Glance 2011," June 24, 2011.
37. School of Public and Environmental Affairs, "The Federal Outsourcing Boom and Why It's Failing Americans," *Washington Post*, January 31, 2014.
38. A selection of these euphemisms is captured in Seamus Milne, *The Revenge of History: The Battle for the 21st Century* (Verso Books, 2012), pp. 84–8.
39. Susan Daly, "CSO Calls Criticism of Census 2011 Contractor 'Irresponsible,'" TheJournal.ie, March 16, 2011.
40. Crouch, *Post-Democracy*, p. 41.
41. James Meek, *Private Island: Why Britain Now Belongs to Someone Else* (Verso, 2014), see Chapter 14 esp.
42. OECD, *Privatization in the Twenty-First Century: Recent Experiences of OECD Countries—Report on Good Practices*, January 2009 (OECD, Paris), pp. 1 and 7.
43. Crouch, *Post-Democracy*, pp. 36–7, drawing in part on Klein.
44. Ibid., pp. 37–8.
45. Reprinted in Milne, *The Revenge of History*, p. 88.
46. Enron: Stiglitz, *The Roaring Nineties*, Chapter 10 esp.
47. Paul Blumenthal, "Read the Bill: The Commodity Futures Modernization Act," Sunlight Foundation, April 1, 2009.
48. Simon Romero, "Worldcom's Collapse: the overview; WorldCom Files for Bankruptcy; Largest US Case," *New York Times*, July 22, 2002.
49. The example is found in Milne, *The Revenge of History*, p. 94.
50. Robin Blackburn, "Capital and Social Europe," pp. 90 and 92.
51. James Meek, *Private Island: Why Britain Now Belongs to Someone Else* (Verso Books, 2014), p. 26.
52. *Citizens United, Appelant, v. Federal Election Commission*, Supreme Court of United States, 130 S.Ct. 876 (2010); see also Nick Bentley, "What Is Citizens United? An Introduction," *Reclaim Democracy*, nd.
53. Ariana Eunjung Cha, "Watchmen Stand Vigil in City's Wealthiest Homes," *Washington Post*, September 10, 2005; Blackwater: Peter Marcuse, "The Threat of Terrorism and

Existential Insecurity: Urban Policy Responses," Conference lecture at the Symposium "Architectures of Fear: Terrorism and the Future of Urbanism in the West," CCCB, May 17–18, 2007; Gussie Glapion, Cooper Newman, "Gussie Glapion: Her Katrina Survival Story and What I Plan to Do About It": http://ccecoopernewman.blogspot.com/2015/11/gussie-glapion-her-katrina-survival.html.

54. See Karen Bakker, "Constructing 'Public' Water: The World Bank, Urban Water Supply, and the Biopolitics of Development," *Environment and Planning D: Society and Space*, 31.2 (2013): 280–300.

55. Cited in Bruce Braun and James McCarthy, "Katrina and Abandoned Being," *Environment & Planning D: Society and Space*, 31.2 (2013): 802–9, p. 802.

56. Cited in Roberts, *The Collapse of Fortress Bush*, p. 140.

57. Bakker, "Constructing 'Public' Water," pp. 798–9.

58. Mike Davis, *Ecology of Fear* (Picador, 2000).

59. Eric Klinenberg, *Heatwave: A Social Autopsy of Disaster in Chicago* (University of Chicago Press, 2002).

60. Loïc Wacquant, "From Slavery to Mass Incarceration," *New Left Review*, 13 (January–February 2002).

61. Mary Bruce, "Full 2007 Video of Obama Emerges of Then-Senator Obama Claiming Federal Discrimination Against New Orleans," ABC NEWS, October 2, 2012.

62. Cited in Greg Grandin, "Katrina Time," *London Review of Books*, January 6, 2011.

63. See Elizabeth Hinton, *From the War on Poverty to the War on Crime: The Making of Mass Incarceration in America* (Harvard University Press, 2016).

64. Joan Wypijeski, "Workless Blues," *New Left Review*, 42 (November–December 2006), p. 144. The postmortem was disguised as a book review and the layoff rates come from the book in question: Louis Uchitelle, *The Disposable American*, also cited here, p. 144.

65. Cited ibid., p. 145. Indianapolis also cited from here, p. 145.

66. For these acts and their cumulative effect, see Brenner, "Structure vs. Conjuncture," *New Left Review*, 43 (January–February 2007), p. 35.

67. Mike Davis, "The Democrats after November," *New Left Review*, 43 (January–February 2007), p. 24.

68. Jim Pickard, "Democrats Failed to Engage on Values, Says Clinton," *Financial Times*, May 11, 2004.

69. At 1.6 percent for the period 1999–2003, is GDP growth rate lagged considerably behind that of the UK and US, which were both on 2.2 percent. See Andrea Boltho, "What's Wrong With Europe," *New Left Review*, 22 (July–August 2003), p. 13.

70. Boltho, ibid., pp. 6–8.

71. Alan Crawford and Tony Czuczka, *Angela Merkel: A Chancellorship Forged in Crisis* (Bloomberg, 2013), pp. 36–8.

72. See Anderson, "A New Germany?," *New Left Review*, 57 (May–June 2009), p. 16.

73. Emily Bickerton, "Sarkozy's Fifth Column," p. 143.

74. Hyperpresidency: Emile Chabal, "Conclusion," in Emile Chabal (ed.), *France Since the 1970s: History, Politics and Memory in an Age of Uncertainty* (Bloomsbury, 2015); On Dati: see Eric Hazan, "Under New Management," *New Left Review*, 48 (November–December 2007), pp. 70–1.

75. See Bickerton, op. cit., p. 147.

76. On French liberalism: *Emile Chabal, A Divided Republic: Nation, State and Citizenship in Contemporary France* (CUP, 2015), pp. 259–60.

77. Eric Hazan, "Under New Management," p. 79.

78. This shifting political landscape is well précised in Susan Watkins, "A Weightless Hegemony," *New Left Review*, 25 (January–February 2004).

79. Alain Supiot, "Possible Europes," *New Left Review* 57 (May–June 2009), p. 58.

80. Robin Blackburn, "Capital and Social Europe," *New Left Review*, 34 (July–August) 2004), pp. 100–1.

81. Ibid., p. 108.

82. Mike Ludwig, "The Year of the Immigrant Rights Movement," Truthout.org, January 6, 2014.

83. Bill Ong Hing and Kevin R. Johnson, "The immigrant rights marches of 2006 and the prospects for a new civil rights movement," *Harvard Civil Rights-Civil Liberties Law Review*, 42 (2007), pp. 100–1.

84. Mark Engler and Paul Engler, "The massive immigrant rights protests in 2006 are still changing politics," *Los Angeles Times*, August 6, 2016.

85. Alan Ingram, "Experimental Geopolitics: Wafaa Bilal's 'Domestic Tension,'" *Geographical Journal*, 178.2 (2012): 123–33.

86. "The Economic Consequences of the War on the US Economy," *Institute for Economics and Peace* (February 2012), p. 15.

87. Katie Connolly, "What Exactly Is the Tea Party?," BBC News, September 6, 2010.

88. Obama received 53 percent of the popular vote, to Reagan's 51 percent and FDR's 57 percent. Moreover this was substantially higher than Bill Clinton's 44 percent before him. For a Democrat, it was a very good showing.

89. Mike Davis, "Obama at Manassas," *New Left Review*, 56 (March–April 2009).

90. For the best single overview of the campaign, from inside and out, see Ryan Lizza, "Battle Plans: How Obama won," *New Yorker*, November 17, 2008.

91. War and debt: Tim Jackson, *Prosperity Without Growth: Economics for a Finite Planet* (Routledge, 2011), p. 27.

Chapter 15: The Great Recession

1. William L. Silber, *Volcker: The Triumph of Persistence* (Bloomsbury, 2013), p. 10.

2. Gregory Gethard, "Falling Giant: A Case Study of AIG," Investopedia, September 14, 2014.

3. Alan Blinder, *After the Music Stopped: The Financial Crisis, the Response, and the Work Ahead* (Penguin, 2016), reprint edn, p. 6.

4. Cited in Mark Scott, "European Banks: The Bailout Continues," Bloomberg, October 7, 2008.

5. Alan Blinder, *After the Music Stopped: The Financial Crisis, the Response, and the Work Ahead*, Chapter 6 esp.

6. Ambrose Evans-Pritchard, "BIS warns of Great Depression dangers from credit spree," *Daily Telegraph*, June 25, 2007. See also, Robert Wade, "The Deep Causes of the First-World Debt Crisis, and the Case for Financial Reregulation," text of Guest Lecture, New Zealand Treasury, March 31, 2008.

7. Yves Smith, *ECONned: How Unenlightened Self Interest Undermined Democracy and Corrupted Capitalism* (Macmillan, 2011).

8. See Steven Kates (ed.), *The Global Financial Crisis: What Have We Learned?* (Edward Elgar, 2011), pp. 138 and 143–4. See esp. Chapter 8, Mervyn K. Lewis, "Monetary Policy During the Financial Crisis: An Appraisal."

9. Blinder, *After the Music Stopped*, p. 58.

10. David Dayen, "Obama Failed to Mitigate Foreclosure Crisis," *Atlantic*, December 14, 2016; see also US Department of Housing and Urban Development, Office of Policy Development and Research, "Report to Congress on the Root Causes of the Foreclosure Crisis," January 2010; racial discrepancies: Gillian B. White, "The Recession's Racial Slant," *Atlantic*, June 24, 2015.

11. Philippe Legrain, *European Spring: Why Our Economies and Politics Are in a Mess: And How to Put Them Right* (CB Books, 2014), p. 65.

12. Federal Reserve Bank of Kansas City, "Housing, Housing Finance, Monetary Policy," Jackson Hole, Wyoming, August 30–September 1, 2007, p. 24; see also Edward M. Gramlich, "Booms and Busts: The Case of Subprime Mortgages," *Federal Reserve Bank of Kansas City: Economic Review*, 92.4 (2007), p. 105.

13. Edmund L. Andrews, "Fed Shrugged as Subprime Crisis Spread," *New York Times*, December 18, 2007; Raghuram Rajan: Laura Wallace, "Finder of Financial Fault Lines," *Finance & Development*, 52.1 (March 2015): 2–5.

14. Niall Ferguson, "Banking Crisis: Don't Blame the Central Banks," September 29, 2007.

15. Robin Blackburn, "The Subprime Crisis," *New Left Review*, 50 (March–April 2008).

16. Borstelmann, *The 1970s*, p. 144.

17. For the problem of markets in capitalist democracy, at least insofar as raised here, see Crouch, "Privatized Keynesianism," and Streeck, *Buying Time: The Delayed Crisis of Democratic Capitalism* (Verso, 2014); cf. Adam Tooze, "A General Logic of Crisis," *London Review of Books*, January 5, 2017.

18. Federal Reserve Bank of Kansas City, "Housing, Housing Finance, Monetary Policy," p. 23.

19. Bernanke wrote widely on this. See, inter alia: Ben S. Bernanke, Thomas Laubach, Frederic S. Mishkin, and Adam S. Posen, *Inflation Targeting: Lessons from the International Experience* (Princeton University Press, 1999).

20. Ben S. Bernanke and Frederic S. Mishkin, "Inflation Targeting: A New Framework for Monetary Policy?," *Journal of Economic Perspectives*, 11.2 (1997): 97–116, p. 97.

21. "abdicated control," "an affluent society," and being on autopilot: Greta Krippner, *Capitalizing on Crisis* (Harvard University Press, 2011), p. 137 and passim.

22. Rubin, of course, was arguing that this was how it should be: that it was all proof you didn't even need a central bank to assert any determined control over the market.

23. Philippe Legrain, *European Spring*, p. 12.

24. Greta Krippner, *Capitalizing on Crisis*, pp. 135–7.

25. Robin Blackburn, "The Subprime Crisis," p. 66. See Blackburn also for Bush's two demands.

26. "property owning" nation: this was in fact an old Rawlsian notion, the "property-owning democracy," originally borrowed from early twentieth-century British conservatives, and now stripped of the "democracy" part altogether. See Amit Ron, "Visions of Democracy in 'Property-Owning Democracy': Skelton to Rawls and Beyond," *Journal of Political Thought*, 29.1 (2008): 89–108, pp. 186–7.

27. See Mauricio Lazzarato, *The Making of Indebted Man: An Essay on the Neoliberal Condition* (Semiotexte, 2012), p. 111.

28. See Mark Levinson, "The Economic Collapse," *Dissent* magazine, Winter 2009.

29. Cited in Mark Levinson, "The Economic Collapse," *Dissent* magazine, Winter 2009.

30. Mervyn Lewis, in Steven Kates (ed.), *The Global Financial Crisis*, p. 139.

31. Cited in Carlo Bastasin, *Saving Europe: How National Politics Nearly Destroyed the Euro* (Brookings Institution, 2012), p. 38.
32. Bruce Crumley, "No Gloating in France on Finance Crisis," *Time* magazine, September 23, 2008.
33. Robin Blackburn, "The Subprime Crisis," p. 63.
34. Ibid.
35. See ibid.
36. Legrain, *European Spring*, pp. 57–9.
37. Vivien A. Schmidt, "What Happened to the State-Influenced Market Economies (SMEs)?," Chapter 9 in Wyn Grant and Graham K. Wilson, *The Consequences of the Global Financial Crisis: The Rhetoric of Reform and Regulation* (OUP, 2012), p. 178. For Spain and Italy see here also.
38. See Philippe Legrain, *Aftershock: Reshaping the World Economy after the Crisis* (Little, Brown, 2010), pp. 72–4.
39. Blinder, *After the Music Stopped*, pp. 166–7.
40. See the timeline by Mauro Guillén, "The global economic and financial crisis: a timeline," The Lauder Institute (University of Pennsylvania, 2009).
41. Mark Levinson "The Economic Collapse," pp. 61–6.
42. Cited in Louis Uchitelle, "Volcker Pushes for Reform, Regretting Past Silence," *New York Times*, July 10, 2010.
43. William L. Silber, *Volcker: The Triumph of Persistence*, p. 6.
44. See Blinder, *After the Music Stopped*, p. 11.
45. "squabbling": Nelson D. Schwartz and Katrin Benhold, "European Leaders Vow to Fight Financial Crisis," *New York Times*, October 4, 2008.
46. Mark Scott, "European Banks: The Bailout Continues," Bloomberg, October 7, 2008; "vow to respond," in Nelson D. Schwartz and Katrin Benhold, ibid.
47. Peter Schwarz, "European Stock Markets in Freefall Following Paris Financial Summit," World Socialist Web Site, October 7, 2008.
48. Martin Heipertz and Amy Verdun, *Ruling Europe: The Politics of the Stability and Growth Pact* (CUP, 2010), p. 188.
49. Ben Hall and Nikki Tait, "Brussels Blocks French Bank Bailout," *Financial Times*, November 28, 2008.
50. Martin Sandbu, *Europe's Orphan: The Future of the Euro and the Politics of Debt* (Princeton University Press, 2015), pp. 103–5.
51. Adam Tooze, *Crashed: How a Decade of Financial Crises Changed the World* (Allen Lane, 2018), p. 287.
52. Peter Schwarz, "European Stock Markets in Freefall Following Paris Financial Summit," World Socialist Web Site, October 7, 2008.
53. Mark Scott, "European Banks: The Bailout Continues," Bloomberg, October 7, 2008.
54. Robert Wade, "The Deep Causes of the First-World Debt Crisis, and the Case for Financial Reregulation," text of Guest Lecture, New Zealand Treasury, March 31, 2008.
55. Cited: Eric Pfanner, "Germans Receive Bush Speech Coldly," *New York Times*, September 25, 2008; swap lines: Tooze, *Crashed*, pp. 210–13.
56. "will lose its status," an "outpost of Euro-Atlanticism," and the Georgian conflagration: Alex Callinicos, *Bonfire of Illusions: The Twin Crises of the Liberal World* (Polity, 2010), pp. 3–6; South Caucasus geopolitics: Emmanuel Karagiannis, "The 2008 Russian–Georgian

War via the lens of Offensive Realism," *European Security*, 22.1 (2013): 74–93; aftermaths: Council of the European Union, *Independent International Fact-Finding Mission on the Conflict in Georgia*, Vols. I–III (September 2009); war details: Michael Schwirtz, Anne Barnard, and C. J. Chivers, "Russia and Georgia Clash Over Separatist Region," *New York Times*, August 8, 2008.

57. "A worrying new world order," *The Economist*, September 11, 2008.

58. Nicolas Sarkozy, cited in Bastasin, *Saving Europe*, p. 8.

59. Cited: Tooze, *Crashed*, p. 218.

60. Sarkozy in New York, Statesman of the Year, Lagarde, and Washington official: Bastasin, *Saving Europe*, pp. 21–2 and p. 7.

61. Angelique Chrisafis, "Nicolas Sarkozy: How a Once Popular President Became Toxic," *Guardian*, February 10, 2012; NATO: Frédéric Bozo, "France and NATO under Sarkozy: End of the French Exception?," *Fondation Pour L'Innovation Politique Working Paper* (March 2008), and Stefan Simons, "France Breaks with De Gaulle and Tradition," *Spiegel Online*, March 12, 2009.

62. Colin I. Bradford, Johannes F. Linn, Paul Martin, "Global Governance Breakthrough: The G20 Summit and the Future Agenda," Brookings Institute, December 17, 2008.

63. See for example, Michael P. Dooley, David Folkerts-Landau, Peter M. Garber, "Why Bretton Woods II Still Defines the International Monetary System," NBER *Working Paper Series*, Working Paper 14731 (February 2009); Jonathan Kirshner, "Dollar Primacy and American Power: What's At Stake," *Review of International Political Economy*, 15.3 (2008): 418–38. On debates as they stood at the time see Robert Zoellick, "The G20 Must Look Beyond Bretton Woods II," *Financial Times*, November 7, 2010, and "Beyond Bretton Woods 2: Is There a Better Way to Organize the World's Currencies," *The Economist*, November 4, 2010.

64. Adam Tooze, *Crashed*, pp. 239–41.

65. Barry Eichengreen, *Exorbitant Privilege: The Rise and Fall of the Dollar* (OUP, 2011), p. 147.

66. China and the continued primacy of the dollar: Adam Tooze, *Crashed*, p. 266–68; see also p. 267 for the 85 percent figure further up.

67. The London G20: ibid., pp. 269–72.

68. Henry Chu and Christian Retzlaff, "Sweeping Bank Bailouts Unite Europe," *Los Angeles Times*, October 14, 2008.

69. Merkel, Berlusconi, and Brown: Bastasin, *Saving Europe*, p. 21; Cameron's response: "Gordon Brown Mocked Over 'Save the World' Slip-Up in Commons," *Daily Telegraph*, editorial, December 10, 2008.

70. Tooze, *Crashed*, p. 332.

71. Sandbu, *Europe's Orphan*, p. 58.

72. Legrain, *European Spring*, p. 71.

73. Ibid., pp. 71–3.

74. Jean Pisani-Ferry, *The Euro Crisis and Its Aftermath* (OUP, 2014), p. 82; Merkel: Franz-Josef Meiers, *Germany's Role in the Euro-Crisis: Berlin's Quest for a More Perfect Monetary Union* (Springer, 2016), p. 25.

75. Jean Pisani-Ferry, *The Euro Crisis*, p. 78.

76. Legrain, *European Spring*, p. 9.

77. Carlo Bastasin, *Saving Europe*, p. 42.

78. Sandbu, *Europe's Orphan*, pp. 80–5.

79. "The True Cost of Austerity and Inequality: Portugal Case Study," Oxfam (September 2013); and "Portugal's Finance Minister and Architect of Austerity Drive Quits," *Financial Times*, July 1, 2013.

80. Thomas Wright, "Merkel May Make Greece a Pariah State," *Newsweek*, July 7, 2015.

81. On the Treuhand comparison: Dirk Laabs, "Why Is Germany So Tough on Greece: Look Back 25 Years," *Guardian*, July 17, 2015. On "enforcement": General Secretariat of the European Council, "Conclusions of the European Council," EUCO 52/1/11 Rev 1, October 23, 2011, p. 3.

82. The ten-point plan: "Euro Summit Statement," Brussels, October 26, 2011, p. 11.

83. Greek, Spain, and Portugal figures: Mark Weisbrot, "Why Has Europe's Economy Done Worse Than the US?," *Guardian*, January 16, 2014; Cypriot banks: Martin Sandbu, *Europe's Orphan*, pp. 15–22.

84. "Finance is a war machine": Lazzarato, *The Making of Indebted Man*, p. 111.

85. Ben Stein, "In Class Warfare, Guess Which Class Is Winning," *New York Times*, November 26, 2006.

86. Wyn Grant and Graham K. Wilson, *The Consequences of the Global Financial Crisis*, p. 219.

87. For these details see Mauro Guillén, "The global economic & financial Crisis: a timeline."

88. World Economic Forum, "Ranking: the top most competitive economies in Europe (2012)."

89. Martin Sandbu, *Europe's Orphan*, p. 123.

90. See Blinder, *After the Music Stopped*, pp. 12–13.

91. Suzanne Casaux and Alessandro Turrini, "Post-Crisis Unemployment Developments: US and EU approaching?" ECFIN Economic Brief 13 (May 2015).

92. Declining share of GDP going to wages: Michael Roberts, *The Long Depression: How It Happened, Why It Happened, and What Happens Next* (Haymarket Books, 2016), p. 146.

93. Ibid., p. 145.

94. See Gary Younge, "A Crisis Decades in the Making," *Guardian*, April 7, 2016.

95. Joe Painter, "We Need to Talk About Money," *Soundings*, 66 (Summer 2017), pp. 34–9.

96. Mark Thomas, Foreword to Mary O'Hara, *Austerity Bites: A Journey to the Sharp End of Cuts in the UK* (Policy, 2015), p. xii.

97. Tola Onanuga, "Emergency Budget: George Osborne's Speech in Full," *Guardian*, June 22, 2010.

98. On general social conditions, see Kerry-Anne Mendoza, *Austerity: The Demolition of the Welfare State and the Rise of the Zombie Economy* (New Internationalist Publications, 2015).

99. See William Keegan, *Mr. Osborne's Economic Experiment: Austerity 1945–51 and 2010* (Searching Finance, 2014), p. 109.

100. Austerity impacts: Mark Blyth, Second Foreword to Mary O'Hara, *Austerity Bites*, p. xv; damp homes and heating: Stewart Lansley and Joanna Mack, *Breadline Britain: The Rise of Mass Poverty* (Oneworld Publications, 2015), p. ix.

101. See Philippe Legrain, *European Spring*, p. xv.

102. Thomas Piketty, *Capital in the Twenty-First Century* (Harvard Belknap, 2014).

103. Tooze, *Crashed*, p. 374.

104. Ibid., p. 455.

105. Cited in Milne, *The Revenge of History*, p. 99.

Chapter 16: Back to the Streets

1. Ian Black, in Toby Manhire (ed.), *The Arab Spring: Rebellion, Revolution, and a New World Order* (Random House, 2012), p. vii.

2. Neil Smith, "Ten Years After," np.

3. Ernesto Castañeda, "The Indignados of Spain: a precedent to occupy Wall Street," *Social Movement Studies*, 11.3/4 (2012): 309–19, p. 309. Reference to the Spanish "economic miracle" ought really to be divided into two separate things. The first miracle was the tourist-driven, post-Franco boom. The second was the housing-driven boom of the postmillennium years. A quick look at any Spanish GDP charts shows the dividing line clearly enough.

4. Castañeda, "The Indignados of Spain," p. 318.

5. Carole Cadwalladr, "The man accused of starting the 2011 riots—and what he did next," *Guardian*, June 26, 2016.

6. Cited in ibid.

7. Lorenzo Zamponi, "'Why don't Italians Occupy?' Hypotheses on a Failed Mobilization," *Social Movement Studies*, 11.3/4 (2012): 416–26, p. 416.

8. Giles Fraser, "Giles Fraser: My Hopes for the Occupy St. Paul's Drama That Puts Me on the Stage," *Guardian*, May 24, 2015.

9. David Graeber, *The Utopia of Rules: On Technology, Stupidity and the Secret Joys of Bureaucracy* (Melville House, 2015), p. 41.

10. Nancy Fraser, "A Triple Movement?," *New Left Review*, 81 (May–June 2013), p. 121.

11. Giles Tremlett, "The Podemos Revolution: How a Small Group of Radical Academics Changed European Politics," *Guardian*, March 31, 2015.

12. Diego Beas, "How Spain's 15-M movement is redefining politics," *Guardian*, October 15, 2011.

13. "The Lure of Technocracy" is from Jürgen Habermas's book of the same name.

14. Cited in Peter Spiegler, "The Leaked Geithner Files," *Financial Times*, November 11, 2014.

15. Deauville: Alan Crawford and Tony Czuczka, *Angela Merkel: A Chancellorship Forged in Crisis* (Bloomberg, 2013), pp. 75–8; Ashoka Mody, "The ghost of Deauville," VOX CEPR's Policy Portal, January 7, 2014; "She's a scientist" and "Mr. Bean": both cited in Steven Erlanger, "Europe's Odd Couple," *New York Times*, January 13, 2011.

16. Merkel was speaking to the Bundestag on May 19; cited in David Marsh, *The Euro: The Battle for the New Global Currency* (Yale, 2011), Chapter 8.

17. Eurobarometer Qualitative Study, "Coping With the Crisis," Aggregate Report, November 2014, p. 51.

18. Rachel Donadio and Niki Kitsantonis, "Thousands in Greece Protest Austerity Bill," *New York Times*, October 19, 2011.

19. Berlusconi's resignation: Rachel Donadio and Elisabeta Povoledo, "Berlusconi Steps Down, and Italy Pulses with Change," *New York Times*, November 12, 2011; not "the will of the people": Ivan Krastev, "Democracy as Self Correction," *Aspen Review*, Issue 01, 2013.

20. Martin Sandbu, *Europe's Orphan*, p. 131. Sandbu provides perhaps the best account of Europe's dalliance with technocracy in Chapter 5.

21. Ibid., p. 132.

22. Cited in Peter Spiegel, "The Leaked Geithner Files."

23. Berlusconi's demise: Martin Sandbu, ibid.; Monti's rise: Bastasin, *Saving Europe*, see esp. Chapter 21.

24. Jean Pisani-Ferry, *The Euro Crisis*, p. 88.

25. Dina Kyriakidou, "Isolated Papandreou Acts Alone in Referendum Gamble," *Reuters*, November 1, 2011; Helena Smith and David Gow, "Papandreou Scraps Greek Referendum as Open Warfare Erupts in His Party," *Guardian*, November 3, 2011; and Philippe Legrain, *European Spring*, p. 154. For details here see also, Crawford and Czuczka, *Angela Merkel: A Chancellorship Forged in Crisis*, pp. 9–17.

26. Smith and Gow, "Papandreou Scraps Greek Referendum"; and Philippe Legrain, *European Spring*, p. 154.

27. "Greek Prime Minister Lucas Papademos resigns, calls May 6 elections," *Australian*, April 12, 2012.

28. Monti's reforms: Hans-Werner Sinn, *The Euro Trap: On Bursting Bubbles, Budgets, and Beliefs* (OUP, 2017), p. 229; "creditocracy": Jean Pisani-Ferry, *The Euro Crisis*, p. 162.

29. Bastasin, *Saving Europe*, see esp. Chapter 22.

30. Duncan McDonnell, "Turn of the Technocrats Tells Us Parties Have Failed," *The Conversation*, May 17, 2013.

31. Baverez, cited in Steven Erlanger, "Euro, Meant to Unite Europe, Seems to Rend It," *New York Times*, October 19, 2011.

32. Philippe Legrain, *European Spring*, p. 151.

33. Phillip Inman, "Eurozone crisis threatens to spread to France as Paris is warned over its debts," *Guardian*, November 10, 2011.

34. Gilbert, *European Integration*, p. 212.

35. David Marsh, *The Euro*; see Chapter 8, note 3.

36. Legrain, *European Spring*, p. 148; "fiscal compact": ECB Monthly Bulletin, March 2012, pp. 101–2.

37. Rocard and the Chinese: David Marsh, *The Euro*; see Chapter 8 and Introduction respectively.

38. Cited in Habermas, *The Lure of Technocracy*, p. 21.

39. Otmar Issing, cited in Marsh, *The Euro*, see Chapter 8.

40. Jean Pisani-Ferry, *The Euro Crisis and Its Aftermath* (OUP, 2014), passim.

41. Hollande, Monti, and the banking union: Bastasin, *Saving Europe*, Chapter 21.

42. Pohl: cited in Marsh, *The Euro*, Chapter 8.

43. Gilbert, *European Integration*, p. 217.

44. Legrain, *European Spring*, p. 80.

45. Martin Sandbu, *Europe's Orphan*, p. 7.

46. Figures: in Bastasin, *Saving Europe*, see Chapter 21.

47. Eurobarometer, "The Future of Europe," No. 413, p. 4.

48. Cited in Kathleen Buer, "Ekstremistekspert om Breivik: Ingen Ensom Galling," *TV2 Nyheter*, July 23, 2011; on the case more generally, see also Simon Reid-Henry, "Beyond Madness," *London Review of Books blog*, August 23, 2012.

49. Cited in: John Hooper, "Ex-Berlusconi Minister Defends Anders Behring Breivik," *Guardian*, July 27, 2011.

50. Yascha Mounk, *The People vs Democracy*, pp. 29–31 and 175.

51. Socioeconomic indicators: Elisabetta Gualmini and Martin Rhodes, "Welfare States in Trouble: Policy Reform in a Period of Crisis," Chapter 11 in Paul M. Heywood, Martin Rhodes, and Ulrich Sedelmeier (eds), *Developments in European Politics 2* (Palgrave, 2011).

52. Arjun Appadurai, *Fear of Small Numbers: An Essay on the Geography of Anger* (Duke, 2006).

53. Migrant figures: *The Economist*, Daily Chart, "Europe's Migrant Acceptance Rates," September 1, 2015.

54. See Louis Proyect, "How Stieg Larsson Exposed the Swedish Far Right," *CounterPunch*, September 19, 2014.

55. Minorities perspective: Sarah Isal, " 'Alarming' Rise in Support for Far-Right European Parties," *Parliament Magazine*, June 10, 2014.

56. Far-right figures and framing: Matthew Goodwin, "Right Response: Understanding and Countering Populist Extremism in Europe," Chatham House, September 1, 2011, p. 10.

57. See Ineke van der Valk (assisted by Froukje Demant), "The Extreme Right: Entry and Exit," *Racism & Extremism Monitor*, Anne Frank House, Leiden University, 2010 (trans. Nancy Forest-Flier).

58. *La Meute*: see inter alia, Brigitte Noël, "La Meute: The Illusions and Delusions of Quebec's 'largest' Right-Wing Group," *VICE* magazine, January 6, 2017; on the New Zealand case: see "Community Perceptions of Migrants and Immigration," NZ Ministry of Business and Unemployment, December 2016.

59. Mazower, *Dark Continent*, p. xi; see also Jan-Werner Müller, "Europe's Twin Dangers," *Eurozine*, November 14, 2014; and Michael Heise, "Overcoming Europe's Twin Growth Challenges," *Project Syndicate*, December 1, 2015.

60. See Hans-George Betz, "Contemporary right-wing radicalism in Europe," *Contemporary European History*, 8.2 (1999): 299–316, pp. 306–8.

61. See Tomas Sardi, "Parliamentary elections in Hungary—the results and political implications," Budapest: CEC Government Relations, 2010, p. 1; for his part Blair was speaking just the day before a bomb attack at Brussels airport in 2015: "One of the problems with the West," observed Blair, "is that it constantly can be made to feel guilty about itself. . . . If you don't give a solution, and you leave people with a choice between what I would call a bit of flabby liberalism and the hardline, they'll take the hardline, I'm afraid."

62. "the new state": cited in Csaba Tóth, "Full Text of Victor Orbán's Speech at Baile Tusnad of July 26, 2014," *Budapest Beacon*, July 29, 2014; the race was on: see Honor Mahony, "Orbán Wants to Build 'Illiberal' State," *EUobserver*, July 28, 2014; on the development of Orbán's politics more generally see Paul Lendvai, *Orbán: Europe's New Strongman* (C. Hurst & Co, 2017).

63. Jan-Werner Müller, "An Interview with Kriszta Bombera," *Hungarian Spectrum*, June 23, 2015.

64. See Jan-Werner Müller, "Trump, Erdoğan, Farage: The attractions of populism for politicians, the dangers for democracy," *Guardian*, September 2, 2016.

65. On some of these features of populism see Peter H. Merkl, "Why are they so strong?," Chapter 1 in Peter H. Merkl and Leonard Weinberg (eds), *The Revival of Right-Wing Extremism in the Nineties* (Routledge, 2014).

66. The point is Nadia Urbinati's, as delivered in her keynote "Democracy, Populism, and Technocracy" at the Challenges to Democracy conference, University of Oslo, November 5, 2015.

67. Filippo Tronconi (ed.), *Beppe Grillo's Five Star Movement: Organization, Communication and Ideology* (Ashgate, 2015), p. 10. On Grillo's embodiment, see for example the expe-

rience of the Citizens' Assemblies in 2006, whereby participatory votes were presented by Grillo to Prodi. See Maria Elisabetta Lanzone, "The 'Post-Modern' Populism in Italy: The Case of the Five Star Movement," in Dwayne Woods and Barbara Wejnert (eds), *The Many Faces of Populism: Current Perspectives* (Emerald Group, 2014), pp. 53–78.

68. Ashoka Mody, *Euro Tragedy: A Drama in Nine Acts* (OUP, 2018), Chapter 9 esp.

69. Lisa Jucca and Gavin Jones, "Italy's Monti calls for EU meeting to tackle anti-euro 'populism,'" Reuters, September 8, 2012.

70. Daniel Ward, "The Telegram That Saved Us from Technocracy," *The Spectator*, January 10, 2015.

71. "Government by Nerds One Step from Tyranny," *Australian*, November 19, 2011.

72. Cited in Peter Spiegler, "The Leaked Geithner Files," *Financial Times*, November 11, 2014.

73. Richard Wolffe, *Revival: The Struggle for Survival Inside the Obama White House* (Broadway Books, 2011), p. 3.

74. Jonathan Oberlander, "Long Time Coming: Why Health Reform Finally Passed," *Health Affairs*, 29.6 (June 2010): 1112–16.

75. Cited in Richard Wolffe, *Revival*, p. 285.

76. Matt Smith, "Obama Signs Bill Warding Off Fiscal Cliff," CNN, January 3, 2013.

77. Samuel Moyn, "Resisting the Juristocracy," *Boston Review*, October 5, 2018.

78. Chuck Todd, *The Stranger: Barack Obama in the White House* (Little, Brown, 2014), p. 12.

79. See Nancy Fraser, "A Triple Movement," *New Left Review*, 81 (May–June) 2013, p. 129.

80. See M. B. Pell, "K Street Cashes In on Bill," *Politico*, May 21, 2010.

81. Cornell W. Clayton and Lucas K. McMillan, "The Supreme Court" in Peele et al. (eds), *Developments in American Politics 7* (Palgrave Macmillan, 2014), p. 155.

82. Gillian Peele et al., *Developments in American Politics 7*, p. 11.

83. Evan Bayh, cited in Sean Theriault, "Polarization We Can Live With. Partisan Warfare Is the Problem," *Washington Post*, January 10, 2014. For other details on these issues see Gillian Peele, "An Emerging Constitutional Debate," in Peele et al. (eds), *Developments in American Politics 7*, pp. 14–31.

84. The professor in question was Chris Cochrane: see Kurt Kleiner, "The Polarisation of Canadian Politics," *University of Toronto News*, November 1, 2012. The other professor was David Moscrop in British Columbia, cited in Jeet Heer, "Why Is Canada's Liberal Party So Dominant?," *New Republic*, October 22, 2015. See also Richard Johnston, "Canada Is Polarizing—and It's Because of the Parties," *Washington Post*, February 18, 2014.

85. Jeet Heer, "Why Is Canada's Liberal Party So Dominant?," *New Republic*, October 22, 2015.

86. Kathy Marks, "The Rise of Populist Politics in Australia," BBC News, March 1, 2017; on the Singapore comparison, see Doug Hendrie, "In Praise of Technocracy: Why Australia Must Imitate Singapore," *Meanjin*, 74.3 (Spring 2015).

87. Steve Bell, "Steve Bell's Political Cartoons of the Year," *Guardian*, December 30, 2010.

88. Culture wars: Giorel Curran and Morgan Gibson, "WikiLeaks Anarchism and Technologies of Dissent," *Antipode: A Radical Journal of Geography*, 45.2 (2013): 294–314, p. 303.

89. Barton Gellman, "Person of the Year: Runners Up—Julian Assange," *Time* magazine, December 15, 2010.

90. Ibid. See also Julian Assange, "Don't shoot the messenger for revealing uncomfortable truths," *Australian*, December 8, 2010. See also Charlie Savage, *Power Wars: Inside Obama's Post-9/11 Presidency* (Little Brown, 2015), p. 391.

91. Charlie Savage, *Power Wars*, pp. 162–6.

92. Ibid., pp. 350 and 362; for Drake: David Wise, "Leaks and the Law: The Story of Thomas Drake," *Smithsonian Magazine*, July–August 2011.

93. Steven Pearlstein, "The Federal Outsourcing Boom and Why It's Failing Americans," *Washington Post*, January 31, 2014.

94. These elements are the same criteria—competence, reliability, and honesty—that Onora O'Neill references in her work on Trust and Trustworthiness. See, for example, her lecture "What We Don't Understand About Trust," *TED*, June 2013.

95. Colin Crouch, *Post-Democracy* (Polity, 2004), p. 16.

96. See Bruce E. Cain and Peter J. Ryan, "Political Parties," in Peele et al. (eds), *Developments in American Politics* 7, pp. 68–74.

97. For this insight, see Gordon Silverstein, *Law's Allure: How Law Shapes, Constrains, Saves and Kills Politics* (Cambridge, 2009), p. 7.

98. The lines are from W. H. Auden's popular poem "Funeral Blues"; their meaning I hope is here restored to the original intent—the fear and political disgust—of its appearance in the play *The Ascent of F6*, by Auden and Christopher Isherwood.

99. Philippe Legrain, *European Spring*, Introduction.

100. Will Hutton, *Them and Us: Changing Britain—Why We Need a Fair Society* (Little, Brown, 2010), p. 3.

101. See Danyl Mclauchlan, "The New Zealand Project Offers a Bold, Urgent, Idealistic Vision. I Found It Deeply Depressing," The Spinoff, April 22, 2017.

102. Charles S. Maier, *Changing Boundaries of the Political: Essays on the Evolving Balance between the State and Society, Public and Private in Europe* (CUP, 1987), pp. 5 and 22.

Chapter 17: Crisis upon Crisis

1. Ivan Krastev, "The Populist Moment," *Eurozine*, September 18, 2007, n.p.

2. This is a point well made by Mark Mazower, "Trump, Le Pen and the Enduring Appeal of Nationalism," *Financial Times*, April 29, 2016.

3. See Torgeir Larsen, "Sikkerhetspolitiske rammebetingelser i bevegelse," Norwegian Institute of International Affairs, Policy Brief 4 (2018); Ole Jacob Sending and Joachim Nahem, "Wielding Influence in a New Governance Architecture: Norway, the G20 and the 2020 Agenda," Norwegian Institute of International Affairs, Policy Brief 6 (2017); Amitav Acharya, "After Liberal Hegemony: The Advent of a Multiplex World Order," *Ethics & International Affairs*, 31:3 (September 2017); Richard Gowan, "The Price of Order," United Nations University, Center for Policy Research, September 23, 2018.

4. See "Mikhail Gorbachev Brought Democracy to Russia and Was Despised for It," Peter Baker, *New York Times*, September 6, 2017.

5. Robert Service, *The Penguin History of Modern Russia: From Tsarism to the Twenty-First Century* (Penguin, 2015), pp. 551–2. The account of Putin that follows is drawn from Service's excellent overview.

6. Ibid., pp. 553–65.

7. Mattias Schepp, Christian Neef, and Uwe Klussmann, "Russian Journalist Murdered: Is Russian Press Freedom Dead?," *Der Spiegel*, October 20, 2006; see also the Committee to Protect Journalists, Russia/Central Europe report: https://cpj.org/europe/russia/.

8. Shaun Walker, "The Murder That Killed Free Media in Russia," *Guardian*, October 5, 2016.

9. Stephen M. Walt, "I Knew the Cold War: This Is No Cold War," *Foreign Policy*, March 12, 2018.

10. Yanukovych and Russian concerns over Ukraine: Sophie Pinkham, "How Annexing Crimea Allowed Putin to Claim He Had Made Russia Great Again," *Guardian*, March 22, 2017; on the global context, see also Christopher Walker, "The New Containment," *World Affairs* (May–June, 2015).

11. Cited in Jan-Werner Müller, "Constitutional Fantasy," *London Review of Books*, June 1, 2017.

12. Odd Arne Westad speaking to Heather Souvaine Horn, "The Problem with 'Cold War' Comparisons," *New Republic*, April 17, 2018; see also Odd Arne Westad, "Has a New Cold War Really Begun?," *Foreign Affairs*, March 27, 2018.

13. See Shani Bar-Tuvia and Marie Walter-Franke, "Why Some EU States Want Hotspots in the Sahel," *Newsdeeply.com*, November 10, 2017; see also Miriam Ticktin, "The Off-shore Camps of the European Union: At the Border of Humanity," *International Affairs Working Paper 2009–03* (March 2009). They were also the very fantasy of some of the most renowned economists writing at the time: to wit Paul Collier and Alexander Betts, *Refuge: Transforming a Broken Refugee System* (Allen Lane, 2017).

14. Gary Younge, "A disaster decades in the making," *Guardian*, July 4, 2016. As Younge pointed out, the result was the worst of all possible worlds: "racism and xenophobia are condemned but never challenged, which leaves those who hold such views feeling silenced and ignored, but never engaged."

15. "Police Charge Leader of Slovak Far-Right Party with Extremism," Reuters, July 28, 2017.

16. "a new mix of cultures": cited in Sylvie Kaufmann, "Europe's Illiberal Democracies," *International New York Times*, March 10, 2016; "Poles of the worst sort": cited in Müller, "Trump, Erdoğan, Farage: The Attractions of Populism for Politicians: The Dangers for Democracy," *Guardian*, September 2, 2016.

17. See, inter alia: Jan-Werner Müller, "The Problem With 'Illiberal Democracy,'" *Project Syndicate*, January 21, 2016, and Jan-Werner Müller, "'Democracy' still matters," *New York Times*, April 5, 2018; Yascha Mounk, *The People vs. Democracy: Why Our Freedom Is in Danger and How to Save it* (Harvard University Press, 2018); and Timothy Snyder, *The Road to Unfreedom: Russia, Europe, America* (Bodley Head, 2018).

18. Jameel Jaffer, former deputy legal director of the ACLU, "How the US justifies drone strikes: targeted killing, secrecy and the law," *Guardian*, November 15, 2016.

19. Drone attack details: Micah Zenko, "Bush and Obama Fought a Failed 'War on Terror.' It's Trump's Turn," *New York Times*, August 25, 2017; see also Alice Ross, "Into the Drone Age," *Bureau for Investigative Research Report*, December 11, 2012; "At this point" and "I think we're looking": Glenn Greenwald, "Key Democrats, Led by Hillary Clinton, Leave No Doubt that Endless War Is Official U.S. Doctrine," *Intercept*, October 7, 2014.

20. Ian Black, in Toby Manhire (ed.), *The Arab Spring: Rebellion, Revolution and a New World Order* (Guardian Books, 2012), p. vi.

21. Michael Lüders, *Blowback: How the West F*cked Up the Middle East* (Old Street Publishing, 2017), p. 52.

22. Lüders, ibid., p. 62; "ill-tempered scenes": "Syria Geneva II peace talks witness bitter exchanges," BBC News, January 22, 2014.

23. James Mann, *The Obamians: The Struggle Inside the White House to Redefine American Power* (Penguin, 2014), p. 140.

24. Lüders, *Blowback*, pp. 74–9.

25. 800 people: Sanya Dosani, "Five Charts That Help Explain Europe's Migrant Crisis," Al Jazeera, May 7, 2015.

26. Lauren Collins, "Europe's Child-Refugee Crisis," *New Yorker*, February 27, 2017.

27. Marcel Fratzscher, "Why Europe Needs to Share the Burden of Migration," *World Economic Forum*, April 11, 2016.

28. See Helen Williams, "Changing the National Narrative: Evolution in Citizenship and Integration in Germany, 2000–10," *Journal of Contemporary History*, 49.1 (2014): 54–74.

29. Patty Culhane, "Will US Step Up to Syrian Refugee Crisis Challenge?," Al Jazeera, September 9, 2015.

30. Markus Dettmer, Carolin Katschak, and Georg Ruppert, "Rx for Prosperity: German Companies See Refugees as Opportunity," *Spiegel* Online International, August 27, 2015.

31. Roderick Parkes, "The Internal–External Nexus: Re-bordering Europe," EUISS Briefing, October 2016.

32. Kondylia Gogou, "The EU–Turkey Deal: Europe's Year of Shame," Amnesty International, March 20, 2017.

33. "Merkel's Refugee Policy Divides Europe," *Der Spiegel*, September 21, 2015.

34. See Fratzscher, op. cit.; Schäuble's new mission: Guy Chazan, "Wolfgang Schäuble to Step Down as German Finance Minister," *Financial Times*, September 27, 2017. See also Adam Tooze, "After the Wars," *London Review of Books*, November 2015.

35. Cited in: Rob Merrick, "Brexit 'Is Not Inevitable' and Can Be Stopped by the Will of the People, Tony Blair Says," *Independent*, February 17, 2017.

36. Newspaper banners, "Whatever Happens Next, We'll Help You Make Sense of It" (*International New York Times*) and "Democracy Dies in Darkness" (*Washington Post*).

37. Margot O'Neill, "Poll Data Reveals Australia's Waning Interest in Politics, Decline in Support for Democracy," ABC News, August 11, 2014.

38. Tony Blair quoted in Thomas L. Friedman, "Tony Blair's Lesson for President Trump," *New York Times*, March 1, 2017.

39. "the British people have had enough": Michael Gove, interview with Faisal Islam, *Sky News*, June 3, 2016; "one of the biggest democratic exercises": UK Foreign Office, cited in Daniel White, "UK Government Rejects Petition for 2nd Brexit Vote," *Time* magazine, July 9, 2016.

40. See e.g. John Detrixhe, "Brexit Negotiations: The Best and Worst Cases for the UK Finance Industry," *Quartz* magazine, June 23, 2017; and the Justice and Home Affairs "opt in" alongside the Schengen "opt out" perusable at both http://www.statewatch .org/news/2017/nov/uk-ho-jha-optouts.htm and https://www.gov.uk/government /publications/jha-opt-in-and-schengen-opt-out-protocols--3.

41. Cited in Joschka Fischer, "The French Election and Europe's Future," *Social Europe*, May 4, 2017. See also Alan Johnson, "Why 'Brexit' Is Essential for Britain," *International New York Times*, March 28, 2017.

42. Timothy Snyder, *On Tyranny: Twenty Lessons from the Twentieth Century* (Bodley Head, 2017), p. 107.

43. Julian Zelizer (ed.), *The Presidency of Barack Obama: A First Historical Assessment* (Princeton University Press, 2018).

44. Cited in Michael Tomasky, "The Dangerous Election," *New York Review of Books*, March 24, 2016; Berlusconi: L. Newman, "Bunga Bunga," *Slate*, April 2017.

45. Cited in Brendan Simms and Charlie Laderman, *Donald Trump: The Making of a Worldview* (I. B. Tauris, 2017), p. 6.

46. Cited in Jan-Werner Müller, "Capitalism in One Family," *London Review of Books*, December 1, 2016.

47. Colin Dueck, *The Obama Doctrine: American Grand Strategy Today* (OUP, 2015), p. 10. On his Jacksonianism: see Simms and Laderman, *Donald Trump*, p. 12.

48. Adam Davidson, "Peter Thiel's Oddly Conventional Defense of Trump," *New Yorker*, November 1, 2016; see also Peter Thiel, "The Education of a Libertarian," *Cato Unbound*, April 13, 2009.

49. Cited ibid.

50. On the interrelation of these in a philosophical sense, rather than their use by Republican strategists, see Martha C. Nussbaum, "Powerlessness and the Politics of Blame," *ABC Religion and Ethics*, November 14, 2016.

51. Cited in: Jennifer Senior, "Through the Lens of the Obama Years, Ta-Nehisi Coates Reckons With Race, Identity, and Trump," *New York Times*, October 1, 2017.

52. Charles Duhigg, "Trump Embraces Tech World Tactics: 'Move Fast and Break Things,'" *New York Times*, March 8, 2017.

53. Roger Cohen, "Daydreaming in Germany," *International New York Times*, October 17, 2017.

54. See "What We Saw as Trump Took Office," *New York Times*, curated selection, January 23, 2017.

55. Roger Cohen, "The Closing of Trump's America," *New York Times*, January 27, 2017.

56. These examples from Peter Baker, "Trump's Impulses Now Carry the Force of the Presidency," *New York Times*, January 25, 2017.

57. John Yoo, "Executive Power Run Amok," *International New York Times*, February 7, 2017.

58. "Saying 'I do' becomes a priority," *International New York Times*, January 4, 2017.

59. David Brooks, "Bonhoeffer, Benedict, or Ford," *New York Times*, February 14, 2017.

60. Cited in Julian Borger, "'Terrifying Nixonian': Comey's Firing Takes Democracy to Dark New Territory," *Guardian*, May 10, 2017.

Chapter 18: Epilogue: The End of an Era?

1. George Freeman, cited in "World Leaders React to Trump's Victory," *Nigerian Tribune*, November 10, 2016, p. 3; and "the European Union is dead," cited in Ivan Krastev, "How Donald Trump might save the E.U.," *International New York Times*, February 21, 2017; Roger Cohen, "A Fractured 2017," *New York Times*, December 4, 2017.

2. These comments from *NY Review of Books* podcast, "Why Populism Now?," June 24, 2016, respectively from Sam Tannenhaus and Pamela Paul.

3. Margaret Canovan, "Trust the People! Populism and the Two Faces of Democracy," in *Political Studies*, 47.1 (1999): 2–16, p. 11.

4. My thanks to Charles Maier for conversations on this point and for the phrase "public institutional commitments."

5. Jan-Werner Müller, "The End of Christian Democracy," *Foreign Affairs*, July 14, 2014; citizens' "dual commitments": Jürgen Habermas, *The Crisis of the European Union: A Response* (Polity, 2013).

6. Reinhold Niebuhr, *Reflections on the End of an Era* (Charles Scribner's Sons, 1934); see also Robert Horwitz, "The Revival of Reinhold Niebuhr: A Foreign Policy Fable," *Public Culture*, 28.1 (2015): 113–18.

7. Democracy, for Niebuhr, is God's "proximate solution for [the] insoluble problems" of

humanity, as Cornel West has put it: see Kate Massinger, "What Would Niebuhr Say?," *Commonweal* magazine, February 15, 2017.

8. Charles S. Maier, "Democracy and Its Discontents," *Foreign Affairs*, 74.3 (July–August 1994).

9. See Jane Mansbridge, "Negotiation in the Crisis of Democracy," *Social Sciences Research Council*, Anxieties of Democracy Series, n.d.

10. Peter A. Hall, "Anxiety about Democracy? Why Now?," Social Sciences Research Council, Essay Forum Collection, Anxieties of Democracy Series, n.d.

11. Fareed Zakaria, *The Future of Freedom: Illiberal Democracy at Home and Abroad* (W. W. Norton, 2007), p. 14.

12. See, inter alia, Engin Isin, *Citizens Without Frontiers* (Bloomsbury, 2012); and Engin F. Isin and Greg M. Nielsen, *Acts of Citizenship* (Zed, 2008).

13. Thomas Meaney and Yascha Mounk, "What Was Democracy?," *Nation*, June 2, 2014.

14. Cornel West, "Goodbye, American Neoliberalism. A New Era Is Here," *Guardian*, November 29, 2016.

15. Tony Judt, "What Is Living and What Is Dead in Social Democracy," Chapter 24 in Tony Judt, *When the Facts Change: Essays, 1995–2010*, Jennifer Homans (ed.) (Penguin, 2015), pp. 319–38.

16. Mark Leonard, "The Rise of Demotic Democracy in Europe," *Project Syndicate*, June 25, 2016.

17. Repressing the catastrophe: Jacques Rancière, *Hatred of Democracy* (Verso, 2009), p. 4; and Pierre Rosanvallon, *Counter-Democracy: Politics in an Age of Distrust* [The Seeley Lectures] (CUP, 2008).

18. Ernesto Cortes, "Why Democracy Needs a Strong Civil Society to Survive," lecture delivered at Queen Mary, University of London, October 16, 2018.

19. Benito Mussolini and Giovanni Gentile, "The Doctrines of Fascism," at https://www.mtholyoke.edu/courses/rschwart/hist151/MUSSOLINI.pdf.

20. Mark Lilla, "The Truth About Our Libertarian Age," *New Republic*, June 18, 2014.

Index

Star Wars missile defense, 195, 235, 248, 491, 509

state: challenges and redefining of, 747–48; as employer, 193; individual vs., 187–89, 203; mistrust of, 688–91; nation state, 30–31, 690; new social contract (1980s), 204–9; ownership and control by, 193; persistence, 743; power and control of, 747–48; privatization and, 429; public sector employees, 193; regulation by, 193–202; social contracts, 477; social functions diminish, 157; social welfare program costs, 193, 194; Thatcher-Reagan anti-statist policies, 193–202

Stein, Herbert, 191, 337–38

Steinbrück, Peer, 618–19

Stenvig, Charles, 49–50

Stevens, John P., 681

Steyn, Johan, 548

Stiglitz, Joseph, 382, 554

Štiks, Igor, 363

Stockman, David, 194, 205

"Sto Diethnes To Magzi" (Hatzis), ix

Stoltenberg, Gerhard, 247

Stoltenberg, Jens, 559, 662, 701

Stoltenberg, Thorvald, 376

Sträng, Gunnar, 123

Strategy for Labor (Gorz), 226

Stråth, Bo, 178

Strauss-Kahn, Dominique, 407, 621, 627

Streeck, Wolfgang, 216, 751

Strong Democracy (Barber), 224

Students for a Democratic Society (SDS), 19, 35–36, 43, 49; Port Huron Statement, 36; Weather Underground radical offshoot, 19, 111

Summers, Larry, 383, 612–13

Supiot, Aslan, 584

Sutherland, Peter, 431

Sweden, 122; anti-terror legislation, 531; austerity-driven discontent, 643; civic trust diminishes, 419; controls inflation, 89; currency devaluation, 90; democracy in, 27; environmental protection, 464; ERM crisis and, 331–32; EU competitive success, 635; EU membership, 343, 409; far-right party in, 485; foreign workers, 75–77; gay migration to, 231; holidays, 560; illegal asylum seekers, 717; immigrant and refugee numbers, 664, 712; internationalization of capital and, 343; peace movement, 134;

recession, 405; rise of right-wing populism, 666–68; social anxieties, 301; social democrats in, 122–23; social welfare reforms, 445; taxation rates, 123, 216; trade unions and, 81, 213; wage bargaining system, 68; as welfare state, 69, 106, 445, 664; women's status in, 132; xenophobia in, 749

Switzerland, 77, 86, 129, 199, 343, 484–85, 634

Sydney, Australia, 459

Syria: civil unrest and war, 1, 699–700, 706–10; refugees from, 712–13, 715; Russia and, 707; Western involvement in, 708; Yom Kippur War and, 62–63

Tancredo, Tom, 540

Tawney, R. H., 684, 784

taxes: antitax sentiment, 194; Bush 43 tax cuts, 558; corporate tax havens, 152; levels of, 123, 193–94, 216; New Zealand cuts, 350; reform, 227; Republican position on cuts, 342; Thatcher-Reagan tax cuts, 193–202, 233

technocracy, 36, 56, 227, 651, 669, 683, 694

Technological Society, The (Ellul), 56

technology: consumer, 391; effect on political economy, 217, 313–14; Google and, 390; laissez-faire and, 396; Microsoft and, 390; mobile telephony, 313–14, 391–92; "new economy" and, 382, 391; publicly funded advances, 393; Silicon Valley and, 390–91

telecommunications, 340–41

television, 34, 228, 467

terrorism: anarchists and, 656; in Barcelona, 719; Charlie Hebdo attacks, 531, 545; as continuing threat, 736; effects on economy, 554–55, 603; far-right movements and, 487; in Indonesia, 542; IRA in Britain and, 394; Islamic extremism and, 512, 542–44, 546, 651, 718–19; Left-wing radicals, 1970s, 108–14; Madrid bombings, 542–43; Mediterranean and, 541; in the Netherlands, 542; in Nice, 719; Norway massacre, 662; Oklahoma City bombing, 487; in Paris, 719; radical right and, 662. See also 9/11 terrorist attack; war on terror

Thatcher, Margaret: accomplishments of, 288–89; anti-statism and privatization, 196–99, 206, 321, 567; Britain's joining ERM and, 329; Bush 41 and, 279, 283; civil society vs., 225; conservative administration,

About the Author

Simon Reid-Henry is an award-winning academic and writer. He is associate professor at Queen Mary, University of London, where he teaches in the School of Geography. Simon is the author of several books, including *The Cuban Cure* and *The Political Origins of Inequality*. He has held visiting positions in history at Columbia University in New York and at the Norwegian Institute of International Affairs and is a former senior researcher at the Peace Research Institute Oslo. He is a recipient of the Philip Leverhulme Prize and has written for the *Guardian, New Statesman*, the *Economist*, the *Times* (London), the *Independent on Sunday*, and the *London Review of Books*. He lives in Oslo with his family and can be contacted at simonreidhenry.com and @sreidhenry.